An introductory housing and interior design program from Goodheart-Willcox

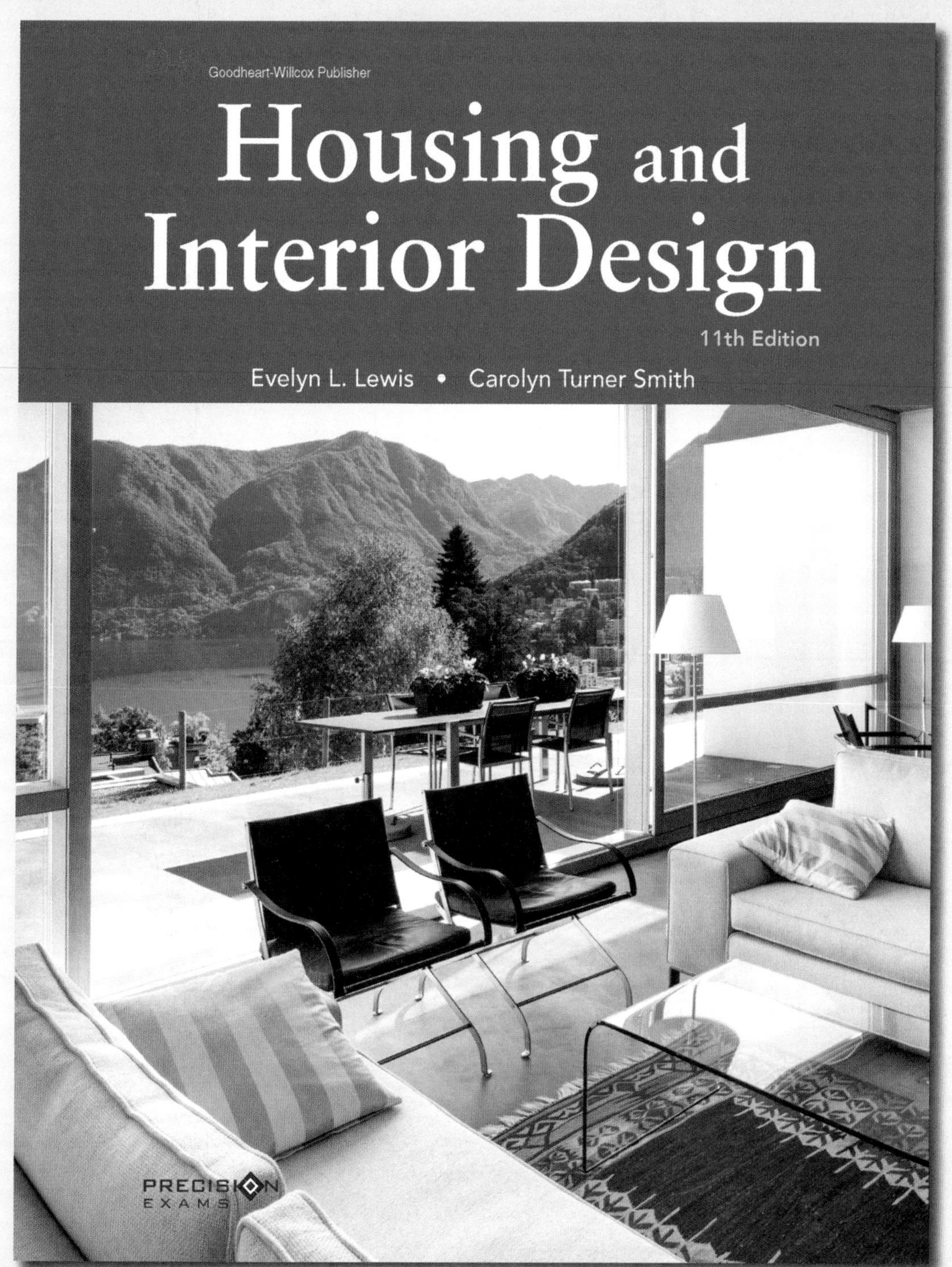

the first step in students' housing-related career pathway

Spotlights diverse careers and career-readiness activities

130 Unit 2 The Built Environment and Space Planning

Career Focus Historic Preservationist

Do you love to shop for antiques and visit old buildings? When you do, are you interested in the history behind them and not just the beauty? Do you wonder what it would take to bring them to life again, maybe for a new use? If so, you may consider exploring a career as an architect or interior designer who specializes in historic preservation.

Interests/Skills: Do you have a love of studying architectural styles in history? Are drawing and sketching a major part of your hobbies? Do you share the value of historical buildings with others and believe that older buildings should be given new life through adaptive reuse? Do you believe it is important for future generations to understand the evolution of such buildings? Exceptional research and organizational skills along with strong presentation and communication skills are necessary to work with others. Skills necessary for this important career also include computer and hand drawing and rendering abilities.

Career Snapshot: Historic preservationists usually have an architecture or interior design background. They choose to specialize in the adaptive reuse of old buildings and commonly work in an architectural or design preservation firm. Historic preservationists also work with local governments and community groups. They help identify buildings with historic significance and are often consulted on the true historic value of a structure. Historic preservationists need to be salespeople, too. It can be difficult to educate and convince others of a structure's importance to the community. The history and style of a building are most important, but the use of materials and applications must also have proven value. For example, paint colors must be authentic to the time period a building was constructed. Preservationists also may work with the restoration of furnishings and fine art.

Education/Training: A bachelor's degree in architecture, design, or urban planning is most often required. A master's degree or postgraduate studies in historic preservation is preferred. Courses of study include the history of architecture, history, art, art history, specific courses in the techniques and research for historic preservation, architecture, and computer programs.

Licensing/Examinations: All states require architects to be licensed. Architects must pass all divisions of the Architect Registration Examination.

photobank.ch/Shutterstock.com

The exterior structure and interior finishes of this space have been historically restored and the interior filled with more modern furniture and architectural features.

Many states require interior designers to be licensed or registered. Interior designers must pass the National Council of Interior Design Qualification (NCIDQ) exam to receive licensure. A supplemental historic preservation certification may be available, depending on the state of residence.

Professional Associations: Membership in the National Trust for Historic Preservation, the American Society of Interior Designers (ASID), and the International Interior Design Association (IIDA) is ideal.

Job Outlook: Current trends for green and sustainable architecture are positive for historic preservationists. Skills in adaptive reuse design methods and techniques to repair and maintain buildings that already exist are valuable.

Sources: The Occupational Outlook Handbook (OOH); the Occupational Information Network (O*NET)

394 Unit 4 The Process of Interior Design

Career Focus Interior Designer

Do you consider yourself artistic and creative? Do you have a flair for design? If you do, a career in interior design may be for you!

Interests/Skills: Do you find yourself very aware of your surroundings when you are dining out in a restaurant, visiting an airport, shopping in a retail store, visiting a new school, or entering a bank? Can you imagine yourself as someone who designs the interiors of homes or businesses? Do you frequently like to think about designing or redesigning your own personal space? Future interior designers answer "yes" to these questions and must possess three important skill sets: artistic and technical skills, interpersonal skills, and management skills.

Career Snapshot: More and more, designers are involved in the architectural detailing as well as the aesthetic design for interior spaces. Designers must be able to read construction documents (blueprints) and understand building codes. Many work with architects and builders to determine layouts and location of elements such as windows, doors, stairways, and hallways. For complex projects, interior designers may submit drawings to a building inspector for approval to make sure the design meets all codes.

Education/Training: Completion of a four- or five-year bachelor's degree through an accredited college or university is preferable and usually qualifies the graduate for a formal design apprenticeship program. Completion of a two-year associate's degree generally qualifies the graduate to be an assistant to an interior designer.

Elena Elisseeva/Shutterstock.com

Licensing/Examinations: After a one- to three-year apprenticeship to gain experience, interior desi graduates can take a licensing examination thr the Council for Interior Design Qualification (C Although only 50 percent of states require lice interior designers, passing the exam is necess obtain a license and have a competitive caree want to identify your state's title and practice a impact interior designers. *Title acts* govern, o the use of a title, such as *certified interior de* but do not require licensing to practice interio States with *practice acts*, however, require li those who practice interior design. These sta

Skills for Interior Designers

Artistic and Technical Skills	• Knows how to plan a space • Can draw a plan and create a model by hand and via computer • Can present a plan visually so the client understands it • Has material and product knowledge for creating and furnishing a space • Knows how texture, color, lighting, and other factors combine and interact to space its "feel" or "look" • Understands the structural requirements of his or her plans • Understands health and safety issues in spaces • Is knowledgeable about building codes and many other technical aspects o
Creative Ability	• Displays innovative and imaginative ability in creating design solutions • Adaptable to trying new design ideas within the parameters of good design • Displays good aesthetic judgment • Takes prudent risks to excel in solving design problems • Executes original/unique design plans to meet customer needs

Chapter 6 Reading Architectural Plans 149

Career Focus Architect

Is the design of buildings—old and new—fascinating to you? Do you ever wonder what it might be like to design such buildings? If you do, a career as an architect might be for you.

Interests/Skills: Architects work as part of a team to produce incredible structures. Interestingly, in larger firms, it is often difficult to tell who is an architect and who is an interior designer or engineer, although each serves a special and important purpose. Architects study and explore concepts, use spatial awareness, and use creativity to meet clients' needs. Skills include a strong background in multiple areas like art, science, and math. They should love to draw, as they do it manually and using computer-aided design. Effective organizational skills, attention to details, along with active listening skills are a must. Strong visual, written, and verbal communication skills are also essential in order to demonstrate problem-solving abilities.

Career Snapshot: Architects plan and design structures, such as private residences, office buildings, factories, theaters, and airports. The buildings they design have to be safe, economical, and must suit the needs of the people who use them. They work on computer programs to help them accomplish this. They prepare many contracts and documents. Architects also supervise the construction of the building or structure to make certain that their design plans are followed. Architects spend a great deal of time explaining their ideas to clients and others. Successful architects must be able to communicate well and get others to "buy-in-on" their ideas.

Education/Training: The completion of a bachelor's degree in architecture and a master's degree in architecture is the most common route for a career in architecture. Someone looking to specialize might also select elective coursework in *gerontology* (the science of aging) or *urban planning*. There are also countless continuing education opportunities which teach the technical, customer service, and business management skills specific to this concentrated area of design.

Monkey Business Images/Shutterstock.com

Licensing/Examinations: Most areas in the U.S. require a professional degree in architecture from a program accredited by the *National Architectural Accrediting Board (NAAB)* in order to take the Architect Registration Examination (ARE) licensure exam developed by the National Council of Architectural Registration Board (NCARB). It also takes approximately three years of documented experience under a registered architectural mentor to qualify.

Many architectural professionals also become LEED Accredited Professionals (Leadership in Energy and Environmental Design) for their particular area of specialization, and may also take the Construction Documents Technologist (CDT) and Certified Construction Contract Administration (CCCA) exams.

Professional Associations: American Institute of Architects (AIA); Construction Specifications Institute (CSI). These are national organizations that offer continued education opportunities and exposure to new products and building methods.

Job Outlook: While the overall professional outlook is very good, it is even better in specialty architectural areas such as schools/education, healthcare, and sustainable design.

Sources: The Occupational Outlook Handbook (OOH); the Occupational Information Network (O*NET); the National Council of Architectural Registration Board (NCARB); the American Institute of Architects (AIA)

Career Focus features give students a closer look at housing and interior design careers.

Design Practice

13. **House design** Imagine you are an architect designing housing in the year 2030. Use computer or hand-drawing techniques to create an exterior design that you think would reflect future design trends. Does your design relate to any previous historical styles or time periods? What features of exterior design, if any, do you think are classic and will be repeated in the future? How does your design relate to changes of lifestyle for future generations? Present your design to the class and provide evidence to support why you think this design reflects future design trends.
14. **Portfolio** Presume you are a contractor who is selecting photos, drawings, and descriptions of the house styles your company builds for a new website. Determine the styles of homes that your business will offer. If the styles are part of a planned housing development or subdivision, describe it as well. Put together a digital storyboard of your offerings in preparation for meeting with a web designer. Save a copy of your digital storyboard for future reference.

Design Practice

14. **Community design** Suppose you are a professional architect who is hired by your community to design a new building for the city's art collection. The design must incorporate examples of as many different lines as possible. Try to include horizontal, vertical, diagonal, and curved, including circular, oval, curvy, and complex free-form. Either by hand or by using CADD software, apply the elements of design to interiors by drawing the interior and exterior of a building that meets these requirements.
15. **Portfolio** Create a digital storyboard with school-approved web-based application to show beautiful room interiors. Each image should clearly show all elements of design. Label the elements of design in each image. Share your digital storyboard with the class and save a copy for your portfolio.

Design Practice

13. **Residential design plan** Illustrate interior design ideas from observation and experience for a room in a residential house, such as a living room, kitchen, master bedroom, bath, or a teen's or child's bedroom. Demonstrate technological applications and effective use of interior design tools and media by creating a visual design presentation board following the phases for planning and presenting a professional design (including interior architectural drawings) described in this chapter. Make an oral presentation explaining the visual solution displayed on your presentation board and the written schedule.
14. **Commercial design plan** Presume you have been selected to design a commercial space, such as a bank lobby, high school lobby, hair salon waiting area, or hotel lobby. Prepare a visual design presentation board demonstrating effective use of interior design tools and media in designing. Presume your class is your "client." Make an oral presentation explaining the design concept displayed on your presentation board and the written schedule.
15. **Portfolio** Add one or more of your design presentation boards and the best samples of your work as portfolio examples of your design capabilities. Write a summary about each project to keep in your portfolio.

Design Practice includes activities that students can collect for their career portfolios.

Reinforces STEM concepts with features and exercises

STEM Math Estimating Perimeter

Perimeter is the distance around a building, room, or other closed space. You need the perimeter of a room if you are installing baseboards and ceiling moldings, or painting the walls.

To calculate perimeter of a quadrilateral or four-sided room, measure each side and add the measurements together. If a room is square, you can estimate its perimeter by measuring one side and multiplying that number by 4. If the room is rectangular in shape, estimate perimeter by adding one short and one long side together, and doubling the sum.

The perimeter of a circle is called the *circumference*. Given the diameter or radius of a circle, you can calculate the circumference. The *diameter* is the line that bisects the circle into two symmetrical parts. The *radius* is a straight line from the center point of a circle to its outer edge; radius is half the diameter.

Circumference = d × π, where *d* is diameter
Circumference = 2 × π × r, where *r* is radius

The symbol π, called *pi*, is approximately equal to 3.141592. It can be rounded to 3.14.

Example: What is the circumference of a circle with a diameter of 8 feet?

Circumference is 8 × π or 8 × 3.14, which equal 25.12 feet

Math Practice

1. Practice measuring perimeter. Measure eac side of the following four-sided rooms and add the measurements together to obtain t perimeter: a classroom, a room in your hor and a bathroom or restroom.
2. Locate several circular objects within your environments. Measure the diameter of ea and then use the above formula to calcula circumference.

action, excitement, and sometimes agitation. Use

STEM Math Symmetry

Objects are often described as being *symmetrical* or *asymmetrical*. An object is symmetrical if a line drawn through it divides it into two matching halves. The dividing line is called the *line of symmetry*.

An object may have one or more lines of symmetry. For example, a rectangle has two lines of symmetry. A circle has an infinite number of lines of symmetry since any line drawn through the center creates a line of symmetry.

An object is asymmetrical if it has zero lines of symmetry; no two halves match. Your hand is asymmetrical; you cannot draw a line that will result in two matching halves.

Symmetry creates balance. Architects and interior designers often incorporate symmetry in their work. For example, the exterior of a Georgian home exhibits symmetry. You can also achieve symmetry by placing matching chairs on both sides of an entryway.

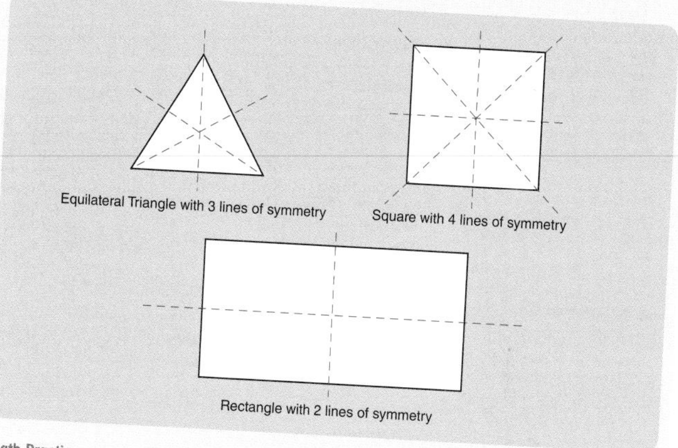

Rectangle with 2 lines of symmetry

Math Practice

Take a walking tour in your neighborhood and carefully observe symmetry in the housing styles as you walk. Select at least six homes you think display symmetry and take digital pictures of the homes (ask the owner's permission). Print the house pictures. On the printed house pictures, carefully draw a vertical line exactly through the middle. Do the houses actually display symmetry? Why or why not? Give an oral report to share your findings with the group.

STEM Math features provide housing-related math formulas and practice activities.

STEM Science & Technology Visible Light and the Electromagnetic Spectrum

Light is a form of energy called *electromagnetic radiation*. It travels through space as oscillating waves. From crest to trough, these waves range in size from large as a building to small as a microscopic particle. *Wavelength* is the distance between the crests of two adjoining waves. *Frequency* is the rate at which a wave oscillates or fluctuates and is measured in hertz. The chart shows the electromagnetic spectrum arranged according to wavelength and frequency in hertz. As the length of a wave increases, its frequency decreases.

Visible light makes up a small part of the electromagnetic spectrum and it's the only part you can see. Visible light consists of the colors you see in a rainbow—red, orange, yellow, green, blue, and violet. These colors form the basis for the color wheel that interior designers use for creating color schemes.

The spectrum also includes other forms of energy you encounter every day: infrared, radio waves, microwaves, X-rays, gamma rays, and ultraviolet rays. Many consumer electronics products utilize the electromagnetic spectrum. Can you identify a few of them?

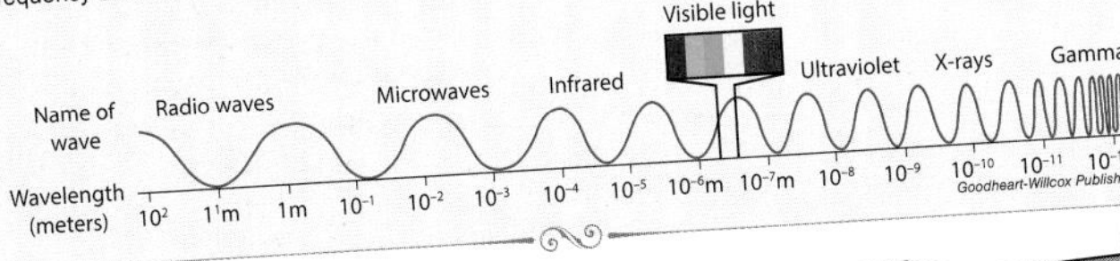

STEM Science & Technology features explore science concepts in housing and examine housing-related technology.

STEM Science & Technology Consumer Electronics Explosion

Between 1975 and 2008, the number of electronic devices in the average American home grew from 1.3 to 25—with numbers continuing to climb in recent years. Examples of these devices are televisions, computers, electronic readers, gaming systems, digital cameras, personal media players, and phones.

Consumers must subscribe or buy services to use some consumer electronic products. Services include cell phone and Internet access, cable television, and satellite radio. Telecommunication industries, which provide these services, transmit voice, data, and images. For example, when you make a phone call, send an e-mail, text, or tweet, you are using telecommunications services. Many of these companies also sell their own products.

Electronic products are merging with each other and with various home appliances. Manufacturers are incorporating Internet connectivity into many televisions and appliances sold today. In the near future, many devices and appliances can be repaired or updated through an Internet connection. Some appliances (and home-related technologies like lighting and security systems) can be controlled and monitored from your cellular phone. This process, or *convergence*, involves the merging of separate products into one. Other merged products include smartphones, personal digital assistants, and touch-screen devices that allow users to read books, visit websites, and download videos. New telecommunications technologies continue to change the way people communicate, work, learn, and have fun.

Engages students with high-interest features

Sociocultural Connections — The Changing American Household

Households by Type: 1970 to 2012 (percent distribution)

	1970	1980	1990	2000	2009	2012
Married couples with children	40.3	30.9	26.3	24.1	21.5	19.6
Married couples without children	30.3	29.9	29.8	28.7	29	29.1
Other family households	10.6	12.9	14.8	16	16.8	17.8
Men living alone	5.6	8.6	9.7	10.7	11.7	12.3
Women living alone	11.5	14	14.9	14.8	15.3	15.2
Other nonfamily households	1.7	3.6	4.6	5.7	5.7	6.1

Source: U.S. Census Bureau, *Current Population Survey, Annual Social and Economic Supplements*, selected years 1970 to 2012.

According to the U.S. Census Bureau, the composition of U.S. households changed between 1970 and 2012. The most significant changes include

- **Reduction of family households.** Family households—two or more members related by birth, marriage, or adoption—accounted for about 66 percent of households instead of 81 percent.
- **Reduction of married-couple households.** The share of married-couple-with-children households decreased from 40 percent to 20 percent of households. Additionally, in 1970 married couples with children outnumbered married couples without children. By 2012, the reverse was true.
- **Increase in nonfamily households.** The proportion of nonfamily households—mostly people who live alone—increased 10 percentage points between 1970 and 2012.

The Census Bureau cites many reasons for these changes. For example, the roles of men and women have changed. More women are working and living on their own. People are marrying and having children later or not at all. Also, people are living longer due to technological innovations. The baby-boom generation—those born between 1946 and 1964, who make up more than 25 percent of the adult population—is moving into retirement.

Changes in the composition of U.S. households bring changes in the housing market. For example, after their children grow up and leave home, many baby boomers choose to downsize into smaller dwellings. Older adults generally prefer single-level homes or buildings with elevators since climbing stairs can be difficult.

Dig Deeper

Use online or print resources to investigate ways that households have changed in your community in the last 25 years. How have these changes influenced the type of housing available in your community? Discuss your findings with the class.

Sociocultural Connections invite students to explore the human aspects of housing. *Dig Deeper* questions promote class discussion.

Sociocultural Connections — Economics: Supply and Demand

The U.S. has an economic system in which businesses are privately owned and operated with limited government regulation. Businesses compete with one another for sales and profits and people generally make their own decisions about what to buy and sell.

In other economic systems, the prices of goods and services, including housing, may be set by the government. In the market economy of the U.S., however, prices are determined by *supply and demand.*

- *Supply* is the quantity of a product or service businesses are willing to provide. According to the *law of supply,* the higher the price at which something can be sold, the more of it businesses want to produce.
- *Demand* is the quantity of a product or service consumers are willing to buy. According to the *law of demand,* the higher the price of something, the less of it consumers want to buy.

When demand is greater than the supply, price rises. This is why airfares are highest during the holidays. More people want to fly then, so airlines can charge a premium. Likewise, when supply is greater than demand, price falls. In the months after the holidays, the same seats on the same planes cost less. Airlines lower their prices to entice people to fly.

Supply and demand help set prices in the housing market as well. Supply is the number of existing homes for sale, and demand is the number of homes sought by home buyers at a given time. For example, a home for sale near the seashore or other desirable area may cost $400,000 or more. In a less desirable area, the same home would sell for substantially less.

Dig Deeper

Use online resources to further investigate the laws of supply and demand in regard to housing prices. At what times of the year are home sales greater? lower? How do seasonal changes impact housing supply and demand? How does supply and demand impact product sales for home interiors?

Green Choices — What Does "Green" Mean?

"Green" refers to making choices about various aspects of housing and interiors that are environmentally friendly. This means making choices to incorporate sound environmental principles of building, materials, and energy use. The basic intent of green choices is to have low negative-environmental impact on air quality, soil quality, or use of natural resources. Environmentally friendly choices include

- using less water
- using less energy
- using nontoxic materials and substances
- choosing materials that can be recycled or have been recycled
- recycling and reusing items

These choices range from such small items as cleaning supplies to all aspects of buildings. Specifically, *green* choices affect consumers and the fields of architecture, landscape architecture, urban design, urban planning, engineering, graphic design, industrial design, and interior design.

Many terms are used when referring to green choices including: environmentally friendly, green design, eco-design, design for the environment, eco-friendly, and sustainable design.

(NOTE: Throughout this text, *Green Choices* features offer ideas and ways to incorporate green concepts for housing consumers and people in the housing and interior design professions.)

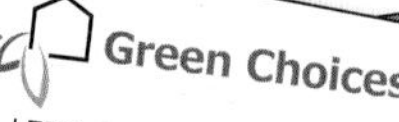

Green Choices — Choose a LEED-Certified Home

LEED stands for *Leadership in Energy and Environmental Design.* A LEED-certified home means that the structure meets the guidelines to be a green and sustainable building. The U.S. Green Building Council sets the guidelines and ratings. The Council has a rating system with four levels that certify that a house is environmentally responsible. The four levels include the following: Certified, Silver, Gold, and Platinum (highest).

The LEED certification means that a home's features promote such green and sustainable design, construction, and operations practices as the following:

- Innovation and design—highest standard for "green" performance
- Environmentally responsible within the larger community
- Sustainable sites—minimal impact of the home on the land
- Water efficiency—indoors and out
- Energy efficient—in the structure and heating and cooling design
- Materials and resources—efficient use of materials, use environmentally preferred materials, and produce less waste in construction
- Indoor environmental quality (IAQ)—reduce the creation of and exposure to pollutants
- Home owner education—how to use and maintain the green features
- Third-party verification—someone other than the builder has certified the green parts of the home

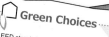

Green Features introduce students to green and sustainable housing efforts.

Housing Health & Safety

Reducing Mold with Paperless Drywall

Mold growing in drywall can be a major concern to the health of a family and the indoor air quality of a home or building. There are many forms of mold, and some are toxic—especially to people with mold allergies. Exposure to water and moisture causes mold spores to multiply. Mold in drywall also impacts the maintenance and value of a home.

Mold thrives on the paper component of traditional drywall. That is why researchers have developed a new paperless drywall. Instead of paper facings, this new product uses fiberglass mats for the facing. The design community considers paperless drywall more sustainable because it

- lasts longer than other wallboards with exposure to moisture
- is mold and moisture resistant
- has the *Greenguard Environmental Institute* certification as a product with low emissions of volatile organic compounds (VOCs)

The U.S. Green Building Council—developers of the Leadership in Energy and Environmental Design (LEED) Green Building rating system—values products with a longer sustaining life. Such products have low VOC emissions and provide good air quality. Builders used this product in reconstructing homes in New Orleans after Hurricane Katrina.

The designer of the basement within the left photo made a sustainable design choice by specifying a mold- and moisture-resistant drywall in the construction. The second designer did not.

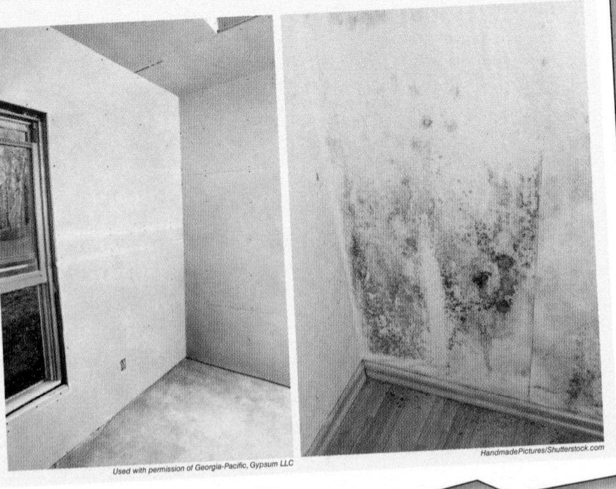

Used with permission of Georgia-Pacific, Gypsum LLC

HandmadePictures/Shutterstock.com

Housing Health & Safety features examine housing designs that help protect the occupants.

Reinforces concepts with review questions and assessment activities

Review & Assessment

1. What is housing?
2. Distinguish between the near environment and total environment.
3. Identify three physical needs people have.
4. What are four psychological needs that people have?
5. Given the chance, how would you change your housing to better meet your need for self-actualization?
6. Give an exampl meet each of th expression; (B) c

Review & Assessment

1. Name two examples of how culture influenced housing.
2. What barriers do new immigrants face in finding suitable housing?
3. What would help new immigrants find safe, suitable housing that reflects culture?

Review & Assessment questions strengthen students' understanding of content throughout the chapter.

Review & Assessment

1. For each of the following home features, list one green product: doors and windows; siding and decking; roofing; heating, cooling, and hot water; and fixtures and appliances.
2. Name four housing concerns, other than energy use and conservation, addressed by the Southface Eco Office and Resource Center.
3. What are the key advantages of Zero Energy Homes?
4. Contrast the features of a Zero Energy Home (ZEH) with an Earthship home.

Terms in Action

1. **Term flash cards** Work in teams to locate small images that visually represent each of the *Content Terms* at the beginning of the chapter. Print the images. To create flash cards, write each term on a note card and paste the image that describes or explains the term on the opposite side. Use the flash cards to review the terms.

Terms in Action

1. **Term antonyms** Individually or with a partner, create a T-chart on a sheet of paper and list each of the *Content* and *Academic Terms* from the beginning of the chapter in the left column. In the right column, list an *antonym* (a word of opposite meaning) for each term. Discuss how understanding antonyms can help reinforce word meanings.

Terms in Action activities invite students to apply their vocabulary knowledge at the end of every chapter.

Core Skills

6. **Writing** Identify 10 househ community that you know w family names private.) For ea of household it is. Also, writ description of each member approximate age, and relati
7. **Writing** Consider your ho examine your home's interio years, has the size of your hou so, how? Did the change result per person? In comparison, do less personal privacy today tha Forecast your household's need from now. What possible chang may occur in the next five year the amount of space per perso the space per person? Write a b your forecast.
8. **Speaking and listening** I adult and ask him or her to de in his or her housing over the y the person's lifestyle and housi other. Is ability to age-in-place this older adult? Why? If poss adult's permission to audio-r and share it with the class.
9. **Research and writing** A people in your community? I town (city) and local charitab are doing to handle this probl do these organizations take to Summarize your findings in a
10. **Writing** In your own words, summary of the chapter conte less. Save your summary for fu
11. **Speaking** Imagine a full a homeless person. Look for tries to convey that experien the information it provides. homelessness surprise you?

type of lay... in the kitchen?

7. **Math practice** Use a ruler or metal tape measure to measure the length and width of this text book. Then draw the configuration of the textbook on a sheet of graph paper using a ¼" = 1'-0" scale. Then use a plain sheet of paper and an architect's scale to draw the dimensions of the text book to scale using the scale of ¼" = 1'-0". Use the STEM Math feature box on page 144 as a guide for using the architect's scale.
8. **Writing** Use Internet or print resources to investigate further information about the Building Information Model (BIM). If possible, interview an architect or builder who uses BIM. What are the best features of this process? Write a brief report and share your findings with the class.
9. **Reading, writing, and speaking** Locate a set of house plans on the Internet or from another source. Read the document carefully. Identify and label the symbols and line types you find on the plan. What schedules and specifications accompany the plan? How do they help convey meaning to the drawings? Show your plan to the class, pointing out the symbols and line types and what they mean.
10. **Reading, sketching, and writing** Locate a house floor plan on the Internet that you like and print a copy. Based on your readings under the *Order of the Documents* on pages 146–147 of this chapter, imagine what a complete set of drawings for this house would look like if this home were to have the master suite renovated. Make a list, sketch, or otherwise determine what type of drawings you think would need to be included in the *Order of Documents* for the renovation. Share your thoughts with the class.
11. **Math practice** Measure the perimeter of your classroom and write down the measurements. Then measure the dimensions of room features such as windows, door, cabinetry, and SMART boards, etc., and write

Core Skills activities boost students' career readiness abilities.

A complete program for students and teachers

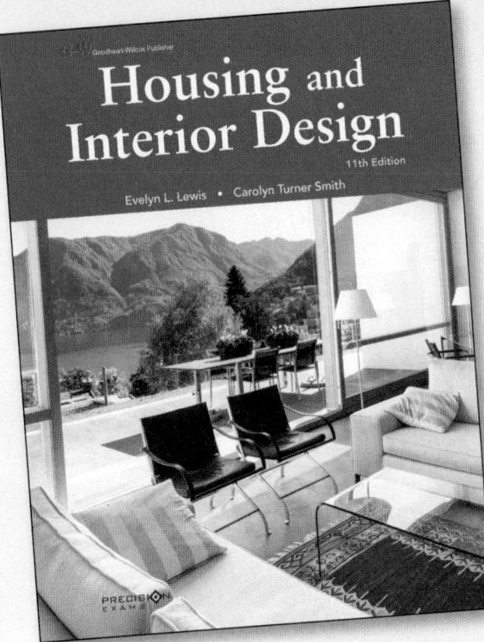

Student Textbook—Print or Online
The student edition of *Housing and Interior Design* is available as a printed textbook or as an interactive online text. Simply choose the format that works best for your students.
www.g-wonlinetextbooks.com

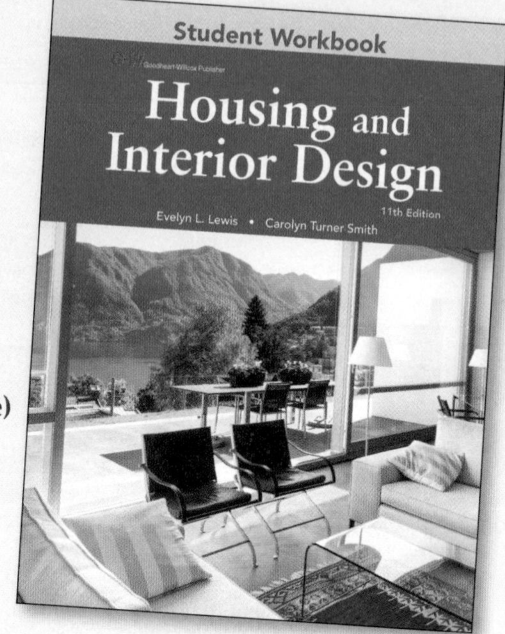

Student Workbook (available in print or online)
Workbook activities reinforce material presented in the textbook, offering students a hands-on learning experience.

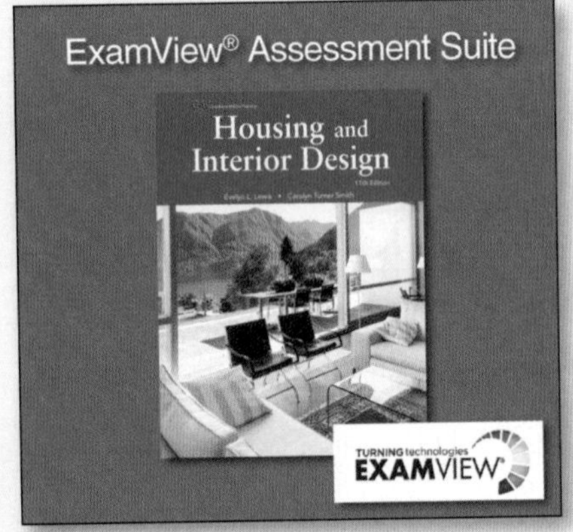

ExamView® Assessment Suite
Quickly and easily prepare and print tests with the ExamView® Assessment Suite. You can choose which questions to include in each test, create multiple versions of a single test, and automatically generate answer keys.

Instructor's Resource CD
Includes lesson plans, reproducible masters, answer keys, and grading rubrics.

Instructor's Presentations for PowerPoint®
Visually reinforce key concepts with prepared lectures. Integrated discussion questions make the presentations interactive.

G-W integrated learning solution

G-W LEARNING.COM

The **G-W Integrated Learning Solution** offers easy-to-use resources for both instructors and students. Both digital and blended (print + digital) teaching and learning content can be accessed through any Internet-enabled device, such as a computer, smartphone, or tablet. From the following options, choose the ones that work best for you and your students.

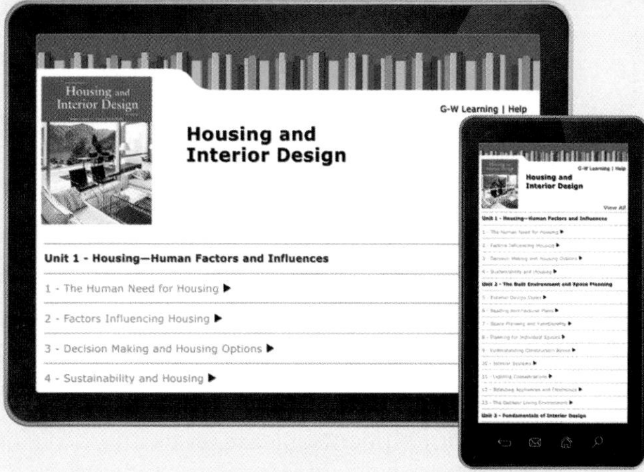

The **G-W Learning Companion Website** for *Housing and Interior Design* accompanies the Student Textbook and provides content to help students build skills and knowledge, extend textbook content, and reinforce learning. The website complements textbook chapters and is available to students at no charge.

The **Online Learning Suite** for *Housing and Interior Design* is available as a classroom subscription. It includes the online student text, the companion website content, and the digital workbook.

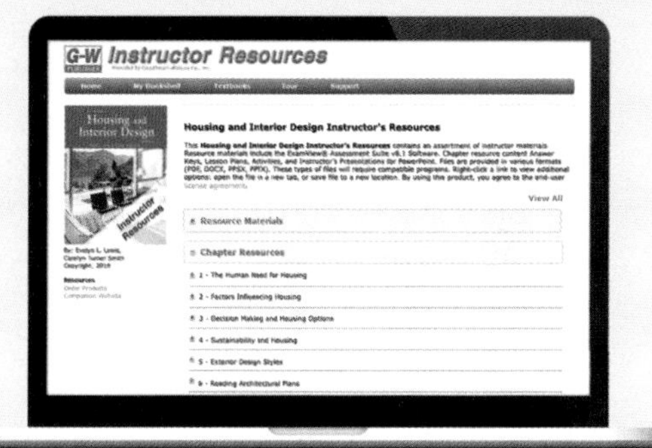

The **Online Instructor Resources** provide extensive support for instructors. Included in the online resources are Answer Keys, Lesson Plans, Instructor's Presentations for PowerPoint®, ExamView® Assessment Suite, and much more. These resources are available as a subscription and can be accessed at school or at home. They are also available on CDs.

Looking for a **Blended Solution**? G-W offers the Online Learning Suite bundled with the printed textbook in one easy-to-access package for school districts and instructors seeking a combination of print and digital tools. With this option, individual students and instructors have the flexibility of using solely print, solely digital, or a combination of print and digital versions of the *Housing and Interior Design* educational materials to best meet their particular learning and teaching styles.

Goodheart-Willcox Publisher Welcomes Your Comments

A leader in educational publishing since 1921, Goodheart-Willcox Publisher offers outstanding print and digital products for Family and Consumer Sciences courses. This new edition of the *Housing and Interior Design* textbook program provides the basis for high school students interested in architecture and interior design career pathways.

If you teach a class in housing and interior design, or any course in the Family and Consumer Sciences Education area, and you have been unable to find a suitable text for your students, please let us know. We are eager to develop high-quality, innovative products that fill educators' unmet needs in the educational market. Your suggestions may lead to the development of digital or print materials that benefit teachers and students across the country.

With each new product, our goal at Goodheart-Willcox Publisher is to deliver superior educational materials that effectively meet the ever-changing, increasingly diverse needs of students and teachers. To that end, we welcome your comments or suggestions regarding *Housing and Interior Design* and its supplemental components.

Please send any comments and suggestions to the managing editor of our Family and Consumer Sciences Editorial Department. You can send an e-mail to editorial@g-w.com, or write to:

Managing Editor—FCS
Goodheart-Willcox Publisher
18604 West Creek Drive
Tinley Park, IL 60477-6243

Housing and Interior Design

11th Edition

by

Evelyn L. Lewis, Ed.D.
Professor Emerita, Home Economics
Northern Arizona University
Flagstaff, Arizona

Carolyn Turner Smith, Ph.D., CFCS
Professor Emerita, Department of Family and Consumer Sciences
North Carolina Agricultural and Technical State University
Greensboro, North Carolina

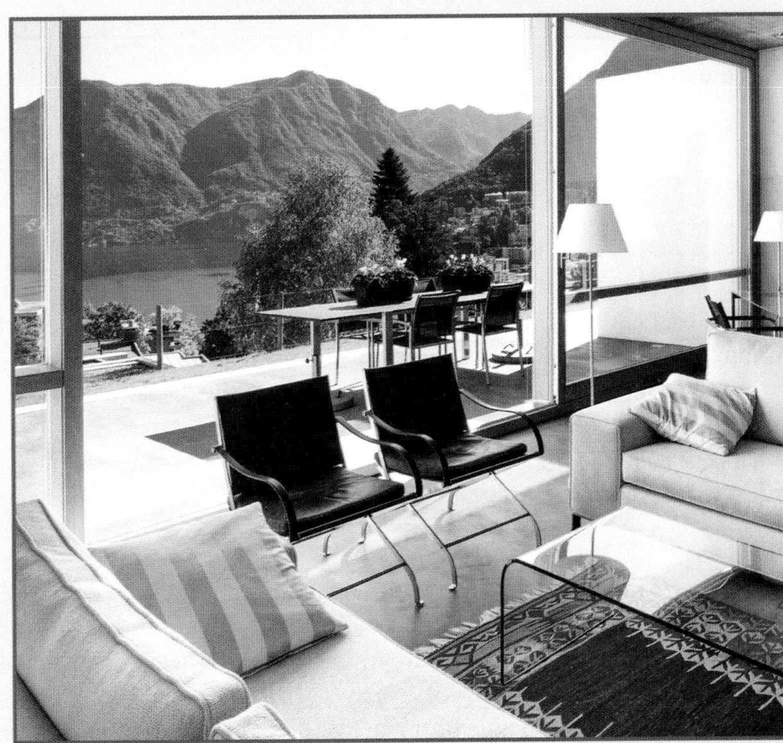

Publisher
Goodheart-Willcox Company, Inc.
Tinley Park, IL
www.g-w.com

Previously published as *Housing Decisions* by Evelyn L. Lewis and Carolyn S. Turner
Previous editions copyright 2012, 2006, 2004, 2000, 1994, 1990, 1987, 1984, 1980, 1978

Manufactured in the United States of America.

ISBN 978-1-63126-567-9

2 3 4 5 6 7 8 9 – 18 – 22 21 20 19 18 17

The Goodheart-Willcox Company, Inc. Brand Disclaimer: Brand names, company names, and illustrations for products and services included in this text are provided for educational purposes only and do not represent or imply endorsement or recommendation by the author or the publisher.

The Goodheart-Willcox Company, Inc. Safety Notice: The reader is expressly advised to carefully read, understand, and apply all safety precautions and warnings described in this book or that might also be indicated in undertaking the activities and exercises described herein to minimize risk of personal injury or injury to others. Common sense and good judgment should also be exercised and applied to help avoid all potential hazards. The reader should always refer to the appropriate manufacturer's technical information, directions, and recommendations; then proceed with care to follow specific equipment operating instructions. The reader should understand these notices and cautions are not exhaustive.

The publisher makes no warranty or representation whatsoever, either expressed or implied, including but not limited to equipment, procedures, and applications described or referred to herein, their quality, performance, merchantability, or fitness for a particular purpose. The publisher assumes no responsibility for any changes, errors, or omissions in this book. The publisher specifically disclaims any liability whatsoever, including any direct, indirect, incidental, consequential, special, or exemplary damages resulting, in whole or in part, from the reader's use or reliance upon the information, instructions, procedures, warnings, cautions, applications, or other matter contained in this book. The publisher assumes no responsibility for the activities of the reader.

The Goodheart-Willcox Company, Inc. Internet Disclaimer: The Internet resources and listings in this Goodheart-Willcox Publisher product are provided solely as a convenience to you. These resources and listings were reviewed at the time of publication to provide you with accurate, safe, and appropriate information. Goodheart-Willcox Publisher has no control over the referenced Web sites and, due to the dynamic nature of the Internet, is not responsible or liable for the content, products, or performance of links to other Web sites or resources. Goodheart-Willcox Publisher makes no representation, either expressed or implied, regarding the content of these Web sites, and such references do not constitute an endorsement or recommendation of the information or content presented. It is your responsibility to take all protective measures to guard against inappropriate content, viruses, or other destructive elements.

Cover credit: lancelot/Shutterstock.com

About the Authors

Dr. Evelyn L. Lewis, Professor Emerita, taught 37 years in primary, secondary, and higher education. She developed curricula for the Arizona Department of Education and prepared training programs for Coconino County career education. Lewis also served Flagstaff's Habitat for Humanity as a volunteer.

Dr. Carolyn Turner Smith is Professor Emerita, Department of Family and Consumer Sciences, North Carolina Agricultural and Technical State University, Greensboro. Currently, she serves as Adjunct Professor in Interior Design at High Point University, High Point, North Carolina, where she teaches a global issues course in international housing. Dr. Smith has taught housing and resource management at the college level, particularly for preparing students to teach courses in high school housing and interior design. Also, she has conducted research on housing for populations with special needs, residential energy efficiency, and renewable energy applications. Smith served on the board of directors as a national officer for the American Association of Family and Consumer Sciences (AAFCS). She is past president of the North Carolina Association of Family and Consumer Sciences and the national Housing Education and Research Association. Dr. Smith has served on the States Energy Advisory Board for the U. S. Department of Energy and on the Executive Advisory Board for the U. S. Department of Homeland Security. She serves on housing boards at the local, state, and national levels.

Acknowledgments

Goodheart-Willcox Publisher and the authors would like to thank the following professionals who reviewed selected chapters and provided valuable input into the development of this textbook program.

Contributing Writers

Jennifer Blanchard Belk, MAE, LEED AP, IIDA
NCIDQ Certified Designer at Belk Construction Management Group
Director and Programming Coordinator at LOOM Coworking
Fort Mill, South Carolina

Judith Brinkley-Berry, ASID
Judith Brinkley-Berry Interior Design
Hilton Head Island, South Carolina

Madge Megliola, ASID
Megliola Beal Interior Design
Greensboro, North Carolina

Instructor Reviewers

Denise Bourdeau
Family and Consumer Sciences Teacher
North Colonie Central School District
Shaker High School
Latham, New York

Leah Bratcher
FCS/CTE High School Teacher
Marina High School
Huntington Beach, California

Anne Dewalt
Family and Consumer Sciences Educator
Manassas Park High School
Manassas Park, Virginia

Jana Din
Interior Design Teacher
Galt High School
Galt, California

Kerry Doll
Instructor
Fountain Valley High School
Fountain Valley, California

Barbara Grenga
Family and Consumer Sciences Instructor
North Syracuse Central School District
North Syracuse, New York

Joyce Harrison
Family and Consumer Sciences Instructor
James Bowie High School
Arlington, Texas

Amanda K. Lucero
Family and Consumer Sciences Instructor
Sharyland High School
Mission, Texas

Kari McDermott
Family and Consumer Sciences Teacher
Austin High School
Austin, Minnesota

Janel Simmons
High School Family and Consumer Sciences Teacher
St. Francis High School
St. Francis, Minnesota

Blair Turner
Family and Consumer Sciences Teacher
Naaman Forest High School, Garland ISD
Garland, Texas

Rhonda Yommer
Family and Consumer Sciences Teacher
York Comprehensive High School
Floyd D. Johnson Technology Center
York, South Carolina

Industry Reviewers

Kathy Andersson
Color Marketing Manager
Chairholder, Color Marketing Group
The Sherwin-Williams Company

Dr. JoAnn Emmel
Associate Professor Emerita
Virginia Tech
Blacksburg, Virginia

Catherine Cauthen Turner
Realtor/Broker
Cottingham Chalk Haynes
Charlotte, North Carolina

Dr. Jane Walker
Professor
Department of Family and Consumer Sciences
North Carolina Agricultural and Technical State University
Greensboro, North Carolina

Steve Windham
Landscape Design and Landscape Services Representative
New Garden Landscaping and Nursery, Inc.
Greensboro, North Carolina

Precision Exams Certification

Housing and Interior Design explores the knowledge and skills needed for successful careers in interior design. Goodheart-Willcox is pleased to partner with Precision Exams by correlating *Housing and Interior Design* to Precision Exams' Interior Design I or Interior Design II Standards. Precision Exams' Standards and Career Skill Exams were created in concert with industry and subject matter experts to match real-world job skills and marketplace demands. Students who pass both the written and performance portions of the exam can earn a Career Skills Certification™. To see how *Housing and Interior Design* correlates to the Precision Exams Standards, please see the *Housing and Interior Design* correlations at www.g-w.com. For more information on Precision Exams, please consult the accompanying *Housing and Interior Design Instructor's Resources* or go to www.precisionexams.com.

I earned a CAREER SKILLS™ Certificate in Interior Design. You can earn one, too!
Career Skills Certificate
This is to certify that
Eve Denton
has demonstrated competency in
Interior Design
CTE
Ask your instructor how you can earn a CAREER SKILLS™ Certificate for your résumé.
800.470.1215
PRECISION EXAMS
precisionexams.com

Wavebreakmedia/istock.com

Brief Contents

Contents

Features

Green Choices

Sociocultural Connections

STEM Science & Technology

STEM Math

Career Focus

Housing Health & Safety

Introduction

With a new look, this edition of *Housing and Interior Design* encourages you to develop foundational knowledge and skills relating to career pathways in housing and interior design. Chapter topics will lead you through many concepts and issues home owners and interior designers and their clients face when selecting and designing living spaces. With a strong emphasis on universal and green or sustainable design, this text offers you many practical ways to put the *design process* into practice.

Through this text, you will learn how to identify and evaluate the wide array of housing and design options to fill human needs. Hundreds of beautiful photos effectively illustrate design concepts you can adapt to fit various structures. The charts and illustrations help demonstrate and clarify important text information about such topics as architectural design, furniture design, and design technology and trends.

With a focus on professional practices and career success, the *Housing and Interior Design* text includes a number of elements that can help you on your career journey. The *Career Focus* features highlight related housing and interior design careers with a bright job outlook. In the chapter review, the *Design Practice* activities offer you a wealth of practical ways to develop your design creation and presentation skills. Because involvement with student and professional organizations is key to career success, the FCCLA activities on every unit opener reinforce teamwork, workplace skills, and community involvement.

Unit 1

Housing—Human Factors and Influences

Rob Marmion/Shutterstock.com

Leadership, Housing, and Human Needs

What do community service and your feelings and attitudes about “home” have in common? Both begin in the heart—with those things you value most. Take a look around your community. What housing-related concerns do you see? Are there people living in homeless shelters or unsafe housing? Are there needs that you could help meet?

Take the lead in planning and implementing an *FCCLA Leadership Service in Action* project that focuses on meeting the needs of those who live in homeless shelters or unsafe housing. For example, consider collecting grooming and personal-hygiene items and donating them to your local homeless shelter.

Use the *FCCLA Planning Process* and related documents to plan, implement, and evaluate your project. See your adviser for information as needed.

Active Citizens Influence Housing

As communities look for ways to improve housing for citizens and protect the environment, opportunities exist for people to take action. How can you get involved? Start by attending one or more meetings of your city council or county board. What housing-related issues are facing your community? Is your community supporting a recycling program or other environmentally friendly practices? On what level can citizens become involved?

Once you have answers to these questions and more, plan and implement an *FCCLA Power of One* project involving a community housing issue. Use the *FCCLA Planning Process* as a guide. Then evaluate your project. See your adviser for information as needed.

Chapter 1

The Human Need for Housing

Content Terms

housing
house
home
near environment
needs
adobe
yurt
beauty
creativity
values
family
roles
lifestyle
household
life cycle

Academic Terms

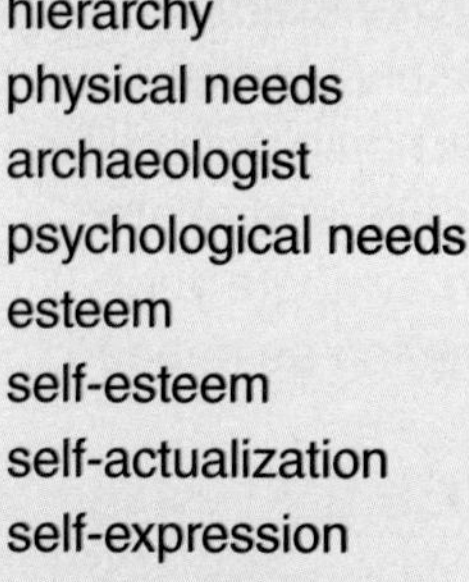

hierarchy
physical needs
archaeologist
psychological needs
esteem
self-esteem
self-actualization
self-expression
quality of life

Learning Outcomes

After studying this chapter, you will be able to

- assess how housing helps people meet their needs.
- analyze human factors that impact housing choices, including values, space, costs, roles, and lifestyle.
- summarize how housing needs change over the life span.
- examine ways housing affects quality of life.

Reading with Purpose

Rewrite each learning outcome as a question. As you read, look for the answers to each question. Write the answers in your own words.

While studying, look for the access icon to:

- **Practice** the *Content* and *Academic Terms* with e-flash cards, matching activities, and vocabulary games.
- **Reinforce** what you learn by completing the *Review & Assessment* questions and e-mailing them to your instructor.

G-WLEARNING.com www.g-wlearning.com/housing/

Monkey Business Images/Shutterstock.com

Housing, good or poor, has a deep and lasting effect on all people. Winston Churchill once said, "We shape our buildings, and then they shape us." This is especially true of the buildings in which people live. First people find shelter to satisfy their needs, and then this shelter affects the way they feel and behave. Housing or interior design professionals have the knowledge, skills, and abilities to impact housing through meeting the needs of all humans. As you read about housing and human needs, think about ways you can start meeting the housing needs of others now.

People and Their Housing

Housing, as this text uses the word, means any dwelling that provides shelter. It refers to what is within and near the shelter, such as furnishings, neighborhood, and community. A **house** is any building that serves as living quarters for one or more families. In contrast, a **home** is any place a person lives. The relationship between people and their housing will be the focus throughout this text.

Housing is the **near environment,** a small and distinct part of the total environment in which people live. Housing includes a dwelling place, the furnishings in the space, the neighborhood, and the immediate community. The *total environment* includes all a person's interactions with people and buildings as well as different geographical areas outside the dwelling place, neighborhood, and local community. Although housing is just one part of an individual's total environment, it is a very important part (Figure 1.1). It has great impact on how a person lives and develops as an individual.

Whether living alone or with others, people interact with their housing. Housing affects people's actions, and in turn, their actions affect their housing. For instance, if an individual lives in a small apartment, he or she will not easily host large parties because there will not be enough room. The neighbors might complain about the noise and lack of accessible parking near the building. If an individual wants to entertain large numbers of guests, choosing to live in a large house that is set apart from other houses may be the best option.

It is also possible to view interaction with housing on a smaller scale. Suppose a person chooses to decorate a room in his or her house with many fragile, expensive accessories. Although this gives a feeling of formality and elegance, this room would not be the place to exercise or dance. If physical fitness is important to an individual's lifestyle, furnishing the room differently—or adapting the housing to match a way of life—is likely the best option.

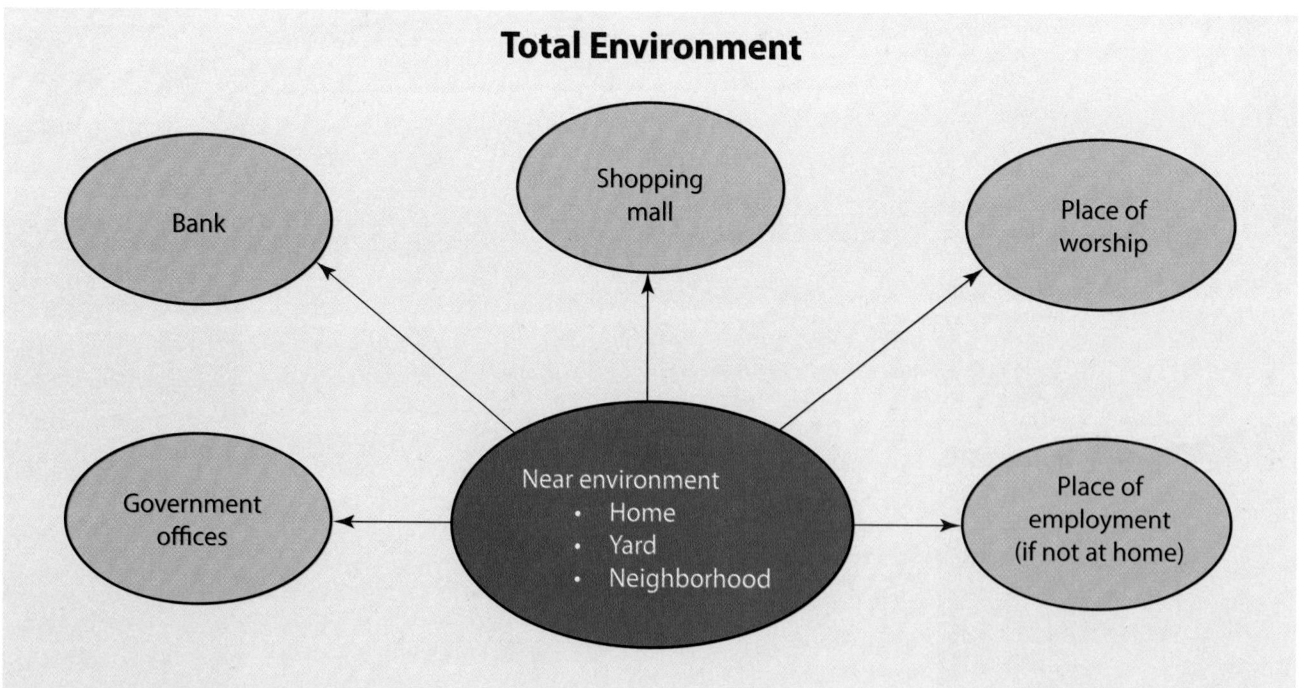

Goodheart-Willcox Publisher

Figure 1.1 The near environment is part of the total environment.

Meeting Needs Through Housing

All aspects of environment impact human well-being. The near environment, in the form of housing, helps people meet their needs. **Needs** are the basic requirements that people must fill to live. All people have physical, psychological, and other needs—sharing the need for shelter in which to eat, sleep, and carry on activities of daily living.

Consider the following observation by the director of a shelter for homeless people. When people came to the shelter for help, their basic needs had not yet been satisfied—they were hungry and could think only of food. Once they had eaten, their next concern was to be comfortable—having a place to sleep and feel safe. Only after meeting their most basic physical needs can people think of their psychological needs.

Psychologist Abraham Maslow identified priorities for human needs (Figure 1.2). According to Maslow, as an individual meets each type of need, he or she progresses up the ***hierarchy*** (a classification or ranking in order) to the next level of need. At the foundation of the hierarchy are the basic physical needs which are important to meet first. When these are satisfied, only then can people think about such other needs as security, love, esteem, and self-actualization.

Physical Needs

Physical needs are the most basic human needs. Because they are essential for survival, physical needs have priority over other needs. Physical needs include shelter, food, water, and rest. Basic or primary needs are other words for physical needs.

Shelter

The need for shelter and protection from the weather has always been met by a dwelling of some type. The findings of archaeologists show this is true. ***Archaeologists*** are social scientists who study ancient cultures by unearthing dwelling places of past civilizations. Their findings reveal how ancient structures were made and used, and how they met the human need for shelter.

Such natural settings as caves and overhanging cliffs are examples of the earliest dwellings (Figure 1.3A and Figure 1.3B). Later, people built crude dwellings from readily available materials. The Pueblo Native Americans used **adobe**, which is a building material consisting of sun-dried earth and straw. They also used rafters made from native materials. The thick walls and flat roofs (Figure 1.3C) provided shelter from the hot climate. Apache Native Americans built houses from tree branches (Figure 1.3D). Cooling breezes circulating through the branches and protection from the scorching sun are key features of Apache homes.

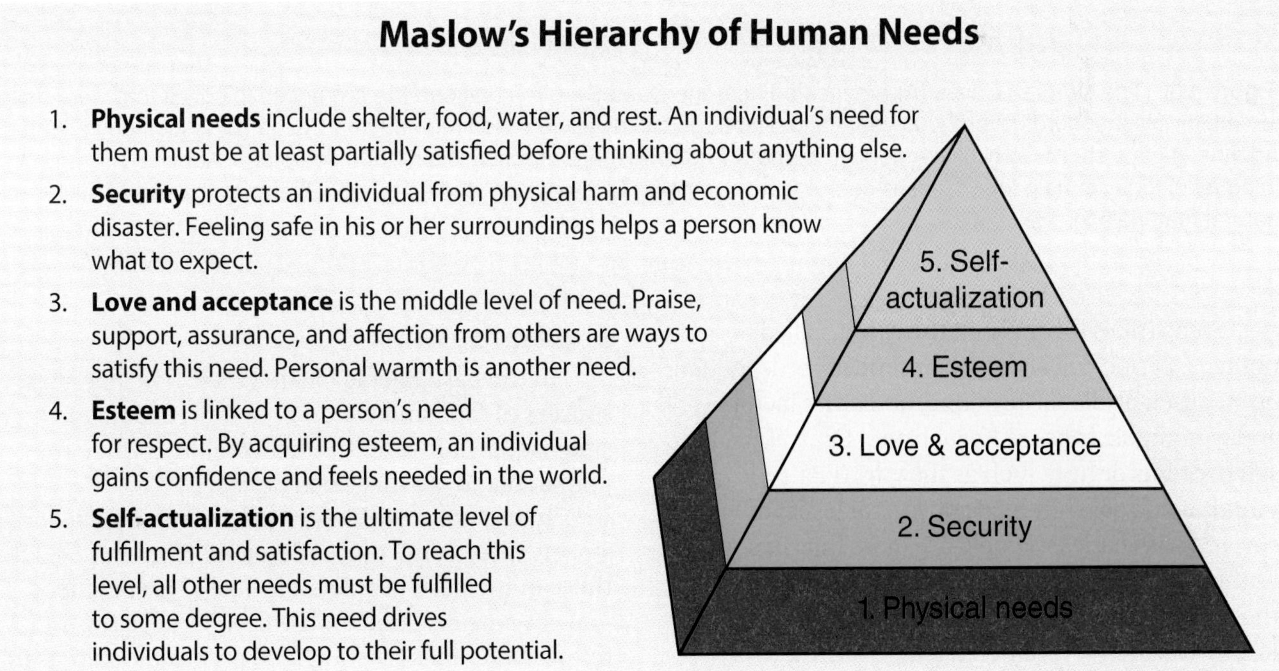

Maslow's Hierarchy of Human Needs
1. Physical needs include shelter, food, water, and rest. An individual's need for them must be at least partially satisfied before thinking about anything else.
2. Security protects an individual from physical harm and economic disaster. Feeling safe in his or her surroundings helps a person know what to expect.
3. Love and acceptance is the middle level of need. Praise, support, assurance, and affection from others are ways to satisfy this need. Personal warmth is another need.
4. Esteem is linked to a person's need for respect. By acquiring esteem, an individual gains confidence and feels needed in the world.
5. Self-actualization is the ultimate level of fulfillment and satisfaction. To reach this level, all other needs must be fulfilled to some degree. This need drives individuals to develop to their full potential.
5. Self-actualization
4. Esteem
3. Love & acceptance
2. Security
1. Physical needs
Goodheart-Willcox Publisher

Figure 1.2 Physical needs are the most basic needs and, therefore, the first step in Maslow's Hierarchy.

A Dejan Gileski/Shutterstock.com B Zack Frank/Shutterstock.com C Tutti Frutti/Shutterstock.com D Maria Dryfhout/Shutterstock.com

Figure 1.3 The Qumran Caves (A) are located near the Dead Sea. You can see the entrances to caves that were used for shelter by shepherds over 2,000 years ago. The large cliff dwelling called Montezuma Castle (B) is located in central Arizona. It gave shelter to Native American farmers who lived there probably over 1,000 years ago. Adobe (C) is still used in housing today to help keep houses cool in warm climates. The American Indian tepee (D) shows the use of sticks and natural materials for the structure.

Some tribes throughout the world, called nomads, periodically move their residences depending on weather, available farmland, and other factors. Today nomadic tribes in Kazakhstan, Central Asia, still use tents or huts such as the yurt (Figure 1.4). A **yurt** is a portable hut made of several layers of felt covered with canvas. People use these huts in summer as they move to more fertile growing areas. In winter, the occupants live in permanent huts with thick walls to stay warm in severely cold temperatures, which stay below 0°F for long periods.

Food and Water

In the past, people located their housing near sources of food and water. They stored food and a small supply of water in their dwellings while they prepared and ate their food outside.

Today, areas within dwellings are set aside for storing, preparing, and eating food (Figure 1.5). Like those in the past, people today like to prepare food and eat outside. Some house designs keep this in mind, sometimes locating food preparation areas in enclosed patios to make outside eating easier.

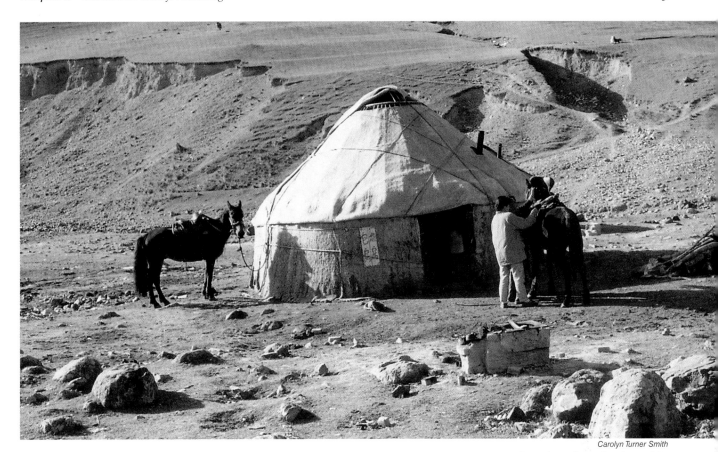

Carolyn Turner Smith

Figure 1.4 A yurt is a portable hut made of several layers of felt covered with canvas. It can be taken down in about 20 minutes and folded to fit on the back of a camel or horse.

Photography Courtesy of Bosch Home Appliances

Figure 1.5 Today's modern kitchen has developed from a simple area for stockpiling food and water to a comfortable room for storing and preparing food and eating meals.

Rest

A basic human need is *rest*—a period of inactivity that allows recovery and growth. Rest can take the form of sleep or relaxing. Rest helps people overcome fatigue and restore energy to the body. The amount of sleep each person needs varies, but most adults sleep seven and one-half to eight hours at night. Rest and relaxation are as important as sleep. After strenuous work, complete rest may be necessary. At other times, people need relaxation or a change of pace. Any activity different from the usual routine can be relaxing. Pleasurable and relaxing activities help a person shed tension and remain robust.

Areas within dwellings are designated for sleep, generally the bedrooms. These areas or others can also provide space for relaxation. Shared common areas, such as family rooms, offer space for group relaxation. Hobby areas and other rooms promote individual relaxation.

Psychological Needs

Once basic physical needs are met, people strive to meet the psychological needs. These needs are higher on Maslow's hierarchy of human needs. ***Psychological needs*** relate to the mind and feelings that people must meet to live a satisfying life.

Security

Housing provides security from the outside world. It offers protection from physical danger and the unknown and helps people feel safe and protected. Living in a dwelling that is well built and located in an area free from crime can help people feel secure.

Love and Acceptance

Housing affects an individual's feelings of love and acceptance. For instance, if you have your own bedroom or private place, you know others care about you and accept you as a person who has needs. When you receive task assignments, it is because of your acceptance as part of a group—and you have responsibilities to fulfill as part of that group.

Esteem

People need to feel ***esteem***, or the respect, admiration, and high regard of others. A person's housing tells other people something about him or her and can help an individual gain esteem. A home that is clean, neat, and attractive will gain the approval and respect of others.

Self-esteem is another need. ***Self-esteem*** is awareness and appreciation of worth. When people have healthy self-esteem, they think well of themselves and are satisfied with their roles and skills (Figure 1.6). Living in a pleasant, satisfying home can help an individual to gain self-esteem.

Self-Actualization

Meeting the need for ***self-actualization*** indicates an individual is developing into his or her full potential as a person and doing what he or she does best. Think about your own efforts in striving toward self-actualization. If your talent is sports, you will be trying to increase your strength, stamina, and athletic skills. If your talent is building furniture, each piece will be of higher quality than the previous one.

For self-actualizing people, housing is more than a place to live. It is the place where each person can progress toward becoming all that he or she is capable of being. Striving toward self-actualization is often a lifelong process.

Other Needs Met Through Housing

Recognizing the levels of human needs as described by Maslow can help you understand how important needs are in relation to housing. Beauty, self-expression, and creativity are also important needs. You can achieve these needs through your housing decisions.

Beauty

Beauty is the quality or qualities that give pleasure to the senses. Your concept of beauty

Fotokostic/Shutterstock.com

Figure 1.6 Ability to maintain a home and its furnishings contributes to a feeling of self-esteem.

is unique. What is beautiful to you may not be beautiful to someone else. In fact, the same objects may not appear beautiful to you as you mature. An appreciation of beauty develops over time as exposure to it increases. Beautiful surroundings, such as those in Figure 1.7, can make you feel content and relaxed. This is important to keep in mind as you think about a possible career as a housing or interior design professional.

Christina Richards/Shutterstock.com

Figure 1.7 Beauty in a room can help you feel happy, content, and peaceful.

Self-Expression

Showing your true personality and taste is self-expression. ***Self-expression*** is evident when choosing a color palette for the design of your home or the home of a client. Those colors are often a clue to an individual's personality. For instance, someone with an outgoing, vibrant personality might show it by using bright, bold colors inside his or her home (Figure 1.8). In contrast, a person with a quiet, subdued personality might show it by using pale, soft colors. Furnishings can also help express personality.

Creativity

Creativity is the ability to use imaginative skill to make something new. Combining two or more things or ideas into a new whole that has beauty or value is another way to describe creativity. You show creativity when you express your ideas to others.

Your housing provides opportunities for you to express your creativity. Primitive people exhibited creativity when they painted pictures on the walls of their cave dwellings. Today, people still use painting to express their creativity. Likewise, some people enjoy gardening and working with flowers. They express their creativity by designing beautiful

J. Banks Design Group

Figure 1.8 What does the use of bright, bold colors tell you about the personalities of the people who live here?

Simone van den Berg/Shutterstock.com

Figure 1.9 This woman, who enjoys gardening, created this space to arrange fresh-cut flowers and repot plants.

gardens or making floral arrangements to display around the house (Figure 1.9). Creative people look to many sources of inspiration, including nature, music, books, and other creative people.

Review & Assessment

1. What is housing?
2. Distinguish between the near environment and total environment.
3. Identify three physical needs people have.
4. What are four psychological needs that people have?
5. Given the chance, how would you change your housing to better meet your need for self-actualization?
6. Give an example of how housing can help you meet each of the following needs: (A) self-expression; (B) creativity.

Factors Affecting Housing Choices

There are many factors that influence choices in housing. These include values, family relationships, space needs, costs, roles, and lifestyle.

Values

Values are strong beliefs or ideas about what is important. They can be views, events, people, places, or objects you prize highly. When you choose something freely and take action on that choice, you are acting on a value. This gives meaning to your life and enhances your growth.

All the values you hold—such as family, friendship, money, status, religion, and independence—form your value system. Your value system is different from anyone else's. You form your value system as a result of experiences you have. The people you know and the activities in which you participate all influence your value system.

Whenever you decide between two or more choices, you use your value system. The choice you make depends on which items you desire most. Suppose you have a choice between sharing an apartment with a friend and living alone. If money is not an issue, your decision depends on how highly you value privacy versus interactions with others.

If you share a home with others, you will find that some of your values differ from theirs. The values that household members have in common will control the thinking and actions of the group. Shared values influence your housing decisions.

How Needs and Values Relate

Your needs and values are closely related. For example, you need a place to sleep. A cot can satisfy this need. However, the cot may not meet your value for comfort. If you have a choice, your value for comfort may cause you to choose a bed with a mattress instead of the cot.

You may also need space in your bedroom for activities other than sleeping. Your values determine whether you choose a large or small bed for the room. While the large bed may provide more comfort, the smaller bed will use less floor space. Some people may want to devote a corner of a bedroom to a play area, desk, or exercise equipment (Figure 1.10).

Space

People have spatial needs. While too much space can make people feel lonely, they need a certain amount of space around them to avoid feeling crowded. They create invisible boundaries around themselves. Others can sense those boundaries and, therefore, know whether they have permission to enter.

Hobbies and activities can influence the need for space. For example, people who like to garden need space for a garden. People who enjoy spending time with friends need space for entertaining.

The way people use space also influences the amount they need. In places where you cannot add or remove space, the right furnishings can make the space seem larger or smaller. For example, reducing the number of furniture pieces in a crowded room can make it more spacious and airy. Likewise, by adding furniture a large room can become warm and cozy.

Photo Courtesy of JELD-WEN Windows and Doors

Figure 1.10 This bed allows part of the room to be used for other activities.

Privacy

People need privacy to maintain good mental health. Sometimes they need to be completely alone, where others cannot see or hear what they are doing. Sometimes, too, they want to avoid seeing and hearing what others are doing. They may want to think, daydream, create, read, or study without being disturbed (Figure 1.11).

Since the need for privacy varies among people, it can be satisfied in a number of ways. One of the most extreme ways is to live alone in a dwelling that is set apart from other dwellings. Another way is to have a private room or some other private place where people can enter only when invited.

Some people may not have the opportunity to live alone or have their own private place. However, they can still meet their need for privacy. Doing a task alone—such as mowing the lawn or driving a car—provides some privacy. A chair that is set apart from other furnishings in a room can create a sense of privacy. Also, solitary activities that require concentration, such as woodworking or piano playing, can free people from interacting with others. Even the sound of a TV or music playing gives some degree of privacy. It isolates a person from sounds made by others.

Family and Group Relationships

If people believe the well-being of their family and other people in the household are important, they consider this factor when making housing

Monkey Business Images/Shutterstock.com

Figure 1.11 This area provides privacy for a teen to work on the computer.

decisions. Families and households that value such relationships make decisions to benefit all members, not just some. A **family** is two or more people living together who are related by birth, marriage, or adoption. A household consists of all persons living together in one dwelling.

When concern for family and group relationships is an important value, several areas of the house can be designed for group living. For example, a great room is useful for family or group activities. A large, eat-in kitchen may be desirable so members can cook and eat together, as in Figure 1.12. An outside area may offer space for group recreation.

Costs

For most people, the cost of housing is an important factor in making housing decisions. Whether people rent or buy housing, it costs money. Additional expenses include the furnishings and equipment that go into a dwelling plus the bills for repair and maintenance. Utilities, such as electricity, gas, and water, also cost money.

When money is very limited, people choose dwellings that provide just enough space for their needs. They buy only the furnishings and equipment they can afford. They save money by conserving energy, as in turning off lights in empty rooms and setting thermostats at moderate temperatures. People can also maintain their homes well since maintenance bills nearly always cost less than repair and replacement costs. These owners do their own home repairs whenever possible.

Roles

Roles are patterns of behavior that people display in their homes, the workplace, and their communities. Usually each person has more than one role. An adult female, for example, may have the roles of a wife, mother, teacher, and hospital volunteer. An adult male may be a husband, father, grandfather, carpenter, and neighborhood soccer coach. You currently balance the roles of a student and son (or daughter). Perhaps you are also a brother (or sister) and even a part-time worker.

The roles people have can affect the type of housing they choose and how the housing is used. To fulfill the role of student, a home needs a quiet area for studying. If young children live in a home, they need space to play with toys and each other. People involved in sports and hobbies need room for their supplies and equipment.

Volt Collection/Shutterstock.com

Figure 1.12 An eating area next to the food preparation center allows family members to spend more time together.

Iriana Shiyan/Shutterstock.com

Figure 1.13 A home office is a common feature of many residences since greater numbers of people are working from their homes.

The role of a wage earner can also impact housing choices. A lawyer may work from home, needing an office for working with a seating area for greeting clients. A professional tailor needs space for storing supplies, cutting fabric, and sewing garments, as well as space for clients trying on and modeling their finished clothing. People whose work involves entertaining at home have other requirements to address before the housing meets their needs. Ideally, housing should meet the needs of all its members in all their roles (Figure 1.13).

Lifestyle

A **lifestyle** is a living pattern or way of life. Together, all the various roles of the occupants make up the lifestyle of a residence. How you live influences the type of housing you choose to enhance your way of life.

When thinking of lifestyles and their influences on housing choices, consider everyday activities in the home. The following questions can help identify activities related to lifestyle:

- Are members involved with hobbies that need space, such as furniture refinishing or indoor gardening?
- What type of entertaining, if any, occurs in the home—both inside and outside?
- Do any adults work from home and need a high-tech office?
- Are the occupants retired, traveling frequently, and not spending much time at home?

The answers to these and other related lifestyle questions determine the type of housing selected. For example, people who love the outdoors seek housing with a view of nature or a private patio or garden. Those who spend little time at home often prefer a maintenance-free residence close to major thoroughfares so they can travel quickly to their various commitments. Retirees may choose a retirement community with a convenient central dining room plus on-site recreation and grooming services (Figure 1.14).

Income also influences lifestyle. Higher incomes allow people to spend more money on their homes. Consider the example of those who enjoy swimming. They can use a local recreation center to enjoy their favorite form of exercise, but if they can afford it, many install a pool at home. Depending on their income, installation of a new pool may be

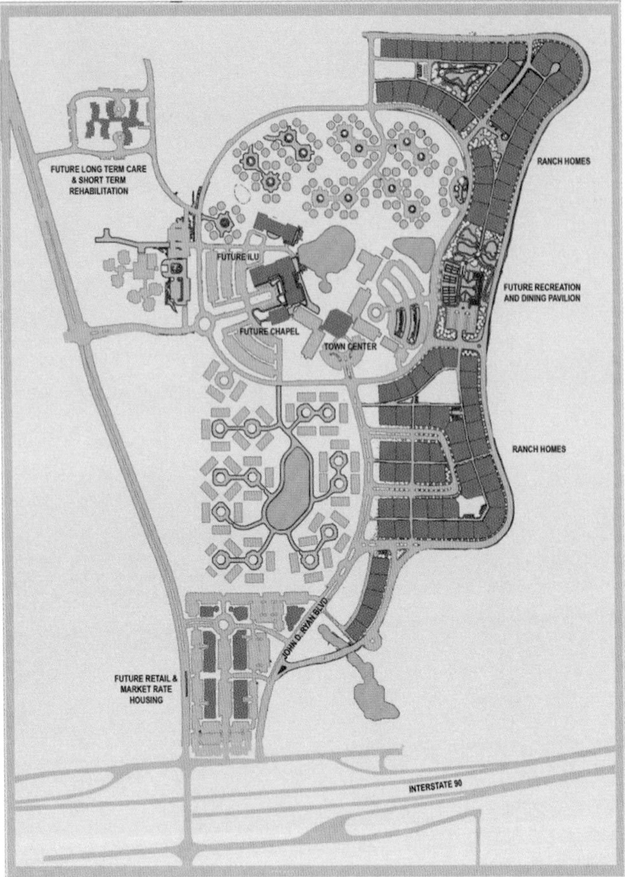

Courtesy of Perkins Eastman

Figure 1.14 This retirement center shows the multi-levels of living for senior citizens. The drawing was used for long-term strategic planning at Blue Skies of Texas West in San Antonio, Texas (formerly known as Air Force Village II).

aboveground, in-ground, or perhaps inside as part of a new wing built onto the home. Income greatly affects the degree to which people add comforts and conveniences to a home to address their lifestyles.

Review & Assessment

1. How does a person form his or her value system?
2. Describe five ways to achieve privacy.
3. How do space and privacy relate?

Housing Needs Through the Life Span

On almost a daily basis, you can be sure of change. Life situations cause change and affect the way you live. They relate to every aspect of your life, and the way you interact with other people and with your housing.

In group housing, people are generally not relatives. Retirement complexes and college residence halls, Figure 1.15, are some common examples. The occupants live in separate units within the group dwelling. In contrast, people in residential dwellings are often relatives.

James R. Martin/Shutterstock.com

Figure 1.15 A residence hall offers group housing to students pursuing an education.

Households

The most common residential dwelling is a household. A **household** includes one or more people who occupy a dwelling, both family and nonfamily members. The household size can vary, but most households contain families. The following describes the five basic family structures:

- **Nuclear family.** This family includes couples and their children. The children are either born into the family or adopted. None of the children are from a previous marriage.
- **Single-parent family.** These families consist of a child (or children) and only one parent, often because a parent has died or left home. Other single-parent families consist of a never-married adult with one or more children.
- **Stepfamily.** This family consists of parents, one or both of whom have been married before. The family also includes one or more children from a previous marriage.
- **Childless family.** These families consist of a couple who has not had children. For some couples this is a temporary condition, delaying the arrival of children until their finances improve. For others, the couple is unable to have children or chooses to remain childless, for whatever reason.
- **Extended family.** There are two basic types of extended families, which form by adding one or more relatives to a household already identified. One type

consists of several generations of a family, such as children, parents, and grandparents. Variations can include aunts, uncles, or cousins as well as their children. A second type of extended family consists of members from the same generation, such as brothers, sisters, and cousins.

The smallest household is a single-person household, which consists of one person living alone in a dwelling. That person may be someone who has never married or whose marriage has ended because of the loss of a spouse through death, desertion, or divorce.

Throughout this text, you will see how an individual's household affects housing decisions. In turn, you will also learn how the decisions you make concerning housing affect your household and possibly the households of clients.

Life Cycles

Life cycles are another way to view your housing needs. A **life cycle** is a series of stages through which an individual or family passes during its lifetime. In each stage, there are new opportunities and new challenges to face. You develop new needs and values and prioritize them according to what is most important to you. These changes relate to your housing.

Individual Life Cycle

Each person follows a pattern of development, or an individual life cycle. It is divided according to age groups into the following four stages with each stage divided into substages:

- **Infancy.** The two substages of infancy include *newborn* (birth to one month old) and *infant* (one month to one year old).
- **Childhood.** The childhood stage has three substages: *early* (one to six years old), *middle* (six to eight years old), and *late* childhood (nine to 12 years old).
- **Youth.** The youth stage has four substages including preteen, early teen, middle teen, and late teen.
- **Adulthood.** Young, mature, and aging adult are the substages of adulthood.

Family Life Cycle

Just as you have a place in an individual life cycle, your family has its place in the family life cycle. A family life cycle has six stages (Figure 1.16). One or more substages may exist within each stage.

- **Beginning stage.** This is the early period of a marriage when a couple is without children (Figure 1.17). The husband and wife make adjustments to married life and to each other.
- **Childbearing stage.** This is the time when a family is growing. It includes the childbearing periods and the years of caring for preschoolers. Depending on the household lifestyle and working arrangements, the family may need child care. If so, the design of the early childhood environment should meet the developmental needs of the child.

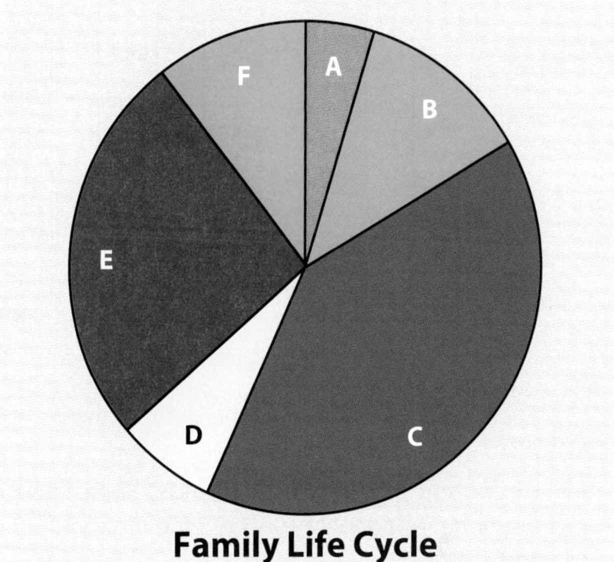

Family Life Cycle

A. **Beginning stage:** Married couple without children
B. **Childbearing stage:** Couple with child(ren) up to 2½ years old; couple with child(ren) 2½ to 6 years old
C. **Parenting stage:** Couple with child(ren) 6 to 13 years old
D. **Launching stage:** Couple with child(ren) leaving home; couple with child(ren) living away from home
E. **Midyears stage:** Couple before retirement, but after all children left home.
F. **Aging stage:** Couple during retirement until death of both spouses

Goodheart-Willcox Publisher

Figure 1.16 The family life cycle includes both stages and substages.

Petinov Sergey Mihilovich/Shutterstock.com

Figure 1.17 These newlyweds are entering the beginning stage of their own family's life cycle.

Sociocultural Connections The Changing American Household

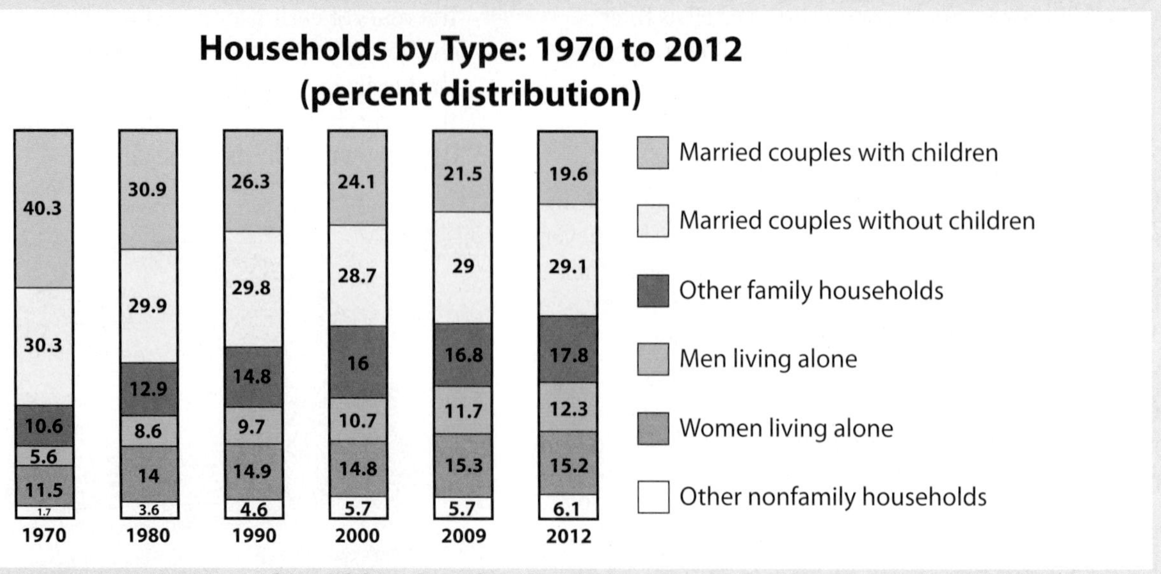

Source: U.S. Census Bureau, Current Population Survey, Annual Social and Economic Supplements, selected years 1970 to 2012.

According to the U.S. Census Bureau, the composition of U.S. households changed between 1970 and 2012. The most significant changes include

- **Reduction of family households.** Family households—two or more members related by birth, marriage, or adoption—accounted for about 66 percent of households instead of 81 percent.
- **Reduction of married-couple households.** The share of married-couple-with-children households decreased from 40 percent to 20 percent of households. Additionally, in 1970 married couples with children outnumbered married couples without children. By 2012, the reverse was true.
- **Increase in nonfamily households.** The proportion of nonfamily households—mostly people who live alone—increased 10 percentage points between 1970 and 2012.

The Census Bureau cites many reasons for these changes. For example, the roles of men and women have changed. More women are working and living on their own. People are marrying and having children later or not at all. Also, people are living longer due to technological innovations. The baby-boom generation—those born between 1946 and 1964, who make up more than 25 percent of the adult population—is moving into retirement.

Changes in the composition of U.S. households bring changes in the housing market. For example, after their children grow up and leave home, many baby boomers choose to downsize into smaller dwellings. Older adults generally prefer single-level homes or buildings with elevators since climbing stairs can be difficult.

Dig Deeper

Use online or print resources to investigate ways that households have changed in your community in the last 25 years. How have these changes influenced the type of housing available in your community? Discuss your findings with the class.

- **Parenting stage.** During this stage, the children are in school. This stage includes the years of caring for school-age children and teens.
- **Launching stage.** Children become adults and leave their parents' homes during this time. They may leave to go to college, take a job, or get married.
- **Midyears stage.** During this time span, the children leave home and the parents retire. When all the children leave home, the couple is again alone.
- **Aging stage.** This stage begins with retirement. Usually, at some point in this stage, one spouse lives alone after the death of the other. As people live longer, the length of this stage increases.

In some cases, the family fits the description of two life-cycle stages. For example, when a family has both a preschool child and a school-age child, the family is in overlapping stages. Other families may have gaps between the stages or substages. An example is a family in which the mother is pregnant and the children are teens.

Life Cycles and Housing Needs

As you move from one stage or substage of a life cycle to another, your housing needs change. When planning housing, consider what stage or substage of the life cycles you are in. If you think about both your present and future needs, your housing can help you live the kind of life you desire.

One example of a need that changes as a person moves through the life cycles is the need for space. During infancy, a baby takes no more space than a small crib. As that baby grows, he or she needs more sleeping space. From the childhood stage through the youth stage, children often sleep in twin or bunk beds (Figure 1.18). As adults, people prefer more spacious beds that provide greater comfort.

Phase4Studios/Shutterstock.com

Figure 1.18 When a child outgrows a crib, he or she may sleep in a bunk bed. This also provides space for playmates to spend the night.

The need for space also changes throughout a family's life cycle. In the beginning stage, a young married couple may not need very much space. Once they enter the childbearing stage, however, their space needs increase. During this stage, the number, ages, genders, and activities of their children will affect their space needs.

With the addition of new members, families require more space. As each member grows, he or she requires even more space. Teens need space for studying and entertaining friends. They also need space to store sports equipment, computer equipment, clothes, and personal belongings.

When family members leave home during the launching stage, they take many of their belongings with them. This leaves more space for the rest of the family. After launching all the children, parents enter the midyears stage and may feel they have too much space. At this time, some couples desire a change of scenery. They may want a smaller home that presents fewer demands.

STEM Math Fraction/Decimal Conversions

How many members of your class are female? male? These questions are asking for proportion, which is the relation of one part to the whole. Proportion is often expressed in fractions.

If 21 out of 28 students in your class are girls, you can represent that with the fraction $^{21}/_{28}$. You can convert fractions to decimal numbers by dividing the fraction's *numerator* (top number) by the *denominator* (bottom number).

Ex: $^{21}/_{28} = 0.75$

You can convert a decimal number to a fraction. The fraction's numerator is simply the decimal number minus the decimal point. The fraction's denominator is the place value of the right-most number.

Ex: $0.75 = {}^{75}/_{100}$

Math Practice

1. Practice expressing proportion as fractions. Count the number of students in your class. How many students in your class are males? Write this number as a fraction. Then convert the fraction to decimal numbers by dividing the numerator by the denominator.
2. Use a separate sheet of paper to convert the following fractions to a decimal:

A. $\frac{3}{5}$

B. $\frac{7}{8}$

C. $\frac{9}{8}$

Other couples, however, prefer to stay in their present homes. They may not want to leave behind the memories linked to their family's home. They may also want to have plenty of room when their children and grandchildren come to visit.

Review & Assessment

1. Provide an example of an extended family that is not a stepfamily.
2. List the four stages of the individual life cycle.
3. Give an example of the way housing needs change as a family moves from one stage of the life cycle to another.
4. Explain how a couple in the beginning stage of the family life cycle differs from a couple in the aging stage.

Housing and Quality of Life

Quality of life is the degree of satisfaction a person obtains from life. Housing is *good* when it provides people with satisfying surroundings that can improve their quality of life.

Personal Quality of Life

Quality of life is important to you as an individual. Just as you are unique, your concept of the quality of life is unique. Your idea of an improved quality of life may not appeal to someone else. Your housing environment helps you meet your needs and values. It also adds satisfaction to your life and, therefore, improves the quality of your life.

Quality of life is also important to the other members of your household. Your household, whether it is your family or some other group, is one part of your life situation. The members play a part in shaping your attitudes and values. In turn, the combined needs and values of the members determine the type of housing environment in which you live (Figure 1.19). If all the members show concern about the well-being of the group as a whole, this action enhances the quality of life for everyone.

Group 3, Architectural and Interior Design, Hilton Head Island, South Carolina. Photography courtesy of John McManus, Savannah, Georgia.

Figure 1.19 The values of the people who live in this home are obvious in the furnishings used in this room.

Green Choices

What Does "Green" Mean?

"Green" refers to making choices about various aspects of housing and interiors that are environmentally friendly. This means making choices to incorporate sound environmental principles of building, materials, and energy use. The basic intent of green choices is to have low negative-environmental impact on air quality, soil quality, or use of natural resources. Environmentally friendly choices include

- using less water
- using less energy
- using nontoxic materials and substances
- choosing materials that can be recycled or have been recycled
- recycling and reusing items

These choices range from such small items as cleaning supplies to all aspects of buildings. Specifically, *green* choices affect consumers and the fields of architecture, landscape architecture, urban design, urban planning, engineering, graphic design, industrial design, and interior design.

Many terms are used when referring to green choices including: environmentally friendly, green design, eco-design, design for the environment, eco-friendly, and sustainable design.

(NOTE: Throughout this text, *Green Choices* features offer ideas and ways to incorporate green concepts for housing consumers and people in the housing and interior design professions.)

Quality of Life for Society

The future of a society depends on individuals and groups who work to make life better for everyone. Some of the work is social in nature, which means groups of people must cooperate to reach a common goal. This goal is to improve the quality of life for society. All people cannot make equal contributions toward any given goal. One example is the plight of people who are homeless. They do not have the resources to secure housing for themselves. In such cases, groups of people work together to make housing available for people without homes.

People must also work together and use their resources of time, money, and energy to maintain and support beautiful surroundings. Examples of such surroundings are well-kept buildings and natural landscapes. These surroundings satisfy the needs and desires of many people in society.

Review & Assessment

1. How does housing help individuals and society meet quality-of-life needs?
2. How can you and others you know make a difference in the quality of life for people who are homeless?

Career Focus Interior Designer—Early Childhood Facilities

Can you imagine a career as an interior designer of early childhood development facilities? If you can, read more about the following details.

Interests/Skills: If you share some of following interests and skills, you may want to consider becoming an interior designer who specializes in designing early childhood development centers. Do your interests include an enjoyment of artistic and creative projects? Do you feel design takes a major role in children's growth and development? In addition, do environments for children interest you? Are your communication skills strong—especially with listening, writing, and speaking? Do you pay attention to details and have a strong background in art? Planning and organizing are essential skills for completing a project.

Career Snapshot: Along with researching and understanding the special needs of the children and adults who use the space, interior designers in this field also need additional training in working with civic contract projects. Designers work closely with a center's director. Together they make sure that all building and interior codes and all classroom needs are met when making design decisions for the project. For example, napping, teaching, circulation, and storage spaces need to fit together and meet certain health and safety standards. Creating a play area where children come to learn and interact requires attention to the details.

Education/Training: Completion of a bachelor's degree is preferred. To specialize in designing spaces for early childhood development, take additional courses in childhood development and psychology.

©2007 Image by Warren Lieb/LS3P Associated, LTD. Children's Center at Carolina Park, Mount Pleasant, South Carolina

Licensing/Examinations: Approximately one-half of the states require interior designers to be licensed. The *Council for Interior Design Qualification (CIDQ)* administers an examination that interior designers must pass to obtain a license and be competitive in their careers.

Professional Associations: The American Society of Interior Designers (ASID); International Interior Design Association (IIDA)

Job Outlook: As long as the population keeps growing, there will be a need for early childhood development centers. Designers who pave a career path to specialize in this particular field will thrive.

Sources: The Occupational Outlook Handbook; the Occupational Information Network (O*NET)

Chapter 1 Assessment

Summary

- People interact with their housing. Their housing affects them, and they affect their housing.
- Housing helps satisfy people's physical and psychological needs and can help them move toward self-actualization.
- Beauty, self-expression, and creativity are other needs people meet through housing.
- Each person's housing reflects the lifestyle he or she has chosen.
- Needs and values are closely related. The needs and values of people and living units vary, however, as they move through the life cycles.
- Housing affects and helps improve the quality of life for both individuals and society.

Terms in Action

1. **Term flash cards** Work in teams to locate small images that visually represent each of the *Content Terms* at the beginning of the chapter. Print the images. To create flash cards, write each term on a note card and paste the image that describes or explains the term on the opposite side. Use the flash cards to review the terms.

Think Critically

2. **Analyze impact** Suppose some family members must manage multiple roles such as parent and worker. Analyze the changes that might need to be made to the interior of a home to meet the needs of a member who works from home.
3. **Assess needs** What needs and values are met by housing? Make a personal assessment and list your needs and values in order of priority. In contrast, if you were to work with a housing or interiors client, what questions might you ask to help your client assess needs and values met by housing?
4. **Analyze space** Analyze and describe how the use of a spare bedroom may change depending on whether the living unit includes the following: small children, teens, people with hobbies, a person working at home, or retirees.
5. **Analyze behavior** In teams, brainstorm actions or behaviors that may be useful for enhancing creativity for interior designers. Discuss your team's ideas with the class.

Core Skills

6. **Writing** Identify 10 households in your community that you know well. (Note: Keep family names private.) For each, identify the type of household it is. Also, write a one-sentence description of each member, identifying gender, approximate age, and relationship to the family.
7. **Writing** Consider your household members and examine your home's interior space. In the last five years, has the size of your household changed? If so, how? Did the change result in more or less space per person? In comparison, do you have more or less personal privacy today than five years ago? Forecast your household's need for space five years from now. What possible changes in the household may occur in the next five years that will increase the amount of space per person? that will decrease the space per person? Write a brief summary of your forecast.
8. **Speaking and listening** Interview an older adult and ask him or her to describe changes in his or her housing over the years. Ask how the person's lifestyle and housing impact each other. Is ability to age-in-place important to this older adult? Why? If possible, ask the older adult's permission to audio-record the interview and share it with the class.
9. **Research and writing** Are there homeless people in your community? Investigate what the town (city) and local charitable organizations are doing to handle this problem. What actions do these organizations take to prevent it? Summarize your findings in a one-page report.
10. **Writing** In your own words, write a brief summary of the chapter content in 15 sentences or less. Save your summary for future reference.
11. **Speaking** Imagine a full day in the life of a homeless person. Look for a website that tries to convey that experience and examine the information it provides. What facts about homelessness surprise you? How many

children and youth are homeless? How does homelessness affect their learning? Look for facts about homeless youth and make a printout of a fact that surprised you. What options exist for preventing homelessness or meeting the needs of homeless people? Give an illustrated oral report to the class of your findings.

12. **Research and speaking** Use reliable online resources to research cliff dwellings. Determine who built them and why they were built. Find out how many different sites containing cliff dwellings exist in Colorado. How many households do these cliff villages contain? Why did the people build their homes in the cliffs? Discuss your findings in class.
13. **CTE career readiness practice** Use a digital camera to photograph examples of housing in your community that address a household's psychological needs. Take separate pictures to demonstrate examples of housing that meet the following four needs: *security, love/acceptance, esteem,* and *self-actualization*. Use presentation software or a school-approved web application to display your examples for the class. Describe why the housing example in each picture meets a particular need.

Design Practice

14. **Design for privacy** Obtain permission to rearrange furniture in a part of your home, or the home of someone else you know, to provide more privacy. How did the new furniture arrangement lead to more privacy? How did household members react to the change? Report your actions and results to the class.
15. **Portfolio** When you apply for a job or perhaps to a college, you may need to describe your qualifications to others. A portfolio is a selection of related materials that you collect and organize. These materials show your qualifications, skills, and talents. There are two common types of portfolios: print and electronic portfolios (e-portfolios). An e-portfolio is also known as a digital portfolio. To learn more about portfolios, do the following:
    A. Use the Internet to search for *print portfolio* and *e-portfolio*. Read two or more articles about each type of portfolio. Then complete an article summary. In your own words briefly describe each type.
    B. You will be creating a portfolio for this class. Which portfolio type would you prefer to create? Write a paragraph describing the type of portfolio you prefer.
16. **Portfolio** Building a quality portfolio about your design experience is essential to having a successful career in housing and interior design. Along with the design examples you will create throughout this course, you will also need to include writing samples that showcase your ability to communicate well in writing. In one page or less, write a *goal statement* about your future career as an interior designer. Why do you want to pursue this career? What aspects of this career ignite your passion for housing and interior design? Use word-processing software to create your goal statement. Save a copy of the document for your electronic and paper portfolios.
17. **Portfolio** Create a storyboard that reflects housing appropriate for a family progressing through the six stages of the family life cycle. Use online photos or images, magazines, or other sources to show the stages. Be sure to cite the sources of your images. Assume the following details about the family:
    - *Beginning*—couple lives on one partner's earnings while the earnings of the other go toward savings and paying college loans
    - *Childbearing*—the family has one full-time wage earner working outside the home, one part-time wage earner working from the home, and two children under age four
    - *Parenting*—the family has saved enough for a down payment on a moderately priced home, the part-time wage earner now works full-time outside the home, and all members are active in sports
    - *Midyears*—couple frequently entertains children and grandchildren on weekends and travels as much as possible
    - *Aging*—one partner lives alone after the death of another

Chapter 2

Factors Influencing Housing

Content Terms

density
row houses
tenement houses
architect
substandard
tract houses
subdivision
planned development
new town
planned community
new urbanism
urban sprawl
pocket development
culture
hogan
baby boomers
dual-career family
teleworking
telecommuting
computer-aided drafting and design (CADD)
three-dimensional printing (3-D)
building codes
zoning regulation
infrastructure

Academic Terms

agrarian
census
demographics
median
gross domestic product (GDP)
Industrial Revolution

Learning Outcomes

After studying this chapter, you will be able to

- relate historical events to housing.
- summarize housing characteristics common to various cultures and regions.
- determine the relationship between societal changes and housing.
- analyze aspects of community planning that impact housing decisions.
- analyze concerns about environmental aspects of housing.
- compare and contrast the impacts of economy and housing on each other, including the relationship of family housing and economics.
- research and describe the effects of technology on current and future housing trends.
- summarize the role of government in housing decisions.

Reading with Purpose

Predict what you think will be covered in this chapter. Make a list of your predictions. After reading the chapter, decide if your predictions were correct. If they were not correct, explain why.

While studying, look for the access icon  **to:**

- **Practice** the *Content* and *Academic Terms* with e-flash cards, matching activities, and vocabulary games.
- **Reinforce** what you learn by completing the *Review & Assessment* questions and e-mailing them to your instructor.

www.g-wlearning.com/housing/

Joseph Sohm/Shutterstock.com

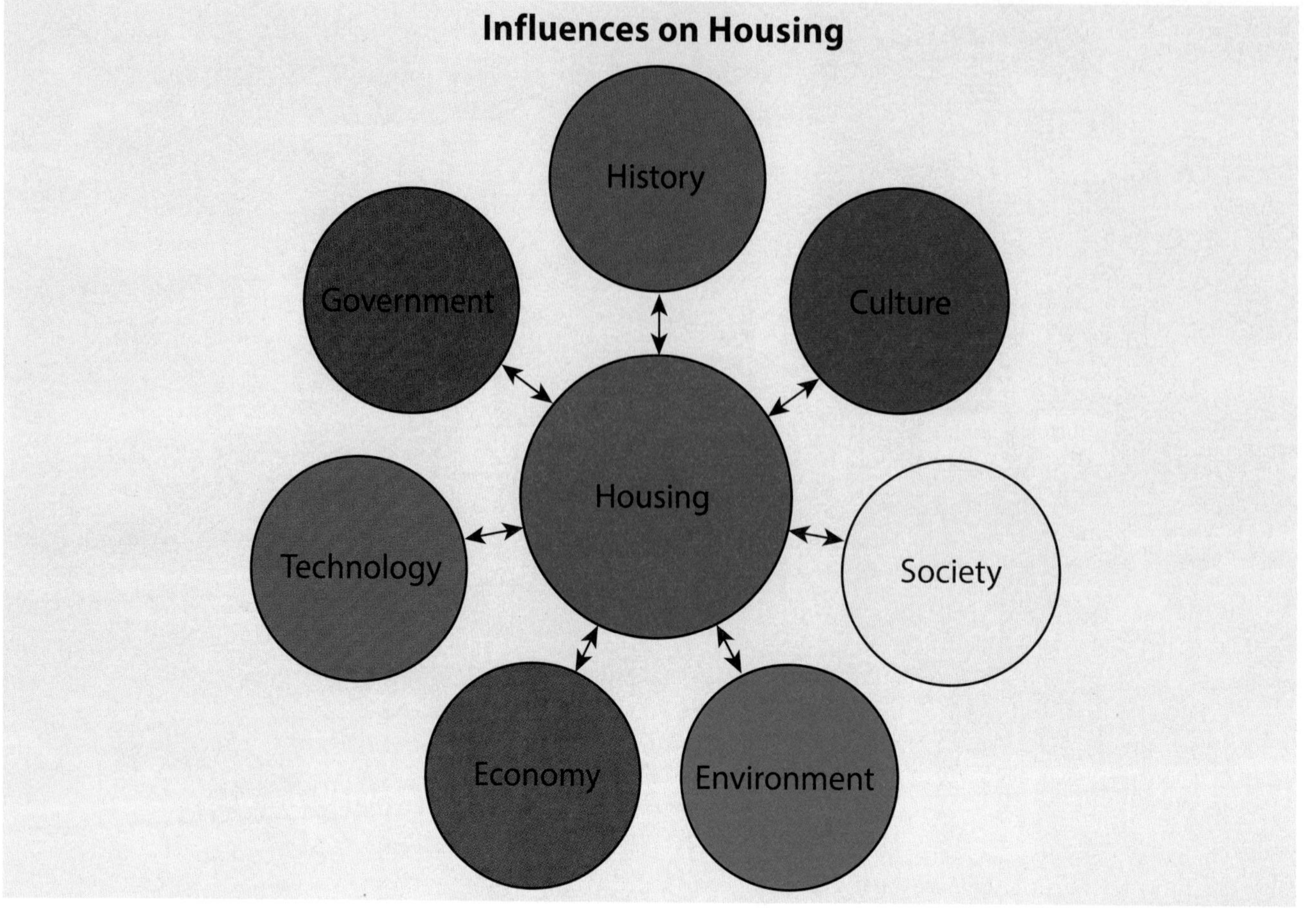

Goodheart-Willcox Publisher

Figure 2.1 This diagram displays the major factors that influence housing. Notice that the arrows point both to housing and then from housing back to each individual factor. This means that the factor affects housing but also that housing affects the factor.

Housing changes occur according to the needs and desires of those who occupy it. Housing also changes because of outside influences. These include historical, cultural, societal, environmental, economic, technological, and governmental influences. Figure 2.1 shows how these factors impact housing.

Historical Influences on Housing

The story of housing in the United States began before the first European settlers established the colonies. There is a sharp contrast between the houses of today and those of early North America.

Early Shelter

Early humans lived in caves that provided a degree of safety and protection from the weather and wild animals. These caves helped people meet the basic need for shelter—a place to sleep and rest.

Another form of early shelter was a *dugout*—a large hole dug in the earth. Dugouts were warm in cold weather and cool in warm weather. Sometimes a dome-shaped covering was added to the dugout to make it roomier. Typical materials for such coverings were animal skins, mud and bark, or mud and branches.

Housing of Native Americans

Some early Native American cliff dwellers often used a crude rock overhang or cliff for housing (review *Figure 1.2*). The overhangs or cliffs were modified for housing by adding an enclosure which gave warmth, privacy, and security to the cliff dwellers. Living in cliffs gave these Native Americans the ability to see great distances—an added advantage to their security.

Native Americans occupied North America before European settlers began to arrive. The materials used for their housing depended on what was available in the section of the country in which they lived. Some lived in huts that were constructed from a framework of poles with coverings of thatch,

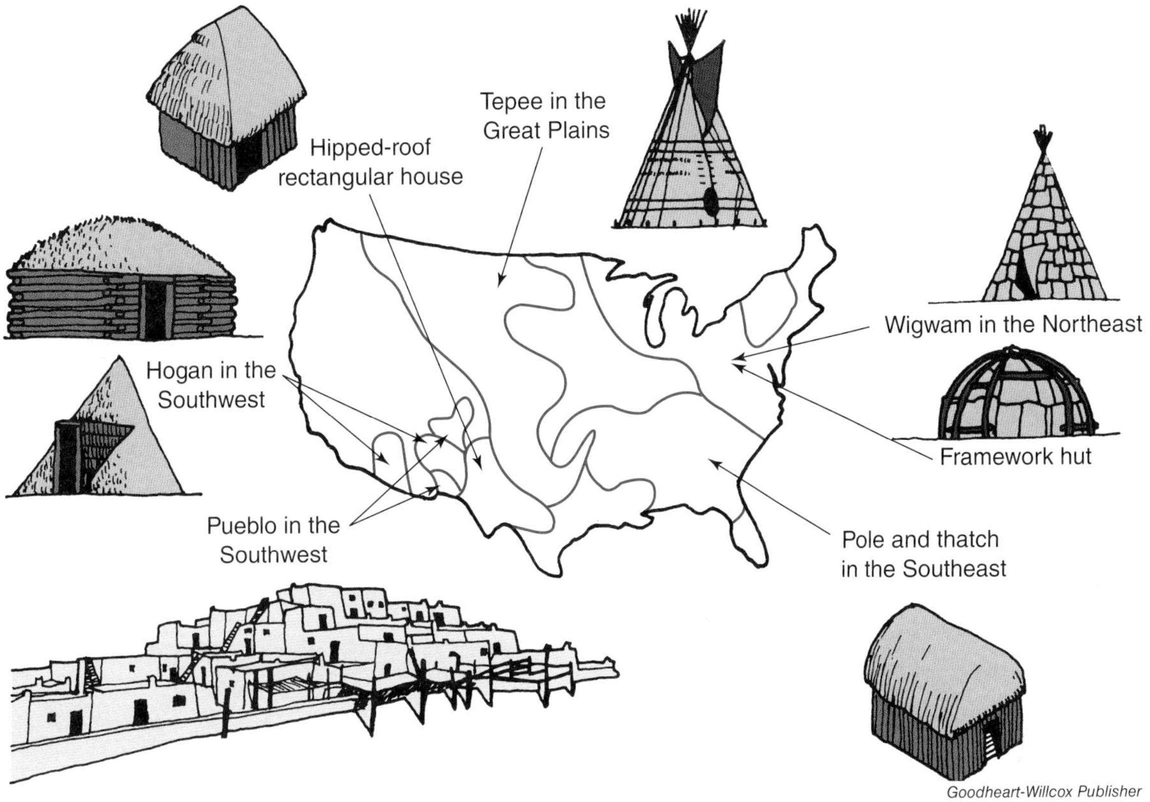

Native American Housing

Hipped-roof rectangular house
Tepee in the Great Plains
Wigwam in the Northeast
Framework hut
Hogan in the Southwest
Pueblo in the Southwest
Pole and thatch in the Southeast

Goodheart-Willcox Publisher

Figure 2.2 Early Native Americans lived in housing that varied according to the region in which they were located.

hides, or mud over the framework. Others lived in tepees and wigwams. Some Native Americans lived in permanent dwellings constructed of adobe. Figure 2.2 shows the different types of Native American dwellings and their locations.

Housing of the Colonists

The first English settlement in North America was established in 1585 on the island of Roanoke in North Carolina. The first shelters used by the European settlers were copied after Native American dwellings. Other houses were built of sod. Dirt floors were common.

The early colonists built their own houses. Sometimes they built them with the help of many neighbors, an event called a *house-raising*. Because many people helped with the work, a house could be built in a short amount of time. The quality of these early dwellings was limited due to the lack of skills, tools, and materials.

After settling in North America, the colonists attempted to replicate the houses from their homelands. The styles, however, had to be adapted to the available materials. Some housing styles of the colonists' homelands did not suit the climate of the new land and consequently were not replicated. For instance, the thatched roof, commonly used in England, was not suited to the cold New England climate (Figure 2.3).

The abundance of trees in the eastern forests made the log cabin convenient to build. It is believed that the first *log cabins* were built about 1640 by Swedish and Finnish colonists. They began as one-room structures with fireplaces for heating and cooking (Figure 2.4). The chimneys were located on the outside of the cabins.

Later, the log cabin was built in a variety of styles. Rooms were often added as families grew larger. Some log cabins were built with three rooms—an entryway, kitchen, and sleeping room, while others were two stories tall. The kitchens in these log cabins were large, so food could be both processed and prepared in the house. Sleeping rooms were small and sometimes located in a loft. If a small log cabin was replaced by a larger dwelling, the small cabin was sometimes used for storage.

The log cabin spread from the Northeast into the South and onto the western frontier. It became a symbol of the early United States.

Most housing in early settlements could be found in group settings with security being the key

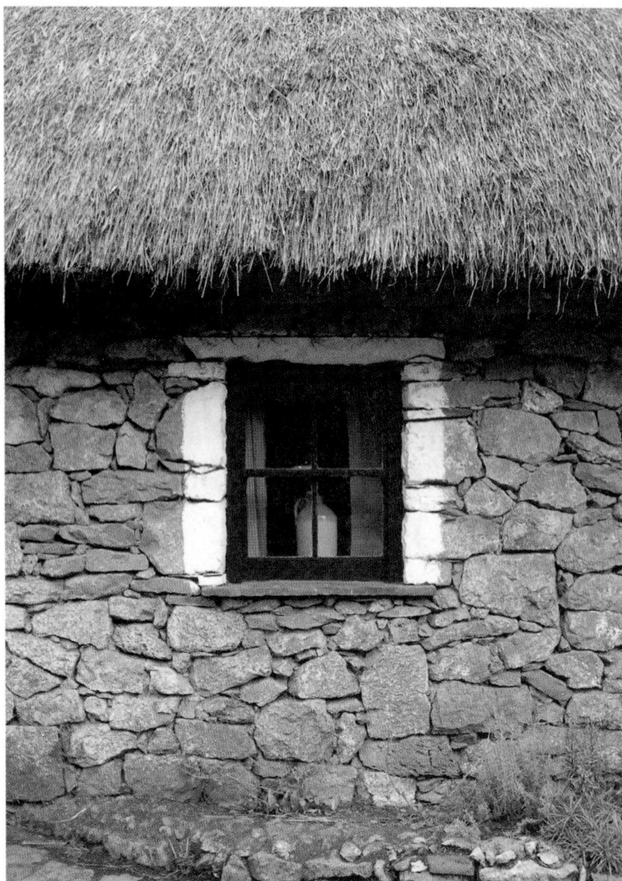

Lindsey Moore/Shutterstock.com

Figure 2.3 The thatched roof, which is not appropriate for cold climates, is very common in warmer climates.

David P. Smith/Shutterstock.com

Figure 2.4 A typical log cabin looked similar to this.

Kevin L. Chesson/Shutterstock.com

Figure 2.5 Plantation houses were common dwellings for large landowners of the South.

reason for building houses close together. Generally square or rectangular in form, many houses had one or two rooms and a fireplace. When other rooms were added around the main room, it became known as the *great room*.

As the country became settled, more people with building skills arrived. They helped build houses and taught others their skills. When logs were cut into lumber, it became a common building material. Other houses also appeared that were built of stone or brick.

Housing of the 1700s and 1800s

Throughout the 1700s and 1800s, many people moved west to settle on large plots of land. They lived on their land in a variety of dwellings. Farmhouses ranged in design and construction from sod houses to log cabins to ranch houses. At the same time, construction of large plantation houses was happening in the South (Figure 2.5).

In the late 1700s, most North America settlers were ***agrarian***, or people who earned their living from the land. By 1890, the rural population had decreased as a result of the Industrial Revolution (1750–1850). The Industrial Revolution brought major changes to the economy and society through the use of new machines and efficient production of goods. The demand for workers grew out of changes in mass production due to use of such machines. Along with immigrants, rural people began moving to the cities looking for jobs. With an increasing birth rate, the cities grew. This increased the demand for housing in the urban areas.

Urban Housing

The housing in cities was built close together and crowded with inhabitants, causing a high density. **Density** is the number of people in a given area. Early urban dwellings included row houses and tenements.

The first row houses were built in the 1820s. **Row houses** are a continuous group of dwellings linked by common sidewalls. Many of them were built to house factory workers (Figure 2.6). Two-story row houses sometimes housed as many as six families at a time.

Eventually, row houses with fewer common walls evolved into dwellings for one family. Two-family dwellings, called *duplexes,* were built and multifamily housing was built for four or six families.

Most houses were frame houses in various designs. A number of **tenement houses**, or early apartments, were built before housing regulations existed. The first tenement houses appeared in New York City around 1840 to house immigrants. Most were built on city lots measuring 25 by 100 feet. A typical tenement house was a five-story building, measuring 25 by 25 feet. Next to each dwelling was another 25-foot square building.

Jorge Salcedo/Shutterstock.com

Figure 2.6 Many people in urban settings lived in these row houses in the late 1800s.

The typical tenement house had as many as 116 two-room apartments. The outdoor toilets were located on the land between the buildings. Conditions were very poor, earning the landlords the title of *slumlords*.

By 1890, government regulations required that each room in a new tenement house have a window. Each apartment was to have running water and a kitchen sink. Community toilets were to be located in the stairway area connecting the floors.

The tenement houses and row houses were the forerunners of modern apartments. Some apartments first appeared during the housing shortage caused by the Industrial Revolution. At the same time, mansions were built for the wealthy (Figure 2.7).

Changes in Housing

Many changes were taking place in housing and the housing industry in the 1700s and 1800s. There were new inventions, machinery, and technology.

Wood- and coal-burning stoves appeared in houses. Steam-heating systems were installed. Oil and gas lamps replaced candles. *Iceboxes* (early refrigeration units) became available. Water supplies, plumbing, and sanitation facilities were improved. Some houses had indoor toilets and bathtubs. Only people with high incomes in typically urban areas, however, could afford to take advantage of these new developments. Rural regions were slow to adopt the improvements.

Machinery, craftspeople, and architects were all important in the housing industry. An **architect** is a person who designs buildings and supervises their

Ella_K/Shutterstock.com

Figure 2.7 Mansions, such as the Alva Vanderbilt Marble House shown here, were often built for wealthy businesspeople in the late 1800s.

construction. Many found inspiration for building designs from designs used in buildings of other countries. Machinery, such as electric saws, helped the buildings go up rapidly. People who were skilled in various crafts or trades—such as carpenters, plumbers, and electricians—contributed to high-quality work. No single housing style dominated the scene.

Housing in the 1900s

During the early 1900s, there was a dramatic increase in the number of immigrants to the United States with many moving to the cities. A housing boom in the early 1900s began to meet this need for housing.

Then during World War I (1914–1918), almost no housing was built except by the federal government, causing a housing shortage. House ownership declined. Housing was overcrowded. There was a shortage of materials and, as a result, structures fell into disrepair. After World War I, about one-third of the population was living in substandard housing. **Substandard** means the housing is not up to the quality living standards prescribed by law that are best for people. For example, substandard conditions often included inadequate light from windows (and sometimes no windows), unheated spaces, limited access to working plumbing for water, and unsanitary means of handling human waste. These homes were often unsound structures with leaky roofs and holes in the floors. During this time, only a halfhearted housing reform was taking place.

By the time of the Great Depression in 1929, more than half the U.S. population lived in cities. The building of houses, however, had slowed down. People of all income levels struggled to meet their housing needs. Private enterprise as well as the government soon saw the need for housing reform and began to lay the foundation for change.

The first census of housing in the United States was taken in 1940. A ***census*** is an official count of the population by the government. The census supported what the people knew—the housing needs of people at all income levels had not been met. The impact of the increased population, World War I, and the Great Depression had left housing conditions in a neglected state.

Solutions to Housing Shortages

In response to housing shortages, factory-produced units emerged as a major type of American housing (Figure 2.8). Depending on the type, units

Photo by Palm Harbor Homes

Figure 2.8 Some manufactured homes must be moved in sections and joined on-site.

were produced to various levels of completion and delivered to a housing site. The advantage of factory-built housing involved the savings in cost as well as in construction time.

Houses that are conventionally built on-site generally take more time to complete. This is because weather-related delays often prolong construction and coordination of many different tradespeople. When factory-building housing on an assembly line, coordination is easier and takes less time to complete. While some units are finished at the factory, others come in parts that need to be put together on-site. All involve a certain amount of labor when being placed on the site. Full descriptions of these housing types appear later in the text.

Factory-built housing units helped with the housing shortage by serving as year-round housing for many people, including defense workers, factory employees, and military personnel. Housing units on wheels provided an affordable solution for home ownership since the cost was considerably less than a conventional house built on a foundation at a housing site. Today, factory-built housing is one of the fastest growing types of affordable housing in the United States.

Following World War II, housing construction resumed. Along with this construction came the appearance of **tract houses,** which are groups of similarly designed houses built on a tract of land. These tract houses had a "cookie cutter" appearance because they all looked alike. They were moderate in size and built to meet the needs of the moderate-income family. The owners of tract houses have adapted them to fit their needs. For example, many have added room extensions and garages, while others have personalized the homes with new exterior materials and colors.

Improvements in Urban Housing

Throughout this period, several new ideas emerged to improve housing. Two of these included *subdivisions* and *new towns.*

A **subdivision** is the division of a tract of land into two or more parcels that make it easier to sell and develop. This division involves laying out a parcel of raw land into lots, blocks, streets, and public areas. As a result, the density and types of buildings are controlled. The focus of a subdivision is on the division of land for various purposes.

Subdivisions are often created from undeveloped land by private investors, or *developers*. Developers must obtain permission to create a subdivision from local government officials, who must consider many factors. One such factor is the impact the new subdivision will have on the amount of traffic it will add to area roads. Other considerations include the potential overcrowding of schools and excess strain on such government services as police and fire protection, a fresh-water supply, waste pick-up, and sewage treatment. In setting up subdivisions, land surveyors play an important role in making sure the lots and roads are properly laid out and that property lines are correct.

A well-thought-out design for a subdivision may include areas to develop for recreational facilities as pools, tennis courts, basketball courts, hiking trails, bike paths, and man-made lakes for boating and fishing. New roads are included in the plan and possibly a new school, too. A well-designed subdivision may also include easy access to shopping centers and medical offices.

There is a distinct difference between a subdivision and a *planned development*. A subdivision is the planning and development of the land itself. Once the division of land occurs, it needs further organization before construction can begin on it. In contrast, a **planned development** has a master plan showing how to use land for various purposes.

A **new town** is an urban development consisting of a small to midsize city with a broad range of housing and planned industrial, commercial, educational, and recreational facilities (Figure 2.9). It covers up to 6,000 acres. The number of residents ranges from 10,000 to 60,000. The industrial facilities provide employment opportunities. A new town is designed to appeal to people of all ages, economic levels, races, educational backgrounds, and religious beliefs.

The idea for new towns dates back to the early 1900s, but it was 1960 before the idea started to gain attention. New towns are carefully planned from the beginning and are usually constructed in an undeveloped area. Because of their structure, they promote the orderly growth of areas with fast-growth potential. The early 1970s saw the beginnings of about 15 new towns. By 1990, at least 60 new towns were in progress in the United States.

The term *new town* is the term used in the initial stages of the movement, but now a new town is referred to as a *planned community*. A **planned community** is the design and implementation of a community, city, or neighborhood with a master plan. A *master plan* includes more than one primary type of zoning area (housing, commercial, and industrial). New towns, planned developments, planned cities, and planned neighborhoods are all examples of planned communities.

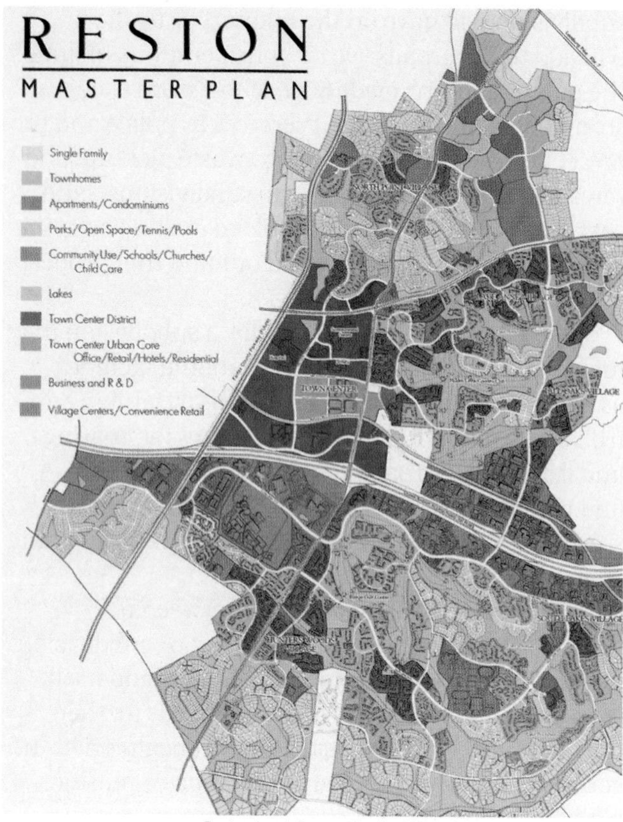

Reston Land Corporation/Archives of the Reston Historic Trust

Figure 2.9 A master plan was used when developing the planned community of Reston, Virginia.

Since the early 1990s, a newer version of planned neighborhood, or *new urbanism,* has gained popularity. **New urbanism** refers to communities that are planned to encourage pedestrian traffic and place more emphasis on the environment—producing most of the energy needed and/or using minimum natural resources. In communities built on the new urbanism concept, everything is within walking distance of the home. These developments are mixed-use, which means shops, offices, apartments, and single-family homes are included in one planned area. Another name for new urbanism communities is *live/work communities.* As a characteristic of these communities, a housing unit is often located above a commercial shop, such as a jewelry store or an insurance office.

The *Congress for the New Urbanism (CNU)* is the leading organization promoting neighborhood-based developments as an alternative to **urban sprawl**—the spreading of urban developments such as housing and shopping centers on undeveloped land near a city. Active members include planners, developers, architects, engineers, public officials, investors, and community activists who create and influence the built environment. Their work brings restorative plans to hurricane-battered communities, turns around failing shopping centers, and reconnects isolated public housing projects with the community. Followers of new urbanism are striving to become leaders in community building.

Planned Communities—the Future

Planned communities are one answer to today's housing problems, and the expectation is they will continue to grow with sustainability as a goal.

Green Choices

Let the Environment Work for You!

The famous American architect, Frank Lloyd Wright, led the way in placing housing on land that takes advantage of the natural environment. (*Review Figure 2.18.*)

Housing that takes advantage of the natural environment is "green" because the house will cost less to heat and cool. Also, there will be fewer disturbances to the natural environment by the construction process. Specifically, home buyers and builders can select or build houses with the following "green" ideas in mind:

- Use natural sunlight as much as possible to heat interior spaces (place most lived in areas on southern side of the home)
- Place rooms that produce heat on the northern side of the home (kitchen, bathrooms, utility rooms)
- Choose landscaping that blocks northern winds from reaching the house (large trees/bushes that keep their leaves all year)
- Build levels of the house to match the natural slope of the land

These strategies can reduce energy costs. They also add to the thermal comfort and views of the home.

Instead of growing by one building at a time, the design of these communities will meet present and future needs. Urban planners and designers give careful consideration to the use of resources and the needs and values of the residents. Community associations govern planned communities. Well-run associations can raise the quality of life as well as property values for residents.

The planned communities of Reston, Virginia, and Irvine, California, have received awards for their promotion of the quality of life of the residents.

Columbia, Maryland is another example of a planned community. This is one of several communities planned by architect James W. Rouse. It is located on 14,000 acres of land between Baltimore and Washington, DC. About 3,200 acres are set aside for parks, lakes, and a golf course. The city of Columbia consists of a cluster of nine residential villages—or *satellite communities*—that surround an urban downtown. Columbia is a culturally diverse community. Homes are available in a wide range of prices and styles, for purchase or rent.

Included in the planning of Columbia were specialists from many fields: architects, sociologists, educators, religious leaders, and doctors. They tried to answer the question, "What should be included in a well-planned community?" See Figure 2.10 for planning factors they considered.

As an example of a planned community with a goal of sustaining the environment, Columbia continues to attract new businesses, employees, and home owners to live, work, and invest in the downtown area. Community members and leaders are working toward making Columbia and Howard County a model green community. In addition to Green Building standards, the Columbia Town Center implemented a *Sustainability Program*. Redevelopment of the Columbia Town Center has the potential to be the single largest effort toward green technologies and sustainability countywide.

A recent approach to planned communities is on a smaller scale and is referred to as **pocket development**, focused more on the small neighborhood concept. The idea is that developers find small land areas, referred to as "pockets," and place close together small homes of about 800–950 square feet. The units face into a common shared courtyard in a small acreage community. The concept is that people will live close to each other and connect as people might have done a century ago. A benefit of this type of development is that small land areas can be used for smaller housing units that may not be usable for housing otherwise.

Adequate housing for everyone has never fully been achieved in the United States and remains one of the nation's greatest challenges (Figure 2.11). Ideally, the housing supply will someday meet the needs of a growing, diverse U.S. population. This includes people with special needs—such as older adults or those with physical or mental limitations—singles, first-time home owners, and people of all cultures, races, and income levels.

Factors for Designing a Planned Community

- The lifestyles desired by the occupants
- Affordable housing
- Easy access to schools, health facilities, places of worship, stores, and government offices
- Recreational facilities that appeal to individuals and groups of all ages
- The use of parks, playgrounds, and green belts to separate space and create neighborhood zones
- Affordable public transportation
- Employment opportunities at all levels
- Education opportunities at all levels
- Effective and affordable health care facilities
- Effective communications about community events and activities

Figure 2.10 These factors were considered when the planned community of Columbia, Maryland, was designed.

Green Choices

What Is Sustainability?

A special term used in referring to "going green" is sustainability. *Sustainability* means meeting the needs of the present without compromising the ability of future generations to meet their own needs. Consequently, sustainability should have no impact environmentally, socially, and economically. It is the ultimate goal of going green. Sustainable designs create the following:

- ***No negative environmental impact.*** This means no use of resources except for what is generated in the structure. For example, zero-energy buildings show this concept. These buildings actually generate their own energy from solar or other renewable energy sources.
- ***No negative social impact.*** This means the design does not cause problems in communities by interfering with the daily living or lifestyles of people in communities.
- ***No economic impact.*** The design does not contribute to economic losses in communities. For example, taking wood for buildings from forests could remove opportunities for local farmers and others to make a living. This would have a negative economic impact.

jdwfoto/Shutterstock.com

Figure 2.11 House by house, Habitat for Humanity International is helping meet one of the greatest needs in the United States—adequate housing for all people.

Review & Assessment

1. Identify three types of early Native American dwellings.
2. Describe the housing of the first European settlers.
3. Why is the log cabin the symbol of the early United States?
4. What was the main cause of the population shift from rural to urban areas in the late 1700s?
5. Identify two housing problems created by the population shift.
6. Contrast row houses and tenements.
7. What three historical events resulted in substandard housing?
8. Summarize the principles behind the concept of new urbanism and community planning.

Cultural Influences on Housing

The beliefs, social customs, and traits of a group of people form their **culture**. A group's culture influences its housing choices, and the housing becomes part of the culture. The following examples illustrate how housing influences culture.

Native American Culture

The Navajo, a Native American tribe of the North-American Southwest, lived in **hogans**, which were buildings made of logs and mud. The windows faced west and a single door faced east. The placement of the door had religious significance. The Navajo believed that the door must face east so the spirit guardians could enter. The tradition exists today, even though the type of housing for many Navajos has changed. Homes built by the Crow, a Native American tribe of the Northwest, also have doors facing east.

The cultures of Native American tribes in North America closely entwined the environment with their religious beliefs. They typically viewed the land and water as common property to which everyone must show respect and use wisely. With the arrival of European settlers in North America came contrasting views. These settlers saw the opportunity for private ownership of the land and water.

With the arrival of the Pilgrims at Plymouth Rock in the winter of 1620, the need for shelter was immediate. They duplicated the housing of the Native Americans. After the winter was over, they began to duplicate the English cottages of their

Sociocultural Connections The Tiny House Movement

Citing environmental and financial concerns as well as a desire for more time and freedom, many people across the country have abandoned traditional homes in favor of a small or tiny house. Known as the *Tiny House Movement*, this lifestyle trend has seen thousands swap space for simplicity.

Tiny houses go by a number of different names like "micro houses," "compact houses," "mini houses," or "little houses." As the different names suggest, they are much smaller than the typical American house.

Compared to the average American house, which is about 2,100 square feet, the average tiny house is only 186 square feet—less than one-tenth of the size of the average American house. Most tiny houses are lofted, with sleeping quarters tucked away from the first floor, which includes a kitchen, bathroom, and general living area.

People in favor of the tiny house movement see many advantages to downsizing including greater mobility to take on adventures, environmental awareness, independence, lower taxes, little or no debt, and lower upkeep costs. Over 68 percent of tiny-house owners do not have a mortgage—the average price of a tiny house is $23,000, which is significantly less than the average U.S. house.

People of all ages buy tiny houses, but 40 percent of all tiny house owners are older than 50 years old. Looking to the future, it seems that younger people are more open to the idea of living in a tiny house. Surveys have found that while nearly 60 percent of those over 55 years old would "definitely not" live in a tiny house, only 30 percent of those 18 to 34 years old would refuse to consider this possibility. Almost 35 percent of 18- to 34-year-olds would at least give it serious thought as opposed to only 15 percent of those older than 50 years old.

From an environmental perspective, a smaller house means less lumber and other building materials, smaller and fewer appliances, fewer rooms to heat or cool, and less electricity and fuel use. Also, given their size, many tiny houses are actually built from recycled materials.

Susan Law Cain/Shutterstock.com

While most people buy a tiny house and use it as their main residence, it does serve other functions as well. For example, some people use their tiny house as a home office or guest house for visiting in-laws or kids who move back home. Cities have also bought tiny houses to help provide shelter to the homeless.

Tiny houses can be purchased across the country, but there are a large number of builders who can be found in CA, CO, FL, TX, and WI.

Dig Deeper

Think about what you have just learned about the tiny house movement. Would you consider living in and designing your own tiny house? Why or why not? Write a short essay explaining your personal views on this movement toward home ownership. Cite the text and other reliable resources to support your views.

homeland. They used wood, which was abundantly available and the traditional building material of their homeland. The first cottages were often crude and made of timber—large, squared-off pieces of wood. They had dirt floors, few windows, and chimneys built of sticks and heavy clay. As better materials and skills became available, the cottages more closely resembled the cottages in England.

As other cultures came to North America from Europe, they also contributed their styles of housing to the American landscape. As mentioned earlier, the Swedish log cabin became a popular form of housing. The Dutch Colonial, Pennsylvania Dutch (German) Colonial, French Normandy, and Italianate housing styles are other examples of European influences on American housing. (You will learn more about these influences later in the text.)

Before regions in the South and Southwest became states, people from Spain settled them. The Spaniards built missions with whitewashed walls

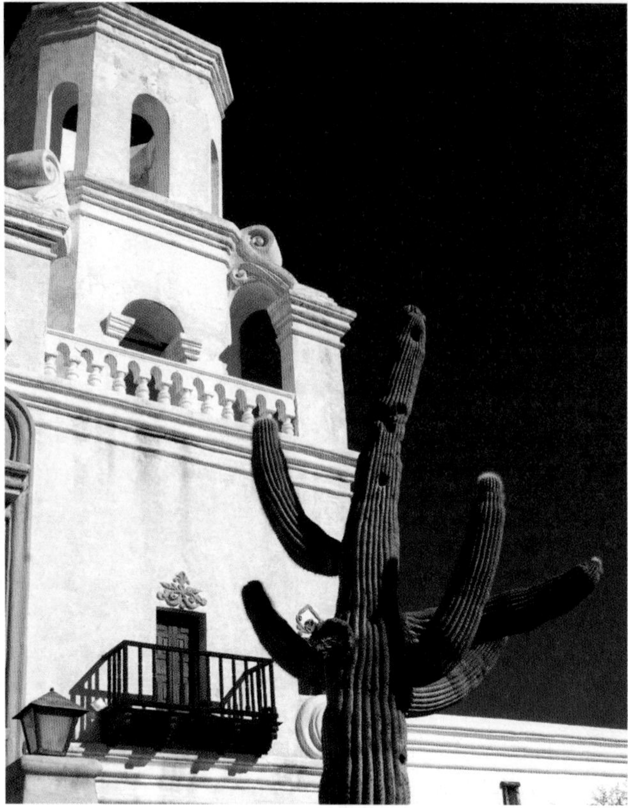

Jim Parkin/Shutterstock.com

Figure 2.12 Spanish missions, such as this one, influence architecture even today.

Monkey Business Images/Shutterstock.com

Figure 2.13 About 67 percent of foreign-born citizens are home owners, which is about the same percent of U.S.-born citizens who own homes.

and red-tiled roofs. The style of the Spanish missions greatly influenced the local architecture. In the early 1900s, there was a revival of Hispanic heritage including architecture. Along with preservation of the old missions came construction of houses and other buildings following details of early Spanish architecture (Figure 2.12). Throughout the nation and the South and Southwest today, much architecture shows Hispanic influence.

Throughout history, houses have been strong indicators of culture. Housing reflects the heritage as well as traditional skills and materials of the builders. As cultures change, the changes are evident in the housing.

New Immigrants

Each year, the United States welcomes thousands of legal immigrants from all over the world. Now, as in the past, these immigrants bring their dreams and expectations for a better life as they adapt to their new homeland. Finding housing that reflects their cultural preferences and personal values is part of that dream.

Many immigrants, for example, are members of large extended families that need extra space in housing for sleeping quarters. Other immigrants may want to have a large yard where they can grow a vegetable or fruit garden, just as they did in their homelands.

Low wages and limited knowledge of the English language can be barriers to finding decent, safe, and affordable housing. Too many new immigrants live in conditions that are substandard and unsafe, jeopardizing their families' desires for better living. To help find suitable housing that reflects their culture in a way that meets housing codes and regulations, new immigrants need simple housing information provided in their own languages.

Not all immigrants fall into the category of low-paid laborers, however. Many new immigrants are skilled workers and professionals such as doctors and lawyers. Others are workers with advanced degrees or exceptional abilities, including university teachers and skilled musicians. Even the majority of low-paid immigrants are eventually able to improve their living conditions and save enough money to buy a home. Acquiring a home, personalizing it, and becoming a part of a community is a desire shared by foreign-born and native-born citizens alike (Figure 2.13).

Review & Assessment

1. Name two examples of how culture influenced housing.
2. What barriers do new immigrants face in finding suitable housing?
3. What would help new immigrants find safe, suitable housing that reflects culture?

Societal Influences on Housing

Signs of societal change are everywhere. You can see them in the growth of the cities and the movement of people to new jobs and locations. You can also see them in relationships and lifestyles. Many of these changes affect housing.

Household Size

The U. S. Census Bureau collects data to provide information on ***demographics***—statistical facts about the human population. Demographic information helps society plan for future needs and understand trends that affect those needs. Demographic information includes such characteristics of individuals as age, income, race, gender, and the relationship of people living in a household.

One important social change that influences housing is the average number of people living in a household. Since the first U.S. Census in 1790, the average number has gradually decreased. This first census showed that most households had between three and seven members. In 1900, the majority had two to five members. The 2010 U.S. census and recent statistics show that two to three people live in most households today.

Household Composition

The decrease in the number of household members is not the only change evident in households. The composition of households has also changed. In 1940, for example, married couples headed 75 percent of all households, and 7 percent were single-person households. By 2013, the percentage of married couples households decreased to 48.7 while the number of single-person households increased to 27.5 percent.

In the past, married couples were more likely than single people to own their own homes. This has changed, however, due in part to an increase in the number of singles. For example, there were 96.6 million single persons 18 years of age or older in 2009. By 2011, there were 102 million single persons 18 years of age or older, representing an increase of over five million in two years. The increase is due to many reasons, such as the tendency to postpone marriage until careers are established and the steady increase in the nation's divorce rate. Recent census figures show that women and men are marrying later than ever before. The percentage of people marrying in their 20s continues to decline.

Some singles choose to live with roommates and share housing costs, while others prefer to live alone (Figure 2.14). Many singles are renters and live in apartments. Others are home owners living in a variety of housing types.

Some singles live with their parents. Never-married singles or single-again adults may return to live with their parents after living on their own for a while. The combined living arrangement may last for a short or extended period.

An Older Population

The continual aging of the population is another change in society that affects housing. The *median* age of the U.S. population is 37.6 years, reflecting the ever-growing number of people in higher age categories. ***Median*** is the mathematical average that divides a group of numbers into two parts with half the numbers above the median and half the numbers below the median.

According to the most recent U.S. census estimates, the fastest growing age group is age 65 and older. In fact, this age group has grown faster than the general population. The members are part of the large segment of the adult population referred to as **baby boomers**. They get their name from the period after World War II called the *baby boom*, which includes births from 1946 through 1964. Since this group is so large, the housing they need as they age is placing high demands on society.

AVAVA/Shutterstock.com

Figure 2.14 Singles who want extra space to pursue a hobby or a business may prefer to live alone rather than share housing with a roommate.

Lindasj22/Shutterstock.com

Figure 2.15 Compact, one-story houses are ideal for senior citizens.

Already the housing needs of older adults are large and growing. Recent U.S. census information indicates that in 2000, about 35 million people were age 65 and older, accounting for 12 percent of the population. By 2010, the number of persons age 65 and older had grown to 40.3 million people, representing 13 percent of the population. This shows a growth of 15.1 percent in the 10-year period of this older age group while the total U.S. population only grew by 9.7 percent. By 2020, the U.S. census projections show the number of people age 65 and older will increase to 55 million, accounting for 16 percent of the total population. The majority of older persons live with a spouse. Among those who live alone, most are women.

Housing needs for older adults differ from those of the general population. Many older people lose some physical abilities as they age. They may have a partial loss of hearing or sight. Some are more sensitive to heat and cold or may no longer be able to use stairs. Many older people live in housing that presents limits or barriers to taking full advantage of their homes. Housing that is adapted or designed to fit the needs of older adults helps them live in their homes longer, thus remaining independent (Figure 2.15).

As a result of the aging population, housing and related services for the older adults are a national concern. Retirement centers, assisted living arrangements, and personal health assistance will need to expand to meet the changing population demands.

People with Special Needs

Many people have physical, sensory, or mental disabilities that limit their activities. A *disability* is an attribute or functional limitation that interferes with a person's ability to carry out daily living activities. For example, such disabilities may interfere with a person's ability to walk, lift, hear, or see. These physical limitations may be temporary or permanent. As a result, an individual will have special housing needs. His or her housing must not restrict the ability to carry out day-to-day activities. According to the latest census data, 19 percent of the population has at least one disability.

When housing limits a person's daily activities, housing professionals must give consideration to ways to build or adapt housing to meet specific needs. Guidelines for meeting these needs will follow in later chapters.

Finding Affordable Housing

Many people live in inadequate housing. In general, housing is inadequate if the occupants pay more than 30 percent of their income for housing or if the housing itself is substandard in some way. Some people with inadequate housing may live on social security benefits or other housing assistance, which provide minimum resources. Some become homeless as a result of unemployment and loss of income.

Inadequate housing has many effects on society. Substandard dwellings become overcrowded, which results in a lack of privacy and increased family conflict. It also contributes to the spread of disease.

The middle-income group is the largest in the United States. Most jobs provide middle-income salaries, and most housing and furniture designs have middle-income families in mind. Today's middle-income individuals and families, however, sometimes have difficulty buying houses. This is because they have excess debt (usually credit-card payments) and incomes that are not rising as fast as housing costs. Oftentimes, they may not have enough savings for a down payment.

In the recent past, families were advised to spend no more than two and one-half times their annual income to purchase a house. Today, the average house in the United States is more costly. The average family spends at least one-third of its income on housing. Some of those who purchase houses may pay up to four times their annual income for an average house. These increases in the cost of housing make single-family homes unaffordable for many.

Since the housing costs have risen faster than income, middle-income families must decide how to balance their housing and lifestyle needs. Instead of buying a single-family house, for example, they may choose to buy a home in a multifamily unit or simply rent an apartment (Figure 2.16).

Alita Bobrov/Shutterstock.com

Figure 2.16 Many families today choose to live in low-maintenance apartments such as these.

Changing Roles

Today, many women work outside the home. Some are working to support themselves. Others are working to support their families, which might include children or older relatives. Many women own their own houses.

When both adults in a family have employment outside the home, they have a **dual-career family**. This common situation is necessary for many families because income does not keep up with the cost of living. While dual-career families may have more income, they may have less time for household tasks. They may desire more convenient housing and timesaving devices.

Planning for Leisure Time

People today are spending more time at various types of work—balancing their jobs with home tasks, child care, and sometimes parent-care responsibilities. This often leaves little time for relaxation and recreation. Consequently, many individuals and families must make time for leisure and use that time wisely.

How you choose to use your leisure time affects your housing decisions. Many people choose housing with low-maintenance requirements to spend less time on upkeep. Others may enjoy decorating or fixing up their homes and view these as leisure or recreational activities.

Some people specifically choose housing that provides opportunities for leisure activities. The house may have a special room, such as an exercise or hobby area. It may be near a golf course, tennis court, or swimming pool. A large backyard may be the place a home owner wants to spend leisure time with family and friends. Also, people can choose to live in housing complexes or other living arrangements that have options for leisure time, which can include clubhouses, swimming pools, tennis courts, and other recreational opportunities.

Working at Home

Due to technological and other changes in the workplace, the number of people working from their homes is increasing. Census data in 2013 indicated an almost 80 percent increase of persons working at home from 2005 to 2012. These individuals may have their own businesses in their homes or may be employees working at home. **Teleworking** refers to the use of technology in various locations to avoid the need for the worker to travel to work. **Telecommuting,** a form of teleworking, involves working at home or another site through an electronic link to a computer network at a central office. In addition, fax machines, e-mail, and the Internet make working at home easier.

STEM Science & Technology: Telecommuting Technology

People who telecommute or run home-based businesses usually rely on the Internet to do their jobs. Using a high-speed Internet connection, or big broadband, enables computer users to send and receive large files, photos, and streaming video, and to perform other business functions. Unfortunately, the U.S. lags behind other industrialized nations in providing big broadband to consumers at affordable prices.

If you plan to telecommute, consider big broadband availability before renting or buying a home. Find out which companies provide Internet service in the area and how that service is delivered. You'll get the fastest speeds if your home is hooked up to a fiber optic network, which is not available in all communities. Fiber optics technology uses narrow glass strands to carry data at the speed of a laser light beam. Telephone and cable companies are replacing their older copper wires and cables with fiber optic cables.

Also ask about upload and download speeds and under what conditions and price you can achieve optimal speeds. Many companies charge more for their highest-speed connections.

The use of the home as the workplace requires creating a work area that is both functional and convenient. This has implications for the design or redesign of the home environment. You will learn more about how to design a workspace that successfully meets the specific needs of a telecommuter in following chapters.

Working at home not only presents challenges for designing the workspace, but also for dealing with distractions that interfere with the work routine. Persons working at home need to develop strategies to deal effectively with difficulties that may arise in family relationships, completion of household tasks, and focusing their job requirements.

A Mobile Society

In a mobile society, people often travel from one location to another. The average vehicle owner travels 15,000 miles a year. Some travel with their portable dwellings (Figure 2.17). The average household moves every four years, which can exceed 17 moves in a lifetime.

Sometimes people move to change from renting to home ownership or vice versa. The main reason for so much movement is to relocate for employment reasons. Other reasons for moving include retirement, a better climate, the desire for larger (or smaller) housing, or the preference for a quieter (or livelier) neighborhood.

Population shifts in the United States are the result of a mobile society. Before 1970, there was a slow, continuing westward movement. People also moved toward large bodies of water such as the oceans, Great Lakes, and Gulf of Mexico. After 1970, people began moving to the Sunbelt. The *Sunbelt* includes the southern and southwestern regions of the United States.

JaySi/Shutterstock.com

Figure 2.17 Many people use motorized recreational vehicles as a home for traveling around the country.

Review & Assessment

1. What are three societal factors regarding households that can influence housing?
2. Name two reasons some older adults have special housing needs.
3. Assess and explain the impact of demographic trends on psychological, physical, and social needs as they relate to housing decisions.
4. How can leisure time impact housing decisions?

Environmental Influences on Housing

Your *environment* is the total of all conditions, objects, places, and people that are around you. People adapt to their environments in the housing they design and build. They are also able to manipulate their environments through their housing choices.

The Natural Environment

Nature provides the *natural environment*. Land, water, trees, and solar energy are elements of the natural environment. The natural environment also includes *climate*, which is the combination of weather conditions in a region over a period of years such as temperature, wind velocity, and precipitation. The altitude and distribution of the land and water help produce the climate.

Shelter varies according to the climate in which it is located. For instance, in areas where it snows or rains often, roofs are sloped to shed snow and rain. In warm, dry areas, roofs may be flat and accessible so people can sleep on the cooler rooftops at night. In cold regions, houses may have smaller doors and fewer windows.

While people want protection from nature, they do not want to be closed off from it. Large windows can frame views of the outdoors while providing protection from the elements. On mild days, patios, swimming pools, and decks provide great opportunities for outdoor living.

A region's *topography*, or the arrangement of physical features of the land, and its climate influence the location and design of dwellings.

Houses with locations and designs that harmonize with the natural setting and climate are more likely to be efficient. For example, placing a house on a location to take advantage of the sun and wind exposure can reduce the amount of energy necessary to heat and cool the interior space and add to occupant comfort.

During the 1950s, integrating houses with the natural environment was explored. Architects designed houses to fit various natural environments. One of the most influential architects concerned with the environment was Frank Lloyd Wright. He broke away from traditional housing designs, saying people should have the courage to follow nature. He used natural settings and many native building materials. For example, Figure 2.18 shows *Fallingwater*—a home Wright designed. Located in Pennsylvania's Laurel Highlands about 90 miles from Pittsburgh, Fallingwater was built over a waterfall between 1936 and 1939. Wright positioned houses to take advantage of natural sunlight and prevailing breezes. He also located them so they had a great deal of privacy. Design for much of today's housing takes advantage of the natural environment.

The Constructed Environment

The *constructed environment* includes the natural environment after changes from human effort. A constructed environment is created when a dwelling is built, landscaped, and heated and/or cooled to control the indoor climate.

Together, natural and constructed environments can provide pleasing surroundings. Highways through the mountains make the beautiful scenery accessible to people. Dwellings located along beaches allow people to enjoy a view of the ocean (Figure 2.19).

The Behavioral Environment

Housing creates an environment in which people can interact with one another. This place of interaction is the *behavioral environment*. Human qualities, such as intelligence, talent, and energy, are one part of this environment. Feelings, such as happiness, loneliness, love, and anger, are another part of it.

The behavioral environment overlaps with the natural and constructed environments. The location of this environment is wherever people interact—in child care centers, schools, shopping centers, neighborhoods, and houses.

Housing fosters social behavior. It may restrict certain types of behavior and permit others. Housing is more than a response to the physical environment. It is a setting for the development of the members of the household.

A positive behavioral environment is desirable for the growth and development of all household

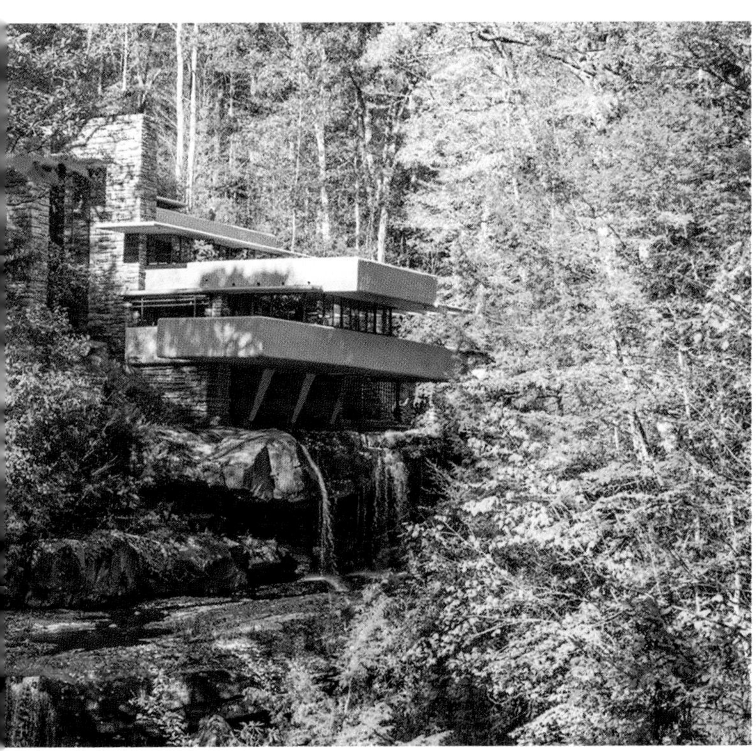

©iStock.com/fdastudillo

Figure 2.18 Frank Lloyd Wright designed this building to visually blend into its hillside environment.

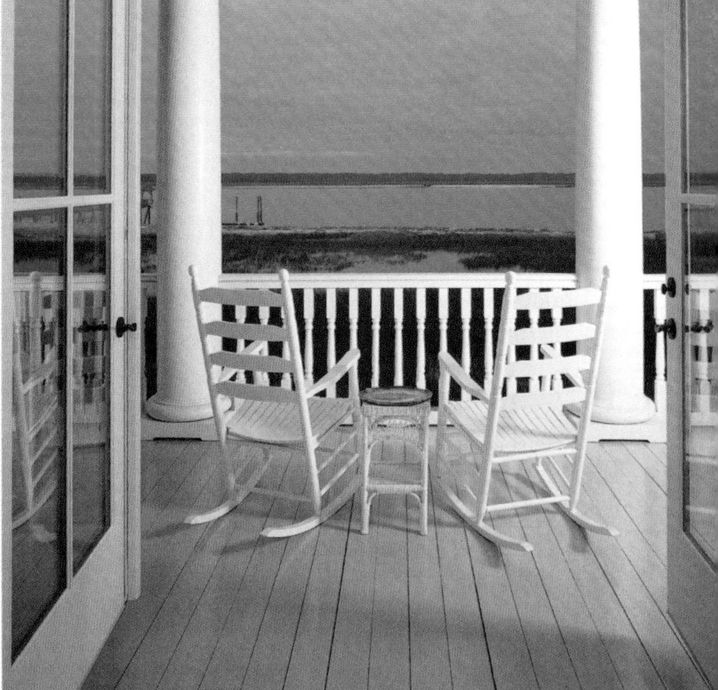

Group 3, Architectural and Interior Design, Hilton Head Island, South Carolina. Photography provided as a courtesy of John McManus, Savannah, Georgia.

Figure 2-19 The people who live in this beach house have easy access to the ocean plus a beautiful view.

Monkey Business Images/Shutterstock.com

Figure 2.20 Many of a person's fondest memories are often linked to the social experiences he or she enjoyed at home.

members. Housing that is safe and adequate contributes to such positive behavior (Figure 2.20). When housing is substandard, however, it can produce a behavioral environment that has a negative effect on household members. For instance, psychological distress due to substandard housing may influence drug addiction, alcoholism, violence, and other negative behaviors among household members.

Interaction of the Environments

Each type of environment affects the other two, causing a chain reaction. One example is a community that has no open space. Houses in this community are built close together, covering most of the land. No land is set aside to preserve part of the natural environment.

The behavioral environment in this type of community can be full of conflict because the constructed and natural environments are not satisfying to the residents. People are simply too crowded and do not have the space they need or the natural beauty they want. Because their environments are not controlled, all their needs and wants cannot be met. Individuals in such environments cannot move toward self-actualization.

Review & Assessment

1. Contrast a constructed environment with the natural environment.
2. What is the behavioral environment? How does it overlap with the natural and constructed environments?
3. Name two negative interactions of natural, constructed, and behavioral environments.

Economic Influences on Housing

The local and global economic influences on housing and interiors involve the production and consumption of goods and services related to housing. These influences include the interaction among consumers, businesses, and government in meeting housing needs.

People make economic decisions every day—decisions concerning how to use their resources to meet their goals. *Resources* are objects, qualities, and personal strengths that people can use to reach a goal. One resource people have is money or purchasing power—a resource they need to achieve for the goal of paying for housing.

Houses are expensive and costs keep rising. According to the National Association of Realtors, the median price of existing homes was $52,200 in 1980. By 1990, the median price rose to $95,500. In 2000, the median price of an existing home was $139,000. By 2007, the National Association of Realtors reported the median housing cost of existing homes was $221,900. Recent reports from this same group, however, indicate that during the housing crisis of 2008–2009, housing prices dropped dramatically. For example, the median price of existing single-family houses dropped to $186,000 in 2008 and to $173,000 in 2009. In 2014, the median price of existing homes rose to $208,900, showing an increase in the health of the overall economy following the 2008 recession.

How Housing Affects the Economy

One way to measure the local economy is to determine the number of families that can afford to buy a median-priced home. High mortgage rates and high unemployment affect the ability of households to purchase housing. According to the U. S. Census Bureau, 52 percent of the total population in 1984 could afford to purchase median-priced homes in their area. By 1995, only 48 percent could afford to buy them. As a result of the economic conditions of 2008–2009, many potential home buyers had reduced incomes and could not buy homes. Although the estimated percentage of buyers who could afford the median-priced existing single-family homes decreased during this period, the affordability is expected to increase slowly from 2009 over the coming years. This is due to the drop in housing prices and housing-loan interest rates.

Another measure of the economy is the number of *housing starts*, or the building of new houses in a given year. In an average year, the housing starts should number around two million, which would meet the demand for new housing. When the economy is up, housing starts will likely reach that number. When the economy is down, the number of housing starts may fall short of expectations.

How the Economy Affects Housing

The economy affects, and is affected by, the production of houses. Many nationally produced goods and services relate to the housing industry. Employment goes up and down in relation to the condition of the housing industry (Figure 2.21). The housing industry employs planners, developers, builders, material suppliers, tradespeople, and financial experts. There are millions of enterprises involved in this industry.

The housing industry depends on the *housing market*, or the transfer of dwellings from the producers to the consumers. The strength of the housing market depends on supply and demand. This is the number of existing houses versus the number needed by the population. The housing market changes considerably from year to year since it follows the general pattern of economic prosperity and decline. War, recession, depression, inflation, and economic uncertainty all negatively impact the housing market.

Housing is traditionally the first major sector of the economy to rebound after an economic slump. Growth in the housing industry has a positive impact on the ***gross domestic product (GDP),*** which is the value of all goods and services produced within a country during a given time period. The GDP is the most accurate indicator of the health of a nation's economy.

Home-loan interest rates and tax advantages affect growth in the housing industry. Interest rates on home loans and inflation seem to increase at the same time.

Sociocultural Connections — Economics: Supply and Demand

The U.S. has an economic system in which businesses are privately owned and operated with limited government regulation. Businesses compete with one another for sales and profits and people generally make their own decisions about what to buy and sell.

In other economic systems, the prices of goods and services, including housing, may be set by the government. In the market economy of the U.S., however, prices are determined by *supply and demand*.

- *Supply* is the quantity of a product or service businesses are willing to provide. According to the *law of supply,* the higher the price at which something can be sold, the more of it businesses want to produce.
- *Demand* is the quantity of a product or service consumers are willing to buy. According to the *law of demand,* the higher the price of something, the less of it consumers want to buy.

When demand is greater than the supply, price rises. This is why airfares are highest during the holidays. More people want to fly then, so airlines can charge a premium. Likewise, when supply is greater than demand, price falls. In the months after the holidays, the same seats on the same planes cost less. Airlines lower their prices to entice people to fly.

Supply and demand help set prices in the housing market as well. Supply is the number of existing homes for sale, and demand is the number of homes sought by home buyers at a given time. For example, a home for sale near the seashore or other desirable area may cost $400,000 or more. In a less desirable area, the same home would sell for substantially less.

Dig Deeper

Use online resources to further investigate the laws of supply and demand in regard to housing prices. At what times of the year are home sales greater? lower? How do seasonal changes impact housing supply and demand? How does supply and demand impact product sales for home interiors?

Blend Images/Shutterstock.com

Figure 2.21 Construction workers have plenty of employment opportunities when demand for housing is strong.

When rates for home loans are low, demand for housing is so high that enough housing may not be available to meet the demand. When rates are high, fewer households invest in new housing.

The federal tax advantages to owning a home include the opportunity to deduct home-loan interest and real estate taxes from your taxable income. Also, home owners are not required to pay taxes on any profits they make from selling their homes, provided they meet a few easy conditions. Finally, those who move because of a job change may have yet another tax advantage.

Review & Assessment

1. What are two ways to measure how housing impacts the local and global economy?
2. What effect does housing growth have on the GDP of a country or nation?
3. Name two tax advantages of owning a home.

Technological Influences on Housing

Technology is the practical application of knowledge. Knowledge of tools, materials, and processes allows people to adapt to their environments. Technology changes over time as new and better ways of meeting human needs are discovered.

Early Technology

Technology began with the early cave dwellers. Caves met the housing needs of the day because they were dry and secure and maintained a moderate temperature. Caves, however, were in short supply and often located far from food and water.

When people evolved from hunting and gathering food to farming, living in caves became less desirable. People then used technology to build dwellings. They constructed their houses with naturally occurring materials, such as logs, sticks, bark, rocks, leaves, grass, mud, and snow. These houses were temporary, lasting only two or three years and were quickly abandoned if the household wanted to move or better housing became available. The main shortcoming of these dwellings was the quality of materials used, not the design.

Over time, technology improved natural materials and new techniques replaced the old. Logs were made into wood planks and stones were chipped into blocks. Animal hides became coverings for windows and doors. Later, methods for developing bricks, tiles, pipes, glass, and cement enhanced the quality of homes.

Industrialization

The ***Industrial Revolution***—a rapid major change in the economy marked by the general introduction of power-driven machinery or the prevailing types and uses of such machines—had a dramatic technological impact on housing. Goods were mass-produced and the railroad system moved them efficiently. Farmers and factories used the railroads to ship their products, which included ready-made housing materials. These ready-made houses became popular because they could be shipped in sections. Between 1908 and 1944, Sears, Roebuck & Company shipped 100,000 mail-order houses. These were "kit" houses ordered from a catalog. All the parts needed for the construction were delivered to the site. Today, some "kit" houses or factory-made houses are available for delivery.

Industrialization changed housing in many ways. Today, many parts of houses, such as doors and windows already in frames, come from the factory ready to install. Factory-produced climate-control units, such as heat pumps, air conditioners, and furnaces, have replaced fireplaces and simple fans. Replacement of hand tools with such laborsaving devices as electric saws and automatic power-nailers made completing such labor-intensive tasks as sawing wood and nailing house frames easier.

The pace of change is increasing faster than ever, fueled by nonstop scientific discoveries. Change is occurring so rapidly that sometimes equipment becomes outdated before it is fully utilized.

Current Technologys

Technology continues to be an ever-changing influence on the trends affecting people's choices regarding housing and interiors. Homes today often include media rooms or home theaters complete with large screens and wireless surround-sound systems that offer a "cinema" feel in the comfort of home (Figure 2.22). Household members extensively use computers, tablets, and other media forms to connect to the Internet for creating documents, research, and many other tasks. People can also use computers to select and locate housing through virtual tours of homes on the web.

Computer technology is the basis for many of the technology-related items found throughout the home. You probably do not even think about the simple computer systems you use, such as a touch-pad on a microwave oven. Computer technology is the reason they operate as they do, and this is true for many other household items. Computers, digital tablets, and cell phones, for example, allow central control of energy management, entertaining, and security systems and promote convenience in living.

LuckyPhoto/Shutterstock.com

Figure 2.22 A current trend in home design is to include media rooms and home theaters.

Many energy-saving and other features on today's appliances result from technology advances. Ranges now have safety locks to protect children and others from unauthorized use. Voice-activated commands assist people with vision disabilities in using appliances. It is now possible to order groceries from a flat-panel computer located on the refrigerator door. Some Wi-Fi enabled refrigerators have the ability to monitor food spoilage and when groceries are needed.

Advances in technology continue to improve building design, assembly systems, and construction materials. For example, treated materials such as wood shingles and asphalt are now made to last at least a half century. Other advances include the use of special roof shingles, in addition to solar panels, to collect energy for electricity. Today's factory-built housing offers higher quality materials, too.

Many architects and interior designers use **computer-aided drafting and design (CADD),** which is software and hardware that creates designs with a computer. CADD is useful in creating housing interiors and house plans. With CADD, designers can quickly adjust plans to conserve materials and improve a building's structure and energy efficiency. They can also more easily make adjustments based on client needs and desires. Consumer versions of CADD are also available for individuals who wish to use their computers to explore possible home modifications or decorating plans (Figure 2.23).

A new technology of use to professionals in the fields of housing and interior design is 3-D printing. **Three-dimensional printing (3-D)**—an additive manufacturing process that uses a 3-D printer to create a three-dimensional solid object/model from a digital file—assists by producing a 3-D model of an object that can be tested or developed more fully. The potential of 3-D printing is being developed for printing actual houses. Ten houses in China were printed full-size in 20 hours. This printing of houses could reduce the speed and cost of building a house as well as use less energy and use recycled materials. See Figure 2.24 for an example of a house model being formed by a 3-D printer.

While technology can solve some problems, it sometimes causes others. One example is a freeway system in a large city that helps people drive quickly and easily between home and work. With increased traffic, however, pollution often develops and decreases air quality.

nahariyani/Shutterstock.com

Figure 2.23 Several brands of computer software in the consumer market can simplify house planning and design.

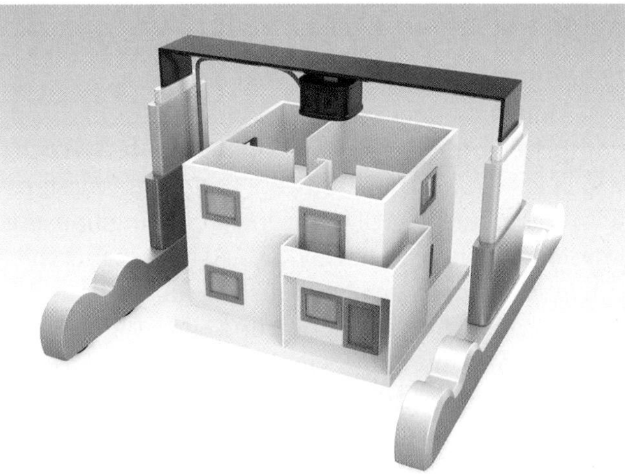

Chesky/Shutterstock.com

Figure 2.24 This photograph shows a 3-D printer actually printing out a house model. The size can be small or the actual size of the house.

Review & Assessment

1. List two forms of early technology that influenced housing.
2. What are two ways the Industrial Revolution influenced housing?
3. How does computer technology influence housing?
4. List two ways that CADD is used to improve housing.
5. What is 3-D printing?

Governmental Influences on Housing

Government at all levels—federal, state, and local—influences housing decisions. This influence began early in U.S. history and continues today. A list of major housing and related legislation appears in the table in Figure 2.25.

Legislation

Laws regulating housing began during colonial times. Some laws prohibited the building of houses on the village green, which was often set aside for government buildings and places of worship. Other laws helped control the spread of fire between adjacent houses. Fireplaces used to cook food and provide heat were often inferior. They caught fire easily and soon the whole house burned. The fire would often spread to other dwellings, and sometimes a single fire would wipe out a whole settlement. In 1649, the British ordered that houses be built of brick or stone and the roofs be made of slate or tile to help prevent the spread of fire.

Over the years, the government has played an increasingly stronger role in safeguarding people and their housing. In the late 1800s, Congress began enacting laws and allocating money for housing. Laws were also introduced at the turn of the twentieth century to control the use of land, prevent overcrowding, and encourage beautification.

Since the 1930s, the federal government has stepped up its efforts to improve housing conditions in the United States. Efforts were made to rebuild the slum areas. The *Federal Housing Administration (FHA)*, an agency that still exists today, was the result of the *Housing Act of 1934*. With the passage of the *Housing Act of 1937*, came the creation of the public-housing program with the objective of providing decent, sanitary housing for families with limited incomes.

Subsequent legislation continued to provide housing programs for families with limited incomes and older citizens. This led to building even more tract houses and numerous apartments and townhouses. In 1965, the *U.S. Department of Housing and Urban Development (HUD)* was formed. This is a cabinet-level, policy-making body whose mission is to promote a decent, safe, and sanitary home, and suitable living environment for every American.

Housing Legislation		
Date	**Legislation**	**Purpose**
1901	**Tenement House Act**	• Improve conditions in tenement houses
1918	**U.S. Housing Corporation**	• Established to provide housing for veterans
1933	**Home Owners' Loan Act of 1933**	• Established corporation to refinance mortgages of distressed home owners; considered successful
1934	**Housing Act of 1934**	• Established *Federal Housing Administration (FHA)* • Established *Federal Savings and Loan Insurance Corporation* to protect deposits • Made possible lower interest rates and longer amortized mortgage periods • Improved housing standards by instituting minimum physical property standards as a basis for FHA participation
1937	**Housing Act of 1937**	• Started public housing program; provided decent, sanitary housing for low-income families • Set forth principle of basing rental payments on an individual family's ability to pay • Provided subsidy by paying difference between rental income and cost of managing the housing units
1942	**National Housing Agency**	• First attempt to coordinate all federal housing programs into one agency
1946	**Veteran's Emergency Housing Act**	• Established the Veteran's Administration program for mortgage insurance
	Farmers' Home Administration	• Now called USDA Rural Development • Created agency in the *U.S. Department of Agriculture* to provide assistance in rural areas to help families obtain housing and offer low-interest loans and grants to limited-income households and the elderly
1947	**"Reorganization Plan No. 3"**	• Created the *Housing and Home Finance* agency. • Placed *Federal Housing Administration,* the *Public Housing Administration,* and the *Home Loan Bank* under the Housing and Home Finance agency
1949	**Housing Act of 1949**	• This very important piece of legislation allowed federal land to be developed by private developers and acknowledged the need for public/private partnership to house the low-income population and to clean/redevelop run-down buildings • Developed the expression of a "decent home and suitable living environment for every American family"
	National Trust for Historic Preservation	• Established a national organization to provide support and encouragement for grassroots preservation of historic buildings • Primary purpose was to acquire and administer National Trust Historic Sites

(Continued)

Figure 2.25 Housing legislation helps safeguard people and their homes. Most legislation relates to quality construction standards, control of land, funding for housing, housing for people in need, and environmental protection.

Housing Legislation *(Figure 2.25, continued)*		
Date	**Legislation**	**Purpose**
1954	**Housing Act of 1954**	• Established the *Urban Planning Assistance Program* • Established the concept of rehabilitation, which is the retention and improvement of essentially sound structures in an urban renewal area • Recognized the need for nonresidential urban renewal to attack blight in business and industrial areas • Broadened concept of rehabilitation to include urban revitalization versus the single goal of good housing
1956	**Housing Act of 1956**	• Established relocation payments for families and businesses, aid for older people, and the *General Neighborhood Renewal Program*
1959	**Housing Act of 1959**	• Established the *Community Renewal Program* and special credit for college and university urban renewal projects
1961	**Housing Act of 1961**	• Shifted more of the financial burden from communities to the federal government for costs associated with removing blight • Established the *Open-Space Program* and the *Mass Transportation Program* • Liberalized various programs of the *Federal Housing Administration*
1964	**Housing Act of 1964**	• Authorized code enforcement of urban renewal projects intended to attack the beginnings of blight in basically sound areas • Authorized low interest loans for residential rehabilitation to support the projects • Liberalized relocation procedures and aid
1965	**Housing and Urban Development Act of 1965**	• Authorized the formation of a cabinet-level federal agency named the *U.S. Department of Housing and Urban Development (HUD)* • Established new approaches to urban renewal including neighborhood facilities, public works and facilities, urban beautification, municipal open spaces, and rehabilitation loans to low-income home owners • Set new public housing policies for rent supplements, leased private housing, and the purchase of existing units
1966	**Demonstration Cities and Metropolitan Development Act of 1966**	Authorized *Model Cities Program* to rebuild to restore extensive blighted areas. Included • "new town" development through FHA financing • new FHA sales housing program for low-income families • grants for surveys of structures and sites to determine historic value • air-rights projects for industrial development
	National Historic Preservation Act—funding	• Established to create federal funding support for the *National Trust for Historic Preservation* (Note: federal funding for the National Trust was terminated in 1996)

(Continued)

Housing Legislation *(Figure 2.25, continued)*		
Date	**Legislation**	**Purpose**
1968	**Housing and Urban Development Act of 1968**	• Added new programs for low- and moderate-income families whose incomes were above the level permitted by public housing; very important piece of legislation
	Civil Rights Act of 1968	• Prohibited discrimination concerning the sale, rental, and financing of housing based on race, religion, natural origin, sex, handicap, and family status • Title VIII of the Act is known as the *Fair Housing Act of 1968*
1970	**Housing and Urban Development Act of 1970**	• Authorized the establishment of a national urban growth policy to encourage and support orderly growth in populated areas
1970	**Office of Fair Housing and Equal Opportunity**	• Established the *Federal Equal Housing Opportunity Council* • Council coordinated equal rights of 50 federal departments and agencies to assure unhindered access to the housing of their choice
	Clean Air Act	• Passed to control smoke pollution and provide environmentally sound treatment of solid waste
1971	**Lead-Based Paint Poisoning Prevention Act**	• Passed in 1971 and amended in 1973; first major lead-based legislation • Addressed lead-based paint in federally funded housing
1974	**Housing and Community Development Act of 1974**	• Established community development block grants to continue urban renewal or neighborhood development programs
	Emergency Housing Act of 1974	• Authorized HUD to buy mortgage loans at below-market interest rates so lenders could offer mortgages at subsidized interest rates
	Real Estate Settlement Procedures Act	• Designed to give consumers more information about costs related to buying or selling a home
	Solar Energy Research, Development and Demonstration Act	• Pursued a vigorous program of research and resource assessment of solar energy as a major source of energy for the nation • Provided the development and demonstration of practical ways of using solar energy on a commercial basis
1975	**Energy Policy and Conservation Act**	• Mandated appliance labeling • *Department of Energy* and *Federal Trade Commission* jointly oversee the implementation of the Act
	Emergency Homeowner's Relief Act of 1975	• Temporary assistance to help defray mortgage payments on homes owned by persons who were temporarily unemployed or underemployed as the result of adverse economic conditions
	National Housing Act	• Amended to increase the maximum loan amounts for the purchase of mobile homes
1976	**Housing Authorization Act of 1976**	• Amended and extended many laws relating to the fields of housing and commercial development

(Continued)

Housing Legislation *(Figure 2.25, continued)*		
Date	**Legislation**	**Purpose**
	Energy Conservation and Production Act	• Required states and localities to adopt Building and Energy Performance Standards
	National Housing Act	• Extended to provide additional subsidized housing • Increased funding for a housing program for the elderly
1977	**Housing and Community Development Act**	• Made it easier for people to buy and improve their dwellings, including raising mortgage loan limits for manufactured homes
	Weatherization Authorization	• U.S. Department of Energy, Community Service Act, and the Farmers Home Administration initiated these programs
	Clean Water Act	• Established a way to regulate discharges of pollutants into U.S. waters
1978	**National Energy Conservation Policy Act**	• Passed to require energy-saving measures nationwide and reduce the country's dependence on oil from other nations. Included: • Utility requirement of information and service to consumers • Availability of energy conservation grants and loans for low- and moderate-income families, rural families, the elderly, and people with special needs • Tax credits for use of renewal energy • Energy efficiency standards for major home appliances
	Consumer Product Safety Commission	• Banned the residential use of lead-based paint
1987	**McKinney Homeless Assistance Act**	• Created to protect and improve the lives and safety of the homes
1988	**Indian Housing Act**	• Legally separated the federal government's efforts for Native Americans from other housing programs
1990	**Cranston-Gonzalez National Affordable Housing Act**	• Passed to help families purchase homes, particularly for first-time home buyers • Made available rental assistance for low-income families
1991	**Cranston-Gonzalez National Affordable Housing Act (revised)**	• Expanded to include war veterans and residents of Indian reservations
1992	**Residential Lead-Based Paint Hazard Act of 1992**	• Requires sellers to warn buyers of presence of lead-based paint
	Energy Policy Act of 1992	• Required that states adopt a residential building code for energy efficiency that meets or exceeds the Council of American Building Officials (CABO) Model Energy Code • Established thermal insulation and energy efficiency standards for manufactured housing similar to standards of some site-built housing • Pilot studies in five states were authorized to study energy efficient mortgages • Required energy efficiency labels on windows and window systems to help consumers make informed decisions

(Continued)

Housing Legislation *(Figure 2.25, continued)*

Date	Legislation	Purpose
1995	**Housing for Older Persons Act of 1995**	• Passed to exempt housing communities of older persons from the *Fair Housing Act* discrimination charges, allowing them to continue to offer services to singles or couples age 55 years or older versus including younger persons or to those with different family arrangements
1996	**Safe Water Drinking Act of 1974 (extended)**	• Extended beyond just safety of water to include source water protection, operator training, funding for water system improvements, and provision of public information
	National Trust for Historic Preservation (funding)	• Federal funding for the *National Trust for Historic Preservation* was terminated; the Trust proceeded on private-sector contributions
1997	**Housing Opportunity and Responsibility Act of 1977**	• Reformed public housing by providing for the demolition of deteriorating public housing and replacement with mixed-income housing through partnership with the public sector
	Clean Air Act	• Amendments established air quality standards
1999	**Federal Omnibus Act of 1987 Act 9 (amended)**	• Amended and expanded to require skilled nursing facilities to provide services to meet the highest practical physical, medical, and psychological well-being of every resident
2000	**American Homeownership and Economic Opportunity Act of 2000**	• Removed barriers to home ownership, making sure that Tribal housing and other special groups were included
2001	**Programs for Older Persons**	• Helped older persons stay in their homes by providing support services; included Tribal communities
2005	**Energy Policy Act of 2005**	• Provided tax breaks for making energy conservation improvements to their homes • Promoted ENERGY STAR compliant technologies for the home • Included tax credits for new energy-efficient homes and for energy-efficient appliances
2008	**Emergency Economic Stabilization Act of 2008**	• Extended many of the consumer tax incentives for energy-efficient existing homes, including renewable energy home applications and systems (solar energy, small wind turbines, geothermal heat pumps)
	Housing and Economic Recovery Act of 2008	• Provided ways to stimulate housing activity to offset conditions that adversely affect consumers and the economy • Provided a tax credit and increased loan limits to assist first-time home buyers
2009	**American Recovery and Reinvestment Act of 2009 (ARRA)**	• Provided stimulus to the U.S. economy due to the recent downturn
	Worker, Homeownership and Business Assistance Act of 2009	• Extended tax credits to home buyers

Due to an economic downturn beginning in 2007, the federal government passed several stimulus packages to offset related economic problems. Sections of the stimulus packages were to assist individuals and families in making payments on their housing loans. These packages included special sections and assistance for renters, home owners, and first-time home buyers.

In 2008, Congress passed and the president signed into law the *Housing and Economic Recovery Act of 2008.* The economic conditions of the United States and its households led to extensive foreclosures on homes throughout the nation. This law provides ways to offset these conditions and to encourage activity in the housing market. The act includes a tax credit and increased loan limits to assist first-time home buyers.

In 2009, Congress passed and the president signed into law the *American Recovery and Reinvestment Act of 2009.* This law has many provisions affecting housing. For example, it includes provisions for first-time home buyer assistance, rental assistance, and construction incentives for housing for people with limited incomes.

Congress continues to pass housing legislation and allocate money for housing programs. States also pass laws that relate to housing, which must conform to federal legislation. The federal government is delegating more and more responsibility for regulating housing in the states.

City or county governments may establish local housing-related ordinances. These regulations must also conform to both federal and state laws. Most local housing legislation falls into one of the following categories:

- standards for quality construction
- control of land and density
- funding for housing
- housing for people in need
- environmental protection

Standards for Quality Construction

Much of the housing legislation sets minimum standards of quality for various areas. Standards are set for land use and dwelling construction. They are also set to control density and separate residences from industry. Other standards are set to protect human health.

Standards include building codes. **Building codes** establish minimum standards for materials and construction methods. There are codes for plumbing, heating, ventilation, and electrical systems (Figure 2.26). Placement of stairways and exits are also included in the codes. The codes help assure healthy, safe, and sanitary conditions. Some standards also relate to appearance. They indicate roof styles or maximum height. Local and state governments formulate and enforce such codes. The latest edition of the *International Building Code* is the most widely adopted model building code in the world. It sets minimum standards for building construction.

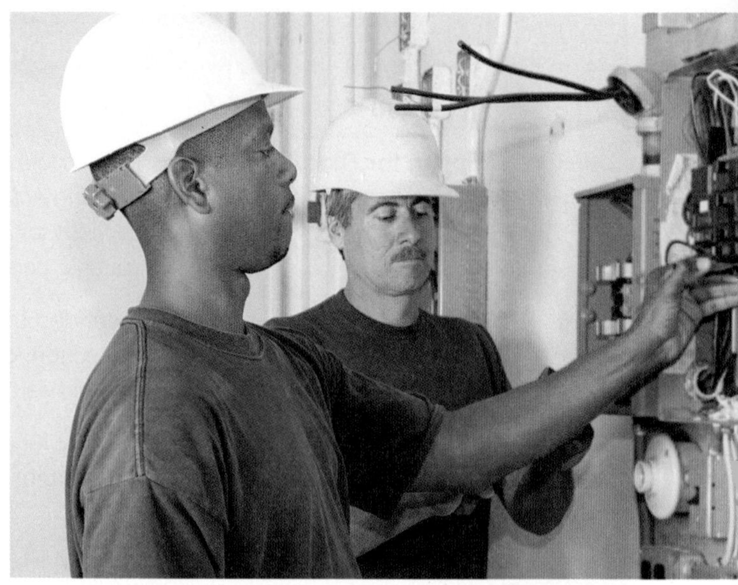

Lisa F. Young/Shutterstock.com

Figure 2.26 Building codes require qualified electricians to install the electrical systems. The same is true for the heating, cooling, and plumbing systems.

Standards become part of the building code only after formal adoption by a broad range of industry experts. Standards help ensure the safety, health, and integrity of materials, products, and services for consumers. Organizations such as the *American National Standards Institute (ANSI)* and the *American Society for Testing and Materials (ASTM)* promote and facilitate standards development.

Some housing codes determine the use, occupancy, and maintenance of buildings. One reason is to prevent overcrowding. Another is to guarantee that major alterations made to a dwelling meet required standards. Enforcement of these codes may be poor in some communities, sometimes because of too few inspection officials. Also, some people resist inspections that will result in exposure of their code breaking, which often involves a fine and/or penalties.

Control of Land and Density

A **zoning regulation** is a government requirement that controls land use. It specifies and

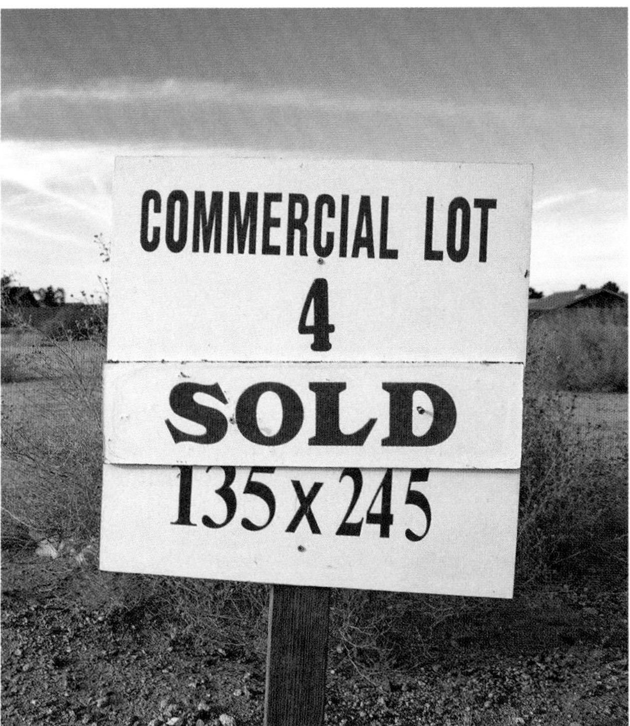

Straight 8 Photography/Shutterstock.com

Figure 2.27 The land under this sign is zoned for commercial purposes only.

permits the type of buildings and activities in a certain area. For example, such regulations may dictate land for residential, commercial, or industrial use. In a residential zone, only residential dwellings can be built. Commercial zones limit structures to stores and office buildings (Figure 2.27). In industrial zones, only construction of factories and other industrial businesses can occur. Sometimes regulations may only permit one type of dwelling within a residential area. Many communities restrict the location of manufactured housing and multifamily dwellings to specific areas. Zoning laws may also specify the minimum size of dwellings in an area.

Zoning regulations also control density. Controlling density reduces the risk of fire and keeps traffic and pollution manageable. It also restricts excessive noise and lighting. Density restrictions also limit lot size and the placement of a building on a lot.

Government controls at all levels tend to increase the cost of housing. However, the intention of building and zoning controls is to serve the best interests of the public.

Funding for Housing

Funding is another example of government involvement in housing. Several government agencies are charged with buying and selling home loans. The government assures some loans, which means it stands behind the lender if home owners do not meet their obligations. The government helps special groups—such as older people, people with disabilities, veterans, families with limited incomes, and first-time home owners—acquire funding. Most of these financial organizations are a part of HUD.

Housing for People in Need

Various forms of government assistance are available to help people who cannot afford housing. HUD provides rent supplements to individuals and families with low incomes. HUD also builds public housing for those unable to fully pay for satisfactory housing. The federal government also gives support to private programs created to help the homeless.

Local governments may donate existing houses that need rehabilitation or may assist with the infrastructure. **Infrastructure** is the underlying foundation or basic framework. In housing, the term often refers to installation of the sewer, water, gas, and electrical lines to make housing livable.

In recent years, the number of homeless people has increased dramatically. Current estimations indicate there are between 500,000 and seven million homeless people in the United States. A large percentage of homeless people are members of families with children and war veterans. Many are newly and temporarily homeless, having suddenly lost a job or the ability to work. Others are chronically homeless, having accepted their homeless condition as a way of life. In addition, the number of homeless people in rural and suburban areas rose dramatically in 2007 and beyond.

People who become homeless do not fit any one description. All people, however, experiencing homelessness have basic needs, including adequate incomes, affordable housing, and health care. Some homeless people may need special services, such as mental health or drug-abuse treatment, to have adequate housing. Preventing homelessness requires meeting all their needs.

Many people have benefited from government housing assistance. There never seems to be enough assistance, however, to accommodate everyone who needs it. Since government assistance cannot meet the total housing-assistance needs in American society, various community partnerships have formed to help meet the housing needs of limited-resource families.

An important example is *Habitat for Humanity*. This is a partnership formed to help eliminate homelessness and substandard housing, not only in the United States, but also in other countries.

Career Focus Industry Researcher and Trend Forecaster

Do you wonder why some things are popular and some things are not? Do you notice trends in interiors and fashion that you encounter? Do you like the idea that you could influence trends in the future? If you do, a career in Industry Research and Trend Forecasting might be for you!

Tashatuvango/Shutterstock.com

Interests/Skills: Curiosity and a love of learning are great starting points for someone interested in *Industry Research and Forecasting.* Researchers must be able to collect information and critically identify consumer patterns. Forecasters must be creative and be able to communicate findings to those who will benefit. They must have what is called consumer empathy, being observant and able to relate to potential customers' wants and needs. Forecasters must enjoy exploring and benefit greatly from being bilingual, as travel is a major part of their work.

Career Snapshot: An industry researcher or trend forecaster might work for a manufacturer, as an independent consultant or for an association or publication. A *market researcher* analyzes trends; examines sales in the various design areas; and collects consumer insights, research innovations, and identify patterns in the industry. A *trend forecaster* attends markets, exhibitions, trade shows, and industry events throughout the world—identifying and tracking trends in interior products and allied industries. The forecaster takes these inspirations and combines them with the market researcher's findings to establish forecasts for consumer preferences often a full two years ahead of time. These forecasts might include colors, themes, materials, shapes, and even entire product categories that will be popular in the future. Manufacturers, design firms, retailers, and individual designers use this information to understand what consumers want and how much they will pay for products which then drive their decisions. If working for a textiles, materials or furniture manufacturer, a forecaster manages product introductions to the public consumer. Some might serve as professional magazine writers or editors of style and design publications or publish what are called "white papers" that design industry members turn to for inspiration and direction.

Education/Training: A bachelor's degree in Interior Design with additional studies in Merchandising and Marketing is a great first step in becoming a design trend forecaster. Many might explore master's degree studies in Psychology, Sociology, Anthropology, or Art History for further preparation for the industry. The research and writing aspects of the profession might require a more concentrated education in the areas of business, marketing, or journalism.

Licensing/Examinations: Although strict certifications are not required, it is beneficial for a trend forecaster to seek certifications in their area of specialization. For instance, if you wanted to specifically track and predict trends in sustainable products and development, it might be wise to become a *LEED Accredited Professional* (Leadership in Energy and Environmental Design). For those more interested in the research and data analysis aspects, there is an exam to be a *Certified Professional in Demand Forecasting (CPDF).*

Professional Associations: The American Society of Interior Designers (ASID); the International Interior Design Association (IIDA); the Color Association of the United States (CAUS); and the Color Marketing Group (CMG).

Job Outlook: As online and international consumption increases, as does the industry's use of data and market research, job opportunities in each facet of research and forecasting will continue to grow much faster than traditional careers.

Sources: The Occupational Outlook Handbook; the Occupational Information Network (O*NET); the Color Association of the US (CAUS); the Color Marketing Group (CMG)

Habitat for Humanity®/Will Crocker

Figure 2.28 These college students spent their spring break as volunteers building new homes for families without adequate housing.

Plamen/Shutterstock.com

Figure 2.29 Safeguarding the natural environment will allow people to enjoy the beauty of nature for generations to come.

Habitat for Humanity relies on volunteers for a number of tasks, including the providing of labor to actually build houses (Figure 2.28). The future home owners must make a generous hands-on donation of labor or similar resources, called "sweat equity," to help produce their own housing. They make a down payment and have low monthly payments. The money goes into a revolving fund to help others obtain housing through the program. Hundreds of volunteers from civic clubs, religious groups, professional organizations, student groups, and institutions regularly join forces with Habitat for Humanity to build housing structures and a true sense of community.

Environmental Protection

Concern for the environment has led to a number of environmental protection laws. In addition, creation of such government agencies as the *U.S. Environmental Protection Agency (EPA)* and the *U.S. Consumer Product Safety Commission (CPSC)* helps foster a positive natural environment. They support research and provide information to consumers so the housing environment, and the total environment, will be safe and protected. The agencies have telephone hotlines to assist consumers with problems concerning the environment.

The job of the Environmental Protection Agency (EPA) is to safeguard the natural environment, including the air, water, and land upon which life depends. Consequently, the agency focuses on the natural environment as well as the quality of air and water within housing (Figure 2.29). EPA also assists with voluntary pollution-prevention programs and energy-conservation methods.

The *Consumer Product Safety Commission (CPSC)* has jurisdiction over more than 15,000 consumer products used in and around the constructed environment. The agency's focus is to save lives and keep families safe by reducing the risk of injuries and deaths associated with consumer products. Examples of products the commission tests include cleaning supplies, small and large household equipment (such as toasters and dishwashers), lamps, and outdoor play equipment. The CPSC has the authority to recall unsafe products or require their repair. The agency also investigates product complaints linked to injuries and deaths and issues safety guidelines and consumer education.

Review & Assessment 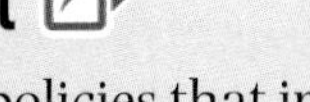

1. Summarize laws and policies that impact housing decisions and costs.
2. Contrast building codes and zoning regulations.
3. Give an example of a nongovernmental partnership that helps meet housing needs.
4. What is the role of the U.S. Environmental Protection Agency?
5. How does the Consumer Product Safety Commission save lives and keep families safe?

Chapter 2 Assessment

Summary

- Many forces work together to influence housing. Some forces involve people. Other forces involve conditions.
- The cultural development of housing in North America began when settlers arrived from all over the world to join the Native Americans, bringing their cultures and housing influences with them.
- Historical events such as the Industrial Revolution, Great Depression, and World Wars I and II impacted how people were housed.
- Societal events—such as changes in household needs, wants, and lifestyles—affected housing designs.
- The Industrial Revolution, population increases, and economic crises all caused housing shortages.
- To ease the shortages, use of technology and government agencies helped develop new solutions for affordable housing.
- Housing is a part of the constructed, natural, and behavioral environments.
- Government legislation establishes building standards, zoning regulations, and environmental protection.
- The government ensures the natural, constructed, and behavioral environments work well together and provides funding for affordable housing.

Terms in Action

1. **Term flash cards** Work with a partner to write the definitions of the *Content Terms* and *Academic Terms* at the beginning of the chapter based on your current understanding before reading the chapter. Then pair up with another pair to discuss your definitions and any discrepancies. Finally, discuss the definitions with the class and ask your instructor for necessary correction or clarification.

Think Critically

2. **Analyze options** Not all people have incomes sufficient to adequately meet their housing needs. In your opinion, should all, part, or none of their housing costs be paid (subsidized) by government sources? If the government is involved, what selection process should be used to determine who is eligible to receive assistance?
3. **Draw conclusions** What could happen to housing if building regulations were suddenly eliminated—allowing anything to be built in any way? In what instances (if any) could the resulting housing be better? In what instances could it be worse? Draw conclusions and share your opinions with the class.
4. **Predict technology** Working with two or three classmates, predict what new technology trends will be used in houses in 20 years. List your ideas with as much detail as possible and share them with the class.

Core Skills

5. **Reading and speaking** Locate and read a biography or autobiography about an Early American settler. What was life like for this individual? What shelter options did this person have? How did these options impact daily living? Give an oral book report to share with the class.
6. **Speaking and listening** Conduct an oral-history interview with an older member of your community to determine housing characteristics common to your region when he or she was growing up. Ask how housing has changed and improved over time. How did housing decisions impact family relationships and management of family, community, and wage-earner roles? Share your findings with the class via an oral report.
7. **Reading and writing** Obtain online advertisements from different housing developers and house builders to analyze aspects of community planning that impact housing decisions. List the advantages they give for the types of houses they promote. Summarize in writing how the advantages relate to the natural, constructed, and behavioral environments.
8. **Research and writing** Suppose a client wants to add a three-season room off the back of his house. Use online or print resources to research information on local building codes to determine what building-code requirements are necessary for this project. How do the local building codes expand on the International

Chapter 2 Assessment

Building Code? Write a summary of your findings to share with the class.

9. **Research and writing** Identify a local problem that involves the environment and housing conditions. Research how this problem could be solved and which government agencies could help you. Write a brief report.
10. **Technology** Search the Internet for new technologies in housing trends. Choose one that interests you and determine the following: What are the benefits of using the technology? What are some possible disadvantages with using this technology? In your opinion, is the technology likely to be used in almost all houses? Why or why not?
11. **Research and speaking** Investigate the harmful health effects that lead-based paint poses to humans. Check out the websites for the National Safety Council or the U.S. Consumer Product Safety Commission for your research. Determine where it is generally found and how it can be removed safely. What groups of people are identified as most affected by lead-based paint? Create a news bulletin and post it to the class web page.
12. **Research and speaking** Choose a topic from the chapter and use images and a presentation software application to show how the topic has influenced housing. Obtain the images off the Internet or take pictures with a digital camera. Add appropriate captions and credits to the photos. Possible topics include: household composition, life expectancy, government influences, and technological advances. Share your presentation with the class.
13. **CTE career readiness practice** As communities look for ways to improve housing for citizens and protect the environment, opportunities exists for people and their employers to take action. Because of your involvement with *Rebuilding Together,* your employer asks you to spearhead a team of employees to help improve living conditions for people in your community. To start the service project, your employer agrees to give participating employees one workday to initiate a project. You and several team members attend a city council meeting to identify housing and environment issues that negatively impact your community. The workday following the council meeting, you do the following:

    A. ***Identify the community concerns to the team.*** Have teams brainstorm ways to address one or more of the problems. Evaluate the list and narrow it to one project on which the team agrees.

    B. ***Have the team set a goal.*** Determine the resources the team needs to meet the goal.

    C. ***Create a plan.*** Determine who, what, where, when, and how your team will accomplish the goal. How can individual members continue to help meet the team goal after the initial action?

    D. ***Carry out the team plan.***

    E. ***Evaluate the results of the team action.*** How was your team able to meet its goal and your employer's goal of getting workers involved in the community? In what ways will team members carry on with the project to meet community needs?

Design Practice

14. **Designing for older adults** Presume that you and have taken on the challenge of redesigning living space for an older adult with moderate mobility problems who still manages all self-care activities. Modifications to the living space will make daily-care activities easier for the older adult. Use resources as needed to complete the following: (A) Write a 300 word proposal indicating design modifications—especially to the living area, kitchen, and bath—that will enable the older adult to better provide self-care. (B) Locate photo examples for your proposed design modifications and use them with your electronic presentation. Obtain facts that support your modifications for the space. (C) Share your presentation with your client (the class).
15. **Portfolio** Walk around your neighborhood and look for ways people have altered the natural environment for housing purposes. Photograph the changes you find. Assess how the constructed environment influenced the alterations to the natural environment and write a short summary of your assessment. Create a digital storyboard to share your findings. Save your presentation on a CD or other storage device for your portfolio.

Chapter 3

Decision Making and Housing Options

Content Terms

region
community
neighborhood
site
orientation
minimum property standards (MPS)
public zone
service zone
private zone
cooperative
condominium
owner-built housing
factory-built housing
site-built house
modular housing
manufactured housing
mobile homes
panelized housing
precut housing
kit housing
aging-in-place
reverse mortgage
assisted-living facility
graduated-care facility
Fair Housing Act

Academic Terms

decision-making process
heterogeneous
homogenous

Learning Outcomes

After studying this chapter, you will be able to

- summarize the different types of decisions and factors affecting these choices.
- identify human and nonhuman resources.
- summarize the steps of the decision-making process.
- demonstrate effective decision-making skills.
- analyze aspects of community planning that impact decisions about housing such as region, community, neighborhood, population, site, and natural restraints.
- identify decisions involved in choosing a site and house.
- compare different types of available housing.
- research and describe housing features and needs for people who have special needs including older adults, people with disabilities, or families with children.
- research and describe current and future housing trends and the effects of technology.

Reading with Purpose

Read the review questions at the end of the chapter *before* you read the chapter. Keep these questions in mind as you read to help determine which information is most important.

G-WLEARNING.com

While studying, look for the access icon  **to:**

- **Practice** the *Content* and *Academic Terms* with e-flash cards, matching activities, and vocabulary games.
- **Reinforce** what you learn by completing the *Review & Assessment* questions and e-mailing them to your instructor.

www.g-wlearning.com/housing/

Alison Hancock/Shutterstock.com

In the first two chapters of this textbook, you read that many decisions affect housing. These decisions relate to your needs, values, life situations, lifestyle, and environmental and governmental influences. Because these factors are constantly changing, you continually face making new decisions. By making these decisions wisely, you and other members of your household will have the chance to grow and develop to full potential. It is important to develop good decision-making skills so you are able to enhance your life and your housing. These skills will also be necessary in any career path you choose to follow whether it is as an interior designer or other housing career.

In this chapter, the decision-making process and the many options for choosing housing are explored. The ***decision-making process*** is a method for selecting logical choices from available solutions to make a decision or solve a problem. This process includes five steps: identify the challenge or problem; list the possible alternatives or solutions; make the best decision; take action on the decision; and evaluate the results. The decision-making process is a clear tool to assist in selecting the options that best meet people's needs.

Types of Decisions

All decisions are not alike. Learning to recognize the different types of decisions will help you develop decision-making skills.

Decisions can be classified into two groups (Figure 3.1). One group consists of those decisions that vary according to the thought and care used in making them. The other group of decisions consists of interrelated decisions and is based on their relationship to other decisions.

Resources for Housing Decisions

As you learned earlier, *resources* are material objects, qualities, or personal strengths you can use to reach a goal. You need resources to carry out any type of decision you make. Resources are available to you in many forms.

Human Resources

Human resources are resources available from people. They include ability, knowledge, attitude, energy, and health (Figure 3.2).

You may have many resources that help you make choices about housing. For instance, if you have the ability to make house repairs, you have *skill* as a human resource. If you are willing to learn how to make house repairs, you have *intelligence* as human resource. When you develop and use these resources, you can make decisions and achieve results.

If you are a person with a high energy level, you may spend time after school and on weekends doing extra projects to improve your housing. If you have a low energy level, you may choose to hire someone to perform maintenance tasks to keep your house in shape.

Good health as a resource enables you to use other human resources to an advantage. For

Types of Decisions	
	Decisions Based on Degree of Thought
Rational Decisions	Solutions are selected only after carefully examining problems. All alternatives and consequences are considered.
Impulse Decisions	Choices made quickly with little thought given to possible outcomes.
Habitual Decisions	Choices made instinctively or routinely without thought. Decisions are required only when new factors arise.
	Decisions Based on Relationships
Central-satellite Decisions	A central, major decision surrounded by related but independent decisions.
Chain Decisions	A series of decisions in which one decision triggers other decisions. All decisions must be made to complete an action.

Figure 3.1 Decisions are classified by the amount of thought devoted to them or by their relationships to other decisions.

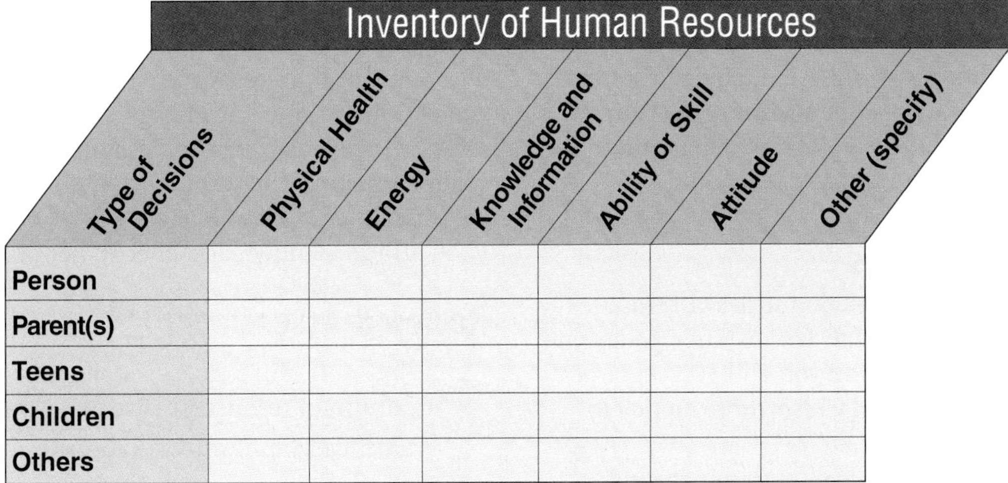

Type of Decisions	Physical Health	Energy	Knowledge and Information	Ability or Skill	Attitude	Other (specify)
Person						
Parent(s)						
Teens						
Children						
Others						

Figure 3.2 Make an inventory of the human resources in your household by preparing a chart similar to this. Rate household members on a scale of 1 to 5, with 5 being the highest rating.

example, when you are healthy you likely have motivation to use your knowledge and skills. You might decide to remodel your kitchen. If you have poor health, you are likely to postpone the project or hire someone to do it for you.

Nonhuman Resources

Nonhuman resources are resources that are not directly supplied by people. They include money, property, time, and community resources.

Money

Consider the use of the nonhuman resource of money in housing. Everyone has some housing expenses. You need money to buy or rent a place to live. You need additional money for furnishings, equipment, utilities, and repairs. You must decide what you can afford to spend for these items. The following factors will determine the amount to spend:

- income
- savings
- lifestyle
- possessions

Property

The property you acquire and the way you use it relate to your housing decisions. Property resources include such items as land, buildings, and furnishings. The choices you have made and the property you already possess partly determine the amount you can afford for housing. Perhaps you are willing to live in a less expensive apartment so you can have new furniture. If you choose a more expensive apartment, the furniture or some other housing feature may need to wait. You may decide to reupholster or repair older furniture rather than replace it.

Time

Time is also a nonhuman resource. How you use time is what counts most. You have 24 hours a day, 365 days a year, just as everyone else has. Time is the only resource all people have in equal amounts. Other resources come in different quantities for different people.

Community Resources

People often take community resources for granted, but these resources can play an important part in your housing decisions. You may base the decision of where you will live on the quality of the community resources available. For example, you may want to have a good public library in your community. This will help you do your homework, prepare for a career, and even find a job. You can also use library resources for recreation.

A city park with a playground and a picnic area is another community resource. If you know that a park is nearby, you may choose housing with a yard smaller than originally planned.

Some community schools and recreation departments offer special classes for self-improvement. By taking advantage of these classes, you can learn such skills as furniture refinishing, upholstering, remodeling, and home maintenance. As interest in do-it-yourself projects increases, many home-improvements stores are also teaching classes on home maintenance as well as some television programming.

Other community resources include hospitals, fire stations, police departments, shopping centers, and sports facilities (Figure 3.3). What community resources are available where you live?

Using Resources

You will have different quantities of resources at different times in your life. For instance, today you may have more energy than you will 30 years from now. In the future, you may have more money to spend than you have now.

Some people have little of both money and energy. To make their resources meet their needs, they must know how to use their knowledge and abilities to save money and energy.

You can choose which resources to spend and which to save. Suppose that you own a house that needs painting. You could paint it yourself, although this would take a lot of time that you may prefer spending in some other way. You may decide to hire someone else to paint the house, such as a professional painter or experienced friend.

Some human resources decrease as you use them, namely time and energy, while others increase with use, such as your abilities and knowledge. You seldom use only one resource at a time since all are closely related. To develop a new skill, you need a good attitude, knowledge, energy, health, and time.

Review & Assessment

1. What is the difference between human and nonhuman resources? Give an example of each.
2. Name five community resources.
3. What one resource is the same for everyone?
4. Give an example of how your use of resources, both human and nonhuman, can change over time.

The Decision-Making Process

To make a wise decision, you must first understand the question, problem, or issue involved.

Anne Kitzman/Shutterstock.com

Figure 3.3 A community pool and picnic shelter is a valuable entertainment resource.

Green Choices

Choose a LEED-Certified Home

LEED stands for *Leadership in Energy and Environmental Design*. A LEED-certified home means that the structure meets the guidelines to be a green and sustainable building. The U.S. Green Building Council sets the guidelines and ratings. The Council has a rating system with four levels that certify that a house is environmentally responsible. The four levels include the following: Certified, Silver, Gold, and Platinum (highest).

The LEED certification means that a home's features promote such green and sustainable design, construction, and operations practices as the following:

- Innovation and design—highest standard for "green" performance
- Environmentally responsible within the larger community
- Sustainable sites—minimal impact of the home on the land
- Water efficiency—indoors and out
- Energy efficient—in the structure and heating and cooling design
- Materials and resources—efficient use of materials, use environmentally preferred materials, and produce less waste in construction
- Indoor environmental quality (IAQ)—reduce the creation of and exposure to pollutants
- Home owner education—how to use and maintain the green features
- Third-party verification—someone other than the builder has certified the green parts of the home

Knowing that, you can then reach a satisfactory answer or solution by following the steps in the decision-making process (Figure 3.4).

1. **Identify the challenge or problem.** The first step in the decision-making process focuses on defining the question or challenge accurately. This is the most important step. If you cannot properly identify the real issue, all the work that follows may be in vain.
2. **List possible alternatives or solutions.** The second step involves exploring possible alternatives or solutions. You look for various ways to address the issue and list each possible alternative. While exploring your options, you would answer the following questions:
   - What is the likely outcome of each possible alternative?
   - Will any alternative provide lasting satisfaction to those involved?
   - What other decisions must you make first?

   During the second step, you must also examine your resources since they affect which decisions you can make. Suppose you plan a backyard get-together with friends. If storms arrive, you must have the resource of sufficient indoor space to use. Without it, you do not have all the resources you need for the get-together.

   Another consideration includes limitations imposed by others. Suppose a student decides to spend the money earned at an after-school job on a used car presuming his family will provide insurance coverage. If his family cannot insure the vehicle, the student must reconsider his options and make a different decision.
3. **Make the best decision.** The third step involves making a decision by choosing which of the alternatives on your list is best. If one option does not clearly stand out as the best choice, you probably need to repeat one or both

Steps in the Decision-Making Process
1. Identify the challenge or problem.
2. List possible alternatives or solutions.
3. Make the best decision.
4. Take action on the decision.
5. Evaluate the results.

Figure 3.4 Following these steps carefully will help you make good decisions.

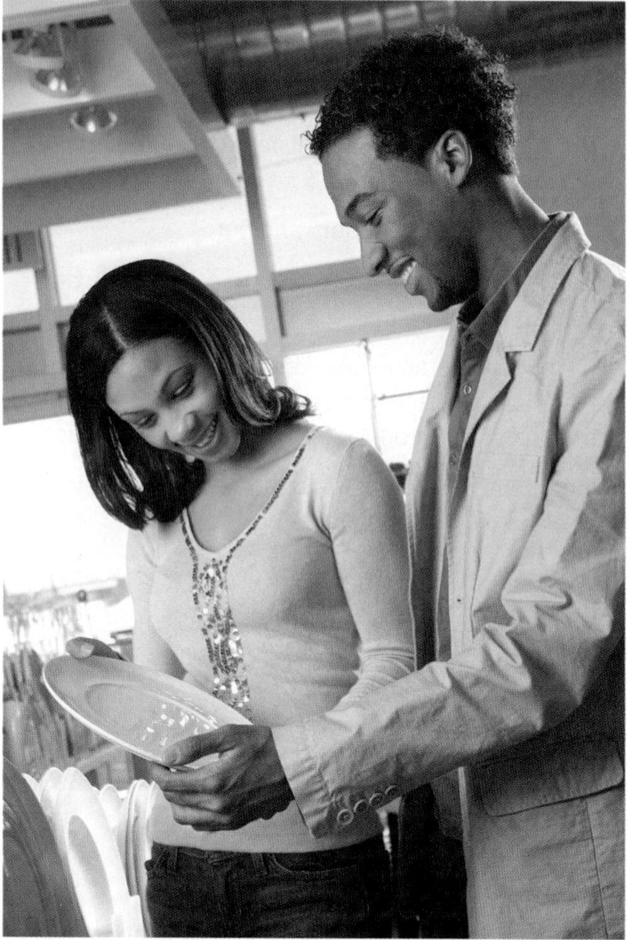

iofoto/Shutterstock.com

Figure 3.5 Shopping for items to fill a specific need forces you to go through the steps of the decision-making process.

of the earlier steps. Then, the best option should be clear (Figure 3.5).

4. **Take action on the decision.** The fourth step involves taking action to *implement* your decision, or put thoughts into action. A plan of action is necessary to fully implement a decision. Before taking action, you need to plan exactly what to do as well as when, where, how, and with whom to do it.
5. **Evaluate the results.** The fifth step is to evaluate the results of your decision. Did everything go as planned? Was the problem or challenge satisfactorily addressed? Did something totally unexpected occur? If so, you may need to plan a new course of action or repeat part or all of the decision-making process.

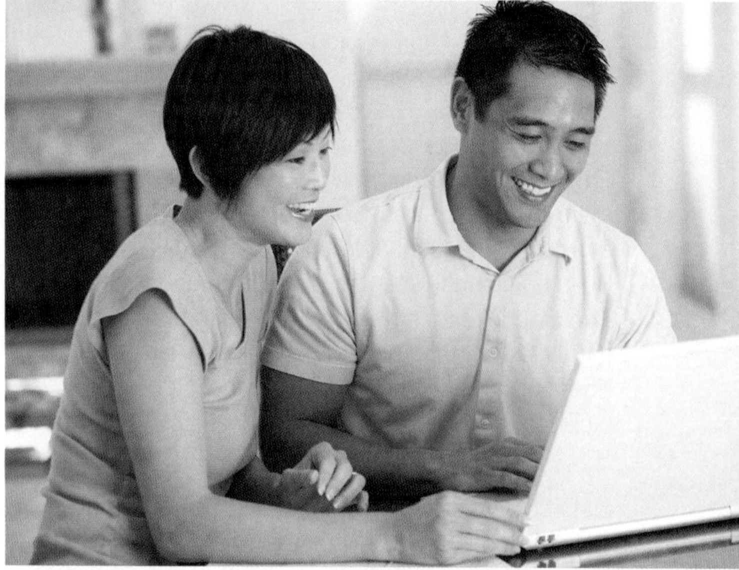

Monkey Business Images/Shutterstock.com

Figure 3.6 This couple is carefully deciding what option will be best for their family.

That last step provides ideas on how to improve your decision making next time. If you are not pleased with the results, ask yourself the following questions: Did I define the problem clearly? Did I think of all possible alternatives? Did I implement my decision in the most desirable way? How could I have made a better decision in this case? How could I have implemented the decision with a better plan of action? Asking such questions is important for all decisions, whether personal or decisions for housing and interiors clients. See Figure 3.6.

Housing Options

You will have many decisions to make when finding a place to live. Some of these decisions will concern the

Green Choices

LEED Accredited Architects and Interior Designers

When you decide to build a home or design the interior of a home with green or sustainable design, a first step is to choose architects and/or interior designers who have the designation of LEED Accredited Professional (LEED AP).

An architect or interior designer who has the LEED AP has passed an exam given by the Green Building Certification Institute, a division of the U.S. Green Building Council. Passing the exam indicates that the architects or interior designers have knowledge of the LEED rating systems that allows them to facilitate the integrated-design process and streamline LEED certification for their projects.

location and type of dwelling to choose. Other decisions will concern choosing a design that meets the needs of all people, including those with special needs.

Location

When choosing a place to live, you will need to carefully consider the following about the location (Figure 3.7):

- the region or area of the world, country, or state
- the community—rural, suburb, or city
- neighborhood or section of the community
- composition of the population
- the site or lot within the neighborhood

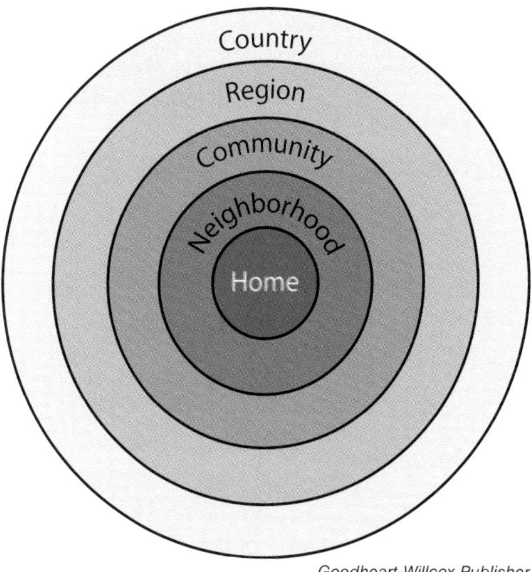

Goodheart-Willcox Publisher

Figure 3.7 Selecting a location in which to live involves considering the country, region, community, neighborhood, and the actual home.

Region

A **region** is a specific part of the world, country, or state in which you live. The reasons for choosing to live in a certain region vary. You may like the scenery. Perhaps the climate is important to you (Figure 3.8). You may want to be close to family members or friends. Employment may also lead you to a certain region. Jobs are usually easier to find in regions with large cities. Figure 3.9 lists several items to consider when choosing a region in which to live. Which describes your ideal region?

Community

A region is divided into communities. A **community** may be a large city, small village, or rural area.

Cities are high-density areas with many people living close together. If you or your housing and interiors clients enjoy living in close proximity to other people, you are *contact* people and may enjoy an urban lifestyle.

A oliveromg/Shutterstock.com

B Carlos Neto/Shutterstock.com

C Alvov/Shutterstock.com

Figure 3.8 Some people choose a place to live that is close to the sports activities they enjoy. For example, they may prefer living where they can spend most of the year (A) playing at the beach, (B) hiking, or (C) snow skiing.

Choosing a Region	
Consideration	**Range of Choices**
General Climate	• Hot to cold • Dry to wet/humid • Constant temperature to varying temperature
Topography	• Flat to mountainous • Desert to forest • Low altitude to high altitude
Cost of Living	• Low to high

Figure 3.9 These are some of the choices that will influence your selection of a region in which to live.

Rural areas and the outskirts of towns and cities are low-density areas. If you or your housing and interiors clients enjoy a less populated area and reduced contact with other people, you are *noncontact* people who prefer a more secluded community.

Specific groups of people often want or require certain types of communities. For instance, older people who no longer work, yet desire the companionship of peers with like interests and values, want the freedom and activities retirement communities have to offer. Planning for university communities must meet the needs of large groups of students and professors. Some businesses develop special communities for employees and their families.

Before choosing a community, you should consider more than just its size and social aspects. You should study the number and type of services a community offers. For instance, what stores are in the community? Does the school have a reputation for high academic standards? Does your religious group have a meeting place? Are there high-quality medical facilities? Will you have adequate fire and police protection? Are resources available for self-improvement? What recreational facilities does the community offer? Are jobs easy to find? If some of these services are not available in the community, how far away are they? What type of public transportation is available?

The information in Figure 3.10 can serve as a guide for evaluating a community. Which factors

Choosing a Community	
Consideration	**Range of Choices**
Type	• Rural to urban/suburban • Residential to industrial/commercial
Size	• Farm to ranch • Village/town to city/metropolis
Population Density	• Low to high
Employment Opportunities	• Few to many • Little variety to varied • Low-paying to high-paying • Seasonal to steady
Public Facilities and Services	• Few to many

Figure 3.10 When you look for the ideal community, these factors are considered.

apply to your present community? Which would you want in your ideal community?

Neighborhood

While regions are divided into communities, communities are divided into neighborhoods. A **neighborhood** consists of a group of houses and people. The buildings in any one neighborhood are usually similar in age, design, and cost. The people in a neighborhood usually have some similarities, too.

Physical Neighborhood

The usage of land and buildings determines the *physical neighborhood.* Some neighborhoods are all residential, with homes occupied by people. Commercial neighborhoods include stores and businesses. A shopping center is a kind of commercial neighborhood while industrial neighborhoods include businesses, factories, warehouses, and industrial plants.

Some neighborhoods combine residential, commercial, and industrial buildings. For instance, when houses surround a local grocery, the neighborhood is a combination of residential and commercial buildings.

Zoning Regulations and Other Restrictions

Zoning regulations control land use in certain areas. A neighborhood may include zones for residential, commercial, or industrial use, or a combination of uses.

Housing *developers* subdivide land and make such improvements as streets and street lighting before building structures. Developers can set additional limits, called restrictions. Figure 3.11, shows a set of restrictions drawn up for a subdivision. These restrictions may control the design and construction of the buildings in an area.

Career Focus Civil Engineer

Can you imagine yourself working as a civil engineer? Read more about this challenging and exciting career.

Interests/Skills: If you share any of the following interests, you may choose to explore a course of study that would lead to a career as a civil engineer. Do you like practical projects that involve hands-on activity? Do you enjoy fact-finding and problem solving? Civil engineers use these skills: mathematics, science, critical thinking, active listening, active learning, complex problem solving, monitoring, judgment and decision-making, and negotiation.

Career Snapshot: Civil engineers design roads, buildings, airports, tunnels, dams, bridges, or water supply and sewage systems. They must consider many factors in their designs, from the costs to making sure the structure will stay intact during bad weather. This is one of the oldest types of engineering. Many civil engineers manage people and projects. A civil engineer may oversee a construction site or be a city engineer. Others may work in design, construction, research, and teaching. There are many specialties within civil engineering, such as structural, construction, environment, and transportation.

Education/Training: Civil engineers typically enter the occupation with a bachelor's degree.

Licensing/Examinations: State licensing is required for civil engineers. A license requires four years of relevant work experience and passing an exam. Beginning engineers often work under an experienced engineer to get their required work experience.

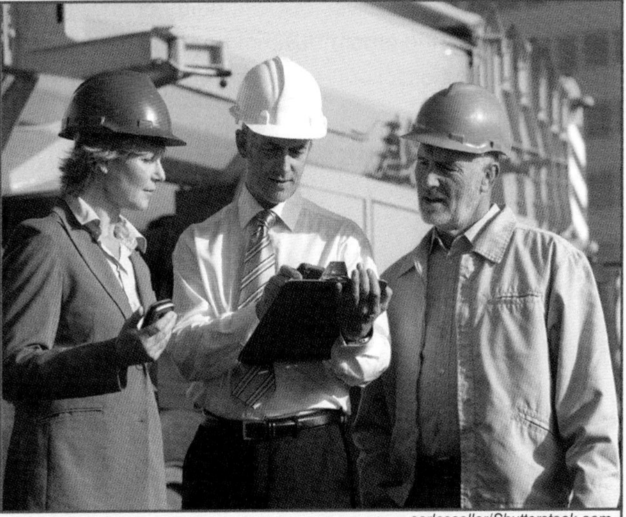
carlosseller/Shutterstock.com

Professional Association: American Society of Civil Engineers (ASCE)

Job Outlook: Jobs for civil engineers are expected to grow 20 percent from 2012 to 2022, faster than the average for all occupations.

Sources: The Occupational Outlook Handbook (OOH); the Occupational Information Net (O*NET)

Declaration of Restrictions for Lawndale Subdivision

1. All of said lots in Lawndale Subdivision shall be known and designated as residential lots and shall not be used for any business purposes whatsoever.
2. No structure other than one private dwelling, together with a private garage or carport for not more than three cars, shall be erected, placed, or allowed to remain on any of the lots.
3. No dwelling house shall be erected which contains less than 1,100 feet of livable space, exclusive of attached garage, porches, patios, breezeways, and other outdoor living spaces. No residence shall be built which exceeds the height of 2½ stories or 30 feet from the curb level. All structures on said lots shall be of new construction and no building shall be moved from any other location onto any of said lots.
4. There shall be no trailer houses or homes built around or incorporating trailer homes. All camper trailers, campers, or boats shall be stored behind the dwelling house or within the garage.
5. There shall be no unused automobiles, machinery, or equipment allowed on these premises outside of enclosed garages. All driveways or parking areas used for parking vehicles shall be constructed of concrete.
6. All clotheslines, equipment, service yards, woodpiles, or storage piles shall be kept screened by adequate planting or fencing to conceal them from views of neighboring lots or streets. All rubbish, trash, or garbage shall be removed from the lots and shall not be allowed to accumulate thereon. All yards shall be kept mowed and all weeds shall be cut. Garbage and refuse containers may be brought to the street not more than 12 hours before collection time and must be removed within 12 hours after collection time.
7. No animals, livestock, or poultry of any kind shall be raised, bred, or kept on any lot. However, dogs, cats, and other household pets may be kept, provided they are not kept, bred, or maintained for commercial purposes, and so long as applicable laws on restraining or controlling animals are observed.
8. No solid wall, hedge, or fence over 2½ feet high shall be constructed or maintained past the front wall line of the house. No side or rear fence shall be constructed more than 6 feet in height.

Figure 3.11 This is a partial list of typical restrictions for a subdivision. Its purpose is to assure all owners maintain a similar style of living.

Consider a Live/Work Community

When considering a place to live, a "green" decision is a live/work community. This is part of the *New Urbanism* movement that began in the 1990s. A live/work community combines where you live with where you work. Often the living quarters are located on the second floor of a building while a business is located on the first floor.

Most live/work communities involve self-contained neighborhoods that have restaurants, laundering services, grocery stores, and other commercial options within walking distance of home. The advantages of a live/work community are the following:

- lower gasoline costs without the need to drive to work
- convenient location of services
- neighborhood activities that create a sense of community and belonging

Figure 3.12 There are several ways to arrange lots, including (A) the traditional "gridiron" arrangement, with all lots the same size and shape; (B) the contour arrangement, with the shape of streets and lots adding variety and interest to the neighborhood; and (C) the cluster layout, with houses placed together in groups to discourage traffic from nonresidents.

They may also limit the type and number of animals that residents can keep in a neighborhood.

After a community government designates a parcel of land as a subdivision, planning begins on how to use the land. A *planned neighborhood* is usually in an area with zoning restrictions. In such neighborhoods, developers organize the subdivision and make decisions about the size and layout of individual lots before constructing dwellings. This creates the shape of the neighborhood. Figure 3.12 shows three ways to arrange lots.

All houses built in a planned neighborhood must fit into the overall community plan. Some planned neighborhoods have single-family houses. Some have only apartment buildings. Others include more than one type of housing with the types grouped together. A recent development in planned communities relates to *live/work communities.* These communities often combine living space and work space.

Communities sometimes control the quality of construction and the types of design in a planned neighborhood. This assures buildings in the neighborhood will not deteriorate because of poor quality materials or workmanship.

Many planned neighborhoods include recreational facilities. Nearby parks and playgrounds offer locations that are convenient to people living in the neighborhood (Figure 3.13). Clubhouses include places for meetings and social activities. *Urban planners* help develop these neighborhoods and areas within a city. See the next page for more information about a career as an urban planner.

Colleen Clabaugh/Shutterstock.com

Figure 3.13 Playgrounds are a part of many planned neighborhoods.

Population Composition

The people who live in any neighborhood may be quite varied. When this happens, the neighborhood is ***heterogeneous,*** meaning dissimilar or culturally diverse. If the residents are very similar to each other, the neighborhood is ***homogeneous***. Some neighborhoods or whole communities have residents of similar age, ethnic background, income level, or occupation. These patterns occur in both rural and urban settings.

Another factor associated with the people in a neighborhood is population density. A low-density neighborhood has more space for each person than a high-density neighborhood. Smaller houses,

Career Focus Urban Planner

Can you imagine yourself as an urban planner? If you can, review the following information about this exciting career.

Interests/Skills: Do you enjoy problem solving and decision making? Do you have the desire to contribute to improving the living conditions of the population and you think it important the communities meet the total needs of all of its members regardless of age and physical abilities? Do you share an interest in creating communities that are both green and sustainable? Urban planners have these skills: complex problem solving, active listening, critical thinking, time management, judgment and decision making, and computer.

Career Snapshot: City or urban planners figure out the best way to use the land in cities and neighborhoods. They report on the best location for houses, stores, and parks. They try to solve a lot of problems. These include such things as traffic problems and increases in air pollution. Planners need to plan where people should drive their cars and where they can park. Planners make new plans when more people move into a community. They might tell community leaders when they need new schools or roads. Planners also are concerned about saving trees and wetlands. They try to find safe places for getting rid of trash.

Education/Training: Job prospects will be best for those with a master's degree and strong computer skills. Bachelor's degree holders may find positions, but advancement opportunities are limited.

Albo/Shutterstock.com

Licensing/Examinations: Most states do not require licensing; however, certification from the American Institute of Certified Planners is recommended. New Jersey is the only state that requires planners to be licensed, although Michigan requires registration to use the title "community planner."

Professional Associations: American Planning Association (APA)

Job Outlook: Faster than average employment growth is projected for urban and regional planners. Most new jobs will be in affluent, rapidly expanding communities. Job prospects will be best for those with a master's degree and strong computer skills.

Sources: The Occupational Outlook Handbook (OOH); the Occupational Information Network (O*NET)

smaller lots, and more people in less space create high-density neighborhoods. Apartment buildings and manufactured-housing parks also fit in the high-density category.

Which kind of neighborhood would you or your potential clients choose? What are the reasons for making that choice? The factors listed in Figure 3.14 can assist with making a decision.

Site

A location within a neighborhood is a site, or lot. A **site** is the piece of land on which the dwelling is built. It extends to the property lines.

Each site has its own characteristics—size, shape, contour (hills and curves), and soil type. What kind of site would be ideal? Would you or your client like to have a house on a hill or on flat land? What kind of view is desirable? Is close proximity to neighbors a preference, or is more privacy a greater preference? Consider these characteristics before choosing a site for a house (Figure 3.15).

If you or your client are buying a house that someone else built, or when renting an apartment, carefully look at the placement of the house on the site. It will have a great effect on the near environment. Placement determines the views, the amount of sunlight, and the amount of protection from wind the dwelling has.

When building a house, you or your client can choose the site and the type of house and also the placement of the house on the site. This gives an opportunity to make the house and site work together to form a satisfying near environment.

When planning a site for yourself or your clients, encountering restraints, or obstacles, is common. Some will be natural restraints while others will be legal restraints.

Natural Restraints

Natural restraints are those that come from nature. To gain the maximum advantage from the site, it is important to consider the topography. *Topography* is the configuration of a surface including its natural and manufactured features showing their relative positions and elevations. One kind of natural restraint is the topography of a site.

Choosing a Neighborhood	
Consideration	**Range of Choices**
Physical Appearance	• Zoned or not zoned • Strictly residential dwellings to some commercial and/or industrial buildings
Organization of Lots	• Attractive to unattractive • Planned to unplanned • Low street traffic to high traffic area • No park/play areas to many park/play areas
Type of Structures	• Single-family to multifamily • Low spread to high spread
Location in Community	• Edge to center
Population Composition (age, income, occupation, educational level, interests, religious beliefs)	• Homogenous (similar) to heterogeneous (varied)
Residents	• Mostly singles to mostly families • No friends/acquaintances to many friends/acquaintances
Prevailing Values (views/beliefs that seem to dominate the thinking and actions of people)	• Very *different* from own values to *similar* to own values

Figure 3.14 Which of these factors are important to you in selecting an ideal neighborhood?

Choosing the Site	
Consideration	**Range of Choices**
Location of Neighborhood	• Edge to center
Orientation to Environment (view, sun, water, wind)	• Does not use natural features well to uses natural features well
Physical Qualities	• Tiny to large size • Rectangular to irregular shape • Flat land to steep slopes • Sandy soil to dense clay • No obstructions to many large trees and/or rocks that must be removed

Figure 3.15 Before you select a site, consider all your choices.

Flat sites make the job of mowing grass easy (Figure 3.16A). Flat lawns are also good places for children's games and lawn furniture. In contrast, hilly sites are more difficult to maintain, but they are often attractive. Some houses, such as split-level houses, look best on hilly sites.

Sites with extremely steep slopes have some disadvantages. For instance, a house built at the top of a slope may be difficult to reach, especially in icy weather. Also, soil may wash away and cause land erosion.

Landscaping is altering the topography and adding decorative plantings to change the appearance of a site (Figure 3.16 B). For instance, building small hills for such plantings makes the site more attractive.

Soil and water can be natural restraints. Soil conditions affect both the site and the house. Poorly drained soil freezes and expands, which can cause sidewalks and driveways to crack and bulge. Plants have difficulty growing in shallow or nonporous topsoil. High water levels can cause swampy yards, wet basements, and poor plant growth.

Orientation can be a restraint or an advantage. **Orientation** refers to placing a structure on a site in consideration of the location of the sun, prevailing winds, water sources, and scenic view. Houses with southern and western exposures receive more sunlight than houses with northern and eastern exposures. In colder regions, houses often have large amounts of glass on the south and west sides of the dwelling. The glass allows sunlight to bring light and warmth into the dwellings.

Because of the earth's changing position in relation to the sun, more sunlight reaches the earth during the summer (Figure 3.17). Some houses may need protection from the intense summer sun. Trees

A

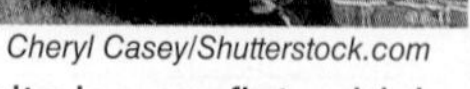

Cheryl Casey/Shutterstock.com

B *Photography Courtesy of Ed Pinckney*

Figure 3.16 The topography of this site is very flat, which makes yard maintenance easy (A). In this landscape plan, brick and stone were used to create terraces and to take advantage of the lot (B).

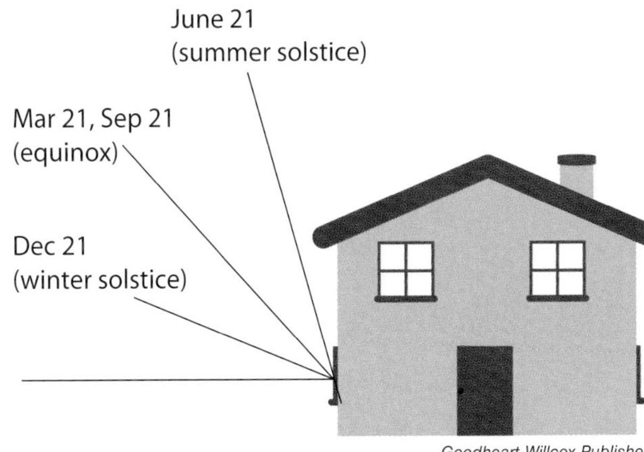
June 21
(summer solstice)
Mar 21, Sep 21
(equinox)
Dec 21
(winter solstice)

Goodheart-Willcox Publisher

Figure 3.17 The sun shines on the south side of a house at different angles depending on the time of the year. By knowing this, architects can plan proper roof overhangs.

shade some houses. Built-in features, such as roof overhangs, can also provide shade. The width of the overhang on a roof affects the amount of sunlight that enters a building. Wider overhangs block out more sunlight.

Orientation to the wind is another natural restraint. Locating houses on the land to protect them from strong winds is essential in some regions. Windbreaks provide some of this protection. Trees and shrubs are natural windbreaks while walls and stone or wood fences are also windbreaks. Placing a garage on the north side of a house usually eliminates drafts from cold winter winds and reduces home-heating costs.

In most regions, the general direction of the wind links to the season of the year. Consider this factor when planning for protection from the wind. The illustration in Figure 3.18 shows a house that is well oriented to both the sun and wind.

Orientation to scenery is also a consideration. A pleasant view is desirable, but nature does not always provide one. If necessary, you can create a nice view through landscaping. Landscapers use gardens, shrubs, trees, and decorative elements to change the scenery.

Legal Restraints

Federal, state, or local laws establish the legal restraints that affect a site. These laws are set for the protection of the population. Many local governments establish density restrictions that can impact the size of lots, placing limits on how small they can be and how close the structure can be to the property line. Local zoning commissions usually administer these restraints.

If a person is seeking a mortgage through the federal government, the housing must meet certain

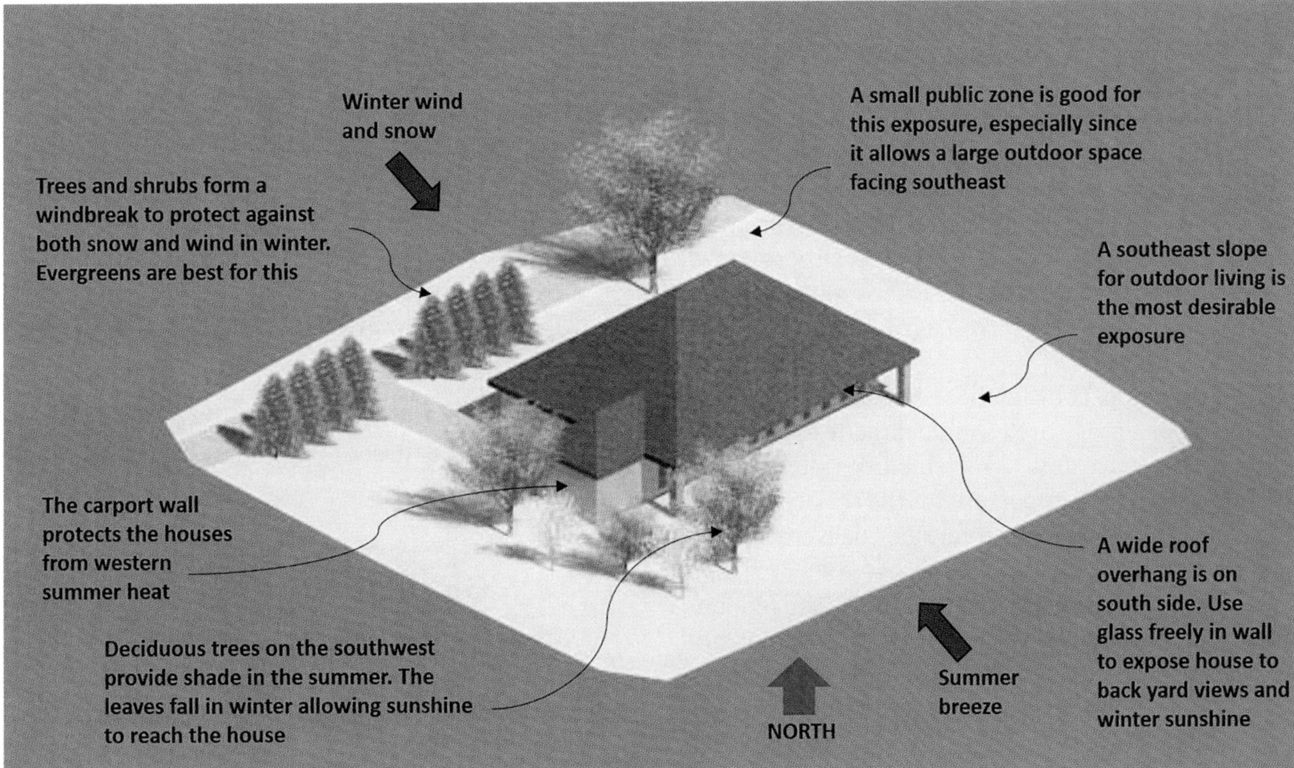
Winter wind and snow
A small public zone is good for this exposure, especially since it allows a large outdoor space facing southeast
Trees and shrubs form a windbreak to protect against both snow and wind in winter. Evergreens are best for this
A southeast slope for outdoor living is the most desirable exposure
The carport wall protects the houses from western summer heat
A wide roof overhang is on south side. Use glass freely in wall to expose house to back yard views and winter sunshine
Deciduous trees on the southwest provide shade in the summer. The leaves fall in winter allowing sunshine to reach the house
NORTH
Summer breeze

Jennifer Blanchard Belk, IIDA, LEED AP

Figure 3.18 Orientation to sun and wind are important factors to consider when deciding the ideal location for a dwelling on a site.

requirements concerning the safety and security of the occupant and the soundness of the structure. The Federal Housing Administration sets **minimum property standards (MPS)** that require the systems and property construction meet durability standards. In addition, housing structures must also meet building codes.

The local government or the developer may set higher standards than the MPS. State and local authorities also establish limits and standards for the quality of construction, water supplies, and disposal of wastes. Do you have a housing authority office in your community? If so, what legal restraints does it enforce? How might this impact a home purchase? How could these standards influence the interior design of a house?

Courtesy of Chief Architect Software

Figure 3.19 This image, showing a swimming pool in the private zone, was created using a computer program.

Zones Within the Site

The part of the site that is not the actual dwelling is divided into three zones—public zone, service zone, and private zone.

The **public zone** is the part of the site people can see from the street or road and is usually in front of the house. If the house is on a corner lot, the public zone is L-shaped and includes the front and side of the lot closest to the street. Since people see the public zone more often than any other part of the site, they want to make it attractive but seldom use it for activities.

If the house is as far forward on the lot as the law permits, the public zone is small. Many people want small public zones because they are easier to maintain.

The **service zone** is the part of the site that household members use for necessary activities. It includes sidewalks, driveways, and storage areas for such items as trash, tools, lawn equipment, firewood, sporting equipment, and automobiles. Others can usually see at least part of the service zone, however, many people choose to screen as much of it as possible from view.

In this zone, convenience is most important. The outdoor service area should directly connect to the indoor service area, which includes kitchen and laundry areas. It is important for the service zone to be accessible from the street since deliveries are usually made in the service zone.

The **private zone** is the part of the site hidden from public view. It provides space for recreation and relaxation (Figure 3.19). Shrubs, hedges, screens, fences, or walls can separate private zones from public zones.

Some households want a large private zone. They may want a place for yard accessories, such as outdoor furniture and barbecue equipment, yard games, or a swimming pool. Other households prefer a small private zone that requires little upkeep. Some want all the available space inside the house and do not want an outdoor private zone. Figure 3.20 shows the placement of a house on the site to provide all three zones—public, service, and private.

Review & Assessment

1. Summarize the five basic steps in the decision-making process. Give an example demonstrating how to make a wise decision using each step of the process.
2. What are five major factors about location to consider when choosing housing?
3. Name three reasons for living in a certain region.
4. Contrast residential, commercial, and industrial neighborhoods.
5. What are two natural restraints that affect sites?
6. What legal restraints affect housing sites? Why?
7. Summarize how the FHA relates to the MPS.
8. Describe the three zones within a site.

Types of Housing

After choosing a region, community, neighborhood, and site, your next decision is to choose a form of housing. As you learned earlier, a *house* is any building that serves as living quarters for one or more families. A *home* is any place a person lives. The two major groups of houses are multifamily and single-family. Within each group are several variations.

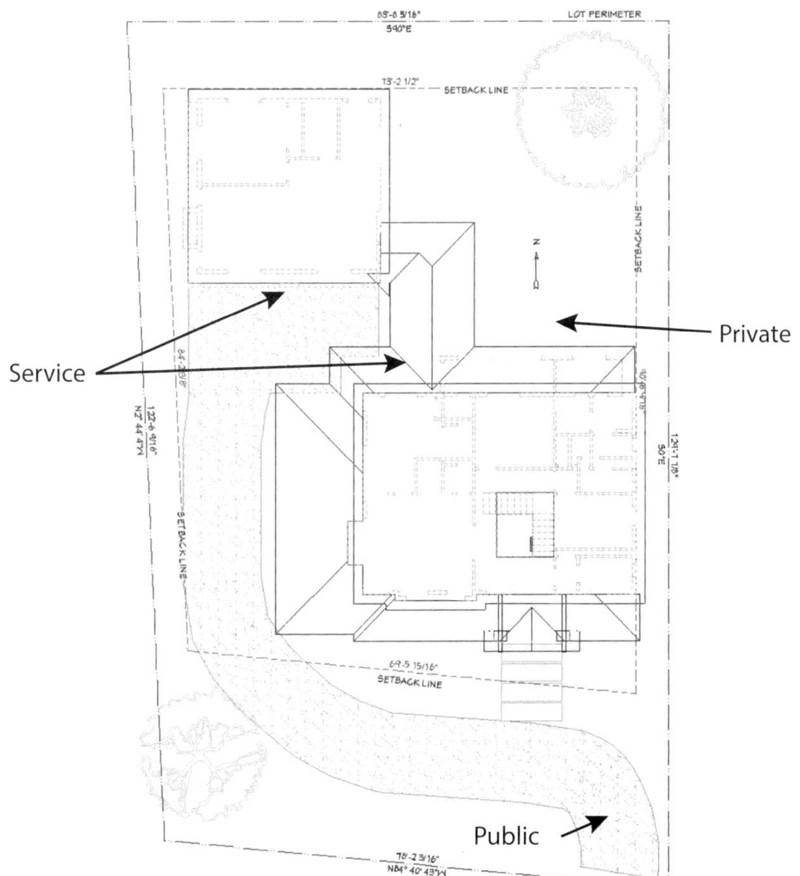

Courtesy of Chief Architect Software

Figure 3.20 The house at the top has a huge private zone. How do the sizes of the public and service zones compare?

Multifamily Houses

A **multifamily house** is a structure that provides housing for more than one household. Each household within the dwelling has its own distinct living quarters.

Today, lifestyles are changing, and the demand for multifamily housing is increasing. In the past, single people, young married couples, and retired people were the primary residents of this type of housing. Now, others are turning to multifamily housing, too. This type of housing is usually less costly and easier to maintain than single-family houses.

Some multifamily housing is in *high-rise buildings*. Other multifamily housing is in low-rise buildings (Figure 3.21). Those in *low-rise* buildings may be *duplexes* (two households), *triplexes* (three households), or *quadplexes* (four households).

Rentals

Rental apartments range from garden apartments to penthouses. Penthouses are suites located at the top of apartment buildings. *Garden apartments* are one-story units with landscaped grounds. Rentals also vary in the number and type of facilities offered. An *efficiency apartment* has one main room, a small kitchen area, and a bathroom. Many apartment buildings have laundry appliances, tennis courts, and swimming pools available to residents. Some large, high-rise buildings are like small cities. They include business offices, stores, recreational facilities, and parking space.

Cooperative Units

The word **cooperative** refers to a type of ownership in which people buy shares of stock in a nonprofit housing corporation. These shares entitle them to occupy a unit in the cooperative building. When people move into a cooperative unit, or co-op, they "buy" their apartment by purchasing shares of stock in the corporation. If a resident wants a larger unit, he or she purchases more stock. Residents have an absolute right to occupy the unit for as long as they own the stock.

Although residents do not own their units, they own an undivided interest in the entire property. They have a voice in how the corporation operates and even get the chance to select their neighbors. When people want to buy shares in the corporation and move into the building, the members of the corporation vote on admitting them.

An advantage of living in a co-op is that neighbors meet regularly and work together to create a pleasant housing environment for all residents. A disadvantage is that anyone who disagrees with the majority on an issue must accept and live with the decision.

Condominium Units

A **condominium** is a type of ownership in which the buyer owns individual living space and *also* has an undivided interest in the common areas and facilities of the multiunit project. In comparison

A nostalgi1@mail.ru/Shutterstock.com

B Philip Lange/Shutterstock.com

Figure 3.21 This is a series of high-rise buildings in Chicago where several hundred families live (A). Low-spread apartment buildings require larger lots per household than high-rise buildings (B).

to co-ops, buyers purchase condominium units as separate dwellings. At the same time, the buyers receive a portion of the common areas. They share the ownership of the site, parking areas, recreational facilities, hallways, and lobbies with the other condominium owners.

Although condominium owners own their units, they must answer to the desires of the entire group of owners for certain items. For instance, the appearance of the outside of their units and their yards may be under the control of the group's management.

Remember, the terms *cooperative* and *condominium* refer to a type of ownership, not a building design. When you look at a multifamily dwelling, you cannot tell if it is a rental, cooperative, or condominium (Figure 3.22).

Single-Family Houses

In spite of the rising trend for multifamily dwellings, the *single-family house*—a dwelling that houses one family—is still popular. People can rent or own single-family houses.

Attached Houses

Some single-family houses are *attached houses*. Each unit holds one household but shares common walls with the houses on each side. End units, however, have only one shared wall. *Townhouses* and *row houses* are names for these houses. A *townhouse* is a unit that has at least two floors.

Usually, these houses share entire sidewalls, but there are variations. The designs of the attached dwellings are often alike. The owners of an attached, single-family house possess the dwelling itself and the land on which it is located. They have their own entrance and yard area.

Freestanding Houses

When single-family houses stand alone, without connections to another unit, they are *freestanding houses*. They vary in size, design, color, features, and cost.

The most individualistic type of house is *custom-designed* and *custom-built* by an architect and a contractor. This kind of house is a dream house and is often expensive and takes a long time to plan and build.

Courtesy of JELD-WEN Windows and Doors

Figure 3.22 This multifamily unit could be rentals, co-ops, or condos. There is no way to know by looking at exteriors.

When custom-designing a house, an architect considers the needs, values, and life situations of the household. He or she then designs a house to "fit" that household's needs and desires.

A *contractor* is a person who contracts, or agrees, to supply certain materials or do certain work for a specific fee. With a custom-built house, a contractor arranges for all the tradespeople to do their various jobs efficiently and on schedule. He or she builds the house according to the architect's plans and owner's wishes. The general contractor is responsible for completing the construction of the house. He or she may arrange with one or more subcontractors to complete certain parts of the construction. A subcontractor can be either an individual person or a firm.

Some houses are custom-built from stock plans. In these cases, people go to a contractor and look at house plans. They choose the plan they want and the contractor builds a house for them on their site. They also incorporate any adjustments or individualized treatments the owner desires. For example, the owner may want larger windows with different locations than the plan indicates (Figure 3.23).

Owner-built housing is for people with lots of spare time, energy, and building skills. This type of house can be less expensive than a custom-built house. There is less investment in money and more investment in such resources as time and energy. Sometimes the owner hires a contractor to construct the house shell while the owner does the interior work. In other cases, the owner builds the entire house, often with volunteer help from friends. Building codes usually require qualified experts to handle some parts of the project, such as electricians and plumbers.

In contrast, developers sometimes build entire neighborhoods at once, creating tract houses. They build these houses before selling them. Repeating one or two sets of plans throughout the development saves money on construction costs. Tract houses lack individuality because there are few variations. However, they are less expensive to buy than custom-built houses.

Factory-built housing is housing constructed in a plant and moved to a site. Some units are fully finished in the plant, while others arrive in parts that are joined at the site (Figure 3.24). All factory-built housing involves some labor for placement on the lot. The advantages of factory-built housing include decreased cost and/or completion time in making a home available. You often cannot tell a site-built house from a factory-built house. A **site-built house** is built on a lot, piece by piece on a foundation, using few factory-built structural components. Five types of factory-built housing in use today include

- modular
- manufactured/mobile
- panelized
- precut
- kit

Modular housing is factory-built in a coordinated series of modules. The wall, floor,

Lindasj22/Shutterstock.com

Figure 3.23 This home's exterior looks like the stock plan, but many changes were made to the inside. The kitchen area was doubled and an office was added to the first floor.

Photography Courtesy of Palm Harbor Homes

Figure 3.24 This modular home was assembled on site by connecting the parts (modules).

ceiling, and roof panels are combined in boxes (or modules) complete with windows, doors, plumbing, and wiring before delivery to the site. When the modules arrive at the housing site, workers place them on the foundation and join them together. These housing units are built to meet local building codes and standards.

Both **manufactured housing** and **mobile homes** are single-family dwellings that are completely built in a controlled factory environment. The completed housing units have attached chassis and wheels and are moved to a lot or housing site. Units built before 1976 are called mobile homes, while those built later are called manufactured housing. Early units first appeared as travel trailers in the 1920s and 1930s, and evolved into house trailers in the 1930s and 1940s.

Manufactured houses are built to federal standards called the HUD Code because the U.S. Department of Housing and Urban Development (HUD) administers it. A manufactured or mobile home is one solution to affordable home ownership since cost is considerably below that for a conventional, site-built house (Figure 3.25).

Manufactured housing is available in many sizes. Smaller homes come in single units, or single-sectional housing. Larger homes come in two or more units, either double-sectional or multi-sectional, that are joined at the site. There are length and width limitations on these larger homes because of transportation requirements for pulling them across highways to their sites.

Although manufactured houses and mobile homes have wheels for moving, less than five percent ever move from their original sites. Each state has laws that movers must follow when moving one of these homes. Some local governments have additional rules, such as zoning regulations that prohibit the placement of these homes in certain areas.

The owners can move single-sectional homes as long as they follow all laws. Larger homes must be moved in parts from the factory to the site. A company specializing in moving manufactured or mobile homes handles the job. Once joined together, double-sectional and multi-sectional units are usually fixed permanently to their sites.

Three other types of manufactured housing include the following:

- **Panelized housing** involves panels of walls, floors, ceilings, or roofs that people can order separately and have assembled at the housing site. The units are usually complete with windows, doors, plumbing, and wiring.
- **Precut housing** refers to housing components that are cut to exact size in the factory and delivered to the building site. A crew then assembles lumber, finish materials, and other components at the site (Figure 3.26).
- **Kit housing** is a type of factory-built housing. Kit houses are shipped to the site in unassembled parts or as a finished shell from the factory. The interior is then completed according to the buyer's wishes.

A kit house is less costly than most other types of factory-built housing. Several factors, such as the size and style of the house, influence the total

Photography Courtesy of Palm Harbor Homes

Figure 3.25 When in place and landscaped, a manufactured home is difficult to distinguish from a site-built home.

Katahdin Cedar Log Homes

Figure 3.26 Many modern-day log homes are precut housing.

Green Choices

Urban Designer's Role in Sustainable Design

Urban designers, working together with architects, have a major role in promoting green and sustainable design by examining ways a developing city can impact the environment. Specifically, urban designers follow these principles in creating green and sustainable communities:

- **Design on a human scale.** Place housing, shops, and cultural resources close together so that residents can walk among these areas.
- **Provide choices.** Arrange for different options in housing, shopping, recreation, transportation, and employment.
- **Encourage mixed-use development.** Integrating different land uses like living and shopping areas in the same building.
- **Preserve urban centers.** Restoring, revitalizing, and infilling neighborhoods and buildings to avoid new building and unnecessary expansion.
- **Vary transportation options.** Giving people the option of walking, biking, and using public transportation.
- **Build vibrant public spaces.** Citizens need welcoming, well-defined public places to stimulate face-to-face interaction, collectively celebrate and mourn, encourage civic participation, admire public art, and gather for public events.
- **Create a neighborhood identity.** A "sense of place" gives neighborhoods a unique character, enhances the walking environment, and creates pride in the community.
- **Protect environmental resources.** A well-designed balance of nature and development.
- **Conserve landscapes.** Open space, farms, and wildlife habitat are essential for environmental, recreational, and cultural reasons.

cost. Another cost factor is the delivery cost, which is based on the distance from the factory to the site. Finally, the cost of a kit house is influenced by whether all the materials and labor for the house are purchased with the kit or separately.

Review & Assessment

1. Contrast the ownership differences among rentals, cooperative units, and condominium units.
2. How do attached houses and freestanding houses differ?
3. What are the roles of the architect and contractor in custom housing?
4. How does a tract house differ from a house custom-built from stock plans?
5. Name the five types of factory-built houses.

More Housing Decisions

Other items to consider when choosing a dwelling include the house's condition (if it is not new), price, size, design features, and appearance on the site. Figure 3.27 can guide you as you make decisions about a house. Other decisions include the needs of those who inhabit the dwelling such as older adults, people who have disabilities, and families with children.

Needs of Older Adults

Many people look forward to retirement. They may plan to enjoy activities they could not pursue much in the past, such as golfing, fishing, traveling, or volunteering. Their retirement plans will likely affect their housing decisions. They may want housing that requires less maintenance or that will be secure while they are away. The situations vary with each older adult, as do their housing choices.

Aging-in-Place

Most adults over age 50 prefer to stay in their homes as they age. According to the Centers for Disease Control, the concept of **aging-in-place** identifies a need for older adults to remain independent and live safely and comfortably in their homes regardless of age, income, or ability level. Having familiar surroundings, community services, and built-in social network are all important to aging well. In order to meet aging-in-place needs, it is important to understand the challenges of aging that influence ability to live successfully.

Choosing the Dwelling	
Considerations	**Range of Choices**
Type of Ownership	• Rental to buyer (cooperative, condominium, or private dwelling)
Type of Dwelling	• Low spread to high rise • Multifamily to single family • Old to newly built • Owner-built versus contractor-built • Stock plans versus custom design • Site-built versus factory-built (modular, manufactured/mobile, panelized, precut, or kit housing)
Landscaping	• Dwelling looks out of place to site harmonizes with dwelling • No landscaping to attractive use of landscaping elements
Size of Outside Zones (public, service, and private)	• Small to large
Structural Quality	• Substandard/deteriorated quality to high quality
Size of Dwelling	• Cramped to spacious
Price	• Affordable to expensive

Figure 3.27 Many options are possible when choosing a home.

As people age, their energy levels often decrease. Perhaps their health declines and they find their houses difficult to maintain. This makes it hard for older people who prefer to *age-in-place,* or stay in their present houses. They need housing that permits easy cleanup and requires little maintenance. Adding functional design features to an existing home or moving to a home designed with such features can make housing more accessible and conducive to aging-in-place.

With appropriate interior design, older adults can remain independent even when aging reduces their mobility. For example, adding a no-step entrance with a wider doorway and nonslip floors are design changes that benefit everyone. They would especially benefit a person with a broken leg using crutches. Even more so, the changes would benefit those in wheelchairs or with permanent impairment from aging.

Reverse Mortgages

For older adults who choose to live on their own, the cost of house ownership can be high. Some may find they are "house rich and cash poor" because their savings went to acquire their houses. With time, their houses may need repair. With limits on income, older adults may not have money for maintenance, repairs, utilities, or taxes. In this case, they would not have extra money to adapt their houses to meet their special needs.

Measures have been taken to assist older adults. Some states allow reverse mortgages. A **reverse mortgage** enables older people to convert the money tied up in their houses into income. They receive a monthly payment as long as they live in the dwelling. When they no longer live in the house, the mortgage company assumes ownership of the dwelling. Reverse mortgages can help older home owners stay in their houses.

There are some disadvantages with reverse mortgages. Although the older adult can pass the house on to heirs, the reverse mortgage cost will be attached to the dwelling. Also, older adults should consider reverse mortgages only if their income is such that they cannot pay bills and plan on living in their homes until death. If older adults take out reverse mortgages and later move, they may end with less money than if they had sold the house originally.

Assisted- and Graduated-Care Facilities

Some older adults find that living in their old neighborhoods is no longer convenient. They may be far from shopping areas and community centers where they can be with their peers. If they have difficulty driving, they may not want to leave home often. This can lead to loneliness, especially if they live alone.

When older adults can no longer live alone due to loneliness or health problems, they usually change housing. They may become a part of another household, perhaps living with a son, daughter, or someone who can help care for them. They may choose to become part of larger group quarters, such as a senior-living community or may choose a retirement home or an assisted-living facility (Figure 3.28).

- **Assisted-living facilities** serve those who need daily living assistance but not constant care. Meals, laundry service, and household cleanup are the most common services these facilities provide.
- **Graduated-care facilities** offer more than one level of care. Older adults may move from individual apartments with no care, to assisted living, or to a nursing-home unit as their needs change. Facilities with good design and optimal administrative services offer comfortable living.

Needs of People with Disabilities

There are many people with disabilities in the United States. They include children, older adults, and adults who work and live on their own or with their families. The types of disabilities vary. Some people have a vision or hearing loss while others have difficulty moving and must use wheelchairs, crutches, or walkers. Others may have learning or developmental disabilities.

Jennifer A. Walz/Shutterstock.com

Figure 3.28 Senior-living communities often include assisted-living facilities.

People with disabilities need housing to meet their needs. They may be unable to live independently in housing built in the past. Appropriate housing can assist people who have disabilities with their daily living. For example, the bathroom in Figure 3.29 has been adapted to meet the needs of a person in a wheelchair.

The **Fair Housing Act** of 1988 is legislation that gives people with disabilities greater freedom to choose a place to live that meets their needs. The Act forbids discrimination in housing and requires multiunits to be accessible to people with disabilities. The law requires accessible entrances, wider doors, and easier installation of grab bars around toilets and bathtubs. Although the law does not address every aspect of making multiunits fully accessible, definite improvements were made. As a result, the law helps provide housing that is safer and easier for everyone to use.

If you or a member of your household has a disability, consider

- a ground-level dwelling
- a building with a minimum 5-foot by 5-foot level entryway or landing that permits entry doors to open easily

Photo Courtesy of Kohler

Figure 3.29 The smooth floor, space around the sink, toilet, and bathtub, and the convenient grab bars make this bathroom accessible to everyone in the household.

- wide interior doorways and hallways
- good lighting for people with low vision
- audio and visual smoke detectors and carbon monoxide detectors
- housing along or near public transportation lines
- housing near shopping areas

When people with disabilities have housing that meets their needs, they can live more independently. If you should build a home someday, you can incorporate features of universal design to extend the house's usage for all conditions of life.

Needs of Families with Children

Children develop physically, mentally, emotionally, and socially. No matter how old they are, they need to live in a safe and healthy housing environment that promotes positive development.

A housing choice that fits the needs and desires of a couple without children may not be satisfactory when a child arrives. Children need room to grow as they learn to crawl and walk. As they grow older, they need additional space for activities (Figure 3.30). An outdoor play area that is protected from street traffic is desirable. This gives children a place to move around and play safely.

Andresr/Shutterstock.com

Figure 3.30 This outdoor play area in front of the house offers the children in this family a space to grow and develop.

The community in which children grow can influence their development. When choosing a place to live, look for communities and neighborhoods that will foster healthy growth and development. Look for good schools, safe neighborhoods, park programs, and recreational facilities.

Often children have pets, which also require special considerations. If you rent a house, you may find that the owner wants neither children nor pets. However, antidiscrimination laws prevent landlords from refusing to rent apartments to families with children. The same is not true for pets.

Review & Assessment

1. Identify three groups of people who have special housing needs.
2. What is aging-in-place?
3. What is the purpose of a reverse mortgage?
4. Contrast assisted-living facilities with graduated-care facilities.
5. Name four housing factors to consider if you or a household member has a disability.
6. What key housing features are important for families with children?

Innovative Housing Solutions

Shifting populations, lifestyle changes, and longer lifespan dictate attention to new alternatives. Housing designs of the future will reflect these and other considerations, such as the needs and values of people.

Home owners are continually seeking new solutions to meet their changing lifestyles, such as redesigning the space within a home. Recent research indicates that most new home owners have less interest in a separate living room that gets little use in comparison to home owners in the past. Instead, many current house plans include great rooms. Will homes of the future eliminate separate living rooms? Will they instead have the increasingly popular entertainment rooms or home theaters? Lifestyle changes dictate the future direction for housing design.

New Living Spaces

Many of today's housing problems relate to space. About 75 percent of the people in the United States are living on less than 10 percent of the land, yet space for housing is difficult to find. It is also expensive. In just 40 years, the cost of land has risen dramatically from about 10 to 25 percent of a home's purchase price. In some areas, the cost will be as much as 50 percent. To solve this problem, some forward-thinking individuals are exploring new sources of living space.

Floating Houses—Living on the Water

Throughout the world, as many as 200 million people live in coastal areas prone to flooding. Many scientists predict an increase in coastal flooding as a consequence of changing climate conditions. Such changes are causing a rise in sea levels and the number of flood-producing storms. From the Netherlands to New Orleans, architects and other experts are designing and developing new types of flood-safe housing for a sustainable way of living.

With the goal of helping provide safe, affordable, and sustainable housing, the *Make It Right Foundation* is funding such developments in the Lower Ninth Ward of New Orleans. When Hurricane Katrina hit the southern coast of the United States in 2005, much of this community was destroyed by flooding. Katrina was one of the costliest natural disasters in U.S. history, killing more than 1,500 people and causing more than $81 billion in damages.

The *Make It Right Foundation* spearheaded the building of 150 single-family homes in a neighborhood heavily damaged by a levee breach. Various architects and design firms are designing the homes. These homes must be able to withstand flooding and be sustainable. Many of the homes rise off the ground on piers or stilts. They are only accessible by flights of stairs that are difficult for some people to climb.

Morphosis Architects and a team of UCLA architecture graduate students came up with a solution to this accessibility problem. They designed a raft-like house that can float in up to 12 feet of water (Figure 3.31). The two-bedroom, 1,000 square feet "FLOAT House" is suitable for affordable housing because its components can be mass-produced and assembled on-site. Energy- and water-conserving elements include

- solar-powered panels that generate power for the house
- a concaved roof that collects rainwater and funnels it to a cistern in the base of the house
- highly insulated structural panels for walls
- energy-efficient appliances and fixtures
- geothermal heating and cooling

The long narrow house, which can have a front porch, resembles the local architectural style (similar in look to a Louisiana shotgun house). Secured to two steel guideposts (that are anchored to two 45-foot deep piles in the ground), the house floats, or rises vertically on the guideposts, only when the water level rises during severe flooding. The home design aims to protect a home owner's investment and limit catastrophic damage. The home occupants, however, must still evacuate during a hurricane or flood.

Although the concept of floating houses is not new in the world, the New Orleans FLOAT House is the first of its kind in the United States. Because of

Courtesy of Morphosis Architects. Photography by Iwan Baan

Figure 3.31 Development of the FLOAT House began to help supply housing that is flood-safe, affordable, and sustainable in the Lower Ninth Ward of New Orleans.

its design and the prefabrication of its component parts, this house is affordable and adaptable for use in many regions in the U.S. and beyond.

Underground and Underwater Housing

Some people think living space could extend downward into the earth. Earth-sheltered housing, caves, cellars, and basements all have their place in the story of housing. The idea of building whole, modern communities underground, however, has not attracted any interest. Underwater hotels now exist but underwater homes have not yet been developed.

Outer Space Settlements

One expanding "frontier" is outer space. Although you may not be able to imagine it, living in a space colony is not impossible. For humans to exist for periods in outer space, extensive testing is a requirement to guide the development of life-support systems as well as new methods of food production and waste management. Ongoing climate research is happening under controlled conditions that simulate outer space.

From 1991 to 1993, the Biosphere 2 project in Arizona investigated ways to grow and harvest plants in climate conditions similar to outer space as well as human reactions to the controlled environment. This project's unique ecosystem was one of the first attempts to simulate plant growing conditions and human living arrangements in outer space and echoes a community of organisms living in nature and their reaction to changed environments. Currently, the Biosphere is an adaptive tool for Earth education and outreach to industry, government, and the public.

Although many people have fantasized about humans from Earth living on another planet, the first attempt to actually have a permanent human settlement in outer space is Mars-One. This effort began in 2011 by a nonprofit group in the Netherlands. The idea is to have a space colony beginning on Mars in 2027. See the rendering of the exterior of the Mars-One units and two interior renderings in Figure 3.32.

The plan provides for a crew of four persons to arrive on Mars in 2027 with a full colony of 20 settlers to be there by 2035. Flight time to Mars is seven months. As planned, initial exploration will be made to determine the site of the colony on Mars and various payloads will be sent ahead of the colonists. Colonists are to be sent every two years after the initial settlement arrivals in 2027.

A

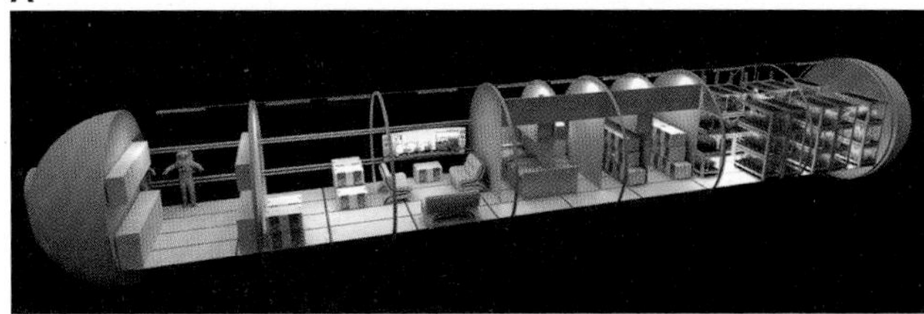
B

C

Mars-One/Bryan Versteeg

Figure 3.32 These are images from Mars-One, the first planned space settlement, showing (A) the exterior, (B) the layout of a complete living unit showing the plant growing area, and (C) a close-up in the living unit.

Despite any criticisms, it is interesting and educational to view the rendering of the space colony exterior as well as an interior view of a living space and plant growing area. A number of persons have applied for this trip to Mars. How would you evaluate this as a viable living environment in the future? Is this a practical option for the future? Time will tell.

Review & Assessment

1. Why are floating houses a benefit in flood-prone areas? Give three features of a "FLOAT House."
2. Why do you think there is little interest in underwater housing?
3. How did the Biosphere 2 project in Arizona set the stage for living on another planet?
4. What are some issues related to developing human settlements in outer space?

Chapter 3 Assessment

Summary

- Three types of decisions grouped according to the amount of thought or care used include rational, impulse, and habitual decisions.
- Other types of decisions are grouped according to the relationships between decisions.
- The use of human resources and nonhuman resources impacts decisions about housing and interior design.
- By following the logical steps of the decision-making process, you are more likely to make wise decisions.
- You will not know if you have made the best decision until after you evaluate results.
- When choosing a place to live, examine the region, neighborhood, site, and zone within the site and the restraints—natural and legal—of the location.
- Types of housing choices vary ranging from multifamily to single-family, attached or freestanding, owner or contractor built, or factory-built housing.
- Other factors to consider when choosing a dwelling include the needs of older adults, people who have disabilities, and families with children.
- Innovative housing solutions focus on the shifting populations, lifestyle changes, and longer lifespan.
- Housing designs of the future need to reflect the needs and values of people along with a sense of adventure.

Terms in Action

1. **Write definitions** Read the text passages that contain the *Content Terms* listed at the beginning of the chapter. Then write the definitions of each term in your own words. Double-check your definitions by re-reading the text and using the text glossary.

Think Critically

2. **Evaluate decisions** Evaluate a recent decision that you made in terms of the success of its outcome. What could have been done differently to yield more successful results? What lesson did you learn to help you improve future decision making?
3. **Analyze decisions** Read the following case study and complete the suggested activities. Andy and Noelle are both students at a community college and plan to marry in June. Both have part-time jobs, will continue in school after the wedding, and graduate after another year. Andy plans to work in an auto repair and welding shop while Noelle wants to continue her job in the college library. In four or five years, they plan to start a family and want two children. Noelle likes music and wants a piano. Andy likes to fish and play golf.
   A. Identify a major housing decision this couple will face.
   B. What resources will be available to them? What are the alternatives they may consider? What are the possible outcomes of each alternative? What other related decisions will they need to make?
   C. Which alternative would you choose as a solution? Give reasons for your choice.
4. **Analyze trends** One trend in housing is to build the total housing or various parts in a factory and move them to the housing site. Analyze the possibility of this trend continuing. Do you think it will ever be predominant? Why or why not?
5. **Assess adaptations** Visit a house that is for sale. Assess the features that need to be adapted for a person with a mobility disability or an older adult who desires to age-in-place. Create a list to discuss in class.

Core Skills

6. **Writing** Divide a sheet of paper into three columns. Label the first column *Decision*, the second column *Type of Decision*, and the third column *Degree of Satisfaction*. In the first column, list three housing decisions made by members of your household. In the second column, identify whether the decision was *rational*, *impulsive*, or *habitual* behavior. In the last column, write + + if much satisfaction resulted from the decision, + if some satisfaction resulted, and – if no satisfaction resulted.
7. **Writing and speaking** In teams, write and present a skit showing how some resources decrease while others increase at the same

Chapter 3 Assessment

time. Create a video recording of the script. Play the video for the class, but first give a brief introduction. Then answer any questions your classmates have after your presentation.

8. **Research and writing** Use Internet or print resources to look up zoning regulations and building codes for your community. Write a summary of the requirements for local housing.
9. **Writing** Contact your local chamber of commerce and obtain the literature it provides to new or prospective area residents. What features of the area might appeal to different types of residents, such as older adults, people with disabilities, families with children, and single persons? Summarize your findings in a short written report.
10. **Speaking, listening, and writing** Survey 10 people in your community and ask what they *like* and *dislike* about living there. Select individuals of both genders and different ages to get a range of responses. Use spreadsheet software to create a display of the information for the class. Keep the identities of the surveyed individuals confidential.
11. **Reading and writing** Read the information about reverse mortgages on the Federal Housing Administration website. Write a summary of your findings to share with the class.
12. **Research and technology** Choose a region beyond your community where you would enjoy living. Locate the website for the area's chamber of commerce and find out more about the community. What are the advantages and disadvantages of living there? Use a school-approved web application to create a digital poster to share on the class web page.
13. **Research and speaking** Use reliable Internet resources—such as the AARP and National Association of Home Builders (NAHB) websites—to research the requirements for becoming a *Certified Aging-in-Place Specialist.* Give an oral report to the class.
14. **CTE career readiness practice** With a classmate, use the Internet to research information about one of the following topics:
    A. housing for older adults who desire to age-in-place
    B. housing for people (either adults or children) with disabilities
    C. housing for children

    Create a digital video news report about your topic. Consider doing an "on the scene" report at a housing site for your topic. Be sure to answer *who, what, when where, why,* and *how* questions related to your topic. Post your news video to the class website.

Design Practice

15. **Design decision** Assume your new clients desire to build a new home for their expanding family. They have two preteen children and are soon expecting a baby. They desire a master bedroom with a sitting area and private bath; however, a full bath for the children is important, too. Space efficiency and green design are very important to your clients. Use Internet or print resources to locate floor plan examples for your clients. Narrow your choices to three. Use the decision-making process to determine why each floor plan would be a great choice for your clients. With two of your classmates acting as your clients, role-play a discussion of options with your client. Present each floor plan and justify the reasons why each would benefit the client.
16. **CADD practice** Using an available CADD software package, draw a dwelling on a site showing the three zones within the site. Print a copy of your drawing or save a copy on a flash drive or other digital device.
17. **Portfolio** Presume that you want to pursue an interior design career after high school. Your dilemma concerns where you want to go to school to obtain a four-year degree in interior design. Search the Internet for three accredited colleges or universities of interest. Use the decision-making process to choose which school to attend. Use word-processing software to record your decisions and actions for each step of the process. Save a copy of your decision for your portfolio.
18. **Portfolio** Put a copy of your CADD drawing from item 16 in your portfolio along with a written description identifying why you positioned the zones in the manner you did on the site.

Chapter 4
Sustainability and Housing

Content Terms

sustainability
sustainable design
home automation
renewable energy sources
nonrenewable energy sources
photovoltaic (PV) system
geothermal energy
cogeneration
fuel cell
microturbine
volatile organic compounds (VOCs)
photovoltaic shingles
graywater
Zero Energy Home (ZEH)
Earthship housing

Academic Terms

bandwidth
off-gassing

Learning Outcomes

After studying this chapter, you will be able to

- define sustainability and sustainable design.
- summarize the importance of sustainable design.
- identify the principles or goals of sustainable design.
- determine reliable information sources for sustainable design.
- review examples of buildings with sustainable features.
- summarize the responsibilities of designers for sustainable design.

Reading with Purpose

Find an article on the *Google News* website that relates to the topics covered in this chapter. Print the article and read it before you read the chapter. Then, as you read the chapter, highlight sections of the news article that relate to the text.

While studying, look for the access icon  **to:**

- **Practice** the *Content* and *Academic Terms* with e-flash cards, matching activities, and vocabulary games.
- **Reinforce** what you learn by completing the *Review & Assessment* questions and e-mailing them to your instructor.

www.g-wlearning.com/housing/

Johnny Habell/Shutterstock.com

The future of the environment depends on how people use and protect natural resources. The term *sustainability* describes the interaction between people and their living environments. This chapter describes sustainability and shows ways that design professionals can and should promote and use sustainable design principles in creating housing and interior spaces.

Defining Sustainability and Sustainable Design

Sustainability is a term that describes human interaction with the resources in the earth's environment. These resources include the air, water, forests, and other materials. Humans use natural resources in creating and designing housing structures and living spaces. They not only use natural resources to build and furnish living spaces, but also to operate structures in heating and cooling spaces as well as heating water.

The idea of sustainability is that people today should responsibly use natural resources to meet their needs in a way that does not affect the ability of people in the next generation to also meet their needs. With sustainability, there is also the expectation of no negative impact on the people, communities, or environment.

Sustainable design refers to incorporating sustainability in the built environment. Sustainable design focuses on the responsible

- use of materials for building and furnishing interiors
- operation of living spaces
- practices in the manufacture of materials and production of buildings

Sustainable design is important because buildings and their interiors have a powerful impact on the environment of the earth. Buildings of all types account for over 40 percent of energy use worldwide. According to the U.S. Energy Information Administration in 2014, 41 percent of U.S. energy consumption was for residential and commercial buildings.

Designers and all professionals in the building industry can have a powerful impact on maintaining the environment. They do this by designing buildings and selecting all materials and systems based on the principles of sustainable design.

Eco-Friendly Labeling and Certification Programs

Many guides assist consumers or professionals in making decisions in finding green housing solutions. When selecting a new house or products for the home, choose an eco-friendly program to guide your choices.

Each of these programs certifies/labels green components in different ways and some are highlighted in *Green Choices* features throughout this textbook. Programs that certify or label green housing and products include

- **ENERGY STAR®**—Identifies products and structures that use at least 30 percent less energy than the standard products and structures (Environmental Protection Agency and U.S. Department of Energy)
- **Energy Guide Label**—Relates the approximate energy consumption and utility cost of operating the products and is required on all ENERGY STAR products (U.S. Environmental Protection Agency and U.S. Department of Energy)
- **LEED Rating System**—Certifies structures that have overall sustainable features (U.S. Green Building Council—USGBC)
- **Forest Stewardship Council (FSC)**—Sets standards for responsible forest management; works with FSC-accredited certifiers to identify companies that follow sustainable practices in wood harvesting and manufacturing
- **WaterSense® Label**—Identifies products that use less water; manufacturers have partnership agreement with the U.S. Environmental Protection Agency and have products certified through an EPA-licensed certifying body
- **Sustainable Furnishings Council**—Tags furniture that was manufactured using sustainable practices; promotes sustainable practices among furniture manufacturers
- **REGREEN**—Provides guidelines for incorporating green in remodeling projects (partnership between ASID and USGBC)
- **Carpet and Rug Institute (CRI)**—Verifies that products (carpet, adhesives, and cushions) have low-emission of VOCs (Indoor Air Quality testing)

Review & Assessment

1. Define sustainability and sustainable design.
2. Explain the importance of sustainability.
3. Why is sustainable design important?

Principles of Sustainable Design

Sustainability is incorporated into buildings through following principles of sustainable design. The principles that guide sustainable design include the following:

- use less energy in the operation of buildings
- use renewable energy sources for living environments
- select materials from renewable sources
- use recycled materials and/or materials that can be recycled
- conserve water use
- protect occupant health and safety
- produce less waste

Use Less Energy

A major principle of sustainable design is to use less energy in the operation of buildings. The interior designer and other building professionals can select equipment that uses less energy. This includes home appliances, space heating and cooling equipment, water heating equipment, and lighting. Specific energy efficient equipment, is covered in the appropriate sections of the text.

Energy-efficient homes are most effective if originally designed to use less energy. Many homes on the market, however, have energy-efficient features. Figure 4.1 provides a checklist of features of an energy-efficient home.

After the energy-efficient appliances and equipment are in the home, one way occupants can manage and control energy use is through **home automation**. Dwellings with home automation have an integrated and centrally controlled system based on computer technology. This system controls all the systems in the home and focuses primarily on one or more of the following areas:

- convenience
- energy management
- entertainment
- safety

Homes built today incorporate many versions and features of "smart" technology. The exteriors of homes with automated systems look like any other homes (Figure 4.2). These homes contain advanced systems, components, and materials—all the result of ongoing technological development.

Historically speaking, electronic houses were something that only appeared in science fiction for much of the twentieth century. In the 1980s, however, the National Research Center of the *National Association of Home Builders (NAHB)* helped the advancement of home automation by initiating The SMART HOUSE Project. The technology wired the home with a single multiconductor cable that included electric power wires, communications cables for telephone and video, and other connections to appliances and lamps. The multiconductor cable was then linked with electronic devices to control the supply of power throughout the home. The SMART HOUSE was designed to respond to the resident's needs by adjusting lighting, temperature, and even music. Currently, NAHB is no longer the leader in marketing home automation, but instead private companies are leading the way for home automation.

The basic idea of home automation, is to employ sensors and control systems to monitor a residence and adjust the systems according to the user's needs. By doing so, the home becomes a safer, more comfortable, and more economical residence. For example, the system can turn off the lights and lower the thermostat after everyone has gone to bed. It can monitor burglar and fire alarms and optimize the operation of the water heater by anticipating hot water usage.

Home automation technologies require broad changes to building construction. These changes may impact house wiring and cabling for power and communications. The development of a new information infrastructure offers many possibilities. For instance, such technology offers greater participation in civic and community activities, access to educational resources, as well as work and entertainment. Higher-bandwidth communication technologies provide the means for electronic community town meetings, distance learning, home shopping, and video-on-demand. ***Bandwidth*** refers to the capacity for data transfer of an electronic communications system.

After meeting technical and organizational challenges, many will find a fine line between an intelligent house that maintains comfort levels and an overbearing house that monitors the inhabitants too closely. Few people object to using a thermostat

Evaluating Energy Efficiency of a House
Use the following questions to evaluate and note the features for home energy efficiency.
Orientation and Landscaping
• What is the orientation of the long side of the house (N, S, E, or W)? • How many windows face east? (Note number and calculate the area in square feet.) • How many windows face west? (Note number and calculate the area in square feet.) • How much shade from landscape features is on east or west sides of the house? • Is the southern exposure unobstructed or shaded by deciduous trees?
Thermal Resistance
• How much insulation is in the attic? (Note the type and thickness.) • Are the walls insulated? If so, how thick is the insulation? • Is there under-floor insulation, especially in homes with crawl spaces, cold basements, and garages under living areas? • Are the heating and cooling ducts, hot water pipes, and hot water heater insulated? • Are the windows double- or triple-glazed (paned) with low-E glass? • Are the doors solid-core wood or insulated metal? • Are there storm doors?
Lighting and Windows
• Is energy-efficient lighting used in work areas (for example, fluorescent or LED)? • Are windows or skylights located in work areas? • Do windows occupy less than 10 percent of the total wall area? (Measure the window area and calculate its percentage of total wall area.)
Appliances
• Are ENERGY STAR appliances used? • Is the refrigerator located away from range, dishwasher, and direct sunlight?
Ventilation
• Are ceiling fans or a whole-house fan used in the house? • Are window and door placements appropriate for cross-ventilation? • Is the attic properly vented with vents near the roof ridge and beneath the eaves? • Is there adequate air infiltration? • Are the windows properly fitted? • Is weather-stripping located around doors, windows, and the attic entry? • Is there adequate caulking around door frames, window frames, and penetrations for pipes and wiring?

Figure 4.1 Use this question list to compare houses for energy efficiency.

to control the temperature in a house. Most cherish, however, the power to set and reset the thermostat. As the hardware and software to control home automation systems become increasingly complex, designers must make it easy for inhabitants to program the house and to override preprogrammed settings.

Use Renewable Energy Sources

A principle of sustainable design is relying more on **renewable energy sources**—those that replenish themselves regularly—in providing energy to operate a building. The housing and interior design professional should have knowledge about the energy sources. In particular, he or she should know about renewable energy sources and how to promote them in buildings.

Fuel provides heat, and people need heat to live. Like all forms of energy, fuel begins as solar energy derived from the sun. Nature converts solar energy to raw materials such as oil and coal. The conversions

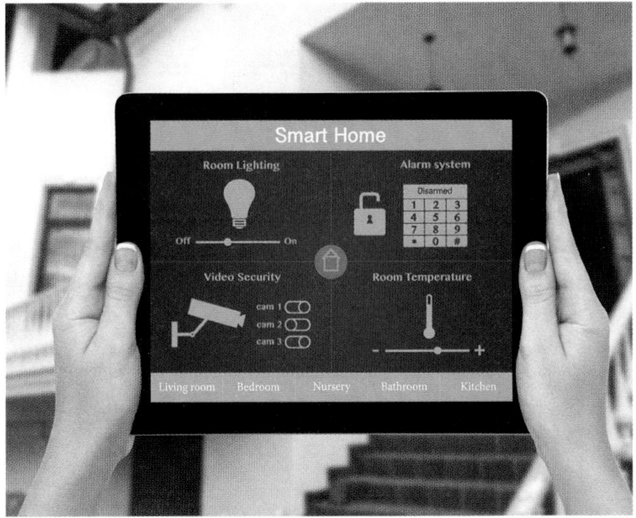

Denys Prykhodov/Shutterstock.com

Figure 4.2 By looking at its exterior, you cannot identify this smart home. The controls shown on the tablet indicate it is a smart home.

take millions of years to complete. The raw materials are then refined and used as fuel for electricity. Figure 4.3 shows coal is the nation's main source of energy. Nuclear energy, hydroelectric power, natural gas, and petroleum are the other leading energy sources in the country.

Nonrenewable energy sources, such as common energy sources of fuel as oil and coal, are depleting in supply. Renewable energy sources, on the other hand, replenish themselves regularly. Renewable sources of energy include the sun, wind, water, and geothermal energy, all of which can be converted to electricity.

The housing and interior design professional can help in promoting the use of renewable sources for energy uses in buildings. This focus is primarily on the use of solar energy, geothermal energy, and wind.

Solar Energy

There are several ways to use solar energy in structures. One way is to use the natural heating effect of the sun by orienting the building to incorporate this heating effect. Designing the structure depends on the climate and other variables and must be done correctly (Figure 4.4). Another way to use solar in structures is to use it to heat the space or heat the hot water (Figure 4.5).

Solar energy could supply a majority of the energy needed to heat and cool buildings throughout the United States. Solar heating systems are usually expensive to install. A major part of the expense is the high cost of the component parts. Ongoing long-term research and development will help reduce costs, improve reliability, and improve performance of technologies that solar programs use.

Despite the high installation cost, those who use solar energy usually see a great reduction in their utility bills. In the long run, solar heating systems usually cost less than conventional systems.

Active solar systems can heat space, heat water, or produce electricity. An active solar system that converts sunlight into electricity is a **photovoltaic (PV) system**. The sun shines on panels (called *arrays*) and converts this solar energy into electricity.

The downside of photovoltaic systems is they generate electricity only when the sun shines. The system's batteries can store enough electricity

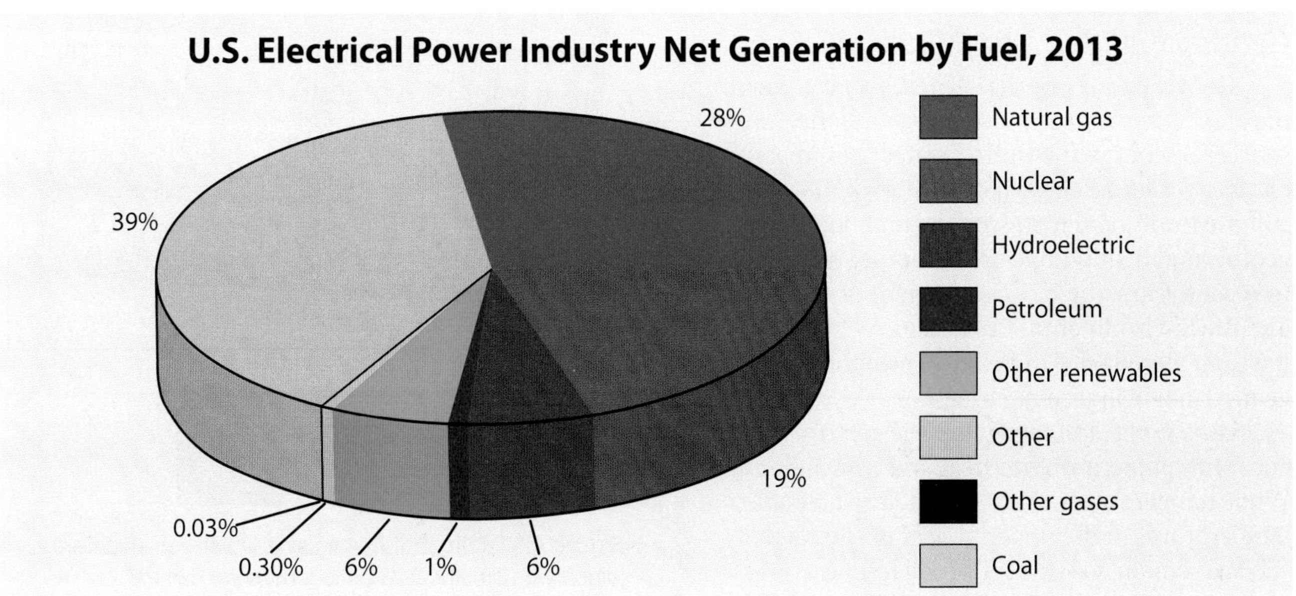

U.S. Energy Information Administration, Electric Power Annual (2013)

Figure 4.3 The United States relies heavily on coal to fuel the generation of electricity for industrial use.

pics721/Shutterstock.com

Figure 4.4 A sunroom is a beautiful and calming space; however, if the orientation is not correct, it can become hot like a greenhouse and be unusable space.

jessicakirsh/Shutterstock.com

Figure 4.5 This house has solar panels on the roof to take advantage of active solar heating.

to power a house for several days, but persistent overcast weather can deplete it. Deluxe systems can match the reliability of power supplied by utility companies, but they are expensive. As the cost of solar electric systems declines, environmentally conscious home owners will likely invest in this technology.

Some solar energy heating systems supply more energy than a home needs. Home owners can sell the excess to a utility company or store it in the lines until needed by the producer. *Net metering* programs also provide consumer investment in renewable energy generation. The plan allows customers to use their own generation to balance their consumption. The electric meters turn backward when they generate electricity in excess of their demand (Figure 4.6).

Geothermal and Wind Energy

Geothermal energy—energy that comes from the earth's core—and wind energy are the primary sources of energy the United States uses in power plants to produce electricity. Although most homes still use traditional furnaces and air conditioners, geothermal heat pumps are becoming more popular. In recent years, the U.S. Department of Energy (DOE) and the Environmental Protection Agency (EPA) have partnered with industry to promote the use of geothermal heat pumps.

Geothermal heat pumps use the earth's constant temperatures to heat and cool buildings. While temperatures above ground are unstable, temperatures in the upper 10 feet of the earth's surface remain constant. The soil temperatures are usually warmer than the air in winter and cooler than the air in summer. The heat pumps transfer heat from the ground (or water) into buildings in winter and reverse the process in the summer.

Geothermal energy has advantages and disadvantages. One advantage is its low cost in comparison to other fuels. It also is a source of heat that does not emit harmful pollutants into the environment. A third advantage is that geothermal energy is a renewable resource.

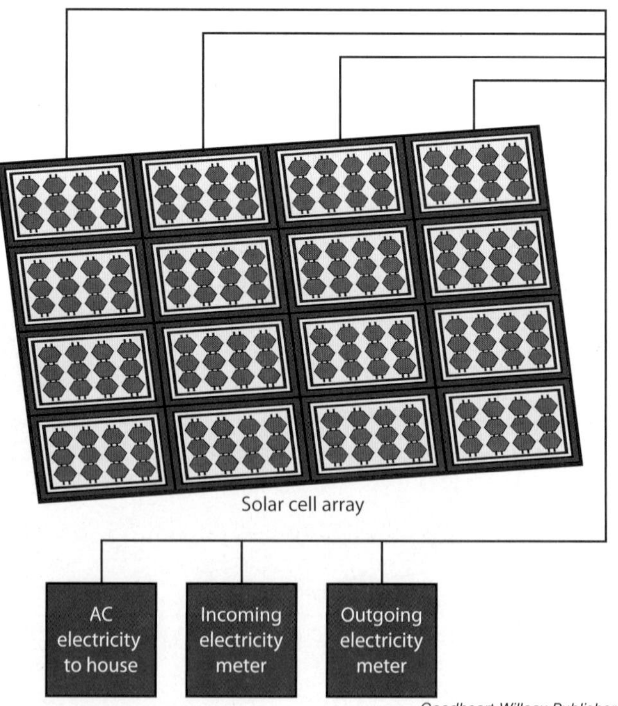

Goodheart-Willcox Publisher

Figure 4.6 In a photovoltaic system, silicon chips are joined with electrical wires to form solar cell arrays. The arrays collect different amounts of solar energy, depending on the season, time of day, and degree of cloudiness.

Career Focus Environmental Scientist

Can you imagine yourself as an environmental scientist? If you can, read more about this challenging and exciting career.

Interests/Skills: If you share any of the following interests, you may choose to explore a course of study that would lead to a career as an environmental scientist. Are you investigative and realistic? Do you enjoy working with ideas, and do you like to search for facts and figure out problems mentally? Do you prefer practical, hands-on problems and solutions? Do you appreciate the outdoors along with plants, animals, and real-world materials like wood, tools, and machinery? Environmental scientists typically have skills in the sciences, have critical-thinking ability, can express themselves to others in writing and speaking, and work well with people.

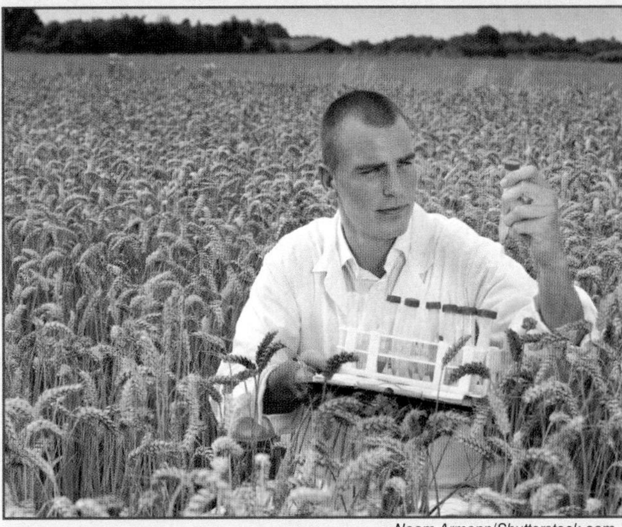

Noam Armonn/Shutterstock.com

Career Snapshot: Environmental scientists find and fix pollution and other environmental problems. They figure out what is in the air, water, and soil to make sure that the environment is safe. They also give advice on how to clean the environment. For example, they might design a safe way to get rid of trash. Some environmental scientists help to make laws about protecting the environment. They also help companies follow the laws. Environmental scientists work in laboratories and offices. They also work outside, taking measurements.

Education/Training: All of these workers need a college degree in such STEM-related areas as environmental science or environmental studies. Some need an advanced degree—either a master's or a doctoral degree.

Licensing/Examinations: (none currently)

Professional Association: National Association of Environmental Professionals (NAEP)

Job Outlook: The number of jobs for environmental scientists is projected to grow 15 percent through 2022, faster than average for all occupations.

Sources: The Occupational Information Network (O*NET); the Occupational Outlook Handbook (OOH); the Bureau of Labor Statistics

There are some disadvantages to using an open-loop geothermal energy pump and pulling directly from the groundwater. Some geothermal waters contain chemicals that require responsible disposal. A second disadvantage is the direct use of geothermal energy can only occur near the production sites. Transportation of hot water over long distances cannot occur without losing heat and turning cold. Closed-loop systems address these problems. The geothermal loop is made of a tough plastic that is extremely durable and buried underground to allow heat to pass through efficiently. The fluid in the loop is water or an environmentally safe antifreeze solution that circulates through the pipes in a closed system.

The use of wind as energy dates back to early civilizations with the use of windmills to pump water and grind grain. Wind is gaining popularity as an energy source. Most wind machines today are the horizontal-axis type. They have blades like airplane propellers. A typical horizontal wind machine stands as tall as a 20-story building and has three blades that span 200 feet across. Wind machines stand tall and wide to capture more wind. A minimum average annual wind speed of 10 miles per hour is necessary to run a wind generator. An average above 12 miles per hour allows the development of an excellent wind system.

Some regions of the United States have strong, shifting winds that are useful for power generation. Wind turbine generators grouped together to form wind farms can convert air motion to electrical current (Figure 4.7). The electrical current that wind machines produce feeds into utility lines or storage systems. The systems keep the power flowing even when the air is still. Use of small wind electric systems for individual residences is possible, but is somewhat limited by a number of variables. One is the requirement of an acre of land for the wind turbine. A potential concern is resistance to what the wind turbine would look like.

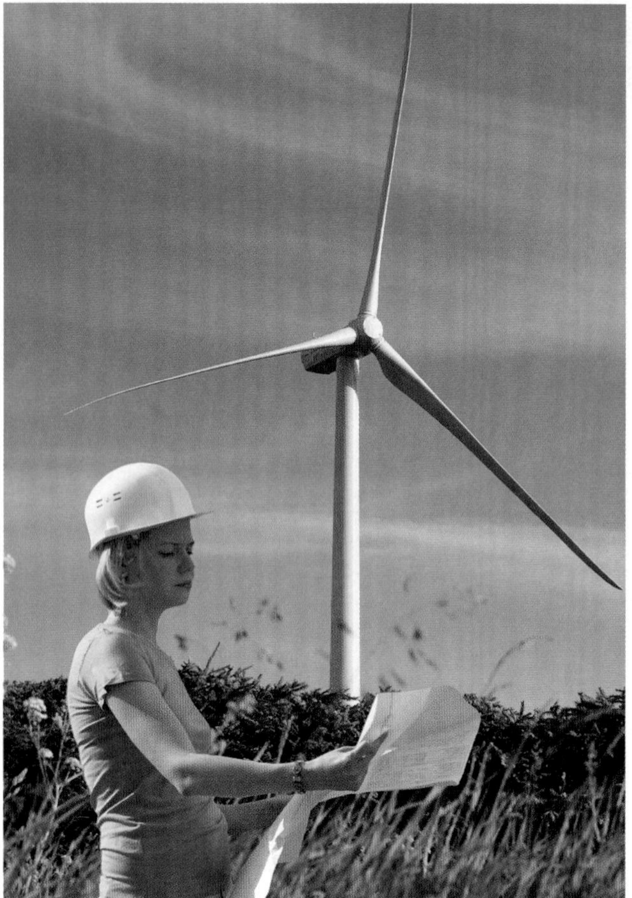

nostal6ie/Shutterstock.com

Figure 4.7 This wind system converts the power from constant breezes to create electricity for nearby residents.

Another drawback is balancing the home energy level needed with the cost involved.

Cogeneration in Residences

Cogeneration—also known as *combined heat and power (CHP)*, and total energy—is an efficient, clean, and reliable approach to generating power and thermal energy from a single fuel source. CHP uses heat that is otherwise waste from conventional power generation to produce thermal energy. This energy provides cooling or heating for industrial facilities, district energy systems, and commercial buildings. The development of new technologies that produce electricity makes this system possible. These developments include photovoltaics, fuel cells, and microturbines.

- A **fuel cell** is an equipment system that produces electricity from the use of chemicals. Research is underway to handle the waste products of heat and water.
- A **microturbine** is a small turbine engine that produces electricity.

Cogeneration systems are available to small-scale users of electricity. Currently, modular systems are useful for commercial and light industrial applications. Several factors could affect CHP growth to more residences. They include the initial cost of buying a cogeneration system, maintenance costs, and environmental control requirements. CHP in residences makes the occupants less dependent on electrical utility companies to provide electricity. This can be helpful especially in blackouts and during natural disasters when electric power may not be available.

Select Renewable Materials

Interior designers can select materials that renew themselves regularly. An example is bamboo, a wood that is prevalent and can be used in flooring, furniture, and other building components (Figure 4.8). Many materials are renewable including wool.

When using wood materials, it is important that the production of the material has certification as environmentally friendly. According to the Forest Stewardship Council Certification guidelines, achieving environmentally friendly certification requires certain practices. These include

- harvesting the wood from the forest in a sustainable way that leaves the forest in good condition and able to grow additional wood

Karkas/Shutterstock.com

Figure 4.8 This bamboo floor serves well as a renewable material, but is also quite durable in this dining space.

- transporting and treating wood using sustainable practices
- keeping production waste to a minimum—possibly using waste products effectively in some future manner

Use Recycled or Recyclable Materials

Using recycled materials is environmentally healthy when new materials are not used for products. This reduces the environmental impact of buildings and interiors.

An example is the use of recycled materials in carpeting. Reclaiming materials from old houses and buildings when tearing them down is another example. A key approach is to use materials that can be recycled if they are no longer needed.

Reusing existing buildings versus tearing down and starting over is a sustainable practice. This reduces waste and also avoids new use of environmental resources such as wood. Historic preservation is a key practice that promotes sustainability.

Protect Occupant Health and Safety

A principle of sustainable design is protecting the health and safety of occupants. To accomplish this, housing and design professionals select nontoxic materials and substances. A major concern is the *indoor air quality (IAQ)* and assuring that no contaminants are released into the space that can have harmful impact on humans. An example includes selecting materials that have low or zero off-gassing. ***Off-gassing*** is the release of fumes and chemicals in the air as a result of the treatment of a product, such as carpeting. Some wallcovering glues have contaminants that affect some people. An important concern for indoor air quality is the provision of natural ventilation and air circulation. Selection of windows that actually open is important (Figure 4.9).

Another strategy to protect occupants of a structure is to select paint that has low **volatile organic compounds (VOCs)**—chemicals that evaporate into the air. VOCs can cause breathing difficulties and health problems for some people.

Produce Less Waste

Interior designers and building professionals can produce less waste by carefully determining the correct amount of materials for a project. Selecting recyclable materials can also produce less waste. A key approach is to use materials that can be recycled if they are no longer needed.

Verkhovynets Taras/Shutterstock.com

Figure 4.9 Usually, skyscrapers do not have operable windows for safety reasons; however, this high-rise condominium has shallow windows to provide natural ventilation and good indoor air quality.

Review & Assessment

1. List the principles of sustainable design.
2. What is home automation, and what areas might this system control?
3. How does a heat pump use geothermal energy?
4. What is cogeneration?
5. Name three environmentally friendly guidelines for using wood materials according to the Forest Stewardship Council.
6. What is off-gassing, and what does it impact?

Features of Sustainable Buildings

As you recall, *green* buildings refer to those structures that use materials and techniques to conserve resources in all aspects of construction and maintenance. The planning of such buildings uses *green design* or *sustainable design*. These buildings use one or more green products or measures in the structure. Green products conserve scarce resources and generally utilize sustainable and recyclable materials. For example, the use of steel in construction more often replaces the use of wood—wood is a limited commodity and thereby is costly. Using bamboo for flooring can be sustainable, depending on the source location and production methods.

Although these homes conserve resources, today's green-built homes are virtually indistinguishable from other homes. The following include some uses of green products and design in today's typical homes:

- **Doors and windows.** Insulation in exterior doors is an energy saver in cold and warm climates. Insulated, low-E glass in windows helps keep homes more comfortable and energy efficient.
- **Siding and decking.** Vinyl and fiber-cement siding reduce the need for cedar, redwood, and other products on exterior walls. Plastic lumber and composite products (made from recycled wood fibers and plastics) are common decking materials.
- **Roofing.** Such roofing materials as metal and fiber-cement are more durable. They reduce the need for frequent roof replacement. Some older-style roofing materials require frequent replacement and are a major source of landfill waste.
- **Heating, cooling, and hot water.** High-efficiency heating, cooling, and water-heating units greatly reduce energy use in most homes. Using passive-solar design takes advantage of the sun's energy to help heat homes through glass features with a southern exposure to the sun. In addition, proper insulation of walls and attics reduces energy loss in homes.
- **Fixtures and appliances.** New energy-efficient dishwashers, refrigerators, and clothes washers require less energy. Look for the ENERGY STAR label. New toilets and faucet aerators use less water to operate (Figure 4.10).

The steps you take to conserve energy lower energy costs, reduce pollution resulting from energy production, and save valuable resources. What are some simple steps you can take to start conserving energy now and in your future work as a housing and design professional? Continue reading to learn more about special programs that promote green and sustainable buildings.

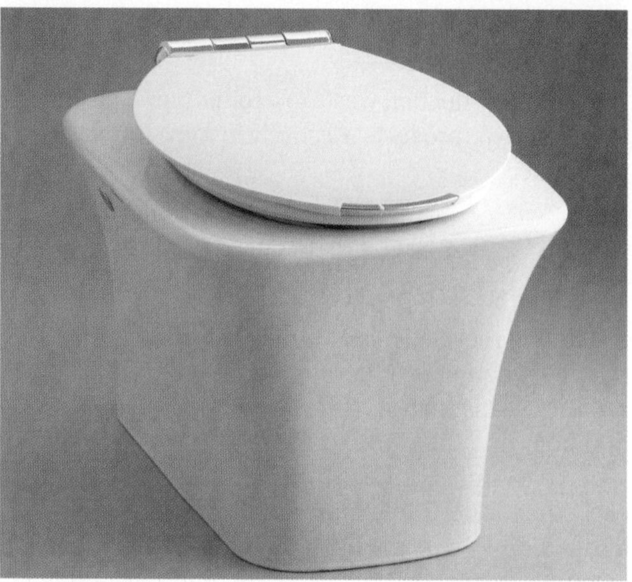

Photo Courtesy of Kohler

Figure 4.10 New plumbing fixtures, such as this toilet, are designed to use less water.

Resources for Producing Sustainable Design

Many programs clearly define and direct the building of structures/interiors that meet the criteria of sustainable design. These certification programs guide professionals as well as consumers in reaching green housing solutions.

There are also many labeling programs that assist professionals and consumers in the selection of green products. Each of these programs certifies/labels green components in different ways and some are highlighted in *Green Choices* features throughout this textbook. See the *Green Choices* box in this chapter for a listing of these eco-friendly labeling and certification programs. A major program is the *Leadership in Energy & Environmental Design (LEED)* rating system. Sponsored by the U.S. Green Building Council, this certification program provides sustainability guidelines for residential, commercial, and other buildings. There are four levels of LEED certification: *Certified, Silver, Gold,* and *Platinum*.

Examples of Sustainable Buildings

As you read the *Green Choices* features throughout this text, you will notice numerous programs and organizations promote green and sustainable housing design. Many provide certification indicating that houses have features that support the environment and sustainability. One such outstanding organization is the *Southface Energy Institute*.

Southface Eco Office and Resource Center

The Southface Energy Institute is a resource for home owners, residential and commercial builders, and people who want to learn more about environmentally friendly design. With a mission to promote sustainable homes, workplaces, and communities, the campus of the Southface Energy Institute headquarters shows many techniques and features of sustainable design. The headquarters—located in Atlanta, Georgia—is a showcase for innovative building designs and techniques. It also has the LEED-Platinum designation (Figure 4.11).

The headquarters consists of a three-story commercial building, the Eco Office, an attached residential building, and the Resource Center. These buildings display many innovative features for homes and commercial structures. The buildings address energy efficiency, thermal comfort, indoor air quality, and accessibility. Also highlighted are ways to reduce waste and use recycled materials. These sustainable designs and technologies include the use of recycled building materials and utility-operating activities (such as energy, water, and waste management).

The headquarters has many energy-related features. These include passive solar heating, cooling solar water heating, and solar-electric systems. A special roof component of the Resource Center includes solar-electric shingles. These shingles are photovoltaic (PV), which means they convert sunlight into electricity. **Photovoltaic shingles** resemble conventional fiberglass roofing shingles. The electricity they produce supplies part

A

B

C

Southface Energy Institute, Atlanta, Georgia; Photos by Jonathan Hillyer

Figure 4.11 The Southface Eco Office and Resource Center buildings have many innovative features for offices and homes (A). Photovoltaic shingles are installed on the roof of the Southface Resource Center to make electricity from the sun's rays (B). The "light shelf" in the window area helps deliver the sunlight deep into this office space (C).

of the facility's electrical needs. As in other solar applications, the PV shingles are on a south-facing roof to receive full sun.

The Southface campus utilizes a well-planned passive solar design and daylighting. This office space takes advantage of sunlight as a prominent light source year-round. Exterior shades block direct sunlight while interior light shelves bounce sunlight deep into the office. The use of daylighting strategies offsets the larger need for artificial lighting and is balanced with light-monitoring sensors.

Other energy-saving measures at the Center include energy-efficient ENERGY STAR appliances (ENERGY STAR products are certified to save energy without sacrificing functionality or features) and a geothermal heat pump. In a practical sense, geothermal energy for heating and cooling involves a heat exchange via a buried, liquid-filled pipe designed in a loop. This creates an ultra-efficient heating and cooling system that utilizes the stable temperature of the surrounding earth. This approach is more efficient than conventional air-exchange systems.

The Center's landscape emphasizes the principles of drought-tolerant landscaping. In addition, the Center uses a rainwater catchment irrigation system for watering and flushing toilets. The landscaping also uses such recycled materials as wood-chip mulch and concrete rubble for stepping-stones. **Graywater** is wastewater from washing machines, showers, and sinks. It is not contaminated with human waste and can be used for landscape watering.

Career Focus Sustainability Coordinator

Do you care about the environment? Are you interested in making people more comfortable and healthy at work and at home? Do you dislike seeing garbage dumpsters full of construction waste? If you do, a career in sustainable design and management might be for you!

Interests/Skills: By far the most important skills in sustainable design coordination and management are communication and teamwork. These professionals must be able to communicate implementation-strategy plans for green initiatives verbally, visually, and in writing with a wide variety of architects, designers, contractors, tradespeople, engineers, and clients involved in the building process. Environmental professionals must think critically about the project goals (increasing natural ventilation, utilizing natural water sources, specifying recycled products, etc.) and come up with logical, but creative ways to meet them. Because this work involves much research and documentation, sustainability coordinators must have excellent organizational skills and pay attention to details.

Career Snapshot: Designers can create sustainable buildings that are more environmentally friendly, healthier for the occupants, use less water and energy, and utilize land and space more efficiently. Often, designers work toward getting their buildings LEED (Leadership in Energy and Environmental Design) certified, which is a method of identifying and awarding construction projects that have employed sustainable practices in site development, indoor environmental quality, water use, energy efficiency, and the use of earth-friendly products. Coordinators help establish overall and specific sustainability goals for construction projects and monitor the progress as the project develops.

Education/Training: The completion of a bachelor's degree in interior design, architecture, engineering, or building science is the minimum for understanding of sustainability. Many schools offer minors and entire degrees in sustainability and environmental design. Some professionals pursue a master's degree in a specific area of sustainability such as indoor air quality or urban planning.

Licensing/Examinations: All interior design graduates who pass the *National Council for Interior Design Qualification (NCIDQ)* licensing examination are tested on their basic knowledge of sustainability, especially for commercial interiors. For those wishing to pursue a more concentrated career, construction and design professionals will become *LEED Accredited Professionals*. This certification comes in two tiers. The first exam allows recent grads to demonstrate their basic knowledge of sustainability concepts. The second exam is for those who have experience with environmentally focused projects and desire to specialize in particular environments such as commercial interiors, residential developments, and existing structures.

Professional Associations: The American Society of Interior Designers (ASID); International Interior Design Association (IIDA); U.S. Green Building Council (initial developer of the LEED certification and accreditation system)

Job Outlook: Due to public interest and a great deal of federal and state funds going toward sustainable building, this segment of the design and construction industry is forecast to grow much above the U.S. employment average.

Sources: The Occupational Outlook Handbook (OOH); the Occupational Information Network (O*NET)

Zero Energy Homes (ZEH)

An example of a sustainable energy home is a Zero Energy Home (ZEH). The **Zero Energy Home (ZEH)** is a home that produces and uses its own energy—as much or more than it needs. A ZEH combines state-of-the-art, energy-efficient construction and appliances with commercially available renewable energy systems. These renewable systems include solar water heating and solar electricity. Even though the home may have a connection to an electrical grid, it has zero energy consumption from the utility company.

The U.S. Department of Energy partners with building professionals and organizations to further develop the ZEH concept. Design features of a Zero Energy Home include

- climate-specific design
- passive solar heating and cooling
- energy-efficient construction
- energy-efficient appliances and lighting
- solar water heating system
- small solar electric system

Specific advantages of Zero Energy Homes are many. They include

- improved comfort—because the energy-efficient structure reduces temperature variations in the home
- reliability—because the home will continue to operate even during blackouts
- energy security—because the home produces its own energy and protects the occupant from fluctuation in energy prices
- environmental sustainability—by saving energy and reducing pollution

Earthship Housing

Another example of sustainable building design is **Earthship housing**. The name of the housing, *Earthship*, suggests the need for housing to be self-sufficient just as a "ship" has to be self-sufficient. This housing uses passive solar and earth-sheltered design along with the use of recycled materials to produce sustainable dwellings. Earthships have the feel you might expect of housing built on another planet. This is because the form of the housing structure does not necessarily follow the angular dimensions people associate with traditional housing (Figure 4.12).

Michael Reynolds, an architect, founded the Earthship concept and the Earthship Biotecture business headquartered in Taos, New Mexico. Near Taos, whole communities of Earthships exist. Earthships have been built in the United States, Canada, Mexico, Honduras, Nicaragua, Bonaire, Jamaica, Bolivia, Scotland, England, France, the Netherlands, Spain, India, and Japan. There are over 3,000 Earthships worldwide.

The houses are all different from the outside, but share a number of features. Figure 4.13 shows the following features:

- building with recycled materials
- water harvesting
- contained sewage treatment
- solar/thermal heating and cooling
- solar and wind electric power
- food production

The southern side of an Earthship house faces the sun and collects the heat of the sun through windows to warm the home. Usually there are two sets of windows. The outer set creates a greenhouse where plants and food are grown. The interior set of windows connects

A

Earthship Biotecture, Taos, New Mexico

B Earthship Biotecture, Taos, New Mexico

Figure 4.12 The Earthship housing has organic and natural shapes not usually found in angular traditional homes (A and B).

Earthship Biotecture, Taos, New Mexico

Figure 4.13 This diagram shows the features of Earthship housing.

to the living space and controls the amount of heat entering the house from the greenhouse space.

The back wall on the north side of the housing is actually built of earth, called a *berm*. The berm stores heat collected from the sun.

Recycled products form the building materials for these homes. For instance, used tires filled with earth form the walls. Then plaster fills in the cracks and forms a smooth surface on the walls. In addition, glass bottles serve as decoration as well as allow light into the houses. The glass bottles are cut crosswise and the bottoms connect to create cylinders. These cylinders are embedded into walls (Figure 4.14). The bottles appear as round lights in the photo.

Usually, owners attend workshops on construction methods and requirements to build the homes. The building of these homes is very labor intensive. In general, all these homes are individualized and reflect the lifestyle and interests of the owner.

Earthship Biotecture, Taos, New Mexico

Figure 4.14 This is the interior of an Earthship bathroom that uses bottles in the walls for decoration and transmission of light. The round "lights" are the bottles.

Review & Assessment

1. For each of the following home features, list one green product: doors and windows; siding and decking; roofing; heating, cooling, and hot water; and fixtures and appliances.
2. Name four housing concerns, other than energy use and conservation, addressed by the Southface Eco Office and Resource Center.
3. What are the key advantages of Zero Energy Homes?
4. Contrast the features of a Zero Energy Home (ZEH) with an Earthship home.

Designer Responsibilities for Sustainable Design

Housing and interiors professionals have the responsibility to promote and use principles of sustainable design. Because of the high use of natural resources in living environments, these professionals encourage the use of sustainability through their design.

Professionals in housing and interior design must know how to incorporate the principles of sustainable design into buildings and interiors. This knowledge includes programs that ensure and verify green or sustainable practices. Some professionals can be certified in these areas.

Using sustainable design is a good thing for maintaining the environment now and for future generations. Also, a trend exists among clients and consumers who want to include these "green" features in their homes, where they work, and where they stay when traveling. Residential designers especially have clients who are requesting green products for their designs and remodeling projects. According to the *Travel Industry Association of America*, many travelers are willing to pay more for accommodations with green features and are more likely to stay at properties that utilize sustainable practices. Figure 4.15 lists some strategies that housing professionals and interior designers use in design projects.

Review & Assessment

1. List at least 10 sustainable practices recommended for interior designers.
2. Why are housing and interior design professionals encouraged to use sustainability in their designs?
3. List two strategies housing and interior design professionals can use to support sustainable design for each of the following: residential design, commercial design, and hospitality design.

<table>
<tr><th colspan="2">Strategies for Sustainable Design Practices</th></tr>
<tr><th>Residential Design</th><th>Commercial Design</th></tr>
<tr><td>
<ul>
<li>Use programs and guidelines for sustainable design such as
<ul>
<li>REGREEN (guidelines for specific sustainable practices for remodeling)</li>
<li>Forest Stewardship Council (FSC) (certification that wood used in furniture and building products was harvested and produced in an ecological manner from forests)</li>
</ul></li>
<li>Select products that do not cause health problems for occupants including
<ul>
<li>paint and other finishing materials with low VOCs</li>
<li>products free of urea formaldehyde, a known carcinogen</li>
</ul></li>
<li>Specify products for flooring and fabrics that are renewable, such as bamboo</li>
<li>Use energy-efficient appliances with the ENERGY STAR™ rating</li>
<li>Work with contractors who use sustainable rating systems such as LEED</li>
<li>Select recyclable materials whenever possible</li>
</ul>
</td><td>
<ul>
<li>Design floor plans that are flexible for different ways to be used now and in the future (to avoid recycling or filling landfills with building products)</li>
<li>Provide for natural lighting to offset reliance on electricity</li>
<li>Provide ample and accessible recycling stations</li>
<li>Select locally manufactured materials (within a 500-mile radius)</li>
<li>Specify carpeting with sustainable results including
<ul>
<li>wool or recycled fibers</li>
<li>recycling existing carpeting (through Carpet America Recovery Effort)</li>
</ul></li>
<li>Be involved in selecting high-quality and energy-efficient lighting</li>
<li>Suggest use of office equipment with the ENERGY STAR™ rating (copiers and computers)</li>
<li>Promote healthy indoor-air quality by
<ul>
<li>selecting low-VOC materials and products</li>
<li>requiring a period of time before occupancy for VOCs to escape a building</li>
</ul></li>
</ul>
</td></tr>
<tr><th colspan="2">Hospitality</th></tr>
<tr><td colspan="2">
<ul>
<li>Use designs that will avoid or delay future renovations (classic, timeless designs since renovations produce recycling)</li>
<li>Select products that promote healthy indoor air environments through reduced off-gassing including
<ul>
<li>paints and other materials with low VOCs</li>
<li>fabrics that are naturally flame-retardant versus fabrics with chemical flame retardants</li>
</ul></li>
<li>Specify occupant sensors for safety and reduced energy consumption including
<ul>
<li>ways to work with lighting when occupants are in a room</li>
<li>use of occupant sensors in public restrooms</li>
</ul></li>
<li>Recycle existing carpeting and wallcovering</li>
<li>Recommend use of equipment with the ENERGY STAR™ rating such as televisions and refrigerators</li>
</ul>
</td></tr>
</table>

Figure 4.15 Housing and interiors professionals have a responsibility to their clients and their profession to utilize sustainable design practices.

Chapter 4 Assessment

Summary

- Sustainability means that present generations use environmental products and resources to meet their needs, but also allows future generations to meet their needs.
- Sustainable design assures that buildings and interiors have less negative impact on the environment and assures consideration of natural resources.
- Principles of sustainable design include using less energy, using renewable energy sources, selecting materials from renewable sources, recycling, conserving water use, protecting occupant health and safety, and producing less waste.
- Many resources exist to guide sustainable design including a number of certification programs and labeling systems.
- Professionals in housing-related and interior design careers have a responsibility to promote and use sustainable design practices in their work.
- Knowledge of the certification programs and other practices that guide sustainable design is essential for all housing and interior design professionals.

Terms in Action

1. **Term antonyms** Individually or with a partner, create a T-chart on a sheet of paper and list each of the *Content* and *Academic Terms* from the beginning of the chapter in the left column. In the right column, list an *antonym* (a word of opposite meaning) for each term. Discuss how understanding antonyms can help reinforce word meanings.

Think Critically

2. **Analyze evidence** In the text, the author indicates that "after use of energy-efficient appliances, one way occupants can manage and control energy use is through *home automation*." Use the text and additional reliable resources to investigate and analyze evidence about home automation. How available is such technology to the average consumer? What are the pros and cons of home automation? Discuss your analysis of this evidence with the class.
3. **Analyze recycling** New uses for recycled materials are continually changing. Make a list of three items that are currently not recycled in your community. Analyze how recycling these items could benefit new housing. Some examples include converting old auto frames into steel beams and other building materials and recycling plastic water bottles into carpeting. What are your ideas? Post your ideas to the class blog for discussion.
4. **Predict consequences** Environmental scientists and others study the impact of housing on the environment. Predict the consequences of failure to build and renovate housing that has little to no impact on the environment. Discuss your predictions with the class.

Core Skills

5. **Technology and speaking** Consult a home builder in your city to find out how he or she uses new technology in constructing houses. This should include sustainable building materials, construction techniques, and equipment. Ask if he or she has built an automated house or a house utilizing green or sustainable building technology. How is this type of housing becoming more affordable in your community? Write a summary of your findings to share with the class.
6. **Photo essay and speaking** Check the buildings in your community to see how many have solar heating systems. Using a digital camera, photograph the visible solar collectors. Compile a photo essay with presentation software complete with written photo descriptions to share with your class. What types of buildings (residential, commercial, or government) seem to use solar power most often? Present your findings to the class with your illustrated report.
7. **Research and writing** Presume you are an investigative writer for a building technology magazine. Your assignment is to research and predict the most common trends for housing

that has little to no environmental impact 50 years from now. Write an article in which you discuss the top five sustainable items. Post your article to the class discussion board.

8. **Research and speaking** In teams, research economic considerations related to sustainability and housing. What are the economic costs to the United States of failure to build and renovate housing that meets sustainability standards? Give an oral report to share your research with the class.
9. **Research and writing** Presume you are an investigative reporter for your school online news network. Your assignment is to research techniques and materials that can be used in housing to promote sustainability. Research the use of cogeneration systems, such as fuel cells and microturbines, for the home. What is the benefit of such systems? How will such systems help home owners become less dependent on energy from other sources outside the home? Write an article summarizing your findings and post it to the online school news network.
10. **Research and speaking** Using information on your community website, determine technological applications that can be used in housing and other buildings to promote sustainability. What are the community's projected goals for use of solar and other sustainable applications in the future? How will such applications impact economics and energy usage in your community? Discuss in class.
11. **CTE college and career readiness** To find out more about LEED certified buildings in your community, survey several architects to determine which community buildings have LEED certification. To learn about sustainable design features and LEED, arrange a tour of one or more LEED buildings for your FCCLA chapter. Use the FCCLA *Planning Process* to plan, carry out, and evaluate your activity. Consider using this tour as part of a project for the FCCLA *Career Connection* program. Write a summary about what you learned during the field trip to share on the school website. How is striving for LEED certification on buildings part of responsible citizenship?

Design Practice

12. **Green interior design** Use your problem-solving skills to analyze and solve the following problem. Presume you have been hired to design a "green" kitchen remodel for a home in your community. You have been involved with the client as extensive renovations to most rooms and all the house systems (heating, cooling, and water) have been done over time. The kitchen size is 16 feet by 24 feet. The client desires an eat-in kitchen that makes use of green products and finishes in the design. Research sustainability practices that affect interior design using the *REGREEN Residential Remodeling Guidelines (ASID/USBGC)* as a resource along with any relevant local building code information. Include the following in your "green" kitchen interior design plan:
    - CADD floor plan drawing that shows the kitchen layout including eating area, food preparation area, and a food storage area with a pantry.
    - CADD elevation drawing to show cabinetry and storage.
    - Sample selections for ceiling, wall, and floor treatments; cabinetry and trim finishes; furnishings (table and chairs); kitchen appliances (range or cooktop/ovens, refrigerator, dishwasher, and microwave or convection oven).

    Then prepare a design presentation board and a written summary about each of the products and finishes you chose for this "green" kitchen design project to share with the client (the class).
13. **Portfolio** Create a digital brochure using presentation software that promotes affordable green and sustainable housing design. Illustrate your presentation with photos or drawings and cite the source of the images. Share your digital brochure with the class and save a copy on a CD or a USB storage device (such as a thumb drive or flash drive) for your portfolio.

Unit 2

The Built Environment and Space Planning

Brandon Bourdages/Shutterstock.com

Citizenship and Historical Preservation

Check out your community's website to find out about a historical preservation group in your area. With your team, attend a meeting of this group to learn more about the group's activities. What needs does the organization have? How can youth get involved?

Report your findings to your FCCLA chapter. Determine if and how your team might work with this organization in your community. Then use the FCCLA *Planning Process* to plan, carry out, and evaluate your project. Use your project for an FCCLA *Illustrated Talk* STAR Event or a project for *Leadership Service in Action.* See your adviser for information as needed.

Citizens in the Know—Universal Design

Prepare an FCCLA *Illustrated Talk* STAR Event on the topic of *universal design* in housing. From a citizen's view, investigate the use of universal design in your community. How does it impact the lives of those who inhabit these structures? How could it make a difference to you?

Use a digital camera to take photos of one or more dwellings (interior and exterior) that utilize universal design in your community. Be sure to obtain written permission to take and use the photographs. Follow the presentation requirements in the *STAR Events Manual*. See your adviser for information as needed.

Chapter 5

Exterior Design Styles

Content Terms

traditional
folk
classic
half-timbered
dormer
stucco
gable roof
pent roof
gambrel roof
Mansard roof
hip roof
pilaster
portico
Palladian window
cornice
belvedere
bungalow
ranch
earth-sheltered
adaptive reuse

Academic Terms

symmetrical
asymmetrical

Learning Outcomes

After studying this chapter, you will be able to

- summarize the development of exterior architectural styles throughout history, including Traditional (both folk and classic), Modern, Postmodern, and Contemporary house styles.
- compare and contrast historical architectural and housing styles.
- identify how exterior home style influences interior characteristics and space layout.
- summarize the value of historical preservation.

Reading with Purpose

As you read this chapter, write a letter to yourself. Imagine that you will receive this letter in a few years when you are working at your future job as an interior designer. What key chapter points will be important to remember from this chapter? In the letter, list these points.

While studying, look for the access icon  **to:**

- **Practice** the *Content* and *Academic Terms* with e-flash cards, matching activities, and vocabulary games.
- **Reinforce** what you learn by completing the *Review & Assessment* questions and e-mailing them to your instructor.

www.g-wlearning.com/housing/

©iStock.com/LUNAMARINA

The evolution of housing exteriors is usually grouped into a number of styles and time periods. The greatest influences on these styles include geographical location and the historical and economic events during the era in which they were built.

To better understand period housing styles, it is important to note that while each time period and style has specific characteristics, some overlapping does exist. Because of this, dates for periods and styles are approximate. For example, in different regions of the country certain design styles could exist at the same time. In addition, not all designs in a certain style or specific era would be identical. The individual architects and builders brought their own personal creativity to their designs. Throughout history styles have been revived, utilizing traditional characteristics by implementing interior spaces and functionality appropriate to modern families. The architectural history of housing was and still is an ongoing process.

Housing in North America began with the Native Americans. They developed a wide variety of housing styles prior to the arrival of foreign explorers and settlers. The styles included hogans, pueblos, tepees, wigwams, pole-and-thatch structures, and others. When immigrant settlers arrived in North America, they brought with them the styles that existed in their homelands. Over time, these styles evolved into new types of housing that have become known as traditional styles.

Traditional Houses

Traditional houses reflect the experiences and traditions of past eras. These designs have adapted and changed over time to meet the needs of their inhabitants. Many house designs in use today were actually created in previous time eras of North American history. Each style has distinct characteristics and features that set it apart from the others.

The two categories of Traditional style design are folk and classic. **Folk** style originates from the common experiences of a group of people, such as common values and concerns. **Classic** style refers to the use of formal architectural elements that have been recognized over time for their enduring design excellence. Various renditions of folk and classic styles appear in many periods of architectural history.

Traditional Folk Houses

The styles of traditional folk houses varied from region to region. In some cold areas such as the Midwest, houses had to withstand heavy snowfalls. In warm climates such as the Southeast, orientation to the cooling breeze was important. In windy locations such as the coastal Northeast, housing needed to withstand heavy gusts.

In addition to the effects of climate and geographical location, the style of traditional folk housing was based on the ethnic experiences and lifestyles of the inhabitants. These housing styles were also shaped by the natural resources available to construct them. Because of this reliance on native materials, there has been a resurgence of these styles due to sustainable design and building practices. Styles described as *Native American, Early English, Spanish, Scandinavian, German, Dutch,* and *French* are types of traditional folk houses.

Native American

The many different styles of Native-American housing have influenced today's housing, as you have learned earlier in the text. Early settlers sometimes copied the eight-sided mud-and-log hogans of the Navajo or the wood frame structures of the Seminole.

The Pueblo in New Mexico still live in apartment-type adobe dwellings (Figure 5.1). The basic design of these adobe dwellings repeats in housing throughout the country, especially the Southwest. Characteristics of Pueblo housing include boxlike construction, flat roofs, and projecting roof beams.

Early English

An architectural style built by English settlers in North America beginning in the early 1600s is *Early English*. Several distinct housing types evolved from this traditional folk architecture. These types include Tidewater South and the New England styles known as Cape Cod, Saltbox, and Garrison.

Paul Matthew Photography/Shutterstock.com

Figure 5.1 The Pueblo live in these adobe dwellings.

The first successful English settlement in North America was established in 1607 in Jamestown, Virginia. Archaeologists think these early English settlers used the *mud-and-stud method* of building. Early records trace this building technique back to Lincolnshire County along the east coast of England. In this building technique, the frame of the house was built from upright forked logs with cross beams. The walls were filled with mud and clay, and the roof was thatched with leaves, tree bark, or bundles of reeds and straw. This technique was later refined and referred to as half-timbered construction. In **half-timbered** houses, the wood frame of the house actually formed part of the outside wall (Figure 5.2). Brick or plaster was used to fill the spaces between the beams.

Tidewater South. Settlements continued to grow in the low-lying coastal lands called Tidewater areas. An architectural style built by early English settlers in the southern coastal regions of what is now the United States is *Tidewater South* (Figure 5.3). The construction style of these homes was simple: a one-room wooden building with a wood or stone chimney at one end. As families grew, house additions were built. The first addition was another room, often built as large as the first. It was added next to the wall with the chimney. Many rural farmhouses throughout the South had similar plans. Covered porches were also added to these simple plans to increase the amount of living area and to provide shelter from the hot sun.

New England. Plymouth, Massachusetts was the second successful English settlement in 1620. By 1640, a number of small English settlements were established along the eastern area of North America. This region of North America, now *New England*, includes the states of Maine, New Hampshire, Vermont, Massachusetts, Connecticut, and Rhode Island.

Photo Courtesy of the Jamestown-Yorktown Foundation

Figure 5.2 This thatched-roof house is an example of half-timbered construction.

Rob Byron/Shutterstock.com

Figure 5.3 The Tidewater South architectural style was commonly built by English settlers along the southern coastal regions of the United States.

Early seventeenth-century English settlers in northern New England commonly built two-story houses. They were constructed of heavy timber frames. In timber framing—or post-and-beam construction—large pieces of wood are joined together with woodworking joints (mortise-and-tenon joints), or with wooden pegs, braces, or trusses. Metal nails were expensive and used sparingly.

Timber frame construction was the construction method for all frame houses in seventeenth- and eighteenth-century America because of the abundance of wood. The house exteriors were covered with shingles, unpainted clapboards, or other wooden siding. A *clapboard* is a board that has one edge thicker than the other and is typically used for exterior horizontal siding. When applied, the board above laps over the thinner edge of the one below. This application is also known as bevel siding or lap siding.

The Cape Cod style grew out of variations on the one-story house design. As a family grew, rooms were added to the basic plan.

- **Cape Cod.** The *Cape Cod* is a small, symmetrical, one- or one-and-one-half-story house with a steep gable roof and side gables. A design is ***symmetrical*** when objects on both sides of a center point are identical. The Cape Cod style has a central entrance and a central chimney with several fireplaces. The eave (lower edge) line of the roof overhangs the exterior wall just above the first-floor windows. The windows are multipaned and usually have shutters. Originally, the siding was made of shingles or unpainted clapboards.

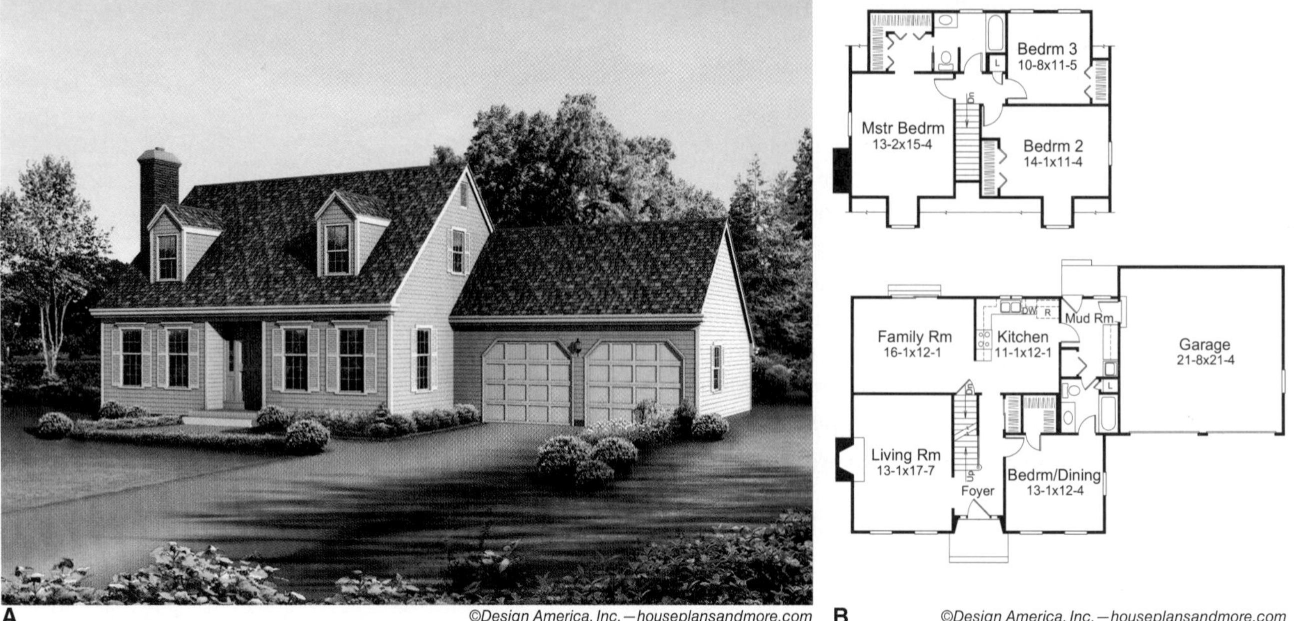

A ©Design America, Inc.—houseplansandmore.com B ©Design America, Inc.—houseplansandmore.com

Figure 5.4 The Cape Cod is a one-and-a-half-story house with a gable roof and dormers (A). The plan of a typical Cape Cod shows the standard centered entrance and the oddly shaped second-story rooms (B).

The loft area of the Cape Cod is usually expanded and made into finished bedrooms with angled ceilings. Openings are then cut in the roof for dormers. **Dormers** are structures with windows that project through a sloping roof in the second story (Figure 5.4). They add light, space, and ventilation to the second story. There was a revival of the Cape Cod after World War II because they were simple and affordable to build.

- **Saltbox.** Another type of home built by the English settlers in the New England area was the Saltbox house. The *Saltbox* is a variation of the Cape Cod (Figure 5.5 A). The earliest Saltbox houses were created when a lean-to addition was built on the rear of the house. The Saltbox house takes its name from the shape of the wooden box in which salt was kept at that time.

  In Saltbox construction, the house has two or two-and-one-half stories in the front, but just one story in the back. It is characterized by a long, steep-pitched gable roof that slopes down from the front to the back. Other typical features are large windows with small panes of glass and a large central chimney.
- **Garrison.** A later design built by the English settlers in New England was the *Garrison* house,

A Jody LaFerriere/Shutterstock.com

B Zack Frank/Shutterstock.com

Figure 5.5 A Saltbox house has narrow wood siding and windows without shutters (A). This Garrison style house, which was originally owned by Paul Revere, features an overhanging second story (B).

named after early garrisons, or forts. Like the old forts, Garrisons have an overhanging second story, (Figure 5.5 B). The overhang allows extra space on the second floor without widening the foundation. It also has a supporting effect, which prevents the second-story floor from sagging in the middle. This supporting effect is created when beams extending out from the first floor support the second floor. The farther the beams extend out, the greater is the support in the center.

The overhang is always on the front of the house and sometimes extends to the sides and rear. Carved drops or pendants below the overhang provide ornamentation. Other characteristics of the Garrison house are symmetrical design, a steep gable roof, and windows that have small panes of glass. Originally, the siding was made of wood shingles or unpainted clapboards.

Roof styles used in housing can vary widely (Figure 5.6) and often influence the layout and ceiling heights within. While most of these styles are used in traditional houses, they can also be used in unique ways for contemporary housing, which will be discussed later in the chapter.

Spanish

The first Europeans to establish colonies in North America were Spaniards. These colonies were mostly in Florida and the Southwest beginning in the 1500s. Florida's Spanish-colonial city of St. Augustine was begun in 1565, making it the oldest continuing permanent European settlement. Between 1565 and 1821, Florida was mostly under Spanish control.

A large portion of what is now the southwestern United States was under Spanish, then Mexican, control from the seventeenth to the mid-nineteenth century. Spanish Texas gained its independence from Mexico in 1836.

The *Spanish* style was developed in areas where the climate was warm and dry. Early Spanish style was characterized by one-story structures with flat or low-pitched red tile roofs. The houses were masonry construction of adobe brick or stone covered in stucco. **Stucco** is a type of plaster applied to the exterior walls of a house. The interior was usually simple with earthen floors, beamed ceilings, and whitewashed plaster walls.

The overall design of Spanish-style housing is ***asymmetrical***. This means that one side of the center point is different from the other. During the seventeenth century, Spanish settlers in California and parts of the Southwest built more elaborate styles.

A Spanish-style house is pictured in Figure 5.7. Specific features include courtyards, enclosed patios, wrought-iron exterior décor, and arched windows and doors.

Scandinavian

Immigrants from Sweden, Finland, Norway, and Denmark were known as *Scandinavians*. Of this group of immigrants, the Swedish settlers are credited with introducing the log cabin to North

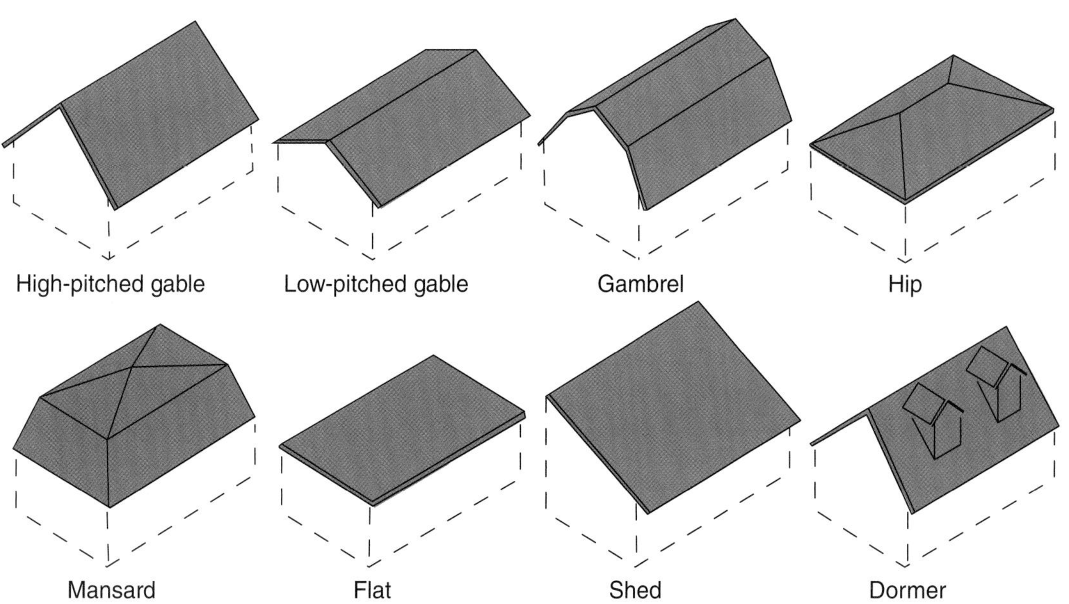

Figure 5.6 Roof styles have a great effect on the exterior design of buildings.

Denise Kappa/Shutterstock.com

Figure 5.7 This house includes many of the traits of the traditional Spanish-style house.

ksb/Shutterstock.com

Figure 5.8 The original log cabins looked very similar to this one.

America in the early 1700s. The *log cabin* was originally a one-room, rectangular house about 10 feet wide and 12 to 20 feet long, which might also include a sleeping loft.

Typical log cabins were built on a stone or rock foundation to keep the logs above the ground. The logs were squared off and notches were cut on the top and bottom of each end. The logs were then stacked with the notched ends fitted together in the corners. *Chinking*—a filling of sticks and wood chips—was used to fill the gaps between the logs and was then covered with a layer of mud to fill the remaining spaces. A door opening and at least one window were then cut into the house. The fireplace was built of stone, and the floor was dirt or gravel that had been raked smooth.

The log cabin had a gable roof. A **gable roof** comes to a high point in the center and slopes on both sides (Figure 5.8). A gable is a triangle formed by a sloping roof.

Log cabins were a popular style for the North American midlands and frontier, where timber was a readily available resource as a building material. They are still popular today in many areas as either a primary residence or for use as a second vacation home. Many companies specializing in manufactured log cabins offer a wide range of floor plans and price ranges. They meet the need that many home owners have for a rustic style that depicts a simpler lifestyle.

German

The majority of early *German* settlers, who traveled from the region called Germany today, arrived in North America in the late seventeenth century. They primarily settled in what is now southeastern Pennsylvania. They built large, durable homes of wood and fieldstone for warmth. The entry led to the kitchen on the first floor. The fireplace was in the center of the first floor with a family room for entertaining located on the opposite side of the fireplace. If the home was large enough, there would be a number of small bedrooms behind the family room. The houses were constructed with gable roofs. Some also had small roof ledges between the first and second floors called **pent roofs** (Figure 5.9).

Dutch

Dutch settlers founded settlements in North America as early as 1614 in what is now known as Albany, New York. A later settlement began in 1626 in New Amsterdam, which became New York City. The first Dutch houses were one-story structures of brick in urban areas, or stone in rural areas. One of the most important characteristics was the front

Photography Courtesy of Bradley S. DeForest of the Skippack Historical Society

Figure 5.9 Germans who settled in Pennsylvania built houses similar to this. Many had a pent roof—a small ledge between the first and second floor.

door, which was divided in half horizontally. This style became known as the *Dutch door*. It was the later Dutch design, however, that left the most long-lasting mark on architecture.

The later style is known today as Dutch Colonial. *Dutch Colonial* is a housing style with a gambrel roof. A **gambrel roof** is a roof with a lower steeper slope and an upper less-steep slope on both of its sides, making use of what would be attic space. Sometimes the lower portion extends over an open porch, which is known as the *Dutch kick*. Houses of this style were often built of fieldstone or brick and in some cases wood. Other characteristics of the Dutch Colonial are dormers, a central entrance, an off-center chimney, chimneys that flank the ends of the house, and windows with small panes (Figure 5.10).

Dutch Colonial homes were most commonly built in northern states such as New York and Delaware. The Dutch did not bring this style from their homeland, but created it after settling in North America. Many residents ran businesses out of these homes, separating the public and private spaces by floors.

MR. INTERIOR/Shutterstock.com

Figure 5.10 This home has features that are typically original to Dutch Colonial homes such as a *gambrel* roof that flares at the bottom.

French

During the colonial period, French settlements formed in the 1700s along the St. Lawrence River, Great Lakes, and Mississippi River. Early French homes were built in the *French Normandy* style, which was brought to North America by the Huguenots. These homes were one-story structures with many narrow door and window openings. The roofs were steeply pitched and either hipped or side-gabled. The walls were stucco, which was usually applied over a half-timbered frame. Porches were added in settlements located in warmer regions. Also, houses in the South were constructed on posts one story above ground. This provided better air circulation in the humid environment and protected the house from floods. The Southern adaptation of this design is the *French Plantation* house.

A distinctive style evolved in New Orleans known as the *Louisiana French* style. The most outstanding characteristics of this style include balconies with elaborate ironwork railings and white stucco walls. The structures were built on raised brick or stone basements to protect them from flooding.

Even after Louisiana became the eighteenth state in the Union in 1812, the French influence continued to impact American architecture in many ways. One example, the *French Manor*, is a symmetrically styled home with wings on each side and a Mansard roof on the main part of the house (Figure 5.11). A **Mansard roof** is a variation of the gambrel roof. Its designer was a French architect named François Mansart. When used on detached single-family dwellings, the roof continues all around the house. Dormers often project from the steeply pitched part of the roof. When used on commercial buildings, the Mansard roof may be used only on one or two sides.

French influence also appears in the house style called *French Provincial*. This style originated in New Orleans and became popular all over the country. It has a delicate, dignified appearance and is usually symmetrical. The windows are a dominant part of the design. The tops of the windows break into the eave line. A French Provincial house can be as tall as two-and-a-half stories.

Classic Traditional Houses

As the early settlements flourished and colonies and states were formed, prosperity brought change and improvement to housing. The quality of building materials improved, and the growth of trade brought new information to the settlers. Architects and house plans from Europe became available. Growing prosperity fostered interest in refined taste (cultivated and genteel) and classic style. Classic traditional homes include the following time periods and styles: *Georgian, Federal, Greek Revival, Southern Colonial,* and *Victorian*.

Georgian

The *Georgian* style (1690 to 1800) was adapted from English architecture. It is called Georgian because it was popular during the era when Kings George I, II, and III ruled England.

Georgian houses have simple exterior lines, dignified appearances, and symmetry. The centrally located front doors have windows with small panes

Steve Holderfield/Shutterstock.com

Figure 5.11 French Manor houses are noted for their stately appearance and *Mansard* roofs.

of glass, and either gable or **hip roofs**—roofs with sloping ends and sides. A flat area with a *balustrade* or railing sometimes tops hip roofs. This area is called a captain's or widow's walk. Georgian houses usually have a tall chimney at each end of the roof, and most have some ornamentation under the eaves. A distinctive type of eave ornamentation, known as *dentil molding*, is still popular today. As a trim board with square, tooth-like blocks, this ornamentation is sometimes mislabeled as "dental" molding (Figure 5.12).

PRILL/Shutterstock.com

Figure 5.12 Georgian houses have simple, dignified lines with ornamentation—or dentil molding—often found under the eaves.

The symmetry of these homes does not stop with the exterior features. The interiors typically have a central hallway with enclosed rooms two deep on either side. This rectangular layout allowed each room to have one side of a double-sided fireplace as well as each to have three to four windows for natural light and ventilation.

As the Georgian style developed, it became more elaborate. Additional ornamentation was given to doors and windows. The front door was often highlighted with a decorative crown over the top with flattened columns, or **pilasters**, on each side. The style also changed according to the region in which it was built.

Wood was used in New England, and stone in the Mid-Atlantic region. In the South, brick was used and a wing was added to each side of the main house.

Federal

Following the American Revolution (1775 to 1783), interest grew in developing distinctly American styles and symbols. National pride was strong, and Americans adopted a new style of architecture that reflected confidence in their newly won independence. The style was named in honor of the Federal form of government in the United States. Federal-style architecture became popular between 1780 and 1840. A house built in the *Federal* style has a box-like shape, is

STEM Math Symmetry

Objects are often described as being *symmetrical* or *asymmetrical*. An object is symmetrical if a line drawn through it divides it into two matching halves. The dividing line is called the *line of symmetry*.

An object may have one or more lines of symmetry. For example, a rectangle has two lines of symmetry. A circle has an infinite number of lines of symmetry since any line drawn through the center creates a line of symmetry.

An object is asymmetrical if it has zero lines of symmetry; no two halves match. Your hand is asymmetrical; you cannot draw a line that will result in two matching halves.

Symmetry creates balance. Architects and interior designers often incorporate symmetry in their work. For example, the exterior of a Georgian home exhibits symmetry. You can also achieve symmetry by placing matching chairs on both sides of an entryway.

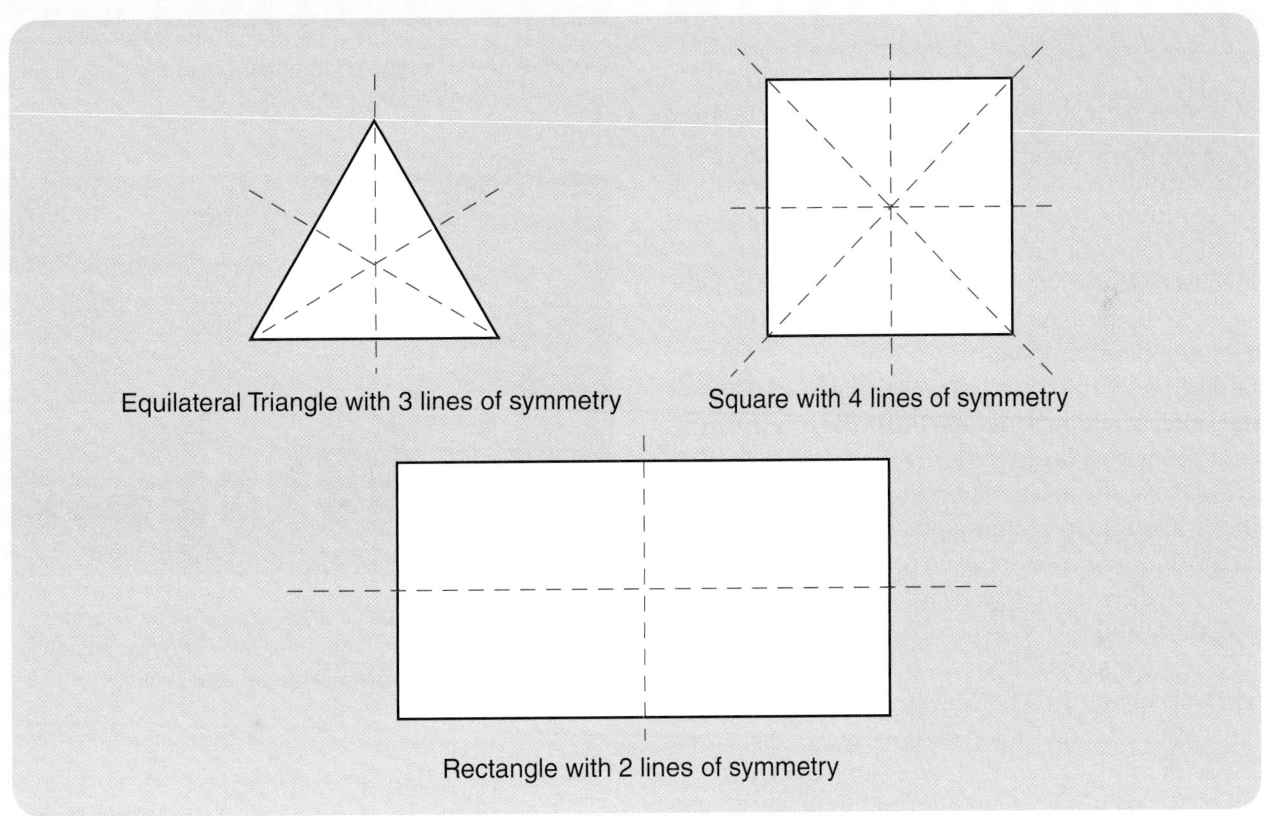

Math Practice

Take a walking tour in your neighborhood and carefully observe symmetry in the housing styles as you walk. Select at least six homes you think display symmetry and take digital pictures of the homes (ask the owner's permission). Print the house pictures. On the printed house pictures, carefully draw a vertical line exactly through the middle. Do the houses actually display symmetry? Why or why not? Give an oral report to share your findings with the group.

symmetrical, has double-hung sash windows, and is at least two stories high (*symmetrical* structures look balanced, corresponding in size, shape, and position on opposite sides of a central dividing line). Sometimes a small portico was added to the main entrance. A **portico** is an open space covered with a roof supported by columns. Federal-style houses also had *pediments*, which are architectural roof-like decorations that are usually found over a portico, window, or door. The pediments can be segmental or triangular (Figure 5.13). During the Federal period, two important architectural styles emerged, Adam style and Early Classical Revival.

Adam style. The *Adam style* of architecture was named after the design work of two Scottish brothers, Robert and James Adam. These talented

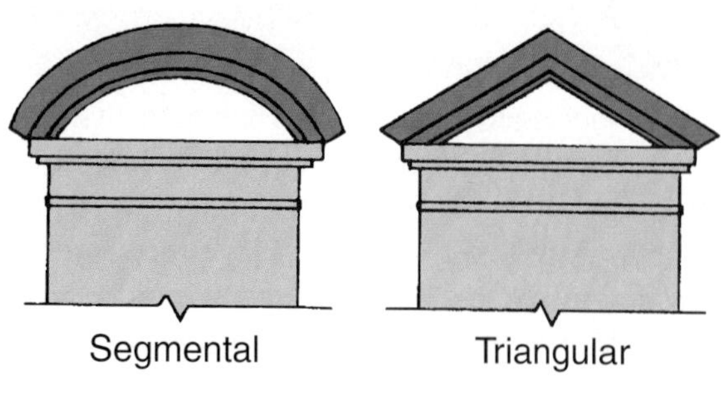

Goodheart-Willcox Publisher

Figure 5.13 Pediments are used over doors and windows to add interest to a design.

Joe Gough/Shutterstock.com

Figure 5.14 The gabled pediment over the door is an example of the Federal influence.

teammates were architects, interior designers, and furniture designers. Their work was based on plans for Italian houses and palaces. The Adam style continued the symmetry of the Georgian style. The types of graceful details that were added to the Georgian-style architecture included swags, garland, urns, and other refined motifs. The main identifying feature of the Adam style is a fanlight over the front entrance (Figure 5.14). Other characteristics include **Palladian windows** (windows with a large center section and two side sections, usually arched), circular or elliptical windows, recessed arches, and oval-shaped rooms. The most famous oval-shaped room in this style is the Oval Office of the President of the United States in Washington, D.C.

Early Classical Revival. During the Federal period, architecture evolved using the classical details of Greek and Italian design, known as *Early Classical Revival.* One of the best examples of this architectural style is *Monticello* (meaning "little mountain" in Italian), the home Thomas Jefferson designed and built for himself (Figure 15.15). He began construction in 1769. Because of the influence of Roman architecture, the architectural style of his home is classified as *Roman Neoclassicism.* (*Neoclassicism* refers to an adaptation or revival of classical details.) Monticello has a large portico on its west front with columns and a triangular pediment gable. Jefferson added the dome in 1800 after being influenced by the French architecture he saw while traveling in France. Jefferson was the founder of the University of Virginia in Charlottesville, Virginia and designed the original campus.

In addition to these major contributions, Jefferson was the principal author of the *Declaration of Independence* and third President of the United States. He was also an inventor and renowned political leader.

©iStock.com/John M. Chase

Figure 5.15 Monticello—the home built by Thomas Jefferson—is found in Charlottesville, Virginia. It is an example of Early Classical Revival architecture.

Greek Revival

Greek Revival (1825 to 1860) is another style of classic traditional design. It developed during a period that embraced, and carefully duplicated, the formal elements found in ancient Greek architecture.

One characteristic of a house in the Greek Revival style is the two-story entry porch across the entire front of the structure. This structure is supported by Greek columns. Another key characteristic is a large triangular gable with a pediment (Figure 5.16). These houses are also symmetrical with bold moldings and heavy **cornices**—which are molded and projecting horizontal members that crown architectural elements such as columns. Houses of this style are large and impressive. The emphasis on the front door meant a wide hallway on the interior, which would be centered and have a very grand scale (Figure 5.17). Some government buildings are designed in the Greek Revival style.

Anne Power/Shutterstock.com

Figure 5.16 A Greek Revival house is characterized by a two-story portico supported by Greek columns with a large triangular pediment.

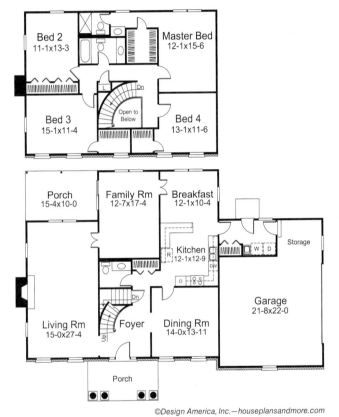

Bed 2
11-1x13-3
Master Bed
12-1x15-6
L
Dn
Open to Below
Bed 3
15-1x11-4
Bed 4
13-1x11-6
Porch
15-4x10-0
Family Rm
12-7x17-4
Breakfast
12-1x10-4
Storage
Kitchen
12-1x12-9
R
W
D
DW
Garage
21-8x22-0
Dn
Living Rm
15-0x27-4
Foyer
Up
Dining Rm
14-0x13-11
Porch

©Design America, Inc.—houseplansandmore.com

Figure 5.17 This plan shows a current adaptation of a typical Greek Revival plan including the main floor and second-story bedrooms. Although there is a garage on one side of the house, the primary front facade is very symmetrical.

Southern Colonial

An offshoot of the Greek Revival style developed in the 1800s is the Southern Colonial. The *Southern Colonial* is a large, two- or three-story brick or frame house of symmetrical design (Figure 5.18 A). Two-story columns extend across the entire front, covered by an extension of the roof that created expansive outdoor living spaces. The roof style is hip or gable. Dormers, shutters, and a belvedere are often included. A **belvedere** is a small room on the roof of a house used as a lookout.

On the interior, there is typically a large central hallway with a grand staircase and doors at either end to help with cross-ventilation. This would be flanked with small fragmented rooms with extensive wood surfaces (Figure 5.18 B). The smaller rooms help in retaining fireplace heat.

A *Sean Pavone/Shutterstock.com*

B *Olivier Le Queinec/Shutterstock.com*

Figure 5.18 The design of this Southern Colonial evolved from the Greek Revival style (A). In addition to the ornate furniture (which you will learn about later), Southern Colonial homes are typically rich in ornate and formal wood and trim work (B).

Victorian

Following the Civil War, growing industrialization greatly influenced architecture of the *Victorian* period—a time during the reign of Queen Victoria of England (1837 to 1901). House styles of the Victorian period, Figure 5.19 A–E, include the following:

- Italianate
- Gothic Revival (wood and masonry)
- American Second Empire (Mansard style)
- Stick style (also called Carpenter Gothic)
- Richardsonian Romanesque
- Eastlake Victorian
- Queen Anne

The main feature of all Victorian housing styles is the abundance of decorative trim (Figure 5.20).

Italianate *Christopher Meder/Shutterstock.com*

Romanesque *Thomas Barrat/Shutterstock.com*

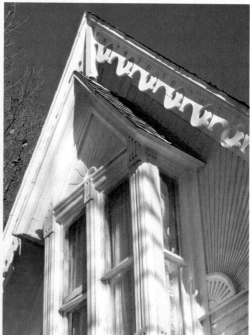

Queen Anne *Donald J. Price/Shutterstock.com*

Gothic Revival *Gary Blakeley/Shutterstock.com*

Gingerbread *Bonita R. Cheshier*

Figure 5.19 These homes show some of the varied features of Victorian homes, including a turret (small tower) with much decorative trim.

Marcin Sylwia Ciesielski/Shutterstock.com

Figure 5.20 The asymmetrical and varied layout of the exterior of a Victorian home often creates interesting shapes for interior rooms.

Other characteristics include high porches, roofs with steep gables, tall windows, high ceilings, dark stairways, long halls, and *turrets,* which are small towers. Not every Victorian house had every feature, but a strong combination of these elements came to be associated with the haunted-house stereotype in horror movies. They also made the interior layouts of the houses much more intricate and varied than most style counterparts (Figure 5.21 A and B).

The interiors of the styles also varied. Italianate homes are asymmetrical and box like. They will typically have small rooms, multiple small porches (rather than a wrap-around) and more subdued colors. Gothic Revival homes are known for tall towers and elevated ceilings with exposed beams. The exterior detailing of Romanesque structures (visually heavy materials, low arches, and round towers) typically extend to the interior finishes and forms. Queen Anne style, the most widely recognized, has large wrapped porches for outdoor living, an asymmetrical layout, and bright and varied colors.

As the Victorian style developed, owners tried to outdo one another in the amount of decorative trim on their houses. Machine-made trim became a sign of prosperity and high style. Quantity became more important than quality. Scrolls and other decorative trim made from wood appeared under eaves and around windows and doors. This came to be known as *gingerbread.*

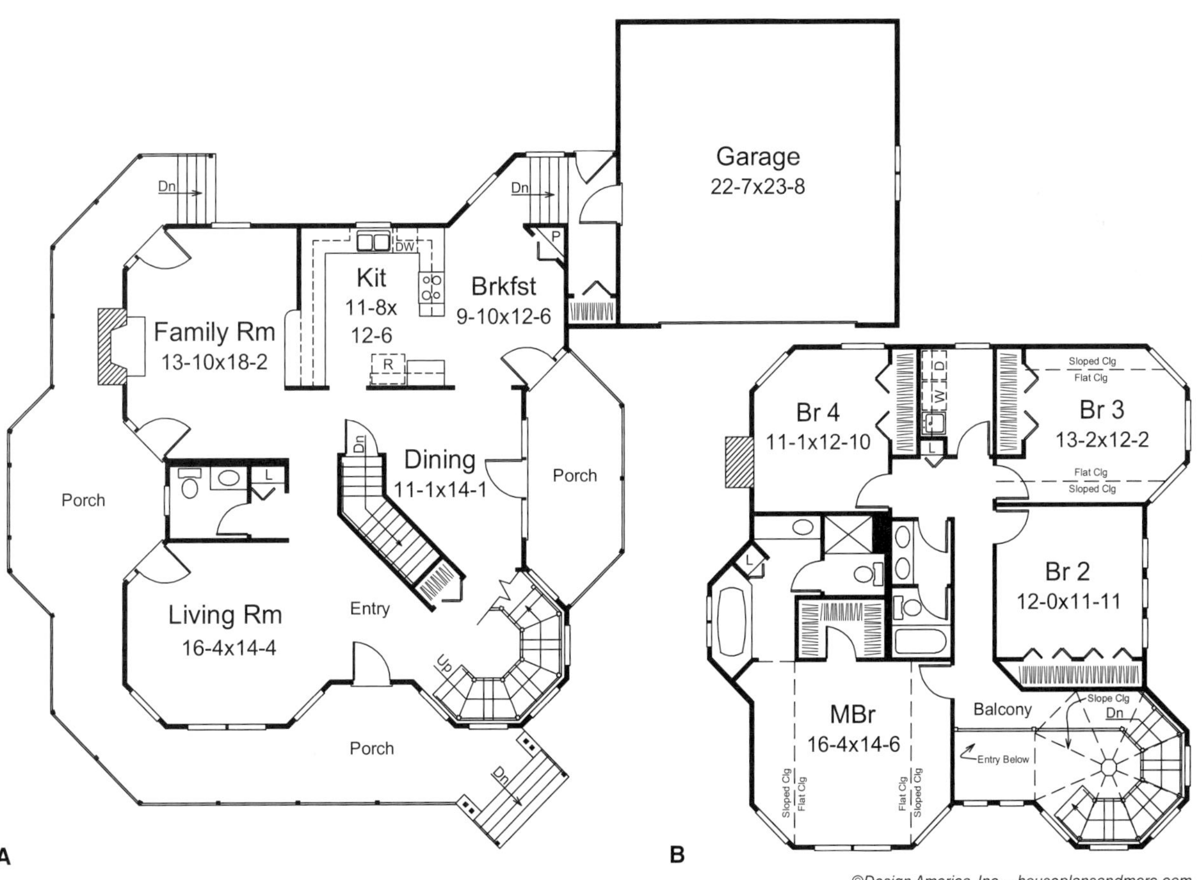

©Design America, Inc.—houseplansandmore.com

Figure 5.21 This plan shows the fragmented nature of both floors of most Victorian homes (A and B) as well as an expansive porch for outdoor living. The garage is a modern addition.

Review & Assessment

1. Red tile roofs, enclosed patios, and arch-shaped windows and doors are characteristics of which style of traditional housing?
2. Contrast the meaning of *folk* and *classic* styles of traditional architecture.
3. Compare and contrast the following styles: Cape Cod, Saltbox, and Garrison.
4. Name two features typical of the Spanish style.
5. What are the similarities and differences between the Dutch Colonial and the French Manor house styles?
6. List three features of a Georgian-style house.
7. What two architectural styles emerged from the Federal period?
8. What is the difference between a *portico* and a *pediment*?
9. How can you identify Greek Revival-style architecture?
10. Identify four characteristics of Victorian houses.

Modern Houses

Housing designs developed in the United States from the early 1900s into the 1980s are classified as the *Modern style*. Compared to the other housing styles discussed so far, these are quite new. Modern styles include the *Prairie style, Arts and Crafts, Bungalow, Spanish Revival, Tudor,* and *International* style. All are very popular, and their use will likely continue in the future.

Prairie Style

Frank Lloyd Wright, who is one of the most noted architects of modern times, designed the Prairie style house. Wright is considered the greatest figure in modern American architecture. He designed a series of Prairie style houses between 1893 and 1920 that were very different from the traditional architecture built before this period (Figure 5.22).

Prairie style houses have strong horizontal lines, low-pitched roofs, and overhanging eaves. Wright believed that a house should strongly relate to its environment, or setting. He liked to create the illusion that the house had actually evolved from the site. Prairie style homes were constructed of wood, stone, plaster, and materials found in nature. Earth-tone colors were used to emphasize the link between the man-built structure and its natural setting.

EQRoy/Shutterstock.com

Figure 5.22 The low-pitched roofs with overhanging eaves, strong horizontal lines, and windows of the Robie House designed by Frank Lloyd Wright are characteristic of the Prairie style.

Previous architectural styles used walls to divide interior space into box-like rooms. Wright reduced the number of walls to allow one room to flow into another, creating an open floor plan, and used a large centralized fireplace to give organization to the space. In addition, this style allowed interior space to visually flow outdoors through porches, terraces, and windows. The horizontal lines of the exterior carry into the interior with the use of ribbon windows. His flexible use of space greatly influenced the design work of European architects.

Arts and Crafts

Arts and Crafts style or Craftsman style houses were built between 1905 and 1930. This popular style had its roots in the Arts and Crafts movement of the 1880s. It celebrated use of natural materials worked by hand. Simple, nature-inspired colors and patterns were often used for interior fabrics and wall coverings. As a response to the overabundance of machine-made gingerbread and other architectural excesses of the Victorian era, English designers such as John Ruskin and William Morris and many others began this movement. In the United States, two brothers from California—Charles Sumner Greene and Henry Mather Greene—designed houses during the Arts and Crafts movement. They were widely praised for creating the "ultimate" bungalow—a larger, sprawling version of the earlier bungalow.

The name "Craftsman" came from the title of a popular magazine published between 1901 and 1916 by Gustav Stickley—the famous furniture designer. At that time, a true Craftsman-style house was built strictly according to plans published by Stickley. Gradually, other magazines, mail-order

A LesPalenik/Shutterstock.com

B MR. INTERIOR/Shutterstock.com

Figure 5.23 Bungalows typically have low-pitched roofs and covered porches as is characteristically found in this California bungalow (A). This Arts and Crafts bungalow interior represents a more casual and informal environment and a use of natural colors, textures, and materials (B).

houses, and builders began to publish plans with their own Craftsman-like details, modifying and often diluting the true Craftsman style.

Characteristics of a Craftsman-style house include a low-pitched roof, wide eaves with triangular brackets, exposed roof rafters, and wood, stone, or stucco siding. Craftsman houses feature stone porch supports with thick, square or round columns and exterior chimneys made of stone. The floor plans are open, with few hallways. These structures use beamed ceilings and many windows. Some windows feature stained glass or leaded-glass designs.

Built between 1905 and 1930, the bungalow style house expressed the simple and economical ideals of the Arts and Crafts movement. A **bungalow** is one-and-a-half stories with a low-pitched roof, horizontal shape, and a covered front porch (Figure 5.23 A). Sometimes the porch is enclosed. The bungalow is usually made of wood or brick. The shingled roof extends beyond the walls. Windows are set high to allow the placement of furniture beneath them. The California bungalow is similar in design, but larger.

Within a bungalow, most of the living spaces are on the ground floor. The floor plan features a front door which leads directly into a living room at the center and connecting rooms without hallways. The design of the floor plan is very efficient with such features as built-in cabinets, shelves, and seats. Interior spaces are very relaxed and informal, utilizing natural colors such as stained wood (Figure 5.23 B).

Tudor

In the 1920s, Tudor homes, those influenced by medieval shapes and decoration, gained popularity in America. These homes are either built of actual heavy timber (which is left exposed and filled in with stucco) or using more contemporary materials with a false facade of thin timber and stucco (Figure 5.24). Emphasizing the height of the exterior and interior spaces, ceilings are highly pitched and architectural elements including fireplaces are substantial (Figure 5.25). Additional accents include patterned brick and stone designs, leaded glass bands of windows, and exposed trusses.

Susan Law Cain/Shutterstock.com

Figure 5.24 The brown and white on many Tudor style homes emphasizes the contrast of the two primary materials, timber and stucco.

Spanish Revival

A Spanish Revival style house is pictured in Figure 5.26 A and B. This is called a revival

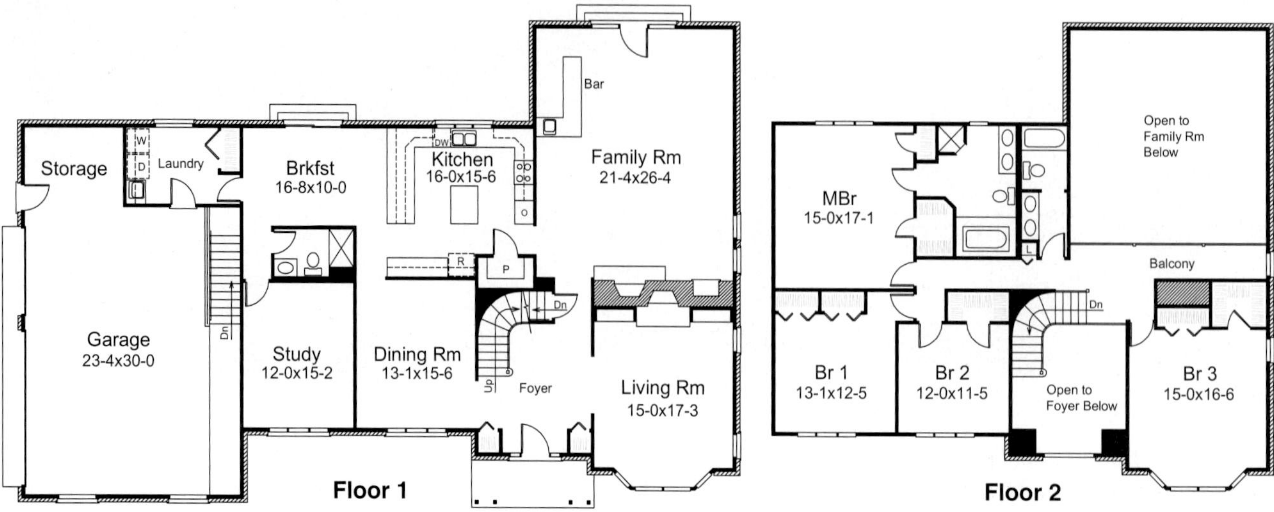

©Design America, Inc.—houseplansandmore.com

Figure 5.25 The plan shown indicates an open, highly pitched ceiling in the social space, a typical characteristic of Tudor homes.

style because it is being used in more modern homes (late 1800s and beyond), but emulates the characteristics of the original style. Specific features include enclosed patios, wrought-iron exterior decor, stucco outside (and often inside), and arched windows and doors. Climate permitting, most have interior courtyards or full one-story porches. This style of housing is widely used in the Southwest (Figure 5.27).

International Style

The most dramatic architectural style of the Modern movement is the *International style*. It is a style of architecture and furniture design that began in the 1900s, influenced strongly by Bauhaus—the German state school of design that merged art and technology. It emphasized the simplicity of design and eliminated unnecessary elements.

Sociocultural Connections — Asian Origins of American Bungalows

Home designers often blend elements of different cultures in their work. The history of the bungalow illustrates how a home, considered by many as the essence of American design, reflects influences from other parts of the world. Bungalow-style homes line the streets of American cities from Los Angeles to Chicago. Although there are regional variations in style, a bungalow is generally a one- or one-and-a-half-story home with a low-pitched roof.

The bungalow originated in a tropical region that is now eastern India and Bangladesh. These early bungalows were thatched-roof huts suited to the climate. They were designed to minimize heat buildup and take advantage of cooling breezes. By the early 1800s, the British controlled India. When British soldiers and merchants settled in the area, they lived in single-family homes that incorporated elements of the Indian huts. The huts, called "bangla" or "banggolo," spread across India and then to the U.S. and Europe.

In the early 1900s, California architects Charles and Henry Greene popularized the bungalow. The Greene brothers, leaders in the Arts and Crafts movement, added Japanese features to their bungalows. For example, interior and exterior spaces were designed to flow into one another. This created an open and airy feel. One of the Greene brothers' masterpieces, the David B. Gamble House, completed in 1909 in Pasadena, California, reflects such Japanese influences.

Dig Deeper

Use reliable resources to dig deeper into the Arts and Crafts designs of the Greene brothers or other leaders in the Arts and Crafts movement. If possible, locate photographs of their designs. Use a school-approved software application to create a digital report to share with the class.

A Pawel Kazmierczak/Shutterstock.com

B Ron Zmiri/Shutterstock.com

Figure 5.26 This house includes many of the traits of the traditional Spanish style house (A). Much of the living spaces in Spanish homes are by way of porches and verandas (B).

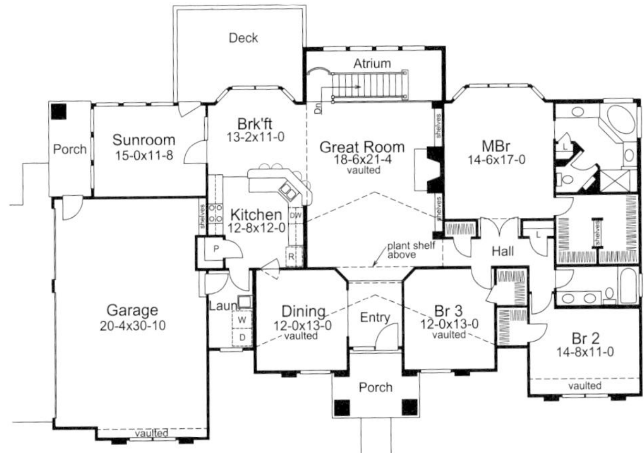

©Design America, Inc.—houseplansandmore.com

Figure 5.27 If Spanish homes are located in climates where a center open courtyard is not practical, they often retain a centralized floor plan where secondary spaces splay out from a grand social area.

International style is a blend of ideas from four leading architects of the early twentieth century:

- Frank Lloyd Wright, American architect
- Walter Gropius, a German architect and founder of the Bauhaus School
- Ludwig Mies van der Rohe, another famous German architect and director of the Bauhaus School
- Le Corbusier, a famous French architect

Geometric shapes and large expanses of glass windows were the foremost features of U.S. houses built in the International style (Figure 5.28 A, B, and C). Emerging technology fostered the use of new building materials and opened new ways of thinking about space, form, and beauty. With this form of construction, flat rooftops were possible and rooftop gardens became commonplace. Many of these houses

A jl661227/Shutterstock.com

B Claudio Divizia/Shutterstock.com

C MR. INTERIOR/Shutterstock.com

Figure 5.28 Many mid-century and International style homes are simply a combination of basic geometric forms (A).This home is an example of the International style of architecture (B). Because of the simplicity of the architecture, much of the personality of International Modern homes is found in the furnishings (C).

were constructed of reinforced white concrete. The exteriors of the houses had little or no ornamentation. Interior furnishings took on a new importance in these types of homes that utilized open, flowing floor plans.

Review & Assessment

1. Who designed the Prairie style house?
2. Name four characteristics of the Craftsman-style house.
3. Describe the features of a bungalow house.
4. What influenced Tudor-style homes in America? Name one feature.
5. List two features of the Spanish Revival style.
6. What two features were characteristic of houses built in the International style in the United States?

Postmodern Houses

Postmodernism is a view about the architectural style of housing that began in the 1970s and continues today. This view often deviates from strict rules of architecture by using building techniques, angles, and styles differently. Postmodern design includes a sense of rebellion to the "less is more" simplicity of modern architecture. In addition, it includes a sense that anything in design is acceptable.

Some features of Postmodernism include residential designs filled with absurd humor or wit. Some architectural critics say that if the "wit" feature is absent from Postmodern design, it may just be modern or some other design style. Unexpected and playful elements are essential in the Postmodern design (Figure 5.29).

Postmodern homes are all unique. The diversity of design also includes some blending of previous styles including traditional, contemporary, and newly invented forms. Details may be exaggerated. Postmodern houses can be bizarre or shocking.

Architects leading this era of Postmodern design include Robert Venturi, Cesar Pelli, and Frank Gehry. Venturi states that although previous architectural styles are easily identified by consistent characteristics, Postmodernism is characterized by its diversity in features.

Review & Assessment

1. What are the key features of Postmodern architecture?
2. Name three characteristics of a Postmodern home.
3. Who are the leading architects of Postmodern design?

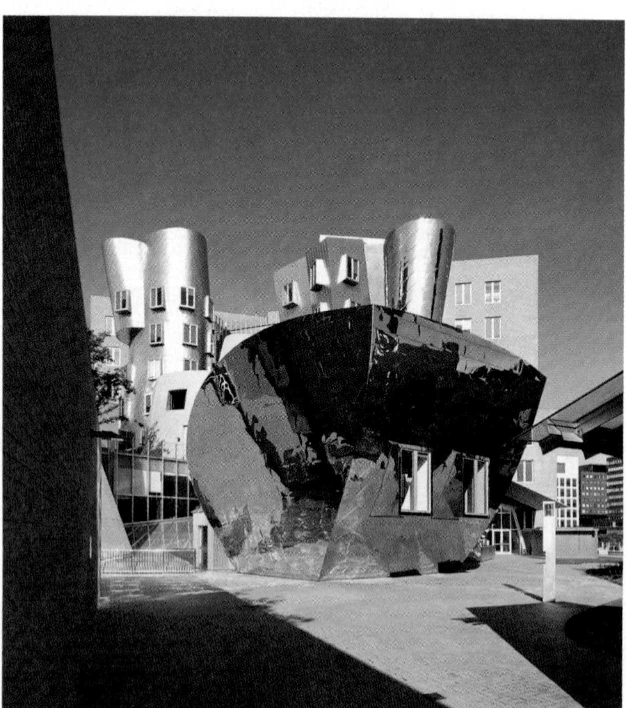

Jorge Salcedo/Shutterstock.com

Figure 5.29 This example of Postmodern design can be seen at the Massachusetts Institute of Technology in Cambridge, Massachusetts.

Contemporary Houses

Contemporary styles are the current or latest house designs constructed today. Many of the styles reflect design features from the traditional styles, both folk and classic. In some cases, current contemporary designs actually combine design features from several traditional architectural styles. There are some

Breadmaker/Shutterstock.com

Figure 5.30 Contemporary residential design cannot be attributed to any style. This newly constructed home has many Arts and Crafts influences yet still fits within its neighborhood's guidelines.

commonly recognized characteristics, however, of contemporary houses. These include a wide variation in ceiling heights, very tall windows with large glass panes, open floor plans, and unusual use of shapes and spaces. The exterior architecture often reflects these elements through such features as rooflines and tall windows.

Some contemporary housing designs may seem surprising or even controversial when compared to the traditional styles of the past. Other contemporary houses may combine both traditional and modern elements in their plans (Figure 5.30). The successful blending of unrelated styles and features requires careful planning to coordinate and harmonize their impact. Because of this, it is not as easy to classify and describe Contemporary-style houses as it is the purely traditional or purely modern styles. Contemporary designs may also vary widely from one to another in shape, material usage, details, and interior layout (Figure 5.31). Many convey a custom or distinctive one-of-a-kind design. The exterior may be brick, siding, stucco, stone, concrete, or a combination of these materials.

In contemporary residential architecture, anything is possible. Any home configuration can have exterior detailing that might be in contrast to the traditional manner of that style. For instance, a basic nondescript rectangular home could have the exterior decoration of a Queen Anne Victorian home without the interior layout of one. With this in mind, it becomes more important to understand how the form of the home affects its appearance, scale, relationship to the site and neighbors, functionality, and design possibilities. Ranch homes, split-level, earth-sheltered, and solar homes all offer their own challenges, restrictions, and design opportunities.

Ranch

A traditional **ranch** house is a one-story structure that may have a basement (Figure 5.32). Ranches often have an asymmetrical facade and entry and a central but not elaborate fireplace. They typically have a more open, rectilinear floor plan but also a centrally placed structural wall which might limit future renovations. Large windows and sliding glass doors that open onto a patio are common. The use of building materials and energy-saving features vary according to each region. For instance, light-colored siding and paint are used to reflect the heat in warm climates. Brick is another common exterior siding choice.

The ranch style began in the West. The informal lifestyle, large plots of land, and generally warm climate made the ranch style ideal for the region. Ranch style homes have since become popular throughout the country and often include garages in colder climates.

Ranch houses vary considerably in size. Small ranch houses may be relatively inexpensive to build, while larger sizes can be expensive. This is due to the large foundations and costly roof areas. Larger ranch style houses are less energy efficient than more compact house plans. One-story ranch houses are easy to maneuver through and maintain. Modified ranch structures are regaining popularity as older adults seek homes with all rooms on one level in an effort to eliminate climbing stairs. One-story ranch houses are also a good choice for incorporating universal design, although two-story versions are available (Figure 5.33 A).

There are many variations of the ranch style. One is the *hillside ranch*, (Figure 5.33 B and C). As

Image courtesy of Chief Architect Software

Figure 5.31 Contemporary space plans are often not dictated by their exterior styles. Homeowners can decide for traditional exterior detailing and materials while having a more modern and flexible interior layout.

rSnapshotPhotos/Shutterstock.com

Figure 5.32 Ranch-style houses began in the West on farms and ranches where space was plentiful. Now they are found in many communities. Becoming popular after WWII, ranch homes were basic and some of the first American homes to come with all appliances included.

A rSnapshotPhotos/Shutterstock.com

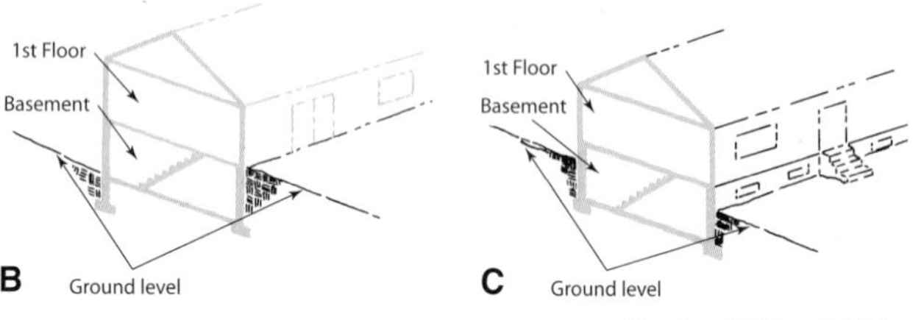

B C

Goodheart-Willcox Publisher

Figure 5.33 Ranch homes can also come in two-story versions but have similar interior layout characteristics as a single story (A). Part of the basement of a hillside ranch is above ground level (B). Since the top part of the basement of a raised ranch is above ground, the basement can be used as a living space (C).

its name implies, the house is built on a hill. It has a basement that is partly exposed, allowing use of natural light and the possibility of an exterior entry. This style of basement is also known as a "walkout" basement. Depending on the layout of the lot, the exposed part of the basement may be anything from a living area to a garage.

Another variation is the raised ranch, or split-entry. It is like a ranch, except the upper half of the basement is aboveground. This allows light to enter the basement through windows. The basement living area can be very pleasant if it is well insulated and waterproof. A disadvantage is that stairs must be climbed to get anywhere in the house. This can be a problem for small children, people with disabilities, and older people.

Split-Level

A split-level house has either three or four levels. The levels can be arranged in many ways (Figure 5.34 A and B). The split-level was developed for sloping lots, although it is occasionally built on flat lots.

One advantage of a split-level house is that traffic into the social, quiet, and service areas can be separated easily. Also, there are few stairs to climb to get from one level to another. However, getting from one level to another always requires climbing stairs. Again, the stairs may present a problem for individuals who are less physically agile.

Solar Houses

Solar energy is energy derived from the sun. Today, many house designs utilize solar energy. They can use either active solar heating systems or passive solar heating systems (Figure 5.35 A).

A rSnapshotPhotos/Shutterstock.com

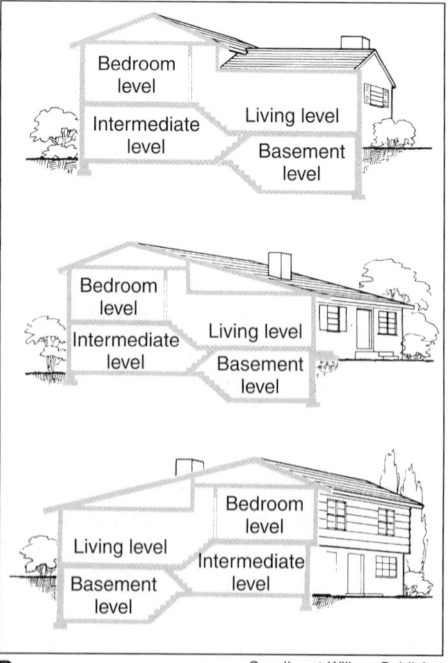

B Goodheart-Willcox Publisher

Figure 5.34 Split-level houses are designed to adapt to sloped sites (A). Changing the arrangement of levels in a split-level house also changes its outside appearance (B).

A ©iStock.com/qingwa

B Photograph by Pamm McFadden, NREL02909

Figure 5.35 This house has both active and passive solar heating systems (A). This earth-sheltered house is partially covered with soil. The soil helps insulate it from heat and cold (B).

Houses with *active solar* heating systems use special equipment, such as panels installed in the roof of the building, to capture the sun's energy. Then, fans and pumps move heated air or liquid from the panels to a storage area or wherever heat is needed.

Passive solar heating systems have no working parts. Instead, they include any design feature or construction material that makes maximum use of the sun for heating. A passive solar house might include large areas of windows on the home's southern side. Reinforced, concrete-pipe columns or dark-colored walls may absorb heat from the sun and gradually transfer it inside.

Earth-Sheltered Houses

Another type of contemporary housing is earth-sheltered housing. **Earth-sheltered** houses are partially covered with soil (Figure 5.35 B). They are energy efficient because the soil is a natural insulation and helps protect the house from weather elements and climate extremes. Some earth-sheltered houses are designed to be partly underground. Other dwellings are built into a hill or have soil compacted against the sides of the building.

A number of earth-sheltered houses are powered in part by solar energy. They may utilize active or passive solar heating systems or both.

Review & Assessment

1. What are four common characteristics of Contemporary style homes?
2. List three characteristics of a one-story ranch home.
3. Contrast a hillside ranch with a split-entry ranch.
4. What is the difference between active and passive solar homes?
5. What is the main advantage of an earth-sheltered home?

Historic Preservation

One trend in housing design is actually a step back in time. Nationally, there is a growing concern for restoring and preserving older buildings and houses (Figure 5.36). Increasingly, various agencies, local governments, and private

holbox/Shutterstock.com

Figure 5.36 As a designated national historic landmark, the preservation of *Beacon Hill* makes this neighborhood one of the most desirable neighborhoods in Boston.

Career Focus Historic Preservationist

Do you love to shop for antiques and visit old buildings? When you do, are you interested in the history behind them and not just the beauty? Do you wonder what it would take to bring them to life again, maybe for a new use? If so, you may consider exploring a career as an architect or interior designer who specializes in historic preservation.

Interests/Skills: Do you have a love of studying architectural styles in history? Are drawing and sketching a major part of your hobbies? Do you share the value of historical buildings with others and believe that older buildings should be given new life through adaptive reuse? Do you believe it is important for future generations to understand the evolution of such buildings? Exceptional research and organizational skills along with strong presentation and communication skills are necessary to work with others. Skills necessary for this important career also include computer and hand drawing and rendering abilities.

Career Snapshot: Historic preservationists usually have an architecture or interior design background. They choose to specialize in the adaptive reuse of old buildings and commonly work in an architectural or design preservation firm. Historic preservationists also work with local governments and community groups. They help identify buildings with historic significance and are often consulted on the true historic value of a structure. Historic preservationists need to be salespeople, too. It can be difficult to educate and convince others of a structure's importance to the community. The history and style of a building are most important, but the use of materials and applications must also have proven value. For example, paint colors must be authentic to the time period a building was constructed. Preservationists also may work with the restoration of furnishings and fine art.

Education/Training: A bachelor's degree in architecture, design, or urban planning is most often required. A master's degree or postgraduate studies in historic preservation is preferred. Courses of study include the history of architecture, history, art, art history, specific courses in the techniques and research for historic preservation, architecture, and computer programs.

Licensing/Examinations: All states require architects to be licensed. Architects must pass all divisions of the Architect Registration Examination.

photobank.ch/Shutterstock.com

The exterior structure and interior finishes of this space have been historically restored and the interior filled with more modern furniture and architectural features.

Many states require interior designers to be licensed or registered. Interior designers must pass the National Council of Interior Design Qualification (NCIDQ) exam to receive licensure. A supplemental historic preservation certification may be available, depending on the state of residence.

Professional Associations: Membership in the National Trust for Historic Preservation, the American Society of Interior Designers (ASID), and the International Interior Design Association (IIDA) is ideal.

Job Outlook: Current trends for green and sustainable architecture are positive for historic preservationists. Skills in adaptive reuse design methods and techniques to repair and maintain buildings that already exist are valuable.

Sources: The Occupational Outlook Handbook (OOH); the Occupational Information Network (O*NET)

Green Choices

Reusing Old Buildings

Old buildings often outlive their original purposes. A way of reusing an old building is called adaptive reuse. This process adapts old buildings for new uses. Designers evaluate the features of an original structure before making design changes. Honoring the historical past of a structure is part of this process. An example of adaptive reuse is converting an old post office to a retail center with many shops.

When the building has historic features, the adaptive reuse retains these features through historic preservation techniques. Adaptive reuse has the following advantages:

- **Environmental sustainability.** Historic preservation is really "recycling" on a large scale and is an effective tool for protecting environmental resources.
- **Economic sustainability.** Reusing old buildings supports the economy of the local community.
- **Social sustainability.** Historic preservation protects and celebrates the social and cultural resources that will enrich communities and their citizen's lives for generations to come.

A Helen Filatova/Shutterstock.com B Photographee.eu/Shutterstock.com

Figure 5.37 Urban developers are bringing abandoned downtown warehouse spaces back to life (A). The second photo shows just one example of an upscale residence created from one such building (B).

organizations are identifying properties that represent architectural value and importance. One such group is the *National Trust for Historical Preservation*. This group identifies such structures and grants them landmark status. Once they become landmarks, these buildings cannot undergo destruction or significant alteration. A person who helps restore these buildings is an *historic preservationist*.

Restoration work follows careful guidelines to ensure that materials, colors, and designs are true to the original era of a building's construction. Another type of renovation called **adaptive reuse** involves updating existing buildings for new and creative uses (Figure 5.37 A and B). In this way, society preserves the best of its past for future generations to experience.

Review & Assessment

1. Summarize the meaning of historic preservation.
2. A person who helps restore historic buildings is called a _____.
3. How is adaptive reuse different from historic preservation?

Chapter 5 Assessment

Summary

- There are many varieties of exterior housing styles in the United States. They evolved from the housing styles of the Native Americans and of the settlers who brought styles from their homelands.
- Traditional folk styles include those from Native Americans, Spanish, Scandinavians, Dutch, Germans, French, and English. During colonial times, other styles unique to the United States began to evolve. They include the Cape Cod, Saltbox, and Garrison styles. Later, the classic traditional styles of Georgian, Federal, Adam, Early Classical Revival, Greek Revival, Southern Colonial, and Victorian were developed.
- During the early to mid-twentieth century, modern homes were designed to fit and take advantage of the environment and changing lifestyles. Modern houses include the Prairie Style, Arts and Crafts, the bungalow, Tudor, Spanish Revival, the International Style, the ranch and its variations.
- Postmodernism is a recent approach to housing design that often combines features of past housing with a new look that sometimes has a jarring effect on the viewer.
- Contemporary homes may use traditional or modern styles, or can be unique, distinctive, and one-of-a-kind designs. Beyond the aesthetic style of a house, the form a home takes on influences how it functions and how it can be modified.
- As housing styles continue to evolve to meet changing trends and lifestyles, preserving the best of the past for future generations is desirable.
- Historical preservation saves outstanding examples of past architectural styles from demolition or significant alteration, and adaptive reuse can breathe new life into neglected buildings.

Terms in Action

1. **Relating words** On a separate sheet of paper, list the *Content* and *Academic Terms* from the beginning of the chapter. Then, work with a partner to explain how these words are related.

Think Critically

2. **Form a hypothesis** Review the styles of architecture from the 1600s to the present time. How are architectural characteristics similar and different throughout the ages and in various regions? What features appear again and again? Form a hypothesis about why certain architectural features are presently popular. What does this say about people and culture?
3. **Identify evidence** When describing the Arts and Crafts movement of the 1880s, the author states: "As a response to the over-abundance of machine-made gingerbread and other architectural excesses of the Victorian era, English designers such as John Ruskin and William Morris and many others began this movement." Use the text and reliable online resources to identify evidence that expresses *why* Ruskin and Morris sought to work with natural materials in a more simple form of design. Write an informative news article on your findings to post to the class website.
4. **Draw conclusions** As many older homes and buildings face destruction in the modern world, many people are striving to preserve the heritage of these older structures. Draw conclusions about why there is growing concern to restore and preserve these older buildings.

Core Skills

5. **Research and speaking** Take a walking tour of one of the oldest residential areas of your community. What styles of architecture do you see? If possible, take a few digital photos of the various architectural styles (be sure to ask permission of the owners). Then, examine the historical records of your community to find out when it was first settled. Who were the earliest inhabitants? Which of the houses in your photos can you track down? Prepare a photo essay and summarize your findings for the class.
6. **Research and writing** Compare the availability of housing alternatives by examining the classified ads about real estate in your local community. Using the information and pictures in the ads, compile a price list of

Chapter 5 Assessment

different styles of homes that are currently on the market. What styles do the ads mention? What are their descriptions? What architectural trends can you identify in the ads? Are older homes more expensive because of historical significance? Are certain styles of homes priced below the market average? Is there a style of house that reflects the greatest value? Write a summary comparing the desirability of these housing alternatives.

7. **Writing** Imagine you and your family were among the early settlers in North America. Pick a style of folk architecture and write a story that describes the lifestyle you and your family might have experienced living in the house. Think in terms of cooking, sleeping, bathing, working, learning, enjoying recreation, and conducting other aspects of daily life. You may wish to illustrate your story. Share your story with the class.
8. **Technology applications** From the early Swedish immigrants to modern time, the log cabin remains a house style appealing to many in the U.S. culture. Trace the roots of the log cabin from its earliest beginnings to present time. How has the technology (the practical application of knowledge in a particular area) for building log cabins changed over the years? What role does computer-aided drafting and design (CADD) and computer-aided manufacturing (CAM) play in building modern-day log cabins? Use presentation software to share your findings with the class.
9. **Research and writing** Choose an architect to research, such as Thomas Jefferson, Frank Lloyd Wright, Robert and James Adams, William Morris, Walter Gropius, Ludwig Mies van der Rohe, Robert Venturi, or Frank Gehry. Write a one-page report summarizing the architectural influence of the architect. Include photos or drawings of this architect's work that represent his/her style. To where would your class need to travel to find the closest example of a building designed by this architect?
10. **Technology and speaking** For many generations, people have used the soil to help protect their homes from severe climate conditions. Investigate ways that digital technology has improved the way people build earth-sheltered structures. How is beauty combined with form and function in such houses? How does 3-D modeling help improve such designs? If possible, use a school-approved modeling application to share your findings with the class.
11. **Writing** Identify the architectural styles exemplified in housing in this chapter. Choose five styles and write a brief summary of the specific features of these styles.
12. **CTE career readiness practice** Presume you are an interior designer who is a *Certified Aging-in-Place Specialist*. Your interpersonal skills—your ability to listen, speak, and empathize—are a great asset in working with clients. Lillian, your new client, has a mobility disability but desires to stay in her historic bungalow house. Write a list of questions you would ask Lillian on a site visit as you observe and evaluate how she functions in her space.

Design Practice

13. **House design** Imagine you are an architect designing housing in the year 2030. Use computer or hand-drawing techniques to create an exterior design that you think would reflect future design trends. Does your design relate to any previous historical styles or time periods? What features of exterior design, if any, do you think are classic and will be repeated in the future? How does your design relate to changes of lifestyle for future generations? Present your design to the class and provide evidence to support why you think this design reflects future design trends.
14. **Portfolio** Presume you are a contractor who is selecting photos, drawings, and descriptions of the house styles your company builds for a new website. Determine the styles of homes that your business will offer. If the styles are part of a planned housing development or subdivision, describe it as well. Put together a digital storyboard of your offerings in preparation for meeting with a web designer. Save a copy of your digital storyboard for future reference.

Chapter 6

Reading Architectural Plans

Content Terms 

architectural drawings
schematic drawings
presentation drawings
construction drawings
schedule
specifications
Building Information Model (BIM)
print
alphabet of lines
symbols
plan view
floor plan
square footage
exterior elevation
elevation view
section view
detail view
rendering
model
isometric drawing

Academic Terms 

symbology
imperative
fabrication

Learning Outcomes 

After studying this chapter, you will be able to

- identify types of architectural drawings in a set of house plans and why they are used.
- interpret architectural drawings including the use of schedules and specifications.
- describe how computers and software are utilized in creating architectural drawings and prints including use of abbreviations, types of lines, and symbols.
- summarize the purposes of various views in architectural drawings including plan views, elevation view, and section and detail views.
- describe the organization of construction documents.
- identify when an architect or interior designer would use renderings, models, and isometric drawings.

Reading with Purpose

Arrange a study session to read the chapter with a classmate. After you read each passage independently, stop and tell each other what you think the main points are in the passage. Continue with each passage until you finish the chapter.

While studying, look for the access icon  **to:**

- **Practice** the *Content* and *Academic Terms* with e-flash cards, matching activities, and vocabulary games.
- **Reinforce** what you learn by completing the *Review & Assessment* questions and e-mailing them to your instructor.

www.g-wlearning.com/housing/

bikeriderlondon/Shutterstock.com

The design and construction of a house involves many people working together. These people include the owner, architect, designer, contractor, banker, and various tradespeople. These people and many others form the design and construction team. Members of the team communicate through house plans. If you are buying or building a house, it is important that you, as a member of the team, be able to interpret the house plans.

Architectural Drawings for a House

Important to the development of house plans are the architectural drawings. **Architectural drawings** contain information about the size, shape, and location of all parts of the house (Figure 6.1). They vary in complexity and depth of information presented according to their intended use. Architectural drawings include the following (Figure 6.2):

- **schematic drawings**—freehand sketches of a proposed plan the designer uses in refining a design
- **presentation drawings**—refined drawings or renderings to use for publication or for showing the design to a client
- **construction drawings**—drawings with detailed instructions to the builder to obtain necessary permits and erect the structure

This universal language of the construction industry uses lines, symbols, views, and notes to convey ideas. To ensure that everyone understands architectural drawings, standard rules of drafting determine the types of lines, symbols, and views, and the location of dimensions. These rules give meaning to each set of architectural drawings. It is important to read all notes and reference all *legends* (lists showing what that project's symbology means), however, to ensure correct understanding of the documents. (Note: ***symbology*** refers to the interpretation of symbols or a system of symbols.)

Another standard that prevents errors on construction drawings is the standardization of lettering. There are a few specific fonts that are typically used by architects and builders and typically these are in all *capital* letters. This helps to ensure that letters and numbers are not misread which can lead to major problems once construction begins. Fortunately, with the use of CADD and BIM, spelling and grammar checkers can also help ensure accuracy.

Architectural drawings are drawn in proportion to actual size. For instance, if a drawing is *half size*, it is one-half as large as the actual object. When an architectural drawing is either smaller or larger than the actual object, it is *drawn to scale*. Drawings for a house are normally drawn at a scale of ¼" = 1'-0". This means that one-fourth inch on the drawing equals one-foot on the house. The scale for each drawing is indicated in a note. Sometimes, a designer uses a graphic scale, such as a person or vehicle, to visually depict the scale. A designer uses a graphic scale when the size of the final print is unknown, such as for presentation drawings.

A ©Design America, Inc.—houseplansandmore.com

B ©Design America, Inc.—houseplansandmore.com

Figure 6.1 The architect has provided both a rendering (A) and a floor plan (B) so his clients can visualize how their new home will look.

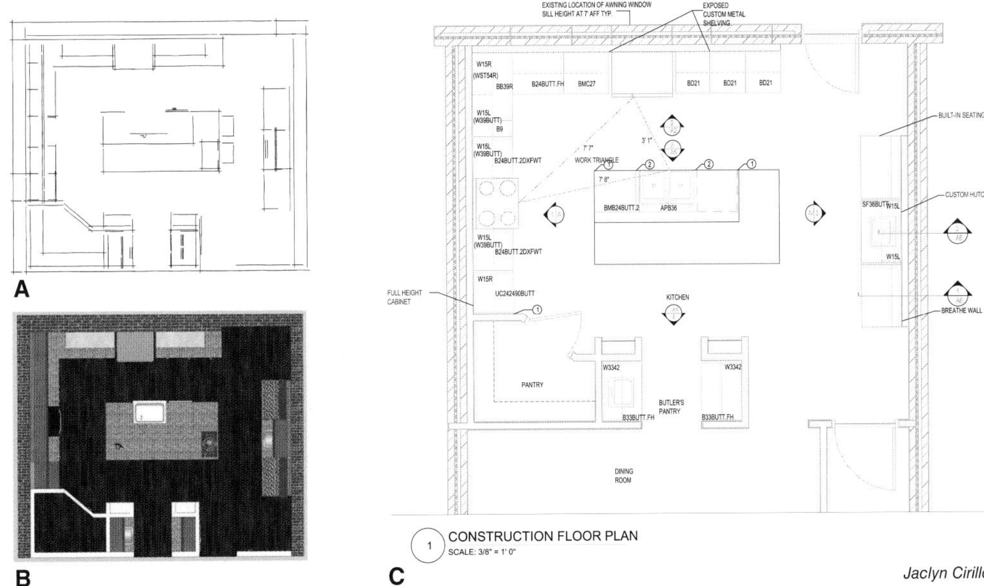

Jaclyn Cirillo

Figure 6.2 The images above represent schematic (A), presentation (B), and construction drawings (C) of a custom kitchen.

STEM Math How to Read a Scale Ruler

Architectural drawings are drawn in proportion to actual size. A floor plan of a room, for example, represents the actual dimensions of the room. This is done by using a scale; one measurement represents another.

A scale ruler is used to create and read these drawings. A six-edged triangular ruler is one of the most common scale rulers. One edge has a 12-in. ruler with each inch divided into 16 units. The other edges have two scales each—one is read from right to left and the other is read from left to right. The scale that reads from left to right is half as large as the scale that reads from right to left.

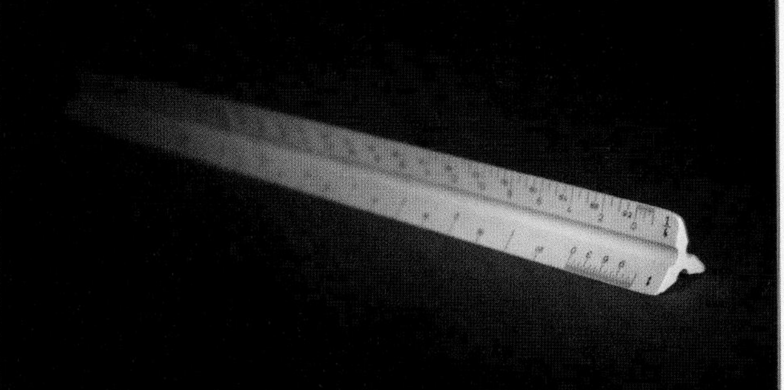

Goodheart-Willcox Publisher

To use the ruler, find the scale you need and make sure you read it from the correct direction (left to right or right to left). House plans are usually drawn at a standard scale of ¼ in. equals 1 ft. Each ¼ in. on the drawing represents 1 ft. on the actual house. Always use zero—not the ruler's edge—as the start point of the measurement.

Example 1: A house plan shows the length of a room as 3 in. How long is the actual room if you use the scale ¼ in. = 1 ft.?

Answer: If ¼ = 1, then 1 = 4; 3 × 4 = 12 ft.

Example 2: A room is 12 ft. wide by 15 ft. long. How would a) width and b) length be expressed in a drawing using the scale ¼ in. = 1 ft.?

Answer:

a. Width. 12 ÷ 4 = 3 in.

b. Length. 15 ÷ 4 = 3.75 in.

Math Practice

Measure the width and length of two rooms in your home or school. Then use a scale ruler to create a floor plan in a scale of ¼" = 1'-0". Use small tick marks to mark off the dimensions and then use a traditional ruler or straightedge to draw the lines. (*Note*: Do not use the scale ruler to draw your lines—doing so can damage the edge and make further measurements inaccurate.)

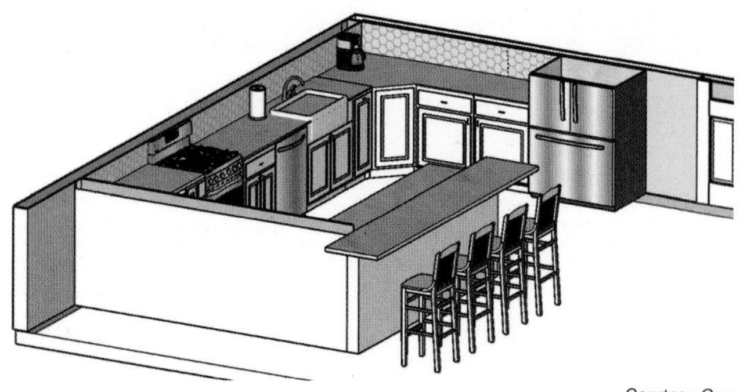

Courtney Guy

Figure 6.3 Floor plans are "sliced" at a height of 4 feet above the floor. This presentation drawing demonstrates how upper cabinets and higher elements are not seen in floor plans.

Another concept important to understanding floor plans is that the height they are viewed from is 4 feet. What this means is that plans will only fully represent what is at or below 4 feet off the floor, as if a model of that house was sliced with a knife half-way down the wall and the top portion removed (Figure 6.3). For this reason, items such as wall cabinetry, the top of a door frame, and ceiling details may or may not appear on a plan.

Architectural drawings cannot convey all information about a house. For example, it is hard to show texture or represent paint color on the drawings. Wall texture and paint color, however, are important to finishing a house. A **schedule** is an organized chart of detailed notes in a ruled enclosure (Figure 6.4). Designers and contractors use schedules to describe large quantities of information in the drawings. Construction drawings define many items by schedules of repetitive or similar items. A typical construction drawing includes schedules for such details as doors and windows, electrical fixtures, plumbing fixtures, door hardware, and finishes. Other information for design and construction relates primarily to construction-quality standards called specifications or *specs*. The **specifications** are detailed documents that tell the types and quality of materials to use and give directions for their use.

Review & Assessment

1. What does an architectural drawing contain?
2. Contrast *schematic*, *presentation*, and *construction drawings*.
3. When is an architectural drawing drawn to scale?
4. Why do designers and contractors use schedules in architectural drawings?
5. What are specifications?
6. Why do ceiling mounted elements not show up on floor plans?

Drawing Methods and Prints of Architectural Drawings

In the past, drafters in architects' or contractors' offices used manual drafting machines and instruments to create most architectural drawings. Today, drafters use *computer-aided drafting and design (CADD)* software to create most drawings. Many CADD programs are available both for the novice and professional. These programs range from simple home-plan design software to very sophisticated professional CADD programs requiring extensive training.

Room Schedule			
Name	**Ceiling Finish**	**Floor Finish**	**Area**
Boys' RR	Paint	Mosaic Tile	120 SF
Breakroom	2x2 Acoustical Tile	Vinyl Composition Tile	145 SF
Children - 5 yrs	1x1 Surface Glued Acoustical Tiles	Loop Carpet	218 SF
Children - 6/7 yrs	1x1 Surface Glued Acoustical Tiles	Loop Carpet	262 SF
Children - 8/10 yrs	1x1 Surface Glued Acoustical Tiles	Loop Carpet	567 SF
Children - 11/12 yrs	1x1 Surface Glued Acoustical Tiles	Vinyl Composition Tile	266 SF
Classroom	Paint	Loop Carpet	128 SF

Jennifer Blanchard Belk, IIDA, LEED AP

Figure 6.4 Because a floor plan cannot show all details, schedules are used to provide specifics about items such as doors, windows, and finishes.

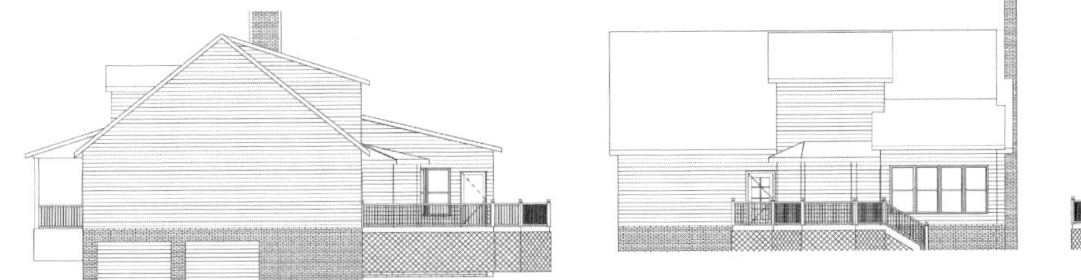

Jennifer Blanchard Belk, IIDA, LEED AP

Figure 6.5 Software that uses the *Building Information Model (BIM)* allows a designer or architect to manipulate or change multiple views of the drawing set simultaneously.

One of the newer tools available to architects, designers, and builders is the **Building Information Model (BIM)**. BIM is an approach to building that embraces every stage of a building's lifecycle: design, construction, maintenance, and sometimes, demolition. Some software programs that utilize BIM help architects, designers, and builders design buildings that are green and sustainable. Before construction begins, software using BIM can evaluate *virtual materials* that have the same properties as real materials (for example, concrete and lumber). Once a *virtual building* is built, the design and building team can analyze the building for structural integrity and environmental impact.

Unlike alternative methods, software using BIM allows a designer or architect to manipulate or change multiple views of the drawing set simultaneously (Figure 6.5). For example, suppose a client decides he or she wants a high ceiling that is 10 feet instead of one that is traditionally 8 feet high. That seems easy; however, a change like that would make walls taller, raise ceiling fans, and likely change the height of the entire house. If done correctly, the designer can make that one ceiling change on one of the associated drawings and the software will shift the size and placement of all other items dictated by the ceiling's placement. In addition, it will update any documents related to the drawings such as the materials list,

Architect's Responsibilities for Sustainable Design

For thousands of years, architects planned buildings using hand-drawn plans. The creation of computer and special software programs streamlined the timely job of hand drawing, saving both time and money.

A new approach available to architects and all professionals involved in a building project is the Building Information Model (BIM). This approach provides consistent and reliable information and leads to improved building performance. Several computer-software programs, such as Autodesk® Revit, for example, incorporate BIM to assist in this process.

BIM helps bring about faster decision making, better documentation, and a way to evaluate building design options. It can also predict how the building will perform in energy use and other "green" and sustainable areas before the first piece of work is done on the project!

Here's what BIM and a computer program can do:

- Provide many three-dimensional (3-D) views at all project stages. This can help the client and designers work together better in producing the final design. For example, a well-built BIM model can show you the before, during, and after stages of construction, in 3-D, and from any angle.
- Improve the design coordination. One of the biggest pushes with BIM is to get architects, engineers, and construction firms talking to each other by using compatible software to share their ideas.
- Analyze the impact of green designs. For example, BIM models are made using "virtual materials." Imagine you are developing plans for a skyscraper. You can choose the materials (for example, steel used in beams and exact type of concrete). The computer software that uses BIM can then analyze both soundness of the structure and impact on the environment.

Use of BIM and the software program that uses it will see more frequent use in the future. Architects using BIM can increase the quality of design and have a positive impact on the environment.

showing that more materials will be needed to construct and finish the extra 2 feet of ceiling height.

Using BIM and compatible software allows architects, designers, and builders to collaborate more easily. Some software even offers a video-conferencing feature to allow team members in different areas to view plans simultaneously.

When the drafter completes a set of architectural drawings, he or she gives copies to all members of the construction team. A **print** is a copy of a drawing. In the past, a reproduction of a drawing consisted of white lines on a dark blue background. Consequently, the term *blueprint* came into being. Today, engineering copiers, or large-format copiers (similar to office photocopiers) and plotters (graphics printers) are used to handle the heavier and much larger sheets of paper for copying these technical drawings.

Publishing drawings to the Internet is also popular. This may be in the form of digital prints that the viewer cannot alter, or may be the actual CADD or BIM files on a protected site. Often, all documents including specifications, contracts, and other valuable information are included. This allows the construction team to access and simultaneously view the latest set of construction documents.

Abbreviations

Within all industries, there is vocabulary that is particular to that line of work. Often, to save space on drawings, designers and architects will utilize abbreviations for common words or statements. Some of them might be easy to understand such as KIT equals KITCHEN or CPT equals CARPET. Others are not so intuitive but are ***imperative*** (necessary) in order to understand the drawings. Here is a list of some probably unfamiliar abbreviations you might find:

ACT	Acoustic Ceiling Tile
AFF	Above Finished Floor
CLG	Ceiling
CLR	Clear
CMU	Concrete Masonry Unit
DEMO	Demolish or Demolition
DIA	Diameter
DIM	Dimension
DWG	Drawing
EQ	Equal
GWB	Gypsum Wall Board
HM	Hollow Metal
HVAC	Heating, Ventilating, and Air Conditioning
MIN	Minimum
NIC	Not In Contract
OC	On Center
RCP	Reflected Ceiling Plan
SIM	Similar
SPEC	Specified OR Specification
T/D	Telephone/Data
TYP	Typical
UNO	Unless Noted Otherwise

Alphabet of Lines

To understand the architectural drawings, you must first understand the lines used on the drawings. Seven different lines, called the **alphabet of lines**, are commonly used on architectural drawings. They allow the drafter to communicate ideas clearly and accurately.

These lines vary in thickness or weight. They may be solid or a combination of dashes and breaks. Figure 6.6 illustrates the following examples:

- *Phantom lines* show alternate positions, repeated details, and paths of motion.
- *Visible lines* or *object lines* show the outline of the building, walls, plumbing fixtures, cabinetry, and any other tangible element that can be seen in the current view. These lines vary in thickness depending on the importance of the object and its distance from the viewer.
- *Hidden lines* show edges of surfaces that are not visible in a specific view of the house. An example would be wall-hung cabinets when viewing a floor plan.
- *Center lines* show the center of an arc or circle. An example would be to indicate the precise center of installment for a ceiling fan.

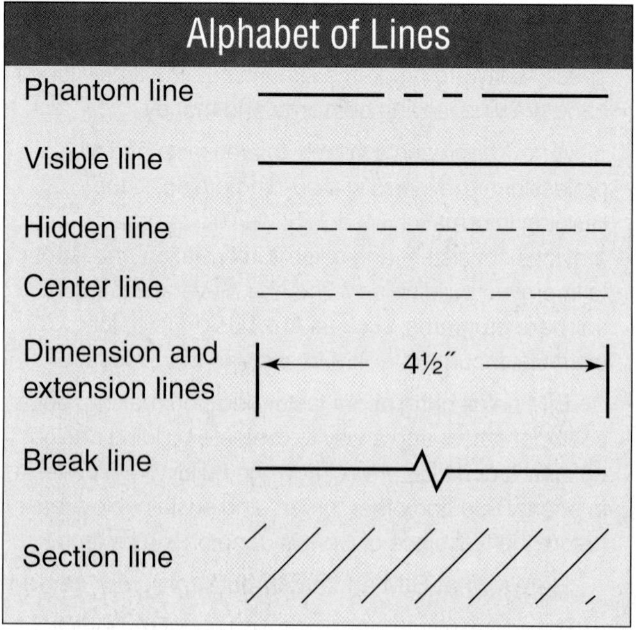

Goodheart-Willcox Publisher

Figure 6.6 The *Alphabet of Lines* shows the basic lines that are used in all architectural drawings.

- *Dimension and extension lines* show the extent and direction of measurements. Dimension lines show the size and location of the dimension. Extension lines show the termination points of a dimension.
- *Break lines* show the object continues on, but the complete view is not shown.
- *Section lines* show a feature that has been sectioned. Another name for these lines is crosshatch lines.

In addition, leader lines are those that point to and join aspects of the plan with explanatory notes.

Symbols

It is almost impossible to draw exactly the many features of a finished product. Because of this, drawings utilize standard symbols. **Symbols** represent plumbing and electrical fixtures, doors, windows, furniture, and other common objects in a house or structure. Drafters may use templates to trace symbols or CADD programs to insert symbols representing common objects. Although typical symbols are often general and not specific to the project, it is important for them to represent the object as closely as possible. For instance, a freestanding claw-foot tub looks and functions differently than a built-in tub/shower, even if they take up the same amount of space. Notes on the drawings, in the form of legends, give additional explanations for symbols. In Figure 6.7, you can see several common symbols.

Symbols for tangible items in the built environment come in the following forms:

- Actual built objects (*representational—a realistic likeness of the object*) such as electrical symbols on a drawing that include light fixtures and appliances which are the shape and size of the piece.
- Actual built objects (*symbolic*) including electrical symbols such as switches and receptacles that are not drawn to the actual size to the actual size and shape of the piece they represent. This ensures they are large enough to be readable and can be differentiated from similar pieces. Hidden lines drawn between switches, fixtures, and receptacles indicate wiring.
- *Door and window symbols* show the type of door or window and the direction each opens.
- *Mechanical symbols* indicate plumbing, heating, and air-conditioning fixtures used on a plan.
- *Materials* (plan or section) including surface materials such as wood flooring or ceramic tile that might be shown on a floor plan. These are typically shown in their actual size.
- *Small-scale sections* (discussed later) may include similar small patterns detailing the specific materials that are being cut through. These may or may not resemble the actual material. For instance, a small dot pattern may represent a particular type of stone even though that stone does not actually have that pattern. These patterns should always be shown on an accompanying legend, such as this wall legend (Figure 6.8).

The most important symbols for being able to understand an entire set of documents are the informational and reference symbols (Figure 6.9). These are symbols that point the viewer to supplemental information in the drawing set. Examples are:

- *Elevation symbols* indicate that an elevation exists of the wall being pointed to, on what page it is located, and what drawing number it is on that page. These can typically be found outside of the home for exterior elevations and inside the home within spaces that have custom elements, such as kitchens and bathrooms.
- *Section symbols* indicate that a section exists of the element being cut through, on what page it is located, and what drawing number it is on that page. These symbols can typically be found on the previous mentioned elevations for detailed cabinetry information or on floor plans to indicate a cross section of the entire building.
- *Detail symbols* indicate that an enlarged plan (or section) of the encircled area exists, on what page it is located, and what drawing number it is on that page. These symbols can typically be found on the previous mentioned details for custom cabinetry information or on floor plans of rooms that are dense with cabinetry or equipment.
- *Column lines* and *bubbles* create a grid at which columns are placed. Similar to the coordinates on a road map, these are a good way of identifying locations on an otherwise open floor plan.
- *General notes* are those that pertain to either the entire set of drawings or simply the page they are on. These notes are general in that they describe standard construction or finish instructions such as "all baseboards to be 4-inch-tall vinyl."
- *Reference* or *Key* notes serve to give specific information on a drawing that is not applicable to the drawing as a whole. Because they are often keyed with a letter or number cross-referenced to a list of notes, they also keep a plan, elevation, or detail from becoming too cluttered. An example might be a special display cabinet in a kitchen

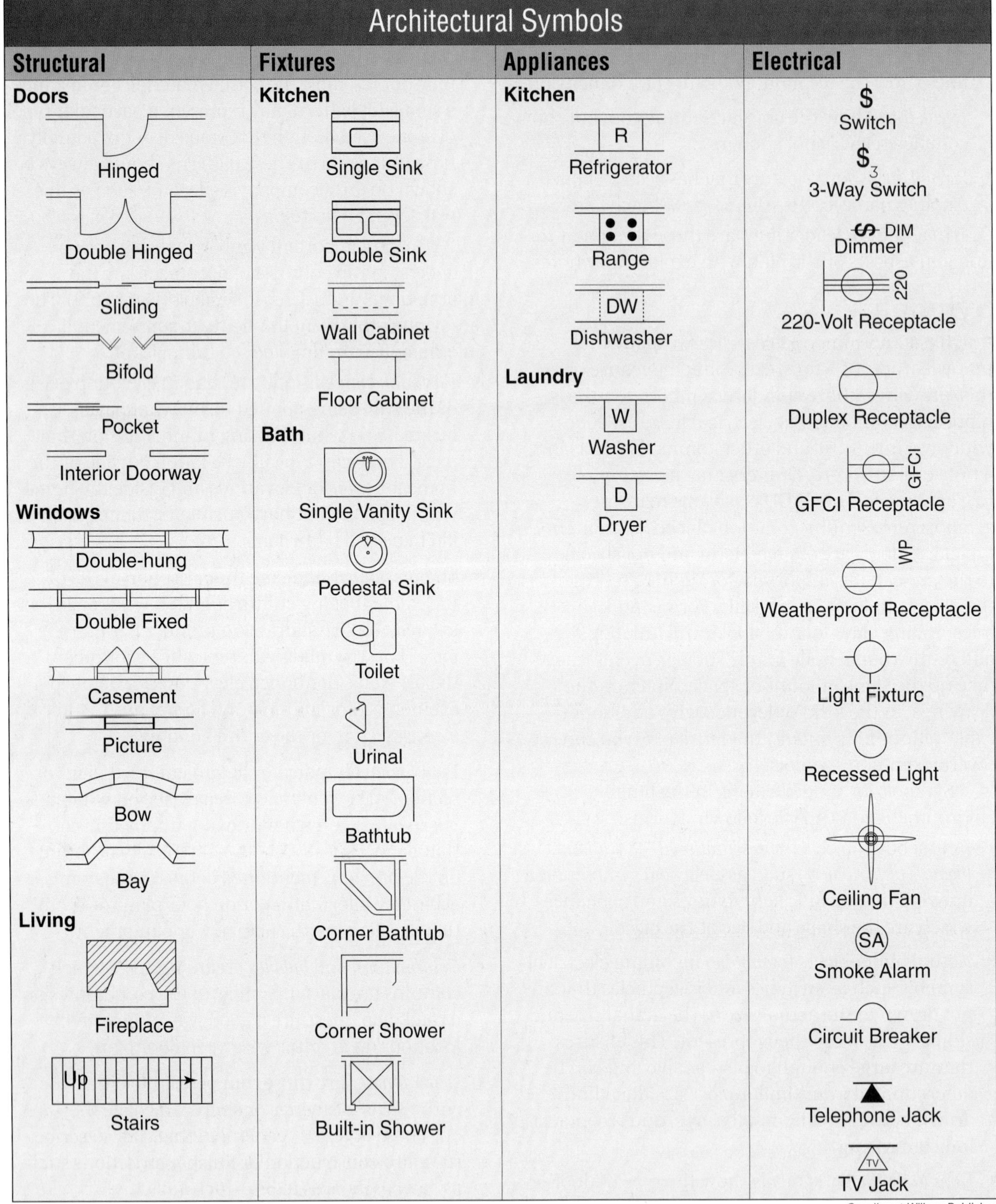

Goodheart-Willcox Publisher

Figure 6.7 These symbols are used on drawings to represent objects in the house.

with a note saying "cabinet to have glass door inserts" when all the other doors are solid wood.

- *Tags* are various symbols used to refer the viewer to specific information (construction, size, materials, etc.) regarding doors, windows, walls, and more.
- *Title lines* identify the order, name, and scale of the drawing it is associated with.

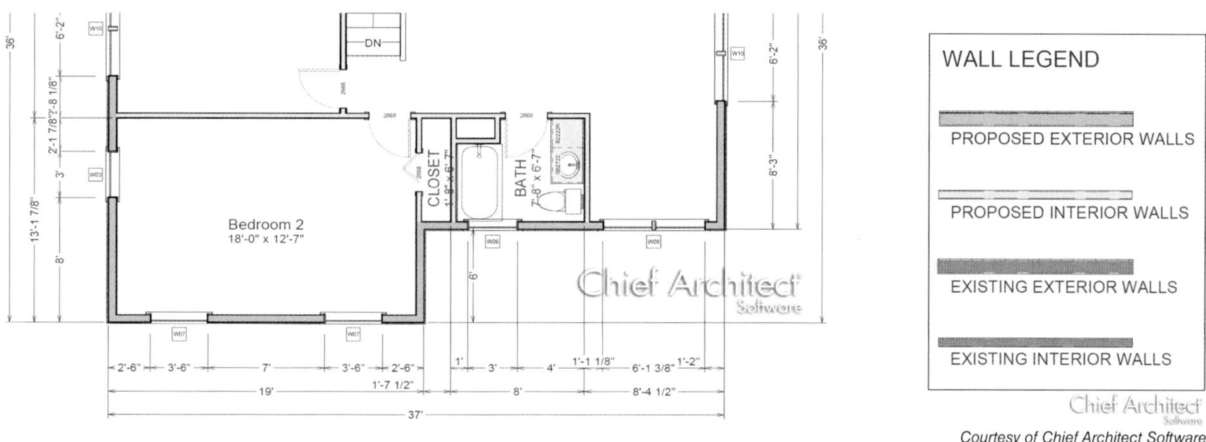

Courtesy of Chief Architect Software

Figure 6.8 A wall legend is one of the many types of legends to help the viewer understand a floor plan.

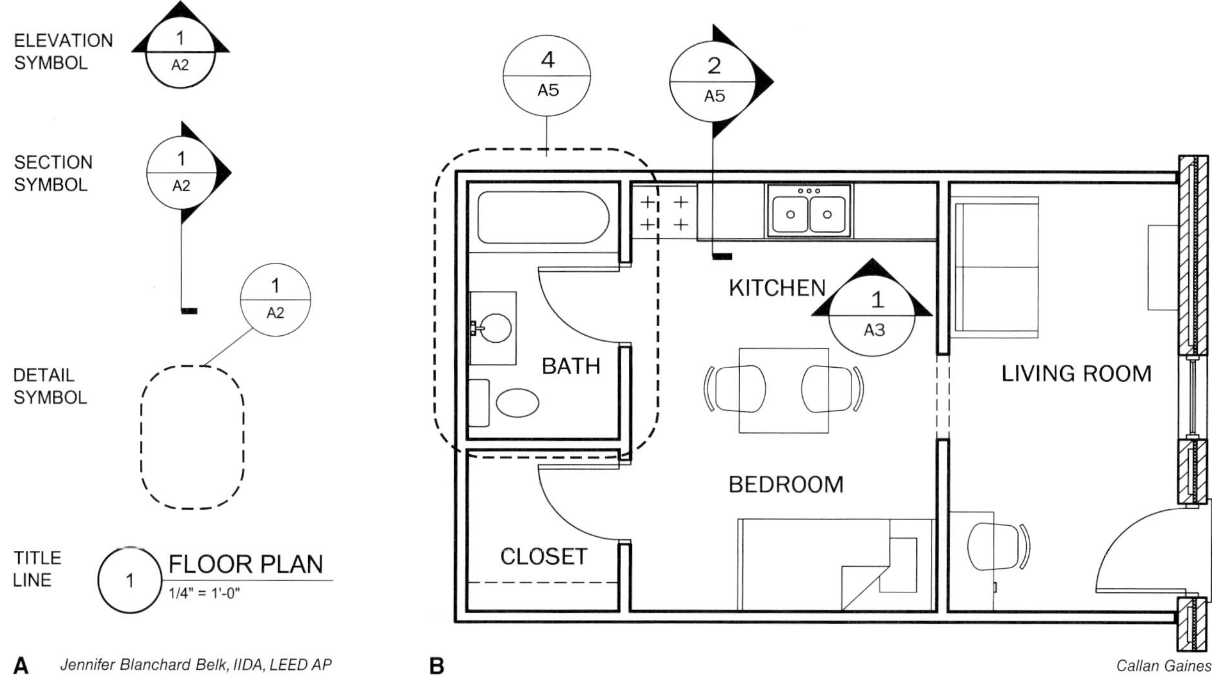

A Jennifer Blanchard Belk, IIDA, LEED AP B Callan Gaines

Figure 6.9 Understanding an architectural drawing is a matter of knowing what the symbols mean (A). Can you determine where you might look for supplemental drawings? What line types can you identify (B)?

Review & Assessment

1. What is the Building Information Model (BIM)? Why is it a benefit for architects and designers?
2. What advantages does software using BIM have over CAD software?
3. Why do designers and architects use abbreviations? Give two examples of abbreviations they might use on their drawings.
4. Name the seven types of lines in the Alphabet of Lines and give a brief description of each.
5. What are four or more types of symbols an architect or interior designer might use in drawings?

Views for Architectural Drawings

Architectural drawings of a house usually include different types of views. Among these are plan views, elevation views, and views of sections and details. Imagine the house enclosed in a large glass box. Each view is projected toward its viewing surface on the glass box, and is then brought into position as though unfolding the sides of the box.

Plan Views

Views taken from the top of the imaginary glass box are **plan views**. The *site plan, floor plan, foundation*

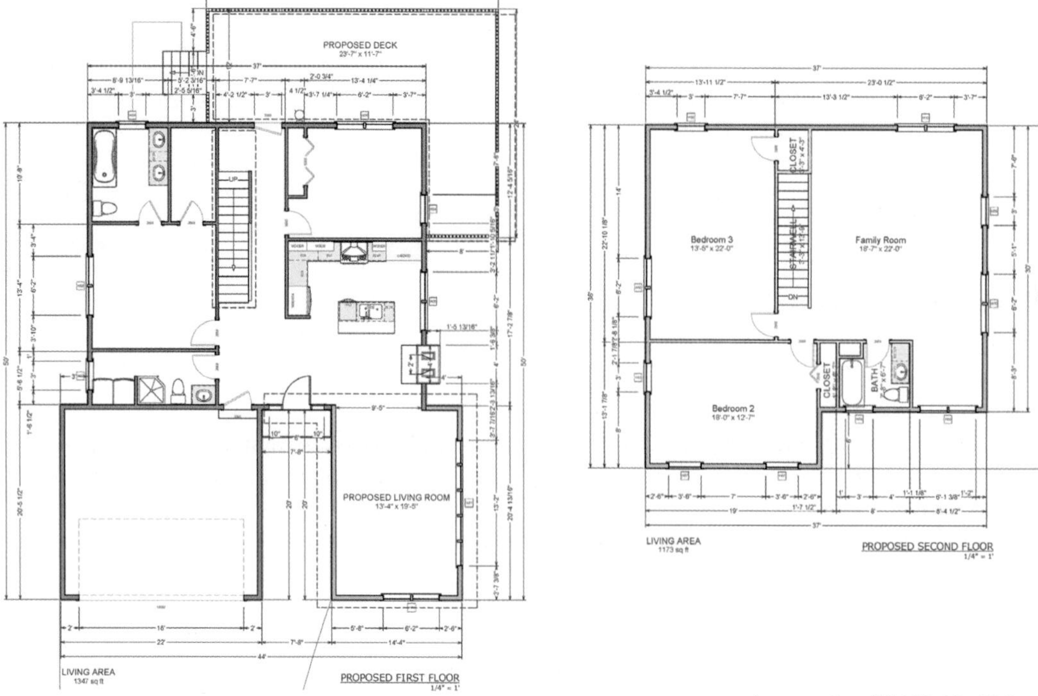

Image courtesy of Chief Architect Software

Figure 6.10 The interior designer can use the dimensions on the floor plan to determine the square footage of the space. What other symbols can you identify on this floor plan?

plan, and *roof plan* are all plan views. The **floor plan** is the most important drawing on a set of house plans. It is a simplified drawing, somewhat like a bird's-eye view, that shows the size and arrangement of rooms, hallways, doors, windows, and storage areas on one floor of a home. In Figure 6.10, you can see the symbols used in the floor plan.

When discussing plan views and describing houses, the design team often uses the term **square footage**—a measurement of house size that refers to the amount of living space in the home. You will use the room dimensions that appear on the floor plan to determine square footage.

STEM Math Determining Square Footage of a Home

Often a house plan or description refers to the total square feet in a home. Square footage is used to compare homes in terms of size. The higher the square footage, the larger the home will be. Likewise, the lower the square footage, the smaller the home will be.

Square footage is the total amount of living space (area) in the home. You can determine the total living space by adding together the square footage space from all rooms. The dimensions of each room appear on the floor plan. Note that closets, other storage space, and garages do not count toward the square footage of a house. Once you find the dimensions on the floor plan, use the following formula to determine the square footage for each room:

Area = Length × Width

If a room is 12 feet long and 10 feet wide, the square footage will be the following:

A = 12 ft. × 10 ft.

A = 120 sq. ft.

To calculate the total square footage of a home, complete the calculation for each room and add them together.

Math Practice

To practice calculating square footage, measure all of the living space in your home. Use the formula above to calculate the square footage of each room. Then add together the square footage for each room to determine the total square footage of the living space in your home.

Elevation Views

Exterior elevations are architectural drawings that show the outside views of the house. A set of drawings usually includes four exterior elevations showing all four sides of the house. If the building is simple, there may be only the front elevation and one side elevation. Interior elevation drawings may show cabinetry or other special areas.

An **elevation view** shows the finished exterior appearance of a given side of the house. Elevations usually show height dimensions. These views help people visualize the completed house and helps contractors to build what was planned. By studying both the floor plan and the elevation views, you can envision the completed structure (Figure 6.11). Even for minor renovations, interior elevations may be required to show the height of interior elements and built-ins (Figure 6.12).

Section Views and Detail Views

To show how individual structural parts of the house fit together, the designer or architect uses section and detail views. For instance, the drafter may want to show the inside of the house. When a view is taken from an imaginary cut through a part of a house, such as a wall, it is called a **section view**. Therefore, the plan view is a *horizontal* slice through the house and the section view is a *vertical* slice. See the example in Figure 6.13. A section view can also be taken of a single room, custom shelving, or a ceiling detail (Figure 6.14).

A **detail view** is usually an enlargement of some construction feature. The detail drawing often uses a larger scale than other drawings. It shows the details of a small part of the house (Figure 6.15).

Katherine West

Figure 6.11 It is important that all elevation views of a house be present on the plans, not just the face of the building.

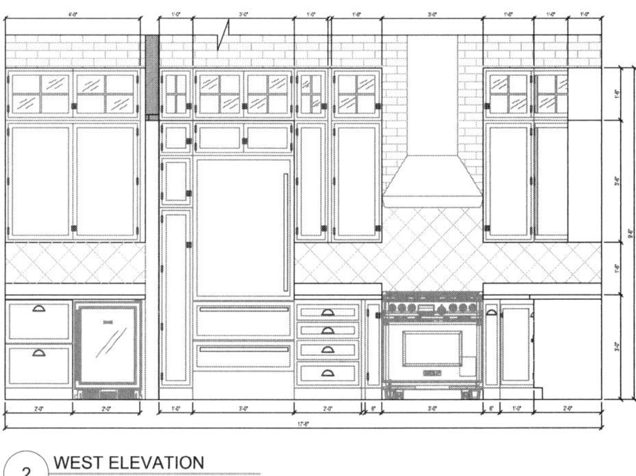

Vanessa Fleming

Figure 6.12 This is an interior cabinetry elevation. The lines to the right of the drawing indicate the heights above the ground.

Katherine West

Figure 6.13 A section of a building gives an understanding of the multiple floors.

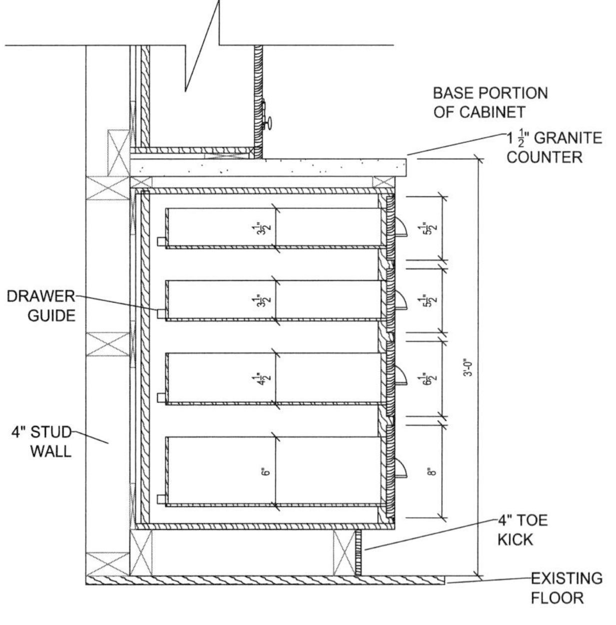

Vanessa Fleming

Figure 6.14 Whether a cabinet or an entire house, a section allows the viewer to see the thickness of building materials and their method of assembly.

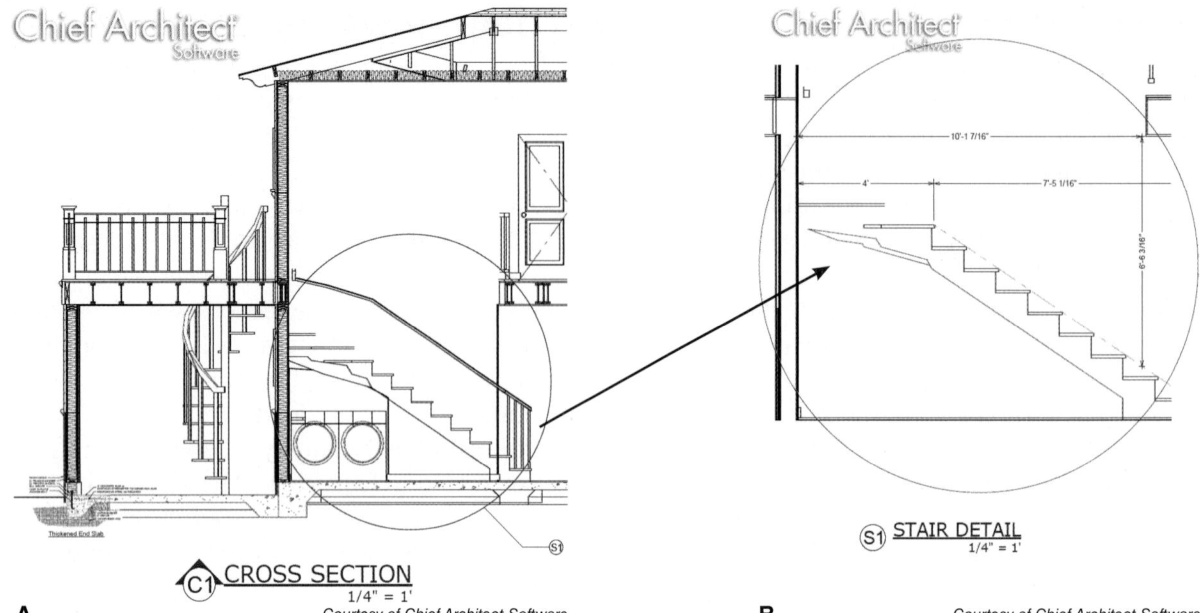

A Courtesy of Chief Architect Software B Courtesy of Chief Architect Software

Figure 6.15 There is a drawing of a set of stairs on the inside of the home that is difficult to understand (A). For this reason, the architect drew a partial section of the home to reveal the stairs and then did an enlargement to show dimensions (B).

Order of the Documents

There is a logical order within a set of construction drawings and standard information you can find in the *title block* (Figure 6.16). The complexity of the project and the variety of trades that have involvement in the project, dictate the number of pages in the set of construction drawings and level of detail in each drawing. A set for a small interior renovation project may be only a page or two in length. A larger, newly constructed building often involves civil and mechanical engineers, architects, designers, and others on the design team, resulting in a set that could be hundreds of pages long. For example, a minor kitchen renovation might include a

- demolition floor plan (what is being removed)
- new construction floor plan
- elevations of the cabinetry walls
- details and sections showing cabinetry construction methods

No matter what the project is, there is a logical order most sets of construction drawings will follow that helps the viewer understand what they are seeing. Larger projects involve more complex organization and more professionals are typically involved. In addition to a cover sheet, a document set for a large custom home might include a title block lettered:

- **G** (General information such as a table of contents, symbols used, etc.)
- **C** (Civil Engineer drawings indicating how the land might be modified to accommodate the home)
- **A** (Architectural drawings, such as dimensioned plans and elevations)
- **S** (Structural drawings)
- **P** (Plumbing drawings)
- **M** (Mechanical drawings, such as heating and air)
- **E** (Electrical drawings)

You may notice that each page also has a number associated with the letter. This is indicating that there are multiple pages from that particular trade. Drawings typically move from general information to specific details. Each of these pages has identifying letters or numbers within the page title block that is easy to understand. For instance, within the *Architectural* pages of a kitchen renovation, pages might include

- A1—Architectural floor plan similar to the one shown (Figure 6.17)
- A2—Electrical plan
- A3—Ceiling plan
- A4—Dimensioned and noted cabinetry elevations
- A5—Cabinetry sections showing materials and construction methods

A5	SCALE: 1/4"= 1'-0" PAGE NAME: FLOOR PLAN DATE: 09/15/2017	CLIENT NAME	PROJECT NAME	FIRM NAME

Jennifer Blanchard Belk, IIDA, LEED AP

Figure 6.16 Although title blocks can vary in layout graphics, they must always include the client name, design firm, and project information.

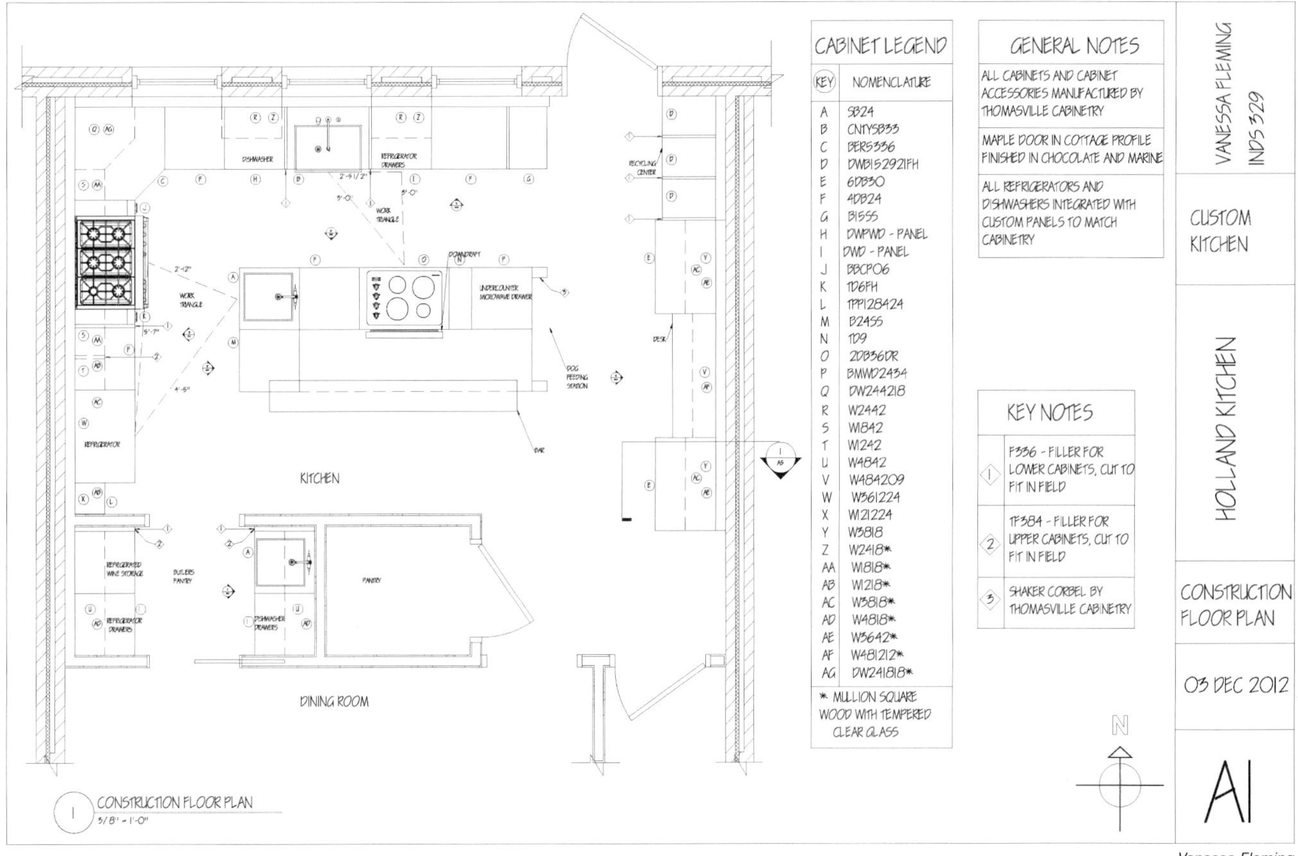

Vanessa Fleming

Figure 6.17 It is standard for the page information to be in the lower-right of the page.

Although each trade is only responsible for its own section of the documents, it is the architect's and the designer's responsibility to make sure the entire set is correct. This ensures that each contractor's work coordinates with and does not conflict with another.

Renderings and Models

To help clients better visualize a finished house, architectural firms frequently produce a rendering. A **rendering** is a presentation drawing—usually with color, texture, and shadows—that shows a realistic view of the completed house. Refer to the top of the image in *Figure 6.1*.

Some architectural firms also develop a model to show all sides of the new house. A **model** is a three-dimensional miniature of a design. A client can view it from different angles and in various lighting conditions to get more realistic views of the house.

Producing renderings and models by hand is very costly in terms of time and materials. It also requires considerable artistic skill. These views usually incorporate landscaping plans and other aspects of the completed house.

Today, architects have a choice in producing renderings and models. Depending on the requirements of the project, they may use CADD. The computer creates very realistic views of the house under various lighting conditions (Figure 6.18). Saving time and accuracy are the biggest advantages of using computers to create housing views.

Some architectural firms use CADD to allow the client to view the structure from many different angles before finalizing the plan. The customer can virtually "walk through" the space and determine if the building's layout meets expectations. If not, the designer can easily make adjustments to the plan, and produce different versions of the plan quickly. CADD brings the plan to life for the client. It also helps architects and builders avoid costly mistakes and verify that the final design meets client expectations.

An **isometric drawing** illustrates a space or product in three dimensions (width + length + height) at the same time. The resulting image is an overhead

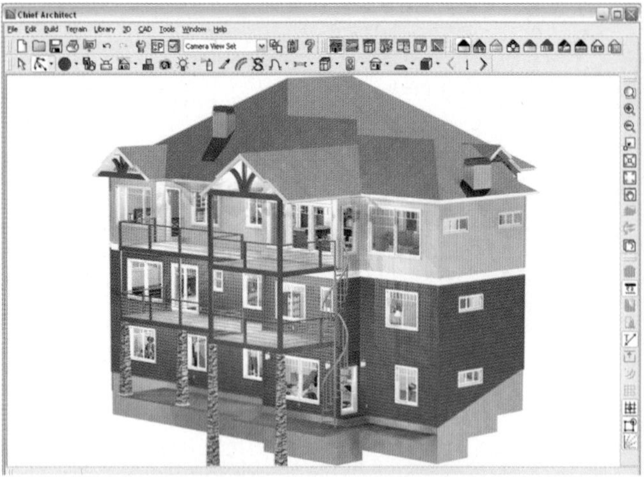
Courtesy of Chief Architect Software

Courtesy of Chief Architect Software

Figure 6.18 The rendering of this house was created by using computer-aided drafting and design (CADD). The rendering shows realistic views of the house under various lighting conditions at different times of the day and night.

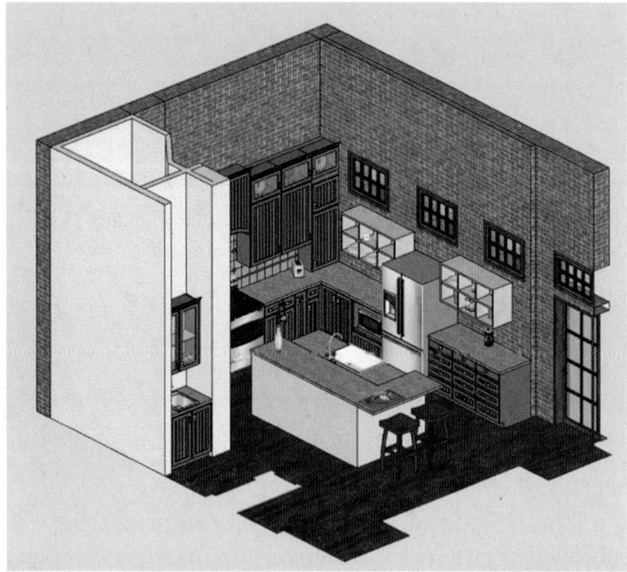
Jaclyn Cirillo

Figure 6.19 An isometric drawing shows a three-dimensional, bird's-eye view of a space at 30-degree angles.

Jaclyn Cirillo

Figure 6.20 Perspective drawings show the three-dimensional volume of a space in two dimensions, giving a client a more realistic view of a space.

view showing depth perception at 30-degree angles (Figure 6.19). It combines information from a plan drawing (width + length) and an elevation drawing (width + height). Designers may use this image to visually communicate the written information in specification documents. It is a valuable tool for ensuring quality construction, ***fabrication*** (to create or manufacture), and installation.

For presentation to a client, however, isometric drawings have their limits. This is because the overhead items are typically removed and there are always walls blocking part of the view, unless the designer also removes these walls. A better use of the designer's time is to prepare perspective drawings to show clients realistic eye-level views of space (Figure 6.20).

Review & Assessment

1. What are plan views? Name four types.
2. Why is the floor plan the most important drawing in a set of house plans?
3. What is square footage?
4. Contrast *elevation view, section view,* and *detail view*.
5. What dictates the number of pages and level of detail in a set of construction drawings?
6. What do the following letters mean in a set of construction drawings: G, C, A, S, P, M, and E?
7. What does the number mean following a page letter in a set of construction drawings?
8. What is the difference between a rendering and a model?
9. What are the features of an isometric drawing? Why do designers use isometric drawings?

Career Focus Architect

Is the design of buildings—old and new—fascinating to you? Do you ever wonder what it might be like to design such buildings? If you do, a career as an architect might be for you.

Interests/Skills: Architects work as part of a team to produce incredible structures. Interestingly, in larger firms, it is often difficult to tell who is an architect and who is an interior designer or engineer, although each serves a special and important purpose. Architects study and explore concepts, use spatial awareness, and use creativity to meet clients' needs. Skills include a strong background in multiple areas like art, science, and math. They should love to draw, as they do it manually and using computer-aided design. Effective organizational skills, attention to details, along with active listening skills are a must. Strong visual, written, and verbal communication skills are also essential in order to demonstrate problem-solving abilities.

Career Snapshot: Architects plan and design structures, such as private residences, office buildings, factories, theaters, and airports. The buildings they design have to be safe, economical, and must suit the needs of the people who use them. They work on computer programs to help them accomplish this. They prepare many contracts and documents. Architects also supervise the construction of the building or structure to make certain that their design plans are followed. Architects spend a great deal of time explaining their ideas to clients and others. Successful architects must be able to communicate well and get others to "buy-in-on" their ideas.

Education/Training: The completion of a bachelor's degree in architecture and a master's degree in architecture is the most common route for a career in architecture. Someone looking to specialize might also select elective coursework in *gerontology* (the science of aging) or *urban planning*. There are also countless continuing education opportunities which teach the technical, customer service, and business management skills specific to this concentrated area of design.

Monkey Business Images/Shutterstock.com

Licensing/Examinations: Most areas in the U.S. require a professional degree in architecture from a program accredited by the *National Architectural Accrediting Board (NAAB)* in order to take the Architect Registration Examination (ARE) licensure exam developed by the National Council of Architectural Registration Board (NCARB). It also takes approximately three years of documented experience under a registered architectural mentor to qualify.

Many architectural professionals also become LEED Accredited Professionals (Leadership in Energy and Environmental Design) for their particular area of specialization, and may also take the Construction Documents Technologist (CDT) and Certified Construction Contract Administration (CCCA) exams.

Professional Associations: American Institute of Architects (AIA); Construction Specifications Institute (CSI). These are national organizations that offer continued education opportunities and exposure to new products and building methods.

Job Outlook: While the overall professional outlook is very good, it is even better in specialty architectural areas such as schools/education, healthcare, and sustainable design.

Sources: The Occupational Outlook Handbook (OOH); the Occupational Information Network (O*NET); the National Council of Architectural Registration Board (NCARB); the American Institute of Architects (AIA)

Chapter 6 Assessment

Summary

- Architectural drawings contain information about the size, shape, and location of all parts of the house and are drawn to scale. There are several types of architectural or design drawings.
- CADD and BIM can assist with producing construction documents as well as isometrics and perspectives.
- When drawings are complete, prints are made which also include schedules and specifications.
- There are standards as to the layout, lettering styles, information, and abbreviations found as well as the order in which the drawings are typically put together in a set of construction documents.
- To understand architectural drawings, it helps to be familiar with the special lines and symbols used.
- Architectural drawings usually include several views of the house including plan views, elevation views, section views, and detail views.
- Understanding the reference symbols and notes will help understand the drawings.
- Construction drawings follow a logical order with pages dedicated to the design and construction teams.
- To help clients understand their house design, architectural firms frequently produce renderings, or presentation drawings, that show a realistic view.
- Some designers also produce a three-dimensional model of a design.

Terms in Action

1. **Graphic definitions** With a partner, use the Internet to locate photos or graphics that depict the *Content* and *Academic Terms* listed at the beginning of the chapter. Use presentation software to show your photos or graphics to the class, describing how they depict the meaning of the terms.

Think Critically

2. **Identify evidence** Suppose you have been asked to produce an entire set of drawings for your own residence. Interior elevations will be needed but not for every wall in the home. Identify four or more walls in the home that would most require drawn elevations for a builder to understand how to build them. Identify evidence to support your choices. Write a brief summary explaining your choices.
3. **Analyze consequences** The author discussed that many different trades will produce drawings that make up an overall set of construction drawings. Why must a designer be familiar enough to have a basic understanding of the other trade's plans? In what ways might a plumber's, electrician's, or mechanical engineer's plans conflict with the architect or designer's plans? What problems could arise from such conflicts? Discuss your analysis in class citing text and other reliable evidence to support your conclusion.
4. **Generate a solution** Suppose you have a new client who wants to build a new home. Based on information your client gave you about the needs and wants for this new home, you have created a proposed floor plan and a few schematic hand sketches and have shown them to your client. Your client, however, is still having trouble envisioning what the house will look like. How could you use plan views, elevation views, and section views and details to convey meaning for your client?

Core Skills

5. **Field trip** Visit a model home in a new subdivision or a nearby housing complex and do the following:
   - A. Obtain a copy of the floor plan and take a walking tour around the home.
   - B. Compare the impression of the house you get from studying the floor plan to the actual experience of touring the house. Were some aspects of the house not conveyed clearly in the floor plan?
   - C. Identify aspects of the floor plan that you would like to change and explain why.
   - D. Write a one-page summary of your answers to items B and C.
6. **Reading** Answer the following questions by examining and reading the details in Figure 6.10:

Chapter 6 Assessment

(A) How many windows are in the house? (B) Where is the furnace located? (C) The house has approximately how many square feet? (D) How many bathrooms does the house have? (E) What type of layout exists in the kitchen?

7. **Math practice** Use a ruler or metal tape measure to measure the length and width of this text book. Then draw the configuration of the textbook on a sheet of graph paper using a ¼" = 1'-0" scale. Then use a plain sheet of paper and an architect's scale to draw the dimensions of the text book to scale using the scale of ¼" = 1'-0". Use the STEM Math feature box on page 144 as a guide for using the architect's scale.
8. **Writing** Use Internet or print resources to investigate further information about the Building Information Model (BIM). If possible, interview an architect or builder who uses BIM. What are the best features of this process? Write a brief report and share your findings with the class.
9. **Reading, writing, and speaking** Locate a set of house plans on the Internet or from another source. Read the document carefully. Identify and label the symbols and line types you find on the plan. What schedules and specifications accompany the plan? How do they help convey meaning to the drawings? Show your plan to the class, pointing out the symbols and line types and what they mean.
10. **Reading, sketching, and writing** Locate a house floor plan on the Internet that you like and print a copy. Based on your readings under the *Order of the Documents* on pages 146–147 of this chapter, imagine what a complete set of drawings for this house would look like if this home were to have the master suite renovated. Make a list, sketch, or otherwise determine what type of drawings you think would need to be included in the *Order of Documents* for the renovation. Share your thoughts with the class.
11. **Math practice** Measure the perimeter of your classroom and write down the measurements. Then measure the dimensions of room features such as windows, door, cabinetry, and SMART boards, etc., and write down these measurements. Then use graph paper or architectural drawing software and a ¼" = 1'-0" scale to draw a floor plan of your classroom. Use the floor plan symbols in *Figure 6.7* to depict windows and doors (drawn to scale). Review your drawing with your instructor, making revisions necessary until you are satisfied with the accuracy of your plan. Then, print (or plot) your drawing to present it to the class.
12. **Writing** Search online for examples of architectural or drafting lettering. Based on what you find, see what font you can find in your desktop publishing software that most resembles that font.
13. **CTE career readiness practice** To enhance your communication skills as a potential housing designer, consider volunteering as a tour guide for a community event, such as a "Parade of Homes." Work alongside community organizers and architects to learn as much as you can about the homes, their floor plans, and architectural details. Use the information you learned in this chapter to help convey information about plan drawings to tourists. Some historical data about the inhabitants of these homes will add interest to the tour.

Design Practice

14. **Draw an elevation** Find a wall of cabinetry in your home or school. If none are available, home improvement stores typically have kitchen cabinet vignettes you could use. Sketch out the plan and elevation views of the cabinets based on examples from this chapter. Make general and key notes about what you see and any renovations or changes you would suggest.
15. **Portfolio** Using one of the house exteriors from the portfolio activity in Chapter 5, create an interior floor plan on graph paper. Apply the symbols and lines discussed in this chapter. Review your floor plan with your instructor, making revisions until you and your instructor are satisfied with the results. Save a hard copy for your portfolio. If desired, scan your floor plan and create a digital file for your e-portfolio.

Chapter 7

Space Planning and Functionality

Content Terms

space planning
functional zone
private area
multipurpose room
work area
social area
alcove
circulation
traffic patterns
built-in storage
common-use storage
anthropometry
scale floor plan
template
clearance space

Academic Terms

proximity
buffer zone
notations
translucent

Learning Outcomes 

After studying this chapter, you will be able to

- apply principles of space utilization, zoning, and traffic patterns in planning and furnishing housing.
- organize space by grouping rooms according to function.
- evaluate storage needs and space.
- analyze ways to arrange furniture effectively.

Reading with Purpose

Arrange a study session to read the chapter with a classmate. After you read each passage independently, stop and tell each other what you think the main points are in the passage. You can use the *Review & Assessment* questions as a guide. Continue with each passage until you finish the chapters.

While studying, look for the access icon  **to:**

- **Practice** the *Content* and *Academic Terms* with e-flash cards, matching activities, and vocabulary games.
- **Reinforce** what you learn by completing the *Review & Assessment* questions and e-mailing them to your instructor.

www.g-wlearning.com/housing/

Diego Cervo/Shutterstock.com

Before fully discussing the concept of **space planning**—the process of placing furnishings for a well-functioning and visually pleasing area—a housing professional, designer, or homebuyer must think about the overall nature of the residence. The type of home and the situation surrounding the home purchase have an immense impact on the space-planning choices the owner will have. Examples might include the following.

- **Is this an existing home or is it new construction?** With new construction, although there are limits, the buyer has more opportunity to customize the space plan and details prior to construction.
- **Is the home move-in ready or are major renovations needed?** If a home requires major renovations, that might be an excellent opportunity for a buyer to create a better space plan than already exists.
- **Is this the first home for this homebuyer or are they upsizing/downsizing from a previous home?** Furnishing a home for the first time can be expensive but it offers a buyer a cleaner slate for creating a design and space plan of his or her liking. Those who have previous furnishings will have to accommodate the size and shape of possibly large pieces of existing furnishings. Newlyweds may need to consider combining and prioritizing a great deal of furniture.
- **Is this a vacation home or a full-time residence?** The space plan of a full-time residence is primarily about daily functionality. The concerns of a vacation home might deal more with accommodating larger groups of occupants.
- **Is the home or apartment already furnished versus unfurnished?** Of course, a furnished home will save the buyer upfront money. Many of the space planning and design decisions will already have been made.

If you select furniture before considering its placement in a home, you may choose items that will not fit or result in good room design. Knowing how to properly arrange furniture will help you choose only the furniture necessary taking the home itself and current belongings into account for either yourself or your client. For the purpose of this chapter, we will discuss the design and planning of a newly constructed home as it allows for the most flexibility and choice.

The Space Within

Now that you understand the drawings for the house, you need to consider planning the space within. The division of space within the house is one of the most basic concerns in housing.

When planning how to use the space within a house, the designer must give consideration to the activities, habits, lifestyles, and life situations of the occupants. Much of this takes place during the initial phase of the project and should include lengthy interviews and observations. You will learn more about these concepts in detail in Chapter 17.

With this information in hand, the designer divides the interior space into areas according to the intended use of each. Optimal space divisions should satisfy the needs and preferences of the occupants.

Grouping by Functional Zones

As you look at floor plans, you will notice that certain rooms of a house are usually located next to one another. This is because certain rooms serve similar purposes, or *functions*. Grouping rooms together by **functional zone** is an efficient way to organize space. Three zones encompass most of the space within a house: a *private area*, *work area*, and *social area*.

The Private Area

The **private area** in most houses consists of bedrooms and bathrooms. These rooms provide space for sleeping, resting, grooming, and dressing (Figure 7.1). The private area of a house offers the

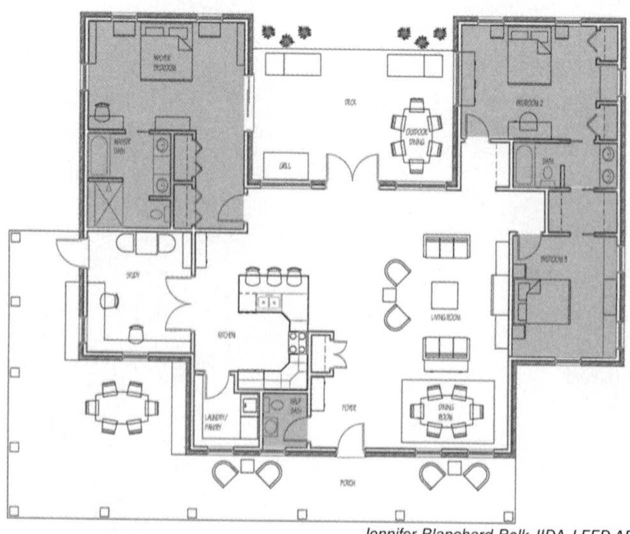

Jennifer Blanchard Belk, IIDA, LEED AP

Figure 7.1 The shaded area of this floor plan represents the private area.

best setting for rest and relaxation. It is usually a comfortable and quiet place.

Because sleep and rest are basic needs, they should be among the first to consider when planning the use of space. In some homes, each person has a separate room. In other homes, this is not possible or desirable. The important goal is to ensure the comfort of each person and put his or her spatial needs ahead of group needs.

Dressing and grooming are other activities that take place in the private area (Figure 7.2). These activities require privacy and space for storing clothes and grooming supplies. Both bedrooms and bathrooms help fulfill these spatial needs.

Some bedrooms may provide space for other activities, such as reading, studying, watching TV, listening to music, and working on hobbies. When this is true, the rooms become **multipurpose rooms**. Household members use them during active periods of the day as well as sleeping hours.

The Work Area

Some rooms in a home are set aside for the work area. The **work area** includes all parts of the house needed to maintain and service the other areas. Sometimes the work area overlaps with the service zone outside the house. Rooms in the work area vary from house to house. The kitchen, laundry area,

Master bath pics721/Shutterstock.com

Full bath Photobank.ch/Shutterstock.com

Half bath Iriana Shiyan/Shutterstock.com

Figure 7.2 No matter what the size of a bathroom (master, full, or half), it must be functional and private.

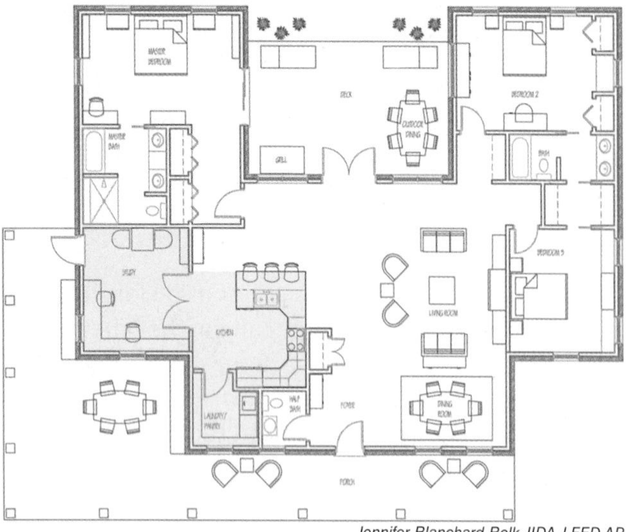

Jennifer Blanchard Belk, IIDA, LEED AP

Figure 7.3 The shaded kitchen and utility room areas represent the work area.

utility room, and garage are generally part of the work area. A workshop, home office, or sewing room may also be part of the work area (Figure 7.3).

If your lifestyle or that of a client requires a home office, you will need to include this space in the work area of the home. When planning office space, the first step is to determine its purpose. Is it for occasional use, such as paying bills and organizing household documents? Will people use the home office frequently, perhaps by children doing homework or adults bringing work home from the office? Will the office receive daily use, perhaps by a household member working from home or telecommuting? Knowing how inhabitants will use the home office helps to determine its location.

The actual space available in the dwelling also affects the location of a home office. Plans for some home offices require a corner of the kitchen or in an alcove. For daily use, a home office generally requires much more space, such as a separate room. However, few households can afford to give that much space to a home office. Instead, most plans for home offices utilize a spare bedroom, the basement, or attic space (Figure 7.4).

Rade Kovac/Shutterstock.com

Figure 7.4 This home office is a functional use for a little used corner of a family room.

After the workspace for the home office is determined on the floor plan, attention can later turn to the next steps. These include selecting and arranging furniture, securing the lighting, and getting the necessary equipment. You will learn more about these topics in Chapter 8.

The Social Area

Members of a household spend much of their time in the social area of the house. The **social area** provides space for daily living, entertaining, and recreation. It includes entrances, dining rooms, living rooms, and family rooms (Figure 7.5).

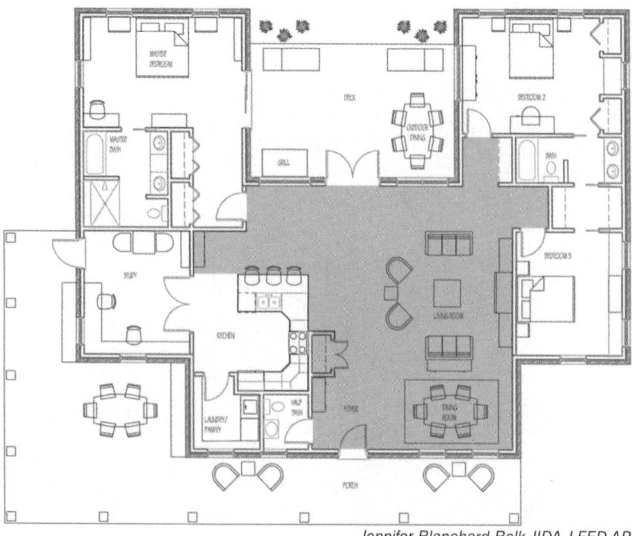

Jennifer Blanchard Belk, IIDA, LEED AP

Figure 7.5 The shaded portion represents the social area of the floor plan.

An entry or entrance is a place where household members identify and greet guests. It is here that guests remove outerwear and place it in nearby coat closets. Entries also help direct the movement of people throughout the house. If a dwelling has more than one entrance, each may have a slightly different purpose; however, each is still part of the social area.

Some houses have separate dining rooms for eating meals and entertaining guests. If a dining room does not get regular use, the cost of having a separate dining room may be too great. In that case, household members may prefer to eat close to where the food is prepared. This can be in the kitchen at a special counter or a separate table. During mild weather, household members often enjoy eating outdoors. When special events are on TV, many families like to eat meals in the family room or living room.

Living rooms provide space for family activities as well as for entertaining guests. If a dwelling has both a living room and a family room, the family room is often more casual. It offers space for recreational activities and relaxation (Figure 7.6).

Outdoor Living Spaces

Outdoor spaces (porches, decks, patios, pools, etc.) can be important and useful extensions of social, work and private zones. Each serves a specific purpose but an outdoor area can also create multiple benefits. Locating these spaces near the kitchen can encourage outdoor dining and grilling. An outdoor space near the social zone promotes entertaining and often can bring a great amount of natural light into a space. A master suite connected to a deck or patio provides a retreat and an excellent place for meditation and relaxation. As you can see, due to its ***proximity*** (closeness), the backyard deck in Figure 7.7 could serve all these purposes.

Breadmaker/Shutterstock.com

Figure 7.6 This living room offers space for family activities and entertaining guests.

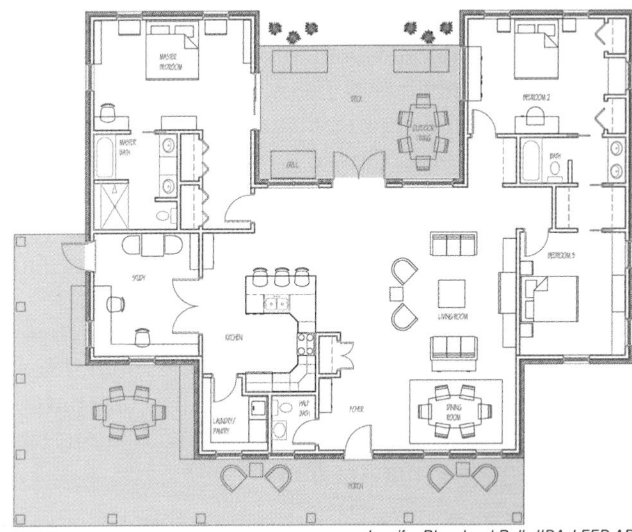

Jennifer Blanchard Belk, IIDA, LEED AP

Figure 7.7 Outdoor areas can provide an extension of a home's social spaces.

Separating Areas and Rooms

There are several ways to separate the private, work, and social areas. One way is to locate different areas on different ends or levels of the house. For instance, the private area may be upstairs, while the social and work areas are on the ground floor.

Hallways are another way to separate areas. Besides physically separating areas, hall space also acts as a ***buffer zone***—a neutral area designed to separate space—for noise. A hallway between the private and social areas makes it possible for some people to rest or sleep, while others are entertaining guests, dining, or watching TV. Near work areas, hallways help reduce the volume of noise from appliances and tools that reach the quiet and social areas. Hallways range from 36 inches to more than 48 inches wide with short halls using the 36-inch width. In contrast, a 42-inch width is customary in very long halls or in halls where wheelchairs are in regular use. A 46-inch width is the most common width used. Hallways must be substantially larger if they are to accommodate furniture or access to large storage areas. Many designers avoid using too many hallways as it is often considered wasteful square footage.

Walls usually separate individual rooms; however, some dwellings have large open areas with divisions into separate areas. For example, **alcoves** (small recessed sections of a room), varied ceiling heights, and balconies sometimes separate spaces for different functions. Screens, freestanding storage units, and careful arrangement of furniture can also separate space according to function. Even when there are no walls dividing a room, you can see that the room design provides for different activities.

An advantage of not separating areas with walls is a large, open area where people can enjoy more than one activity at a time. For instance, the kitchen may be open to the family room or living room. The open space allows those preparing food to take part in other activities, such as conversing with family members or entertaining guests.

Room Relationships

The nearness of and connections between various rooms is important to convenience and ease of use. For example, kitchens should be close to the dining room to make food service faster and more efficient. A garage or parking area should be close to the kitchen to make carrying in groceries easier. Bathrooms should be close to the bedrooms for convenience. Outdoor living areas should be close to the social areas to allow guests to enter the house without going through the work or private areas. Considering how to use the space and its closeness to related activities will improve the functionality of the living space (Figure 7.8).

Types of Circulation Activities

There are four types of **circulation**, or movement, activities that impact living space: *family*, *guest*, *work*, and *service*. These circulation activities have specific considerations and will be discussed in more detail in the next chapter:

- **Family.** Family members should be able to move freely between living areas without having to pass through a bedroom to get to another part of the house. High-frequency routes are short and direct.
- **Guest.** Guest circulation provides access to a coat closet, living room, and dining room without having to walk through the work areas or private areas of a home. There should also be a bath close by for guests.
- **Work.** To meet this circulation need, the kitchen should be located near the service entrance and have easy access to basement, garage, and laundry/utility areas.
- **Service.** This type of circulation refers to movement of persons into and out of the home including repairmen and service people. Service circulation also includes taking garbage out and bringing in groceries.

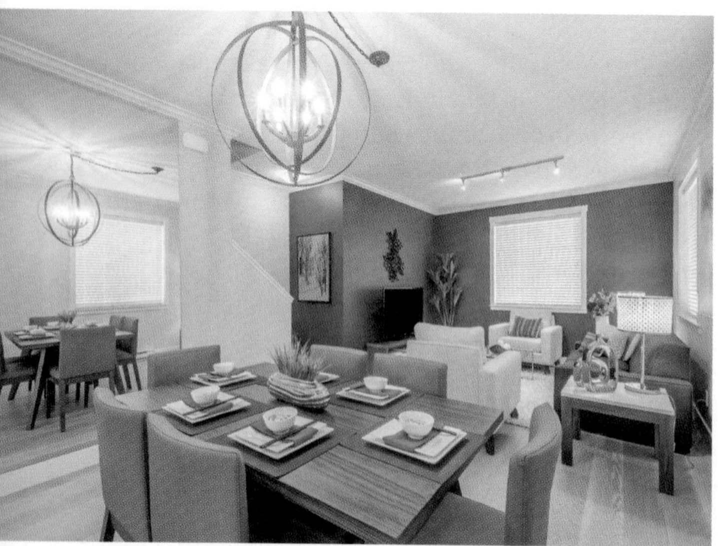

karamysh/Shutterstock.com

Figure 7.8 This casual living space and dining room are part of the social area of the home.

Traffic Patterns

Have you ever been in a traffic jam after leaving a football game or concert? Often the police relieve the congestion by directing traffic and creating alternate routes.

Traffic planning also helps reduce or prevent congestion throughout a house. It relates to the types of circulation activities that occur throughout the home. When organization of a space is effective, people move easily within a room, from room to room, or to the outdoors. **Traffic patterns** are the paths they follow. Within more open spaces, furniture naturally funnels people onto particular paths.

Traffic patterns require enough space for people to move about freely. However, it is wasteful to use more space than is needed. As a rule, traffic patterns should be about 40 inches wide with extra width in areas where major traffic patterns intersect.

The design of traffic patterns should allow people to move throughout a house without disturbing other activities. For example, major traffic patterns should avoid the private area of a home so it can remain quiet. Work areas are unsafe if people frequently walk through them. To avoid accidents, traffic patterns should lead to work areas, but not through them. Also, traffic patterns should not be located through the center of social areas, since this can interrupt conversation, study, and TV viewing.

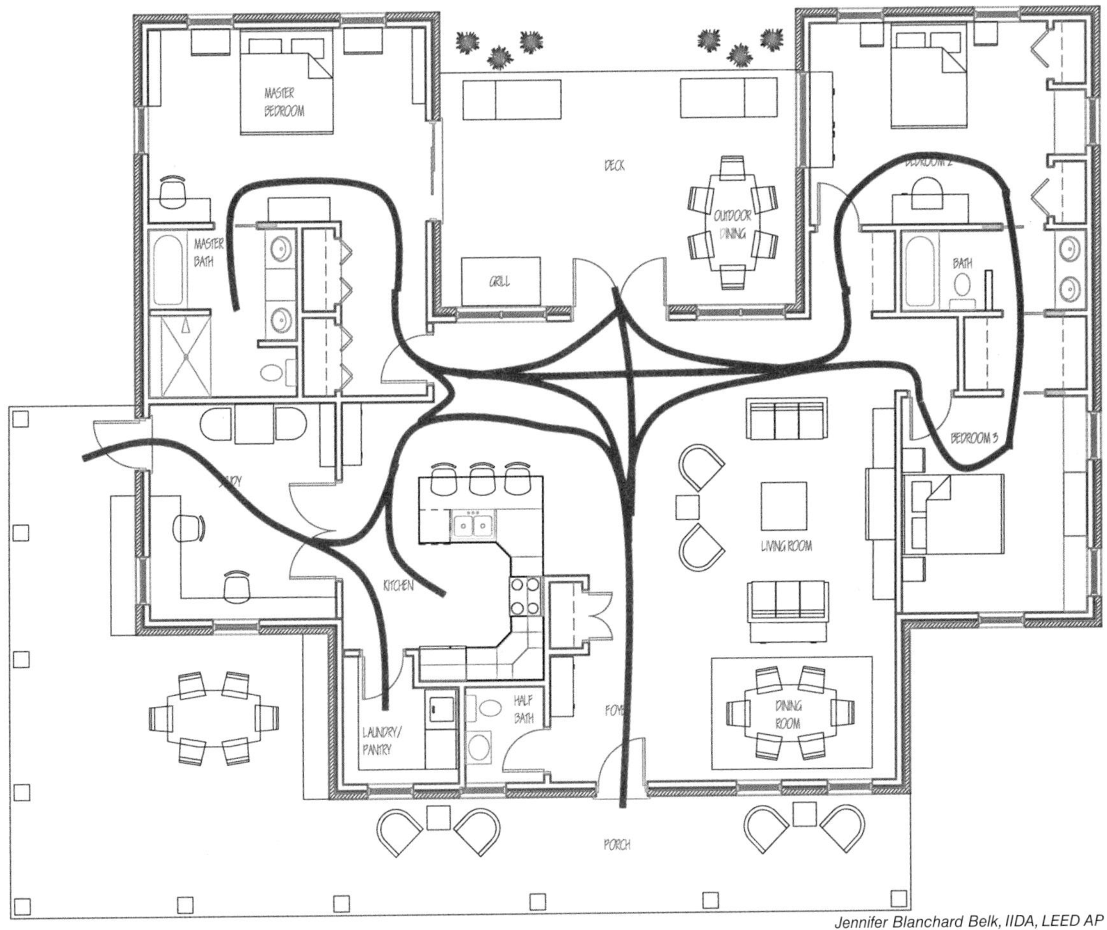

Jennifer Blanchard Belk, IIDA, LEED AP

Figure 7.9 The open floor plan of this home permits traffic to flow smoothly in many directions.

The easiest way to evaluate traffic patterns is to study floor plans. Look at the examples in Figure 7.9. Do the traffic patterns use the following guidelines for safety and convenience? Traffic patterns should

- be convenient and direct
- provide adequate space without wasting it
- provide easy access from the entrances to other parts of the house
- separate traffic to the work area from traffic to the private and social areas
- avoid cutting through the middle of rooms
- avoid interfering with a good furniture arrangement or interrupting activities within a room
- avoid interfering with privacy in areas of the house where privacy is expected
- avoid cutting through a kitchen, work area, or any other hazardous area
- give the kitchen easy access to all areas of the home
- provide a direct access from the service entrance to a cleanup area
- provide access from a service entrance to the private area without going through the social area
- provide direct access from utility area to the outside service zone
- provide direct access from the main entrance to social areas without going through work or private areas

Space for Doors

Outside doors and doors between rooms also help determine the flow of traffic. Other doors within a room may conceal storage. It is important that the space in front of these doors remain free. Blocked doors will stop traffic and cut off access to stored items.

Not only should the space immediately in front of doors be free, but there should also be space for doors to swing and stand open. Figure 7.10 shows the space requirements that different types of

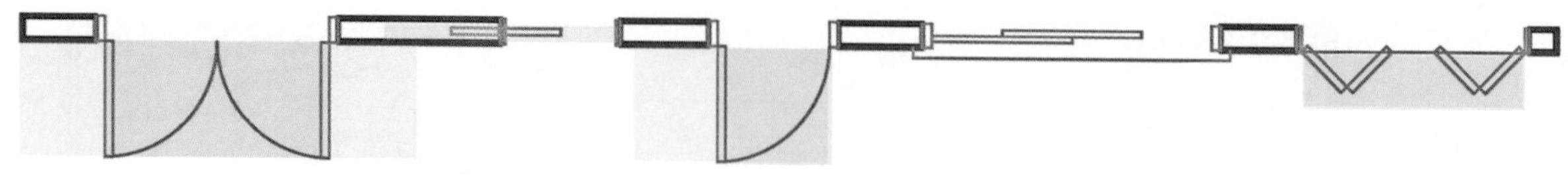

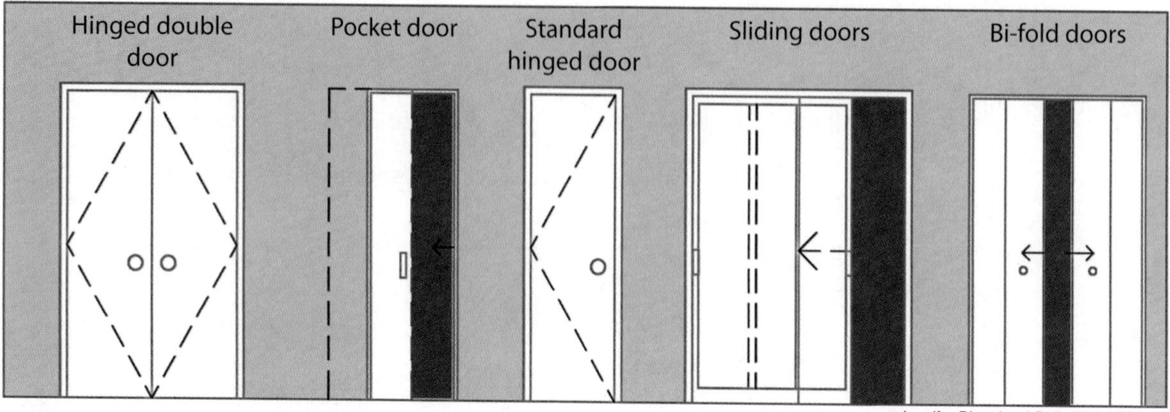

Jennifer Blanchard Belk, IIDA, LEED AP

Figure 7.10 For each of the floor-plan symbols directly above each door drawing, note that the darker shaded areas show the amount of space that must be kept clear around each type of door. The lighter shaded areas indicate the space needed for full swing doors.

doors need to swing open. People also need space to approach the doors, go through the doors or to use storage areas. When planning specialty doors like pocket doors, designers must remember that there cannot be plumbing or electrical planned for the pocket side of the door.

Many factors determine door sizing. Exterior and high-traffic areas should have at least 36 inches for openings. Bedrooms and walk-in closets require at least 32 inches. Linen closet doors may be as small as 18 inches. In addition to these minimums, consider opening sizes for moving large furniture and appliances.

Survey the Storage Space

It is important to have plenty of storage space scattered throughout a house. When looking at house plans, look at what storage space is available. Make sure there is enough space to store all belongings. Check to see if the storage space is located in convenient places. If you or your client plan to use some rooms for more than one activity, make sure they have the storage space you need. For instance, you may plan to use the dining room as both a study area and a place to eat. In this case, you will need space to store paper, pens, and reference books as well as dishes and table linens.

Looking at floor plans can help you evaluate the storage space of a home. A floor plan, such as the one in Figure 7.11, shows the location of built-in storage units. **Built-in storage** includes shelves and drawers that are built into a housing unit. You cannot sell, replace, or move built-in storage

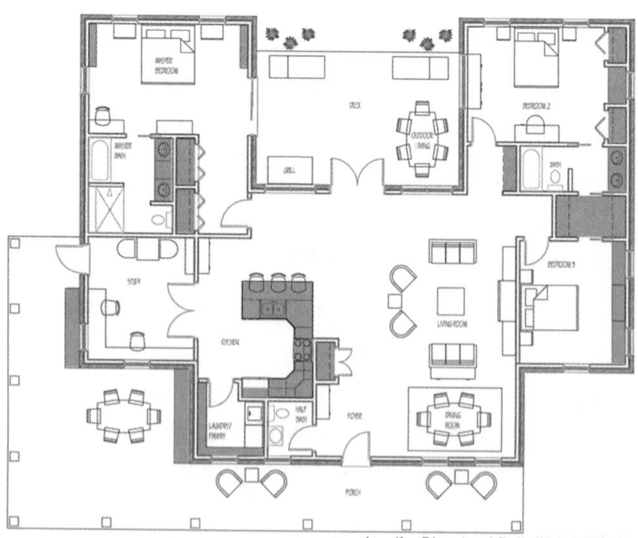

Jennifer Blanchard Belk, IIDA, LEED AP

Figure 7.11 This floor plan shows the location of closets, a pantry, cabinetry, and shelving throughout the home, which are all forms of built-in storage.

like pieces of furniture. A section view will show the number of shelves and drawers in the storage unit. Floor plans also show how much floor space is available for additional storage, such as shelves and bookcases.

Planning for Storage

If you or a client plan to build a house, planning for storage is essential. First, determine the storage needs of each member of the household. A rule-of-thumb to follow is to devote 10 percent of the floor space to storage. Then plan for **common-use storage**—storage which is used by all who live in a house. It includes the storage near the entrance where household members keep outerwear and storage for food, tools, and other items for sharing.

You can add to the amount of built-in storage available in a dwelling with storage units and storage furniture. Storage furniture includes desks, chests, armoires, and dressers (Figure 7.12). Storage furniture is easy to move to other locations in the house and occupants can take it with them if they leave or move to a new dwelling. Some units may require disassembly.

Photography Courtesy of Pottery Barn

Figure 7.12 Baskets under tables can be used in addition to built-in storage to hold household items.

Built-in storage, storage units, and storage furniture also have advantages. Because you cannot take built-in storage with you when you move, you will not have the cost of moving it. Also, a home increases in value if it includes built-in storage.

Evaluating the Floor Plan

When considering a floor plan on paper, on a computer screen, or by walking through a home, evaluate the layout carefully. Ask yourself the questions in Figure 7.13. By answering these questions, you can identify any areas that may present future problems.

No floor plan is perfect for everyone so your ideal plan may present problems to someone else. A plan that fits your immediate lifestyle needs or those of your client may not work as your lifestyles change. You can solve problems in a floor plan by making changes to the construction of the space or by *adapting the space.* When you adapt a space, you use it for something other than the original purpose. Sometimes, too, using interior design treatments may help solve floor-plan problems.

Evaluating a Floor Plan

Answering "yes" to the following questions indicates a well-designed floor plan. Any "no" answers may indicate a need to modify the floor plan.

- Would all members of your household have enough space to satisfy their needs?
- Are rooms grouped according to function?
- Are private areas away from public view and traffic?
- If a multipurpose room exists, can it be used for all the intended purposes?
- Are eating areas close to the kitchen?
- Is space provided for entertaining as well as day-to-day living?
- Are the entrances conveniently located?
- Are the traffic patterns safe and convenient?
- Is storage adequate and convenient?
- Is the house free of barriers?

Figure 7.13 Can you think of other questions you would ask yourself when evaluating a floor plan?

Sociocultural Connections Anthropometrics

What factors influence building codes for such parts of a structure as minimum doorway height, depth of a kitchen cabinet, or the height at which a handrail is attached along a stairway? To answer this question, a designer must not only know building codes, but must also understand the bodily dimensions of the average person who will enter the doorway, store items in the cabinet, and use the handrail. Measurements of height, weight, and arm reach are some of the data available from researchers in anthropometry. **Anthropometry** is the scientific study of human body measurements on a comparative basis.

Researchers working for the government, universities, and businesses usually collect this data. One of the largest databases of anthropometric data, collected by the U.S. military, is based on men and women in the U.S. armed services. The U.S. government also collected data on children. Designers and manufacturers use data averages to create building materials, appliances, and home furnishings to fit the general population.

Design professionals can access much of this data in tables or on the Internet free of charge. However, there are some limits to this data. For example, data from measurements of healthy young adults may have less usefulness to someone designing housing for older adults or people with disabilities. Also, data collected decades ago may not reflect the changes in average weight and size of populations over time. It does not reflect changing demographics.

Anthropometric data is expensive to collect. Some businesses sell it. New technology is revolutionizing how to collect and use this data. For example, designers can take their own measurements of virtual bodies scanned by researchers using 3-D body scans. The types of measurements that can be collected in this way are limitless.

Dig Deeper

Suppose you are a new furniture designer for a small furniture manufacturing company. Your company wants to design a line of simple, yet supportive and comfortable desk chairs for home use. Investigate what anthropometric data you need to be able to design several chairs. Your supervisor expects to see at least two preliminary sketches by the end of the week. After you collect your data, create two desk chair sketches you think will meet the needs of today's customer.

Review & Assessment

1. Why does it matter if a home is the first or second for a homebuyer? new construction or existing?
2. What are the three functional zones that divide the space of a house?
3. How does considering the use of a space and its closeness to related activities improve functionality? Give an example.
4. Name four types of circulation activities.
5. List five guidelines for functional traffic patterns.
6. Name one advantage of each: built-in storage and storage furniture.

Arranging Furniture

Before selecting furniture for a room, you need to plan how to arrange it. The first step in this process is *space planning*. To plan a space, first measure the dimensions of the room. Room measurements let you know how much space is available in the room and how much furniture will fit in it. After taking measurements, several design tools can help you develop a space plan for a functional and attractive furniture arrangement.

Developing a Scale Floor Plan

To begin space planning, measure the length and width of each room. Then measure and determine the location of all the existing room features, such as doors and windows (to the inside of the frames), electrical outlets, heating and cooling vents, and air intakes. In addition, measure the dimensions of any alcoves or other permanent features, such as fireplaces, cabinets, or built-in furniture pieces, too. All measurements should include the floor placement of the features as well as ***notations*** (characters, symbols, or abbreviated expressions used in math to express technical facts or quantities) about their wall height.

Before arranging furniture, you need to develop a scale floor plan. A **scale floor plan** is a reduced-size drawing that is directly proportional to the actual size and shape of a space or room. A common floor plan scale is ¼ inch equals 1 foot. This means that ¼ inch on the drawing is equal to 1 foot in real life. You can create a scale floor plan from house plans used to build a home, as described in Chapter 6.

If the house plans are not available, there are two ways to create a scale floor plan. One way involves a manual process of using graph paper and templates. The second involves using a computer aided drafting and design (CADD) program to assist you. You will learn more about how interior designers use the CADD method in Chapter 18. A third method for drawing an accurate floor plan involves using an architectural scale, a mechanical pencil, a T-square or parallel bar, an angle or triangle, and a secured piece of paper. Using the side edge of a table or drawing board, a T-square creates a horizontal edge to draw against. Sliding a triangle along the horizontal helps to create precise vertical lines. Whichever method you choose, use the common scale for residential floor plans of *¼ inch equals 1 foot* (¼" = 1'-0"). A larger house, however, may not fit on standard-size paper and a smaller scale such as ⅛" = 1'-0" can be used.

Graph Paper and Templates

To begin, draw the room on graph paper and include the features and dimension measurements. Use the symbols from *Figure 6.7* to indicate the doors, windows, electrical outlets, and other features in the plan.

After creating a scale floor plan, you can use furniture templates to represent the furniture in the room. A **template** is a small piece of paper or plastic scaled to the actual dimensions of the furniture piece it represents. Manufactured plastic templates allow you to simply trace the shape of the furniture onto your plan. If you do not have access to manufactured templates, you can create your own by cutting small pieces of paper scaled to the actual dimensions of the furniture it represents. You can also use paper that is slightly ***translucent*** (clear, allowing light to pass through) and trace the furniture rather than cutting it out. All templates must be the same scale as the floor plan, which usually is *¼-inch equals 1 foot*.

To create furniture templates, measure the length and width of the furniture you want to use. You may choose different colors of paper for different pieces of furniture. Cut them out and arrange the templates on the scale floor plan until you find the best arrangement (Figure 7.14). Sometimes all the planned furniture pieces fit well. At other times, they may not. If you are purchasing furniture and the furniture comes in different standard sizes, such as beds, create a template for each possible size. For example, if it is appropriate, it may be easier to accommodate two twin beds rather than one king size. This is a much easier way to determine good furniture placement than actually moving heavy pieces of furniture back and forth.

Factors to Consider When Arranging Furniture

Several questions will help you develop the best space plan for a furniture arrangement. How will you or a client use the furniture? What space does it need? How will room features and traffic flow affect furniture placement? Also consider the principles of design.

Furniture and Room Use

How furniture is arranged depends on how it is used. Each piece of furniture has one or more specific uses and requires a certain amount of space as a result. For instance, a chest of drawers takes up floor space and wall space. Clearance space is also needed in front to open the drawers. **Clearance space** is a measurement term for the amount of space to leave unobstructed around furniture to allow for ease of use and a good traffic

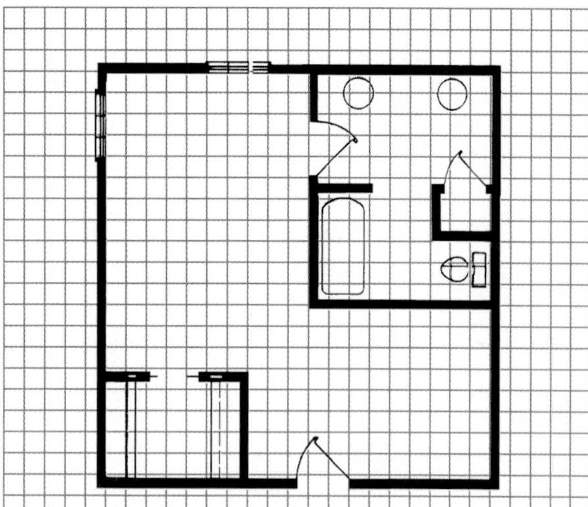

Step 1. Draw the dimensions of the bedroom on graph paper showing windows and doors in their correct positions.

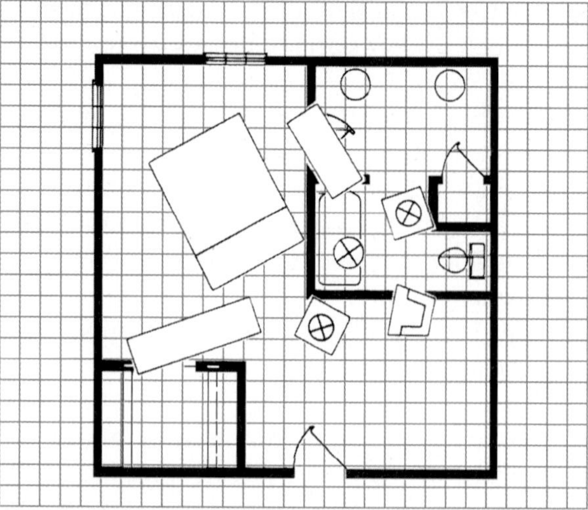

Step 2. Make furniture templates to be placed in the room, and cut them out.

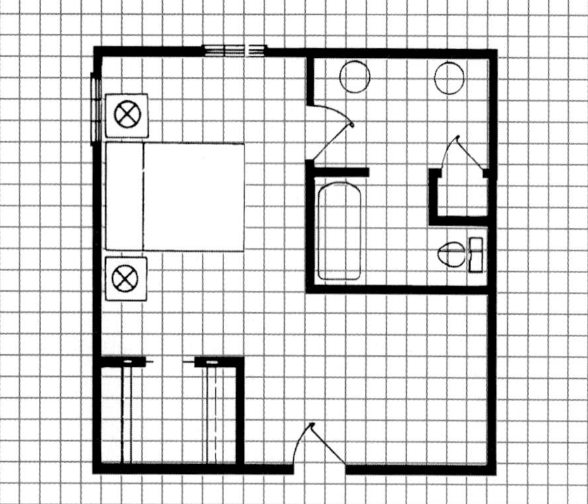

Step 3. Place the bed first.

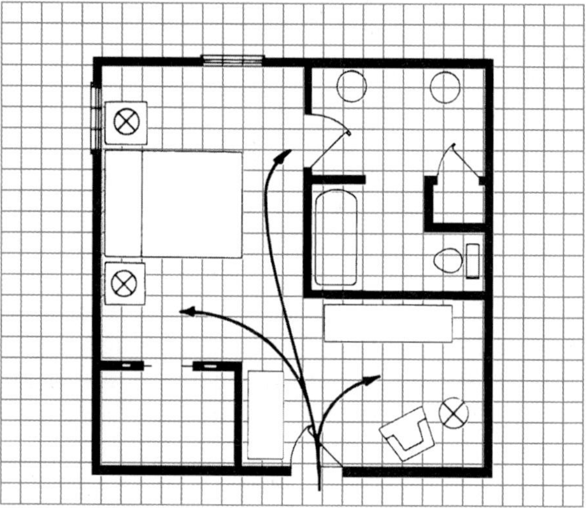

Step 4. Place the remaining furniture, keeping circulation paths clear.

Goodheart-Willcox Publisher

Figure 7.14 Using a scale floor plan makes planning furniture arrangements easy.

pattern. See Figure 7.15 for a list of clearance space requirements for furniture.

A furniture arrangement also depends on the room use. Before arranging furniture in a room, think about the activities that will take place there and the amount of space available. Then consider where within the room each activity will focus.

List the basic furnishings needed for each activity area, and determine the amount of space the furniture will occupy. For instance, you might want to create a conversation area in the living room (Figure 7.16). A furniture grouping of chairs, sofas, tables, and lamps should be no more than 8 to 10 feet across, measuring from the fronts of the seats. To encourage conversation, the area should form part or all of a circle. In the grouping, conveniently arrange lamps and other accessories in relation to their use. Give attention to the availability of electric outlets in planning the placement of lamps.

Room Features

When developing a space plan, arrange furniture so it does not interfere with the features of the room such as windows, doors, outlets, and air vents. Do not place furniture where a door will hit it, and try not to block electrical outlets or air vents. Also, avoid placing furniture in front of a functioning window, which makes opening and closing the window difficult. In addition, plan furniture arrangements around special architectural features. For example, furniture should not block a fireplace or built-in bookshelves.

Standard Clearance Spaces	
Room	**Clearance Space in Inches**
Living Room	
Around seating, such as chairs and sofas	18–30
Between sofa and coffee table	15–30
For minor traffic pattern area	18–48
For major traffic pattern area	48–72
Dining Room	
Between chair backs and wall or buffet (for diners remaining seated)	18–24
Between chair backs and wall or buffet (for self-service or host/hostess service)	30–36
Between table edge and wall or buffet (for self-service or host/hostess service)	18–30
For leg room in front of chair	48
Kitchen	
Between oven and opposite workspace (opening door)	40 minimum
Between refrigerator and opposite workspace (opening door)	36 minimum
Between dishwasher and opposite workspace (opening door)	40 minimum
For circulation space	24
For work zone space between counter and nearby obstacle	48
Bath	
For activity zone in front of sink	18
For circulation space	24
Between front of sink and opposite wall or obstacle	40 minimum
Bedroom	
For activity zone in front of dresser to allow for work space and opening	42–48
For work zone space for making beds	26–40
For circulation space	24
Between twin beds	24

Figure 7.15 In the process of space planning, you must maintain adequate clearance space for proper traffic circulation.

By using a scale floor plan, you can see the placement of the features. If you have trouble visualizing furniture placement in relation to the features, add walls to your plan and indicate the features (Figure 7.17).

Traffic Patterns

As you recall from earlier in the chapter, traffic patterns need to provide enough space for people to move about freely. Place each piece of furniture so people can circulate easily

Career Focus In-house Commercial Designer

Have you ever wondered what goes into building huge facilities like malls, high-rise offices, and hospitals? If so, a career as an in-house interior designer or facilities manager might be for you!

Interests/Skills: Facility design and management requires an appreciation for the balance of beauty and function, often to a very large scale! These professionals must be able to analyze situations, visualize creative solutions to extremely intricate space planning problems and document those creations for use by a wide variety of tradespeople. Those who have an ability to work under pressure with enthusiasm while maintaining an attention to detail, good time management, and organizational skills would be a good fit for this industry. Facilities personnel must be able to communicate and collaborate with large groups of architects, engineers, furniture vendors, department managers, and contractors.

Career Snapshot: Designers who work directly for the public and private clients they serve (rather than independently or for a design firm) are considered in-house or facilities designers. Interior design graduates can serve as in-house facility designers for:

- Large corporation and commercial office developers
- Colleges and universities
- Federal, state and local government institutions (school systems, military bases)
- Health-care facilities (hospitals, clinics, senior living)
- Hospitality companies (hotel and restaurant chains, conference centers, cruise ships)
- Retail companies (store chains, shopping malls)

Facility designers handle a wide range of projects from multistory building designs to the replacement of a single ergonomic office chair. These designers often have the power to impact the furniture, space planning, and finish standards for that company's buildings around the world, which can lead to interesting travel opportunities. Managers may also handle security, property finances, and contracts.

Education/Training: The completion of a bachelor's degree in interior design or architecture is typically sufficient for a designer but a business minor is beneficial to those seeking management positions. Students should seek exposure to a variety of courses including electrical and mechanical systems, accounting, space planning, energy management and property development.

logoboom/Shutterstock.com

Licensing/Examinations: Due to the incredibly vast nature of this segment of the industry, facility designers and managers have many choices when it comes to voluntary licensing, in addition to the National Council for Interior Design Qualification (NCIDQ). The National Association of Industrial and Office Properties (NAIOP), a commercial real estate development association, CoreNet Global, and the International Facility Management Association (IFMA) administer certification exams. These certifications ensure companies that a designer is sufficiently trained in dealing with issues particular to large corporations or organizations. Many professionals will also become LEED Accredited Professionals for their particular area of specialization.

Professional Associations: In addition to more general organizations such as The American Society of Interior Designers (ASID) and the International Interior Design Association (IIDA), involvement in The National Association of Industrial and Office Properties (NAIOP), the International Facility Management Association (IFMA), the U.S. Green Building Council (USGBC), CoreNet Global, and Commercial Real Estate Women (CREW) are beneficial.

Job Outlook: Facility managers should anticipate an average increase in job opportunities compared to all occupations in the United States, although designers may benefit by aligning themselves with high growth segments such as environments for the aging and sustainable projects.

Sources: The Occupational Outlook Handbook; the Occupational Information Network (O*NET); International Facility Management Association (IFMA); US Green Building Council (USGBC)

Breadmaker/Shutterstock.com

Figure 7.16 The furniture in this grouping is arranged to encourage conversation.

Ksenia Palimski/Shutterstock.com

Figure 7.17 From a simple scale floor plan, free online or professional space planning software can be used to produce a 3-D view of a room or home. This helps homebuyers envision their space more easily.

throughout the room. To accomplish this, you must maintain proper clearance space around each piece of furniture. When placing furniture in a high-traffic area, consider increasing the clearance space. A furniture placement should not create an obstacle course or block traffic patterns between rooms.

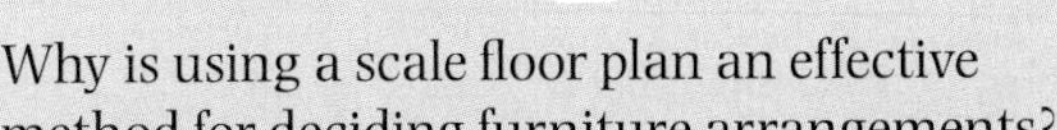

Review & Assessment

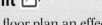

1. Why is using a scale floor plan an effective method for deciding furniture arrangements?
2. Identify three factors to consider when planning a furniture arrangement.
3. Why are traffic patterns and clearance space important to creating effective furniture arrangements?

Chapter 7 Assessment

Summary

- After evaluating drawings, consider the actual space needs within a house.
- Many factors regarding a homebuyer's situation impact the level of future space planning choices. Consider all variables whether an individual is new to home ownership, if it is a vacation home, or if it will require renovation.
- Rooms are usually grouped by function, room relationship, and circulation activities.
- Space is divided into three different areas—for privacy, work, and socializing.
- Planning traffic patterns help reduce and prevent traffic congestion and provide enough space for opening doors.
- Organizing space to provide plenty of storage is also important.
- Using a scale floor plan aids in arranging furniture. It shows the dimensions and features of a room and allows the movement of furniture templates to create the best space plan.
- Good furniture arrangement is dependent on how the furniture and the room are used.
- Arrangements should provide for adequate clearance space to avoid interfering with room features and traffic patterns.

Terms in Action

1. **Graphic definitions** With a partner, use the Internet to locate photos or graphics that depict the *Content* and *Academic Terms* listed at the beginning of the chapter. Use presentation software to show your graphics to the class, describing how they depict the meanings of the terms.

Think Critically

2. **Identify issues** Consider how you and those you live with use your public spaces. Are there any functions that seem to be too far apart? any activities that do not have enough space to function well? Would you prefer the environment be more open or closed?
3. **Deconstruct evidence** In the text the author states that "Grouping rooms together by functional zone is an efficient way to organize space." Use the text and other reliable resources to validate this statement. Is the statement biased or true? What supporting values and evidence support this statement? Discuss your reasoning and cite your sources for the class.
4. **Analyze traffic patterns** Suppose you analyze the traffic patterns in a home you plan to buy and see potential problems between the private and social areas. Otherwise, the house is very pleasing and convenient to use. Would you buy the house with the idea of changing the traffic patterns later, or would you keep looking for a better floor plan? Use the text information and other reliable resources to provide evidence to support your choice.

Core Skills

5. **Research and writing** Visit a local furniture store. Evaluate the furniture vignettes to determine if they meet the minimum standard clearance distances between furniture pieces. Document your findings in writing to present to the class.
6. **Observing and speaking** Ask a neighbor if they would like for you to evaluate their home environment. While the family cooks dinner, cleans the house, etc., observe any traffic pattern issues. When do they get in each other's way? Is there anything that could be easily changed to make the situation more functional? Give them a brief explanation and document your findings.
7. **Research and speaking** Locate a floor plan on the Internet that you like and print a copy. Use the floor plan to do each of the following: (A) Shade the private, social, and work areas with different-colored pencils. Determine if the areas are divided appropriately and justify your decision. (B) Trace the traffic patterns, and check them with the guidelines listed in this chapter. Explain if they are safe and convenient. (C) Identify which storage is for individual use and which is for common use.

    Then prepare an oral/visual presentation with your floor plan, that shows your creation of visual solutions based on your experience and imagination, to share with the class. Point out the private, social, and work areas and present

Chapter 7 Assessment

your justification for item A. Then do the same for traffic patterns and storage.

8. **Writing** Use a desktop publishing program or school-approved web-based application to develop a flyer that shows safety issues in housing plans. Develop a list of safety considerations for adults and children in the following areas of a floor plan: the home's entrances, traffic patterns in kitchens, and placement of interior doors. Present your print flyer to the class or post your digital flyer to the class web page for discussion.
9. **Research and speaking** Use Internet or print resources to investigate ways that anthropometric measurements are used in house design. Locate images that help support your findings. Then prepare a digital photo essay to share your research with the class.
10. **Math practice** Use a metal tape measure to measure the perimeter of your classroom or another space in the school. Measure the doors and windows and their distances and placement on the walls. Measure the tables or desks and their placement in the classroom. Record your measurements. Then draw a scale floor plan on graph paper using a 1/4" = 1'-0" scale by hand. Accurately place furnishings in their proper locations according to your measurements. Identify the typical traffic patterns in the classroom. Have your instructor check your floor plan and revise as needed for accuracy.
11. **Technology practice** Use a school-approved CADD design program to create a scale floor plan and furniture arrangement for a living room that measures 20 feet by 18 feet. Show the placement of one door and three windows. Place furniture pieces—such as a sofa, two chairs, two side tables, and a coffee table—in the room in three different arrangements. You may decide to delete or add more furniture keeping in mind the best quality available within your client's budget constraints. Use the chart in *Figure 7.15* to check the clearance-space measurements between furniture pieces in your designs. Do your designs meet recommendations? If not, redesign the arrangements as necessary to meet the recommended clearances until you and your instructor are satisfied with the results.
12. **Space-planning practice** Older adults need interaction with other people, especially those who live in group settings or spend their days in an adult day services center. Activity-space arrangements can stimulate interaction or hinder it. As part of community service project, do the following: (A) Contact the director of a long-term care facility or adult day services center in your community. Make arrangements to visit the facility. (B) Discuss with the director ways that you and your team can encourage interaction with the older adults or meet some other needs. Ideas may be as simple as rearranging an activity room or adding decorative accessories that invite interaction. (C) Take measurements of the facility or activity room. Then create scale floor plans offering at least three different ways to use the space more effectively. (D) In addition, identify ways that you and your team might have regular interaction with these adults. (E) Share your ideas with the director of the facility and implement if possible.
13. **CTE career readiness practice** Suppose your new clients called you with a need to renovate the social and work areas of their home. They say they want these spaces to be more user-friendly. Your first effort to creatively solving their design problem is to ask questions. As you are preparing for your first client interview, you know you need to dig deeper into the problem. Create a list of questions—*Who, What, When, Where, Why,* and *How*—that focus on the client's design problem.

Design Practice

14. **Scale floor plan** Select and measure one room in your home or in a home of someone you know to apply principles of space utilization in housing. Following the chapter guidelines, draw a scale floor plan of the space on graph paper. Make scale templates of either existing furniture or new furniture, and create two different plans for arranging the furniture. Carefully consider clearance space and allow for traffic patterns.
15. **Portfolio** Review the floor plans you have created for this chapter. Refine the plans. Then use presentation software to create a design presentation suitable for client review. Save your presentation as an example of your work.

Chapter 8

Planning for Individual Spaces

Content Terms

quantitative information
qualitative needs
accessibility
physical limitation
adaptability
universal design (UD)
vision disability
hearing disability
hand limitation
mobility limitation
adjacencies
micro-adjacencies
work triangle
landing space
butler's pantry

Academic Terms

tangible
innate
pragmatics

Learning Outcomes

After studying this chapter, you will be able to

- summarize the importance of developing a deep knowledge of individual occupant needs.
- explain the differences among ways to address housing needs: accessibility, adaptability, and universal design (UD).
- research and describe housing features for individuals with special needs, including ways to modify housing for accessibility for people with physical limitations and make a home safe and secure for people with vision and hearing disabilities.
- summarize the principles of universal design (UD) and features that meet the needs of all people, including those with special needs.
- evaluate any characteristics of an existing home that would impact space planning.
- summarize space needs for individual rooms within a home.

Reading with Purpose

Before reading the chapter, skim the illustrations and their captions. As you read, determine how these concepts contribute to the ideas presented in the text.

While studying, look for the access icon  **to:**

- **Practice** the *Content* and *Academic Terms* with e-flash cards, matching activities, and vocabulary games.
- **Reinforce** what you learn by completing the *Review & Assessment* questions and e-mailing them to your instructor.

www.g-wlearning.com/housing/

Katherine West

In previous chapters, you learned about functional zones, room relationships, circulation, and traffic patterns. Now, you will use this information in more detail for individual room planning. Earlier you learned about the different scenarios for home occupants (new construction, vacation home, or rental) and how they might affect what can and cannot be done in a home. This chapter will discuss the design and space planning of individual rooms of an existing home.

Existing structures bring with them opportunities and restrictions not as evident in new construction. As a future housing professional or designer, you may be involved in helping a client actually select a home, so knowing their needs in a deep and personal way will allow you to help them find a perfect match. In this chapter, you will learn ways to see the potential in each room of a home and explore strategies for making any home accommodate a variety of occupants.

Clients and Their Needs

By far, the most important interactions a designer and client have are during the early part of the design process. Whether documented in written or graphic form, in as much depth as possible, the goal is to explore the needs and wishes of the client in a *quantitative* and *qualitative* way. As you may assume, it is essential that the designer know that there needs to be six dining chairs, three bedrooms, two bathrooms, etc., which is **quantitative information**—a characteristic of an object or interior that can be measured with numbers (size, quantity, temperature). Also important is meeting the client's **qualitative needs**, characteristics (quality needs) of an object or interior that cannot be measured such as the need for privacy, security, and control.

Without exposure to different types and scales of residences, housing professionals, designers, and clients may have a very narrow view of what a home should be and what the possibilities are. The number of spaces they have visited or the few homes they have lived in may limit their impression of what a home should be. It is better to explore the reasoning behind requests than to simply put their perceived needs on a wish list. For instance, a client might say they must have a guest room. Once you delve deeper, however, you find that the client rarely has guests and when they do, it is several nieces and nephews. You might suggest that it would be wiser to make sure there are multiple convertible sofas in the basement family room, leaving the additional room upstairs for a more practical use such as a home office or studio.

In another situation, a client might request a home office. Once you explore more, however, you find that, not only does the client work outside the home 75 percent of the time, but when home is very mobile and uses only a small laptop. You might suggest that a small area of the living room, kitchen, or bedroom provide a place for this technology and supplies, as well as make sure appropriate power outlets and glare control are available throughout the house (Figure 8.1).

An essential practice is walking through a client's existing space, viewing the current living situation and belongings, and discussing daily activities and use of each individual space. This helps to distinguish needs brought to light by current inadequate facilities versus making assumptions about needs. Further discussions help you anticipate future needs and the essential accommodations for family growth and change.

Although it is important to get some basic information about the spatial and square footage needs, it is even more important to understand the lifestyle, activities, and interests of individual occupants. People have some distinctive needs such as for order, identity, privacy, security, and others that are, to differing degrees, common to everyone. Primarily, the designer needs to investigate what makes these occupants differ from what is often typical. Does this client have an excessive book or art collection? Do any of the occupants have emotional

ID1974/Shutterstock.com

Figure 8.1 Mixed-use rooms are a great way to combine two rooms that might not be used frequently, such as a guest room and office.

needs that give them a higher than normal need for security or privacy? Are there belongings, such as antique cars, which require specialized spaces? Are there any current or future accessibility concerns?

This chapter will explore how to not only meet ***tangible*** (capable of being precisely identified) needs within areas of the home, but also meet ***innate*** (belonging to the essential nature of something) psychological needs that are often forgotten. First and foremost, it is important to address physical needs.

Review & Assessment

1. What is the goal of the early part of the process of design when working with clients?
2. Contrast quantitative information with qualitative needs.
3. Why is exposure to many different types of homes important for housing professionals and designers?
4. What information can housing professionals or designers gain from walking through a client's existing space?
5. What are some of the intangible, psychological needs a home can provide?

Design for All

Meeting the needs of all occupants, now and in the future, is important. This is done through using the concepts of *accessibility*, *adaptability*, and *universal design*. Housing professionals and interior designers need to understand these concepts and how they are used in residences. One way to look at these terms is to see them on a continuum of designing spaces (Figure 8.2).

Accessibility---------	Adaptability---------	Universal Design
(design to meet special needs)	(design to make future modifications easier)	(design when built to meet all needs)

Goodheart-Willcox Publisher

Figure 8.2 The concepts of accessibility, adaptability, and universal design are essential for housing professionals and designers to understand and use when designing residences.

Accessibility, Adaptability, and Universal Design

Accessibility is the ability to reach something and use it. In reference to interiors, it is the ability to fully use the entry by people with a wide range of disabilities, specifically wheelchair users. Accessibility describes the way that a building structure meets specific special needs. Laws, such as the *Americans with Disabilities Act*, exist for public buildings and government-sponsored housing that requires accommodating spaces for special needs including **physical limitations** such as mobility, vision, and hearing disabilities. These conditions limit how people can use or interact with the living environment. **Adaptability** refers to the ability to change or fit different circumstances. In reference to interiors, it means the ability of an interior to meet the changing accessibility needs of the occupants without excessive cost or inconvenience. An example is fortifying bathroom walls later so that grab bars can be added when needed. **Universal design (UD)** is a design concept that focuses on making living environments, and the products used to create them, without special adaptations. These living environments meet the needs of all people when they are built so they will not require future alterations.

Accessibility—Housing Modifications for People with Special Needs

Housing should provide convenience, safety, and accessibility for all members of the household. This includes people with special needs, including physical limitations, vision disabilities, and hearing disabilities.

Houses for people with physical limitations can be attractive and affordable. By spending approximately two percent above the base cost on a new house, builders can incorporate design features to make it barrier free. Also, you can modify the exterior, Figure 8.3, and interior, Figure 8.4, of existing features at a reasonable cost to meet the needs of people with physical limitations. For example, modifications in a kitchen can make the cooking and cleanup areas more accessible to household members with limited reach.

Accessibility for Exteriors

The exteriors of houses for people with physical disabilities should be as safe and accessible as possible. When building or choosing a house, keep the following points in mind:

- Choose flat lots for easy access.
- Plan the entrance to face south, so ice and snow on sidewalks and driveways melt faster.
- Utilize nonskid surfaces, such as textured asphalt or concrete for sidewalks, driveways, and garage floors. (Keep oil and debris off these surfaces.)
- Make driveways and garages wide enough to park cars and to move in and around wheelchairs.
- Use garage door openers that automatically light garages.
- Install appropriately sloped ramps with handrails for easy access to the house.
- Make sidewalks, ramps, and entries wide enough for wheelchairs to move easily. To allow for enough room on each side of a wheelchair, sidewalks should be four or five feet wide and entries should be three feet wide.
- Make thresholds as level as possible to prevent stumbling.
- Consider push-button or automatically operated doors because they are the easiest to use.
- Equip doors with levers or handles, which are easier to grasp and turn than conventional knobs.
- Install effective lighting outdoors and at entry areas.

Figure 8.3 Safe and accessible housing exteriors and entrances can be attractive and affordable.

Accessibility for Interiors

Since people spend most of their time inside, safety and accessibility are important. When choosing housing that eliminates barriers for people with physical limitations, some key features are very important. Barrier-free homes should include the following:

- Stairs with an easy rise (not too steep) and steady handrails, thin enough to grip securely.
- Floors and stairs with wood or hard-surface coverings for easy mobility. If carpet is used, it should have a low pile.
- Floor plans that accommodate use of a walker or wheelchair.
- Open traffic lanes that lead directly to specific areas.
- Halls at least four feet wide to permit a wheelchair to enter into a room.
- Rooms with adequate turnaround space for wheelchairs, usually a five-foot radius circle.
- Doors that swing both ways or fold for ease of use, with doorways that are at least 32 inches wide for clearance.
- Storage space, equipment, and appliances are within easy reach.
- Electrical outlets are 18 inches to 48 inches off the floor and switches no higher than 48 inches.
- Light switches that can be pressed to operate versus moving up and down.
- A home elevator or staircase-lift if the living quarters are on more than one level of the house.

Figure 8.4 Barrier-free homes that are safe are essential for people with physical limitations.

Vision Disability

A person with a **vision disability** may have any degree of vision loss. For most people, changes in vision begin after the age of 40. These changes often become more severe after age 65. One of 20 people over the age of 85 is legally blind. People with a vision disability live most comfortably and safely in familiar surroundings. Adapt living areas to the needs of a person with a vision disability with the following measures:

- Prominently mark changes in floor levels and countertop levels.
- Place furniture away from traffic lanes.
- Increase the amount of lighting and make sure it is evenly distributed.
- Use highly visible colors, such as yellow-orange and red.
- Avoid using similar colors together. Instead, use contrasting colors to visually separate items.
- Keep a consistent light level in bedrooms and halls. Use night-lights.
- Where appropriate, use braille or tactile markings in cookbooks and on controls.

The checklist in Figure 8.5 will help you analyze how well a home is adapted for the needs of people with vision disability.

Hearing Disability

The most common disability among older people is hearing loss. Hearing ability declines gradually, so a person with a **hearing disability** may have any degree of hearing loss. People with hearing disability may need a communication system that complements their hearing ability. Amplifying devices on doorbells and phones may be sufficient. People with a total hearing loss will need visual signals, such as a flashing light.

Hand Limitation

A **hand limitation** results from arthritis and other conditions limiting movement and gripping

Meeting the Needs of People with Visual Impairments

- ✓ Are raised numbers or letters used on entrance doors, especially in apartment dwellings? (Note: They should be at least three feet above the floor.)
- ✓ Are hanging objects higher than the person with poor vision?
- ✓ Are obstructions removed from major traffic areas?
- ✓ Are sliding doors used on closets and elsewhere to eliminate walking into an edge of an opened door?
- ✓ Are handles treated with knurling (or a special adhesive) on doors that lead directly to steps or other potentially dangerous areas?
- ✓ Are push-button controls identifiable by touch?
- ✓ Are all control dials marked or shaped so fingers can feel different positions and know what settings they are? (In some cases, click stops may be substituted.) The important controls to mark are
  - ✓ range
  - ✓ oven
  - ✓ mixer
  - ✓ faucets
  - ✓ washer
  - ✓ dryer
- ✓ Is storage adequate so items can be stored separately on adjustable shelves or similar items can be stacked without piling too high?
- ✓ Do water faucets always have hot water on the left and cold water on the right of the user?

Figure 8.5 This checklist helps people adapt living spaces for people with vision loss.

Career Focus Universal Design and Aging-in-Place Specialist

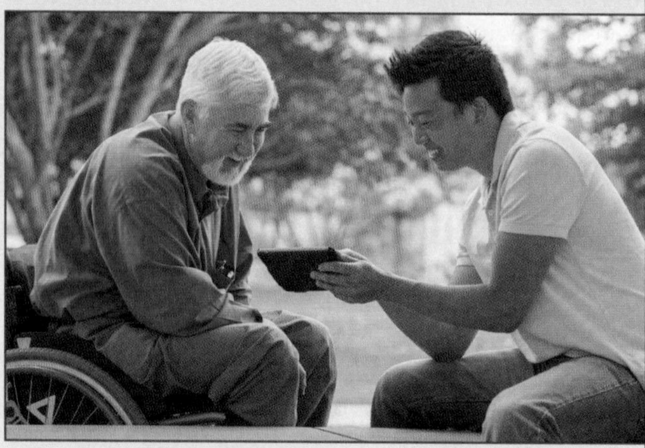
Huntstock.com/Shutterstock.com

Do you notice when someone with a disability has trouble entering or using a space? Do you see improvements you could make to allow everyone equal accommodations? Do you remember ever having to help an aging family member perform basic tasks in their home? If you do, a career in universal design might be for you!

Interests/Skills: Designers specializing in universal accessible design and modifications should be critical thinkers and creative problem solvers. They should also be empathetic to clients' needs, understanding the difficulty many occupants of an environment may have, and have excellent communication and customer service skills. These designers should be able to see the big picture and see into the future. What does that mean? Seeing the big picture is being able to identify universal design barriers in an environment that might impede not only the elderly and those in wheelchairs but also those who are visually, audibly, or cognitively impaired; children, and those of short or tall stature. Seeing into the future means a designer can anticipate the needs of the changing or aging occupants.

Career Snapshot: All interior designers, architects, builders, and engineers must be well-versed in mandatory accessibility guidelines, especially those relative to commercial interiors. However, the goal ultimately is to not only meet government regulations for access but to also ensure full and equal access to amenities, activities, products, and services for all. A designer specializing in universal design might work as a consultant or within a larger firm evaluating built environments, accessible technologies, and proposed plans for compliance and suitability. Those who practice aging-in-place design work specifically with residential projects helping older adults maintain independent living and allowing their homes to adapt to their needs as they age. They not only meet with clients but also create plans for construction and renovation and may oversee construction. A designer more interested in the technical aspects might serve as an accessibility compliance officer for a district, a large corporation, or a senior living community.

Education/Training: The completion of a bachelor's degree in interior design, architecture, or building science is typically sufficient. Someone looking to specialize might also select elective coursework in gerontology (the science of aging) and special education or pursue a master's degree.

Licensing/Examinations: All interior design graduates who pass the licensing examination through the National Council for Interior Design Qualification (NCIDQ) are thoroughly prepared to deal with accessible design issues, especially for commercial interiors. For those who want a more concentrated certification in residential design, The Certified Aging-in-Place Specialist (CAPS) designation was developed by the National Association of Home Builders (NAHB) Remodelors™ Council, in collaboration with the AARP, NAHB Research Center, and NAHB Seniors Housing Council.

Professional Associations: The American Society of Interior Designers (ASID); International Interior Design Association (IIDA); National Association of Home Builders (NAHB); International Association of Accessibility Professionals (IAAP)

Job Outlook: Research shows that by 2030, approximately 20% of Americans will be over age 65. Aging citizens prefer to live in their own homes instead of moving to assisted living communities. Seniors with expendable income are investing money to achieve low-maintenance but luxurious homes as well as beach or mountain vacation properties. Those who do move to senior communities expect to have hospitality and amenities not available to previous generations. For all of these reasons, design for the aging has a better than average employment outlook.

Sources: The Occupational Outlook Handbook; the Occupational Information Network (O*NET); Americans with Disabilities Act; Age-in-Place Networks; The Center for Universal Design (CUD)

ability. These individuals need large lever-type controls on doors and faucets. Special faucets are also available with proximity sensors or electric eyes that turn them on and off. Electronic touch controls on appliances are often easier to use than knobs, which require grasping and turning. Light switches that an individual can press are easier to use than those that move up and down. On outside doors, keyless push-button locks are good.

Mobility Limitations

A person who has a **mobility limitation** has difficulty walking from one location to another. Living spaces that are all on one level will eliminate the need for using stairs. For climbing and descending stairs well, they must be easy to use. Stairways must have secure handrails and a nonskid surface on each step. Ideally, people with limited mobility should use stairways with shorter, wider steps.

Some people with mobility impairments move well with the use of a walker. Other people require a wheelchair. Accessibility requirements change drastically when interior designers take the needs of a person using a walker or wheelchair into account. Determine if your house can provide a comfortable and convenient environment to a person with limited physical ability.

Adaptability—Providing for Aging-in-Place

Forecasting is a huge aspect of interior design. Anticipating how a client's needs may change allows them to appreciate and utilize the home for years to come. Creating environments with this in mind eases issues created by changes in vision, hearing, strength, color perception, memory, and orientation in the elderly. Housing adaptability takes the concepts of accessibility and universal design and merges them with the understanding of how the body and mind age and the desire to limit costs for renovations later in life. In addition to the universal design concepts in this chapter, examples might include the following:

- Single-story living.
- In case of a two-story home, a main floor master suite that might serve as a guest space or family room with a second master suite on the second floor.
- Walk-in closets approximately five feet by five feet on both the first and second stories so that the home could potentially later be retrofitted with a residential elevator.
- Blocking or structure inside the bathroom walls so that grab bars can be easily installed later.

Universal Design—Design for All People

In recent years, housing has become a much-discussed issue. Government officials, builders, housing developers, and the general public expressed a growing need for safe, decent, affordable housing for all people. Initially, groups of people with special requirements were the focus, such as older adults, people of all ages who have disabilities, and households with children. Today, many housing designs utilize universal design to accommodate the needs of all people. The focus of universal design is to make housing more usable by all people, even those with physical limitations, for little to no extra cost.

Ronald Mace from the *Center for Universal Design* at North Carolina State University developed the concept of universal design. Mace realized that, through careful design, products and environments could be usable by more people at little or no extra cost. Mace named the design concept *universal* since it simplified living for practically everyone.

The universal design concept targets the needs of all people, regardless of age, physical characteristics, or ability. By contrast, accessible or adaptable design benefits only certain people, such as persons with mobility limitations.

When universal design principles are used, every building and product within is developed to provide greater usefulness to as many people as possible (Figure 8.6). This includes every faucet, light fixture, shower stall, public telephone, entrance, and all other implements people use in everyday life. The principles of universal design also apply to the spaces everyone uses for daily activities.

Many universal design features are structural and must be built into the house. Other nonstructural features are items that are easy to add to existing housing. Some universal design features are regularly built in homes of today, especially by request of the occupants (Figure 8.7).

The Principles of Universal Design

1. **Equitable Use:** The design is useful and marketable to people with diverse abilities.
2. **Flexibility in Use:** The design accommodates a wide range of individual preferences and abilities.
3. **Simple and Intuitive Use:** Use of the design is easy to understand, regardless of the user's experience, knowledge, languages, skills, or current concentration level.
4. **Perceptible Information:** The design communicates necessary information effectively to the user, regardless of ambient conditions or the user's sensory abilities.
5. **Tolerance for Error:** The design minimizes hazards and the adverse consequences of accidental or unintended actions.
6. **Low Physical Effort:** The design can be used efficiently and comfortably and with minimum fatigue.
7. **Size and Space for Approach and Use:** Appropriate size and space are provided for approach, reach, manipulation, and use regardless of user's body size, posture, or mobility.

Figure 8.6 The *Principles of Universal Design* were developed by The Center for Universal Design in collaboration with researchers and professionals across the United States.

Benefits of Universal Design—The General Interior

The benefits of universal design to people with physical limitations are obvious. The benefits to others, however, may not be as apparent. Here are some examples of how universal design benefits people who do not have physical limitations.

Minimum door opening of 32 inches

- improves circulation throughout the house, especially when guests are visiting
- reduces damage to the door frame when moving furniture or equipment through doorways

Lever-style door handles

- are easier for everyone to use
- permit owners to open the doors with just an elbow or knee when hands are filled
- add an elegant touch at little or no extra cost

Adjustable-height closet rods

- make closets usable by children
- increase storage by creating room for a second-tier closet rod or other types of organizers
- tailor closets to individual wardrobe needs

Tall windows placed low on the wall

- provide a good view for everyone, especially children and seated adults
- add more natural light and elegance to the room
- are easier for a child to open
- require less reaching to open, close, and lock (24 to 36 inches from the floor)

Electrical receptacles 18 inches from the floor

- are easier to find than those low to the floor and are easier to reach without bending
- are located conveniently for electric cords to be removed correctly—by grasping the plug, not pulling on the cord

These and other universal design features are generally standard features in all types of new housing. However, considerations can also be made for the special needs of older adults, people who have disabilities, and families with children.

Figure 8.7 The use of universal design in the general interior of a home benefits all people, those with and without disabilities.

Review & Assessment

1. Contrast accessibility with adaptability. Give an example of each.
2. What is universal design (UD)?
3. List three ways to adapt the living area for a person with a vision disability.
4. Name one accommodation for each of the following disabilities: hearing disability, hand limitation, and mobility limitation.
5. What are three adaptations that can be made to a home to allow for aging-in-place?
6. What is the purpose of universal design?

Existing Home Characteristics

Once you understand a client and their needs, the next task is to evaluate the characteristics of the home. With existing homes, there are structural elements and architectural characteristics that are difficult to change and can dictate a great deal of your space planning. In order to determine the use of each room, this evaluation might include the following topics.

Pragmatics

Pragmatics means dealing realistically with things that cannot be changed easily. Even unfinished, an interior gives subtle and obvious information as to how people should use it. If major renovations are not in the budget, the current kitchen and bath locations and layout will likely not change. Unless there are easy solutions, the front entry will likely remain where it is. Rearrangement of movable elements and even minor changes to interior openings, however, can drastically affect the usability of spaces.

Spaces that do not have semipermanent architectural features (such as plumbing and connection to the outdoors) are where your creative mind can begin to see the alternative space uses and possibilities within a home. As you learned earlier in the text, the number of levels in a home also affects the implied floor plan by segmenting public, private, and recreational areas on different floors.

Interior Landmarks

Structural columns and stairs are also very expensive to move. Although they do not dictate the spaces they are within (as plumbing does), they can affect circulation. Flooring material and wall color can imply a division of space even within an open floor plan and are fairly inexpensive alterations. Ceiling height changes and floor elevations can also segment an open space but are much more challenging to change. Rooms with an awkward shape require extra attention when space planning (Figure 8.8).

Window Analysis

Existing windows can tell a lot about the possibilities of room use, although changing window types is not quite as expensive of a change. The amount of light entering a room may be more or less desirable for particular room uses. Windows that are low to the floor may be preferable in living rooms and dining rooms but might make space planning difficult in kitchens and rooms with a great deal of wall-based furniture (such as a bedroom). It is also important to note that for a room to be designated a bedroom, an operable window must be present.

Circulation and Proportion

Based on the existing (unfurnished) space plan, where are the main traffic patterns? Do you pass through the spaces, pass by the spaces, or does your path terminate at the space? Would changes in furniture arrangement allow you to alter these patterns and make the spaces more efficient?

It is also important to understand that not all square footage is created equally. For instance, a 400-square-foot room could be:

- **Twenty feet by twenty feet (20' × 20').** Square rooms can be considered awkward to plan as it is difficult to avoid circulation through the conversation areas or have extra space in the middle of the room.

Karen Armstrong

Figure 8.8 This sloping ceiling limits bed placement against the wall in this room. Placing the bed at an angle against the corner of the room offers enough head clearance at the slope and adds interest to the room.

- **Ten feet by forty feet (10' × 40').** Overly long rooms waste a disproportionate amount of square footage on circulation and can feel like a bowling alley.
- **Sixteen feet by twenty-five feet (16' × 25').** This ratio is near 40 percent to 60 percent, which is not only a pleasing proportion but also allows for multiple activity zones such as a kitchen/breakfast room combination.

In addition to the points above, pay attention to the overall layout of the home which may give you an indication of potential uses. Some plans appear to radiate from a center room, which implies that the room might work well as public gathering space. A long, linear plan might imply that the spaces increase in needed privacy the farther they get from the front entrance, terminating in the most private zone of the home.

Defining Space

Open floor plans create a great deal of flexibility but can be difficult when a client or designer tries to determine the space plan and furniture arrangement needed. Not having frequent walls to push furniture up against requires creative solutions to space delineation. Consider the following suggestions:

- **Using planes.** Vertical planes, such as shelving units, columns, and partial walls, can separate spaces physically without blocking natural light and visual connection.
- **Texture and color changes.** Even in an extremely open environment, a colorful accent wall or area rug can designate and differentiate uses of space (Figure 8.9).

Photographee.eu/Shutterstock.com

Figure 8.9 This dining space (which is an extension of the kitchen counter) is defined from the rest of the open space by the use of a bold accent color on the wall and floor.

- **Furnishings.** An implied conversation circle created from chairs or an area rug can designate space use.
- **Lighting.** Varying levels of light pooling over certain areas of an open plan can differentiate spaces.

In some cases, spaces may not need definition. Occupants may use multiuse spaces simultaneously or will rotate their use throughout the day. A client's need for order and control over the environment should dictate the appropriateness of such spaces.

Review & Assessment

1. What is the meaning of pragmatics? Give an example related to housing and interiors.
2. Name an example of a change to interior landmarks that are fairly inexpensive alterations.
3. Why is it important to understand that not all square footage is created equal?
4. List two suggestions for creatively defining space.

Considerations for Individual Spaces

Whether designing and building from scratch or evaluating an existing structure, consider each room individually and as part of the whole of the home. Think about room sizes and proportion in addition to distinct space amenities and layout. For instance, living areas of the home (entry, living, dining, plus recreation area, sunroom, great room, den, and more) typically make up about one third of the square footage of a home. Although these are generalizations, they can certainly give an idea of relative sizes of spaces.

Typical Space Sizes

Building codes determine the bare minimum size individual rooms should be. As homes differ greatly in size, so do the rooms within. The National Association of Home Builders, however, prescribes a space allocation that is helpful no matter the overall square footage of the home. The recommended space per room is approximately the percentage of finished (conditioned) space as shown in the pie chart in Figure 8.10.

When discussing individual spaces, consider the possible space allotments based on a 1,000-, 2,000-, and 3,000-square-foot home. These suggested square footages for the three different sizes of homes appear in the table in Figure 8.11.

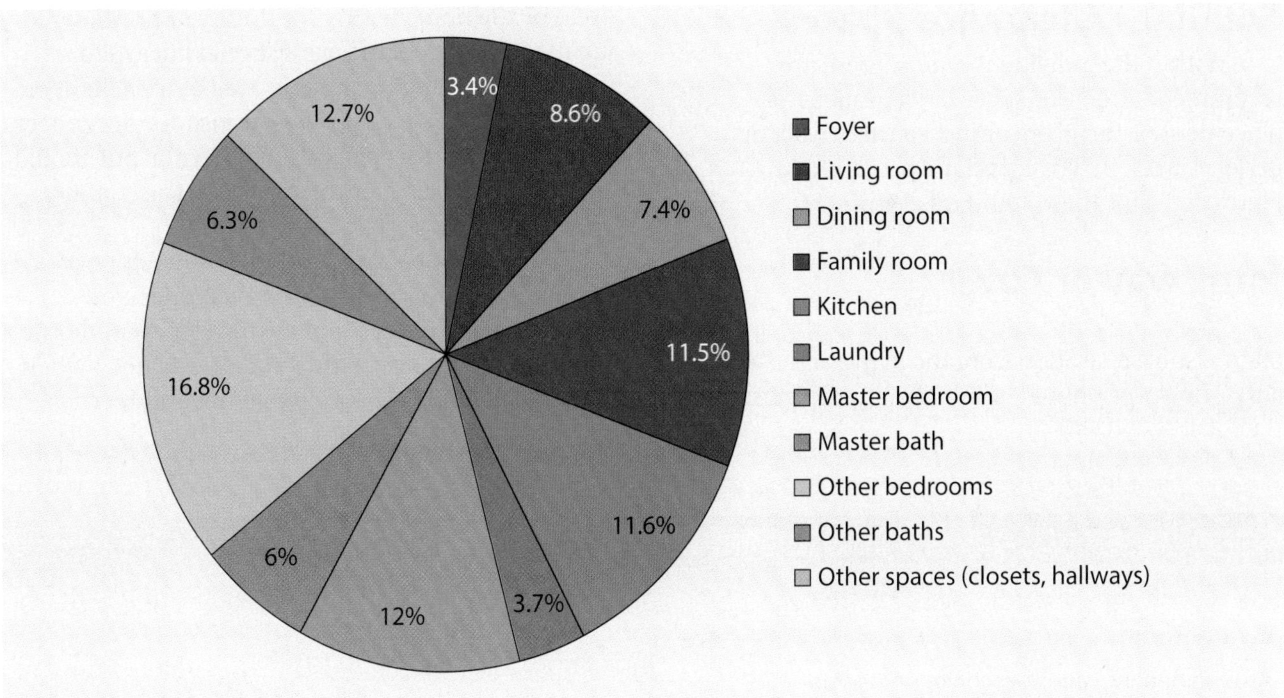

Source: National Association of Home Builders (NAHB)

Figure 8.10 This pie chart shows the percentage of floor space recommended by the National Association of Home Builders to be allocated to rooms in a house.

Housing Space Allocations				
Room	**Percentage of Home**	**1,000-Square-foot Home**	**2,000-Square-foot Home**	**3,000-Square-foot Home**
Foyer	3.4%	34	68	102
Living Room	8.6%	86	172	258
Dining Room	7.4%	74	148	222
Kitchen	11.6%	116	232	348
Laundry	3.7%	37	74	111
Family Room	11.5%	115	230	345
Master Bedroom	12.0%	120	240	360
Master Bath	6.0%	60	120	180
Other Bedrooms	16.8%	168	336	504
Other Baths	6.3%	63	126	189
Other Spaces (breakfast, closets, and hallways)	12.7%	127	254	381

Source: National Association of Home Builders (NAHB)

Figure 8.11 This chart shows the square footage recommendations for three different house sizes. The square footage is the percentage per house recommended by the National Association of Home Builders.

Standard Clearance Spaces

Within the individual rooms, there are recommendations for space or clearances for placement of furniture or just space to walk or perform work in a residential structure. See Figure 8.12 for these standard clearances.

Entryway or Foyer

People prefer an entryway to have physical and often visual separation from the living areas. The entry, however, should be adjacent to the most public areas of the home with a continuity of finishes and furnishing styles. Entryways should have indoor and outdoor standing areas as well as a sidelight or peephole through which to view visitors. Secondary entranceways are typically not as formal but should allow for easy transport of groceries, trash, and otherhousehold tasks.

The entry space should have some type of storage for coats, access to convenience and security lighting, and a place to set keys and other belongings that occupants and guests need when exiting the home. Many clients have concerns

Standard Clearance Spaces	
Room	**Clearance Space in Inches**
Living Room	
Around seating, such as chairs and sofas	18–30
Between sofa and coffee table	15–30
For minor traffic pattern area	18–48
For major traffic pattern area	48–72
Dining Room	
Between chair backs and wall or buffet (for diners remaining seated)	18–24
Between chair backs and wall or buffet (for self-service or host/hostess service)	30–36
Between table edge and wall or buffet (for self-service or host/hostess service)	18–30
For leg room in front of chair	48
Kitchen	
Between oven and opposite work space (opening door)	40 minimum
Between refrigerator and opposite work space (opening door)	36 minimum
Between dishwasher and opposite work space (opening door)	40 minimum
For circulation space	24
For work zone space between counter and nearby obstacle	48
Bath	
For activity zone in front of sink	18
For circulation space	24
Between front of sink and opposite wall or obstacle	40 minimum
Bedroom	
For activity zone in front of dresser to allow for work space and opening	42–48
For work zone space for making beds	26–40
For circulation space	24
Between twin beds	24

Figure 8.12 In the process of space planning, you must maintain adequate clearance space for proper traffic circulation.

Benefits of Universal Design—Entrances
Here are some examples of how universal design at entrances benefits people who do not have physical limitations.
Level and accessible entrances • are easier to enter with groceries and packages • pose fewer hazards when wet or icy • are easier to repair and maintain than steps • are easier to clear of snow, ice, and leaves • provide more convenience for moving furniture, appliances, baby strollers, and bicycles in and out
Covered entries • provide less damage to the door's finish from the weather • offer sheltered space for receiving a package delivery or waiting for a school bus
Full-length side window at entry door • increases the natural light in the foyer • allows everyone to see who is at the door before opening it

Figure 8.13 The use of universal design at entrances benefits all users.

about environmental particles and allergies and request a space to remove and store shoes near the door. Unless there is space at a secondary private or utility entrance, many families will also request some form of storage cubbies for children's school supplies and belongings. Because of visitors, entryways are one of the major places to implement universal design (Figure 8.13).

Living Room

Living rooms and family rooms can take on many different forms. The living habits of the occupants influence the functions these rooms serve. The purpose and needed furnishings determine room size and layout. In the past, homes would usually have a formal living room that served as a type of receiving parlor for guests. Today, either to conserve space or to have a more cohesive, open environment, families prefer a more comfortable and inviting living environment. They may use such spaces to entertain guests, to watch television, play games, and for other daily interactions (Figure 8.14). Clients often request a secondary family room or bonus to meet the needs of children, extensive audio/visual systems, or game systems.

Living rooms should be centrally located, near or convenient to an entrance. This does not necessarily have to be the primary entrance but should have a connection to the other public areas of the home. Whether a closed or open floor plan, because of the amount of time spent in these areas and the multifunctional purpose of the space, having a good line of site to the remaining public areas and the outside spaces helps to keep family members aware of children's activities and be able to communicate.

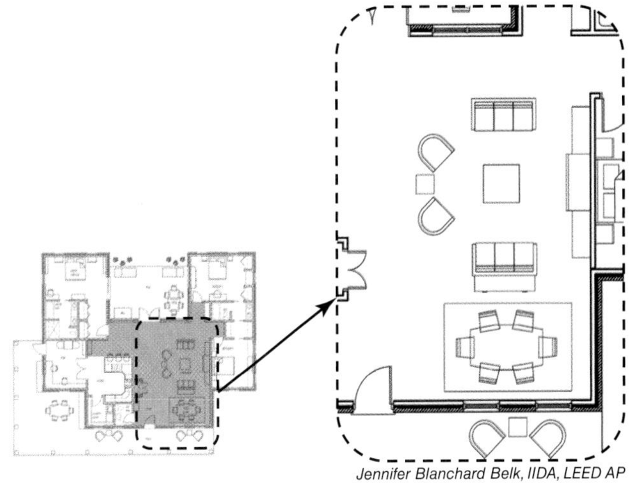

Jennifer Blanchard Belk, IIDA, LEED AP

Figure 8.14 Using the zoning plan from the previous chapter, explore the needs of each individual room. Here you see the public zone.

While there are endless configurations and furniture types, the scale and layout of the space should accommodate a sensible furniture arrangement. Even within a large space, comfortable and intimate seating clusters should be accomplished by separating into multiple conversation areas. They should accommodate four to six people with flexibility to bring in more. Personal discussions take place at about a four foot distance while other discussions take place within 10 feet, or else the occupants will be too far away from each other (Figure 8.15). Regardless of room scale, it is always best not to have traffic patterns passing through conversation areas.

Furniture needed in a living room varies but here are some typical items:

- Seating should be a mix of types. At least one piece should be a long sofa that could accommodate three people or one lying down. You can achieve balance by mirroring the large sofa or creating an "L" with other smaller single chairs. Movable pieces allow for a variety of types of entertaining.
- Low coffee tables are similar to the height of a sofa's seat because the occupant leans over to place a beverage.
- Side tables are similar to the height of the sofa arm to be a natural transition for placing a beverage to the side.
- Sofa tables are placed behind the sofa and are at the height of the rear surface.
- Lamps give occupants control of the space without leaving the configuration and are more appropriate for reading.
- Area rugs help anchor a seating arrangement within a great room.

KUPRYNENKO ANDRII/Shutterstock.com

Figure 8.15 Appropriate clearances make conversation comfortable and functional.

The television or fireplace typically becomes the focal point within the room with furniture oriented in their direction. With a fireplace, the main considerations are the overall size of the room and the level of heat produced versus occupant comfort. With a television, the size of the unit influences the layout. Larger TVs require a farther viewing distance. Manufacturers provide guidelines for the prescribed distance. An entertainment center should accommodate audio-visual equipment, game systems, digital media, and other items. Also consider secondary functions when determining storage needs such as additional dining, games, magazines, and books (Figure 8.16).

Family Room

Many alternative spaces, or spaces not always included in a home, are considered semiprivate. They may be accessible to guests but they are more physically separated and occupied by guests less frequently. A family room may be a bit more casual for less formal, more personal entertaining (Figure 8.17). The furniture is often flexible and geared to the multimedia experience. There may be a wet bar especially where basement spaces open onto backyard entertaining. As these spaces are very actively used by occupants, finishes and surfaces should be durable.

Bonus Spaces

Family rooms are often multipurpose and have varied needs related to the activities at hand. Ideally, these activities have their own dedicated rooms, possibly created from an unused bedroom or previously unfinished space.

- **Study or office.** If your lifestyle or that of a client requires a home office, you will need to

A Karen Armstrong  B Karen Armstrong

Figure 8.16 Fireplaces and televisions are the most common focal points in a living room. This large space is separated so that one area is oriented toward the well-appointed entertainment center (A) while a quiet reading area is created at the fireplace (B).

Low Chin Han/Shutterstock.com

Figure 8.17 This family room contains flexible furnishings great for movie watching or family game night.

include this space in the work area of the home (Figure 8.18A). When planning office space, the first step is to determine its purpose. Knowing how inhabitants will use the home office helps to determine its location.

Is it for occasional use, such as paying bills and organizing household documents? Will people use the home office frequently, perhaps by children doing homework or adults bringing work home from the office? Will the office receive daily use, perhaps by a household member working from home or telecommuting?

- **Library.** This may be a separate, formal room, or be in a family room, master suite, great room, or another location in the home. Appropriate and flexible storage is necessary for the types of books and other articles on display. It is preferable to have control of acoustical privacy and lighting.

A MR. INTERIOR/Shutterstock.com

B Paul Matthew Photography/Shutterstock.com

Figure 8.18 If a home is large enough, extra spaces can be used for a variety of activities including office space (A), a library, media room, music room, game room (B), or home gym.

- **Media and entertainment rooms.** These rooms may include space for a home theater, music making, dancing, games such as billiards or ping-pong, video games, and a snack bar (Figure 8.18B). Acoustical privacy and adjustable light control are required as well as comfortable seating.
- **Hobby and special-use areas.** Sewing, music, crafts, and other special interests are encouraged by well-planned spaces dedicated to the activity. There should be appropriate and flexible storage for supplies for order and access as well as adequate but adjustable lighting.
- **Home gym.** Special care should be taken if mingling home gym equipment in with other family room activities. This equipment can generate a great deal of noise, so it is best if these activities do not take place simultaneously.

  Gym areas should have adequate ventilation, floor space, and overall clearances for the full movement of the equipment and the occupant. Flooring should be water- and slip-resistant.
- **Game room.** These rooms are typically dictated by large gaming tables and the clearances around them for use. For instance, a pool table takes approximately four times the square footage for total maneuverability and use compared to the actual size of the table. Table tennis, darts, and standard seating at game tables for card and board games are also common.

Dining

Dining areas are sensibly located in relation to the kitchen. A butler's pantry may house china and serving pieces, act as a vestibule between the dining room and kitchen, and may also be a secondary prep location and bar. In the dining room, there should be space for the dining table, good lighting, and enough space to move around the table for seating and serving. The size and layout of the room are often determined by purpose and level of formality and the number of guests being served (Figure 8.19). There may be access to outdoor dining or other entertaining areas.

The furnishings needed and available are a major consideration in planning. These include the following:

- **Table and chairs.** A good rule of thumb for a rectangular table is one linear foot per person. For instance, if you would like to comfortably fit eight people, make sure the table is a least eight feet long with no awkward leg placement. This gives each person two feet of space. Chair arrangements could include four chairs on each side (leaving the ends for a high chair) or three on each side with two on the ends. Increase the spacing for larger chairs or chairs with arms.

  A table that is too wide or large and round may become difficult for reaching across to pass food. For accessibility, leave an open end to the table without a chair with plenty of navigation and approach space.
- **Table leaves and space for additional chairs.** Many formal dining tables have leaves (inserts) which allow them to expand for holidays and entertaining. Consider additional chairs beyond those for daily use with this plan.

A Rodenberg Photography/Shutterstock.com B Pixachi/Shutterstock.com

Figure 8.19 Formal dining spaces are separate from, but close to, the kitchen for serving food (A). Informal dining spaces are often physically and visually connected to the kitchen and may offer table seating or seating connected to a kitchen island or peninsula (B).

- **Buffet or sideboard.** A serving area created by these pieces can assist with extra platters from the table as well as facilitating self-service.
- **China cabinet.** This piece allows for storage of everyday and/or special occasion china, flatware and serving pieces, place mats and tablecloths. If it is strictly for display, large glass front storage pieces may have internal lighting.

Some people may forego a formal dining room in exchange for an office, study, music room, den, or guest space if the informal dining or breakfast room is plentiful enough. An informal dining space may also serve as a work or prep area, office, and homework area, although take specific care to select something durable for their uses.

Kitchen

In most homes, the kitchen receives more use than any other room (Figure 8.20). It is important to delve into the specific needs of your client in relation to the use of the kitchen. These are just a few types of questions that could be asked:

- How much socializing is expected within the space? What type of entertaining is done?

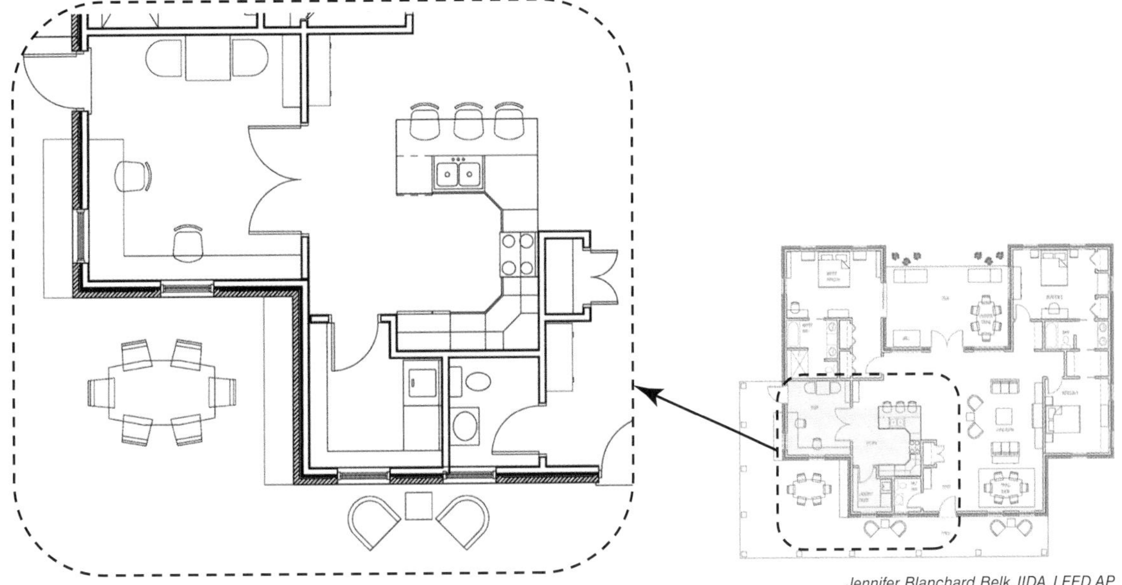

Jennifer Blanchard Belk, IIDA, LEED AP

Figure 8.20 This partial plan represents the work zone of a home.

- How often and what type of cooking takes place in the current kitchen?
- Is a visual connection to the other public spaces a requirement?
- Does the client want a kitchen island or peninsula for food prep and in-kitchen dining?
- Are there any special requests related to the appliances (for example, a side-by-side refrigerator/freezer, a refrigerator with a bottom freezer, or a separate freezer)?
- Is there a need for a prep or bar sink in addition to the main kitchen sink?
- Will there be a need for a walk-in pantry or a standard-depth pantry in the cabinetry?

A Day in the Life

When determining **adjacencies** (the nearness of two or more rooms or functions) within a kitchen, it is often helpful to think about the process that a cook or an item goes through over the course of a day. Follow the physical path of:

- **Groceries.** A bottle of spaghetti sauce is brought in with the groceries and put away in the pantry. When needed, it is retrieved and used at the cooktop. After use, it is rinsed in the sink and put in the primary or secondary recycling.
- **Utensils.** Prior to a meal, utensils are removed from the utensil drawer and placed on the table. After use, they are used to scrape plate scraps into the pet's bowl or the trash and then placed in the sink. They are then rinsed and placed in the dishwasher. After the wash, they are finally placed back in the utensil drawer.

What this method of thought demonstrates is the importance of logical placement and adjacencies within a kitchen. Inappropriate placement of items used on a daily basis can cause inefficiencies and chaos during the meal-making process. Use this method for considering **micro-adjacencies** (the nearness of two or more tasks or tools within a room). For example, a micro-adjacency for a kitchen would be to place wall cabinets for drinking glasses between the refrigerator and the dishwasher, making them easy to fill before a meal and easy to put away after washing. Elsewhere in the home, consider micro-adjacencies for "a day in the life" of a shirt or towel (considering the laundering process) or a child's backpack.

Tools of the Trade

The foundation of kitchen design involves knowledge about the furnishings, tools, and appliances that are available for use. Visiting different homes and touring home-improvement stores is a great way to gain exposure to the building blocks of kitchen design. The knowledge of typical cabinet sizes (upper cabinets are 12 inches deep, lower cabinets are 24 inches deep), and an understanding of how they are used for food and equipment storage, can make kitchen design a fun and fulfilling task. Arm yourself with a pad of grid paper and make sketches of unique and interesting kitchen designs you find.

The Primary Work Areas

The kitchen has the following three primary areas of activity or work centers:

- food preparation and storage center (associated with the refrigerator)
- cleanup center (associated with the sink and dishwasher)
- cooking and serving center (associated with the range and oven)

The imaginary line that connects these three centers forms a **work triangle**. Anyone preparing a meal in a kitchen will walk along the lines of the triangle several times before the meal is ready. In a well-designed kitchen, the total length of all sides of the work triangle does not exceed 26 feet (Figure 8.21). A work triangle that is too large can be inefficient. If the overall space is too large to accommodate an appropriate size work triangle, creation of a secondary work triangle for another worker can sub-section the room. Figure 8.22 summarizes the advantages and disadvantages of each.

In addition to emphasizing the work triangle concept, the *National Kitchen and Bath Association (NKBA)* uses 40 guidelines to describe what they deem appropriate design of kitchen environments in terms of safety and functionality. It is up to you to determine the unique needs of the occupants and plan the kitchen accordingly, but the following tips are here to help.

Clearances

In most cases, assume that at one time or another, there will be more than one person working in a kitchen at once doing multiple tasks simultaneously. Due to this factor, it is best to

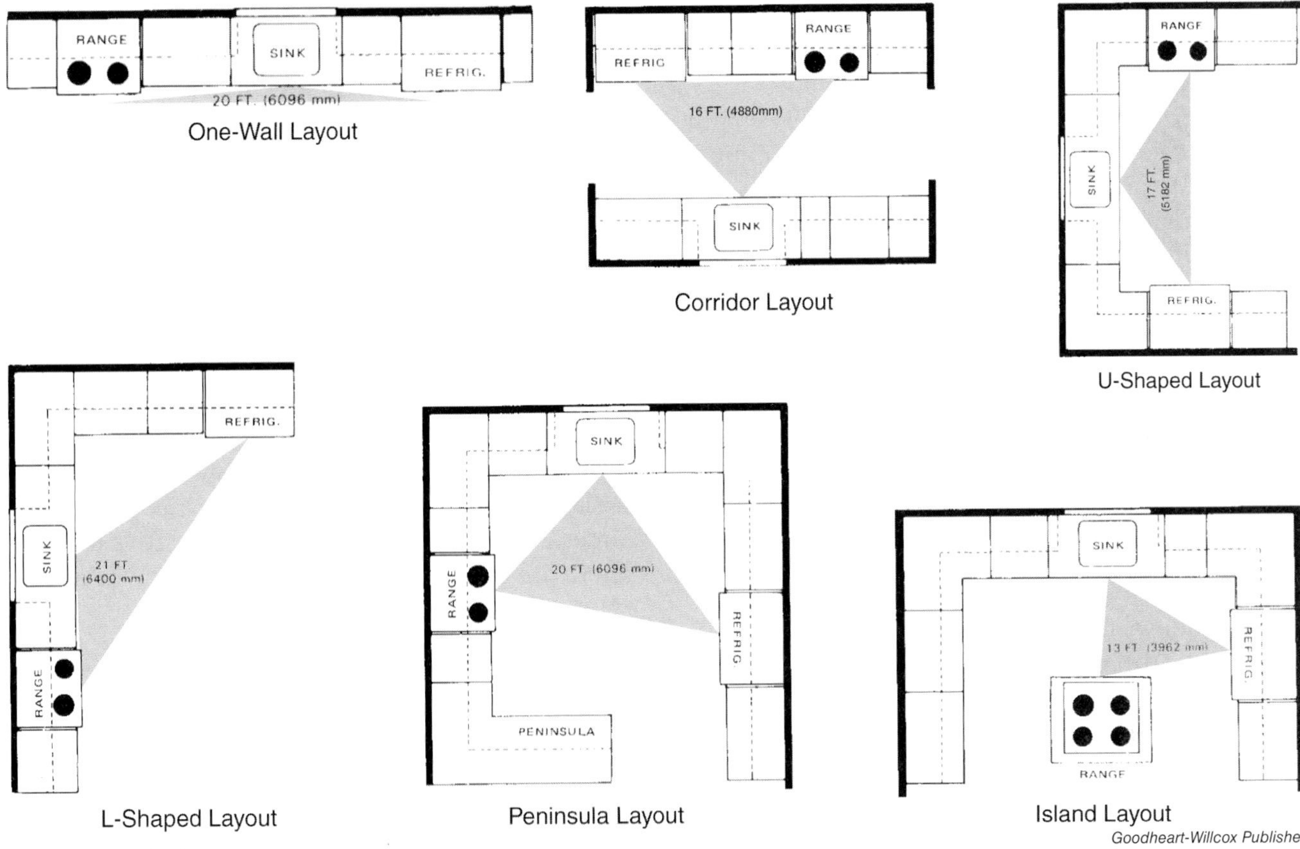

Figure 8.21 The distance around the work triangle in each of these kitchen layouts is less than 26 feet.

Advantages and Disadvantages of Kitchen Layouts		
Kitchen Layout	**Advantages**	**Disadvantages**
One-Wall	Uses space most efficiently; can be easily added into other rooms	Limits countertop work area
Corridor or Galley	Can use space efficiently	Any traffic entering the room will cross the work triangle
L-Shaped	Allows traffic flow into the kitchen without entering the work triangle; the work areas on the two adjoining walls use square footage efficiently	Offers less countertop work space than other kitchen designs
U-Shaped	Uses space efficiently in work areas; allows traffic into the kitchen without entering the work triangle	Depending on door location, traffic may enter the work triangle and interfere with task completion
Peninsula or G-Shaped	Adds a countertop to use as either extra work space or as eating space with chairs or stools	May hinder movement into and out of the kitchen work area
Island	Allows ample countertop area for activities that do not enter the work triangle	May require more square footage than other designs

Figure 8.22 Each type of kitchen layout has advantages and disadvantages.

increase the typical 42-inch clearance between rows of facing cabinets to 48 inches. Housing professionals and designers should also consider clearances at breakfast-bar seating and table seating as well as clearances at appliances when their doors are open. Although it may be impossible to prevent some circulation through a kitchen, never let a major traffic pattern cut through the work triangle.

Landing Space

On each side of each work center, there should be adequate **landing space**—the area on either side or across from an appliance or other functional kitchen piece that serves as a space to set cooking tools, hot food, or oversized items. For instance, you should have space on either side of the sink to place dishes to be washed and dishes that are drying. Space on either side of a cooktop allows for spoon rests, ingredients, and tools while also protecting neighboring surfaces from heat. On at least one side and across from the refrigerator, you should be able to place large platters. Supplemental appliances should also have their own landing areas.

Other Appliances and Their Placement

It is imperative not to forget the supplemental appliances. These might include the following:

- **Microwave oven.** More and more, the microwave plays a primary role in meal preparation. It may also serve as part of a secondary work triangle where another cook or assistant might work. Many microwaves are located directly over the cooktop under a short wall cabinet. This is not optimum because it conflicts with a primary work center. Another option is placing the microwave on a counter, however, this wastes valuable counter space. The most preferable options are in a wall cabinet away from the cooktop, in a tall cabinet grouped with the primary or secondary oven, or just under the countertop in a base cabinet.
- **Dishwasher.** When open, a person should be able to stand to one side of the dishwasher. He or she should be able to load the dishwasher while standing at the sink and have a surface on which to place the clean dishes or the ability to put them immediately in the appropriate cabinet.
- **Additional oven.** Many homes have a supplemental or specialty oven outside of the main work triangle. This can be helpful for two-cook families.
- **Countertop appliances.** Most homes regardless of size have some counter space occupied by small appliances. These might include a coffeemaker, toaster, toaster oven, food processor, and many others.

Larger homes may also include special beverage storage, a built-in ice maker, and warming drawers. Also to be accounted is the storage and surface needed for large countertop and specialty appliances such as an indoor grill.

Cooking Surface Safety

Safety is also a great concern of the NKBA. A range hood provides exhaust ventilation to the cooktop. It can be in the form of an inconspicuous under-cabinet vent or as a large decorative hood. There are also cooktops with built-in downdraft exhaust systems when using an overhead is undesirable or impossible. Another safety recommendation from NKBA is to avoid operable windows or window coverings near a cooking surface.

Counter and Storage Space

The larger the kitchen, the more storage and counter space it needs. The assumption is that a larger kitchen is there to accommodate a larger family and more entertaining and, therefore, there would be a need for more dishes, food storage, prep space, etc. Investigate special cabinetry features such as divided flatware drawers, spice racks, plate slots, pull-out drawers, and deep drawers in base cabinets for cookware (Figure 8.23). Also consider the adjacency of these pieces to the appliances they serve, such as cookie sheet storage near the oven. There are a great variety of choices when it comes to sizes and stacking options of upper cabinets to tailor the storage to the client's needs and stature.

Corner and Tall Storage

When considering kitchen shapes, note that corner cabinets can be either an opportunity or an inefficient use of space. These cabinets are deep and can be difficult to access. For this reason, it is important to consider cabinet additions such as a rotating *lazy Susan* or hinged sliding shelves in order to access items in the back of the cabinet. Peninsula cabinets also allow access from the back side. Tall, full-depth cabinets are also an efficient use of space if interior organization is accomplished. Use tall cabinets sparingly and on the outside of the work triangle so as not to interrupt valuable counter surfaces.

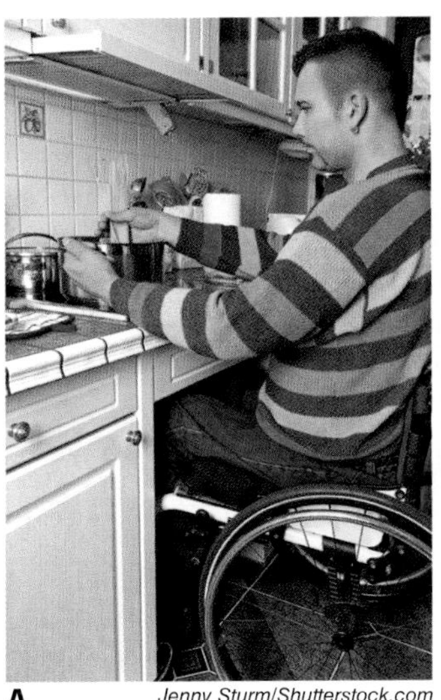
A Jenny Sturm/Shutterstock.com

B OmiStudio/Shutterstock.com

C adpePhoto/Shutterstock.com

Figure 8.23 Instead of installing storage cabinets under this sink and cooktop, the space was left open to accommodate a wheelchair (A). Various in-cabinet organizational devices, such as pull-out shelves and drawers, can accommodate a wide variety of kitchen storage and help make the space accessible (B and C).

Lighting

Lighting is an essential component in kitchen design. A well thought out lighting plan can increase the safety at each task area of the kitchen, can add to the aesthetic qualities, and can increase psychological comfort. You will learn more about lighting later in the text.

Waste and Recycling

At least one trash receptacle is necessary in a kitchen. More than one, however, is helpful if there are multiple work triangles or a **butler's pantry**—a service room between the kitchen and dining room. Recycling may be a small container in the kitchen with a larger sorting container in the garage or mudroom.

Accessibility and Universal Design in Kitchens

Features in kitchens can be designed to meet the requirement of accessibility and universal design. See Figure 8.24 for information on accessibility and universal design for kitchens.

Breakfast Room

An informal dining space, a breakfast room or nook may also serve as work or prep area, office, or homework space. This is often the location for everyday dining and breakfast and may have a view of a television. In contrast, a more serene and casual breakfast area could be a soft seating area in a quiet part of the home such as an area of the master bedroom or living room.

Breakfast areas are typically not much larger than the table and chairs with maneuvering space since there are usually not serving and storage pieces due to adjacency to the kitchen. Adjacent to the kitchen for serving and monitoring food prep, living spaces, outdoors, and possibly the garage, the breakfast area can be a very multipurpose space. Seating can be a combination of built-in booth, multi-seat bench, and individual chairs. If a home lacks the appropriate square footage, an eating counter/bar in the kitchen with stools can replace a breakfast room.

In order to bring families closer together and avoid the fragmentation that can come from a home with too many separate rooms, including a *great room* has become increasingly popular. A great room is one that serves several functions such as a dining room, living room, and family room, combining all the public areas of the home together in one space.

Laundry and Utility Room

No longer strictly a basement space, the laundry room is now a major component of the work zone of a home. It is often in close proximity to the kitchen to allow for work efficiencies or to serve as a mudroom entrance. Newer trends place the laundry within the private zones, where dirty clothes are stored and where they return to

Benefits of Universal Design—Kitchens
Here are some examples of how universal design benefits people who do not have physical limitations in kitchens.
Knee space under sink and cooktop • provides a space to store a serving cart or recycling bins • allows people to work while sitting on a stool
Lever-type water controls • permit easier adjustment of water temperature and volume • can be operated with use of a single hand or elbow • have fewer parts than other types of controls, so are less costly to repair • are easier to keep clean because of few crevices
Variable-height work surfaces • make it easier to designate counter space for different functions • allow family members of all heights to help with meal preparation
Contrasting borders on countertops • makes it easier to repair damaged edges without repairing the entire countertop • reduces the likelihood of spills because the ends of counters are easier to see
Pull-out shelves, trays, and drawers in cabinets • make it possible to reach items stored in the back without stretching • permit easier maneuvering of large items in and out of the cabinet
Pantry cabinet with full-length shelves • provides storage that can be reached from all heights • offers the maximum storage per square foot of floor space
Appliances with front touch controls • make use of appliances easier versus knobs that require grasping and turning

Figure 8.24 Pull-out storage is convenient for everyone, especially people with disabilities.

once clean. This may be in a bathroom or off the hallway. Knowing the location, amenities, and adjacencies a client prefers is essential.

The larger the home, the more amenities the laundry room can provide (Figure 8.25). While all facilities should have a washer and dryer, more elaborate laundry spaces may have the following items:

- laundry sink for stain removal and hand-washing
- folding and ironing area
- an area for hanging clothes
- storage for cleaning and pet supplies
- drop zone for school books, coats, and shoes
- craft area and supply storage

Iriana Shiyan/Shutterstock.com

Figure 8.25 A multipurpose laundry room should provide adequate storage for cleaning products, pet supplies, craft materials, and much more.

Private Zones

When beginning discussions regarding bedrooms and bathrooms, it is important to have the client elaborate on the functions they believe these spaces serve in addition to sleeping and bathing (Figure 8.26). Their answers will greatly change the direction of the design.

If functionality is a client desire, design requests might center on creating order. For instance, a design should provide enough storage space and separate sinks so toiletries do not co-mingle. If having a retreat is a desire, the environment should meet client needs to relax, meditate, read, and have uninterrupted sleep. A soaking tub or steam shower may be on the request list. Some clients will ask for privacy, acoustic control, and possibly secondary living areas such as a terrace or reading nook.

A Image Courtesy of Chief Architect Software

B Rodenberg Photography/Shutterstock.com

C Pavel L Photo and Video/Shutterstock.com

Figure 8.26 The design and furnishings of a bedroom are dictated by the purpose. Special attention can be paid to functionality and storage (A), luxury and peace (B), or self-expression (C).

If having their own space is a desire, client requests might focus on providing a place for personal expression and individuality away from the common areas of the home. These aesthetic needs may deal more with identity and less with beauty. Privacy, security, and control will be high on the list of priorities. These conversations will be very different when discussing guest bedrooms, additional bathrooms, and children's spaces.

Furniture choices and room function generally dictate bedroom size. Local and national codes set minimum room sizes but knowing if a client requires a queen- or king-size bed will affect the plans. Bedrooms can be grouped together as the quiet zone of the home or segmented by occupant—master, guest, and children (Figure 8.27).

Providing multiple furniture arrangement options can allow families to grow and change within the same environment. This could include making sure there is more than one wall in each room that could accommodate the head of a bed (due to window and door placement). A bedroom typically includes

- bed(s) with size depending on client need and preference
- side tables with reading lamps and electrical outlets
- clothing storage by way of low or high dresser or armoire, which can also serve as a surface for a television and other audio-visual equipment
- hanging storage by way of closet (required; typically two feet deep)
- at least one operable window as a means of egress (required) with additional windows for ventilation and light

Master Bedroom

A master bedroom has an attached bathroom and typically a walk-in closet or dressing area. It is generally more luxurious than the other private areas. The master bedroom may contain personal reading and conversation areas,

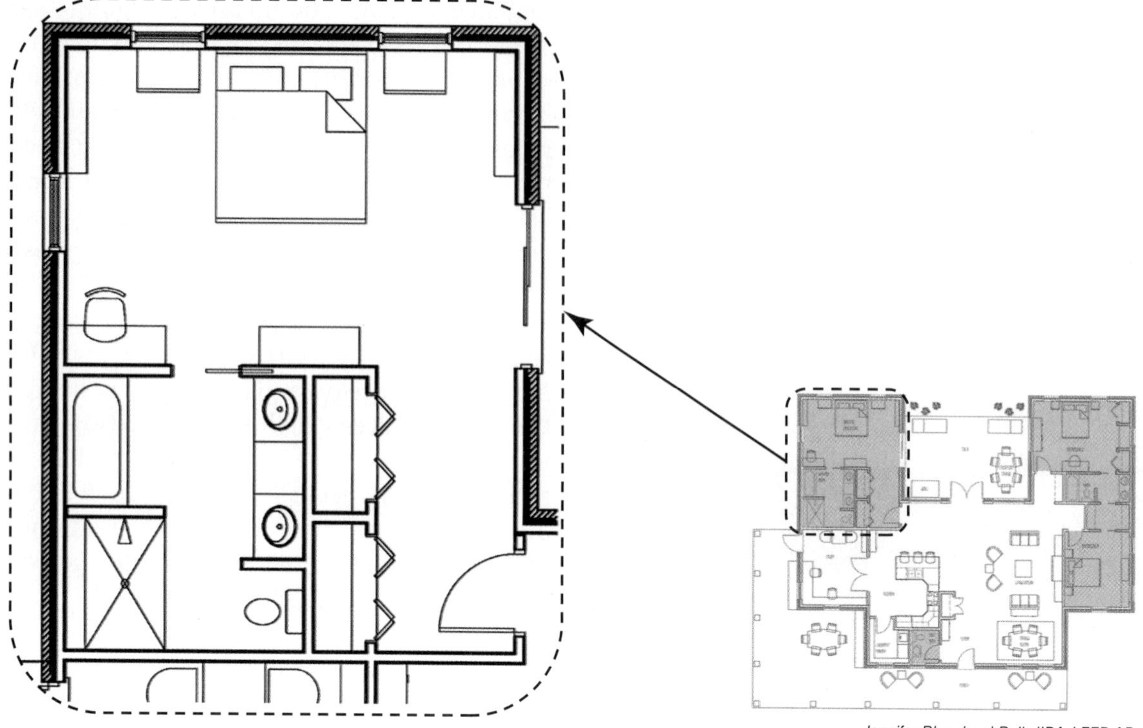
Jennifer Blanchard Belk, IIDA, LEED AP

Figure 8.27 A master suite works well as a secluded wing of a home.

entertainment and exercise equipment, and a spa (Figure 8.28). Closet storage should fit the needs of the occupants. Closet shelves and rods should be at appropriate heights and depths for individual belongings. A dressing area may be in the bedroom, inside the master closet, or in the bathroom. Regardless of location, it should include an appropriate counter, drawer and hanging storage, a mirror and lighting, and a chair.

EPSTOCK/Shutterstock.com

Figure 8.28 A common client request for a master suite is access to outdoor living and a private lounge space.

It is desirable to lay out master bedrooms as a suite to maintain maximum privacy but also to have a small foyer into the suite. This prevents a line of sight into the room from public areas. A wall of closets or a bookcase can act as a sound barrier between the bedrooms and louder spaces.

Other Bedrooms

Children's spaces should accommodate not only sleeping, dressing, and storage but also playing, studying, and personal entertainment (Figure 8.29). Children have a need for independence and personal space. Having a room that meets their needs and that they had a part in designing is an integral part of that. Storage should evolve as they grow, changing from toys in the early years to displays, books, and media in their teens (Figure 8.30). Accommodating friends or relatives via bunk or trundle beds can help conserve space.

Guest bedrooms may serve a secondary purpose as a home office or craft space. Most guest rooms have one queen-size bed or two twin beds. Alternative sleeping arrangements are also an option, such as using a convertible sofa, futon, or *Murphy bed*—a bed that folds into a closet or wall. The space must have a closet and an operable window to count as a bedroom. The closet should hold additional linens. In addition to standard bedroom accessories, guest rooms also benefit from having a ceiling fan to regulate temperature, window coverings for light

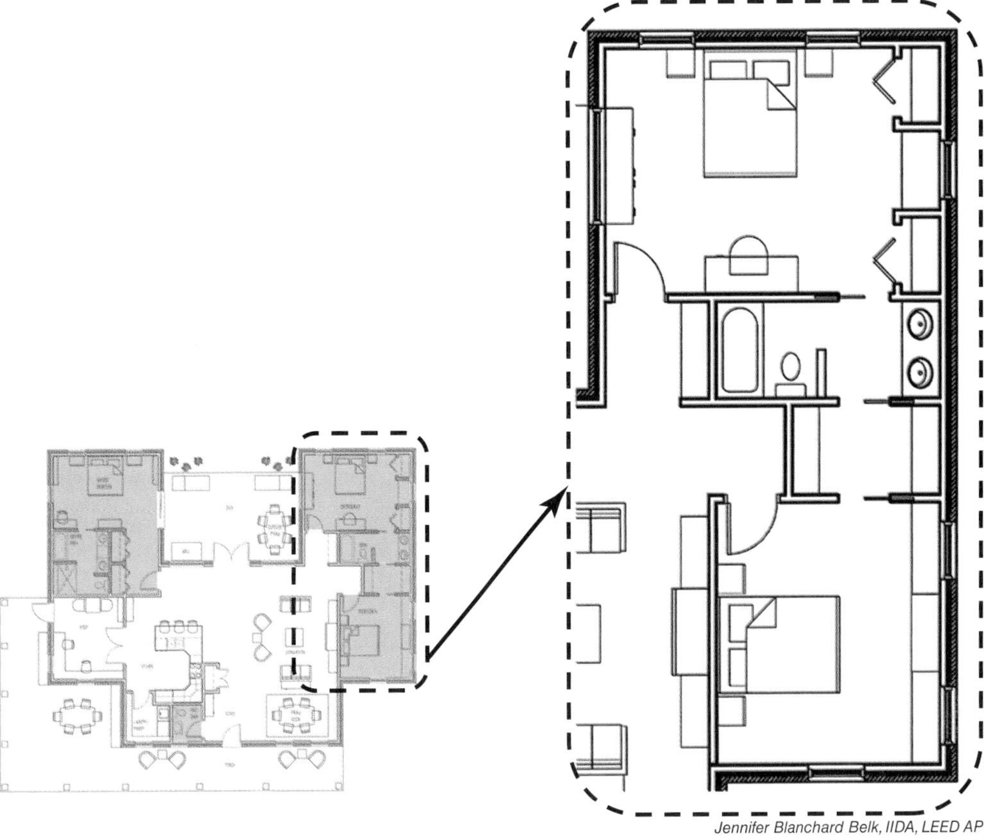

Jennifer Blanchard Belk, IIDA, LEED AP

Figure 8.29 Children's and guest spaces can share amenities such as bathrooms.

Iriana Shiyan/Shutterstock.com

Pavel L Photo and Video/Shutterstock.com

Figure 8.30 Children's rooms should allow for age-appropriate storage and layout as children grow.

control, and a small work or dressing area. Drawer storage is not as important as space for open luggage and luggage storage (Figure 8.31).

Master Bath and Other Bathrooms

Bathrooms are located throughout the house and should provide the required fixtures, a functional layout, and adequate storage. While master bathrooms can be totally private, full and half baths for guests should be accessible from the living areas of the home. A bathroom to accommodate multiple users should provide privacy to more than one user simultaneously. Enclosing the shower and toilet areas meets this need.

Fixtures within a full bathroom (minimum size of 5 feet by 8 feet) include the toilet, sink, and shower/tub combination. A half bath (minimum size of 3 feet by 7 feet) only contains a sink and

Thomas Barrat/Shutterstock.com

Figure 8.31 This bench in the guest room serves as a seating area, but also provides a functional surface for luggage.

toilet (Figure 8.32). The sink could be wall-hung, providing accessibility. Other options include a pedestal sink providing a space-saving appearance or countertop with cabinet for additional storage.

There are also many varieties of prefabricated and custom baths and shower enclosures. Accessories in a bath, depending on size, include hampers, bath mats, door hooks, towel bars, shelf and cabinet storage, mirrors, and counter space. Larger homes and master baths may include a garden tub, multiple sinks, heated towel rack, and a separate shower (Figure 8.33).

Accessibility and Universal Design in Bathrooms

Features in bathrooms can be designed to meet the requirement of accessibility and universal design. See Figure 8.34 for accessibility and Figure 8.35 for universal design in bathrooms.

Other Spaces

Although not discussed individually, it is important to allocate space for essential storage and common areas that might not be associated with a specific room or activity.

Photographee.eu/Shutterstock.com

Figure 8.32 A shallow lavatory is a great solution for a limited space half bath.

Karen Armstrong

Figure 8.33 Luxury can also be functional. This master bath has dual sinks and bathing options to accommodate two users as well as elevated counters and cabinets due to the occupants' tall stature.

Accessibility for Bathrooms
Accessible bathrooms include • sinks and toilets mounted at heights for easy access • showers or bathtubs with doors for easy access • grab bars conveniently located at toilets and bathtubs or showers • lever handles, rather than knobs, for easy grasp and use

Figure 8.34 These features increase accessibility for users who have physical limitations.

Garage or Carport

Depending on climate and location, a home may or may not have a garage or carport. If it does, the size must accommodate vehicles and other furnishings to be functional. For a single car, a good rule of thumb is 15 feet by 20 feet. For a double garage, 22 feet by 22 feet is practical. It is important to take hobbies and other functions into account because workbenches, bicycles, recycling areas, and other storage can take a lot of space. The carport or garage may be attached to the house or separate with an optional breezeway.

Benefits of Universal Design—Bathrooms
Here are some examples of how universal design benefits people who do not have physical limitations in bathrooms.
Adjustable-height showerhead • can be adjusted to suit the height of different users • makes it possible to avoid wetting a bandage, cast, hairdo, or anything else that should remain dry • can be used for massaging one's back, rinsing hair, and washing the dog
Grab bars in tub or shower • can double as a towel bar when hung horizontally • make it easier and safer to enter and exit a tub or shower
Over-sink mirror extending down to backsplash • allows children and seated adults to have a view of the mirror while using the sink • reduces water damage to the wall behind the sink • makes it easier to clean behind the faucet • makes the room seem more spacious

Figure 8.35 People without disabilities can enjoy the benefits of universal design in bathrooms.

Review & Assessment

1. What determines the minimum size of rooms in a home?
2. Give an example of clearance space requirements for two areas of the home.
3. What features are most important for the main entry of a home?
4. Why is it important to pay attention to distance between seating pieces in a living room?
5. What is a good rule of thumb for determining needed dining table length?
6. Name at least three questions to ask a housing client about use of the kitchen space.
7. Contrast adjacencies and micro-adjacencies.
8. What are the six basic kitchen designs and maximum length for the work triangle? Give an advantage and disadvantage of each.
9. Contrast the basic design needs for the master bedroom with bedrooms for children.

Chapter 8 Assessment

Summary

- For the design of a home, it is essential to meet a client's qualitative, quantitative, and psychological needs.
- Anticipating how client needs will change can direct design decisions and allows a client to appreciate and utilize the home for years to come.
- Accessibility, adaptability, and universal design (UD) play important roles in housing design.
- Accessibility to the exterior and interior space of a house sometimes requires modifications to meet the needs of a household member who has physical limitations, such as those who have mobility, vision, and hearing disabilities.
- If a house is convenient, safe, and accessible for people with physical disabilities, it will meet the needs of any occupant.
- Universal design features in housing help make housing safer as well as easier and more convenient to use for all people.
- Evaluating the characteristics of the home through questions can inform housing professionals and designers about space planning possibilities.
- Room circulation and proportion can affect the efficiency and definition of spaces.
- When space planning, give specific considerations to the size and planning of individual spaces.
- Public (*entries and living areas*), work (*kitchen and laundry areas*), and private areas (*bedrooms and bathrooms*) of the home have typical space needs; however, it is important for housing and design professionals to be mindful about individual needs and wants of current and future occupants.

Terms in Action

1. **Term communication** Divide into two teams. Play charades to act out the meaning of each of the *Content* and *Academic Terms* at the beginning of the chapter. Each team member will draw a slip of paper with a term prepared by your instructor. As team members identify the terms, the team gets a point. The team that acts out and identifies the most terms within 15 minutes wins the game.

Think Critically

2. **Draw conclusions** Housing should be adaptable to meet the needs of changes in life circumstances and the family life cycle. Imagine having a home with flexible features such as movable walls and adjustable kitchen countertops. Draw conclusions about why you think this *is* or *is not* a good idea. Discuss your conclusions in class.
3. **Analyze evidence** Analyze the benefits of universal design in terms of accessibility and adaptability for each of the following areas of a home: entrance, kitchen, general living areas, bathrooms, and bedrooms. Write an essay about your analysis indicating why you think universal design benefits all people.
4. **Analyze criteria** Suppose you have been asked to plan a dining room that seats 10 people. The client owns two pieces of serving furniture that are two feet deep. Based on what you know about furniture clearances and determining table length, what size room (length and width) will you need to accommodate the client? Analyze the criteria based on text information and write a summary of your analysis.
5. **Make inferences** Of the psychological needs that a master bedroom can provide, infer which is most important to you. Can you determine why? What have you done in your current living space to meet that need? Transfer this personal knowledge to make inferences about how you might query a client about psychological needs to inform space planning needs for the room. What strategic questions would you ask a client? Write a list. Discuss your questions with the class.

Core Skills

6. **Math practice** Measure a large room in your home or a friend's home. Draw it out on grid paper and determine the square footage. Take the same amount of square footage and re-proportion the room to make it squarer, an extremely elongated rectangle, etc. Draw in the same existing furniture to determine which shape room is the best layout. Then create a digital poster of your drawings and summarize your conclusions about the best layout. Upload your poster to the class web page for review.

Chapter 8 Assessment

7. **Reading and speaking** Use online resources to locate either an apartment or home that has photos of features specifically designed for people who need a walker or wheelchair for mobility. How does the home apply principles of space utilization, zoning, and traffic patterns in the design? What other features would make the housing more usable to these occupants? Create a digital presentation using a school-approved application to show and describe these features to the class.
8. **Research and writing** Visit the kitchen department of a local home improvement center or hardware store. Select one of the display kitchens that has product literature available. Investigate any storage accessories or special features in the display and find examples of these pieces in your literature. Write a summary of your findings to share with the class and include the product literature.
9. **Research and speaking** Use Internet or print resources to research the link between universal design (UD) and the *Americans with Disabilities Act (ADA)*. What role does universal design play in developing barrier-free environments for people with limitations and disabilities? How does the ADA law link to universal design? Present your findings to the class in an oral report.
10. **Floor plan practice** Locate a floor plan that you like on the Internet and print a copy. Use the floor plan and the principles of space planning and traffic patterns to do each of the following:
    A. Shade the quiet, social, and work areas with different-colored pencils or markers. Determine if the areas are divided appropriately and justify your decision.
    B. Trace the traffic patterns, and check them with the guidelines and clearances listed in this chapter. Explain if they are safe and convenient.
    C. Identify which storage is for individual use and which is for common use.
11. **Math practice** Locate a copy of a floor plan online and print it. Highlight the walls or architectural features that would be very expensive or impossible to move. Estimate the percentage of the home which you could easily and less expensively renovate. How would these factors impact space planning?
12. **CTE career readiness practice** Imagine you are a housing professional with a client who is considering a home that has 2,400 square feet. Use the statistical information in *Figures 8.10* and *8.11* to estimate about how large the individual spaces should be within. Write a summary of your estimations.

Design Practice

13. **Space planning practice** Suppose you have a new client whose favorite hobby is sewing and making other crafts. Your client wants to convert an 8'-0" × 10'-0" utility room with one entry door, one closet door, and two windows into a room for sewing and crafts. List the furnishings, equipment, and accessories that might be needed to create a room especially for this purpose. Note sizes of the pieces and the clearances needed. Sketch your ideas for how this sewing and craft room might accommodate the necessary furnishings and equipment. Present and discuss your sketches to the client (your instructor) and refine until you and the client are satisfied with the results.
14. **Space plan analysis** Consider yourself at age five versus the age you are now. On grid paper, draw a basic shaped room that is approximately 195 square feet (12'-0" × 15'-0"). Duplicate that plan. Draw in the needed furnishings for the five-year-old you and the current you on the two separate plans and label each piece. How did your needs change? Are there any furniture pieces or accessories that would work well in both scenarios? Write a summary of your analysis.
15. **Portfolio** Your portfolio should showcase your academic accomplishments and your technical skills for this class. Write a paper describing the technical skills you are learning (space planning, computer skills, etc.) and revise it as you learn new skills. Save this paper along with your work for items 7 through 12 in your portfolio. If using an electronic portfolio, scan all hard copy documents.

Chapter 9

Understanding Construction Basics

Content Terms

foundation
footing
concrete
foundation wall
moisture barrier
pressure preservative treated (PT)
joist
girder
subflooring
plywood sheet
stud
bearing wall
nonbearing wall
header
rafter
siding
masonry
veneer wall
shingle
flashing
gypsum wallboard
paneling
synthetic
plaster
acoustical

Academic Terms

penetrates
veneers
noncombustible
rigid
porous
clad
substrate

Learning Outcomes

After studying this chapter, you will be able to

- summarize house construction including the parts of the foundation and frame of a house.
- compare the advantages and disadvantages of different types of materials used for exterior and interior construction.
- distinguish between basic types of windows and different types of doors used in houses.
- summarize how technology can assist the house-construction process.

Reading with Purpose

As you read this chapter, take notes in presentation software. Make one slide for each of the main headings. List three to four main points on each slide. Use your finished presentation to study for tests.

G-WLEARNING.COM

While studying, look for the access icon  **to:**

- **Practice** the *Content* and *Academic Terms* with e-flash cards, matching activities, and vocabulary games.
- **Reinforce** what you learn by completing the *Review & Assessment* questions and e-mailing them to your instructor.

www.g-wlearning.com/housing/

Anton Foltin/Shutterstock.com

When buying a pre-owned house or building a new one, it is helpful to understand basic house construction. Familiarity with housing construction and determining the availability of construction materials in your area help you make good decisions when selecting a place to live. Poor decisions, however, can result in poor investments and/or expensive repair costs.

The Foundation and Frame

The foundation and frame are the basic structure of the house. Understanding how they are constructed is the first step in making an informed housing decision. When buying a pre-owned house, you may be able to inspect the foundation and frame for defects and needed repairs. When building a house, you will be able to observe the construction and make sure it is done correctly.

The Foundation

The **foundation** is the underlying base of the house. There are three types of foundation construction. Houses may be constructed with a basement, a crawl space with a pier foundation, or a slab-on-grade foundation. The foundation consists of foundation walls and the footing. The **footing** is the very bottom of the foundation (Figure 9.1). Footings are usually made from **concrete**, which is a strong, durable, hard building material consisting of cement, sand, and gravel with water.

For added strength, a system of horizontal bars—or rebar—reinforces the footings. The concrete and steel footings should be strong enough to support the rest of the foundation and the house it will support. The footings need to be the correct width and thickness to support the weight of the foundation and house.

Foundation walls support the load of the house between the footing and the floor. They form an enclosure for basements or crawl spaces. Concrete or concrete block are the most common foundation-wall materials. Some *permanent wood foundations (PWF)* utilize pressure-treated lumber. The thickness of the foundation wall varies from 6 to 10 inches with 8 inches being the most common thickness. Local building codes normally control wall thickness and reinforcement requirements.

Footings are placed on undisturbed, compacted soil below the frost line. The *frost line* is the depth to which frost ***penetrates*** (enters or goes through) soil in the area. If the footing is above the frost line, the soil under it freezes and expands. This expansion causes the foundation to crack until the soil is compact again. It also causes cracks to appear in the foundation wall. In extreme cases, cracks will appear on inside walls. This cracking and settling will continue for years. During this time, the cracks will

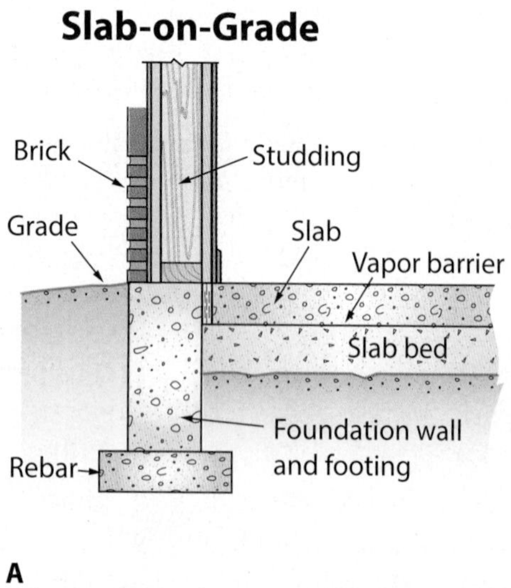

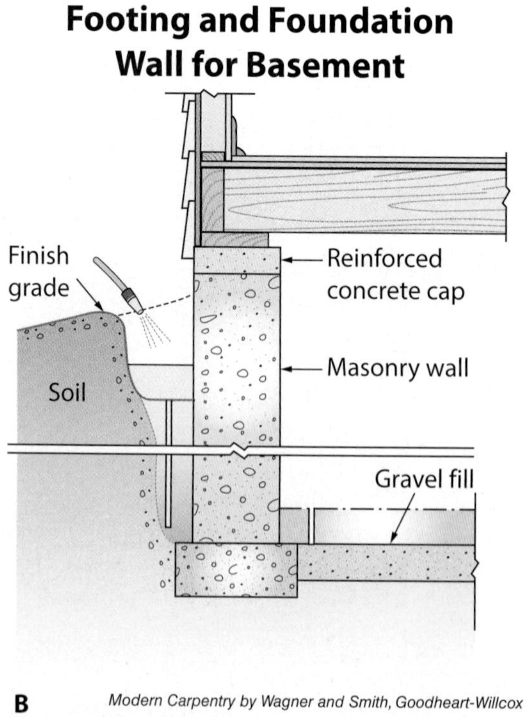

Modern Carpentry by Wagner and Smith, Goodheart-Willcox

Figure 9.1 The footing is a wide concrete base that supports the foundation and the rest of the house. The footings for both the slab-on-grade (A) and basement (B) must be below the frost line to prevent damage to the foundation.

continue to expand and lengthen. The local building code may specify how deep the foundation must be according to soil conditions and the depth to which the ground freezes.

Most foundations settle evenly as the house adjusts to the ground. The foundation and walls may show hairline cracks, which are cracks less than ⅛-inch wide. Cracks greater than ⅛ inch are excessive. The builder is required to surface-patch these cracks.

Stress cracks differ from hairline cracks and are signs of possible structural problems. They are usually wider at one end than the other. Stress cracks can occur when the footing settles more at one point and the foundation pulls apart from underneath. They can also indicate that one side of the house is settling more than the other.

Stress-crack repair depends on the extent of the damage and usually requires leveling the house and reinforcing the footing. This is a costly procedure. Unless the purchase price of the house is low enough to cover the cost of this problem, the potential buyer should not purchase a house with this problem.

When looking at a pre-owned house, make sure the foundation walls are straight and square at the corners. They should not have major stress cracks.

imging/Shutterstock.com

Figure 9.2 This Mediterranean ranch-style house is built on a slab-on-grade foundation.

A house with a *slab-on-grade* foundation has no basement or crawl space (Figure 9.2). This type of construction is particularly useful when building ranch-style homes in areas in which the ground does not freeze. The earth beneath the slab must be very hard and compact. Before pouring the slab, the contractor first grades or levels the ground at the site. Usually, some fill material is brought in to raise the foundation above the existing grade. The contractor then spreads the filler, which is usually gravel or stone. This allows any groundwater to

STEM Science & Technology Designing for Disaster: Earthquakes

An earthquake is a sudden and sometimes violent shaking of the earth's crust or outer layer. The crust consists of large jigsaw-like pieces called *tectonic plates*. These plates float on a layer of rock melted by the high temperatures and pressure deep inside the earth. The plates are in constant motion, usually moving only a few centimeters a year. Volcanic action or a sudden release of energy along points of stress between and within the plates, however, can cause intense shaking or earthquakes.

The number of earthquakes in the United States between 2000 and 2012 ranged from 2,342 to 8,496 according to the U.S. Geological Survey (USGS). The USGS is the federal agency that records and reports U.S. earthquake activity. Fortunately, most earthquakes are mild and cause little or no damage. They can, however, be extremely destructive and lethal. In 2008 for example, an earthquake in Sichuan, China, caused more than 5 million buildings to collapse and killed an estimated 87,587 people. In 2010, another earthquake killed multitudes of people in Haiti. Many lost their lives in their homes, schools, and other buildings from falling debris. The goal for design and construction in earthquake-prone areas is to minimize damage to homes and other structures and to prevent deaths. Designers and builders use such resources as the following:

- **International Residential Code (IRC).** In the United States, this is the principal building code for residential construction. It includes recommendations by the National Earthquake Hazards Reduction Program (NEHRP).
- ***Homebuilders' Guide to Earthquake-Resistant Design and Construction.*** This document, published by the Federal Emergency Management Agency (FEMA), offers construction guidance and provides supplemental information to the IRC. This guide also presents some "above code recommendations" and low-cost construction measures to increase building performance and functionality during and after an earthquake.

For more information about the theory of plate tectonics and earthquakes, go to the U.S. Geological Survey's website. Use the key words *plate tectonics* and *earthquakes* to learn more.

dissolve without causing damage to the slab. A **moisture barrier**, or a sheet of 6- to 10-millimeter polyethylene (pahl-ee-EH-thuh-leen)—a type of plastic—is then spread across the filler. Parts of the heating and plumbing systems are actually put in place before pouring the slab. Concrete is poured over the moisture barrier, forming a slab that is about 4 inches thick. The slab has a turned-down footing that totals approximately 16 inches in depth. Rebar reinforcements strengthen the concrete slab and discourage cracking.

The Frame

The frame of the house is the skeleton around which the builder constructs the rest of the house. It consists of joists, studs, and rafters fastened together to support the house and its contents (Figure 9.3). When assembled and covered with sheet materials, the frame forms floors, walls, and roof surfaces.

Floor Frame

After completing the foundation walls, construction of the floor frame occurs. First, the builder places a *sill* (bottom layer) sealer and sometimes a termite shield on top of the foundation walls. Next, the installation of the first piece of lumber, or *sill plate*, occurs. When the sill plate comes in contact with hard building material combined with mortar, it must consist of pressure preservative treated (PT) lumber. The process for creating **pressure preservative treated (PT)** lumber forces chemical preservatives into the cellular structure of the wood under pressure. This process preserves the wood from mold, mildew, termites, and other insects.

David Lee/Shutterstock.com

Figure 9.3 The framing members of the house provide the skeletal structure.

The sill plates support the outside walls of the house. *Anchor bolts* secure the sill plate to the foundation walls. Local building codes will determine the spacing between the anchor bolts to meet uplift requirements to withstand tornadoes and hurricanes. Anchor bolts are set into the concrete of the foundation walls before the concrete hardens.

If the foundation wall consists of concrete block, the top two cores (or layers) of the blocks are first filled with *mortar*—a mixture of sand, cement, and water. Then the builder embeds anchor bolts into the mortar to bolt down the sill plate.

The floor frame is built on top of the sill plate or on top of wall frames when a second or third floor is desired. It consists of joists, girders, and subflooring. **Joists** are lightweight horizontal support members. Header joists and rim joists form the perimeter of the floor framing. The ends of the floor joists are nailed to the header joists at 16- to 24-inch intervals. In some homes, a wood or steel girder supports the joists. A **girder** is a large horizontal member in the floor that takes the load of joists. It supports the load of the floor joists and the weight of the floor or roof above it. Girders may be solid lumber, built-up lumber (often three wooden planks fastened together with nails or screws), engineered wood (layers of wood secured with strong adhesives), or steel beams.

Subflooring covers the floor-framing members. **Subflooring** consists of a covering of plywood or oriented strand board (OSB) sheets directly glued and nailed to the floor joists. **Plywood sheets** are layers of thin wood ***veneers*** (thin layers of material) that have been glued and pressed together. *Oriented strand board (OSB)* is made by layering wood chips and fiber in a crosshatch pattern and gluing them together to form a sheet. The better the construction of the floor frame, the less likely it is to develop problems. Squeaky floors usually indicate problems with floor-framing construction. Because normal vibrations over a period of time may loosen the subflooring, some houses develop floor squeaks, especially in heavy traffic areas. Refer to Figure 9.4 to see the components of a floor frame and wall frame.

Wall Frame

The wall frame is built on top of the floor frame. Traditionally, lumber is used to construct the wall frame. Lumber that is 2 inches by 4 inches or 2 inches by 6 inches forms the vertical framing members, or **studs**, and the plates, or the horizontal framing members. Wall frames have a single *sole plate* on the bottom and a double *top plate* that supports the ceiling joists and roof members. Exterior and interior walls are generally built by laying them flat

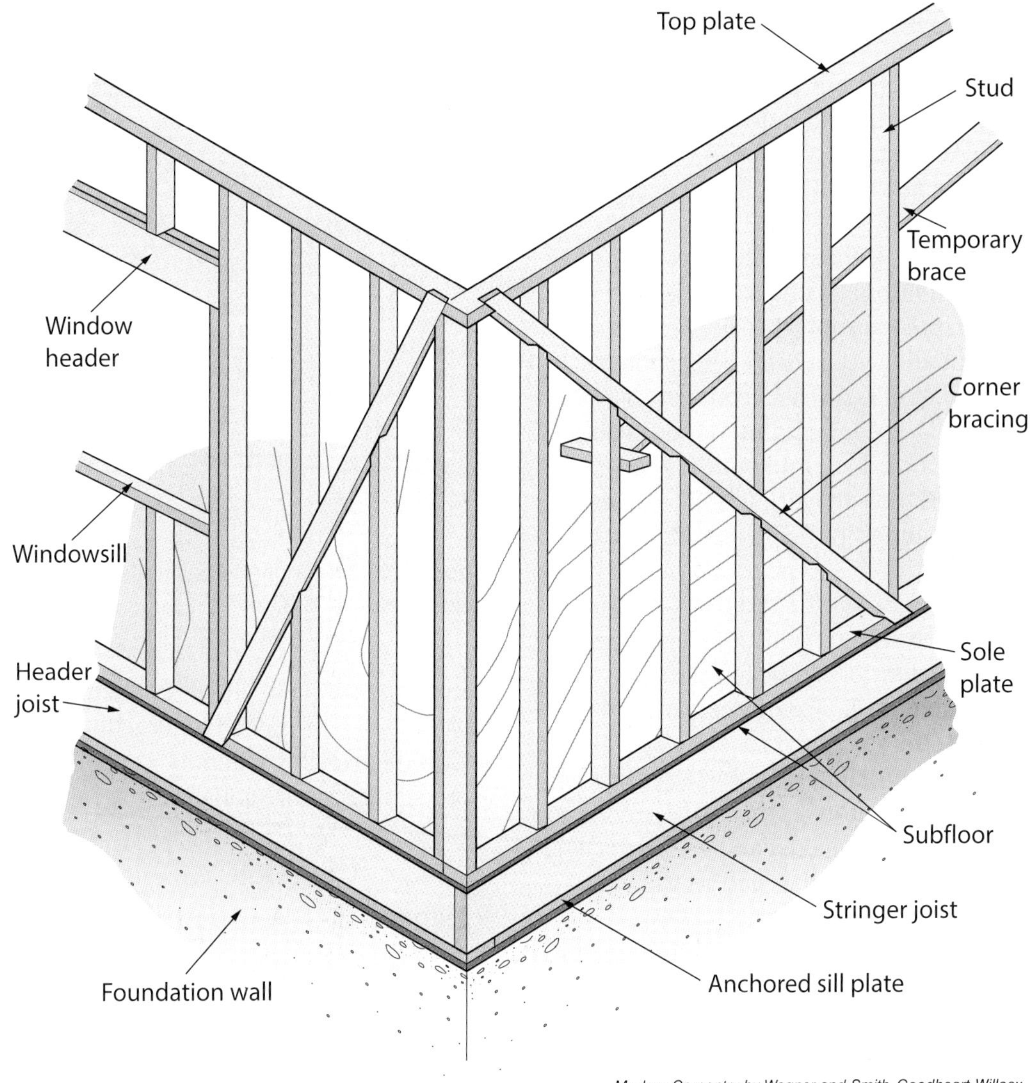

Modern Carpentry by Wagner and Smith, Goodheart-Willcox

Figure 9.4 The floor and wall framing consists of joists, studs, girders (not shown), plates, headers, and subflooring.

on the subfloor. The builder then raises and nails them into position on the floor frame.

Wall frames are either bearing or nonload bearing. A **bearing wall** supports some weight from the ceiling or roof of the structure. A **nonbearing wall** does not support any weight from the structure beyond its own weight. Exterior frame walls are usually bearing walls. Interior frame walls are called *partitions* to distinguish them from exterior walls. While some main partitions are also bearing walls, most interior partitions are nonbearing.

Headers are small, built-up beams that carry the load of the structure over door and window openings. For a 6-inch-thick outside wall, headers are made from 2-inch by 10-inch lumber on edge with a piece of 1/2-inch thick plywood between them. This forms a header that is 3 1/2 inches thick. (See Chapter 20 for a discussion on finishes for interior walls.)

Cracks, waves, or buckles in these wall frames indicate shifting of the wood frame or an incorrectly installed wall covering, such as wallpaper or vinyl. Also, stains on the wall covering may indicate moisture from a leaky roof or leaks around windows and doors. It is important to correct any such area to prevent the growth of mold in the structure.

Alternatives to traditional wood wall framing for the exterior walls of houses include the use of autoclaved aerated concrete (AAC), insulated concrete forms (ICF), and metal framing systems.

Autoclaved aerated concrete (AAC) block construction involves mixing sand, fly ash, cement, and water with aluminum powder—an expansion agent. The mixture is cast into a mold and then cut into blocks. It cures under pressure and heat for 8 to 12 hours at the manufacturing plant. The builder assembles the finished blocks at the job site to create the framing system of the house. The result is an ultralightweight concrete building material that is energy efficient, very strong, sound absorbent, and not harmful to the environment. AAC systems have been used in Europe for many years and have gained acceptance in the U.S. market.

AAC masonry block construction has many advantages over traditional wood framing. Because it is ***noncombustible*** (cannot be easily burned), home owners can reduce the cost of their home owner's insurance. It also resists termite or insect attack. In addition, it is a low-maintenance product and cannot rot as wood does, and builders can use traditional hand tools to work with it. You can expect to see more homes in the future built with this material.

Insulated concrete forms (ICF) consist of ***rigid*** (stiff; not flexible) polystyrene (plastic) foam forms with internal plastic for ties. These forms stack together like building blocks. Reinforcing steel is put into the ICF during the stacking process. Concrete is poured into the open middle, forming a reinforced concrete wall with insulation on the face. Exterior finishes, such as stucco or wood, can be used to cover this system. Traditional materials can be used to cover interior walls.

Contractors may also use metal framing systems very much like wood framing; however, they fasten metal framing together with screws. An advantage of these systems is that they are fireproof and rot resistant. The cost of alternative framing systems depends on several factors. These factors include the location in which you are building and the training of the workforce in your area.

Roof Frame

The roof frame consists of a series of beams, or **rafters**, that support the weight of the roof. They extend from the exterior walls to the ridge (Figure 9.5). The *ridge board* is the horizontal member at which the two slopes of the roof meet. It is the highest point of the roof frame.

In modern houses, most roof framing utilizes truss rafters. A *truss rafter* is a group of members forming a rigid-triangular framework for the roof. They are assembled at a factory and delivered to the job site. The builder then attaches them directly to the double top plate. Truss rafters usually span the distance between exterior walls.

As you evaluate the frame of the house, remember to look for stress cracks and hairline cracks. If you notice a sagging ceiling, it could indicate use of the wrong size or type of lumber. New houses will not show problems until they have settled. Pre-owned houses have had time to settle and probably will not crack further unless remodeling or more construction takes place.

Roof and Ceiling Frame

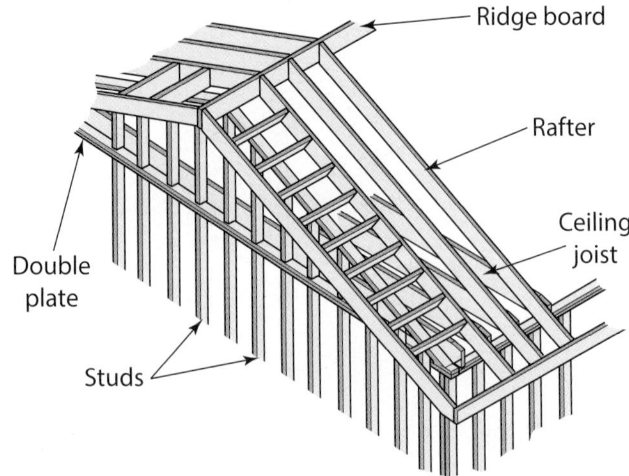

Modern Carpentry by Wagner and Smith, Goodheart-Willcox

Figure 9.5 The roof and ceiling framing consists of plates, joists, rafters, and the ridge board.

Review & Assessment

1. What are footings? Why do footings need to be placed on undisturbed, compact soil below the frost line?
2. What structural problems might cause stress cracks?
3. Identify the three main parts of the frame that work together to support the house and its contents.

Materials Used for Exterior Construction

After the foundation and frame are built, the exterior walls and the roof coverings are put in place. The materials used for exterior construction vary. The first layer applied is the *sheathing*, or protective covering. It may be wood, nail-base fiberboard, OSB, or plywood that is nailed to the studs. The sheathing is then usually covered with a thin plastic sheet called *house wrap* or a water-resistant paper called *building paper*. It is important for house wrap or building paper to form a water-resistant membrane but remain permeable enough to allow water vapor to pass through it.

Christina Richards/Shutterstock.com

Figure 9.6 Fiber-cement siding is being applied to the side of this new house.

Next is the siding application. **Siding** is the material forming the exposed surface of outside walls of a house. It is applied in strips, as shown in Figure 9.6. The most common types of siding are wood, aluminum, vinyl, pressed wood (OSB or fiberboard), or fiber-cement siding. Other siding materials include **masonry**—a hard building material, such as brick, concrete block, stucco, or natural stone, bonded together with mortar. The selection of materials depends on their availability in the area, the cost of the materials, and the preference of the home owners. Siding materials present different advantages and challenges.

Wood Siding

Wood is a common material used for siding. Wood siding is milled from cedar, redwood, pine, and cypress. It is suitable for a wide variety of exterior styles. Sustainable or green wood siding materials come from forests in which the highest ethical, social, and environmental practices are used in forest management.

Wood has some distinct advantages as a siding material. It has a relatively low cost and is an excellent nonconductor of heat. It is also easy to cut and assemble. The ease of working with and fastening wood together with simple tools provides flexibility without extensive redesigning. Wood does, however, expand and contract with changes in temperature or humidity.

With wood siding, routine inspections for rot and pest invasion (such as termites or carpenter ants) must occur to check for damage. Another disadvantage of wood is the maintenance cost of frequent painting or staining. Some parts of the country have climates that require painting every four years. However, periodic painting does give home owners the flexibility of changing house colors as they see fit.

When inspecting the exterior siding of a house, look for putty marks covered with paint. This may indicate poor siding application or repair. Also, a house that has siding covered up with putty and paint may have other problems that have been disguised.

Green Choices

Forest Stewardship Council®

Why is the Forest Stewardship Council (FSC®) considered green? This international, nonprofit Council is green because it promotes responsible forestry standards. The FSC certification provides a label certifying that certain wood products for use in building houses and furniture come from forests that are managed to meet the needs of present and future generations.

Forests provide clean water and fresh air. Preserving them is an important factor in making sure the world is sustainable through protection of its natural resources. In many forests, however, certain timbering practices still contribute to habitat destruction, water pollution, and more.

FSC®

The FSC label certifies the wood products come from forest timbering that supports the highest social and environmental principles of conservation of natural forests. For a company or organization to earn the right to use the FSC label, it must first comply with all applicable FSC requirements. Also, the FSC labeled wood products meet the requirements of the Green Building Council's certified LEED program.

Plywood siding is another type of wood siding. It can be applied horizontally or vertically. It covers large areas and saves installation time. Plywood siding must also be painted or stained, then sealed. It is also susceptible to termite damage and climatic changes.

Manufactured Siding

Siding materials also make use of such products as aluminum, vinyl, pressed wood, and fiber-cement products. These different materials have varying advantages and disadvantages.

The advantages of *aluminum siding* are its durability and lack of need for repainting. It often has weather- and corrosion-resistant finishes. Aluminum siding does dent, however, as often occurs in hailstorms, and may conduct electricity.

Vinyl siding is also durable and does not conduct electricity. It can expand and contract with changes in the temperature and humidity, but it is not the most sustainable of products. Like aluminum, it does not require painting. Vinyl siding will, however, show dents.

Pressed wood siding is made from oriented strand board (OSB) or primed fiberboard. As you know, OSB is made by layering wood chips and fiber in a crosshatch pattern. Fiberboard has similar construction but uses longer strands of fiber. Both products are easy to paint but cannot be stained. They are less expensive than plywood siding. Special surface treatments are available, such as brushed, texture-embossed, and V-grooves. A V-groove surface treatment creates a "V-shaped" groove in the board that adds interest and looks like a more expensive treatment of two separate boards put together.

Fiber-cement siding is made from a calcium-silicate material that is evenly dispersed with reinforcing fibers. It is dimensionally stable, and resists moisture, mold and mildew development, and pests. It will not burn and has a zero smoke-development rating. It is less expensive than brick but has all the benefits. Fiber-cement siding can be ordered with a factory-primed finish. It requires painting but holds paint two to three times longer than wood.

Masonry Siding

Construction of the exterior wall sometimes utilizes brick, clay tile, concrete block, natural stone, or exterior stucco. As you learned earlier, stucco is a type of plaster (Figure 9.7). *Brick* is a block molded from moist clay and hardened with heat. *Natural stone* is hardened earth or mineral matter.

Paul Matthew Photography/Shutterstock.com

Figure 9.7 Stucco homes have remained popular throughout the years.

Builders sometimes use a brick veneer wall to create the look of a masonry wall. A **veneer wall** is a nonsupporting wall. House wrap covers the sheathing on the wall frame and thin sheet-metal ties secure the veneer wall to the sheathing. There is about a 1-inch space between the veneer and sheathing to allow any moisture to flow to the bottom of the structure and out *weep holes* (holes created for water removal). Masonry construction is ***porous*** (allows substances to pass through) by nature, so control of water in the wall design is very important. In many areas of the country, usage of masonry veneer walls is common.

Masonry products have distinct advantages. The products are strong, durable, and usually inexpensive to maintain. Also, they generally last a long time. The disadvantage of masonry products is the initial cost. They are usually hand-laid, which is one reason for their expense.

Masonry materials are available in a wide range of sizes, colors, and textures to produce different architectural effects. The *pattern bond*, or the pattern formed by masonry units and the mortar joints on the face of the wall, can create other interesting effects. By varying the bonds and the depth and shape of mortar joints between units, additional depth dimensions and shadows add to the masonry wall.

When you examine a masonry house, make sure to look for cracks or bows in the walls. Hairline cracks in the joints are normal expansion cracks.

Green Choices

Builder Responsibilities for Sustainable Design

Builders play an important role in creating houses that have a positive impact on the environment. A good source of builder information on green and sustainable design is the *Model Home Building Guidelines* from the National Association of Home Builders (NAHB). Many local home-builders associations across the nation are developing programs that use these guidelines.

Builders with concerns for the environment can obtain these guidelines and use them in their construction projects. Also, builders can acquire the *Certified Green Professional Designation* from the NAHB by attending 24 hours of special training and continuing education every two years.

Builders can follow green design principles by doing the following:

- Use the natural environment in lot preparation to enhance the home's long-term performance.
- Use advanced framing techniques to get the most from building materials.
- Focus on the best ways to handle waste from construction.
- Build more energy-efficient structures and incorporate more energy-efficient mechanical systems, appliances, and lighting into a home.
- Use methods to reduce indoor and outdoor water usage.
- Control moisture, ventilation, and other issues to create a more comfortable and healthier indoor living environment.
- Inform the home owner on green aspects of the home and how to best operate and maintain the home.

Larger cracks, however, can break bricks as they continue up or down the wall.

Roofing Materials

Common roofing materials include asphalt, fiberglass, vinyl, wood, tile, slate, concrete, and metal. These materials provide color and texture that make the exterior of the house more attractive. These materials, however, must also provide a protective, watertight covering to keep out rain and snow. If the roof leaks, the seepage can damage the house structure and its contents.

Most houses have sloping roofs with a covering of shingles. **Shingles** are thin pieces of building material that lay in overlapping rows on roofs. Asphalt shingles are the most common roofing material. In warmer regions, usage of shingles that combine asphalt and fiberglass helps keep the house cooler. Asphalt shingles range in price from inexpensive to more costly depending on the composition, warranty, and quality of the product (Figure 9.8). Vinyl shingles are similar to asphalt shingles and come in a variety of textures and colors. Shingle color is a consideration factor depending on the climate. Dark roof colors tend to absorb heat and light colors tend to reflect heat.

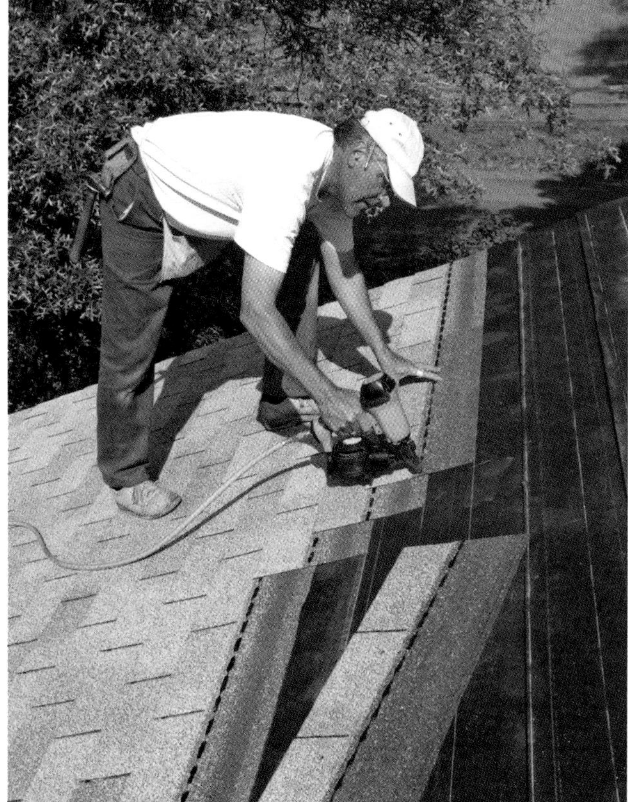

Christina Richards/Shutterstock.com

Figure 9.8 Many roofs are covered with asphalt or asphalt-and-fiberglass shingles.

Dimedrol68/Shutterstock.com

Figure 9.9 Roof tiles weigh about ten pounds each. This heavy load requires stronger rafters and other framing members to support the total weight of the roof.

Wood shingles as well as *shakes*—thicker, less uniform shingles—are more costly than asphalt shingles. Treatment with fire-retardant and decay-resistant chemicals is important for durability. Shingles and shakes are popular because of their natural colors. Usage of these shingles is most common where cedar, redwood, and cypress trees grow.

In parts of the country with hot sun and little snowfall, clay or fiberglass tile, slate, and concrete roofing materials are often used. These materials are heavy and require proper roof design and structure to support the extra weight (Figure 9.9). Also, they are expensive. Clay or fiberglass tile, slate, and concrete roofing materials are very durable and will last a lifetime.

Metal roofing materials are also available. Sheets of metal roofing are obtainable in aluminum, zinc-plated steel, *terneplate* (a lead-tin coating on steel), and stainless steel. Copper may be used on an entire roof or as an accent to a small area. The price of metal roofing varies depending on the quality. Metal roofing materials are more costly than asphalt and vinyl shingles, but are not as expensive as tile.

The application of most roofing materials occurs in the same manner. First the builder covers the roof frame with sheathing. Then an application of a heavy building paper or roofing felt is added to help keep out a limited amount of rain. After installation of a metal *drip edge* along the eaves, the builder applies a starter strip of shingles along the roof bottom and then fastens the rest of the shingles in straight lines. When complete, a shingled roof should have a uniform appearance in the pattern of application.

When inspecting an existing roof, it is important to ask about reasons for every roof repair. A change in shingle color may indicate patching instead of reroofing. Problems that lead to patching usually resurface at a later date. In addition, it is important to pay close attention to the materials used for flashing and their installation. **Flashing** is a water-resistant sheet metal used to help keep the roof watertight. It is used in valleys—the junctions that form where two sloping roofs meet at an angle. It is

STEM Math Polygons

A *polygon* is a plane figure bounded by straight lines on three or more sides. Polygons are classified by the number of sides and the angles they contain. For example, a five-sided polygon is a *pentagon* (*penta-* means *five*). An angle is where two sides meet. There are five angles inside the pentagon. A regular polygon is one in which all sides are of equal length and all interior angles are equal. You can use a formula to calculate the size of an interior angle of a regular polygon. If x is the number of sides, the size of each interior angle is $(x - 2) \times 180° \div x$.

Math Practice

1. Calculate the size of interior angles for a polygon that has 11 sides.
2. Calculate the size of interior angles for a polygon that has 15 sides.

Regular Polygons

Name	Number of Sides	Number and Size of Interior Angles
Triangle	3	3, 60°
Quadrilateral	4	4, 90°
Pentagon	5	5, 108°
Hexagon	6	6, 120°
Heptagon	7	7, 128.57°
Octagon	8	8, 135°
Nonagon	9	9, 140°
Decagon	10	10, 144°

also used where a roof meets a vertical surface such as a wall or chimney. If the flashing is a substandard material or installed incorrectly, leaks can occur.

Give special attention to inspecting flat areas of the roof. These areas should have a covering that consists of a buildup of layers of roofing felt and asphalt or a membrane product such as heavy rubber sheeting. If the sheeting is used, it should have few or no seams. Inspect such flat areas on a roof carefully because they are very prone to leaks. All flat areas must be sloped to drain areas that collect standing water to help prevent leaks.

The remaining components of a roof system are the gutters and downspouts. A *gutter* is a horizontal open trough located under the perimeter of the roof to channel away water. A *downspout* is a vertical pipe that connects the gutter system to the ground to carry rainwater away from the home's foundation. The construction of gutters and downspouts uses aluminum or vinyl materials. The color is baked onto aluminum, but exists throughout vinyl. The advantage of both materials is that they do not require painting. Aluminum has one additional advantage over vinyl—gutter extrusion can actually happen on-site for a seamless installation.

TFoxFoto/Shutterstock.com

Figure 9.10 The installer is checking to be sure the rough opening is the correct size for the window installation. Note the waterproof house wrap on this structure.

Review & Assessment

1. What are three advantages of wood siding?
2. Contrast the advantages and disadvantages of each of the four types of manufactured siding discussed in the chapter.
3. What are five types of roofing materials?

Windows and Doors

As the exterior walls are built, spaces are also created for windows and door frames. These spaces are an integral part of the housing design and structure.

When people first built dwellings, a window was an opening that provided ventilation. A door was an opening for entry and security. In the past, windows and doors did not fit houses well and allowed heat to escape from houses. They also provided very little insulation. Over time, many new types of windows and doors were developed. They were built to prevent air from escaping and to provide better insulation (Figure 9.10). Today, a wide range of styles, shapes, and special options are available for both windows and doors.

Windows

Windows have many uses in a house. From the interior, they provide natural light, air circulation, and a view. They can also serve as a point of emphasis in a room or as a part of the background. On the exterior, their size, shape, and placement affect the appearance of the house. In addition, some windows have built-in features or special coatings that conserve energy, are UV resistant, and prevent heat transference. Also, high-impact glass panes add protection from breakage by flying objects during storms or high winds. These windows are more costly because of the additional features. Certain regions of the country, however, such as coastal areas, are adopting building codes that require windows with special coatings or features in new construction.

Windows have many parts (Figure 9.11). These parts include the following:

- **Frame.** The frame is the perimeter of the window that fits into the window opening and is nailed

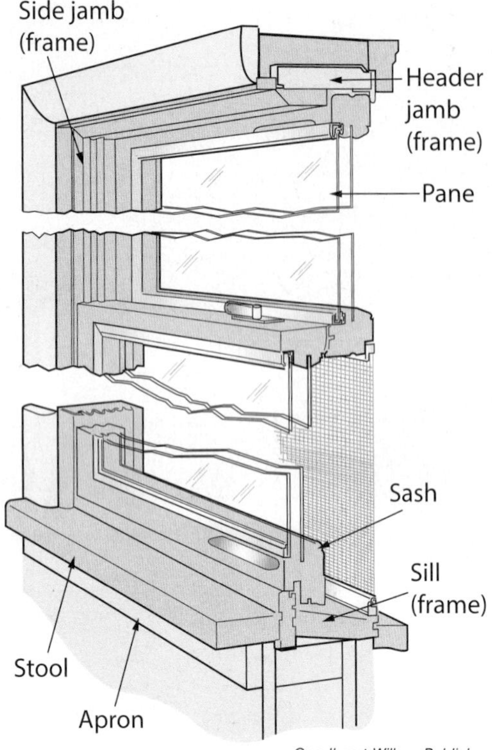

Goodheart-Willcox Publisher

Figure 9.11 The five main parts of a window are the frame, sash, pane, stool, and apron.

or screwed into place. The sides of the frame are called *jambs*. The top of the window frame is the *header*, and the bottom of the window frame is the *sill*.

- **Pane.** The pane is the window glass.
- **Sash.** The sash is the framework that holds the glass in the window. The sash swings or slides open. *Muntins* are vertical and horizontal dividers that separate different panes of glass in a window. Originally made of wood, muntins divide the pane of glass into smaller sections. Muntins in modern insulated windows are an overlay on a large sheet of glass. They no longer separate or support small panes of glass.
- **Stool.** The stool is the horizontal trim member located on the bottom of the interior window frame.
- **Apron.** The apron is a strip of decorative interior trim that is below the stool.

Originally, window frames were made from either wood or aluminum. Today, windows are often ***clad*** (covered) with aluminum or vinyl for low maintenance or are made from vinyl extrusions. As a result of strict local and national energy codes, more energy-efficient materials are used in the construction of window units.

There are three basic types of windows: sliding, swinging, and fixed windows. All other window styles are based on these three types. The type chosen for a house depends on the exterior style of the house, building codes, and personal preference. A traditional design, such as a Southern Colonial or French Provincial, looks best with a sliding window with muntins. A contemporary house may feature large expanses of fixed windows.

Sliding Windows

Sliding windows can operate either vertically or horizontally. A *double-hung window* is a vertical sliding window, as shown in Figure 9.12. It provides an opening of about one-half the size of the window.

Horizontal-sliding windows have two or three sashes. Two-sash windows have one sash that slides and the other that stays fixed (Figure 9.13). On a three-sash window, the center sash is fixed and the two outside sashes slide toward the center. Screens are mounted on the outside.

John Wollwerth/Shutterstock.com

Figure 9.12 The windows in this bathroom are double-hung sliding.

photobank.ch/Shutterstock.com

Figure 9.13 One sash is operable in this two-sash, horizontal-sliding window.

ThomBal/Shutterstock.com

Figure 9.15 This dormer includes one casement and two fixed windows. The curve of the windows adds interest.

Swinging Windows

There are four types of swinging windows. They are casement, awning, hopper, and jalousie windows (Figure 9.14).

Casement windows open and close with a crank and swing outward (Figure 9.15). Usually, the entire window area can be opened for ventilation.

Awning windows swing outward at the bottom and are hinged at the top. This provides protection from rain. A similar window is the *hopper window*. It is hinged at the bottom to allow the top of the sash to swing inward.

Jalousie windows are a series of horizontal, adjustable glass slats fastened into a metal frame. They open and close with a crank and are used where ventilation is needed. Screens and storm windows are located on the interior.

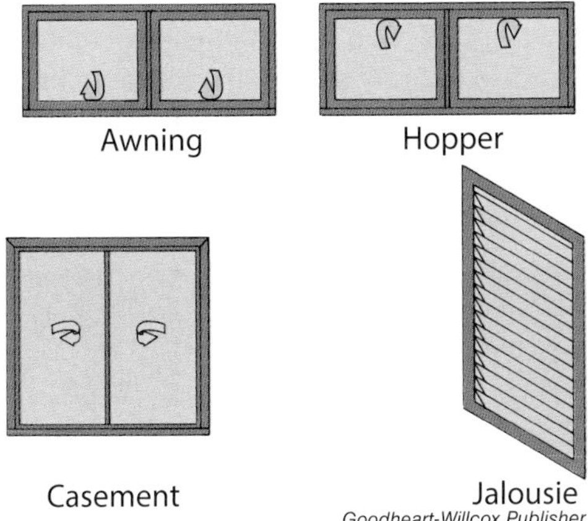

Goodheart-Willcox Publisher

Figure 9.14 Awning, hopper, casement, and jalousie windows swing out to provide excellent ventilation. The arrows indicate the direction of swing.

Fixed Windows

Fixed windows admit light and provide a view. They do not open, however. Fixed windows come in many shapes and sizes, including rectangular, oval, half-round, round, and arched. Glass blocks are fixed windows that provide light while preserving visual privacy, (Figure 9.16).

Combination Windows

Fixed windows used with other types of windows are called *combination windows*. For example, hopper windows are often used above a fixed window. A large fixed window can have a casement window on either side.

A *bay window* is a combination window that projects outward from the exterior wall of the house. It often has a large fixed window in the center and double-hung windows on both sides.

Skylights and Clerestory Windows

Using skylights and clerestory windows helps let light into areas that get little or no natural light. They can also offer additional light to give a room an airy appearance. *Skylights* are normally located in the ceiling or roof (Figure 9.17). They are usually square or rectangular and come in various sizes. *Light tubes* are an economical and energy-efficient form of skylight. They have a small clear plastic dome on the roof and a shiny metal

A Image Courtesy of Anderson Corporation B Tony Marinella Photography/Shutterstock.com

Figure 9.16 The fixed-window unit in image A creates a dramatic focal point in the room. The glass-block windows in image B admit light but provide privacy.

tube that connects to a lens with a light diffuser in the ceiling. Placement of *clerestory* windows is generally high on an outside wall. They can be standard or custom-made windows.

PlusONE/Shutterstock.com

Figure 9.17 The large window and skylights play an important part in the interior design of this house.

Doors

Doors provide access, protection, safety, and privacy. They also provide a barrier against sound, extreme temperatures, and light. Exterior doors are made from wood or wood covered with metal or vinyl. Interior doors are made from wood, metal, or wood covered with vinyl. Interior doors may also include louvered doors (similar to shutters) for spaces requiring ventilation.

Doors are often classified by their method of operation (Figure 9.18). *Swinging doors* operate on hinges and usually swing open in one direction

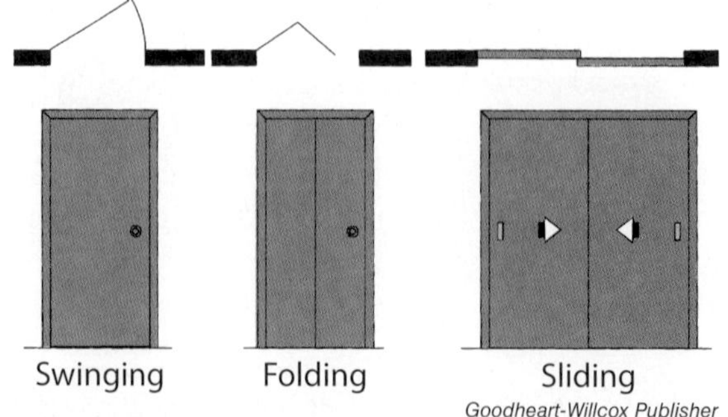

Goodheart-Willcox Publisher

Figure 9.18 Doors operate in three different ways—by swinging, folding, or sliding.

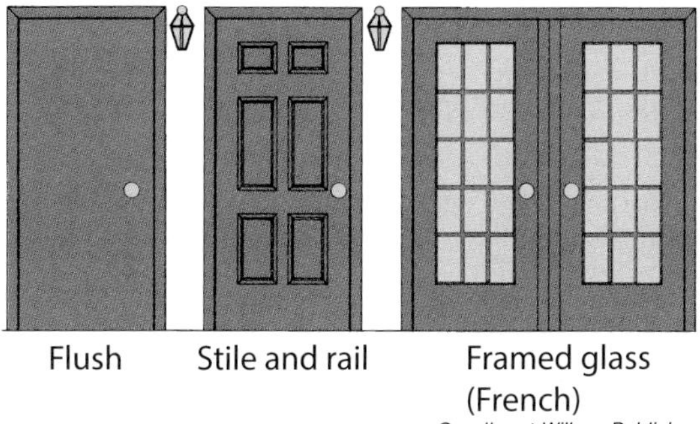

Figure 9.19 Doors can be constructed in many different ways, including these three methods.

(although double-action doors are available). Enough room needs to be allowed for the door to swing open and close. *Sliding doors* are set on a track and open or close by gliding on the track. Exterior use includes sliding glass patio doors. Interior use includes pocket, bypass, and barn-style doors (doors that slide over the face of a wall). A pocket door requires that the wall be free of any outlets, light switches, or plumbing. When open, a *folding door* folds into a multisection stack. Folding doors are typically used in interior construction, and include bi-fold and accordion-style doors. Revolving doors are also available but are typically only used in commercial construction. Classification of doors also occurs by their method of construction and assembly (Figure 9.19).

Stile and Rail Doors

Stile and rail doors consist of *stiles* (solid vertical members), *rails* (solid horizontal members), and panels (material that fills the space between stiles and rails). The panels may be decorative or glass. They may be raised or flat. Raised panels are cut from solid wood, and flat panels are usually cut from plywood. The number of panel combinations is limitless.

Flush Doors

Construction of flush doors requires covering a framework core with wood or other material, such as metal or vinyl. There are two basic types of cores—solid and hollow. A solid-core door consists of tightly fitted blocks of wood covered with veneer. Some doors utilize particleboard as the core. These doors are heavy and are used mainly for exterior doors and for interior doors where sound control is a consideration. A hollow-core door has a heavier outside frame combined with wood strips, stiff cardboard, or paper honeycomb as the core. This type of door is lightweight and is used mainly as an interior door.

Figure 9.20 These dramatic French doors create both a division and a transition between spaces.

Framed-Glass Doors

Framed-glass doors are stile and rail doors with glass panels. The glass may be single-pane or insulating glass. French doors are framed-glass doors with the glass divided with muntins into small sections. Installation of French doors is usually in pairs (Figure 9.20). Sliding glass doors are another example of a framed-glass door. They often take the place of windows in small or medium-sized houses.

Review & Assessment

1. For each of the following, identify whether the window is fixed, sliding, or swinging: (A) jalousie; (B) double-hung; (C) awning; (D) half-round; (E) horizontal-sliding; (F) casement; (G) hopper.
2. How is an interior door construction different from an exterior door?
3. Contrast a solid-core with a hollow-core door.

Interior Construction

Walls, ceilings, and floors provide protection from the outdoors, reduce the amount of noise entering a room, and provide a ***substrate*** (base) for millwork and finishes. (You will learn more about surface finishes in Chapter 20.) Factors in determining appropriate materials might include thermal and acoustical comfort, durability, level of formality, fire-resistive characteristics, and compatibility with other interior materials.

Walls

When designing interior spaces, considering the type of wall construction is an important factor. Builders use a variety of materials to construct interior walls. Interior walls may be wood or steel studs, masonry, or concrete and constructed similarly to exterior walls as previously discussed (Figure 9.21). Walls hide pipes, wiring, and insulation and may include extra interior studs to assist with fireproofing and cabinetry installation. They also divide space within a dwelling and provide privacy. They may be covered with gypsum wallboard, plastic wallboard, paneling, plaster, or masonry. The materials used in wall construction will help determine what type of finish treatments can be used.

Gypsum Wallboard

Gypsum wallboard is the most common building material used for interior walls and ceilings. Other names for this product include *drywall* and *Sheetrock*™ (the manufacturer name). It comes in panels that are 4 feet by 8, 9, 10, or 12 feet and can be run sideways if needed. The use of larger panels minimizes the number of joints or seams. To achieve a seamless wall surface, installers use joint tape and a fast-drying joint compound to cover the drywall seams. A smooth wall surface often requires sanding and applying several coats of joint compound. Then the walls are ready for such surface finish treatments as paint, tile, wall coverings, or fabric. Structural walls constructed of concrete or masonry often have an additional layer (called furring) of wood or metal strips and interior gypsum wallboard to make finish application and fixture attachment easier. Gypsum is also available in water-resistant forms for use in bathrooms.

Plastic Wallboard

Plastic wallboard is a building material with a durable decorative finish that contractors commonly use for interior walls. It comes in both enamel and plastic laminate finishes, which makes it easy to maintain. Its primary use is in bathrooms and kitchens or in commercial applications.

Paneling

Paneling is a building material that is usually made of plywood but can be produced from a synthetic material. A **synthetic** material is a manufactured material that imitates or replaces another substance. Paneling comes in many different colors and textures, and is commonly available in 4-foot by 8-foot panels. Builders can apply it directly to the wall frame. To achieve a more substantial wall installation, they can also apply the paneling over gypsum wallboard.

Christina Richards/Shutterstock.com

B Brown/Shutterstock.com

Figure 9.21 Interior walls, floors, and ceilings must accommodate plumbing, electrical lines, and framing for fixtures that will be installed later in the construction process. These photos show the difference between wood and metal studs as well as a partial gypsum drywall application.

Housing Health & Safety

Reducing Mold with Paperless Drywall

Mold growing in drywall can be a major concern to the health of a family and the indoor air quality of a home or building. There are many forms of mold, and some are toxic—especially to people with mold allergies. Exposure to water and moisture causes mold spores to multiply. Mold in drywall also impacts the maintenance and value of a home.

Mold thrives on the paper component of traditional drywall. That is why researchers have developed a new paperless drywall. Instead of paper facings, this new product uses fiberglass mats for the facing. The design community considers paperless drywall more sustainable because it

- lasts longer than other wallboards with exposure to moisture
- is mold and moisture resistant
- has the *Greenguard Environmental Institute* certification as a product with low emissions of volatile organic compounds (VOCs)

The U.S. Green Building Council—developers of the Leadership in Energy and Environmental Design (LEED) Green Building rating system—values products with a longer sustaining life. Such products have low VOC emissions and provide good air quality. Builders used this product in reconstructing homes in New Orleans after Hurricane Katrina.

The designer of the basement within the left photo made a sustainable design choice by specifying a mold- and moisture-resistant drywall in the construction. The second designer did not.

Used with permission of Georgia-Pacific, Gypsum LLC

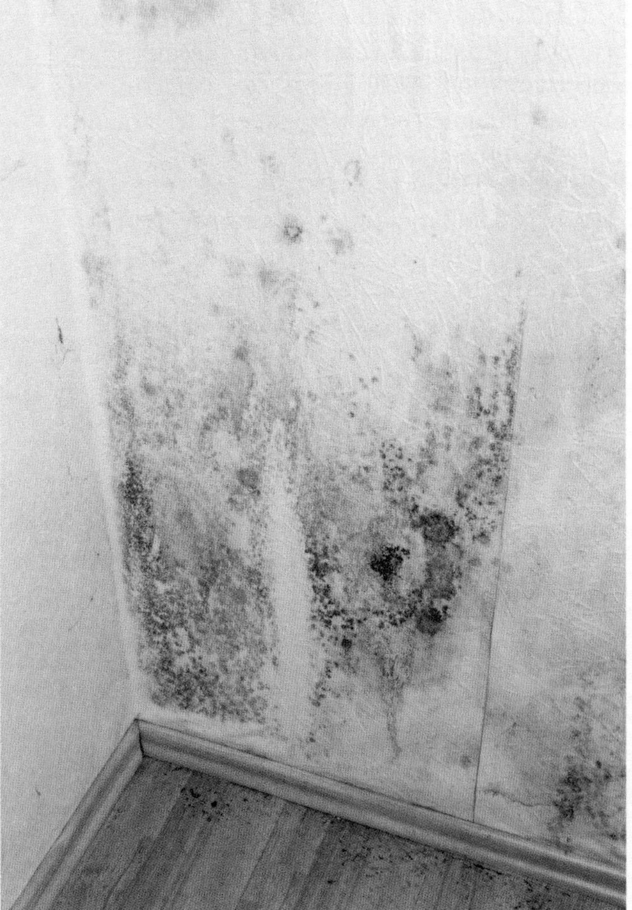

HandmadePictures/Shutterstock.com

Plaster

Plaster is a paste used for coating walls and ceilings that hardens as it dries. Plastered surfaces can be either smooth or rough, and usually have a finish coat of paint. Applying plaster requires special skills and equipment, so it costs more than most other types of walls. Usage of this product is rare except in older homes and some commercial buildings.

Masonry

Masonry walls can serve as both exterior and interior walls. Cement blocks are a commonly used form of masonry. Sometimes they are painted. Since cement blocks are large, they belong in large rooms decorated with large pieces of furniture, rough textures, and bold colors.

Brick or *stone* may form entire walls—primarily decorative walls and fireplace walls. They are beautiful and durable, and they require little or no upkeep. However, they are costly to install. Interior designers often use both brick and stone for informal settings (Figure 9.22).

Some of the materials used in wall construction can also serve as the wall treatment. Because they are decorative in their original state, paneling, bricks, and stones do not need additional wall treatment.

Specialty Walls

Movable and modular walls can be a great way of adding flexibility to an interior environment. Interior walls may also be constructed using glass-block and fixed-glass windows to create spatial definition while allowing light to filter into adjacent spaces.

Ceilings and Floors

The materials and techniques used in ceiling and floor construction can affect future decisions regarding finishes and fixtures. For instance, a client might choose to leave a ceiling exposed to the framing components (joints, girders, etc.) or even leave concrete foundations unfinished within a space.

The ceiling of a room is often the surface people notice least, but it performs many tasks and may account for 30 percent of the room's surfaces. It holds and conceals insulating materials that help control the house temperature. It hides electrical wiring. Some ceilings also hide water lines and gas lines. Finished ceilings may create a very formal atmosphere. Ceilings left unfinished (with exposed structure and/or building systems) can give a rustic, historic, or industrial look. See Figure 9.23.

The height of the ceiling can help create certain moods. Minimum and most typical ceilings are 8 feet from the floor. Higher ceilings give a feeling of spaciousness. The five most common materials used for ceilings are plaster, acoustical plaster, acoustical tile, wood, and gypsum wallboard. **Acoustical** means that the material will reduce or absorb sound.

- *Plaster* is one of the earliest forms of ceiling treatments. People seldom use it today except in restorations of older houses. Its surface can be either smooth or rough.

Irina Borsuchenko/Shutterstock.com

Figure 9.22 This photo demonstrates a variety of interior wall materials including gypsum drywall and masonry, as well as wood cabinetry and trim work.

imging/Shutterstock.com

Figure 9.23 Leaving a ceiling structure exposed (yet finishing it appropriately) can create drama and relate to pieces within the room.

- *Acoustical plaster* has a rough texture. It helps absorb sound and thus reduces the noise in a room. Application of this plaster requires spraying it onto the ceiling's surface. Acoustical plaster is difficult to paint, clean, and repair.
- *Acoustical tile* is decorative and functional. It comes in many patterns and colors. It absorbs sound and is easy to clean. Application of these tiles generally involves hanging them from a grid to hide mechanical, plumbing, and electrical components above the ceiling.
- *Wood ceilings* may come in the form of planks or bead-board similar to those used on floors and walls. Bead-board is a thin but large sheet of wood with close and evenly spaced grooves that mimic strips of wood. Wood ceilings can be stained to match interior furnishings or other finishes.
- *Gypsum wallboard* is a common ceiling treatment. It can be finished with a smooth surface or with a rough texture that resembles plaster. Manufacturers produce thicker and more rigid wallboard for ceilings to resist sagging. As with other wallboard applications, paint is usually the final finish.

Regardless of the future finish, floor framing is typically covered with a substrate such as plywood. This gives a surface to which other materials can be adhered. Concrete floors may be left exposed but are typically stained and sealed. As with the wall and ceiling finishes above, these options will be discussed in Chapter 20.

Stairs

Although stair sizing and layout are dictated by building code, there are many decisions related to their design and construction materials. Stairs can be in a variety of configurations (straight, L, U, winder, curved, spiral). They can be constructed in different ways (closed or open) and have a range of materials used on the vertical and horizontal elements as well as on the various parts of the stair railing. Stairs and railings should be designed to coordinate with the materials, lines, and style of cabinetry and furnishings on both of the levels they connect (Figure 9.24).

Dinga/Shutterstock.com

Figure 9.24 In addition to meeting functional and ecological goals, a designer must consider the aesthetic continuity of stairs, railings, and casework.

Interior Millwork

Interior millwork (woodwork completed at a mill) includes any cabinetry or trim work included in the construction of a home. Cabinetry may be within kitchens and bathrooms but will also occur as built-in storage in entertainment rooms, closets, window seats, and other functional spaces within a home. Trim work such as baseboards and crown molding can be found throughout the home but is typically more plentiful in public formal areas such as the dining room.

Considering millwork is important because it typically represents a large portion of a new construction or renovation budget and is less frequently replaced than interior surface finishes. Design decisions related to millwork include:

- Frame type (Cabinetry with an integral frame will be more sturdy than frameless cabinetry. Also, the countertop selected may require the cabinetry to be framed.)
- Joinery, or the art of joining pieces of wood
- Door style
- Types of drawers and shelves
- Hinges and hardware

The criteria for evaluating millwork construction and materials may be functional, aesthetic, and ecologically based. These factors are very similar to those related to furniture construction, which is covered in Chapter 21.

Review & Assessment

1. What purposes do walls, ceilings, and floors have other than to divide spaces?
2. What are the five most common materials used for ceilings?
3. Why are decisions related to millwork of great importance to the budget of a project?

Computer Applications in Construction

Most architects, engineers, building contractors, and interior designers use technology applications to assist them with decisions related to house construction. Computer applications usually speed the process of creating exterior and interior architectural drawings to help to assure the accuracy of the designs. Another advantage of technology is the realistic view it provides of the final product—the house. Since most people cannot visualize how a finished house will look from architectural plans, seeing a lifelike picture can help avoid disappointed clients. House designers use computer applications in three basic ways—to analyze the strength and appropriateness of planned materials, to select construction components, and to manage the building process.

Analyzing Components of Construction

The designer of a house must assure the structural integrity of the design. For instance, the design of the steep roof on the home in Figure 9.25 helps prevent the buildup of snow. Besides providing the support needed under normal conditions, the house design will also need to withstand heavy snowfalls of several feet at a time.

Pete Spiro/Shutterstock.com

Figure 9.25 The builder of this house used special windows with insulated glass. The roof was engineered to withstand heavy snow.

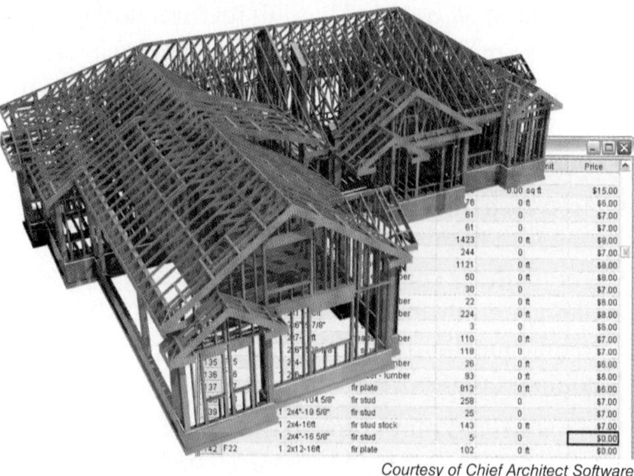

Courtesy of Chief Architect Software

Figure 9.26 This image clearly shows the structural parts of the frame. The designer can identify and solve problems before construction begins.

Specialized computer software can analyze the planned materials and structural supports. It can also examine the stress these materials will undergo as a result of conditions in the geographic area, such as high heat and humidity. Software programs also allow the designer to "test" various designs and materials to assure the safety and effectiveness of the structure before it is built. See Figure 9.26 for an example of how technology can be used to analyze structural components.

Selecting Components of Construction

Housing components that are available in a wide variety of choices, such as windows, are best selected with the help of technology. Housing designers and builders, for example, can view various window options and different placement combinations by using designer websites or special CD-ROMs. Designer websites are the primary resource for such material selections.

Designer websites usually provide product photos, price charts, sizing charts, design templates, and order forms. Window companies, cabinet manufacturers, and providers of other construction components may also make CD-ROMs available. You can obtain the most up-to-date information about these companies by going online to their websites.

Career Focus Building Inspector

SpeedKingz/Shutterstock.com

Are you fascinated with buildings and how they are constructed? Are you interested in how things work in a building, such as the electrical, mechanical, plumbing, and HVAC systems? Do you enjoy working on construction projects such as building and working with your hands? If so, a career as a building inspector may be right for you.

Interests/Skills: A genuine interest in the safety of others is an important start for building inspectors. Detail-oriented people with knowledge of interior systems of a building and compliance rules and regulations are essential. Building inspectors must also have advanced math and writing skills.

Career Snapshot: Building inspectors determine the structural soundness of buildings. They must also ensure that the structures are safe and meet all local building codes, regulations, and specifications. Their inspections may be general in nature or may be limited to such specific areas as the footings, foundation, framing, electrical, and plumbing. Building inspectors work with a number of professionals and others in allied careers such as a cost estimator, brick mason, roofer, construction carpenter, drywall installer, plasterer, and cabinetmaker.

Education/Training: Most employers require at least a high school diploma or the equivalent, even for workers with considerable experience. More often, employers look for people who have studied engineering or architecture. A growing number of construction and building inspectors enter the occupation with a bachelor's degree.

Licensing/Examinations: Many states and local jurisdictions require some type of license or certification for employment as a construction and building inspector. Requirements vary by state or local municipality.

Professional Associations: National Association of Home Inspectors (NAHI); American Institute of Inspectors (AII); American Society of Home Inspectors (ASHI); and the National Association of Certified Home Inspectors (NACHI).

Job Outlook: Inspectors should experience average employment growth. Job opportunities in construction and building inspection should be best for highly experienced supervisors and construction craft workers who have some college education, engineering or architectural training, or certification as inspectors or plan examiners.

Sources: The Occupational Outlook Handbook (OOH); the Occupational Information Network (O*NET); U.S. Bureau of Labor Statistics (BLS)

Managing the Construction

Computer programs can assist the designer and builder in developing plans that identify the sequence of steps required to construct the house. To ensure house completion in a timely and cost-effective manner, programs can develop a timetable for the project. You will learn more about computer-aided design and drafting (CADD) and other assistive software in later chapters.

Review & Assessment 

1. What are three benefits of computer applications in construction?
2. How can computer applications help analyze components of construction?
3. How can computer programs help manage the construction timetable of a project?

Chapter 9 Assessment

Summary

- Understanding house construction helps house buyers, designers, and other housing professionals make good decisions.
- The foundation and the frame are the basic structure of the house. The foundation supports the frame structure above it. It needs to be constructed correctly to prevent uneven settling.
- Once the foundation and frame are built, the exterior walls and the roof are added. A variety of materials is used.
- Windows and doors complete the basic construction of the house. The three main types of windows are sliding, swinging, and fixed. Other windows are variations of these three types or combinations of them.
- Doors are classified by their method of operation—swinging, sliding, or folding. They are also classified by the method of construction used to make them.
- Interior construction includes the walls, floors, ceilings, millwork, and stairs that define and connect spaces. Their materials may be chosen for functional, aesthetic, or ecological reasons.
- With the help of technology, designers and builders can work more efficiently.

Terms in Action

1. **Chapter summary** Write a brief chapter summary to an adult who is interested in working in housing construction. In your summary, include each *Content Term* listed at the beginning of this chapter.

Think Critically

2. **Assess buildings** Presume you have been hired by the local government as a building inspector. Develop a house evaluation form that will help you inspect buildings and assess them for problems. Use additional online or print resources to help develop your evaluation. Share your results with the class through the class website or through an oral report.
3. **Analyze information** Assume your client is building a home in the northwest region of the United States. Sustainable design and construction is an important factor for your client. Use online or print resources to locate and evaluate information on construction materials and the availability of them. Include the best window and siding options for this region in your search. Then analyze which options support your client's value for sustainable design and construction. Write a summary outlining the availability of the best options and provide evidence regarding why these options are best.

Core Skills

4. **Construction observation** Observe a house under construction and identify as many of the structural and framing components discussed in this chapter as you can. If the project is further along, note the surface materials used and determine the reasoning for their selection. If possible, take photographs of the house under construction. Report your findings to the class.
5. **Research, writing, and speaking** Make a list of the door and window sizes in one room of your house or from the house of someone you know. Take this list to a building supply company and obtain costs for replacing these windows and doors with energy-efficient units. Compare the costs of two manufacturers. Also find out the labor cost for installing them. As an alternative, use the websites of two building supply companies to do your comparison. Use school-approved presentation software to create an illustrated report to share your findings with the class.
6. **Researching and writing** Review the website for your state's attorney general regarding information about problems with new home construction or remodeling that home owners report. Also, check the cautionary information to home owners that these offices provide. Use the information and desktop publishing software to create a consumer flyer noting a list of brief steps to help home owners avoid potential problems when building or remodeling.

Chapter 9 Assessment

7. **Math practice** Imagine you are a contractor hired by a family to build their new home. The house plan they have selected contains a total of 1,800 square feet of heated space. Your clients want a rough estimate of how much it will cost to build this plan before they proceed with contract discussion. How would you determine the cost? Contact a number of builders in your community, and ask them what the building costs currently are per square foot of space. Find the average and multiply it by 1,800 square feet. What is your estimate?
8. **Research and writing** Use the Internet to examine information about the process for creating pressure-treated lumber and engineered wood beams. What environmental and safety factors are involved in the manufacture of this lumber? Is it sustainable? Why or why not? Write a summary of your findings.
9. **Technology** Determine if your school has housing-design software similar to what is used in the housing industry. If so, explore the program(s) and determine how the software can assist a builder. Print out a drawing from the computer and present it to the class along with a summary of your findings, or create a digital report to share your information with the class.
10. **Research and speaking** Use the website of a major window manufacturer to identify photos of various window styles, shapes, and special options to share with the class. Use a school-approved web application to create a digital poster of your findings. Upload your poster to the class website for peer review. Be sure to credit the window manufacturer in your poster presentation.
11. **Research** Search online using the key term *house construction* to find a site containing photos of houses under construction. Identify the various stages of construction.
12. **Reading and writing** Using reliable online resources, research one career related to housing construction that is not already presented in this chapter. Provide a summary of that career, including interests and skills needed for the job, a career snapshot or overview, education and training needed, licensing and examinations required, professional associations for the career, and job outlook. Cite all sources you used in your research.
13. **CTE career readiness practice** Suppose you work in a manufacturing facility that utilizes heavy machinery. Safe actions are important to prevent employee injuries. In an effort to promote employee safety and health, the company strictly follows a random drug testing policy. One of your coworkers often brags to you about his off-hours alcohol and drug use—the effects of which showed in his near-accident recently. You wonder whether his actions were responsible, especially in light of the type of work and machinery he uses on the job. You go about your work without saying anything to anyone. After your coworker misses three days of work, you ask your boss about him. All that your boss reveals is "he won't be back." You wonder if he failed his drug test. Then you begin to ask yourself, "Am I acting responsibly in this situation by not talking to my boss about my coworker's behavior? Are my coworkers in danger because of this lack of action? How should I handle such situations in the future? What is the responsible way to behave in such situations and how should I handle them?" Write a response to this scenario addressing each question.

Design Practice

14. **Frame design** Use a CADD software program to draft the footing and foundation design for a home. Apply local building codes and guidelines for house construction in your area. Print a copy of your design to keep in your portfolio.
15. **Portfolio** Choose a house design discussed in Chapter 6. Then draw the foundation and frame of the house using a ¼-inch to 1-foot scale. Label each part of your design. Then select the types of windows and doors you would suggest for it. Include drawings, photos from magazines or websites, or pictures from sales brochures to illustrate your selections. Write a summary about your proposal. Keep your project in your portfolio for future reference.

Chapter 10

Interior Systems

Content Terms

system
electric current
conductor
circuit
ampere (amp)
voltage
watts
conduit
service drop
meter
overcurrent protection devices
fuse
circuit breaker
ground fault circuit interrupter (GFCI)
home generators
vent stack
soil stack
trap
HVAC
forced warm-air system
duct
insulation
weather stripping

Academic Terms

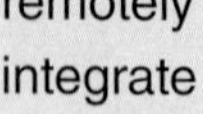

remotely
integrate
decompose
impermeable

Learning Outcomes

After studying this chapter, you will be able to

- summarize the parts of the electrical system.
- distinguish between the use of natural gas and liquid propane gas in households.
- summarize the functions of the two main parts of the plumbing system.
- compare and contrast the different types of heating systems.
- summarize how cooling systems work.
- determine materials and techniques used in housing to conserve household energy.

Reading with Purpose

Find a news article that relates to a topic covered in this chapter. Print the article and read it before reading the chapter. As you read the chapter, highlight passages in the news article that relate to the text.

While studying, look for the access icon  **to:**

- **Practice** the *Content* and *Academic Terms* with e-flash cards, matching activities, and vocabulary games.
- **Reinforce** what you learn by completing the *Review & Assessment* questions and e-mailing them to your instructor.

www.g-wlearning.com/housing/

adbePhoto/Shutterstock.com

Almost every house has systems within it to make it physically comfortable. A **system** is an interacting or interdependent group of items forming a unified whole. The systems in a house—or *mechanical systems*—control the interior temperature and relative humidity, and provide electricity, gas, and water to the house.

Basic housing considerations regarding the interior systems may include the following questions: Will I have gas or electric appliances, or both? How can I make the house more energy efficient? How much insulation do I need? What window type is best for the climate? What new technologies do today's houses use? These questions will be easier to answer after studying this chapter.

Electrical Systems

Almost all houses in the United States have electrical power. Electricity provides energy for lighting and the operation of appliances. It also powers the operation of most of the systems within the house (Figure 10.1).

Around your house, perhaps you have noticed words like *watts*, *volts*, or *amperes (amps)* on electrical appliances or even lightbulbs. Knowledge of basic electricity will help you understand these terms and how the electrical system functions.

Electrical Terms

Electricity is the movement of electrons along a conductor. Another name for electricity is **electric current**. The **conductor** allows the flow of electricity and is usually a wire. This movement takes place at about the speed of light. A **circuit** forms when electrons follow a path from the source of electricity to the device and back to the source. The circuit is composed of a delivery wire and a return wire.

Harry Hu/Shutterstock.com

Figure 10.1 Electricity provides the capacity to watch TV in a well-lighted room.

The greater the number of electrons passing a given point in a circuit, the greater is the current. The measure of the amount of electricity passing through a conductor per unit of time is the **ampere (amp)**. For example, a 100-watt incandescent lightbulb requires almost one ampere (0.83 amps) of current to make it work properly.

Voltage is a measure of the pressure used to push the electrical current along a conductor. This pressure is present in wiring circuits whether electricity is in use or not.

The electrical utility company delivers electricity to your house at a voltage that will operate your lighting, electrical appliances, and other electrical equipment. Lighting and most small appliances require 110 volts. Larger appliances—such as an electric kitchen range, electric water heater, electric clothes dryer, and furnace—require 220 volts.

The amount of electrical power used is measured in **watts**. When operating a device, watts tell consumers how much electrical power the device will use. For example, the usage of one watt of power occurs when one ampere lights a 100-watt incandescent lightbulb in a circuit with a force of one volt. The following equation helps show this concept:

$$\text{watts} = \text{amperes} \times \text{volts}$$

Electrical Power Generation

Electrical power comes from a variety of sources. Power plants usually generate electrical current by converting the energy from falling water, atomic fission, or burning fossil fuels into electricity. A *fossil fuel* is a fuel that forms in the earth from plant or animal remains. Fossil fuels include natural gas, propane, gasoline, coal, charcoal, and wood. Burning of these energy sources produces steam that turns turbines in generators to produce electricity.

Another form of electrical power generation comes from the wind. How does this renewable source of energy produce electricity? Modern-day wind turbines (similar to the old-style windmills) capture wind energy. The large blades of the wind turbines rotate as wind flows over them. While rotating, the blades move a drive shaft that runs an electric generator to make electricity.

Power plants transmit electricity at high voltages in wires held high by steel towers. When the electricity reaches the community, a transformer reduces the voltage and increases the current. Distribution of electricity occurs throughout a neighborhood via wires on poles or buried

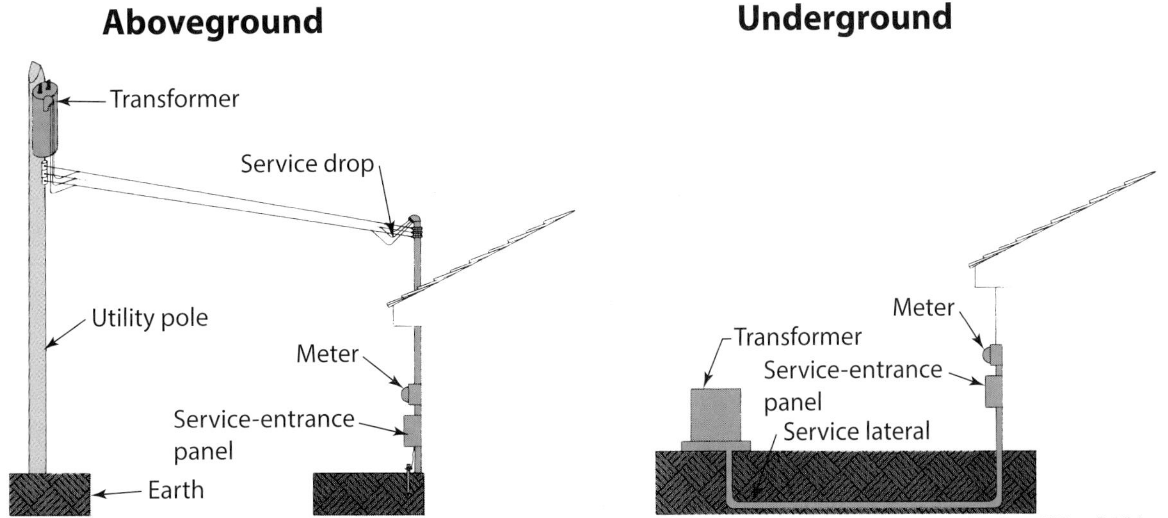

Figure 10.2 Electricity travels from the power plant to your house through conductors that carry the electric current.

underground in a conduit. A **conduit** is a metal or plastic pipe that surrounds and protects the wires.

Before the electricity reaches your house, another transformer lowers the voltage even further. A three-wire line from the transformer provides both 110 and 220 voltages for the house.

Electricity in the House

At the house, the electric company installs a service drop. A **service drop** contains the wires connecting the utility pole transformer to the point of entry to the customer's house (Figure 10.2). The wires can also run underground to the house through a *service lateral*. In both instances, the three wires run to the electric meter for the house. The **meter** monitors electrical usage. A power company representative periodically checks the meter to determine power usage for the house. In some locations, the power company uses a computer program to read the meter ***remotely*** (at a distance) from a central office.

The *service entrance panel* is a large metal box that receives power from the electric company's service drop or service lateral. It divides the power into individual circuits. These circuits provide electricity to each room or combination of rooms in the house (Figure 10.3).

Overcurrent Protection

An **overcurrent protection device** protects each circuit by stopping the excessive flow of electrical current in the circuit. This situation occurs when appliances or other electrical items on a circuit draw too much current. Most large electrical appliances—such as refrigerators or dishwashers—require their own circuit (or dedicated circuit). This means no other appliances should be on this circuit.

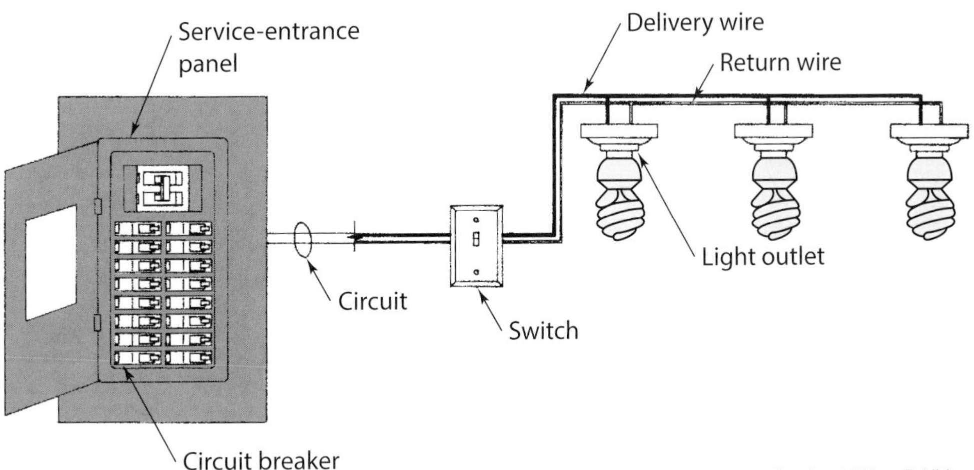

Figure 10.3 A circuit carries electricity from the service entrance panel to the electrical devices in your home.

Two types of overcurrent protective devices exist: a fuse and a circuit breaker. A **fuse** is a device that includes a wire or strip of fusible metal that melts and interrupts a circuit when an electrical-current overload occurs. A **circuit breaker** is a switch that automatically trips and interrupts the flow of electrical current in the event of an abnormal condition. If trouble develops on one circuit, only that circuit will be out of operation when the fuse blows or circuit breaker trips. Usage of fuses mainly occurs in older houses, while newer houses utilize circuit breakers.

In addition to fuses and circuit breakers, **ground fault circuit interrupters (GFCIs)** are special electrical devices that stop the flow of electrical current in a circuit as a safety precaution. (A *ground fault* is an unintentional electrical path between a current source and a grounded surface.) GFCIs help protect people from burns or electrical-shock injuries that are severe or fatal. The National Electrical Code requires installation of GFCIs in kitchens, bathrooms, new garages, and other areas where water may be present.

Installation

Electricians install the wiring inside the house from the service entrance panel to the points of electrical power use. Wiring installation happens while the wall framing is open and accessible. An electrical code authority must inspect the wiring installation while it is still visible.

Deciding where to place electrical outlets and other electrical connections requires advance planning of each room's use. The electrician will need to know the placement of such specific items as the range, refrigerator, furnace, and water heater. Knowing furniture placement is very useful, too. Furniture placement helps determine where connections for cables, TVs, and lamps will go. As a general guideline, each room should have at least three outlets (receptacles). Also, no point along the base of a wall should be more than 6 feet from an outlet.

STEM Science & Technology GFCIs for Household Use

There are three types of GFCIs available for household use. They include the following:

- **Circuit breaker GFCI.** Installation of this special circuit breaker is in the electrical service panel and replaces ordinary circuit breakers. They are much more sensitive to abnormal electrical conditions.
- **Receptacle GFCI.** This type of GFCI replaces a standard receptacle near the kitchen or bathroom sink. Test and reset buttons are in the middle of the receptacle. Although available for use in any house, houses that have a service entrance panel with fuses must use receptacle GFCIs.
- **Portable GFCI.** The most common type of portable GFCI combines an extension cord with a GFCI. You might use a portable GFCI for appliances where installation of GFCI receptacles is not practical.

Circuit breaker GFCI

Photograph Courtesy of Siemens Industry, Inc.

Receptacle GFCI

Goodheart-Willcox Publisher

Portable GFCI

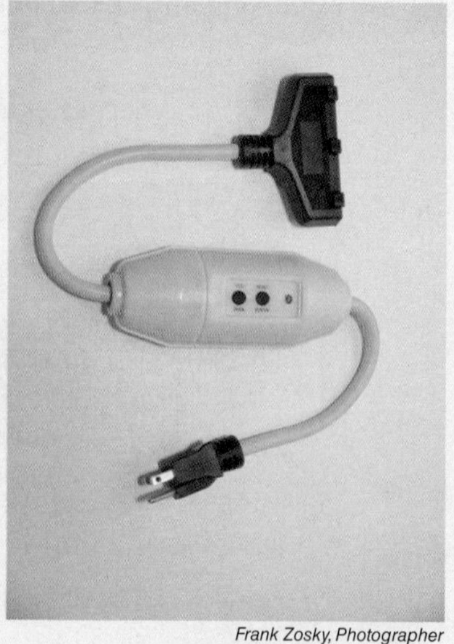

Frank Zosky, Photographer

With greater use of electronic communications and home automation, homes may need integrated wiring schemes (or *structured cabling*) to be able to use electricity-dependent technologies. Existing homes may need rewiring or additional wiring. Often both options are expensive. In new or remodeled homes, however, installation of the integrated wiring can easily occur during the construction process. This is an affordable way to prepare for electrical needs. However, more and more technology supports wireless applications that do not require additional hard-wired connections.

Integrated wiring includes threading coaxial cabling and telephone connections through a central plastic pipe extending vertically to all floors. *Coaxial cabling* allows transmission of high-frequency signals at high speeds in a protective covering that prevents interference and thus provides more effective and efficient transmission. The purpose of wiring in this manner is to ***integrate***, or join, all the systems in the home. This integration offers occupants additional convenience in home entertainment, safety, communications, and home management.

- **Entertainment.** Occupants can program the same video and audio selections throughout the house from one location. They can also operate entertainment systems separately.
- **Safety.** Integrated systems enhance safety because occupants can view visitors on their TV monitors before answering the door. Likewise, they can monitor strangers near the house. They can also control and monitor smoke and carbon monoxide detectors for exit strategies in event of smoke, fire, or carbon monoxide.
- **Communication.** The home computer links to a variety of home services, including banking and shopping.
- **Home management.** Integrated wiring makes installation and repair of home systems easier. For appliance maintenance, a manufacturer can monitor the equipment through a remote computer system to alert the owner of what steps to take for a repair. The computer system also lets occupants control and monitor activities and systems in the home, including lighting and room temperatures.

In response to electric power outages that result from severe weather or other causes, some homes now have backup generators, or **home generators**. These home generators can turn on automatically to create electricity when the electric power fails. Power sources for home generators include natural and propane gas. See Figure 10.4.

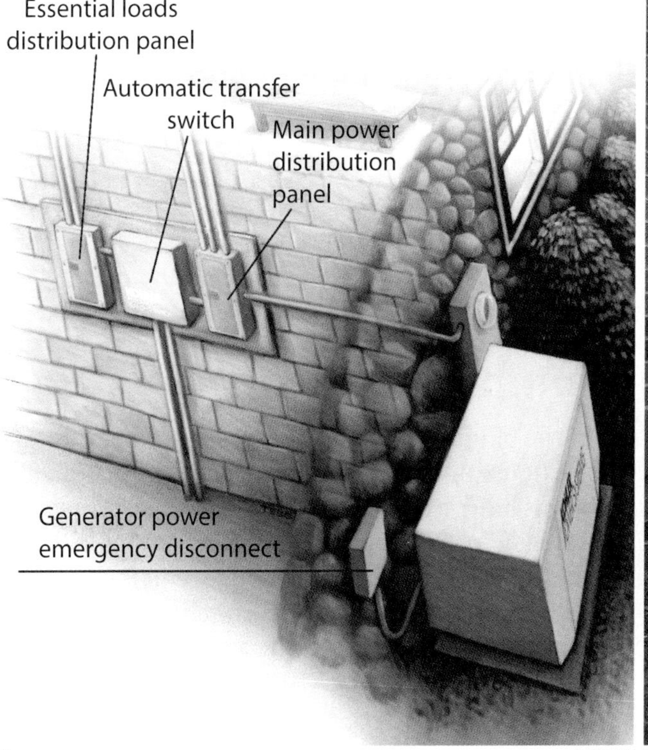

A KOHLER

B KOHLER

Figure 10.4 This illustration shows how a home generator works (A). It comes on automatically when there is electric utility failure and provides seamless electricity for the home. The home occupants do not need to worry when the utility power goes off because this home generator provides the necessary backup electricity (B).

Review & Assessment

1. What is electricity? What role do conductors and circuits play in electricity?
2. Contrast *ampere*, *voltage*, and *watt*.
3. What is the function of the service entrance panel?
4. Explain the differences between a *fuse*, *circuit breaker*, and *GFCI*.
5. What is the benefit of an integrated wiring scheme?

Gas as an Energy Source

Many houses use gas as an additional source of energy. It is a popular fuel for cooking, heating water, and heating the air. Gas fuels include natural gas, which is piped from a gas main to your house, and liquid propane gas, which is delivered in pressurized tanks to your house.

Natural Gas

Natural gas comes from wells in the ground. From the gas fields, high-pressure pumps force the gas through large pipelines to communities (Figure 10.5). After reducing the pressure, the gas company distributes the gas throughout the community in pipes called *gas mains*. To furnish gas to your house, the gas company taps the main and lays an underground pipe to your house. The company then places a gas meter where the line enters your house. Like an electric meter, it records the amount of fuel usage.

In the house, the plumber installs branch lines to all gas-burning appliances. Branch lines consist of black pipe and fittings. Usage of a pipe-thread compound prevents the leakage of natural gas on all fittings. The plumber checks the system for leaks before it is used.

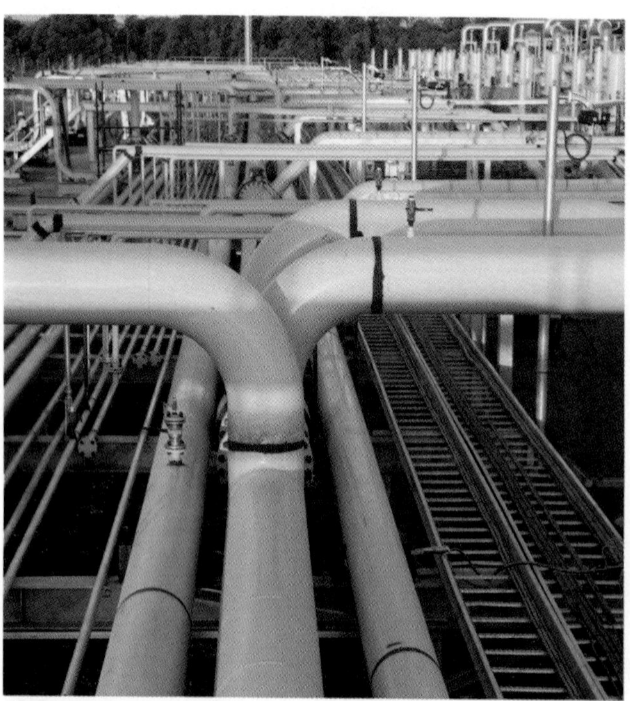

GTS Productions/Shutterstock.com

Figure 10.5 Natural gas is transported in large pipes to communities where it is distributed to houses through gas mains.

Liquid Propane Gas

Propane is a colorless, odorless gas. Houses that normally do not have access to a natural gas line use propane as fuel. Oil refineries produce propane from natural gas, crude oil, or oil refinery gases. Gas supply companies then deliver the *liquid propane gas* (LG or LPG) in tanker trucks to each house as needed. Storage of LPG must be in large, pressurized metal tanks on concrete pads near the house, but not next to it. Then the gas line from the house connects to the tank. LPG has about twice the heating value of natural gas per cubic foot. With the delivery cost and storage requirements, however, it is normally more expensive than natural gas.

Review & Assessment

1. For what functions is gas used in a residential home?
2. What are the key differences between natural gas and liquid propane gas (LPG)?
3. Why are gas lines checked before they are used?

Plumbing Systems

The plumbing system in a house provides water to the house and removes waterborne waste from it. (The gas lines are also part of the plumbing system.) A water supply system provides sufficient hot and cold water so fixtures and appliances can function properly. A wastewater removal system removes waste and used water, depositing them into a sewer line or private septic tank.

Water Supply System

Water flows under pressure to your house from a community water main or a private well or system. It enters the house through a pipe called the *building main*. Inside the house, the water may pass through a water softener, filter, or another treatment device. It then flows to separate cold and hot water mains. The hot water main starts at the water heater. Hot and cold water-branch lines travel throughout the house to each fixture or appliance that needs water.

Piping for the water supply system is located in the floor, walls, or ceiling of a house. Water lines are usually made of $\frac{1}{2}$- or $\frac{3}{8}$-inch-diameter pipes of copper, plastic, or galvanized steel (Figure 10.6). Copper water pipes are the most popular, but are expensive. Various types of plastic are also used. They include the following:

- PEX (cross-linked polyethylene) is commonly used because it is economical, easy to install, and flexible in a large range of temperatures.
- CPVC (chlorinated polyvinyl chloride) is also widely used and is very economical.

Because of serious failure issues, PVC (polyvinyl chloride) water pipe is *not* used for water lines. Local codes may restrict the use of certain types of pipe. The lines are usually under a pressure of 45 to 60 *pounds per square inch (psi)*.

Installation of a shutoff valve at the water meter in a convenient place near or in the building is necessary to turn off the water to the house. Additional shutoffs on each branch line next to fixtures or appliances make it possible to repair separate parts of the system without shutting off the water for the entire house. A leak in the main water line requires closing the valve at the meter.

TFoxFoto/Shutterstock.com

Figure 10.6 The small metal pipes are the hot and cold water lines. The large white pipes are the waste disposal pipe and vent stack.

Wastewater Removal System

In the house, waterborne waste comes mainly from bathrooms, kitchens, and laundry areas. Since it tends to ***decompose*** (break down) quickly, removal of waste should happen before it causes odors or becomes hazardous to human health.

Waste disposal pipes are completely separate from the water supply system. They are much larger (generally $1\frac{1}{2}$ to 4 inches in diameter) than water

Green Choices
Conserving Water in the Bathroom

Saving water in the bathroom requires a few small steps that can make a big difference in water consumption. Consider these tips for using less water every day.

- Turn off the faucet while brushing your teeth, and rinse out the sink when you are done.
- While you are waiting for the water temperature to change, capture water from the shower. Use the captured water for watering plants.
- Save hot water by plugging the tub drain plug and adjusting the water temperature as you fill the tub.
- Flush the toilet when disposing of sanitary waste only. Do not flush garbage.
- Fill the bottom of the sink with a few inches of water to rinse your razor when saving. Do not run the water while shaving.

Bathrooms and kitchens are two of the busiest rooms in the home. Over one-fourth of the water used in an average home is flushed down the toilet. When you are building or if it is time to remodel, consider using water-conserving products, fixtures, and technologies to help reduce wastewater and lower your water bill.

supply lines and are not pressurized. Instead, they rely on gravity to remove waste. The number and type of plumbing fixtures that discharge into the line determine the size of wastewater piping. Piping such as plastic, cast iron, copper, and brass alloy are used. Local codes specify the types and sizes of pipes required in the area.

As the wastewater leaves the house, it moves either to the community sewer lines or a private septic tank. When connected to a community sewer line, wastewater goes through a treatment system. Then it usually is recycled and used for industrial and irrigation purposes.

When community sewer lines are unavailable, homes use septic tanks to dispose of wastewater. A *septic tank* is an underground tank that decomposes waste through the action of bacteria. The wastewater flows into the tank where bacteria dissolve much of what settles to the bottom. The liquid wastewater at the top of the tank flows into a system of perforated (punctured with holes) underground pipes called a *drainfield*. There, wastewater disperses into the soil.

Removal of gases that result from the wastewater removal system must also occur. A **vent stack** is a vertical pipe that extends through the roof to release gases and odors outdoors. It connects to the drain lines or soil stack that carries the wastewater. The **soil stack** is the main vertical pipe that receives waste matter from all plumbing fixtures. In the use of a combination waste and vent (CWV), the vent also acts as the soil stack. The pipe channels the water and waste to drain down and away from the house. Every house has at least one soil stack for each toilet.

Each plumbing fixture has a **trap**—a bend in the pipe within or just below a fixture that catches and holds a quantity of water. This pocket of water prevents sewage gases from seeping back into the house. Installation of a trap is necessary at each fixture unless the fixture has a built-in trap, such as a toilet. Notice the trap under the sink in Figure 10.7.

In remote cabins or isolated cottages, sometimes a water source and sewage system for installing a toilet is not available. Installing a toilet in places such as basements, workshops, and garages may also be difficult. In these cases, one option is a composting toilet. A *composting toilet* is a self-contained, stand-alone toilet. These units require no water or external plumbing. The system operates like a garden compost pile, transforming waste into a stable end product.

Lisa F. Young/Shutterstock.com

Figure 10.7 The trap under this sink catches and holds a pocket of water that prevents sewage gas from backing into the house.

Plumbing Fixtures

A plumbing fixture is a device that connects to the plumbing system. Plumbing fixtures include kitchen sinks, lavatories, toilets, and bathtubs. Modern plumbing fixtures are made from a variety of materials. They include enameled cast iron, enameled steel, stainless steel, fiberglass, and plastics. These materials are durable, corrosion-resistant, nonabsorbent, and have smooth, easy-to-clean surfaces (Figure 10.8). Industrial designers often design these fixtures.

Plumbing fixtures have a variety of characteristics and purposes. Plumbing fixtures include the following:

- **Kitchen sink.** A kitchen sink is a flat-bottomed plumbing fixture used for food preparation and cleanup. Sinks are available in a large variety of sizes and shapes. The most common is the double-compartment sink installed in a cabinet countertop.
- **Lavatory.** A *lavatory* is a plumbing fixture designed for washing hands and faces in bathrooms. Lavatories come in a variety of colors, sizes, and shapes. They are available in wall-hung, countertop, and pedestal models (Figure 10.9).
- **Toilet.** A toilet is a water-flushed plumbing fixture designed to receive human waste. Toilets are usually made of a ceramic material called *porcelain*. They are installed directly on the floor or suspended from the wall.

Green Choices: Conserving Water in the Kitchen

To save water in the kitchen, use the following steps to reduce your water usage:

- Use as little water as possible when washing dishes by hand. Use only the necessary amount of dish liquid.
- Rinse the dishes in a rack all together to reduce rinse-water usage. Use a sprayer with short bursts to rinse. Avoid letting the water run.
- Use appropriate water and energy-efficient settings when using the dishwasher.
- Keep a container of drinking water on hand in the refrigerator. Doing so wastes less water than waiting for running water to cool down for each glass.
- Use the microwave oven to defrost food or defrost in the refrigerator instead of using running water.
- Use only the required amount of water for cooking such foods as pasta or vegetables.

Career Focus: Industrial Designer

Are you artistic, realistic, and enterprising? Do you enjoy working with forms, designs, and patterns in a way that requires self-expression? Do you enjoy practical, hands-on problems and solutions? If so, a career as an industrial designer may interest you.

Interests/Skills: Industrial designers are skilled in the fields of art, business, and engineering. Many have an appreciation for plants, animals, and real-world materials like wood, tools, and machinery. They must be able to start up and carry out projects. Industrial designers have these skills: creativity; artistic ability; detail-orientation; and problem-solving, communication, and technology skills.

Career Snapshot: Industrial designers are engineers who design the products people use every day. These designers are responsible for the style, function, quality, and safety of almost every manufactured product. Usually designers specialize in one particular product category, such as automobiles, appliances, electronics, medical equipment, furniture, toys, tools and construction equipment, or housewares.

Education/Training: A bachelor's degree is required for most entry-level commercial and industrial design positions. Many designers also pursue a master's degree to increase their employment opportunities.

Licensing/Examinations: None.

Professional Association: Industrial Designers Society of America (IDSA)

Job Outlook: Employment of industrial designers is expected to grow two percent, slower than average for all occupations, through the year 2024. Competition for jobs is expected; those with strong backgrounds in engineering and computer-aided drafting and design and extensive business expertise will have the best prospects. Consumer demand for new products and product styles will help sustain the demand for industrial designers.

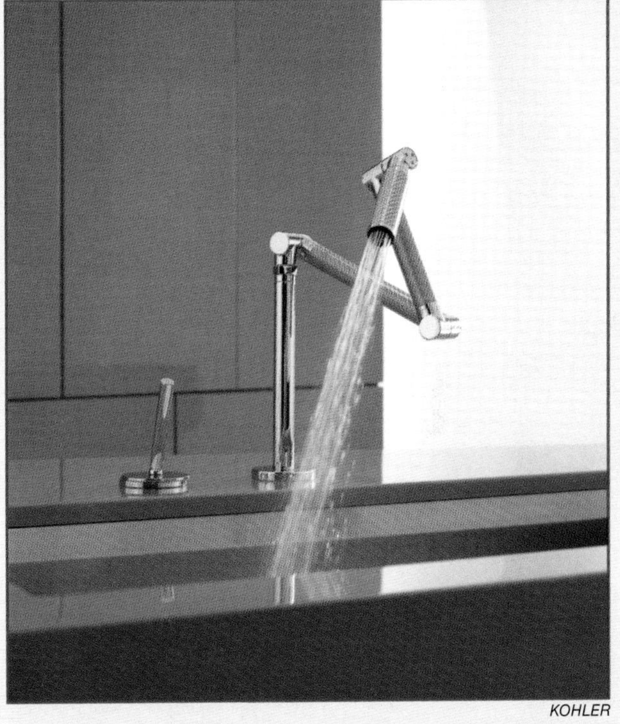

KOHLER

Sources: The Occupational Outlook Handbook (OOH); the Occupational Information Network (O*NET)

Pottery Barn

Figure 10.8 The surfaces of plumbing fixtures should be extremely durable and stain resistant.

© iStock.com/skodonnell

Figure 10.9 Sinks can be plain or quite fancy, as this beautiful design shows.

- **Bathtub.** A bathtub is a fixed tub that holds water for bathing. It comes in a variety of shapes, but the most common is rectangular. Overhead installation of showerheads is common in many bathtubs. Separate showering units are available.

Review & Assessment

1. Describe how the water supply system functions.
2. How does the waste removal system function?
3. Name four common plumbing fixtures.

Heating Systems

Heating a house may occur by using one of four conventional heating systems. They are forced warm-air, hydronic, electric radiant, and central heat-pump systems. Nonconventional heating systems—such as solar heat, fireplaces, and stoves—can also heat a house. **HVAC** (heating, ventilating, and air-conditioning) is a common term that refers to systems that condition the living space for thermal comfort.

Conventional Heating Systems

Conventional heating systems may use electricity, gas, oil, or coal as fuel. The use of coal is rare in newly built houses. The choice of which energy source to use is based on availability and the cost of fuel and operation. Environmental concerns also influence the fuel choice.

Forced Warm-Air System

In the **forced warm-air system**, the furnace heats and delivers the air to the rooms through supply ducts. A **duct** is a large round tube or rectangular boxlike structure that delivers heated (and air-conditioned) air to distant rooms or spaces. Ducts are located beneath floors and along ceilings. Ducts connect the heating (or cooling) system to vents in or near the ceiling or floor (Figure 10.10). The heating unit consists of a heater (and/or cooler) and a blower section that connects to the duct system.

A furnace uses gas, oil, or electricity to heat the air. A blower moves the heated air through the supply ducts to the living quarters. A separate set of ducts, or air return, carries the cool air from each room back to the furnace. This periodic movement of warm air into cold spaces continues until rooms reach the desired temperature.

The indoor temperature is controlled in the living area with a thermostat that is wired to the furnace. A *thermostat* is a device for regulating room temperature. Furnace filters trap dust to prevent blowing it throughout the house. Forced warm-air systems are very common because they are economical and easy to install. However, some

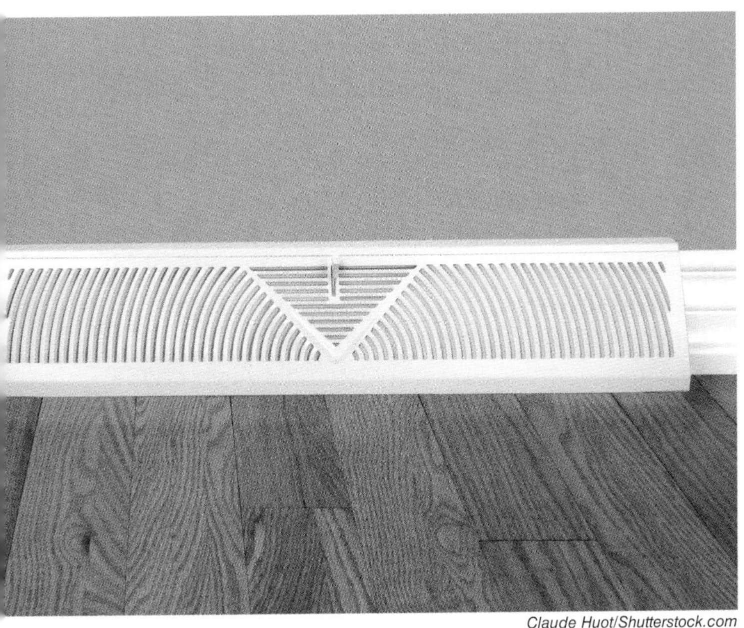
Claude Huot/Shutterstock.com

Figure 10.10 This heating vent delivers warm air to a room and is connected to a heating duct below the floor.

people dislike the sound and feel of the rapid air movement the system causes.

Hydronic Heating System

Circulating hot water systems are called *hydronic heating systems*. Water heats in a boiler to a preset temperature, usually 180°F to 210°F. When the water reaches the proper temperature, a pump circulates it through pipes to radiators (Figure 10.11). As the water cools, it returns to the boiler for reheating. Radiators are located throughout the living areas, usually along the outside walls to reduce cold air drafts and increase comfort.

A *radiant-hydronic heating system* circulates hot water through copper or plastic tubing embedded in a coil or grid pattern in a concrete floor, wood floor, or plaster ceiling. As the water circulates, heat radiates from the floor or ceiling into the room. Usage of this system is common in mild climates and also as a backup heating system.

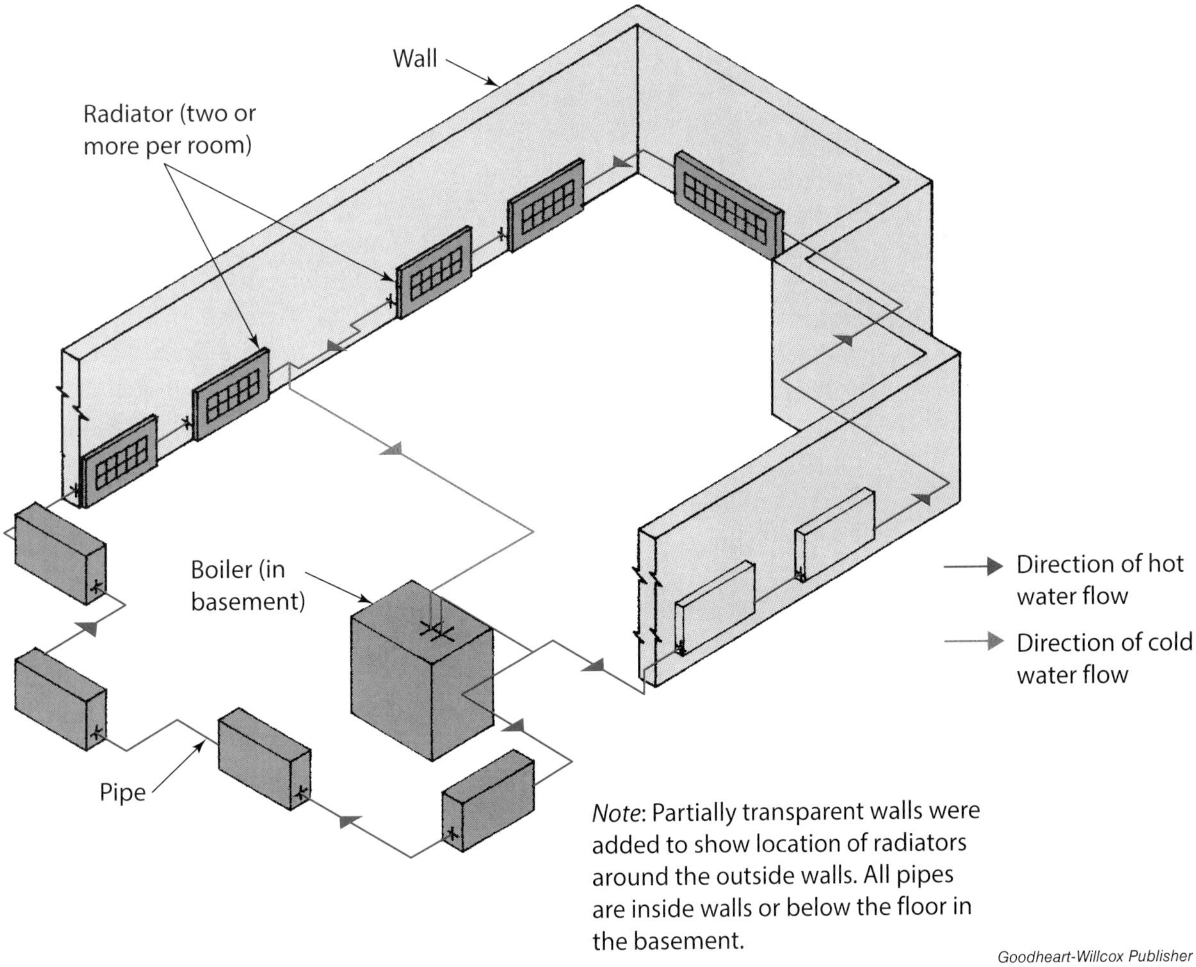

Wall
Radiator (two or more per room)
Boiler (in basement)
Pipe
Direction of hot water flow
Direction of cold water flow

Note: Partially transparent walls were added to show location of radiators around the outside walls. All pipes are inside walls or below the floor in the basement.

Goodheart-Willcox Publisher

Figure 10.11 Hot water is pumped from the boiler to the radiators in individual rooms. Cool water is returned to the boiler for reheating.

Career Focus General Contractors and Allied Tradespeople

Do you often wonder how something is assembled or built? Do you notice when something is built or works well? Do you see improvements that could be made in the craftsmanship of a room? If you do, a career in a variety of construction trades might be for you!

Interests/Skills: General and subcontractors rely on mathematical and critical-thinking skills to estimate costs, develop contracts, and maintain budgets. Leadership, time-management, organization, and communication skills are imperative to manage construction schedules as well as to anticipate and deal with delays and unexpected issues on job sites. All contractors should be self-motivated, dependable, and have an excellent attention to detail in order to provide timely and professional results for their customers. Basic business skills are essential.

Career Snapshot: General contractors organize construction teams, maintain budgets, and oversee all aspects of construction projects from beginning to end. They typically work in the field rather than inside an office and may supervise multiple projects simultaneously. General contractors collaborate with multiple entities including architects, engineers, interior designers, and multiple subcontractors. Subcontractors represent all of the various allied trades that do the actual construction, including painters, millworkers, brick masons, flooring installers, etc. They also work with electricians, HVAC mechanical installers, and various engineers. They must be aware and ensure compliance with all safety codes and accessibility laws. General contractors and the allied trades typically work full-time, but often work alternative schedules to accommodate tight construction schedules and odd hours when building sites are available.

Education/Training: For a general contractor, an associate's or bachelor's degree in building science, construction management, or architecture is essential for success in larger firms. These programs will typically cover construction materials and methods, project management and budgeting, interior systems, and safety codes and standards. For subcontractors and other tradespeople, certificate and training programs are available in a wide range of specialties. Apprenticeships and internships are a great way to gain experience in construction while under the watchful eye of an experienced manager or tradesperson.

Licensing/Examinations: Licensing and certification requirements differ within each state, but seeking certification certainly increases employment opportunities. Those states who do require licensure may call for not only educational credentials, but also extensive hands-on industry experience. The *Construction Management Association of America (CMAA)* and the *American Institute of Constructors (AMC)* are organizations with certifications for general contractors and managers. These certifications must be renewed every few years to ensure professionals are up to date on building regulations. There are dozens of separate certifications for allied trades including plumbing and electrical subcontractors, those that deal with the removal of hazardous waste, and even basic framing and construction. Requirements often include passing an exam and providing proof of experience and letters of recommendation from former supervisors. Many construction professionals become LEED Accredited Professionals (Leadership in Energy and Environmental Design) for their particular area of specialization. Contractors may also take the *Construction Documents Technologist (CDT)* and *Certified Construction Contract Administration (CCCA)* exams.

Professional Associations: Associations include the *Construction Management Association of America (CMAA)*; the *American Institute of Constructors (AMC)*; and the *Construction Specifications Institute (CSI)*. These are national organizations that not only provide licensure, but also offer continued education opportunities and exposure to new products and building methods.

Job Outlook: Employment for construction managers is projected to be about five percent through 2024, which is about as fast as average for all occupations. The employment outlook for tradespeople (construction, electrical, plumbing, and HVAC) is expected to range from 12 to 14 percent, which is faster than average growth for all occupations. Those with an education and experience in sustainable design, technology, and engineering have the best employment prospects.

Sources: The Occupational Outlook Handbook (OOH); the Occupational Information Network (O*NET)

Hydronic heating is a quiet, clean, and efficient type of system that does not create drafts. A disadvantage, however, is that it takes longer to raise a room's temperature to a comfortable level. Also, if installed in a concrete floor that cracks for any reason, repairs are costly. Hydronic heating systems normally do not provide for cooling, air filtration, humidification, or dehumidification.

Electric Radiant-Heating System

Electric radiant-heating systems use resistance wiring to produce heat in the wire. The placement of wires may be in the ceiling, floor, or baseboards. Since heat travels from hot to cooler objects, the heat moves from the wiring through the air molecules. Individual thermostats control the temperature in each room.

The electric radiant-heating system allows complete freedom in furniture and drapery placement. There is no introduction of air, no radiator usage, and air movement from the system is almost nonexistent. Disadvantages of the electric radiant-heating system include the high cost of electrical energy and the installation costs. Installation of this type of system generally occurs during house construction.

Central Heat-Pump System

A *central heat-pump system* is an electric refrigeration unit used to either heat or cool the house. It removes heat from the outside air or ground in cold weather. In warm weather, it removes heat from the air in the house. The heat pump consists of liquid refrigerant, a compressor, and heat exchangers. A fan circulates the heated or cooled air through the house (Figure 10.12).

A central heat-pump system is most efficient in areas with moderate to mild winter climates, where temperatures stay above 20°F. It usually costs more than other heating systems. However, it costs less than buying both a heating system and an air-conditioning unit.

Solar Heating Systems

Solar heating systems use energy from the sun to provide heating and sometimes hot water for a house. A house that uses a solar heating system often has a backup heating system such as a stove to compensate for long periods of cloudy weather. The two main types of solar heating systems are active and passive. Both systems consist of a collector and a storage area.

Active Systems

Active systems have solar collector panels on the roof of the house. This type of system requires pumps, fans, or other devices to move the heat from the collectors to a storage area or the space requiring heat.

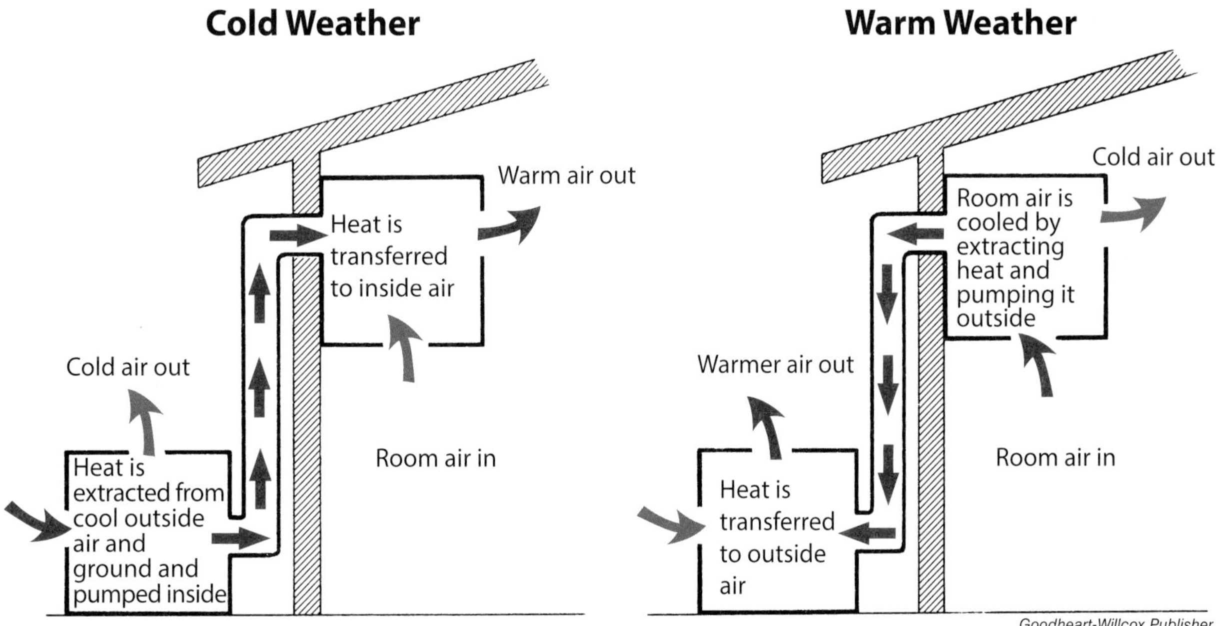

Figure 10.12 In cold weather, the heat pump absorbs heat from the air and ground outside and pumps it inside. In warm weather, the heat pump absorbs heat from the air inside the house and pumps it outside.

Passive Systems

Passive systems have no solar panels. Instead, they rely on the construction materials to collect and store the sun's heat. Windows, doorways, greenhouses, or skylights act as solar collectors. Walls and floors made from masonry materials such as concrete, concrete block, brick, stone, and adobe absorb the heat and act as the storage areas. Water-storage walls or tanks also store heat effectively.

Fireplaces and Stoves

Fireplaces and stoves are sources of heat as well as focal points. They differ from models of the past because they are safer, cleaner, and more efficient. Wood-burning fireplaces and stoves, however, still require cutting, splitting, and stacking of firewood. Moving wood indoors can leave debris on the floor. Also, after prolonged use, most stoves and fireplaces produce a light film of smoke residue in the room.

Fireplaces

Careful design and construction of fireplaces is necessary for them to operate correctly and prevent heat loss when not in use. Most fireplaces today have a single opening, or *face*, in the front. Some also have two or three openings. Contemporary houses often have freestanding fireplaces.

Traditional fireplaces are made from masonry, while newer models are often made from metal. Metal fireplaces may have a covering of brick or other materials so they look like solid masonry. Although many of these new units are wood burning, some use electricity or gas to give the appearance of a log fire.

A fireplace consists of a hearth, firebox, damper, smoke shelf, chimney, and flue (Figure 10.13). The *hearth* is the flat area where you build the fire, and the apron is in front of the fire area. The *firebox* is the combustion chamber. Firebrick—which is made from fire-resistant clay—lines the firebox. A *damper* is a metal device that closes off the airflow when the fireplace is not in use. The *smoke shelf* is where the smoke collects before going up the chimney. The smoke shelf also prevents outside air currents from forcing smoke back into the room. The *flue* carries smoke outdoors and creates a draft for the fire. Special tiles or metal liners that resist high temperatures line the flue. The chimney pipes the smoke out of the house. A variety of tiles can be used to create the fireplace surround (Figure 10.14).

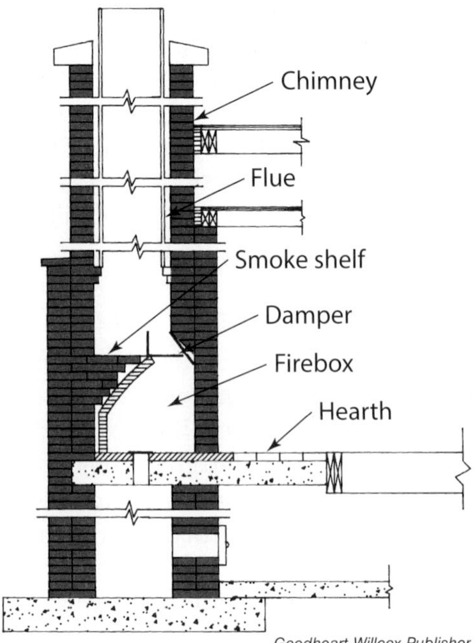

Goodheart-Willcox Publisher

Figure 10.13 Each part of the fireplace plays an important role in the efficient burning of wood and removal of smoke.

Phase4Studios/Shutterstock.com

Figure 10.14 This beautiful fireplace design was created by using quality wall and decorative tile and demonstrates the use of a fireplace for outdoor entertaining.

A *fireplace insert* is a metal device that fits into an existing fireplace and attaches to the chimney liner. The fireplace may be made of masonry or be factory-built. A fireplace insert transforms a drafty fireplace into a more energy-efficient heat source.

The insert draws the room's air into the fireplace, circulates it around a heat exchanger, and returns it to the room. Heat-detecting sensors on the insert automatically shut off the blower when the room reaches a desired temperature. This can reduce heating costs since fireplaces with inserts normally have efficiency ratings near 70 percent. Fireplaces without inserts have an efficiency rating of 15 to 35 percent.

Stoves

Stoves usually produce more heat than fireplaces. They generally use coal or wood to generate heat. There are two main types of stoves. *Radiant stoves* produce heat that radiates through the room to cooler objects (Figure 10.15). The surfaces of these stoves are extremely hot. You must keep flammable materials away from them.

In *circulating stoves*, a compartment separates the main fire area from the outside of the stove. Air circulates into and out of the compartment, transferring heat into the room. Sometimes a fan helps the air move through the compartment.

Paul Maguire/Shutterstock.com

Figure 10.15 A radiant stove is a highly efficient and functional heating unit. The one shown here is wood burning.

A thermostat controls the level of heat entering the room. These stoves are safer than radiant stoves because they produce less smoke and their exposed surfaces are cooler.

Another type of stove is the *pellet stove*. It burns waste wood or other organic materials such as agricultural waste. Waste wood refers to "left-over" materials not used in production processes such as furniture making. The waste materials are compressed into pellets resembling rabbit food. One ton of pellets will generate about 17 million British thermal units (Btu) of heat. A wood-burning stove generates about 8 to 10 million Btu per cord of firewood. The pellet-stove hopper (a receptacle that holds pellets) may hold 35 to 130 pounds of pellets—enough to heat a home for about one day. These stoves usually burn a handful of pellets at a time. This results in high-combustion efficiency, which means less ash and no visible smoke. Instead of the conventional chimney, a pellet stove requires a vent.

Today, stoves are more efficient and clean burning because of standards established by the U.S. Environmental Protection Agency (EPA). One standard limits the amount of smoke released per hour through the chimney. Another requires stoves to produce more heat per unit of fuel used. These two standards help to assure a cleaner and safer environment.

Review & Assessment

1. List advantages and disadvantages of the four types of conventional heating systems.
2. Why might someone choose a radiant-heating system instead of a forced warm-air heating system?
3. Describe a fireplace, wood stove, and pellet stove. Explain which you would choose for a new house.

Cooling Systems

Cooling systems provide cool, clean, moisture-free air during hot, humid weather. Usage of a central air conditioner is the most frequent cooling system in houses. Room air conditioners are also used for cooling certain rooms. The most common cooling system is the compressor-cycle system. It uses a compressed refrigerant (a liquid) to absorb heat, which cools the air. The refrigerant absorbs heat as it passes through an evaporator coil and changes from a liquid to a gas. The gas passes through the compressor, where it is pressurized. The hot, pressurized gas passes through the condenser coil, where it gives up heat and changes back to a liquid. Moving through the liquid line, it passes through a metering device into the evaporator coil to begin the cycle again (Figure 10.16).

When cooling a room, moisture in the air condenses on the fins of the condenser and drains away. This process dehumidifies the air and increases the comfort level. The cooler air moves to various parts of the living space through a system of ducts. A blower or air handler usually moves the air through the heating system's ducts.

In a central air-conditioning system, the compressor and the condenser unit are placed outside the building while the air handler is located inside the house. With a room air conditioner, all components are contained in one unit. A part of this unit extends outside through a window or wall opening.

Review & Assessment

1. What is the most common cooling system? Briefly explain how it works.
2. How does air become dehumidified as a room is being cooled with a compressor-cycle system?
3. Where is the equipment of a central-air conditioning system placed?
4. How many pieces of equipment are used with a room air conditioner?

Conserving Energy

Housing consumes about one-fifth of all the energy usage in the United States. Efforts to improve the energy-efficient construction of houses are underway. The U.S. Department of Energy (DOE) has the goal of reducing household energy consumption of both new and existing houses. Energy codes, as part of state building codes, can accomplish this goal by requiring

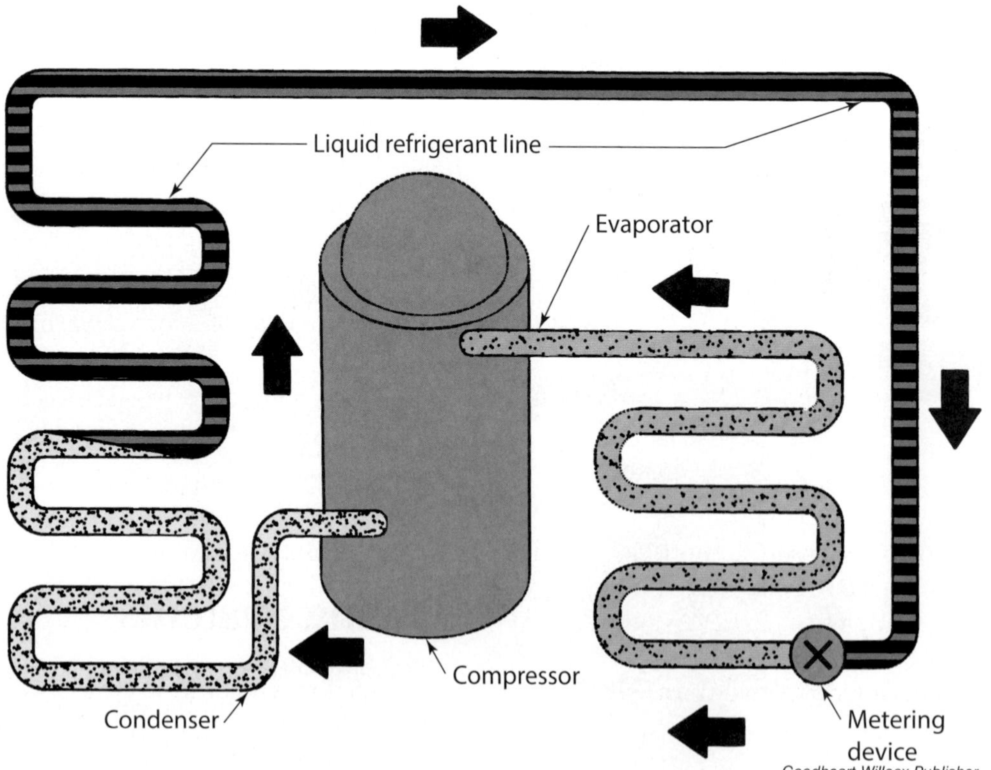

Figure 10.16 This diagram shows the path the refrigerant takes as it moves through the compressor-cycle system of air conditioning.

Engineer Responsibilities for Green and Sustainable Design

During the building process, architects begin by creating a design. Then engineers add equipment and systems for heating, cooling, electricity, plumbing, and other parts of the structure. In the past, lack of communication between architects and engineers led to such problems as buildings that were not durable, comfortable, or energy efficient and were expensive to operate.

Now engineers collaborate with the architects and other industry members in the initial planning stage of the building. This collaboration is possible because of the BIM (Building Information Model), and the software programs that utilize the BIM.

Mechanical, electrical, and plumbing systems (MEP systems) represent one-third of the building cost. Well-engineered MEP systems are vital for the longevity and sustainability of the buildings.

Responsibilities of engineers for green and sustainable design include the following:

- keeping up-to-date on energy efficiency and environmental principles in heating, ventilating, and air-conditioning equipment and design
- choosing new, innovative, and high-performance products from the lighting industries that reduce the amount of energy used for lighting
- selecting plumbing fixtures that can reduce water usage by 30 percent or more
- including rainwater-collection systems for irrigation or toilet flushing while at the same time reducing storm water runoff

improved construction materials and techniques. Thus, building-code authorities are promoting the inclusion of energy codes in state building codes to help reduce household energy consumption. The National Association of Home Builders (NAHB) is a leader in this effort. The ultimate homes in energy efficiency are the zero-energy-use homes, which are part of the push for sustainability and green housing.

In addition, ENERGY STAR®—a joint program of the EPA and DOE—informs consumers about how to save money and protect the environment by choosing the most energy-efficient housing, materials, and appliances on the market. Consumers can achieve the greatest energy savings by choosing products with the ENERGY STAR label. See Chapter 12 for more information about the ENERGY STAR program and household appliances.

Controlling room temperature through heating and cooling systems accounts for most of the energy used in a home. Heating water is the next greatest energy user. Together, space conditioning and hot water systems account for over two-thirds of the energy used in homes.

There are many ways to use less energy at home and thus, reduce energy bills. Although there are many ways to save, one major focus is to improve the air-tightness of the building and install energy-efficient equipment. The remainder of this chapter examines ways to save energy with insulation, energy-efficient windows and doors, and computerized energy management.

Sealing and Insulation

Air leakage is one of the largest wastes of energy in houses. The first step in reducing air leakage is to seal a house with building wrap and apply weather stripping and sealant on windows. The next step in conserving home-energy usage is to surround the living space with proper insulation during house construction. **Insulation** is a material that restricts the flow of air between a house's interior and the outdoors. Insulation has millions of tiny air pockets that resist the flow of heat through it. Insulation materials keep heated air indoors in winter and outdoors in summer. How well a material insulates is measured by its *R-value*. The greater the R-value, the more resistant the material is to the movement of heat (Figure 10.17).

Insulation is made from a variety of materials that differ in efficiency, quality, and safety. These materials include fibrous glass, rock wool, cellulose, urethane, and polystyrene. Insulation is available in blanket, board, loose-fill, and spray-foam forms. Each

R-Values of Common Insulation Materials

Note: The higher the R-value, the better the material blocks transfer of heat per one inch of thickness. Values are averages.

Insulation Material	R-Value Per Inch
Batts or Blankets	
• Fiberglass	• 2.9–3.8
• Rock Wool	• 3.7
Foam Board	
• Molded Expanded Polystyrene	• 3.8–4.4
• Extruded Expanded Polystyrene	• 5.0
• Polyisocyanurate and Polyurethane	• 5.6–8.0
Loose Fill (poured in)	
• Fiberglass	• 2.2–2.7
• Rock Wool	• 3.0–3.3
• Cellulosic Fiber	• 3.2–3.8
Spray Foam	
• Open-Cell Polyurethane (permeable)	• 3.6
• Closed-Cell Polyurethane (non-permeable)	• 6.5

Source: U.S. Department of Energy

Figure 10.17 This chart compares the R-values of common insulating materials.

wavebreakmedia/Shutterstock.com

Figure 10.18 Blanket insulation is used here to insulate a wall.

has different uses and shapes and meets different requirements.

- *Blanket insulation* comes in long rolls, or *batts,* which are shorter rolls usually 4 to 8 feet long. Both rolls and batts come in 16- to 24-inch widths and in various thicknesses. The thicker the insulation is, the shorter the roll. Common usage of blanket insulation occurs in floors, walls, and around pipes and ducts (Figure 10.18).
- *Foam board* insulation is made from rigid-foamed plastics. It is available in sheets 1½-inches to 4-inches thick. It is usually 2 by 4 feet or 4 by 8 feet in size. Foam board insulation is higher in R-value per inch of thickness than other forms of insulation. However, foam board insulation also tends to be more expensive. It is used between concrete and earth, around foundation walls, and on one side of the footing. It is also used on the outside of studs as sheathing.
- *Loose fill* is used in spaces where other types of insulation are difficult to install. It may also be used in attics, inside frame walls, in cores of concrete block, and as filler between other types of insulation. It comes in bags and may be poured or blown into place (Figure 10.19). Loose fill insulation tends to compact over time, however, and loses some of its insulating quality.
- *Spray-foam* insulation is becoming more commonplace and is very effective at both insulating and sealing a house. Spray foam comes in two forms—permeable and ***impermeable*** (material that does not allow substances to pass through). The permeable type allows moisture vapor to pass through while impermeable does not. Advanced designers and builders now insulate the entire envelope of a house, from the underside of the roof to the crawl space or basement. This allows greater efficiency with the HVAC systems in semi-conditioned spaces.

Installing more insulation usually slows the escape of heated air in winter and cooled air in summer. This helps to lower energy use, which lowers heating and cooling bills. Some areas of the country need insulation to combat intensely hot summers, extremely cold winters, or a mix of both.

Ozgur Coskun/Shutterstock.com

Figure 10.19 Here, recycled cellulose insulation is being blown into the attic area. It is excellent for sound control, fire protection, and energy savings.

Both heating and air conditioning needs contribute to the recommended R-values shown in Figure 10.20. These figures reflect national, state, and local recommendations. To use the information, look at the map and find the zone that covers your area. Then read the various R-values shown for that zone to determine your insulation needs.

Having insulation of the proper R-value is very important for promoting energy efficiency and comfort. Equally important is the proper installation of insulation. Consumers should use skillful installers from companies with a reputation for doing high-quality work.

Targeted Air Sealing

One major way to control energy use in a residence is to block conditioned air from leaving the living area. The top of the building should receive first priority, followed by the bottom of the building. Give attention to any leakage from the ducts in forced warm-air heating systems and target walls, windows, and doors last. A special test can help identify air leakage from the home (Figure 10.21). Designers can then develop an appropriate strategy and design to reduce energy loss.

Windows and Doors

Heat loss around windows and doors and through glass panes is an energy problem. Adding weather stripping to windows and doors helps prevent drafts and heat transfer. **Weather stripping** is a strip of material that covers the edges of a window or door to prevent moisture and air from entering the house. Another way to conserve energy is to install storm windows over single-pane glass windows. The airspace between the windows acts as an insulator.

Windows that have double or triple the insulation value of single-pane windows are available. Window ratings assist the consumer in evaluating the expected energy performance of specific types of windows.

Many types of energy-efficient windows contain two or three gas-filled insulating chambers that block almost all the sun's ultraviolet rays. They provide more daylight with less winter heat loss and less summer heat gain. Very energy-efficient windows are available, including *low-emission glass* (low-e) and other window technologies (Figure 10.22). Consumers can also add a film to windows to control excessive heat transfer and damaging rays. Frequent exposure to sun rays can fade and/or weaken fibers and wood finishes.

The need for energy efficiency is not limited to windows. Sliding patio doors feature the same double- and triple-pane window systems. Door construction has evolved so that many attractive doors are also extremely durable and energy efficient.

Energy Conservation Through Technology

An inexpensive device for controlling heating and cooling levels is a programmable thermostat, which uses a computer chip. You can set programmable units to automatically adjust temperatures around your personal schedule—a comfortable setting when you are home and an energy-saving setting when you are

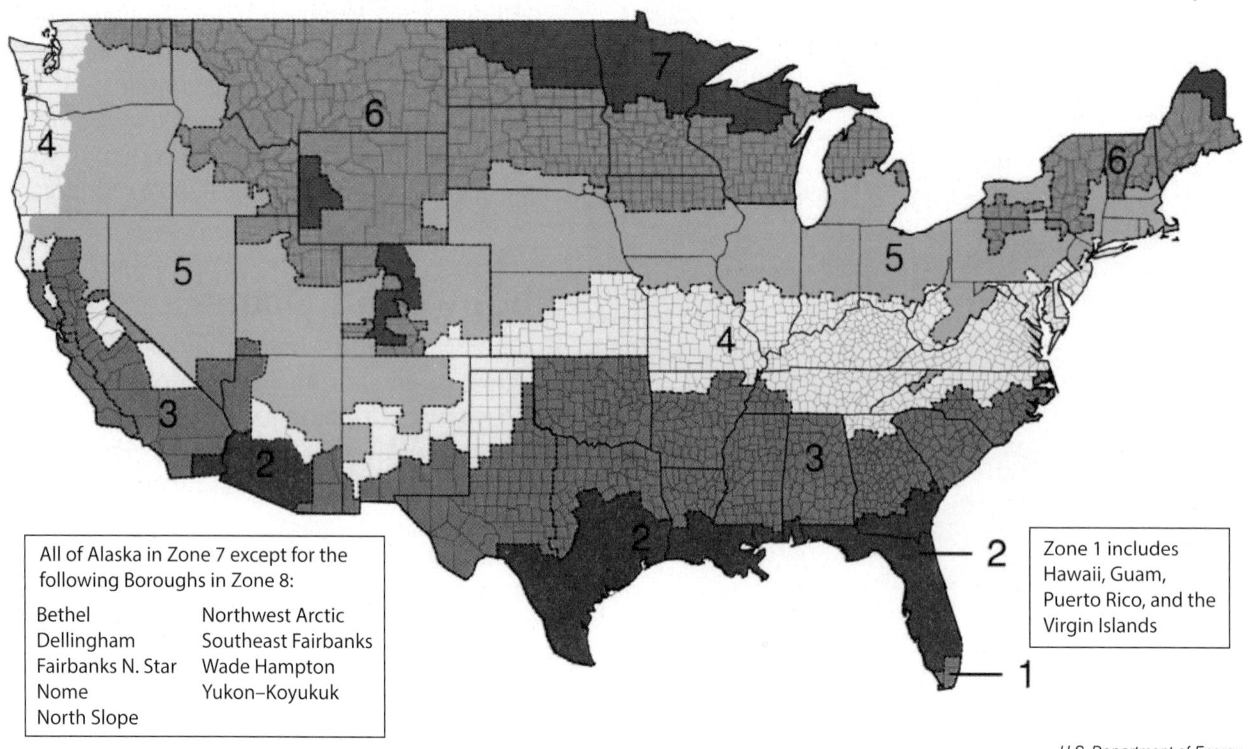

Recommended R-Values for Zones

New Wood-framed Homes

Zone	Heating System	Attic	Cathedral Ceiling	Walls		Floor
				Cavity	Insulation Sheathing	
1	All	R30–R49	R22–R38	R13–R15	None	R13
2	Gas, Oil, Heat Pump, Electric Furnace	R30–R60	R22–R38	R13–R15	None	R13
						R19–R25
3	Gas, Oil, Heat Pump, Electric Furnace	R30–R60	R22–R38	R13–R15	None	R25
					R2.5–R5	
4	Gas, Oil, Heat Pump, Electric Furnace	R30–R60	R22–R38	R13–R15	R2.5–R6	R25–R30
					R5–R6	
5	Gas, Oil, Heat Pump, Electric Furnace	R30–R60	R22–R38	R13–R15	R2.5–R6	R25–R30
			R30–R60	R13–R21	R5–R6	
6	All	R49–R60	R30–R60	R13–R21	R5–R6	R25–R30
7	All	R49–R60	R30–R60	R13–R21	R5–R6	R25–R30
8	All	R49–R60	R30–R60	R13–R21	R5–R6	R25–R30

(Continued)

Figure 10.20 The different heating zones in the states are numbered 1 to 8. The charts show the R-values recommended for house insulation in each zone for both new construction and renovations.

Recommended R-Values for Zones (Figure 10.20, continued)			
Existing Wood-framed Homes			
Zone	Add Insulation to Attic		Floor
	Uninsulated Attic	Existing 3-4 Inches of Insulation	
1	R30–R49	R25–R30	R13
2	R30–R60	R25–R38	R13–R19
3	R30–R60	R25–R38	R19–R25
4	R38–R60	R38	R25–R30
5–8	R49–R60	R38–R49	R25–R30

Wall Insulation: Whenever exterior siding is removed on an

Uninsulated wood-frame wall:

- Drill holes in the sheathing and blow insulation into the empty wall cavity before installing the new siding, and
- Zones 3–4: Add R5 insulative wall sheathing beneath the new siding.
- Zones 5–8: Add R5 to R6 insulative wall sheathing beneath the new siding.

Insulated wood-frame wall:

- For Zones 4 to 8: Add R5 insulative sheathing before installing the new siding.

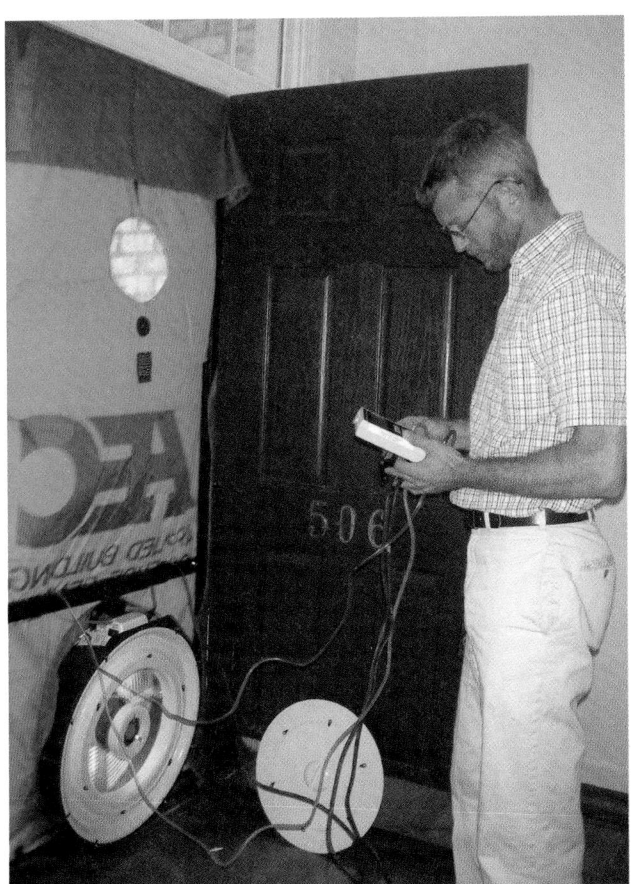

Advanced Energy, Raleigh, North Carolina

Figure 10.21 Trained heating and cooling technicians use a blower-door test to check air leakage in a home.

Image courtesy of JELD-WEN Windows & Doors

Figure 10.22 This remodeling contractor is installing quality windows that provide energy efficiency and reduce the harmful effects of ultraviolet rays on interior furnishings.

STEM Math Calculating Percentages and Energy Savings

Home owners can save a substantial amount of money by making their homes energy efficient. By plugging a zip code into the U.S. Department of Energy's *Home Energy Saver calculator*, you can find out exactly how much you can save. The calculator estimates the annual energy costs for two homes in a zip code—an average home and an energy-efficient home. Use the calculator to find the estimates for two homes in your zip code.

For example, home owner A with an average home in Riverside, Illinois, paid about $1,615 in energy costs last year. How much money did home owner B save by having an energy-efficient home? For the same time and place, home owner B paid $969, or $646 less than home owner A.

With these estimates, you can calculate home owner B's savings in terms of percent. Divide the amount that home owner B saved by the total amount that home owner A paid:

$$646 \div 1,615 = 0.40$$

Convert the decimal number into a percentage by multiplying the decimal by 100 and adding the percent sign (%):

$$0.40 \times 100 = 40\%$$

Home owner B, therefore, enjoyed a 40% savings in average energy costs that year. The Home Energy Saver calculator on the U.S. Department of Energy website also allows users to input detailed facts about their homes to calculate more accurate estimates.

Math Practice

1. Suppose home owner A paid $2,107 in energy costs last year, while home owner B paid $1,148. How much money did home owner B save compared to home owner A last year?
2. Use the same data in the previous question to calculate the percentage home owner B saved in cost compared to home owner A.

away. Most climate controls can be set to change temperatures four times during a 24-hour period—when you wake, leave for work, return home, and go to bed. A programmable thermostat is inexpensive and generally pays for itself in a short period of time.

The trend toward more powerful comfort controls, which in housing is so much more than older models. The new controls can reduce energy use 20 to 40 percent by monitoring electronics used in the home (Figure 10.23). Electronic items include appliances

Christian Delbert/Shutterstock.com

Figure 10.23 Besides regulating the home's lighting, this center also manages home security and messages.

as well as communications, HVAC, and electronic equipment. Computerized controls can manage the lighting, interior climate, and maintenance systems in the following ways:

- turn lights on and off automatically as people enter and leave rooms
- roll shades up and down automatically to admit sun or block cold air
- adjust heating, ventilation, and air-conditioning systems to outdoor weather conditions
- adjust the interior temperature according to activities in the house
- report maintenance and equipment problems automatically so total climate comfort and maximum use of equipment are maintained
- monitor the climate-control system for dirty filters to maximize the efficiency of this system

Trends in the advanced comfort-control centers provide all the features previously discussed in addition to the ability to regulate the home's system from anywhere inside or outside the building. Since the control system links wirelessly to the Internet, home owners can make adjustments to their settings from anywhere they can access the Internet.

Conserving Water

The quality and availability of water is increasingly becoming an important environmental issue. Some areas of the country have severe rainfall shortages that affect how people use water in their homes.

When you are selecting plumbing fixtures for homes such as faucets and toilets, consider choosing from the many products on the market that reduce water usage. These include low-flow showerheads, high-efficiency toilets that reduce water use by 20 percent over standard 1.6 gallon toilets, and water-efficient faucets.

To assist consumers and professionals in making choices about water-efficient products, the EPA has developed a program and label called WaterSense®. Products showing this label undergo independent, third-party testing. This assures consumers that these products meet the EPA's criteria to use at least 20 percent less water than conventional models while still performing well (Figure 10.24).

Image Courtesy of the Environmental Protection Agency

Figure 10.24 The EPA provides this WaterSense® label to help consumers identify products that use water efficiently.

Review & Assessment

1. Contrast *blanket, foam board, loose fill,* and *spray foam* forms of insulation.
2. Identify three ways to save energy with windows and doors.
3. How can technology systems help conserve energy in a house?
4. Why is conserving water important?

Chapter 10 Assessment

Summary

- Interior systems provide electricity, gas, and water to the house to make it more comfortable. There are several options for each system type.
- Electricity provides energy for operating lights, appliances, and most of the systems within the house.
- Gas is another source of energy for the home. It can be in the form of natural gas, which reaches the house from a gas main. Liquid propane gas, which is delivered to the house in pressurized tanks, is another option.
- The plumbing system brings water to and through the house via the water supply system. Waterborne waste is removed from the house through the wastewater removal system.
- The four types of conventional heating systems used to heat houses are the forced warm-air, hydronic, electric radiant, and central heat-pump systems. Nonconventional heating systems include solar heat, fireplaces, and stoves.
- Central air conditioners and room air conditioners provide cool, clean, dehumidified air during hot, humid weather.
- When choosing systems for your house, look for those that conserve energy.
- Use the proper insulation to keep the house warm in cold weather and cool in warm weather.
- Energy-efficient windows and doors also provide insulation.
- Computer systems can help conserve energy in your home by controlling lighting and interior climate, and by maintaining the systems.

Terms in Action

1. **Term comparison** With a partner, choose two related terms from the *Content Terms* listed at the beginning in this chapter. Create a Venn diagram to compare these terms. Write one term above the left circle and the other term above the right circle. Where the circles overlap, write three characteristics the terms have in common. Also write differences of the terms in each term's respective outer circle.

Think Critically

2. **Compare and contrast** Suppose you bought a house with an elaborate digital program to manage its systems. Make a list of what home systems you would like to control with the technology system. Contrast the advantages and disadvantages of using such a system.
3. **Predict outcomes** In your lifetime, to what extent do you believe the United States can totally become reliant on domestic energy sources rather than foreign energy sources? Predict what new or renewable energy sources are needed for such independence.
4. **Identify and assess** Assess the type of overcurrent protection devices you have in your house and where they are located. Summarize what to do when a circuit breaker trips.
5. **Analyze and assess** Locate online or print ads for windows and doors that claim to be energy efficient. Then use reliable resources to determine characteristics consumers should look for in energy-efficient windows. Display the ads on a bulletin board or with presentation software for others to compare. How can you assess if the information the ad claims are true? Discuss your findings with the class.
6. **Identify and create** Create a floor plan of your home. Locate the water shutoff valves for each water-using fixture in your house and mark their locations on the floor plan. Post your floor plan in a place that family members can easily find.

Core Skills

7. **Research and writing** Suppose you have a new client who wants to build a family room and a home office in the unfinished basement of their home (an open space that is 30 feet by 20 feet). Your client works several days per week from home and uses a computer, printer/scanner, and digital camera. Your client's family desires room for watching movies and playing with their game systems. Both rooms will require special electrical wiring and structured cabling. Investigate the type of wiring installation to recommend for your client. What wiring is needed? How many switches and electrical receptacles will the space

Chapter 10 Assessment

need? Where will ground fault circuit interrupters be required for safety? Write a summary of your plan to present to your client that is effective and conserves energy.

8. **Science and writing** Composting toilet systems are one option for homes located in remote areas. Use reliable online and print resources to locate information about how these systems work. What scientific facts support such systems for remote areas? What is your initial reaction to this type of waste management? What questions do you have that are not answered in the information provided by companies selling these toilets? Write a summary of your findings.
9. **Math practice** Survey your classmates to determine all the types of heating systems used in their homes. Create a pie chart to show the systems and the percentage used by classmates. Which types of heating systems are used most frequently? Which, if any, are not used? Share your findings with the class.
10. **Research and technology** New technologies for use in home construction are always under development. Search online for five examples of household equipment or computer programs that relate to this chapter. Analyze which needs such new technology meets in a home. Obtain photos, if available, and develop an electronic brochure to present to your classmates. To extend this activity, investigate how these new technologies are also used in commercial construction.
11. **Research and writing** Use online or print resources to research the cost of installing a system to conserve energy use by the systems in a house. Write a brief report and share your findings with the class.
12. **Writing** Use the *Home Energy Audit* website to complete an online energy audit for your home. Write a summary about your findings to share with the class.
13. **Reading** Use the Energy Savers website to locate information on the *blower door tests* that professional home-energy auditors use to determine the air-tightness of a home. What information do consumers need to know about quality blower door tests? Use the website to locate reliable energy auditors in your area. If possible, contact a local energy auditor about observing a blower door test. Share your findings with the class using presentation software.
14. **Writing** Use the *Carbon Footprint Calculator* on the Environmental Protection Agency website to determine the emissions from energy used at your home and in your travels. How does your household compare to that of the average U.S. household? What might you do to help lower the carbon emissions of your household? Write a summary of your findings.
15. **CTE career readiness practice** As citizens look to the future, finding and using alternative energy systems to heat and cool their homes is important to creating a sustainable environment. What alternative energy forms interest you most? Select one form of alternative energy to research in depth. How can homes benefit from this type of energy? Are there disadvantages? Write a report on your research to share with the class.

Design Practice

16. **Designing for energy efficiency** Presume you have a client who has hired you to create a house renovation plan to maximize the energy efficiency of a home in Vermont. The 1,200 square-foot home was built in the late 1960s. It has single-pane windows, a 25-year-old furnace in the unfinished walk-out basement, and no attic insulation. The client desires to finish the basement to create a family room.
    A. Create a plan that includes a list of features and products you would recommend to maximize the energy efficiency of this home.
    B. Identify your rationale for allocating resources and choosing each product.
    C. Create a digital plan presentation to share with your client (the class).
17. **Portfolio** Continue working on the home you chose for the Chapter 9 portfolio project. Create plans for the electrical, gas, plumbing, and heating and cooling systems of the home. Review your plan with your instructor and make revisions as necessary. Keep a copy of your best plan in your portfolio.

Chapter 11

Lighting Considerations

Content Terms

incandescent light
lumen
tungsten-halogen (quartz) light
fluorescent light
compact fluorescent lamp (CFL)
fiber optic lighting
light-emitting diode (LED)
reflected light
absorbed light
diffused light
color temperature
color rendering index (CRI)
general lighting
direct lighting
indirect lighting
task lighting
wattage
foot-candle
accent lighting
structural light fixture
nonstructural lighting

Academic Terms

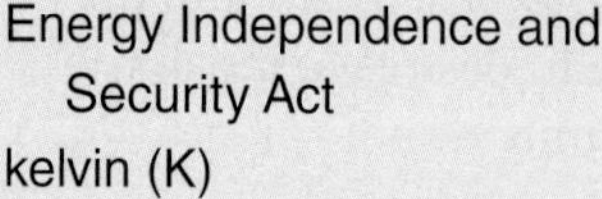

Energy Independence and Security Act
kelvin (K)

Learning Outcomes

After studying this chapter, you will be able to

- compare artificial lighting types and methods of control available for residential and nonresidential uses.
- summarize the properties of light.
- analyze the functions and principles of lighting.
- recommend lighting applications for specific interior needs, including safety, conservation, and sustainability.
- plan residential lighting for visual comfort, safety, and beauty.
- distinguish between structural and nonstructural lighting.
- determine appropriate lighting for residential and nonresidential interiors.

Reading with Purpose

Write the main headings in the chapter on a sheet of paper, leaving space under each heading. As you read the chapter, write three or more main points that you learned as you read each passage.

G-WLEARNING.com

While studying, look for the access icon  **to:**

- **Practice** the *Content* and *Academic Terms* with e-flash cards, matching activities, and vocabulary games.
- **Reinforce** what you learn by completing the *Review & Assessment* questions and e-mailing them to your instructor.

www.g-wlearning.com/housing/

Petinov Sergey Mihilovich/Shutterstock.com

One of the final steps for furnishing a room is providing good and appropriate lighting. You will continue to use the elements and principles of design that you learned in earlier chapters as you learn to add the finishing touches with lighting to a design scheme.

It is important to know the types of lighting available and also to be aware of how different types of artificial lighting affect surfaces and surroundings. Selecting the type and level of lighting is crucial to achieve a pleasing and comfortable indoor environment.

Types of Artificial Light

Natural light is not always available so artificial light is also needed. Previously, the two main kinds of artificial light used in homes were incandescent and fluorescent light. However, other types of light sources are replacing old technologies and are becoming more available to consumers.

Incandescent Light

Incandescent light is produced when electric current passes through a fine tungsten filament inside a bulb. The electricity heats the filament until it glows and gives off light (Figure 11.1). Over time, the filament deteriorates, leaving a dark coating on the bulb. This coating lowers the light level coming from the bulb, making it very inefficient. Incandescent bulbs vary in shape and size, but they all work the same way.

Incandescent lightbulbs used in homes range from 15 to 250 watts. As you recall, the amount of electrical power used is measured in *watts*. When comparing two incandescent bulbs, the one with the higher wattage will give more light. For two incandescent bulbs with the same wattage, compare the lumen output of the bulbs. A **lumen** is a measurement of the amount of light a bulb produces. A higher lumen number means the bulb emits more light, therefore, making it a more efficient choice. Incandescent bulbs, in general, are not very efficient sources of light. They produce very little light for the energy used, and use most of their energy for the production of heat.

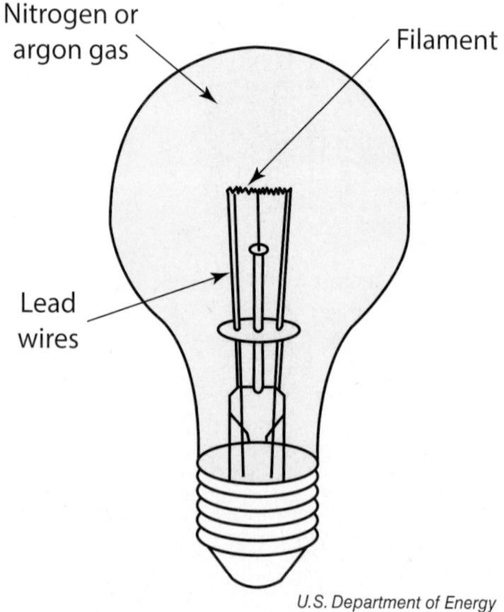

Figure 11.1 Inside an incandescent lightbulb, nitrogen or argon gas surrounds a filament. Electric current heats the filament and makes it glow.

Most incandescent bulbs for home use have a *frost finish* that covers the entire inside surface of the bulb. The main purpose of the frost finish is to reduce glare and make shadows appear softer. Some people prefer to use clear bulbs that do not have the frost coating in some light fixtures. Bulbs without a frost finish produce a great deal of glare. To eliminate the glare, use them only in fixtures that hide the bulbs completely from view.

Many kinds of special incandescent bulbs are available. One is the *three-way bulb*. Sets of filaments operate separately or together to produce different amounts of light. For example, a three-way bulb may have the light-level options of 50, 100, and 150 watts. Some bulbs have silver or aluminum coatings on the sides of the bulb which focuses the light in one direction. Other bulbs have a silicone coating. This coating prevents the glass from shattering if the bulb breaks.

In the coming years, incandescent bulbs will become a thing of the past. In 2007, the ***Energy Independence and Security Act*** passed in the United States established energy efficiency standards for many types of lightbulbs. These include incandescent bulbs and the proposed phase-out of incandescent and other inefficient bulbs over time. The law required that all lightbulbs had to use 25 to 30 percent less energy by 2014. The act was subsequently defunded in 2012 but by that time, U.S. lightbulb manufacturers had already altered their technologies and marketed their efforts.

A **tungsten-halogen (quartz) light** is another form of incandescent lighting. In this type of bulb, halogen gas combines with tungsten molecules to activate a filament inside a quartz enclosure. Halogen bulbs burn more intensely than standard incandescent bulbs.

Tungsten-halogen bulbs have many advantages over regular incandescent bulbs. They produce a whiter type of light. The amount of light in an aging tungsten-halogen bulb does not decrease as much as in regular bulbs. Also, tungsten-halogen bulbs last up to three times longer than regular incandescent bulbs. Tungsten-halogen bulbs are less energy efficient than fluorescent lights, but more energy efficient than other types of incandescent lights. These lights, however, become extremely hot. Care should be taken when handling them or placing them near combustible materials.

Fluorescent Light

Fluorescent light is produced in a glass tube by releasing electricity through a mercury vapor to make invisible ultraviolet rays. A coating of fluorescent material on the inside of the glass tube converts these rays into visible light rays. There is a delay between the release of electric current and the production of light.

Fluorescent light is more energy efficient than incandescent light. A fluorescent tube produces about four times as much light as an incandescent bulb of the same wattage.

Fluorescent tubes are more expensive than incandescent bulbs, but they last longer and are less expensive to use. Fluorescent tubes can last up to 20,000 hours and use about 40 watts of electricity. Fluorescent tubes are straight or circular, and available in various sizes.

The color of light from a fluorescent tube varies by changing the coating of fluorescent material in the tube. The two types of tubes are cool-white light which intensifies cool colors like blues and greens and warm-white light which intensifies yellows, reds, and oranges. Common uses for both types of lights are often in kitchens, bathrooms, and workshops. Deluxe cool-white light closely imitates natural daylight. Full-spectrum fluorescent tubes are designed to replicate natural daylight.

The **compact fluorescent lamp (CFL)** is a type of fluorescent lamp that is replacing old incandescent bulbs. Compact fluorescent bulbs screw into regular lightbulb sockets and come in many sizes and shapes (Figure 11.2). Some CFLs have a cork-screw shape and newer models look like standard incandescent bulbs. CFLs produce light differently than incandescent bulbs. With an incandescent bulb, electric current runs through a wire filament and heats the filament until it starts to glow. In a CFL, electric current runs through a tube containing argon gas and a small amount of mercury vapor. This generates *invisible* ultraviolet light that excites a fluorescent (or phosphor) coating on the inside of the tube. When this coating is excited, it emits *visible* light. CFLs use about 75 percent less energy and operate for nearly 9,000 hours while using fewer watts of electricity (Figure 11.3).

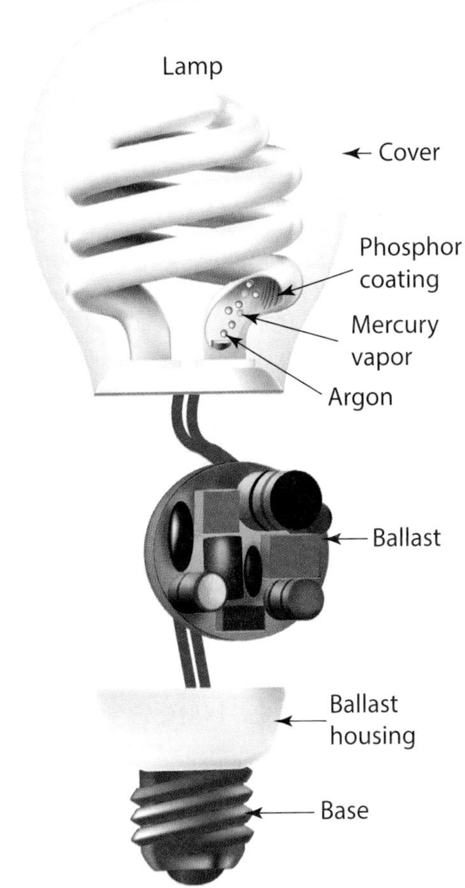

Provided by ENERGY STAR at www.energystar.gov

Figure 11.2 Although compact fluorescent bulbs look and function differently from regular incandescent lightbulbs, you can use them in the same fixtures.

Comparing Incandescent and CFL Lamps

Incandescent Bulbs (Watts)	Minimum Light Output (Lumens)	ENERGY STAR Qualified Equivalent CFLs (Watts)
40	450	9 to 13
60	800	13 to 15
75	1,100	18 to 25
100	1,600	23 to 30
150	2,600	30 to 52

Figure 11.3 This chart compares incandescent and CFL lamps. Notice that the CFLs use less energy but provide the same lumen output.

Housing Health & Safety

Handling CFLs

Handle CFLs carefully when taking them home after purchase. Broken CFLs can emit a small amount of dangerous mercury, a risk to human health. Do not throw CFLs into the regular trash to avoid contaminating landfills with mercury, a hazardous waste. You must recycle or properly dispose of CFLs according to your community's hazardous waste removal guidelines. Many home-improvement stores and community agencies also offer free recycling for CFLs.

Compact fluorescent lamps help the environment. Overall, CFLs create less energy during manufacturing. For example, it takes just as much time to produce six to 10 incandescent bulbs as it takes to make one CFL. During the life of a CFL, it will use four times less energy than six to 10 incandescent bulbs in the same time period. The electricity you save by replacing an incandescent bulb with a CFL equals the energy produced by burning about 450 pounds of coal.

Green Choices

Saving Resources with Lighting

When it comes to lighting, environmental friendliness and sustainability does not just mean using efficient bulbs. Housing professionals and designers can use multiple strategies to not only reduce electrical consumption but also save money, conserve resources, and increase occupant well-being. Here are just a few:

- Give as many people as possible the ability to control the amount of light they use. You will find that most people prefer less than industry standard.
- Use occupancy sensors to turn lighting on and off in rooms with natural light. These will automatically turn off lighting when the room is light or unoccupied.
- Make a plan for smaller lighting zones. Even for ambient lighting, create smaller clusters of fixtures for maximum control.
- Use salvaged decorative lighting and accessories, ensuring they have been rewired for fire safety.
- Provide daylight and views for as many occupants as possible while redirecting light and preventing glare.
- Limit use and use timers on exterior lighting. This reduces light pollution and is kinder to native animal life.
- Use computer-simulation modeling to estimate fixture needs in a space. You may often find that your original plans result in over-illumination (Figure A).

A *Julia Woodside*

B *Jennifer Blanchard Belk, IIDA, LEED AP*

As more sustainable innovations become more commonplace, you will begin to see environmental initiatives being employed in all types of buildings and spaces. Many hotels are already using a form of occupancy sensor (Figure B). When you enter, you must use your key to activate the lighting and electricity in your room. Therefore, you cannot help but turn everything off when you leave.

Lighting from Fiber Optics

Fiber optic lighting is a type of heatless light produced by passing an electric current through a cable containing very fine strands of glass. These cables are primarily used in communications (such as Internet and TV), but are also useful for lighting. Optical fibers permit such transmissions over longer distances and at higher bandwidths than other forms of communication. *Bandwidth* refers to how much data you can send through a network connection. Fiber optic lighting gives off no heat or ultraviolet rays that can distort colors.

Fiber optic lighting lends a dramatic effect in interior spaces. In museums, it can recreate star constellations on ceilings as well as give finishing effects to exhibits. Using fiber optic lights can also provide energy-efficient and somewhat unique decorative lighting at home.

Light-Emitting Diodes (LED)

Extremely long-lasting bulbs are made from **light-emitting diodes (LED)**. LEDs are composed of crystals on silicon chips about the size of a grain of salt. These crystals produce light when a low electric current passes through them. An LED bulb can last 100,000 hours or more. In comparison with other bulbs, it will last about 10 times longer than CFLs and over 100 times longer than incandescent bulbs. The initial cost of LED lighting is currently a little more costly than incandescent lighting. LED lighting, however, lasts longer, consumes less energy, is more durable, and gives off less heat than other traditional lighting methods. LED lighting is beginning to replace many other types of lighting sources in the future.

The small size and flexibility of LEDs make them a good option for a number of general lighting purposes. For example, with interior spaces you may use LEDs for recessed down lights, under-cabinet lighting in the kitchen, and as portable desk/ task lighting. LED lights are also useful in outdoor lighting especially for landscaping. They can provide necessary surface brightness while using less energy and requiring less maintenance.

Review & Assessment

1. What is a lumen?
2. How do incandescent lights differ from fluorescent lights in terms of purchasing cost and operating cost?
3. List two energy-efficient types of lightbulbs.

The Properties of Light

You can use light to achieve several different effects in residential and nonresidential environments. To do this, you first need to understand the various properties of light. Objects and surfaces can absorb or reflect light. It can shine directly on a certain spot or lighten a whole room. By knowing the properties of light, you can make light work for you.

Reflected Light

Light, color, and texture are closely related. Without light, there is no color. In turn, colors reflect and absorb various amounts of light. Surfaces with rough textures look dark because tiny shadows form where the light does not reach. Together, light, color, and texture greatly affect the appearance of rooms.

Reflected light is light that bounces off surfaces. It seems to come from these surfaces as well as from its source. Light colors and smooth, shiny surfaces on objects and surfaces all reflect light. Surface treatments in the home also reflect light. Some surfaces reflect so much light that they produce glare or bright light shining in a person's eyes. It is best to avoid lighting placement that creates glare. See Figure 11.4 to learn how much light various surfaces can reflect.

Absorbed Light

Absorbed light is light that is drawn in by a surface. Rough textures and dark colors absorb most of the available light rays. If light is absorbed, it cannot be reflected. For example, suppose you use rough textures and dark colors in large areas of your home. Because

Reflected Light

Background Surface	Minimum	Maximum
Ceilings		
Pale color tints	60%	90%
Walls		
Natural wood	5%	50%
Light colors	70%	80%
Medium colors	35%	60%
Dark colors	5%	25%
Floors		
Carpeting, tile, woods	15%	35%
Countertops	30%	50%

Figure 11.4 This chart gives minimum and maximum amounts of reflected light.

these rough textures and dark colors absorb light, the areas appear smaller. A room with many dark surfaces may need additional light for certain activities.

Diffused Light

Diffused light is light that scatters over a large area. It has no glare, which is the most troublesome aspect of lighting. Instead, it creates a soft appearance. Devices that diffuse light—or *diffusers*—spread the light evenly. An example of a diffuser is the frosted or white finish on incandescent and fluorescent bulbs. Other diffusers are more apparent, such as the covers for light fixtures. These diffusers are usually made of frosted or translucent glass. Lamp shades also serve as diffusers.

Light Temperature

The light given off by various light sources differs in **color temperature**. The color of a light is rated in ***kelvin (K)***—the base unit of temperature (a scale) used to measure light temperature. Light from these sources is divided into the following three general tones:

- Orange (incandescent), which is 2700–3000°K
- White (halogen), which is 3000–3600°K
- Blue (fluorescent), which is 3000°K for warm, and 4000°K for cool

The color of the light affects how things will appear in that light. When selecting lights for a certain purpose or space, keep in mind how the light will affect the surfaces around it. For example, skin tones are best viewed by light with a color temperature in the warm range of about 2800–3500°K. Color temperatures are listed with most light sources.

The **color rendering index (CRI)** of light indicates how well light from a source will bring out the true color. The CRI scale is from 1–100, with 100 equaling the color rendering of daylight. A CRI of 80 or above is good. The closer the CRI of a light source is to 100, the more accurately the light will reproduce color. Information for many light sources will list it as a CRI rating. Having the best CRI possible is especially important in rooms such as the kitchen (for food safety), bathrooms (for grooming and makeup application), and closets (to accurately represent clothing colors).

Review & Assessment

1. Contrast reflected and absorbed light. Give an example of each.
2. What is color temperature and why is it important?
3. What is the color rendering index (CRI)? Why is CRI important?

Functions of Lighting

Lighting serves several purposes. It illuminates areas that may pose a safety hazard. Lighting also focuses attention on beautiful objects or attractive architectural features. The most common use of lighting, however, is illuminating the environment so people can comfortably see, especially when performing certain tasks.

Lighting for Visual Comfort

To create visual comfort in a home, you need two basic types of lighting: *general* (ambient) and *task*. The type and amount needed vary from room to room. Accent lighting, used to create beauty and emphasis, will be discussed later.

General Lighting (Ambient)

General lighting, or ambient lighting, provides a uniform level of light throughout a room. Achievement of general lighting occurs through either of two ways: direct or indirect lighting.

- **Direct lighting.** When lighting shines directly toward an object, it is called **direct lighting.** It provides the most light possible to a specific area, such as when using a lamp in a room (Figure 11.5). If used alone, direct lighting creates a sharp contrast between light and dark areas, which can cause eye fatigue. Therefore, if you need direct lighting for a task, use other lights in the room, too.
- **Indirect lighting.** You can also achieve general lighting through indirect lighting. **Indirect lighting** is directed toward a surface, such as a ceiling or wall that reflects the light into the room (Figure 11.6). Indirect lighting may provide soft light for a large area. It does not provide enough light for detailed work.

General lighting should light a room well enough for occupants to see objects clearly and move about safely. The amount of general lighting needed depends on the shape, size, and use of the room.

Task Lighting

General lighting does not always supply enough light for visual comfort. In such cases, you can supplement with task lighting. **Task lighting** is lighting used in areas where specific activities require more light. Using the right amount of task lighting helps prevent eyestrain.

The amount of task lighting you need depends on the activity. The finer the detail or the faster the action taking place, the more light you need. For instance, playing table tennis requires more light than shooting pool. Tasks such as writing letters, carving wood, or

Breadmaker/Shutterstock.com

Figure 11.5 The use of direct lighting in this kitchen helps make food preparation and cooking easier and safer.

EpicStockMedia/Shutterstock.com

Figure 11.6 Indirect lighting can give a glow that lifts the appearance of the ceiling.

sewing require higher levels of task lighting to assure that you can see well enough to perform the task.

Task lighting in one part of a room can serve as general lighting for another part. For instance, if you are reading in one corner of a family room, the lamp that you use for task lighting adds to the general lighting of the entire room.

To get the right amount of good quality light, combine general and task lighting. Together, they give adequate light without sharp contrast.

Task lighting related to the use of computers can be difficult. In addition to glare, you must consider who uses the equipment and for how long. With the prevalence of mobile technology, any room could be for computer use. Giving people flexibility with lighting use and ability to dim the lighting helps ensure eye comfort.

Measuring Light

The following terms are important to the measurement of light. **Wattage** is the amount of electricity a bulb uses. As you recall, a *lumen* is a measurement of the amount of light a bulb produces. One lumen is the amount of light produced by a source equaling the intensity of one standard candle. **Foot-candle** is a measurement of how much light reaches an object or a surface. One foot-candle is the amount of light a standard candle gives to an object one foot away. *One foot-candle equals one lumen per square foot.* You can measure the amount of light reaching a surface (foot-candle) with a light meter.

In 2011, the Federal Trade Commission changed the label regulation on what should appear on lightbulbs to help purchasers know the level of lighting and other features of the bulb. Required is the number of lumens, which measures the amount of actual light. See Figure 11.7 for lumens

Residential Lighting Recommendations

Room/Task in Residence	Recommended Level of Lumens
Living Room	1500–3000 ambient
Reading	400 (minimum)
Dining Room	3000–6000 ambient
Kitchen	5000–10,000 ambient
Sink/range	450 (minimum)
Bathrooms	4000–8000 ambient
At mirror	1700 (minimum)
Front Entry	1000–2000 ambient
Pathways	300 (minimum)
Bedrooms	2000–4000 ambient
Reading	500 (minimum)
Closet	400 (minimum)
Home Office	3000–6000 ambient
Desk	1200 (minimum)
Entries and Stairwell	1200–4000 ambient
Hallway	1200–2500 ambient

Figure 11.7 Use this chart to determine the approximate amount of light needed for certain rooms and activities.

Housing Health & Safety

Lighting Levels for the Home

Improper lighting can have implications on occupant health and safety for many reasons. There are things a designer and a homeowner can do with lighting to reduce the likelihood of discomfort, injuries, or death.

- **Sufficient light levels and intensity.** Illumination that is appropriate for the task at hand, the occupants, or the surrounding materials can help prevent headaches, eyestrain, prevent slips and falls, limit harsh shadows and glare, and reduce the time needed for eyes to adjust to light levels.
- **Lighting for safe exiting.** General design recommendations indicate there be at least one foot-candle of illumination at floor level in any area along a path toward an exit. Should power be lost, certain manufacturers make glow-in-the-dark materials such as vinyl baseboard that can illuminate the way to an exit.
- **Fire ratings.** Light fixtures in fire-rated walls must be airtight. No fixtures should come in direct contact with flammable materials such as insulation.
- **Emergency power.** Although not a requirement for residential environments, having backup or generator power can help prevent injuries due to loss of power.
- **Wet locations.** Building codes require that only those fixtures rated for damp locations be placed within bathrooms or other humid locations. Another suggestion is to not place hanging lights in areas such as bathrooms.
- **Effortless control.** Having motion sensors or remote controls on lighting limits the amount of movement needed to turn lighting on when needed.
- **Fixture placement.** For occupant safety, avoid wall or ceiling mounted fixtures that protrude into a path of travel. These can cause head injuries.
- **Flicker prevention.** Flicker is a strobe-like effect created by lighting. It can happen due to varying frequencies of a bulb, which can be prevented by changing bulbs before they blow. It can also be caused by incorrect placement of fixtures. If a ceiling fan is placed between down-lighting and an occupant, a harsh flicker will result, which can actually be a cause of seizures in humans.

Rather than considering only the negative effects bad lighting can cause, it is important to know that excellent lighting conditions can actually improve health. Utilizing and making the most of natural light by way of space planning, window placement, and treatment can lower blood pressure and stimulate energy and healing. Studies have shown that both natural and artificial lighting, used in higher, warmer, and varying levels, can increase alertness and comfort. It can also help regulate sleep patterns, elevate mood, and even decrease the need for pain medications in occupants.

recommended for various rooms and tasks in residential settings as well as expected lumens from the wattage of incandescent lightbulbs.

With the emphasis on using less energy, the recent labeling also allows the user to know how efficient the lightbulb is, in other words, how much energy it uses to produce the lighting. The newer lightbulbs have longer life expectancy and use less energy.

Lighting for Safety

Lighting for safety is very important. It can help prevent accidents and fires. Accidents can occur in dim and dark areas. To guard against accidents, plan lighting where it will work best for you. If you can answer "yes" to the following questions, you will know your lighting promotes safety. Can you

- light your way as you go from room to room?
- switch lights on or off from each doorway?
- turn on stairway lighting as you go up or down stairs?
- light entrances as you enter?
- control garage or carport lighting from inside or outside the house?
- control outside lighting from inside the house?

UL (Underwriters Laboratories)

Figure 11.8 A seal on a lamp showing UL or CSA assures you the lamp was made according to safety guidelines.

Another aspect of lighting for safety concerns is safe wiring. If wiring is unsafe, it can start fires in the home. To assure safety, the wiring used for lighting should meet standards set by various groups. For example, the National Electrical Code® is a standard with which all wiring should comply. Often there are local requirements, too.

When you purchase electrical lighting fixtures, buy only those with a safety seal from a safety-testing organization such as *Underwriters Laboratories (UL)* (Figure 11.8). The seal tells you that the light was manufactured according to safety standards. A safety seal, however, does not guarantee that the parts will remain safe. You need to use lights safely and watch for possible dangers. Always read and follow the instructions for the use and care of the lights. This includes using bulbs of the correct wattage for the fixture as the manufacturer specifies. Using a larger wattage bulb than specified could possibly lead to overheating and a fire or damage to the light fixture.

Lighting for Beauty

While all light can be decorative, the purpose of some lighting is for beauty alone. Soft light can create a quiet, restful mood. Sharp light can highlight the focal point in a room. When lighting serves as a highlight, it is called **accent lighting**. Some lighting is decorative merely because of lighting fixture design, which adds beauty to a space. In other cases, this lighting serves the purpose of drawing attention to fine art and collectibles. Fixtures should be chosen and placed wisely so as not to distract from or damage the art (Figure 11.9).

You can also use decorative lighting outside the home (Figure 11.10). Homes may have yard lights next to the street. Lights near entrances are also common. Lighting patios for night use adds to the outdoor living space, which makes the lighting functional as well as decorative. In such areas, the light should be attractive. Avoid harsh and glaring light that you and your neighbors may find annoying. With the right choices, you can have pleasant, glowing light.

Cynthia Taylor

Figure 11.9 These pendants create perfect scallops of light to accent the art.

photobank.ch/Shutterstock.com

Figure 11.10 Exterior lighting gives this stylish home a dramatic appearance.

Review & Assessment

1. What are three purposes of light?
2. Why do homes need both general (ambient) and task lighting?
3. Contrast direct lighting with indirect lighting. Give an example of when you might use each.

4. What is task lighting and why is it important?
5. How do wattage, lumens, and foot-candles impact the measurement of light?
6. Name three questions to ask to determine whether lighting promotes safety.
7. What is accent lighting? Give an example.

Structural and Nonstructural Lighting

Lighting affects the appearance of a room. So does the delivery of light to a room. The two ways of delivering light are through structural and nonstructural lighting.

Structural Lighting

A **structural light fixture** is one that is permanently built into a home. It is either included in the original plans or added during a remodeling project.

When you choose structural light fixtures, keep them in harmony with other aspects of the room's design. When choosing fixtures, consider the following points:

- Diffused light gives more visual comfort than exposed bulbs, which can produce glare.
- Fixtures that can change position allow for usage in more than one way. Some fixtures you can raise or lower. Others swing or swivel for a variety of effects.
- Fixtures that provide different light levels—such as three-way bulbs or dimmer switches—allow for more flexibility with light levels in the home.

There are many types of structural lighting fixtures. See Figure 11.11.

Ceiling mounted fixtures are the most common, least expensive, and easiest to install. They can be used in rooms with lower ceilings and can come as part of a fan/light combination.

Valance lighting fixtures are mounted over windows and hidden by the window valance. Since the window valance is open at the top and bottom, fluorescent light is directed upward and downward, giving both direct and indirect lighting.

Bracket lighting fixtures and *sconces* are similar to valance lighting fixtures, except they are used on walls or over work areas. The fluorescent light shines upward and downward. Bracket lighting can serve as general or accent lighting.

Cornice lighting fixtures are concealed sources of light that are mounted to the wall near the ceiling. Fluorescent light shines downward, giving direct light only. You can use cornice lighting on almost any wall for a variety of effects.

Cove lighting fixtures are also mounted near the ceiling. Fluorescent light is directed upward, giving indirect light only. Cove lighting provides good general lighting; however, you must supplement it with local lighting. It also gives a room a feeling of height.

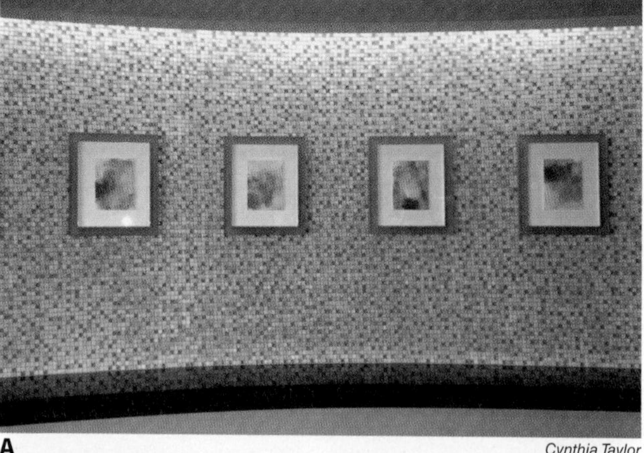

A Cynthia Taylor

B Nickolay Khoroshkov/Shutterstock.com C Carolos Yudica/Shutterstock.com

D Napoom08/Shutterstock.com

Figure 11.11 There are many options for structural lighting. Wall washers (A), sconces (B), track lighting (C), and chandeliers are just a few types (D).

Career Focus Lighting Designer

Do you notice the mood change when a restaurant dims its lights for dinner? Do you see improvements you could make in the way clothing is highlighted in a retail store? If you do, a career in Lighting Design might be for you!

lightpoet/Shutterstock.com

Interests/Skills: Lighting designers must have both technical and artistic skills. They should have good 3-D visualization skills to help them produce computer- or hand-generated presentation drawings. Good communication skills are necessary for interacting with clients and contractors. Math and technical writing skills are important since much of lighting design deals with determining and documenting the quantity of light needed for a space.

Career Snapshot: Designers with a lighting specialty develop the quantity, intensity, direction, purity, and color of the illumination within interiors. Their creations can affect the mood in hospitality design or give emphasis to products in a retail setting. Each must consider the existing environment, its quantity of natural light, and the reflectance of interior materials. Lighting designers typically work in collaboration with an interior designer, art consultant, or visual merchandiser to design lighting systems, develop plans and renderings, and ensure the quality of installations on the build site. For projects with a sustainability focus, lighting specialists work with engineers and architects to produce studies (for instance, computer renderings or animations) of proposed buildings to determine the optimum mix of natural and artificial light. Theatrical design is a subset of this specialty.

Education/Training: The completion of a bachelor's degree in interior design, architecture, or building science is typically sufficient, but a concentration in lighting or theater design is beneficial. Someone looking to specialize might also select elective coursework in fine art and engineering or may pursue a master's degree. An internship and having a helpful mentor is extremely valuable.

Licensing/Examinations: All interior design graduates who pass the licensing examination through the National Council for Interior Design Qualification (NCIDQ) are thoroughly prepared to deal with typical lighting design issues, especially for commercial interiors. For those wishing to pursue a more concentrated specialty, the Lighting Certification (LC) exam is administered by the National Council on Qualifications for the Lighting Professions (NCQLP). Designers may also seek LEED Accreditation (Leadership in Energy and Environmental Design) as that exam tests a great deal of lighting and energy efficiency knowledge.

Professional Associations: The American Society of Interior Designers (ASID); the International Interior Design Association (IIDA); the International Association of Lighting Designers (IALD); the Illuminating Engineering Society of North America (IESNA); and the American Lighting Association (ALA)

Job Outlook: Statistics show that lighting design employment is projected to be similar to the U.S. average, although specialists may benefit by aligning themselves with high growth segments such as environments for the aging and sustainable projects.

Sources: The Occupational Outlook Handbook (OOH); the Occupational Information Network (O*NET); National Council on Qualifications for the Lighting Professions (NCQLP); International Association of Lighting Designers (IALD); Illuminating Engineering Society of North America (IESNA); the American Lighting Association (ALA)

Pendant lighting fixtures are those that hang from a chain, tube, rope, or rod from an overhead surface. They can provide both ambient and task lighting. The shape and material of the shade determine the quality, direction, and color of light.

Chandeliers are large pendant fixtures with multiple bulbs typically used for general ambient illumination. In addition to providing light, they are a major aesthetic component within dining rooms and entrance foyers. Depending on the shape of the fixture and shades (if used), it can provide direct and/or indirect light.

Recessed downlights are small, circular lights installed in the ceiling. Using several of these lights spaced throughout the ceiling offers good general lighting. Too many recessed lights, however, can give a "Swiss cheese" effect to the ceiling. Using just a few creates effective accent lighting. The typical scalloped pattern of light and shadow produced by recessed downlights gives a dramatic look to a wall.

Wall washers are also installed in the ceiling. They have a contoured inner reflector that directs nearly uniform light on walls from ceiling to floor. This gives walls a smooth look. If the wall-washer fixtures are located closer to the wall, they can emphasize a textured wall surface.

Soffit lighting fixtures consist of an enclosed box attached to the ceiling. Often, a plastic panel at the bottom of the soffit box diffuses the light as it shines downward. Soffit lighting is used where a large amount of local light is needed, such as over a kitchen or bathroom sink.

Strip lighting is a structure consisting of a strip of receptacles that hold a series of incandescent lightbulbs. It is often used around mirrors in a bathroom or dressing room to provide good task lighting.

Track lighting consists of several light fixtures mounted on a metal strip. You can arrange the fixtures in varying positions to shine in different directions and create different effects.

Nonstructural Lighting

Nonstructural lighting is lighting that is not a structural part of the house. You can move, change, and replace these lights more easily than any other form of lighting.

Lamps are the most common type of nonstructural lighting. They can serve decorative purposes as well as provide good general and task lighting. When choosing lamps, keep the following points in mind:

- A sturdy or heavy lamp base prevents tipping.
- Some have a diffusing bowl that prevents glare.
- A harp makes it possible to change the height of the lampshade. A harp is a metal hoop or arch that supports a lampshade.
- The colors and textures of lamps and lampshades should harmonize.
- Light-colored, translucent lampshades give the most light.
- Adjustable lamps are the most practical. You can raise or lower some, such as swag lamps. Some have swinging arms and some use three-way bulbs.

foamfoto/Shutterstock.com

Figure 11.12 Lamps, recessed downlights, and accent lighting provide artificial light for this room. A large window area provides natural light during the day.

You can combine structural and nonstructural lighting in many different ways (Figure 11.12). The goal is always to achieve good lighting throughout the dwelling.

Lighting Layout Throughout the Home

Lighting, electrical, and reflected ceiling plans can assist in explaining the plans for illumination in a home (Figure 11.13). Structural lighting will be shown on the lighting plan, while electrical outlet placement on an electrical plan shows where lamps could be easily placed. A *reflected ceiling plan* is one that includes not only lighting but also anything that affects the ceiling, including

- ceiling material changes
- height changes
- air supply
- brackets for televisions
- smoke detectors
- full-height cabinetry

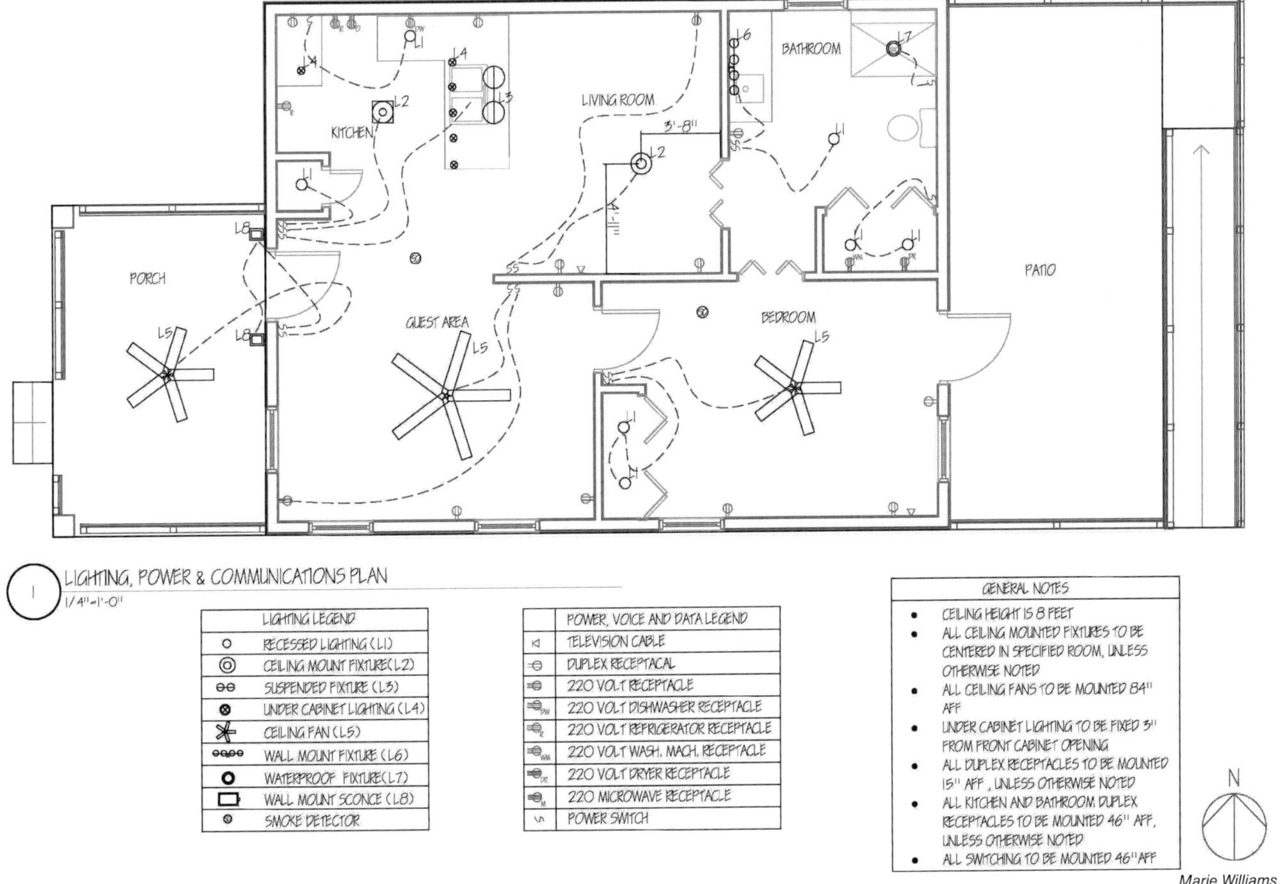

Figure 11.13 Can you determine what types of fixtures are in each room?

Legends explain the lighting symbols and may reference separate specifications with actual manufacturer and ordering information.

When considering where to put the lighting fixtures, think about the furniture placement in the rooms. If there is an open floor plan with many furniture arrangement options, include a more general lighting placement rather than one that is specific to a particular furniture layout. For instance, if a floor plan is inflexible and there is no choice where to locate the dining table, then a center hanging fixture would be appropriate. If the space is wide open with multiple possible locations for the table, a more general lighting plan accented with nonstructural fixtures might be better.

Determining where to locate switches is important because it affects traffic flow into and out of spaces. Consider how someone would enter and leave a room. Larger rooms with multiple entrances might require multiple switches (called three- and four-way switches). Also, make sure there is adequate wall space in a convenient location for the switch placement. Frequent electrical outlets to accommodate lamps throughout the space are important, too.

Each room of the home has individual lighting and switching needs (Figure 11.14). Although everyone uses spaces differently, there are basic guidelines. Use the following guidelines for either laying out a lighting plan for a new home or for evaluating the appropriateness of an existing home's lighting plan. The following passages will get you thinking about practical and functional placement.

Foyer or Entry

Usually one central ceiling fixture is adequate. In addition to a switch for the interior fixture, there should always be a way to control exterior lighting from the interior space.

Living Room or Great Room

A large entertaining space needs plenty of illumination but also needs the ability to vary lighting levels and effects (Figure 11.15). You can achieve this by incorporating a combination of ceiling fixtures, cove lighting, accent lights, and table and floor lamps. Having ability to dim the lighting is important, too. Even if the room does not have a central light, consider the installation of at least one

Lighting Controls	
Forms of Switches	• Standard switches—toggle switch or button • Dimmers—dial or slide • Pull cords directly on lighting fixture • Electronic panel with preprogrammed settings
Special Operations	• Dimming—assists with setting a mood and personal choice of light level • Motion sensors—should be placed in most active or task-oriented area of room • Photo sensors—activated by lower natural light levels; should be located near occupants rather than directly by windows for optimum performance • Timers—helpful in areas that are sporadically used; may also include a heat lamp
Manipulation	• Occupant turns them on by hand • Remote control located near seating, bed, etc. • App or software for whole-house environmental controls

Figure 11.14 Understanding different types of lighting controls helps you determine the best choices for occupant needs.

Santiago Cornejo/Shutterstock.com

Figure 11.15 Having multiple types of illumination that can be controlled separately takes advantage of the natural light within the room.

Breadmaker/Shutterstock.com

Figure 11.16 Here you can see the use of task, accent, and ambient lighting.

ceiling fan. Pay special attention to accent lighting for art or areas of emphasis, as well as preventing glare on television screens. Excessive switching is challenging in these types of spaces so make sure to group switches together as much as possible.

Dining Room

A formal dining room typically has a centrally located ceiling fixture or a cohesive series of fixtures that appear as one form. Since dining rooms often have multiple entrances, consider using a three-way switch.

Kitchen

Appropriate and varied lighting in a kitchen is imperative. Provide general lighting plus accent lights over task areas such as the sink, island, prep areas, and casual dining zones (Figure 11.16). You can achieve this by mounting pendant fixtures closer to the work surface or by using under-cabinet lighting. Place general switches at entrances while

Patryk Kosmider/Shutterstock.com

Figure 11.17 The lighting in the niches and along the wall draws your attention up and away from the heavier floor.

pics721/Shutterstock.com

Figure 11.18 This vanity lighting is optimum for even illumination in the mirror.

switches for accent and track lighting should be close to the area of use. Use lighting and switching in similar ways for utility and laundry spaces.

Halls and Stairs

Because of the confined area, most hallways do not have elaborate fixtures that hang low or protrude from the walls. Place basic ceiling lights no more than 12 feet apart. Stairwells often have single pendants or chandeliers in proportion to the overall size of the room. Switching is required at either end of a hall or stairwell.

Bedrooms

Standard-size bedrooms typically have one central ceiling fixture which may be in combination with a fan. Accommodating the use of side-table lamps requires locating at least two outlets on each potential bed wall of the room. Consider using accent lighting in larger rooms, those with significant built-ins, and those with dressing areas (Figure 11.17). Bedrooms may also have switch controls at the room entrance to turn on lamps. Dimmable fixtures are preferable for most occupants.

Bathrooms

There should be individual lighting within each enclosed or separated area including toilets, bathtubs, and showers. Several of these may be combination fixtures that include exhaust fans. When planning vanity and mirror lighting, it is better to have illumination from both sides (by using wall sconces) rather than straight down onto the occupant, creating harsh shadows (Figure 11.18).

Closets

Shallow hall or linen closets typically do not have their own fixtures. Large or walk-in closets can often have enough illumination by using only a single ceiling fixture. Take special care to ensure realistic color rendition and minimize shadows, which may require alternative light placement.

Garage Lighting

One lighting fixture per garage bay is usually sufficient for most garages. The garage door-opener kit may incorporate this lighting. Additional lighting is helpful at task areas such as workbenches.

Exterior Lighting

In addition to having at least one light fixture outside each entry (switched from inside), home exteriors should have sufficient illumination at walks, drives, patios, and decks.

Review & Assessment

1. What is structural lighting?
2. Name and describe five types of structural lighting.
3. What is nonstructural lighting?
4. What do you need to consider when determining where to put lighting fixtures in a room?
5. What factors impact where to locate light switches in a room?
6. Name four areas of a house and list the possible lighting needs for each.

Chapter 11 Assessment

Summary

- Understanding the principles and functions of lighting is important to effective design.
- Artificial lighting supplements natural light or daylight.
- Types of artificial lighting include incandescent, fluorescent lighting, compact fluorescent, and light-emitting diodes (LED). Each type has its advantages and disadvantages.
- Light can be used to achieve different effects.
- General and task lighting helps create visual comfort.
- As you work with lighting, you need to consider using it for safety and beauty.
- Some lighting is structural, and fixtures are a part of the house. Other lighting fixtures are nonstructural and are separate from the house structure. The choice depends on the type of lighting you or your client needs or desires.
- When determining lighting needs and fixture placement, consider traffic flow, furniture arrangement, and future use of the room.
- Use standard layout guidelines and then supplement lighting to fit the individual needs of the occupant.

Terms in Action

1. **Term flash cards** Work in small teams to locate small images online that visually describe or explain each of the *Content Terms* at the beginning of the chapter. Use the images to create flash cards. Write each term on a note card and paste the image that describes or explains the term on the opposite side.

Think Critically

2. **Identify evidence** The author states in the text that LED lighting "... lasts long, consumes less energy, is more durable, and gives off less heat than other traditional lighting methods." Use the text and reliable online sources to verify this evidence. Which sustainable, energy-efficient form of lighting is more popular with consumers, CFL or LED lighting? Why? How do you see LED lighting being used in the future in residential and commercial lighting design? Create an illustrated report of your findings to share with the class.
3. **Analyze central issues** Analyze one of the rooms in your home or the home of someone you know. Identify which surfaces reflect light and which absorb it. Under what circumstances is the reflected light helpful? When does it create problems? How does the light that is absorbed affect the look of the room? If possible, take digital photos of the lighting situations you have identified and create an illustrated report to share with the class.

Core Skills

4. **Research and speaking** Use Internet or print resources to investigate *light temperature*—both warm and cool—and *color rendition* as it relates to light. What system is used for measuring light temperature? color rendition? How is this information used on lighting packaging? How can light temperature and color rendition impact your lighting choices as an interior designer? Use a school-approved web application to create an illustrated report of your findings to share with the class.
5. **Research and speaking** Use Internet or print resources to read about the *Energy Independence and Security Act of 2007*. What principles are outlined in this legislation? How did mandated energy requirements help consumers? How does it impact the availability of different types of energy-saving lighting? How do consumers and housing professionals benefit? Give an oral report of your findings.
6. **Lamp research and writing** Visit a local home improvement store and find an example of the following types of light sources: frosted incandescent bulb, clear incandescent bulb, CFL, fluorescent tube, halogen bulb, and LED lamp. On a sheet of paper, make a chart to compare their wattage, lumens, cost, and hours of life. Also add CRI and color temperature as

Chapter 11 Assessment

listed on the packaging. How do the different types of light compare? Write a summary to post on your class blog or web page.

7. **Interview, listening, and writing** Interview a lighting specialist about the functions of lighting and guidelines for determining lighting needs for various tasks in a house. How is lighting measured for various spaces? What calculations does the specialist use in determining the amount of lighting and fixtures needed for a room or space? Write a summary about what you learned for future reference.
8. **Lighting evaluation and speaking** Take a tour of your school building and grounds. Determine which areas have lighting that is adequate for safety. Identify specific areas that you feel have inadequate lighting. What solutions would you recommend to improve the lighting for safety? Share your recommendations with the class in an oral report.
9. **Research and writing** Research your local electrical wiring code requirements. Find out who is responsible for inspection. What problems would you anticipate if there were no requirements or inspections? Write a brief summary of your findings to post to the class web page.
10. **Technology** Visit the *American Lighting Association* website. Click on "Lighting Your Home" and then click on the lighting design videos. Choose at least three videos on trends in lighting design to view and compare. What do the lighting specialists indicate as current trends in lighting design for the home? How do these trends impact the functions of lighting and methods of lighting control? Write an article for the class blog regarding what you learned about trends in lighting design.
11. **Research and speaking** Suppose your client is building a new home and has asked you to recommend specific lighting applications and fixtures. Your client wants to include structural lighting fixtures for lighting throughout the home that not only provide beauty but also enhance safety and are energy efficient. The rooms in the new home include the entry, living room, and eat-in kitchen, master bedroom and bath, guest bedroom, and a half-bath. Based on what you know regarding the properties and functions of light, choose structural fixtures to recommend for each room or space. Use online lighting resources to select image examples to share with your client. Write a summary for each fixture, explaining the details about the fixture and why it is a good choice for the space.
12. **CTE career readiness practice** Suppose you are interested in a career as a lighting designer in the Design/Pre-construction career pathway. You have done your research in regard to educational requirements for such a career and this fits with your personal and career goals. You feel, however, that you are missing the first-hand experiential knowledge that is necessary to commit to such a career. Locate a person with a local company or firm who is an expert in lighting design. Make arrangements to job shadow or work with this individual as a mentor as you pursue your career. How can you benefit from having such a mentor? Keep a journal about your mentoring experience, recording details about what you learn along the way.

Design Practice

13. **Lighting design plan** Suppose a new client asks you to plan the lighting for her bedroom scheme. She has a 16- by 20-inch piece of custom art and a few family photos she wants to include, but the rest is up to you. There are only two available walls in the bedroom: one is 11 feet by 8 feet and the other is 14 feet by 8 feet. Develop a design plan that includes an analysis of the functions and principles of lighting. Create wall elevations to show your lighting plans. Write a summary to accompany your design plan that explains the details to your client.
14. **Portfolio** Create a floor plan for a kitchen or bathroom that includes recommendations for structural and nonstructural lighting. Explain the reasons for your selections.

Chapter 12

Selecting Appliances and Electronics

Content Terms

appliance
EnergyGuide label
ENERGY STAR® label
warranty
full warranty
limited warranty
extended warranty
induction cooktop
self-cleaning oven
convection oven
microwave oven
dehumidifier
humidifier

Academic Terms

kilowatt hour (kWh)
British thermal unit (Btu)

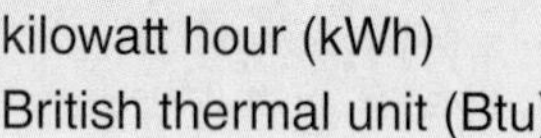

Learning Outcomes

After studying this chapter, you will be able to

- determine the role of appliances and electronics in interior design for residential and nonresidential settings.
- analyze the selection process of appliances and electronics.
- evaluate choices in styles and features of various kitchen, laundry, and climate control appliances, including manufacturers, materials, care, maintenance, trends, and special needs.
- appraise other appliances and electronics for safety, cost, and quality.
- select appliances and electronics to meet specific needs including those of people with special needs.

Reading with Purpose

Before reading this chapter, skim the chapter and examine its organization. Look at the bold or italic words, headings of different colors and sizes, bulleted lists or numbered lists, tables, charts, captions, and features.

While studying, look for the access icon  **to:**

- **Practice** the *Content* and *Academic Terms* with e-flash cards, matching activities, and vocabulary games.
- **Reinforce** what you learn by completing the *Review & Assessment* questions and e-mailing them to your instructor.

www.g-wlearning.com/housing/

Photography Courtesy of Bosch Home Appliances

Creating an attractive interior design is only part of the inside story. To meet needs and values, a home or commercial space must also be functional. Appliances greatly increase the usefulness of various areas in the home or workplace.

Appliances are devices powered by gas or electricity that serve a specific use or function. Large appliances, such as refrigerators and ranges, are major appliances. Smaller appliances, such as toasters and hair dryers, are small or portable appliances. Appliances play a significant role in the kitchen and laundry area. They are also used in other areas throughout a home or workspace. Appliances help people meet their basic needs. Choosing appliances carefully can help create a home or workplace environment that is safe, comfortable, attractive, healthy, and efficient.

User Satisfaction and Appliance Considerations

Satisfaction with appliances depends largely on user choices. Appliance manufacturers and retailers, however, will also affect user satisfaction.

As a consumer or a housing professional or interior designer, you have a responsibility to obtain information about the appliances you buy or recommend to your clients (Figure 12.1). You need to know the various options that are available.

Photography Courtesy of Bosch Home Appliances

Figure 12.1 Matching appliance choices with household needs, lifestyle, and budget leads to satisfaction with appliances.

Appliance options should match the needs, lifestyle, and desires of the people in a household. Determining the amount of money you or a client can afford to spend on an appliance is an early priority. In addition, you should understand the warranties and service available for appliances. Reading and understanding use and care information before operating an appliance is essential. You cannot depend on the new appliance operating like the previous one. Fulfilling these responsibilities helps improve user satisfaction with appliances.

Manufacturers have a goal of preserving their reputations and keeping their residential and commercial customers happy. When appliance buyers are content with their purchases, they become repeat buyers and share this opinion with others. Unsatisfied customers and returned merchandise can put a manufacturer out of business.

To assure satisfaction, manufacturers strive to make appliances safe, dependable, easy to use, easy to clean, water and energy efficient, and affordable. They provide a variety of models that meet varying consumer needs and preferences. Appliances generally conform to safety standards set by the *American National Standards Institute (ANSI)*. Manufacturers give warranties and detailed instructions about the use of their appliances—either in print or on the Internet. Many manufacturers also offer free cookbooks or cooking suggestions and toll-free phone numbers. Their helpful websites provide more information about their products and how to use them, as well as instructions for proper installation.

The success of retail appliance businesses also relies on customer satisfaction. To meet the various needs of different consumers, retailers provide a selection of models. Responsible retailers train their salespeople to clearly explain the features of all models. Most retailers deliver and install appliances, and offer maintenance services, too. Some retailers offer free classes and demonstrations. Reputable retailers serve as a go-between for the customer with the manufacturer to make sure the conditions of the warranty are met.

Consumers can expect most major appliances to last 10 years or more. When buying appliances, considering both present and future needs is important. Here are some questions about which to think:

- Will the number of household members or employees increase or decrease in the next decade?
- Is the household or employer planning to move in the near future?

Tomasz Markowski/Shutterstock.com

Figure 12.2 A fully equipped kitchen is a convenient, but costly part of housing.

- If a move is in the future, will the appliances be taken to the new home or place of business?

Major appliances account for a large part of a housing budget. This is especially true when completely equipping a home (Figure 12.2). If you rent a home that has appliances in it, part of your rent goes toward the cost of appliance maintenance. Because appliances are so costly, their purchase requires careful consideration. Purchase and operating costs, features, functions, size, safety, aesthetics, and quality are among the factors consumers should consider.

Purchase Price

When considering a major appliance purchase, think about whether the appliance cost fits the household or the business budget. The cost of appliances varies greatly from brand to brand and from model to model. Larger appliances with many features cost more than smaller, more basic models. The materials from which appliances are made can also impact the price. For example, stainless steel is typically more costly than more traditional appliance materials. Prices also vary from one retailer to another. Consequently, smart consumers shop around and compare prices. Some vendors will actually price match their competitors and offer an additional discount to savvy buyers.

The purchase price of an appliance is only part of its true cost. When shopping, inquire about delivery and installation charges and extra fees for hauling away old appliances. Finance charges may also be applicable when buying an appliance on an installment plan.

Energy Cost

Energy costs are another part of the expense of major appliances. The wise consumer must consider the long-term operating costs. Purchase price plus operating cost reveals the true lifetime cost of an appliance. When examining appliance energy usage, two labels are helpful to consumers. The EnergyGuide label and the ENERGY STAR label offer different information.

The two energy labels calculate and organize energy use information that aids professionals and consumers in product selection. The actual operating cost of an appliance can also be individually determined on a yearly basis by using the formula to calculate the ***kilowatt hour (kWh)***—a unit of measure to determine energy use per hour (one kilowatt equals 1000 watts). See the STEM Math box on page 273 which shows an example using this formula.

wattage × (hours used per day) × (days per year) ÷ 1000 = annual kilowatt-hour (kWh) consumption

Green Choices

Environmentally Friendly Appliance Decisions

Many companies now offer environmentally friendly products and buildings. As a consumer or interior design professional, how can you be sure that products or buildings will perform as advertised? In other words: will a certain washing machine use less water? or will a house require less energy to operate?

You can rely on testing labels and certification programs to help answer these questions. An example of using a verified label is the ENERGY STAR label for appliances. Choosing household appliances with the ENERGY STAR label makes saving energy easier. The energy-efficiency percentage is different for various products, but ENERGY STAR qualified appliances use at least 10 percent less energy than the average appliance without the label.

The bright yellow and black **EnergyGuide label** states the average yearly energy use and operating cost of an appliance. The U.S. government requires these labels on new refrigerators, refrigerator-freezers, freezers, dishwashers, clothes washers and dryers, and water heaters because these appliances can vary greatly in energy use between brands or models. Room air conditioners and furnaces have an energy efficiency rating versus a label.

EnergyGuide labels enable you to compare average cost estimates for similar appliances (Figure 12.3). This helps you determine which appliances are the most *energy efficient*, or use the least amount of energy. Of course, those that use the least energy are the least costly to operate.

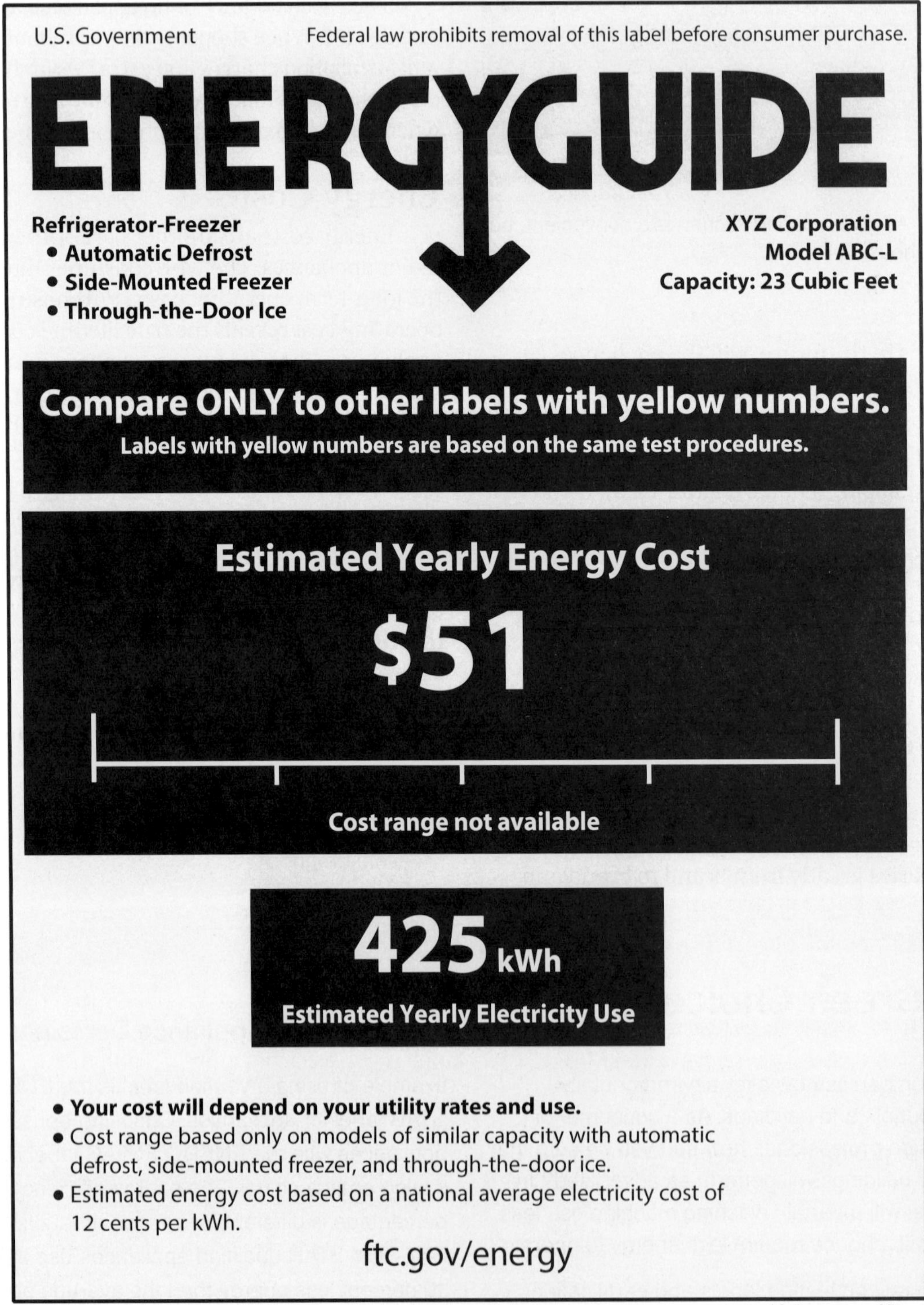

U.S. Department of Energy

Figure 12.3 EnergyGuide labels allow consumers to compare the average yearly energy costs of similar major appliances.

STEM Math Estimating Appliance Energy Consumption

You can estimate the amount and cost of electricity used by appliances and consumer electronic products. As you recall, energy use is measured in *watts*. Energy use is expressed in *kilowatt-hours (kWh)*. On its website, the U.S. Department of Energy gives the following formula to calculate energy used by a product each year:

(wattage × hours used per day) × (days used per year) ÷ 1000 = annual kilowatt-hour (kWh) consumption

Suppose you want to know how much it costs to operate a refrigerator during a year's time. Products are marked with the maximum wattage they draw. Suppose the refrigerator is marked 725, meaning it draws a maximum of 725 watts. Since refrigerators cycle on and off and do not operate continuously at maximum wattage, divide the hours used per day by 3. If you plug the information you have into the equation, you get:

(725 × 8 × 365) ÷ 1000 = 2117 kilowatt-hour (kWh) per year

To figure out what this would cost, look up the current rate—given in cents per kWh—charged by your electric utility provider. If the utility charges $.0917/kWh, you would calculate the following:

(2117 kWh used per year) × ($.0917 per kWh) = $194.13 yearly cost

It would cost approximately $194.13 to operate the refrigerator for a year. For more information, visit the U.S. Department of Energy's *Energy Savers* website and click on *Appliances and Electronics, Estimating Energy Use*.

Math Practice

1. Use the formulas above to calculate the energy cost of using one of your kitchen appliances—refrigerator, range, or dishwasher—based on usage and the current rate charged by your electricity provider.
2. Choose a personal electronic device or television you use regularly and calculate the operating cost using the above formulas.

To roughly estimate the cost of 10 years of operation, for example, multiply the operating cost figure on the EnergyGuide label by 10. You will notice that many inexpensive, "no-frills" appliances usually cost the most to operate. In contrast, more expensive appliances, with all the features customers might want, will cost less to operate over time. This means the money you or clients save when purchasing some less-expensive models you may eventually use to pay the extra energy costs needed over their lifetime. Of course, buying an energy-efficient appliance on sale represents even more savings. When buying appliances for the long-term, therefore, consider both purchase price and operating costs.

The **ENERGY STAR® label** is not a requirement, but it serves as an easy-to-use energy guide for consumers. ENERGY STAR qualified appliances are the most energy efficient in their group. Typically these products are at least 10 percent more energy efficient than similar products that meet minimum government energy standards. For example, ENERGY STAR qualified clothes washers use about 30 percent less energy and use over 50 percent less water than regular clothes washers. An ENERGY STAR qualified refrigerator uses 20 percent less energy than a new non-ENERGY STAR qualified model.

The requirements for meeting ENERGY STAR designation change over time for many reasons. One good reason is that more appliance companies are improving the energy efficiency of their products. As a result, the government modifies the ENERGY STAR requirements to remain a meaningful energy-efficiency guide to consumers. The U.S. Environmental Protection Agency (EPA) and the U.S. Department of Energy (DOE) sponsor the ENERGY STAR program.

The ENERGY STAR label makes it easy to locate energy-efficient products without giving up features, quality, or personal comfort. You can find the label on products in 30 different categories, including appliances, electronics, office equipment, lighting, heating and cooling equipment, windows, and even new homes. Consumers can save money monthly on their utility bills by choosing ENERGY STAR products.

Using products with an ENERGY STAR label not only saves money in operating costs, but also helps save the environment. Effective environmental product design focuses on reducing water use, promoting cleaner air, and using construction materials wisely.

Finishes and Features

Appliances are available with a wide range of finishes and features. Careful planning will help you choose the look and features that best compliment your design plan and meet your needs. When shopping, ask yourself some of the following questions: Is it available in the color you want? Will it coordinate with the other furnishings and appliances in the room? A particular design trend for consumer kitchens in recent years is the look of a "commercial kitchen." Designers label this the "Professional Look." For appliances, this means selecting models with a stainless steel finish (Figure 12.4).

When deciding what appliance features you need, consider the people who will use it. Is the appliance easy to use and understand? Does it perform all the tasks the household requires? Does it have extra features that household members will not use? Extras add to the price. Consider convenience features such as buzzers to tell you when a cycle is completed or if a refrigerator door is left open accidently.

A feature being incorporated into many household appliances is the use of steam. Steam ovens and counter-installed units produce moist food and preserve nutrients. Steam in clothes washers removes stains and provides added cleaning power. Some clothes dryers use steam to reduce wrinkles and refresh clothing. In addition, steam provides added cleaning power and eliminates prewashing in dishwashers.

Does anyone in the household have special needs? For instance, people who use wheelchairs cannot reach as high or as far as others. Front-mounted controls are ideal for these appliance buyers. People with difficulty grasping or turning knobs, for example, may find electronic touch pads easier to use. Does the household include small children? If yes, look for features like lock-out controls that will limit a child's access to an appliance.

After deciding which appliance features meet the household's needs, not just wants, consider items that have these features to find the best purchase. Although consumers can add some features later—such as icemakers—factory installed components are preferable.

Elena Elisseeva/Shutterstock.com

Figure 12.4 The sleek look of stainless steel is apparent in the refrigerator, cooktop and hood, and the double ovens.

Size

Size is another consideration when purchasing a major appliance. How large should the appliance be to meet the needs of the household? How many people will be using the appliance now and in the future? Does the household need a large or extra-large model, or something more compact? Will the appliance fit the space planned for it? Does it fit through doorways and hallways?

Safety

When purchasing a new appliance from a reputable dealer, you can be sure that it meets current safety standards. In contrast, appliances (usually portable appliances) purchased at flea markets or garage sales often do not meet current safety standards. In addition, a bargain appliance with an unfamiliar brand name may mean that the appliance does not meet safety standards.

Usually the first page of any owner's guide addresses appliance safety. Look for a seal certifying that the appliance conforms to safety standards. Consumers can find these seals on the back of major appliances, on the nameplate, and in the use and care materials. On small electric appliances, the seal is usually on the nameplate or attached to the electrical cord. Common safety seals found on electric or gas appliances include:

- *UL* from Underwriters Laboratory
- *ETL* of Intertek Testing Services Ltd.
- *CSA Group* testing and certifying services (Canada and United States)

With safety as the common goal, many groups join forces to develop safety standards. Appliance manufacturers, safety-testing organizations, and the U.S. Consumer Product Safety Commission lead the way in such efforts. Safety standards exist for each appliance category and undergo periodic review.

In addition, manufacturers often include ground fault circuit interrupters (GFCI) on the cords of some small appliances for safety. As you recall, GFCIs are safety devices in outlets or on electrical cords that prevent electrical shock. They interrupt the unintentional flow of electricity to avoid shock, burns, and possible fatalities in the home. See Chapters 10 and 24 for more information about GFCIs.

In the home, appliance safety depends primarily on proper installation and use (Figure 12.5). The literature that accompanies the appliance identifies these requirements. Always install tip-over prevention hardware provided by the manufacturer. Make sure the house has the correct electrical or gas connections. A 120-volt, major electrical appliance should have a three-prong plug. The third (round) prong grounds the appliance. If a grounded appliance has damaged wiring, electric current will flow to the ground rather than through your body. Because the grounding prong prevents electrical shock, appliance owners should not remove it. Also, avoid circuit overload by making sure the home has adequate electrical service for the appliance before installation.

Some appliances provide additional safety in the form of extra features. For example, some ranges provide childproof control locks, which prevent children from turning on the oven or burners. Some consumers regard such extra safety features as a need.

Photography Courtesy of Whirlpool Corporation

Figure 12.5 An important safety issue with microwave ovens is using the right model for over-the-range installation. This model is designed specifically for that purpose.

Quality

The quality of an appliance is a key purchase consideration. Appliances that require frequent repairs are costly and troublesome to operate. You want appliances that will work dependably for many years.

Asking a few questions may help evaluate quality. Here are some question examples:

- Is the appliance well constructed?
- Is the manufacturer reputable?

Housing Health & Safety

Eliminate Hazards for Appliance Safety

Almost any household item can pose a hazard to unsupervised infants and children. Appliance entrapment and tip-over hazards are high on the list. Sadly, some children suffocate or are crushed by heavy appliances when playing with items in ways that are contrary to the manufacturer's instructions. Here are some safety concerns that deserve special attention.

- **Eliminate entrapment hazards.** Current law and voluntary safety standards require that the doors of refrigerators and chest freezers easily push open from the inside to keep from trapping children. Yet people often keep chest freezers made before 1970 with the old hook-and-latch lock as spare storage containers long after they stop operating. Tragically, when children use such an appliance as a hiding place, they cannot escape. As a safety precaution, owners should remove one part of the locking mechanism to disable chest-type freezers. Your state may also require removal of the freezer cover before you can discard it.
- **Eliminate appliance tip-overs.** When buying new appliances, make sure installers use anti-tip hardware and follow the safety instructions manufacturers provide. For example, installers should secure a free-standing range to a wall to keep it from tipping forward if a child leans, sits, or stands on an open oven door.

To prevent appliance related accidents in the home, supervising young children and using items safely are key.

- Is the use and care manual thorough and easy to understand?
- Does the retailer or manufacturer offer after-sale service?

Assessing quality also involves reading the warranty. A **warranty** is a manufacturer's written promise that a product will meet certain performance and quality standards as outlined in the warranty. When reading a warranty, be sure to find out how long the warranty lasts and what it covers—the entire product or only certain parts. Does the warranty include labor fees?

A warranty may be full or limited. A **full warranty** provides the consumer with free repair or replacement of a warranted product or part if any defect occurs during the warranty period. Under a **limited warranty**, a warrantor provides service, repairs, and replacements only under certain conditions. For example, the warrantors can charge for repairs. Consumers may also be responsible for shipping the item back to the warrantor or taking other steps to get repairs.

In addition to the full and limited warranties, one option to consider is the **extended warranty**. For an extra fee, the consumer can add several years to the manufacturer's warranty. Read an extended warranty document very carefully to decide if it is necessary and worth the extra cost. Many times, extended warranties are not a wise purchase.

Choosing Kitchen Appliances

All aspects of food storage, preparation, and cleanup require the use of kitchen appliances (Figure 12.6). The purchase considerations already discussed pertain to all these appliances. Use the following information to help select appliances wisely.

Refrigerators

Refrigerators are a necessity for storing fresh and frozen foods. Perhaps that is why nearly every home in the United States has at least one refrigerator.

Styles

Refrigerators are available in a few basic styles. A *one-door refrigerator* has a single door and does not have a freezer. One example of the one-door refrigerator is the *compact refrigerator*. It is suitable for use in college dorm rooms, hotel rooms, and small apartments. Consumers can purchase or rent them at a low price. Compact models may be capable of freezing ice cubes but are usually not suitable for storing frozen foods. Specialized refrigeration units, like wine coolers, can also fit into this category. In the higher-end market there are also what is referred to as single use units which are the size of a standard refrigerator and dedicated to either all fresh food refrigeration or all freezer.

Review & Assessment

1. To assure user satisfaction, what qualities do manufacturers strive to achieve with making appliances?
2. To what safety standards do appliances conform?
3. What factors should users consider when choosing appliances?
4. What is the difference between the EnergyGuide label and the ENERGY STAR label?
5. What should users think about when deciding on appliance features?
6. What three safety seals indicate an appliance conforms to safety standards?
7. What is a warranty?
8. Contrast full warranty, limited warranty, and extended warranty.

Photography Courtesy of Bosch Home Appliances

Figure 12.6 The tasks of storing food, cooking meals, and washing dishes are all made easier with the help of appliances.

Most refrigerators available today are *two-door refrigerator-freezers*. These models have separate freezer sections that freeze food. The freezer section temperature remains about 0°F. The freezer section may be above, below, or at the side of the fresh food section of the refrigerator. *French door refrigerators* have two upper refrigerator doors that open from the middle and a freezer drawer on the bottom (Figure 12.7).

Most refrigerator-freezers are free-standing, which means it is possible to move them. Free-standing units can be either standard depth or counter depth. The consumer can choose a built-in refrigerator, which is the same depth as the kitchen counter and is actually bolted to the cabinets. These refrigerators allow the addition of panels to match the cabinets, making the refrigerator appear to be part of the cabinetry.

The refrigerator drawer is a new option that saves floor space. The drawer unit—which can be a refrigerator or freezer or a combination of the two—is installed in place of a base cabinet. These innovative refrigerators are convenient for small kitchens, efficiency apartments, recreation rooms, or even master bedrooms.

Photography Courtesy of Bosch Home Appliances

Figure 12.7 Some refrigerator-freezer owners prefer having the refrigerator section on top and the less-used freezer at the bottom.

Features to Consider

Refrigerators and refrigerator-freezers are generally available in several basic colors to fit the wide range of design schemes. Special features include individual compartments and temperature controls for meat, produce, and dairy products (Figure 12.8 A). Adjustable shelves allow easy storage of large items. Another option on some models is a reversible door that hinges on either side of the refrigerator. The ability to change hinge location can allow better access to adjacent counter space. A reversible door is particularly helpful when moving a refrigerator to a new residence that may present different traffic patterns from the current location. Ice and water dispensers also are features that many people want.

The refrigerator's defrost system is a feature to consider. In general, one-door compact models usually require *manual defrosting*. This means that frost accumulates inside the refrigerator, reducing the efficiency of the appliance. When the frost becomes ¼-inch thick, the appliance must be turned off so the frost can melt. This usually requires emptying the appliance and drying the compartments before turning it on again.

Today, most refrigerator-freezers are *automatic defrosting* models where no frost accumulates. These frost-free models are convenient, but are more costly. They may also use more electricity, but the convenience may be worth the cost.

Storage space is another important consideration. The measurement of space inside a refrigerator is in cubic feet. An 18-cubic-foot refrigerator-freezer may be the ideal size for a family that shops frequently or eats out often. In contrast, the same appliance may be too small for a family that shops less frequently or buys food in bulk.

The amount of refrigeration versus freezer space is another important consideration. All 12-cubic-foot models, for example, do not have same-size fresh food and freezer sections. Make sure both compartments provide the necessary storage space. Check the interior dimensions and the shelf sizes (Figure 12.8 B). Will the storage accommodate all needed items? A range of sizes is available to meet the needs of various households.

Another consideration is the amount of kitchen space available for a refrigerator. Measure the height, width, and depth of the space you have. If you select the counter depth style, which does not protrude

A Photography Courtesy of Bosch Home Appliances

B Photography Courtesy of Bosch Home Appliances

Figure 12.8 The temperature control is located on the outside of the refrigerator and is convenient to adjust (A). Storage should not be a problem with the many compartments of this refrigerator (B).

into the work area, keep in mind that less depth means less storage space for the household. Take the measurements with you when you shop. A checklist for buying refrigerators is shown in Figure 12.9.

Freezers

When more freezer space is a requirement, buyers may want to purchase a separate freezer. The size necessary depends on how consumers will use it. Will it simply provide backup storage or will extra freezer space be a regular need? People who preserve homegrown fruits and vegetables, buy food in bulk quantities, or freeze make-ahead meals usually need more freezer space.

Styles

The two styles of freezers are chest and upright. Large, bulky packages are easier to store in a chest model. Chest freezers use less electricity because less cold air escapes when opening the door. One disadvantage of chest freezers is that they require more floor space. Another is that users must lift the food when removing it from the freezer. Chest freezers usually require manual defrosting.

Food is easier to see and remove in an upright freezer. These freezers only require a small amount of floor space, but they cost more to operate.

Features to Consider

You can choose an upright freezer with either a *manual defrost* or a *full automatic-defrost* system. Full automatic defrost models are convenient, but the purchase price and operating costs are higher. Figure 12.10 shows a checklist for freezers.

Ranges

Recent years have seen many changes in ranges. These changes are due to advances in technology and consumer interest in the speed of cooking and cleanability. You or your client will have several factors to consider when choosing a range.

A first decision concerns the energy source. The fuel choice of either electricity or gas depends on the availability and cost of each as well as personal preference.

Electric Ranges

Electric ranges offer several styles of cooking surfaces. The *conventional coil* cooktop has wires encased in coils. The electric current flows through the coils to produce heat, and the heat transfers to cookware by conduction and radiation. This type of cooking element is usually found in the very basic style of appliances and is less expensive.

Checklist for Refrigerators

- Does the refrigerator require defrosting?
- Are interior and door shelves adjustable for more flexible use of space?
- Is space available for heavy and tall bottles and large items like pizza boxes?
- Is the interior well lighted?
- Is the refrigerator interior easy to clean?
- Are shelves made of strong, noncorrosive, rust-resistant materials such as glass?
- Are all interior parts easy to remove and/or accessible for cleaning?
- Is the fresh-food section easy to reach, use, clean, and organize?
- Are door shelf retaining bars strong and securely attached?
- Is crisper space adequate? Is it designed to keep moisture inside?
- Is the freezer section easy to reach, use, clean, and organize?
- Is the refrigerator easy to move for cleaning?
- Is the refrigerator's energy consumption, as shown on the EnergyGuide label, reasonable for its size and features?

Figure 12.9 Consider these points before choosing a refrigerator.

Checklist for Freezers

- Will model fit your floor space and weight limitations?
- Will the type of door opening be convenient in its location?
- Are shelves and/or baskets adjustable?
- Are all sections readily accessible?
- Is the interior well lighted?
- Does it have a safety signal light to let you know that power is on?
- Is the freezer frost-free? If not, does it have a fast-defrost system?
- Does it have easy-to-read and accessible controls?
- Does it have magnetic gaskets around the door frame to seal cold air in more completely?

Figure 12.10 Consider these points before choosing a food freezer.

A very popular style of electric range features a smooth *glass-ceramic* cooktop, which makes the range easy to clean. This surface usually hides radiant heating elements that radiate heat through the glass to the cookware. Because the glass is also heated, it is important that the cookware be very flat in order to conduct heat and cook efficiently. The induction cooktops also use a glass-ceramic surface.

Induction cooktops use a magnetic field below a glass-ceramic surface to generate heat in the bottom of cookware. The cookware *must* be magnetic. Cast iron and some stainless steel cookware work well because they offer resistance to the passage of the magnetic waves, which generates heat. Heat from the cookware then transfers to food. The range surface does not heat up. To determine whether or not cookware is appropriate for an induction surface, check to see if a magnet will cling to the bottom surface. If it does, the cookware can be used on the induction surface. Cleanup is easy because spills do not burn.

Gas Ranges

The combustion process between gas and oxygen in the air produces the heat in gas ranges. Regulating the flow of gas through a valve controls the heat. More gas causes a higher flame and hotter temperatures. In the past, users had to light a pilot light to use the burner. Current standards require electronic ignitions on all new ranges powered by natural gas or propane gas.

Most gas cooking surfaces today incorporate the sealed burner surface where no opening exists between the burners and the cooktop surface. This makes cleanup easier. The energy usage of gas

Career Focus Interior Designer—Kitchens and Baths

Can you imagine yourself as an interior designer who specializes in kitchen and bath design? If you can, read more about this challenging and appealing career.

Interests/Skills: Do you enjoy cooking and realize how important proper space planning is to creating an efficient food preparation area? Do you consider the kitchen a great space for family interaction? Skills include a vision for what a space could look like and balancing it with the rest of the home. When working with existing space, measurements and problem solving are very important.

Career Snapshot: Some residential interior designers specialize in designing kitchens and baths. The finished product needs to be a style that fits seamlessly with the rest of the home. Kitchens require a different approach to interior design than a living room or dining room. Designers must research products and select materials that provide for a safe environment. In kitchen design, they must be able to create a kitchen with properly placed work centers for storage, preparation, cooking, cleanup, and mixing. For bathrooms, the designer works with the client to determine what will work best to meet individual and family needs. In designing both kitchens and baths, special attention must be given to the placement of electrical outlets, lighting, and ventilation, as well as features that create a safe and functional space. The designer must meet all local building codes.

Education/Training: A bachelor's degree is most often required. In addition, Certified Kitchen Designers (CKD) and Certified Bath Designers (CBD) are certified through the National Kitchen & Bath Association (NKBA).

KOHLER

Licensing/Examinations: Approximately one-half of the states require interior designers to be licensed. The National Council for Interior Design Qualification (NCIDQ) administers an examination that interior designers must pass in order to obtain a license. In addition, designers specializing in kitchen and bath design would need to pass either the Certified Kitchen Designer (CKD) or the Certified Bath Designer (CBD) exam, both administered by the NKBA.

Professional Associations: American Society of Interior Designers (ASID); International Interior Design Association (IIDA); the National Kitchen & Bath Association (NKBA)

Job Outlook: Customers often look to specialized positions for the best quality of service. Although not as qualified as an architect to do complex plans, a Certified Kitchen Designer can perform most similar services at a lower cost.

Sources: Occupational Outlook Handbook (OOH); Occupational Information Network (O*NET)

burners is measured in ***British thermal units (Btu)***, with larger burners consuming more Btus. Gas ranges or cooktops can include from four to six burners with a variety of Btu output, including high-powered and low-Btu keep-warm burners.

Styles

Ranges come in several styles and sizes. A consumer's choice depends on the capacity requirement and the available space. All ranges have a cooking surface with one or two ovens. *Freestanding* models are the most common, with many size, color, and feature options. The controls are usually located on the range backsplash at the back of the range, but they can also be on the front panel of the range. These ranges may stand alone or you can place them between cabinets for a built-in look (Figure 12.11).

Slide-in and *drop-in* range models either slide into a space or rest on a base cabinet. They fit snugly between kitchen cabinets and counters. Chrome strips often cover the side edges and provide a built-in look.

Michael Higginson/Shutterstock.com

Figure 12.11 This quality freestanding range becomes a focal point in the kitchen.

Lorraine Kourafas/Shutterstock.com

Figure 12.12 A warming drawer is an ideal appliance for someone who does a lot of baking or cooking.

The controls for these models are on the cooktop surface because these models do not include a backsplash.

Built-in models provide cooking surfaces separate from the oven. This allows flexible kitchen arrangements. Installation of surface units is in a countertop, often a kitchen island. Oven installation is in a wall cabinet or below the countertop. Some built-in ovens are double ovens. Many built-ins are single ovens installed above or below a microwave oven and/or a warming drawer. A *warming drawer* keeps hot food warm until serving time. Also, it warms up dinner plates and serving pieces. Some warming drawers have humidity controls to keep selected foods moist (Figure 12.12).

Features to Consider

Many consumers want a self-cleaning feature for the oven. **Self-cleaning ovens** operate at extremely high temperatures to burn away spatters and spills. The user simply wipes away the small amount of remaining ash. Because these ovens reach very high temperatures during cleaning, they have extra insulation. This also helps save energy during normal baking periods. The self-cleaning feature adds to the price of the range, but the cost of operating the cleaning cycle is less than the cost of chemical oven cleaners. Such ovens generally use three to four kilowatt-hours of electricity during the self-cleaning cycle.

A surface-cooking option to consider is the ceramic cooktop. These cooktops may have a variety of different element sizes including dual elements that give multiple size options. In addition, warm-and-serve elements that operate at very low temperatures to keep food warm without overcooking are also optional. Some have modular surface units the user can interchange with a grill or griddle (Figure 12.13).

robophobic/Shutterstock.com

Figure 12.13 The modular surface units in this cooktop have been replaced with a grill.

Single-purpose modular units can also be installed in the countertop. Such units might include a deep fat fryer, steam well, single or double elements/burners, or an induction element. Newer glass-ceramic cooktops do not use knobs, but instead have electronic touch controls that are part of the glass surface. With no knobs to clean, the surface is very easy to clean.

Other range features to consider include clocks, timers, and programmable cooking cycles. Delay and time-bake cycles allow you to start and stop the cooking process while away. Study the checklist for ranges in Figure 12.14.

Convection Ovens

Convection ovens bake foods in a stream of heated air. Because these ovens continually force heated air directly onto the food, it browns the food and seals in juices. Convection ovens cook in about two-thirds the time and with less energy than conventional cooking. The user may need to adjust the cooking times for favorite recipes for convection cooking.

A convection oven can be part of a range, but can also be a separate built-in oven or countertop model. You can use most convection ovens in the convection mode, as well as the conventional mode without the fan. These ovens typically come with a "convection bake" option for baked items and a "convection roast" option for meats.

Checklist for Ranges

- Is the range suitable for cooking needs and kitchen space?
- Are cooktop burners or units an adequate size for the pans you will use?
- Is oven capacity adequate to meet regular cooking needs?
- Are controls placed for convenient and safe use?
- Are control settings and numbers easy to read?
- Is the range designed to simplify cleaning? Does it have a smooth backsplash, an absence of grooves and crevices, removable burners or units, and a self-cleaning oven?
- Does the range offer features that are important to family needs and use?

Figure 12.14 Consider these points before choosing a range.

Steam Ovens

Another style of oven now available is the steam oven. These ovens are typically smaller ovens that use steam to cook the food. Steam cooking not only produces moist products, but it cooks quickly and preserves nutrients. Some manufacturers are combining steam with convection forced air in their ovens.

Microwave Ovens

Microwave ovens cook food with high-frequency energy waves called *microwaves*. These appliances can cook, defrost, and reheat foods in a fraction of the time required for conventional ovens. Microwave cooking can also save up to 75 percent of the energy used by conventional ovens, depending on the type and amount of food cooked.

As food absorbs microwaves, the molecules within the food vibrate against one another. The friction produced creates the heat that cooks the food.

The time requirement to cook foods depends on the type of food and the power level used for cooking. Most microwave ovens have 10 power levels. Protein foods—such as eggs, cheese, and meats—and thickening sauces require low power levels, as does defrosting. For most other foods, you can use medium and high power levels.

For even and efficient cooking, it is important to use cookware items that allow microwaves to pass through them. Generally, glass, ceramic, and some plastics allow microwaves to pass through them better than other types of cooking materials.

Users should carefully select cookware and containers to use in the microwave oven. The owner's manual generally recommends cookware and containers that are appropriate to use. For safety, use only cookware manufactured for use in the microwave oven. Glass, ceramic, and plastic containers that are safe are usually labeled as safe for microwave use. A general recommendation is to avoid placing metal (metal pans, metal trim, utensils, foil decorations on wrappers, etc.) in the microwave because of potential fire or damage to the microwave oven. Also avoid using plastic dinnerware and storage containers for microwave cooking.

Styles

Several styles of microwave ovens are available. Countertop models are the most popular and offer a large number of features. Users can place them on a countertop, table, or cart. Microwave ovens are available in a variety of sizes and oven wattages.

MR. INTERIOR/Shutterstock.com

Figure 12.15 Microwave ovens built for over-the-range installation have vent systems, too.

Checklist for Microwaves
• Is the oven cavity the right size and shape for your needs?
• Does it have the power settings and pre-timed buttons you need?
• Is there a signal when the microwave oven finishes cooking and shuts off?
• Does it have a timer? If so, does the timer have enough minutes to allow you the flexibility you need?
• Are the controls mechanical (knobs and push buttons) or electronic (touchpad)?
• Are the controls easy to understand?
• Does a cookbook come with the microwave oven?

Figure 12.16 Consider these points before choosing a microwave oven.

Microwave ovens with ventilation hoods are attached to the wall and cabinet above a range. These models are similar to countertop models; however, they may have less capacity (Figure 12.15).

A microwave feature is sometimes built into "speed cook" ovens. The microwave mode can be used alone or together with convection air or light energy in a cooking cycle. In these ovens, the *microwave mode* cooks the food quickly and the *heat mode* browns and crisps it.

Features to Consider

Features available on microwave ovens include automatic programming, automatic settings, sensor cooking, temperature probes, and turntables (Figure 12.16). These features do the following:

- **Automatic programming.** This feature automatically shifts the microwave oven power levels at preset times. It allows you to program the oven to do several operations in sequence. For instance, you can set this oven to defrost a food product, cook it, and then keep it warm. Pre-timed settings, as for popping popcorn, are available on many microwave oven models.
- **Automatic settings.** These settings, available on some models, determine cooking times and correct power levels for you. You just set the controls for the type and amount of food, and the oven does the rest.
- **Sensor cooking.** This feature determines food doneness by either sensing the temperature or moisture levels in the oven. The oven will stop when it determines the food is cooked.
- **Temperature probes.** This probe is a type of food sensor that helps you control cooking. It automatically turns off the oven or switches to a warm setting when food reaches a preset temperature.

Range Hoods

Hoods over cooking appliances help vent heat, moisture, toxins, smoke, grease, and odors from the kitchen (Figure 12.17). Installers can vent hoods to the outside, and if using gas cooking appliances, this is the best type of hood to install. Unvented models use a special screen to collect grease, and sometimes a charcoal filter to remove smoke and odors. The unvented design does not remove moisture, heat, or toxins. Systems that vent to the outdoors do a more complete job of removing all pollutants produced in the home kitchen.

An alternative to a hood is a *downdraft ventilation system*. A fan below the cooktop pulls fumes down into a vent. The downdraft units are vented to outdoors.

Quieter operation of the exhaust fans comes with modern range hoods. You can also find remote fans in which the fan is not part of the hood itself, but outside the house. Many new styles and sizes of hoods are available. Some are focal points in the kitchen and make a strong design statement.

Photography Courtesy of Bosch Home Appliances

Figure 12.17 This slim range hood is interesting and effective in removing odors and heat out of the kitchen.

Jennifer Blanchard Belk, IIDA, LEED AP

Figure 12.18 This two-drawer design for a dishwasher allows faster cleaning of small loads of dishes.

Dishwashers

A dishwasher can save the homeowner time, energy, and water. It also has the ability to clean dishes better than hand washing because it uses hotter water and stronger detergents. Dishwashers also dry dishes, which avoids wiping them with towels that may carry pathogens.

Styles

Most dishwashers are built into the cabinetry, but some are portable/convertible models. Portable/convertible models are on casters, so users can move them easily to the sink from a storage area in the kitchen. Hoses in the back of the dishwasher connect to the sink for operation. With removal of the casters, users can convert this model into a built-in model. Newer types of dishwashing appliances include the dishwasher drawer, Figure 12.18, and compact countertop models.

Features to Consider

Dishwashers often feature a variety of design options and cycles to meet various cleaning needs. Many door designs and finishes are available. The consumer can choose between molded plastic and stainless steel for the interior liner. In recent years a significant improvement in dishwasher operation is quiet operation. In addition to less noise, here are some other features you or your clients may find of value:

- special cycles for scrubbing pans, sterilizing items (like baby bottles), or washing fine china
- adjustable upper rack to wash large or odd-sized items along with baskets for small items
- continuous bottom racks for more capacity and adjustable rack tines for convenience
- top-rack only wash, hidden controls and heating elements, and a preheat cycle to heat water to the ideal temperature
- a third rack for flatware or flat items, automatic detergent dispenser, or a food disposer to eliminate food particles

Many models offer energy-saving features, such as a non-heat drying cycle. This can save up to one-third the electricity usage in a normal drying cycle, but dishes may not dry completely. See the checklist in Figure 12.19 before choosing a dishwasher.

Trash Compactors

Trash compactors compress household trash to a fraction of its original volume. Compactors use heavy-duty plastic bags or special plastic-lined paper bags to collect trash. They are typically built into base cabinets.

Checklist for Dishwashers

- Are the tub and door linings durable and stain resistant?
- Does the wash system have two or more levels? (A single system takes considerable loading care to get all the dishes clean.)
- Will it hold at least 10 place settings? Do your favorite pots and pans fit?
- Does it offer more than one cycle, such as rinse/hold or prerinse cycles?
- Is there a preheat setting that will heat water to the appropriate temperature for better cleaning?
- Is an automatic wetting agent dispenser provided?
- Is the dishwasher insulated to eliminate excessive noise and heat?
- Does it have an energy saver switch to turn the heating element partially or completely off during some cycles?

Figure 12.19 Consider these points before selecting a new dishwasher.

Trash compactors handle almost any kind of nonfood trash, including bottles, cans, and plastic containers.

Compactors are not intended for food scraps, due to the growth of bacteria and odor development. Also, they should not be used to dispose of highly flammable materials and aerosol cans. These items present safety concerns and should be discarded separately. With an increasing emphasis on recycling, trash compactors are less popular than in the past.

Food Waste Disposers

A food waste disposer easily eliminates the smell and mess of food scraps. With installation below the kitchen sink, this appliance catches and grinds most types of food scraps. It connects to a sewer line or drains into a septic tank.

Both batch-feed and continuous-feed models are available, with continuous feed the most popular. In *batch-feed* models, scrape the food down the drain opening into the grinding chamber. Then put the drain cover in place, turn on the cold water, and twist the drain cover to activate the disposer. When the scraps flush away, turn off the water and remove the cover. Do not overfill the disposer. Instead, process many small batches. In *continuous-feed* models, add food scraps to the disposer while it runs. This disposer is usually activated by a wall switch and also utilizes a stream of cold water to help grind the scraps and flush them through the drain. Flushing the drain with more cold water is important to ensure food does not stay in the drain and cause unpleasant odors.

Review & Assessment

1. Name two types of refrigerator styles available.
2. What styles of freezers are available? Which is more energy efficient?
3. What type of material is used to make cookware for an induction cooktop? Why?
4. Explain why a convection oven cooks food faster and at a lower temperature than a conventional oven.
5. What cookware materials are generally safe for microwave cooking? Which should users avoid?
6. Summarize the key features of a dishwasher.

Choosing Laundry Appliances

Doing laundry is a routine household task. Having a washer and dryer in a home is highly convenient. Users can do laundry whenever time allows without the trouble and expense of taking it to a self-service laundry. Placement of laundry appliances can vary from the kitchen, a utility area, or in a second-floor laundry closet (Figure 12.20 A).

Washers

Size is one of the most important variables in washers. Does the household do small loads of laundry on a frequent basis, or fewer, bigger loads? Will a full-size or compact unit meet family needs? Is a side-by-side washer/dryer pair or a stackable washer and dryer preferable (Figure 12.20 B)? In small homes, stackable laundry appliances may be the best option because they take up less floor space or can be incorporated into a closet. A style reintroduced to the market is the combination washer/dryer. It is one appliance that serves as both a washer and dryer.

Styles

There are two basic types of washers for the home: top-loading and front-loading models. The

A

B Photography Courtesy of Bosch Home Appliances

Figure 12.20 Placing the washer and dryer in a clothing closet adds convenience (A). A stackable washer and dryer is a good choice where floor space is limited (B).

top-loading models, or *vertical-axis machines*, have a door on the top of the appliance. This style has been the one preferred by most American consumers. A standard top-loading model has an agitator in the center of the wash tub. Clothes wash in a tub partially full of water. The agitator moves the clothes around in the water to remove soil.

Several companies offer new water- and energy-efficient top-loading models. These models load from the top, but the wash action is very different from the standard models. Instead of having an agitator in the middle, they have another means for "tossing" clothes in the wash tub with only a small amount of water. Clothes rinse in a shower of water. These models use much less water than the typical top-loading models.

Front-loading models are also called *horizontal-axis washers* (Figure 12.21). Because these models load from the front, they require more bending of the user than the top-loaders unless they are elevated with special pedestals available from manufacturers. While they cost more to purchase than traditional washers, front-loading models are highly efficient and use *much* less water and save energy, too. Horizontal-axis machines have a faster spin speed that wrings out more water. Less water means a shorter drying time. They also use less detergent, but require special low-sudsing, high-efficiency detergents. Look for "he" on the detergent label. Because there is no agitator, front-loading models are gentle on clothing.

Photography Courtesy of Bosch Home Appliances

Figure 12.21 This home owner chose to use the front-loading washer and dryer. Notice the convenient sink and clothing-hanging area.

To suit a variety of fabrics, washers have cycles, such as heavy-duty, normal, permanent press, and delicate. All cycles have the same basic steps: fill, wash, spin (drain), rinse, and spin again. Cycles vary in the length of time, amount of agitation or movement, water temperature, and number of rinses.

Features to Consider

Features on washers include dispensers that release detergent, bleach, and fabric softener into the wash water at the right times. Top-loaders also feature a control that lets the user match the water level to the load size. Front-loading machines weigh the load to determine the water use. Some washers have a water temperature control for the wash water.

Porcelain-coated and stainless-steel tubs are rust-resistant and smooth enough to protect fine fabrics. If chipped, however, porcelain-enamel tubs can form rust spots. Plastic tubs are durable and rust-resistant, but may develop rough spots over time which may snag clothes. See the checklist in Figure 12.22 when buying a washer and dryer.

Dryers

Clothes dryers are often bought at the same time as washers. They are usually available in matching sets. Dryers should be large enough to dry a full load from the washer. An advantage of buying a matching pair is the dryer design handles the same load size as the washer. For easy loading, arrange the dryer so that the open door faces the clothes washer. This is especially important in the front-loading models.

Dryers operate on gas or electricity. Compare installation and operating costs as well as purchase prices before you buy.

Basic clothes dryer models have preset temperatures that are safe for most fabrics. A permanent press feature prevents wrinkles from forming by tumbling clothes without heat at the end of the drying time. An *air-dry* option may be available to fluff items without using heat.

Most models of dryers have a timer control, and some have either a temperature sensor or a *moisture-sensing system.* These sensors shut the dryer off when clothes reach a selected temperature or degree of dryness. Another feature of deluxe models guards against wrinkles. Some reverse the drum direction periodically to mix up the clothes. Others tumble dry clothes without heat for a few seconds every few minutes until they are unloaded.

Checklist for Washers and Dryers	
Washers	**Dryers**
• Will the washer fit your space limitations?	• Is the lint trap in a convenient place for ease in removing, cleaning, or replacing?
• Does the washer have a self-cleaning lint filter?	• Is the control panel lighted? the interior?
• Does the top-loading model have a water-level selector?	• Is there a signal (buzzer or bell) at the end of the drying period?
• Is there a water temperature selector?	• Is there a safety button to start the dryer?
• Does it have a minimum of regular, delicate, and permanent-press cycles?	• Does the dryer offer one heat setting or a choice?
• Is a presoak cycle available? a permanent-press cycle? a knit cycle? a delicate cycle?	• Does the dryer have an automatic sensor to prevent overdrying?
• Does the washer have a control to stop the machine and signal when the load is unbalanced?	• Does it offer a wrinkle-guard feature? an air-only, no-heat setting?
• Does the model have dispensers for bleach, fabric softener, and detergent?	• Does it have a touch-up cycle to remove creases in dry clothes?
• Does the washer have an optional second rinse selector?	
• Is the tub and lid made of porcelain enamel or stainless steel?	

Figure 12.22 Before buying a washer and dryer, consider these points.

Review & Assessment

1. Contrast the features of top-loading washers and front-loading clothes washers. Which tends to be more energy efficient?
2. Why should detergents labeled "he" only be used in front-loading washers?
3. Name three features available on clothes dryers.

Andrey_Popov/Shutterstock.com

Figure 12.23 Room air conditioners come in different sizes both to fit the window space and also to handle the cooling requirements of different rooms or areas.

Choosing Climate-Control Appliances

Appliances can help control the climate in your home. They can maintain humidity levels and temperatures that increase the comfort of the indoor environment.

Dehumidifiers and Humidifiers

The humidity level of the air in a home will determine the need for a dehumidifier or a humidifier. A **dehumidifier** is an appliance that removes moisture from the air. Excess humidity can cause discomfort as well as mildew, musty odors, rust, and other problems. If a home has an air conditioning unit, there may not be a need for a dehumidifier because the air conditioner removes moisture as well as heat. Many households place a dehumidifier in a basement area where more moisture may accumulate because of its location underground.

A **humidifier** performs the opposite function of a dehumidifier. It adds moisture to the air. Dry air is a problem in some climates, especially during winter months when homes are heated. Static electricity and splintering wood floors and furniture are signs the air is dry. In addition, some health problems can be associated with extremely dry air.

Dehumidifiers and humidifiers can be portable or part of the heating-cooling system. When purchasing a new unit, follow the recommendations of a manufacturer that offers a wide variety to locate a type and size for a particular home.

Room Air Conditioners

A room air conditioner is an appliance for cooling a room or small area when a whole-house cooling unit is not available. There are three types of room air conditioners: window units, built-in wall units, and portable units. Regardless of the type, the air conditioner should have the cooling capacity appropriate for the needs of the room or area. Window units must fit the window opening for installation (Figure 12.23). Built-in models fit an opening in an exterior wall. When it is not possible to use window units or built-in models, portable air conditioning units are the remaining option. These units are on castors and users can move them from room to room. They tend to be more costly than window or built-in models and may be less efficient.

When you shop for room air conditioners, you will need to know your cooling needs in detail. You can pick up a helpful form from a retailer that includes all the key questions to answer. For example, what direction does the room face? South and west exposures receive more sunlight and, therefore, require greater cooling capacity. What are the size and shape of the area requiring cooling? How many people normally use the space at the same time? How much glass and insulation are in the area? Greater glass area builds up heat while greater insulation will control heat/cool air exchange.

The answers to these and other questions help in calculating the cooling needs of a home. A retailer or heating/cooling specialist can help with this step. Cooling needs and the cooling capacity of room air conditioners are expressed in British thermal units (Btu). Once the Btu range is known, check the EnergyGuide labels of similar models to compare *energy-efficiency ratings (EERs)*. Models with higher EERs use less energy and, therefore, cost less to operate. In addition, look for the ENERGY STAR label, too.

Also check the controls. Are they easy to reach and use? Can the user change the level of cooling to meet his or her needs? Can the user program it to change cooling levels automatically? Check the louvers for air direction. If possible, turn on the unit to check the noise level. Most units include a filter that must be cleaned or replaced periodically.

Many homes today have whole-house air conditioners as part of their HVAC system. For more information, refer to Chapter 9.

Portable Space Heaters

A portable space heater is an appliance used for heating a room or small area. Numerous types of space heaters are available including those that rest on the floor and baseboard heating. There are also heaters that can be wall mounted and some heaters can rest on tables or other furniture.

A major energy source for space heaters is electricity, either in the form of electric space heaters, electric oil or water radiators, and electric baseboard heaters. Some space heaters also use kerosene or propane for fuel, but some cities do not permit this use. For example, the District of Columbia Fire Code strictly prohibits the use of kerosene heaters in any location of Washington, D.C. Before considering one of these fuel based heaters, be aware of all safety considerations related to indoor air quality and fire. Only buy units with safety seals and carefully read the manufacturer's use instructions and warnings.

Features in portable space heaters are numerous, with safety and operational controls of top importance. These features may include

- an automatic cut-off when the heater is off balance or tips over
- an automatic cut-off when overheating of the unit occurs
- thermostatic controls with variable temperature settings and a remote control to adjust settings
- an oscillating fan to distribute warmth throughout the space

Review & Assessment

1. Explain the difference between a dehumidifier and a humidifier.
2. What questions should a person have answers to when shopping for room air conditioners?
3. What are four safety and operational features of a portable space heater?

Choosing Other Appliances

Many other appliances, both essential and optional, are available for home use. Water heaters, vacuum cleaners, personal computers, and a variety of portable appliances are among those that people might consider buying.

Water Heaters

Many tasks in a home require hot water, including bathing, laundry, and a variety of cooking and cleaning tasks. Water heaters use either gas or electricity to heat water. The type of water heater you (or a client) choose will depend on the home heating system. For example, homes with gas heating will utilize a gas hot water heater. In contrast, homes with electric heating systems use electric hot water heaters.

When purchasing a water heater, considering size capacity is important. This will depend on the amount of hot water a household uses. The more people who live in a home, the higher the demand will be for hot water. Other appliances that require large amounts of hot water, namely a dishwasher and an automatic clothes washer, also influence water heater size.

Heating water adds to home energy costs. Therefore, it is wise to properly insulate the water heater, especially if the water heater is located in an unconditioned space such as a garage or crawl space. To do this, simply wrap an insulating jacket around the water heater to provide more insulation. Insulating hot water pipes to reduce heat loss is also important. Set the water heater thermostat at 120°F; however, if you have a dishwasher without a preheat feature, set the water heater thermostat at 140°F. Most new water heaters are preset at the factory to 120°F, and alterations to this temperature are not possible. In this case, make sure the dishwasher has a preheat feature. If possible, install the water heater near the kitchen and laundry areas. These steps will help save energy, too.

Additional types of water heating systems to consider include solar and tankless/instantaneous. Solar systems use panels that collect the sun's heat energy to heat the water for the home. Tankless/instantaneous water heaters heat water on demand by the user. These units can service an entire house or heat water at a single use area, such as the kitchen sink or a bathroom. This type of water heater is used extensively in other parts of the world.

Vacuum Cleaners

A vacuum cleaner is a useful appliance for removing loose dirt from rugs and carpets. Uses also include cleaning hard-surface floors, draperies, and upholstery. Attachments allow vacuum cleaners to perform other cleaning tasks, too.

Some vacuum cleaners use a High-Efficiency Particulate Arresting filter, or HEPA filter. A HEPA filter removes additional allergens from the air before recirculating the air into the room. The fact a vacuum includes a HEPA filter does not ensure healthy air quality or good cleaning performance. These vary with manufacturer and model.

A consumer's choice of a vacuum cleaner depends on what he or she wants it to do. There are many types available. These include canisters, uprights, minicanisters, stick, handheld, and wet/dry vacuums. Some people choose to own more than one type to meet their various needs. The vacuum can either use a disposable bag to collect soil or be of the bagless type where soil collects in a reservoir that can be emptied.

Canisters

Canister vacuums are easy to handle and do a good job of house cleaning (Figure 12.24). They are effective on bare floors, stairs, and upholstery. Canister cleaners can be straight suction models, or they may feature a power nozzle attachment that increases the carpet cleaning capability with rotating beaters and brushes.

Uprights

Upright cleaners are the choice of many people purchasing vacuum cleaners. Their primary usage is to clean carpets, but many are also designed to clean hard floors. Most are adjustable for all types of carpet pile. Some adjust automatically, while others are set manually. Uprights are available in self-propelled models. Nearly all uprights have attachments for other cleaning tasks, such as removing dust from furniture, draperies, or stairs. Stick-type designs are smaller in size for light-duty floor cleaning.

Central Vacuum Systems

A central vacuum is a built-in system with a heavy motor and dirt collection container that stay in one place, usually a garage or basement. The user carries a flexible, lightweight hose from room to room and inserts it into wall outlets in convenient locations. Newer models have hoses that are stored in the wall and pulled out when in use. The system can also have a power attachment and special cleaning attachments. The air is filtered to the outside of the home. Floor level outlets on these systems allow the user to sweep dirt over to the outlet, such as in a kitchen, and it is suctioned away.

A auremar/Shutterstock.com

B Kornfoto/Shutterstock.com

Figure 12.24 The lightweight vacuum cleaner can easily be carried throughout the home (A). A robotic vacuum cleaner cleans while you do other tasks (B).

Portable Appliances

Portable appliances allow the user to move them easily from one area to another. They include everything from toasters to electric blankets to hair dryers.

Rudy Umans/Shutterstock.com

Figure 12.25 Portable appliances are available for a wide range of food preparation and cooking tasks.

In today's society, many consider major appliances to be basic necessities. Living without a refrigerator or water heater, for instance, would require a big adjustment in lifestyle. The same is not true for portable appliances. These small appliances provide many conveniences, but are not necessary in many situations.

Portable appliances tend to be less costly than major appliances. However, the procedure for choosing them is much like choosing major appliances. The first step is determining the specific needs of household members and household resources. Then shop and compare. Choose portable appliances to meet the specific needs of household members.

Check construction details, warranties, and prices. Decide which of the latest features you want and can afford. Determine whether a small appliance is necessary and whether it performs multiple functions. For example, can a mini-food processor chop nuts and grind coffee as well as grate vegetables? Look for recognizable brands, and be sure appliances have a seal indicating they meet safety standards. Read use and care information to help you select appliances that are easy to operate, clean, and maintain. As with other equipment, consider and plan for where and how to store portable appliances. Following these guidelines will help you make wise appliance choices (Figure 12.25).

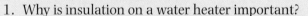

Review & Assessment

1. Why is insulation on a water heater important?
2. How does air filtering on a central vacuum system differ from that on most canister and upright vacuum cleaners?
3. What factors should a person consider before buying small appliances?

Choosing Electronics

Electronics differ from appliances in that they operate only on electricity or batteries. Appliances, as you recall, operate with gas or electricity. Electronics serve many purposes in the home and workplace including education, communications, and entertainment. The electronic devices having the greatest impact on interior design schemes include computers, televisions, and their accompanying components or peripheral devices. Some computers and digital devices require additional furniture or mounting components.

Televisions

With the arrival of all-digital television broadcasts, many people are replacing their older box-like TVs with sleeker flat panel sets, most of which are *high-definition TV (HDTV)* units. High-definition means the screen incorporates more pixels and therefore projects clearer images. The impact of this transition for interior design varies. Flat panel sets and the components that accompany them—cable and satellite TV boxes, gaming systems, and digital video recorders—require space. Some households choose to wall-mount their flat panel sets and use wall shelving for components. Others choose to set it on a freestanding furniture unit or shelf. Because HDTV sets and their components use much electricity, appropriate electrical wiring, cable connections, and electrical outlets are essential. Newer technologies incorporated into televisions include the "smart" technology that allows you to download media from the Internet, 3-D (three-dimensional picture) units, and the 4K Ultra HD, which has four times the pixel quality of a standard HD set and therefore a very sharp image (Figure 12.26).

Computers and Digital Devices

A versatile electronic device typical in most homes and commercial environments is the computer. Desktop and portable laptop computers can meet an array of user space needs. Computers serve a number of purposes including tutoring students, entertaining children, and organizing entrepreneurs. Other common uses include sending and receiving communications and playing games. Developing household budgets, online bill-paying, managing household records, controlling household systems, and activating appliances are other computer-related activities.

When purchasing computers and digital devices such as tablets for home or office, the first decision involves what the user wants it to do. *Software programs* and *applications* (or app—a type of self-contained software program) are instructions that tell computers and digital devices what to do. For example, the operating system software controls the basic functions of a computer or digital device. When the user opens another software program or application, it runs inside the operating system until the user closes the program.

Consumers can customize their computers and digital devices by purchasing additional software programs or applications. Software programs (or applications) can perform specific tasks to meet practically every need, whether creating a household budget or analyzing the nutritional value of meals. Review the software applications for the tasks you want to perform. Then find out what type of computer or digital device and how much memory capacity you need to operate these applications.

When buying computers and other digital devices, consider everyone who might use them and all the ways they might use these devices. Find out if the device memory capacity can expand to meet future needs. Ask whether telephone or online support service is available when questions arise. Investigating the purchase of computers and digital devices carefully will help you get the most use and value from these products.

Setting Up a Home Office

In addition to determining computer needs, also consider workspace setup and location. When setting up the home office, the purpose for the space will determine furnishings, equipment, and supportive wiring needs (Figure 12.27). In addition to a

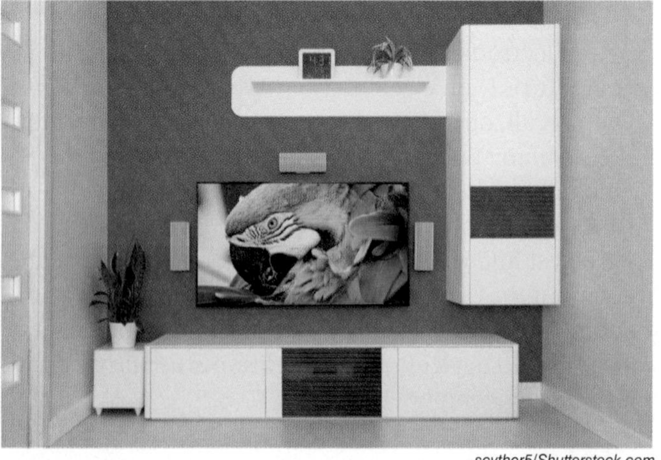

scyther5/Shutterstock.com

Piotr Adamowicz/Shutterstock.com

Figure 12.26 The space requirements for high-definition televisions vary depending on user needs and wants.

STEM Science & Technology Consumer Electronics Explosion

Between 1975 and 2008, the number of electronic devices in the average American home grew from 1.3 to 25—with numbers continuing to climb in recent years. Examples of these devices are televisions, computers, electronic readers, gaming systems, digital cameras, personal media players, and phones.

Consumers must subscribe or buy services to use some consumer electronic products. Services include cell phone and Internet access, cable television, and satellite radio. Telecommunication industries, which provide these services, transmit voice, data, and images. For example, when you make a phone call, send an e-mail, text, or tweet, you are using telecommunications services. Many of these companies also sell their own products.

Electronic products are merging with each other and with various home appliances. Manufacturers are incorporating Internet connectivity into many televisions and appliances sold today. In the near future, many devices and appliances can be repaired or updated through an Internet connection. Some appliances (and home-related technologies like lighting and security systems) can be controlled and monitored from your cellular phone. This process, or *convergence*, involves the merging of separate products into one. Other merged products include smartphones, personal digital assistants, and touch-screen devices that allow users to read books, visit websites, and download videos. New telecommunications technologies continue to change the way people communicate, work, learn, and have fun.

A GaudiLab/Shutterstock.com

B Stephen Coburn/Shutterstock.com

Figure 12.27 Telecommuters frequently use the computers and other digital devices to communicate coworkers (A). Placing a personal computer in a kitchen work area helps keep household records organized (B).

powerful computer, perhaps many of the following items are required: a telephone, digital tablet, Internet connection, shredder, fax machine, copier, scanner, and printer. Often, one piece of peripheral equipment combines the functions of faxing, copying, scanning, and printing. Such multipurpose office equipment reduces surface-space needs. Most importantly, give attention to purchasing adequate surge protection, appropriate electrical wiring, cable connections, and electrical outlets.

Review & Assessment

1. Identify one way the transition to high-definition TV units and their components impacts interior design.
2. Name two purposes that computers and digital devices serve.
3. What are two factors to consider when setting up a home office?

Chapter 12 Assessment

Summary

- Choosing household equipment, including major and portable appliances, is part of housing and design decisions for you or your client.
- Choosing appliances that meet specific needs for you or your clients results in satisfactory performance.
- Consider cost, features, size, safety, care, energy use, and quality when making appliance purchases.
- Kitchen appliances include refrigerators, freezers, ranges, convection and microwave ovens, dishwashers, trash compactors, and food waste disposers. These appliances are available in a range of styles and features.
- Careful consideration of styles and features helps in selecting appliances that best meet the needs of you or your client.
- Other appliances, including those used for laundry and climate control, must also be chosen with user needs in mind.
- Although they are a big investment, appliances can improve the convenience, efficiency, comfort, and safety of the user's household.
- Electronics perform a variety of functions in the home and workplace.
- Televisions, computers, and other digital devices can be a source of education, communication, and entertainment; however, they can impact the interior design of a space.

Terms in Action

1. **Writing definition** Read the text passages that contain each of the *Content* and *Academic Terms* at the beginning of the chapter. Then write the definitions of each term in your own words. Double-check your definitions by re-reading the text and using the text glossary.

Think Critically

2. **Analyze risks** Suppose you found a small appliance (such as a toaster) for sale at a flea market or yard sale. It looked rather new, but it had no information about the use and care or warranty information. Analyze the potential risks of buying the small appliance.
3. **Draw conclusions** Major appliances play a significant role in modern-day homes. For instance, most American homes have a clothes washer, range, and refrigerator. Use of these appliances is a part of everyday life. In contrast, many households tend to collect small appliances that are used infrequently. Draw conclusions about reasons for this fact.
4. **Analyze marketing** Analyze a TV infomercial for a household appliance or consumer electronics item. Summarize your observations by answering the following questions: What is the appliance or consumer electronics item and what does it do? According to the infomercial, why is it better than competing products on the market (if there are any)? How much does it cost? How persuasive is the infomercial? Give a report of your observations to the class. If possible, show a video clip of the infomercial.

Core Skills

5. **Technology and speaking** Review the website of a local store that sells major appliances. Compare the prices, energy costs, performance features, aesthetics, size, safety features, warranties, care, and quality of two brands of similar major appliances. Use the checklists given in this chapter to help you evaluate the two products. Share your findings with the class in an oral report.
6. **Reading and writing** Locate a use and care manual for a major appliance. Summarize the kinds of use and care information that it provides in a written report.
7. **Reading and speaking** Locate and read two magazine or newspaper articles on new types of appliances or new appliance features coming in the future. Research trends in safety, care, designs, and the latest technological advancements in appliances. Use a school-approved application to create a digital poster of your findings and upload it to the class website for peer review. As an alternative, read two

Chapter 12 Assessment

articles about consumer electronics and how they impact the interior design space in a home. Also, explain your findings about the safe use and care of appliances to the class (including current trends).

8. **Reading and speaking** Read two or more articles about tankless water heaters. Use reliable resources such as the websites for ENERGY STAR, the U.S. Department of Energy, the U.S. Environmental Protection Agency, or a magazine such as *Consumer Reports*. What are the key features of tankless water heaters? How do materials and installation labor costs compare to the savings in energy? Give an oral report of your findings to the class.
9. **Math practice** Suppose you are creating a design plan for a new kitchen for a client. Your client wants you to select two range models and two refrigerator models and compare the energy costs for each model for one year. Review the EnergyGuide labels for each range and refrigerator. Calculate the energy usage in kilowatt hours based on your local energy rates using the following formula:

   Wattage × (Hours Used Per Day) × (Days Used Per Year) ÷ 1000 = Daily kilowatt-hour (kWh) consumption

10. **Technology and speaking** Choose a kitchen or laundry appliance and investigate the technology trends used in the most current models. How does the appliance work? What are the pros and cons of the appliance? How do organizations such as ENERGY STAR and Consumer Reports rate the appliance? What conditions must the appliance meet to have an ENERGY STAR label? Put together your findings using presentation software and give your report to the class.
11. **Research and writing** Locate a website that provides helpful comparisons of appliance features—including aesthetic aspects—and prices for consumers. Review and analyze the information for two models of an appliance (large or small) or consumer electronics item of your choice. Use a school-approved web application to write a blog describing the appliance review. Share your blog on the class web page. Based on the information presented, which model would you buy? Explain your decision.
12. **CTE career readiness practice** Suppose you are a public relations specialist who works for an electronics manufacturer. To capture consumer attention, your supervisor has assigned you to write the advertising copy for their new 4K HD television and its technological advancements. After reviewing the company's product information, write the copy and submit it to your supervisor (your instructor) for review.

Design Practice

13. **Home office design** Presume you are designing a home office for a client's small business. The available space is 16 ft. by 20 ft. The painting and carpet installation are complete—both are warm neutral hues. A work surface and computer are essential. Your client also wants a small presentation area within the office space. The presentation area will require TV and component equipment. Use CADD software to design the floor plan showing the locations of the work and presentation areas. Then select photos of equipment and furnishings to best meet the client's needs. Write a summary of your recommendations to accompany the floor plan for your client.
14. **Portfolio** A family you know is trying to decide what new refrigerator to buy. The household currently has an 18-cubic-foot refrigerator-freezer that all members of this five-member household use. The family shops for groceries once per week, and refrigerated items usually fill all available space. They purchase few frozen foods. One of the family's three children uses a wheelchair. Everyone makes frequent trips to the refrigerator for ice and the pitcher of chilled water. Research the available options—including use, care, and current trends—and make a recommendation. Keep a copy of your research and recommendation in your portfolio.

Chapter 13

The Outdoor Living Environment

Content Terms

landscape
natural landscape elements
annuals
biennials
perennials
ground cover
hardscape
manufactured landscape elements
enclosure elements
landscape zones
conservation
water conservation
xeriscape
soil conservation
sunroom
landscape architect

Academic Terms

organic matter
staggering

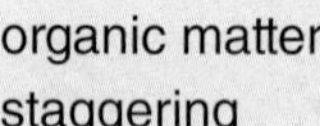

Learning Outcomes 

After studying this chapter, you will be able to

- summarize the goals of landscaping.
- identify natural and manufactured landscape elements.
- determine zones in a landscape site.
- select furnishings for outdoor living.
- summarize sustainable and conservation measures for landscaping.
- design an outdoor living space.

Reading with Purpose

Locate a magazine article on www.magportal.com that relates to the chapter topic. Read the article and write five questions that you have about the article. Next, read the textbook chapter. Based on your reading, try to answer the questions you had about the magazine article.

While studying, look for the access icon  **to:**

- **Practice** the *Content* and *Academic Terms* with e-flash cards, matching activities, and vocabulary games.
- **Reinforce** what you learn by completing the *Review & Assessment* questions and e-mailing them to your instructor.

www.g-wlearning.com/housing/

debr22pics/Shutterstock.com

The beauty of nature surrounds you. When making housing decisions, you should find ways to enhance and enjoy this beauty. People spend much of their time indoors—in schools, offices, and homes. The **landscape** is the outdoor living space. A beautifully landscaped area or even a small balcony in city housing can draw people outdoors. Everyone can find ways to enjoy the beauty of nature.

When preparing a site for construction, many disruptions occur in the natural surroundings. The construction process often changes the layout of the land.

If you leave the landscape alone after construction, it may never bring you pleasure. If you work in partnership with nature, however, you can have an outdoor living space that is psychologically rewarding. Note how the landscaping shown in Figure 13.1 enhances the appearance of the home. A pleasing outdoor living space should encourage the positive development of each member of your household.

Goals for Planning the Landscape

The basic goal of landscaping is to create outdoor spaces to complement various activities. The landscape should be private, comfortable, attractive, safe, and convenient. If you or your client are like most people, the area should be easy to maintain and designed with sustainable features. It is possible to achieve any or all of these qualities in a well-planned landscape.

You will have more successful results if you identify your landscaping goals. Some of your goals may include

- recreation and entertainment—including areas for playing and/or socializing
- privacy—attained by enclosures and screens that shield the space from the public
- comfort—which allows people to relax in an inviting space
- beauty—which highlights attractive areas and draws attention away from less interesting areas
- safety—achieved by installing landscaping elements correctly and providing adequate lighting
- creativity—evident in the ways that you use your landscape to express yourself
- ease of maintenance—which incorporates laborsaving ideas, such as raised planters, watering systems, and ground covers that require no mowing
- conservation and sustainability—incorporating a "green" element into the landscape through the use of drought-tolerant plants, less turf, and water-conserving recycling methods

Considering everyone's needs and values in the planning process allows for the creation of a satisfying environment for all household members. Take time to identify your goals before you start your plan. Before designing an outdoor living space, ask

A New Garden Landscaping & Nursery—Steve Windham

B New Garden Landscaping & Nursery—Steve Windham

Figure 13.1 After construction is complete, landscaping can make a site more attractive. Image A shows a swimming pool and landscaping under way. Image B shows the finished pool and landscaping.

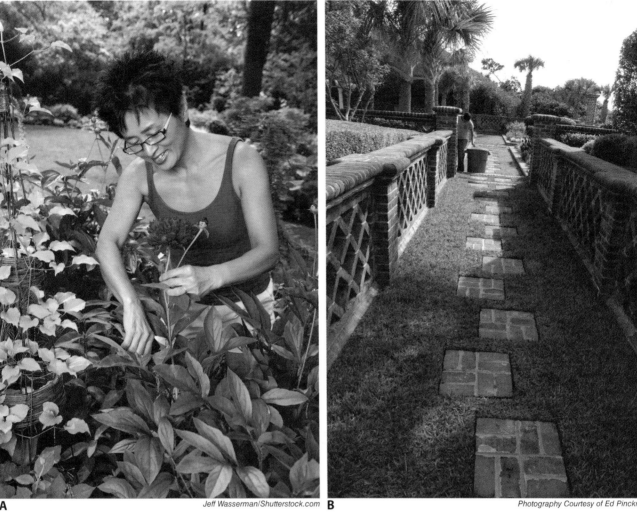

A Jeff Wasserman/Shutterstock.com B Photography Courtesy of Ed Pinckney

Figure 13.2 Some people prefer to maintain their own landscape (A). A consideration in this attractive brick walk is the cost in time or money for maintaining the edging around the bricks (B).

yourself or your client the following questions as you formulate your goals:

- What is the lifestyle of your household? Are there children and pets to consider?
- How much time, money, and effort are you willing to spend (Figure 13.2)?
- What is the cost of maintaining the plan?
- If you are concentrating on one area of the site, how will it affect other areas? Will the addition of a patio, deck, or swimming pool reduce the lawn area too much?
- Do you know what types of materials to consider for your plans?
- What activities are likely for the area?
- How much open space do you want to maintain?
- What measures can you take to save water and energy over the long term?

Review & Assessment 

1. What is the basic goal of landscaping?
2. Name at least five goals for landscaping.
3. List four questions to ask yourself or your client when planning the landscaping for a residence.

Landscape Elements

Before planning a landscape, become familiar with various landscape elements. There are two basic types of landscape elements: natural elements and manufactured elements.

Natural Landscape Elements

Natural landscape elements are those found in the natural environment. The terrain and soil are natural elements that are already on the site. Other natural elements include trees, shrubs, flowers, ground covers, boulders, stones, wood, bark, water, sun, and wind. Change is not possible for some elements, such as a natural stream. Alterations to other elements can happen to a certain degree. For instance, you can add or remove trees, shrubs, and large rocks from the landscape.

An important consideration in the selection of plants is to choose plants, trees, shrubs, flowers, and ground covers that are appropriate for the particular zone. A plant hardiness zone map appears in Figure 13.3.

Topography

The topography, or contour of the land, is basic to the landscape. Level land is the easiest and the least expensive to landscape. The ideal topography is a gentle, rolling terrain with natural drainage.

Soil

Good soil encourages plant growth and provides plants with the right nutrients. It has a proper balance of sand, silt, and clay. The soil must drain well, yet hold enough water to sustain plant life.

Trees and Shrubs

Trees and shrubs range in size from small to large. Trees can provide shade as well as shelter from wind. Evergreen trees and shrubs remain green all year. Deciduous trees and shrubs, on the other hand, lose foliage in the fall and sprout new leaves in spring. Trees and shrubs can also provide privacy (Figure 13.4).

Flowers

Flowers add fragrance and color to the landscape. There are three types of flowers: annuals, biennials, and perennials. **Annuals** and **biennials** last one and two years respectively. Most of these flowers require yearly planting. In

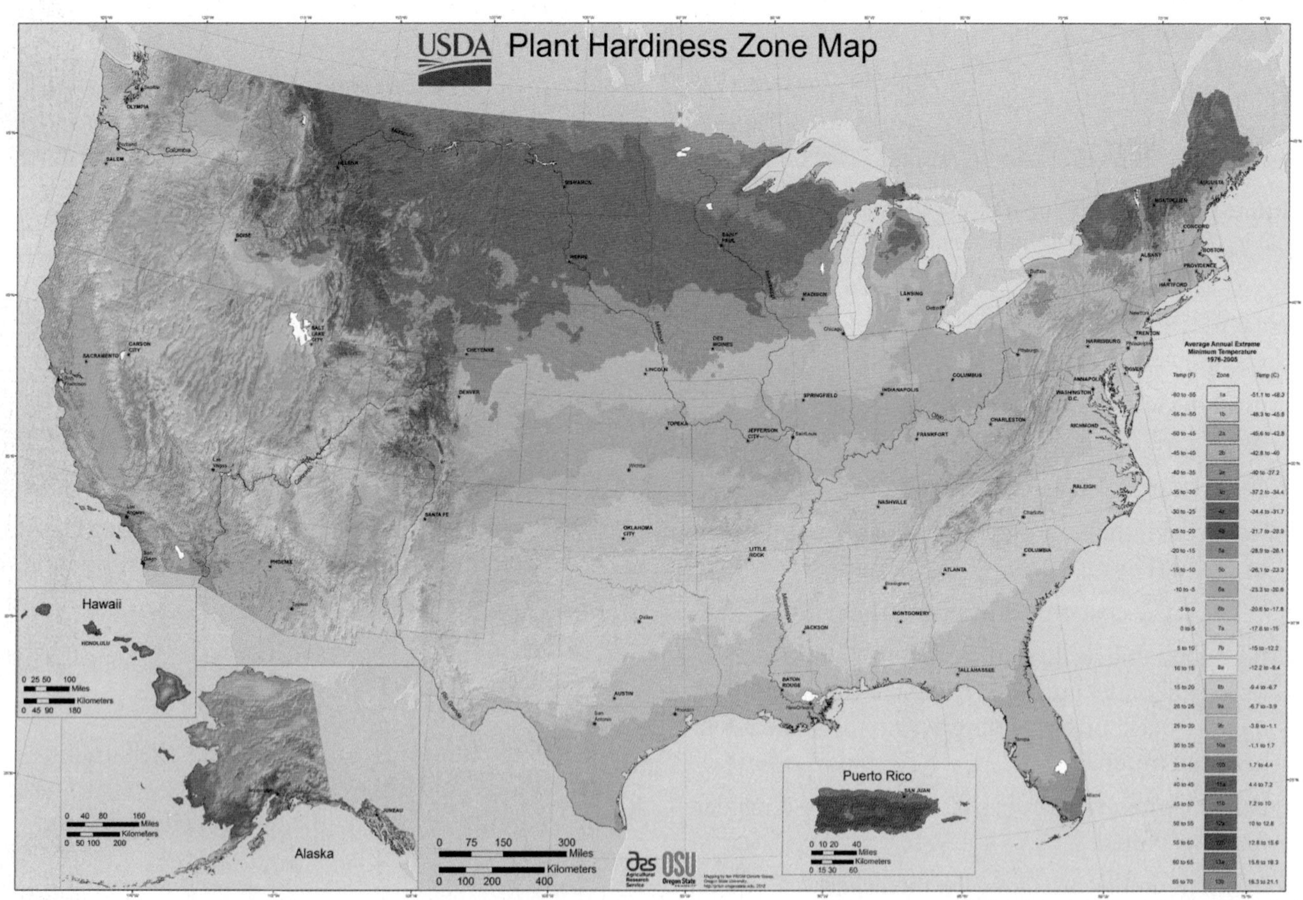

United States Department of Agriculture (USDA)

Figure 13.3 This *Plant Hardiness Zone Map* provides information on zones, which is important in making sure that landscaping plants will thrive in a particular region of the United States.

Photography Courtesy of Ed Pinckney

Figure 13.4 The hedges behind the fence provide privacy. A major consideration is the eventual height of the hedge.

V. J. Matthew/Shutterstock.com

Figure 13.5 This professionally designed landscape combines evergreen and deciduous trees and shrubs with annual and perennial flowers.

contrast, **perennials** last for many years without replanting. Some perennials never need replanting (Figure 13.5). Many gardeners prefer perennials because they require less work than annuals or biennials.

Most flowers grow from seeds or bulbs. If you desire, however, you can plant seedlings. *Seedlings* are young plants started from seeds. You can start the seedlings yourself or purchase them from a nursery. Many home owners start flowers from small starter plants or seedlings they get from a nursery. With the right choices, you can have flowers blooming throughout the growing season. In some geographical areas, it is possible to develop landscape plans that provide year-round color.

Ground Covers

A variety of ground covers are available for use in landscaping. **Ground covers** include grasses and various types of low-growing plants. *Grass* is the most common ground cover and many types are available for lawns. Some are more appropriate for use in warm climates, while others thrive in cool climates. The growth cycle of grasses varies with the climate. Some grow well in the shade. Others need full sun. Some grasses can stand heavy traffic, while others will tolerate very little.

Other ground covers include *low-growing plants* that are useful in places where grass is not desirable or maintainable. You can purchase ground covers in the form of vines, woody plants, or herb-like plants. Some are evergreen and others are deciduous, but all are perennials. Use ground covers when low maintenance is a need or requirement. Also, use ground covers in places that are difficult to maintain. Most ground covers are not suitable for high-traffic areas.

Boulders and Stones

Usage of boulders and stones—available in various sizes—is common in landscaping. Boulders with unusual forms, textures, or colors will add interest to any landscape. Such additions to the landscape plan are the hardscape of the plan. **Hardscape** is anything in the landscape other than vegetation and outdoor furniture.

Water, Sun, and Wind

Water, sun, and wind will always be a part of the outdoors. They are natural landscape elements. Water is a basic need of any plant life, but high water levels can cause swampy yards, wet basements, and poor plant growth. Orientation to the sun and wind affect the use of outdoor living areas. At times, you need protection from these elements and you want to take advantage of them.

Manufactured Landscape Elements

Manufactured landscape elements are those elements not found in the natural environment. They are, however, a common sight in most landscapes.

Photography Courtesy of Ed Pinckney

Figure 13.6 A variety of manufactured landscape elements are used in this setting. Notice the pergola at the right.

These elements include hard surfaces, such as walks, driveways, steps, and various structures such as walls, fences, patios, and decks. These items are also a type of hardscape (Figure 13.6). Numerous other items, such as lighting and outdoor furnishings, are landscape elements.

Hard Surfaces

When hard surfaces are a requirement, you can create them with *brick or concrete.* Concrete can form brick-like blocks, stepping-stones, and slabs (Figure 13.7). You can purchase these items ready to use, or you can make your own by placing the concrete into forms. *Asphalt paving* produces a hard surface and is relatively inexpensive to apply. In some cases, soil is compact enough to create a hard surface. *Flagstone,* shown in Figure 13.8, is a flat stone found in certain areas of the country. It can be set in concrete or placed on a bed of sand. Such surfaces are also part of the hardscape in the landscape plan.

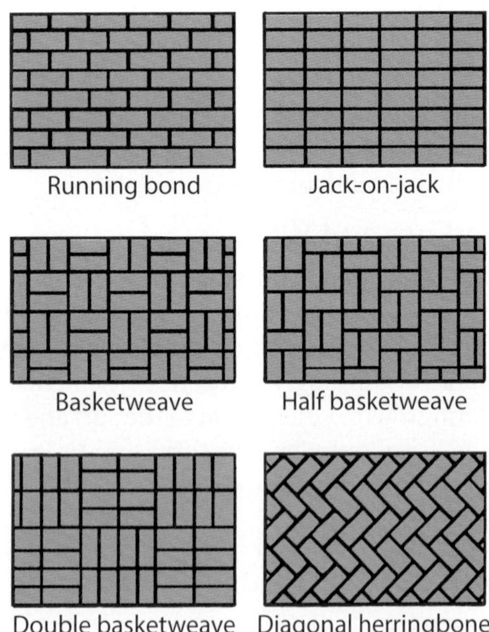

Goodheart-Willcox Publisher

Figure 13.7 Bricks can be placed to form a variety of designs.

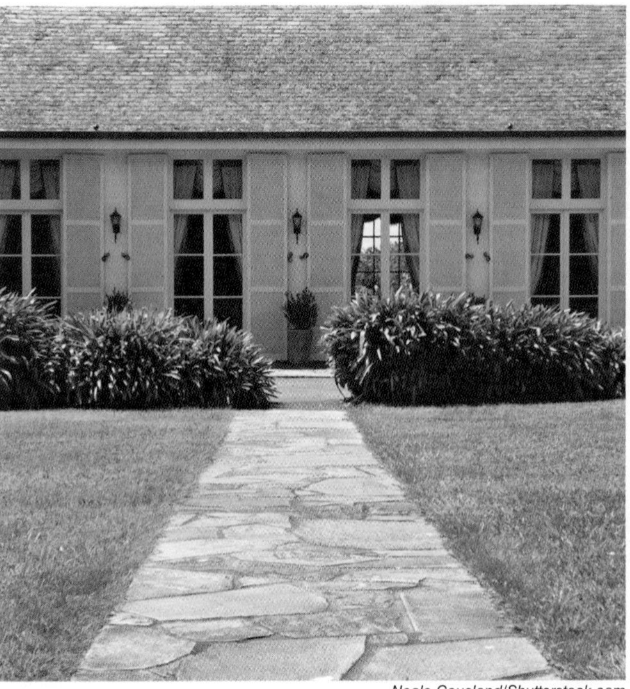

Neale Cousland/Shutterstock.com

Figure 13.8 This attractive walk is constructed of flagstone.

Enclosure Elements

Walls and fences are **enclosure elements**, or features that enclose a space. They are useful for keeping children or pets in a secure place. They can also keep out unwanted visitors. Enclosure elements consist of various materials—wood, brick, block, stone, concrete, plastic, metal, or a combination of these. A "green" approach to creating fencing and decking is to use a unique combination of wood and plastic fibers. To make such fence and deck products, manufacturers use wood materials "left over" from other manufacturing, such as wood pellets from furniture manufacture, and recyclable plastic grocery bags (Figure 13.9A).

Landscapers and home owners often use *freestanding walls* along property lines. These walls give privacy and serve as boundaries. *Retaining walls* have soil against one side (Figure 13.9B). They are useful for terracing and forming boundaries for yards and planting beds.

A *fence* is usually less expensive than a wall and is easy to construct. Fences are available in many styles and several heights. Figure 13.9C shows several styles. Most fences do not provide as much privacy as walls. Some local city, county, or municipalities place restrictions on fences, such as the height of a fence.

Unlike a row of hedges or trees, enclosure elements do not need time to grow. After construction or installation, both walls and fences are available for immediate use. There may be times, however, when hiding an unpleasant view or gaining full privacy is not possible with a fence due to height restrictions. In such instances, planting hedges and trees may provide a screen. Be sure to consider the

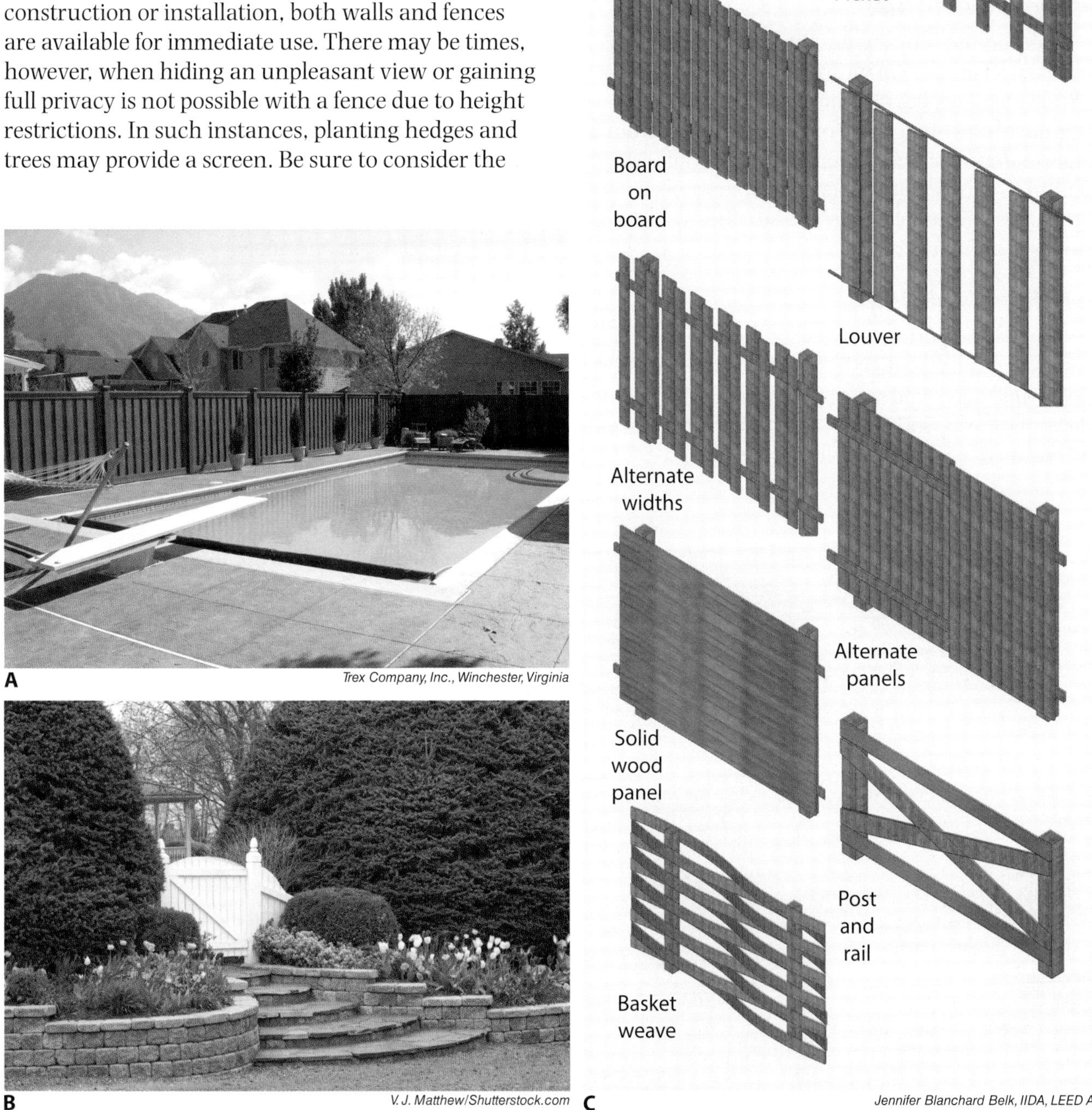

Figure 13.9 The fencing provides privacy around the pool. A special "green" bonus is that the manufacturer makes this fencing by combining recycled wood and plastic (A). Retaining walls are used to hold soil in place (B). Fences are available in a variety of designs. Nine popular styles are shown (C).

eventual height of such hedges and trees. What will they look like in five years?

There are many other types of structures used in landscaping. You may build them or buy them ready to put in place. Courtyards, patios, decks, and terraces can enhance and extend an outdoor living space. Other structures to consider include fountains, barbecue pits, gazebos, playhouses, and storage structures. A variety of containers with plants also adds beauty to a landscape.

Outdoor Furniture

Outdoor furniture is another manufactured landscape element. Furniture materials usually include metal, wood, fiberglass, plastic, or glass. Manufacturers often make outdoor furniture from a single material or a combination of materials. Many furniture styles are available to meet most needs. Sometimes enclosure elements and other structures also serve as furniture.

Artificial Lighting

Another important element of the landscape is artificial lighting. Outdoor lighting should be functional and provide safety and security (Figure 13.10). Lighting allows nighttime work or leisure activities. It can also add beauty to an outdoor setting.

Photography Courtesy of Palm Harbor Homes

Figure 13.10 The outdoor lighting plan of this home provides excellent safety and security.

Floodlights, spotlights, and underlighting can be useful in accenting a landscape site. *Automatic timers* are available for security lighting. These timers turn lighting on and off at predetermined times. *Photoelectric cells* turn lights on at dusk and off at dawn. *Motion detectors* activate lights when there is movement within a certain area. Some lights conserve energy. For example, many manufacturers produce low-voltage outdoor lighting kits that operate on 12 or 24 volts. Lights that use solar energy store it directly from the sun. Also, improved technology in LED bulbs and fixtures not only provide good lighting quality, but also use less electricity.

The location of a property predetermines some natural landscape elements. Household members can choose other natural elements, as well as all manufactured elements. Recognizing the elements available can help you design an outdoor living space that meets all needs and goals.

Review & Assessment

1. Name three examples of natural landscape elements.
2. How do perennials differ from annuals and biennials?
3. What are two types of ground cover? When and where should you use them?
4. List five examples of manufactured landscape elements.
5. What is the purpose of artificial lighting for the outdoor landscape?

Designing Outdoor Living Spaces

Designing a landscape is similar to designing the interior of a home. You can design the space yourself or you can hire a landscape architect. Designers and landscape architects think of landscape areas as outdoor rooms. As you may recall from Chapter 3, divisions (or zones) inside of a house relate to certain activities. The exterior grounds have three divisions, or **landscape zones**, as well, that relate to outdoor activities. Landscape zones include the

- *public zone*—a part of the site that can be seen from the street

Housing Health & Safety

Monitoring Outdoor Air Quality

The quality of the air you breathe depends on where you live and can vary from one day to the next or one hour to the next. The U.S. Environmental Protection Agency (EPA)—along with state, local, and tribal agencies—monitors and forecasts levels of air pollutants across the country. The Air Quality Index (AQI) alerts the public to dangerous levels of five air pollutants. These are

- *particulate matter*—dirt, dust, ash, soot, pollen, mold spores, chemicals, and acids suspended in the air; comes from vehicle exhaust, power plants, wood burning, wildfires, and other sources
- *carbon monoxide*—a colorless and odorless gas; a by-product of fuel burning, especially vehicle exhaust
- *sulfur dioxide*—a gas released when sulfur-containing coal and oil are burned; mostly produced at power plants and other industrial sites
- *nitrogen oxide*—a gas created by burning such fuels as coal, oil, or natural gas; higher concentrations occur near busy roadways
- *ground-level ozone*—a gas formed by chemical reactions of pollutants, including nitrogen oxide, in sunlight

These pollutants, especially ground-level ozone and particulate matter, are most harmful to human health. They can cause and aggravate health problems, especially in children, older adults, and people with asthma and other chronic illnesses.

The AQI is often cited in news and weather reports. You can also check the current and forecasted AQI in your area by going to the Air Now government website. The higher the index—which runs from 0 to 500—the more unhealthy the air. The index is divided into five color-coded levels for easier reading.

- *private zone*—a part of the site for recreation and relaxation that is generally separated from the public zone
- *service zone*—the part of the site that includes sidewalks, driveways, and storage areas for tools, trash cans, lawn equipment, and other items

Only the home owner and designer can decide how much landscaping is desirable for each zone. The landscape plan should include backgrounds and accents. Be sure to allow for activities and traffic. Innovation is important to the use of landscape elements when planning the zones of an outdoor living space (Figure 13.11).

Review the elements and principles of design and incorporate them into the zones or areas of a landscape. In addition, some home owner associations in housing communities have special landscaping requirements. Recall the ways to use color effectively. You can apply what you have learned to the form, line, color, and texture of the landscape elements you choose. The landscaped space should have unity and balance. Landscape elements should be in proportion to one another and to the structures they surround.

Image provided courtesy of JELD-WEN Windows & Doors

Figure 13.11 This family's love of private outdoor meals and relaxation influenced their desire for a beautiful, yet functional, deck.

Landscape Backgrounds

The backgrounds for landscaping include the soil and topography, the hard surfaces, and the ground covers. They provide an important foundation to any landscape plan.

STEM Math Calculating Volume for Landscape Design

Volume is the amount of space occupied by a three-dimensional object. It is measured in cubic units, such as cubic feet (cu. ft.) and cubic yards (cu. yd.). A cu. ft. is a space that is 1 ft. wide by 1 ft. long by 1 ft. deep. A cu. yd. is 3 ft. wide by 3 ft. long by 3 ft. deep, or 27 cu. ft.

The volume of a three-dimensional square or rectangle is calculated by multiplying length times width times height (depth). Other mathematical formulas calculate the volumes of pyramids, cones, spheres, and cylinders.

Landscape architects and other design professionals use volume calculations in their work. For example, suppose a 15 ft. by 20 ft. brick patio is being installed in a grassy yard. The grass and dirt covering the patio site must be dug up and removed. The brick pavers and sand will rest on 6 in. (or .5 ft.) of gravel. A volume calculation gives the amount of gravel needed to install the pavers.

Volume = 15 ft. × 20 ft. × .5 ft. = 150 cu. ft.

Gravel is ordered in cubic yards.

Cu. yd. = cu. ft. ÷ 27
150 cu. ft. ÷ 27 cu. ft. = 5.6 cu. yd. of gravel

Math Practice

Suppose your client wants to include a backyard playground for the family day care she provides out of her home. Because there will be climbing equipment, your client wants a well-cushioned play surface. The playground area will be 16 feet by 24 feet. You suggest a rubber-based cushion material. The manufacturer recommends 2 inches of the rubber material over 4 inches of gravel. What is the total volume of the playground site?

You may not have good soil on the site. If not, with knowledge and effort, you can improve it. The use of compost and mulch can improve soil. *Compost* forms from decomposing or rotting natural material. Working compost into the soil replenishes nutrients. *Mulch* is an organic material, such as straw, peat moss, bark, or leaves. Landscapers and gardeners use it to cover the soil, usually around plants, to prevent weed growth. Both compost and mulch are important to building soil. They increase the penetration of water and air, help the soil hold water, and control soil temperatures. If you plan to include grass or any other plants in your landscape, the condition of the soil is important.

Grass is one of the most appealing parts of the landscape. It creates a pleasing ground covering for the landscape site and can provide recreational areas for household members. It also prevents soil erosion and supplies oxygen to the air. After mowing the grass, use the clippings to produce ***organic matter*** (compost or mulch) to replenish the soil. Grass unifies or connects all parts of the landscape.

Use a variety of plants other than grass as ground cover in areas where there is no traffic. These plantings typically do not need as much care as grass (Figure 13.12). Local factors may limit choices since some plants will grow only in certain soil, temperature, and sunlight conditions.

Andrew Zarivny/Shutterstock.com

Figure 13.12 Native plants with colorful flowers or foliage can create a beautiful front yard requiring less care than grass.

Loose aggregate, such as sand, gravel, cinders, wood chips, and bark, is suitable for sections of the site that have poor soil or are difficult to water. Use loose aggregate when low maintenance is desirable or water is scarce. Sometimes it serves as mulch in planting areas.

Sections of the landscape's floor will have pavement or other coverings consisting of hard materials. For example, common surfaces include driveways and sidewalks. Hard surfaces on a lot

Denise Kappa/Shutterstock.com

Figure 13.13 A walk does not have to be placed in a straight line. This walk was designed to complement the landscape.

Zoltan Major/Shutterstock.com

Figure 13.14 A wrought iron gate can be attractive and functional.

should slope away from the house to provide proper water drainage. Standing or freezing water on a driveway and sidewalk is a hazard.

Walks are one of the easiest landscape elements to construct. They can consist of any durable material and often serve as borders. Walks divide the landscape site into separate areas and act as pathways to these areas (Figure 13.13). You should choose an attractive pattern for the walk. If the ground level varies, include steps in the route. Most walks are long-lasting. However, changes are sometimes necessary when plant life matures and becomes larger. If you anticipate changing the route at some point in the future, use stepping-stones to form a walkway. They are easier to move than most other materials used for walk construction.

Trees, shrubs, walls, and fences create the boundaries of the landscape. Walls can act as a screen, giving visual privacy (Figure 13.14). They also curb noise and serve as windbreaks. You must decide which areas to enclose with walls. If there is a good view in one direction, consider taking advantage of it by leaving the area open.

Consider planting suitable shrubs or evergreens close together to form a wall. For a dense grouping, combine trees with shrubs. For example, plant short shrubs among the tall trees. Also consider planting two rows of trees, ***staggering*** (arranging in various zigzags or alternations) the plantings to make a continuous barrier.

The original function of property walls was to keep enemies away. Today, they serve different functions. Walls may separate one property from another, provide privacy, and block wind. Many walls are decorative, using wood, stone, or concrete.

Fences often serve the same purposes as walls. Some are solid, while others have openings. Fences that allow others to see into a private space often have coverings of vines for more privacy.

Gates are part of the landscape's wall. They can add an interesting touch to the enclosure. Gates must blend with the walls of the landscape.

Trees not only create shade, but also create interesting shadows and patterns as the sun shines through. The spreading branches of some trees give a canopy effect. For this reason, some landscape architects put trees in specific locations for the shade they produce. Outdoor structures, such as *pergolas*, can also add partial shade (Figure 13.15). Overhead structures can also provide necessary shade. Such materials as canvas, bamboo, fiberglass, louvers, or lath can form ceilings or overhead structures.

Accents

Landscape accents form the finishing touches. They include colorful flowers, the interesting boulders, and the other special features. Some accents become background elements for smaller accents. For example, a boulder may serve as a background for a cluster of flowering plants. Include a variety of accents in every landscape plan.

A Photography by Ed Pinckney

B abimages/Shutterstock.com

Figure 13.15 The trees along this walk create a pleasing design as the sun shines on and through the trees (A). A pergola as part of the landscape background provides partial shade (B).

Flowers are not a permanent landscape element. Because they die in dormant seasons, flowers generally serve as an accent. When in bloom, they are spectacular in their color and showiness. There are many forms, heights, and colors of flowers from which to choose (Figure 13.16).

Flower plantings should be simple. Too many types or colors in a single bed will produce a disorganized appearance. Some flowers need full sunlight. Others do well in the shade or partial sunlight. Find out which flowers will do best in your landscaping project.

Planting beds are good choices for flowers. These beds are the spaces that are set aside for plants. Raised beds or planters are effective. They are ideal for older people or people who use wheelchairs. Home owners can move portable planters from one outside area to another, and then move them inside during the cold season.

Photography by Ed Pinckney

Figure 13.16 The potted red, yellow, white, and purple flowers create a splash of color as an accent on this terrace.

Choices of materials for planters include wood, plastic, glass, metal, concrete, and glazed ceramics. Look for planters that are durable and decorative. In areas with freezing temperatures, avoid planters containing glass, ceramic, and other materials that shatter when the moisture in soil freezes.

Landscape architects and home owners often choose boulders and stones as accent pieces. Informal placement of these items in the landscape creates a casual look (Figure 13.17). They have a more formal appearance when they serve as borders along paths and flowerbeds. Place boulders and stones to show off their interesting features. Rock gardens are popular in landscaping.

Sculptures, murals, and mosaics can enhance a landscape design. The selection of these accents is very personal. They express household member's tastes, and consider form, color, and texture. A landscape will have a cluttered appearance with the use of too many accents. Place most accents at eye level. Sculpture fits well against a background of foliage. You may, however, want to combine it with some type of structure.

Other Landscape Features

Throughout a landscape, you can use many different features. You can have fun planning them and may even enjoy building some of them.

Some home owners might want a *gazebo* in the landscape. A gazebo is a raised platform that has

Landysh/Shutterstock.com

Figure 13.17 The boulders in this flowerbed serve as both an accent and a background.

four, six, or eight open sides. Relaxing in a gazebo is a wonderful way to enjoy the landscape. A gazebo can also double as a playhouse. Some gazebos have a protective roof. Others have lattice or vine-covered roofs. Gazebos are easy to adapt to fit the home owner's desires. In addition, outdoor fireplaces and fire pits are popular.

Water features are other popular landscape items. Water features can be very enjoyable. The sound and sight of running water has a soothing effect (Figure 13.18). Having water fall from a high level produces pleasing sounds. Jets, bubbles, and sprays can also make soothing water sounds.

Water in motion has a special attraction. Installation of a small, inexpensive circulating pump in the water feature can move water. Be sure to recycle water that you use in a landscape element. Use it again in the landscape or to water plant life. An important consideration in adding water features is the additional maintenance requirements of water features.

Some people want to attract birds to their property. To do this, include a pool or pond in the landscape. The pool can be small or large. Small pools work best if they are near a group of plantings.

Hanging feeders and birdhouses will also attract birds to a yard. For those who enjoy watching birds, plan the landscape to attract them. The local cooperative extension service provides information about what plants in a given area attract birds. Be sure there are good places for nests in the landscape.

Gerald Hng/Shutterstock.com

Figure 13.18 A water feature can add a soothing effect to any landscape.

Furnishing Outdoor Living Spaces

Outdoor furnishings can extend the living space since they invite people outside. The furnishings can help make the landscape site enjoyable and functional for the entire household.

Outdoor furnishings generally include tables, chairs, accessories, and cooking equipment. Furnishings that are durable and weather resistant are best for outdoor use. They should have high-quality construction. Choose furnishings that resist the deterioration caused by temperature extremes, sunlight, wind, and water. Furnishings should also be soil resistant. Figure 13.19 describes materials commonly used in outdoor furniture and other outdoor accessories.

If you plan to move the outdoor furniture frequently, it should not be too heavy. When selecting furnishings, use what you have learned about organizing space and traffic patterns. The principles apply to outdoor living spaces as well as indoor spaces.

You may want to store the furniture during the off-season or use it in another location. Some furniture is appropriate for both indoor and outdoor

Materials for Outdoor Furniture		
Materials	**Types**	**Descriptions**
Metal	Aluminum	• Lightweight and rustproof • Sometimes has a finish to prevent corrosion
	Wrought iron	• Heavy and not very portable • Rusts without the proper finish
	Molded cast iron	• Heavier than wrought iron • Brittle • Rusts, cracks, and breaks easily
	Steel	• Strong and durable • Weather resistant
Wood and Woody Plants	Cedar, cypress, and redwood	• Needs a protective coating to prevent deterioration
	Rattan, wicker, and bamboo	• Cannot be finished to withstand continuous outdoor conditions • Works well for sunroom furnishings
Plastics	Urethane	• Durable • Requires minimal maintenance • Used for molded items
	Polyester and acrylic	• Used for furniture tops
Glass	Fiberglass	• Lightweight • Strong and durable • Weather resistant • Can be designed to fit contours
	Glass	• Common for tabletops • Must be high quality

Figure 13.19 Outdoor furniture is made from a variety of materials.

use. If you want furniture for dual-purpose use, keep this in mind when making your selection (Figure 13.20).

Carpeting is sometimes part of the outdoor furnishings. It is best if outdoor carpeting consists of 100 percent synthetic fiber. Olefin, acrylic, and nylon are suitable fibers for outdoor use. The best outdoor carpeting uses needle-punched or tufted construction. The needle-punch process produces felt-like carpeting. Tufting produces loops. The loops may or may not be cut. Glue or tape either type of carpeting securely to a hard surface. For more information on carpet construction, see Chapter 20.

Additional furnishings include decorative and functional accessories. Accessories add the finishing touches to the furnished area. Common examples of decorative accessories include wind chimes, sculpture, driftwood, and urns. Examples of functional accessories include pillows and cushions, cooking equipment, and waste containers.

Josh B. James

Figure 13.20 This attractive, lightweight furniture can be used for both exteriors and interiors.

Fabrics for outdoor pillows and cushions usually consist of woven or knitted synthetic fibers. The fillers for pillows and cushions must be weather-resistant. These materials can usually withstand moisture. Nevertheless, protect pillows and cushions from standing water.

Accessories often set the mood for the landscape area. There is no end to the choices you have when you select accessories. Coordinate the style and color of your outdoor furnishings and accessories. Consider accessory needs and determine where and how to use them. When you are selecting furnishings and accessories for outdoors, consider the comfort, convenience, durability, portability, storability, quality, design, and maintenance of these items.

Outdoor living spaces may not seem complete without the addition of cooking equipment (Figure 13.21). Portable or stationary units are available. Position a portable unit so it does not interfere with the landscape. Locate it in an area that provides protection from strong winds and hot sun. Users will not want the smoke from the unit to be a bother. Keep portable equipment in outdoor storage when not in use.

If you choose stationary cooking equipment, place it in a convenient spot. However, do not allow it to detract from its surroundings. A well-planned unit can add pleasure to the landscape. Fuels for cooking equipment include charcoal, natural gas, or propane. Cooking equipment that uses propane or natural gas is generally more convenient than equipment using charcoal as fuel.

Lighting the Outdoor Living Space

Lighting can create a type of magic in the landscape. It can extend the use of the outdoor living space and invite you outside at night. Lights also enhance the view from inside the house (Figure 13.22).

Appropriate lighting is important for each area of a property. Outside lighting should illuminate the sidewalks and driveways. It should provide a clear view to and from the house. At the same time, lighting should discourage intruders. Lighting at entryways can help home dwellers see who is approaching.

While spotlights are good for lighting specific features, floodlights are useful for large areas. You can highlight a garden sculpture or flowing water with a spotlight. Uplighting is especially appropriate for small areas. *Uplighting* is the practice of directing the light upward from the ground level into plants or other landscape features. Uplighting a large tree, for example, can create a spectacular focal point in a night landscape plan.

If possible, situate light fixtures to hide them from view. Place ground-level lights behind plants or structures. Install higher fixtures under eaves or on rooftops.

imging/Shutterstock.com

Figure 13.21 The addition of an outdoor kitchen enhances the usability of the exterior space.

Alexey Stiop/Shutterstock.com

Figure 13.22 Well-planned outdoor lighting can help extend the use of outdoor living spaces.

Review & Assessment

1. How is designing a landscape similar to designing the interior of a home?
2. Name the three landscape zones.
3. What is the purpose of using compost and mulch in the landscape?
4. Name three functions of the "walls" of a landscape design.
5. What are three accents used in landscaping?
6. Name three other types of landscape features home owners or residential clients might desire.
7. List five factors to consider when selecting outdoor furniture.
8. What is uplighting for landscaping?

Carolyn Turner Smith

Figure 13.23 The orange fencing material is used to prevent soil erosion during the construction of a new home.

Landscaping for Sustainability and Conservation

Sustainability in landscaping includes the principles of design to have minimal impact on the environment. This involves decisions to conserve soil, water, and energy. **Conservation** is the process of protecting or saving something. Efforts at conservation should begin when a house is under construction (Figure 13.23). Disturbances to the soil occur during construction. Planting ground covers at this time helps prevent erosion of the topsoil. In steep areas, building terraces can prevent erosion, too. Measures can be taken to help prevent the decline in trees during and after construction. An effort to protect trees and root zones can be achieved by fencing around a tree to the drip line with a fence and mulch. This would help keep bulldozers and other equipment from damaging the roots of the trees. Builders should be encouraged to employ these and other conservation measures.

Once construction is complete, permanent conservation efforts can begin. Even if you or a client have been in a home for some time, it is possible to make significant contributions to conservation. The lifestyle of a household is probably the most important factor in conservation. Environmentally conscious households want to conserve natural resources.

Home owners want their outdoor space to be comfortable and attractive. They can accomplish this and still conserve natural resources through landscaping.

Green Choices

GreenScaping: What Is It?

According to the U. S. Environmental Protection Agency (EPA), GreenScaping is a set of landscaping practices that can improve the health and appearance of your lawn and garden while protecting and preserving natural resources. The practices focus on the "4 Rs"—reduce, reuse, recycle, and rebuy.

By adopting simple landscape changes, it is possible to create a GreenScape—that over time—can save time and money while protecting the environment. Here are some simple steps for effective GreenScaping:

- Eliminate unnecessary water and chemical use.
- Use landscaping plants that require less care.
- Conserve water supplies by choosing plants native to your area and those that use less water.
- Use chemicals properly and only when necessary to keep waterways and drinking water clean.
- Reduce yard waste by recycling yard trimmings into free fertilizer, compost, and mulch.

Water and Soil Conservation

Awareness is the first step in conserving water. **Water conservation** includes reducing water use and eliminating water waste. If you live in a dry part of the country, you realize how important it is to conserve water. People throughout the United States are becoming more aware of the need to conserve water. In many places, water prices have increased substantially while available water supplies have decreased. This is forcing consumers to review their water use habits.

A concept that serves as a reminder with water conservation is "*Right Plant, Right Space*." This means selecting plants that match the area of the planting. For example, if the space is shady, select plantings that do well in shade. Likewise, choosing plants that require less water not only reduces water use but contributes to easy maintenance.

Planning a water-efficient landscape design is one answer. **Xeriscape** refers to a landscaping method that utilizes water-conserving techniques. Originally developed for arid or semiarid climates, xeriscaping is becoming more prevalent in other climates, too. Xeriscaping involves choosing and grouping plants native to an area according to the amount of water and sunlight they need. Watering deeply and less often encourages plants to develop deep roots. Using mulches and adding more trees and grass promotes water retention.

Plan to use the most water in areas that receive the most use. These areas often include the lawn, play areas, and gardens. Using runoff water from roofs and gutters can reduce water costs.

Patios and similar areas need water only for accent plants. Areas near the property boundary may require little or no watering. If you use native plants, you should have low water use. Native plants are better adapted to the climate and usually need less watering than other plants (Figure 13.24).

Watering, if needed, should supply plants with enough moisture to live. Too much water can lead to plant disease. Excess water also prevents plants from developing properly. It is better to water less often but deeply. Deep watering can help roots grow better and make plants more drought resistant.

The most effective watering method is trickle irrigation, or *drip irrigation*. This technique involves delivering water directly to the base of the plants, reducing evaporation and runoff. Some trickle irrigation systems use narrow tubing routed under the ground. Other systems deliver water to plants through a porous hose aboveground.

Mariusz S. Jurgielewicz/Shutterstock.com

Figure 13.24 The native plants in this landscape require very little water.

The most common watering method involves the use of sprinklers. Sprinklers spray plants with water droplets or a fine mist. You can move portable sprinklers to various positions in the landscape. Built-in sprinkler systems have several stationary sprinkler heads in various locations throughout the landscape. Because they require no moving, built-in systems are generally more convenient than portable sprinklers. A considerable amount of water is lost to evaporation when using sprinklers, particularly those that spray fine mists. If sprinklers are not controlled, water runoff can be excessive (Figure 13.25). Rain sensors are useful to prevent timed sprinklers from coming on unnecessarily. Existing water codes and certification are important considerations.

topseller/Shutterstock.com

Figure 13.25 The sprinklers in this built-in system are controlled to conserve water.

Irrigating at night saves water. However, with night watering, some plants are susceptible to certain diseases. Know the characteristics of your plants. Irrigating when the wind is calm will help reduce evaporation. A system controlled by a timer will also help save water. If possible, try to recycle water. You can use water from a pond to water grass or plants. Can you think of other ways to recycle water?

Soil conservation includes improving and maintaining the soil. Organic matter is the result of decaying plant or animal material. For example, leaves and manure are organic matter. Analyzing the soil is a very important part of soil conservation. Home owners can send soil samples away for testing or analyze them on-site. The results of these tests will determine what to do to improve the soil. Usually, soil improvement is a project most home owners can handle with advice from an expert. For large or complex projects, however, a garden center or yard maintenance service can handle the job.

Mixing organic matter with the native soil can improve the soil. The organic matter creates air space in the soil. It also retains moisture and requires less watering. Improved soil increases the chances for good plant growth.

Soil conservation also includes taking steps to avoid erosion. The topography of the yard must encourage a natural drain pattern so water drains away from the house slowly. This gives moving water enough time to penetrate the earth, instead of eroding it. Improper grading and leveling of the lot encourages water to form streams, carry dirt off the lot, and create gullies.

Give special care to installing perforated plastic pipes to the ends of the downspouts. Burying these pipes underground to direct the water away from the foundation of the house has several benefits. One benefit of channeling water underground is soil conservation since water will not run off the downspouts to cause erosion and gullies. Another benefit reduces the risk of basement flooding since underground piping directs the water away from the house's foundation.

The plants you select for planting and the plan you develop for their placement can further prevent erosion and conserve the soil. To accomplish this, select plants and trees with good root systems and give careful consideration to their placement in the landscape plan. When planning a landscape, it is important to consider both water and soil conservation. Rain gardens can take advantage of wet areas in yards by allowing excess water to drain into the rain garden and preventing erosion or rain runoff. Special plants are selected for rain gardens.

Energy Conservation

Home owner interest in conserving energy through landscaping continues to increase. The proper use of landscape elements helps modify the climate in and around a home. For example, good landscaping helps reduce heat gains in the summer and heat losses in the winter. In areas that require the use of air conditioning, effective landscaping can reduce cooling as much as 75 percent. Landscaping that provides plenty of summer shade helps reduce these costs. In regions that do not require the use of air conditioning, landscaping can help make the home interior more comfortable.

Properly placed vegetation and manufactured landscape elements can block prevailing winds. Windbreaks can save enough energy to lower heating bills by 10 to 15 percent.

Trees with high branches and many leaves provide summer cooling by blocking the sunlight. Tall trees provide less shade than those that are widespread. Since deciduous trees lose their leaves in the winter, they provide summer cooling and still allow you to benefit from the warmth of the winter sun. Deciduous trees are a good choice for placement on the south and east sides of buildings. Evergreen trees are good as windbreaks on the north and west sides of buildings because those sides get more sunlight all year long. The types of trees that do best vary from region to region.

Shrubs and vines provide good shade for the walls of a house. Most walls retain heat in the summer sun. Shrubs and vines act as insulation to reduce the heat reaching the walls. Evergreen shrubs and vines will also help prevent heat loss in the winter. If you plan enclosures to collect heat from the winter sun, use deciduous plantings.

Overhangs and roof extensions offer shade, too. Architects and designers can plan them to shut out summer sun and take in winter sun.

A **sunroom**, or garden room, is another structure that can use energy more efficiently. A sunroom structure uses energy from sunlight to heat a living space. Tile floors absorb energy from the sun, and in turn release heat into the room. The room may be part of a house or entirely separate.

To ensure a sunroom conserves energy, it must be in the correct position. For instance, it should face south, away from any shade cast by nearby trees or shrubs. In addition, use window treatments to regulate the amount of sunlight that enters the room during the day. They can act as insulation during the night to contain the heat (Figure 13.26).

Flashon Studio/Shutterstock.com

Figure 13.26 The tile floor of this sunroom absorbs energy from the sun during the day and releases the heat during the night.

Conserving natural resources for future generations is everyone's concern. You can do your part, too. Information is available to help you make decisions about conservation. Before deciding which measures to include in a landscape, learn all you can. Since the role of landscaping varies from region to region and season to season, gather information specific to your area.

Information about conservation measures is available from landscape dealers or the cooperative extension service in your county. Look for publications from the U.S. Department of Agriculture (USDA). Most large communities have at least one garden club. Members of these clubs can guide you to helpful conservation resources in your area. Libraries and the Internet are also excellent sources of information.

Review & Assessment

1. What conservation efforts should be taken when a house is under construction?
2. What is the benefit of the xeriscape landscaping method?
3. What is the most effective watering method for landscape plants?
4. Name two ways soil conservation benefits the landscape.
5. How does effective landscaping help conserve energy?

Completing a Scaled Plan

Awareness of what you have and how you want to use it is essential to developing a good outdoor plan. Be sure to consider the needs, interests, and desires of a household. In addition, consider the site's climate, topography, soil conditions, and orientation to the sun. What is attractive and what is unattractive about your outside environment? Determine the best natural resources on the site. Note the sunny and shady areas (Figure 13.27).

Image provided courtesy of JELD-WEN Windows & Doors

Figure 13.27 Thought was given to this well-designed landscape plan in that it provides enjoyment from the interior as well as the exterior.

After compiling all the necessary information, you are ready to develop a scaled plan, or *site plan*, for designing a landscaping. The northern edge of the site should be at the top of the plan. It is a good idea to begin a plan for the outdoor space with a map of the entire property. A landscaping plan should include the following information:

- property boundaries
- location of the residence, showing windows and doors
- location of other structures
- orientation to the sun and wind
- location of the driveway and sidewalks
- position of both underground and aboveground utilities
- location of existing plant life, rocks, and other natural features

Developing the Landscape Design

As with interior design plans, you can produce scaled plans of a landscape site either manually or with a CADD computer program. Whichever method you use, draw the plan to scale. To show the greatest detail, use this scale: *1/4 inch equals 1 foot*. When you need less

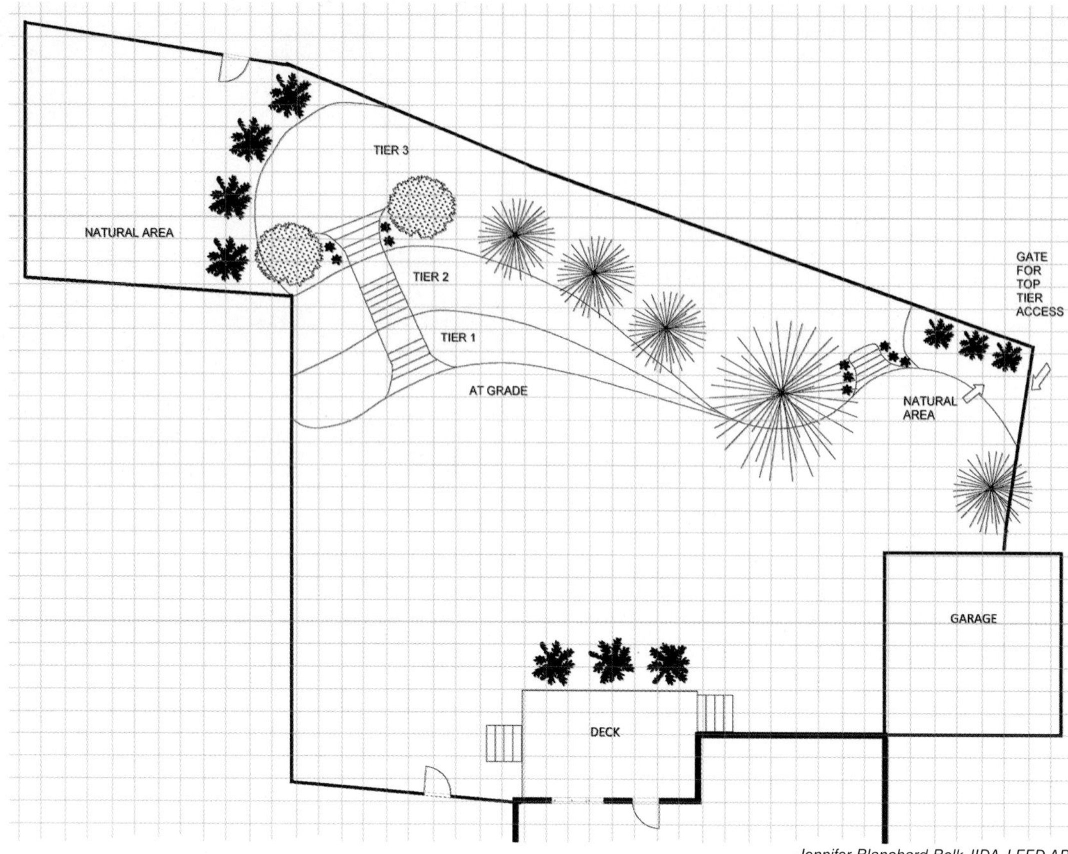

Jennifer Blanchard Belk, IIDA, LEED AP

Figure 13.28 Landscape plans can be drawn on graph paper.

detail, it may be possible to use one of the following scales: *1 inch equals 10 feet or 1 inch equals 20 feet.*

Drafting

Using graph paper, you can produce a drawing similar to Figure 13.28. You can also create several overlays to decide which plan you prefer. When drawing plans entirely by hand, the drafting process can be very time-consuming. Some landscape planning kits have ready-made symbols that designers can use to mark landscape elements.

Computer-Aided Drafting and Design (CADD)

With a computer and landscaping software, a designer can create scaled plans. A designer can draw the grounds area and all items on the premises with computer graphics. Besides designing the landscape plan, a computer-aided drafting and design (CADD) program can create a realistic view of how a completed design will look (Figure 13.29). Some software programs allow you to view designs for the yard and outdoor living area from a walk-through perspective.

It is possible to learn some landscaping software in several hours. More complicated versions, usually used by landscape architects, will take longer. However, spending the time to learn a CADD program usually results in more designs and more views to help you or a client better visualize possible results.

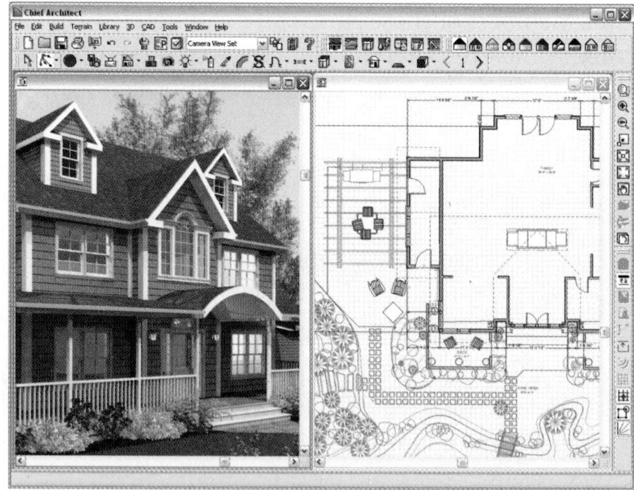

Courtesy of Chief Architect Software

Figure 13.29 A CADD computer program can be used to plan and visualize the landscaping around the home.

Regardless of which tool you use to create a design, feel free to experiment. Produce several designs

Career Focus Landscape Architect

Do you like to work with soil and plants? Do you enjoy beautiful outdoor spaces? If you do, perhaps a career as a landscape architect is for you.

Interests/Skills: Do you think about important environment questions and believe it is important to preserve and sustain the environment? Do you enjoy spending time outdoors and sketching drawings? Perhaps you appreciate attractive parks and plazas and would like to create similar places that provide a balance between people and the environment. People who like this job enjoy working with their hands and being creative and artistic. Landscape architects need good communication skills. They have to explain their ideas to other people and talk to groups. It also helps to have good computer skills along with effective writing skills.

Career Snapshot: Landscape architects make outdoor places more beautiful and useful. They decide where to put flowers, trees, walkways, and other landscape details. They keep sports fields from getting soggy, and work with architects, surveyors, and engineers to find the best place to put roads and buildings. They also work with environmental scientists to find the best way to conserve or restore natural resources.

Education/Training: Most professionals have a four- or five-year college degree in landscape architecture or a related subject. This career requires continuing education and training.

Scott E. Feuer/Shutterstock.com

Licensing/Examinations: Nearly all states (49) require landscape architects to be licensed or registered.

Professional Association: The American Society of Landscape Architects (ASLA)

Job Outlook: Jobs for landscape architects are expected to grow faster than the average (about 20 percent) for all occupations through the year 2018.

Sources: The Occupational Outlook Handbook (OOH); Occupational Information Network (O*NET); Bureau of Labor Statistics (BLS); and the American Society of Landscape Architects (ASLA)

and consider different placements for the features. Clearly mark spaces for specific uses. Complete the design by arranging the outdoor furnishings. Remember to allow for traffic and convenience when planning furnishing arrangements.

Once you have decided on a landscape plan, it is time to roll up your sleeves and go to work. You and other family members may enjoy working together to create your outdoor living environment. As an alternative, you may choose to hire a landscape firm to carry out your entire plan or just the difficult parts. Many nursery owners have training in landscape design. They are knowledgeable about plants and can help you with the planning.

Another alternative is to hire a landscape architect to design your plan. A **landscape architect** is professionally trained to create designs that function well and are aesthetically pleasing. Members of professional groups such as the *American Society of Landscape Architects (ASLA)* are the most qualified experts in this field. If you desire, you can hire specialists to care for your outdoor living area. Maintenance companies will establish a service contract with you to mow the lawn, keep flower beds free of weeds, and prune shrubbery. They can provide periodic fertilizer applications to your lawn and garden.

Review & Assessment

1. List five items to include on a landscaping plan.
2. What are two ways to draw a landscape plan?
3. What is a landscape architect?

Chapter 13 Assessment

Summary

- When planning the outdoor living area of a home, first identify household goals. These will depend on the lifestyle, needs, and desires of the household.
- Recognizing the types of landscaping elements and their uses will help you make plans.
- You must determine which natural elements are suitable for the landscaping site and then choose the manufactured elements that fit the situation.
- Planning a landscape is much like planning the rooms inside a house.
- Just as a house is divided into several areas, the landscape site is divided into three zones—private, public, and service. Each zone requires different treatment.
- When planning the landscape rooms, consider the floors, walls, ceilings, furnishings, and accents. Also, include lighting in the outdoor living area to make it usable at night.
- Knowing the topography and the soil condition of the site is important. This information helps individuals conserve soil, water, and energy.
- Detailed plans of the outdoor rooms and landscape zones are a requirement for a successful landscape design.
- For accuracy, draw landscaping plans to scale.
- You can use various resources to help make landscaping decisions and incorporate them into the site.

Terms in Action

1. **Visual communication** In teams, play *picture charades* to identify each of the *Content* and *Academic Terms* listed at the beginning of the chapter. Write the terms on separate slips of paper and put the slips into a basket. Choose a team member to be the *sketcher*. The sketcher pulls a term from the basket and creates quick drawings or graphics to represent the term until the team guesses the term. Rotate turns as sketcher until the team identifies all terms.

Think Critically

2. **Make recommendations** Assume your neighbor, a new design client, lives in a three-year-old home. The front of the home has a southern exposure. The home has a lawn and a few shrubs, but no mature landscaping. Your neighbor is concerned about how warm the rooms in the front of the home get, especially during the summer. Make some recommendations about how your neighbor might use landscaping to help keep the home cooler in the summer.
3. **Draw conclusions** The author states that conserving natural resources, such as water and energy, is important for both present and future generations. Draw conclusions about what could happen if individuals and communities did not use wise conservation practices. What would it be like to live permanently in a drought-stricken environment? How could this become a worldwide problem? Discuss your conclusions with the class.

Core Skills

4. **Research and writing** Use Internet or print resources to research newspaper and magazine articles for landscaping and gardening news. Write a report about landscaping ideas that are suitable for your area. Share your report on the class website or blog.
5. **Reading, writing, and speaking** Read through the seed catalogs at a local gardening store or online. Find five annuals and five perennials that grow well in your area. Note how they can be purchased (seeds, bulbs, plants). How might you use these plants in a landscape design? Then use a school-approved web application to create a digital poster of your findings to share with the class.
6. **Writing** Imagine that you are a reporter for a local newspaper, and there is a water shortage in the area. Your assignment is to write an article on effective water conservation practices. Use Internet and print resources for your research. Also, consider interviewing people

in the community who are using good water conservation practices. Write the news article determining techniques to use in housing to conserve water and other resources, and post it to the class or school website.

7. **CADD practice** Use a CADD program to complete the site plan of a house familiar to you. Draw a floor plan of the dwelling's ground level. Divide it into zones. Then design the outdoor living space. In a separate document, describe and evaluate the effects of each landscape element you selected on the house and larger environment.
8. **Research and writing** Search the Internet for two photos of houses that are nicely landscaped. Print a copy of each. Determine the types of manufactured material items used in the design and describe how they affect it. Do the items make the design more attractive, safer, more private, easier to maintain, and more conserving of resources? Write a brief report evaluating the effects of landscaping on housing and on the larger environment.
9. **Technology and speaking** Use a digital camera to take pictures of the different types of enclosures and fencing used at local schools, child care centers, libraries, and other public buildings. Incorporate your digital photos into presentation software and share your findings with the class. Discuss the likely goal of each type of enclosure and how well the goal for each was achieved. As an alternative, take photos of effective landscape backgrounds. Use a digital application to create a visual report to share with the class.
10. **CTE career readiness practice** Suppose you are directing a landscape beautification project in your community with a team of classmates. Do the following to carry out your plan.
    A. Identify areas of need in your community. (It could be your school grounds, a community park, a government building, an assisted living home, the local library, or another well-known building.) Meet with community members to brainstorm some projects and decide on a project.
    B. Set a goal. Determine what resources your team needs to carry out the project.
    C. Obtain the assistance of a local nursery to sponsor your project, or create fund-raising projects to meet your goal.
    D. Plan the area to be planted with a professional landscape designer serving as a volunteer. Use the principles of design discussed in this chapter along with conservation techniques.
    E. Carry out the plan. Have your classmates roll up their sleeves and help with the planting.
    F. Evaluate the results. How was your team able to meet its goal? Describe ways team members carried out the project to meet community needs.

Design Practice

11. **Outdoor design** Suppose friends asked you to help them develop a private outdoor space around their home. How would you advise them on the following items: where to locate the space, what plants to install to block views from neighbors, and how to make the area easy to maintain? What resources would you use and suggest they review? What special considerations would you make if they lived in an apartment? Then use CADD software to create your design plan to share with your friends.
12. **Portfolio** Your new client wants you to create a backyard landscape design for his long, narrow backyard. The yard measures 16 feet wide by 40 feet long. Your client wants to include an area for entertaining that includes cooking and seating areas along with a small play area for two young children. Use a CADD program to draw the layout of the backyard to scale (¼ in. equals 1 ft.). Select natural and manufactured landscape elements, furniture, cooking equipment, and appropriate play equipment for the children. Save a copy of your landscape design in your portfolio.

Unit 3

Fundamentals of Interior Design

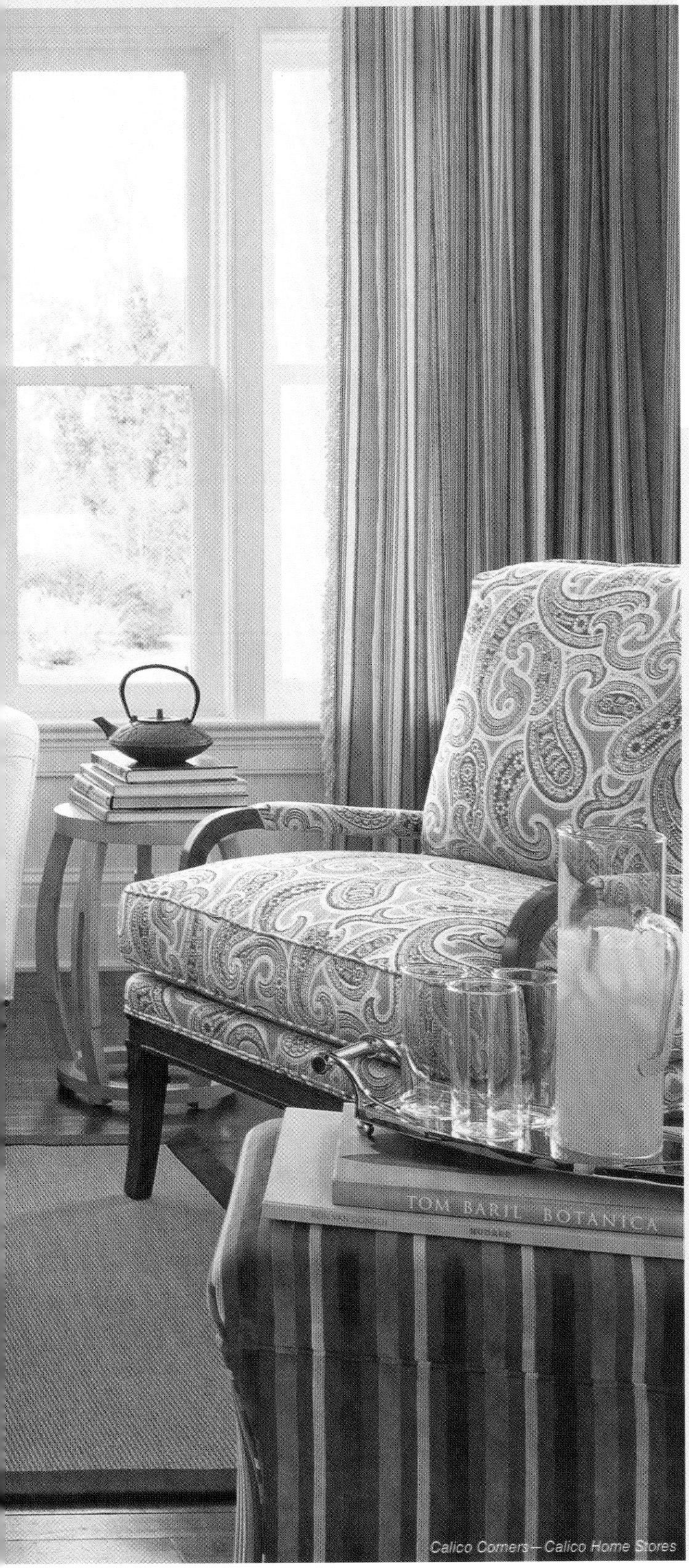

Leadership in the Workplace

To learn more about interior design careers—specifically the use of the elements of design—complete an FCCLA *Power of One* unit called *Working on Working.* Contact an interior designer in your community. Make arrangements to job-shadow him or her for a day. Focus on how the designer uses the elements of design in daily work. How does working knowledge of the elements of design help the designer lead clients effectively in planning interiors?

Use the FCCLA *Planning Process* and the *Working on Working* unit activities to plan, carry out, and evaluate your project. See your adviser for information as needed.

Using the Elements and Principles of Design

Prepare an FCCLA STAR Event *Illustrated Talk* on a topic related to using the elements and principles of design. For example, you might use the elements and principles of design to organize a presentation about a low-cost design for a child's bedroom, a teen's room, or a room for an older adult.

Use the *Illustrated Talk* guidelines found in the FCCLA *STAR Events Manual* on the FCCLA website. See your adviser for information as needed.

Calico Corners—Calico Home Stores

Chapter 14
Elements of Design

Content Terms 

visual imagery
design
function
construction
line
horizontal lines
vertical lines
diagonal lines
curved line
form
realistic form
abstract form
geometric form
free form
space
mass
high mass
low mass
texture
tactile texture
visual texture

Academic Terms 

verbal communication
nonverbal communication
aesthetics

Learning Outcomes 

After studying this chapter, you will be able to

- identify the meaning of design and the use of visual imagery.
- summarize the characteristics of good design.
- evaluate the use of the elements of design in residential and commercial interiors.
- analyze the psychological impact of the elements of design on people.
- analyze the effects the elements of design have on aesthetics and function.

Reading with Purpose

Before reading the chapter, make a list of five things you already know about the elements of design. Leaf through the pages of the chapter and note the heading topics. Predict five things you will learn about using the elements of design.

While studying, look for the access icon  **to:**

- **Practice** the *Content* and *Academic Terms* with e-flash cards, matching activities, and vocabulary games.
- **Reinforce** what you learn by completing the *Review & Assessment* questions and e-mailing them to your instructor.

www.g-wlearning.com/housing/

ShortPhotos/Shutterstock.com

Communication takes place in many ways. It can be verbal or nonverbal. ***Verbal communication*** forms include expressing yourself by talking, writing a letter, or singing a song. ***Nonverbal communication*** includes using sign language or body language such as a smile, a grimace, a shrug of the shoulders, or making a "high five" sign. In order for people to understand each other, they must understand the language. For example, the sender and the receiver must both know the sign for "high five" and its meaning.

Visual imagery is a type of nonverbal communication. It is the language of sight. When you see an item of clothing, a piece of furniture, or an unusual object, you see a visual image. This image communicates a feeling to you. Look at Figure 14.1 and Figure 14.2. Each room's visual image communicates a certain personality or mood and can have a psychological impact on the room's occupants. Design is the basis for this visual image. Understanding and creating good design requires knowing design characteristics and the *elements of design*.

The word *design* has many meanings. Interior designers refer to **design** as the entire process used to develop a specific project. The project might be an object, room, or building. Design also refers to the product or result of the process.

robinimages2013/Shutterstock.com

Figure 14.1 What message does this room communicate to you?

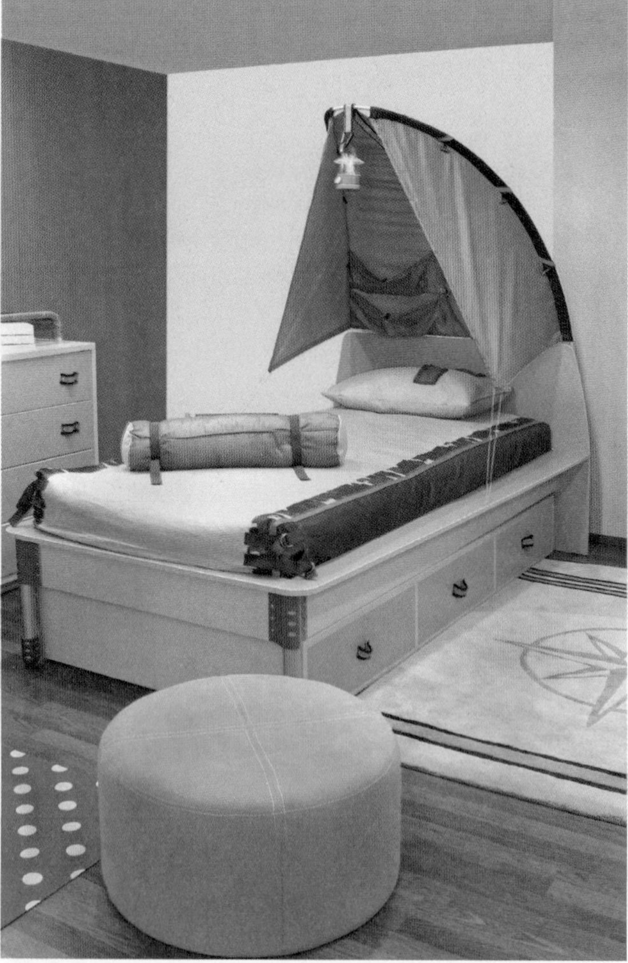

Ttatty/Shutterstock.com

Figure 14.2 How does the visual image of this room differ from that in Figure 14.1?

Design Characteristics

Design has three characteristics: *function*, *construction*, and *aesthetics*. Designers use all three guidelines in creating and evaluating any design.

The first characteristic is **function**, or how a design works. A design's function includes usefulness, convenience, and organization. Good design makes a product or room better or easier to use. It considers the needs of people using the item. Good functional design also accommodates the ages, sizes, and physical abilities of the users. Successful functional design provides easy access for all people and eliminates barriers.

The second characteristic of design is **construction**. Construction includes materials and structure. *Materials* are the different kinds of fabrics, woods, metals, plastics, or stones used to build a product or room. Choosing appropriate materials is necessary to support the room's function. When selecting materials, you should consider design function, quality, initial cost, maintenance, environmental implications, and such long-term costs as repair and replacement. Materials also need to meet industry standards, government codes, and regulations.

Structure refers to the assembly of materials. Products need to be safe, durable, and well made. The assembly method must also be appropriate for the intended use of the product or space. Like materials, structures must meet industry standards, government codes, and regulations.

The third characteristic of design is ***aesthetics***, or beauty, which is a pleasing appearance or effect. Because each person has his or her own personal taste, aesthetics, or what is beautiful, is difficult to define. Good aesthetic design, however, is pleasing to many people. It may stimulate an emotion or communicate a message, such as excitement or relaxation, humor or seriousness (Figure 14.3). Personalized design reflects the aesthetics a person wants to express in a room.

Designers must consider function, construction, and aesthetics to create a successful design. For example, a room that is aesthetically pleasing but does not function well and is poorly constructed is not good design.

Review & Assessment

1. How does visual imagery relate to room design?
2. What is the meaning of design?
3. Contrast the three characteristics of design: *function, construction,* and *aesthetics*. Why are all three important to good design?

Elements of Design

Successful designers use tools to create designs. These tools—or the elements of design—include *line, form, space, mass, texture,* and *color*. Because color involves such a detailed discussion, you will read about it later in the text. All the elements of design are necessary to describe, plan, and evaluate housing interiors.

Vitaly Titov & Maria Sidelnikova/Shutterstock.com

Figure 14.3 This room's pleasing casual appearance communicates a feeling of relaxation. What room features enhance this feeling?

Line

A **line** is the most basic element of design. It forms when two dots are connected. Lines connect the edges or outlines of objects and areas. They also show direction and cause the eyes to move from one point to another. For example, a line can cause you to look from objects on one end of a shelf to objects at the other end.

Types of Lines

The two major types of lines are *straight* and *curved* lines. The different types of lines create varying emotional responses.

There are three types of straight lines, including horizontal, vertical, or diagonal.

- **Horizontal lines.** Parallel to the ground, **horizontal lines** direct your eyes across a space (Figure 14.4A). These lines communicate feelings of peace, relaxation, calmness, and restfulness.

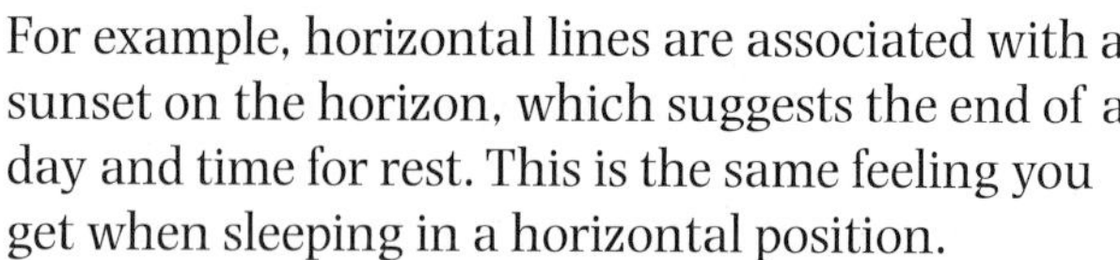

For example, horizontal lines are associated with a sunset on the horizon, which suggests the end of a day and time for rest. This is the same feeling you get when sleeping in a horizontal position.

Many home furnishings utilize horizontal lines. You can see them in fireplace mantels, bookcases, long sofas, shelving, fabrics, or wallcoverings that embellish a room.

- **Vertical lines.** Because they are perpendicular to the ground, **vertical lines** cause your eyes to move up and down. This movement suggests height, strength, dignity, formality, permanence, and stability. In Figure 14.4B, notice how the columns visually communicate height. This is because the vertical lines direct your eyes upward. Since the columns support the porch roof, these vertical lines communicate a feeling of strength. In addition, the columns stand straight and tall and communicate a feeling of dignity. Vertical lines that rest on the ground convey stability.

Vertical lines appear in many home furnishings. Look for vertical lines in window treatments, striped wallcoverings, and decorative trims that carry your eyes upward. Grandfather clocks, highboys, armoires, and tall mirrors have vertical lines.

- **Diagonal lines.** Lines that angle between horizontal and vertical lines are **diagonal lines**. They communicate different levels of activity, ranging from a low- to high-level of energy (Figure 14.4C). The level depends on the degree of the angle and total number of angles. For example, the symbol for a bolt of lightning has several sharp diagonal lines. This symbol communicates

A *Image provided courtesy of JELD-WEN Windows & Doors*

B 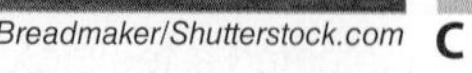 *Breadmaker/Shutterstock.com*

C *foamfoto/Shutterstock.com*

Figure 14.4 *Horizontal* lines (A) can make a room feel more relaxing and informal, while the *vertical* lines (B) in these columns give the front of this house the feeling of height, strength, dignity, and stability. The *diagonal* lines (C) created by this parquet floor create interest and movement and work to balance the vertical lines created by the display case.

STEM Math Estimating Perimeter

Perimeter is the distance around a building, room, or other closed space. You need the perimeter of a room if you are installing baseboards and ceiling moldings, or painting the walls.

To calculate perimeter of a quadrilateral or four-sided room, measure each side and add the measurements together. If a room is square, you can estimate its perimeter by measuring one side and multiplying that number by 4. If the room is rectangular in shape, estimate perimeter by adding one short and one long side together, and doubling the sum.

The perimeter of a circle is called the *circumference*. Given the diameter or radius of a circle, you can calculate the circumference. The *diameter* is the line that bisects the circle into two symmetrical parts. The *radius* is a straight line from the center point of a circle to its outer edge; radius is half the diameter.

Circumference = $d \times \pi$, where d is diameter

Circumference = $2 \times \pi \times r$, where r is radius

The symbol π, called *pi*, is approximately equal to 3.141592. It can be rounded to 3.14.

Example: What is the circumference of a circle with a diameter of 8 feet?

Circumference is $8 \times \pi$ or 8×3.14, which equals 25.12 feet

Math Practice

1. Practice measuring perimeter. Measure each side of the following four-sided rooms and add the measurements together to obtain the perimeter: a classroom, a room in your home, and a bathroom or restroom.
2. Locate several circular objects within your interior environments. Measure the diameter of each and then use the above formula to calculate the circumference.

action, excitement, and sometimes agitation. Use of diagonal furniture placement in floor plans not only brings movement, interest, and excitement, but can also enhance conversational areas.

In home furnishings, diagonal lines create a feeling of transition from one level to another. They appear in rooflines, cathedral ceilings, staircases, lampshades, and various fabrics and paintings.

Curved lines are the second major type of line. A **curved line** is part of a circle. If you completely extend and connect a perfectly curved line, it becomes a circle. You can also modify the curved line and extend it to form an oval. Curved lines can also take a free-form shape and range from slightly curvy to very curvy.

The different degrees of curves in lines communicate different ideas. Generally, curved lines seem softer than straight lines. A circle or oval reflects organization, eternity, and uniformity. Slightly curved, free-form lines have a natural, soothing, and flowing movement. They communicate softness, freedom, and openness (Figure 14.5).

Image provided courtesy of JELD-WEN Windows & Doors

Figure 14.5 The *curved* lines of the doorway and these accessories convey a calm, organized feeling. The curved lines in their decorative patterns are flowing and active.

Using Lines in Housing and Interior Decisions

Applying different types of lines to specific interior design situations can result in different effects. For example, a space can appear larger,

robinimages2013/Shutterstock.com

Figure 14.6 Combining horizontal, vertical, diagonal, and curved lines can be very pleasing to the eyes.

John Wollwerth/Shutterstock.com

Figure 14.7 The floral image on this ceramic tile kitchen wall is an example of realistic form.

smaller, calmer, or busier just by using different types of lines. Repeating straight lines or curved lines can create a strong, intense statement. To create a more subtle and diverse look, combine various types of lines.

Observe the use of various straight, diagonal, and curved lines in Figure 14.6. The vertical lines of the windows and wallcovering draw the eyes upward. The horizontal lines of the sofa appear to make the space seem wider. Diagonal lines in the hardwood flooring create a feeling of movement as you view the room and move within it. Finally, curved lines of the sofa table and accessories help soften the many straight lines in the room.

Form

Form is the physical shape of objects. It outlines the edges of a three-dimensional object and contains volume and mass. Form also has height, width, and depth. Form can have a great psychological impact on the feelings individuals have when they enter a room or area.

Types of Form

There are four different types of form: *realistic, abstract, geometric,* and *free* form. When a form looks very much like the real thing, it has **realistic form**. Realistic form communicates a lifelike, traditional, and familiar feeling (Figure 14.7). For example, a common chair has realistic form because of its specific form. It is easily recognizable as a chair.

- **Abstract form** rearranges or stylizes a recognizable object. The abstract item has traits that look like the real item, but altered. Abstract form communicates a contemporary, changing, creative, and artistic feeling.
- **Geometric form** uses squares, rectangles, circles, and other geometric figures to create form. It communicates organization, order, planning, and a tailored look. You can find geometric forms in home furnishings, such as square tables, round lampshades, and various shapes of pillows.
- **Free form** is random and flowing. You can find it in nature—in plants, stones, and wood. It does not have geometric design. Free form communicates a sense of freedom. Free form is untraditional, unfamiliar, and different from realistic form.

Using Form in Housing and Interior Design Decisions

There are three guidelines to follow to help use form wisely in housing design. They include

- Form follows function.
- Related forms are more agreeable and pleasing than unrelated forms.
- A gradual change in form smoothly directs the eyes.

With the first guideline, consider the function of an object first in developing the design concept. Then choose the form. For instance, chairs for a family room should have a form that lets people sit comfortably and relax. If chairs have seats that slant to one side or legs that are too tall, they will not be comfortable. The unusual form would not function well as a chair.

According to the second guideline, your eyes feel comfortable looking at similar forms. For instance, square forms dominate the room in Figure 14.8. The use of such forms throughout this room gives it a crisp, organized look.

The third guideline means seeing a smooth transition from one form to another to direct the eye also leads to comfort. An abrupt change in form or too many different forms together may be unpleasant and confusing. When forms change, your eyes work harder to follow the different shapes. Sometimes, however, a change in form can cause excitement.

OmiStudio/Shutterstock.com

Figure 14.8 The related square forms used in this bath create a pleasing look.

Space

Space refers to the area around a form, such as the area around a table. It also refers to the area inside a form, such as the area inside a room. When discussing space, consider these two closely related factors: the size of the space and its arrangement.

Size of the Space

Height, length, and width often define the size of interior space. The size affects who will use the space and how they will use it. For example, a bedroom that is 10 by 12 feet is probably too small for two teenagers who each need a bed, dresser, desk, and chair. In contrast, the same size bedroom is likely adequate for two small children who only need beds and one shared dresser.

The size of a space can also communicate positive or negative feelings. For example, a large space can communicate feelings of openness, grandeur, or freedom (Figure 14.9). A large space, in

yampi/Shutterstock.com

Figure 14.9 This cathedral ceiling creates an open and visually expanding space.

Sociocultural Connections Proxemics

If you are like most people, you maintain a bubble of personal space around yourself. When someone breaches that bubble—as when a stranger brushes against you—you are uncomfortable and may even back away. Researchers in the field of *proxemics* study this social-distancing behavior. Among other things, they measure the physical distances people maintain between themselves and others. A person's distance requirements vary by situation and by relationship. For example, close friends and family members are usually allowed to get closer than strangers. Strangers crowded into an elevator tolerate the situation because they know it is temporary. They maintain social distance by avoiding eye contact.

The father of proxemics, anthropologist Edward T. Hall, found that the size of each person's bubble of space depends on cultural background. For example, South Americans generally tolerate more physical closeness than North Americans. People in many South American countries are accustomed to people, even strangers, moving very close to them during a conversation. That same interaction would probably require more distance between two North Americans or two Japanese people.

Designers apply proxemics in their work. When interior designers create a conversation area in a living room, for example, they must consider how far apart to place the seating. If the arrangement of furniture forces people to sit too close, they will be uncomfortable. If furniture is placed too far apart, people will also feel uneasy. They may be unable to hear one another or miss important nonverbal cues such as facial expressions. As a result, the general rule is to place chairs within 10 to 12 feet of each other.

Dig Deeper

Use reliable Internet resources to investigate more details regarding proxemics or social-distances that impact design. Create a digital report of your findings. Locate digital photo examples of each type of distance and explain why it is important to consider in design.

contrast, such as a sports arena, may make a person feel small, lost, or overwhelmed.

Small spaces can offer a cozy, intimate, or comfortable feeling in a space. Adding more people and furnishings to a small room, however, might feel very crowded.

Arrangement of the Space

When using space in design, first evaluate the space and decide what design effects you want to achieve. By arranging the space differently, you can achieve various effects or feelings about a space. For instance, you can arrange space to make large spaces look smaller and small spaces look larger.

To open and expand spaces, you can enlarge a window area, use mirrors, or remove walls. To create the feeling of cozy quarters, designers can divide the space into separate areas. Using area rugs, grouping furniture, or even building a kitchen island can physically and visually divide space (Figure 14.10). Take great

bikeriderlondon/Shutterstock.com

Figure 14.10 These furnishings and their arrangement create a cozy setting in this open, expansive space.

Career Focus Interior Designer—Community Libraries

Can you imagine yourself as the interior designer of a community library? If you can, read more about this interesting career.

Interests/Skills: Do you have a strong desire to improve the quality of life in your community? Do you love books and learning? Have you ever wondered what could be done to reduce the noise volume in a library? Or perhaps, you noted the lighting is not adequate and have wondered how it could be improved. You may have thought the space could be rearranged so that the room functioned better for the staff and the public. Designers who work with library design must have knowledge of construction and design and know how libraries must function. In addition, their marketing skills for library design can bring all ages together and compete with the modern bookstore/coffee shops. Superior writing, speaking, and active listening skills are critical for interior designers to communicate ideas to other people. Strong math skills and computer skills are a necessity.

Career Snapshot: Library interior design requires detailed preparation before plans are drawn. Designers must consider the needs of the library patrons and the atmosphere library personnel want to convey to the visitors when planning the design. Bookstore features such as nice, comfortable chairs and coffee services entice visitors to stay longer. To compete effectively, modern libraries need to be equally enticing. Designers must work closely with librarians and architects to understand how to plan the space. The library needs to function for members of all ages and abilities. Special areas for small children, meeting rooms for public use by local clubs and groups, and efficient and comfortable staff work areas are important design considerations. Designers need to advise clients on such factors as space planning, use of furnishings and equipment, and color coordination. As in all areas of interior design, they must demonstrate and apply the principles of universal design and meet all local building and fire codes. Since funding for most libraries comes from local tax dollars, it is very important for designers to keep costs down without compromising quality or safety.

Tyler Olson/Shutterstock.com

Education/Training: Completion of a bachelor's or master's degree is preferred. Classes include business management, lighting, computer technology, color theory, textiles, and CADD. Additional courses in library science and psychology help make the designer more competitive in the job market.

Licensing/Examinations: Approximately one-half of the states require interior designers to be licensed. The National Council for Interior Design Qualification (NCIDQ) administers an examination that interior designers must pass in order to obtain a license and to be competitive in their careers.

Professional Associations: The American Society of Interior Designers (ASID); the International Interior Design Association (IIDA)

Job Outlook: Job growth is expected to be as fast as average through 2022. Outlook will be especially good for designers who specialize in unique areas such as ergonomic design, or green and sustainable design.

Sources: The Occupational Outlook Handbook (OOH); Occupational Information Network (O*NET)

care when planning space arrangements. Poor divisions of space can create an unorganized or confused feeling.

Mass

Mass is the amount of pattern or objects in a space. It also refers to how crowded or empty a space appears. A space can have high mass or low mass.

High Mass

High mass refers to a space that is visually crowded. Fabrics with a high-mass design have a lot of pattern or lines. A room with high mass has many items in it and may look congested. High-mass rooms may reflect a full, crowded, or cluttered feeling (Figure 14.11). High mass may communicate an impression of formality and weightiness.

Low Mass

Low mass refers to a space that is simple and sparse. It is the opposite of high mass. Low-mass designs use only the most essential furnishings. Low mass communicates clean and airy feelings. The traditional design style called *Minimalism* reflects low mass. Shaker furniture also reflects minimalism in design. The room in Figure 14.12 is an example.

Jacek_Kadaj/Shutterstock.com

Figure 14.11 The use of high mass evident in the patterned wallcovering, black accent wall, and heavy furniture gives this room a formal feeling.

Using Mass in Housing and Interior Design Decisions

Designers can use either high mass or low mass to create a strong design statement. Blending high and low mass can create variety in a room design. For example, placing a low-mass design above a high-mass design creates a very open feeling in the room. The two extremes often complement each other.

Texture

Texture refers to the way a surface feels or appears to feel. There are two kinds of texture: *tactile* and *visual* texture.

Tactile Texture

Tactile texture is the way a surface feels to the touch. You can see and feel tactile texture. For instance, think of yourself standing next to a stone wall. You can see the ridges and crevices in the stone with your eyes, and you can feel its coolness

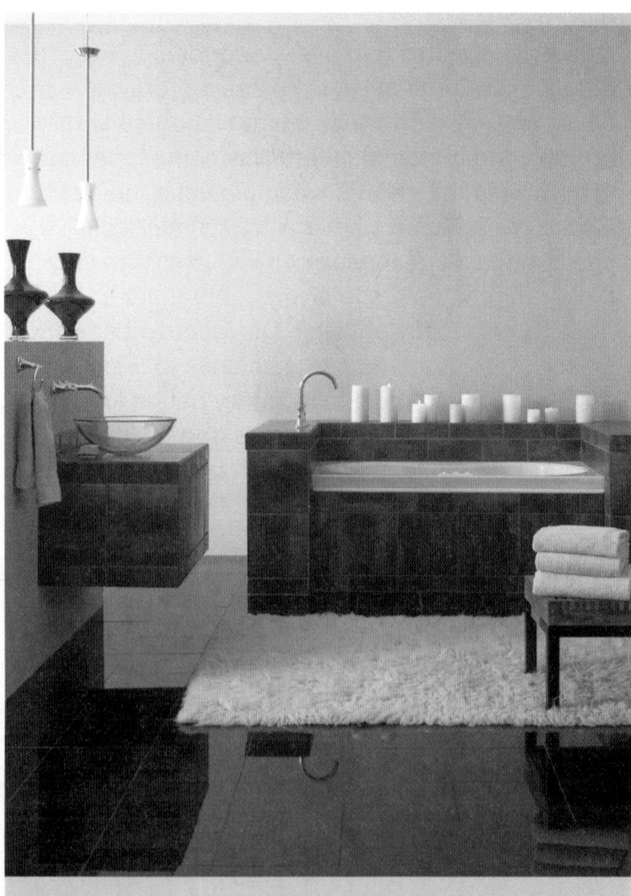

Copyright, The Sherwin-Williams Company, Cleveland, Ohio.

Figure 14.12 The plain lines and lack of ornamentation give this bathroom a sparse but airy feeling.

and roughness with your hand. A stone wall has tactile texture.

There are many tactile textures used in design. For instance, a surface might feel *bumpy, rough, soft, smooth, grainy, porous,* or *hard*. When selecting items for a residence, consider the way they feel. For example, some fabrics may be too rough and uncomfortable to use in upholstery. Tactile textures can also be functional, such as those used in slip-resistant flooring.

Visual Texture

Visual texture is texture that you see, but cannot feel. You can find it in scenic wallcoverings or pattern design in fabric. A plaid pattern in a fabric has visual texture although the tactile texture of the fabric could still be smooth to the touch. Visual texture is also evident in photography. In a photograph of a stone fireplace, for instance, you can visually see the texture without feeling its coolness and roughness, as you do with actual stone. Instead, you only feel the smoothness of the photo.

Using Texture in Housing and Interior Design Decisions

Use of specific textures can communicate different feelings in a room. For instance, rough surfaces, such as textured plaster or paint treatments, can create a more casual feeling. Smooth surfaces, such as glass, polished wood, or brass, may communicate an elegant feeling. Polished stone or marble can communicate both elegance and strength. Terms used to describe the roughness or smoothness of texture include *nubby, crinkled, quilted, ribbed, uneven,* and *even*. Terms that describe the hardness and softness of texture include *rigid, crisp, harsh, flexible,* and *limp*.

The use of textures can impact the visual size of a room. Heavy or rough textures absorb more light than smooth textures. They do not reflect light throughout the room, so the room looks smaller. In contrast, smooth surfaces make small rooms look larger. The light reflects off the smooth surface, creating the illusion of a larger space.

You can create *variety* by using both visual and tactile textures. When a designer uses more than one texture in a room, the room has a more interesting look (Figures 14.13 and 14.14). Too many kinds of textures in one room, however, may be a distraction.

Iriana Shiyan/Shutterstock.com

Figure 14.13 The wide range of textures used in this room creates both variety and interest.

Iriana Shiyan/Shutterstock.com

Figure 14.14 Visual and tactile textures create interest in a room. What texture do you find most pleasing in this photograph?

Review & Assessment 

1. Describe the different types of lines. What feeling does each communicate?
2. Identify the type of form described by each of the following: (A) lifelike, normal, and traditional; (B) random and flowing; (C) organized, ordered, planned, and tailored; (D) rearranged or stylized
3. List three guidelines for using form in design.
4. Why are related forms more agreeable than unrelated forms?
5. How can you use space to create a cozy feeling in a room?
6. Give an example of an object with high mass and one with low mass.
7. Contrast tactile and visual texture. Give an example of how you might use each in a room.

Chapter 14 Assessment

Summary

- Visual imagery is the language of sight that communicates different feelings.
- Foundational to understanding visual imagery is knowing the design characteristics and elements of design.
- Function, construction, and aesthetics are the three characteristics of design that provide guidelines for creating and evaluating design.
- The tools used to create good design are *color, line, form, space, mass,* and *texture.*
- Using different types of straight and curved lines can create different emotions and visual effects in a room.
- The four types of form and the three guidelines for using form inspire countless design ideas.
- When using space—the area inside and around a form—consider its size and arrangement.
- Designers use high mass or low mass to create a strong design statement.
- High mass and low mass can be used together in a room to create variety.
- Using textures in a space can communicate different feelings and influence the visual size of a space.

Terms in Action

1. **Term attributes** For each of the *Content* and *Academic Terms* at the beginning of the chapter, identify a word or group of words describing a quality of the term—an *attribute.* Pair up with a classmate and discuss your list of attributes. Then discuss your list of attributes with the whole class to increase understanding.

Think Critically

2. **Draw conclusions** The elements of design in a dwelling can have a psychological impact on its occupants. Apply the elements of design as you draw conclusions about how each element might psychologically impact the occupants of a residence. Cite text and other reliable examples to support your conclusions.
3. **Predict outcome** For each of the three characteristics of design—*function, construction,* and *aesthetics*—predict at least two possible outcomes of poor design. Use text and Internet resources to validate your predictions and share your findings with the class.
4. **Make generalizations** Select any room in your school and evaluate whether form follows function. Make a list of five generalizations about the items in the room that address the room's function. Make a separate list of five generalizations of items that address form. What recommendations would you make to improve both the form and function of the space? Discuss with the class.

Core Skills

5. **Compare and contrast design elements** Choose a room in your school, home, or a community building and evaluate how well each element of design is used and its impact on the users. Divide a sheet of paper into two columns. List the elements of design in the left column. In the right column, rate each element on a scale of 1 to 5: *1 = very poor* and *5 = very good.* Cite at least one reason to support your rating of each element. Total the score and discuss your evaluation with your classmates.
6. **Research and speaking** Use Internet resources to locate at least four pictures of rooms in a house, each illustrating several elements of design discussed in the chapter. Use a school-approved online poster application to create a digital poster using the pictures you located. Label the design elements observable in each image. Present your room pictures and the elements of design used in each to the class. Cite reasons why these photos clearly depict each element of design.
7. **Research and writing** Research how proxemics influence design in at least three different cultures. How do proxemics influence communication in each culture? How might

Chapter 14 Assessment

this knowledge influence how you would design a conversation space in a living area for each culture? Write a summary of each culture indicating how proxemics influences communication and design.

8. **Texture collage** Choose a word that describes a texture. Write the word in the middle of a large sheet of poster board or construction paper. Locate examples of this texture—such as pieces of fabric, wood, or stone as well as pictures representing the word—and mount your examples on the poster board. Share your texture collage with the class and explain why each artifact is an example of the texture. Identify ways each texture can be used in a room design.
9. **Writing** Think about an attractive and inviting room you have recently seen. How did the elements of design impact your feelings about the room? Write a short description comparing and contrasting how each element of design was used in the room using industry terminology. If possible, post your description to the class blog or website.
10. **Reading and writing** Locate an article about the elements of design in a popular magazine such as *This Old House, Architectural Digest, Dwell,* or *Country Living.* Read the article. Compare and contrast the use of interior design elements in the article. How do the design plans shown use industry terminology? Write a short article review identifying at least five additional concepts you learned about the elements of design. How do these concepts relate to what you already know about the elements? Be sure to note the name of the article, the writer, and date of publication, and magazine title on your summary page.
11. **Research and speaking** Search the Internet for the term *interior design* and find a site that provides useful ideas dealing with a room's size and space. What interior design techniques are recommended for changing the perception of a room's size and space? What design choices can make a room appear smaller? appear larger? How does mass influence the space? Create a digital presentation using the design examples you found to show the class, and identify the product or service offered by the website sponsor. Cite your source and credit the images.
12. **Speaking** Select a favorite photo in the text outside this chapter. Use a video camera or digital camera with a video-recording option to develop a short video presentation about your photo selection. In your video, apply your oral communication skills concisely to identify the photo you selected and summarize how the room's line, form, mass, space, and texture convey good interior design. Upload your video to the class website.
13. **CTE career readiness practice** The ability to read and interpret information is an important workplace skill. Presume you work for a large home improvement retailer in public relations. One of your assignments is the monthly newsletter for customers. This month your employer wants you to write an article related to good kitchen design and how the employer's products support good design. Locate three reliable sources on the latest information and read and interpret the information. Then write your newsletter article linking your findings to the company products.

Design Practice

14. **Community design** Suppose you are a professional architect who is hired by your community to design a new building for the city's art collection. The design must incorporate examples of as many different lines as possible. Try to include horizontal, vertical, diagonal, and curved, including circular, oval, curvy, and complex free-form. Either by hand or by using CADD software, apply the elements of design to interiors by drawing the interior and exterior of a building that meets these requirements.
15. **Portfolio** Create a digital storyboard with school-approved web-based application to show beautiful room interiors. Each image should clearly show all elements of design. Label the elements of design in each image. Share your digital storyboard with the class and save a copy for your portfolio.

Chapter 15

Color in Design

Content Terms 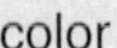

color
color spectrum
color wheel
primary colors
secondary colors
tertiary colors
hue
value
tint
shade
tone
intensity
complement
pigment
warm colors
cool colors
color harmony
monochromatic color harmony
complementary color harmony
split-complementary color harmony
double-complementary color harmony
analogous color harmony
triadic color harmony
neutral color harmonies
color scheme

Academic Terms 

advancing
receding

Learning Outcomes 

After studying this chapter, you will be able to

- analyze the psychological impact and meaning of different colors.
- summarize how color influences human behavior.
- analyze and describe the relationships between colors on the color wheel.
- evaluate the use of color harmonies in planning interior designs.

Reading with Purpose

On a separate sheet of paper, write the main headings from this chapter. Leave space for note-taking under each heading. As you read the chapter, write down three key points you learn from each section. Then answer the following: How does this information relate to what I already know about color?

While studying, look for the access icon  **to:**

- **Practice** the *Content* and *Academic Terms* with e-flash cards, matching activities, and vocabulary games.
- **Reinforce** what you learn by completing the *Review & Assessment* questions and e-mailing them to your instructor.

www.g-wlearning.com/housing/

daylightistanbul studio/Shutterstock.com

In the previous chapter, you learned about the elements of design—line, form, space, mass, and texture. In this chapter, you will learn about another element of design—color. Color is likely the most important element of design. Deciding what color to use is usually the first decision made when designing a room. It is one of the first things others notice about your design. Color sets the mood in a room and leaves a lasting impression with most people.

Understanding Color

Color is an element or property of light. It can help you create certain moods in your home by communicating excitement, calmness, mystery, or other sensations and emotions. When you understand the effects of color, you can use it to make your personal living space attractive and satisfying (Figure 15.1).

The Psychology of Color

Each color has certain psychological effects on people and can evoke certain feelings. Factors that can influence peoples' reactions to color include age, gender, culture, and life experiences. Although there is no single specific system for identifying ways all people respond to color, some of the effects for each of the following colors may include:

Photography Courtesy of Calico Corners—Calico Home Stores

Figure 15.1 The combination of colors used in this child's room creates a cheerful space.

- *Red* is associated with power, danger, fire, strength, and passion. It is bold, aggressive, exciting, and warm. It demands attention. Red can make you feel energetic. However, too much red in a room can be overpowering.
- *Orange* is hopeful, cheerful, warm, and less aggressive than red. It expresses courage and hospitality. It can make a room feel energetic and friendly.
- *Yellow* is friendly, happy, and warm. It is associated with sympathy, sunlight, prosperity, cowardice, and wisdom. Yellow rooms are cheerful, light, and airy. However, pure yellow draws attention due to its brightness, so take care when using it in large amounts.
- *Green* is the color of nature. Consequently, it is refreshing, friendly, cool, and peaceful. Additional meanings include hope, good luck, and envy. Green mixes well with other colors and looks especially good next to white.
- *Blue* is cool, quiet, and reserved. It is associated with tranquility, serenity, and formality. Blue can be soothing and peaceful. It can be especially pleasing when used with white. However, too much blue in a room can be depressing.
- *Violet* is a royal color. It is dignified and dramatic. It works well with most other colors.
- *Black* is sophisticated and mysterious. It is associated with wisdom, evil, and death. Small amounts of black help ground a room, or may add a timeless, classic elegance. When used in large quantities, however, black may be oppressive.
- *White* is fresh, peaceful, and pure. It is associated with youth, innocence, and faith. White can make rooms look crisper and livelier.

People feel most comfortable when colors in their surroundings reflect their personalities. For instance, outgoing people might choose bright red or yellow for the main color in a room. Shy people might feel awkward in a red room. Instead, they might prefer a room that features a soft blue or green.

When making color decisions for your home or the home of a client, consider the preferences of each family member. No single color will satisfy everyone. The color and design of the social area of the home, however, should make all members feel as comfortable as possible. Use individual color preferences in personalized sleeping areas and other private work or play spaces.

The Color Spectrum

The **color spectrum** is the full range of all existing colors. A beam of white light produces *spectral colors* as it passes through a prism. Although limitless in number, more than 10 million colors have been identified in the color spectrum. Each distinct color derives from a few basic colors. The rainbow in Figure 15.2 is the ideal example in nature of how sunlight can separate into a continuous band of colors, or a *spectrum*. In the case of a rainbow, the raindrops themselves serve as tiny prisms separating the light.

The variety of colors possible in nature is virtually limitless. Paint manufacturers have translated the spectrum into several hundreds of different paint colors (Figure 15.3).

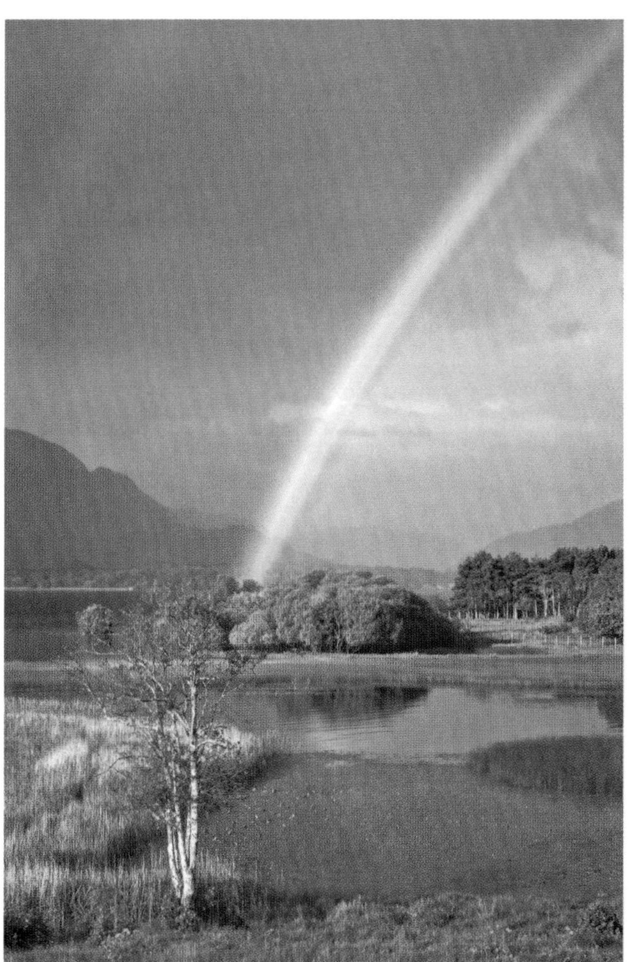

Jane McIlroy/Shutterstock.com

Figure 15.2 The water droplets in a rainbow separate light into its many colors.

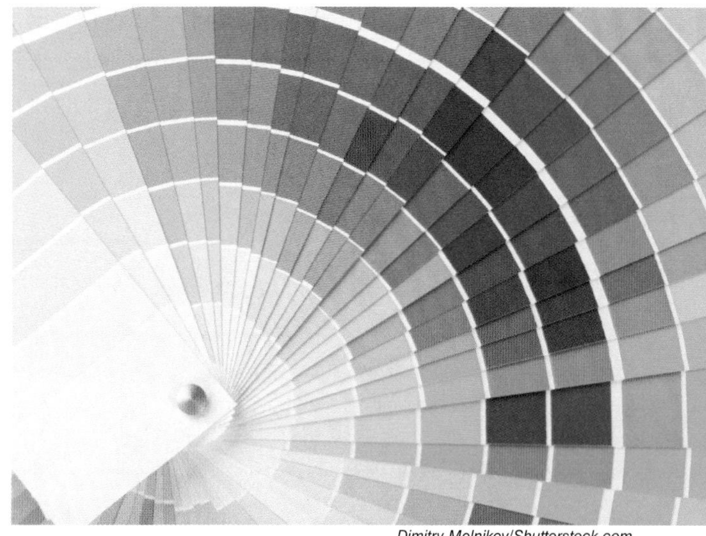

Dimitry Melnikov/Shutterstock.com

Figure 15.3 This fan of different paint colors represents a portion of the many colors that exist in nature.

Review & Assessment

1. What is color?
2. What factors influence the psychological impact color has on people?
3. Summarize the effects the following colors evoke in people: red, orange, yellow, green, blue, violet, black, and white.
4. When are people most comfortable in their surroundings? Give an example.
5. What is the color spectrum?

The Color Wheel

Color relationships are easy to understand when you learn a few basic principles. The standard color wheel is the tool used to best illustrate these principles. The **color wheel**, Figure 15.4, is the most commonly used tool to understand the basis of all color relationships. It is made of three concentric rings: an outer, middle, and inner ring. The middle ring of the color wheel consists of three types of colors: primary, secondary, and tertiary.

Yellow, red, and blue are the **primary colors**. They are the basic colors and you cannot create them by mixing other colors. However, mixing, lightening, or darkening the primary colors can make all other colors.

Orange, green, and violet are the **secondary colors**. Mixing equal amounts of two primary colors produces these colors. Orange is a mixture

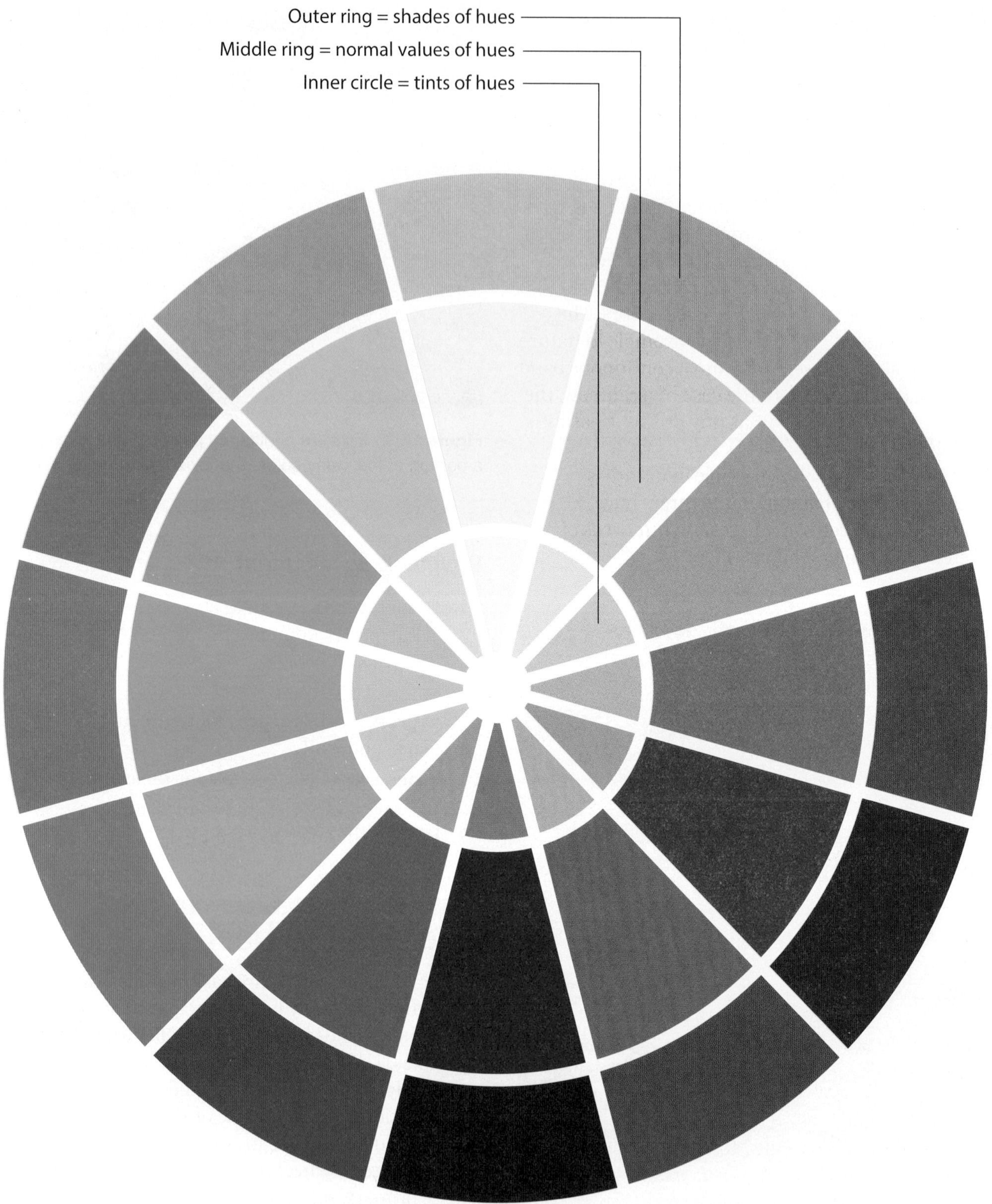

Figure 15.4 The arrangement in a color wheel provides a basis for all color relationships.

of red and yellow. Green is a mixture of yellow and blue. Violet is a mixture of blue and red. Look again at the color wheel. Notice each secondary color is located halfway between the two primary colors used to make it.

The other colors in the middle ring of the color wheel—yellow-green, blue-green, blue-violet, red-violet, red-orange, and yellow-orange—are the **tertiary colors**, or the third level of colors. Another name for the tertiary colors is *intermediate*

Sociocultural Connections — Color Psychology at Work

Color is a vital tool for interior designers because it impacts how people feel. Vibrant colors, especially oranges and reds, enliven the seating areas of many fast-food restaurants. They tend to stimulate customers' appetites.

Designers working for clients in various industries use color to achieve other goals. For example, designers of airplane interiors avoid using large expanses of fast-food reds and oranges. Their goal is not to stimulate appetites, but to create a relaxing environment for passengers. Neutrals and muted shades often work well. In hospital rooms, color is used to create spaces that do not raise anxiety or trigger depression among ill or injured people.

In residential settings, designers often use the color blue in bedrooms because it has a calming and peaceful effect.

Dig Deeper

Use online and print resources to research the effects of color for people in other cultures. Choose at least three cultures to research other than your own. How do people react to these colors in each culture? What are the color meanings in these cultures and how do they differ from those in the United States? Write a summary of your findings to post to the class website.

colors. The names of tertiary colors reflect the names of the two colors used to make them—an equal mixture of a primary color with a secondary color adjacent to it on the color wheel. Note that their names always have the primary color listed first. For example, blue-green is correct but not "green-blue."

The lightest color on the color wheel is yellow and it is always at the top of the wheel for that reason. Violet is the darkest color on the color wheel. It is directly opposite from yellow at the bottom of the wheel.

Color Characteristics

Each color has three characteristics: hue, value, and intensity. Various tools illustrate these characteristics. For example, the color wheel shows hues and some values. Separate scales, such as the

STEM Science & Technology — Visible Light and the Electromagnetic Spectrum

Light is a form of energy called *electromagnetic radiation*. It travels through space as oscillating waves. From crest to trough, these waves range in size from large as a building to small as a microscopic particle. *Wavelength* is the distance between the crests of two adjoining waves. *Frequency* is the rate at which a wave oscillates or fluctuates and is measured in hertz. The chart shows the electromagnetic spectrum arranged according to wavelength and frequency in hertz. As the length of a wave increases, its frequency decreases.

Visible light makes up a small part of the electromagnetic spectrum and it's the only part you can see. Visible light consists of the colors you see in a rainbow—red, orange, yellow, green, blue, and violet. These colors form the basis for the color wheel that interior designers use for creating color schemes.

The spectrum also includes other forms of energy you encounter every day: infrared, radio waves, microwaves, X-rays, gamma rays, and ultraviolet rays. Many consumer electronics products utilize the electromagnetic spectrum. Can you identify a few of them?

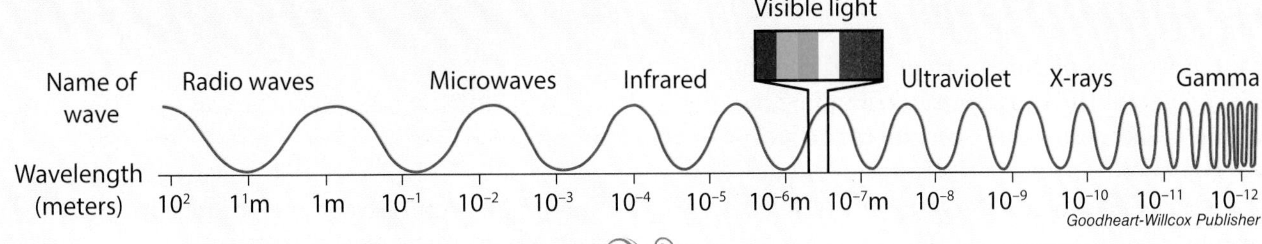

Goodheart-Willcox Publisher

color rendering index (CRI), show color values more completely as well as color intensity.

Hue

A **hue**, or color name, is the color in its purest form, with no added black, gray, or white. It is the one characteristic that makes a color unique. It is what makes red different from blue and green different from yellow. It is the specific, individual nature of each color.

Value

The **value** of a hue is the relative lightness or darkness of a hue. The middle ring of the color wheel shows the normal values of hues. The normal values of some hues are lighter than the normal values of others. For instance, yellow has the lightest normal value of any color in the middle ring of the wheel. As you move away from yellow on the color wheel, the normal values of hues become darker. Violet has the darkest normal value.

Adding white to a hue makes it lighter. The addition of white to a hue produces a **tint**. For instance, pink is a tint of red. Adding white to red creates pink. Adding white to blue creates baby blue, a tint of blue. Peach is a tint of orange. Lavender is a tint of violet. The innermost ring of the color wheel shows the tints. Lighter tints require the addition of more white.

You can make the value of a hue darker by adding black. The addition of black to a hue produces a **shade**. For instance, burgundy is a shade of red. Adding black to red creates this shade. Navy blue is a shade of blue and is created by adding black to blue. Darker shades require the addition of more black. The outer ring of the color wheel shows the shades. Refer again to the color wheel to identify the normal value of hues, tints, and shades.

Adding gray softens the value of a hue, which produces a **tone**. Rose is a tone of red. Wedgwood blue is a tone of blue, created by adding gray to blue. Note that adding light gray to a hue causes confusion with a tint. Likewise, adding dark gray to a hue can cause confusion with a shade. However, there is a difference. Medium grays, of course, are the easiest to recognize as tones when mixed with hues.

Figure 15.5 pictures a *value scale*. The left column shows the range of tints obtained by adding greater amounts of white to the blue color. The right column shows the range of shades obtained by adding greater amounts of black to the blue.

Goodheart-Willcox Publisher

Figure 15.5 Values for the color blue, ranging from tints to shades, are shown on this value scale.

Intensity

Intensity refers to the brightness or dullness of a hue. The middle ring of the color wheel shows the normal intensity of each hue.

One way to dull a hue, or lower its intensity, is to add some of its complement. The **complement** of a hue is the hue opposite it on the color wheel. For instance, blue is the complement of orange. To lower the intensity of orange, you add varying amounts of blue, as shown in Figure 15.6. To lower the intensity

Goodheart-Willcox Publisher

Figure 15.6 Adding blue to orange reduces the intensity of orange, making it a duller color.

of red, you add small amounts of its complement, green. Examples of high-intensity colors include hot pink and fire-engine red. Smoky blue and rust are examples of low-intensity colors. Another way to lower the intensity of a hue is to add gray, making the color a tone.

Neutrals

Although neutrals are not really colors, they are usually classified as colors when discussing design. Black, white, and gray are neutrals. Black is the combination of all colors when it exists as a pigment. A **pigment** is a coloring agent used in paint and printed materials. In contrast to black, white used as a pigment has no color. Gray is a combination of black and white. Brown and its tints and shades are also neutrals. Combining equal amounts of complementary colors forms a brown color.

By adding a neutral color to a hue, the value of the hue changes to either a tint or a shade. This makes the hue less intense. With any of these changes, neutralization of the hue occurs. Neutralized hues blend better with other colors.

Warm and Cool Colors

Colors can be classified as either warm or cool. Although the actual temperature may be the same throughout an entire home, some rooms may seem cooler or warmer due to the usage of certain colors in decorating.

Warm colors include yellow, orange, red, and the colors near them on the color wheel, with red being the warmest. They are called warm colors because they remind us of fire and the sun.

Warm colors are ***advancing***—meaning they appear to move forward. Warm-colored objects appear closer to you. Warm-colored walls look closer together. For example, a room painted red, yellow, or orange appears smaller than its actual size.

Warm colors attract your attention. They can make you feel happy, energetic, and full of excitement. Research shows the color red actually stimulates the nervous system and can increase blood pressure, heartbeats, and breathing rate. Many advertisements use warm colors to make you notice them. Restaurants use warm colors to increase your appetite. Locker rooms use them to generate excitement. Warm colors in homes make household members feel lively and cheerful. An overuse of warm colors, however, may make people feel nervous or tense, especially if they are full-intensity colors.

Cool colors are opposite the warm colors on the color wheel. These include blue, green, violet, and the colors near them. They are cool colors because they remind people of water, grass, and trees.

Cool colors are ***receding***—meaning they make objects seem smaller and walls seem farther away than they really are. Decorating a small room in cool colors can make it appear larger than in actuality.

Cool colors are quiet and restful. Hospitals often use them to help patients relax and feel calm. They are also popular for bedrooms. With overuse, however, cool colors may make people feel depressed.

Warm and cool colors create different moods that make people feel differently (Figure 15.7). For

A *xJJx/Shutterstock.com*

B *MaxFX/Shutterstock.com*

Figure 15.7 By comparing these two living rooms, you can sense the warmth created by the use of yellow and red (A) and the feeling of coolness generated by the use of green and blue (B).

example, workers in an office complained their lunchroom was always cold. When the employer changed the light blue room to orange, the complaints stopped even though the temperature never changed.

Review & Assessment

1. What is the color wheel?
2. Name the secondary colors. What primary colors, in what proportions, are used to make each?
3. Which color name is listed first in the name of a tertiary color?
4. Contrast value and intensity.
5. What are the differences among a tint, shade, and tone?
6. Summarize how to neutralize a hue.
7. List the characteristics of warm and cool colors. Give an example of each.

Color Harmonies

To achieve optimal success when using color in design, follow one of the standard color harmonies. A **color harmony** is a pleasing combination of colors based on their respective positions on the color wheel. There are seven basic color harmonies: monochromatic, complementary, split-complementary, double-complementary, analogous, triadic, and neutral. Established color harmonies bring colors together in combinations that are very satisfying to the eyes.

Monochromatic Color Harmony

A **monochromatic color harmony** is the simplest color harmony. It uses a single hue from the standard color wheel. The hue selected for the monochromatic color harmony in Figure 15.8 is pink (a tint of red).

You can achieve variation in a monochromatic color harmony by changing the value and/or intensity of the hue. For example, you could use light blue, gray blue, and navy blue—a tint, a tone, and a shade of the same hue. A paint fan deck will usually show five to seven values of the same hue. To add interest to the color scheme, use accents of neutral colors. Using a monochromatic color harmony can make a room appear larger. It can also unify the furnishings and accessories used in the space. The monochromatic color scheme is the most restful of all, because it has the least contrast or drama.

Complementary Color Harmony

Selecting two colors that are directly opposite each other on the standard color wheel creates a **complementary color harmony**. Complementary colors are sometimes called

Avoid Greenwashing

Are "green" products always "green?" Some companies and agencies may be less than truthful about the "green" aspects of their products and services. These companies and agencies realize that more consumers are looking for green products and are easily influenced by terms relating to green features. They may use terms that mislead consumers and professionals about the "green" features of their products. Some environmental product claims are false while others are misleading. The term for this deceptive way of doing business is *greenwashing*.

An example of greenwashing involves low- or zero-volatile organic compound (VOC) paints. Because they are less toxic to humans and the environment, these paints are catching on quickly with consumers. Several reliable paint suppliers produce these paints. Other companies are putting "green" on the labels, but their paint may actually be neither low- or zero-VOC products.

Before buying any green products, check a number of websites that provide information on the validity of products that indicate green features. See the websites for the following:

- GreenBiz
- EDC—(the official magazine for LEED® Professionals)
- GreenGuard (part of the UL Environment; a business of Underwriters Laboratories)

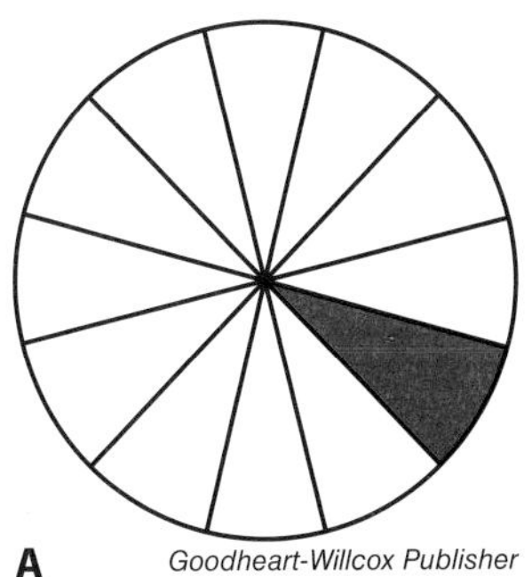
A Goodheart-Willcox Publisher

B © 2015 The Sherwin-Williams Company

Figure 15.8 Pink, (a tint of red—A), is the basis for this monochromatic color harmony (B).

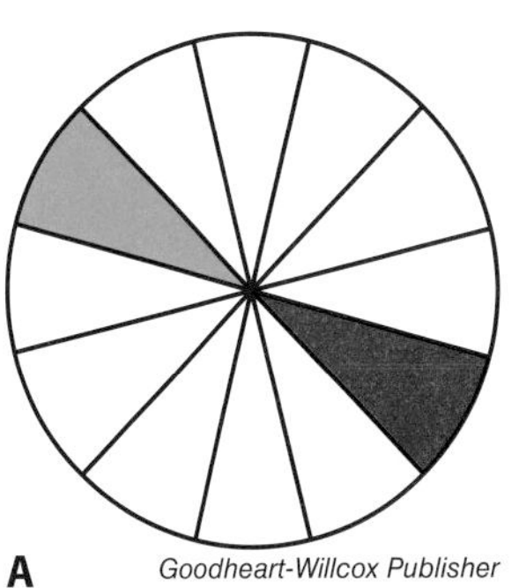
A Goodheart-Willcox Publisher

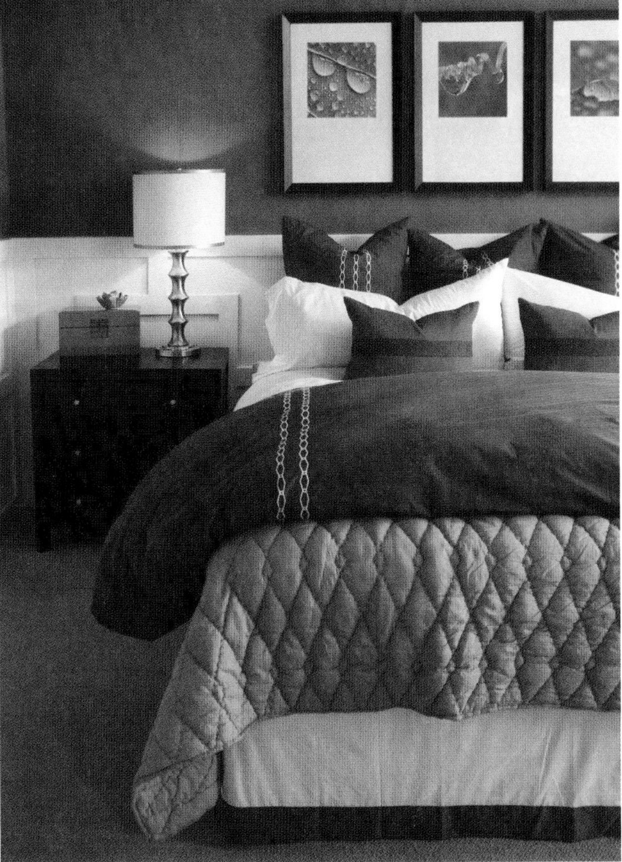
B Beata Becla/Shutterstock.com

Figure 15.9 Red and green are complementary colors (A). Shades of green and red are used in this contemporary bedroom to create a complementary color harmony (B).

contrasting colors because they make each other look brighter and more intense. For example, when using blue next to orange, the blue looks bluer, and the orange looks stronger. A complementary color harmony can make a room look bright and dramatic.

Although such a sharp contrast is fine for some rooms, most rooms are more comfortable with less contrast. Varying the values and intensities of the colors can do this along with varying the amounts of the colors (Figure 15.9). The more one color dominates the other, the less noticeable the contrast.

Split-Complementary Color Harmony

Using one hue with the two hues adjacent to its complement creates a **split-complementary color harmony**. As a variation of the complementary color harmony, the split-complementary harmony uses *three* colors. For example, if you choose the blue hue first, you would look directly across the color wheel to find orange, its complement. You would then select the colors on both sides of orange to establish your split-complementary color harmony. The resulting color harmony uses

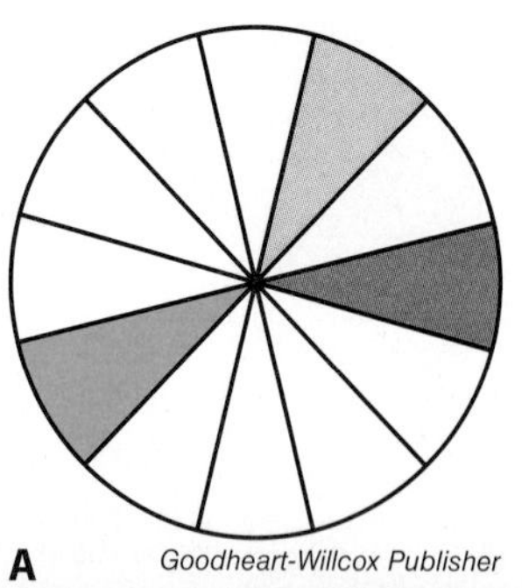
A Goodheart-Willcox Publisher

B Omegafoto/Shutterstock.com

Figure 15.10 A split-complementary color harmony uses a main color (blue) with the colors on both sides of its complement (yellow-orange and red-orange) (A). How is the split-complementary color harmony used in this photo (B)?

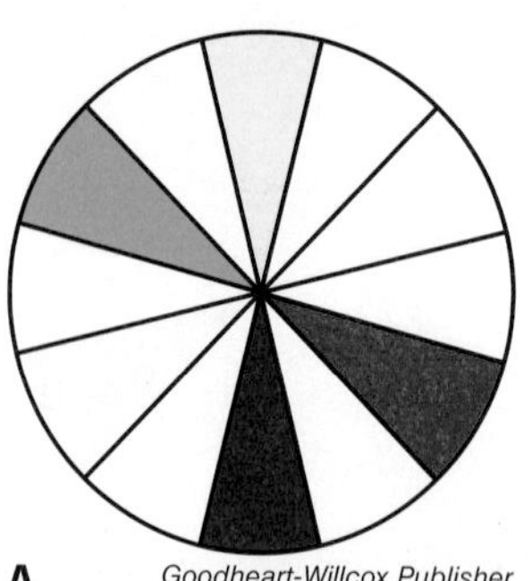
A Goodheart-Willcox Publisher

B Alexey Kashin/Shutterstock.com

Figure 15.11 A double-complementary color harmony is made of two sets of complementary color schemes (A). Which complementary schemes are represented in this photo (B)?

blue, yellow-orange, and red-orange (Figure 15.10). With this color selection, blue will likely be the dominant color, while yellow-orange and red-orange provide lively contrast.

Double-Complementary Color Harmony

Selecting two colors and their complements from the standard color wheel creates a **double-complementary color harmony**. In this way, you use four colors to create the color harmony. One example of a double-complementary color harmony results from pairing red and green with violet and yellow (Figure 15.11). As long as each pair is composed of complementary colors, you may use any combination of pairs.

Analogous Color Harmony

Selecting related hues from the standard color wheel creates an **analogous color harmony**. These are hues that are next to each other on the color wheel. In an analogous color harmony, usually three to five hues are used. Since they are related, they blend together well. One color seems to merge into another. Even when the colors in an analogous color harmony are all warm, the room will be more restful than one that uses colors from both sides of the color wheel. Figure 15.12 shows an example of an analogous color harmony.

An analogous color harmony will look best if you choose one color as the dominant color and use smaller amounts of the others to add interest and variety. You may also want to use a tiny amount of an unrelated color as an accent.

Triadic Color Harmony

A **triadic color harmony** uses any three colors that are equally distant from each other on

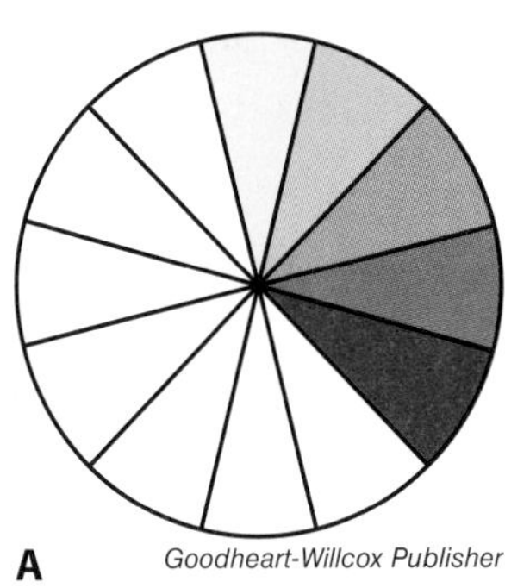

A Goodheart-Willcox Publisher

B Johnny Lye/Shutterstock.com

Figure 15.12 An analogous color harmony uses hues next to each other on the color wheel (A). The analogous color harmony using yellow, yellow-orange, orange, red-orange, and red, gives this room a vibrant appearance (B).

Career Focus Color Designer

If you share some of the following interests, you may want to consider a career as a color designer.

Interests/Skills: Do you like to experiment with the colors of your clothing and accessories? Do you realize that color plays an important role by having a positive or negative impact on emotions? Do you enjoy being in spaces where the colors give you a sense of peace? Have you found enjoyment working with colors and paint throughout your education? Skill requirements for a color specialist include: an excellent eye for color; thorough understanding of color psychology, the color wheel, and how to use different color harmonies; and the ability to organize details and research information. In addition, excellent speaking, writing, and listening skills are needed to communicate with a client.

Career Snapshot: Color designers work with manufacturers and interior designers. They provide many different design services as well as marketing. A color designer must have a strong combination of the two. They consult manufacturers about colors that will work best for trends in new furniture, paint, wall coverings, fabrics, rugs, and other accessories. For example, a color designer may work for a textile firm and may recommend yarn colors that will be the most popular and marketable. Color designers must be able to recognize very subtle differences in colors. They must stay current in their research to predict color trends.

Education/Training: A bachelor's or a master's degree is preferred. Courses include color theory, psychology of color, art, art history, interior design, and computer programs.

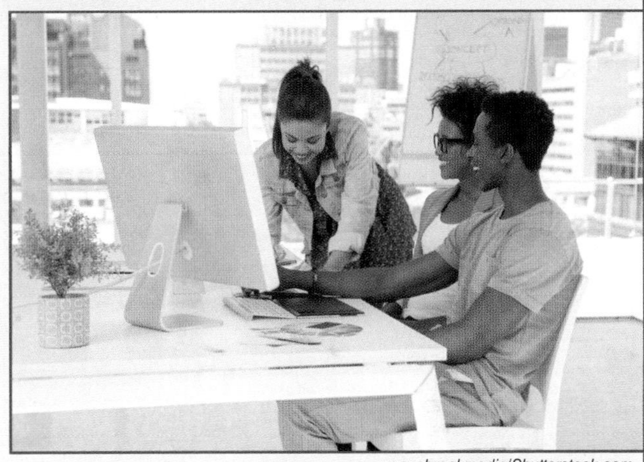

wavebreakmedia/Shutterstock.com

Licensing/Examinations: No license required.

Professional Associations: The Color Marketing Group (CMG); The American Society of Interior Designers (ASID); the International Interior Design Association (IIDA); the Inter-Society Color Council (ISCC)

Job Outlook: The many career possibilities for a color designer in interior design will grow about four percent, slower than average through 2024. Color designers may work for a large firm that specializes in color design, an interior designer specializing in color design, or an individual company as a consultant. Some choose freelance work for projects of interest.

Sources: The Occupational Outlook Handbook (OOH); Occupational Information Network (O*NET)

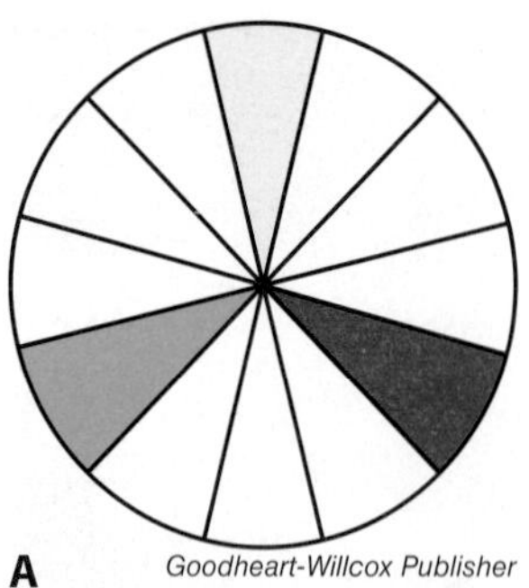
A Goodheart-Willcox Publisher

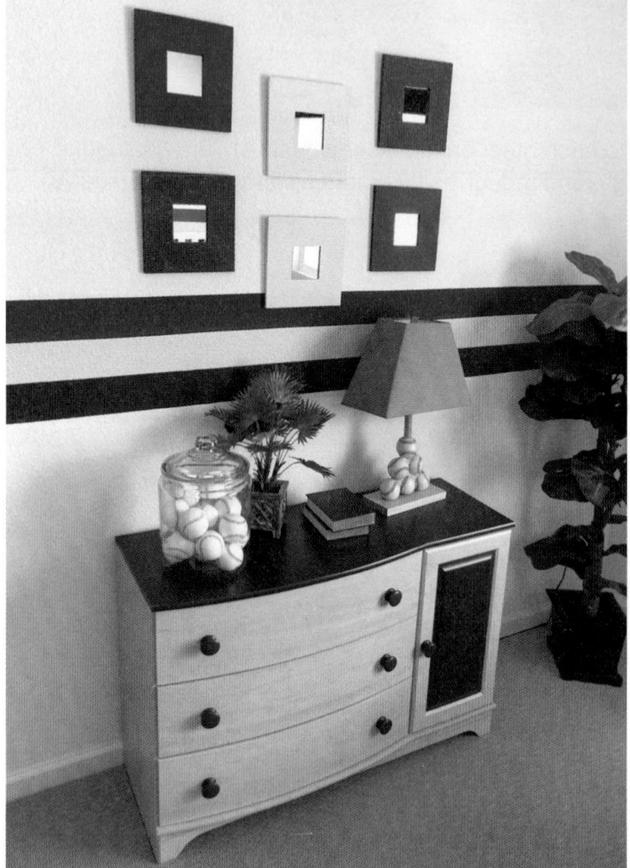
B Stephen Coburn/Shutterstock.com

Figure 15.13 Triadic color harmonies use three colors that are equidistant from each other on the color wheel (A). Triadic color harmonies are often used in children's bedrooms (B).

the standard color wheel. The triadic color harmony will follow a pattern of using every fourth color on the color wheel. For example, yellow, blue, and red—the primary colors—form a triadic color harmony (Figure 15.13). The secondary colors—green, orange, and violet—also create a triadic color harmony. The two other possible color combinations are: yellow-orange, red-violet, and blue-green; or red-orange, blue-violet, and yellow-green. Designers use great care and skill to achieve pleasing triadic harmonies. Changing values and intensities can lessen the sharp contrasts.

Carunfu/Shutterstock.com

Figure 15.14 Combinations of black, gray, and white create neutral color schemes. Small splashes of accent colors can add interest.

Neutral Color Harmony

Although black and white are not hues on the standard color wheel, they are the basis for **neutral color harmonies**. Combinations of black, white, and gray create neutral color harmonies. Brown, tan, and beige can also be used. Sometimes adding small amounts of other colors to neutral color schemes gives the room more interest (Figure 15.14).

Review & Assessment

1. What is a color harmony?
2. What is the purpose of using established color harmonies?
3. Name the seven color harmonies and identify an example of each.

Using Color Harmonies

Now that you have learned about color and the color harmonies, you can begin to use this information to create interior design color schemes for a home. A **color scheme** is the combination of colors selected for the design of a room or house. When designing a room, choose colors that you like seeing together. The chosen colors probably look good together because they conform to an established color harmony.

A well-planned color scheme will use color harmonies to blend and unify the design of the home as you transition from one room to another.

STEM Science & Technology The Anatomy of Color

Objects absorb and reflect light. The color that you see depends on the wavelength and frequency of the reflected waves. Red has the longest wavelength; violet has the shortest.

Humans have *trichromatic color vision*. The key part of the eye responsible for color vision is the retina. This area, at the back of the eye, contains millions of light-sensitive nerve cells called rod and cone cells. *Rod cells* enable you to see in low light. *Cone cells* enable you to see color and detail.

The *tri* in trichromatic refers to the three types of cone cells. Each type is sensitive to waves of a different part of the visible light spectrum. "Blue cone cells" react to the shorter waves on the blue end of the color spectrum. "Red cone cells" react to longer waves on the red end of the spectrum. "Green cone cells" react to medium-length waves in the green spectrum.

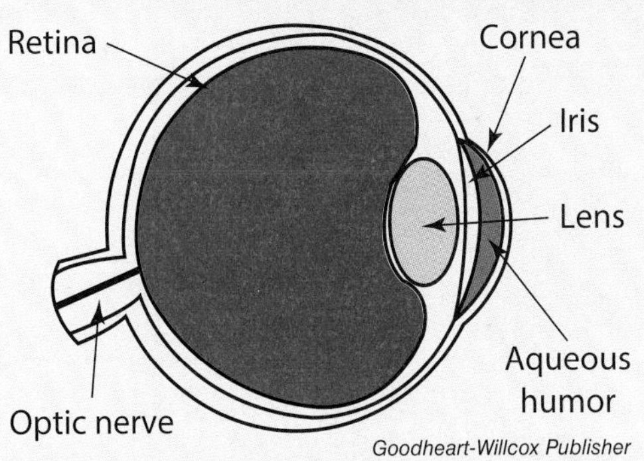

Goodheart-Willcox Publisher

When light enters the eyes and hits the retina, it stimulates the cone cells and sends electronic impulses to the brain. The signals from the cone cells are transmitted to the brain. In a complex process that researchers are still trying to understand, the human brain collects and processes this and other information to produce a color image.

It will also consider the function of the room. As you will see, even if you love red, it may be a poor choice for a bedroom because of its intensity. By following important guidelines, you can create a color scheme that will enhance the near environment and increase the enjoyment of a home (Figure 15.15).

Choosing the Right Colors

The color harmonies you choose for the color scheme of a home depend on several factors. They include what mood or style a person wants, the lifestyle of the family members, the function or the way the occupants will use the room, the items in the room, and the room's location.

Abketta Sangasaeng/Shutterstock.com

Figure 15.15 Colors found in nature were the inspiration for the earthy color scheme in this bedroom.

Moods and Styles

You can create a variety of moods in a room through the use of color. For example, you may want a room to feel restful, or you may want it to appear exciting. Choosing cool colors that have similar values will create a restful mood in the room, such as in Figure 15.16 on the next page. Choosing warm colors with contrasting values will make the room feel exciting.

You can also choose colors that will create a certain style in a room. Different styles, such as southwestern or country, often suggest the use of specific colors. You can use these colors in different color harmonies to achieve the style you want.

In a southwestern-style room, for example, you may choose warm desert colors, such as rust, sunset orange, brick, and sand. In a country-style room, you may choose low-intensity shades of reds, blues, oranges, and yellows.

Lifestyles

Some people have active lifestyles while others lead quieter lives. The colors you choose depend on the lifestyles of household members. For instance, with small children, give consideration to darker colors and shades that do not show dirt easily. In contrast, a household of adults may choose lighter

Software by Chief Architect

Figure 15.16 By using a CADD program, you can test how a paint color will look in a room to see the warmth or coolness it creates.

colors for the walls and upholstery because upkeep is less of a concern.

The colors you choose for each room also depend on how they are used. Primary and secondary colors of normal intensity are fine for a child's room, such as in Figure 15.17. If you use the same hues in an adult's bedroom, however, softer tints or tones at lower intensity levels are preferable.

Room27/Shutterstock.com

Figure 15.17 The use of primary and secondary colors in this child's room gives the room a feeling of fun and excitement.

Function of the Room

While teens may sleep, study, and socialize in their bedrooms, most adults use their bedrooms for rest and relaxation. In this case, cooler colors and less drama are more conducive to good sleep. A den or family room where everyone meets and socializes is often more appropriate in warm colors. For a writer or an accountant that works alone from home, the home office may be best in cool colors. In contrast, a salesperson who talks on the phone most of the day may perform best in warm colors. When choosing colors and color schemes, be sure to give thoughtful attention to colors that support the function and purpose of a room.

Items in the Room

Another way to choose color harmonies is to consider the usage of all items in the room plan. For instance, plans for a room may include an area rug, sofa, or favorite picture. To create a color scheme around any of these items, you need to select one color used in the object. This color becomes the base, or main color. After choosing the base color, use your knowledge of color harmonies,

Stephen Coburn/Shutterstock.com

Figure 15.18 A neutral base color and harmony in this room provide a backdrop for the existing art collection.

values, and intensities to select colors to go with it (Figure 15.18).

You also need to consider the type of lighting used in the room. The colors you select must work well during both day and night. This means you must view the intended colors during daylight hours in natural light and at night under the influence of artificial light. Always make your final color selections in the actual room and under the lighting conditions where you will use them. Many people experience disasters after selecting a paint color in a retail store under lighting that differs from the actual lighting in their space.

Most homes have some combination of natural, incandescent, and fluorescent lighting. However, some homes now are using the newer and more energy efficient lighting such as compact fluorescent lighting (CFL), light-emitting diodes (LED), and fiber optic lighting. Incandescent lighting can bring dullness to some colors and fluorescent lighting can completely distort color. Incandescent lighting generally makes colors appear warmer. Fluorescent lighting makes colors appear warmer or cooler, depending on the color of the lightbulb or tube. In general, most fluorescent lighting will make colors appear cooler compared to incandescent lighting. Halogen lighting renders the truest presentation of colors. *Compact florescent lighting* affects colors in various ways, depending on the color rating of the bulb. The chart, Figure 15.19, shows the impact of various lighting types on colors.

Location of the Room

The direction the room faces—north, south, east, or west—must be taken into consideration when choosing the base color and color harmony.

Color and Artificial Lighting					
Type of Artificial Lighting	**Yellow**	**Orange**	**Red**	**Blue**	**Green**
Standard Incandescent	Warms	Strengthens	Enriches	Dulls	Darkens
Tungsten-Halogen Incandescent	Warms	Strengthens	Enriches	Dulls slightly	Darkens slightly
Deluxe Cool-White Fluorescent	Enriches and intensifies	Close to true hue	Warms	Enriches	Brightens
Deluxe Warm-White Fluorescent	Brightens	Strengthens	Enriches	Darkens and enriches	Enriches
Cool-White, Bright-White CFL	Enriches and intensifies	Close to true hue	Warms	Enriches	Brightens
Warm-White, Soft-White CFL	Warms	Strengthens	Enriches	Dulls	Darkens

Figure 15.19 Colors change when viewed under different types of artificial light.

If a bedroom is located on the north side of a house, the subdued light of the northern exposure may make colors appear cooler. To make the room appear warmer, choose a color harmony that uses warm colors. A southern exposure receives the most sunlight and generally makes colors appear bright and warm. Sometimes cool colors are preferred for rooms with southern exposures (Figure 15.20).

You cannot assume, however, the quality of light entering a room from a specific direction is always the same. The light entering a bedroom with a northern exposure will change significantly, for example, if it reflects off a bright white house next door. Also, a room with a southern exposure will not be sunny if a covered porch overhangs the windows and doors. Even the light that filters through trees outside a window can change the quality of sunlight entering the room. Consequently, the best rule of thumb is to view a color sample in the actual room at different times of day and night to examine all lighting factors.

When considering location, you also need to think about the colors used in adjoining rooms. The new colors you choose should blend with those used in adjoining rooms. In general, color should not change abruptly from room to room. Instead, it should make a gradual transition from one space to another.

If the location of a dining room is next to the living room, you can use the same base color in both rooms. You might use an analogous color harmony with yellow as the base color of the color scheme in both rooms. In the living room, consider selecting yellow as the dominant color with the other analogous hues playing secondary roles. Then use the same analogous color harmony in the dining room but expand the harmony from three to five hues and add interest by changing the tints or shades of the hues selected. You might also choose to have yellow play a less-dominant role in the dining room than it did in the living room. Introducing a color in the split-complementary color harmony with yellow as an accent will add excitement to the room. Since yellow is the base color of all the harmonies in both rooms, it provides a smooth transition.

WorldWide/Shutterstock.com

Figure 15.20 Because this bedroom has a southern exposure, the designer chose cool colors to decorate the room. These colors keep this room looking serene, light, and airy.

There is an exception to the rule of blending colors in adjoining rooms. In homes using contemporary design, the walls of adjoining rooms may intentionally have different, bold colors. Devote special care, however, to applying the basic rules of color harmonies so the abrupt transitions result in good design.

Using Color Correctly

As you work with color, the following guidelines will help you use color well:

- Applying colors to large areas makes them appear to gain intensity. Because of this, a color you select from a paint chip may appear too intense or dark when painted on all four walls of a room. At other times, a paint chip that appears soft and easy on the eye will fade to nothing when you apply it to the four walls of a room. It is advisable to paint a large swatch of the color on the wall or piece of foam board to help visualize how a paint color will appear on a wall.
- Using contrasting colors draws attention. For example, bright accent pillows against a neutral sofa will draw more attention than those of the same hue or tone (Figure 15.21). While you may want to avoid a totally neutral room, remember, too many strong contrasts in a room can be confusing and tiring.
- Color harmonies are easier on the eye when one color, the base color, is dominant. The dominant color should cover about two-thirds of the room area. When you use equal amounts of two or more colors in a room, your color selections can become a distraction and appear cluttered as each color competes for attention.

Naphat_Jorjee/Shutterstock.com

Figure 15.21 Color harmonies look best when your base color dominates the room. The dominate color should cover at least two-thirds of a space.

- When choosing colors for large areas, such as walls and floors, select low-intensity colors. If you use high-intensity colors in large amounts, they can become overpowering. Instead, use high-intensity colors in small amounts as accent colors in accessories or small pieces of furniture.
- Heavily textured surfaces make colors appear dark. This is because the light strikes the surface at different angles, making the item appear to have greater depth (Figure 15.22). When trying to match fabrics, it is important to have samples of the fabrics you are matching. For example, if you are matching drapery fabric to carpet, make sure you have samples of the carpet with you.

Khumnoo/Shutterstock.com

Figure 15.22 Although the trim work and furniture have the same wood tone, the textures on the chair and the bamboo curtains make the room look darker and heavier.

Iriana Shiyan/Shutterstock.com

Figure 15.23 Using the color guidelines to choose the right colors and create pleasing color harmonies is important for you or a client.

- If a room is very large, consider choosing colors that will make it look smaller. Shades, high-intensity colors, and warm hues that have advancing qualities make a room appear smaller.
- If a room is small, color can make the room appear larger. Tints, low-intensity colors, a monochromatic or analogous color scheme, or cool hues that have receding qualities make a room look larger.

Choosing the right colors, creating color harmonies, and following the color guidelines are important (Figure 15.23). This will help you make color work well for you, your home, or your customer.

Review & Assessment 

1. What is a color scheme and on what is it based?
2. What factors influence the way color harmonies are used in planning an interior design?
3. How does lifestyle influence the way colors are chosen for children and adults? Give an example.
4. Why do you need to consider the type of lighting used in a room when choosing colors?
5. Give an example of how room location can impact choice of base color and color harmony.
6. Name four guidelines to follow to use color correctly.

Chapter 15 Assessment

Summary

- Color is one of the most important elements of design. It can create and communicate different moods.
- Color has its own physiological and psychological effects on people.
- The basis of all color relationships is the color wheel.
- Colors in the middle ring of the color wheel are primary, secondary, or intermediate colors.
- Color has three characteristics—*hue, value* and *intensity.*
- The cool colors are located on one side of the wheel, and the warm colors are on the other.
- Using colors together in a pleasing manner creates color harmonies.
- The color harmonies are monochromatic, complementary, split-complementary, double-complementary, analogous, triadic, or neutral. Colors in the neutral harmony are black, white, gray, tan, beige, and brown.
- When choosing a color harmony for a personal color scheme or that of a client, first choose the right colors for a home and the lifestyle of the occupants. Then following certain guidelines will coordinate the colors you select into good design.

Terms in Action

1. **Term attributes** Create a T-chart on a separate sheet of paper and list each of the *Content* and *Academic Terms* in the left column. Identify a word or group of words describing a quality of the term—an attribute. Pair up with a classmate and discuss your list of attributes. Then discuss your list of attributes with the entire class to increase understanding.

Think Critically

2. **Draw conclusions** No two people perceive color in exactly the same way and indeed some people are unable to distinguish between certain colors at all. How could these behaviors pose an obstacle to an interior designer's presentation to a committee in charge of finalizing selections for new corporate offices? Draw conclusions about what techniques the designer could use to overcome objections.
3. **Identify alternatives** Assume you are working with two clients who want to redesign the master bedroom in their home. The room has a northern exposure with little natural lighting. One client prefers warm, intense hues while the other prefers cool hues. In addition to sleeping, your clients also use the room for reading. What color alternatives would you suggest that both clients will find pleasing? How can lighting impact your color choices?

Core Skills

4. **Research, writing, and speaking** Tour a model home to research and observe the use of color. Record your observations and, if possible, take digital pictures of the site. Be sure to get permission to take pictures. Did the colors match your preferences? Did the colors reflect current trends? How were colors used to create mood in various rooms? Identify several psychological impacts the colors may have on some people. Use a school-approved web application to create a digital poster to summarize your findings. Upload your poster to the class website for peer review.
5. **Research, writing, and speaking** Analyze the color scheme of a room in your home or in the home of someone you know. Which of the colors used is your favorite? How long has this room had this appearance? What color scheme was used before? If you could redecorate next week, what colors would you select? What do you think your color preferences reveal about your personality? Take one or more pictures of this room with a digital camera to place in an electronic presentation. Include examples and colors you might want to use in the future. Share your electronic presentation with the class.
6. **Writing** Locate a home or business in the community whose exterior has a pleasing

combination of colors. Identify the colors used and how they were used. Also, identify a building's exterior that represents the opposite of pleasing to you. What colors are used? Which colors would you change if you had the job of updating the look of the building on a budget? Write a summary of your update suggestions citing a rationale for your thinking.

7. **Research and speaking** Search the Internet for current color trends in residential design. What cultural influences, elements of nature, or other factors inspire the new color trends? How strongly does culture influence color? Which of the new color trends do you find most appealing? Why? Why do you think color trends change from year to year? Share your findings during a small group discussion.
8. **Research and writing** Presume you are a reporter for a design magazine. Your supervisor has assigned you to investigate how *light reflectance value (LRV)* can influence an interior designer's choice of colors for a room design. How might LRV influence the aesthetics and function of a room design? Use online or print resources for your research. Write the article citing your sources and post the article for your supervisor's review (your instructor).
9. **Photo essay and speaking** Use a digital camera to take pictures of 10 rooms that display good interior design. (Perhaps some are in your home or in historical homes that you have visited.) For each room, identify the type of color harmony that predominates. Also, analyze possible reasons for the color harmonies selected, given the purpose of each room. Using presentation software, combine your photographs and explanations to share with the class.
10. **CTE career readiness practice** Do you find the psychology of color fascinating? Are you interested in the impact of color on overall room design? If you are, consider joining forces with a community organization, such as Rebuilding Together® for a community service project. Such groups repair and modify homes for people with limited incomes, including older adults, people with disabilities, and veterans. Join forces with your classmates to consult a leader in the organization about working with one or more clients to create a functional and aesthetically pleasing color palette for a room or entire home.

Design Practice

11. **Computer design project** Use technological applications (CADD, etc.) to create an architectural interior drawing. Create drawings of two small rooms of the same dimensions. Cover the walls of one room with light, dull, cool colors. Cover the walls of the other room with dark, bright, warm colors. Analyze which room looks larger and which looks smaller. Why? Print a copy of the room colors for each room. Write a brief report summarizing your analysis.
12. **Color consulting** Imagine you are a professional color consultant who has been hired to help select the room colors for a new community center in your neighborhood. Based on your knowledge of the psychological effect color has on people, what colors would you use in each of the following spaces? Why? Use your written communication skills to convincingly justify your choices (actions) in a socially acceptable manner that is easily understood by others.
    - children's recreation room
    - reading room for older adults
    - hospitality room with a snack bar
    - small nature museum room
    - drama room for theatrical rehearsals
13. **Portfolio** Continue the storyboard for the elements of design you started in Chapter 14. Add color as a design element and provide samples of all color harmonies, labeling the colors used. Keep a copy of your storyboard in your portfolio.

Chapter 16

Principles of Design

Content Terms 

golden mean
golden section
golden rectangle
scale
visual weight
balance
formal balance (symmetry)
informal balance (asymmetrical)
emphasis
rhythm
repetition
gradation
radiation
opposition
transition
harmony
unity
sensory design

Academic Terms 

proportion
subdued

Learning Outcomes 

After studying this chapter, you will be able to

- evaluate the use of the principles of design in residential and nonresidential interior environments.
- demonstrate effective use of decision-making skills in applying principles of design and space to residential and nonresidential interior environments.
- summarize the goals of design.
- analyze the effects of sensory design.

Reading with Purpose

After reading each passage of this chapter, answer the following question: If you were explaining the information in this chapter to a friend who is not taking this class, what would you tell him or her?

While studying, look for the access icon  **to:**

- **Practice** the *Content* and *Academic Terms* with e-flash cards, matching activities, and vocabulary games.
- **Reinforce** what you learn by completing the *Review & Assessment* questions and e-mailing them to your instructor.

www.g-wlearning.com/housing/

Photographee.eu/Shutterstock.com

In the previous two chapters, you learned about the elements of design. When the elements of design are applied *using* the principles of design, you can achieve the goals of design. In this chapter, you will learn how to use this process to create well-designed rooms.

The Principles of Design

The principles of design are guidelines for working with the elements of design. When you understand the principles of design, you can use the elements of design successfully. The principles of design are proportion and scale, balance, emphasis, and rhythm.

Proportion and Scale

Proportion and scale are closely related but different. They both describe size, shape, and amount. They are both concerned with the relationships of objects and parts of objects.

Proportion

Proportion is the ratio of one part to another part or of one part to the whole. It is an important factor when selecting and positioning furniture and accessories in a room. For example, proportion is a consideration when choosing a shade for a lamp. The lamp base and the lampshade need to be in proportion to each other (parts of the same object). Proportion is also a factor to consider when choosing the surface on which to place the lamp. The lamp and table need to be in proportion to each other (different objects in the same group). The accessories that surround the lamp are also considered. The accessories must be in proper proportion to both the lamp and the table (different objects in the same group).

When developing a design scheme, ratios such as 3:5, 5:8, and 8:13 are more effective than ratios of 1:1 or 1:2. For instance, a rectangle has more pleasing proportions than a square. These ratios also apply to rooms, furniture, and accessories (Figure 16.1).

The Greeks were masters of the use of proportion. They developed guidelines that have been used for centuries. Study Figure 16.2 as you read about the Greek guidelines for developing pleasing proportions:

- The **golden mean** is the division of a line midway between one-half and one-third of its length. This

A photosphobos/Shutterstock.com

B oksana perkins/Shutterstock.com

Figure 16.1 Good proportion is important when furnishing a room. The chairs, the table, and the pendant light should be thought of as one element when designing a dining room. Notice in the first dining room (A), the light fixture is too large and overwhelms the space, while the light in the second dining room (B) is more proportionate and in keeping with the style of furnishings.

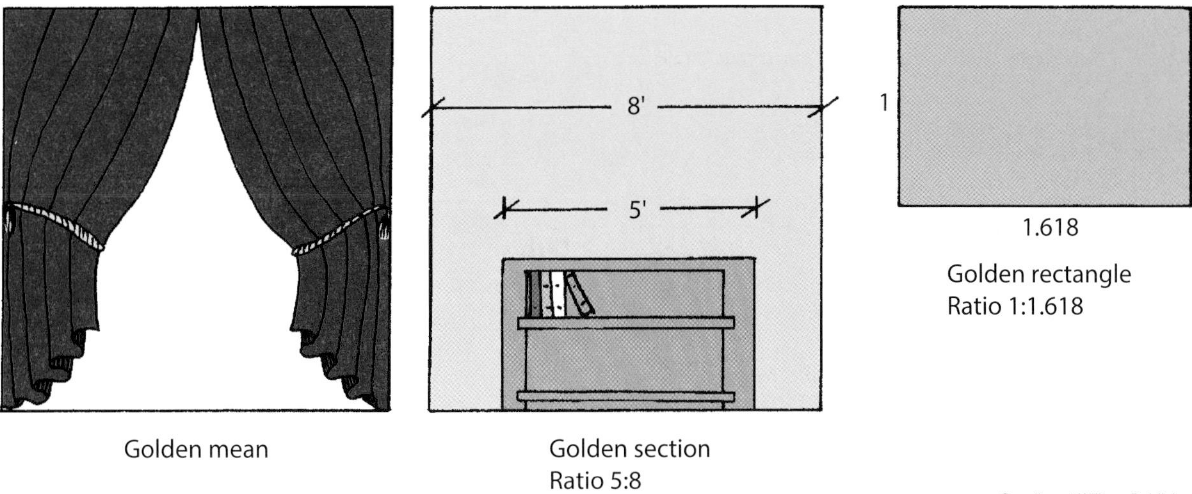

Figure 16.2 The golden mean, golden section, and golden rectangle are all guidelines to help you achieve good proportion.

unequal division is more pleasing visually than an equal division or a division at a point that is less than one-third of the line's length. Interior designers often apply the golden mean when planning wall arrangements, tying draperies, and hanging pictures.

- The **golden section** is the division of a line or form in such a way that the ratio of the smaller section to the larger section is equal to the ratio of the larger section to the whole. This relationship is based on the progression of the numbers 1, 1, 2, 3, 5, 8, 13, 21, 34, 55 and so forth. Notice that the number 2 and each number following is the sum of the two previous numbers.

  When using the golden section to plan a design, you will find that the ratio of 3:5 is about the same as the ratio 8:13 and other similar ratios. Using the concept of the golden section can help you develop more pleasing proportions in your designs.
- The **golden rectangle** has sides in a ratio of 1 to 1.618. It is based on the ratio of the golden section. To form a golden rectangle, divide two equal lines following the golden section. Then combine the short segments and long segments to form the rectangle. One example of the golden rectangle is the Parthenon in Athens. The golden rectangle is frequently an aspect of good design. You can find many examples of the golden rectangle in houses and their furnishings.

Most people do not actually measure proportions. They can tell by looking at a rug on a floor if it is in the proper proportion. Likewise, they can tell if a bed or sofa visually "fits" its room. People tend to develop an awareness or sense of proportion based on their own visual perceptions.

Scale

Scale refers to the relative size of an object in relation to other objects. For example, a chair is a small piece of furniture in comparison to a bed. A twin bed is small in comparison to a king-size bed. The twin bed, however, is still larger than the chair.

When the scale of furnishings relate to the space they occupy, they are visually pleasing. For example, large rooms require large-scale furnishings. A king-size bed is appropriate in a large bedroom; however, it might seem too large for a small room. Small rooms require small-scale furniture.

The furnishings within a room should be in scale with one another. For example, a large sofa requires a large coffee table. A small sofa would not go well with a large coffee table.

Furnishings also need to be in scale to the people using them. A large person will feel more comfortable in a chair of substantial size. Likewise, a child will feel more comfortable in a chair in scale to his or her size (Figure 16.3). This aspect of scale relates to an understanding of *human scale*, or anthropometrics. Human scale is one of the most important considerations in designing a space—either interior or exterior plans. Although Maslow did not mention human scale in his *Hierarchy of Human Needs*, several terms he mentions can strongly relate to human scale. These terms

Calico Corners—Calico Home Stores

Figure 16.3 The reduced size of the chair shown provides greater comfort and accessibility for children although it is out of scale with the other furnishings in the room.

include fulfillment, dignity, relationships, security, protection, and shelter. Peoples' personal size, capabilities, and limits influence how they interact with their environments.

Human scale influences such common everyday objects as the standard door that is 6-feet 8-inches tall by 3-feet wide, steps and ramps that are easy to ascend, or residential elevators that are wide enough to accommodate a wheelchair. Human scale also influences how you feel in a space. For example, think about how differently you feel when you compare the ceiling of a concert hall to the ceiling in your home. Understanding of the subtle aspects of human scale is one of the most important skills to develop in any of the environmental design professions.

Another aspect of scale is **visual weight**. Visual weight is the perception that an object weighs more or less than it really does. For example, a wooden chair and an upholstered chair may have the same dimensions. However, the upholstered chair will look larger and heavier than the wooden chair. Thick lines, bold colors, coarse textures, and large patterns add to visual weight.

When creating a design plan for a small room, choose furniture that has light visual weight. This will prevent the furniture from making the room look crowded. Likewise, choose accessories that are in scale to the furniture. In a small room, it is wise to "think small" in regard to furniture and accessories.

Balance

Balance implies equilibrium among parts of a design. It is a perception of the way arrangements are seen. When there is balance, there is a sense of equal weight on both sides of a center point (Figure 16.4). There is not a visual pull in one direction more than the other. Balance can be either formal or informal. Both types of balance can be used in the same room or space.

In **formal balance**, or symmetry, there is identical proportion and arrangement of objects on both sides of a center point. *Symmetry* is another name for formal balance. Elegant and formal rooms often use this type of balance (Figure 16.5). It is especially appropriate for traditional design styles. It is also useful in exterior design. Formal balance is easy to achieve and makes people feel comfortable because of its orderliness.

With **informal balance**, there is an arrangement of different but equivalent objects on each side of a center point. *Asymmetrical balance* is another name for informal balance. Although the sides are not alike, neither side overpowers the other. This creates a feeling of equilibrium.

You can achieve informal balance in various ways. In order to balance a heavy object and a light object, place the heavier object closer to the center line than the light object. Several smaller objects can balance a single, large one. If objects are the same size but are of unequal distance from you, the object closest to you will appear larger.

An object that has visual weight can also balance a single, large object. Color, texture, and form all create visual weight (Figure 16.6). Bold, warm colors will appear heavier than ***subdued*** (lacking vitality, intensity, or strength) cool colors. Decorations added to an object give it visual weight. Typically, large objects appear heavier than small objects.

Balance is a very important principle to follow when arranging accessories and furnishings. The furnishings on each half of a wall or opposite walls should balance with each other. Likewise, the accessories chosen for display on a table or in a bookcase should also balance with each other. The type of balance used helps determine the mood of a room. Formal balance creates an air of formality.

A *Africa Studio/Shutterstock.com*  **B** *Africa Studio/Shutterstock.com*

Figure 16.4 The same accessories can be arranged in many different ways to create balance on either side of a center point. Image A shows the use of formal balance while image B shows the use of informal balance. Both give the feeling of equal weight on either side of the center point.

Group 3, Architectural and Interior Design, Hilton Head Island, South Carolina. Photography provided as a courtesy of John McManus, Savannah, Georgia.

Figure 16.5 The symmetry created in the entrance to this dining room is an excellent example of formal balance.

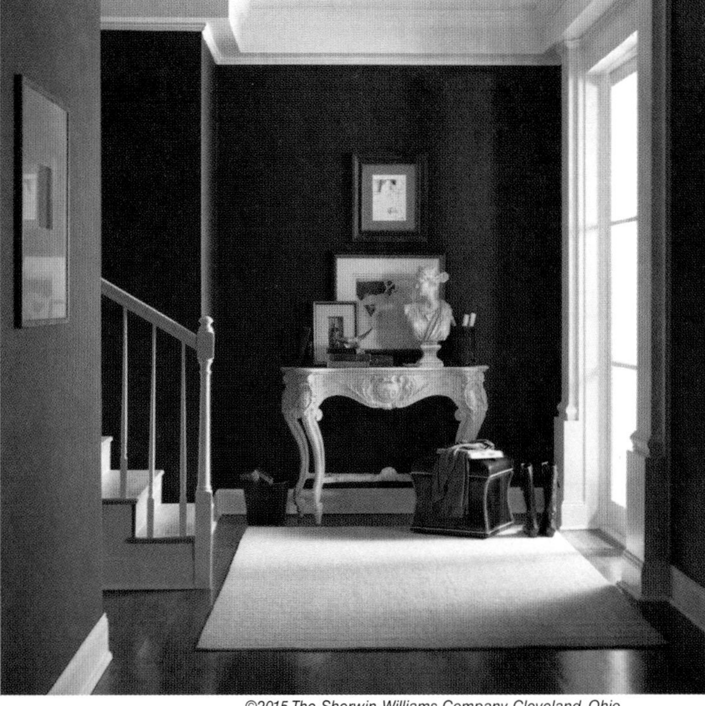

©2015 The Sherwin-Williams Company, Cleveland, Ohio

Figure 16.6 The accessories on the table at the end of the hall create informal balance.

pics721/Shutterstock.com

Figure 16.7 The structure of the doorway and placement of furnishings and accessories in this space represent both formal and informal balance.

Informal balance creates a casual atmosphere. In Figure 16.7, the double doors in the entry create formal balance. Also in this image, the arrangement of furniture and accessories illustrate informal balance.

Emphasis

Emphasis creates a center of interest or focal point in a room. It is the feature that people see first and repeatedly draws attention. Every well-designed room has a focal point. With one area of emphasis, the eyes immediately focus on that point when entering the room. This gives a feeling of stability and unity to the room. When planning a focal point, keep the following guidelines in mind. The focal point should

- be worthy of the attention it will receive
- dominate the room, but not overpower it or the design
- not compete with other features, which results in confusion

Architectural features, such as picture windows and fireplaces, can provide a focal point for a room. Likewise, you can create a focal point through the use or special placement of various items. These include furniture groupings, colorful rugs, striking works of art, mirrors, shelves of books, or other collections (Figure 16.8). Unusual accessories and objects, or their placement in a room, can also serve as focal points. For example, a beautiful piece of antique furniture in a contemporary setting is eye-catching. Similarly, the inclusion of contemporary sculpture as an accessory in a very traditional setting could create a prominent focal point. Special lighting cast upon a significant object can also create a focal point.

The focal point gives order and direction to a room. Everything else in the setting should relate to it through color, texture, proportion, scale, and theme.

Color is usually the first aspect of a focal point to catch one's attention. Carrying it throughout the room in accessories, window treatments, and upholstery fabric can further emphasize the color. You can emphasize the texture of the focal point throughout the room in similar ways.

The size of the point of interest should be in proportion and scale to the room and its furnishings. A massive focal point will be too large for a small room. A large room or a room with a cathedral

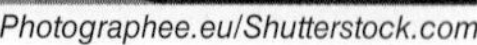
Photographee.eu/Shutterstock.com

Breadmaker/Shutterstock.com

Figure 16.8 Although these two living rooms have many stylistic similarities, the room symmetry, furniture direction, and contrast of materials puts a much greater emphasis on the fireplace in the second photo.

ceiling, however, demands a focal point that will not be dwarfed by the room size.

The usage of a room determines the theme of the room. The focal point should set the stage for the furnishings. For example, the common use of a living room is for socializing. If the fireplace is the focal point, group comfortable seating that permits socializing around the fireplace.

Rhythm

Rhythm smoothly leads the eyes from one area to another in a design. Rhythm results when an element of design forms an organized pattern. For example, a continuous line found in window and door frames produces rhythm. You can achieve rhythm in a room design through repetition, gradation, radiation, opposition, and transition.

Repetition is the basis for all types of rhythm. Repeating an element of design—such as color, line, form, or texture—creates rhythm by **repetition**. Repetition is one of the easiest ways to achieve rhythm in a design. For instance, you can create rhythm by repeating a dominant color throughout a room. The repeating lines in bookcase shelves or structural members create rhythm (Figure 16.9). Repetition of form occurs when you use rectangular end tables and a rectangular coffee table in the same setting. Texture may be repeated in fabrics used in draperies and upholstery.

Gradation is the type of rhythm created by a gradual increase or decrease of similar elements of design. The eyes travel through the levels of progression. For example, color value can change from dark to light or from light to dark. Lines can vary from thick to thin in a design. Objects that have the same form can increase or decrease in size (Figure 16.10). Textures can range from smooth to rough.

In rhythm by **radiation**, lines flow outward from a central point as in a wagon wheel (Figure 16.11). Sunburst designs are examples of rhythm by radiation. Accessories usually show radiation in home furnishings. For example, a flower arrangement or a cushion may have radiating lines. A window that forms a half-circle with a sunburst design is a good example of rhythm by radiation. A round table with surrounding chairs whether in a residential or commercial setting also shows radiation.

In rhythm by **opposition**, lines meet to form right angles. You will often find rhythm by opposition in the construction of a room as well as in the furnishings. For example, you can find it at the corners of windowpanes, picture frames, fireplaces, tables, and other furniture. Rhythm by opposition also exists

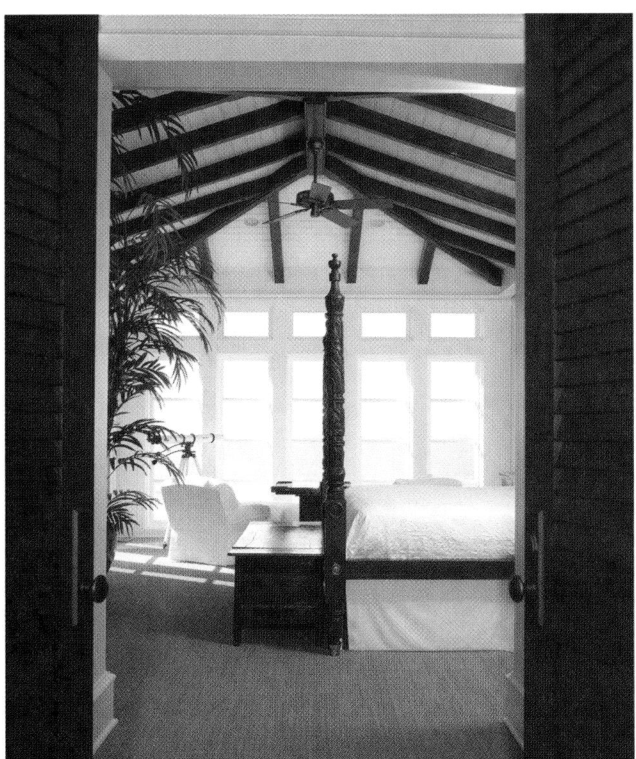

Group 3, Architectural and Interior Design. Hilton Head Island, South Carolina. Photography provided as a courtesy of John McManus, Savannah, Georgia.

Figure 16.9 The beams in this bedroom create rhythm by repetition.

Dave Green/Shutterstock.com

Figure 16.10 These nesting tables are a good example of rhythm by gradation. The eyes move from the largest table to the smallest.

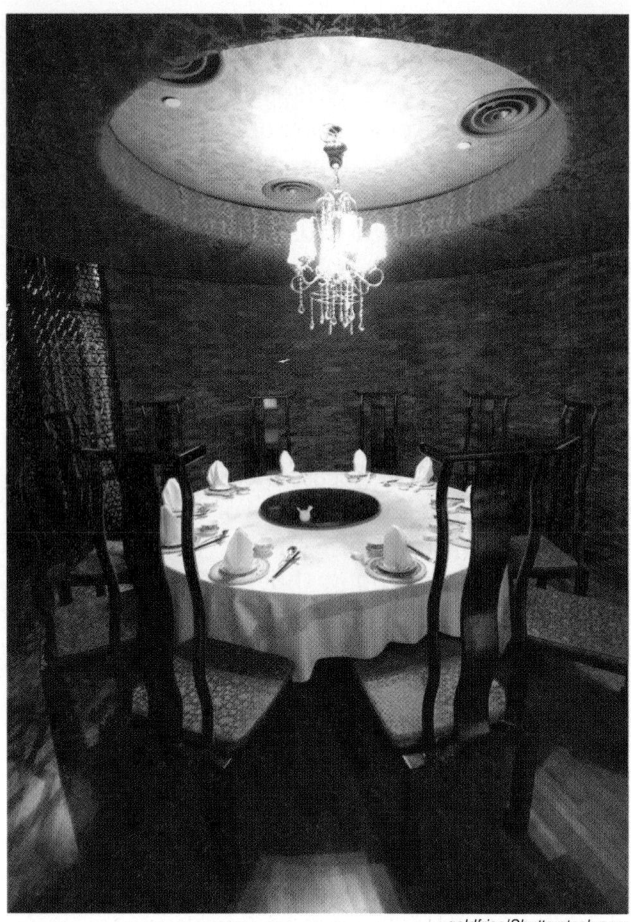

goldfries/Shutterstock.com

Figure 16.11 The circular chair layout in this dining room shows rhythm by radiation.

in floor treatments (Figure 16.12). The simple ways you accessorize and decorate can also create rhythm by opposition. For instance, three books lying on their sides may hold a row of books in place. The three books form a right angle to the other books on the shelf.

Iriana Shiyan/Shutterstock.com

Figure 16.12 The corners of the block pattern used in this floor treatment create rhythm by opposition. The varied nature of the slate tiles gives variety and an unlimited palette of color for developing color schemes.

Image courtesy of Andersen Corporation.

Figure 16.13 These vertical and horizontal lines in this custom window design are an example of rhythm by transition. The vertical lines lead the eyes up to the top of the window while the horizontal lines in the windows lead the eyes around the room.

Curved and horizontal lines that carry the eyes from one part of an object or room to another part create rhythm by **transition**. See Figure 16.13. Transition leads the eyes in, through, and over an object until they have seen the whole object. You can find curved and horizontal lines in architectural features and in furnishings. An arched window will lead your eyes from one side to the other. A drapery swag will draw your attention from one part of the drapery to another. Repeated lines and patterns in stained glass also transition your attention from one part of the room to another.

Review & Assessment

1. Contrast proportion and scale.
2. Which is more pleasing, a sofa with an adjacent coffee table in a 1:2 ratio or in a 2:3 ratio? Why?
3. Large-scale furnishings need ______-scale accessories.
4. How does human scale influence design?
5. Contrast formal balance and informal balance. Sketch an example of each.
6. How can a designer use emphasis to create a focal point? Give an example.
7. What are the five kinds of rhythm?

Goals of Design

As you work with the elements and principles of design, you need to keep in mind the goals of design. The goals of design are function and appropriateness, harmony with unity and variety, and beauty. These goals help make sure that your design works together as a whole. Also consider the use, convenience, and satisfaction of the household as you work to achieve the goals of design that meet individual and family wants and needs.

Function and Appropriateness

Function and appropriateness are closely related. If furnishings serve their various functions (or purposes), they are appropriate and suitable. The people who live in a dwelling determine the functions of rooms and furnishings within the rooms. When furnishings provide service, comfort, and pleasure

Career Focus Interior Designer—Restaurants

Do you enjoy eating out in a comfortable, pleasing, relaxed atmosphere? If you do, creating designs for restaurant and other commercial hospitality interiors may be for you!

Interests/Skills: Do your interests include enjoying working on artistic and creative projects? Are you interested in food preparation, cooking, and food presentation? When you enter a restaurant for the first time, do you study the décor? Along with effective communication and presentation skills, interior designers for restaurants and other hospitality facilities need a strong understanding of how restaurants operate to make logical design decisions. For example, understanding the flow of food from kitchen to a customer's table helps in circulation design. As a designer, you have to work well with your client and their ideas. Effective marketing and research skills are especially important for designers of these facilities.

Career Snapshot: To offer relaxing vacation opportunities for families and individuals, hospitality interior designers create pleasing spaces for restaurants, resorts, hotels, cruise ships, and airplanes. Their designs enhance local community and urban plans. More and more people depend on having good meals away from home. Restaurant dining has become a way to relax and unwind. Because the food industry has a lot of interest and money, it is important for industry to develop trends that impact customers. This includes interior designs that appeal to potential and current clients. A unique design can help set the tone for a restaurant or other hospitality facility. It can achieve a certain mood. Well-planned interiors contribute to the success and the profits of any establishment.

Education/Training: Completion of a bachelor's or master's degree is preferred. Classes include

ariadna de raadt/Shutterstock.com

business management, lighting, computer technology, color theory, textiles, and CADD. Additional courses in culinary arts and psychology would make the designer more competitive in the job market.

Licensing/Examinations: Approximately one half of the states require interior designers to be licensed. The National Council for Interior Design Qualification (NCIDQ) administers an examination that interior designers must pass in order to obtain a license and to be competitive in their career.

Professional Associations: The American Society of Interior Designers (ASID); the International Interior Design Association (IIDA)

Job Outlook: Jobs are expected to grow at a rate of four percent through 2024. The job outlook for designers who specialize in such areas as healthcare, hospitality, and commercial or corporate design is projected to increase eight percent through 2024.

Sources: The Occupational Outlook Handbook (OOH); the Occupational Information Network (O*NET)

with minimum care, they are functional and appropriate. There are three guidelines to follow when thinking about function and appropriateness in the home.

- Furnishings should be appropriate for the function of the dwelling. For example, formal dining room furniture is not appropriate for a vacation cabin.
- Furnishings should be appropriate for each room. For instance, a living room is not an appropriate place for a refrigerator.
- The form of furnishings should be appropriate for their function. Their designs should adapt to the structure of the human body. Their arrangements should meet the needs to reach, stand, sit, and move within a room.

Above all, a home should be appropriate and functional for all members of the household. It should fit the personalities, lifestyles, needs, and wants of those who live there.

Harmony with Unity and Variety

Harmony is an agreement among the parts. Using the elements of design effectively according to the principles of design creates harmony. A designer uses one idea and carries it throughout the design.

Think about harmony in design as it compares to the beautiful sounds of an orchestra in concert. The instruments or "elements" are in tune, so the resulting sound is harmonious. The total effect is more important than any of the parts.

Harmony results when there is unity among the elements. **Unity** occurs when all parts of a design relate to one design idea. When unity is present in a design, you see the room as a whole—not as separate pieces (Figure 16.14). By repeating

ShortPhotos/Shutterstock.com

Figure 16.14 When the elements and principles of design are used effectively, a harmonious room such as this is created.

similar elements of design, you can achieve unity. For example, the furnishings and accessories in a room may all be square or rectangular. This ties the room together.

It would be monotonous, however, for the room to have only square and rectangular furnishings and accessories. Adding a few circular or triangular accessories creates variety. Unity with some variety makes a design more interesting. Without variety, the limitations on the elements and principles of design can result in an uninteresting, lifeless room.

While an area or room needs some variety, too much variety can cause confusion. Variation is like seasoning in food. The right amount of seasoning makes food tasty. Too little or too much may make it unacceptable. Consequently, the goal of good design is unity with some variation.

When working to achieve harmony, let only one type of each element of design dominate. For example, one color should dominate. This color can be the base color of your color harmony. Smaller amounts of a coordinating color can be used as an accent. This will assure harmony and unity with variety in the design. The overall appearance of a room will be pleasing. If you use several colors in equal amounts in a room, the room may be a confusing combination of parts.

Planning a Harmonious Color Scheme

When planning a color scheme, there are several steps to creating an integrated and coordinated look among the rooms. These steps include the following:

Step 1: Select two or three colors that will convey the mood or "feel" you want in the space. Each of these colors will serve different purposes in different rooms; however, just one color at a time is usually dominant in a particular space. The other colors you choose may have vivid impact and strong contrast, or they may blend softly with slight contrast.

Step 2: Add a neutral tone. The neutral tone allows for separation of the major colors, making them more powerful and noticeable. This enhances the visual depth and dimension of the space. The neutral color should relate to the major colors and therefore add to their harmony. Neutrals add unity when appearing consistently on similar surfaces, such as wood moldings, doors, and ceilings. As you learned in Chapter 15, neutral tones are combinations of black, gray, and white. You can also use brown, tan, and beige.

Step 3: Add an additional color in a very controlled way. This additional color will give a "punch" to specific areas and create variety. Successful punches of contrasting color help to make a space memorable. The word "punch" describes an eye-catching color. It gets your attention right away—and it may be the first thing you notice in a room. A strong contrast catches your eyes. Punch occurs by color, through shape, and by using other design elements.

In order to use a coordinated color scheme effectively, it is important to plan the application of color for each room or space. As the colors trade places and emphasis in each room, they create different personalities for each space.

The following two photograph examples involve a living room with the adjacent dining room and den. The color scheme consists of three colors with strong contrast. The designer chose them to convey a "spring garden" effect: yellow, red, and green. Neutral ivory is the neutral tone. A strong, clear blue gives the punch. This is how the color scheme works in these rooms.

In the formal "dressy" living room, Figure 16.15 A, you can easily identify yellow as the dominant color covering the sofa and tall walls. This provides a soft, sunny backdrop for the stronger garden colors. Neutral ivory predominates in the rug, and its lightness relates the floor to the walls. The rich supporting reds and greens of the chairs rest comfortably against the light, sunny background. The play of the same colors in the sofa pillows, candles, and floral arrangement on the coffee table strengthens the harmony. Note that the reddish-brown finish of the wood furniture is a purposeful choice, adding to the overall coordination of the room. Finally, the designer adds the "punch" with limited dashes of a strong, clear blue.

In the den, Figure 16.15 B, the yellow walls and neutral floor again combine to create a unified backdrop of dominant color. A collage of pictures and plates in light and dark neutrals offers interesting contrast and a definable pattern to the

A Photos Courtesy of Madge Megliola, ASID

B Photos Courtesy of Madge Megliola, ASID

Figure 16.15 Effectively choosing a color scheme helps create interest with unity and variety in a design. (A) Note the major colors in this formal living room are yellow, red, and green. The blue sofa pillows and rug motif add variety. (B) The major colors in this den are yellow, red, and green. They bring unity and coordinate with the colors in Figure A. Note the colors in the den are not as strong and create a softer, more relaxed feel.

tall walls. The softer reds and greens and plentiful neutrals of the large, sectional sofa allow the busy upholstery pattern to exist with the wall collage. The energetic color and pattern of this side of the room is in balance with the simplified blocks of color on the opposing wall. Note the large, neutral club chairs stand out against a solid cherry wall and mantle with a deep-green marble fireplace surround. Airy greenery, strategically placed throughout the room, accents and lightens the look of the heavy walls and furniture, contributing to an inviting, relaxing look.

Beauty

In addition to being a characteristic of design, beauty is also a goal of design. Each person has a unique concept of beauty. The word beauty, however, generally describes well-designed and aesthetically pleasing objects.

The development of elements and principles of design is the result of studying objects that most people consider beautiful. If the arrangement of the elements of design follows the principles of design, the result will appear beautiful to most people. The separate elements enhance one another and heighten the overall effect of beauty. Beauty gives a house, its furnishings, and its surroundings a distinction. Although beauty is not the only goal in planning and furnishing a home, it is what makes the visual appearance memorable.

Review & Assessment

1. How are the design goals of function and appropriateness related?
2. What are three guidelines to follow to make sure that a design is functional and appropriate?
3. How do unity and variety impact harmony?
4. Identify three steps to use when planning a color scheme for a room.
5. What is the relationship between beauty and the elements and principles of design?

Sensory Design

Good design responds to all sensory needs and serves people of all ages, sizes, and physical capabilities. Design that considers the senses enriches the total environment. **Sensory design** is the application of design that affects the senses of sight, hearing, smell, and touch. It helps make housing more accessible and functional for people with limitations as well as those without limitations.

Most types of design affect the sense of sight. People can tell if they like a design by how it looks. With housing design, however, the other senses need consideration, too. Using specific materials in construction and design can control the noise levels in a room. For instance, hard and smooth

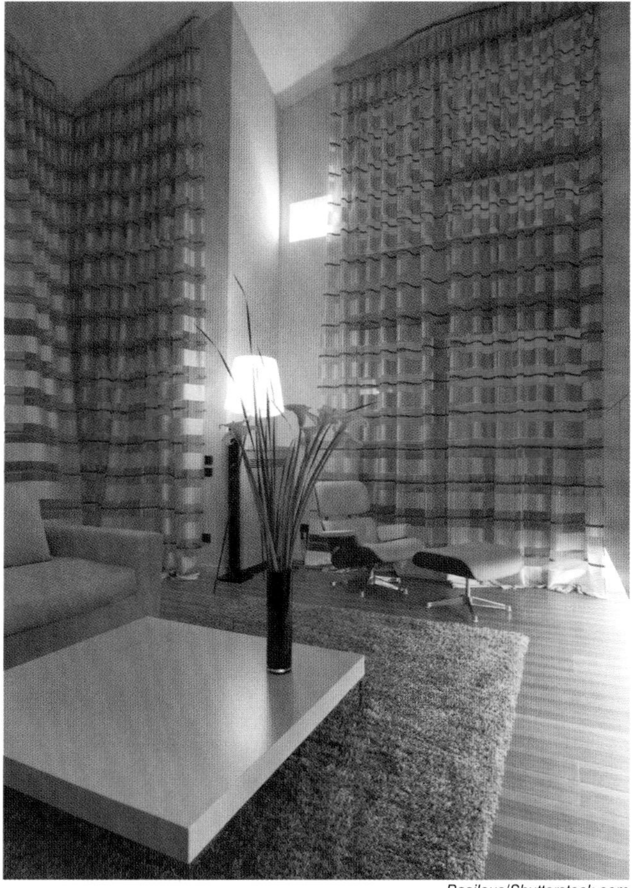

Basileus/Shutterstock.com

Figure 16.16 Modern interiors can have extensive acoustic issues and can feel sterile because of the sleek, flat surfaces. The designer of this living room introduced a rug, curtains and even plants to give a more comfortable feel and to absorb sound.

Juriah Mosin/Shutterstock.com

Figure 16.17 Placing fresh flowers and fruit in these accessories enhances the sensory design of the room.

surfaces make sounds louder by reverberating or bouncing them around a space. Rough and soft surfaces absorb sound, which creates a quiet atmosphere (Figure 16.16). As you design a room, think about what kinds of sounds you want to hear in the room. Then think about the kinds of materials you need to include in your design to create this atmosphere.

The smell of a room can evoke feelings and emotions. Fresh flowers placed in a room may provide a fragrance that many associate with elegance (Figure 16.17). A lemon scent used in cleaners can create the impression of freshness. Pine reminds people of the outdoors. Candles, herbs, and spices used as accessories in design can create certain atmospheres in a room.

The sense of touch also affects your response to design. The texture of various materials used in design can communicate specific feelings. Marble is cold and hard, silk can be soft, and wood can be rough or smooth. People who are visually impaired rely on their sense of touch to direct them. For example, braille used in elevators helps them identify specific floors.

The temperature of a room also affects design. As you know, the choice of colors for a room can convey either warmth or coolness. In addition, people are sensitive to actual temperature changes, which can affect their comfort level. Heating and cooling systems help keep a room comfortable.

Review & Assessment

1. What is sensory design?
2. How does each of the following senses impact design: hearing, smell, and touch?
3. Give an example of how sensory design can benefit you.

Chapter 16 Assessment

Summary

- The design principles guide the application of the elements of design. The principles of design are proportion and scale, balance, emphasis, and rhythm.
- Proportion and scale both describe size, shape, and amount. They are also concerned with the relationships of objects and parts of objects.
- Guidelines for using proportion are the golden rectangle, the golden mean, and the golden section.
- Visual weight, an aspect of scale, is a perception that an object weighs more or less than it really does.
- Balance can be formal or informal. It is a perception that both sides of an imaginary centerline are equal.
- Balance can be attained through the arrangement of objects and the use of color, texture, and form.
- Emphasis creates a focal point in a design. The focal point gives order and direction to a setting.
- Rhythm leads the eyes from one area to another in several ways.
- The goals of design can be achieved when the elements and principles of design are used together well.
- The goals of design are function and appropriateness, harmony with unity and variety, and beauty.
- Using harmony with unity and variety helps create a color-scheme plan that coordinates the look between rooms.
- Sensory design responds to the needs of people of all ages and incorporates the senses into design.

Terms in Action

1. **Relating words** On a separate sheet of paper, list the *Content* and *Academic Terms* from the beginning of the chapter. Then, work with a partner to explain how these words are related.

Think Critically

2. **Analyze design priorities** Imagine that you have just rented a new apartment and need to design your living room, which currently is empty. Analyze your lifestyle (needs and wants), personal preferences, and budget in relation to your design priorities. What would you select for the focal point of this room? What other accessories would you include in the room to complement the focal point? Compare and contrast your use of the interior design principles in your personal design plans using industry terminology.
3. **Recognize alternatives** Suppose a client hired you to create a room design which involved purchasing several new pieces of furniture and some accessories. You worked with the client to be sure these selections fit the client's needs, wants, preferences, and budget. Within days of completing the project and a positive client walk-through, you receive a complaint call from the client regarding a new mantel clock that ticks too loudly and a new chair that has scratchy upholstery and an uncomfortable fit—both of which were special order items. Your client wants you to replace the items, claiming poor design. (Note your client signed a letter of agreement which indicates there are no returns on special orders.) What alternatives can you recognize for solving your client's problem? Your client is an influential community member whose business you greatly value.
4. **Compare and contrast** Think about the design of a space in your community that you find particularly pleasing. Compare and contrast the use of interior design principles in the design plan of the room using industry terminology. What effect do the principles of design have on the aesthetics (beauty) and function of the room?
5. **Evaluate design** Tour a model home (or furniture store with designer room displays). Obtain permission to take digital pictures of the home. Pay special attention to the interior design of the living room, dining room, and master bedroom. Compare and contrast how the principles of design are represented in the home (or room displays). List the principles and explain how they are represented. Does the home (or room displays) meet the goals of design? Give examples of how each goal is or is not met. Create a digital visual presentation to share with the class.

Chapter 16 Assessment

Core Skills

6. **Writing** Look around your school or place of employment and identify where the golden mean, golden section, and golden rectangle are used. If they are not used, make suggestions where they could be applied. Write a one-page report on your observations.
7. **Reading and writing** Research the use of golden section and golden rectangle in music and art by such noteworthy historical figures as Chopin and Leonardo da Vinci. Locate one or more examples to share with the class.
8. **Math** Investigate the relationship between the golden section, golden rectangle, and the *Fibonacci sequence* of numbers. What is the application to interior design? Write a summary of your findings.
9. **Speaking** Working with a team of classmates, assemble a variety of room accessories such as books, bookends, plants, clocks, pictures, photographs, baskets, sculptures, and vases. Choose items with varying cultural influence as well. Then do the following:
   A. Create an area in your classroom for display, such as a long desk or bookshelf. Take turns arranging the accessories in different ways to give examples of both *formal* and *informal* balance.
   B. Use a digital camera to take photos of each design. Identify how the principles of proportion, scale, balance, emphasis, and rhythm are displayed in each photo.
   C. Combine your images in a photo-essay format using presentation software. As your team presents its photos to the class, discuss what you notice about the visual weight of the accessories as you change their position in each arrangement.
10. **Research and speaking** Search the Internet for two room examples that effectively use the principles of design. Then locate two contrasting examples—those that show poor use of the principles of design. Present your examples to the class and give supporting reasons as to why the room designs effectively or ineffectively utilize the principles of design to achieve the goals of design.
11. **CTE career readiness practice** Interview a community member who has a special need or physical limitation. Determine ways that good housing design can make his or her housing more accessible, functional, and appropriate—enhancing the quality of his or her life. Write a detailed summary of your interview and outline suggestions regarding how sensory design could make his or her home more accessible and increase the enjoyment of the space.

Design Practice

12. **Design for human scale** Suppose a client has hired you to create a design for a very small living room that measures 10 ft. by 12 ft. Expanding the space is not an option because the dwelling is part of a condominium complex. Because previous furnishings have been uncomfortable, your client's greatest concern is that the furnishings "fit" his or her 5 ft. 3 in. stature. Create a floor plan for the room layout. Select photos of furnishings that meet your client's requirements. Write a proposal for your client summarizing how the proportion and scale of the furnishings fit both your client and the room.
13. **Wall design** Use a CADD software program to design a wall against which you need to place a large piece of storage furniture (as is used in a dining room or bedroom). Create five different designs, making sure to utilize each of the design principles. Print a copy of each design. Mount your designs on poster board to share with the class. Explain how each design arrangement effectively uses the principles of design.
14. **Design for harmony** Use online resources to locate three photos of living room designs that effectively use harmony with unity and variety. Analyze the photos. Use a school-approved web application to create a digital poster and summarize the items in each photo that help bring harmony with unity and variety to each design.
15. **Portfolio** Because good organizational skills are important for an interior designer, use word-processing software to create a checklist that includes the elements and principles of design and a brief explanation of each. Use your checklist as an organizational tool for further design projects.

Unit 4

The Process of Interior Design

Chapter 17 The Process of Design
Chapter 18 Design Communication

wavebreakmedia/Shutterstock.com

Using the Principles and Elements of Design

Prepare an FCCLA STAR Event *Illustrated Talk* on a topic related to using the principles and elements of design. For example, you might use the principles and elements of design to organize a presentation about a low-cost design for a child's bedroom, a teen's room, or a room for an older adult.

Use the *Illustrated Talk* guidelines found in the FCCLA *STAR Events Manual* on the Internet. See your adviser for information as needed.

Teamwork in Interior Design

In a team, use the FCCLA *Planning Process* to plan, carry out, and evaluate a project for the FCCLA *Interior Design* STAR Event. The event conditions and requirements include

- writing a family profile and creating a display board illustrating the family profile
- selecting a floor plan that meets the family's needs
- designing furniture arrangements and color schemes
- selecting materials, furnishings, and surface treatments and other items
- creating a design board which includes elevation drawings and materials samples

Use the *STAR Events Manual* on the FCCLA website to identify specific competition requirements for your project. See your adviser for information as needed.

Chapter 17

The Process of Design

Content Terms

design process
letter of agreement
retainer
Programming phase
profile
adjacency matrix
criteria matrix
Schematic Design phase
schematic drawings
memo sample
cutting for approval (CFA)
Design Development phase
bid
change order
Contract Documents phase
Contract Administration phase
outsource
liaison
punch list

Academic Terms

business culture
jurisdiction
critical path schedule

Learning Outcomes

After studying this chapter, you will be able to

- summarize the phases of the interior design process as effective practice used to evaluate residential and nonresidential interiors.
- differentiate between the contract and financial elements for developing an interior design project.
- use effective design practices to differentiate individual (client) and business needs, goals, and resources in creating design plans for residential housing and furnishings or for commercial interiors.

Reading with Purpose

Read all parts of the chapter and write three key points for each heading. Then write a summary describing how this chapter will help you apply concepts you learned in previous chapters.

While studying, look for the access icon  **to:**

- **Practice** the *Content* and *Academic Terms* with e-flash cards, matching activities, and vocabulary games.
- **Reinforce** what you learn by completing the *Review & Assessment* questions and e-mailing them to your instructor.

G-WLEARNING.COM www.g-wlearning.com/housing/

alicedaniel/Shutterstock.com

The goal of an interior designer is to help solve a client's design problem by producing a usable, safe, and attractive space. The designer may begin with an empty new room or may redesign an existing space. The designer may also collaborate with builders, architects, and other tradespeople to create a new space. To create this new space, the interior designer follows an orderly process.

As you read this chapter, imagine yourself as an interior designer who is working with a client to develop a design concept for a room or area. Think about how each aspect of the design process and your prior learning will influence the decisions you make for your client's design plan. This chapter will help you link previously learned information to the organization of the designer's tasks.

What Is the Design Process?

In order to reach a client's goals, you will use the design process. The **design process** is a series of organized phases a designer uses to carry out a project in an orderly manner (Figure 17.1). Following the design process will help assure your clients that a design plan will help meet their desired results. The design process includes the following five phases:

Phase 1. Programming—gathering information from the client and other sources to guide the actual design

Phase 2. Schematic design—designer prepares preliminary sketches and compiles drawings, samples, and furniture photos to present as ideas to the client

Phase 3. Design development—the designer prepares the final design drawings and puts together a presentation board to obtain the client's approval on the complete design

Phase 4. Contract documents—designer prepares final construction drawings and product specifications, involves appropriate professionals for the project, and possibly initiates the bidding process for the final contract

Phase 5. Contract administration—designer makes purchases for the client which involves actual construction and interior finishes, and ordering and installing furnishings and equipment

Not all design projects fit neatly into phases that have precise beginnings and endings. Indeed, the phases often overlap or occur at the same time. In addition, some designers argue that not all projects go through all steps in the phases. Regardless of the size or extent of a project, all projects involve some parts of all the phases in the design process. The remainder of this chapter provides details on how to complete phases of the design process. These phases apply to both residential and commercial projects. *Residential* refers to where people live, such as homes and apartments. *Commercial* refers to business spaces where people go for services, such as hotels, restaurants, hospitals, day care centers, and banks.

Before beginning the design process, you will often have a consultation with the client about his or her needs, goals, and resources for the project. Careful listening is extremely important. You will need to understand the client's expectations for creating an attractive, functional environment for a home or business. It is also during this meeting that the designer evaluates whether he or she has the experiences, skills, resources, time, and interest in completing the design with the potential client.

During an initial consultation, you and your client may sign a letter of agreement. The **letter of agreement** spells out the scope of project services and the responsibilities of each party. The designer's responsibilities include planning and carrying out a design plan and informing the client about fees. The client's responsibilities include providing the designer with necessary budget information, approving the design plan, and paying the designer's fees.

The letter of agreement generally requires the client to put down a **retainer**—an upfront fee the client pays to engage the services of a designer. Usually, the designer deducts the retainer from the balance due at the end of the project. After initial consultations and interviews, you will draw up an official contract that includes very specific details about the project. Doing this early, before you spend time considering and documenting project solutions, will protect you from wasting time on a project that does not develop. You will learn more about methods a designer uses to establish fees later in the chapter.

Designer Tasks During the Design Process	
The following is a brief list of tasks that typically take place within the course of a design project. Individual projects vary by scope and size, so not all of these will take place in each project and often not in this same order.	
Process Phase	**Designer Tasks**
Programming	• Meet with the client(s) to investigate the design problems to be solved as well their specific needs and wants. This may include functional goals as well as stylistic and aesthetic needs. • Analyze the project to understand the full scope of the design work and the tasks needed to complete the project. • Determine the need for additional experts such as lighting consultants, landscapers, engineers, etc. • Collect additional pertinent information through surveys, observation, and other user-specific research. • Compile all gathered information into a programming document for client approval. This may include a chart of individual space needs and typical square footages. • Assist client with selection of a space or building if one has not already been selected. • Obtain as-built drawings for an existing space from the client or consultant. Measure the space to confirm accuracy of drawings. • Perform an inventory of previously owned furniture, equipment, art, etc., and note the condition of the items. • Analyze the building use, location, construction type, etc. to determine what life safety, accessibility, or other building codes will need to be addressed. Meet with the appropriate officials regarding any conflicting or incomplete information. • Determine a preliminary schedule and budget based on the client's needs and available time and funds. Discuss any objectives or goals that are affected by these constraints. • Administrate a letter of agreement or contract with client.
Schematic Design	• Based on the goals and objectives stated in the programming document, develop a *concept statement*. • Prepare conceptual diagrams including bubble diagrams and adjacency matrices based on programming information. • Develop digitally or by hand initial space drawings to include space allocations, built elements, and basic furniture placement. Prepare additional visuals such as perspectives and elevations where appropriate. • Select initial interior finishes (and exterior, if appropriate), colors, furniture, and equipment. • Solidify selections and plan decisions through multiple communications with client, getting approval before proceeding to further phases. This may take several rounds of meetings. • Consult with appropriate experts about any building code, construction, or budgetary implications of your design. • Evaluate the preliminary budget in light of the furnishings and finishes selected and the amount of construction to occur.

(Continued)

Figure 17.1 Throughout the design process, interior designers perform many tasks. Here are just a few.

Designer Tasks During the Design Process *(Figure 17.1, continued)*	

Design Development	• Refine and complete space plans based on client feedback and approval.
	• Produce all preliminary drawings for:
	  • Demolition and new construction
	  • Architectural finishes and furnishings
	  • Electrical and lighting
	  • Custom cabinetry or furniture
	• Prepare any essential visuals such as rendered perspectives and elevations.
	• Construct tangible or digital boards as needed for client approval of:
	  • Finishes
	  • Furnishings
	  • Equipment
	  • Lighting
	  • Accessories and art
	• Make more detailed presentations to client using boards and drawings.
	• Construct a more complete budget based on refined selections and plans.
	• Obtain approvals on all the above items before proceeding to next phase.

Contract Documents	• Develop schedules for all selections made while qualifying and ensuring availability of products from manufacturers. • Complete construction drawings started in previous phase. Supplement with additional furniture, equipment, and art installation drawings, and construction method detailing as necessary. • Prepare all written and visual specifications for materials, finishes, furniture, and equipment. Ensure all correlate with information within previously developed schedules and drawings. • If part of scope, assist client in the preparation of all documents needed for and the acquisition of contractor bids and building permits.
Contract Administration	• Based on bids received, help client select contractors. • Work with client and contractors to maintain close adherence of project to budget and schedule. • Oversee the entire construction, installation and (if appropriate) building inspection processes. Ensure that the work adheres to the prepared plans, schedules, and specifications through frequent visits to the site. • Purchase (or assist the client in the purchase of) all furniture, furnishings and accessories for the space. This may involve a separate bid process from furniture vendors. • Manage move-in and oversee all furniture and equipment installations. • Performs *punch-list* activities and ensures contractors address issues. • Administer or assist with all project closeout measures including vendor and contractor payments, certification for occupancy by the building codes office, and any post-occupancy evaluations.

Review & Assessment

1. Summarize the five phases of the design process.
2. What is the difference between residential and commercial design?
3. Describe a letter of agreement.
4. What is a retainer and why is it important?

Phase 1: Programming

The main purposes of the **Programming phase** include identifying client objectives and requirements, gathering information from the client such as a review of existing spaces and inventories of existing furnishings, developing a client contract and overall budget, and preparing a broad concept statement to guide the actual design. You will need to understand what the client wants in as much detail as possible. This usually requires meeting with the client to acquire this information; however, some designers have the client complete a questionnaire (Figure 17.2). Either way, you need to ask very specific questions and discuss options that will help meet your client's unique needs and wants. With commercial clients, it is important to do a little research about that particular industry prior to the meeting. This gives you a better understanding of how the business space must function.

Monkey Business Images/Shutterstock.com

Figure 17.2 Meeting with your clients to acquire information about their design project is an essential part of the design process.

Gathering Client Information

During this part of the process, you will gather information about everyone who may use a space. This may include reviewing quantitative and qualitative information. In planning the interior space of a house, this includes the number of family members, guests, and friends. Do any occupants have special needs the space must fulfill? For example, do older adults or anyone with a disability live in the home? How much privacy does each person require? You will generally create a profile for each occupant of the home along with profiles of guests and friends. A **profile** is a concise biographical sketch (or word picture) that portrays the key characteristics about the client. A residential client profile will include details about lifestyle, space functions, household activity needs, design style preferences, and future needs.

A commercial client profile includes details about ***business culture*** (a company's beliefs and actions that indicate how employees and management deal with clients and customers and with each other) as well as space functions and design style preferences. Other business requirements a designer must consider include

- **Location of offices.** The designer needs to know the location of work spaces and how close they must to be to one another. For example, the designer must know whether a manager's administrative assistant is close to the manager or is located in a pool of assistants in a central location. Work flow and the needs of various departments also impact the arrangement of offices and their closeness.
- **Accessibility of services.** For example, does the client prefer services such as printing and photocopying in a central location or in other strategic areas of the office?
- **Employee hierarchy.** Hierarchy within an office often determines the location of offices. For example, a top manager's office may be located the farthest from the entry while the receptionist is within a few feet of the entry.

An adjacency matrix and a criteria matrix are tools to assist the designer in locating the rooms and space according to client needs. An **adjacency matrix** shows the desired relationship of room and space locations (Figure 17.3). A **criteria matrix** looks at the impact of specific needs on various spaces. These specific needs include the need to control noise or provide visual privacy.

The details you require depend on the size and complexity of the project. Factors to consider when gathering client information also include codes that

Adjacency Matrix							
Location of Spaces in Apartment	Bathroom	Bedroom	Balcony	Living Room	Kitchen	Toilet	Entry Hall
Entry Hall	3	3	3	1	1	1	
Toilet	3	3	3	2	2		
Kitchen	3	3	2	1			
Living Room	3	2	1				
Balcony	3	1					
Bedroom	1						
Bathroom							

A

Jennifer Blanchard Belk, IIDA, LEED AP

1 = Close adjacency
2 = Moderate adjacency
3 = Remote adjacency or not applicable

Criteria Matrix			
Factors within Space	Natural Light	Sound/Insulation	Ventilation Control
Entry Hall	3	2	3
Toilet	3	1	1
Kitchen	2	3	1
Living Room	1	2	3
Balcony	3	3	3
Bedroom	1	1	3
Bathroom	3	1	1

B

Jennifer Blanchard Belk, IIDA, LEED AP

1 = Important
2 = Minor importance
3 = Not desirable or not applicable

Figure 17.3 An adjacency matrix (A) helps an interior designer show the desired relationships between room locations and space to meet client needs. A criteria matrix (B) establishes the importance of particular aspects of the environment such as the presence of natural light.

might affect the space design. These codes include construction, fire safety, general safety, mechanical, plumbing, and accessibility codes.

Lifestyle and Function

The client's lifestyle includes all the various activities that occur in the home or space. As an interior designer, you must identify how the client thinks about *home*. Is home a place of rest and rejuvenation? Is it a place of constant activity? Is it a social place where many people gather for formal or informal meals, games, music, or media activities? How much space do household members need for privacy and interaction? For example, you will need to know if your clients use the bedrooms for more activities than sleeping, such as studying or watching television. What family history or cultural factors may influence the design? All this and more will help you create the best possible design concept for your client.

Space Requirements

When designing a functional and pleasing space, you must know how much space to allow for each of the activities and functions that occur in the home. Traffic patterns and standard dimensions of furnishings are important parts to solving the design puzzle. Storage needs to be adequate for all of the client's belongings. Taking inventories of household equipment, sports equipment, furnishings, clothing, musical instruments, and other items for all occupants of the dwelling is important for allocating storage space. In addition, many homes today are sites of cottage industries and home offices that require more storage.

Design Preferences

Good communication is key to assessing your client's design preferences. Whether you are designing one room or a whole house, learning the likes and dislikes of each occupant helps to develop a design concept pleasing to all. In addition, visiting the client's home will give you great insight into the client's style needs, wants, preferences, cultural factors, and tastes. What might you learn by viewing a client's living space? The following factors provide clues for a successful design plan:

- What types of things surround a client's living space? Is the space uncluttered and does it have clean surfaces?

- How does the space make the client feel? Is it energizing or restful? close and cozy, or spacious and private?
- What color-scheme preferences does the client have? What backgrounds, lighting, and accessories bring comfort to the client?
- What new or existing furniture will the client want to use?
- What cultural artifacts and psychological elements seem to influence the client's taste?
- Is the client's style traditional or contemporary? Does your client prefer a vintage style?

Future Needs

Although clients generally have very specific ideas for their spaces today, the needs and goals for a home or office often change over the years. For example, when developing a design plan for a young family, a key goal may include accommodating play space for the whole family. How might this goal change as the family grows and children leave home?

Assessing the Environment

As you directly observe a client's living space, you will assess a number of environmental factors about the space. Noting even the smallest details will help you effectively meet the design needs, goals, and solutions for your client. The details to notice include the following:

- **Location of functional areas.** Where are the private, social, and work areas located? How do these areas relate to each other? How much space does the client allocate to each functional area? See Figure 17.4.
- **Number and arrangement of rooms.** Whether your client wants to develop a new design plan for a single room or for the whole house, it is important to know the number of rooms and their arrangement in the space. For example, design plans for one room can impact another adjacent room.
- **Storage.** Does every bedroom have adequate closet space? Where are other storage areas located throughout the dwelling? Is there adequate space for bed and bath linens? Does kitchen storage adequately meet client needs? Does your client require special storage, perhaps for sports equipment or musical instruments?
- **Background surfaces.** What ceiling, wall, and flooring backgrounds are in your client's current space? Does your client prefer paint or wall coverings, hardwood floors or carpeting, and drapery or non-drapery window treatments?

TZIDO SUN/Shutterstock.com

Figure 17.4 The well-defined relationships among the food preparation, dining, and living areas takes into consideration the client's needs for multiple activities in a space.

- **Furnishings.** What style does your client prefer in furnishings? Is the current style traditional or eclectic? Does your client prefer furniture designs from previous eras, such as the Victorian or Craftsman periods? Perhaps your client prefers contemporary furnishings with a futuristic edge. What items will help address functional and aesthetic needs?
- **Energy and environmental needs.** What energy needs and environmental factors does your client want to meet? Is replacement of windows with insulated windows and low-E glass on the agenda? Is an upgrade to a high-efficiency ENERGY STAR model for the heating and cooling system in order? Perhaps your client wants to install an active solar system or insulated window treatments.
- **Traffic patterns.** How do household members move through the house? Are there features that interfere with good traffic flow? What traffic flow needs does the client want to accomplish? How does traffic flow impact furniture arrangement?
- **Health and safety.** Creating a design that meets all codes and health and safety factors is essential.

Establishing a Preliminary Project Budget

Once you take all of the measurements required for the design concept, you will need to make many financial decisions. These include establishing fees and developing a project budget, and proposing

kristian sekulic/Shutterstock.com

Figure 17.5 Designer fees will need to be part of the total budget for a project.

strategies for controlling costs throughout the project. Many factors enter into establishing a preliminary project budget. The costs for products, furnishings, labor, and services vary for every project. You will need to consider whether there is a need for other consultants such as those who, for example, specialize in planning licensed child care facilities. In addition, the costs involved for other professionals, such as architects, carpenters, and electricians also affect the total project budget. The first step in planning a project budget is establishing designer fees and a payment schedule (Figure 17.5).

Designer Fees and Payment Schedule

Interior designers are unique in their talents, skills, knowledge, experience, personalities, specialty areas, and reputations. Likewise, fees and payment schedules also differ from one designer to the next. As a result, there is no usual fee for interior design services. The designer's experience and the project complexity usually influence fees and payment arrangements. Although some interior designers may negotiate their fees to suit a client's needs, most use one of the following methods, or combination of methods, to set their fees:

- **Fixed (or flat) fee.** With this fee method, you identify a specific sum to cover costs. One total fee applies to the complete range of services, from conceptual development through layouts, specifications, purchases, and final installation. This requires knowing in advance every cost, the time involvement for services, and the appropriate profit margin for the complete project.
- **Hourly fee.** For this form of compensation, you base the fee on the actual time you spend on a project or specific service. Hourly fees for interior designers can range from $60.00 to $200.00 per hour or more depending on the designer's experience and the project complexity. Note that this is the client cost, not the hourly pay of a design-firm employee, which is about one-third the hourly rate.
- **Cost plus.** With this fee method, you purchase materials, furnishings, and services (such as carpentry, drapery workroom time, picture framing, and more) at cost. Then you sell these items to the client at cost plus a specific percentage agreed to with the client to compensate for your time and effort.
- **Retail.** The retail method relates to the cost plus method because the client purchases products from the designer. In this method, the client pays the manufacturer's recommended price for the item as sold in stores or by the interior designer. You as the designer will keep the actual markup profit on the items, which can be 100 percent, while ordering items at the lower professional rate.
- **Per square foot.** For larger commercial projects, you may calculate costs on a per square foot basis, based on the area of the project.

The Preliminary Budget

Before beginning to develop a client's design concept, you must have a basic idea about what the client wants to spend and accomplish in the project. In addition to the designer's fees, there are other costs to consider when developing a preliminary project budget. The preliminary budget includes the amount of money the client allocates to spend on the design project. Developing a preliminary project budget that satisfies both the client and designer is a major factor in the designer/client relationship (Figure 17.6). The more complex the project is, the later in the project phases the designer will develop a preliminary budget due to the multitude of space planning and construction decisions the designer and client must make.

When beginning a project with a client, it is important to understand the different ways clients approach setting a project budget. Clients may do the following:

- Ask you to make a budget estimate for completing the specific design concept. Such clients may react to your budget by accepting it fully or by asking you to adjust it to a lower or higher figure.
- Tell you the amount of money they are able to spend on the design project at the first meeting. The clients ask you to develop a concept within this budget.

Determining Budget Allocations	
Mary's client has an overall budget of $50,000. The couple would like to redesign their kitchen as well as replace the carpet in the downstairs of their home (approximately 900 square feet or 100 square yards). Mary can use her past experience to estimate how much of the budget can be allocated toward the kitchen renovation because she recently re-carpeted another similar home for approximately $30.00 per square yard. After estimating for the carpet, her design fees, and a contingency (an amount set aside for unexpected expenses or delays), she can give her client a better idea of the remaining funds available for the kitchen renovation. Review the following allocations.	
Available Total Budget Amount	$50,000.00
• Carpeting (materials plus installation)	–$3,000.00
• Interior design services (fees; approximately 15% of total budget)	–$7,500.00
• Contingency (approximately 10% of total budget)	–$5,000.00
• Kitchen renovation (total budget available)	$34,500.00

Jennifer Blanchard Belk, IIDA, LEED AP

Figure 17.6 Initial budget discussions focus on the basic distribution of a client's funds.

- Work with you as funds become available. Clients may spread the work over a period of time or perhaps approach the design project one room or area at a time.
- Set no predetermined budget figure. The client simply wants you to work without any limitations. A designer may have this type of job once in a lifetime.

When setting a project budget, there are three key areas on which you and a client must agree. These areas include the following budget allocations (Figure 17.7):

- direct costs, such as furnishings, product manufacturing or fabrication, installation, construction, materials and finishes, and delivery services, as well as unusual travel costs the client or project may require of the designer
- indirect costs, such as sales taxes and contractor/delivery delays
- interior designer compensation

If you realize that the available budget will not accomplish the client's design project goals, you have several options. Revise the design to fit within the client's budget, if possible. You can also advise the client to increase the budget to accomplish what he or she wants. If you cannot reach a compromise on the budget and the quality that you must deliver,

Preliminary Budget Sample—Kitchen Wall Finishes

Item	Quantity	Color/Style	Estimated Cost	Notes
Wall Paint	2 gal.	Taupe, flat latex	$72.00	Painter supplies paint
Ceiling Paint **Trim Paint**	1 gal. + 2 qt. 1 gal. + 2 qt.	Ceiling white, flat latex Ivory, semi-gloss oil-based	$33.00 $65.00	Painter supplies paint
Painter, Labor (hourly rate)	36 hours		$1,800.00 (@ $50.00 per hour)	
Designer Fee (hourly rate)	8 hours		$480.00 (@ $60.00 per hour)	Paint/color selection, client consultation; oversee project

Figure 17.7 A preliminary budget provides the client with a breakdown of costs for an interior design project.

then you should tactfully remove yourself from the project. It is important that both the designer and client are clear on their expectations of each other.

Recording Project Needs

Once you have all necessary project details from your client, it is important to put this information in writing and create the client project file. Begin with a general statement about the design concept. Then you can put much of the program research you acquire into an organized chart. For example, you will want to note how many people will use the space along with their names and ages. You will also want to note the functions of all areas. Identify room relationships along with needs relating to the environment, mechanical systems (heating, cooling, electrical), and the cultural and psychological factors that influence the comfort of the space. It is important to have the clients sign off on the program plan to indicate their agreement with the collection of information prior to proceeding with the project.

Review & Assessment

1. Define the Programming phase of interior design.
2. Contrast the information a designer gathers for a residential profile with a commercial client profile.
3. How does an adjacency matrix differ from a criteria matrix?
4. Summarize the details a designer should propose to effectively meet the design needs and goals of a client including strategies for controlling costs.
5. Describe the following ways interior designers establish fees for budgeting purposes: (A) fixed, (B) hourly, (C) cost plus, (D) retail, and (E) per square foot.
6. What are three key areas on which a designer and client must agree regarding the project budget?

Phase 2: Schematic Design

During the **Schematic Design phase**, the designer creates diagrams (matrices and bubble/stacking/block diagrams) to develop solutions, create conceptual space plans, and select initial furniture and finishes. Designers may produce a number of **schematic drawings**—or quick, freehand sketches and drawings to show space arrangements for the project. They also produce various sketches and other documents for client review and approval. Be sure to keep a physical or digital file folder for each room or area that you will be designing. Compile drawings, samples, and photographs of furniture and accessories in these separate folders for each area. Place an itemized list of all items for a room or area in each folder. Organizing the design details in this manner will be very helpful when it comes to developing the preliminary project budget.

Developing Space Arrangements

During this phase, you will create a visual idea of what the project will look like. Begin with using your imagination and brainstorming many ideas. The illustrations can be in two or three dimensions. Two dimensions show only the width and length. Three dimensions show the width, length, and height or depth. Here are some types of drawings you are likely to produce during the schematic phase.

- **Bubble diagrams.** Bubble diagrams are simple, loosely connected circles or bubbles that show the relationships of the various zones (private, work, and social) in residential designs. In commercial designs, these diagrams may show the proximities of offices or services.
- **Rough sketches and floor plans.** After discussing possible ways to arrange the zones, you will create two-dimensional rough sketches and floor plans showing how the space will look. These sketches will show wall locations with fixture and furniture arrangement possibilities.
- **Thumbnail perspectives.** These small, three-dimensional drawings will show exactly how the drawing looks (Figure 17.8). Many designers use one-point and two-point perspective drawings.

Once you have the rough sketches and floor plans, you need to plan how to arrange furniture before you actually select it. As you recall from Chapter 7, space planning involves placing furnishings for a well-functioning and visually pleasing area. If working with new construction, you and your client may collaborate with an architect or contractor to determine dimensions. If working with an existing space, you will need to accurately measure it. Area measurements let you know how much space is available in the room, an important factor to consider in how much furniture can be added. After taking measurements, several design tools can help you develop a space plan for a functional and attractive furniture arrangement (Figure 17.9). The designer may also take measurements during the Programming phase if the designer is considering billing the client by the square foot.

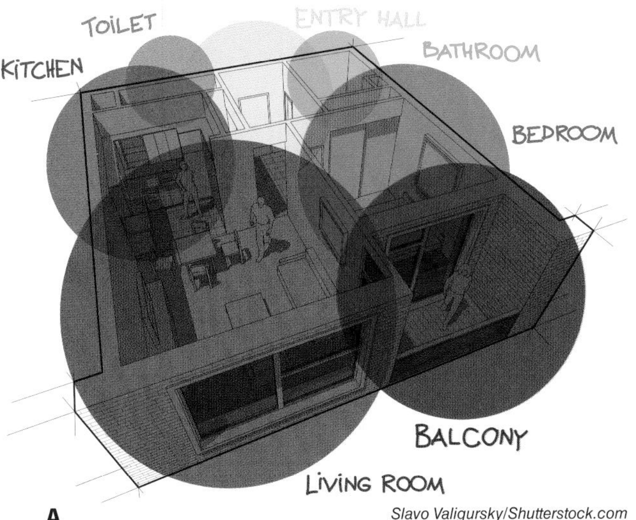

A Slavo Valigursky/Shutterstock.com

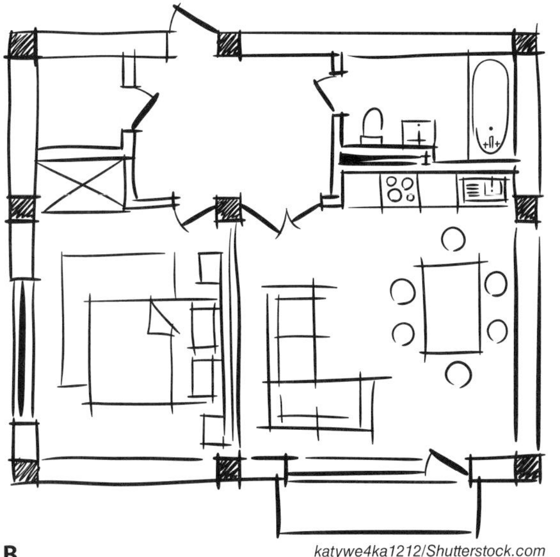

B katywe4ka1212/Shutterstock.com

C Iriana Rogova/Shutterstock.com

Figure 17.8 During the Schematic phase, designers consider adjacencies and other criteria when creating bubble diagrams (A), rough sketch floor plans (B), and thumbnail perspectives (C).

Measurements for a Scale Floor Plan

Before developing your scale floor plan, measure the length and width of each room. Then measure and note the location of all the existing room features, such as doors, windows, columns, electrical outlets, heating and cooling vents, and air intakes. In addition, measure any alcoves or other permanent features, such as fireplaces, closets, cabinets, or built-in furniture pieces, too. All measurements should include the floor placement of the features as well as their wall height. Note whether the room or area involves an open or closed floor plan because this can also impact furniture arrangement. Use the standard scale of ¼ *inch equals 1 foot* (¼" = 1'-0").

Arranging Furniture

To help create furniture arrangements for residential or commercial projects, refer back to your client profile and all of the information about how the client uses the space. How will your client use the furniture? What space does it need? How will room features and traffic flow impact furniture placement? In addition, keep in mind the elements and principles of design discussed in Chapters 14, 15, and 16.

Furniture and Room Use

Furniture use greatly impacts its arrangement. Every furniture piece has specific uses and requires a certain amount of space. Furniture arrangement also depends on room use. Before arranging furniture in a room, consider the activities that will take place there and the amount of space available. Then determine where within the room each activity will focus.

Maintain a list of furniture needs for each activity area, and determine the amount of space the furniture will occupy. For instance, if a room requires a conversation area, group chairs, sofas, tables, and lamps in a full or partial circle. In the grouping, arrange lamps and other accessories conveniently in relation to their use. Give attention to the availability of electric outlets in planning the lamp placement. In some cases, electrical outlets may need to be added to accommodate good lighting design.

Room Features

Be sure to plan furniture arrangements around special architectural features. For example, furniture should not block a built-in entertainment center or a fireplace. A scale floor plan allows you to see the placement of the features.

Interior Designer's Tool Kit

Interior designers use the following tools to develop their designs:

- Computer
- Design software
- Printer
- Graphing paper (thin like tracing paper, marked off in squares, erases easily)
- Tracing paper
- Mechanical pencil and pencil lead
- Eraser
- Scale ruler
- Adjustable triangle
- Circle template
- T-square (or drafting board with a parallel bar)
- Retractable metal tape measure
- Flexible plastic tape measure
- Watercolor paint, colored pencils, or watercolor markers for renderings
- Designer color wheel/paint-fan decks
- Resource file with photos or samples of fabrics, wall treatments and coverings, floor coverings, cabinetry, hardware, furniture, wood finishes, fixtures, appliances and electronics, lighting, and accessories

Figure 17.9 These specialized tools help an interior designer create quality designs throughout the phases of the design process.

If you have trouble visualizing furniture location in relation to the features, add wall elevations to your plan and indicate the features. When using CADD, you can view interior wall elevations. By using CADD, you can also create a three-dimensional view of the furniture placement (Figure 17.10).

Urostom/Shutterstock.com

Figure 17.10 Because of the speed and accuracy of CADD software, many interior designers use such software to create their designs.

Traffic Patterns

When arranging furniture, plan traffic patterns to include space for people to move about freely. People should be able to easily circulate throughout an entire area. Maintaining proper clearance space around each piece of furniture is essential. When placing furniture in high-traffic areas, you may want to increase the amount of clearance space. Keep function and safety in mind to avoid creating obstacles within traffic patterns.

Choosing a Color Scheme

Once you know the dimensions of the space, furnishing requirements, and your client's preferences, it is time to choose a style and a color scheme for the project. As you learned in Chapter 15, using color effectively is an important part of any design plan. Begin with the preferences noted in your client profile. Does your client prefer warm or cool colors? Does your client want the space to be calm and relaxing or vibrant and exciting? Will the client's preferred design style (such as Victorian, Craftsman, or Contemporary) influence the color scheme? With the color wheel as your guide, consider selecting several color-scheme options from which your client can choose. Colors should coordinate with existing finishes elsewhere in the home or space.

Selecting Finishes, Furniture, Lighting, and Accessories

Once you and your client agree on a style and color scheme, you can begin selecting background finishes, furniture, lighting, and accessories. Consider the following factors when making your choices:

- **Background finishes.** Background treatments for floors, walls, and windows set the stage for all other details of your design. Depending on your design plan, you may be selecting paint or wall covering, carpeting or resilient flooring, and blinds or curtains and draperies. Your client may want to see a **memo sample** of wall covering—a sample that is large enough to show an entire pattern repeat. In addition, your client may want to see a small sample of the actual dye lot—a **cutting for approval (CFA)**—to confirm the actual color.
- **Furniture.** Design style, usage, color, and fabric types will influence furniture selections. Your client may choose to order all new furniture, or may keep one piece and have you select options that complement it.
- **Lighting.** Lighting provides visual comfort, safety, and beauty in a room. How will lighting options fulfill functional needs for reading, crafts, or watching movies? How will lighting enhance decorative pieces or fine art?
- **Accessories.** Remember to consider the useful and decorative aspects of accessories. How will the accessories reflect client personality and culture? How will the accessories help tie together the design plan?

Review & Assessment

1. What are schematic drawings?
2. Name three types of drawings an interior designer might use during the Schematic Design phase.
3. What measurements does a designer need to take before developing a scale floor plan?
4. What factors influence a designer's choice in color scheme for a design plan?
5. Summarize the factors a designer should consider when selecting finishes, furniture, lighting, and accessories.

Phase 3: Design Development

In the **Design Development phase**, the designer creates, develops, and refines drawings and specifications based on observation, imagination, and experiences, and effectively using interior design tools and media for drawing, painting, and printmaking. He or she also makes final decisions, evaluates the budget, and communicates solutions to the client. As part of this phase, the designer produces final drawings and details on color schemes and other selections for final client approval (Figure 17.11). Whether you create hand drawings or use CADD software, your final drawings will include

- floor plans
- elevations
- renderings

For larger projects and for ground-up construction, many designers will create either physical 3-D models or will utilize various CADD programs to develop digital models and walk-throughs (Figure 17.12).

In addition, specifications for all the work are included (presented by way of a presentation board) along with details for custom design work. The designer confirms that preliminary space plans and design concepts are safe, functional, and are aesthetically appropriate. They should also meet all public health and safety requirements. This includes code, accessibility, environmental, and sustainability guidelines.

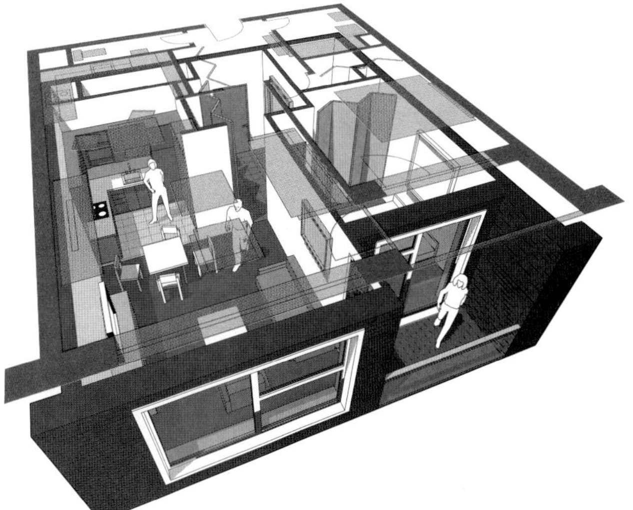

Slavo Valigursky/Shutterstock.com

Figure 17.11 During Design Development, designers finalize previous schematic floor plans for use in attaining client approval.

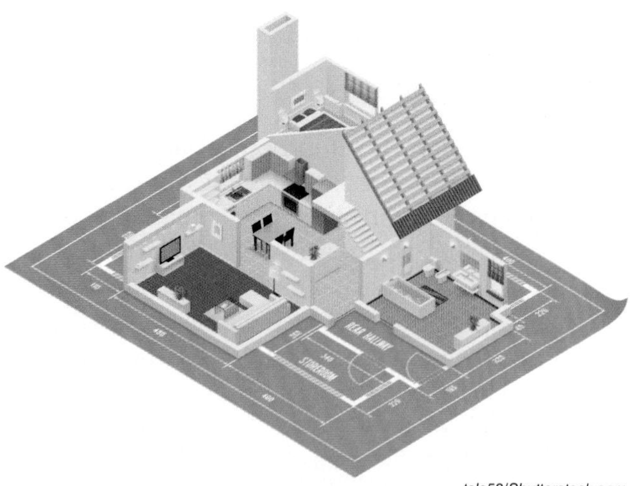

tele52/Shutterstock.com

Figure 17.12 With CADD, you can also create three-dimensional views of a design. This illustration shows a three-dimensional model projected from a two-dimensional floor plan.

Finalizing the Project Budget

After selecting all products, finishes, furnishings, lighting, and accessories, you will need to finalize the project budget (Figure 17.13). Some parts of the preliminary budget may require adjustments due to changes in materials costs or labor.

Estimating Costs

Estimating material and labor costs may be one of the most challenging factors in determining fees for your client. It is essential to provide clients with itemized details of all costs for materials and labor charges. Regardless of the method you use for setting fees, you will need to include overhead costs (such as business supplies and office rent and utilities) and build in profit to your budget estimation. Remember, your budget is a financial plan for coordinating available resources and expenditures, so it is essential that you are working with a complete list of needed furnishings, finishes, and equipment (Figure 17.14).

Because labor costs vary greatly in different regions of the United States, you may need to check several sources for information about these costs. Obtaining price lists from quality contractors, product suppliers, tradespeople, and drapery and upholstery workrooms will help you create accurate estimates. It is also important to determine who will pay for freight, shipping, and handling. Some factors that influence labor costs include scheduling, location and equipment needs, economics, region or city, and clean-up costs. In addition, you may find prices of labor are higher when jobs are plentiful and lower when jobs are scarce, which follows the basic economic principles of supply and

Final Budget Sample—Kitchen Wall Finishes

Item	Quantity	Color/Style	Estimated Cost	Actual Cost	Notes
Wall Paint	2 gal.	Taupe, flat latex (include manufacturer and color number for accuracy of actual cost)	$72.00	$77.04	Sales tax
Ceiling Paint	1 gal. + 2 qt.	Ceiling white, flat latex	$33.00	$35.31	Sales tax
Trim Paint	1 gal. + 2 qt.	Ivory, semi-gloss oil-based	$65.00	$69.55	Sales tax
Painter, Labor (hourly rate)	36 hours		$1,800.00 (@ $50.00 per hour)	$1,926.00	2.5 hours additional labor
Designer Fee (hourly rate)	8 hours		$480.00 (@ $60.00 per hour)	$480.00 (@ $60.00 per hour)	Paint/color selection, client consultation; oversee project

Figure 17.13 Finalizing the preliminary budget may require adjustments to some costs because of changes in material or labor costs.

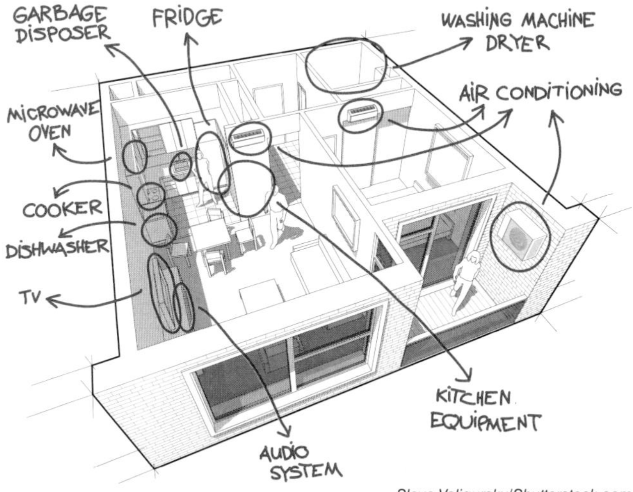

Slavo Valigursky/Shutterstock.com

Figure 17.14 During Design Development, designers must identify and specify all equipment that will be purchased and installed later.

demand. For example, landscaping work might be less expensive during fall and winter when fewer people are planning renovations for outdoor living. It is very important to work closely with trusted building professionals to get an accurate account of renovation costs prior to commencing construction. Here are some points to remember when estimating labor costs for the following:

- **Construction.** Before any finishes can be applied, all other construction must be complete! For example, the basic construction of a new wall would involve framing and drywall contractors. These, along with cabinets and other millwork, are typically billed related to how many linear feet are constructed. In many instances, this work might also involve the use of electrical and plumbing contractors who will usually charge per item installed.
- **Paint.** Professional painters generally base labor charges on the amount of time it takes to paint 100 square feet. The amount of time is then multiplied by an hourly rate. Factors, such as the need for scaffolding, or other special equipment also influence labor costs for painting.
- **Wall coverings.** Labor charges for hanging wall coverings are generally on a per-roll basis. For example, hanging wall coverings may cost anywhere from $16.00 to $50.00 per single roll depending on the wall covering type and quality and the room layout.
- **Carpeting.** Professional carpet installers may base installation fees per square foot or per square yard. Note that installers will charge additional fees for removing old carpeting, moving furniture, or carpeting stairs. Installation fees will also be greater in major markets, such as New York, Chicago, and Los Angeles. If the carpet requires padding, be sure to get the "installed" price.
- **Window treatments.** There are two labor costs for window treatments: workroom or fabrication costs and the installer's costs. In addition, there will be costs for fabrics (per yard), rods (per foot), and hardware for hanging window treatments. Because costs vary, it is best to obtain a price sheet from a reputable drapery workroom. Fabrication time (manufacturing time) can vary depending on how long it takes for the workroom to obtain the correct fabrics and the complexity of the drapery order. Four to six weeks or more is not uncommon for creating custom window treatments.
- **Upholstery.** Professional upholsterers have shop rates based on an hourly rate plus the amount of time required to remove and replace fabric. Repairing frames and springs or applying special accessory trims also adds time to labor estimates. An experienced upholsterer will be able to calculate to the minute, how much time it will take to reupholster a furniture piece.

Creating a Bid

After updating the preliminary budget, the designer then creates the final **bid**—or statement including products, work, and fees for the project. A bid includes the *actual costs* for the project. Fees and expenses that were initially "estimates" need to become final cost figures. The bid must be specific as to the furnishings, wall treatments, window treatments, floor treatments, lighting, and accessories you are selecting for the client and installing in the space. The bid must clearly list and explain the cost of your services and fees over the length of the project. Depending on the project length and complexity, you may want to develop the bid in such a way as to bill your design fee on a monthly basis. In addition, the bid must include the following:

- **Consultant fees and services.** If the design plan requires the services of outside consultants, such as architects and lighting specialists, the bid must include a list of their services and their fees for the job (Figure 17.15).
- **Subcontractor fees and services.** If the project requires construction, the final bid must spell out the work and actual fees for the

Rawpixel/Shutterstock.com

Figure 17.15 The number of consultants can vary greatly based on the project complexity.

subcontractors who will be doing the work. You may recommend that your client obtain several bids from subcontractors in a competitive bidding process. However, the subcontractor and your client should sign the final bid and contract for these services separately. You as a designer should never place yourself in a position in which you are legally responsible for the quality of work another person performs, and some ***jurisdictions*** (governing authorities) may not allow you to do so unless you are also a licensed contractor.

It is critical for the final bid to include all of the work necessary to complete the project to the designer's and client's expectations in a timely manner. Oversights in creating the bid—such as failing to build in time for late shipments—can lead to project delays and misunderstandings between the designer and client. Adequate planning and extremely good organization help avoid such problems.

As the project begins, it is unrealistic to think that clients never change their minds. Changes often occur, especially in the case of new construction or remodeling projects. Unexpected situations may arise that require changes to the bid. For instance, interior demolition of a space may reveal unforeseen mold or termite infestation with which the designer and client must deal before construction begins. In such cases, the designer or contractor prepares a **change order**—a document that outlines the details of the plan changes. The change order will list the services, materials, or design changes to which the client and designer and/or contractor agree (Figure 17.16).There is usually a fee for change orders. The contract should state in advance, how to handle changes once work on a design contract begins.

When you present the bid to a client, you must be able to anticipate and answer all of the client's questions. This is the time to discuss and make adjustments in the bid. Once the bid is final,

Goodluz/Shutterstock.com

Figure 17.16 It is not unusual for clients to change their minds about part of a design as the project moves through the phases. This young couple is discussing a color change with their interior designers.

Kaspars Grinvalds/Shutterstock.com

Figure 17.17 Interior designers may produce construction plans by hand or using CADD.

you will present the client with a final contract. After the designer and client sign the contract (and the client signs any additional contracts with subcontractors and consultants), work on the design project begins.

Review & Assessment

1. What tasks does the designer do during the Design Development phase?
2. What costs must a designer provide to the client for the final budget?
3. Summarize the points a designer should consider when estimating labor costs.
4. In addition to products' costs and the designer's services, what other fees are included on a bid?
5. Contrast a bid with a change order.

Phase 4: Contract Documents

Once your client approves all aspects of the design project, the **Contract Documents phase** begins. During this phase, the designer prepares documents that relate to interior construction. These plans—including demolition, architectural plans, floor plans, furniture plans, reflected ceiling plans, finishes, electrical plans, elevations, and detail drawings—are accompanied by schedules and specifications. This phase also involves getting the appropriate professionals involved in the project. Development of the contract documents (final construction drawings and specifications) uses the construction drawings and the specifications selections prepared during the Design Development phase (Figure 17.17).

Schedules and Specifications

Prepare organized charts of detailed notes, or *schedules*, for all items that correspond to the code numbers and letters on the floor plan. Your schedules may include features for doors and windows, electrical and plumbing fixtures, door hardware, and finishes for ceilings, walls, and floors. These schedules will also include *specifications*, or plans for the types and quality of materials to use, such as manufacturer and color numbers and names along with application information for finish treatments.

To obtain or order fabrication of interior design products, the designer needs a way to communicate exact descriptions of these products to suppliers. He or she prepares written specifications to identify the name, quantity, dimensions, color, construction features, design details, and more for each item. The designer may record the specifications on standard hard-copy or online forms, or on custom spreadsheets he or she develops for individual projects. Subcontractors can use the specification document for bidding purposes and easily convert the information to order forms.

You will also need to prepare specifications for individual pieces of furniture, identifying manufacturers, finishes, dimensions, costs, and any other important details. The specifications also identify the manufacturers, materials, fibers, and fabric content of all the upholstery pieces, window treatments, and floor treatments. Organize your presentation board and write your schedules and specifications clearly to communicate well and anticipate any questions your client may have about the visual design concept.

Whether your design plan is a residential or commercial project will influence how you prepare the contract document. In either case, good communications with material and furnishings sales representatives is beneficial, since they can often provide the bulk of your specification information and answer difficult questions.

Residential Project

You as the interior designer may act as a purchasing agent for your client and hire and supervise various contractors. For example, you may hire the drapery and upholstery workrooms that fabricate window treatments and upholstered furnishings. You may also hire painters, wall-covering hangers, and contractors who specialize in faux finishes for ceilings, walls, and floors. Usually, you will sell these services to your client using the *cost-plus method* or the *retail method* at a marked-up cost.

Commercial Project

With commercial interior design projects, you will often use a bidding process before developing the final contract. In the bidding process, all the various contractors (carpenters, plumbers, electricians, painters, etc.) have a chance to submit proposals on how they would complete the job. Each bidding contractor must submit construction drawings and specifications for each part of the project, such as shop drawings for custom kitchen cabinetry (Figure 17.18).

Several factors will influence which bidder gets the contract for the project. For some clients, the bidder offering the lowest cost is the one who obtains the contract and completes the work. This process reduces all qualifications to cost, which is not always in the best interest of the client and designer. For other clients, cost may not be the biggest factor. When competing contractors have reputations for quality work, it is often neither the lowest nor highest bidder who gets the contract. A contractor with a middle bid and a reputation for meeting all deadlines may win a contract over others who do quality work, but may not always

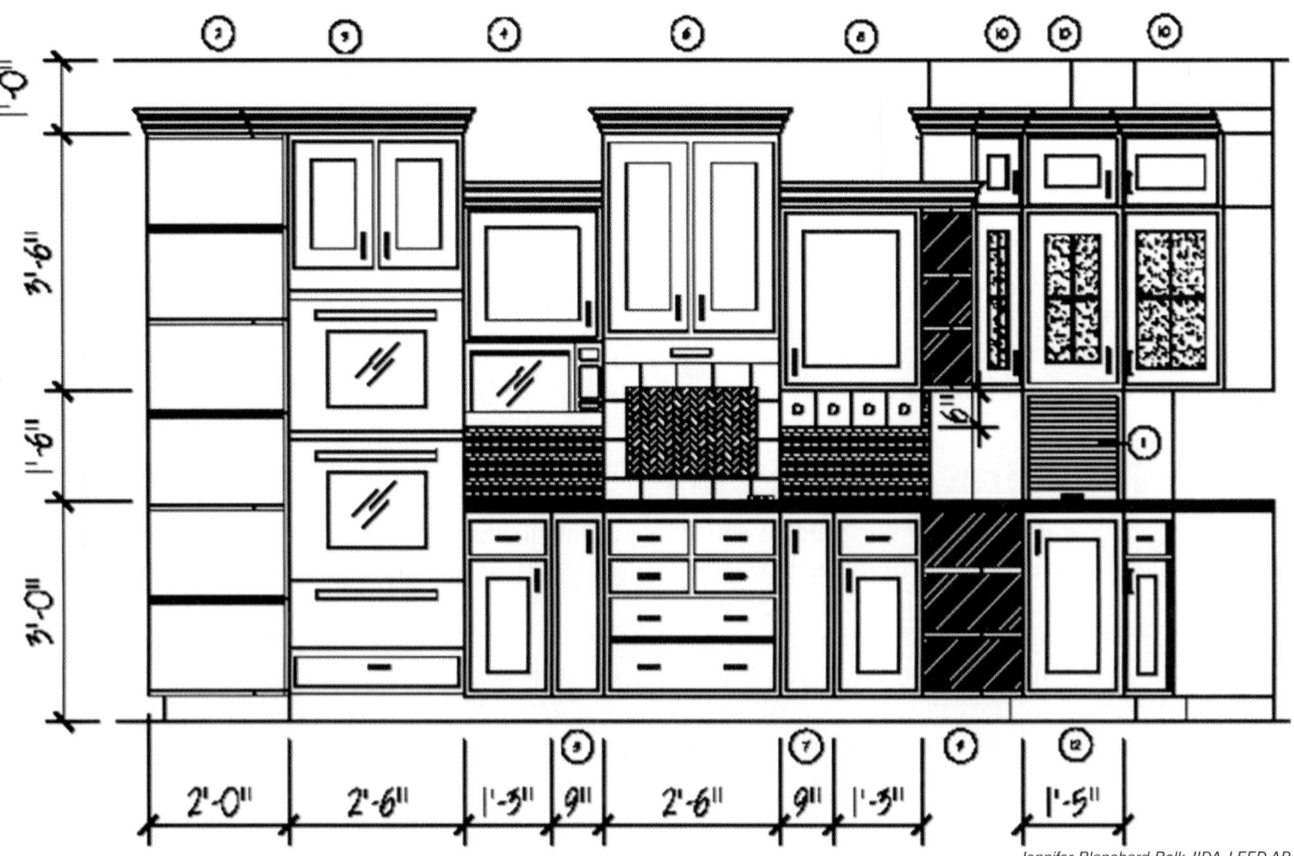

Jennifer Blanchard Belk, IIDA, LEED AP

Figure 17.18 Interior designers are often responsible for the production of all non-structural drawings including custom cabinet details.

complete it on time. When all of the contractors submit bids for the client's response and the client makes a choice, this part of the design process is complete.

Review & Assessment

1. Define the Contract Documents phase.
2. Contrast schedules and specifications.
3. Summarize the differences between contracts for residential projects and commercial projects.

Phase 5: Contract Administration

In phase five of the design process, or the **Contract Administration phase**, the designer facilitates the project by issuing bid documents and receiving proposals, purchasing products, performing site visits, and overseeing construction, holding project meetings for coordination, and executing project completion. During this phase, the interior designer needs to prepare a ***critical path schedule***—a plan that identifies each task within the design and implementation process, the time required for each task, task relationships with other tasks, and the effect that completing tasks ahead or behind schedule has on the entire project.

The critical path schedule shows beginning and ending dates for each task and step of the project (Figure 17.19). This includes any construction as well as the ordering and installing of furniture, furnishings, and equipment. Remember, some contractors will need to do their work before others. For example, electricians and plumbers must do their basic installations before a builder hangs drywall. Wall painting and trim finishes must be complete before installing window treatments and carpeting.

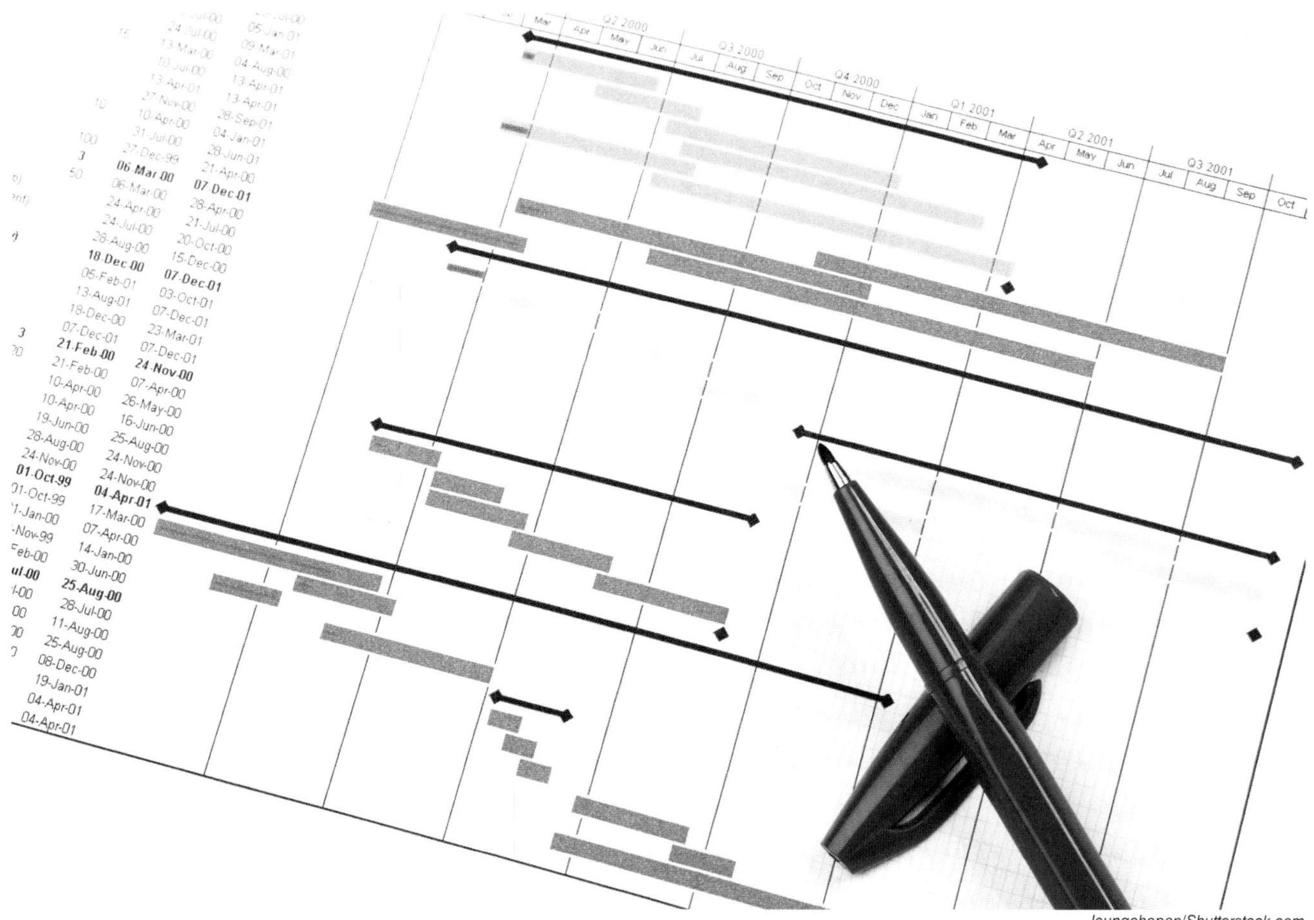

leungchopan/Shutterstock.com

Figure 17.19 A critical path schedule is an essential tool for ensuring adherence to deadlines of multiple contractors during any project.

Career Focus Interior Designer

Do you consider yourself artistic and creative? Do you have a flair for design? If you do, a career in interior design may be for you!

Interests/Skills: Do you find yourself very aware of your surroundings when you are dining out in a restaurant, visiting an airport, shopping in a retail store, visiting a new school, or entering a bank? Can you imagine yourself as someone who designs the interiors of homes or businesses? Do you frequently like to think about designing or redesigning your own personal space? Future interior designers answer "yes" to these questions and must possess three important skill sets: artistic and technical skills, interpersonal skills, and management skills.

Career Snapshot: More and more, designers are involved in the architectural detailing as well as the aesthetic design for interior spaces. Designers must be able to read construction documents (blueprints) and understand building codes. Many work with architects and builders to determine layouts and location of elements such as windows, doors, stairways, and hallways. For complex projects, interior designers may submit drawings to a building inspector for approval to make sure the design meets all codes.

Education/Training: Completion of a four- or five-year bachelor's degree through an accredited college or university is preferable and usually qualifies the graduate for a formal design apprenticeship program. Completion of a two-year associate's degree generally qualifies the graduate to be an assistant to an interior designer.

Elena Elisseeva/Shutterstock.com

Licensing/Examinations: After a one- to three-year apprenticeship to gain experience, interior design graduates can take a licensing examination through the Council for Interior Design Qualification (CIDQ). Although only 50 percent of states require licensing for interior designers, passing the exam is necessary to obtain a license and have a competitive career. You will want to identify your state's title and practice acts that impact interior designers. *Title acts* govern, or control, the use of a title, such as *certified interior designer*, but do not require licensing to practice interior design. States with *practice acts*, however, require licensing for those who practice interior design. These states also

Skills for Interior Designers	
Artistic and Technical Skills	• Knows how to plan a space • Can draw a plan and create a model by hand and via computer • Can present a plan visually so the client understands it • Has material and product knowledge for creating and furnishing a space • Knows how texture, color, lighting, and other factors combine and interact to give a space its "feel" or "look" • Understands the structural requirements of his or her plans • Understands health and safety issues in spaces • Is knowledgeable about building codes and many other technical aspects of buildings
Creative Ability	• Displays innovative and imaginative ability in creating design solutions • Adaptable to trying new design ideas within the parameters of good design • Displays good aesthetic judgment • Takes prudent risks to excel in solving design problems • Executes original/unique design plans to meet customer needs

(Continued)

Skills for Interior Designers *(continued)*	
Interpersonal Skills	• Feels comfortable in meeting and dealing with many kinds of people • Communicates clearly and listens closely • Maintains good client relationships • Works well with architects and other professionals on projects • Negotiates and mediates problems • Creates proposals and presentations that are clear, informative, and persuasive
Management Skills	• Handles more than one project at a time • Works under demanding time lines • Looks for new clients while working on other projects • Develops and implements a business plan in order to protect and grow the practice • Manages business budgets • Manages the budget for each client's project • Knows how to market oneself and interior design services to clients

govern who can call him- or herself an interior designer. Practice acts generally do allow new professionals to practice interior design under the supervision of a licensed professional. Once new designers gain the necessary years of experience and professional skills, they are eligible to pursue licensing.

Professional Associations: The American Society of Interior Designers (ASID); the International Interior Design Association (IIDA)

Job Outlook: Although competition will be intense, the demand for interior designers is expected to grow about four percent through 2024. Those in specialty areas may see a projected eight-percent growth by 2024. Employment opportunities are subject to fluctuations in the economy.

Sources: The Occupational Outlook Handbook (OOH); the Occupational Information Network (O*NET)

Careers in Commercial Interior Design		
Specialty Area	**Facility Possibilities**	
Health Care Designers Specialize in designing interior space within the health care profession	Hospitals Cancer treatment centers Office reception areas (doctors and dentists) Orthopedic sports centers	Assisted living homes Intensive care units (ICU) Birthing centers
Hospitality Designers Specialize in designing interior spaces within the hospitality industry	Restaurants Resorts Hotels and motels	Cruise ships Airplanes
Civic Contract Designers Specialize in designing interior places for public use	Museums Fire stations City halls	Early childhood education centers Elementary, middle, and high schools
Government Designers Specialize in designing buildings and offices for federal and state governments	Courthouses Police stations Detention centers	Prisons Training centers
Retail Contract Designers Specialize in designing interior involved in commercial sales	Large stores Small shops and boutiques	Showrooms/galleries Shopping malls
Office Contract Designers Specialize in designing business interiors	Bank offices and lobbies Accounting firms	Legal firms Corporate offices

Quality Control and Relationships

Sometimes the interior designer or design firm sells furniture, furnishings, equipment, and labor for the project. In these cases, the designer must be able to address some legal responsibilities that go along with such sales. For example, problems may arise that relate to faulty workmanship, equipment failure, warranties, product failure, customer service, repairs, returns, delivery and pickup, and approval policies. The contract document should spell out what the designer is responsible for and for how long.

In order for designers to implement their design plans, they must have access to suppliers, artisans, and tradespeople who offer the types of goods and services they require. Many designers **outsource**, or hire out much of the implementation work to subcontractors who specialize in particular tasks. Painters, faux-finishers, wall-covering installers, millworkers, upholsterers, and other craftspeople are excellent resources to trade professionals who design and specify only.

Similarly, designers use outsourcing to obtain fabrics and furnishings for their clients. Building and maintaining good relationships with quality manufacturers, their representatives, and other suppliers is highly important to the designer. Developing strong relationships with such sources is a good investment of the designer's time.

Usually the interior designer reviews and inspects work for quality, workmanship, and finishes. The interior designer serves as a **liaison**—or connecting agent—between the client and the other persons involved in the project. Supervision of construction and installation of built-ins often requires special certification and knowledge (Figure 17.20). As a result, some states do not allow interior designers to supervise construction and installations.

In this phase, project completion occurs through the following activities:

- completion of paperwork to make purchases, finalizing bids, and preparing necessary drawings and specifications
- completion of construction
- installation of furniture, furnishings, and equipment
- submission of bills to the interior designer, who in turn bills the client for payment
- completion of a walk-through to make sure all work is complete and satisfactory to the client (most commercial jobs require a formal walk-through)
- notation on a **punch list**—a document the designer creates during a walk-through that lists unfinished tasks, missing items or damaged goods, or subpar craftsmanship that a contractor must complete prior to final payment
- obtain and replace missing or damaged goods
- initiation of final payments to the designer and to the contractors after all remaining items of the project are complete

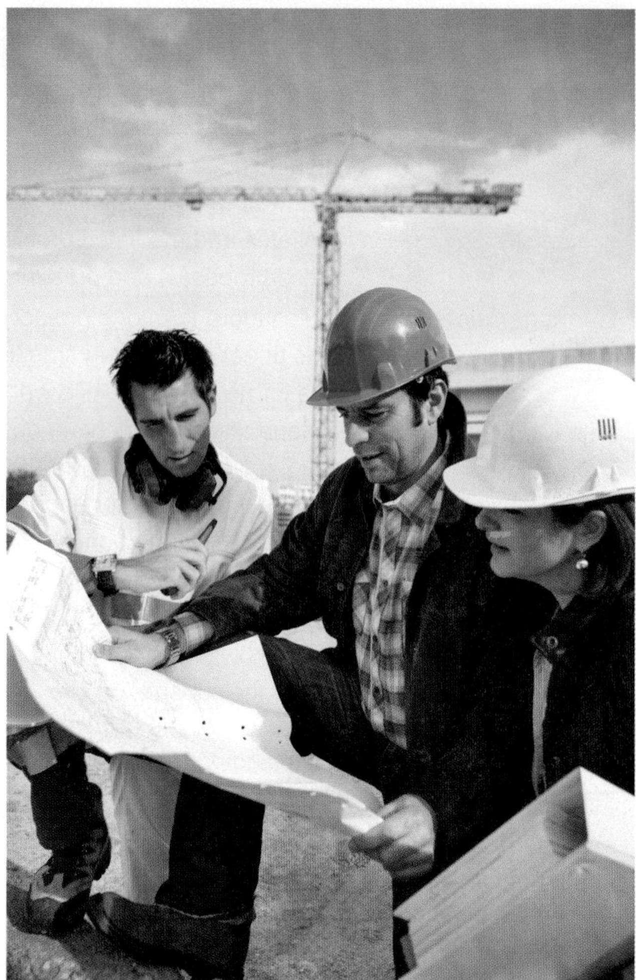

auremar/Shutterstock.com

Figure 17.20 Part of an interior designer's job is to inspect work on his or her projects for quality and adherence to approved drawings.

Project and Time Management

As an interior designer, you will manage a project for overall performance in terms of the time schedule, costs, and quality. The ability or inability to develop the organizational skills for project and time management can either make or break the path to career success. The following identifies some additional tasks that require project and time management skills of the designer:

Monkey Business Images/Shutterstock.com

Figure 17.21 Calling vendors to schedule delivery and installation of products is part of the interior designer's project-management responsibilities during Contract Administration.

- overseeing and coordinating the work of different tradespeople, such as the plumbers and painters
- scheduling the delivery and installation of all purchased items (Figure 17.21)
- inspecting all purchases to ensure that they are of the quality expected when you placed the order
- reviewing and approving all invoices and bills upon receipt

In addition, the designer must be careful that this supervision does not take up more time than noted in the bid for her or his own design services. Successful designers work on multiple projects at one time while still marketing their businesses and contacting new clients.

Review & Assessment 

1. What tasks does the designer do during the Contract Administration phase?
2. What is a critical path schedule?
3. Why is it important for designers or design firms to address legal responsibilities in the contract document when selling furniture, furnishings, equipment, and labor for a project?
4. Give an example of what work an interior designer might outsource.
5. What does a designer note on a punch list?
6. What is the interior designer's responsibility for project and time management?

Chapter 17 Assessment

Summary

- An interior designer uses the design process to carry out an orderly project to meet individual, business, and special needs of the client project.
- The phases of the design process include Programming, Schematic Design, Design Development, Contract Documents, and Contract Administration.
- During Programming, the designer gathers client information.
- Applying the principles and elements of design for all aspects of the project is crucial during the Schematic Design phase. After initial design approval, the designer continues work in the Design Development phase.
- Handling Contract Documents includes making purchases, acquiring bids, and coordinating all professionals on the project.
- Project completion occurs during the Contract Administration phase.

Terms in Action

1. **Term flash cards** Working in small teams, locate a small image online that visually describes or explains each of the *Content* and *Academic Terms* at the beginning of the chapter. To create flash cards, write each term on a note card and paste the image that describes or explains the term on the opposite side.

Think Critically

2. **Recognize values** Suppose a client has hired you to create a design plan for a family room renovation. In teams, discuss how creating profiles for all household members can help you recognize what they value most about the space and how they use it. How might this recognition help you create a realistic design plan?
3. **Assess details** What details should you assess about a client's environment? How can this assessment lead to a better interior design? Write a summary of your responses.
4. **Evaluate information** Product literature includes a wealth of information. Some of this is essential to include in a specification to ensure the appropriate items are ordered. Look up a fabric or finish online store or visit a local store or showroom. Select two products. Evaluate the product literature to determine what information is necessary or required in an actual specification for ordering. Give an oral report of your findings to the class.
5. **Analyze pros and cons** Make a list of all the possible ways clients may decide to approach setting a project budget. Analyze the pros and cons of each approach. How can analyzing and understanding all approaches help you better guide clients in establishing project budgets?

Core Skills

6. **Reading and writing** Read at least three articles about *letters of agreement* for interior design services from reliable sources. Write a summary of each article noting key facts that answer the questions *who, what, when, where,* and *why* about letters of agreement.
7. **Writing** Imagine you are creating an interior design plan for relatives who are building a new house. Begin by making a list of questions you will ask your relatives in regard to how they use their space. Use your questions to gather information about your relatives/clients and write a profile outlining their lifestyle, functions of their space, design preferences, and future needs.
8. **Writing** Presume a family member or friend is a new client who desires a kitchen renovation. Sit and watch your client tackle a kitchen task such as preparing a meal. Take note of any activities that your client has difficulty completing such as reaching high cabinetry, walking too much between work areas, or limited cabinet or countertop space. From your direct observation, create a list of programming needs and illustrate visual solutions for your ideas to address with the client.
9. **Speaking and listening** Imagine you are assisting a client with a complete renovation of her family room. Your client's family consists of herself, her husband, and two children who are in primary school. Use word-processing software to create a list of at least *ten* questions

Chapter 17 Assessment

you would ask the client via an initial interview or questionnaire during the Programming phase of the design process. Review your questions with a peer and then discuss in class. How could you improve your questions to obtain the specific qualitative and quantitative information needed for the project? How can such information help you accurately review qualitative and quantitative work processes and end products?

10. **Math practice** Use applications to create a bill of materials (bid). Propose strategies for budgeting and controlling costs for the following situation. Presume you are an interior designer who is working with a client on a kitchen renovation which includes five new appliances—refrigerator, gas range, range hood, microwave oven, and dishwasher. Use online resources to price the appliances. Then create a bill of materials for the appliances including your fee of five percent of the total cost.
11. **Research and writing** Presume you are starting your own interior design business. You need to establish business relationships with service providers (such as upholstery and drapery workrooms, builders, and painters) and product suppliers (such as paint, textiles, and furnishings). Research service providers and suppliers in your area. What services or products do they provide? What are their fees? Do they offer discounts to other businesses? How can you judge the quality of the services or products? Write a summary of your findings.
12. **CTE career readiness practice** Make an appointment to job-shadow an interior designer in your area. Observe tasks the designer performs and how he or she interacts with clients, and note your observations. What aspects of interior design does the designer find most challenging? most rewarding? What is the designer's view on pricing methods? What strategies does the designer propose for controlling costs and allocating resources? How much time, effort, and experience does it take to become proficient in this career? Share an oral summary of your observations with the class.

Design Practice

13. **Design task list** Suppose you are assisting a client with a full bathroom renovation, including new finishes, fixtures (tub, shower, sink/vanity, and toilet), and accessories. Create a to-do list of designer tasks for completing the design in chronological order using the phases of the design process to meet client (individual) and business needs. Consider what information to gather, types of product selections to make, vendor and contractor coordination and communication, time to oversee project development, and more. Use spreadsheet software to develop your task list.
14. **Punch list preparation** Prior to the client occupying a space, the designer will typically produce a punch list that identifies outstanding project items to address. This list might include finish details to address such as a wall that requires another coat of paint or repairing scratches on furniture. To practice punch list preparation, do the following: (A) Select a room in your home, school, or public space that is a fairly new build or renovation. Neatly hand sketch the overall room layout on grid paper including all doors, windows, furnishings, built-ins, HVAC vents, etc. (B) Carefully observe and critique the issues through the space that would appear on your own punch list if you had been the project designer. Create a list with enough specifics about items to address to instruct the contractor. (C) Identify on your plan sketch the exact location of each of the items in need to address and number or letter each item clearly. Create a key to the numbers or letters that correlates to the items on your punch list.
15. **Portfolio** Keeping your portfolio work organized and well preserved is important. For your hard-copy items, choose a method to keep the items clean, safe, and organized (use a three-ring binder). Store your digital items on a flash drive or your own computer. Then do the following: (A) Choose a method for storing your hard-copy items. Write a paragraph explaining how you will label and store your work. (B) Create a folder on a network drive or flash drive in which to save your digital files. Write a paragraph explaining how you will name folders and subfolders for storing your portfolio materials.

Chapter 18

Design Communication

Content Terms

oral communication
written communication
visual communication
inventory
permit
electronic workflow
title block
horizon line
vanishing point
alignment
proximity
adhesives
storyboard
keystoning
marketing presentation
project presentation
body language
powerless language

Academic Terms

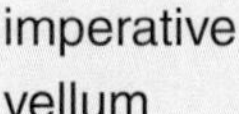

imperative
vellum

Learning Outcomes

After studying this chapter, you will be able to

- understand and apply the different forms of oral, written, and visual communication that designers use during different project phases.
- recognize the various types of CADD drafting and drawing programs, and other software programs integral to interior design.
- determine elements and principles present in all forms of visual communication for designers.
- create an interior design presentation board, model, and portfolio.
- apply design knowledge, skills, processes, and oral, written, and visual presentation skills to communicate design ideas in a manner that others easily understand.

Reading with Purpose

Before reading the chapter, make a list of five things you already know about methods designers use to communicate and who they have to communicate with. Leaf through the pages of the chapter and note the heading topics. Predict five things you will learn about how designers communicate with their oral, written, and visual communication skills. How do designers use these skills to convincingly justify their actions in a socially acceptable manner that others easily understand?

While studying, look for the access icon 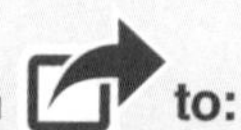 **to:**

- **Practice** the *Content* and *Academic Terms* with e-flash cards, matching activities, and vocabulary games.
- **Reinforce** what you learn by completing the *Review & Assessment* questions and e-mailing them to your instructor.

www.g-wlearning.com/housing/

wavebreakmedia/Shutterstock.com

The goal of an interior designer is not only to solve a client's design problem but to be able to communicate that solution to the client as well as contractors and tradespeople. Ways this information is communicated might include talking with, corresponding via e-mail, or giving drawings and renderings to people involved with the project. The designer may produce visuals by hand or by computerized methods but should be proficient in both. To create this new space and to communicate the plans to the client, the interior designer continues to utilize the same elements and principles discussed in previous chapters.

As you read this chapter, imagine yourself as an interior designer who is working with a client to develop a design concept for a room or area. Consider all the different ways your solution might be communicated and with whom you would be communicating.

Communication During the Design Process

During the design process, there is continuous communication among the designer, client, vendors, contractors, building officials, and other professionals. Each takes place in different forms and at different times. This communication includes the following:

- **Oral communication**—The transmission of ideas through speech. In design, examples of oral communication include verbal presentations and conversations on the phone or in person.
- **Written communication**—The transmission of ideas through a medium that people can read. In design, examples of written communication include contracts, meeting minutes, e-mail correspondence, or purchase orders.
- **Visual communication**—The transmission of ideas through a medium that people can see or view. In design, examples of visual communication include schematic plans, construction drawings, renderings, models, finish boards, or a combination of all.

Programming

The initial communications between a designer and the client are the most important to the success of the project. During programming, the designer conducts:

- interviews to determine needs and goals
- meetings to ensure the client understands the scope of the designer's services (via a contract)
- an **inventory**, or a complete listing of property or belongings of a person or company such as existing furniture, fixtures, or equipment to determine what might or might not be reused (Figure 18.1)
- meetings to determine style, color, and other preferences

In addition, the designer will take this time to communicate with building code officials. The main concern with building code officials regards any accessibility or safety issues associated with the project. Measurements of existing spaces will be taken. These measurements will be used to produce drawings later for estimating construction and materials. Finally, the designer will communicate

Home Inventory

Location	Description	Qty	Size: W x	D x	H	Keep	Restore	Remove	Replace	Purchase	Notes/Issues	Photo?
Home Office	Task Chairs	1				x						x
Home Office	Computer	2						x			New Laptops	
Home Office	Desk	1	72	30	30				x			x
Family Room	Bookcases	NA	60	15	?					x	Accommodate 5 bx of books	
Family Room	Chairs	2	30	30	30		x				Reupholster	x
Family Room	Sofa	1	84	30	30				x			x
Family Room	Ent. center	1	60	24	60	x						x
Family Room	Tables	NA	36	36	18					x		
Family Room	Rugs	1	96	60					x		Larger needed 120x96 needed	x

Jennifer Blanchard Belk, IIDA, LEED AP

Figure 18.1 Having an itemized list of furnishings that are needed or need repair will make the project smoother and more cost efficient.

with the client and other potential consultants to write the proposed schedule, budget, and design program for the project.

Schematic Design

During this early phase, the designer communicates often with the client. The designer is seeking feedback on preliminary plans, sketches, and bubble diagrams as well as initial material and furniture selections. At this stage, usually the presentation does not include a presentation board but does show a large collection of potential choices (Figure 18.2). The designer will also begin discussions at this time with a variety of consultants, vendors, and building officials to determine any issues or opportunities (budget, schedule, scope) related to the project.

Design Development

In this phase, the designer communicates with the clients for approval of the final plans and selections. They will communicate this plan by presenting floor plans and other details, renderings and other presentation drawings, and finish boards (Figure 18.3). This is also when the designer connects with consultants and vendors to be able to accurately communicate the costs of the project to the client.

Contract Documents

An important communication during this phase is what and how designers and architects will complete the project. This communication includes drawings, specifications, and schedules for construction and completion of the space (Figure 18.4). When these are complete, the designer connects with many different contractors to obtain bids or quotes for the desired work and seeks final client approval on all items before construction begins or purchases are made.

Naphat_Jorjee/Shutterstock.com

Figure 18.3 Quick hand- or computer-rendered perspectives are helpful to assist clients with visualizing a designer's solutions.

Maxx-Studio/Shutterstock.com

Figure 18.2 During the Schematic Design phase, discussions about finishes typically do not include presentation boards. Loose presentations allow designers to easily present alternatives to clients.

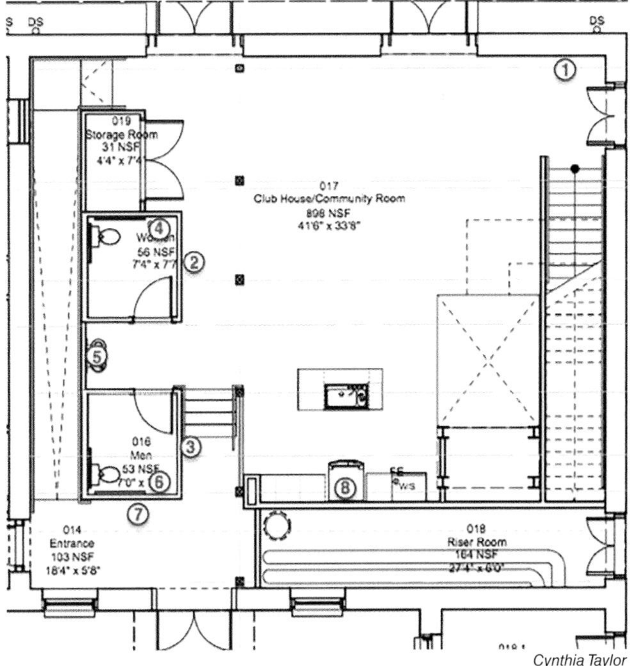

Cynthia Taylor

Figure 18.4 Creating keyed installation plans for items like artwork help make sure of correct placement and any other details of installation. This would be accompanied by a list of instructions and thumbnail pictures of the artwork.

Processes for Procuring Client Products	
Process	**Description**
Credit Applications	• Allows the designer to get items on credit from a vendor while waiting for client payment
Purchase Agreement (a legal contract)	• Provides the necessary requirements for ordering merchandise or contracting for custom items • Requires the client signature before purchases can be made • Includes all pertinent information about products to be ordered
Purchase Order (contract between designer and manufacturer)	• Allows for the sale of products directly to the designer
Work Order (contract between designer and vendor)	• Allows for creation of custom work such as window coverings and reupholstering
Acknowledgments	• Acknowledges/confirms the specifics of an order by the manufacturer or vendor to the designer
Invoice	• Billing a designer receives from a manufacturer • Billing a client receives from a designer
Bill of Lading (delivery ticket)	• Provides a packing list, freight bill, and paperwork associated with the completed delivery of product from a manufacturer

Figure 18.5 Interior designers must be knowledgeable about many business practices and processes when procuring products for clients.

Contract Administration

During this last phase, a designer is in constant communication with contractors and consultants to provide project management supervision of the job site. This includes having dialog with all parties, including the client, about staying on schedule and budget. This is also when the designer produces paperwork for the ordering, shipment, and installation of furniture from manufacturers.

One of the benefits of being an interior designer is that you can purchase furnishings and materials directly from manufacturers at a greatly reduced rate. When a designer assists a client with purchases related to his or her project, there are many processes that take place to communicate the approvals and payment information. See Figure 18.5.

The designer and architect are responsible for connecting with local building officials regarding getting building **permits** (documentation proving permission has been received from a local authority to build or renovate a building) and codes inspections throughout the construction process (Figure 18.6). At completion of the project, the designer may also be in charge of confirming payment of all parties and doing evaluations with the client regarding the quality of the work.

Jim Parkin/Shutterstock.com

Figure 18.6 During construction, a sign must be posted on the jobsite indicating the project information, contractor, and any building permit and inspection facts.

Review & Assessment

1. Describe three types of communication interior designers use to communicate with clients, vendors, and other design-team professionals.
2. Name four essential communication tasks the designer performs during Programming. How does the designer apply oral communication skills to justify his or her actions and decisions?
3. What are two primary tasks the designer performs during the Schematic Design phase?
4. Contrast designer communication tasks during the Contract Documents and Contract Administration phases.

Communicating Through Technology

Some interior designers may draw their scale floor plans by hand on graph paper. Most interior designers, however, typically use such technological applications as computer-aided drafting and design (CADD) software for creating an architectural interior drawing such as a scale floor plan.

Types of CADD Programs

A number of different CADD software products are available for interior designers. Some of the most popular two-dimensional (2-D) and three-dimensional (3-D) options are

- AutoCAD® and AutoCAD LT® by AUTODESK
- Architecture® by AUTODESK
- Revit® by AUTODESK
- MicroStation™ by Bentley
- SketchUp™ by Trimble
- TurboCAD™ by IMSI/Design
- VectorWorks® by Nemetscheck Company
- CorelCAD™ by Corel

Others are geared toward interior-design industry specialties such as 2020™ which has programs focused on the kitchen and bath, commercial furnishings, and retail markets. Some not only allow you to draw a floor plan to scale but may also include features for estimating materials and ordering products.

Many people have difficulty visualizing how a finished room will actually look from a floor plan. With the assistance of a computer, you can position furniture in a room and move it around to consider different arrangements. Also, most software allows you to produce interior wall elevations of the room. With some programs, you can view the spaces by way of a video walk-through. A walk-through provides a more realistic picture that allows you and your client to judge how well the furniture positions, selected finishes, and architectural features meet expectations. For instance, an area may seem more crowded in the walk-through view than it appears when only looking at the floor-scale drawing.

SketchUp™ by Trimble and other 3-D modeling programs are rather easy to learn and are typically free to the public. They offer a quick and user-friendly way to do everything from a conceptual model to an entire building or community, or to create detailed renderings of a single room. Online sources are available to provide millions of uploads of furniture pieces, accessories, architectural elements, and entire buildings. Because these programs are not produced specifically for interior designers, however, the models are made up of basic surfaces and lines, rather than actual interiors and architectural components. For this reason, these open-access programs are excellent for initial design phases but are not typically appropriate for projects that involve construction documents.

BIM, or *Building Information Modeling*, most notably provided by Revit® software from AUTODESK, allows for all of the above and much more. These programs provide interactive real-time changes so you can immediately see the effect moving a wall might have on elevations, electrical layout, HVAC plans, material costs, and more. It also has tools to diagnose any conflicts that might be happening between what two consultants or engineers may have put into the model.

Usually, it saves time to generate the floor plans with a computer (Figure 18.7). Not only can you develop the plans more quickly, but you can also use other options to view the plan in many different ways. Learning how to use a computer software package may take some time, especially for the more complicated programs. Learning how to use such a program, however, can be worthwhile if you are planning several room arrangements, working with a very challenging floor plan, or working with multiple clients.

Matching the Project Needs with Appropriate Software

Determining what software or combinations of software are most appropriate for each individual project can be a challenge for designers

LDprod/Shutterstock.com

Figure 18.7 CADD, BIM and mobile devices make it easy for designers and architects to make changes while in face-to-face discussions with clients or when on site visits.

(Figure 18.8). **Electronic workflow** is the process a project team uses to methodically utilize multiple software packages in a particular order for certain tasks to create successful, coordinated, and efficient design documents for a project. A simple, single-room interiors project which deals primarily with finishes may only need quick hand-sketched plans and thumbnail perspectives. Integrating BIM would be more complicated than what is required. A large project, however, where many changes and consultants are anticipated would be cumbersome, time consuming, limiting, and less accurate using basic 2-D software. Aspects to consider include the following:

- How large and complex is the project?
- What deliverables does the client expect (the types and quality of drawings, visuals, and data that are expected)?
- Which phases of the design process are included in the project scope and what services is the designer providing?

CADD programs are not the only helpful software programs within project development and execution. Many others can assist a designer with production of presentation materials, photo manipulation, data collection and analysis, and research. With advances in technology, more and more designers prepare their presentations with computers and design software. Become comfortable with photo-editing and design-presentation software early in your design career.

Best Practices for Successful CADD Files

Beyond making sure to demonstrate good design, there are many ways to make sure your 2-D and 3-D CADD drawings are as informative, accurate, and easy to produce as possible.

The entire purpose for creating digital drawings is to be informative for the client or contractor and communicate the intent of the design and the instructions for construction. As you learned in Chapter 6, symbols and line types all have meanings so using the right ones is ***imperative*** (necessary). No drawing should ever be produced without a **title block** (a box of information that at a minimum includes the project title, author, drawing name, scale, and date), even if there is not an actual formal title block present.

Accuracy is essential when dealing with CADD documents and files. Utilize the tools which allow you to ensure straight lines and defined intersections, using digital guidelines if needed. Take advantage of commands that allow you to type exact measurements rather than visually estimating the size of objects. Do not forget that most programs also have a spell-check feature and ability to customize screen menus to fit specific problems or needs.

Always consider your productivity. If you have heard the saying, "work smart, not hard," this is extremely applicable to CADD work. Use your *help menu* to assist you through commands with which you are having trouble, and use online design, construction, and manufacturer sites for free downloads and sample files of products. Create progress prints often because line weights and text sizes are not always clear when you view them on a computer screen. For example, the smaller the scale of the drawing, the larger the text must be to remain readable.

The worst thing that can happen is to lose a project you have worked hard to produce. Save your files frequently and back up all of your work to cloud-based storage, rather than relying on a portable drive which you might misplace or damage. Name the

Visual Communication Software Usage in Interior Design	Phase 1 = Programming 2 = Schematics 3 = Design Development 4 = Construction Documentation 5 = Contract Administration	Analysis of Program	Inventories and Data Collection	Conceptual Sketches	Bubble Diagrams	Study Models	Thumbnail Sketches/Perspectives	Preliminary Plans and Elevations	3D Walk-throughs	Realistic Renderings	Detailed Plans and Elevations/Sections	Finish Boards	Complete Construction Drawings	Specifications and Schedules	Project/Construction Management
	Phase	1	1	2	2	2	2	2	3	3	3	3	4	4	5
Small interior, finish oriented project	Hand drawing/assembly														
	SketchUp														
	Basic CAD software (AutoDesk AutoCAD)														
	3D CAD (AutoDesk Architecture)														
	BIM (Revit)														
Basic residential or commercial renovation project with construction	Hand drawing/assembly														
	SketchUp														
	Basic CAD software (AutoDesk AutoCAD)														
	3D CAD (AutoDesk Architecture)														
	BIM (Revit)														
Large residential ground up or commercial interiors project	Hand drawing/assembly														
	SketchUp														
	Basic CAD software (AutoDesk AutoCAD)														
	3D CAD (AutoDesk Architecture)														
	BIM (Revit)														

Software Usage in Interior Design	Phase 1 = Programming 2 = Schematics 3 = Design Development 4 = Construction Documentation 5 = Contract Administration	Case study and Programming Research	Analysis of Program	Inventories and Data Collection	Client Presentations	Bubble Diagrams	Thumbnail Sketches/Perspectives	Realistic Renderings	Developing Custom Elements	Pricing Estimates	Product selection and documentation	Sustainability Analysis	Finish Boards	Specifications and Schedules	Project/Construction Management
	Phase	1	1	1	1-3	2	2	3	3	3	3	3	3	4	5
Additional digital resources	Adobe PhotoShop														
	Microsoft Powerpoint or Adobe InDesign														
	Microsoft Office (Excel, Word, Access)														
	Internet Sources														

Jennifer Blanchard Belk, IIDA, LEED AP

Figure 18.8 The use of different drawing techniques and software depends on the current phase of design as well as the size and scope of the project itself.

files in a logical manner based on the project title, class, or date. Save frequently so you can go back to a previous version of your project if necessary.

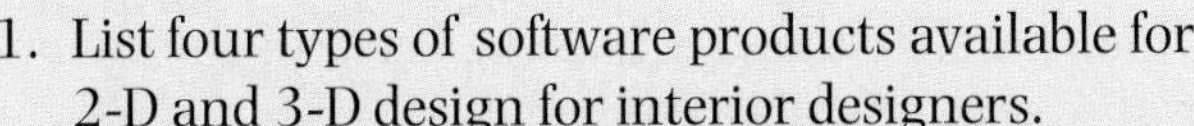

Review & Assessment

1. List four types of software products available for 2-D and 3-D design for interior designers.
2. Why are programs like SketchUp typically not appropriate for projects that involve construction documents?
3. What is electronic workflow? When is it most useful?
4. Why are certain CADD programs more suitable for large and complex projects?
5. What is the purpose for creating digital drawings for interior designs?
6. What can you do to accurately deal with CADD documents and files?

Creating 3-D Drawings

All computer-aided drafting and design (CADD) images as well as hand drawings are done by creating lines and shapes either in 2-D or 3-D. Although the techniques differ greatly, understanding the basics of spatial layout helps with orientation and visualization. Customizing screen menus to fit specific problems or needs may also be necessary.

Drawing Lines and Shapes with CADD

Whichever program you use, understanding which *axis* is being drawn is essential. In 2-D drawings, this is very similar to reading a graph in math class. In CADD, unlike hand drawing, you do not typically consider scale until it is time to print a drawing, since the designer draws items using their actual dimensions. For instance, the *red* axis you see

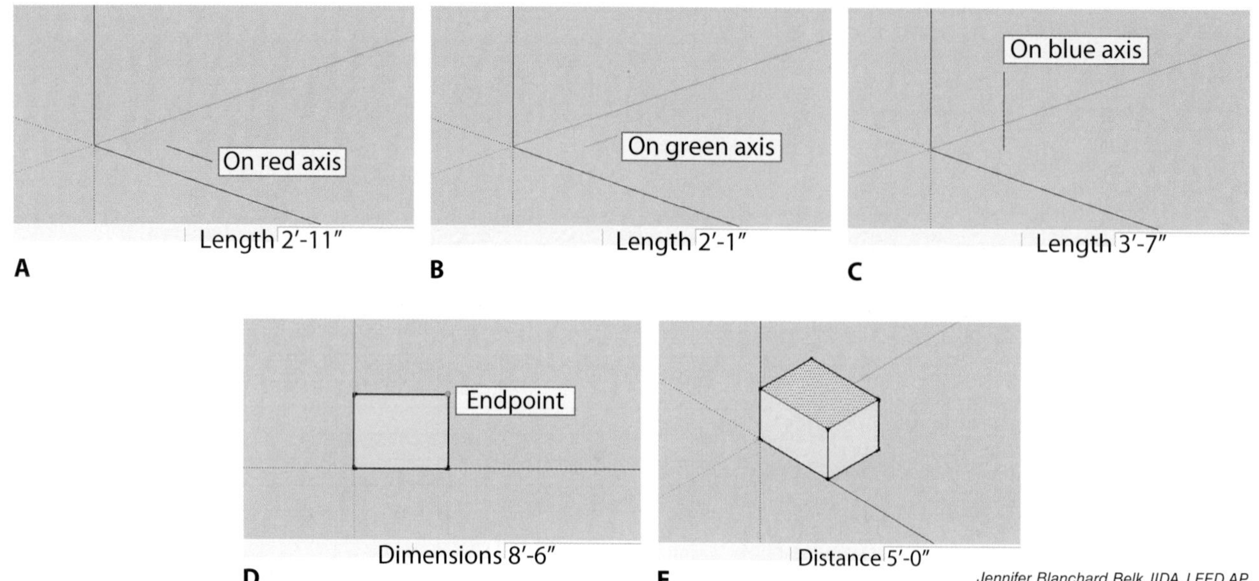

Jennifer Blanchard Belk, IIDA, LEED AP

Figure 18.9 Drawing lines and shapes in CADD is similar to reading graphs in math class.

in Figure 18.9A (some programs call this the *X axis*) indicates lines that lie horizontally on your paper or screen. The line drawn here is 2'-11" in length. The *green* axis you see in Figure 18.9B (some programs call this the *Y axis*) indicates lines that lie vertically on your paper or screen. The line drawn here is 2'-1" in length.

For drawing in 3-D, the *blue* axis you see in Figure 18.9C (some programs call this the *Z axis*) indicates lines that represent height or run perpendicular to the drawing plane. The line drawn here is 3'-7" in length.

Shapes such as rectangles are created by indicating their size based on a starting point and end point. The rectangle shape in Figure 18.9D is drawn at 8'-0" (*red/X axis*) × 6'-0" (*green/Y axis*) from the starting point or origin.

You can give any shape height by extruding or pulling it a particular distance on the *blue* or *Z axis*. This rectangular solid (cube) in Figure 18.9E is now 5'-0" high.

Creating Isometric and Perspective Drawings

Once a designer constructs 3-D objects in CADD, he or she can print unlimited types and angles of 3-D drawings by simply placing and adjusting camera views. Creating 3-D drawings by hand is more time intensive and must be developed for each needed angle but can have a softer quality many clients prefer.

Creating a floor plan and then a 3-D (isometric or perspective) drawing in CADD or by hand requires a designer to begin with accurate room and furniture measurements. The 12'-0" × 9'-0" room in Figure 18.10A is drawn on grid paper and has a sofa, two chairs, and a coffee table.

An isometric drawing is a 3-D representation of a space that does not have a sense of perspective and therefore does not appear as realistic. This type of drawing is created by placing a copy of the grid and floor plan at a 30-degree angle (represented by the *red* and *green axes*) and then projecting lines vertically (*blue axis*) to represent the height of the pieces.

Isometric drawings are easier to hand-draw than more complicated perspectives because all items can be drawn directly off of a scale floor plan with standard tools and any item on the plan can be directly measured for accuracy (Figure 18.10B).

In a perspective drawing, objects that are closer to a viewer appear larger than those that are farther away. This makes these types of drawings appear more realistic. Perspectives are constructed using a **horizon line** (indicating the eye level of the viewer) and a **vanishing point** that represents the point at which parallel lines, such as the backs of the chairs or the ends of a table, converge.

A one-point perspective begins with an elevation of the back wall of a space and includes only one vanishing point. All lines perpendicular to the viewer continue on the *red/X axis* while vertical lines continue on the *blue/Z axis*. All lines on the *green/Y axis* that are traveling away from the viewer aim toward the vanishing point (Figure 18.10C).

A two-point perspective begins with a corner of a space and includes two vanishing points. All vertical lines continue on the *blue/Z axis*. All lines, however, on the *red/X* or *green/Y axis* aim toward their respective vanishing points (Figure 18.10D).

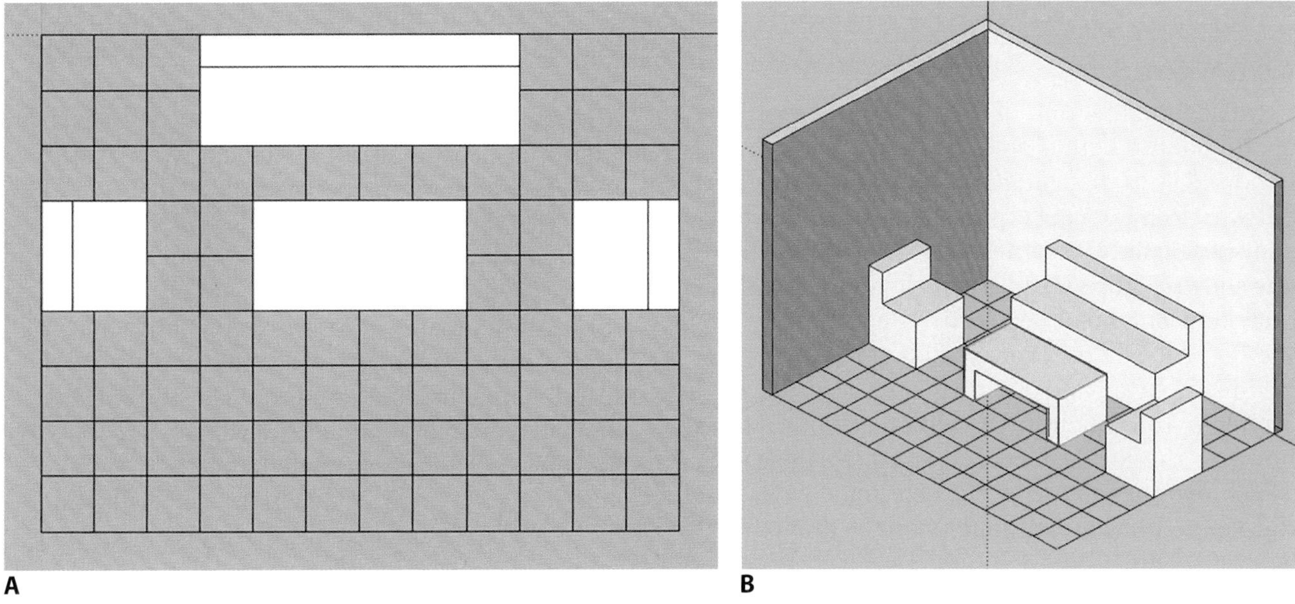

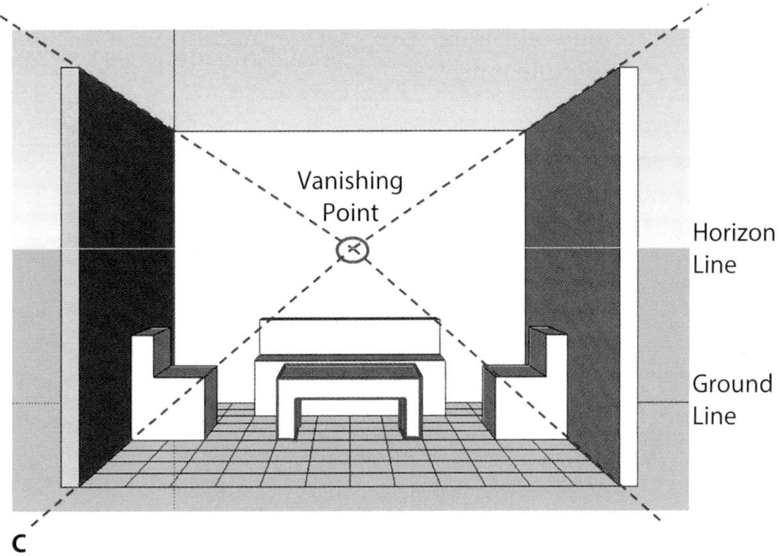

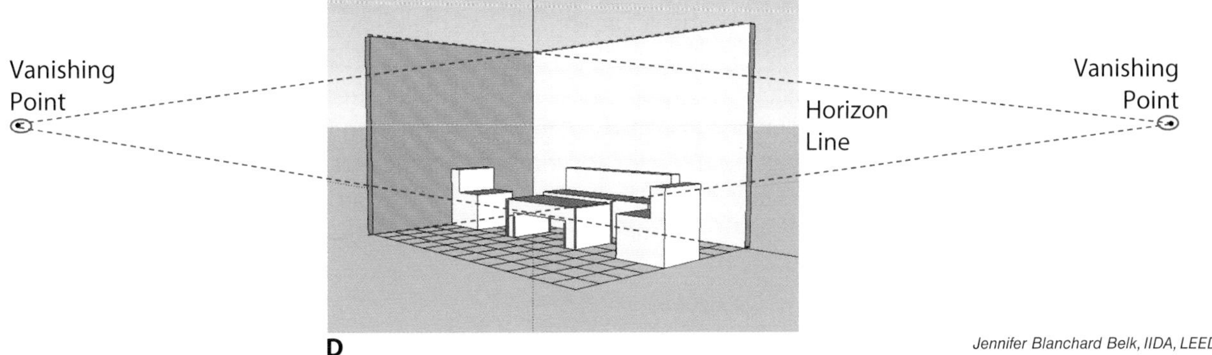

Jennifer Blanchard Belk, IIDA, LEED AP

Figure 18.10 A floor plan on a grid (A) is the foundation for an isometric drawing (B). One-point (C) and two-point (D) perspective drawings help give the client a more realistic view of a design.

Creating One-Point Perspective Drawings by Hand

The fundamentals of a one-point perspective are the same whether produced via CADD or by hand. All lines that run parallel to your view project outward from, or converge back toward, a central vanishing point. Drawing a kitchen, such as the one shown Figure 18.11, is excellent practice for drawing a one-point perspective since most of the elements are rectilinear solids and it often has grid-like flooring and other repeated decorative elements. You can draw this with mechanical tools; however, the goal is to become so comfortable with sketching that you are able to determine angles and the depth of objects without having to draw them so specifically.

When creating a hand-sketched (freehand) one-point perspective, begin with a 2-D elevation of the focal point or back wall of the room. Draw all elements that are either on or against the back wall. Determine where you are standing and how high your eye level is, thus creating your vanishing point and horizon line. Experiment with different eye levels to determine a view that gives the most realistic and informative view of the space. Objects that are closest to you will appear the largest, so be careful selecting where you will stand to sketch. A large piece of furniture could block your view of important pieces in the room.

Once you draw the back wall, project the horizontal lines that are parallel to your view (such as the side walls, door header, or side of cabinet) outward by aligning with your vanishing point. All vertical lines remain vertical (such as the curtains) and all horizontal lines that are perpendicular to you will remain horizontal (such as the front edge of the counters). Block out each item as a basic, solid shape—such as a cube or cylinder—before adding detail or carving out complex forms. Use a light hand pressure or a light lead pencil so that you can emphasize the early lines you sketch more precisely later. Understanding what you *should* see is as important as drawing what you *think* you should see. Some rules of thumb include the following:

- Items will *morph* (change) as they move away from you. For instance, a recessed downlight overhead

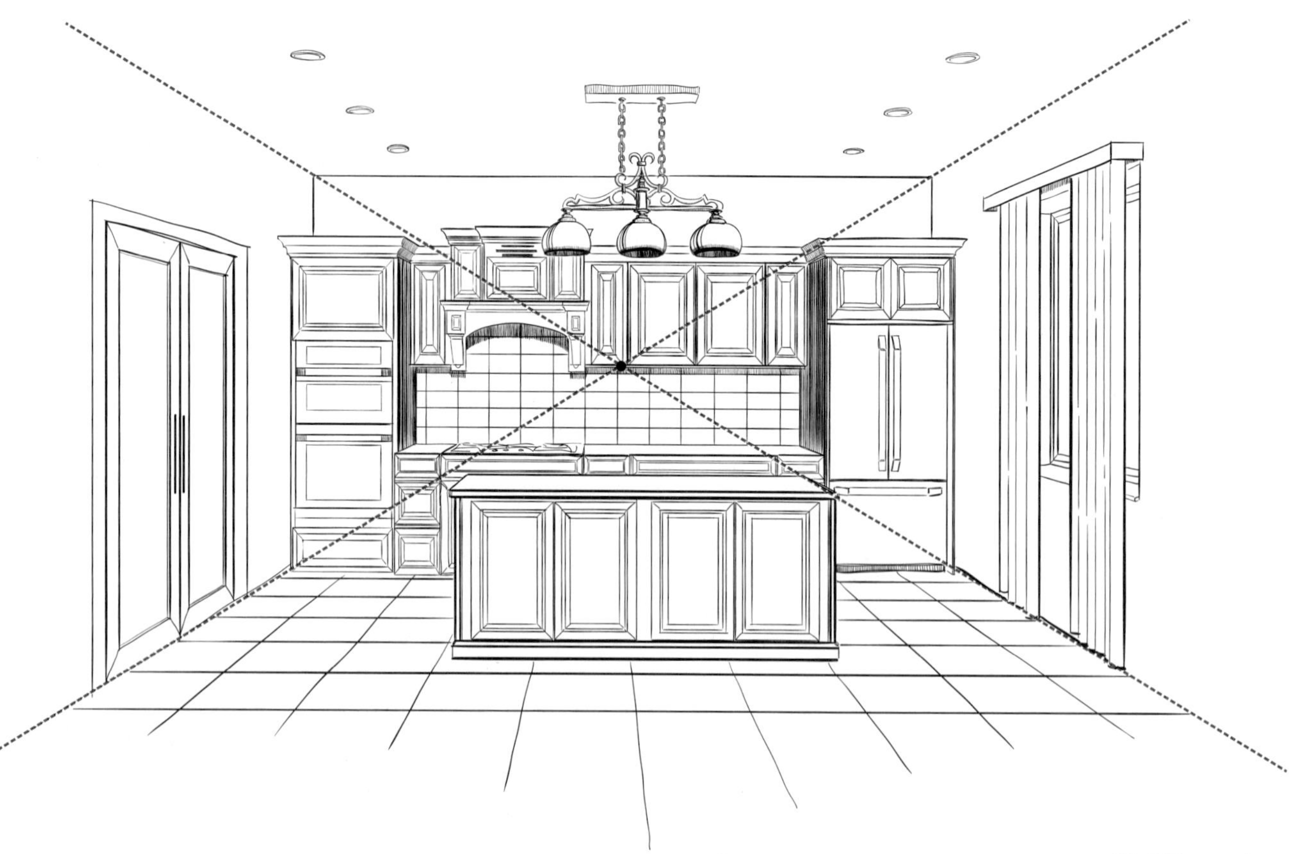

AVD_88/Shutterstock.com

Figure 18.11 Practicing one-point perspective drawings using a kitchen is easier since most of the elements are rectangular, solid shapes.

might be round, but if you view it from across the room, it will appear more elliptical. As you move away from the lights, they will appear to become more flat but still remain symmetrical.

- In a one-point perspective, you will never see more than two sides of a regular-shaped object. For instance, you see the front and top of the kitchen island but not the sides. You see the front and side of the refrigerator but not the top.
- You will only see the top side of items that are below your horizon line (such as the countertops) but will see the underside of items above your horizon line (such as the pendant light globes).
- You may only see one side of an item that is on or near your horizon line (such as the center wall cabinet).
- Objects on parallel walls (such as doors or window frames) may appear painted on and flat if the minor thicknesses are not projected out from the wall.

Review & Assessment

1. What does each of the following represent in CADD software: red axis, green axis, blue axis?
2. What are isometric and perspective drawings?
3. What are the horizon line and vanishing point in regard to perspective drawings?
4. What are the key differences between one-point perspectives and two-point perspectives?
5. Briefly describe how to draw a one-point perspective.
6. Name three rules of thumb to remember about one-point perspective drawings.

Fundamentals of Visual Presentation Materials

Utilizing the elements and principles discussed in earlier chapters for presentation design will lead to success, no matter whether you are preparing a finish board, marketing materials, poster, website, or portfolio (Figure 18.12). Proportion, scale, emphasis, rhythm, harmony, and balance are essential. Draw or sketch your composition before you begin. Draw several ways to compose the board or other visual and then evaluate the best one to use.

When considering the overall layout before getting to any of the details, consider balance and flow of the piece. Determine the orientation (horizontal or vertical) and create a grid or guidelines to give order to the drawing and take the time to

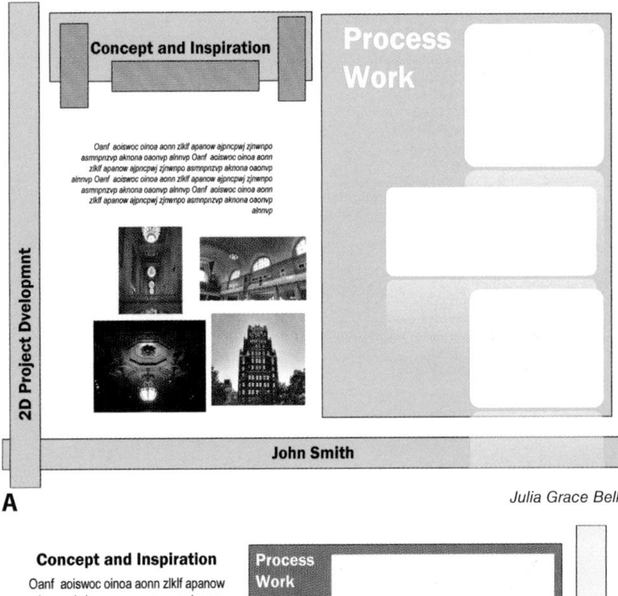

A Julia Grace Belk

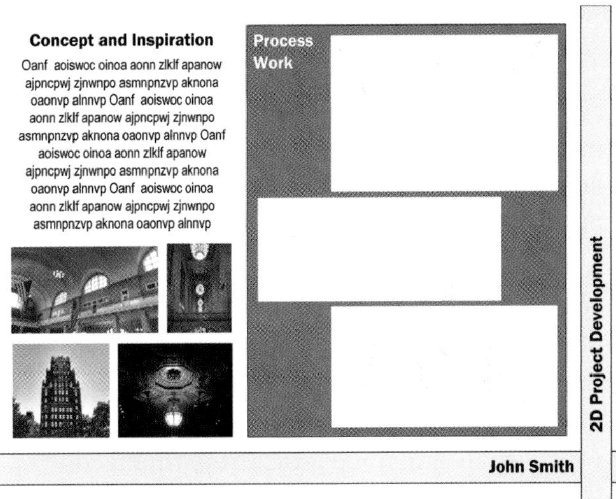

B Julia Grace Belk

Figure 18.12 While reading this section, consider the reasons for the suggested changes between the poor presentation layout (A) and the improved one (B).

experiment with different configurations. These are a few basic rules:

- Place the center-of-gravity slightly below center so that it does not feel top-heavy.
- Lay out content chronologically left to right because it is natural (in western societies) to read left-to-right and top-down. This might mean starting with general items and then getting to specifics or perhaps placing items in the order you would experience when walking through the home.
- Place the title information or consistent logo at the bottom or bottom right of the board or page. This helps to keep the viewer focused on the board and prevents straying.
- Place an element, such as a floor plan, in the center of the board. A layout that radiates from the center of the composition implies growth and ties all elements back to the central element.

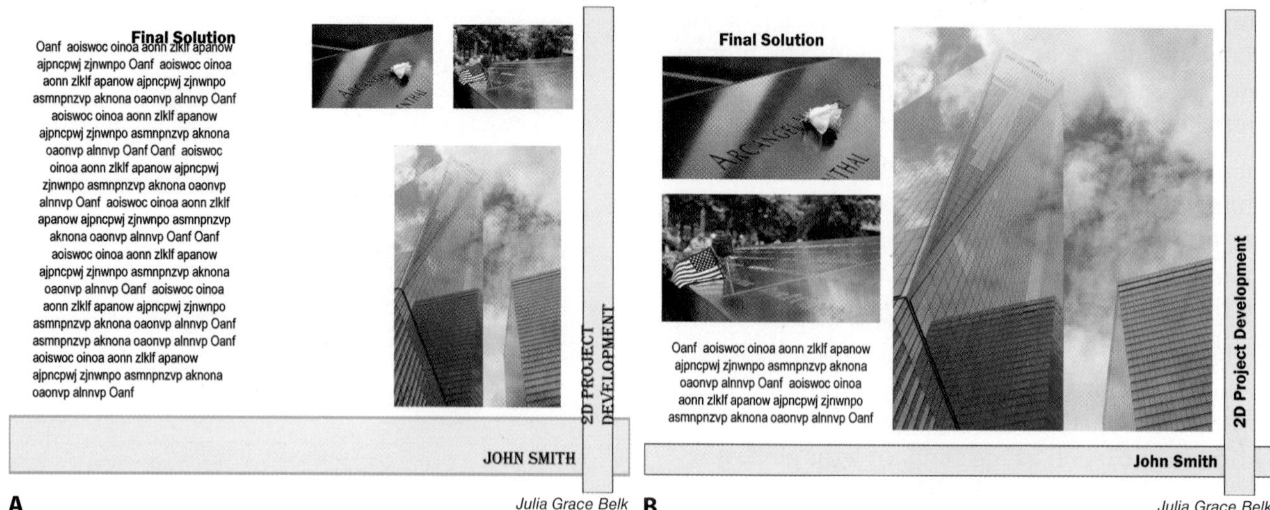

A Julia Grace Belk B Julia Grace Belk

Figure 18.13 What changes or corrections can you identify between presentation A and presentation B?

- Consider spatial relationships. Show lighting higher on the board or page than walls. Show floor patterns and coverings lower on the presentation.
- Use contrast effectively with visuals and text content. Lack of effective contrast creates murky-looking contents, making it difficult for the viewer to recognize details.
- Keep the layout and graphics simple to enhance your visuals and not distract from them. For this reason, light backgrounds are best for pictures, renderings, or any materials with a pattern. Choose only a few accent colors to use for borders and framing, and be consistent with their use.
- Use proximity to group items that go together to help the viewer understand where items are used and keep the board from looking spotty with endless individual square visuals.

    Groupings may be room by room or may be by product (flooring versus furniture versus paints). Overlapping and stacking some items can solidify their relationship and avoid any confusion. For instance, place a chair next to the upholstery to be used. With so many elements within a composition, try to provide some free negative space on your boards. Items should be close, but regardless of the distance, the layout should be consistent.
- Utilize repetition to unify your design and to give harmony to a set of boards, portfolio pages, or web pages. By repeating colors, line types, fonts, methods of bordering, logos, etc, you can create a consistency to your boards which gives harmony to not only the composition but also the elements within (Figure 18.13).
- Use the same background color, size, and orientation for each item to unify the package whether presenting individual boards or each slide of a digital presentation. Borders, spacing, and any effects (such as digital shadowing of visuals) should also be consistent.
- Ensure multiple complementary items are the same *scale* when showing them together on a board or page. For instance, if there is a sofa shown next to a coffee table, you want the comparative scale of those two pieces to appear as they would in reality.
- Use verbiage intelligently on your boards or digital presentations. Fonts should be simple (such as Arial) and consistent. Much of the success of the project visuals relies on the information that accompanies the images.
- Use capitalization only when necessary and never as running text. Vary text size to differentiate headings, subheadings, labels, and text, and make sure the color has much contrast with the background.
- Effective alignment of text and graphics creates strong lines and a sense of organization on your boards or pages (Figure 18.14). Creating a grid or structural skeleton for the layout makes the layout of visuals easier but also makes sure text has a consistent place on the board or page and between elements.

An unprofessional visual can keep a design professional from taking the time to review a portfolio for an intern or new hire. With the

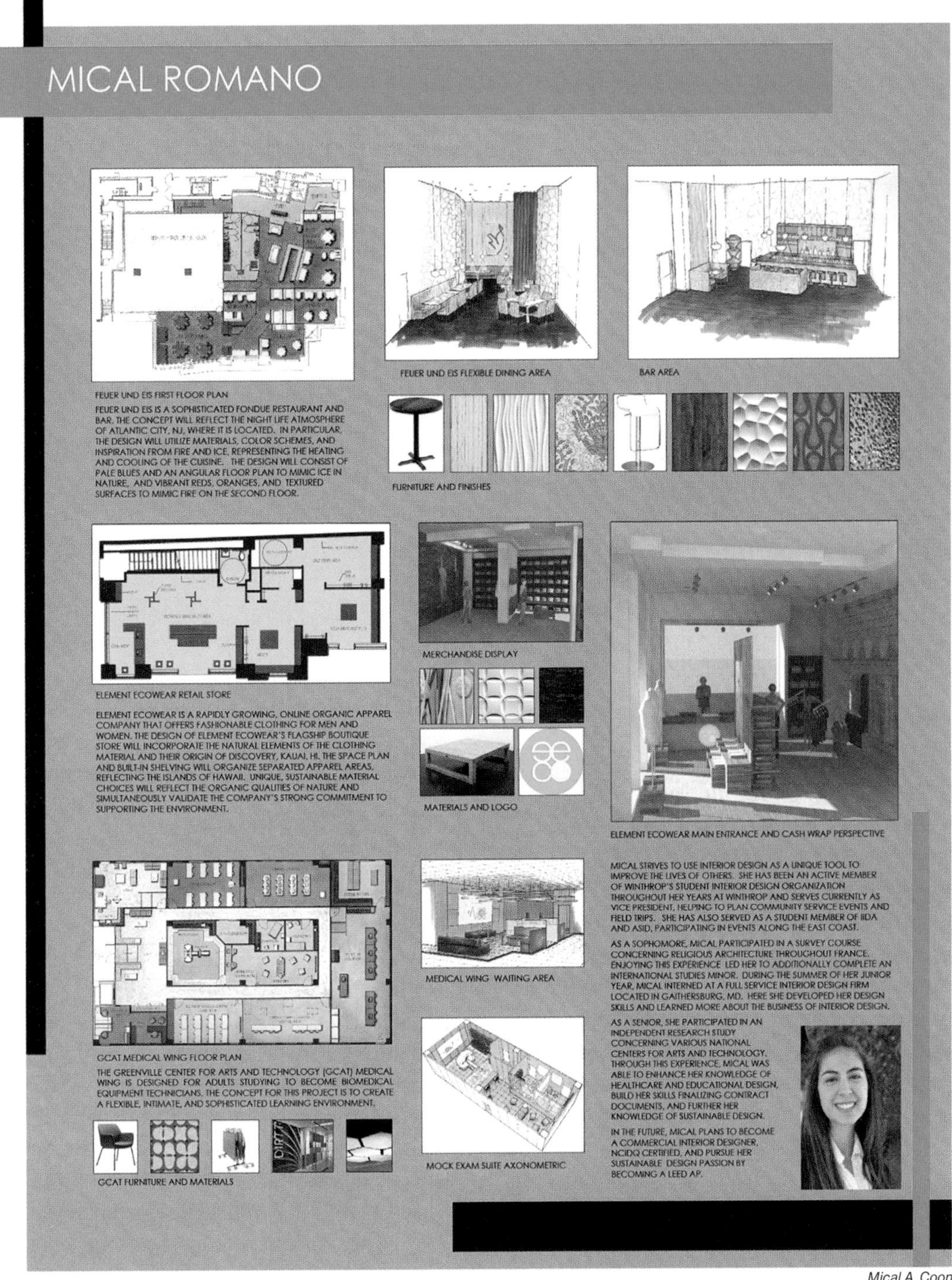

Mical A. Coon

Figure 18.14 Even a large, digitally produced gallery poster can employ the same design fundamentals as a small portfolio.

tools that programs now have, there is no excuse for turning something in with spelling errors. Repeated words and errors in grammar are easy to avoid. Proof your work before gluing or printing, and have someone else review your work as well.

The most important elements on your board or presentation are photos and drawings. These must be the focal point of each layout and given the great majority of the space. Ensure the picture quality is excellent but also consider the size at which viewers will see the image (if the visual will be small when printed, there is no need for it to have resolution that is too high). Use photo editing tools to adjust saturation, brightness, and contrast in photos.

Review & Assessment

1. In what ways can the elements and principles of design be applied to the design of *any* form of presentation material?
2. List 10 basic rules to follow when creating visual presentation materials.
3. What is the drawback to unprofessional visual presentations?
4. What are the most important elements on a board or presentation?

Different Types of Visual Presentation Methods

Although there are commonalities between all types of visual presentations, there are concepts, tips and guidelines relative to each. In combination with the previous section, the following information will help you make all your visual communications successful.

Creating Presentation Boards

Presentation boards can be produced manually, digitally, or a combination of both (Figure 18.15). Either way, make sure to apply the design strategies previously discussed. *Alignment*, contrast, *proximity* and repetition will help your board have harmony and allow you to tell the story that you desire. **Alignment** refers to the quality of two or more visual elements to be in a straight line or arranged in a parallel manner, while **proximity** is the nearness or closeness of two or more items or people. Craft is of utmost importance, so always use rulers and straightedges (handheld or digital tools). Never rely on eyeballing measurements or 90-degree angles to be precise. Always strive for accuracy and precision in all design work, especially when creating client presentations.

Planning Your Board

As with other methods of visual communication, planning is essential. Before constructing your board, make a sketch plan of your board (to scale). Then you will want to cut and prepare all of the separate components and lay them in place. When you feel that you have completed the board (or image or presentation), but before actually adhering anything, step away to the distance your viewer will be seeing it from. Are the drawings and other text readable? Does the order of the board make sense? Are the items you want to emphasize apparent?

Katherine West

Figure 18.15 Digital presentation boards are helpful as they allow you to easily make changes throughout your schooling as you learn new skills. This excellent digital rendering produced with BIM and photo manipulation software could replace the hand-rendered perspective previously produced by this student.

To prepare your professional presentation board (or sample board), you will need a large mat board or illustration board, typically 18 inches by 24 inches or 20 inches by 30 inches. These sizes are optimal because they are half the size of the typical mat board you can purchase at an art supply store. If the color board you prefer is not available, you can purchase large-format colored paper to mount onto a backer board before adhering any materials. You will identify the project by placing the name of your firm or business and the name of your client on the board.

When mounting items on your board, frame individual pieces or groupings of related materials and furnishings with a different, but consistent-color board or card. Black tape can also be used to create an edge on the board itself. Only utilize the front of the board unless you are putting supplemental information just for your use or an envelope for loose materials on the back. Cut fabrics to a finished edge or wrap them neatly around a small piece of foam core before mounting.

Coding and Labeling Presentation Boards

Code and label each part of your floor plan with letters and/or numbers. For example, you may label the furniture with letters (A, B, C, and so forth) and the walls, window treatments, accessories, and light fixtures with numbers (1, 2, 3, and so forth). Label each sample with the same letter or number code that you place on the floor plan. If you label a sofa with the letter "A," you will also label its sample upholstery fabric and photo with "A." As you finish your presentation board, each sample on the board will have a code that shows its use and appearance in the space. You can use this labeling system to cross-reference to future specifications and purchase orders.

When labeling your presentation boards, it is important to consider your method. If your board is relatively light in color, you can print labels on clear vinyl with a sticker back. Carefully and neatly cut the labels from the sheet and apply directly to the board. If your background is darker, however, this method will not work due to lack of contrast. Print the labels using a computer, and then mount each label on foam core as you would a drawing. It is preferable to present your ideas in short, but informative statements or bullet points of key words rather than put essays or paragraphs on presentation boards. It is better to present the details in your oral presentation.

Mounting Floor Plans, Elevations, and Renderings

Mount the floor-plan drawing and any elevations or renderings on the board to show the placement of all structural details, such as the locations of doors, windows, partitions, columns, cabinetry, closets, and storage. These scale drawings will also show the placement and installation of all the furniture and lighting in the room(s). Do not mount your original drawings because glues and tape will show through the ***vellum*** (a strong, translucent, cream-colored paper) and you do not want to risk damaging the piece. Scan the drawing and then print it in color before mounting it to a backing. Only after adhering it to the backing should you cut both the drawing and the backing to size. This ensures that both image and backing are exactly the same size prior to mounting them to the large board.

Selecting and Mounting Samples

Mount on the board samples of each of the following items on which you and the client agree (Figure 18.16):

- paint and wall covering samples for the walls and trim
- wood finish samples for furniture, cabinetry, and millwork (doors, windows, and trims)
- flooring finishes and materials samples
- photographs or drawings showing furniture styles, window treatments (shades, blinds, or curtains and draperies), light fixtures, bath fixtures, and accessories

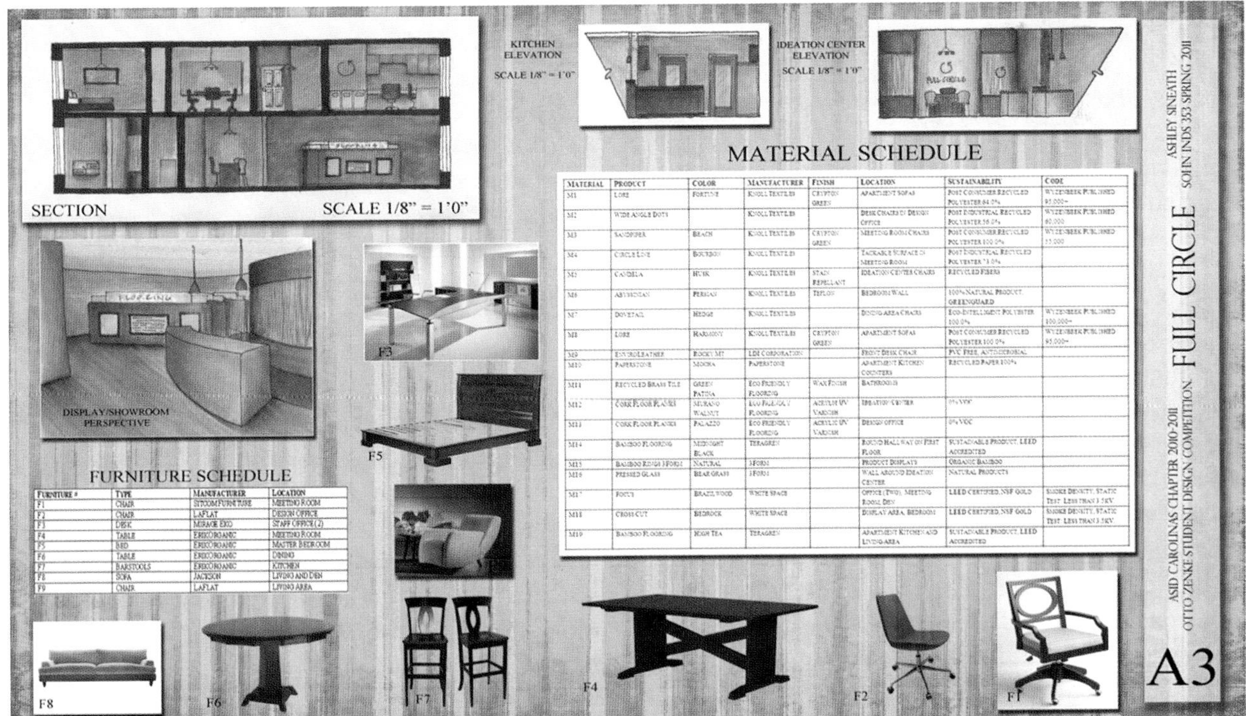

FURNITURE #	TYPE	MANUFACTURER	LOCATION
F1	CHAIR	SITCOM FURNITURE	MEETING ROOM
F2	CHAIR	LAFLAT	DESIGN OFFICE
F3	DESK	MIRAGE EKO	STAFF OFFICE (2)
F4	TABLE	ERIKORGANIC	MEETING ROOM
F5	BED	ERIKORGANIC	MASTER BEDROOM
F6	TABLE	ERIKORGANIC	DINING
F7	BARSTOOLS	ERIKORGANIC	KITCHEN
F8	SOFA	JACKSON	LIVING AND DEN
F9	CHAIR	LAFLAT	LIVING AREA

Ashley Sineath

Figure 18.16 To communicate furniture and finish information to clients and vendors, schedules can be incorporated into presentation boards and keyed graphics.

- fabric swatches and trims for window treatments and each piece of upholstery
- carpeting samples and/or photographs of the rugs you propose for the space

There are many helpful tips for cutting. If you do not have a large-scale paper slicer, a craft knife will work; however, never use scissors to trim images and other samples because this method is not as precise. The main goal is to keep your blades sharp which means changing the blades in your craft knife often. For thicker items like foam core, make two to three passes at the cut to get through the material without chewing up the edges.

There are many options regarding **adhesives** (substances such as hot glue, rubber cement, and spray mount that stick materials together). Whichever you use, it is essential to allow enough time for the adhesive to dry prior to transporting your board. *Spray mount* is the sheerest form of adhesive and the most consistent way to fasten any type of paper to the backing material or frame. For samples and heavier items, use white glue, double-sided tape, or hot glue. You can mount tactile pieces, such as carpet and fabrics, with hook-and-loop tape since you may want to remove the samples to allow the client to feel textures.

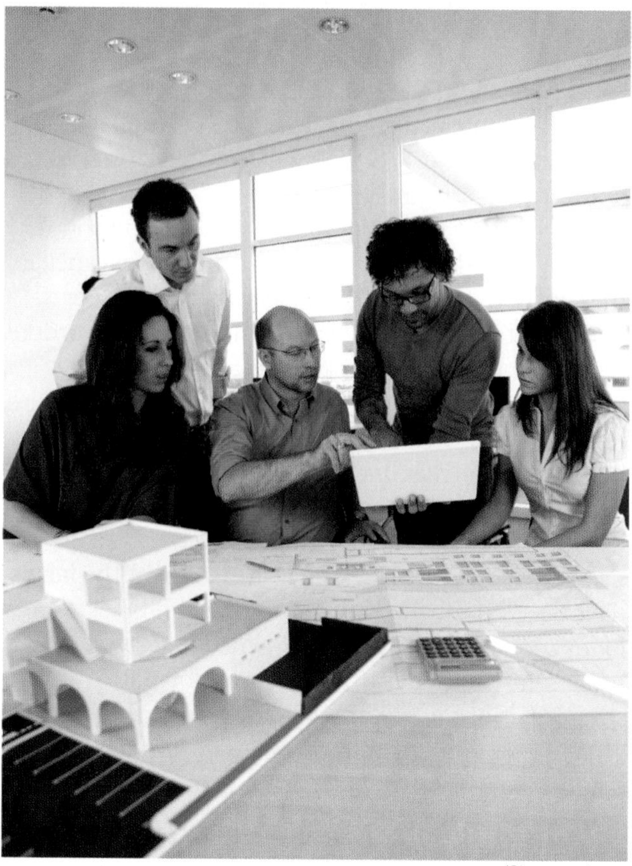

auremar/Shutterstock.com

Figure 18.17 Study or concept models allow designers and design students to understand the volume 3-D character of a building, not just the 2-D floor plan.

Making Models

When planning a model, understanding its purpose is essential. If photo-realism is the goal, the model will require precision, craft, and expensive, realistic materials and textures. If the model's purpose is to express a concept or form, neutral or white materials can work well, using additional drawings, photos, and material samples to supplement the model later. Basic materials such as foam core board are easier to manipulate as well (Figure 18.17). Many materials and techniques are similar to making presentation boards.

Tools that are essential to model making include triangles, templates, scales, cutting tools, T-square, and a metal straightedge. Construction materials vary greatly, but most popular are the many types of boards (chipboard, museum board, mat board, cardboard, and foam core), woods (such as balsa wood sheets or wooden dowels), and materials you can sculpt such as Styrofoam® or clear materials such as Plexiglas® and acetate.

When creating a plan or model, one of the first decisions is determining what scale to use for the model. The structure you plan to build, how much detail it requires, and any restrictions you have on overall size of the model are the basis for determining scale. If you want to show a large area, perhaps for a context model of a site or large property, you must choose a smaller scale. If you need to show detail of a small space, choose a larger scale. See Figure 18.18 for typical model scales for different types of models.

With any project that requires cutting, clean and sharp blades as well as a self-healing cutting mat are essential to ensure craft, safety, and protection of other surfaces. Use a heavy-duty blade for thicker boards but smaller and lighter blades for more delicate materials and curves. When cutting, utilize a metal ruler with a cork back to avoid slipping and accidental slicing of materials. Plan all cuts by sketching the plan and elevation views using actual measurements and explore different joining techniques throughout the model.

Your choice of adhesives can make a huge difference in the success of your model. Regardless of what you choose, make sure to be flexible, inventive, and patient with the work. Here are some tips related to different types of adhesives:

- Use several thin layers when using white glue.
- Use rubber cement to adhere paper and fabrics to a board.

Scales for Making Models (Based on a model size of 12" × 12" × 12")		
Model Subject	**Maximum Subject Size**	**Scale**
Coffee table or chair	4'-0" square	3" = 1'-0"
Dining table	8'-0" square	1½" = 1'-0"
Small bedroom	12'-0" square	1" = 1'-0"
Large bedroom	16'-0" square	¾" = 1'-0"
Master suite	24'-0" square	½" = 1'-0"
Small apartment or two-story home	32'-0" square	⅜" = 1'-0"
Large, two-story home	48'-0" square	¼" = 1'-0"
Multi-story or multi-unit apartment building	64'-0" square	3⁄16" = 1'-0"
Model of home on approximately ¼ acre of land	96'-0" square	⅛" = 1'-0"

Figure 18.18 Determining what scale to use for a model is one of the first decisions you make before creating a model. This table offers scale options for various items.

- Use of hot glue is fast, but unforgiving. It can leave strings and it not easy to remove. It also can melt delicate materials like foam core.
- Protect adjacent surfaces and open a window for fresh air when using spray adhesives. Obtain a brand which allows you to reposition materials. Be careful to avoid oversaturating materials with spray adhesives.
- Use painter's tape to avoid damage to the surfaces of materials.
- Use double-sided tape if you need to attach and layer sheets of paper and foam core.
- Use of straight pins, although they are visible, gives great structure and alignment to a model.

Monkey Business Images/Shutterstock.com

Figure 18.19 For quick prototypes and modeling, architects, designers, and engineers utilize 3-D printers.

Ideally, it is best to be realistic about what you can achieve with your time, materials, and equipment. It is always better to be "less ambitious" but complete a model with great precision and craft. If fast prototypes or multiple models are a need, 3-D printers can be extremely beneficial to turn CADD drawings into detailed models (Figure 18.19).

Creating Portfolios and Websites

If you choose to create a digital portfolio or have a website for your work, there are countless programs you can use to develop your portfolio. Having a *digital copy* (one that you can show on a projection screen, computer, or website) as well as a *print copy* (to thumb through with an employer) is beneficial. No matter what software you use to create your portfolio, save the final version as a PDF file. In this way, if someone with different software opens the file, your layout and fonts remain the same. You can continually add to and improve the original file and then save to PDF when needed.

Your portfolio or website should illustrate not only your strengths and interests, but also what position or scholarship for which you are applying. Consider the audience or who you are presenting it to. If it is primarily a kitchen and bath design firm, you will want to concentrate on those types of projects plus anything else that deals with residential design and cabinetry detailing.

Size and Format for Print Portfolios

The size and format of your tangible print portfolio is up to you. To avoid making a trip to the office supply store each time you need a print, choose a size that is convenient for printing (plotting) and copying. Oversized prints can be costly. An 11-inch by 17-inch print size is a happy medium and is large enough to show most visuals in enough detail. There is no real benefit of using landscape versus portrait orientation. As long as you ensure that the format is consistent, you can look to the typical orientation of your presentation boards and drawings to help you decide.

Presentation Enclosures for Print Portfolios

With portfolios, the actual physical enclosure you select for your work can take on many forms. It can be a presentation case, a custom-made box, a well-made three-ring binder, or a large folder. The main considerations are its ability to display and protect your work. If you are using original artwork, that will dictate the size and type of portfolio. It is a good idea to select something that has flexibility for reorganization. You can use your portfolio for many different purposes, so having something you can rearrange for various audiences can be beneficial.

As you are planning your portfolio or website, look to magazines and websites that attract you visually (Figure 18.20). What line types, colors, fonts, and layouts do you think best coordinate with your work and your style? Refer to text pages 411–413 for layout guidelines.

Selection and Quantity of Work to Display

The quantity and selection of work is up to you; however, there are some general guidelines to consider. Only show your best work. These should be pieces you are proud of and can speak confidently about. Your work should show a progression. Even if you eventually take early fundamental work out of your portfolio, employers like seeing your progression and growth. You may include any side projects you may have done as long as the clients grant you permission. Many students choose to include information and photos from travels, hobbies, and extracurricular activities. This shows that you are an observer and a learner.

Arranging Your Portfolio

Once you make a decision on what pieces to use, consider sketching a **storyboard** (quick, small-scale sketches of the layout and components of pages within a portfolio, typically in sequential order) of your work to determine the arrangement. Some professionals prefer this chronological approach to show the development and growth of your work. Be careful with this technique. If an interview ends abruptly for some reason, a potential employer

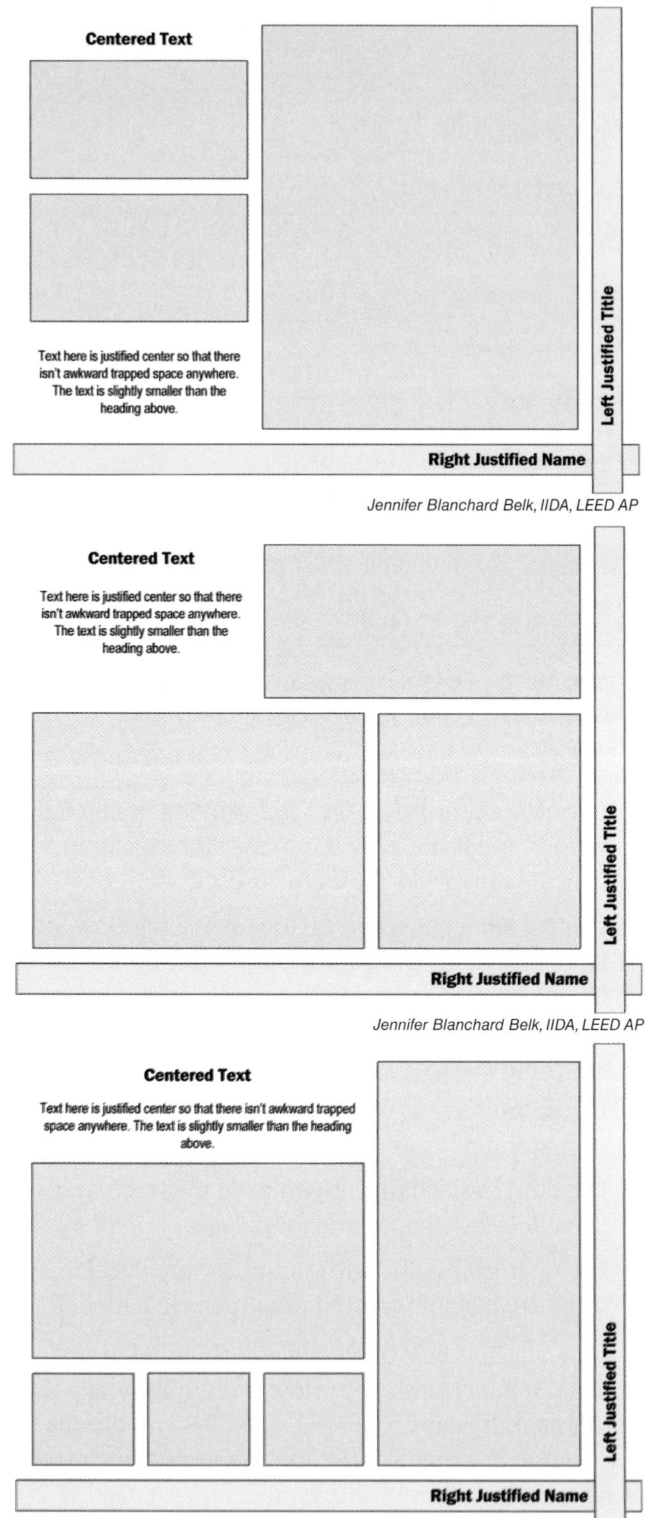

Figure 18.20 A structural grid can be helpful in ensuring consistency from page to page of a portfolio. It is a framework but does not mean you cannot purposefully step outside of the grid.

will miss the best of your work at the end of your portfolio. Many suggest that you "bookend" the portfolio by putting your two best projects at the beginning and end. This gives a good first and last impression of your work.

For school projects, look to your project assignment sheets and any related written work to come up with any verbiage in your portfolio. Make image descriptions brief but informative, as others may view this portfolio electronically and you will not be there to explain your work. Grammar, good writing, and great design are imperative. Also, make sure to give credit on anything you did not produce, such as other components of a group project.

For digital portfolios and web pages, work to make them as clean and graphically consistent as possible. Most programs will allow you to create a template in order to make sure each page is identical in graphic layout, font use, etc. Use tools such as guidelines and digital rulers (Figure 18.21). Always be careful to ensure the files do not get too large which can make them difficult to load and send. Seek tips from the program's *help* menu for limiting size of visuals while still maintaining quality.

Using Photography

Before putting a board together of your own work, you must successfully photograph your previous art and design projects. Using a digital camera makes photographing your work easy. You can view the photos immediately and retake them as needed. Acquire the best camera you can afford.

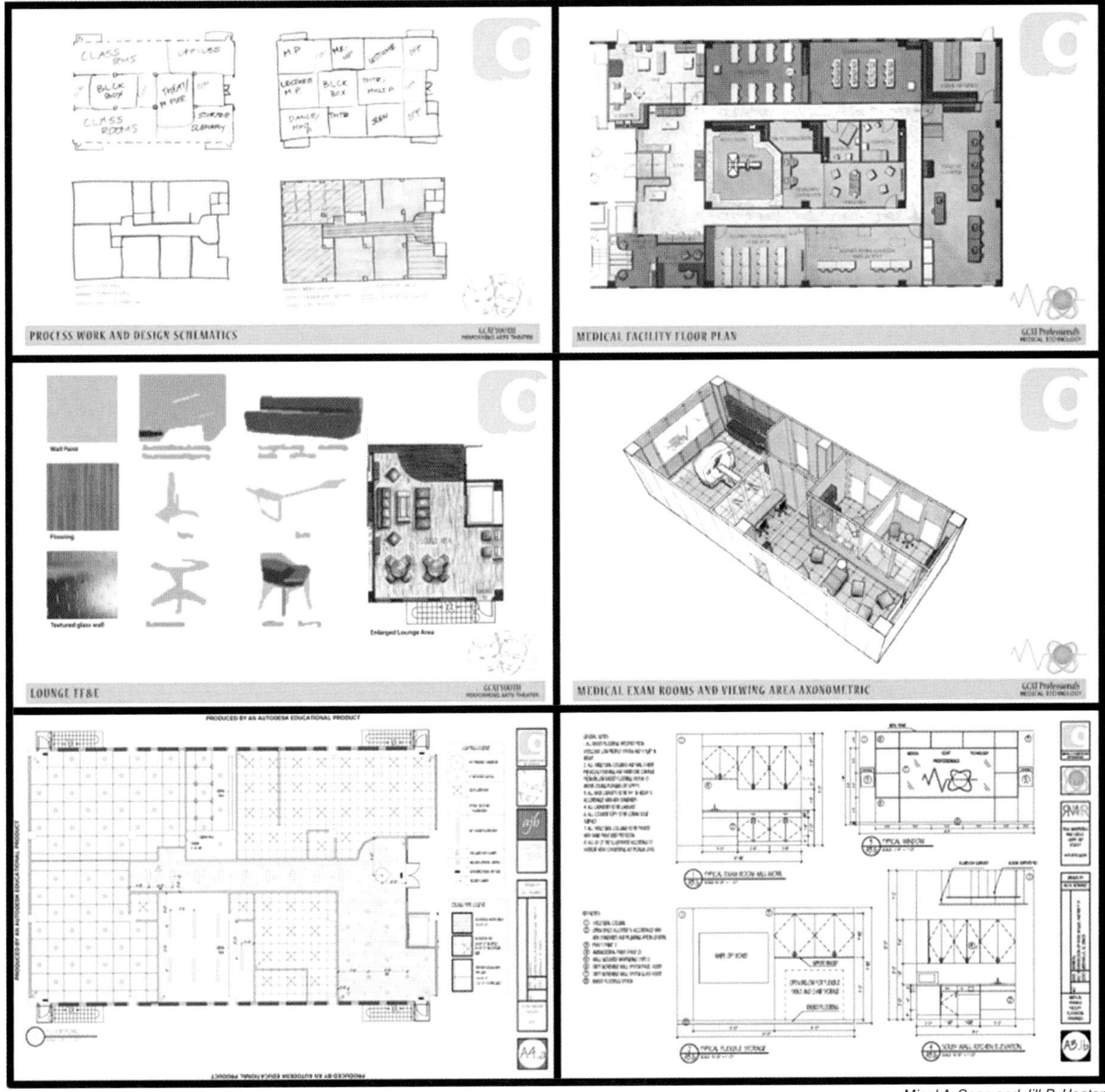

Mical A. Coon and Jill B. Heaton

Figure 18.21 With team projects, it is often difficult to maintain a consistent visual layout. Creating a template and standard graphics allowed these students to create unique but unified presentation slides.

This rarely means using your cell phone's camera. If you do not have a tripod, make sure you hold the camera as steady as possible, using a table or other object to steady yourself.

The angle at which you photograph your pieces is important (Figure 18.22). With a model or sculpture, as long as the angle focuses on the elements of the model, there is no right or wrong. Take multiple views to compare and contrast. With a flat piece like a drawing or presentation board, centering and aligning is key. Scanning such pieces to a computer is always best. If that is not an option, make sure that the piece is on a level surface and you place yourself as central as possible (top to bottom and side to side) when taking the photograph. This will help prevent the perspective distortion of the photograph, or **keystoning**, the effect by which the picture seems to get larger at the top and/or bottom.

A Photobank.ch/Shutterstock.com

B Photobank.ch/Shutterstock.com

Figure 18.22 Whether drawing a perspective by hand or photographing an existing space, select a view angle that gives the most information regarding the connection of spaces and visual elements. In what ways do you feel angle (A) is not as successful as angle (B)?

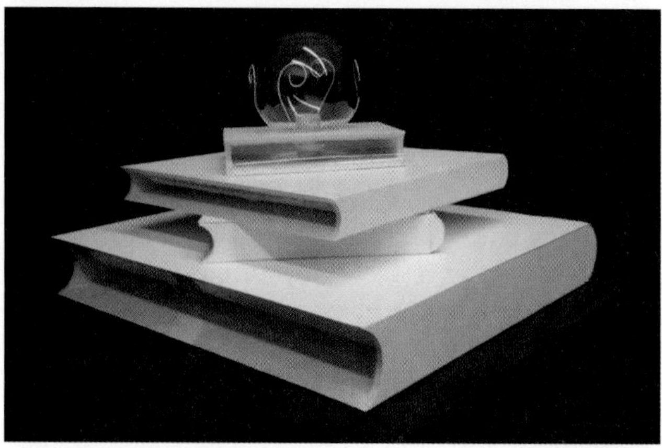

Victoria Waddington

Figure 18.23 Neutral materials are typically used for study modeling so as not to draw attention away from the concept. This also makes it easier to get true color representation when photographing.

Lighting is the biggest factor in whether your photo turns out successfully. Using natural, indirect light will help give your colors the truest appearance and will avoid light spots and glare (Figure 18.23). When using artificial lighting, make sure to have at least two at different angles to avoid shadows. It is best not to use a flash because it will often give a bleaching effect.

Review & Assessment

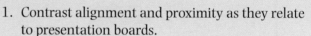

1. Contrast alignment and proximity as they relate to presentation boards.
2. Before adhering items to your presentation board, what should you do and what questions should you ask?
3. Summarize the coding and labeling system to use for presentation boards.
4. What samples should you select to print and mount to your presentation board?
5. List five useful tips for adhesives when making models.
6. Name two guidelines to consider when selecting work to display in your portfolio or website.
7. What is a storyboard and how would you use it?
8. What are three key factors of using photography for presentations, portfolios, and websites?

Presenting Your Design

There are many different kinds of presentations. A **marketing presentation** for a designer is very much like a job interview or portfolio review

Career Focus Interior Design Marketing

Do you enjoy selling people on your ideas and qualifications? Are you a people person? Do you ever wonder why people choose to purchase one product or work with one company and not all the others? If so, a career as an interior design marketing professional might be for you.

Interests/Skills: Marketing professionals must be persuasive, ambitious and personable. They should be able to relate to a variety of client types, be approachable and be able to speak and think on their feet. They must be able to multitask and deal with deadlines but also be very people oriented. Effective organizational skills, attention to detail, along with active listening skills are a must. Strong visual, written and verbal communication skills are also essential.

Career Snapshot: Marketing professionals, no matter what their area of concentration, deal with product, place, promotion and price. Design marketers seek to present a firm's skills and aptitudes to potential clients and collaborators for future job opportunities. They will develop printed and online promotional materials geared toward a target audience. They will develop presentations as a response to Request for Proposals (RFPs) that large corporations and organizations put out when they are ready to start a major building project. Design marketing professionals will typically work for larger architecture and interior design firms since smaller firms will rarely have enough need to sustain a full-time employee in this position. Outside consultants are less likely because it might lead to a conflict of interest serving multiple but similar clients. Either way, a large part of their job is networking with potential clients and following up on prospects.

Education/Training: A higher education degree in either marketing or interior design is typically required. Someone with a marketing degree would then benefit from apprenticeships or internships within design and architecture firms. Someone with a design degree would benefit from an apprenticeship or internship in a marketing firm or in a large design firm under the head of marketing. Most professionals seek other

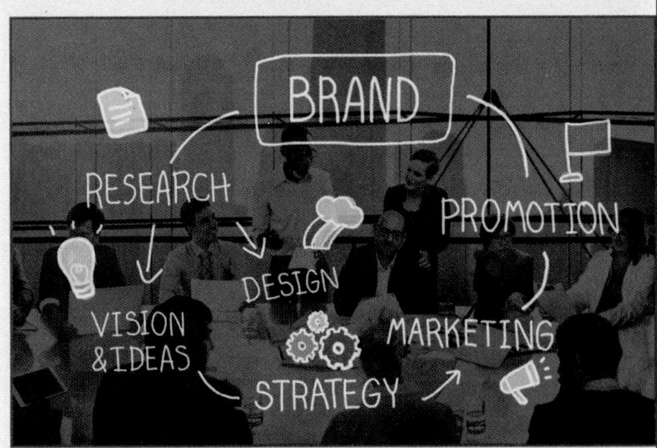

Rawpixel.com/Shutterstock.com

continuing education in a variety of topics including graphic design, technical writing, and psychology.

Licensing/Examinations: Due to the incredibly vast nature of this segment of the industry, marketing professionals have many choices when it comes to voluntary licensing, in addition to the National Council for Interior Design Qualification (NCIDQ). The American Marketing Association has a general certification called a PMC, Professional Certified Marketer. Many professionals will also become LEED Accredited Professionals (Leadership in Energy and Environmental Design) in order to better sell the environmental aspects of their firm.

Professional Associations: In addition to more general organizations such as The American Society of Interior Designers (ASID), American Institute of Architects (AIA), and the International Interior Design Association (IIDA), involvement in the American Marketing Association (AMA) and the Business Marketing Association (BMA) can be a benefit. These national organizations offer continuing education opportunities and exposure to trends and industry research.

Job Outlook: While the overall professional outlook is very good, it is even better in specialty architectural areas such as schools/education/ healthcare, and sustainable design.

Sources: The Occupational Outlook Handbook (OOH); the Occupational Information Network (O*NET)

(Figure 18.24). You are not necessarily presenting solutions to a problem but rather selling the quality of your future services to a potential client, clarifying your experience and abilities.

The goal of a **project presentation** is to educate the client and obtain their approval on the design choices you have made. As the designer, you may need to encourage and coax your client to understand the details and importance of how and why you made your selections. You may need to give your client more details about your selections, such as the *life cycles* (how long items will last and when they

Jennifer Blanchard Belk, IIDA, LEED AP

Figure 18.24 Presentations are not only used for client and class projects; portfolio reviews and scholarship interviews will often require you to show and present the breadth of your work.

might need to be replaced), functions, maintenance, performance, environmental features, and safety. Talk about the process you went through to arrive at your solution. Know your reasoning and criteria for your material and furniture selections, tying them all back to the initial goals set forth for the project.

Personal Preparation

Preparation is key for a presentation. Ready yourself by having a good night's sleep, a healthy breakfast, appropriate dress, and a well-practiced presentation. Your manner of dress will differ depending on the environment, but it is always better to overdress rather than dress too casually. For presentations, however, there are a few guidelines. In addition to being neat and clean, anticipate temperature differences as this can be a distraction or embarrassment. The room might be too cold, so make sure to have a cardigan or jacket. If the room is too warm, perspiration could become a problem. If you remove a jacket, you must make sure that you are not showing underarms or any inappropriate clothing. See Chapter 27 for further suggestions on professional attire.

Find out where you will be presenting so that you know what technology you will have available, how much space you will have, if you need to bring an easel, etc. Know who will be there and who the actual decision makers are. One client may be the person paying the bill while another might actually have the final say on design decisions. If many people are present, you may need to bring a pointer or have extra copies of presentation materials (Figure 18.25).

Organizing Your Presentation

Have a logical order to your presentation. Just like a term paper, your presentation should do the following:

- define an overall purpose and goal
- give background and solutions
- conclude with a summary of the project

Jennifer Blanchard Belk, IIDA, LEED AP

Figure 18.25 In school, you may be required to do project presentations for teachers, professionals, and classmates.

As with a finish board or set of construction documents, it should proceed from general to specific (detailed). Discussing individual finishes will not make sense until you have reviewed the overall floor plan and general color scheme. It is also better not to start with handouts because many clients will get distracted and will try to review them while you are speaking.

Practicing and Executing Your Presentation

Practice is essential for an effective presentation. Many suggest practicing with someone who knows nothing about the project such as a roommate or sibling. This helps to ensure that you do not skim over important facts or ideas—which could easily happen when practicing with a coworker or classmate. Know how much time you will have for the presentation (including question and answer time) so that you understand how in depth your descriptions can be.

Although you should be professional in your oral presentation, it is always best to involve the client by asking questions and confirming their understanding during the presentation. Use a relaxed manner when presenting your design—your client will view this as confidence. Incorporating visuals, both your original drawings and any inspiration or idea files you have, will take some of the pressure off and make the presentation more interactive.

Body language is a form of *non-verbal communication* (communicating without words using facial expressions and gestures). Some body language can give the wrong impression to a client. Examples include

- poor posture—can imply laziness or lack of confidence
- lack of eye contact—may suggest dishonesty
- crossed arms—can infer closed-mindedness or dislike
- harsh facial expressions—may imply criticism or concern

In addition to telling clients about your personality, your body movements can either help or hurt your presentation. Arm movements can direct clients to particular visuals or emphasize a point. Excessive movement, however, can be distracting and repetitive. Leaning close to a client can exhibit warmth, enthusiasm, and interest; however, you should always beware of invading his or her personal space. Pointing to the presentation board as you describe your design can ensure the client is following you (Figure 18.26). Standing on the wrong side of the board, however, may cause you to unintentionally turn your back to the client or block his or her view of your board.

Syda Productions/Shutterstock.com

Figure 18.26 Posture, eye contact, and facial expressions tell as much about your abilities as the solutions that you present.

Always use specific language when reviewing your presentation boards. For instance, say a fabric has "sheen" instead of saying it is "shiny." Say a chair has an "organic" shape rather than saying it is "curvy." Incorporate your knowledge of elements and principles. Avoid **powerless language**—words that do not add depth or content to your presentations and explanations—such as *umm, like, okay,* and *whatnot,* and vague or simple terms such as *nice, good,* and *pretty*. Practice different transitions and vocabulary you could use to describe your selections more precisely rather than using vague terms.

Either at the end or throughout your presentation, your client may disagree with your solutions. Remember, the client may have financial concerns as well as insecurities and uncertainties. It is your responsibility to walk them through such issues. It is important to never tell them they are wrong; rather, allow them to voice the concerns in detail. Once they voice their concerns, restate their concern, clarify any misunderstandings, and give supplemental information that might help them to better understand your solutions. You should always be prepared, however, to discuss alternative choices.

Review & Assessment 

1. Contrast a marketing presentation with a project presentation.
2. How can you prepare yourself for a presentation?
3. How is an organized presentation like a term paper?
4. What is body language? Give an example of body language that gives the wrong impression.
5. What is powerless language? Give an example.
6. If a client voices concerns or uncertainties during a presentation, what should you do?

Chapter 18 Assessment

Summary

- During the design process, there is continuous oral, written, and visual communication among the designer, client, vendors, building officials, and other professionals during different phases of the process.
- Most interior designers typically use computer-aided drafting and design (CADD) software and a computer for creating a scale floor plan.
- A designer must determine what software, or combinations of software are most appropriate for each individual project.
- Beyond making sure to demonstrate good design, there are many ways to make sure your 2-D and 3-D CADD drawings are as informative, accurate, and easy to produce as possible.
- Utilizing the elements and principles of design for presentation design leads to success, regardless whether you are preparing a finish board, marketing materials, poster, website, or portfolio.
- Effectively use contrast, proximity, repetition, and alignment to achieve proportion, scale, emphasis, rhythm, harmony, and balance.
- Although there are commonalities among all types of visual presentations, there are concepts, tips and guidelines individually relative to boards, models, portfolios, and digital presentations. These might include appropriate content, labeling, cutting techniques, suggested adhesives, or form.
- The goal of a project presentation is to educate the client and get their approval on the design choices.
- Personal preparation, practice, logical order and process, professional dress, and body language all contribute to the success of a design presentation.

Terms in Action

1. **Graphic vocabulary** With a partner, use the Internet to locate photos or graphics that depict the *Content* and *Academic Terms* at the beginning of the chapter. Use presentation software to show your graphics to the class, describing how they depict the meaning of the term(s).

Think Critically

2. **Assess communication** The author indicates that oral, written, and visual communication are continuous among the designer, clients, vendors, contractors, building officials, and other professionals. Use the text and other reliable materials to assess common traits of successful communication. Then apply your skills to give an example that demonstrates each form of communication (oral, written, and visual) to clearly and convincingly justify actions and decisions in a socially acceptable manner that others can easily understand.
3. **Assess needs** Imagine you have clients who would like to renovate their existing home and add a very large addition, too. It will involve not only finishes but structural changes. What combination of CADD and other software programs do you think would be the best combination to use on this project? Write a summary explaining your answers.
4. **Analyze pros and cons** Make a list of the advantages and disadvantages of creating a digital portfolio versus a traditional portfolio with original work. In what scenarios might your opinion change? Discuss your response in small groups.

Core Skills

5. **Math practice and technology** Construct lines and other geometric forms using computer-aided design methods for the following. Using two rooms in your home or the home of someone you know measure the room dimensions and create a floor plan design for each room. Be sure to include precise measurements for windows, doors, and any other room features. Transfer your measurements to your digital floor plan. Be sure to customize your screen menus to fit your specific needs.
6. **Writing and drawing** Presume you have been hired to design the waiting room for a new doctor's office in your community. All patients are adults, and a calm and comfortable atmosphere is important to your client. Before committing to a design plan, your client wants you to create two visual ideas about how the waiting room might look. Use your imagination

Chapter 18 Assessment

to create bubble diagrams, rough sketches and floor plans, and simple, freehand one-point perspectives to present your ideas in print using either CADD software or hand drawings, striving for accuracy and precision. Write a proposal to accompany your drawings.

7. **Drawing and speaking** Choose several rooms in your home or school to create several freehand, simple one-point perspective drawings. Use the text directions and any supplemental online drawing videos suggested by your instructor. In addition, consult the user videos or "help" link in your school-provided drawing software.
8. **Drawing, writing, and speaking** Use a school-provided CADD software program to create a scale floor plan, isometric drawing, perspective drawing, elevation drawing, and rendering of a room in your home or the home of someone you know. What design preferences do you prefer to use in this room? Then, print (plot) your drawings. Write a summary of the plans. Effectively apply your oral communication skills in presenting the drawings and your plans to the class, concisely and convincingly explaining your actions and design decisions.
9. **Math practice and speaking** You have been assigned to sculpt a model for class. The instructor needs you to build a replica of your classroom that will fit in a 12" × 12" shoe box. Measure the overall size of the room and determine the largest scale you could use for the model based on the guidelines in this chapter. Apply your oral communication skills to explain actions.
10. **Writing, speaking, and listening** Imagine you have completed the schematic design for the doctor's office in item 6. It is now time for the initial presentation to the client. Write a detailed outline for the presentation contents. Discuss this outline with a classmate and get feedback before revising the final presentation.
11. **Writing and technology** Select an exercise you have previously completed in this text. Create a five-minute presentation about the project to give to one classmate while another video records the presentation. When complete, watch the video and write a critique based on oral presentation skills, body language, and other aspects discussed in this chapter.
12. **CTE career readiness practice** Suppose through this class you have become interested in a career as an interior designer. You have done your research in regard to educational requirements and think this career path fits your personal and career goals. You feel, however, you are missing the first-hand experiential knowledge necessary to commit to such a career. Make an appointment with an interior designer or design firm in your area. Let them know you would like to observe them in a formal or informal presentation. While he or she is presenting, take notes on the details of the presentation. How did he or she prepare? What did he or she bring? How did the environment affect the presentation? Did her or his manner of dress help or hinder the presentation? Share an oral summary with the class.

Design Practice

13. **Residential design plan** Illustrate interior design ideas from observation and experience for a room in a residential house, such as a living room, kitchen, master bedroom, bath, or a teen's or child's bedroom. Demonstrate technological applications and effective use of interior design tools and media by creating a visual design presentation board following the phases for planning and presenting a professional design (including interior architectural drawings) described in this chapter. Make an oral presentation explaining the visual solution displayed on your presentation board and the written schedule.
14. **Commercial design plan** Presume you have been selected to design a commercial space, such as a bank lobby, high school lobby, hair salon waiting area, or hotel lobby. Prepare a visual design presentation board demonstrating effective use of interior design tools and media in designing. Presume your class is your "client." Make an oral presentation explaining the design concept displayed on your presentation board and the written schedule.
15. **Portfolio** Add one or more of your design presentation boards and the best samples of your work as portfolio examples of your design capabilities. Write a summary about each project to keep in your portfolio.

Unit 5

Interior Surfaces, Materials, and Furnishings

Informing Citizens About Eco-Friendly Textiles

Are you concerned about the environmental impact of textiles in your home and surroundings? What sustainable methods do manufacturers use for producing textiles for the home? What should consumers know about the environmental impact of textiles they choose for their homes? How can consumers benefit from choosing eco-friendly textiles?

Using the speaking and presentation guidelines for the FCCLA *Interior Design or Illustrated Talk STAR Event*, prepare an oral and visual presentation about eco-friendly textiles for home use. Follow the FCCLA *Planning Process* as you develop your presentation. Get the word out to as many groups as possible. See your adviser for information as needed.

Taking the Lead—Providing Furniture to People in Need

Many communities have nonprofit agencies that collect gently used furniture and redistribute it to people in need at low or no cost. Local social service agencies generally provide lists of people in need of furniture to such organizations.

As an FCCLA *Leadership Service in Action* project, use your leadership skills and the FCCLA *Planning Process* to develop a project related to providing furniture to people in need. Perhaps you can work with a local group or start a service of your own. If you decide to start a service of your own, consider stepping up to an FCCLA STAR Event project on *Entrepreneurship.* See your adviser for information as needed.

Khongkit Wiriyachan/Shutterstock.com

Chapter 19

Textiles for Environments

Content Terms

textiles
fiber
cellulosic natural fiber
protein natural fiber
manufactured fiber
polymer
generic name
trade name
extrusion
spinneret
yarn
blend
combination yarn
weaving
warp yarn
grain
weft yarn
wale
nap
knitting
bonded fabrics
structural design
applied design
finishes
upholstery
window treatments

Academic Terms 

resiliency
hypoallergenic
opaque
flammable

Learning Outcomes 

After studying this chapter, you will be able to

- analyze factors about fiber, yarn, and fabric manufacturing for use in textile products for residential and commercial environments.
- evaluate characteristics of textiles for use in residential and commercial environments.
- summarize features of textiles for floor treatments, including methods of care and maintenance.
- analyze appropriate textiles for upholstery and window treatments.
- summarize characteristics of textiles suitable for the kitchen, bathroom, and bedroom.
- summarize the key features of textile laws that protect consumers.

Reading with Purpose

Imagine that you own a textile supply business and have several employees working for you. As you read the chapter, think about what information you would like your employees to know about textiles. When you finish reading, write a memo to your employees and include key information from the chapter.

While studying, look for the access icon  **to:**

- **Practice** the *Content* and *Academic Terms* with e-flash cards, matching activities, and vocabulary games.
- **Reinforce** what you learn by completing the *Review & Assessment* questions and e-mailing them to your instructor.

www.g-wlearning.com/housing/

Calico Corners—Calico Home Stores

Textiles are flexible materials made of thin films or of fibers, yarns, or fabrics. You come in contact with a variety of textiles in your home and other environments every day. Your clothes are made from textiles. Carpets, rugs, upholstery, curtains, table linens, towels, and sheets are also made from textiles.

Choose textile products carefully when designing interiors and making furnishing decisions for yourself and potential clients. It is important to understand the characteristics of the many fibers and fabrics used in textiles. You also need to know how to maintain and care for them.

Understanding Fibers, Yarns, and Fabrics

To understand how to use and care for textiles properly, it is important to know how they are made. Textiles begin as fibers. Manufacturers spin fibers into yarns, which are then made into fabrics and other textile products.

Fibers

Fibers are the raw materials of which yarns and fabric consist. They are long, thin, and hair-like. Fibers are obtained from either natural or manufactured sources.

Natural Fibers

Natural fibers come from plant or animal sources. There are two categories of natural fibers—cellulosic natural fibers and protein natural fibers.

Cellulosic natural fibers come from the cellulose (a substance from plant cell walls) in plants. In general, they are highly absorbent, launder well, and seldom experience insect damage. They burn easily, however, and mildew can stain them. Also, prolonged exposure to sunlight can cause yellowing. The fibers are low in elasticity and may wrinkle easily. See Figure 19.1

Cellulosic Natural Fibers			
Fiber	**Source**	**Characteristics**	**Uses**
Cotton	Cotton plant	• Absorbent • Strong • Dyes well • Shrinks in hot water	• Sheets • Bedspreads/comforters • Rugs • Towels • Upholstery • Draperies
Flax (Linen is the fabric name)	Flax plant	• Absorbent • Strong • Wears well	• Table linens • Upholstery • Bedspreads/comforters • Kitchen towels • Draperies
Ramie	China grass	• Dyes well • High gloss or shine • Shrinks	• Table linens
Kapok	Ceiba tree	• Light • Soft • Not washable	• Pillows and pad filling
Bamboo	Bamboo plant	• Soft • Absorbent	• Kitchen towels • Bath towels
Sisal	Sisal plant	• Strong • Durable	• Carpet • Rugs

Goodheart-Willcox Publisher

Figure 19.1 Cellulosic natural fibers come from a variety of plant sources.

for specific traits and uses of some cellulosic natural fibers.

Protein natural fibers come from animal sources. These fibers burn slowly and have good elasticity. They also have ***resiliency***, an ability to return to the original size and shape. These fibers require careful cleaning, however, and they often need to be dry-cleaned. See Figure 19.2 for characteristics and uses of some natural protein fibers.

Manufactured Fibers

Wood cellulose, oil products, and other chemicals make up **manufactured fibers**. There are three classifications of manufactured fibers—regenerated, synthetic, and inorganic. The main differences among the three categories are the raw materials and chemical processes used to make the fiber. *Regenerated fibers* consist of cellulose or protein, which are naturally occurring polymers. A **polymer** is a chemical compound that forms from the union of small molecules that contain repeating structural units. *Synthetic fibers* often come from petroleum-based materials and consist of polymers or simple molecules. *Inorganic fibers* are sometimes classified as synthetic fibers. Inorganic fibers come from natural mineral sources or inorganic and mineral salts. Inorganic fibers have limited importance for textile uses.

Each fiber has a **generic name**, which describes a group of fibers with similar chemical compositions. **Trade names** are names companies use to identify the specific fibers they develop.

Making most manufactured fibers requires using an **extrusion** process to form and shape the fibers. Raw materials for manufactured fibers consist of thick solutions. These solutions form by dissolving the raw materials in chemicals. The process and chemicals used vary according to the type of fiber in production. Once the solution formation is complete, the solution is forced through an opening in a spinneret to form a fiber. The **spinneret** is a small nozzle with tiny holes that is much like a showerhead. Each hole in the spinneret extrudes one fiber. Once the fiber exits the spinneret, it solidifies.

Each manufactured fiber has its own characteristics. However, all manufactured fibers have some traits in common. For example, they generally dry-clean or launder well and are resistant to insects, fungi, and rot. They are ***hypoallergenic***, which means you are not likely to develop an allergy to them. See Figure 19.3 for some common manufactured fibers and their traits and uses.

Yarns

Fibers are spun or twisted into yarns. A **yarn** is a continuous strand of fibers that may consist of

Protein Natural Fibers			
Fiber	**Source**	**Characteristics**	**Uses**
Silk	Silkworm cocoon	• Strong • Absorbent • Dyes well • Lustrous • Water spots easily • Poor resistance to prolonged sunlight exposure	• Draperies • Lampshades • Wall hangings • Upholstery
Wool	Hair of sheep and lambs (also many specialty hair fibers, such as from angora goats, cashmere goats, alpaca, camel, llama, and vicuna)	• Absorbent • Wrinkle resistant • Not moth resistant • Shrinks	• Rugs • Carpets • Curtains • Blankets • Draperies • Upholstery

Goodheart-Willcox Publisher

Figure 19.2 Protein natural fibers are strong and absorbent.

Manufactured Fibers			
Generic Name (Some Trade Names)	**Type**	**Characteristics**	**Uses**
Acetate (Celanese, Chromspun, Estron)	Regenerated cellulosic	• Drapes well • Dyes easily • Weak • Heat sensitive • Poor abrasion resistance	• Bedspreads • Draperies • Upholstery • Sheers
Acrylic (Acrilan, Creslan, Duraspun)	Synthetic	• Warm • Lightweight • Resists wrinkles • Low absorbency • Heat sensitive	• Blankets • Carpets • Draperies • Rugs • Upholstery
Glass (Fiberglas)	Inorganic	• Strong • Resists sun fading • Nonabsorbent	• Curtains • Draperies • Insulation
Lyocell (Tencel)	Regenerated cellulosic	• Stronger than other cellulosic fibers • Absorbent • Drapes well • Soft • Wrinkle resistant	• Bedding • Draperies • Slipcovers • Upholstery
Metallic (Lurex, Chromoflex)	Inorganic	• Resists shrinking • Durable • Nonabsorbent • Increases fabric stiffness	• Drapes • Rugs • Tablecloths • Upholstery
Modacrylic (SEF)	Synthetic	• Warm • Dyes easily • Resists flames and wrinkling • Weak • Nonabsorbent • Heat sensitive	• Blankets • Carpets • Curtains • Draperies • Rugs
Nylon (Anso, Antron)	Synthetic	• Strong • Resistant to chemical damage and abrasion • Does not stretch, shrink, or absorb water • Creates static electricity	• Carpets • Curtains • Draperies • Slipcovers • Table linens • Upholstery

(Continued)

Figure 19.3 Each manufactured fiber has its own unique traits.

Manufactured Fibers (Figure 19.3, continued)			
Generic Name (Some Trade Names)	**Type**	**Characteristics**	**Uses**
Olefin (Essera, Herculon)	Synthetic	• Lightweight • Strong • Resistant to abrasion • Heat sensitive • Nonabsorbent	• Carpet backs • Carpets • Slipcovers • Upholstery
Polyester (ColorGuard, Dacron, Fortrel)	Synthetic	• Strong • Resistant to abrasion, creases, and shrinkage • Holds its shape • Low absorbency • Heat sensitive	• Bedding • Carpet • Curtains • Draperies • Rugs • Table linens • Upholstery • Wall coverings
Rayon (Lenzing Modal, Zantrel)	Regenerated cellulosic	• Highly absorbent • Soft • Dyes easily • Drapes well • Weak	• Bedding • Bath towels • Draperies • Slipcovers • Table linens • Upholstery

kuruneko/Shutterstock.com

Figure 19.4 Cotton fibers are staple fibers that are twisted and pulled into small strands to make fine yarns.

staple fibers (short fibers) and/or filaments (long, continuous fibers). Many natural fibers are staple fibers (Figure 19.4), while many manufactured fibers are filaments. A yarn may consist of a single type of fiber like wool or nylon. Combining two or more different fibers in making yarn—such as cotton and polyester—forms a **blend**. Blends bring out the good qualities of each fiber and minimize the less-favorable characteristics. Combining two or more different yarns creates a **combination yarn**.

Fabric Construction

The type, amount, and size of fibers along with their usage help determine fabric traits. How fabrics are constructed is also important. Fabric construction methods include weaving, knitting, felting, and bonding.

Woven Fabrics

Many fabrics for home use are woven (Figure 19.5). **Weaving** is the interlacing of two sets of yarns at right angles. The **warp yarns** run the lengthwise direction and form the lengthwise grain. **Grain** is the direction threads

Phase4Studios/Shutterstock.com

Figure 19.5 Many woven fabrics are used in this room. They are found in the sofa and ottoman upholstery, as well as in the window treatment and pillows.

run in a woven fabric. Extra warp yarns form the *selvage*, which is the lengthwise woven edge of the fabric. The **weft yarns** are the filling yarns that run in the crosswise direction. They form the crosswise grain.

Manufacturers generally use one of three basic weaves to form woven fabrics. They are the plain weave, twill weave, and satin weave. Each weave varies according to how the yarns are crossed or interlaced. All other weaves are variations on these three basic weaves (Figure 19.6).

- **Plain weave.** The plain weave is the simplest weave. The weft yarn goes over and under each warp yarn. A variation of the plain weave is the basket weave. Two or more weft yarns are interlaced with two or more warp yarns. The rib weave is another variation of the plain weave. Coarser weft yarns are combined with regular warp yarns to give a corded effect.
- **Twill weave.** In the twill weave, the warp or weft yarn passes over two or more yarns. Each succeeding pass begins one yarn above or below the last one. The result is a **wale**, which is a diagonal rib or cord pattern. A twill weave can be even or uneven. Weaving the weft yarns over and under the same number of warp yarns creates an even twill weave. When the number of the weft yarns and the warp yarns are not the same, an uneven-twill weave forms. Twill weave fabrics are stronger than plain weave fabrics and tend to show soil less quickly.
- **Satin weave.** The satin weave has long *floats*, or segments of yarn on the surface of the fabric. Either the warp yarns or weft yarns float over four or more opposite yarns, and then go under one. Each successive float begins two yarns away from the beginning of the last one. The satin weave is smooth and slippery. It drapes

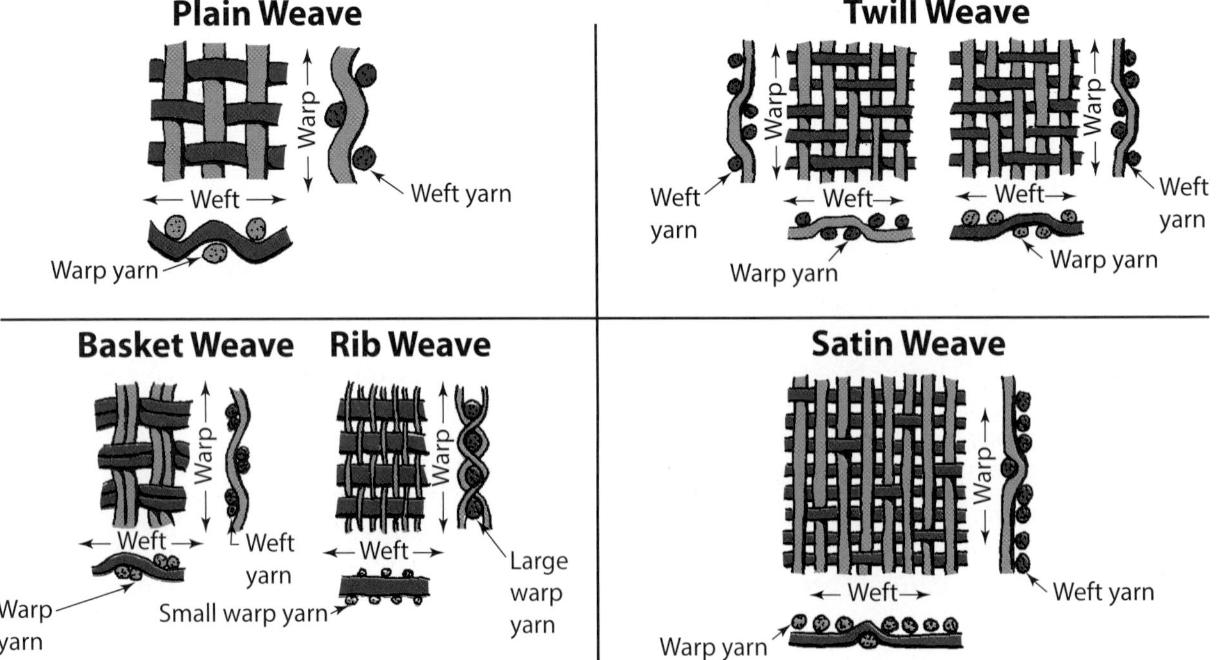

Goodheart-Willcox Publisher

Figure 19.6 Each weave is constructed differently. This gives each type of fabric a different look and feel.

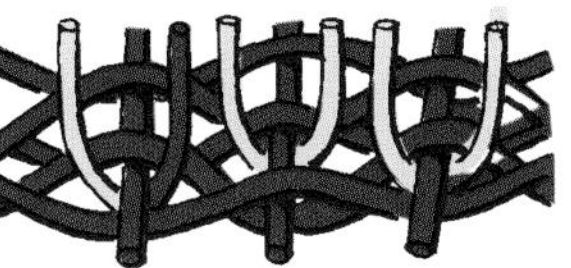

Goodheart-Willcox Publisher

Figure 19.7 A pile-weave fabric has additional yarn covering the surface.

Lorraine Kourafas/Shutterstock.com

Figure 19.8 The tapestry fabric used on these chairs is an example of a jacquard weave.

Leno Weave

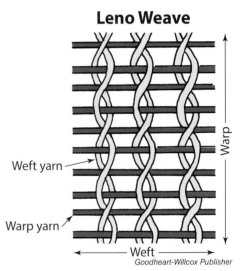

Weft yarn

Warp yarn

Warp

Weft

Goodheart-Willcox Publisher

Figure 19.9 The leno weave is loosely woven and has open spaces.

well and is good for linings. However, satin weave fabrics are less durable than fabrics in other basic weaves because the long floats tend to snag easily.

The pile weave is a variation of the plain and twill weaves. Pile fabrics have yarn loops or cut yarns that stand away from the base of the fabric. In Figure 19.7, you can compare a plain weave, loop-pile weave, and a cut-pile weave. Examples of pile-weave fabrics are velvet, velveteen, corduroy, terry cloth, and frieze.

Pile fabrics have a **nap**, which is a layer of fiber ends that stand up from the surface of the fabric. The nap appears different when you view it from varying directions. It is important to verify that the nap runs in the same direction throughout a product. For example, if you make draperies that have two or more panels, the nap of the pile fabric needs to run in the same direction on all of the panels.

Usage of two other weaves—the jacquard and leno weaves—is common in home-furnishings fabrics. Damask, tapestry, and brocade fabrics are examples of the jacquard weave you will often find in upholstery, draperies, and table linens (Figure 19.8). Fabrics for curtains and thermal blankets often use the leno weave (Figure 19.9). In addition, weaving small geometric shapes such as diamonds or squares into fabric is an example of the dobby weave. The primary use of the dobby weave is for upholstery fabrics and some drapery fabrics.

Knitted Fabrics

Knitting is the looping of yarns together. The size of the loops and how close together they are varies, as well as the way the loops are joined (Figure 19.10). Depending on whether one or two needles are used, knits can be single or double knits.

Weft knits are either circular or flat. They produce single knits, double knits, jersey, rib knits, and jacquard. Warp knits are flat. They are generally tighter, flatter, and less elastic than weft knits.

The main use for knitted fabrics is as backing for other fabrics for the home. This is because they lack the stability and body needed for many

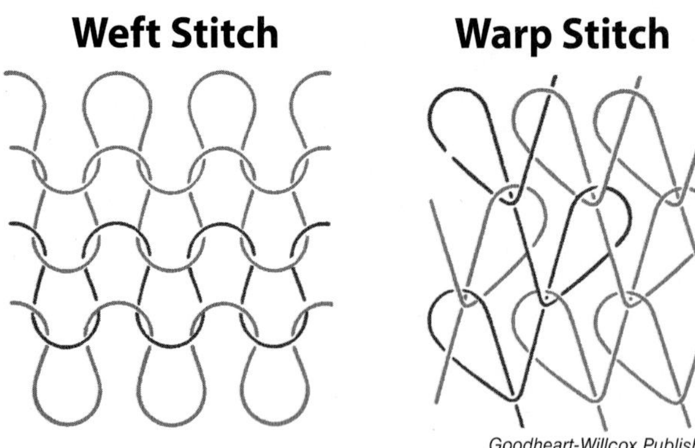

Figure 19.10 Knitted fabrics vary according to yarn size, yarn texture, and loop construction. The weft stitch allows more stretch than the warp stitch.

home textiles. There is increasing use of knitted fabrics, however, for upholstery.

Other Types of Fabrics

There are other fabrics used in residential and commercial interiors that are not woven or knitted. They vary in method of construction.

Manufacturers make nonwoven fabrics by joining fibers together with adhesives or by entangling fibers with heat fusion. During these processes, the masses of fibers interlock and hold together. Felt and fusible interfacing are examples of nonwoven fabrics. Nonwoven fabrics are generally not as strong as woven or knitted fabrics, and they do not have as much stretch.

Vinyl and other plastic materials are not made from fibers. Instead, they are thin, nonwoven sheets. The finishing processes for these sheets can make them look like woven fabrics or leather. Vinyl usually has a knit-fabric backing to give it stability and strength.

Leather is sometimes classified as a nonwoven fabric. The process of tanning leather requires use of a complex acid compound, or tannin, which causes the leather to become soft and resistant to stains, fading, and cracking. Its strength and durability makes it ideal for some home and commercial uses.

Bonded fabrics consist of two layers of fabric that are permanently joined together with an adhesive. Heat sets the bond. Sometimes a face fabric is bonded to a lining. At other times, a face fabric is bonded to synthetic foam. When bonded to another fabric, the face fabric typically has a better appearance and will form the outside of a textile product such as upholstery.

Fabric Modifications

Manufacturers can modify fabrics to improve their appearance, feel, performance, and durability. They can make these changes through design, dye, and finishes.

Design

Designs in fabrics may be structural or applied. Fabric producers make **structural designs** by varying the yarns while weaving or knitting the fabric. The size, texture, and placement of the yarns all affect the final pattern. **Applied designs** are printed onto the surface of the fabric. You can see them distinctly only on one side of the fabric.

Dye

Dyes give color to fabric. There are four main methods of dyeing fabric, depending on when color is added. Applying color to fibers, yarn, or fabric occurs through the following methods:

- **Stock dyeing.** Adding color to the fibers, or stock dyeing, is done before spinning the fibers into yarn. The method of dyeing is uniform and long lasting.
- **Solution dyeing.** Adding color to manufactured fiber solutions before forcing them through the spinneret creates a consistent color throughout the fiber.
- **Yarn dyeing.** Adding color to the yarn before making it into fabric—or yarn dyeing—is one of the oldest dyeing methods. This method is widely used and color absorption is good.
- **Piece dyeing.** The easiest and least expensive method of dyeing is adding color to the fabric, or piece dyeing. It usually requires using a single color.

Finishes

Finishes can improve the appearance, texture, or performance of the fiber, yarn, or fabric. They are often applied to the fabric. Manufacturers are able to produce many finishes for fabrics. See Figure 19.11 for a description of common fabric finishes and the wide variety of benefits they provide.

Basic Textile Finishes	
Type of Finish	**Benefits**
Antibacterial; Antimicrobial	Prevents growth of bacteria, mold, and mildew; prevents odor
Antistatic	Prevents buildup of static electricity
Bleaching	Whitens natural fabric from the mill
Crease Resistant	Prevents fabric from wrinkling
Durable Press	Prevents fabric from wrinkling
Flame-resistant; Flame-retardant	Reduces fabric burning and flaming from exposure to flames or high heat
Moth Resistance	Discourages moths and carpet beetles from attacking wool fibers
Napping	Produces a raised surface by lifting fiber ends
Preshrinking	Prevents fabric from shrinking more than a small amount
Sizing	Provides extra body and weight to fabric through a solution of starch
Soil Release	Makes stain removal easy
Stain Resistance (soil resistance)	Makes fibers less absorbent so stain removal is easier
Waterproof	Prevents water from soaking into the fabric
Water Repellent	Resists water but does not make fabric waterproof

Figure 19.11 The application of finishes to fabrics can improve their appearance, durability, maintenance, and comfort.

Review & Assessment

1. What is the difference between cellulosic natural and protein natural fibers? Name two examples of each type of fiber.
2. Distinguish between natural and manufactured fibers.
3. List five manufactured fibers and two characteristics of each.
4. How do fibers and yarns differ?
5. Contrast weaving and knitting.
6. How are bonded fabrics made?
7. What is the benefit of fabric modifications?

Textiles for Residential and Commercial Use

Textiles are fabrics for use in residential and commercial buildings. The textiles you choose for yourself or for potential clients will depend on where and how you will use them. Consider the appearance, durability, maintenance, and comfort of the fabric. Also think about the ease of working with the fabric and the cost. Your knowledge about fabric types and construction will help you make these decisions.

Appearance

Appearance is the overall visual effect. For instance, a fabric may appear soft or stiff. It may also appear bulky or sheer, light or dark, rough or smooth, or bright or dull. Fabrics can make a room appear elegant or invite relaxation. See the two examples in Figure 19.12.

Durability

Durability is the capacity to be long lasting under normal conditions. You want fabrics to last as long as possible to limit replacement costs. Fabrics that receive heavy use, especially those for commercial environments, need to withstand wear. Tightly woven fabrics or fabrics with bulky yarns have the most durability.

A Calico Corners—Calico Home Stores B Natalie Adamov/Shutterstock.com

Figure 19.12 Fabrics can convey different moods, as demonstrated by different collections of pillows. The atmosphere can range from cheerful and formal (A) to relaxed (B).

Maintenance

Maintenance is the care fabrics require to keep them clean and looking their best. Following instructions and using proper cleaning techniques—either laundering or dry cleaning—ensure good results with fabric care. Also consider the cost of maintaining fabrics. Choosing textiles to launder at home can help avoid the high costs of dry cleaning—both financial and environmental. Most textiles have suggested care instructions. Those for commercial use must also withstand frequent cleaning with disinfectant solutions.

Comfort

Most people want fabrics that make them feel comfortable. Comfort is a psychological consideration and is different for each person. A fabric can give visual comfort if you like its appearance. It can give physical comfort if it is soft or pleasant to the touch.

Ease of Construction

If you are going to sew some textiles yourself, you need to consider the ease with which you can manage the fabric. Heavy, closely-woven fabrics are harder to handle than lightweight, loosely woven fabrics. However, loosely woven fabrics tend to catch on objects and snag easily. Also, stitching is more difficult to see on dark fabric than light fabric.

Cost

Cost is always an important consideration, but do not base your decision on cost alone. Buy the best fabric for its use. A good-quality fabric at a high price may be more economical in the long run than buying a low-quality fabric at a low price. Also, keep in mind the costs of installation, maintenance, and replacement in addition to the initial price. Evaluate fabrics based on these important factors before you make a purchase.

Career Focus Textiles and Furniture Designer

Do you notice patterns in fabrics and finishes that you encounter? Do you see improvements you could make in the furniture you see or sit on? If you do, a career in textiles or furniture design might be for you!

Interests/Skills: Textiles and furniture designers are artistic and creative individuals. They have a good eye for all design elements and principles and are comfortable with the use of computer design software. Attention to detail is another important aspect of this profession. Sewing, weaving, woodworking, and welding skills help designers understand the construction of the products. Most importantly, textiles and furniture designers should listen to client needs, communicate with a client regarding design solutions, and use critical-thinking skills for problem solving.

Career Snapshot: Textile and furniture designers create two-dimensional designs that can be used, often as a repeat design, in the production of commercial and residential fabrics and textile products including carpet and furnishings. Many work with outside designers to create new colorways or versions of current fabric, furniture, or carpet lines. Other designers may deal only with original designs. They prepare sketches of ideas to present to the client and detailed drawings for use in manufacturing. These designers collaborate with marketing forecasting, production, sales departments, and customers to evaluate design concepts. Together, these groups determine the feasibility of design ideas, based on factors such as aesthetics, safety, function, maintainability, production costs and methods, and market trends. Once their proposals are accepted, textile and furniture designers direct and coordinate the fabrication of models or samples and the production of working drawings and specification sheets from these sketches.

Education/Training: Completion of a Bachelor of Fine Arts is ideal, but a Bachelor's or Associate's degree in Interior Design, Textiles Design/Engineering/Merchandising, Industrial Design, Furniture Design, Fiber and Textile Arts, or another allied major will prepare a graduate for an introductory position with a firm or manufacturer.

Victoria Andreas/Shutterstock.com

Licensing/Examinations: Although there are no required certifications in these areas, many designers find it helpful to seek certification as a LEED Accredited Professional, indicating that they have expertise in the sustainability aspects of design, manufacturing, and installation of the products they design.

Professional Associations: Surface Design Association (SDA); International Textile and Apparel Association (ITAA); Association for Contract Textiles (ACT); International Furnishings and Design Association (IFDA); and American Home Furnishings Alliance (AHFA)

Job Outlook: Although the employment outlook fluctuates, it is most common that textiles and furniture designers will work in-house directly for a manufacturer or be self-employed and be contracted as needed by these same companies. Designers with an understanding of ergonomics, market analysis, and environmental practices will progress faster in this specialty.

Sources: The *Occupational Outlook Handbook* (OOH); the Occupational Information Network (O*NET); and The Art Career Project

Review & Assessment

1. Why are the factors of appearance, maintenance, and comfort important when choosing textiles for home or commercial use?
2. Why is it important to select durable fabrics for commercial use?
3. In addition to the initial price, what three costs are important to consider before buying textiles? Why?

Woven Carpet or Rug

Goodheart-Willcox Publisher

Figure 19.13 The carpeting construction method affects the appearance and durability of the carpeting.

Textiles for Floor Treatments

Buying carpets and rugs for residential and commercial use is a major purchase. There are many different construction methods, textures, fibers, finishes, and green options from which to choose. To make a good decision, it is important to know what choices are available.

Construction Methods

There are several methods manufacturers use to construct carpets and rugs, including weaving, tufting, and needle-punching (Figure 19.13). Each of these methods combines the pile yarn, which is the part you walk on, with the backing material. The backing material holds the yarn together.

- **Weaving.** Much like fabrics, manufacturers use looms to weave carpets and rugs. The pile yarns and the backing are interwoven. Velvet and Wilton are the main types of weaves carpet producers use to make woven carpets and rugs. Usage of wool yarns or wool-blend yarns is common with these carpet weaves.
- **Tufting.** Looping the yarns into a backing material and securing them to the backing with an adhesive (often a rubberized latex compound) is a process carpet producers use to make *tufted* carpets and rugs. Tufting is easy to do and is less expensive than weaving and is the most common method of producing carpet and rugs today.
- **Needle-punching.** The process of interlocking fibers by using felting needles is called *needle-punching*. This process produces a flat carpet that resembles felt. Its main use is for indoor/outdoor carpets and rugs.

Green Choices

Consider Environmentally Friendly Carpet

New carpeting often releases volatile organic compounds (VOCs) (compounds with high vapor pressure and low water solubility) into the air as gases. If people inhale them, these gases can have a negative impact on health. These gases are often associated with the smell of new carpeting and can last for weeks to months in an interior environment.

Use the following tips for selecting carpeting that is consumer friendly and environmentally friendly:

- Check the label to ensure carpeting components have undergone testing by the Carpet and Rug Institute (CRI) in its indoor air quality testing program. The Green Label and the Green Label Plus (icons within a small green house) indicate that the product has been tested and that it meets the CRI's standard for low emissions.
- Air out the carpet before installing. Often the installer can do this for you before it is delivered to your home.
- Use felt padding instead of rubber padding.
- Use low-emitting, non-solvent adhesives if carpet installation requires gluing it down.
- Follow proper carpet cleaning guidelines. Improper cleaning can trap VOCs, dust mites, and allergens.

Textures

Pile is another name for carpet texture. Carpet producers create different textures in carpets and rugs when the yarns are cut, left uncut, twisted, untwisted, or cut in different lengths. Examples of types of pile that result from these processes are cut, level loop, multilevel loop, cut and loop, and shag. Level loop pile wears the best. Multilevel loop pile results from a combination of cut and looped yarns.

Twisting the pile yarns can also achieve texture. At other times, the addition of flecks of color results in the appearance of texture.

The thickness of the yarns affects texture, too. Thicker yarns create more plush carpeting and rugs. Density refers to the number of tufts or yarns per square inch. Carpets with a high density look better and are more durable.

Fiber Content

Fiber content greatly affects the quality of carpets and rugs. Wool, nylon, acrylic, polyester, olefin, and cotton are the major fibers manufacturers use for carpets and rugs. Each fiber has unique traits that affect carpeting and rug products.

Wool is an ideal fiber for carpets and rugs because it is very resilient. It is also durable and resistant to soil and stains. Wool, however, is expensive. Therefore, manufacturers generally use wool only for luxury carpets and rugs (Figure 19.14).

Photography Courtesy of Karastan

Figure 19.14 This wool carpet is both durable and resistant to stains and is a good selection for a dining room.

Nylon is the most commonly used fiber for carpets and rugs. It is very durable, resilient, and soil resistant, but oily stains are difficult to remove. Nylon is less costly than wool.

Kitchen, bathroom, and outdoor carpets often consist of olefin fiber. It is very durable and resistant to soil and stains. Olefin is also fairly resilient and resists mold and mildew. Prices for olefin carpets range from medium to low.

Polyester fibers offer a soft, luxurious texture to cut-pile carpets and rugs. These fibers have good color clarity and resist fading. They are easy to clean and stain resistant.

Acrylic looks like wool. It also has good resilience, durability, and soil-resistance like wool. However, oily stains are difficult to remove. Acrylic costs less than wool but more than nylon.

Rayon carpets and rugs are attractive, but not very practical. They are low in resilience, durability, and soil resistance. Rayon rugs are, however, low in price and used when quality is not an important factor. Scatter rugs and inexpensive room-sized rugs are sometimes made of rayon.

Cotton rugs are attractive and durable, but low in resilience and soil resistance. Prices vary according to the type of cotton, but are generally low. The most common use of cotton is for washable scatter rugs for bathrooms and kitchens.

Finishes

The application of finishes to carpets and rugs is mainly for functional reasons. For example, an antistatic finish reduces static buildup. A flame-resistant finish prevents the fabric from burning easily. Stain-resistant and soil-release finishes make carpet care easier.

Review & Assessment

1. Describe the weaving and tufting processes used in carpet construction.
2. Describe pile. How are manufacturers able to adjust carpet texture?
3. Name three fibers and the type of carpet or rug made from each.

Textiles for Upholstered Furniture

Upholstered furniture has full or partial coverings of fabric (Figure 19.15). **Upholstery** is the fabric, padding, or other material manufacturers use to make a soft covering for furniture. When you choose upholstery fabric, consider where and how you will use the furniture.

For furniture that will receive constant wear, choose fabrics that are durable, stain-resistant, and easy to clean. Wool, mohair, and some manufactured fibers, such as nylon and acrylic, are very durable. They are often available in blends. Upholstery for commercial use may require a higher level of durability than that for residential use.

By knowing the fabric content, you will know how well the fabric will clean and withstand wear. The fibers and finishes manufacturers use to produce these fabrics influence cleaning and durability.

Another consideration for choosing upholstery fabrics is their use in formal and informal settings.

Rodenberg Photography/Shutterstock.com

Figure 19.15 The chairs in this room are partially upholstered, while the sofa is completely upholstered.

Formal rooms have an elegant appearance. Designers and manufacturers most often use such fabrics as plain or textured satins, damask, velvet, velveteen, brocade, faille, mohair, or matelassé in formal settings. These fabrics often consist of silk or a blend of natural and manufactured fibers (Figure 19.16).

STEM Science & Technology — Nanotechnology and Household Products

A technological revolution is taking place involving objects so small they cannot be seen through most microscopes. Researchers have been exploring the properties and behaviors of objects at the nanoscale, which ranges from 1 to 100 nanometers. There are 25.4 million nanometers in 1 inch. Using what they learned, scientists and engineers are creating new materials and endowing already existing ones with amazing new properties.

Some of the products you use every day were probably created using nanotechnologies. These include UV-ray-blocking sunscreens; wrinkle- and stain- resistant clothing, bedding, and towels; and even certain foods and beverages. In addition to producing consumer products, cutting-edge nanotechnologies in health care help doctors treat some diseases more effectively.

One of the most popular nanotechnology applications so far is the creation of household products with built-in disinfectants. Many of these products—from refrigerators and cutting boards to bathroom fixtures and bath towels—contain nanoparticles of silver metal, which has germ-killing properties. In addition to textiles with stain and germ-fighting properties, fiber scientists are creating fabrics that may

- repel mosquitoes without pesticides
- absorb and neutralize harmful airborne chemicals, such as indoor air pollutants
- hold color without the use of dyes

Many governments and industries are helping to fund nanotechnology research and development. Some believe that the world's most pressing problems—including pollution, disease, and energy—can be significantly and positively impacted using nanotechnologies.

Other experts, however, believe more research must be directed toward analyzing safety and environmental issues related to nanoparticles. The long-term effects of using some products made with nanotechnologies are unknown.

It is hard to know which products contain nanoparticles and which do not. There is currently no requirement for manufacturers to print this information on consumer product labels. Visit the consumer products inventory page on the *Project on Emerging Nanotechnologies* website to view a list of nanotechnology-based consumer products. Also visit the *U.S. National Nanotechnology Initiative* online to learn more about nanotechnology.

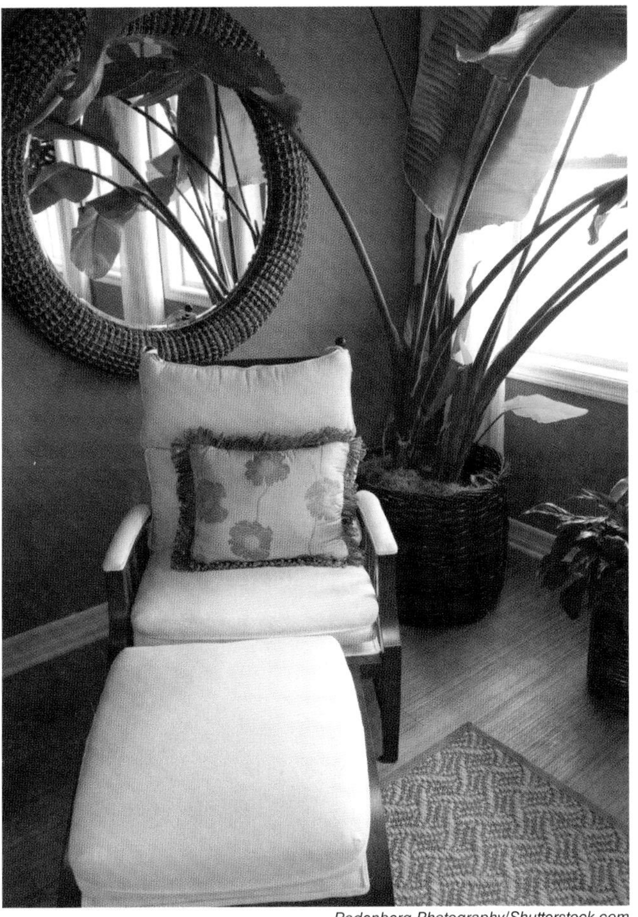

Rodenberg Photography/Shutterstock.com

Figure 19.16 You can add an accent to a simple piece of upholstered furniture by adding a contrasting pillow.

For informal or casual settings, patterns can range from a very small print to a large scenic design. You can use a wide variety of fabrics, including chintz, polished cotton, gingham, sailcloth, burlap, denim, poplin, or corduroy.

If your client wants a new piece of upholstered furniture, you may need to determine how much fabric it will require. Factory-made upholstered furniture is usually less costly than custom pieces. For custom pieces, the fabric cost per yard and the upholstery-workroom labor cost greatly influence the total price of a furniture piece. Most furniture and upholstery fabric companies have fabric estimation charts that can help guide your plans for the project budget. Figure 19.17 shows fabric estimations for a few key pieces of upholstery. For custom pieces, the fabric cost per yard and the upholstery-workroom labor cost greatly influence the total price of a furniture piece.

Suppose your client decides to *reupholster*—or update fabric, padding, and springs for a piece of furniture he or she wants to keep. If your client agrees, involve a reputable upholsterer to determine the material and labor costs for the work. Generally, you can give the upholsterer the following information and he or she can determine the fabric yardage the project requires:

- height and width of the furniture piece
- number of cushions (seat and back)

Standard Upholstery Yardages (No Pattern Repeat)*	
Furniture Type	**Upholstery Yardage**
Traditional sofa (6 ft. long)	10 to 12 yd.
Traditional sofa (6 ft. long)	10 to 12 yd.
Traditional sofa (7 ft. long)	11 to 14 yd.
Traditional sofa (9 ft. long)	13 to 18 yd.
Sectional sofa (3 pieces)	30 to 34 yd.
Chaise lounge	6 to 8 yd.
Club chair	7 to 8 yd.
Slipper chair (armless)	4 to 5 yd.
Wing chair	5 to 7 yd.
Dining chair (upholstered seat and back)	2 to 2.5 yd.
Small ottoman	2 to 2.5 yd.
Medium ottoman	2.5 to 3 yd.
Large ottoman	5 + yd.
*Upholstery yardage is based on a standard 54-in. width of fabric. Estimates may vary with factors associated with such design or construction details as tufting, number and style of cushions, shirting, etc.	

Figure 19.17 Using standard upholstery yardages allows you to do quick upholstery estimates when working with clients or a project of your own.

STEM Math Taking Measurements; Calculating Materials

An important part of successful design development is taking careful measurements. Accurate measurements will help you calculate or verify the amounts of materials to order for a client's design concept. Creating a rough sketch of the floor plan for an area and marking the measurements on the floor plan will help you accurately keep track of measurements.

Remember to use good measuring techniques, such as keeping the tape level when measuring horizontally. When measuring wall length, for example, run the tape measure along the floor next to the wall. When you cannot move furniture, track the tape along a straight floor seam or use a straightedge. For taking most measurements, use a retractable metal tape measure that is marked in feet, inch, and sixteenth-inch graduations for the most accuracy. As a designer, you will often need to calculate paint, wall coverings, flooring, window treatments, and upholstery materials.

Many variables can impact measurements. For example, a reupholstery job will require more fabric if the fabric of choice has a pattern repeat than if the fabric is plain. Likewise, covering existing walls painted a deep red will require more paint. Every design project will have its own unique set of characteristics and variables that can impact the measurements you take.

Math Practice

Locate a chair with an upholstered seat cushion. Create a sketch of the cushion shape. Measure the length, width, and depth of the cushion and record your measurements on the sketch. If you chose an upholstery fabric that was 58 inches wide, how much fabric might you need to order to reupholster the cushion? Record your estimations on your sketch.

- arms and legs, if any, and whether they are exposed
- skirting and piping requirements
- fabric width and pattern repeat

A common practice is to add 10 percent or more fabric to the estimate to account for seams, decorative trims, and *stretchers* (fabric pieces used for pulling upholstery taut to the frame). If the fabric of choice has a pattern, the upholsterer will likely increase the yardage to account for the length of the pattern repeat. Note that pattern repeats can run anywhere from 3 to 50 inches, which will increase fabric yardage by 10 to 40 percent.

Review & Assessment

1. Define upholstery.
2. List three factors to consider when choosing upholstery fabrics.
3. How does a formal setting affect upholstery selection?

Textiles for Window Treatments

Window treatments are applications added to window units, either for helping to control the home environment or for purely decorative purposes. Window treatments—such as draperies and curtains—require the use of fabric. When making your selections, consider the purpose and style of the room in either residential or commercial settings. Also consider the colors and patterns in use throughout the room. Finally, consider the cost of the fabric and its care requirements.

Purpose and Style of Rooms

A window covering can regulate the natural light that enters a room. Sheer fabrics will filter the light (Figure 19.18). They offer a feeling of privacy in the daytime. You will be able to see out, but others will not be able to see into the room. Sheers do not provide privacy at night, however.

When closed, ***opaque*** (not see-through; does not let light through) window treatments will not allow you to see out. They can shut out light and provide privacy both during the day and night. This is an important consideration when choosing fabrics for some rooms, such as bedrooms. Opaque fabrics are usually heavy and thick. Lighter-weight fabrics may not give the privacy you or your client desire.

As you choose window treatments, consider the styles of the rooms in which they are used. In work or informal areas, denim, poplin, and other casual fabrics are good choices. In more formal settings, you may use damask, antique satin, or similar fabrics.

Paul Matthew Photography/Shutterstock.com

Figure 19.18 The sheer fabric selected for this window treatment softly filters the light entering the room.

Calico Corners—Calico Home Stores

Figure 19.19 The colors and patterns in this window treatment complement the other fabrics and furnishings in the room.

Colors and Patterns

The fabric colors and patterns in window treatments should match or complement the room furnishings, as in Figure 19.19. You may choose a dominant color for window treatments. It could be a color that is in the upholstery or carpet. When choosing patterns for textiles, select large patterns for large rooms and small prints for small rooms.

Cost and Care

You can buy ready-made or made-to-order window treatments. You can also purchase fabric and make them yourself. However, it is important to remember that the more fabric and detail a window treatment requires, the more it will cost.

Cost is a factor when considering window treatments. Most draperies and some curtains require dry cleaning, which can be expensive. Other window treatments consist of washable fabrics that you can launder at home. Very large window treatments, however, require professional laundering because of their size.

Review & Assessment

1. What purposes influence the selection of window treatments?
2. Why are opaque window treatments a better choice for a bedroom than sheer window treatments?
3. Describe why care is a consideration in window treatment selection.

Textiles for Kitchen, Bath, and Bed

Textiles for use in the kitchen, bathroom, and bedroom are called linens, although few actually consist of linen fiber today. Consider their appearance, durability, and care requirements when making selection and purchasing decisions.

Kitchen

The main linens used in the kitchen or dining room are table coverings and towels. Easy care and durability are key characteristics for these linens.

Table Coverings

Table coverings include tablecloths, place mats, and napkins (Figure 19.20). Silence cloths that go under the tablecloths to reduce noise are also a form of table covering.

Thinking about how you will use table coverings will help you choose the best type. Is the table

Natalie Adamov/Shutterstock.com

Figure 19.20 Table linens and napkins often coordinate with the tableware.

covering intended for use every day or only for special occasions? Will you use the table linens for a formal dining room or a breakfast nook? Will the table linens be used in a commercial setting such as a restaurant? Knowing answers to these basic questions will help you select an appropriate fabric.

Linen was the preferred fabric for table coverings, but it requires ironing. Easy-care fabrics are most popular with people today. Many table coverings are available in fabrics that require little or no ironing and have soil-release finishes.

Towels

Kitchen towels are usually made of either cotton, a blend of polyester and cotton, or linen. Linen is good for lint-free towels because it does not have a nap and dries more quickly than cotton; however, linen is not used as much now as in the past. All towels you choose should have the following qualities. They should

- absorb water quickly and easily
- provide durability
- be easy to launder
- look attractive

Towels are available in a variety of colors and patterns. Some have borders and woven designs. Any additional decoration—such as special borders or monograms—will increase the cost of towels. These details, however, do not make them better-quality towels.

Bathroom

Linens for use in a residential or commercial bathroom include towels, bath mats, and shower curtains.

Towels

Bathroom towels come in several sizes. These include a bath sheet (extra large), a bath towel (large), a hand towel (medium), and a washcloth (small). Sometimes even smaller towels—guest towels or fingertip towels—are also available. Bath towels often come in sets. You may use a variety of towel colors to coordinate with other colors in a room design (Figure 19.21).

Manufacturers make many towels from cotton terry cloth because it is absorbent. Also, the loops absorb moisture well. Some towels are a cotton and polyester blend. The polyester decreases drying time, adds strength, and reduces shrinkage. The tighter the fabric's weave, the more durable and absorbent are the towels. Velour terry cloth towels have a cut pile on one side, which gives the towels a velvet-like appearance.

Bath Mats

Some bath mats consist of a fabric resembling towels but are heavier. Others are tufted and have latex backing to keep them from slipping. Still others

Image provided courtesy of JELD-WEN Windows & Doors

Figure 19.21 The blue and white towels coordinate with the color of the sliding pocket door and the wall covering in the room.

Career Focus Materials Scientist

Have you wondered why fabrics have certain characteristics such as flame resistance and durability? When something goes wrong in an experiment, do you like to try to find out what happened and fix it? Then you may be interested in a career as a materials scientist who develops new or improved textiles for use in the interior environment.

Interests/Skills: Materials scientists like to ask questions and solve problems, particularly using math. They are creative individuals who look at different ways of solving problems. Materials scientists need critical-thinking skills because they use logic and reasoning to identify the strengths and weaknesses of alternative solutions, conclusions, and approaches to problems. They need good reading and listening skills. A scientist developing materials in a laboratory also needs to manage his or her own time and the time of others.

Career Snapshot: Materials scientists research and study the structures and chemical properties of various natural and manmade materials. They work in laboratories to develop projects and procedures to solve problems, strengthen and combine materials, or make new products in textiles or other materials. These natural and manmade textiles are used in a wide range of products and structures from airplanes to clothing and household goods. Materials scientists observe, receive, and obtain information from all pertinent sources. They analyze information and evaluate results to choose the best solution to problems. They communicate with supervisors and colleagues, often in teams, to solve problems. They must be very exact or highly accurate in performing the job. There is usually freedom to make decisions and to structure work. Materials scientists write reports of their experiments, findings, and conclusions, and publish their research.

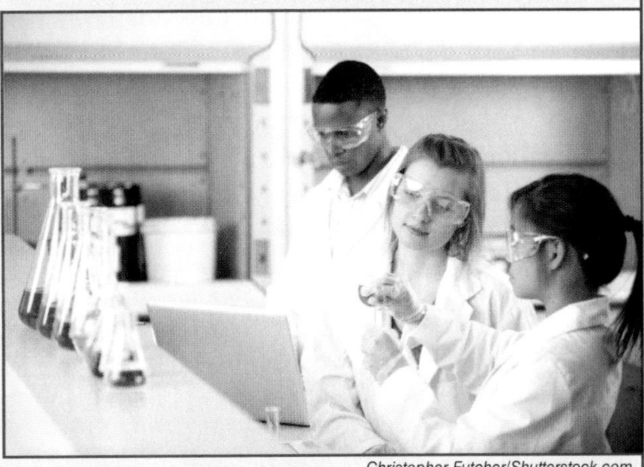

Christopher Futcher/Shutterstock.com

Education/Training: A bachelor's degree is required in chemistry or a related field, such as engineering, that requires extensive background and knowledge in chemistry. Most jobs as a materials scientist require a master's degree or a Ph.D. There may be some on-the-job training, but most jobs assume the person will already have the required skills, knowledge, work-related experience and/or training. Persons interested in materials science should seek experience in academic laboratories or through internships, fellowships, or work-study programs in industry. Most employers prefer to hire individuals with several years of postdoctoral experience.

Professional Associations: The American Chemical Society (ACS); the Materials Research Society (MRS)

Job Outlook: Employment of materials scientists is expected to be slower than the average for all occupations. Job opportunities are more favorable for individuals with a master's degree or Ph.D.

Sources: The *Occupational Outlook Handbook* (OOH); the Occupational Information Network (O*NET)

are made of yarn sewn onto a backing. You may see bath mats made from braided fabrics. Fibers used to make bath rugs include cotton, rayon, and various blends. They often have colors that match or coordinate with the bath towels.

Shower Curtains

Shower curtains prevent water from spraying outside the shower area. They are made from plastic or fabric that has a waterproof finish. Shower curtains have a wide variety of colors and patterns. Often they coordinate with bath towels, bath mats, wall coverings, and window treatments.

Bedroom

Bedding—or linens for bedroom use—includes sheets, pillowcases, blankets, bedspreads, comforters, and duvets. Accessories such as shams, pillows, and dust ruffles are also considered bedding.

Bed Linens

Sheets and pillowcases are usually available in matching sets. The sheets may be flat or fitted. A flat sheet can serve as the top or bottom sheet. A fitted sheet snugly fits the shape of the mattress and functions only as a bottom sheet. Sheets and pillowcases are available in various sizes to fit the different bed sizes. These range in size from standard (for twin and full-size beds) to queen and king sizes. Sheets designed to fit waterbeds are also available.

Sheets and pillowcases are usually made of cotton or a cotton/polyester blend. Cotton sheets are more absorbent, but polyester reduces wrinkling. Sometimes sheets are made from acetate or nylon. Classifications for cotton sheets are usually percale, muslin, or flannel.

- Percale is a high-quality, lightweight, tightly woven plain-weave cotton or cotton/polyester fabric. It has a smooth, silk-like feel and launders easily.
- Muslin is also a plain-weave cotton fabric that ranges from lightweight to heavyweight. Muslin sheets are not as smooth as percale.
- Flannel has a napped surface that provides extra warmth.

When you are buying sheets and pillowcases, be sure to read the thread count on the package label. The higher the thread count, the more closely together the fabric is woven. Closely woven fabrics have a softer and smoother feel. Fine percale sheets cost more and may have a thread count of 200 to 300. Lower thread-count sheets are lower in price.

Washability of sheets and pillowcases for both residential and commercial uses is another factor when selecting bed linens. Since they require frequent laundering, sheets and pillowcases need to be colorfast and durable. For use in such commercial institutions as hotels and hospitals, sheets and pillowcases must also be durable enough to withstand disinfectants.

Blankets, Bedspreads, and Comforters

Blanket items come in weights suitable for different seasons of the year. In certain climates and air-conditioned homes or commercial buildings, using blankets all year is a requirement. Light cotton or rayon blankets are ideal for summer. They are easy to launder and less expensive than heavy blankets. Thermal blankets made by using the leno weave are often a good choice. The open spaces in the weave form pockets that trap air and serve as insulation. Wool, acrylic, or a wool and acrylic blend are good for cold winter nights. Again, comfort, attractiveness, and durability are considerations in choosing blankets. For commercial uses, blankets must utilize washable fabrics and be able to withstand the use of disinfectants.

Most people purchase bedspreads for their attractiveness. They come in a variety of fabrics. You can make a satisfying choice if you know your fabrics. While some bedspreads are washable, many require dry cleaning.

In addition to attractiveness, a bedspread should be the correct size for the bed. It should also harmonize with the other furnishings in the room. Matching bedspread, window treatments, and sheet sets are available for residential and commercial settings.

Comforters (or *duvets*) are thick bed coverings that consist of two layers of fabric with filling sandwiched between them. People choose them for their attractiveness and warmth. The fabric layers make a comforter covering attractive (Figure 19.22). Rayon, acetate, and silk comforter coverings look and feel luxurious. Comforter coverings made from sateen, polished cotton, and challis do not have the same luxurious appearance and feel. However, they are more durable and very attractive.

The filling makes the comforter warm. The warmest comforters have wool or down filling. Down is the soft, fine feathers from ducks or geese. Down is light and resilient, but quite expensive. As a result, manufacturers sometimes use lower-quality feathers instead. Other comforter fillings include polyester or cotton and kapok, which tend to mat or clump.

Calico Corners—Calico Home Stores

Figure 19.22 The comforter and its coordinating pillows and upholstered head- and footboard make this bed very attractive and comfortable.

Review & Assessment

1. What fabrics and their characteristics are suitable for kitchen table coverings and towels?
2. What fabrics are suitable for bath towels? Why?
3. Which fibers and fabrics would you choose for sheets, blankets, and bed coverings for a cold climate? a warm climate? for commercial use?

Textile Laws

There are many laws in the United States that regulate textiles. The intention of these laws is to inform and protect consumers from false labeling and advertising (Figure 19.23). The following is a summary that addresses three major textile acts that apply to household textiles.

Textile Fiber Products Identification Act

According to this law, textile labels must list fibers in a textile product in order of predominance by weight. If the fibers make up less than five percent of a fabric, the manufacturer can list them as "other fiber or fibers." Fabric producers must list natural and manufactured fibers by their generic names, but may also include the trade names. The product information labels must be attached to the product. Certain items, however, such as already installed upholstery fabrics, mattress materials, and carpet backings, are exempt. In addition, the content label must identify the manufacturer and where a product is processed or manufactured.

Wool Products Labeling Act

This law requires all products containing any quantity of wool to include a label identifying the kind and amount of wool used. Wool products must be labeled as one of the following types:

- New or virgin wool—wool fiber that has never been used or reclaimed from a product or used by a consumer.
- Recycled wool—wool fiber recovered from woven or felted-wool products that may have had consumer use. (Felted wool consists of wool fibers held together by moisture, heat, pressure, and chemicals.)

Products made from wool must have labels identifying the percentage of each type of wool used. The product labels also require the name of the manufacturer and must list the name of the country where the wool or wool product was processed and manufactured.

Flammable Fabrics Act

This law prohibits the sale of fabrics that burn quickly, or ***flammable*** fabrics. The *Flammable Fabrics Act* covers fabrics in textile products home use, such as carpets, rugs, mattresses, mattress pads, blankets, draperies, and upholstery. As the result of this law, many new flame-resistant finishes were developed to protect consumers.

Review & Assessment

1. Briefly summarize the Textile Fiber Products Identification Act.
2. What are the two classifications of wool products?
3. Briefly describe the Flammable Fabrics Act.

Dmitry Melnikov/Shutterstock.com

Christi Tolbert/Shutterstock.com

Figure 19.23 As you shop, read labels to learn what fibers and finishes are used in the various fabrics.

Chapter 19 Assessment

Summary

- Fibers come from plant and animal sources, wood cellulose, oil products, and other chemicals.
- Each fiber has its own traits. You can make wise fabric choices by understanding fiber traits and the ways used to construct fabrics.
- Fabrics can be woven, knitted, felted, tanned, or bonded.
- Other factors to consider when choosing fabrics are the design, color, and finishes.
- Uses for some textiles include floor treatments, upholstery, and window treatments. Other textiles are used as various types of linens in the kitchen, bathroom, and bedroom.
- Consider how the fabrics will look with other furnishings in the room. Also, consider durability, maintenance, comfort, ease of use, and cost.
- Various textile laws inform and protect consumers including the *Textile Products Information Act*, the *Wool Products Labeling Act*, and the *Flammable Fabrics Act*.

Terms in Action

1. **Term relation** Select ten terms from the *Content* and *Academic Terms* lists at the beginning of this chapter. Explain how these ten terms are related to each other. Create a graphic organizer or write one or two paragraphs to explain or illustrate how the terms relate.

Think Critically

2. **Analyze characteristics** Imagine you and your college roommate want a new area rug for your dormitory room. Your budget is limited and you want to buy a rug that will be durable, affordable, resilient, and soil resistant. To accomplish these goals, analyze the following characteristics: construction method—weaving, tufting, or needle-punching; type of pile and density; and fiber content and finish. Write a summary indicating your choice of characteristics and reasons supporting your choices.
3. **Draw conclusions** The U.S. Government has created many laws to inform consumers and protect them from such dangers as fabrics that burn too quickly. Suppose you were shopping one weekend at a neighbor's yard sale. Draw conclusions about whether you would feel comfortable buying blankets or draperies that no longer had labels showing fiber content and flammability ratings. Explain your reasons for either making or not making such a purchase.
4. **Evaluate labels** Choose five textile products from one room of your house. Read any labels you find on them. Record the information required by law that appears on each. Evaluate how the label information benefits consumers. Share your findings with the class.
5. **Assess products** Visit a store or showroom for a local supplier of residential and commercial textiles. If this is not possible, use online or print resources for suppliers of home textiles to research and list descriptions of the fiber content, cost, and care requirements for fabrics suitable for each of the following:

   A. upholstery
   B. window treatment
   C. bedroom linens
6. **Analyze options** Presume you are choosing new carpeting for the family room of a home. Because the family actively uses the room as a media room and game room, durability is very important. Compare the criteria for use, selection, and care of floor coverings. Determine what fiber type, construction method, texture, and finish you want for the carpeting. Then review the websites of carpet suppliers in your community. What choices are available to meet your needs? Print a copy of your choice to share with the class. Summarize the carpet features that meet the family's needs.

Core Skills

7. **Writing** As a consumer reporter for a local TV station, you have been assigned to write a consumer report that explains the important factors consumers should know before buying carpeting. If possible, use images identifying carpeting features to enhance your report. Post your report to the class website, if possible, and have the class critique the usefulness of the information in your report.

Chapter 19 Assessment

8. **Science** Use online or print resources—such as the website for the American Chemical Society (ACS)—to research the role of polymer chemists in developing new textiles and modifying performance features of existing textiles. How do demands for recyclable and degradable fibers impact the work of polymer chemists? Write a report or present your findings to the class using presentation software.
9. **Speaking** Use the Internet to research which countries are the largest suppliers of various natural and manufactured fibers. How many metric tons were produced globally of the 10 most commonly used fibers in today's homes? For what percentage of fiber production is the United States responsible? Use presentation software to create a chart or graph showing your findings. Share your findings with the class.
10. **Reading and writing** Review the basic textile finishes listed in Figure 19.11 of the text. Select one type of fabric finish to research in depth. How was this type of finish developed? What types of fabrics most often have this type of finish? Is this type of finish often combined with other finishes? Write an essay to report your findings. Cite any sources used and then proofread your essay for proper spelling, grammar, and punctuation.
11. **Reading, science, and technology** Further investigate the use of nanotechnology in the manufacture of textiles for residential and commercial use. What are the key features? What are the benefits to consumers? What new textile products are on the horizon for residential and commercial consumers? What are some of the drawbacks consumers should consider? Summarize your findings in an oral report for the class.
12. **Listening** Interview someone who has recently purchased upholstered furniture; carpeting; window treatments; or products with textiles for the kitchen, bathroom, or bedroom. Ask this person what factors impacted the purchasing decision. Practice active listening skills and jot down the speaker's responses. Then share a summary of your interview with the class.
13. **CTE career readiness practice** Use reliable online or print resources to investigate the issues surrounding products that are high in volatile organic compounds (VOCs). Read two or more articles and summarize your findings in writing. When evaluating the reliability of the information, remember the following:
    - **Identify author/writer credibility.** Who is the author or writer? Is the author, writer, or publisher known for reliable facts?
    - **Verify details.** Can you verify the facts in the article from other sources (government, medical, or educational institutions)? Is the information current? Is the copyright recent?
    - **Identify bias.** Is the information presented from only one point of view? Is it from a scientific, medical, or well-known educational institution? Avoid articles that lack objectivity.

Design Practice

14. **Renovation project** Presume a client has hired you to select the textiles for room renovations occurring in three rooms of her house—kitchen, bathroom, and master bedroom. List the textile items needed for each room. Use online or print resources (such as supplier catalogs) to locate photos of each textile item on your list. Mount the photos by room on poster board. Label each textile photo with a brief description of the textile features. Then have a classmate serve as your client. Role-play the presentation of your textile choices to your client during class. What evidence did you give to support your choices?
15. **Office textiles** A client in your community wants you to select upholstery and carpeting for an office renovation. The office areas include a meeting room that holds 12 people around the conference table, the owner's office which adjoins the meeting room, and a reception area. All three areas require upholstered seating and carpeting. Locate samples for three design options. Mount them on poster board to share with your client.
16. **Portfolio** Create a vignette of fabrics you would choose for a bedroom design for a future apartment. Label each fabric, identifying its fiber content, finishes, care method, and proposed use.

Chapter 20

Understanding Surface Materials and Treatments

Content Terms 

floor treatment
flooring materials
ceramic tile
porcelain tile
floor coverings
soft floor covering
resilient floor covering
laminate
cork
wall treatment
paint
faux finish
stenciling
wall covering
ceiling treatment
countertop
engineered quartz
butcher block

Academic Terms 

deciduous
rectilinear
reclamation
abrasion
impervious

Learning Outcomes 

After studying this chapter, you will be able to

- compare criteria for selection, use, and care of floor treatments.
- evaluate criteria for selection, use, and care of materials for wall treatments.
- evaluate the selection and care of various ceiling treatments and how they serve as interior backgrounds.
- evaluate countertop materials for kitchens and bathrooms.
- choose appropriate background surface materials to plan satisfying interiors for various residential and nonresidential settings.

Reading with Purpose

Write all of the chapter terms on a sheet of paper. Highlight the words that you do not know. Before you begin reading the chapter, look up the highlighted words in the glossary and write the definitions.

While studying, look for the access icon  **to:**

- **Practice** the *Content* and *Academic Terms* with e-flash cards, matching activities, and vocabulary games.
- **Reinforce** what you learn by completing the *Review & Assessment* questions and e-mailing them to your instructor.

www.g-wlearning.com/housing/

Santiago Cornejo/Shutterstock.com

Floors, walls, and ceilings create interior backgrounds for furnishings and accessories in rooms. They also hide construction details and provide insulation. How they are treated helps to determine the total look of the room and create a desired mood. *Surface treatment* refers to the manner in which floors, walls, ceilings, and countertops are finished with materials or other design applications. The materials you select should reflect careful consideration of both sustainable and green design.

Floor Treatments

The floor treatment is usually the first background surface interior designers will plan for a room. **Floor treatments** consist of flooring materials and floor coverings. There are many types of flooring materials and floor coverings from which to choose. Before you choose a floor treatment, however, consider its appearance, comfort, durability, cost, sustainability, safety, and maintenance. Consider how floor treatments will be used, where they will be used, and how much of the material will be needed.

Flooring Materials

Flooring materials are materials that form the top surface of a floor. They do not include the subflooring; however, part of the installation process is to secure the flooring materials to the subfloor, making it fairly permanent. Common flooring materials include wood, tile, concrete, and brick.

Wood

Wood has always been a popular flooring material. With an appropriate finish, it can coordinate with all styles of furniture. It offers beauty and warmth to a room (Figure 20.1). Wood

STEM Math — Estimating Wood Flooring Cost

This exercise will show you how to estimate the cost of wood planks for a new floor. Suppose a rectangular-shaped room has a length of 14 ft. 0 in. and a width of 11 ft. 7 in. It also has a closet that is 4 ft. by 3 ft. In this example, the hardwood planks are sold in boxes of 24 sq. ft. per box. Each box costs $82.00, not including taxes and the cost of installation supplies.

1. When measurements contain inches, round up to the nearest foot.

   Round up 11 ft. 7 in. to 12 ft.

2. Figure the square footage of the floor space you will cover. Identify the rectangles in your space, figure the area of each, and total the square footage. The formula for calculating the area of a rectangle is length multiplied by width, or l × w.

   The area of the room is 14 ft. × 12 ft. = 168 sq. ft. The area of the closet is 4 ft. × 3 ft. or 12 sq. ft. Add 168 and 12 to get 180 sq. ft.

3. Experts recommend adding about 10 percent to total square footage because of variations in the grain and coloring of wood flooring. Installers want to avoid dramatic changes in coloring from one plank to the next. They achieve a natural look by matching each plank for color with surrounding planks. Also, some leftover planks should be stored in case one or more planks need replacing in the future.

   If you purchase an extra 10 percent of wood flooring (10 percent of 180 = 18), you'll need 180 + 18, or 198 sq. ft. total.

4. Calculate how many boxes of wood planks you will need. Divide the square footage of the floor by square feet per box.

   For example, 198 sq. ft. ÷ 24 = 8.25 boxes. You cannot buy a fraction of a box, so round up to 9 boxes.

5. Calculate the total cost for the wood planks.

   If each box costs $82.00, 9 boxes will cost $738.00.

Math Practice

Assume your family will be installing wood flooring in the family room, a rectangular-shaped room that has a length of 15 ft. 0 in. and a width of 13 ft. 4 in. The hardwood planks are sold in boxes of 24 sq. ft. per box. Each box costs $75.00.

1. What is the square footage of the floor space you will cover?
2. If you purchase an additional 10 percent of the total square footage, how much footage will you purchase in total?
3. How many boxes of wood planks will you need to purchase?
4. What is the cost of the wood planks?

foamfoto/Shutterstock.com

Figure 20.1 This hardwood floor adds warmth and beauty to the room.

has some resilience and is durable, but can be scratched and dented.

Types of Wood Flooring

There are several types of wood used for wood flooring. The cost of wood flooring is moderate to high, depending on the type and quality of wood chosen. Hardwoods, which are from ***deciduous*** trees (trees that lose their leaves once each year) are typically more expensive than softwoods (woods from evergreens). Oak, hard maple, beech, birch, hickory, mahogany, cherry, and teak are common hardwoods used for floors. Oak is the most common because of its beauty, warmth, cost, and durability. Hard maple is also common because it is smooth, strong, and hard.

Southern yellow pine, Douglas fir, hemlock, and larch are common softwoods used for floors. Use of redwood, cedar, cypress, and eastern white pine occurs where they are readily available. Bamboo, which is actually a form of grass, is a sustainable alternative to many wood products. There are two different kinds of wood floor installations. They include unfinished solid wood and prefinished engineered wood flooring.

Installation

When installing solid wood floors that require finishing, the floors must have enough time to adjust to the house environment. Wood that needs finishing will expand and contract during fluctuations in humidity and temperature. The floor finishing process requires multiple steps of repeated sanding and staining. The last step involves sealing the floor surface with a protective coating.

An alternative to a solid wood floor is a floor made of engineered wood, available in many styles and finishes. These floors are prefinished at the factory and, therefore, already sanded and stained. You can install engineered wood floors over concrete and wooden subfloors. Solid wood floors, however, require a plywood underlayment when installing them over concrete. The construction method for making engineered wood floors helps them withstand moisture. They have more stability than solid wood and will expand and contract less with seasonal changes in the environment.

Construction of certain types of engineered wood flooring may involve layering, or laminating, woods of different quality. This process can lower the cost of the product and increase its structural integrity. It also offers a more earth-friendly solution to the use of other flooring materials. Infusion of a substance such as acrylic into this laminate flooring gives it greater durability.

Strip flooring is the most common method of installing engineered wood floors which involves nailing down thin strips of wood that are tongue-and-grooved to keep them close together. *Plank flooring* is a similar installation method that utilizes wider widths of wood. Another style of wood flooring is *parquet flooring*. Creating decorative patterns—such as alternate plank and parquetry as shown in Figure 20.2—adds interest to a wood floor, but should be used sparingly.

Use and Care for Wood Flooring

Wood species and installation type are not the only decisions. When selecting a wood floor, you must also consider how each stain color will act differently on each wood species. For example, a cherry stain will look different on oak than it will on maple. Graining is also an issue. Designers are more likely to use woods with little to no graining for contemporary interiors.

Mladen Mitrinovic/Shutterstock.com

Figure 20.2 The use of parquet flooring adds interest to any room.

Wood finishes of polyurethane, plastic, wax, and oil make the task of maintaining wood floors easy. They protect the wood from moisture, stains, and wear. If properly maintained, a quality wood floor can last the lifetime of the house.

Proper care of wood floors begins with determining the finish on the wood floor. If the floor has a urethane or other glossy finish, wax should not be used on the surface. Also, proper care involves using only products that are designed for wood floors because using products for other surfaces (like furniture) could permanently damage the floor surface. Dusting and sweeping floors to remove gravel and dirt is important for wood floors as the surface can be scratched or marked if not properly removed. Another care guide is not using water as a cleaning method or pouring water directly on the floor to clean it. If water or other spills occur, they should be removed immediately with a paper towel or soft dry cloth. In addition, ammonia should not be used on wood floors.

General care of wood floors involves avoiding the dragging of furniture across the floor. Use felt pads under furniture to move the item. Also, chair and table legs should use felt pads under them to prevent scratching and gouging of the flooring material.

Tile

Tile is a flat piece of kiln-fired clay or natural stone that is available in a wide range of sizes, colors, finishes, and patterns. Tile feels cool to the touch and is therefore more popular in Sunbelt areas than in colder climates. The primary tile choices for residential use are ceramic, porcelain, natural stone, and quarry. Because of the amount of labor installation required, tile can be expensive to install. As with most hard surfaces, consider safety when selecting such products in regard to slip resistance for your interior design projects.

Ceramic Tile

Ceramic tile is a flat piece of kiln-fired clay coated with a protective glaze. High-quality ceramic tile is harder, more durable, and more expensive than ceramic tile of lesser quality. Ceramic tile is a durable choice for a floor treatment, but quality and cost of product and installation can vary considerably. Small tiles and mosaics will be less expensive to install than larger 12-inch by 12-inch or 18-inch by 18-inch tiles. Keep this factor in mind when choosing ceramic tile for yourself or a client.

Glazed ceramic tile is water- and stain-resistant, which makes it easy to maintain. To further protect the floor, you can seal the grout to make it resistant to stains, too. *Grout* is the cement-like mortar substance that fills the spaces between the tiles. Consider the grout color and characteristics alongside your tile. Darker grout that matches the tiles (rather than white) will remain attractive longer. Grout can also be specified to be stain, mildew, and chemical resistant. Tiles can also come in unglazed versions.

Maintaining clean ceramic floor tile requires sweeping or vacuuming with a soft brush head to remove dust and dirt from tiles. Follow with mopping with soapy water. As always, follow manufacturer recommendations for cleaning products.

In the past, the common use of ceramic tile was in bathrooms and entryways. Current interior design trends, however, often promote using ceramic tile for flooring throughout a house or structure (Figure 20.3). Manufacturers can produce ceramic tile in almost any color, pattern, or finish. Ceramic tile is also available in bull-nose (rounded) tiles and strips to ensure a clean transition to other flooring and wall surfaces. Recent advances in computer imaging and glazing techniques enable the creation of ceramic tile to resemble natural stone and marble.

Porcelain Tile

Porcelain tile is the highest quality ceramic tile made. The tile has a white or light clay-colored body that is kiln-fired at a very high temperature. The result is a very strong and durable product. Because of its strength, porcelain tile withstands freezing temperatures, which makes it suitable for indoor and outdoor use. Avoid using tiles with a smooth, high-gloss surface for outdoor living spaces, however, because they become very slippery when wet.

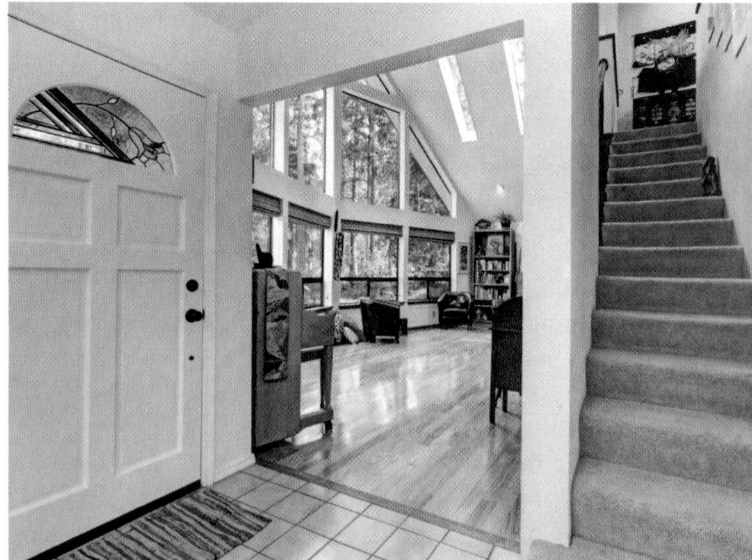

Iriana Shiyan/Shutterstock.com

Figure 20.3 Although the floor plan is open and inviting, there is a lack of continuity of floor coverings and wood tones.

The color of a porcelain tile often penetrates the tile's entire thickness. In contrast, the color of a ceramic tile is only on the surface. Porcelain tile is more expensive than ceramic tile.

Care of porcelain tile involves frequent sweeping (recommended daily) to remove dirt and dust, as dirt and dust can damage the surface. Mopping the porcelain tile with water is essential for light soiling. If there is heavy soiling, however, spray household bleach on the floor before mopping with water. Sealing the surface annually is recommended to avoid permanent staining in the tiles.

Quarry Tile

Quarry tile is available in black and a range of gold hues, beiges, reds, browns, and grays. Manufacturers make quarry tile from clay mixture (the consistency of dough) that goes through an extrusion process and is kiln-fired at a high temperature. For example, manufacturers use a terra-cotta clay mixture to form red tile. Quarry tile is very strong and durable. It resists grease, chemicals, moisture, and changes in temperature. The shapes and textures of quarry tile vary, and it can be glazed or unglazed. Glazed quarry tile is easy to maintain with soapy water. Applying a protective sealer to unglazed tile will make it as easy to clean as glazed tile.

Caring for quarry-tile flooring involves vacuuming with a soft bristle head. The soft head is necessary to avoid damaging the flooring. The quarry floor then needs to be mopped with a cleaner designed for quarry tile floors. The cleaner will help remove grease and odors. Rinse the floor with water. It is important to use distilled water because tap water may leave mineral deposits and a film on the floor. Wipe dry with towels. If there is a residue (film or haze) on the tiles, wipe them down with water and white vinegar, and again dry with towels.

Natural Stone

Natural stone floors are beautiful and durable, but are usually costly to purchase and install. Stone comes in a variety of types, sizes, and qualities. Five types of stone, commonly available in the following colors, are very popular for home use:

- **limestone**—comes in taupe, white, light and dark brown, and gray; with gold or light green veins
- **travertine**—usually cream or beige; contains porous holes so it should have a cement fill and be sealed
- **granite**—comes in almost any color and may have crystals or granules in it
- **marble**—comes in almost any color and should be polished
- **slate**—comes in a wide range of colors typically with a dark base of gray or green; varies in tone and texture

For your interior design background surfaces, you may choose to use stones in their natural shapes or those cut into geometric shapes. You can achieve attractive designs by mixing different types and shapes of stone together. The texture of stone tile may be rough or polished. Polished stone creates a formal appearance while rough stone has a more rustic and informal look.

A sealer protects stone floors from grease, oil, and household stains. You can use stone floors throughout the house, including entryways, kitchens, living and dining rooms, and bathrooms.

Stone floors are fairly easy to maintain by regular sweeping to remove dirt. Pre-mop a stone floor with water before adding a cleaning solution. The pre-mopping makes the cleaning solution more effective and avoids residue development on the stones. Then mop with a solution of white vinegar and water, or use a cleaning solution recommended by the manufacturer.

Concrete

Concrete can have a smooth or textured surface. You can use a smooth surface as a finished floor. Adding color in powder form when mixing concrete blends the color throughout the floor. Installers can also add color by painting concrete with a special paint.

Concrete is extremely sturdy and durable, but uncomfortable to stand on for long periods. Entryways, basements, patios, and garages are common uses for concrete floors. For easy maintenance, apply a coat of nonslip wax on indoor concrete floors. Concrete floors are relatively inexpensive because they do not require subflooring.

Caring for a concrete floor can be fairly easy—especially if there is a glazing applied to the surface. Sweeping or vacuuming regularly will avoid a buildup of soil that is more difficult later when ground into the concrete. Mopping with a recommended cleaner will keep the concrete clean with an acceptable surface finish.

Brick

Brick floors are beautiful, durable, and costly. They look best in informal design settings (Figure 20.4). Because bricks come in many sizes,

pic721/Shutterstock.com

Figure 20.4 Since brick is traditionally an exterior material, it is a wise choice for flooring in this sunroom as it visually and functionally acts as a transition between the interior and exterior of the home.

robinimages2013/Shutterstock.com

Figure 20.5 Wall-to-wall carpeting is an example of a soft floor covering.

colors, and textures, you can use them in a wide variety of patterns. The care of brick floors is similar to that of stone floors—as a covering, it may not require mortar, but as a structural floor it would.

The care of brick flooring involves regular sweeping and then mopping with a recommended product for brick cleaning. If there is grout, glazing of the grout periodically will help prevent discoloring of the grout and make cleaning easier.

Floor Coverings

Floor coverings are surfaces placed over the structural floor. Although they may adhere to the floor, they are not part of the structure. Floor coverings last several years and are expensive. However, they are not as expensive as other flooring materials and many people change them more often than in the past. Floor coverings include soft floor coverings and resilient floor coverings.

Soft Floor Coverings

Carpets and rugs are types of **soft floor coverings**. As you may recall, these are floor treatments that consist of manufactured or natural fibers. Manufactured fibers include nylon and olefin, while natural fibers include wool, cotton, bamboo, and sisal. Carpets and rugs insulate cold floors, provide sound control and walking comfort, and add color and texture to a room (Figure 20.5). They vary in their methods of construction as well as their textures and finishes.

Soft floor coverings can cover the entire floor or portions of it. Floor coverings are classified by how much floor they cover. Common soft floor coverings are wall-to-wall carpeting (broadloom and modular), room-size rugs, and area rugs.

- *Wall-to-wall carpeting* covers an entire floor, making rooms appear large and luxurious. You can typically purchase it on a roll (broadloom). It can hide any damage or faults in the floor surface. Maintain wall-to-wall carpeting with routine vacuuming. Remove stains by applying an appropriate cleaning product as suggested by the manufacturer.
- *Modular carpeting*, or carpet tiles, has similar characteristics to broadloom, but is in the form of smaller square or ***rectilinear*** (made with straight lines) pieces. It typically has a built-in cushion and is easy to install. It gives owners the opportunity to replace small areas (due to stain or wear) without replacing the flooring in an entire space. It is typically patterned, which can mask stains. Modular carpeting can also be used to create a pattern. Alternating tiles can be turned to create a basket weave appearance.
- *Room-size rugs* expose a small border of floor. They can enhance the appearance of a beautiful wood floor while keeping the warmth and comfort of the soft floor covering (Figure 20.6). Maintain room-size rugs in the same manner used for maintaining wall-to-wall carpeting. One disadvantage to using a room-size rug, however, is that the rug and the adjacent floor require separate cleaning procedures.
- *Area rugs* vary in size, but are not as large as room-size rugs. Interior designers often use area rugs to define areas of a room, add interest, and even serve as a focal point (Figure 20.7). You can move them from one furniture grouping to

Breadmaker/Shutterstock.com

Figure 20.6 A room-size rug provides comfort without covering the beauty of the floor beneath.

A MR. INTERIOR/Shutterstock.com

B Iriana Shiyan/Shutterstock.com

C bikeriderlondon/Shutterstock.com

Figure 20.7 These area rugs are examples of three different design styles: traditional (A), abstract contemporary (B), and geometric contemporary (C).

another to create a new look. Maintain area rugs with routine vacuuming and spot-stain removal. One big advantage of area rugs is they are portable—you or a client can move them easily to other locations. Sending them out for professional cleaning is also an option.

Manufacturers generally recommend the use of padding under carpeting and rugs to reduce wear and increase resilience. It also adds luxury and warmth. Padding is made of hair, jute, sponge, or foam rubber. Different types of carpeting and rugs require the use of specific products for padding. Always check the carpet or rug manufacturer's recommendations when buying padding.

As time passes, carpeting and rugs will show wear and dirt in areas of highest traffic. Scheduling a professional cleaning service to do a thorough cleaning or renting the proper equipment and following the manufacturer's care directions are two options of carpeting and rug maintenance.

The carpet industry was one of the first to understand sustainable practices and their part in ecological issues and landfills. Many carpet companies are implementing ***reclamation*** (getting back; reclaiming) programs, reprinting carpet systems, and recycling backing and fibers. They are also encouraging the use of carpet tiles instead of broadloom to reduce the impact of carpet in landfills.

Resilient Floor Coverings

Resilient floor coverings are floor treatments that are generally nonabsorbent, durable, easy to maintain, and fairly inexpensive. They provide some cushioning for walking comfort and noise control. Vinyl floor coverings, laminate floor coverings,

STEM Math Resilient Flooring and Carpeting Calculations

Before taking measurements, create a rough sketch of the room or area in which your client wants resilient flooring or carpeting. There are several factors to remember about these flooring coverings. The standard width of most resilient flooring and carpeting is 12 feet. Some resilient flooring has a pattern that influences the direction to lay the flooring. In addition, all carpeting has a grain or nap—the direction in which the fibers run. Installing carpeting so that the grain runs in the same direction as the entrance (or main entrance in case of multiple doors) to the room helps ensure the carpeting will wear better and last longer.

You will likely work with a floor covering supplier or installer to consider the best way to lay the resilient flooring or carpeting in the room so that the pattern or grain flows with the traffic pattern. This will also help determine where the seams (if any) will fall in the floor covering. Planning the layout helps reduce the amount of waste and often saves the client money. A flooring seam should *never* run down the middle of a room. This is not pleasing to the eye and may cause the resilient flooring or carpeting to wear faster.

When taking floor-covering measurements, use the standard formula for calculating the room area (square footage). Then divide the square footage by 9, or the number of square feet in a square yard. (*Note:* Resilient flooring and carpeting often sells by the square yard rather than square foot.)

When a wall measurement includes a fraction of a foot, always round up the measurement to the next whole foot. For example, if the width of a room measures 14.5 feet, round up to 15 feet before calculating square footage of the room. It is always better to have a little extra than not enough carpeting.

Suppose your client intends to carpet a great room that measures 16.5 feet by 24 feet. How many square yards of carpeting will you need to order?

Step 1: 17 ft. × 24 ft. = 408 sq. ft.

Step 2: 408 sq. ft. ÷ 9 = 45.33 sq. yd. (round up to 45.5 sq. yd.)

Math Practice

Suppose your client would like to install new laminate flooring in his kitchen. The kitchen measures 15.3 ft. by 18.6 ft.

1. What is the total square footage of his kitchen?
2. Calculate how many square yards of laminate flooring you will need to order.

linoleum, and cork tile are types of resilient floor coverings. They are available in a wide range of colors and patterns to enhance any interior design scheme.

Vinyl floor coverings, as shown in Figure 20.8, are available in many colors, patterns, and textures. The quality of the flooring varies with the cost.

stocksolutions/Shutterstock.com

Figure 20.8 This vinyl floor covering is attractive and easy to keep clean.

Vinyl floor coverings resist wear and stains, but ***abrasion*** (damage caused by wearing, rubbing, or scraping) can damage the surfaces of the flooring. They are available in either tile or sheet form. Vinyl tile is typically 12-inch by 12-inch while sheet vinyl can range from 6 feet to 12 feet wide. Sheet vinyl can also be heat welded together so seams are virtually invisible and the flooring becomes ***impervious*** (nonporous) to liquid. These floor coverings need little or no waxing. Some sheet vinyl has a layer of vinyl foam on the bottom, resulting in a floor with good walking comfort and sound absorption.

Solid vinyl floor coverings are growing in popularity. They are a higher quality than sheet vinyl because of their all-vinyl composition. In contrast, sheet vinyl only has a vinyl top layer. Solid vinyl flooring products are available in many striking colors, styles, and patterns. These floors may have the appearance of fine hardwood, elegant stone, marble, slate, granite, or a geometric pattern. They are available in planks, tiles, blocks, or squares. Interior designers often combine these different shapes and patterns in the same floor to provide an endless opportunity for creative custom designs.

Laminate floors vary in quality, depending on their construction. Manufacturers make **laminate** products by uniting one or more different layers, usually a decorative surface, to a sturdy core. To make the best laminate floors, manufacturers fuse four layers of materials under intense heat and pressure. This process creates a single unit with a decorative surface and a sturdy core. The layers consist of a moisture-guard backing, a core of high-density material for structure, the pattern design, and a wear- and stain-resistant finish. The final product resists traffic wear, stains, and fading (Figure 20.9). Laminate floors are easy to clean, comfortable for walking, and good at sound absorption. They are not, however, as resilient and durable as quality solid vinyl flooring.

Because of its environmentally friendly manufacturing process, linoleum is regaining popularity. Made with all natural products, primarily linseed oil, limestone, powdered cork, resins, and wood powder, it is naturally static resistant, biodegradable, and antibacterial. It also resists gouges and scratches.

Linoleum is also available in a wide variety of colors and patterns. This product is durable and provides a cushion for tired feet. It also does not introduce toxic chemicals into interior environments as do many man-made materials.

Cork is the woody bark tissue of a sustainable plant. Manufacturers use this bark to create *cork tiles* that are rich in appearance and good for walking comfort and sound control. An application of a protective coating helps keep cork tile water resistant, durable, and easy to maintain. Without a protective coating, cork wears rapidly, dents easily, is difficult to maintain, and is susceptible to grease stains.

AGITA LEIMANE/Shutterstock.com

Figure 20.9 Laminate flooring is durable and easy to clean.

Cork is not a resilient floor covering without the protective coating. Care of resilient floor coverings involves mopping with water and a cleaning product recommended by the various manufacturers.

Review & Assessment 

1. What is a surface treatment?
2. Contrast flooring materials and floor coverings. Give an example of each.
3. Give an example of when you would use each of the following flooring materials: wood, tile, natural stone, concrete, and brick.
4. Name four ways to care for wood floors.
5. What are five types of natural stone commonly used for floors?
6. How does caring for porcelain tile differ from caring for quarry tile?
7. What is the difference between soft floor coverings and resilient floor coverings?

Wall Treatments

A **wall treatment** is a surface treatment that is applied to an interior wall. Common wall treatments are paint, wall covering, fabric, cork, ceramic tile, mirrors, glass, and reflective metals. Applying these wall treatments varies from easy to difficult. Some treatments are inexpensive while others are high in cost.

As you choose a wall treatment for an interior design project, keep in mind that it should harmonize with the floor and ceiling. It should add to the general mood of the room. Most of all, it should reflect the personalities of the people who use the room.

Paint

Paint is an interior design media that is a mixture of pigment and liquid that thinly coats and covers a surface. It is the fastest and least costly way to cover wall surfaces and change the look of a room (Figure 20.10). There are two categories of paint: water-based and solvent-based. Most designers and paint professionals choose water-based paint—either vinyl or acrylic latex—for interior wall surfaces because it is easy to apply and dries quickly. Equipment cleanup is also easy. Solvent-based paint—or oil-based or alkyd paint—is thinner and takes longer to dry. Also, it is much harder to clean the paint equipment when using a solvent-based paint.

When you choose paint, choose a color that is slightly lighter than the color you want. When

STEM Math Paint Calculations

When a design plan requires painting a room, most interior designers obtain an estimate from a quality painter. The designer determines the paint colors and the type of paint (such as flat or eggshell, semigloss or gloss) and gives this information to the painter. The painter determines how much paint a job requires. Because most painters purchase paint at a reduced cost from their suppliers, you will often get a better deal for the job if the painter supplies the paint. When developing an estimate, the painter

- evaluates how many coats a room will need for coverage (note that covering deep reds and yellows on existing walls often requires extra coats of paint)
- determines the amount of primer and whether to tint the primer the same color as the finish paint (note that tinting the primer may reduce the number of coats a room requires)
- calculates trim paint separately if the trim paint is different from the wall paint (trim includes crown and base moldings, door and window casings, and often doors)

To verify the accuracy of a painter's estimate, you may want to take your own room measurements. Keep in mind that one gallon of paint usually covers 350 square feet of wall space. Divide the total square footage of a room by 350 square feet to estimate the amount of paint. If the result is less than 0.5 gallon, generally two quarts will do. If the result is greater than 0.5 gallon, a gallon is usually more economical.

Ceiling Paint. When calculating the amount of ceiling paint, multiply the ceiling width by the ceiling length to determine the square footage of the area. Divide the square footage by 350 to identify how many gallons the job requires, rounding up your answer to the nearest gallon. Use the following formula for your estimate:

Area = Width × Length

Wall Paint. To calculate the amount of wall paint to order, add together the lengths of the room walls (the perimeter) and multiply the total length by the room height to get the total area (square footage) using the following formula:

Area = Perimeter × Height

Once you know the total area (square footage) of the walls, subtract the square footage of door and window openings (Area = Width × Length). Divide the total by 350 to obtain the total gallons of paint.

For example, how much wall paint is required for a room measuring 13 ft. wide by 16 ft. long by 8 ft. high with one door (3 ft. wide by 7 ft. high) and two windows (3 ft. wide by 4 ft. long)?

Step 1: Calculate the perimeter. P = 13 ft. + 16 ft. + 13 ft. + 16 ft. = 58 ft.

Step 2: Calculate the room area square footage. A = 58 ft. × 8 ft. = 464 sq. ft. (total wall area)

Step 3: Calculate the door opening square footage. A = 3 ft. × 7 ft. (door height) = 21 sq. ft. (total door area)

Step 4: Calculate the window opening square footage. A = (3 ft. × 4 ft.) × 2 (window area) = 24 sq. ft. (total window area)

Step 5: Calculate the total square footage occupied by windows and doors. 21 sq. ft. + 24 sq. ft. = 45 sq. ft. (total window/door area)

Step 6: Subtract the window and door square footage area from the total room square footage. 464 sq. ft. – 45 sq. ft. = 419 sq. ft. (total wall area)

Step 7: Calculate the total gallons of paint needed. 419 sq. ft. ÷ 350 = 1.19 gallons (round up to 1.5)

Because the answer includes 1 whole gallon and a fraction of a gallon less than 0.5, you will need 1 gallon plus 2 quarts of paint. (*Note:* Because of the minimal cost difference, it may be a good idea to round up to the next gallon to allow for touch-ups or to add another coat if necessary.)

Math Practice

Calculate the amount of wall paint required for a room measuring 15 ft. wide by 18 ft. long by 10 ft. high with one door (3 ft. wide by 7 ft. high) and one bay window (6 ft. wide by 7 ft. long). Show your work for each step.

applying the paint color to walls, the paint appears stronger and darker than the color on the paint chip. This is because you see so much more of the color on the wall than on the sample. When painting a lighter color over an existing dark color or when applying paint to a new wall, it is essential to apply a primer coat before you begin to paint.

Textured paints give walls a rough surface. You can use them to cover cracks or irregularities in walls and ceilings. Refer to the label directions before

Iriana Shiyan/Shutterstock.com

Figure 20.10 Paint gives this room a cheerful, light, and airy appearance.

applying texturizing paints. Application of these paints can also minimize the appearance of other designs.

Keeping a record of paint type and color is important. Retaining a chip from the paint company is one way to accomplish this. Sometimes paint chips are not available, particularly if the paint is custom mixed. One way to secure this information for your records is to paint one side of an index card once a room is painted. On the reverse side, write the brand name and color name and formula of the paint. This information can make color matching more efficient in the future. In addition, it will make it easier when coordinating window treatments, floor treatments, or furniture.

Surface Finishes

Paints vary in how glossy or shiny their surfaces look. Paint surface finishes include enamel, semigloss, satin or eggshell, and flat wall paints.

- *Enamel paints* have the most gloss. They give a protective and decorative finish to kitchen and bathroom walls, wood trim, windowsills, radiators, masonry, and heating pipes.
- *Semigloss paints* have less gloss and are slightly less durable than enamel paints. You can use them in most of the same places as enamel paints.
- *Satin or eggshell paint* finishes have a slight sheen. Paint professionals usually use them on walls. They are slightly less durable than semigloss paints.
- *Flat wall paints* have no gloss. They give a soft finish to walls and ceilings. Do not use them for windowsills or kitchen or bathroom walls and woodwork, which are susceptible to moisture, mold, and mildew. Flat paints are usually the least expensive and the most difficult to clean.

Faux Finishes

Paint is usually associated with walls finished in solid colors. A number of different textures and patterns, however, create decorative wall finishes through special applications, or **faux finishes**. (*Faux* comes from the French word meaning *false* or *fictitious.*) Paint professionals can achieve faux finishes by applying paint to the wall with tools other than a common paintbrush. For example, *sponging* is a faux finish that requires dipping a sponge in paint and dabbing it on the wall to add pattern. *Ragging* is another faux finish by which you apply paint with pieces of cloth. *Combing* involves using a rubber comb or other combing device to create a faux finish that results in stripes, swirls, or other unique patterns. A finishing technique called *marbleizing* creates a wall treatment that looks like marble stone. Many other faux finishes are available to create a unique look. See Figure 20.11.

© 2009 Sherwin-Williams

Figure 20.11 To achieve this look, the room was painted with the same base color to seal the tape and avoid bleeding. A glazing liquid was then painted in a thick layer into the taped-off areas. Once dried, the tape was peeled off, giving a rich wall covering effect. The walls appear to have a wall covering, but the stripes are actually examples of a faux-finish technique called *combing*. In addition to traditional paint brushes and rollers, alternative tools can be used to create faux-finishes and textures.

The application of paint in an artistic manner can also create a wall scene or mural so lifelike that it "fools the eye." The name of this technique is *trompe l'oeil*, which means *illusion* in French. Designers and painters can use this technique to turn a plain wall into a grand three-dimensional garden, complete with stone walls, fountains, and beautiful plants (Figure 20.12). The same technique can be used to paint the four walls of a child's playroom with beach scenes showing blue sky, sand, water, swimming fish, and dancing dolphins. Faux finishes and trompe l'oeil can create endless possibilities, but good results require patience and talent.

Stenciling Finishes

In addition to faux finishes, paint professionals can apply paint with a stenciling technique to add interest to a wall. **Stenciling** is applying paint by using a cutout form to outline a design or lettering. You can either create these stencil patterns or purchase them ready-made. For a professional finish, apply paint to the open area of the stencil to transfer the design to the wall. The designs may vary from simple to complex and may entail one coat of paint or many to achieve the proper detail.

Caring for Painted Surfaces

Maintaining painted walls and surfaces is necessary to keep them looking good. Wipe dust off walls periodically with a soft, cloth mop or vacuum with a soft brush attachment. Walls can be washed with water and a small amount of liquid soap or other cleaner recommended by the manufacturer. Soak a soft sponge in the soapy water, wring it out completely, and then wipe walls or other surfaces with very light pressure and a circular motion to avoid damaging the paint. For walls, begin washing at the bottom of the walls and work your way up. This prevents your cleaning solution from running down dirty walls and causing difficult-to-remove streaks.

Wall Covering

A **wall covering** is decorative paper or vinyl applied to a wall with a special paste or adhesive. It can copy the look of almost any surface, such as brick, stone, wood, and leather. Wall coverings can bring the look of the outdoors in through the creation of murals showing outdoor scenes. Larger repetitive patterns require the purchase of a larger quantity to ensure the pattern matches during installation. Because of the variety of patterns available, the use of wall coverings can enhance any room and create any style (Figure 20.13).

A Lost Mountain Studio/Shutterstock.com

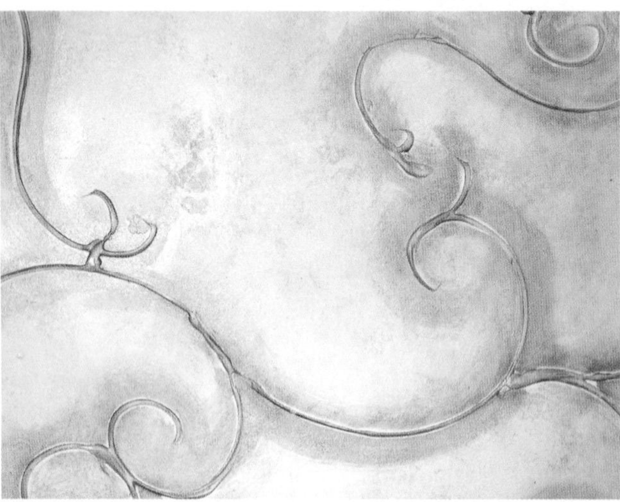

B Sheri Herbert/Shutterstock.com

Figure 20.12 In addition to traditional paint brushes and rollers, alternative tools can be used to create faux finishes and textures (A). A faux finish was applied to this wall to create a trompe l'oeil illusion of a carved scroll pattern in a wall (B).

Software by Chief Architect

Figure 20.13 Consumers and interior designers can coordinate wall covering selections with paint colors by using a CADD system.

STEM Math Wall Covering Calculations

Similar to estimating materials and labor for room paint, interior designers often work with professional wall covering hangers to determine the material and labor requirements for hanging wall covering. Because these professionals work with wall coverings and their variables on a daily basis, they can efficiently estimate these costs. Once a client chooses a wall covering, the interior designer gives this information to the wall covering hanger. Factors that impact the amount of wall covering a job requires include

- type of wall covering (for example vinyl-coated paper or solid vinyl, prepasted or not)
- size of pattern and length of pattern repeat in the wall covering (pattern repeat impacts the usable yield of wall covering—a longer repeat reduces the usable square footage)

To confirm the wall covering estimate, calculate wall covering needs with the same formula for calculating wall area for paint. (*Note:* A single roll of wall covering covers about 30 square feet. Most suppliers sell wall covering in double rolls.)

Divide the total square footage of a room by 30 to determine the number of single rolls of wall covering. If your calculations reveal a fraction of a roll, round up to the next roll. Many experts do not subtract the square footage for door and window openings when estimating wall coverings.

Suppose your client decides to use a wall covering with no pattern repeat for the 13 ft. by 16 ft. room by 8 ft. in height (464 sq. ft.) instead of paint on the walls. How many double rolls of wall covering would you need to order for this room?

Step 1: 464 sq. ft. ÷ 30 = 15.5 rolls

Step 2: 15.5 rolls ÷ 2 = 7.75 double rolls (round up to 8 double rolls)

Math Practice

Calculate the amount of wall covering required for a room measuring 15 ft. wide by 18 ft. long by 10 ft. high. Show your work for each step.

Wall coverings are practical as well as beautiful. Due to cost and difficulty of removal, however, selecting wall covering (as opposed to paint) can be a longer term commitment. Appearance, washability, durability, and flammability are typical selection criteria.

Some wall coverings have a thick vinyl coating, which makes them durable and easy to clean. Other wall coverings consist of solid vinyl. Vinyl-coated or solid vinyl wall coverings are often desirable for kitchens and bathrooms because they resist stains and water. Wall coverings can also be embossed to mask imperfections or have special properties to combat mildew on the wall beneath.

Fabric

Fabric is another product you can use to cover walls. You can use special adhesive, tape, or staples to attach fabrics to walls. Other applications include stretching it over a frame and hanging it on the wall, or stretching it between curtain rods at the ceiling and floor. Fabric can add color, warmth, texture, and interest to a room.

Closely woven, medium-weight fabrics are the best choices for wall treatments. Look for fabric that will not fade, stain, shrink, or mildew. Because fabric applied to walls can be difficult to clean and maintain, it can trigger allergic reactions. It can, however, assist with acoustic issues in a space.

Wall coverings can also be created by attaching fabrics to a paper or vinyl backing. This allows for fabrics to be used that might otherwise be too delicate or unstable to hang. Natural textiles like grass cloth and silk are the most commonly used.

Cork and Ceramic Tile

Cork makes a good wall treatment for rooms that require sound insulation. Cork also adds warmth and textural interest to a room.

Ceramic tile comes in a wide variety of sizes, shapes, and patterns (Figure 20.14). You can use it to create many different styles and designs. The tiles are durable and easy to maintain. Decorative ceramic tiles on a wall can be the point of emphasis in a room.

Mirrors, Glass, and Reflective Metals

Using large mirrors, glass, and reflective metal tiles or strips on all or part of a wall can add interesting design details to a room. Because of repeating reflections in a room, mirrors can make rooms look larger. Covering an entire wall with mirrors will make a room look twice its actual size.

Large expanses of glass in windows and glass doors also serve as a type of wall treatment. This

Housing Health & Safety

Avoiding Lead Paint Dangers

At the time of the lead-based paint ban in 1978, lead-based paint was present in more than 38 million homes in the United States. Even small amounts of lead in dust, dirt, or water can be dangerous. This toxic metal can cause nerve damage, behavioral problems, learning disabilities, reduced IQ, and other serious health problems, particularly in infants, young children, and people with high blood pressure. Lead can cause seizures and death. Pets are also subject to lead poisoning.

Although today's household paints are lead-free, it is possible to release lead trapped in old layers of paint—especially when renovating pre-1978 homes. For example, such projects as sanding surfaces, puncturing walls, and replacing old windows can cause lead contamination of homes and yards. Children can swallow paint chips. Invisible lead dust from paint and lead-contaminated soil is easy to inhale or ingest. Before starting any renovations, interior designers and owners of older homes may want to have these homes tested for lead.

After April 2010, contractors who disturb painted surfaces in pre-1978 homes must be lead-certified by the U.S. Environmental Protection Agency. Consumers should ask to see the contractor's license. Contractors must also follow specific work practices to prevent lead contamination.

For more information, go to the EPA website and the National Lead Information Center.

is because they occupy wall space. Using glass extends the indoor space and brings the outdoors in, creating the illusion of a larger space. For example, the use of glass blocks allows light to enter a space while preventing a clear view into the room. An application such as this is suitable for a bathroom window area where light and privacy are requirements. All large sheets of glass, whether used on the interior or exterior, must be *tempered*, meaning created to be less breakable and less likely to injure inhabitants if it does break.

The application of reflective metal tiles or strips to a wall also allows the reflection of light into a space. The effect of mirrors, reflective metal, and glass wall treatments can be dramatic (Figure 20.15). These wall treatments are especially popular in spaces with a contemporary design. These treatments, however, are more expensive than other wall treatments such as paint and wall coverings. Take care to assure that the reflected image enhances the design of the room.

As you have learned, the various walls and wall treatments provide many different looks. Each one has its advantages and disadvantages. Choose the one that fits the mood of the room and best meets the needs and wants of you or a client. (Mirrors as decorative accessories will be discussed later in the text.)

Caring for Wall Coverings

To care for wall coverings, vacuum the surfaces with a soft brush attachment or dust with

© iStock.com/IPGGutenbergUKLtd

Figure 20.14 The installation of the glass tile backsplash and the stone flooring and counter create this sophisticated design.

gualtiero boffi/Shutterstock.com

Figure 20.15 The reflective metal backsplash on the wall brings a sense of drama to this kitchen.

a soft cloth. Use detergents or cleaning solutions recommended by the manufacturer with water. Dip a soft sponge in the solution, wring it out, and gently wipe down the walls as with painted surfaces. For textured wall coverings, some fabrics, or grass cloth coverings, consult the manufacturer's instructions for removing dirt and stains.

Review & Assessment

1. Describe the difference between wall treatment and wall covering.
2. List the four surface finishes of wall paints.
3. What is a faux finish? Give an example.
4. How should painted surfaces be cared for?
5. Name four types of wall coverings.
6. Evaluate and describe the care of wall coverings.

Ceiling Treatments

A **ceiling treatment** is a coating, covering, or building material applied to the ceiling area. The most common materials used to build ceilings—plaster, acoustical plaster, acoustical tile, wood, and gypsum wallboard—were discussed in a previous chapter. Ceilings should be given just as much importance in the scheme of a space as walls and floors. Oftentimes, when a space is furnished, people see more of the ceiling than the floors! Depending on the room size and height, a ceiling may be comprised of many levels as well as many materials.

In addition to the materials used to construct the ceiling, other surfaces can be mounted to the substrate, a track system, or directly over the drywall. Wood planks and metal panels are inventive ways to give interest and texture to ceilings as well as break up large expanses of ceiling surface.

Paint is another option for ceiling treatment. You can create the feeling of a higher ceiling by painting it a light color. You can also create the illusion of height by using vertical lines on the walls. (*Note:* Painting a ceiling requires an extension handle for the paint roller. The extension handle allows an individual to paint a ceiling without using a ladder, which is safer.) Flat paint is the usual surface covering for gypsum drywall and plaster ceilings.

Lower ceilings make rooms seem smaller and usually create an informal mood. Painting the ceiling a dark color or adding patterned materials will make it appear lower. Another way to make ceilings look lower is to use horizontal lines on the walls.

When you plan background surface treatments for interior design projects, remember to keep the principles and goals of design in mind. This helps achieve pleasing results in any room throughout a dwelling.

Caring for ceiling treatments involves dusting with a soft cloth and possibly using a vacuum cleaner with a soft brush. Be careful to brush in one direction to avoid grinding soil into the ceiling. Metal ceiling panels can be washed with soap and water.

Review & Assessment 

1. Define ceiling treatment.
2. How can you make a ceiling appear higher than it actually is?
3. How can you make a ceiling appear lower than it actually is?
4. What is the recommendation for caring for ceiling treatments?

Countertops

A **countertop** is a durable work surface installed on a base cabinet. Cabinets with countertops are found in kitchens, bathrooms, and play and work areas. Countertops should be functional and attractive. Because they involve a substantial financial investment, you cannot replace them as easily as the paint on a wall. Therefore, use special care when making countertop selections.

For the kitchen area, countertops should be stain-, scratch-, and heat-resistant. Perhaps no surfaces in a home will receive as much wear and tear as those in the kitchen. Common countertop materials include laminates, ceramic and porcelain tiles, and wood (such as butcher block). Popular countertop choices on the market today include solid surfaces, engineered quartz, stone such as granite, and metal.

Laminate

One of the more affordable countertop choices is laminate (Figure 20.16). Manufacturers achieve the colors, textures, and designs by combining decorative surface papers with resins (substances used to make plastics and other materials) that they bond under heat and pressure with other materials. This process forms a single unit with a decorative surface on a rigid base. The typical edge finish is a 90-degree angle, but *beveling* or rounding, though more expensive, can mask the backing materials at joints.

Career Focus Interior Products Sales Representative

Do you have a great ability to convince people to think your way? Do you enjoy problem solving and finding the best solution for a project? If you do, a career as an interior products sales representative might be for you.

Interests/Skills: Product reps must have excellent communication and business skills. They should have the ability to listen and empathize with clients and designers. Attention to detail and critical thinking are imperative. Enthusiasm and passion for the industry as well as their own product lines makes those with design skills into great salespeople.

Career Snapshot: Some of the best interior product salespeople were first trained as designers! Since they understand a designer's goals, they are able to assist in the selection of materials and furnishings. Since projects and design firms are often worldwide, salespeople often have the opportunity for travel to meet with clients, visit project sites, and attend trade shows. Product reps spend a great deal of time explaining their ideas and new product offerings to clients and end users. Successful salespeople must be able to communicate well and get others to "buy" their ideas.

Education/Training: The completion of a bachelor's degree in interior design is the most common route. Someone looking to go into sales would benefit from a minor or concentrated study in business, especially marketing. There are also countless continuing education opportunities which teach the technical, customer service, and business management skills specific to this concentrated area of design.

Licensing/Examinations: Although there are no national standards for certification in product sales, manufacturers have their own training programs that

GWImages/Shutterstock.com

salespeople must complete. Many professionals also become LEED Accredited Professionals (Leadership in Energy and Environmental Design) since most product lines are now heavily focused on sustainability.

Professional Associations: American Society of Interior Designers (ASID), and the International Interior Design Association (IIDA) are the most common. It is also suggested that product reps associate with local and regional real estate organizations and those most closely associated to the markets they serve (healthcare, hospitality, etc.) for acquiring project leads and contacts.

Job Outlook: While the overall professional outlook is very good, it is even better in specialty architectural areas such as schools/education/healthcare and sustainable design.

Allied Careers: Allied trades and careers include painters, carpet/flooring installers, and tile/marble setters.

Sources: The Occupational Outlook Handbook (OOH); the Occupational Information Network (O*NET)

Laminate countertops come in a wide range of colors and textures. Designs include solid colors, various patterns, and finishes that resemble metal, stone, or wood. Patterned laminates can mask seams and stains better than solids. As with other products, there are different quality grades on the market. Less expensive laminates will not offer the durability of more expensive, name brand laminates.

Laminates are relatively easy to maintain by wiping with a damp cloth or sponge. The product will show seams in the installation where sections are joined. It is best to select a product that comes in significant sheet size to minimize the need for seams. Some textured-laminate surfaces may be scratch-resistant. New products are available that are more resistant to stains than laminate surfaces produced in the past. If stains occur, application of a mild household cleaner to the area and gentle rubbing with a soft brush generally removes the stains. It is difficult or impossible, however, to repair such damage to laminate countertops as chipping and burns. No laminate countertop is an appropriate cutting surface.

General care of laminate countertops involves wiping down daily with a soft cloth and mild cleaning products. Do not use an abrasive cleaner because it can scratch the surface of the countertop.

Elena Elisseeva/Shutterstock.com

Figure 20.16 Quality laminate countertops are very attractive and affordable. There are hundreds of different colors and patterns from which to choose.

Solid Surface Material

A *solid surface* is a durable countertop material that contains the color and pattern of the surface throughout. Manufacturers construct this product with an advanced blend of materials and minerals in an acrylic or polyester compound. Solid-surface countertops are easy to clean and available in many colors, but are much more expensive than laminates. When installed, the surface appears continuous, showing no seams. Also, solid surfaces can blend seamlessly into sinks of the same material. Because the product can be shaped and molded, various custom edges are available.

Solid surfaces are scratch-, stain-, and heat-resistant. If damage does occur, these surfaces are repairable and renewable. They do not require sealing and are bacteria-resistant. Solid surfaces are available in many colors. New additions to the market look like natural stone.

Care of solid surface countertops involves wiping down with a damp soft cloth. For more soiled areas, wipe with soapy water and dry with a towel. For shiny surfaces, a mild abrasive cleaning solution can be used. For matte finishes, a very mild abrasive cleaner or baking soda can be used to clean the surfaces. Always dry with a towel.

Ceramic and Porcelain Tile

Tile can be expensive due to the labor costs for installation. Ceramic tiles come in many colors and patterns. They are easy to maintain and are heat- and scratch-resistant. To prevent staining, sealing the surface of the grout is essential. Also, ceramic tile is subject to chipping if struck by a heavy object.

Likewise, porcelain tiles are expensive to install and require sealing. Since the surface color usually penetrates porcelain tile, however, it can keep a like-new appearance in spite of scratches. Be sure to use stain- and mildew-proof grout when using porcelain tile in a kitchen.

Care of ceramic and porcelain tile requires cleaning with a window-cleaning product. Do not use abrasive products or cleaning instruments as the surfaces may be scratched or marred.

Natural Stone

Natural stone, such as granite and marble, is elegant and expensive (Figure 20.17). Since stone is porous, it requires sealing to make it stain-resistant. In addition, stone countertops are prone to scratching and can break if struck with a heavy object. Due to the weight of stone, install natural stone countertops on very sturdy cabinet bases.

Natural stone is not the type of counter material you can select from a catalog, since every slab is different in color and pattern. Once the needed measurements are available, a home owner should always visit the quarry or distributor and select the actual slab to be used.

Care of granite and marble involves removing spilled items quickly to avoid staining and discoloring. Clean the countertops with a weak solution of dish liquid and rinse thoroughly. Avoid using vinegar or acid-type cleaners since they can make the surface dull.

Engineered Quartz

A popular type of countertop that looks like natural granite or marble is **engineered quartz**. It is a stone-like countertop material that is a combination of quartz particles with a mixture of binders.

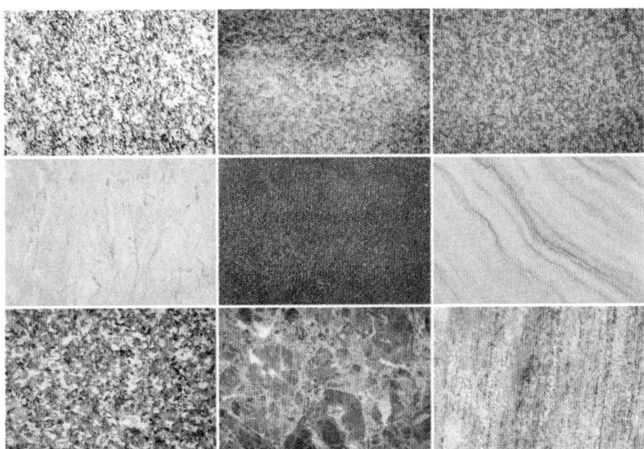

Thailand Travel and Stock/Shutterstock.com

Figure 20.17 Natural stone is available in endless colors and patterns. Each stone type has an identifiable pattern, though there are no two identical pieces.

Manufacturers subject the mixture to a high-tech compression and heating process. The surface has a polished granite or marble appearance and does not require a sealant as is needed with granite or marble.

Engineered quartz surfaces are popular for several reasons. They are less costly than granite and marble; easy to maintain; and much more heat-, stain-, and scratch-resistant. Manufacturers usually guarantee these surfaces against defects by a limited warranty, which is not available with natural stone.

The care of engineered quartz is relatively easy to accomplish. Use mild soapy water and a soft cloth or paper towel. Wiping up spills immediately protects the surface. Harsh cleaning products or metal cleaning tools should not be used on these surfaces.

Metal Surfaces

Use of metal surfaces for countertops is more common in commercial kitchens than in residential kitchens. The most common metal surface is stainless steel, but use of zinc and copper are also common for countertops. Metal countertop surfaces are expensive. Stainless is easy to clean, but can scratch. It is a good idea to use a cutting board with stainless steel counters, although stainless steel can endure scouring.

Care of stainless steel is accomplished through washing with soapy warm water, rinsing, and drying with a dry towel. Avoid using abrasive scrubbing instruments as the surface of the stainless steel can be damaged. Scrubbing in one direction with soft pads can avoid the cross-scrubbing and marking of the metal surface. Avoid leaving acid food items on the surface as the surface can be stained.

Butcher Block

Butcher block is a work surface made by fusing a stack of long, thin hardwood strips. The exposed sides form the countertop surface. Butcher block countertop is not heat-resistant and stain-resistant and is less durable than most other countertops. Also, it can harbor any food bacteria that come in contact with it.

Care of a butcher block requires immediate attention when a spill occurs as the wood absorbs and stains easily. Wipe with a paper towel or soft cloth. When finished using the block, scrub with soap and wipe with a towel to remove all food particles. One way to maintain the sanitation is to keep a spray bottle of vinegar nearby and spray after use. The vinegar helps kill unhealthy bacteria.

Fiberglass

Bathroom countertops use many of the materials used in kitchens. There is an additional product to consider for that room, however. Manufacturers mold *cultured marble* countertops from fiberglass compounds. They are more expensive than laminates, but less expensive than solid-surface, tile, and stone countertops. As in the case of solid-surface materials, you can obtain a bathroom sink and countertop all in one unit. Cultured marble countertops are scratch- and stain-resistant, easy to maintain, and durable if cared for properly. They come in solid colors, marble-like patterns, and polished or matte finishes.

Review & Assessment

1. What three types of durability features should kitchen countertops have?
2. What are three benefits of laminate countertops?
3. What are three features of solid surface countertops?
4. Why does a natural stone countertop require sealing?
5. Give an example showing when you would use each of the following countertop materials and treatments: laminate, solid surface, ceramic and porcelain tile, natural stone, engineered quartz, metal, butcher block, and fiberglass.

Planning Background Surface Treatments

The background surfaces used to create interior design schemes set the stage for the furnishings you choose. Although surface treatments do not need to be costly, they do require careful planning. This is especially important for floor and wall treatments.

Preliminary Budget for Surface Materials

A tool in planning for the purchasing of surface materials is a preliminary budget. The preliminary budget has categories that identify the quantity of surface material needed and the estimated cost. This preliminary budget allows you to change to different materials if the cost is higher than anticipated. See Figure 20.18 for an example of what to include in a preliminary budget.

Planning Floors

Floor treatments receive more wear than other surface treatments. They are usually more expensive, too. Unless design plans require replacing a floor covering within a couple years, choose one that is

Career Focus Interior Designer—Schools

Do you believe design can affect relationships between teachers and their students? Have you thought about better ways to navigate the crowded hallways between classes or how to make the cafeteria more functional for students and staff? Can you imagine yourself as the interior designer for a school in your community? If you can, you may want to consider a career as a civic contract designer who designs schools.

Interests/Skills: Civic designers are artistic individuals with attention to detail. Project organization and time-management skills are essential for civic designers. Designers must be able to convey their thoughts and ideas so others understand them. For example, effective communication about design plans between designers, architects, and school board members helps improve the quality of education.

Career Snapshot: Designers need to know the age group for whom they are designing. Educational buildings constantly and rapidly need to be brought up to current codes and standards. For these types of projects, designers need experience with designing existing spaces. Current trends point the way to eco-friendly design and using sustainable products that promote a healthy environment. As a result, designers must constantly update their education.

Education/Training: Completion of a bachelor's or master's degree is preferred. Classes include business management, lighting, textiles, and CADD. To specialize in designing spaces for schools, additional courses in education, ergonomics, and the psychology of learning are essential. Continuing education is a career-long requirement.

Licensing/Examinations: Approximately one-half of the states require interior designers to be licensed.

Anna Baburkina/Shutterstock.com

The National Council for Interior Design Accreditation administers an examination that interior designers must pass in order to obtain a license and to be competitive.

Professional Associations: The American Society of Interior Designers (ASID); the International Interior Design Association (IIDA)

Job Outlook: Jobs are expected to grow at a slower than average rate. Outlook will be especially good for designers who specialize in ergonomic design or sustainable design. Also, because of the large number of aging schools, the job market will be strong for designers with knowledge of the special needs of this sector.

Sources: The Occupational Outlook Handbook (OOH); the Occupational Information Network (O*NET)

durable. Try to choose a color and style that is neutral enough to allow changes to an interior design scheme.

The floor treatment accents the entire room and helps tie the many parts of the room together. Choosing different floor treatments for each separate area of the house causes a lack of design continuity and the spaces will not flow well. Using a single treatment such as carpeting or hardwood throughout some houses may be preferable—doing so can make the house seem larger and more unified. This can be especially important if your house is small. Selecting one uniform floor covering or pattern, however, may not be practical. Consider a balance between aesthetics, cost, maintenance, and durability. In contrast, for larger, open-plan spaces, varied flooring can help define areas that serve different functions.

Planning Walls

Classic wall treatments are those that continue to be in style year after year. Choosing a classic wall treatment will save the cost of changing the wall treatment as styles change. Off-white is a classic wall-treatment color. As a background, it lets you use a great variety of colors and designs in a room. It also helps make rooms appear more spacious. Since paint colors are easy and relatively inexpensive to change, however, experimenting with

Preliminary Budget—Surface Materials for Great Room

Presume your clients want you to redesign the great room of their kitchen. The room dimensions are 18 ft. wide by 24 ft. long and 8 ft. high. This room is a place where the family gathers to relax, watch movies, and play games. The clients plan to keep their traditional sectional sofa, but want it reupholstered. Your clients know they need additional seating, lighting, window treatments, and accessories. Below is the preliminary budget you have developed for this project.

Item	Quantity	Style/Color	Estimated Cost	Notes
Bamboo Flooring	432 sq. ft.	Natural bamboo with satin finish sealer	$13,000.00 installed	Existing subfloor in good condition
Paint				Painter to supply paint
Walls	2 gal.	Taupe, flat latex	$72.00	
Ceiling	1 gal. + 2 qt.	Ceiling white, flat latex	$33.00	
Trim	1 gal. + 2 qt.	Ivory, semigloss oil-base	$65.00	
Painter, Labor	36 hours @ $50.00 per hour	NA	$1,800.00	Two coats on walls and trim; one coat on ceiling; all surfaces in good condition, no prep work required

Figure 20.18 A preliminary budget is a planning tool that helps guide the selection of background surface treatments.

A Ina Raschke/Shutterstock.com

B Jennifer Blanchard Belk, IIDA, LEED AP

Figure 20.19 Choosing surface materials, such as the slate tile options shown, that have a variety of colors creates endless opportunities for selection of paint and other finishes.

alternate schemes is a great way to utilize your creativity and create interest (Figure 20.19).

Bold, bright wall treatments can give a room a dramatic look. Painted graphic designs, murals, and wall coverings with bold patterns make colorful focal points. Bold treatments tend to make rooms look smaller, so use them carefully. Be sure to choose wall treatments and furnishings that do not compete for attention.

The most common wall treatment is paint. It is important to choose the right paint for the room. Use washable paints in rooms that receive much use, such as kitchens and children's bedrooms. Keep painted surfaces clean to avoid repainting as often. Enamel and semigloss paints are easier to clean than flat paints.

Wall coverings are available in a wide variety of types and designs. Professional wall-covering installers generally hang wall coverings. You can save on installation costs, however, if you or a client chooses to hang the wall coverings. Either way, wall covering is a larger investment and cannot be changed as easily.

Planning Countertops

Apply the same careful attention to countertops as you give to floors, walls, and ceilings. Countertops impact the visual effect of your interior design scheme as much as decisions on any other surface treatment. Countertops also have an important impact on how a space functions and how easy it is to maintain.

As with all design decisions, make countertop choices after considering the total appearance of the room. Walls, countertops, floors, and ceilings must

Green Choices

Be Kind to the Environment—Select Nontoxic Paint

According to the U.S. Environmental Protection Agency (EPA), indoor air is more polluted than outside air. Indoor air quality is one of the top five hazards to human health. Paints and finishes are among the major causes of this hazard.

Low-level toxic fumes and chemicals move into the air for years after painting with certain paints. Most of these toxins come from the volatile organic compounds (VOCs)—in the form of solvents in the paint. In the past, the VOCs were necessary for the paint to do well over time.

Through new environmental regulations and consumer demand, low-VOC and zero-VOC paints and finishes are now available. Most paint manufacturers now produce one or more of these nontoxic paints. In addition, following the environmental disaster of Hurricane Katrina, new paint products are now available that have nontoxic, antimicrobial ingredients to inhibit the growth of mold on paint surfaces. This provides for a healthier air quality and interior environment. These new paints are durable, reasonable in cost, and are less harmful to human and environmental health.

Final Budget—Surface Materials for Great Room

Now that you have considered the materials, use the scenario from the Preliminary Surface Materials Budget and finalize the budget.

Item	Description	Quantity	Style/Color	Estimated Cost	Actual Cost	Notes
Bamboo Flooring (materials, installation)	Natural bamboo with satin finish sealer	432 sq. ft.	Natural bamboo	$13,000.00	$13,867.20	$12,960.00 (slight price reduction) + sales tax
Paint						
Walls	Latex flat	2 gal.	Medium taupe	$72.00	$77.04	Sales tax
Ceiling	Latex flat	1 gal. + 2 qt.	Ceiling white	$33.00	$35.31	Sales tax
Trim	Oil-base semigloss	1 gal. + 2 qt.	Ivory	$65.00	$69.55	Sales tax
Painter, Labor	2 coats, walls and trim; 1 coat ceiling	38.5 hours labor @ $50.00 per hour	NA	$1,800.00	$1,926.00	2.5 additional hours labor

Figure 20.20 A final budget notes the preliminary cost estimates and any adjustments made for final costs.

all work well together to create a pleasing design scheme that functions successfully.

Final Budget for Surface Materials

As previously discussed, a preliminary budget allows control of spending on the project by identifying the amount of surface materials needed for a project and the associated cost. The final budget goes further by guiding the spending on the project and keeps the spending in line with the intended costs. See Figure 20.20 for an example of the final budget.

Review & Assessment 

1. Why is a preliminary budget important when planning for background surface treatments?
2. Why is it a good idea to use neutral floor surfaces in a home?
3. What is the result of bold wall treatments in a room?
4. Why should you pay just as much attention to countertop treatments as you do to other interior surface treatments?

Chapter 20 Assessment

Summary

- Floors, walls, and ceilings serve as backgrounds for the furnishings and accessories in a room.
- Floor treatments include flooring materials or floor coverings. Flooring materials include hardwoods, softwoods, tile, natural stone, concrete, and brick. Floor coverings consist of soft floor coverings and resilient floor coverings.
- Wall construction provides the basis for wall treatments. Finish applications for wall treatments include paint and wall coverings, including fabric, cork, tile, mirrors, glass, and reflective metals.
- The height and the treatment of ceilings are important factors. High ceilings give the feeling of formality and openness. Low ceilings create an informal, close feeling. Different ceiling treatments can create the illusion of higher or lower ceilings.
- Countertops are another consideration when designing surface treatments. They should be functional, yet attractive and durable.
- Interior surfaces last for several years and involve much cost. Designers work with clients to set preliminary and final budgets to meet client needs.
- Select material treatments for countertops, walls, floors, and ceilings so they set the stage for furnishings and accessories.

Terms in Action

1. **Categorization** In teams, create categories for the *Content* and *Academic Terms*. Classify as many of the terms as possible. Then, discuss your ideas with the remainder of the class.

Think Critically

2. **Analyze interior treatments** Economics often influences the choices people make for interior background surfaces. Presume you have the job of designing an affordable and durable interior for a new home built by *Habitat for Humanity*. A family with two daughters under age 10 will occupy the home. What treatments would you select for the flooring, walls, ceilings, and countertops? Analyze interior selections. Explain your choices.
3. **Prioritize** Imagine you have a client who is tired of her kitchen design. She wants to change either the flooring or the countertops, but cannot afford both. Which treatment would you encourage her to replace? Explain your choices.

Core Skills

4. **Research and speaking** Research websites for local stores or manufacturers that sell flooring materials and floor coverings. Print photographs showing examples of products with information about their cost, warranties, and durability. Make two collages—one showing various flooring materials, and one showing several floor coverings. Display your collages as you summarize your findings.
5. **Speaking** Visit a store that sells wall treatments. Obtain samples of six or more different wall coverings—three for residential use and three for commercial use. Display your samples to the class, and explain the effect of each if it were installed in your classroom.
6. **Research and speaking** The use of wall, floor, and ceiling treatments changed continually throughout history. Select a specific country and historical period, and research the types of interior background surfaces that were used. Create a visual digital report with school-approved presentation software describing the social, environmental, historical, and geographical influences that shaped the creation of these background surface treatments. Share your report with the class.
7. **Research and writing** Investigate the process paint manufacturers use to create paint products that have low emissions of volatile organic compounds (VOCs). Why should interior designers promote the use of such products with their clients? Write a summary of your findings.
8. **Math practice** Follow text guidelines to calculate the amount of paint to order for a room that measures 14 feet wide by 18 feet long by 8 feet high and requires two coats of paint. Then, calculate how much paint you would need if one 14 feet by 8 feet wall is an accent color. Assume each gallon of paint covers 350 square feet.

Chapter 20 Assessment

9. **Reading and writing** Use online resources to investigate technological advances in manufacturing eco-friendly wall coverings. Evaluate the features of these products including care and maintenance. Write a summary of your findings to share with the class.
10. **Paint practice** To demonstrate effective use of interior design media in painting, practice applying paint on a 4 ft. by 4 ft. drywall surface. Demonstrate the following painting techniques: traditional application of paint to a wall using a brush and roller, faux finish, and stenciling.
11. **Math practice** Presume a client wants you to prepare a preliminary cost estimate for three types of flooring for use in a kitchen. The floor measurements are 12 feet wide by 16 feet long. Your client wants to compare the prices for hardwood (maple), wood laminate, ceramic tile, and sheet vinyl. Use a spreadsheet program to create a cost estimate for each flooring type. Use realistic prices from flooring companies. Be sure to include separate categories for materials and labor. Share your spreadsheet with the class.
12. **Speaking** The director of the community service group for which you volunteer overheard you explaining methods for selecting interior treatments for walls and ceilings. The director asks you to demonstrate selection methods for wall treatments at the next remodeling project. Prepare a presentation with visual aids for how to evaluate and select wall and ceiling treatments. Think about the following as you prepare your demonstration: cost considerations, durability, and the elements and principles of design.
13. **CTE career readiness** As communities look for ways to improve housing for citizens and protect the environment, opportunities exist for people and their employers to take action. Because of your involvement with *Rebuilding Together*, your employer asks you to lead a team of employees to help improve living conditions for people in your community. In a group, complete the following steps:
    A. Identify community concerns. Examples can include insufficient housing or outdated housing. Then, have the team brainstorm possible ways to address one or more of the problems. Evaluate the list and narrow it down to one project on which the majority of team members agree.
    B. Have the team set a goal. Determine what resources your team needs to meet the goal.
    C. Create a plan for achieving the goal. Determine who, what, where, when, and how your team will accomplish its goal. How can individual team members continue to help meet the team goal after the initial action?
    D. Carry out the team plan.
    E. Evaluate the results of the team action. How was your team able to meet its goal and your employer's goal of improving community housing?

Design Practice

14. **Residential surfaces** As part of a renovation project, your client has asked you to identify several wall, ceiling, and floor treatments to use in the kitchen, family room, and master bathroom. For each treatment, your client wants information about special features, durability, and care requirements. Use presentation software to assemble photos and descriptions of each of your surface choices. Share your plans with your client (the class).
15. **Commercial surfaces** Presume you have been contracted to specify the surface materials for use in the cafeteria and library of a new high school. School officials desire a classic design scheme with a contemporary edge. What wall, ceiling, and flooring choices would you make for each area? Why? What use and care features make your choices especially appropriate for the cafeteria and library surfaces?
16. **Portfolio** Select examples of each type of surface material described in this chapter. Collect and mount samples of flooring materials, floor coverings, wall treatments, ceiling treatments, and countertop treatments. Label each treatment type and note the appropriate features, use, and care of each. Save your materials collection in your portfolio for use with future design projects.

Chapter 21

Furniture Styles and Window Treatments

Content Terms 

Casual style
Country style
Eclectic style
antique
collectible
reproduction
case good
wood grain
solid wood
bonded wood
veneered wood
pressed wood
mortise-and-tenon joint
double-dowel joint
dovetail joint
tongue-and-groove joint
butt joint
corner block
innerspring mattress
foam mattress
memory foam mattress
waterbed
box springs
draperies
curtains
shades
shutters
blinds

Academic Terms

influx
gilt
pliability
stark
coniferous

Learning Outcomes

After studying this chapter, you will be able to

- distinguish among various characteristics of period furniture styles throughout history.
- evaluate quality furniture construction.
- summarize care of quality furniture.
- evaluate use and suitability of various window treatments.
- evaluate treatment options and suitability with window size and location.
- summarize consumer protections for buying furniture and window treatments.

Reading with Purpose

As you read the chapter, record any questions that come to mind. Indicate where the answer to your question can be found: within the text, from your teacher, in another book, online, or by thinking about your personal experiences. Pursue the answers to your questions.

While studying, look for the access icon  **to:**

- **Practice** the *Content* and *Academic Terms* with e-flash cards, matching activities, and vocabulary games.
- **Reinforce** what you learn by completing the *Review & Assessment* questions and e-mailing them to your instructor.

www.g-wlearning.com/housing/

Artashes/Shutterstock.com

Once you select surface materials and treatments for a design scheme, continue the process by deciding how to furnish the interior design space. The first two steps in furnishing an interior space are choosing furniture styles and evaluating furniture construction. You will learn about selecting furniture for a design scheme in chapter 22. Continue to enhance the mood of a room by selecting from a variety of window treatments.

As you recall, design has three characteristics: function, construction, and aesthetics. This chapter focuses on two of those characteristics as they relate to furniture—aesthetics and construction. By focusing on the aesthetics of furniture, you will learn to recognize the physical characteristics that make individual styles unique and appealing. In addition, you will learn about the history and evolution of different furniture styles. Then you will learn to evaluate the quality of the construction.

Understanding Furniture Styles

Choosing furniture styles is a matter of taste, or personal preference. There is no right or wrong furniture—just furniture that is best for you or an interior design client. Studying the various styles can give you a good idea of which styles are pleasing and fit a design plan. Learning furniture styles will also help you use each piece of furniture to its best design advantage.

Furniture style refers to design only. It does not refer to the cost or the quality of construction. Any style, from Queen Anne to Contemporary, can be

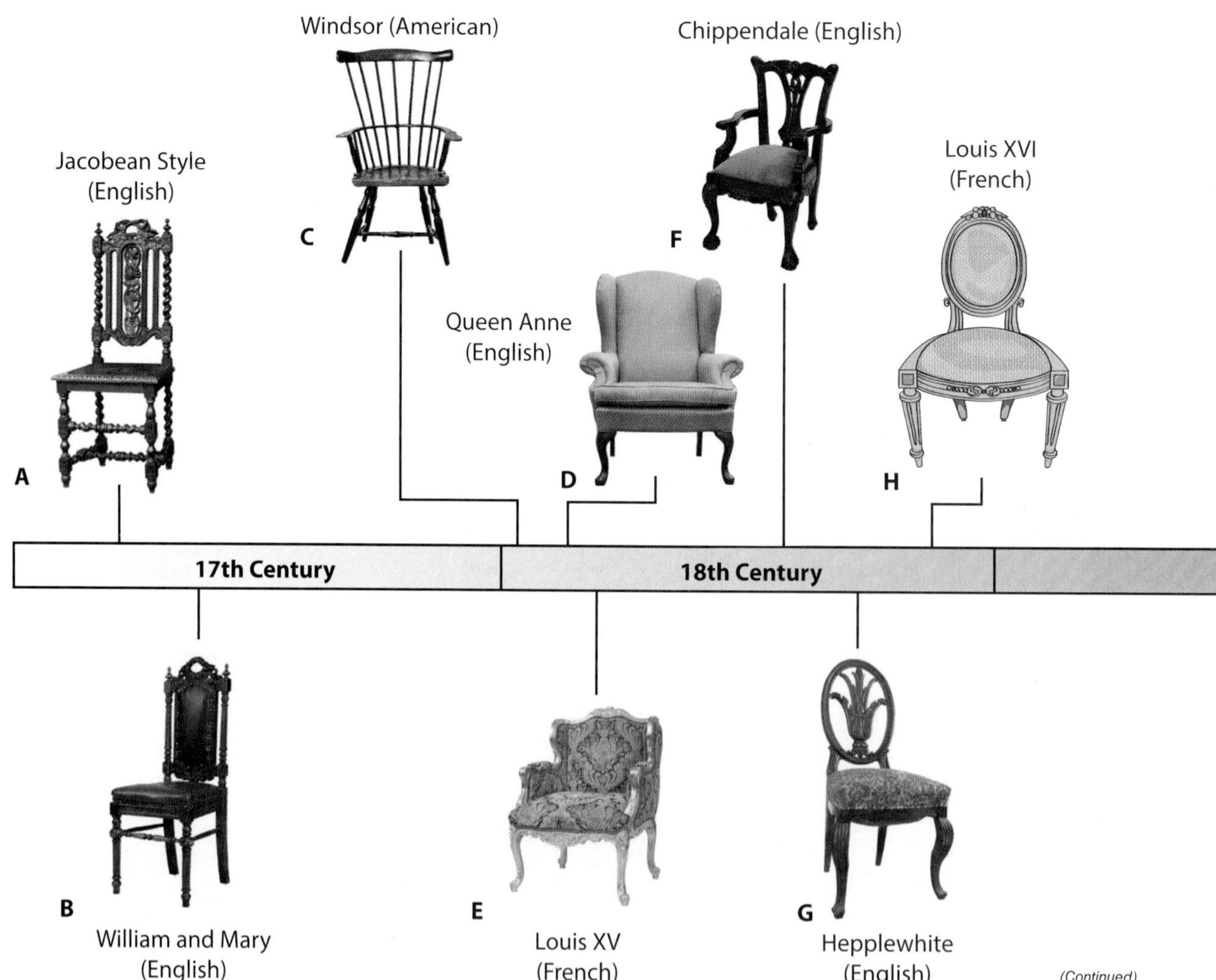

(Continued)

Figure 21.1 Furniture design styles have changed throughout history. Available resources (including technology), lifestyle, and the styles and tastes of an era all influence furnishings. Many period styles continue to influence furniture and interior design today.

made of good or poor materials using good or poor construction methods.

Ancient History of Fine Furniture

The first documented fine furniture styles were those of the Ancient Egyptians in 3000 B.C. Fine quality Oriental furniture dates back to 300 B.C. Styles from Ancient Rome can be documented from 700 B.C., while styles from Ancient Greece date back to 1100 B.C.

For about 800 years (400 to 1200 A.D.), fine furniture making almost became a lost skill. It began its recovery in the 1200s with the emergence of Gothic art in Western Europe. Gothic art influenced both architecture and furniture design with the use of arches and columns. Many furniture styles used today date back to the traditional designs from the early 1600s.

Traditional Furniture Styles

Traditional or period furniture styles were developed during different periods of history. Traditional furniture styles are designs created in the past that have survived the test of time and are still in use today. This chapter discusses traditional styles from France, England, and the United States. Figure 21.1 shows a general time reference for some traditional and nontraditional furniture styles. Most furniture styles are named after the rulers of the era or the craftsmen who actually created them.

Traditional Styles from France

While Louis XIII was King of France, 1610–1643, furniture styles were grand and formal. Rich inlays, carvings, and classical motifs were typical.

At the end of the Renaissance period, Louis XIV, the Sun King, ruled France from 1643–1715. He built

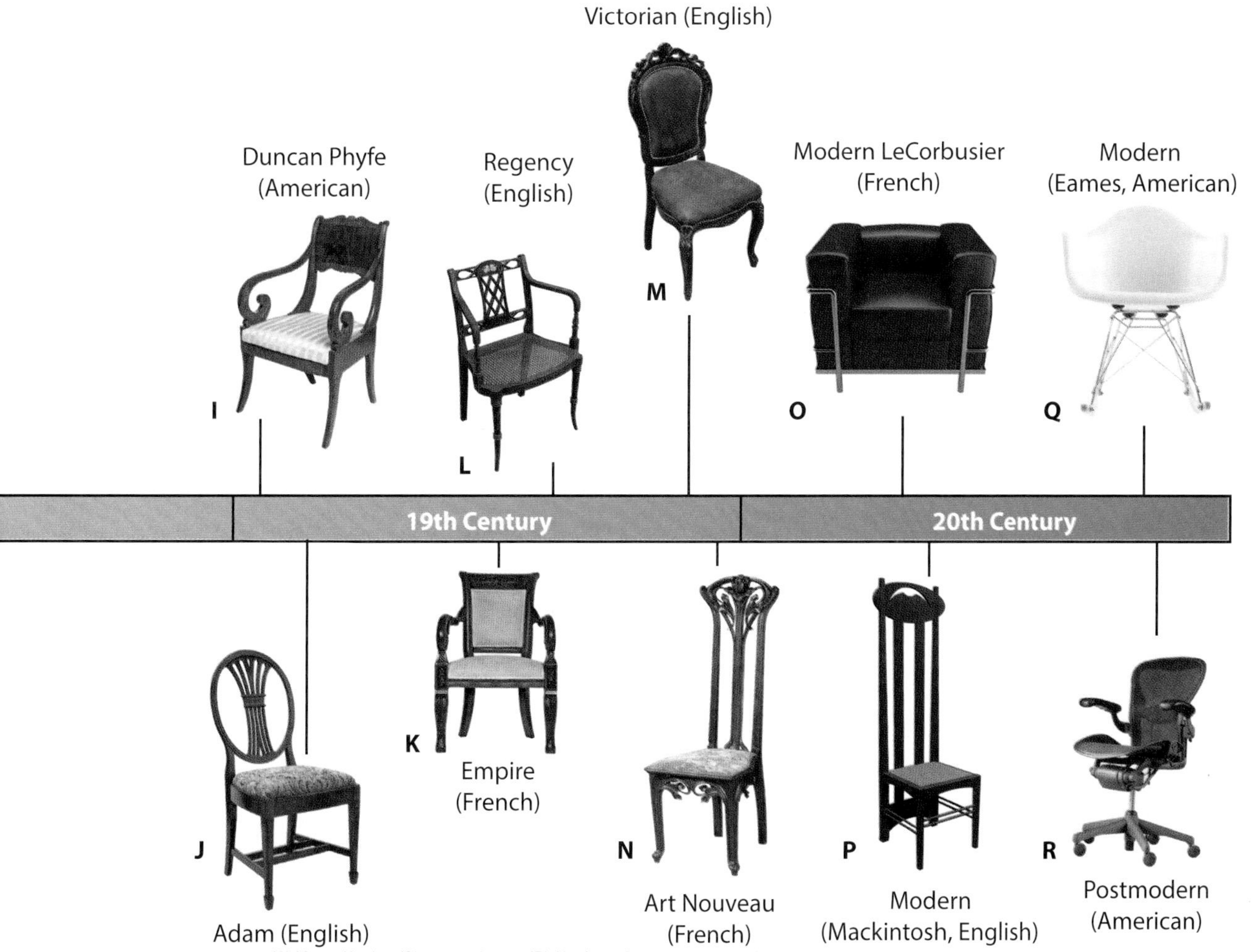

(A) Margo Harrison/Shutterstock.com; (B) AlexAvich/Shutterstock.com; (C) bartzuza/Shutterstock.com; (D) James Marvin Phelps/Shutterstock.com; (E) AlexAvich/Shutterstock.com; (F) Mountain Light Studios/Shutterstock.com; (G) Olemac/Shutterstock.com; (H) ©iStock.com/richcat; (I) AlexAvich/Shutterstock.com; (J) AlexAvich/Shutterstock.com; (K) Arsgera/Shutterstock.com; (L) sgame/Shutterstock.com; (M) Marko Bradic/Shutterstock.com; (N) 300dpi/Shutterstock.com; (O) 3dimentii/Shutterstock.com; (P) Michael Ransburg/Shutterstock.com; (Q) joingate/Shutterstock.com; (R) Le Do/Shutterstock.com

the Palace of Versailles and filled it with extravagant furnishings. The furnishings had heavy ornamentation and gold overlays. These characteristics mark the influential *French Baroque* period.

During the reign of Louis XV, 1715–1774, furniture styles had smaller proportions and became more delicate. Curved lines and soft colors were dominant.

Before the French Revolution, Louis XVI and Marie Antoinette ruled France, 1774–1792. Simple, straight lines and classic motifs, such as fluted columns, were popular in furniture.

When Napoleon ruled France, 1804–1815, he dominated everything—even furniture styles. The dignified style called *Empire* became popular. The furniture was large and heavy. Ornamentation included Napoleon's initial and military symbols. Usage of Egyptian, Greek, and Roman motifs was also common.

During the seventeenth and eighteenth centuries, artisans began copying styles that were popular in the court at Paris. The *French Provincial* style was practical, functional, and comfortable. Usage of local woods and simplified decorations was characteristic of these furniture copies (Figure 21.2).

Calico Corners—Calico Home Stores

Figure 21.2 Country French style of furniture is used frequently today. It is an interpretation of the French Provincial style.

Traditional Styles from England

During the reigns of James I and Charles I, 1603–1649, *Jacobean* furniture became popular. The decorative features of this heavy oak furniture utilized the techniques of turning and fluting. *Turning* is an ornamental detail used on furniture legs and other pieces made by rotating wood on a lathe to create a spiral effect. *Fluting* is another ornamental detail made by carving parallel grooves into the wood.

During the reign of Queen Anne, 1702–1714, there was an Oriental influence in furniture. The use of cabriole legs in the *Queen Anne* style represents the Chinese influence. A *cabriole leg* has a gentle S-shaped curve that ends in a decorative foot. Carved fans and shells are also characteristic of this graceful and comfortable style.

Several furniture styles became popular during the reigns of Kings George I, II, and III, 1714–1820. *Georgian* is the style name people sometimes use for furnishings of this era. Styles from this era, however, are often labeled to reflect the names of their designers—Thomas *Chippendale*, the *Adam* Brothers, George *Hepplewhite*, and Thomas *Sheraton*.

Thomas Chippendale was the first person to publish a book entirely about furniture designs, and his designs became popular worldwide. Gothic and Chinese influences were part of the Chippendale design. Details such as the use of splat-back chairs and curved top edges on the backs of chairs and sofas were typical. Early Chippendale furniture has S-shaped legs with claw and ball feet (Figure 21.3). Later, due to Chinese influence, his furniture had straight legs.

Furniture from the Adam Brothers, Robert and James, was designed to complement their architectural designs. The furniture was classic and symmetrical. The pieces had simple outlines, rectangular shapes, and tapered, straight legs.

George Hepplewhite is most famous for his graceful chair designs. The backs of the chairs had shield, oval, and heart shapes (Figure 21.4).

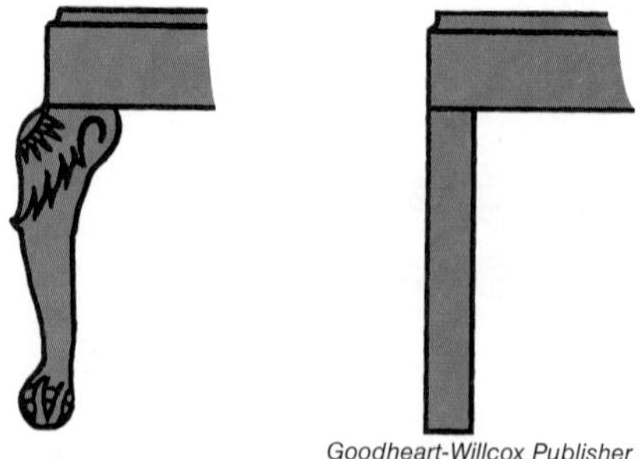

Goodheart-Willcox Publisher

Figure 21.3 Curved legs with claw and ball feet were early Chippendale designs. His later designs had straight legs.

SchneiderStockImages/Shutterstock.com

Figure 21.4 This chair has a shield back, which is characteristic of Hepplewhite.

Marko Bradic/Shutterstock.com

Figure 21.5 This vintage example of Victorian furniture is still found in many American homes today.

The furniture designs by Thomas Sheraton had characteristic straight lines. He included motifs of urns, swags, and leaves. Mechanical devices—such as disappearing drawers, folding tables, and secret compartments—were key features of his furniture.

The *Regency* furniture style, 1810–1837, is named after the Prince of Wales whose reign as regent was nine years. The style reflects an interest in the ancient cultures of Greece, Rome, and Egypt. Bold, curved lines were dominant.

During the reign of Queen Victoria, 1837–1901, the *Victorian* furniture style became popular. Machines could make detailed pieces of furniture quickly and easily. This led to the excessive use of ornamentation that was typical of the style (Figure 21.5). Massive proportions and dark colors were also features of this style.

Traditional American Styles

The first European settlers in North America built sturdy, practical furniture. These *Early American* furnishings were simplified versions of the Jacobean style, which was popular at that time in England. The colonists used native woods, such as maple, pine, and oak. They began making furniture with less massive proportions. Ladder-back chairs and canopy beds were common. Windsor chairs were also popular (Figure 21.6).

Simon Krzic/Shutterstock.com

Figure 21.6 The Windsor chair is typical of Early American furnishings.

Daniel Botha/Shutterstock.com

Figure 21.7 The upholstered wingback chair was popular in the American colonies.

Everett Historical/Shutterstock.com

Figure 21.8 This chair and desk are typical of the simplicity of the Shaker style.

Later the Colonial style became popular. England's Queen Anne and Georgian styles were the basis for this furniture.

The fully upholstered wingback chair became popular in the colonies during this period. The chair design featured a high back with winglike sides that provided protection from drafts (Figure 21.7). Graceful lines, S-shaped legs, and comfortable forms were characteristics of this period.

After the American Revolution, England's influence declined in all areas, including furniture styles. The *Federal* style became popular in the United States. It combined classic influences with patriotic symbols, such as eagles, stars, and stripes.

Duncan Phyfe was a major furniture designer of this period. His most notable design utilized the lyre motif in chair backs. Other features of his designs include brass-tipped dog feet, curved legs, and rolled-top rails on chair and sofa backs.

In the early 1800s, the Shakers—a religious group—gained recognition for their use of the circular saw in making furniture. *Shaker* furniture was very plain in design, but often painted in bright colors. Although Shakers are best known for their side chairs and rockers, they made other furniture, too (Figure 21.8).

Twentieth-Century Furniture Styles

At the beginning of the twentieth century, designers reacted against the cluttered look of the Victorian era. Instead, they wished to create furniture designs that represented a more modern lifestyle. They designed furniture with simpler lines and forms. The primary characteristic of Modern furniture was the use of abstract form. A strong influence on these furniture styles was the ability of manufacturing companies to mass-produce pieces of furniture with automated machinery.

Also significant to the styles of this period was the ***influx*** (inward flow) of many architects into the field of furniture design. The leading architects included Gerrit Rietveld, Walter Gropius, and Frank Lloyd Wright. Twentieth-century design also benefited from a vast international influence. Significant styles of the Modern period include Art Nouveau, De Stijl, Bauhaus, Organic, Art Deco, and Modern Scandinavian.

Art Nouveau

The *Art Nouveau* style began as a revolt against historical revival styles. *Art Nouveau* is French for *New Art*. The movement actually began in the 1800s and lasted until the early 1900s. The rejection of traditional styles by the Art Nouveau movement greatly influenced furniture design in the 1900s. Reflecting a revival of interest in the decorative arts, the use of Japanese motifs was characteristic of this style. Other characteristics include long, slightly curved lines that reflect natural growing forms of plants, such as blossoms, vines, and stalks. These lines typically end abruptly in sharp whip-like curves. The use of curved lines was common in chair legs and backs. Pieces with this design are still popular today. You will typically find them in modern homes and restaurants.

De Stijl

De Stijl, which means *The Style*, began as an art movement around 1917 in the Netherlands. Gerrit Rietveld—a Dutch architect and furniture designer—led the movement. With abstract art as an influencing factor, the furniture style utilized geometric forms such as rectangles. The only colors Rietveld used were the three primary colors of yellow, blue, and red. His work influenced many later furniture styles in the 1900s.

Bauhaus

In the early 1900s, the German *Bauhaus* movement strongly influenced the direction of furniture design. Architect Walter Gropius established the Bauhaus school of design in Weimar, Germany in 1919. The Bauhaus philosophy was simple—*form follows function*. In other words, if the intention for a furniture piece was sitting (as in the example of a chair), it was given a form that made that function possible.

Typical Bauhaus furniture designs were very simple. For chairs, use of chrome-plated steel tubing for support with seats and backs of canvas, wood, cane, or leather was common. Famous examples of this movement are the chair designs by Marcel Breuer and Ludwig Mies van der Rohe. Their designs became popular worldwide. Production and use of these designs in this Classic Modern style continues today (Figure 21.9).

Arts and Crafts

As you may recall from an earlier chapter, John Ruskin (1819–1900) and William Morris (1834–1896) began the *Arts and Crafts* movement in protest to the shoddy industrial production of goods in Victorian design. Ruskin and Morris urged a return to creative, quality handwork by craftsmen who use materials honestly and with less elaborate detail (Figure 21.10). In post-Civil War America,

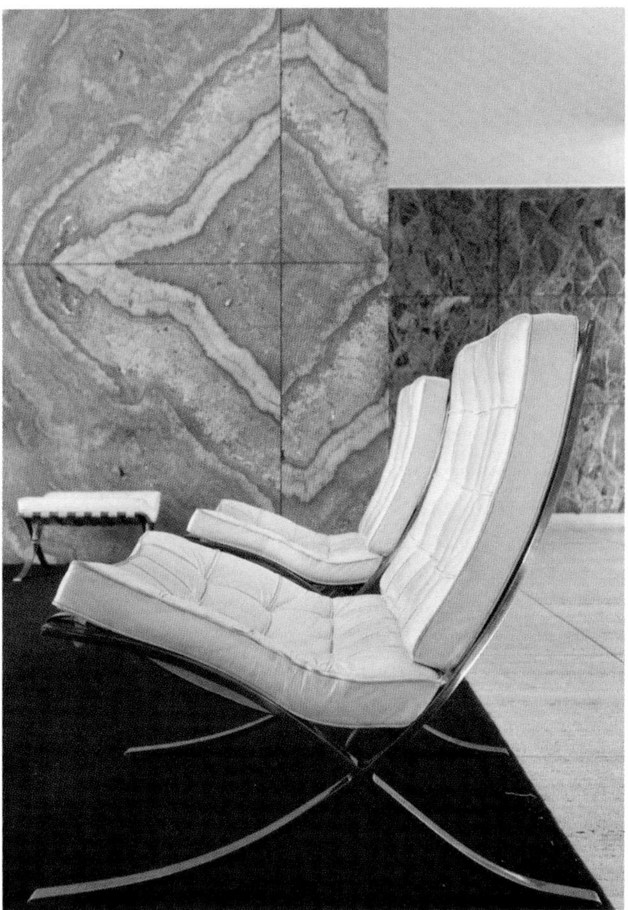

Cosmin Dragomir/Shutterstock.com

Figure 21.9 This photo shows two Barcelona chairs, by designer Mies van de Rohe, in a contemporary setting.

lynnette/Shutterstock.com

Figure 21.10 As a classic example of Arts and Crafts era furniture, this Morris-style chair displays quality craftsmanship and simplicity.

the name of the Arts and Crafts movement was shortened to the *Craftsman* movement. The name *Craftsman* came from the title of a popular magazine publication by a famous furniture designer, Gustav Stickley (1858–1942). The first issue of his magazine in 1901 was dedicated to William Morris. The second edition was devoted to John Ruskin.

Other names for Stickley's furniture are *Mission* or *Golden Oak* style. His furniture expressed his unique design sense and mastery of form, proportion, and color. The furniture designs were simple, functional, and sturdy. He placed emphasis on the details of *joinery*—the art of joining pieces of wood. Tenon and key joints, exposed tenons, and visible dowels gave Stickley furniture a handmade appearance. Through furniture design reform and with his well-made, well-designed furniture, Stickley created an authentic body of work with enduring qualities.

Organic Design

Organic style denotes the furniture designs by American architect Frank Lloyd Wright (l869–1959) and his followers. Wright was known for his Prairie style architecture. His home and structure designs complement their natural surroundings. Wright positioned his houses to work within the natural terrain of the land and take advantage of sunlight and prevailing breezes. These structures utilize basic materials such as wood, masonry, and glass.

Wright believed that furniture should fit easily and naturally into its surroundings. He created furniture designs specifically to fit the design of each house. While the furniture designs varied according to each specific house, Wright's use of geometric shapes, flat surfaces, and slats were common elements in his furniture.

Art Deco

The most popular international decorative style in the 1920s and 1930s was *Art Deco* (Figure 21.11). Images suggesting public interest in speed, such as fast-moving trains, ocean liners, and cars were characteristic of this style. Unusual combinations of industrial materials and traditional luxury materials in the construction of Art Deco pieces supported this interest. For example, manufacturers often paired brushed steel with exotic wood, ivory, or gilt bronzes. (***Gilt*** refers to the application of gold or a material that looks like gold onto a surface.) Other diverse styles—such as mechanical design and Native American, Ancient Egyptian, and African art—were influential on these furniture designs.

Gorin/Shutterstock.com

Figure 21.11 Unusual combinations of industrial materials and traditional luxury materials are typical in Art Deco design.

Modern Scandinavian

Modern Scandinavian design began in Denmark, Norway, and Sweden in the late 1920s. During the twentieth century, the influence of the Modern Scandinavian style on furniture design is evident in chairs consisting of molded wood seats or arms. The perfection and first application of this technique—shaping many veneers of wood by applying steam or heat—was in the construction of molded snow skis. White birch was a typical wood choice because of its hard surface and firmness, but unusual ***pliability*** (ability to bend and twist). Clean, simple lines and natural wood were key features of this style, as were simple upholstery fabrics of wool, cotton, or linen.

The furniture style was very popular because it was warm, natural, and easy to maintain. It was considered functional and elegant. The smaller scale of the pieces worked well in apartments and smaller homes.

Late Twentieth-Century Styles

Later styles of furniture in the twentieth century include the *Retro, Radical Modern,* and *Postmodern* styles. The Retro style of the 1950s and 1960s utilized many of the same elements that were popular in the early 1900s. The use of triangular, boomerang, and rhomboid shapes is characteristic of this style. (As you may recall, a *rhombus* is a slanted parallelogram.)

The single most important furniture design of the late twentieth century was a simple chrome and

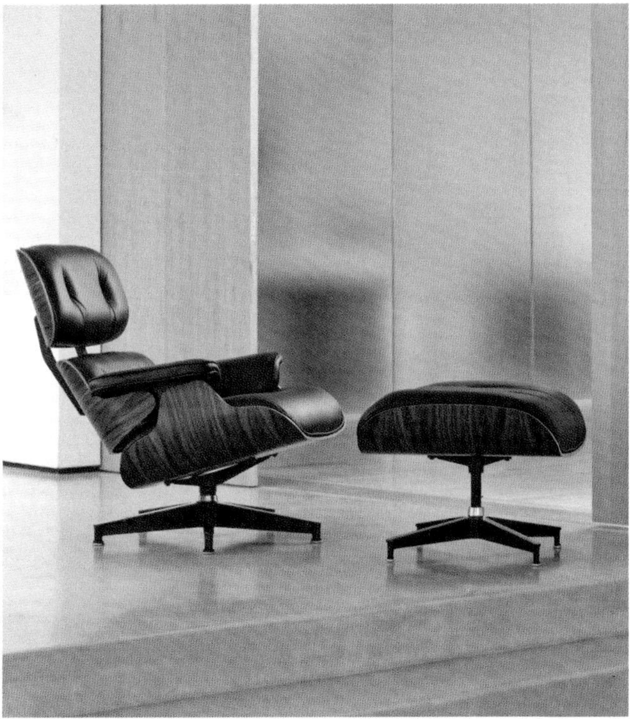

Photography Courtesy of Herman Miller, Inc.

Figure 21.12 This is the basic Eames molded plywood chair design. It is functional and beautifully simple.

molded-plywood chair designed by the American designer Charles Eames (Figure 21.12). Because of the importance of this design, some consider Eames as part of the Classic Modern group. His work, however, came many years after the Bauhaus and International style.

Some retro armchairs feature forms that hug the body. One such design was the *butterfly chair* by Harry Bertoia, an American sculptor and designer.

Modular furniture units also evolved during this period. These units were composed of separate seating pieces in standardized sizes. Because of great flexibility in space planning, designers could group these pieces together or separately in a variety of seating arrangements. Polyfoam™ was used in these pieces instead of the typical coil springs and webbing. By using the Polyfoam, the modular units weighed less and were easier to move. Also, the Polyfoam was less costly than the typical coils and webbing.

Radical Modern design was popular in the late 1960s. Furniture of this style was inexpensive and serviceable, but not long-lasting. One such style was the *beanbag chair*. It was constructed of vinyl, leather, or cloth, and was filled with plastic beads. This chair design conforms to the body of the seated person.

The *Postmodern* design style of the late 1900s (1970 and beyond) used traditional shapes from other styles of furniture, but constructed them in different materials and finishes. Examples of the Postmodern style are the chairs created by American architect Robert Venturi. He designed a Queen Anne chair of bent plywood. He also created bent plywood versions of a Sheraton chair and an Art Deco chair. The results were artistic and light-hearted reinterpretations of historical design.

Other furniture designers of this period purposely designed furniture that machines could not produce. The goal of this movement was to remove furniture design from a factory manufacturing process and return it to the realm of art.

Twenty-First Century Furniture Styles

Currently there are many furniture styles popular in the United States. Popular styles include Contemporary (Modern), Traditional, Casual, Transitional, Country (Shabby Chic), and Eclectic (Figure 21.13). Furniture is available in many different price ranges and levels of construction quality.

Advances in technology impact today's furniture. Wood coatings have added a level of durability and protection to wood surfaces. The variety of materials used to make furniture has expanded to include plastic and sustainable woods such as bamboo. Technology has allowed the adjustment of seating and other furniture items to fit different body types and comfort needs. Through technology, designers are able to incorporate ergonomic factors into furniture such as home office chairs and electric home bedding. The development of furniture glue that limits off-gassing of harmful products has improved indoor air quality.

Contemporary

Contemporary furniture style is composed of designs that are the very latest introductions to the market. They take advantage of the newest materials and manufacturing methods. Many Contemporary designs trace their origin to the Modern or International style designs created during the twentieth century, when function was an important influence.

Usage of plastics, metals, wood, and glass create an endless range of visual effects. Pieces of Contemporary furniture have simple lines and forms. The feeling is streamlined and sleek. Geometric shapes such as circles, rectangles, triangles, cylinders, and cubes are often part of these designs.

A Marko Poplasen/Shutterstock.com B Tad Denson/Shutterstock.com C Rodenberg Photography/Shutterstock.com D MR. INTERIOR/Shutterstock.com E brodtcast/Shutterstock.com F Dinga/Shutterstock.com

Figure 21.13 These rooms show examples of furniture styles that are currently popular in the United States. The furniture designs include Contemporary (A), Traditional (B), Casual (C), Transitional (D), Country/Shabby Chic styles (E), and Eclectic (F).

Colorful fabrics and accessories add beauty and variety to contemporary rooms by enhancing the furniture's simple lines.

In other room designs, Contemporary furniture may appear very ***stark*** (plain, empty). In such a case, the use of color and accessories may be minimal.

Traditional

The Traditional furniture made today continues to be inspired by the early designs of French, English, and American periods. Symmetry and graceful, carved curves are key characteristics of this furniture style. The fabric colors are rich, and the wood finish tends to be dark with a polished sheen. Use of this style of furniture conveys a sense of elegance.

Casual

Casual style furniture is a style that emphasizes comfort and informality. The feeling this type of furniture creates is opposite the elegant mood created by traditional furniture. The emphasis is on comfort, and often the sofas and chairs have an overstuffed look. Fabric designs are carefree in both look and function. Pine, ash, oak, and maple are the common types of wood used. This furniture style is an evolution of the American lifestyle. Its beginnings do not date back to any single historical period of design.

Transitional

Transitional style furniture takes the best aspects of the previous styles and merges them together. With very simple but classical lines, attractive but comfortable and livable fabrics, these furnishings can adapt to a range of interior environments. Without the heavier upholsteries of traditional furniture or the cold metal and glass often found in contemporary interiors, this furniture relies on warm neutrals with color accents, rich woods, and interesting textures. Transitional furniture is a typical choice for model homes and furnished apartments as it is more gender neutral and easy to combine with varied client preferences.

Country

Country style furniture traces its origins to the lifestyles of rural areas. Today, many people call this style *Shabby Chic*. There are many subcategories of Country style furniture depending on the country that influenced the particular design. These styles include American, English, Italian, French, and Irish Country. Characteristics of the style may vary somewhat between countries.

In general, Country style furniture uses painted or distressed wood finishes that convey a feeling of age. Natural pine, cherry, and oak are also used. The chairs and sofas are plump and comfortable. Fabric designs also convey a timeworn appearance.

Eclectic

In the **Eclectic style**, furniture and fabrics cross over styles and periods. The style can be a mix of different ethnic, historical, and international influences as well as works by different artisans or manufacturers. Since an eclectic room may use a variety of furnishing styles, effective use of the principles of design helps create a unified look. For example, the furnishings in an eclectic room should be in proportion to one another and somewhat related in mood. Carefully considering the combinations of textures and colors also helps unify the design scheme.

Antiques, Collectibles, and Reproductions

To help complement the dominant furniture styles of Contemporary, Casual, Transitional, Country, Traditional, and Eclectic, interior designers may also select antiques, collectibles, and reproductions to design a room. Such purchases can mix well with many styles of furniture.

Antiques

Antiques are pieces of furniture made over 100 years ago in the style of the period. As furniture styles become outdated, good-quality pieces have become hard to locate. Some antiques are reasonable in cost. Furniture that is very old and reflects good construction, however, can be quite costly. Fine antiques are those of good quality. The very finest antiques are museum quality as in Figure 21.14. Such pieces are very rare and expensive.

Collectibles

Collectibles are highly valued furnishings less than 100 years old, but no longer made. If kept long enough, they will become antiques. Collectibles are usually located in retail stores such as antique stores.

Reproductions

Reproductions are copies of antique originals. Manufacturers sometimes make them to look worn

Maryunin Yury Vasilevich/Shutterstock.com

Figure 21.14 The antique furniture in this room is museum quality.

Hickory Chair

Figure 21.15 This elegant reproduction chest has a serpentine front that flares out on both sides ending in fluted pilasters. It is made of maple solids and figured "tiger" maple veneers and features custom reproduction solid brass hardware.

or used. For example, manufacturers may add false wormholes to the finish for an older appearance. Reproductions may or may not be accurate imitations. Determining whether a furniture piece is authentic or a reproduction requires careful inspection and research. See Figure 21.15 for an example of an accurate reproduction.

Review & Assessment

1. Summarize three traditional styles of furniture.
2. Which following furniture style is not a Traditional style: (A) Louis XV; (B) Chippendale; (C) Colonial; (D) Organic?
3. What factors influence the unity of an eclectic design style?
4. Summarize the difference between an antique and a collectible.

Evaluating Furniture Construction

Many furniture styles are made with wood, plastic, metal, wicker, or glass. The materials can be used alone or in combination with other materials. The furniture you select for a design scheme depends on the desires of the household, the mood of the room, and money available to carry out the design. Evaluating the functional quality of furniture for usefulness, convenience, and organization is vital for a successful design. You will also need to evaluate furniture's aesthetic value, such as its pleasing appearance or effect. (The elements of design also apply to furniture.)

Knowing how to evaluate the quality of furniture construction is very important. The materials used in the construction of the furniture should meet industry standards and be the highest quality a person can afford. Furniture should also be safe and durable. Understanding furniture construction can help you choose the highest-quality furniture for the money available (Figure 21.16).

Wood in Furniture

Wood is the most common material used in furniture construction. A **case good** is a furniture piece in which wood is the primary construction material. Such furniture includes tables, desks, dressers, headboards, and chests. Fine wood may also be part of the structural framework of furniture that has a covering of another material, such as upholstery.

Wood used in furniture construction can be classified according to the following factors:

- type and quality of wood grain
- hardwood versus softwood
- solid versus bonded wood
- type of wood joints
- finished versus unfinished wood

r.martens/Shutterstock.com

Figure 21.16 If you buy furniture made by a well-known company, you can be assured that high quality wood was used.

These factors affect the quality of the piece. When looking at furniture, be sure to consider each factor to determine if the price reflects the quality.

Grain

A **wood grain**, or pattern, forms as a tree grows (Figure 21.17). The stump or base of a tree has a beautiful, irregular grain caused by the twisted and irregular growth of the tree's roots. Crotch wood has a special grain caused by branches growing out from the trunk of a tree. Burls, which are woody, flattened outgrowths on trees, have a unique and highly prized grain. It is important to evaluate the appearance of the grain when you are selecting a case good.

Lumber is cut to showcase the grain. The way it is cut can affect the appearance of wood grain in furniture. Quarter slicing, rotary cutting, and flat cutting are methods that create different looks with the same kind of wood.

Hardwood and Softwood

Furniture makers can construct furniture entirely from hardwood, softwood, or a combination. Hardwood comes from deciduous trees, or trees that lose their leaves. The most popular hardwoods used for quality furniture include walnut, mahogany, pecan, cherry, maple, and oak. Hardwood does not dent easily. It is usually stronger than softwood and is more costly.

Softwood comes from ***coniferous*** trees, or evergreen trees that do not shed their leaves. Softwood does not have as beautiful a grain as hardwood, and it dents easily. Cedar, redwood, pine, fir, and spruce are the most common softwoods used for furniture. Some softwood is harder than some hardwood, so the names may be somewhat deceiving. Figure 21.18 shows examples of various wood species.

Solid Wood and Bonded Wood

Solid wood means that all exposed parts of a piece of furniture are made of whole pieces of wood. Such furniture is usually expensive, especially if it is made of hardwood. The disadvantage of solid wood is that it has a tendency to warp, swell, and crack.

The application of glue and pressure to several layers of wood forms **bonded wood**. Bonded woods include veneered wood and pressed wood. Bonding three, five, or seven thin layers of wood to one another,

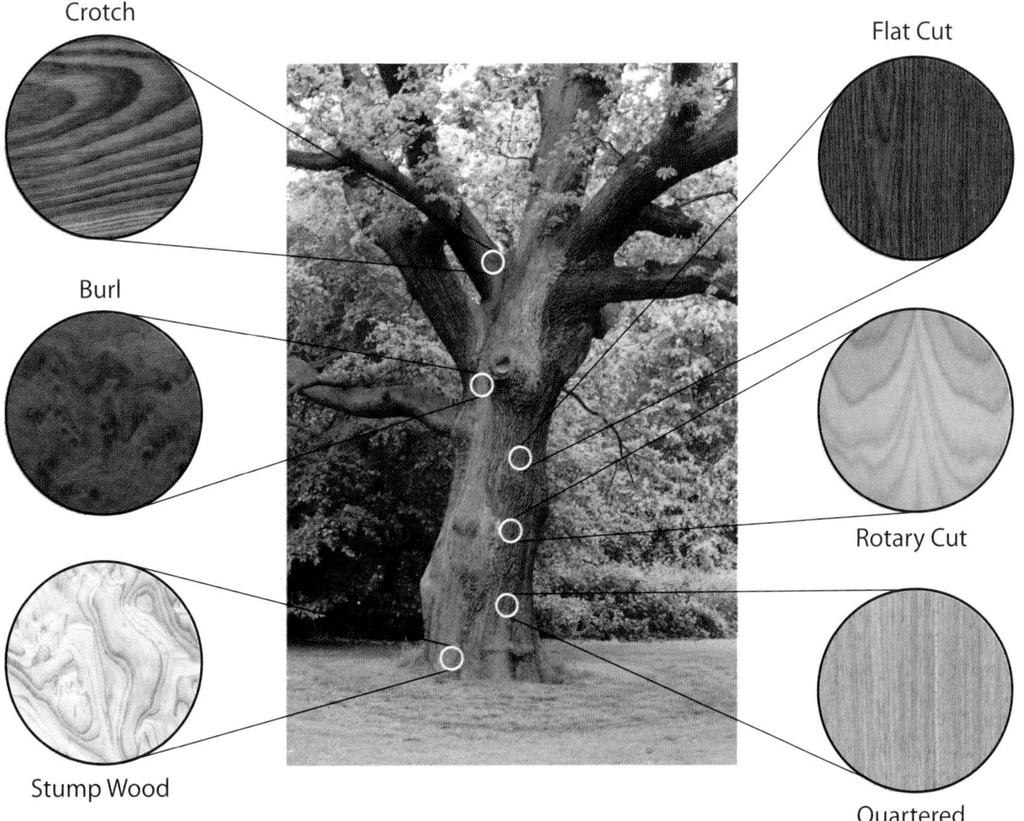

Left to right: Hal_P/Shutterstock.com; Richard Williamson/Shutterstock.com; Bambuh/Shutterstock.com; Tom Curtis/Shutterstock.com; Bambuh/Shutterstock.com; ksb/Shutterstock.com; Bambuh/Shutterstock.com

Figure 21.17 Wood grain varies according to the part of the tree from which the lumber comes (crotch, burl, or stump wood) or the way it is cut (flat, rotary, or quartered).

Photography Courtesy of JELD-WEN Windows & Doors

Figure 21.18 Notice the differences in the wood grain and the colors of these woods. In furniture, each of these woods provides a different look.

to a solid wood core, or to a pressed wood core creates **veneered wood**, or plywood (Figure 21.19). Fine woods make up the outside layers. Less expensive woods make up the inside layers or core.

Since the outside layer of veneered wood utilizes more expensive woods, veneering makes fine woods available at a moderate cost. Rare woods and beautiful grains are also available. Veneering permits the use of fragile woods, since the inside layers add strength. A disadvantage of veneered wood is the adhesive may not stick permanently, causing the veneer to loosen and chip.

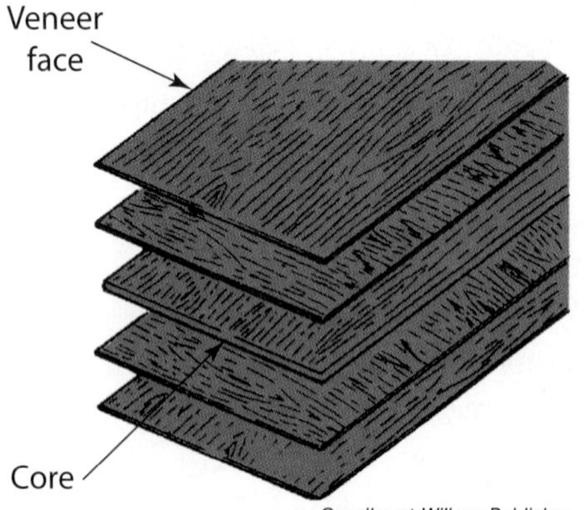

Goodheart-Willcox Publisher

Figure 21.19 In plywood, the grains of alternate veneers run at right angles to one another. This adds strength to the plywood.

Most of the furniture made since 1900 is partly veneered. Today, veneered furniture is more common than solid wood furniture.

Pressed wood is made of shavings, veneer scraps, chips, and other small pieces of wood. Other names for pressed wood include *particleboard, wafer board,* or *composite board*. These wood types are less expensive than solid or veneered wood. Furniture makers often use pressed woods on parts of furniture that do not show. Furnishings that need a tough, durable surface may have a top layer of more expensive wood or plastic laminate.

Wood Joints

When selecting furniture, especially case goods, pay close attention to the method used for fastening, or joining, the wood pieces. Furniture makers can use many different ways to fasten wood pieces, including the use of wood joints. Figure 21.20 shows common wood joints. Usage of glue on all wood joints adds strength and durability. Common wood joints include the following:

- **Mortise-and-tenon joints** are some of the strongest joints used for furniture. The glued tenon fits tightly into the mortise, or hole. This method of joinery uses no nails or screws. Common uses for mortise-and-tenon joints include joining legs or rails to tables, chairs, and headboards.

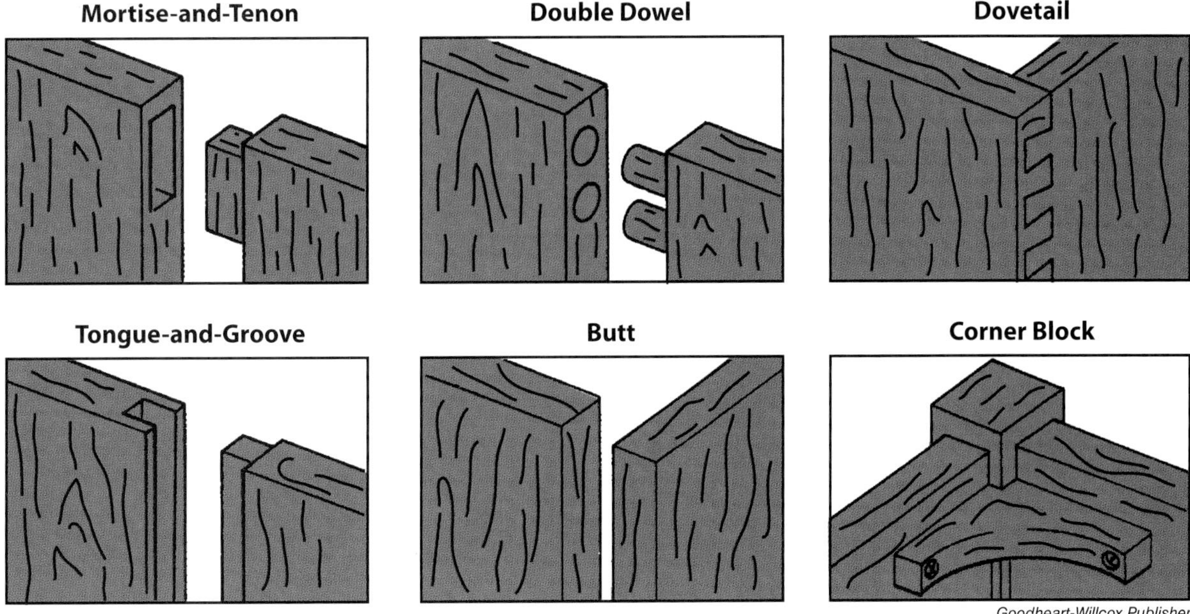

Figure 21.20 Joints are an important factor in determining the quality of furniture pieces.

- **Double-dowel joints** are very common and very strong. Glued wooden dowels fit into drilled holes in both pieces of wood.
- **Dovetail joints** fasten wood pieces at corner joints. These joints utilize flaring tenons and mortises which fit tightly, interlocking two pieces of wood. You can find them in drawers of good-quality furniture.
- **Tongue-and-groove joints** form by fitting a tongue cut on one edge of a board into a matching groove cut on the edge of another board. These joints are invisible if they are made skillfully. They are used where several boards are joined lengthwise, such as in making tabletops.
- **Butt joints** involve gluing or nailing one board flush to another board. They are the weakest of the wood joints.
- **Corner blocks** are small pieces of wood attached between corner boards. They support and reinforce the joint. Furniture makers use them in the construction of chairs and tables. They keep one side from pulling away from the other.

Finished and Unfinished Wood

You can purchase wood furniture finished or unfinished. Most furniture pieces are already finished. Manufacturers may use one or more ways to treat finished furniture to protect and improve the appearance of the wood surface. Some finishes include stains, sealers, waxes, and paints. Water-based stains and oil-based stains bring out the natural beauty of hardwoods and softwoods respectively. Sealers can be penetrating sealers or surface sealers. Plastic sealers resist moisture and are frequently used. Use of wax preserves the wood and gives it an attractive finish. Paint finishes can hide surfaces that are unattractive. Paint can also enhance an existing furniture piece by applying decorative finishes.

The wood in unfinished furniture is in its natural state following construction. Untreated wood surfaces appeal to those who want to finish the furniture themselves, often to achieve a unique look. The initial cost of unfinished furniture is low. Before buying such furniture, it is important to factor in the finishing costs in money, time, and effort.

You or a client may choose to finish furniture by applying a wood stain and a sealer or wax. Paint is another finish choice. Consider applying the paint in a solid color application or in a custom and novel application of a faux finish, such as sponging or ragging. Marbleizing a plain wooden table surface creates the impression of a marble stone top. Applying trompe l'oeil painting techniques to unfinished furniture can add an interesting effect. For example, creative painting can transform a plain wooden chest into a seaside scene with a sailing ship. These paint treatments can turn a bargain piece of unfinished furniture into a custom work of art.

When buying wood furniture, check the quality characteristics in Figure 21.21. You should also read the labels carefully. They offer information

Wood Furniture Checklist

- Do doors shut tightly without sticking?
- Are corner blocks used for reinforcement?
- Are dust panels provided between drawers?
- Do drawers slide easily?
- Are legs attached with mortise-and-tenon or dowel joints?
- Do legs stand squarely on the floor?
- Have insides of drawers, backs of chests, and undersides of tables and chairs been sanded and finished?
- Are surfaces smooth?
- Are surfaces solid, veneered, or laminated?
- Has a protective plastic coating been used on surfaces that will receive hard wear?
- Will the furniture piece fulfill your use, style, color, and size requirements?
- Is the furniture affordable?

Figure 21.21 A checklist is a useful tool when evaluating wood furniture.

about the finishes, the purpose of the finishes, and the care they should receive. It is important to understand all the terms on the labels. For instance, *solid walnut* means the exposed wood (in this case, walnut) is the same wood used throughout the entire piece. *Genuine walnut* means that walnut is the face veneer, but other woods form the core. *Walnut finish* means the piece of furniture has been finished to look like walnut.

Other Materials Used in Furniture Construction

Plastic, metal, rattan, wicker, bamboo, and glass are other materials used in furniture construction. Evaluate all materials for quality when buying furniture.

Plastic

Plastic furniture is usually less costly than wood. It is lightweight, sturdy, and easy to clean. Generally, it looks best in Modern and Contemporary settings.

Plastic used for furniture should not imitate other materials, such as wood. Instead, the furniture design should take advantage of the special properties of plastic. When evaluating plastic furniture, ask yourself the following questions:

- Is the piece strong and durable?
- Are the edges smooth and the surfaces flawless?
- Are color and gloss uniform?
- Are the reinforcement parts (that are not part of the design) hidden?

Metal

Metal is popular for both indoor and outdoor furniture. Wrought iron, steel, cast aluminum, and chrome are all used for different furnishings. Manufacturers often combine metals with other materials, such as wood, fabric, glass, or marble

Determining "Sustainability" in Furniture and Furnishings

Consumers, interior designers, and retailers now have a way to select furniture and furnishings constructed using environmentally friendly practices and materials. The *Sustainable Furnishings Council* has established standards for "Best Practices for Sustainability" in the furniture and home furnishings industry. Over 400 companies are members of the council and display a seal on their labels marketing materials, and advertisements. In addition, those members with significant achievement in sustainability receive authorization to use the Council's hangtag on their products.

The seal assures the furniture manufacturer has steps taken to reduce carbon emissions, reduce waste, and reduce nonrecyclable materials. Further, the hangtag designates exemplary principles used in producing the product from the forest to the showroom floor.

Visit the Sustainable Furnishings Council website to learn more about their standards and members.

Photo Courtesy of Pottery Barn

Figure 21.22 The free-standing storage piece in this bathroom is made of polished nickel-plated steel with marble shelves. Notice the side rails that help secure the accessories.

(Figure 21.22). When evaluating metal furniture, ask yourself the following questions:

- Is the metal or metallic finish rustproof?
- Is the surface smooth?
- Are sharp edges coated or covered?

Rattan, Wicker, and Bamboo

Rattan, wicker, and bamboo furniture combine natural wood frames with woven stems or branches. Rattan furniture utilizes the stringy, tough stems of different kinds of palm trees. These stems bend easily and are strong. Rattan furniture works well in casual or informal room settings.

Popular since the 1800s, the original use of wicker furniture was for outdoor furniture. Construction of wicker furniture requires loosely weaving thin, flexible branches (often from willow trees) around a frame. After the weaving is complete, paint, lacquer, or varnish are common finishes for wicker furniture. Wicker is lightweight and durable. It is also water resistant and has a natural gloss. Use of wicker furniture is now common in both indoor and outdoor settings (Figure 21.23).

Photo Courtesy of Karastan

Figure 21.23 Wicker furniture is popular for informal indoor settings.

Construction of bamboo furniture uses various woody, mostly tall tropical grasses including some with strong hollow stems. These stems, or canes, form the frame of the furniture. Some manufacturers combine bamboo and rattan in one piece of furniture. For example, bamboo can form a chair frame and woven rattan can form the seat. Use of bamboo is most common in casual room settings. When evaluating rattan, wicker, or bamboo furniture, ask yourself the following questions:

- Are the strands smooth and unbroken?
- Are the joints well wrapped and secure?
- Is the finish a high quality?

Glass

Glass is usually combined with metal or wood. It is popular for tabletops and cabinet doors. When glass is a part of the furniture you are choosing, ask yourself the following questions:

- Does the furniture use tempered glass for safety and durability?
- Does the furniture design hold the glass firmly in place?
- Are glass surfaces free from bubbles, scratches, and other defects?

Upholstered Furniture

Another name for chairs, sofas, and other pieces of padded furniture is upholstered furniture. Most or all exposed surfaces of a furniture piece have a covering of fabric (Figure 21.24). This

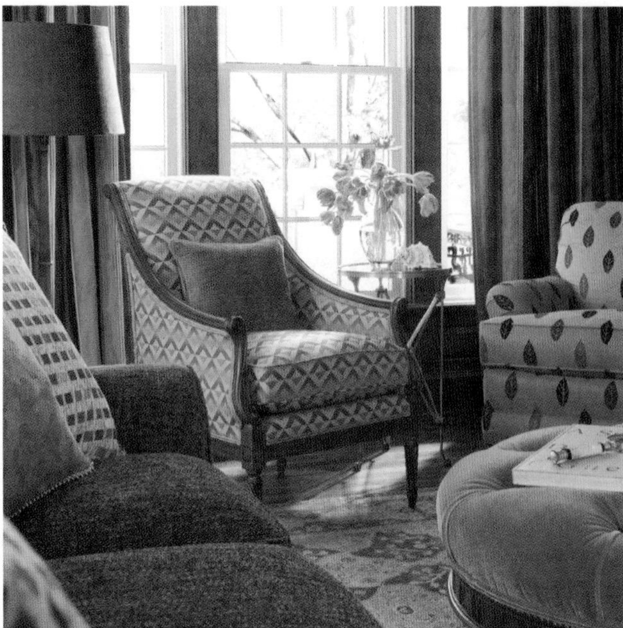

Calico Corners—Calico Home Stores

Figure 21.24 Upholstered furniture may be completely covered in fabric or some wood may be exposed.

outer covering hides the inner construction details. Because you cannot see these details, choosing good-quality upholstered furniture can be difficult. The information that follows will help you evaluate upholstered furniture.

Upholstery Fabrics

Fabric is an important part of upholstered furniture. It is also a clue to the overall quality of a piece. Good-quality furniture has durable, well-tailored upholstery fabric.

Upholstery fabrics are made primarily of blends or combination yarns. Manufacturers weave yarns to create fabrics with different patterns and designs. Upholstery fabrics come in many attractive colors and interesting textures. They can be heavy-, medium-, or lightweight, although lightweight fabrics do not wear as well as the others. When choosing upholstery fabrics, consider the following points:

- Woven fabrics with close, tight weaves are better quality than fabrics with open, loose weaves.
- Long floats, such as in the satin weave, tend to snag.
- Fabrics with equal number and size of warp and weft yarns are more durable.
- Flame-resistant fabrics are safer than untreated fabrics.
- Stain-resistant finishes make woven fabrics easier to clean.
- Colorfast materials are preferred.

Image supplied by LEE Industries

Figure 21.25 This earth-friendly sofa has very soft back cushions that are made from recycled plastic drink bottles.

- Medium to dark colors, patterned materials, tweeds, and textured fabrics do not show soil easily.
- Labels on fabric samples give content and care information.
- Fabrics using earth-friendly products contribute to sustainability (Figure 21.25).

Upholstery Tailoring

When evaluating upholstered furniture, look at the tailoring details. A quick way to check tailoring details is to evaluate a cushion cover. If the cover can be removed, check the seams and filling material, and see if it has an inside casing.

For a more thorough evaluation, check the entire piece of furniture. The more *yes* answers you have to the questions in the following checklist, the better tailored the upholstery:

- Is expert sewing evident?
- Are threads secure and trimmed?

Housing Health & Safety

Furniture Design and Ergonomics

Furniture, particularly workplace and home office furniture, is sometimes described as *ergonomic*. The manufacturer or retailer claims certain furniture designs use principles from the science of ergonomics. The goals of ergonomics are to minimize injury and maximize comfort and efficiency of use. Interior designers and consumers should beware, however, because any product can be labeled as ergonomic. Ergonomics guidelines have been developed by the Business and Institutional Furniture Manufacturer's Association (BIFMA).

True ergonomic products require designers to understand both the physical and psychological characteristics and special needs of their users. They consult anthropometric data, or human body measurements, and study how people interact with furniture and other elements of their environments.

As a result, ergonomic furniture is often adjustable and can be comfortably and safely used by people of different sizes. Controls are simple to use and easy to reach and manipulate without straining. Seats and chair arms are usually padded and covered with nonslip breathable coverings. Many include lower-back supports that maintain the lumbar curve in the lower spine. Ergonomic tables are designed with adjustable-height legs.

Ergonomics is a broad and varied field that covers much more than furniture design. For more information about ergonomics and ergonomic products visit the websites of the following organizations:

- Business and Institutional Furniture Manufacturer's Association
- Human Factors and Ergonomics Society
- U.S. Department of Labor's Occupational Safety & Health Administration (OSHA)

Africa Studio/Shutterstock.com

- Is the fabric smooth, tight, and free from puckers?
- Does the fabric pattern, such as stripes and plaids, match?
- Are curved shapes and corners smooth?
- Are skirts lined and do they hang straight?
- Are buttons and trims securely fastened?
- Are staples and tacks concealed?

Frames, Springs, and Cushions

Upholstered furniture frames are made of wood or metal. As you evaluate the frames, keep in mind the points for choosing wood or metal furniture. You should choose a solid hardwood frame that is heavy and substantial. The joints should be secure, utilizing screws and corner blocks.

Springs are a part of the inner construction. The type and number of springs in a seat base help determine the quality. There are two types of springs: coil and flat (Figure 21.26). *Coil springs* have a spiral shape without padding and covering. Heavier furniture utilizes coil springs. An average-size chair generally has nine to twelve springs per seat. Up to eight ties per spring securely attach the springs to steel bands or webbing. This construction method provides support and enhances durability in a high-quality upholstered piece.

Lightweight pieces of furniture with sleek lines usually have flat or zigzag springs. *Flat springs* are flat, S-shaped springs that may have metal support strips banded across them. They offer firm comfort at lower cost.

Cushions need to be the proper size and should fit snugly into the furniture. They need to give body

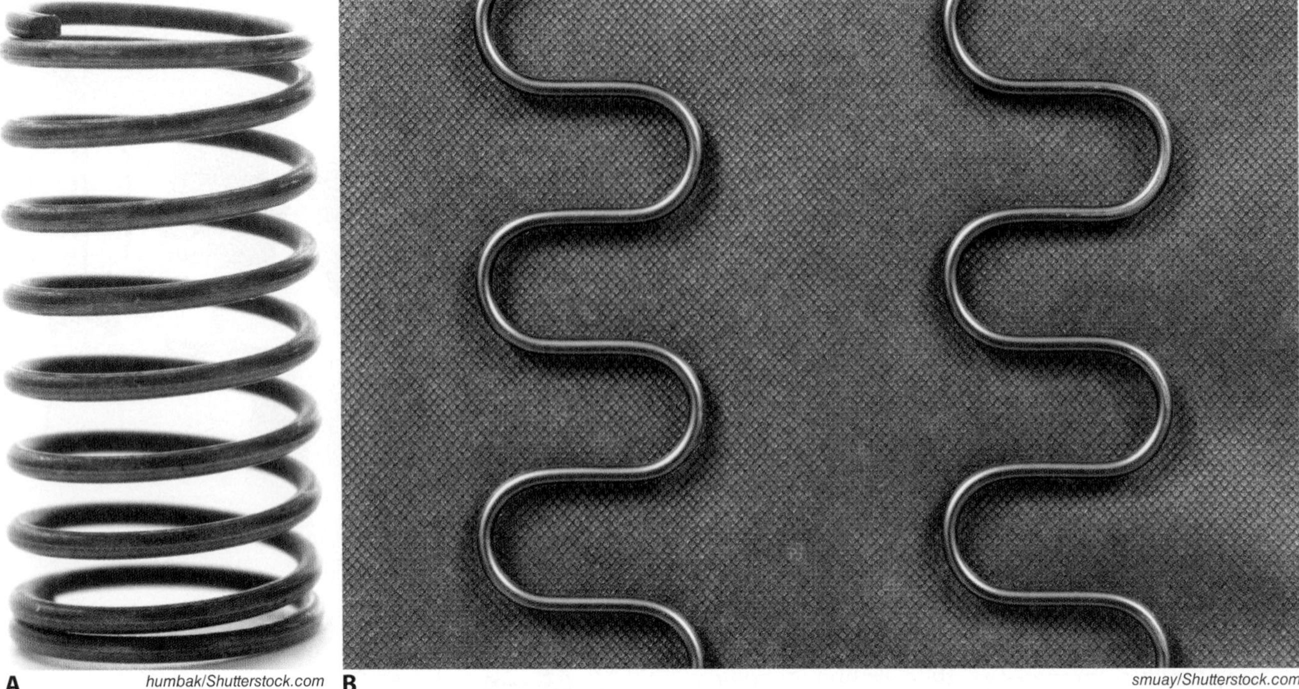

A humbak/Shutterstock.com B smuay/Shutterstock.com

Figure 21.26 Coil springs are used in heavy furniture (A). Flat or zigzag springs are used when a minimum of bulk is desired (B).

support. Cushions often consist of urethane foam or foam rubber, but some manufacturers are now making seat cushions from a 20 to 30 percent soy-based material that is biodegradable (an alternative to petroleum-based materials that are not biodegradable). These materials are durable, lightweight, and resilient. Manufacturers can mold these materials into many shapes, sizes, and degrees of firmness to meet the functional aspects of furniture, including features that meet special needs requirements.

Covered or pocketed coils are sometimes used in cushions. They usually have a covering of a thin layer of foam rubber and a layer of fabric. Other cushions may have a filling of down and feathers. These are very comfortable, but are less durable than foam. They are also more costly.

Cushion filling can also be in the form of loose fill. Shredded foam, kapok, and polyester fiberfill are all types of loose fill. These options are less expensive than the shaped fillers. However, because loose fill takes the shape of the casing, it may not retain its original shape. Furniture styles that have soft pillow cushions use loose fill. In addition, back cushions often use an ultrasoft fiber filling derived from recycled plastic drink bottles.

The cutaway illustration in Figure 21.27 shows the inner construction of an upholstered chair. You can see how the combination of different materials provides seating comfort.

When choosing upholstered furniture, comfort is a very important factor to consider. For example, a sofa that does not feel comfortable is a poor buy. In making furniture selections, sit on a sofa or chair as you would at home. Check the height and depth of the seat. Check the height of the back and arms. Be sure it fits your body's proportions. If you are working with an interior design client, be sure your client has an opportunity to check out the comfort of potential furnishings, too. See the list in Figure 21.28 for other points to consider when selecting upholstered furniture.

Beds

People spend about one-third of their lives sleeping. Therefore, choosing the best bed you or a client can afford is important. A bed includes a mattress, frame, and springs. Addition of a headboard and footboard can help increase the charm of a design scheme (Figure 21.29). Comfort is important when choosing a bed. Before buying a bed, a person should lie on it. That is the only way to determine if it is comfortable.

Since the inside construction of a mattress or box spring is not visible, choose a reliable brand. Many manufacturers have illustrations or miniature mattresses and box springs available for inspection when visiting a dealer. Check samples for support and durability.

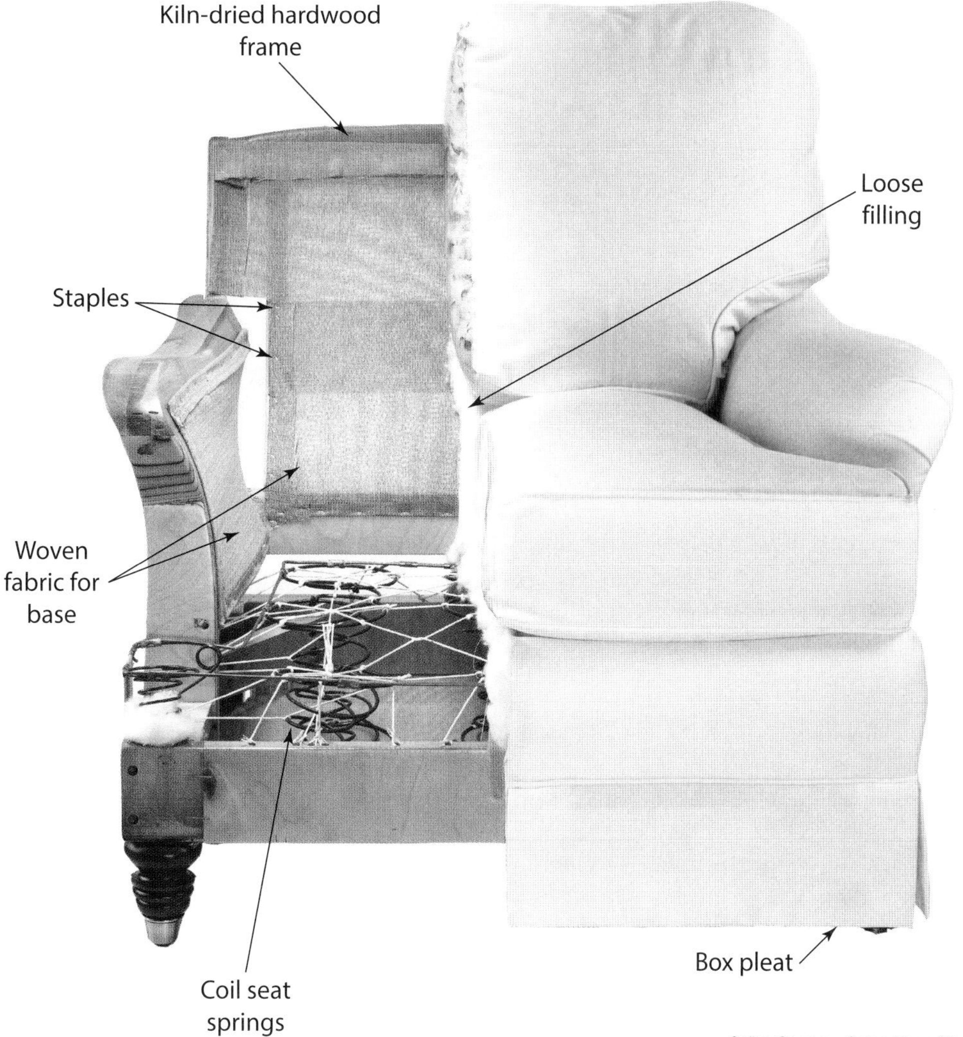

Calico Corners—Calico Home Stores

Figure 21.27 Making a chair durable, yet comfortable and attractive requires several work steps.

Upholstered Furniture Checklist

- Are the legs and joints securely attached?
- What kinds of springs have been used?
- What are the cushion materials and how are they constructed?
- Are the cushions reversible?
- Does the outer covering have a well-tailored appearance?
- Will the outer covering give good wearability for the intended purpose?
- Does the outer covering have a stain-resistant finish?
- Is it appropriate in style, design, and color for the room design?
- Is the furniture affordable for you or a client?

Figure 21.28 Check these points before you buy pieces of upholstered furniture.

Eviled/Shutterstock.com

Figure 21.29 The use of the headboard in this photo adds color, height, and interest while also visually anchoring the bed to the wall.

Career Focus Upholsterer

Do you like to make things with your hands? Are you interested in creating or repairing the fabrics and cushioning on furniture? Do you like using math to solve problems? Do you like to create new things? Perhaps you would like to create final products in household furniture pieces by becoming an upholsterer.

Interests/Skills: Upholsterers are creative individuals who need excellent math skills to estimate yardage needed in repairing or redoing the fabric on a piece of furniture. Knowledge of fabric types and behaviors is important. Skill in using tools, equipment, and machines is required.

Career Snapshot: An upholsterer makes repairs or replaces upholstery or coverings of household or institutional furniture. This involves estimating the amount of material needed and accurately quoting a bid based on labor and materials. It involves knowing the characteristics of fabrics, including their ease of using in upholstery and also the durability over time. A good upholsterer pays close attention to detail and design to create a high quality product.

Education/Training: Although a college degree is not required, serving as an apprentice is essential to develop the knowledge and skills needed on the job. This training may take up to ten years to learn all the essentials to be a skilled and accomplished upholsterer.

Job Outlook: Employment of upholsterers is projected to have little change through 2022. The largest source of positions is in household and institutional furniture manufacturing.

Goodluz/Shutterstock.com

Sources: The Occupational Outlook Handbook (OOH); the U.S. Bureau of Labor Statistics (BLS); the Occupational Information Network (O*NET)

Mattresses

There are many types of mattresses available. One of the most popular types is the innerspring mattress. An **innerspring mattress** contains a series of springs covered with padding (Figure 21.30A).

The springs vary in number, size, placement, wire thickness (gauge), and whether they are individually pocketed. These factors determine the firmness and comfort of the mattress. Manufacturers say a good quality full-size innerspring mattress should have the following features:

- at least 300 firmly anchored, heavy coils
- good padding and insulation placed over and between coils
- a tightly woven cover with a border that does not sag

Foam mattresses are made of latex or polyurethane foam. The foam is cut or molded to shape and usually has a tightly woven covering of cotton cloth. The mattress may be solid foam or the more pliable molded foam. Foam mattresses are lightweight, less durable, and less costly than innerspring mattresses. They vary in thickness, firmness, and quality. A good quality mattress will be about 9 inches thick. It will have some holes or cores in it. The greater the number of cores, the softer the mattress will be. People with allergies often prefer foam mattresses or mattresses with hypoallergenic padding.

The newest foam mattress is the memory foam mattress. A **memory foam mattress** molds to the body during sleep, but quickly returns to its original shape once a person gets out of bed (Figure 21.30B).

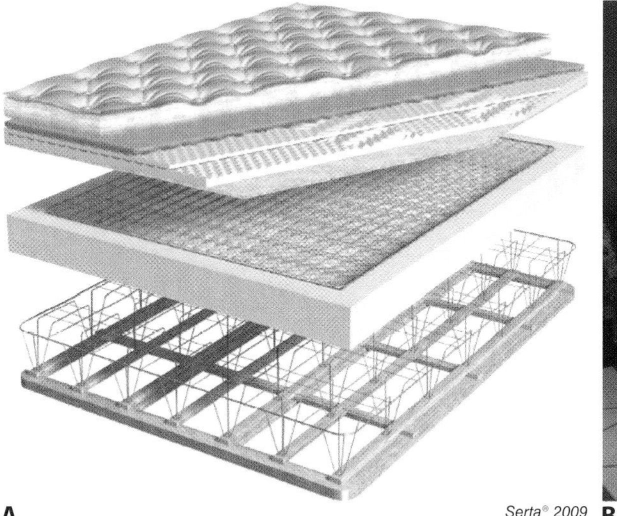

A Serta® 2009

B Serta® 2009

Figure 21.30 When buying a mattress, it is important to check the quality of its construction, as shown in the layering of this high-quality mattress (A). Memory foam mattresses offer good support during sleep (B).

In the 1970s, the National Aeronautics and Space Administration (NASA) developed this foam for use by astronauts in space. NASA never used this foam in space, however, but instead sold the technology to a company that has since developed the foam for consumer use.

A **waterbed** is a bed with a mattress consisting of a plastic bag or tubes filled with water. It conforms exactly to body curves and provides good, firm support. There are two types of waterbeds: hard sided and soft sided.

- *Hard-sided waterbeds* consist of a heavy-duty plastic water bag, a wood frame, a watertight liner between the mattress and frame to contain any leaks, and a water-heating device. Waterbeds range from full-motion to waveless types and require special bed linens. When a queen-size waterbed is full of water, it weighs about 1,600 pounds.
- *Soft-sided waterbeds* consist of a firm foam frame that surrounds the water-filled mattress. The mattress sits on a platform and looks much like a traditional innerspring mattress. One advantage of a soft-sided waterbed is that the owners can use traditional bed linens.

Buildings must have strong foundations to support waterbeds. Some rental properties prohibit waterbeds.

Air mattresses are easy to fill and empty. When empty, they require very little storage space. For these reasons, they make good portable beds. Camping is the primary use for air mattresses, but they are also handy for overnight guests.

Springs

Most conventional beds have springs to support the mattress. Bedsprings have three basic forms: box, coil, and flat. Most people prefer box springs even though they are the most expensive. **Box springs** consist of a series of coils attached to a base and covered with padding. The coils may vary in number, size, placement, and gauge. Coil springs are between box springs and flat springs in terms of quality and cost. Flat springs are the least expensive.

When buying an innerspring mattress and springs, buy them in a matching set. When purchasing them as a set, the coils in the mattress line up with the coils in the springs. This makes the bed more comfortable.

Frames

There are many types of bed frames. The most common type is a metal frame on top of which you place a box spring and mattress. Sometimes springs, usually flat springs, are already built into the frame (Figure 21.31). An electric adjustable bed is like a metal frame bed, except a person can adjust the frame up and down according to his or her needs. It is more expensive than a conventional metal frame.

Some bed frames, such as futons and sofa beds, have a dual purpose. In addition to sleeping, you can also use them for seating. A futon frame is a wooden bed frame that is low to the ground. A cotton mattress is placed on top of it to make a bed. Futons can be folded up to make a chair or sofa. In the case of a sofa bed, pulling out a concealed mattress converts a sofa into a bed.

Group 3, Architecture and Interior Design, Hilton Head, South Carolina. Photography provided as a courtesy of John McManus, Savannah, Georgia.

Figure 21.31 Many people find traditional metal bed frames appealing and comfortable. When would you make a different choice?

Review & Assessment

1. Contrast a case good with an upholstered piece of furniture.
2. Summarize the differences between hardwood and softwood.
3. What are the benefits of using veneered wood for furniture?
4. List six joints used to fasten the structural pieces of wood furniture. Which is the weakest and which is the strongest?
5. What is the difference between solid wood and genuine wood?
6. Which furniture material is popular for indoor and outdoor use?
7. What questions should you ask when evaluating the quality of the following types of furniture: (A) plastic; (B) metal; (C) rattan, wicker, and bamboo; and (D) glass?
8. What characteristics indicate quality in an upholstered piece of furniture?
9. Contrast coil springs and flat springs in terms of bed comfort and cost.

Caring for Furniture

Furniture is a large investment. Regular care will help maintain furniture and prolong use. Furniture pieces need to be dusted frequently and cleaned periodically to remove dirt buildup.

Wood Furniture

Water and regular cleaning supplies should not be used on high-quality wood furniture surfaces. Instead, use products designed for wood surfaces. Before using a product, test it on an inconspicuous area of the furniture to make sure it does not damage the finish. Wax or furniture polish applied periodically will preserve and protect the wood surface.

Upholstered Furniture

Upholstered furniture should be vacuumed regularly to remove loose dirt. Use a hose attachment to vacuum the piece from top to bottom using short strokes. Soak stains up immediately with a white cloth or towel. Before using any cleaning solution, check the upholstery for colorfastness in an unnoticeable area. Stains on many fabrics may be cleaned with a damp cloth and gentle cleanser, such as dish soap. Avoid using too much water, which may cause fabric to shrink. Some fabrics can be water-stained and should only be cleaned with dry-cleaning solvents. Avoid getting water or solvents on metal or wood pieces.

Mattresses and Bedding

Mattresses should be vacuumed regularly. Use your vacuum's hose attachment to vacuum the tops and sides of mattresses in overlapping strokes. Rotate mattresses periodically to help promote even wear. Some mattresses should also be flipped seasonally. Mattresses with pillow tops cannot be flipped. Bedding should be laundered on a regular basis. Sheets and pillowcases should be washed weekly, while blankets and comforters should be washed every few weeks.

Review & Assessment

1. Why should a cleaner be tested on an inconspicuous area before being used on wood furniture?
2. Why should you avoid using water to clean upholstered fabric?
3. How often should sheets and pillowcases be laundered?

Selecting Types of Window Treatments

Window treatments are applications added to window units either for home environment control or for purely decorative purposes. Consider the style, size, and location of windows when choosing window treatments. Other very important considerations for selecting window treatments include the need to control sunlight and noise, and to provide the ventilation, privacy, and insulation for each room.

Window treatments include draperies, curtains, shades, shutters, blinds, and decorative top treatments. The right window treatments can enhance the appearance of a room. Certain treatments can also camouflage windows that are not in proportion to the rest of the room.

Some window treatments can help control the amount of natural light that enters a room by blocking all or part of the light from entering. For example, a treatment should provide both sun control and privacy in a sleeping area for adults or children. However, privacy and sun control may be less important for a child's playroom. For a sunroom, window treatments should allow as much light and air ventilation as possible. In contrast, a media room or home theater requires window treatments to regulate or block the amount of sunlight entering the room.

Sometimes windows require no treatments, especially when privacy is not a concern. If the shape of the window is too difficult to treat or if the window itself is an important architectural focal point of the room, you may choose to leave it untreated. In Figure 21.32, the uniquely shaped windows are left uncovered to give the room a dramatic look and let light enter freely. Furthermore, if windows provide a beautiful view of the outdoors, you may prefer having no window treatments.

Another consideration in the selection of the type of window treatment is the feeling you wish to create in the room. Is the mood of the room to be formal or informal? Is the style of the space to be Traditional or Contemporary? Depending on the design of the window treatment, an interior designer can create many different moods and effects.

Other important considerations for the selection of window treatments deal with the initial cost of purchasing the treatments and the subsequent cost of maintaining them. Keep in mind that custom or made-to-measure window treatments are more costly than ready-made treatments that are mass-produced. In today's market, more and more attractive ready-made styles and options are available. Also, pattern companies offer many designs for creating your own window treatments or for hiring a drapery workroom to do so.

Image Courtesy of Andersen Corporation

Figure 21.32 These striking windows need no treatment.

Whether you purchase or create your own window treatments, give careful consideration to the fabrics you select. Are they colorfast? Do they require dry cleaning or laundering? Can simple dusting or vacuuming maintain the appearance of the treatments? Do not invest in a window treatment that you or a client have neither the time nor money to maintain.

Draperies and Curtains

Draperies and curtains are the most common window treatments. They are extremely versatile and can fit into any décor. The type of draperies or curtains you choose depends on the room's décor and the function of the windows.

Draperies

Draperies are fabric panels with pleats that cover windows completely or are pulled to the side. Depending on the design and type of fabric, draperies

STEM Math Curtain and Drapery Calculations

Curtains and draperies are soft window treatments you can use to enhance the beauty of a room and help tie together the design details. Most curtain and drapery fabrics are 54 inches wide. Curtains or draperies may require 2 or 3 panels or widths of fabric per window depending on the fullness the client desires, pattern repeat, and whether the treatment needs lining. Some styles of window treatments—such as pleated draperies versus tab-top draperies—require more or less fabric than others. To obtain the basic yardage requirements for curtains and draperies, you will need to measure the area these treatments will cover. Take these measurements in inches using the following steps:

Step 1: Measure the width of the window and any wall space the treatments will cover. Then multiply this measurement by the number of fabric widths the client desires. For example, suppose your client wants full, sheer curtains on the living room picture window. The fabric type is sheer Georgette with no pattern repeat. The window measures 72 inches in width. Multiply this measurement by 3 for adequate fullness; then divide this number by 54 to determine the number of fabric widths.

72 in. × 3 = 216 in.
216 in. ÷ 54 in. = 4 fabric widths (panels)

Step 2: Measure the length of the window treatment from the top of the rod (usually 2 to 3 inches above the top window trim). Add 12 to 16 inches to this length to allow for top and bottom hems of the curtains or draperies. Assume your client wants the curtains to touch the floor and have deep hems. Your measurement is 92 inches finished length. Add together the total length and hem allowance. Then divide this total by 36 inches (the length of 1 yard of fabric).

92 in. + 16 in. = 108 in. (length)
108 in. ÷ 36 in. = 3 yd. (per panel)

Step 3: Multiply the number of yards-per-panel by the number of panels you need to obtain the total yardage for the curtains or draperies.

3 yd. × 4 = 12 yd. (fabric)

Math Practice

Suppose your client wants full curtains in the dining room that overlooks a single-door balcony. The fabric type is satin with no pattern repeat. The window measures 36 inches in width and 84 inches in height.

1. How many fabric widths (panels) will you need for this window?
2. Allow an additional 12 inches to the length for top and bottom hems. About how many yards per panel will you need? Round your answer to the nearest whole number.
3. Calculate the total yardage needed for the curtains.

can fit in any style décor. Draperies can be opaque or translucent. Opaque draperies block light, while translucent draperies permit the passage of light. Draperies can be lined or unlined. Lining draperies blocks some sunlight from entering the room and protects the draperies from sun fading. The lining also adds body, makes draperies hang or drape better, and increases their ability to insulate.

You can use draperies alone or with other window treatments, such as curtains, shades, blinds, and decorative top treatments. In Figure 21.33, center draw-drapery panels were the designer selection for this window. Opening them during the day allows light to enter the room. Closing them at night provides complete privacy and helps insulate the room. A decorative top treatment hides the drapery hardware.

The names of different types of draperies represent how they operate. *Draw draperies* open and close from the center or side with a pull stick or cord on one end of the curtain rod. You cannot open or close *stationary draperies*. Permanent placement of stationary draperies is usually at one or both sides of a window.

Curtains

Curtains are flat fabric panels that hang to the left and right of a window or may completely cover it. Like draperies, the design and fabric selected for the curtains impacts the style and mood of the room. Curtains usually have a rod-pocket hem at the top. You slip the curtain onto the curtain rod through the rod pocket and gather it to the desired fullness.

Calico Corners—Calico Home Stores

Figure 21.33 These drapery panels provide sunlight during the day and privacy at night. The valance top treatment is both decorative and functional since it hides hardware.

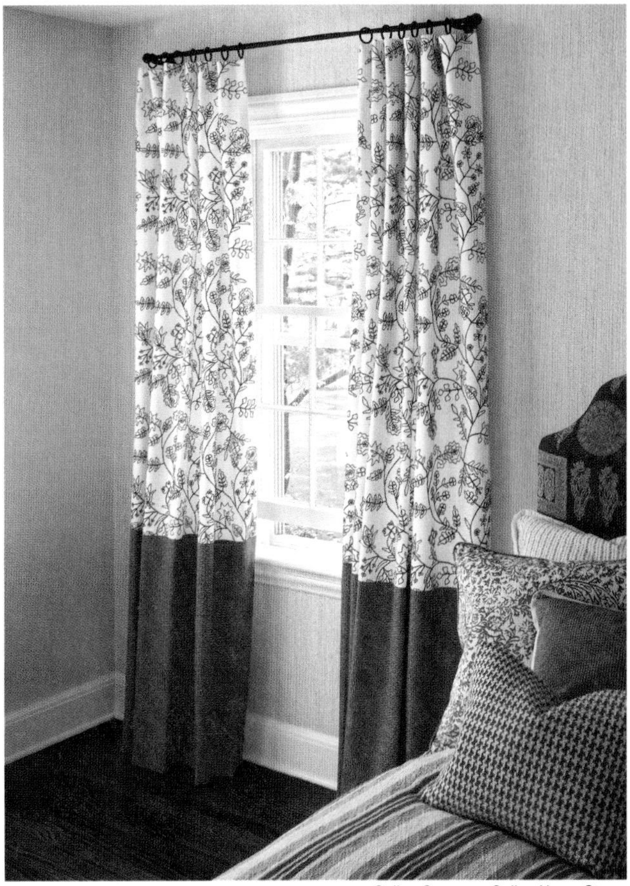

Calico Corners—Calico Home Stores

Figure 21.34 These bedroom curtains are mounted on a metal rod and are attached with metal rings. The designer used two fabrics—a floral pattern and a solid—to create this beautiful installation.

Some curtains may hang from the curtain rod with decorative drapery hardware or tabs of sewn fabric. The rod itself may be plain or decorative, such as a grooved wooden pole or a pole of brushed nickel or wrought iron (Figure 21.34). Ruffles, bands of fabric, and trim can add interest to the panels. The use of tiebacks to pull the curtain panel away from the window gives a curvy shape to the panel instead of simply a straight line.

The amount of light, insulation, or privacy curtains provide depends on the fabric. Curtains from sheer fabric give a room a light, airy feeling. For more privacy, use heavier fabrics. Using heavier fabrics, however, may make the room appear darker.

Café curtains are horizontal panels hung in tiers to cover part of a window. The top of each panel is joined to rings that slip over a curtain rod. Café curtains do not have a draw cord as do draw draperies. Instead, you open café curtains by pushing them to the window sides to control air, light, and privacy. With café curtains, one tier generally covers only the bottom half of the window. More than one tier can completely cover a window. By changing the width or the number of tiers, you can achieve a variety of looks with café curtains. Use café curtains in an informal setting.

The length of draperies and curtains should fall to *stool length, apron length,* or *floor length.* If the bottom edge of a window treatment falls at any other place, it will look either too short or too long. To correctly measure the length of draperies and curtains, use the methods in Figure 21.35.

Caring for Draperies and Curtains

Regular care for draperies and curtains helps keep them looking good. Care is based on fabric type and manufacturers recommendations.

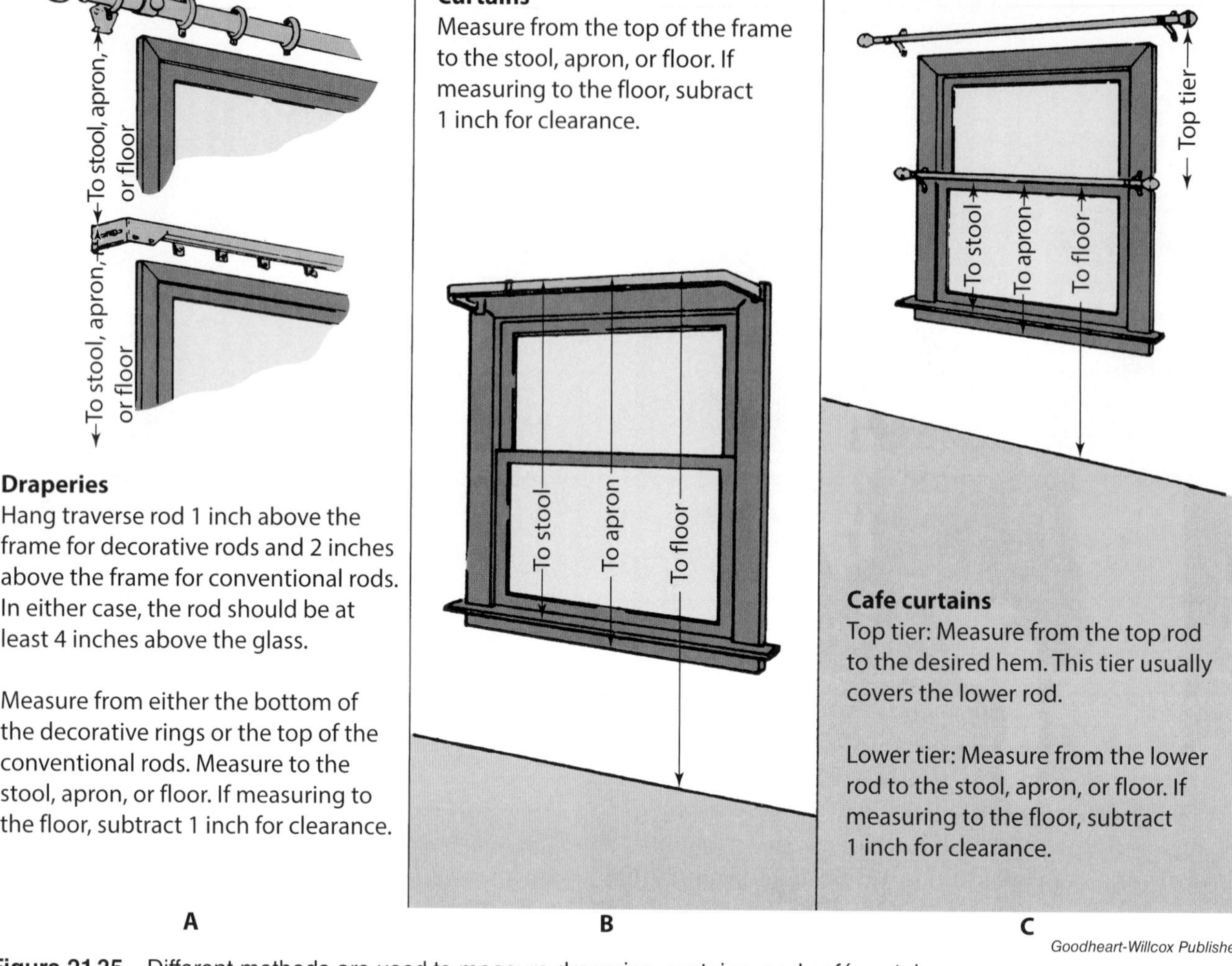

To stool, apron, or floor
To stool, apron, or floor
Draperies
Hang traverse rod 1 inch above the frame for decorative rods and 2 inches above the frame for conventional rods. In either case, the rod should be at least 4 inches above the glass.
Measure from either the bottom of the decorative rings or the top of the conventional rods. Measure to the stool, apron, or floor. If measuring to the floor, subtract 1 inch for clearance.
Curtains
Measure from the top of the frame to the stool, apron, or floor. If measuring to the floor, subract 1 inch for clearance.
To stool
To apron
To floor
Top tier
To stool
To apron
To floor
Cafe curtains
Top tier: Measure from the top rod to the desired hem. This tier usually covers the lower rod.
Lower tier: Measure from the lower rod to the stool, apron, or floor. If measuring to the floor, subtract 1 inch for clearance.
A
B
C
Goodheart-Willcox Publisher

Figure 21.35 Different methods are used to measure draperies, curtains, and café curtains.

Approximately once per month, vacuum draperies with a soft brush attachment to remove dust and dirt. Most draperies—especially pleated draperies—require professional dry cleaning. You can wash draperies only when labeled *washable* by the manufacturer, following their specific directions for hand- or machine-washing.

Be sure to read the laundering instructions provided by the manufacturer before laundering curtains. Many curtains can be machine-washed using cold water, a mild detergent, and a gentle machine cycle. Dry according to directions—either tumble dry on low heat or line dry.

Shades, Shutters, and Blinds

Shades block unwanted light, such as intense sunlight in the afternoon or streetlight at night. They are simple to operate and can cover all or part of a window. Shades vary in appearance to go with almost any décor. The fabric and other materials used in their construction affect the amount of light control, insulation, and privacy they provide.

- *Roller shades* are typically made of a vinyl material and roll over a rod to be easily raised and lowered. These shades come in various colors. They also come in various degrees of opaqueness. Many people commonly use these shades in informal rooms.
- *Roman shades* are fabric window treatments that stack into horizontal pleats when they are raised, but hang flat when closed. Installation of most Roman shades is generally within the window molding. Depending on the fabric choice, they can adapt to many design styles.
- *Balloon shades* are also of fabric construction and form soft poufs along the bottom, Figure 21.36.

Calico Corners—Calico Home Stores

Figure 21.36 The weight of fabric selected for balloon shades determines the amount of sun control, insulation, and privacy.

These shades are similar in operation to Roman shades. They received their name from the balloon shape they take when they are raised. Balloon shades are also very adaptable to different design styles depending on the choice of fabric and pattern.

- *Pleated shades* are very popular in today's market. Manufacturers use synthetic materials to construct them, and they are available in accordion or honeycomb styles. Like Roman and balloon shades, pleated shades are raised and lowered with a cord. They are available in many solid colors, patterns, and textures. They may be opaque or translucent. The honeycomb style shades offer excellent insulation qualities due to an insulating channel of air between the shade layers. They work extremely well in Contemporary settings.

Because some window treatments block air movement, you cannot use them on windows that provide ventilation. Shutters are appropriate choices for these windows. **Shutters** are vertical panels that are hinged together to open and close much like a folding door. They are constructed of wood or synthetic materials. Within the frames of the vertical panels are movable horizontal slats or louvers. The louvers are adjustable to allow sunlight control, ventilation, and privacy. The width of wooden louvers in shutters may vary from 1½ to 4½ inches. They adapt well to both formal and informal room settings.

Blinds are window treatments with slats that can be tilted, raised and lowered, or moved to the side. They are often made of wood, metal, plastic, or fabric. Blinds can be custom-made to fit windows with unusual shapes or placements (Figure 21.37). There are three basic styles of blinds:

- *Miniblinds* are horizontal blinds with narrow 1-inch slats. They operate exactly like other horizontal blinds in regard to raising and lowering and adjusting the slats. They also are most often used in informal rooms.
- *Horizontal blinds*, or venetian blinds, can be raised completely to uncover a window. Adjustments to the angle of the slats help control the amount of air and light entering the room. The slat widths vary from 2 inches to 3 inches. Horizontal blinds appear most often in informal settings.
- *Vertical blinds* have slats that move to one side to uncover a window. The slats are generally 4 inches wide and vary in length. To control the amounts of air and light that enter a room, the angle of the slats can be adjusted. Usage of vertical blinds is more common in Contemporary designs.

Caring for Blinds and Shades

Although some blinds and shades are made from materials that repel dust and dirt, regular cleaning keeps them looking good and wearing well. Regular dusting with a soft cloth or gentle vacuuming with a soft brush attachment is essential for keeping blinds and shades clean. You can spot clean blinds and shades with a soft cloth or sponge that you lightly moisten with warm water. When wiping blinds, be sure to wipe the top side and underside of the slats. Use cleaning solutions as recommended by the manufacturer. Some fabric shades require professional cleaning.

A Nicolaas Weber/Shutterstock.com B © istock.com/MaximShebeko C Kevin-Hsieh/Shutterstock.com

Figure 21.37 By adjusting these miniblinds, a person enjoying this space can have privacy or a wonderful view of the neighborhood (A). The wooden blinds installed in these windows are a complement to the masculine feeling of the room (B). These custom vertical blinds provide an excellent treatment for patio doors and floor-to-ceiling windows (C).

Decorative Window-Top Treatments

Decorative window-top treatments easily combine with draperies, curtains, shades, shutters, or blinds to add interest to the window installation. Such decorative top treatments include the following:

- **Swag.** A *swag* treatment has softly pleated fabric hanging in a curve across the top of the window.
- **Valance.** A *valance* is a horizontal treatment across the top of the window. It can hide the drapery or curtain hardware. The many styles of valances depend on the cut and construction of the fabric, the degree of gathering, and the installation hardware used. (Refer again to Figure 21.33.)
- **Cornice.** A *cornice* is also a horizontal treatment that is usually constructed of wood. The wood is then padded and covered with fabric. Some formal cornices may actually be wood that has been carved in an attractive design. Other more informal cornices may have been painted or stenciled with a design.
- **Lambrequin.** The construction of a *lambrequin* follows the same manner as a cornice, but also extends down the left and right sides of the window.

Decorative window-top treatments may use matching or complementary fabrics and designs to add interest to the treatment. Also, using such trims as decorative braid, tassels, and cording can add a custom touch. Depending on the fabric choices, you can use these top treatments in many different room styles.

STEM Math Measurements for Shades and Blinds

Many styles of non-drapery shades and blinds are available to enhance the look of windows, block light, and provide privacy and insulating qualities. There are two ways to install shades and blinds: inside the window frame or over the window frame and trim.

If you are ordering shades or blinds for more than one window, number or letter the windows on a room or area sketch to make sure each window gets the appropriate shade or blind. When writing measurements for shades and blinds, *always* note the width measurement first and the length measurement second to avoid confusion about how to install these window treatments.

Inside Mount. Measurements for mounting shades and blinds inside the window frame require absolute precision. Use the following steps to take inside-mount measurements:

Step 1: Measure the window width inside the window frame from left to right. Take three width measurements from the top, middle, and bottom of the window. Use the narrowest measurement for the width of inside-mount shades and blinds.

Step 2: Measure the length (or drop) of the window from the top of the frame to the stool on the left and right sides of the window and the middle. If the client does not want the shade or blind to touch the stool, subtract ¼ inch from your length measurement.

Outside Mount. Mounting shades and blinds outside the window trim offers greater privacy and light-blocking properties especially for bedrooms. Use the following steps for taking outside-mount measurements:

Step 1: Measure the window width from the outside edge of the trim on the left to the outside edge of the trim on the right along the top of the window. Add 3 or more inches to the width measurement on each side of the window for adequate coverage.

Step 2: Measure from a point at least 2 inches above the top of the window trim to the appropriate length (or drop) below the window apron. The 2-inch space above the window trim allows room for the mounting brackets.

Math Practice

Select one window to measure at home. Create a hand sketch of the window. Use the inside-mount measuring steps to measure the space needed for shades and blinds. Record the length and width on your window sketch.

Review & Assessment

1. Contrast draperies and curtains.
2. Why are shutters and blinds appropriate for windows that are used for ventilation?
3. Identify and describe two decorative window-top treatments.

Protecting Consumers

Buying furniture is a big investment. Selecting window treatments can also be costly. To help protect the investment, the government has agencies that protect consumers. The Federal Trade Commission (FTC) monitors advertising for truthfulness, while the Consumer Product Safety Commission (CPSC) oversees product safety.

In addition, federal laws also provide consumer protection. The Flammable Fabrics Act prohibits the sale of highly flammable fabrics for apparel and home furnishings. The Textile Fiber Products Identification Act requires a listing of fibers in their order of predominance by weight. It also requires generic names of fibers to appear on labels of all textile products, such as upholstery, carpets, and draperies.

Some fiber producers, fabric manufacturers, and furniture companies set their own high standards to surpass government requirements and industry standards. These companies guarantee the durability and performance of their products after consumers buy them. Information about guarantees and superior-quality materials appear on furniture labels. It is the consumer's responsibility to read the labels before buying any furnishings to know what to expect from the product.

Review & Assessment

1. Identify two government agencies that protect consumer interests when buying furniture, and briefly explain what each does.
2. Identify two laws that provide consumer protection against textile products.
3. True or false? Furniture companies never set their own standards to surpass government standards.

Chapter 21 Assessment

Summary

- Furniture styles are always changing. Many styles link to a certain country or historical period.
- Traditional designs are styles with enduring qualities that make them popular yet today.
- Characteristics of twentieth century furniture styles, or Modern styles, are in opposition to Traditional styles.
- Current furniture styles include Contemporary, Traditional, Casual, Transitional, Country, and Eclectic.
- Understanding furniture construction and materials can help you evaluate the selection, use, and care of quality furniture.
- Plastic, metal, rattan, wicker, and glass are other materials used to make furniture.
- There are a variety of window treatments available, including draperies, curtains, shades, shutters, blinds, and decorative window-top treatments. All can be made from a variety of fabrics and materials.
- Government agencies and federal laws concerning consumer goods and textiles protect the consumer's furniture investment.

Terms in Action

1. **Chapter summary** Write a brief chapter summary to someone who is interested in working in the furniture industry, either as a manufacturer, interior designer, or upholsterer. In your summary, include the aesthetic and functional aspects of furniture (including for special needs) and include each *Content Term* listed in this chapter.

Think Critically

2. **Draw conclusions** Select and research a historical period of furniture design. Draw conclusions about how social, economical, political, technological, and artistic trends of the era influenced the furniture design. Include illustrations of furniture design characteristics that distinguish this furniture design from the characteristics of other period styles throughout history. Apply your oral communication skills concisely and convincingly to explain your actions (choices) in a socially acceptable manner that is easily understood by others.
3. **Analyze upholstery** Different pieces of furniture require different considerations when selecting upholstery fabric that impacts care, aesthetic, and functional aspects including ergonomics and special needs. Analyze the guidelines to follow in selecting fabric for a family room sofa for an active family with small children. How might the guidelines change for a retired couple who is selecting new sofa fabric for a formal living room that is functional and meets their aesthetic and special needs? If possible, obtain samples of fabrics that you would recommend for each setting. Defend your analysis with the class.
4. **Evaluate window treatments** Imagine you have just signed a lease for an apartment on the third floor of a five-story building, across a noisy street from a same-size apartment building. All your windows face the street. Evaluate the selection of types, use, and care of suitable window treatments you would choose and prioritize a buying plan. Your new apartment has the following windows: bedroom—large double-hung window; bathroom—small awning window; kitchen—jalousie window over the sink; and living room—sliding patio doors leading to a balcony.
5. **Identify characteristics** Take a field trip to a store that sells antique furniture or reproductions of antique furniture. With the help of a salesperson, distinguish as many different historical period styles by their characteristics as you can. Note the types of furniture, the countries of origin or association, and the characteristics the furniture possesses of a specific historical period. What influence have these period styles had on interior design throughout history? After your trip, answer the following: How can understanding the availability, characteristics, and popularity of certain antiques and reproductions benefit you in an interior design career?
6. **Finish comparison** Visit a building supply store and examine the selection of wood stain available. Look for a display that shows the application of the same color stain to different types of wood.

Chapter 21 Assessment

How do finishes, such as a polyurethane sealer or wax, cause differences in appearance? Note all variations in appearance. What factors influence the differences in appearance? What factors influence the care of quality furniture? Share your findings with the class.

Core Skills

7. **Research and speaking** Select one of the furniture styles shown in Figure 21.1 and investigate its origin. Where was the style originally crafted and used? What local materials were used? Point out the identifying design features in a presentation to the class.
8. **Writing** Write an article for a consumer website summarizing the care of quality furniture for residential and nonresidential settings. Use text and reliable online resources and present your article to the class for peer review.
9. **Listening and reading** With a classmate, interview a furniture salesperson about the details of furniture construction in the products he or she sells. Check the labels on three items. What consumer information do the labels offer?
10. **Writing** Suppose you have an interior design client who wants you to design his family room based on a photo of an Arts and Crafts period bookcase. You feel it is your responsibility to give your client as much information about this style as possible, including aesthetics and functional aspects of the furniture, before committing to a design plan. Research information about the Arts and Crafts movement to share with your client. Locate photos to help illustrate the information you find. Then use desktop-publishing software to create an illustrated report for your client.
11. **Research and speaking** Research the Federal Trade Commission website to identify laws and label requirements that protect consumers when buying a mattress. What do the various label colors mean? Give an illustrated report of your findings to the class.
12. **Technology** Use the text and online resources to research the impact of technology on furniture, including current trends. Based on your research, describe the impact of technology on furniture, including trends. Write a blog about your findings to post to the class web page.
13. **Career and readiness practice** The ability to read and interpret information is an important workplace skill. Presume you work for a furniture company that would like to add an environmentally-friendly upholstered chair to its product line. They have asked you to evaluate and interpret some research on trends for environmentally friendly and sustainable materials. Locate three reliable sources of information on this topic. Read and interpret the information and write a report summarizing your findings in an organized manner.

Design Practice

14. **CADD furniture design** Use a school-provided CADD furniture-design software program to design and draw a unique chair. Your chair design should display good functional aspects, including ergonomics, aesthetics, and quality construction. Determine the material you will use for this chair. If you choose to use wood, identify whether you will use a hardwood or softwood, solid versus bonded wood, and the type of wood finish. Show details about the wood joints used in the chair. Share your design plan with the class.
15. **Future furniture design** Imagine it is the year 2050, and you are designing furniture for use in a home. Will the furniture be completely different from anything ever designed before, or will it have design features from earlier eras. How will current trends and technology influence the furniture? Then use CADD software to sketch different pieces of furniture for this future period. Share your designs with the class. How are they relevant for future lifestyles?
16. **Portfolio** Locate pictures of different furniture styles for residential and nonresidential use. Create two storyboards—one for residential and one for nonresidential—showing a chronological timetable of the furniture styles throughout history. Organize them by date and country of origin. Note how these styles influenced interior design throughout history. Save your storyboard in your portfolio for future reference.

Chapter 22

Selection of Furnishings, Accessories, and Art

Content Terms

ergonomics
comparison shopping
loss leader
seasonal sale
closeout sale
accessories
multipurpose furniture
unassembled furniture

Academic Terms

prioritize
fad
entice
utilitarian
repurpose
recycle
restore
renew

Learning Outcomes

After studying this chapter, you will be able to

- summarize how to select quality, appropriate furnishings.
- identify types of accessories and criteria for selecting accessories.
- analyze guidelines for the use, placement, and care of accessories.
- summarize guidelines for selecting and placing of mass-produced and fine art.
- determine ways to stretch available furnishings dollars.
- understand opportunities for recycling, restoring, and repurposing furniture, accessories, and art.

Reading with Purpose

After reading each passage (separated by main headings), stop and write a four-sentence summary of what you just read. Be sure to paraphrase using your own words.

While studying, look for the access icon  **to:**

- **Practice** the *Content* and *Academic Terms* with e-flash cards, matching activities, and vocabulary games.
- **Reinforce** what you learn by completing the *Review & Assessment* questions and e-mailing them to your instructor.

www.g-wlearning.com/housing/

Volt Collection/Shutterstock.com

In the previous chapter, you learned about furniture styles and ways to identify quality in construction and materials. This chapter explores the next steps in furnishing a home—selecting furniture, accessories, and art. It will also help you or a client get the most from your budget and consider environmental options for furniture, accessories, and art.

Selecting Furniture

In Chapter 18, we discussed the importance of documenting what is needed and not needed within a space. This documentation is done by creating a home inventory. An inventory helps you or your client understand what furniture needs to be accommodated in the new space (Figure 22.1). This includes determining what furniture pieces need to be restored or removed, what pieces need to be replaced, and what new types of pieces need to be purchased.

Once you know how much space is available and the plans for using it, you can begin selecting furniture. This process involves several steps. These steps include

- prioritizing furniture needs
- determining how much to spend
- identifying lifestyle needs
- identifying furniture style preferences
- determining design preferences
- deciding where and how to shop
- choosing when to shop

By following these steps, you can approach the furniture selection process in an organized manner. Such organization will help make the experience both time-efficient and enjoyable.

Prioritizing Furniture Needs

Even after considering the reuse of or restoration of existing furniture pieces, few people can afford to buy all the furniture they need at once. Consequently, the first step in selecting furniture is prioritizing furniture needs. To ***prioritize*** means to rank goals in order of importance. This means deciding which pieces are first on the priority list, such as furniture for sleeping, eating, seating, working, and storage. It is important to purchase priority items first. When the budget allows, buy the furniture used less often and accessories that accent the large furniture pieces.

When selecting home office furniture, allow enough space for a continuous counter plus adequate cabinet and file storage. Most importantly, select a desk chair with *ergonomic* design. **Ergonomics** involves the design of consumer products and environments to promote user comfort, efficiency, and safety. For example, an ergonomically designed chair has a tilting chair back and adjustable seat height and arm rests. These features take the strain off your muscles when you work at a desk or computer.

A Pattie Steib/Shutterstock.com

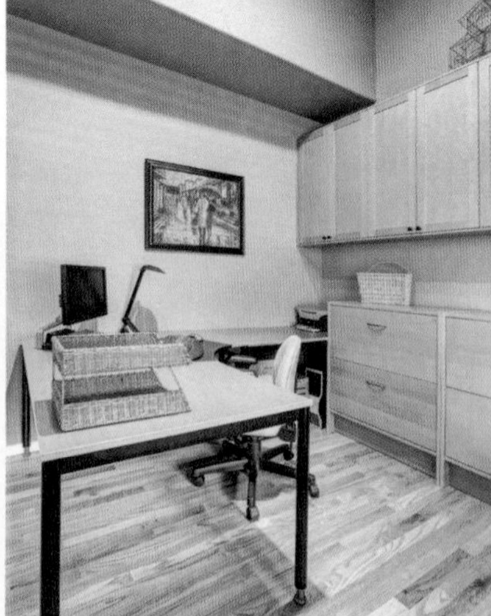

B Iriana Shiyan/Shutterstock.com

C Naphat_Jorjee/Shutterstock.com

Figure 22.1 Home inventories reveal that home owners request a formal home office less frequently today than in the past. This type of environment does not function well for other purposes, such as a play area (A). More often, clients will expect a functional office space with significant storage and layout space (B) or no designated space at all (C), due to the prevalence of laptops and other mobile devices.

Discuss furniture priorities with all household members and ask for their input. This will allow you to make decisions that satisfy everyone. Listing all ideas on paper will help prevent misunderstandings and make the priorities clear.

Determining How Much to Spend

After prioritizing furniture needs, the next step is deciding how much money to spend. Identifying a specific dollar amount will clarify how many items on your list you can afford. All members of the household should express their views on this decision.

As with other projects, the first step is to develop a preliminary budget (Figure 22.2). Then, at a later date, create a final budget that includes actual costs and additional details. As discussed earlier, these budgets identify a number of categories to determine in considering a project.

Smart shoppers buy the best merchandise for the best price. Sometimes, however, trade-offs are made. For example, spending more money for a kitchen table than budgeted will require adjusting the spending plan. This may require cuts in other areas, which may mean waiting longer than planned until making the next purchase, or eliminating one or more items from the list (Figure 22.3).

Identifying Lifestyle Needs

Choose furniture that fits the household lifestyle. Consider the following when making furniture selections to fit lifestyle needs:

- **Family.** Consider the size or projected size of the family. If a person is single, are there plans to marry in the near future? Do young married couples plan to have children? If so, furniture selections must be durable and withstand wear.

Preliminary Furnishings and Accessories Budget

Presume your clients want you to redesign the great room of their kitchen. The room dimensions are 18 ft. wide, 24 ft. long, and 8 ft. high. This room is a place where the family gathers to relax, watch movies, and play games. They plan to keep their traditional sectional sofa, but want it reupholstered. Your clients know they need additional seating, lighting, window treatments, and accessories. Here is the preliminary budget you have developed for this project.

Item/Product	Quantity	Style/Color	Estimated Cost	Notes
Chairs	2	Fully upholstered matching club chairs, taupe multi-linen weave	$3,800.00	
End Tables	2	Two-tier classic end table with center drawer, premium black walnut finish, and small gallery and castors in tarnished silver finish: 21w × 24d × 26h	$1,100.00	
Coffee Table	1	42 in. square glass top with tarnished silver finish metal frame, tapered legs	$1,000.00	
Table Lamps	2	30 in. round ceramic, ivory with brown wood base; ivory silk shades with brown linen trim	$700.00	
Freight			$40.00	Freight is for custom order of lamps
Recessed Ceiling Lights	6	4 in. halogen bulb, white baffle	$450.00	Ceiling is prepared to receive housing; electrical conduit in place for connection
Installation			$450.00	

Figure 22.2 Creating a preliminary budget can help you manage your furnishing expenses.

Green Choices

Green Furniture

Although many green products are in the marketplace, shoppers and professionals now have the opportunity to buy "green" furniture. Of course, this does not refer to the furniture's color, but to its materials and construction practices. Look for furniture on the market that has a label or seal that includes the following green items:

- certified sustainable wood frames (produced from wood secured from forests using environmentally sound methods)
- water-based finishes (versus the finishes that cause harm in the atmosphere)
- soybean cushions (versus foam)
- organic and natural fibers
- company's mission to plant a tree for each purchased furniture piece

Iriana Shiyan/Shutterstock.com

Iriana Shiyan/Shutterstock.com

MR. INTERIOR/Shutterstock.com

romakoma/Shutterstock.com

Figure 22.3 Starting with basic, neutral furnishings allows the client to buy very few pieces. Customize the room with rich color through the use of accessories, paint, and art. If the furniture is well maintained, using colors and accessories is also an easy and economical way to rejuvenate the design over the years.

- **Health.** Does a family member have special health considerations or challenges that impact family lifestyle? Such conditions may require purchasing certain materials, fabrics, or finishes. For instance, if a family member has joint issues, well-made chairs and sofas with arms will make sitting and standing easier. Also, a home that must accommodate a wheelchair may require the specification of slimmer, more space-saving furniture and accessories.

- **Pets.** Are pets a part of the household? An emphasis on durability and space allocation for pet beds and feeding dishes are also requirements.
- **Entertainment.** What type of entertaining do household members usually do: formal, informal, or both? If a household does not entertain with formal meals very often, having a formal dining room set is likely a waste of money and space. Furniture has little value if it is not used.
- **Relocation.** Does one or more household members have careers that may subject them to transfers and moves? If so, it is necessary to make furniture selections that are adaptable to many spaces.

Determining Design Preferences

When identifying design preferences, apply the design information studied in earlier chapters. Browse through interior design magazines and assemble picture files of fabrics, wall coverings, accessories, and other items of interest and assess aesthetic aspects. Do the same on popular social media and design sites by marking folders or boards for these categories. Make a list of favorite colors, go to a paint store and select sample color chips, or obtain a paint fan deck from a favorite paint supplier. What materials, patterns, and textures do you and others find appealing? Examining and gathering samples of fabrics and wall coverings can give you a sense of your own personal design preferences (Figure 22.4). Understanding your own preferences will also help you understand the preferences of others.

Become familiar with interior design and decorating trends. This will help you spot a ***fad***, or a style that is popular only for a limited amount of time. Certain trends have a lasting appeal, but fads do not. Think about how long certain selections will remain enjoyable. Furniture and design selections can be costly. Most people are not able to replace these selections with the same frequency as they would buy new clothes. Accessories like bathroom textiles and sofa pillows are less expensive to replace than furniture, so using bold or trendy colors with these items is more economical. Gathering input from all household members is important to ensure the design will be one that everyone enjoys.

Sociocultural Connections — What Is Feng Shui?

Feng shui [fuhng SHWAY] is a Chinese art and philosophy that began over 8,000 years ago and spread throughout Asia. The words literally mean *wind* and *water*. Millions of people use feng shui in their everyday lives with the belief that it helps bring harmony, happiness, and balance to their surroundings. Practitioners also believe it involves qi [CHEE], a kind of energy that can affect the quality of life. As part of the philosophy, certain colors, materials, and designs encourage greater harmony and balance to those who enter a building and the people within.

Some aspects of feng shui, particularly the feng shui of furniture arrangement, have caught on in the West. Here are a few examples that show how this art may be used in the home:

- Place the bed so the door is visible without directly facing the door. If the bed directly aligns with the door, it is thought that the flow of qi may disturb sleep.
- Place an even number of chairs around a dining table to promote good luck.
- Make the front entry door inviting and accessible to visitors.
- Arrange the kitchen so that the cook can see everyone who enters.

Many retailers sell feng shui books and decorative items. Some colleges offer feng shui classes. A few U.S. corporations hire feng shui consultants to plan the construction and interior décor of buildings and resorts. Many people market themselves as experts, but consumers should be skeptical.

Dig Deeper

Further explore how feng shui is used in the United States and around the world to determine how this design philosophy influences interior design. Create a digital poster showing pictorial examples of the use of feng shui in interior design. Be sure to document your image sources. Use a school-approved web application to share your digital poster on the class website.

severija/Shutterstock.com

Figure 22.4 Creating a collection of inspirational items is a great way to gain a sense of personal design preferences. Sources of inspiration could be photos or items representing colors, textures, patterns, and shapes.

Identifying Furniture Style Preferences

Determine which types of furniture styles you prefer or your client prefers. To begin, review the twenty-first century furniture styles discussed in Chapter 21. Design magazines, store advertisements, and furniture brochures are other sources of style information. In addition, you can look at product catalogs of name brand furniture online. It is often helpful to compile a notebook of pictures showing examples of furniture that you consider attractive. Are you most comfortable with Casual, Contemporary, Country, Traditional, Transitional, or Eclectic styles? Keep in mind that good design is timeless. The newest styles do not necessarily convey good design.

Deciding Where and How to Shop

Many different types of stores sell furniture and accessories. Generally, the more services a store provides, the higher the prices are. Before buying, doing some comparison shopping can save money. **Comparison shopping** means comparing the qualities, prices, and services linked to similar items in different stores. You can save time and energy by checking prices online.

Retail Stores

Retail stores, such as department or furniture stores, offer the most services to customers. For example, retail stores typically will deliver, unpack, and set up the merchandise in a customer's home. However, the prices are usually higher to pay for these services. Some stores provide interior design and decorating services. Design professionals do scale floor plans, evaluate a customer's home, show a wide selection of furniture, and take custom orders. Most furniture retailers require placement of custom-furniture orders one to three months in advance.

Shop at retail stores which provide reliable service for furniture. Select furniture from manufacturers with good reputations. A good store will back up the merchandise it sells, and the manufacturer will replace defective products (Figure 22.5).

Furniture stores usually have a larger selection of furniture than department stores. Both types of stores can order furniture they do not have in stock. Allow extra delivery time for custom furniture.

Some retail stores offer their products at discounted prices. To give discounts, these stores

T.W. van Urk/Shutterstock.com

Figure 22.5 Research a furniture company's reputation before selecting furniture from that company. Companies with a history of good customer service, a plentiful selection, the ability to customize furniture, and quality furniture construction will be worth the investment.

may offer less service. You may need to wait for assistance in the store or for delivery of your purchase. Delivery services for larger items may be unavailable, or available only for an extra charge. If you find a problem with the product, service may be limited. If you are willing to forego convenience for lower prices, you may be able to find bargains at these stores.

Warehouse Showrooms

Generally, showrooms handle only a few brands of merchandise. In addition to brand names, they may also sell off-brands. With ready-made furniture, you will have fewer fabric choices. The advantages of shopping in warehouse showrooms are savings and quick service. You can take the item with you or have it delivered in a few days.

Online and Catalog Shopping

Catalogs let you shop by mail from any location. By shopping from catalogs or online, you can shop, purchase, and order furniture without ever leaving home. You can find store-brand merchandise as well as name-brand merchandise. Some online shopping and catalog sources may give you access to closeout items that have lower prices.

The main disadvantage of online and catalog shopping is inability to inspect the furniture for quality or comfort. In addition, the actual color of the wood and upholstery may look quite different from its picture. Before ordering, request actual fabric samples and finishes for inspection. You can also order furnishings online from retailers who also have physical stores. This allows you to test the comfort and view the finishes and then order online for convenience and price.

Additionally, it is important to research the supplier's reputation. What is the return policy and how helpful is the customer service department? Since the items require shipping, damage could occur in transit. If damage occurs, what is the company's responsibility and what is the customer's responsibility? Also, keep in mind that shipping fees will add to the cost of the product (Figure 22.6).

Other Furniture Sources

Salvage stores, garage sales, auctions, and flea markets can provide great bargains if you have time to shop carefully. Some items may need repairs or refinishing. You can decide whether a price is low enough to make fix-up and freshen-up efforts worthwhile.

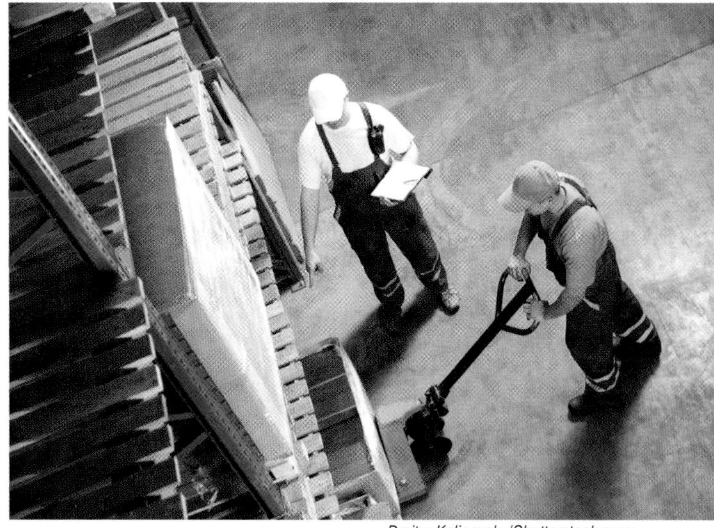

Dmitry Kalinovsky/Shutterstock.com

Figure 22.6 Make sure to check a company's return policy before ordering products. Many companies charge a restocking fee, often 25 percent of the purchase price, to account for the time and labor involved in returning merchandise and preparing it for resale.

Deciding When to Shop

When to shop is as important as *where* and *how* to shop. If people are hurried, tired, or shopping in crowded conditions, they may not make the best decisions and end up with purchases they do not really want. The choice of a time to shop depends on personal circumstances and desires. Wise consumers budget their time with the same care they budget their money. Some shoppers enjoy doing lots of research and browsing or comparison shopping before they buy. Others recognize what they like and buy it.

Shopping at certain times can save money. Stores sometimes have high-quality furniture on sale. Some sales can significantly lower prices. There are many different types of sales, and understanding each can help consumers spend money more wisely.

Loss-Leader Sales

Loss leaders are items priced well below normal cost to ***entice*** (to attract) people into a store to buy them plus items not on sale. The store management hopes people who come for the sales will also buy several other items that are not on sale. When shopping this kind of sale, buy only those items offered at a good price. For instance, you may find a chair is on sale, but the matching sofa is not.

If you want to buy only the chair, it may be a good bargain. If you want to buy the chair and matching sofa, however, you may be able to get a better deal somewhere else.

Seasonal Sales

Stores hold **seasonal sales** at the end of a selling season to eliminate old stock and make room for new items. For instance, patio furniture is often on sale in August to make room for furniture for college dorm rooms. During seasonal sales, consumers will find many discounts on high-quality products (Figure 22.7).

Closeout Sales

If a store is moving to another location or going out of business, management often holds a **closeout sale**. It is better for the store to sell the merchandise at a low price or even at a loss than to move many heavy goods. It is even more important to sell all the merchandise if the store is closing.

When buying furniture from a company that is going out of business, do not expect any after-sale customer service. Customers generally must deal directly with the product manufacturer if a problem arises.

Sales of Damaged and Discontinued Items

Many stores mark down prices on items with slight damage. Make sure you know where and how bad the damage is. A desk with a surface scratch may be a good bargain if the price is low. If the drawers do not open easily, however, the desk may not be a bargain.

Discontinued items for sale offer high-quality goods at low prices because the seller wants to eliminate items no longer in production. However, once the sale items are gone, you will not be able to purchase matching items. For example, you may find a discontinued wall covering on sale. If there is enough for you to cover a complete area, it is a bargain. If you need more, however, this is not a good bargain.

When shopping at sales, keep in mind the saying, "Let the buyer beware." When prices are below the normal cost of items, there is always a reason. It is up to the buyer to learn why and decide whether the lower price really represents a good value.

Bargain Months for Furnishings		
January	**February**	**March**
Appliances, blankets, carpets and rugs, furniture, home furnishings, housewares, and white goods	Air conditioners, carpets and rugs, curtains and draperies, furniture, home furnishings, housewares, and storm windows	Laundry appliances and storm windows
April	**May**	**June**
Gardening specials	Blankets, carpets and rugs, linens, and TV sets	Building materials, furniture, lumber, and TV sets
July	**August**	**September**
Air conditioners, appliances, carpets and rugs, fabrics, freezers and refrigerators, stereos, white goods	Air conditioners, bedding, carpets and rugs, curtains and draperies, fans, gardening equipment, home furnishings, housewares, summer furniture, and white goods	Appliances, paint, and TVs
October	**November**	**December**
China and silverware	Blankets, housewares, and home improvement supplies	Blankets and housewares

Figure 22.7 Good bargains are often available when people wait for seasonal sales.

Review & Assessment

1. Explain the importance of prioritizing furniture needs.
2. Why should consumers decide on the amount of money to spend for furniture before shopping begins?
3. Summarize a lifestyle need that may impact how to select appropriate furniture.
4. List three places to shop for furniture and give one advantage of each.
5. Identify possible shopping drawbacks with each of the following types of sales: (A) loss leader; (B) seasonal; (C) closeout; (D) damaged and discontinued items.

Selecting Accessories

Accessories are items smaller than furnishings that accent the design of a room or area. An accessory should have a purpose in the room; it should not just fill a space. Accessories can be decorative or functional. *Decorative accessories* add beauty to a room. Some examples of decorative accessories are plants, floral arrangements, pictures, paintings, sculptures, wall hangings, and figurines. *Functional accessories* accent the room while serving another purpose. They may include such items as pillows, quilts, lamps, mirrors, books, bookends, candles, candlesticks, and clocks. Some accessories serve both purposes.

Whether for a residential or commercial design, it is a common practice to use functional and decorative accessories together. An example of an accessory that is both decorative and functional is a lampshade of a special design.

Accessories often reflect the personalities of those who use the space. They can show a preference for such items as pictures, clocks, antiques, or treasured objects from other countries or cultures. Some items may have sentimental value such as photographs, souvenirs, or trophies. Others may be parts of collections such as rare coins or antique porcelain plates.

Mirrors

Mirrors are an accessory that can accentuate any interior. A simple change of frame, placement, or orientation can give it new life. Just as with art, a mirror's size should be determined based on the size of the wall on which it will be used and the scale of the other furniture pieces and accessories in the room.

A mirror can be functional in many ways including

- assisting in grooming and dressing in a bedroom, bathroom, or foyer
- creating a sense of spaciousness by visually expanding the perceived size of a room, such as a narrow hallway
- bouncing natural or artificial light and increasing the effect of the illumination
- creating, if angled correctly, a line of site toward an obstructed entry to give a feeling of security

Specific care must be taken in the placement of mirrors. Although mirrors can be used to reflect and therefore double the visual impact of a color, piece of art, or accessory, they can also create problems. Since mirrors reflect the opposite angle, a mirror that is visible from a public path of travel may make a private area unpleasantly visible (Figure 22.8).

Green Accessories

Sustainability, recycling, and repurposing are all ways to create a green environment. When trying to accessorize sustainably, try to find out what a material is made of, how it was made, and where it comes from. Make sure the item isn't made of anything endangered, no harmful ingredients were used or created in its production, and minimal waste and fuel were made or used for its transport. The best scenario is usually a handmade product purchased and produced locally.

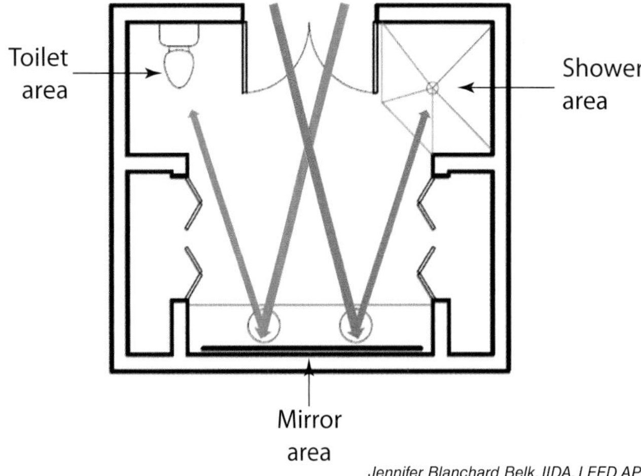

Jennifer Blanchard Belk, IIDA, LEED AP

Figure 22.8 Note the angles of reflection that a passerby might see with these mirror placements.

The following are creative ideas for using green accessories:

- Use old suitcases for extra storage, side tables, and display (Figure 22.9).
- Create new pillows or recover old ones by purchasing scrap fabrics from craft stores. Use a pattern on one side and a solid on the other to increase options for use.
- Lean or mount a ladder against a wall as an inventive display piece or a functional accessory for a bathroom or office.
- Mount functional, secondhand, or unusable musical instruments to a wall to create a unique display in a music room.
- Use salvaged pallets from warehouses and shipping companies to create a variety of accessories and small furniture pieces.
- Use door and cabinet knobs as simple but interesting hooks for coats, purses, and bathrobes.
- Use multiple salvaged doors or shutters and hinge them together to create a room divider for an open floor plan.

Stacy Perzinski

Figure 22.9 These family-owned suitcases were modified and mounted to serve as display shelves.

For some items, all they need is a new finish to look new. Chalkboard paint is an excellent example of how a simple surface finish can repurpose an item to be a functional and decorative accessory.

One of the most creative and fulfilling methods is to use souvenirs from personal family or work-related travels (Figure 22.10). Displaying decorative items or using functional accessories purchased on a trip can be interesting ways of individualizing and giving identity to your environment. These pieces are great conversation starters and purchasing them stimulates the local economies of the places you have visited.

Green Choices

Considerations for Green or Sustainable Products

When developing a design plan for a client, interior designers should ask themselves the following questions when evaluating green or sustainable products:

- Does the manufacturer follow practices to reduce or reuse materials in the manufacturing process, then recycle?
- Is energy efficiency a principle in the manufacturing process?
- Are voluntary testing programs followed?
- To what extent are by-products harmful substances to humans or the environment?
- If raw materials are used, what is the source of the materials?
- Are renewable resources used to make the product?
- Is the product healthy and safe regarding use of any adhesives, coatings, and finishes?
- Does the product perform well?
- To what extent is the safety, health, and well-being of building occupants secured or promoted by using this product?

A Mehmet Cetin/Shutterstock.com
B Angelo Giampiccolo/Shutterstock.com
C clicksahead/Shutterstock.com
D Cococinema/Shutterstock.com
E Curioso/Shutterstock.com
F Carles Navarro/Shutterstock.com

Figure 22.10 An inexpensive and meaningful way to add interest and color into a home is to accessorize using collectibles and souvenirs from an owner's travels or family heritage. Examples might be Greek décor used as a ceiling fan chain (A), an Indian wall hanging (B), ceramics from the Middle East (C), Chinese lanterns (D), pottery from Africa (E), or a South American hammock (F).

Lastly, you may have heard the phrase, "the most environmentally friendly item is one that is never made." This statement implies that repurposing an item is more sustainable than buying a new one. This also means to avoid accessorizing too much. Having a few eye-catching pieces will be much more successful than overwhelming a space and losing emphasis on the important pieces.

Arranging Accessories

Whether an accessory is functional or decorative, it should blend with the style and period of the room (Figure 22.11). Sometimes an accessory may be useful, beautiful, or meaningful to a person, but does not fit the purpose or scheme of the room. At that point, you should ask yourself if it really "belongs." If the item adds a special statement about individuality to the room, you may choose to include it.

If an accessory detracts from the overall room design, consider placing it somewhere else in the home or structure. For example, some people have a personal collection of plaques awarded for excellence in sports. This collection is important, but it may not fit the design of a formal living room. The plaques are more suitable for display in a family or recreation room.

Accessories that are near one another should have something in common. The common factor may be color, texture, style, or purpose. This shared element will help tie the furnishings in a room together. Determine other decisions on the placement and arrangement of accessories by applying the elements and principles of design.

Acquiring Accessories

When acquiring and purchasing accessories, give some thought to the price of the initial investment. Setting priorities about what you (or a client) want and can afford is essential. Select accessories that are both functional and decorative first. Then consider accessories that are versatile and could be used in different rooms and spaces. Later, you may wish to start a collection of accessories based more on their decorative value for a specific space, such as a collection of landscape photographs for use in a study or office.

Also, give consideration to the replacement cost of the accessories. A collection of expensive, fragile, hand-painted figurines is not practical to display within reach of small children. Store such purchases safely out of reach, or postpone the investment until the children are older.

A Petinov Sergey Mihilovich/Shutterstock.com B EmmaAi/Shutterstock.com C StudioSmart/Shutterstock.com D Venus Angel/Shutterstock.com

Figure 22.11 Floor lamps are an example of accessories that are both decorative and functional. The styles shown are Industrial (A), Modern (B), Traditional (C), and Contemporary (D).

Caring for Accessories

In addition to thinking about cost, function, and versatility, think about the maintenance accessories require. For example, a display of silver serving pieces may look lovely on a dining room table. However, you must be certain that you want to dedicate the time it takes to dust, polish, and maintain the silver before purchasing such items. Architectural and decorative lighting fixtures typically need special attention such as regularly cleaning and removing dust shades and bulbs for aesthetics and fire safety. You can clean many accessories with a soft cloth or electrostatic duster. Depending on size and durability, some accessories may be vacuumed with a soft brush attachment. Refer to manufacturer directions when it comes to using special cleaners or polishes to make sure these items will not damage accessory surfaces.

Review & Assessment

1. Explain the difference between functional and decorative accessories.
2. How can a mirror placement be problematic?
3. Why should accessories placed near one another have something in common?
4. Analyze and briefly describe how to care for accessories.

Selecting Art for the Home

Art, a type of accessory, can mean different things to different people. Regardless of individual taste, there are ways to utilize elements and principles to successfully select and display wall art, sculptures, mirrors, ***utilitarian*** pieces (items that are useful or designed for a purpose), and entire collections. When considering a single piece of art, your own love for *and* interest in the piece is the first priority. No matter the framing and placement, a piece that holds sentimental value, is intriguing, or has an interesting story will withstand the test of time in a home. Beyond these factors, consider the value, color scheme, subject matter, framing style, size, and other factors in your decision making.

Purchasing Art

Purchasing mass-produced art (as opposed to fine art prints or originals) can be very similar to purchasing furniture. Before making a purchase, investigate options and the reputations of retailers and understand the guidelines regarding returns.

Art dealers and fine-art retailers typically represent a variety of individual artists, just as furniture showrooms sell only particular manufacturers. To help ensure quality and authenticity of originals or approved reproductions, it is best to buy directly from artists or from authorized art dealers. Know what you are looking for and know the important vocabulary. You will not be able to know if something is an appropriate price if you do not understand the quality or the technique in which it was made.

Auction and estate sales are other options for purchasing art pieces. Estate sales are usually more casual, and it is often difficult or impossible to confirm authenticity of pieces, if that is a concern for you or a client. Auctions are better for those who want more information on the background of the piece or the artist. Be aware, however, of additional charges and fees that are often associated with auction purchases.

With either mass-produced or fine art, know that matting and framing can often cost as much or more than the actual art piece. For this reason, it is important to factor these costs into your overall budget. It is best, when possible, to purchase standard-size pieces so you can then purchase precut mats and standard-size frames. This will be much less expensive than framing for custom sizes. Standard sizes typically include the following sizes:

- 5 × 7 inches
- 8 × 10 inches
- 11 × 14 inches
- 16 × 20 inches
- 18 × 24 inches
- 22 × 28 inches
- 24 × 36 inches

Placing Art

Art and architectural features can work as one. Associating a piece with interior columns, moldings, mantles, and other elements can create an impact in a room much larger than the piece on its own (Figure 22.12). When dealing with art framing and placement, there are a few rules of thumb that will help make any selection successful. Consider the following design elements:

- **Scale.** How large is the piece compared to the wall? Too much wall space will overwhelm a small piece of art (Figure 22.13A).
- **Shape and orientation.** Mixing shapes can be interesting. Mixing orientations between the art and the wall can either cause interest or tension.

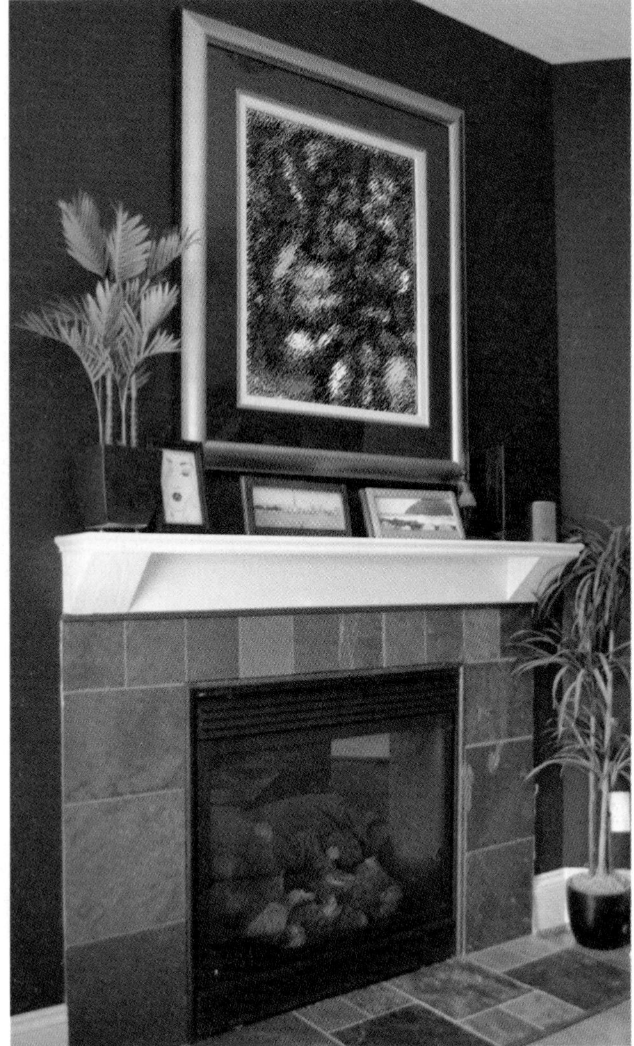

Jennifer Blanchard Belk, IIDA, LEED AP

Figure 22.12 Art over a fireplace is typically seen as a small but important part of an entire composition.

- **Contrast.** Having two adjacent materials that lack contrast makes it difficult to distinguish frame, mat, and wall. Layers of contrasting materials focus the eyes on the art itself (Figure 22.13B).
- **Height.** Depending on the size of the piece, the focal point should be near eye level. For larger pieces or for a series, finding a common horizontal line (like the header of a door frame) can give a good reference line to offer consistency in hanging heights.
- **Balance.** Earlier, you learned about formal and informal balance. Two identically sized pieces that are similar in tone and subject provide formal balance. This is not always the case, however. You can create informal balance by utilizing complementary accessories in different sizes and placements (Figure 22.14).

Most people are comfortable with centering and hanging a single piece of art. When multiple pieces are involved, however, placement and treatment become more complicated. Keep the following points in mind when arranging multiple pieces of art:

- Consider the grouping and room placement of art pieces based on a common subject or theme. For example, all art in a personal office or study could be vintage photos or drawings related to the owner's profession.
- Identify an owner's preferred style. An owner will most likely have a variety of subjects in art

goodday28/Shutterstock.com

goodday28/Shutterstock.com

Figure 22.13 The scale and orientation of a piece to the wall can affect its success (A). Without the right amount of contrast, this painting gets lost in the dark tone of the frame and mat (B).

Cynthia Taylor

Figure 22.14 Furniture and accessories can be used to create asymmetrical balance within art groupings, even if the art pieces themselves have formal balance.

pieces, but possibly a common art style (Abstract, Expressionism, etc.) or a preferred color palette (Figure 22.15).

- Develop an element that can be used as a bonding feature. Since rectangular pieces are most common, a less common shape, such as a square, might be the common bond between art pieces.
- Consider consistency in frame selections. Frames are available in an unlimited number of finishes and styles. Determining a consistent style, color, or material frame to use consistently will not only unify the pieces in a room, but also make rotating art around a home easier (Figure 22.16).

Cynthia Taylor

Figure 22.15 Although different pieces, these three panels with their similar style and size read as one piece.

Irina Fischer/Shutterstock.com

Figure 22.16 Frames can be many different sizes and shapes, but for continuity, there should be a common color, finish, or style used.

When placing art pieces, understand how the pieces create a composition on their own or lend repetition to elements around them. Internal lines are created when pieces are placed a consistent distance apart and have a balanced or unbalanced axis (Figure 22.17A). An external line, like the angle of a staircase, can be mimicked by creative placement of complementary frames (Figure 22.17B). Lastly, multiple related visuals can be grouped together to create a single basic shape and read as a single piece (Figure 22.17C). When using grouped artwork, assure that the arrangement blends with the furnishings layout and basic design of the space. For example, Figure 22.17D shows a grouping of art that fits well with the chairs and table.

Considering Economic and Environmental Options

Being economical with art is not difficult. Recycling and ***repurposing*** (changing the original use of an object to another use that meets an expanded or new need) is an excellent way to breathe new life into an object. Salvaged elements such as a window sash can be an excellent and appropriate frame for an owner's amateur photography (Figure 22.18).

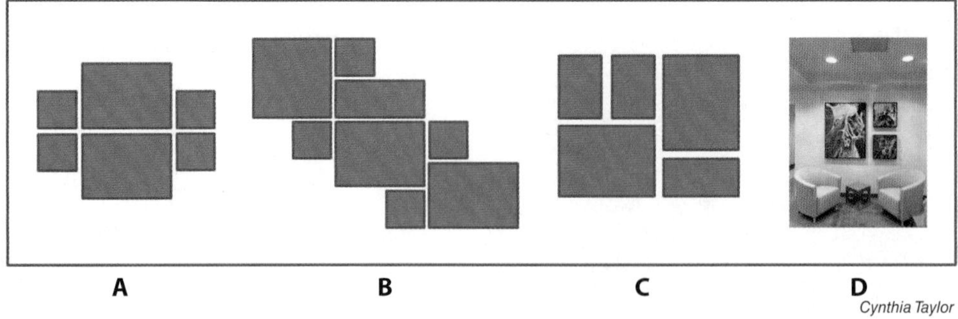

Figure 22.17 Consider not only the composition of the art pieces to the wall and neighboring accessories (A, B, and C), but also the composition of art pieces in a grouping (D).

Figure 22.18 Creative framing techniques can be inexpensive and economical ways of displaying personal photography.

Other economic and environmental ways to populate a home with art include the following:

- Purchase frames in bulk so buying matching frames at a later date isn't a problem. Change the orientation, mat colors, and groupings for variety.
- Have personal photos enlarged or even printed on canvases. A photo on canvas gives an interesting texture to the image and does not need to be framed.
- Frame colorful vinyl record album covers, CD art, poster art, or greeting cards. You can do this in an unlimited number of configurations.
- Visit local high school art shows and purchase original works.
- Buy interesting fabrics and stretch them tightly around tack boards or acoustical panels. This will allow you to arrange displays like bulletin boards, which will also help with noise absorption.
- Visit rummage sales and antiques shows to find interesting items that can be used in alternative ways. Old store signs and metal ceiling panels make intriguing wall hangings.

Review & Assessment

1. Why is it more economical to purchase standard-size art?
2. Which five design elements must be kept in mind when arranging art?
3. Name four examples of creative ways of providing art for a home.

Identifying Information Sources

Before making final furnishings selections, consult various sources for information on items of interest. These sources will provide information on the quality and reliability of the furniture and accessories. They will also help you become familiar with other furnishings that are available. Begin by checking for important information online or at local, reputable furniture and art dealers. Searching for information online is a tremendous opportunity to research and compare products.

Retailers

Retailers rarely carry only their own product lines. Instead they may carry dozens of manufacturers who have similar or complementary styles or costs. This broadens buyer choices (Figure 22.19). Going to retailers and making

Career Focus Visual Merchandising and Exhibit Design

Do you find retail display windows fascinating? Do you ever wonder what it might be like to create the ever-changing and exciting exhibits within stores? If you do, a career as a visual merchandiser might be for you.

fiphoto/Shutterstock.com

Interests/Skills: Creativity and ingenuity are a must for merchandising professionals, who find new ways to display products season to season and use materials in new and inventive ways. Effective organizational skills, attention to detail, and active listening skills are necessary. Strong visual and written and verbal communication skills are also essential to demonstrate problem-solving abilities, visualize a solution, sketch or render perspectives, and work with others. A basic understanding of photography and psychology are also helpful.

Career Snapshot: Visual merchandisers plan displays within retail environments to entice customers. They arrange furniture, merchandise, backdrops, lighting, and signage to best highlight and sell merchandise. Knowledge about methods of sales and marketing as well as a fundamental understanding of design elements and principles are essential. Merchandising professionals may work for a major retailer, working specifically within one store, or they may work for the product line, dealing with the display of those products in stores all over a region. These professionals may also be hired by manufacturers to design booths and showrooms for annual product trade shows and conventions.

Education/Training: A higher education degree is not required, but is helpful for a career in visual merchandising. Having a background as a retail sales associate with experience under a merchandising professional is a great start. Most professionals seek technical education and/or an associate's or bachelor's degree. They may also continue their education in art and design fundamentals, fashion and textiles, interior design, marketing, business strategies, accessible design, and psychology.

Licensing/Examinations: Due to the incredibly vast nature of this segment of the industry, merchandisers have many choices when it comes to voluntary licensing, in addition to the National Council for Interior Design Qualification (NCIDQ). Many professionals also become LEED Accredited Professionals (Leadership in Energy and Environmental Design).

Professional Associations: In addition to more general organizations such as the American Society of Interior Designers (ASID) and the International Interior Design Association (IIDA), other related professional associations include the Exhibit Designers & Producers Association (EDPA), National Association for Retail Marketing Services, Retail Design Institute (RDI), and the Trade Show Exhibitors Association (TSEA). These are national organizations that offer continued education opportunities and exposure to trends and products.

Job Outlook: While the overall professional outlook is very good, designers may also benefit by aligning themselves with high-growth retail goods and manufacturers.

Allied Careers: Allied trades and careers include designers for photo and online retail ads; staging professionals; retail lighting designers; and wayfinding, signage, and graphics professionals.

Sources: The Occupational Outlook Handbook (OOH); the Occupational Information Network (O*NET)

Air Images/Shutterstock.com

Figure 22.19 When shopping retail furniture stores, be aware that many furniture pieces—such as an upholstered sofa—may only come standard in a few neutral colors. Anything different may be considered an upgrade or custom order.

notes of particular furniture manufacturers that occur at multiple retailers is a good way to identity established, reputable lines. Also knowing furniture manufacturers in stores can help identify where there is likely competitive pricing in other stores and online.

Books and Magazines

Home furnishing books and magazines can be great sources of information. Some books and articles tell how to refinish furniture. Some provide ideas on furniture selection and arrangement and many often include money-saving ideas. Others offer great advice for how to accessorize an area. Be careful when considering any printed pricing or availability information, however, because these sources become dated quickly.

Product-Rating Organizations

Consumer Reports is a publication from an organization that tests and rates products. This resource provides information about quality, price, and other factors, such as warranty information. The reports are available as monthly magazines and annual buying guides. You can find these and other product-rating reports online, in a library, or at a bookstore.

Advertisements

Advertisements in newspapers, magazines, radio broadcasts, TV programs, and websites often contain useful information. Use advertisements to compare brand names, features, and prices. It is important to know, however, that what is said in advertisements is only partial information and the details of any deal should be discussed directly with a retailer and documented in writing.

Labels and Seals

Labels on furniture may contain information about the materials used, coverings, fillings, country of manufacture, and origin of style. For example, if the product is made in the United States, the label will state "Danish Style" rather than "Danish." The label may indicate that the materials used are *all new* or *partly made from used materials*. Labels also include care information. Other labels and seals indicate whether furniture is rated green or sustainable.

Better Business Bureau

The *Better Business Bureau (BBB)* is a nonprofit organization sponsored by private businesses. It publishes information on how to shop wisely for products and services. Your local BBB can give you information about stores and businesspeople in the area. The BBB also maintains a record of consumer complaints against local businesses and tries to settle disputes.

Review & Assessment

1. What are five sources of information useful for selecting furniture? Choose one and summarize why it will be useful to you.
2. Why should you be cautious of printed pricing or availability information found in books and magazines?
3. How does the BBB help consumers?

Stretching Your Dollars

Stretching your dollars can help you acquire more furniture and accessories for your money. There are many reasons you may need to do this. You or a client may not have much funding available to spend on furnishings. For example, when you move into your first home, your take-home pay may not cover many furnishing needs.

You may find it necessary to furnish your home with rented or used pieces until you can afford new furniture.

Another reason for stretching your dollar is the likelihood of housing costs increasing as the size of your household increases. Consequently, finding ways to save money on furniture may become more important as you move through the life cycle.

You can stretch your furnishing dollars by doing the following:

- shopping for bargains
- using multipurpose and flexible furniture
- buying unassembled furniture
- reusing old furniture
- creating an eclectic look

Shopping for Bargains

A good way to find furniture bargains is to buy furniture on sale. You can often find bargains at loss-leader sales, seasonal sales, closeout sales, and with sales of damaged or discounted items. No matter how much the item costs on sale, however, it is not a bargain unless you need it and can afford it. Also, the item is not a bargain if you would really prefer something else. A true bargain improves the quality of your life.

Sometimes what seems like a bargain may not be a bargain at all. One item may cost less than a similar item, but it may require more time or effort to acquire or maintain. For instance, a lower-quality floor tile may be less expensive initially, but if it requires more frequent waxing than a slightly higher-quality type, it may be a better investment in the long run to purchase the higher-grade flooring.

Simple furniture may not seem like a bargain, but because of its durability, it usually is. In contrast, complex furniture is often more expensive than simple furniture. Carving, latticework, turnings, and other extras add to the cost of furniture. You can easily update the appearance of furniture with simple lines and colors by changing accessories.

STEM Math Buying Furniture on Credit

The purchase of new furniture can be costly. People who do not have cash often make purchases using credit. Many furniture stores offer financing plans. Customers take furniture home after signing a contract agreeing to make regular payments for a specific period of time or before a certain date. Some stores require that people make a down payment, which is a portion of the purchase price. The down payment amount is subtracted from the total owed.

Buying on credit is more expensive than buying with cash because a finance charge is added. The charge is calculated by the creditor or the lender and consists of interest plus fees. There are several different formulas for calculating a finance charge. It is expressed as a percentage; the higher the percentage, the more costly the credit.

For example, suppose a $500 coffee table is purchased on credit and must be paid in 12 months. The finance charge will vary depending on the percentage. Suppose that interest paid in a year is

$50.08 at 18%

$58.72 at 21%

$67.36 at 24%

At 24 percent, a customer using credit would pay about $67 more for the coffee table than a cash-paying customer. Before you use credit, take time to read the contract carefully and make sure you understand the terms before you sign. A number of groups, including American Consumer Credit Counseling, provide online calculators to help consumers figure the cost of financing.

Math Practice

Suppose the new bedroom set you want is on sale for 40 percent off the original price for a cost of $1,695.00. The credit card interest rate is 16.9%. The credit card company requires a minimum payment of 2% of the total purchase; however, you are able to pay $150.00 per month toward the bill. Use the *Credit Card Interest Calculator* on the American Consumer Credit Counseling website to calculate the cost of financing the sofa. How many months will it take you to pay for the sofa? How much will the total interest cost? What are the pros and cons of buying the sofa with credit?

Using Multipurpose and Flexible Furniture

Multipurpose furniture is furniture that serves more than one purpose. For example, you can use a sofa bed for sitting or sleeping. Flat-topped trunks and chests make usable end tables and coffee tables while functioning as storage pieces. Modular furniture, which is made in separate interchangeable pieces, gives buyers the ability to disassemble and rearrange the furniture for different uses and placement in the future (Figure 22.20).

Unassembled Furniture

Unassembled furniture, which is furniture sold in parts that require assembly, may or may not be finished. It is often a lower quality than most assembled furniture. By assembling furniture yourself, you save money. Since packaging for unassembled furniture is usually very compact, you can save delivery costs by transporting it home yourself.

Reusing Furniture

After acquiring new furniture, you can still reuse your old furniture. This will help you stretch your dollars even further. To reuse your furniture, you can recycle, restore, or renew it.

Recycling Furniture

To ***recycle*** means to adapt to a new use. Recycling furniture means using furniture for a new use after it no longer serves its original purpose. For instance, in a first home, some people may use outdoor furniture in a living room, dining room, or family room. As their budget allows, they replace the outdoor furniture with indoor furniture and then use the outdoor furniture to decorate a patio. Consider recycling furniture pieces in your own home or passing them on to others to use. You can also buy used furniture from other sources to recycle in your home. Good sources of used furniture include garage sales, secondhand stores, and relatives.

Recycling can also mean creatively assembling pieces from items not normally considered furniture (Figure 22.21). For example, bricks and boards easily combine to make bookshelves. Covering a round piece of board with a large circular cloth makes an attractive table. You can also assemble plastic or wooden cubes in a wide variety of ways to create furniture. Combine them

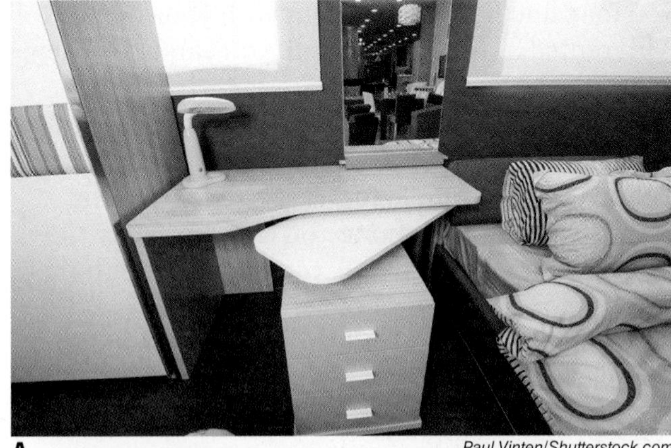

A Paul Vinten/Shutterstock.com

B © iStock.com/ttatty

C Jennifer Blanchard Belk, IIDA, LEED AP

Figure 22.20 With the trends toward downsizing and being environmental, having furniture that serves multiple purposes can conserve space, materials, and money. Typical storage and upholstered pieces can convert into surfaces for writing and dining (A). Furniture such as bookcases can provide storage while also acting as a divider within open-plan environments (B). This custom entertainment center was created so that the three modular pieces can be slid apart, rotated, and rearranged to fit the evolving needs of the owner (C).

jovana veljkovic/Shutterstock.com

Figure 22.21 An economical and sustainable way to furnish a home is to reuse existing materials in new and innovative ways. Much of the furniture in this renovated loft was created from recycled shipping palettes.

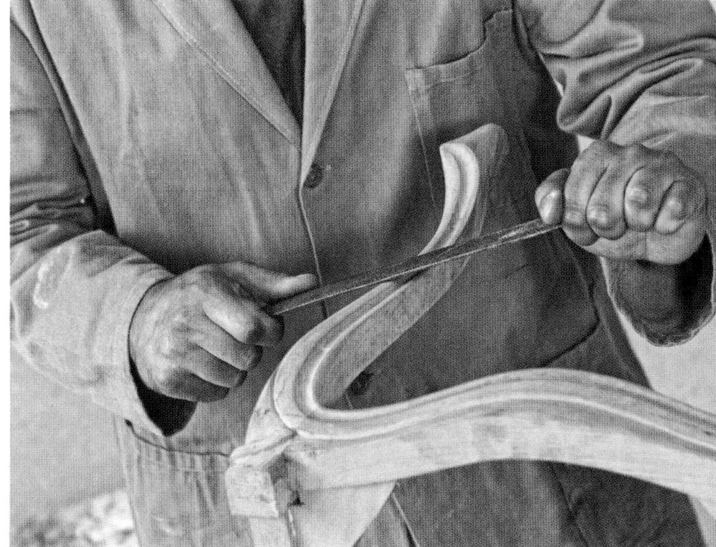

gualtiero boffi/Shutterstock.com

Figure 22.22 Some furniture renovations require the help of a professional.

to create shelves, tables, desks, and seats. Divide some cubes for shelf space or to accommodate drawers. Although plastic cubes come in many colors, you can paint wooden cubes to coordinate your interior design scheme.

Reusing other materials to create furniture is another form of recycling. Look at a material or piece for what it does or is rather than assuming it can only be used for its original purpose. For example, a flat surface can display items, a hollow vessel can hold items, and a small, sturdy item might be used for sitting. Examples of furnishings created from alternative products include

- a bed headboard created from a salvaged fireplace mantle
- a jewelry, flatware, or art supplies storage and organization unit created from an old library card catalog
- a coffee table created from a reclaimed door covered with glass

Renovating Furniture

People often renovate furniture by either restoring or renewing it. It usually costs less to renovate an old piece of quality furniture than to buy low-quality, new furniture. You can choose to renovate furniture yourself or hire a professional (Figure 22.22). If you choose to do it yourself, keep in mind that it takes time, patience, and work. It also takes money for supplies and equipment.

When considering whether to renovate a piece of used furniture, answer the following questions:

- Is it well designed?
- Will it blend well with the other furnishings?
- Is it well constructed and worth repairing?
- Can it be used as is?
- Do you have the time, patience, and energy to do a good job?
- Do you have the necessary equipment and supplies to do the job or the money to buy them?
- Do you have a suitable place to work?

When you ***restore*** a piece of furniture, you return it to its original state as much as possible. There are several steps to restoring a piece of furniture, including repairing, refinishing, and possibly reupholstering. For example, suppose you want to restore an antique chair. Using the following steps will help you effectively complete this task:

1. Remove the paint and sand the finish off the wood furniture's surfaces.
2. Make any necessary repairs, such as redoing, repairing, and reinforcing the joints.
3. Apply a wood finish or paint as close to the original as possible. Seal the finish if necessary.
4. Do any needed reupholstering. Carefully remove the original upholstery fabric and

use it as a pattern for the new upholstery. New filler or padding may be required. For a proper restoration, select an upholstery fabric pattern that is similar in design to the type of fabric original to the piece. The replacement fabric can be secured with an upholstering stapler, tack nails, or something exposed such as decorative brass tacks. Use the securing pieces that are most appropriate and authentic.

This process takes much time and skill. You must have a strong interest in restoring furniture to make it worthwhile.

If a furniture piece is in good condition, but the upholstery or finish is worn or out of date, you can ***renew*** it. To renew furniture means to give it a new look. The steps in this process are similar to those followed in restoration, with one important difference—when you renew furniture, you update it and do not attempt to restore it to its original condition. Based on the fabric and/or paint finish you select, an old piece of furniture can take on a totally different appearance.

Creating an Eclectic Look

Another way to stretch your dollar is to create an eclectic look in your home (Figure 22.23). As you may recall, Eclectic is a design style based on a mixture of furnishings from different periods, styles, and countries. You can use this look while you are acquiring furniture piece by piece, or you can use it on a permanent basis.

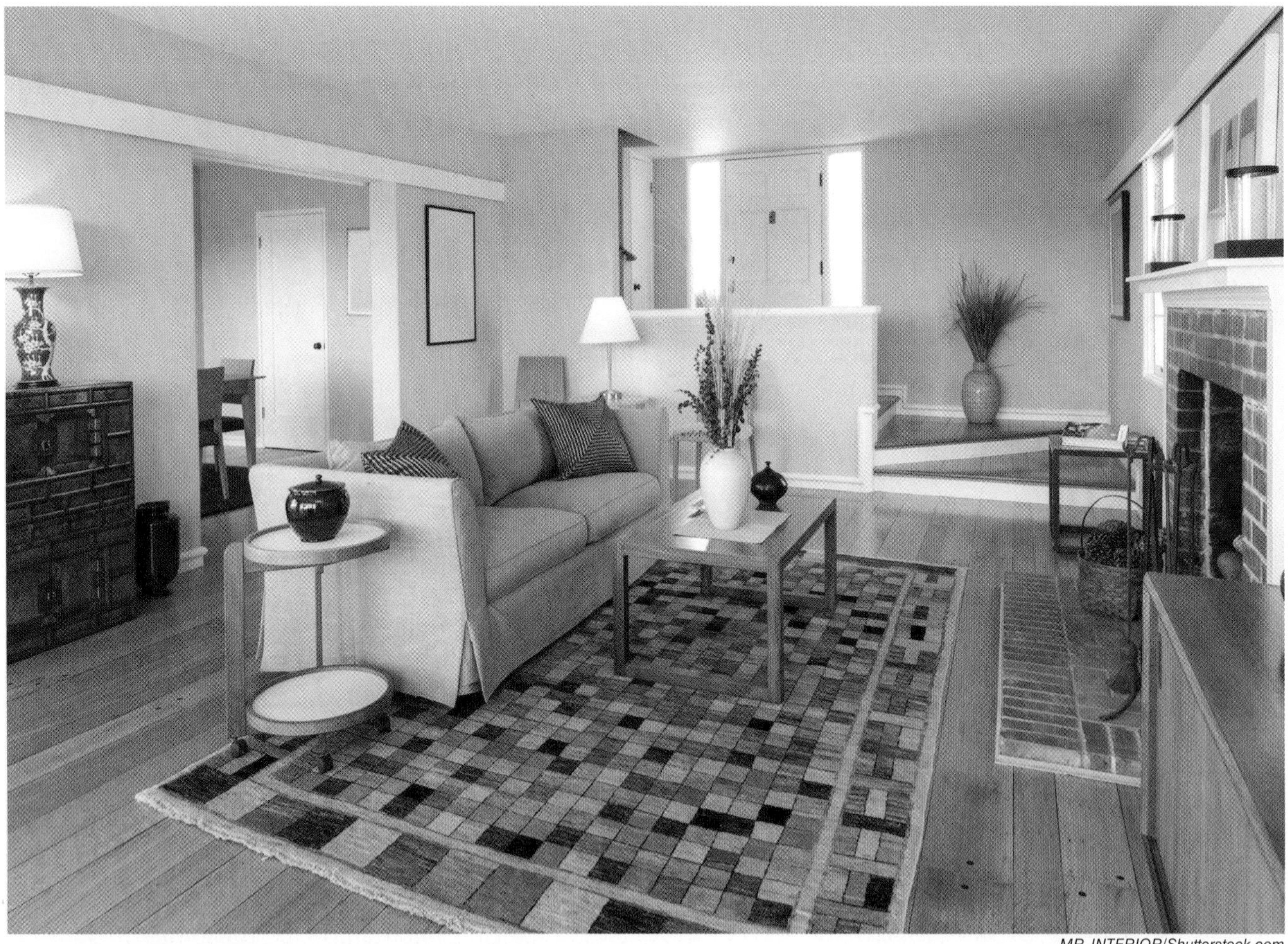

MR. INTERIOR/Shutterstock.com

Figure 22.23 Mixing Traditional and Contemporary furnishings and accessories can create an eclectic look. Using the Eclectic style is also an excellent way to deal with a client's existing collection of furnishings and accessories or the merging of two households.

Final Furniture and Accessories Budget						
Item/Product	**Description**	**Quantity**	**Style/Color**	**Estimated Cost**	**Actual Cost**	**Notes**
Chairs	Club style, fully upholstered, loose seat and back cushions	2	Taupe/multi, cotton/linen	$3,800.00	$4,066.00	Sales tax
End Tables	Classic 2-tiered table, premium finish, with metal gallery and castors 21w × 24d × 26h	2	Premium black walnut finish with tarnished silver metal trim	$1,100.00	$1,177.00	Sales tax
Coffee Table	42 in. square glass top with metal frame	1	Tarnished silver metal frame with tapered legs	$1,000.00	$1,070.00	Sales tax
Table Lamps	30 in. high large round ceramic lamp	2	Ivory ceramic on brown wood base and ivory silk shade w/ brown linen trim	$700.00	$802.50	$750.00 (alternate supplier necessary for exact color) + Sales tax
Freight				$40.00	$42.18	
Recessed Ceiling Lights	4 in. halogen	6	White baffle and trim	$900.00 includes installation	$963.00	Sales tax
Lighting Installation	Direct install; no new circuitry or switching required					

Figure 22.24 Now that you have considered the actual furnishings, review how the scenario from the *Preliminary Furniture and Accessories Budget* (Figure 22.2) changes as selections, specification criteria, and costs become final.

Evaluating Your Budget

Before making the final purchasing decisions on furniture and other home furnishings, the preliminary budget should be adjusted to form the final budget. In the process of selecting furniture and other home furnishings, choices change and dollar amounts can shift, which can affect other decisions. Figure 22.24 shows an example of what a final budget for home furnishings looks like.

Review & Assessment 

1. Name five ways to stretch furnishings dollars.
2. When is renovating a piece of furniture most cost-effective?
3. Contrast restoring furniture with renewing it. When might you do each?
4. Summarize the steps in restoring furniture.
5. Why does the Eclectic design style help people stretch their furnishings dollars?

Chapter 22 Assessment

Summary

- Begin selecting furniture by prioritizing furniture needs. Then decide how much you or your client can afford, the lifestyle, furniture styles and design preferences, and where, when, and how to shop.
- Accessories are part of the design scheme. They can be decorative, functional, or a combination.
- Recycling and repurposing objects as well as highlighting personal items is a low-cost way to furnish and give individuality to a home.
- Shopping for bargains, choosing multipurpose furnishings, or buying furnishings that require finishing or assembly can save money.
- Develop a preliminary budget and then finalize it before purchasing begins to keep spending in line with the project goals.

Terms in Action

1. **Word association** Write each of the *Content* and *Academic Terms* from the beginning of the chapter on a separate note card. For each term, quickly write a word you think relates to the term. In small groups, have each person in the group explain a term on the list. Take turns until all terms have been explained.

Think Critically

2. **Assess aesthetic aspects** Suppose you have a new interior design client. You do not have any information about your client's furniture-style preferences. What approach would you take in assessing your client's aesthetic preferences? What questions might you ask? Write a short paper summarizing your approach to assessing your client's preferences and aesthetic aspects of furniture.
3. **Analyze priorities** A client of yours needs assistance in furnishing a small two-bedroom apartment. The kitchen, dining, and living areas are open to one another. The family has one school-age child who plays soccer for a community team. Your client has beds and dressers, and a limited budget for making furniture and accessory purchases. Assess functional aspects of furniture and accessory items that are priorities for your client. Analyze the care of furniture and accessories. What items are lower on the priority list? Propose a criteria for your client to effectively allocate and control resources for this project.
4. **Recognize value** In what ways can you recognize whether a piece of furniture is a quality piece? Write your response in a one-page paper. Support your response with appropriate examples, summarizing the selection of quality furniture and accessories.

Core Skills

5. **Research and speaking** Compare prices on identical pieces of furniture of the same brand and manufacturer—such as a sofa or dining room table—by visiting two different local stores. Search online to locate sources for the same pieces of furniture, and identify the prices and the shipping costs. Are the prices similar or different? What factors impact price differences or similarities? Which location has the best price? Share your findings with the class.
6. **Research and writing** Visit a local store that sells home accessories. Make a list of the accessories you would buy if you had a budget of $300.00. Consider lifestyle and interests as you make your selections. Would all of these accessories work together in the same room? If not, which rooms would you use them in? Analyze the care these accessories might take. Does the care fit your lifestyle? If your budget was cut to $150.00, which accessories would you eliminate and which would you keep? What factors influenced your decision about these selections? Write a summary.
7. **Writing** You are a reporter for a local news publication. Your assignment is to evaluate sofas and chairs from a manufacturer of your choice. Evaluate the quality of the product construction and materials used in manufacturing. In addition, analyze the care and maintenance methods recommended by the manufacturer and the customer service policies. How can this information benefit consumers and interior designers alike? Write a report summarizing your findings.
8. **Research and speaking** Use online or print resources to investigate how eco-friendly fibers

Chapter 22 Assessment

and fabrics go through the manufacturing process from the farm to the furnishings and accessories in a home. What factors about the growing process make these fabrics *organic* or eco-friendly? What processes do fiber and fabric manufacturers use to create these eco-friendly materials for home use? How do these materials benefit consumers? society? Share an oral summary with the class.

9. **Math practice** Suppose the sectional sofa you want for your new family room design is on sale at a local furniture store. The sofa cost is $1,295.00—a 30 percent savings off the original price, but you have not budgeted for this cost. You decide to use a credit card to make the purchase. The interest rate is 13.9%. The credit card company requires a minimum payment of 2% of the total purchase; however, you are able to pay $100.00 per month toward the bill. Use the *Credit Card Interest Calculator* on the American Consumer Credit Counseling website to calculate the cost of financing the sofa. How many months will it take you to pay for the sofa? How much is the total interest cost? What are the pros and cons of buying the sofa with credit?
10. **Math practice** Create a list of furniture pieces and accessories you need to order for a client's family room that is 12 feet by 14 feet. Keep aesthetics, functionality, ergonomics, trends, and eco-friendliness in mind. Use online resources to locate prices for each item on your list. Use a 20 percent markup with the "cost plus" method for your design fees to calculate the cost of each furniture or accessory piece.
11. **Research and writing** Search for furniture manufacturers that sell furniture online. Locate the customer service policies of the companies on their websites. Identify whether the following questions are answered: (A) How does the company handle returned items? (B) How does the company handle items damaged in shipping? (C) What are the shipping costs? Based on what you find, how would you advise a client who is considering shopping for furniture online? Write a summary of your advice.
12. **Research and writing** Investigate resources for buying furniture online. What options do consumers have? How do costs differ for online buying? How might a consumer determine which online shopping sites are reliable? Summarize your findings on the class website.
13. **CTE career readiness practice** Understanding consumer trends is an important job readiness skill. Because many consumers today desire products that are *green* or *sustainable*, some furniture stores are offering options to meet consumer preferences. Visit one or more furniture stores in your community to investigate the availability of green furniture products, art, and accessories. What options are available? How does technology impact this furniture trend? Interview a sales associate regarding green purchasing trends at the store or in the community. Write a summary of your findings.

Design Practice

14. **Furniture schemes** In previous chapters, you have space-planned and selected finishes for rooms of your design. Select one of these assignments. Using one online retailer, select the room's furnishings and accessories from at least three different manufacturer lines. Coordinate finishes and furniture styles learned in previous chapters. Then create a budget for acquiring these products—including quantity, product descriptions, colors, fabrics and finishes.
15. **Art coordination** Choose three to five individual pieces of art online to purchase for the room selected in the previous activity. Plan and sketch appropriate matting and framing for these art pieces by customizing your CADD screen menus to create your drawings. Finally, key the placement of the art to a copy of the floor plan. Use your written communication skills to effectively, clearly, concisely, and convincingly justify your matting and framing selections in a socially acceptable manner that is easy to understand by others.
16. **Portfolio** Review the floor plans you have created for this chapter. Refine the plans. Then use presentation software to create a design presentation suitable for client review. Save your presentation in your portfolio.

Unit 6

Housing Choices

Take the Lead in Financing Your Future

Although it may be a while before you are ready to rent or buy your own place, it is not too soon to start preparing financially. Through the FCCLA *Financial Fitness* peer education program, plan and carry out a project related to the *Financing Your Future* unit. What do you need to know to become a wise financial manager and a savvy consumer? How can this help you when it is time to rent or buy a place of your own?

Use the FCCLA *Planning Process* and other related documentation to develop, carry out, and evaluate your innovative project. See your adviser for information as needed. Check out the application requirements to receive FCCLA national recognition for outstanding *Financial Fitness* projects.

Building Teamwork Skills by Helping Others

Keeping up with cleaning and home maintenance requires a lot of energy. Some people, including older adults and those with physical challenges, find it difficult to keep up with many home maintenance tasks—especially outdoors. Although some may hire the help they need, many others have limited resources. They may opt to forgo outdoor cleanup and maintenance or rely on the kindness of others for help.

As an FCCLA chapter, use the FCCLA *Planning Process* to organize one or more fall or spring cleanup days for neighborhood citizens in need around your school. Consider preparing a flyer about the service (including a list of items chapter members can do) and distributing it to neighborhood homes. Include a contact phone number to schedule your service days. Be sure to take photos of your work and the people you serve.

Use your fall or spring cleanup project for one of the *Chapter Service* STAR Events—*Chapter Service Project Display* or *Chapter Service Project Manual*. Follow the guidelines for these events in the FCCLA *STAR Events Manual* on the FCCLA website. See your adviser for information as needed.

Khongkit Wiriyachan/Shutterstock.com

Chapter 23
Acquiring Housing

Content Terms

down payment
interest
installment buying
finance charge
security deposit
lease
lessor
lessee
sublet
breach of contract
eviction
equity
foreclosure
gross income
housing-to-income ratio
debt-to-income ratio
credit history
bid
mortgage
amortize
earnest money
agreement of sale
home inspection
appraisal
title
deed

Academic Terms

hedge
contingencies
peril

Learning Outcomes

After studying this chapter, you will be able to

- analyze the advantages and disadvantages of renting and buying housing.
- contrast the impact of needs and wants on housing costs.
- analyze legal and financial aspects related to renting or leasing housing.
- analyze the legal and financial aspects related to purchasing housing.
- summarize the home-buying process.
- contrast buying condominium units with cooperative units.
- compare the different ways to move.

Reading with Purpose

Take two-column notes as you read the chapter. Fold a sheet of paper in half lengthwise. On the left side of the paper, write the main ideas. On the right side, write subtopics and detailed information. After reading the chapter, use your notes to study. Fold the paper in half so you only see the main ideas. Quiz yourself on the subtopics and details.

G-WLEARNING.COM

While studying, look for the access icon  **to:**

- **Practice** the *Content* and *Academic Terms* with e-flash cards, matching activities, and vocabulary games.
- **Reinforce** what you learn by completing the *Review & Assessment* questions and e-mailing them to your instructor.

www.g-wlearning.com/housing/

Hurst Photo/Shutterstock.com

At some point, you will decide how to spend money for housing. You can choose between renting and purchasing a house. You will also decide several other related choices. Your choices will depend on your lifestyle, stage of the life cycle, and other life situations. Finally, you will make decisions regarding the various moving options possible.

Acquiring a Place to Live—Costs and Decisions

People make many decisions in the process of acquiring a place to live. *Process* refers to the method used to accomplish a task. Housing decisions are part of a process beginning with the decision to rent or buy housing, followed by a determination of how to pay for the housing choice and moving. Additional decisions are required later for operating the unit as well as replacing and adapting it through time (Figure 23.1).

In thinking about the process of acquiring housing, can you describe how your family acquired the housing in which you live? Was it purchased or rented? If purchased, was it new or pre-owned? Was the housing built for a previous owner or for your family?

After choosing to either rent or buy, you will make additional decisions in the process about how to operate and maintain the housing. You need to make arrangements to have the water, electricity, and/or gas turned on. You need to arrange to move your belongings to your house. You also need to repair or replace parts of the dwelling from time to time. Repairs may involve something as simple as replacing a worn seal in a leaky water faucet or something as complex as adding a second floor.

You will need to decide how to pay for these housing expenses. You can pay for expenses in the following ways:

- Pay the full amount now with cash, a check, transfer of funds from another account, or by debit card. (A *debit card* is similar to a credit card but immediately releases money from your account when you use it.)
- Postpone payment by using a credit card. (Use caution when using this form of payment.)
- Pay part of the total now, or make a **down payment**, to secure a purchase. You then pay the remainder in regular installments.

Human and Nonhuman Resources

When considering housing costs, it is important to recognize the many factors that affect them. Cost is the amount of human and nonhuman resources used to achieve something. The money you spend for rent or house payments, utilities, and home maintenance is part of your housing costs. The other resources you must spend, such as time, energy, and skills for running the household, are other forms of housing costs (Figure 23.2).

For example, consider what is involved in adding plumbing to a house. First, you need to pay for materials. Additional costs involve the time and energy you would spend installing the new plumbing. If you do not have the necessary skills to install it yourself, or cannot spend the time and

The Process of Acquisition	
Possession Choices	**Financing Choices**
• **Own**—buy, build, own to rent • **Rent**—privately owned, publicly owned, company owned	• **Cash**—currency, check • **Loan terms**—short-term, long-term • **Sources of financing**—current income, savings, private loan, commercial loan, government loan

Operating Choices	Replacement Choices	Adaption Choices
• Furnish • Maintain • Repair	• Sell • Trade • Abandon	• Remodel • Refinish • Redecorate

Figure 23.1 When acquiring housing, you will want to consider all available choices.

iofoto/Shutterstock.com

Figure 23.2 This new home owner had the time and energy to paint her home. She is using these personal resources rather than money resources to hire a professional painter.

energy required, you would need to pay for the labor of an expert.

Usually the cost of materials for a house is far lower than the human costs involved. Human costs can involve planning the work, ordering materials, and delivering them plus handling their installation, maintenance, and repair.

Needs Versus Wants

When considering the costs associated with acquiring housing, it is important to know the difference between your housing needs and wants. *Needs* are basic necessities, while *wants* are things you desire. Wants almost always cost more than needs. Sometimes people have wants that cost far more than they can afford with their current incomes.

For example, first-time home buyers who want the home of their dreams need to align their wants with what they need. In reality, they only need adequate shelter that protects them from the elements. As they search for housing, they will likely find that what they want is not what they can afford. They must examine their priorities and identify which of their preferences they can afford. It is a good idea to determine in advance the amount to spend for housing, and then refuse to go over that amount.

Costs Involved in Payment Methods

When you pay cash for an item, such as a lamp, you know its exact cost. When you pay by check, debit card, credit card, or automatic transfer of funds, however, you may have some banking costs. Some banks charge for checks and for providing various banking services.

Sometimes people use credit cards to make a purchase. A *credit card* is an extension of money to the cardholder based on an agreement to repay. The cost of using a credit card varies. Some companies charge an annual fee, while others are free. If you

STEM Math Calculating Finance Charges

Over the life of a loan, finance charges often total more than the principal, or the loan amount itself. Finance charges increase with the annual percentage rate (APR), the amount borrowed, and the length of the repayment period. Given this information, you can calculate the finance charge.

For example, the finance charge on a $165,000 30-year mortgage with a 6 percent APR and a monthly payment of $989 is calculated as follows:

1. Calculate how many payments must be made over the 30-year life of the mortgage. There are 360 months in 30 years.
2. Calculate the total amount of all payments made over the life of the mortgage. If $989 is paid per month for 360 months, the amount equals $356,040.
3. To calculate total finance charges paid, subtract the amount borrowed from the total payments made over the life of the loan. For example:

   $356,040 – $165,000 = $191,040
   (total finance charges paid over 30 years)

Math Practice

Assume you have purchased a condominium for $115,000. You were approved for a 20-year mortgage with a 5% APR. Your monthly payment is $750. Calculate the finance charge you will have paid by the end of the 20-year loan period. Show your work.

make only the minimum payment by the bill's deadline, the company will add interest to the rest of the amount you owe. **Interest** is the price you pay for the use of someone else's money. By law, the credit card company must tell you exactly how much interest it will charge you. You can avoid paying interest by paying the entire amount of the bill by the due date. To determine the cost of a credit card, ask the following questions:

- How much is the annual fee?
- What is the interest rate?
- Is this an introductory interest rate?
- What may cause the interest rate to increase?
- Do interest charges begin at the time of purchase?

Installment buying is the process of buying something by making a series of payments during a given length of time (Figure 23.3). Installment buying often costs more to use than most other methods. This is because a person, company, or bank is *financing*, or providing credit to you. The lender has paid your bill and is willing to wait for you to repay the amount. In addition to the original cost of the merchandise, you must pay extra for the privilege of using the lender's money.

This extra amount charged, or **finance charge**, includes the interest and any other service fee. The finance charge is stated as an annual percentage rate (APR) of the amount borrowed. You can pay back the money you borrow over a short or long period of time. The longer you take, the more interest you will pay. Most home owners purchase houses with *long-term financing*. You can take up to 40 years to pay back the money you borrow for a house. With long-term financing, however, the total interest you eventually pay may far exceed the cost of the dwelling itself.

GWImages/Shutterstock.com

Figure 23.3 Whenever you consider spreading the cost of a purchase over time, find out about the extra charges you may encounter, such as interest rates and fees.

It is important to know all the costs associated with any housing consideration and figure them into the purchase decision. For instance, it may be better to wait to buy a lamp with cash rather than pay extra for credit card fees. However, few people could ever afford to buy a house if they had to save all the money needed to make a cash purchase. For them, paying some extra interest each month is the only way to afford such a costly purchase.

Green Choices

Consumer Responsibility in Green and Sustainable Design

Whether choosing to rent or buy a place to live, consider the many choices and how these choices affect the environment. Consider the following "green" factors:

- Does the house have a "green" or "sustainable" certification or designation? This means the unit is more environmentally friendly.
- To what extent does the house use the natural environment to reduce energy cost? For example, is there use of the natural sunlight or landscaping that shades the southern side of the house in summer?
- Do the appliances have ENERGY STAR® ratings? This means they use 30 percent less energy than the standard appliances.
- How does the house rate in its "carbon footprint" as compared to the average house? (Check the Environmental Protection Agency website for a carbon-footprint calculator.) This will determine the number of pounds of carbon dioxide the house might emit into the atmosphere.

These are just a few items to consider. "Green" decisions not only affect the environment, but also benefit the consumer with reduced utility costs.

Renting Versus Buying	
Renting Advantages	**Renting Disadvantages**
• Rent is usually less than a mortgage • Down payment is lower • Total housing costs are clearer • Greater mobility—renters can relocate more easily • Few maintenance responsibilities; no repair responsibilities	• No tax benefit • No equity build-up in property • Rent can increase frequently • Little control of living space (e.g., having pets, decorating living space) • Eviction possibility
Buying Advantages	**Buying Disadvantages**
• Usually a good investment for increasing wealth • Equity builds; potential for selling at a profit • Tax benefits—ability to deduct mortgage interest and property taxes on federal income tax • Greater stability and sense of security • Greater control—more choice in space arrangement and decorating	• Monthly mortgage and housing expenses usually cost more • Payment on some types of mortgages can increase • Responsibility for property taxes, maintenance, and repairs • Less mobility since homes usually can't be sold quickly • Possibility of equity loss due to foreclosure for failure to pay • Cash is tied up in house

Figure 23.4 To make a wise decision about where to live, consider the advantages and disadvantages of both renting and buying.

Deciding to Rent or Buy

The first decision in selecting housing is whether to rent or buy. There are advantages and disadvantages to both. Figure 23.4 outlines some of the major considerations in renting versus buying. It is important to remember, however, that if you choose to buy a house, you will begin to examine your finances immediately. These considerations will become clearer as you read the chapter.

Review & Assessment

1. Besides money, what are other types of resources used in covering housing costs?
2. How do needs and wants impact housing costs?
3. Define finance charge.

Renting

About one-third of all people in the United States rent their housing. The majority of these people are single people, young married couples, and older adults. Many in this group have very mobile lifestyles.

The terms *renting* and *leasing* are almost identical in meaning in that they both refer to the use of residential property for a specified time. There may be slight differences regarding the period of time. Renting can occur on a more flexible "month-to-month" basis and can be accomplished through oral communication or through a written rental agreement, agreed on by both parties. Leasing generally refers to a set period of time also but usually for a longer time period than some rental agreements, such as six months to a year, and definitely involves a lease. A *lease* is a legal document signed by both parties that spells out the parts of the rental agreement. Note that in this section, the term *renting* applies to both renting and leasing, unless otherwise indicated.

Renters usually pay for their housing in monthly installments. When they first move into a building, the owner or building manager usually requests a security deposit in addition to the first month's rent. The **security deposit** is a payment that ensures the owner against financial loss caused by the renter. For example, the renter may damage the property during his or her tenancy. Part or all of the security deposit would then be used to pay for the damage. The amount of the security deposit commonly includes one month's rent and may include an additional amount.

Renting has a number of advantages. Renters have more freedom to relocate as they desire. They do not need to worry about the value of property going up or down or about buying and selling. They have a clear idea of what housing will cost them. There are no hidden costs, such as roof repairs, that often come with ownership. Since renters do not own the dwelling, they do not need to budget money for maintenance and repairs. These are the responsibilities of the building's owner.

Darren K. Fisher/Shutterstock.com

Figure 23.5 The lease clearly states the responsibilities of the property owner and the renter. If you choose to rent, be sure to read the lease carefully.

Rental Units

Although rentals can be many types of housing, the most common are multifamily dwellings. Renters usually occupy duplexes, triplexes, and apartment buildings. People can rent single-family houses and vacation houses, too.

As a renter, examine a rental unit closely before you move into it. Many community governments and rental agencies have helpful rental inspection guides. These guides outline the basic features of apartments and other rentals in a checklist form. You can use these guides to evaluate each rental unit and to compare several units. In addition to items on your checklist, ask the unit owner the following questions:

- How much is the rent per month? How and when is it to be paid? Is a security deposit required? If so, how much is it? Under what conditions will it be returned?
- Will rent increase if real estate taxes or other expenses rise for the property owner?
- What are the expenses/fees besides rent? (These may include utilities, storage space, parking space, Internet and TV services, use of recreational areas, installation of special appliances, and late rent fees.)
- Is loud noise prohibited at certain hours?

Be sure to obtain a complete answer to each question—and make sure you are happy with these answers. You want your housing to bring you satisfaction, not frustration.

The Written Lease

Rental agreements can be on a month-to-month basis or for a specific length of time, such as one year. As previously mentioned, an oral agreement is possible, but a written agreement between renter and owner is ideal (Figure 23.5).

A **lease** is a legal document spelling out the conditions of the rental agreement. It lists the rights and responsibilities of both the property owner, or **lessor**, and the **lessee**, who agrees to pay rent for a place to live. Other names for lessor and lessee are *landlord* and *renter*, respectively.

Always read a written lease carefully. It should include the following information:

- **Location.** The lease should clearly state the location of dwelling, including the address and apartment number.
- **Rental amount.** This section should include the cost of rent and when and where it should it be paid. It should also include the penalties, if any, for late payment.
- **Security deposit.** The lease should state whether a security deposit is required and the amount of deposit. It should also identify the conditions that must be met before it is returned and when it will be returned.
- **Lease period.** The date of occupation and length of lease should be part of the lease. It should also include a statement on lease renewal—when to renew or give notice of nonrenewal. The document should also indicate what happens if you must leave before the lease expires. Can you assign or sublet the lease?
- **Appliances, furnishings, services, and amenities.** The lease should include a statement about what appliances, furnishings, services, and amenities (pool, workout room, laundry

facilities) are included in the rent. Are there cable TV, telephone, and Internet hookups? What items may cost extra? Who is responsible for such items as shoveling snow, mowing the lawn, or painting the walls?

- **Utilities.** The lease should state who is responsible for paying utilities, such as water, electricity, and gas, and recycling and waste pickup. (If you are responsible for payment, ask to see a record of previous billings.)
- **Upkeep, maintenance, and repairs.** The lease should clearly state who is responsible for specific upkeep, maintenance, and repairs. What can either party do if one or the other fails to carry out their responsibilities? An entry clause allowing the landlord to enter the apartment for specific reasons (with notice) or in an emergency is also part of the lease.
- **Legal issues.** The lease should outline what legal remedies are available if either party breaks the lease in some way. For example, what will happen if the landlord fails to make repairs or the renter fails to pay rent on time? What legal actions are available to resolve disagreements? Who pays the legal fees?
- **Conditions of use.** Any special conditions should be described in the lease. For example, can you keep pets? Are there any parking restrictions? Can you paint, hang wallpaper, or decorate the dwelling? Can you have a roommate? The lease should also outline any specific costs involved with any conditions of use. For example, landlords who allow pets may charge an additional fee, or security deposit, to cover any pet damage.
- **Special clauses.** The lease should include a clause stating the final inspection of the premises will be made in the renter's presence. It should also state that the lease cannot be changed without the written approval of both landlord and renter.
- **Signatures.** Both the renter(s) and landlord should sign the lease agreement.

If the renter does not like one or more of the provisions in the lease, he or she should try to have them removed from the lease. Similarly, if the renter desires additional provisions in the lease, he or she should request to have them written and added to the original lease. Such provisions might include necessary repairs, additional furniture, or the installation of appliances. The lease should include a specific date and time by which the landlord will make all changes.

Leases vary greatly. Be sure you are aware of any special restrictions in a lease before you sign it. Sometimes the words in a lease are hard to understand. Assistance for renters is often available from a renter's association in the community or state. A member of the renter's association will be glad to explain the unfamiliar terms. Do not sign a lease until you understand everything in it.

Assigning or Subletting a Lease

If you have signed a lease, but you wish to move out early, you have the following three options:

- continue rent payments until the lease expires
- assign the lease
- sublet the lease

To *assign* the lease, you transfer the entire unexpired portion of the lease to someone else. After the assignment is transacted, you are no longer held responsible for the lease.

To **sublet** the lease, you transfer part interest in the property to someone else. For instance, you could turn over your apartment to another person for a period of time. Both you and the other person would be responsible to the landlord for all terms of the lease.

If you do not prefer any of these options, talk with the landlord to see if other options exist (Figure 23.6). Most states have laws to protect renters. Usually, renters can pay to get out of the lease—sometimes three or six months' rent. Become familiar with the laws of your state before talking to the landlord.

Rob Marmion/Shutterstock.com

Figure 23.6 If you have signed a lease and need to move for some reason, be sure to talk with your landlord about your options.

Responsibilities and Rights of Renting

Both landlords and renters have responsibilities and rights in the rental relationship. The lease agreement states these responsibilities. Two legal consequences can occur when there is a violation of the responsibilities of the lease—breach of contract and eviction.

Breach of Contract

Landlords and renters are sometimes unable to fulfill promises. When this happens there is a **breach of contract**. This is a legal term for failure to meet all terms of a contract or agreement. If you cannot keep your agreement, try to work out the issue with your landlord. Be aware that a landlord could file a lawsuit against you for breach of contract. Responding to lawsuits is costly and time-consuming.

The most common breach of contract on the part of the renter is failure to pay rent. For example, if you lose your job, you may not be able to pay the rent on schedule. Make arrangements with your landlord, if possible, to allow for a late rent payment.

A landlord may also be guilty of breach of contract. If the landlord has failed to provide water or a means of heating your dwelling, the landlord has violated the contract. Major repairs are usually the responsibility of the owner. If your dwelling needs such repairs, you should give written notice to your landlord. If he or she does not make the repairs, you will have grounds for breach of contract.

Eviction

If a renter fails to live up to his or her responsibilities, the landlord can evict the renter. **Eviction** is a legal procedure that forces a renter to leave the property before the rental agreement expires. Landlords may begin a court action leading to eviction only after a renter fails to live up to his or her responsibilities.

The eviction process varies from state to state. Nearly all states, however, require that the renter receive a warning before eviction. The warning is a written legal notice.

Renter's Insurance

As a renter, you need to have insurance to protect against the loss of your personal property due to theft, fire, natural disasters, or other causes (Figure 23.7). Rental insurance also offers some liability protection. For example, suppose your friend comes to visit. He or she slips on the floor and breaks an ankle. Your rental insurance may include payment for medical expenses of a nonresident. This helps protect you against unexpected loss.

LSqrd42/Shutterstock.com

Figure 23.7 Renter's insurance helps protect you against loss of your personal property due to such causes as fire and theft.

You can obtain renter's insurance for a reasonable price. In some cases, college students can obtain a rider on their parents' home owner's policy. It provides a sense of security in event of loss of personal property.

Review & Assessment 

1. List four advantages of renting housing alternatives.
2. Name eight items a written lease should include.
3. Contrast assigning and subletting an apartment.
4. What happens if a renter fails to pay the rent?

Buying

About two-thirds of the people in the United States own their own houses. Instead of renting, these people prefer to buy a house and stay in one place for several years. House ownership has many advantages. It provides a sense of freedom. For example, home owners know they have a place to live. Eviction is not likely unless they fall behind in their house payments. Also, they can make decisions about their housing and do not need to depend on another person such as an apartment owner.

Sociocultural Connections Dealing with Foreclosure

Suppose you secure a home loan and buy a house. It will probably be the largest purchase you ever make. You agree to make monthly payments for many years, often decades. What happens if you lose your job or became ill and cannot pay your house payments?

Legally, the lender could foreclose on your loan and take possession of the property. To recover the money you borrowed but cannot repay, the lender could then sell the property.

It is extremely important to notify your lender about problems that prevent you from making payments on time. If possible, make a personal visit to the lender to try to agree on an alternative payment plan until your situation improves. The possibility of losing your home is at stake. You may ask for an extension of time. Know your financial situation and be prepared to answer these questions:

- Why did you miss your payments?
- From where are you currently getting income?
- When will you begin payments again?
- When can you pay the payments you missed?

Dig Deeper

Research several mortgage lender websites and review their policies on what home owners must do if they are unable to make a mortgage payment. What do the lenders tell potential home owners upfront about such situations? How do lenders work with home owners who are having temporary financial difficulties? What guidelines do lenders have in place to protect the lending institution and the home owner from foreclosure?

Financial advantages also exist with house ownership. A house can be a ***hedge*** (something that provides protection) against inflation, which means the house probably will increase in value at a higher rate than the rate of inflation. People who pay rent must make higher payments for the same housing as inflation rises. Depending on the condition of the economy, houses tend to increase in value over time.

As the value of your house increases, and you make payments on the *principal* (the original sum you borrowed) of the home loan, you build up equity. **Equity** is the money value of a house beyond what you owe on it. Renters are not able to build equity in their housing. Home owners can gain from equity if they sell or refinance their houses.

House ownership also offers a tax advantage. The federal government permits deductions for annual real estate taxes on a house and the interest paid on the home loan. Some states allow these deductions, too.

Although there are many attractions to home ownership, it is not for everyone. Buying a house is a complex, time-consuming, and costly process that brings many ongoing responsibilities.

One possible drawback to home ownership is the potential strain on finances. Usually, you can expect to pay more for your housing per month than you did for rent, at least for the first several years. Even if your house payments are less than you paid previously in rent, you must pay property taxes, home owner's insurance, utilities, and maintenance expenses.

Another possible drawback to home ownership is the potential for foreclosure on the home. **Foreclosure** is a legal proceeding in which a lending firm takes possession of the property. This occurs when the borrower fails to make monthly house payments on a timely basis or does not fulfill the agreements related to the loan. The agency that lent the money to buy the home may take the property and sell it (Figure 23.8).

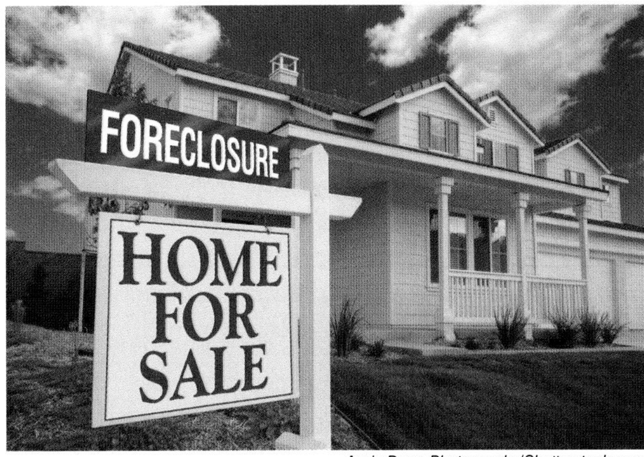

Andy Dean Photography/Shutterstock.com

Figure 23.8 Notify your lender if a personal situation arises that could cause you to lose your home. In some cases, foreclosure can be avoided.

Home owners tend to have less mobility than renters. The owner of a house cannot simply move away and stop making the house payment. He or she must fulfill the terms of the loan contract and pay all real estate taxes. These responsibilities continue until a new owner buys the property. If a person is expecting a transfer within the next year or two, this might not be a good time to buy a house.

Handling maintenance and repairs is a necessary part of owning a single-family house. Some home owners prefer to avoid maintenance requirements, such as mowing the grass, by owning a condominium unit. Condominium owners pay a monthly fee for routine upkeep of the entire property.

When people decide to seek home ownership, a number of people, agencies, and organizations are available to assist them. Each of the many participants in the home-buying process offers different services. See Figure 23.9 for a listing of the primary participants and services they provide. If you decide to buy a house, you will work with these professionals on your journey to home ownership.

Examine Your Finances

Buying the right house is not a simple task. You want a house that makes you feel comfortable and happy. It must also be one that you can afford.

The ability to afford home ownership begins with a realistic assessment of your finances—your income, the size of your savings account, and your debts. Most people do not have the cash to buy a house outright and must borrow a substantial amount of money. The financial institution you choose will make the ultimate decision about your ability to buy a house.

Moneylenders want to deal with responsible borrowers who will pay them back. They carefully screen applicants to avoid future home foreclosures. They will determine how much you can afford for a house while still meeting your other financial obligations. Lenders examine how high your

STEM Math: Meeting Lender Guidelines

Suppose a couple wants to buy a house. They have an annual combined income of $75,000 with a gross monthly income of $6,250. The potential house payment is $825 monthly. The other monthly housing-related costs total $700—which covers property taxes, home owner's insurance, utilities, repairs, and maintenance. The couple owes $600 monthly on long-term debts for two car loans, college education costs, and a dining room set. Would this couple meet approval guidelines to obtain a loan for the house?

To answer this question, the couple must meet two ratios.

1. Housing-to-Income Ratio (must be 28% or less)

To calculate the housing-to-income ratio, use the following formula:

Total Housing Costs ÷ Gross Income = (result) × 100 = Housing-to-Income Ratio

$1,525 ÷ $6,250 = 0.244 × 100 = 24% (rounded) Housing-to-Income Ratio

Conclusion: The couple's housing-to-income ratio is 24%. They meet this guideline.

2. Debt-to-Income Ratio (must be 36% or less)

To calculate the debt-to-income ratio, first add together the total housing costs and long-term debt. Then use the following formula:

Total Debt ÷ Gross Income = (result) × 100 = Debt-to-Income Ratio

$2,125 ÷ $6,250 = 0.34 × 100 = 34% Debt-to-Income Ratio

Conclusion: The couple's debt-to-income ratio is 34%. The couple meets this guideline.

Because the couple meets both ratios, the couple will likely get approval for a house loan with a monthly house payment of $825. In addition to these guidelines, the couple will also need to have a good credit history to get approval for a home loan.

Math Practice

The Clemsons are a newlywed couple interested in purchasing their first home. They have an annual combined income of $66,000 with a gross monthly income of $5,500. The potential house payment is $1,000 monthly. The other monthly housing-related costs total $850—which covers property taxes, home owner's insurance, utilities, repairs, and maintenance. The couple owes $300 monthly for college education costs. Would this couple meet approval guidelines to obtain a loan for the house? Show your calculations.

People Involved in the Home-Buying Process	
Title	**Description and Service Provided**
Appraiser	• A qualified professional who is certified to evaluate real estate property and determine the fair market value.
Attorney (lawyer)	• A person legally appointed or empowered to act on behalf of another—giving legal advice and providing court representation. He or she reviews real estate sale documents and may make arrangements for the title search, funds disbursement, and legal transfer of ownership.
Borrower (mortgagor)	• A person who borrows money to buy a home. • This person pledges to repay the money with interest and maintain hazard insurance on the property.
Government Program Representatives	• First-time home buyer programs vary from one community to the next. A local Housing and Urban Development (HUD) office is a good place to search for programs in your area. • State and local government agencies may offer some assistance with the down payment and extra tax credits through special housing programs.
Home Buyer Counselor	• A person who provides education and assistance to first-time home buyers with all aspects of the home-buying process. HUD funds many home-counseling programs.
Home Inspector	• A professional who evaluates a home for structural defects, such as problems with the roof, wiring, plumbing, or heating and cooling systems. Some states require a separate termite inspector to evaluate the home for insect damage.
Homeowner's Insurance Representative	• A person who provides hazard insurance to protect the home owner and the lender against physical damage (from fire, wind, and vandalism) and other liabilities to a property.
Lender (mortgagee)	• An institution or person that lends mortgage money and uses the property as security for debt payment.
Loan Servicer	• An institution or person that actually collects mortgage payments. The original lender may not provide service for a mortgage.
Mortgage Insurer	• An institution that insures the lender against loss in case the borrower defaults on the loan. This *private mortgage insurance* (PMI) is usually a requirement when home buyers have a down payment that is less than 20 percent of the appraised value.
Real Estate Professional (broker or agent)	• A person licensed to negotiate and complete the sale of real estate. • The broker or agent may be an *exclusive buyer agent* (one who works only with buyers) or a *seller's agent* (one who works only with sellers). Some brokers or agents do both.
Title Company Representative	• A person who arranges for a title search, disbursement of funds, and legal transfer of property ownership.

Figure 23.9 A number of persons providing various services are involved in the home-buying process.

monthly house payments can go and, therefore, how much they can safely lend you.

There are three general guidelines for determining the price range of a house you can afford. One is a general rule for estimating house affordability. The other two guidelines examine your current expenses as ratios to determine how much of your income can go toward a house purchase. These guidelines provide a fairly clear picture of what house price is best for you.

Estimate What You Can Afford

One way to quickly determine the price range you can afford in buying a home is to use a simple rule. Multiply two-and-one-half times your annual **gross income**, or income before deductions. This provides a general idea of the maximum house price you can afford. If you have an annual income of $50,000, for example, you should be able to afford up to $125,000 for a place to live.

Remember, though, this rule for measuring house affordability provides just a "ballpark" figure. A lender will take into account the other debts and responsibilities the buyer has that may make it difficult to repay a loan. Consequently, a person with many debts may not receive approval for a loan to acquire housing valued at two-and-one-half times his or her gross income.

Estimate How Much Money You Can Borrow

For most home loans, the buyer must make a down payment that cannot be part of the loan. This is usually at least 5 percent of the cost of the home, but may vary depending on the loan requirements. Obtaining a loan from a lending institution then pays the unpaid balance on the home.

Your earnings and existing debt will determine the loan size you can obtain. Most lenders use a computer program to determine the eligibility for a loan. The program includes the applicant's income, debts, and other financial factors. Some lenders use two guidelines, or ratios, to determine the size of the loan that an applicant can afford. A good way to determine if you qualify for a loan is to calculate the following two ratios:

- **Housing-to-income ratio.** Your monthly housing costs should total no more than 28 percent of your gross monthly income. These housing costs include the house payment, property taxes, insurance, utilities (such as gas, water, and electricity), repairs, maintenance, and a cooperative or condominium fee, if applicable.

  To obtain your **housing-to-income ratio**, divide your total housing costs by your gross income. Then multiply your decimal result by 100 to obtain the percentage.
- **Debt-to-income ratio.** This second guideline compares total monthly debt to total monthly income. Your monthly housing costs plus other long-term debts should total no more than 36 percent of your monthly gross income. *Long-term debts* are those debts that will take 10 or more months to repay. To obtain your **debt-to-income ratio**, divide your total debt (debt + housing costs) by your gross income. Then multiply the decimal result by 100 to obtain the percentage.

If you can meet these ratios, you will probably qualify for a loan. These ratios may vary slightly depending on the specific type of loan. Other factors also enter into the decision to receive a loan to buy housing. A major factor is the credit history of the potential buyer.

Know Your Credit History

The **credit history** of a person includes the past payment record and a profile of outstanding debts. The credit history includes a person's credit score. A *credit score* is a complex mathematical calculation that evaluates the information in a person's credit history. Lenders use this information to determine whether a person qualifies for a particular form of credit.

Three consumer-reporting companies keep and monitor a person's credit history. The Federal Trade Commission (FTC) requires each of the nationwide consumer-reporting companies—*Equifax, Experian,* and *TransUnion*—to provide a free copy of a person's credit report, at his or her request, once every 12 months.

The credit reports include the past payment record as well as a profile of outstanding debts. The credit history gives a bank or other lending agencies information about whether a person is likely to repay a loan. People are considered "high risk" if their credit history indicates frequent late payments and high debt.

Decisions to Buy or Build

Once you know how much you can afford to spend for a house, decide whether to buy a newly built house, buy a pre-owned house, or build a new house. All options have their advantages and disadvantages. Home buyers need to weigh these options as they make a decision.

Choose an ENERGY STAR Qualified Home

When selecting a new house that has green and sustainable features or certification, choose an eco-friendly program to guide your decision making. Such a program assures you that there are green components in a home. For example, the U.S. Environmental Protection Agency (EPA) sets the guidelines for the *Energy Star® Qualified Home* program. The guidelines state these homes are 20 to 30 percent more energy efficient than the standard home. Home features that lead to lower energy demand and reduced air pollution include

- properly installed insulation
- high-performance windows
- tight construction and ducts
- efficient heating and cooling equipment
- efficient products (appliances, lighting)
- third-party verification (independent rating)

Buying a New House

If you want a new house, but do not want to build it, you can buy a recently built home (Figure 23.10). This process requires much less time than buying land and having a house built on it.

Buying a new house has some unique advantages. One is that you can move in right after closing the deal, or after settling all legal and financial matters. Another advantage is that you can see the finished product before you buy it. If you are a person who cannot visualize a finished house by studying the plans, you may prefer a new house already built.

Buying a Pre-Owned House

For various reasons, many buyers choose previously occupied houses. The same amount of space usually costs less in a pre-owned house rather than a new one. Often you can see how previous owners made use of the space (Figure 23.11). When you look at furnished rooms, you can get a better idea of how much usable space exists. This can help you visualize how your furniture will fit into the same space.

Photo Courtesy of JELD-WEN Windows and Doors

Figure 23.11 A pre-owned house may include mature landscaping that does not come with new homes.

Photo courtesy of Palm Harbor Homes

Figure 23.10 Sometimes contractors build houses that are ready for sale. What traditional features do you find in this new home?

In addition, some items that usually do not come with a new house may be included with a pre-owned one. The previous owner usually leaves the window coverings and their hardware. The lot may have mature trees and shrubs. Fences, walls, and screens may have been added. These are costly in time, money, and effort if you add them yourself.

While you may find that some pre-owned houses are bargains, others are not. No house is perfect. You need to know the flaws before you buy. If you do not find out about the shortcomings until after you move in, it can be a shock. The shock becomes greater when you realize how much they cost to fix.

Before you sign a contract agreeing to buy a pre-owned house, check the house carefully. Look for serious defects, such as the following:

- **Cracked foundation.** A cracked foundation indicates that the house will probably sag or shift, which will weaken the structure.

- **Rotten or sagging interiors or exteriors.** Rotten or sagging roofs, walls, or supports are signs of major construction defects or poor care. All are costly to repair.
- **Insect damage.** Insect damage may be serious enough to require major repairs. It may also mean defects exist that are not visible to the inexperienced observer.

You can repair less serious conditions if you want to spend the time, money, and effort. To learn about the home ahead of time, schedule a home inspection.

Building a House

If you choose to build a house, there are several ways to accomplish it. First you may choose to work with an architect to build a custom-designed house. Another option is to choose from a number of standard house designs. If you choose the second option, you can have an architect or contractor make additional changes to the plans to fit your needs. As a consumer, you need to especially be aware of the green or sustainable aspects of the home's design.

If building a house is your choice, you will need to buy a lot (a portion of land) and then build the house. This involves four steps, accomplished in the following order:

1. **Location.** Choose a region, community, neighborhood, and site. Finding the right location may take weeks or months. Review the considerations for housing site selection described in Chapter 3.
2. **House plan.** Find a house plan you like that fits the site and your lifestyle. The plan may be custom-designed by an architect or chosen from stock plans (Figure 23.12). Changes can be made to either set of plans. In addition, you can include elements of green or sustainable design into the plans.
3. **Select the contractor.** Check the reputation and character of each contractor you are considering by obtaining a list of references of recently completed jobs. Let each contractor examine your plans, the list of materials for the house, and their type and quality of the materials. When you have narrowed your choices to a few contractors, ask each contractor for a **bid**, or the fee each would charge to build the house. The bid should include the cost for both materials and labor. You also need to find out when work can start and how long the job will take.

studioeyes/Shutterstock.com

Figure 23.12 An architect or contractor can help you choose a house plan that best meets your housing needs.

4. **Financing.** Obtain enough money to pay for the house. If you do not have enough cash, you must borrow more money. When you apply for a loan, you must provide the appraised value of the dwelling. You can estimate the home's value by using the information given in your house plans. Generally, financing a new home happens in two parts. The first loan will be for construction of the house. After the house is finished, you can receive a long-term loan.

Review & Assessment

1. What is a general way to determine the cost of a house that a person or family can afford?
2. As the new owner of a mortgaged house, which of the following items should you consider when figuring your monthly housing costs: (A) income tax; (B) mortgage loan payments; (C) house insurance payments; (D) heating bill; (E) car payments; (F) real estate taxes; (G) maintenance allowance?
3. Identify three serious defects to look for when considering the purchase of a pre-owned home.

The Home-Buying Process

Once potential home buyers examine their finances and determine whether to buy a new or pre-owned house, the home-buying process begins in earnest. There are several parts in this process,

Sociocultural Connections: The Housing Bubble Burst

Suppose you purchased a single-family house in Illinois for $250,000 during the housing bubble in the third quarter of 2006. Six years later in the third quarter of 2012, it was worth about $195,574. By the third quarter of 2015, the value of the home was $225,064.

Buying a home has long been part of the American dream. Generations of Americans put their savings into a home and were rewarded with an asset that grew slowly but steadily in value over the years. For many people, purchasing real estate was a sure and safe way to create wealth.

In the mid-1990s, home values skyrocketed in many parts of the United States and around the world. The boom in housing markets—especially in California, Florida, Arizona, and Nevada—was fueled by many factors. Historically low interest rates decreased the cost of borrowing. Low unemployment increased the pool of prospective home buyers.

Perhaps the most important factor for the housing boom was psychological—people believed that housing prices would continue to climb steeply indefinitely. This belief led people, businesses, and investors to take unwise financial risks. For example, many home buyers bought homes that were priced too high. To pay for their homes, they took out loans they did not understand and could not afford. Many financial institutions relaxed lending requirements—sometimes waiving customary requirements for down payments and borrowers' proof of employment—which allowed many more people to qualify for loans.

A market developed in mortgage-backed securities. After making loans to home buyers, many financial institutions sold them to other financial institutions and investors. Large numbers of mortgages were packaged and then bought and sold like stocks and bonds.

An asset "bubble" forms when excess demand drives up the value of assets. Like most bubbles, the housing market bubble eventually burst. By 2005, the rate at which home prices rose began to level off and decline. By 2007, house prices began to fall around the country. Interest rates rose. A growing number of home owners could not pay their mortgages and lost their homes. By the end of 2009, almost one in four borrowers were *underwater*, or owed more on their mortgages than the properties were worth. Housing markets across the United States became clogged with foreclosed homes that drove down the value of all homes.

Some people were able to continue paying their mortgages even though they were underwater. By 2015, many home owners were starting to see the value of their homes begin to recover as noted in the chart.

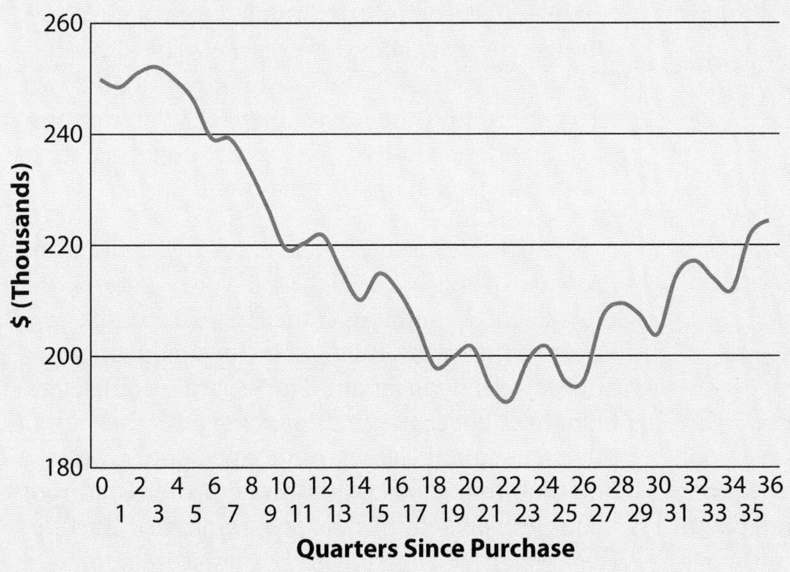

$ (Thousands)

Quarters Since Purchase

Source: HPI (Housing Price Indicator), Federal Housing Finance Agency

Dig Deeper

Research magazine and news articles about families during the housing bubble burst that occurred after 2006. Analyze the impact of these housing decisions on the management of wage-earner roles. For those families who were able to survive the decline in their home values, what management techniques helped them to do so? Discuss your findings in class.

the first of which is selecting a mortgage lender, type of mortgage, and gaining preapproval for a loan. Because of the housing bubble burst in the U.S. economy, many real estate agents require home buyers to have preapproval before shopping for a home. After home buyers gain preapproval and search for a house, the remaining parts of the process occur at the same time.

Mortgage Selection and Preapproval

A **mortgage** is a pledge of property that a borrower gives to a lender as security for a loan with which to buy the property. The borrower agrees to gradually **amortize**, or pay off, the loan (the principal with interest) in monthly installments for a given number of years. If he or she fails to pay, the lender can repossess the home. The lender is usually a bank, savings bank, credit union, or mortgage company. The seller may also be the lender.

Because mortgage loans can vary between lenders and from state to state, it is wise for potential home buyers to examine all loan options. There are many types of home mortgages.

Types of Mortgages

For many years, the standard home mortgage has been a long-term, fixed-rate loan. This means that the mortgage was usually written for a specific period of time with the interest rate and monthly payments constant. Several mortgage options exist for borrowers today. They include conventional fixed-rate mortgages, adjustable-rate mortgages (ARM), and government-backed loans that are FHA-insured or VA-guaranteed.

- **Conventional mortgage.** A two-party contract between a borrower and a lender is a *conventional mortgage*. A conventional loan is a long-term, fixed-rate loan. The typical term lengths for conventional loans are 15, 20, and 30 years, although some lenders may write mortgages for 10 or 40 years. The down payment on a conventional loan may vary from 5 to 20 percent, with many lenders requiring 20 percent. When the home buyer does not have a 20 percent down payment, the lender may require the home buyer to purchase *private mortgage insurance (PMI)*—insurance that protects the lender if the borrower fails to pay. The government does not insure this type of mortgage.
- **Adjustable rate mortgage.** With an *adjustable rate mortgage (ARM)*, the interest rate is adjusted up or down periodically according to a national interest rate index. Depending on interest rate changes, monthly payments may increase or decrease. Initially, some lenders offer these loans at a lower interest rate than fixed-rate mortgages. Also, some of these mortgages have rate caps. This means the interest rate will never exceed a certain rate regardless of the national interest rate index.
- **FHA-insured mortgage.** A three-party contract that involves the borrower, a lender, and the Federal Housing Administration (FHA) is an *FHA-insured mortgage*. This government agency is part of the U.S. Department of Housing and Urban Development (HUD). FHA does not make loans, but it insures the lender against the borrower's possible default, or inability to pay. Anyone can apply for an FHA-insured loan by going to an approved lending institution. In comparison to conventional loans, a home buyer can often secure an FHA-insured loan with a smaller down payment.
- **VA-guaranteed mortgage.** A three-party loan involving the borrower (who is a veteran of the U.S. Armed Forces), a lending firm, and the Veterans Administration (VA) is a *VA-guaranteed mortgage*. These mortgages generally cost less than the other types of common, fixed-rate mortgages. Veterans may apply for a VA-guaranteed loan at a lending institution. The lender submits the applications to a VA office for approval. Congress sets the eligibility requirements. The VA does not require a down payment, but the lender may. The veteran and the lender decide the size of the down payment and the length of the repayment period.

Other alternative house-financing options are presented in Figure 23.13. One type of financing is available to limited-income, first-time home buyers who are taking a home buyer education and counseling program. The program counselors help these buyers secure financing after they attend buyer education classes, reduce personal debts, and maintain good credit ratings. To find out more about housing counseling programs, visit the U.S. Department of Housing and Urban Development website.

House financing alternatives vary from state to state and lender to lender. Research all the options to find the method of financing that is best for you.

Alternative Home-Financing Options	
Type	**Description**
Balloon Mortgage	Monthly payments based on a fixed interest rate, usually short term. Payments may cover interest only, with principal due in full at term's end.
Assumable Mortgage	Buyer takes over seller's original, below-market interest rate mortgage.
Land Contract (or contract for deed)	Seller retains original mortgage. No transfer of title until loan is fully paid. Equal monthly payments based on below-market interest rate with any unpaid principal due at loan's end.
Rent with Option to Buy	Renter pays an option fee for the right to purchase property at specified time and agreed-upon price. Rent may or may not be applied to sales price.
Secondary Financing (or second mortgage)	Financing the buyer secures to reduce the amount of funds required for down payment and/or closing costs.
Biweekly Mortgage	With this type of mortgage, instead of making a monthly payment, the home owner makes a payment every two weeks. This results in making an extra mortgage payment per year, leading to a slightly shorter mortgage term.

Figure 23.13 Many alternative home-financing options exist to meet the varying needs of buyers and sellers.

Shopping for a Mortgage Lender

Because so many mortgage options exist today, it is best to compare at least three different lenders about their mortgage options and interest rates. Also, consider getting information from different types of lenders, including commercial banks, credit unions, online lenders, and mortgage companies.

Dealing with reputable companies is essential because mortgage applications require so much personal information. This is especially true for online lenders. Look for a lender that is financially stable with a strong reputation for providing quality customer service. Lenders who try to push you to use just one lender are cause for suspicion—they may not have your best interests in mind.

Comparing the same information for each lender—the loan amount, the interest rate, the length of the loan, and the type of loan—helps you make sound decisions. Some of this information is available in the real estate sections of your local newspaper. You can obtain other information about fees and costs directly from the lenders. In addition, ask each lender about the following:

- What is the down payment requirement for each loan? Will the lender require private mortgage insurance (PMI) if your down payment is less than the requirement?
- Is the interest rate fixed or adjustable? Also ask about the loan's APR.
- Do the loan costs involve *points*, or fees paid to the lender for the loan (usually one point equals one percent of the loan)?

As you shop for a mortgage and mortgage lender, do not be afraid to negotiate the best deal. This includes making lenders or brokers compete with each other for your business. Smart consumers take time to shop for a mortgage and gather all the facts before making a final decision. Also be aware of fair lending laws, Figure 23.14. To find further information on fair lending laws, visit the U.S. Department of Housing and Urban Development's website.

Obtaining Preapproval for a Loan

Although you can shop for a home and then apply for a mortgage, it is to your advantage (and often a requirement) to seek preapproval for a loan first. *Preapproval* means that the home buyer has gone through a preliminary approval process in which the lender verifies employment and checks tax records, bank references, and the borrower's credit history. The lender then gives the buyer a *preapproval letter* indicating commitment. Preapproval gives the buyer a definite amount to spend on housing. It also gives the buyer

Fair Lending Laws Protect Consumers	
Laws	**Key Provisions**
The Equal Credit Opportunity Act	Prohibits lenders from discriminating against credit applications in any part of the credit transaction based on race, color, religion, national origin, sex, marital status, age, or whether part of an applicant's income comes from a public assistance program.
The Fair Housing Act	Prohibits discrimination in residential real estate transactions based on race, color, religion, sex, handicap, family status, or national origin.

Figure 23.14 Fair lending laws help prevent discrimination against potential home buyers.

negotiating power with sellers because it shows the buyer has serious intentions. Once a home buyer finds a house, he or she will need to finish the approval process to meet other requirements and conditions of the lender.

Searching for a Home

When you know what type of house you want and can afford, it is time to go shopping.

Rachel Sanchez Real Estate

200 E. Main Street, OPEN HOUSE,
Saturday and Sunday, April 22–23,
1–4 p.m., $250,000

Remodeled, updated, and delightful! 4-bedroom brick ranch with fireplace, 2½ baths, utility room, 2½-car garage, and sunroom off master bedroom. Great layout. Quiet location plus a bonus—160-ft. lake frontage on South Lake. Get your fishing pole ready! Take Rt. 50 to Western. Turn west at 3rd Street, north at Walnut, and east at Main Street. Signs are posted.

Goodheart-Willcox Publisher

Figure 23.15 Advertisements in local newspapers can help you find real estate firms.

You can locate a home through real estate firms, websites, and the real estate section of newspapers. You can also learn about homes for sale through word-of-mouth. Finally, you can drive through neighborhoods looking for sale signs.

Using a Real Estate Firm

Real estate firms are in the business of selling land and buildings. They often advertise properties in free shopping guides, in the real estate section of newspapers, and online (Figure 23.15). Most real estate firms are part of a larger network called the *multiple listing service* (MLS). This service provides a combined list of all area houses for sale by network real estate firms.

STEM Math: Calculating Price per Square Foot

Before making an offer to buy a home, home buyers evaluate a seller's asking price. Is the price fair or is the seller asking for too much? Home buyers can compare the home's price to that of a comparable home in the same neighborhood that recently sold. The calculation of price per square foot enables buyer to make a comparison.

For example, House A, which has 1,500 square feet of living space, has an asking price of $200,000. In the same neighborhood, a comparable home, House B, recently sold for $230,000. House B has 2,200 square feet of living space. Calculate the price per square foot of each home.

(House A) $200,000 ÷ 1,500 square feet = $133.33 per square foot

(House B) $230,000 ÷ 2,200 square feet = $104.55 per square foot

House A has a much higher price per square foot than House B. House A is probably priced too high.

Math Practice

Suppose you are interested in buying a townhouse in a popular housing complex. Two homes are available for sale within this complex. House Y has 2,000 square feet of living space and has an asking price of $285,000. House Z recently sold for $301,500 and has 2,500 square feet of living space. Calculate the price per square foot of each home. Does House Y appear to be priced fairly?

Career Focus Real Estate Sales Agent

kurhan/Shutterstock.com

Do you like to bring people together to make decisions and reconcile differences? Do you enjoy interpreting and sharing information effectively with others? Are you flexible and able to adjust your actions in relation to the actions of other people? Can you image yourself as a real estate agent who assists homebuyers locate and purchase homes or sell their existing home? If so, you may enjoy a career as a real estate sales agent.

Interests/Skills: Real estate sales agents must have excellent listening skills. They must take the time to understand the points being made and ask questions as necessary. They must also have strong sales and marketing skills, effective communication skills, and strong ethics and organizational skills. They need technology skills for communications and photography.

Career Snapshot: Real estate sales agents are involved in a number of activities involving persons interested in either buying, renting, or selling properties. The agents present purchase offers to sellers for consideration. They serve as the intermediary in negotiations between buyers and sellers and generally represent one or the other. Agents compare similar properties recently sold to determine the competitive market value. Agents provide advice to clients on market conditions, prices, mortgages, legal requirements, and related matters. A frequent activity of agents involves the sale promotion of properties through advertisements, open houses, and participation in multiple listing services.

Education/Training: Most positions require career and technical education training, on-the-job training, or an associate's degree. All states require a high school diploma and completion of a number of hours of real estate courses.

Licensing/Examinations: Licensing is necessary for real estate agents, generally through the state in which they work. Although requirements vary by state, all states require agents to pass a licensing exam.

Professional Associations: Local associations of realtors help realtors be more profitable and successful. The local associations are connected to a state and national association.

Job Outlook: Jobs for real estate sales agents are expected to grow slower than the average for all occupations. More job openings become available as the economy expands.

Sources: The Occupational Outlook Handbook (OOH); the Occupational Information Network (O*NET)

Real estate agents, who are members of the *National Association of Realtors*, are called *Realtors*. Realtors pay fees to join the Association and must adhere to a code of ethics, which protects the seller and the buyer. Realtors can give you information about the community and neighborhood that you are considering. They can screen out places that would not appeal to you. Sometimes they can help you get financing.

Realtors and real estate agents charge a commission, or fee, for their services. The commission ranges from 5 percent to 10 percent of the selling price. The seller usually pays the real estate fee. The seller may raise the price of the house to cover this cost. It is important to hire a real estate agent that represents you—the buyer— and not the seller. This person is also known as the "buyer's agent."

Locating Homes for Sale

As well as working with a realtor, you can also find homes for sale on your own. Several options exist and can save you time during the search process. They include the following:

- **Online shopping.** Many real estate agents and Realtors offer online home-shopping sites that include floor plans plus inside and outside photos of housing for sale. You can search for housing by specifying such options as the number of bedrooms, the geographic area, and price range. Detailed information about the homes you select will include property taxes and the location of schools. Some sites offer virtual tours that allow you to "walk through" or see 360-degree views of each room. Prospective buyers can use this information to narrow down choices before spending time to actually visit different units.

- **Newspapers.** As well as newspaper listings by real estate firms, you may find homes for sale by owner. This means that you buy directly from the owner. It also means that the price of the house is not inflated to cover the fees the seller must pay to a real estate agent or Realtor.
- **Word-of-mouth.** When shopping for a house, tell friends and acquaintances that you are looking for a home to buy. They may know about certain houses that you would like. They may even know about houses that will be up for sale in the near future.
- **For sale signs.** In general, driving or walking past houses you like is a good way to become familiar with a neighborhood. You may find places with *For Sale* signs that are easy to overlook in real estate ads (Figure 23.16). You may also find a model house on display or find houses that are not advertised anywhere else.

Shopping on your own without a real estate agent takes a great deal of time and knowledge. If you do not have knowledge about real estate deals, the mistakes you might make could be much more costly than any money you might save.

Making an Offer—the Sales Contract

When you find a house that you like in your price range, it is time to make a formal offer on the property. Your real estate agent can give you information about prices of comparable homes that are for sale or have sold in that area. With this information in mind, you can make an *offer to purchase* to the seller. When you make the offer, you will include a check for the earnest money. **Earnest money** is a deposit, or a sum of money you pay to show that you are serious about buying the house. The money is held in trust until the closing of the deal. When the deal goes through, the earnest money is applied toward the payment of the total price. If you cannot get a loan, the money is refunded. You may lose the earnest money if you back out of the agreement for other reasons.

The **agreement of sale** (also known as *offer to purchase, contract of purchase, purchase agreement,* or *sales agreement*) gives a detailed description of the property and its legal location and all specific terms and conditions of the real estate sale. It includes the total purchase price, the amount of the down payment, and the possession date of property. In addition, it states that the seller must have clear title to the property to complete the sale (Figure 23.17).

rSnapshotPhotos/Shutterstock.com

Figure 23.16 Walking through a neighborhood and identifying additional "for sale" signs, increases your options and helps you get to know the neighborhood.

Scott Waldron/Shutterstock.com

Figure 23.17 Making an offer on a home involves completing an agreement of sale. Many experts recommend that home buyers consult a lawyer about real estate transactions before signing any documents.

The agreement of sale will also spell out any specific ***contingencies***, or terms and conditions of the sale. For instance, an owner may agree to leave the draperies, carpeting, range, and refrigerator in the house. The agreement will list such items. This way, you know exactly what you are buying. Other specific terms the document should explain include how the payment of property taxes will be divided and who bears the risk of loss to the property. Loss may occur as a result of fire, wind, and other disasters during completion of the deal.

When the buyer and seller agree to a negotiated price for the house, both sign the agreement of sale making the document legal and binding. Read all of the fine print before signing it. At this time, the buyer moves forward with securing financing and home owner's insurance and having a survey, appraisal, and title search.

Finalizing the Financing

If you have gone through the preapproval process for a mortgage before your home search, the final approval of the loan generally moves swiftly. At this point, the lender provides the buyer with a *lock-in* on the interest rate, or a written agreement guaranteeing the interest rate. You will need to present the sales contract to the lender and complete an application and any other documentation the lender requires. If you do not have preapproval, you will need to find a lender and apply for a loan. When applying for a loan, the lender will require

- tax documentation for the previous two years with W-2s
- two or more paycheck stubs
- debt information
- several recent bank statements
- proof of other assets or income (for example, life insurance policies with cash value)
- the address and property description you want to buy
- a copy of the signed agreement of sale

Obtaining Home Owner's Insurance

While your home loan is in progress, you will need to find home owner's (hazard) insurance. Home owner's insurance helps protect your investment and can save you from financial loss. Most mortgage holders require the home buyer to protect the house from loss with insurance against fire and other hazards. The lender will also want to be listed as the mortgage holder on the property. At the time of closing, the lender will require documentation that an insurance policy is paid in full for one year.

When looking for insurance, be sure to find a licensed company and agent (Figure 23.18). You will want to make sure that you purchase enough insurance to rebuild the home at replacement construction costs—not the current value of the home. You also want to purchase enough insurance to replace your personal belongings. You can insure your personal items for *actual cash value* (with depreciation) or *replacement cost* (without depreciation). To find an affordable policy that covers your needs, be sure to obtain estimates from several providers before making your choice.

Although types of policies can vary from state to state, basic insurance coverage includes property and personal liability coverage.

- **Property coverage.** This insurance pays for physical damage to your house, personal property (furnishings, clothes, etc.), garage, and

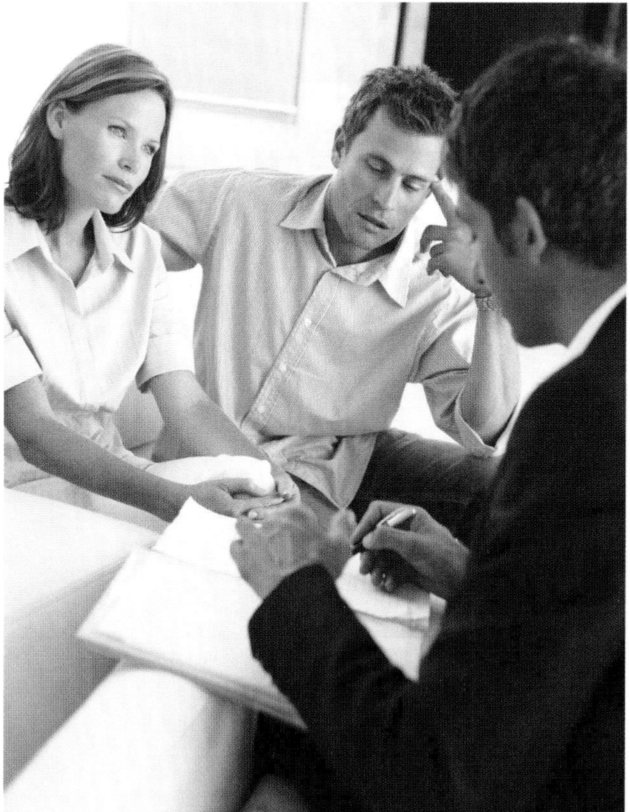

Yuri Arcurs/Shutterstock.com

Figure 23.18 Meeting with an insurance agent to acquire home owner's hazard insurance is a step along the path of the home-buying process.

other detached items such as a garden shed or fence. ***Perils*** (dangers) that cause sudden and accidental damage to your home and property include fire, wind, vandalism, and theft. Your policy will spell out the specific details about items it covers. In addition, your policy may cover living expenses (such as motel and restaurant costs) that occur if you must leave your home temporarily for repairs.

- **Personal liability coverage.** If another person has an accident on your property, this insurance pays for bodily injuries. It will pay for a person's medical expenses for the accidental injury up to the limit of medical coverage you buy. In addition, liability coverage generally pays for damage to another's property for which you or a family member is responsible.

Home owner's insurance *does not* cover every type of property loss. When evaluating insurance policies, it is important to look at the *exclusions*—items that policies do not cover. Most policies do not cover such catastrophic events as flood, earthquake, war, or nuclear disaster (Figure 23.19). Additional exclusions may include: property covered by other policies (cars, boats), damage due to wear and tear on the property, damage from sewer backup or sump-pump overflow, and other hazards, such as injuries by pets.

For some exclusions, home owners can buy additional insurance options—or *endorsements*—to meet their needs. For example, if home owners live in earthquake- or flood-prone areas, they can buy additional protection for their property.

Tony Campbell/Shutterstock.com

Figure 23.19 Be sure to find out what types of property losses home owner's insurance does not cover. Natural disasters such as potential flooding require home owners to purchase additional property protection.

Obtaining a Home Inspection

A **home inspection** is an evaluation of the construction and present condition of the house. The inspection will reveal if any existing defects will impact the value of the home and ultimately the sales price. Some states also require inspections for termites or mold. If the inspections identify any problems with the property, the buyer can renegotiate the terms and conditions of the sale with the seller (if agreeable) or in most cases back out of the deal.

Scheduling a Survey and Appraisal

Many mortgage lenders (and home buyers) require a professional survey of the property. A property survey identifies on a map the property lines indicating where the house, driveway, garage, and other features such as fences are located. This assures the mortgage lender and home buyer that the building is actually located on the land identified in the legal description.

In addition to a survey, lenders require a house appraisal before you buy it (whether the house is pre-owned or new). An **appraisal** is an expert estimate of the quality and value of the property given by a licensed appraiser. The appraiser tours the property and researches properties with comparable sales data in the area. The appraiser then sends a report to the lender about the property value.

When the sale closes, the title passes to the new owner. The **title** is a document that gives proof of the rights of ownership and possession of a particular property. A **deed** is the legal document that shows the transfer of title from one person to another. The deed describes the property being sold. It is signed and witnessed according to the laws of the state in which the property is located. The following types of deeds indicate transfer of property:

- **General warranty deed.** This type of deed transfers the title of the property to the buyer. It guarantees that the title is clear of any claims against it (Figure 23.20). If any mortgage, tax, or title claims are made against the property, the buyer may hold the seller liable for them. This type of deed offers the greatest legal protection to the buyer.

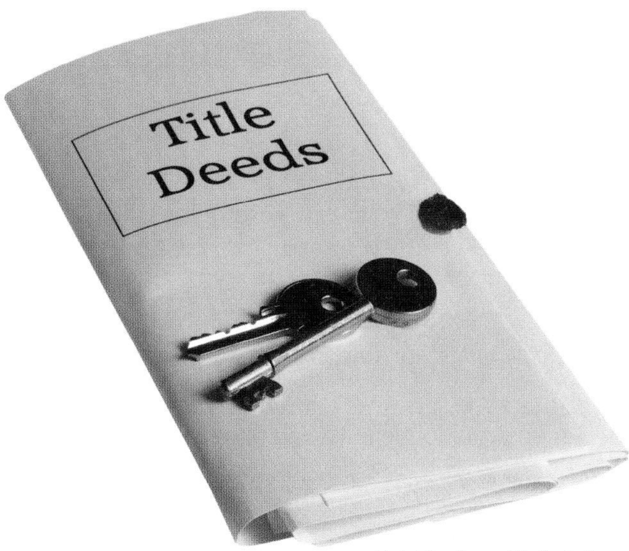

Linda Macpherson/Shutterstock.com

Figure 23.20 A general warranty deed transfers the title of the property to the new owner(s) and guarantees the title is clear of any claims.

- **Special warranty deed.** This deed also transfers the title to the buyer. However, it guarantees that during the time the seller held the title to the property, the seller did nothing that would, or will in the future, impair the buyer's title.
- **Quitclaim deed.** This legal document transfers whatever interest the seller has in the property without providing a guarantee or warranty of title. By accepting such a deed, the buyer assumes all legal and financial risks for the property.

Closing the Sale of a Home

Before a real estate sale is final, payment of fees and charges for settling the legal and financial matters—or *closing costs*—must occur. These closing costs can amount to several thousand dollars (Figure 23.21). Closing costs may include

- recording fees for the deed and mortgage.
- attorney's fee or fee to a title company.
- abstract of title and title insurance.
- appraisal fee.
- survey charge.
- origination fee. This fee is paid to the lender for processing the loan. It usually is one percent of the mortgage loan.
- escrow fees. These are funds paid to an escrow agent to hold until a specified event occurs. After the event has occurred, the funds are released to designated people. In practice, this often means that when the home owner makes mortgage payments, he or she pays an additional sum that is placed in a trust fund. This extra money is used to pay other expenses, such as taxes, insurance premiums, and special assessments.
- points. This refers to a type of interest paid to offset interest lost by the lender. One point usually equals one percent of the mortgage loan.
- miscellaneous fees. Other costs include flood insurance, termite inspection, a credit report, tax services, the underwriter's charge, and application fees.

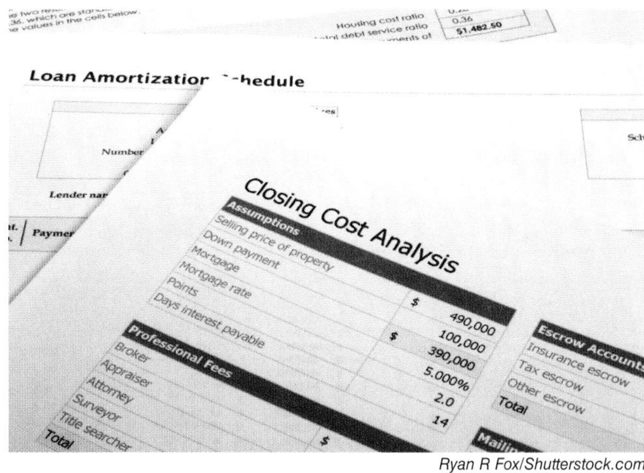

Ryan R Fox/Shutterstock.com

Figure 23.21 Home buyers should come to the closing table with enough money (either cash or cashier's check) to pay the closing costs for their real estate deal.

The seller also has some closing costs. They may include the real estate commission and his or her share of the year's taxes, insurance, and any special assessments. Both the buyer and seller pay the taxes, insurance, and special assessments for the portion of the year they own the property. The seller's closing costs may actually be higher than those of the buyer. He or she may raise the price of the house to cover them.

After you have lived in your new home awhile, you may notice that mortgage interest rates are lower or you may desire to do some home remodeling. Because of these factors, you may decide to *refinance* your mortgage. Refinancing means closing your existing mortgage loan and beginning a new loan. The main idea is to save money with a lower interest rate on the loan or reducing the monthly mortgage payment (or both). Making the decision to refinance requires weighing many options and reevaluating your financial situation. See Figure 23.22 for more information on refinancing.

Refinancing a Mortgage
Reasons to Refinance
• Have lower monthly payments • Take advantage of lower interest rates (one percent or more below your rate) • Make home improvements
Actions to Take

• **Shop for the best rate.** Begin with your current lender to possibly eliminate some costs (such as closing costs).
• **Ask questions before making a decision to refinance.** Get answers to the following questions:
  • Is there a prepayment penalty? Will paying off the old mortgage early cost more?
  • Is a title search, appraisal, survey, or inspection required? How much will they cost?
  • Are there other costs?
  • Who pays the recording and escrow fees?
  • How much will monthly payments change?
  • How many months will it take to recover the cost of refinancing?

Figure 23.22 Some home owners choose to refinance their mortgages for a number of reasons after a period of time.

Review & Assessment

1. Compare and contrast the following types of mortgages: conventional, fixed-rate, and adjustable rate.
2. Name five items included in an agreement of sale.
3. Summarize how fair lending laws protect consumers.
4. What information will an appraiser give you?
5. How are the terms *title* and *deed* related?

Special Ownership Considerations

The home-buying process is much the same for all types of housing. Several types of home ownership, however, require special considerations on the part of the buyer. These include condominium and cooperative ownership.

Condominium Ownership

Buying a condominium unit is similar to buying any other house. You will need to choose a location you like and a unit you can afford. You must decide between a new and pre-owned unit. You will probably work with either a real estate agent or developer. You will sign an agreement of sale, make a down payment, secure a mortgage, pay closing costs, and sign a deed.

Condominium owners have the same financial advantages conventional home owners have. They are investing in real estate and can take advantage of certain income tax deductions. They also build equity in their property.

Condominium units are usually less costly to build than freestanding, single-family houses. Because of the extras you buy, however, the price may be high. Extras may include access to such recreational facilities as a clubhouse, swimming pool, and tennis courts (Figure 23.23).

Approach the purchase of a condominium unit with care. First, be sure to read the *declaration of ownership*. It contains the conditions and restrictions of the sale, ownership, and use of the property within a particular group of condominium units. Check to see that you can sell your unit at any time and that you are liable for only the mortgage and taxes for your unit. Then find out who controls the management of the units.

Antonio M. Magdaraog/Shutterstock.com

Figure 23.23 A swimming pool may be part of the common-use area when a condominium unit is the buyer's choice.

Lastly, get a detailed breakdown of your monthly payments. Besides mortgage payments and taxes, you must pay utilities, insurance, and maintenance fees. Maintenance fees are used for the repair and maintenance of the common areas of the complex. They vary widely and are usually subject to change. Check to see that the fee seems reasonable.

Cooperative Ownership

Buying a cooperative unit is different from buying a house. The first step, finding a unit, may be the most difficult one. Although the concept of cooperative dwellings is increasing, most exist in large urban areas.

The legal and financial aspects of cooperative housing are unique. When a corporation buys an entire building or a lot to begin a cooperative housing project, it secures a mortgage on the property. When you move into a cooperative building, you *cannot* get a traditional mortgage. This is because you are buying stock, not real estate.

In some cases, you will need to pay the full price of the stock in cash. You will not pay closing costs, however, since you are dealing directly with the corporation.

The tax advantages of living in a cooperative unit differ from those for other types of house ownership. In a cooperative situation, the corporation owns the building. It pays real estate taxes and makes the mortgage payments. As a stockholder, you can deduct from your income tax a certain portion of what the corporation pays in real estate taxes and mortgage interest.

When you live in a cooperative dwelling, you will pay a monthly fee. This money helps pay for maintenance and taxes. It also helps pay the corporation's mortgage payments on the property. If some residents fail to pay this fee for any length of time, the corporation might be unable to make mortgage payments and, therefore, face the possibility of foreclosure. Because of this risk, check the financial stability of the cooperative corporation before you buy any stock.

Review & Assessment

1. Identify two types of housing that require special ownership considerations.
2. Describe the information that can be found in a declaration of ownership.
3. When living in a cooperative dwelling, what types of expenses do monthly fees typically cover?

Moving to a New Home

Sometimes a household moves from one house to another within the same neighborhood or community. Many families expect such short moves as they end one stage of the life cycle and enter another. Changes in lifestyle, occupation, socioeconomic status, or other life situations—such as buying a home—also cause people to move. Use the moving expense checklist in Figure 23.24 to be sure you have all the records you need to claim a tax deduction.

Once you decide to move, decide how to do it. You have two alternatives: moving yourself or hiring a moving company.

Moving Yourself

About two-thirds of all moves are do-it-yourself efforts. If you do not own a truck or trailer, you can rent one and move yourself. There are many good reasons for tackling the job on your own. First,

Moving Expense Checklist
Keep the following records pertaining to your move in your possession at all times. Put them in a place you can easily access as some items may be tax deductible.
House-Hunting Trip Receipts
• Transportation costs (air, bus, train, automobile) • Meals • Lodging
Residence Replacement Records
• Advertising expense • Real estate commissions • Attorney fees • Appraisal fees • Mortgage expenses (title fees, points, escrow fees) • State transfer taxes • Lease settlement costs
Mover's Documents
• Bill of lading • Inventory • Packing and unpacking certificates • Weight certificates
Receipts for Temporary Living Quarters
• Lodging • Meals

Figure 23.24 A moving-expense checklist helps when you move. Some items may be tax deductible.

the cost is about one-third of what a professional mover charges. Second, you can move on your own schedule. Third, you and your goods arrive at the same time.

In comparison, realize what you save in money will cost you in time and energy. You will do all the packing, loading, unloading, and unpacking yourself. Family and friends can help if the move is only a short distance. They can also help with packing and loading for a long move.

As you rent moving equipment, such as a truck, dollies, and other supplies, check on liability and damage insurance for it. Find out the cost of insuring your belongings. Sometimes your home owner's or renter's policy covers your goods. If not, you may buy supplemental insurance to cover them. Get a written estimate from the insurance company and ask if there will be additional charges.

You can begin packing early. As you pack, take an inventory of your household items. An inventory will help you check the arrival of your belongings at your new house. It will also provide information you may need to collect insurance if you lose or damage any of your goods (Figure 23.25).

Hiring a Moving Company

Thousands of moving companies exist in the United States. Choose only licensed movers and obtain at least three written estimates to compare.

After choosing a moving company, ask about insurance. Be sure to read the fine print and ask

Rob Marmion/Shutterstock.com

Figure 23.25 Many people choose to pack their own household possessions and move the materials themselves.

Dragon Images/Shutterstock.com

Figure 23.26 When children take an active part in the family move, they adjust better and more quickly.

about additional costs. Also, ask about discounted moves, which offer a lower cost for moving during the off-peak season. Most people move between May 15 and September 30—the peak season. If you move during an off-peak season, be sure the cost is the only item that changes.

The next step is deciding how much, if any, of the packing and unpacking you will do. The cost of the packing boxes and the service of packing and unpacking are not included in the actual moving expense. The extra cost, however, can be worth it. Packing takes time and can be hard work. It is a good idea to photograph expensive pieces to prove their condition and value.

When you are moving with children, you will need to make special considerations. Moving may be traumatic for them. It is helpful to involve children in the move as much as possible (Figure 23.26). Tell them about the move early and let them decide what to pack.

When the moving van arrives at the new house, be sure the dwelling is ready for occupancy. Clean or paint ahead of time since both are difficult to do in a house filled with moving cartons. Decide how you want your furniture arranged and supervise its placement. Be sure items that were taken apart are reassembled.

As your belongings are unloaded from the van, check for damaged or missing items. List any of these items on the driver's copy and your copy of the *bill of lading*, which is a receipt listing the goods shipped.

Moving can be difficult. Therefore, it is important to weigh the advantages and disadvantages of the different ways to move. This will help you decide whether to move yourself or hire a moving company.

Review & Assessment

1. What are the advantages of moving yourself?
2. What are the advantages of hiring a moving company?
3. What is a bill of lading?

Chapter 23 Assessment

Summary

- When acquiring a house, there are various processes and costs involved.
- You may decide to rent or lease your housing.
- Carefully inspect the dwelling you choose before you sign a lease. Learn about assigning or subletting, breach of contract, and eviction.
- If you decide to buy housing, know how much you can spend. Calculate your housing-to-income ratio and debt-to-income ratio.
- Before shopping for a home, evaluate different types of mortgage loans and lenders.
- Obtain preapproval for a mortgage before you shop to help identify what you can spend and to show sellers you are serious about buying.
- After you find the house, you will need to make an offer; secure financing; acquire home owner's insurance; have a home inspection, survey, and appraisal; and pay the closing costs.
- After choosing a place to live or buying a home, decide how to move to it.

Terms in Action

1. **Synthesize terms** Review the list of *Content Terms* at the beginning of this chapter. Couple the terms together to create 10 total pairs of terms. Explain how the two terms you paired together relate to each other. Create a graphic organizer or write a brief description to explain or illustrate how the pairs relate.

Think Critically

2. **Analyze roles** Consider the many housing decisions you or you and other family must make. Analyze the impact of such housing decisions on the management of wage-earner roles. How does the choice to rent or purchase housing influence such roles? Use the text and other resources to defend your analysis.
3. **Analyze a lease** Visit an apartment leasing office and ask for a copy of the lease the landlord uses. Does it include all the important points listed in this chapter? Does it include any additional restrictions? How do your needs and wants impact the cost of housing? Analyze the legal aspects of leasing or renting housing. What are the lease and lessor responsibilities and rights? Discuss your findings in small groups.
4. **Draw conclusions** Sometimes home inspectors evaluate a home that is about to be purchased and discover problems in the foundation, heating system, or windows. Draw conclusions about whether or not you think the new owner should fix the items. Discuss evidence to support your conclusions in class.
5. **Analyze pros and cons** Ask the manager of a condominium complex for a copy of the declaration of ownership. Analyze the pros and cons of condominium ownership. Summarize your findings for the class.
6. **Analyze financial aspects** Locate a local classified ad offering a house for sale. Investigate the monthly cost of buying it using three different types of loans. Compare and contrast the loans for the interest rate, monthly payment, duration of the loan, and any conditions or restrictions. Analyze the legal aspects of purchasing housing. Share your findings with the class.
7. **Determine risk** When moving from one place to another, one way to save money is to have friends help you move. Would you accept the risk of possible damage to furniture or the new home due to accidents caused by your friends? Why or why not? What could you do to help prevent any damage?

Core Skills

8. **Research and writing** Research the consumer rights and responsibilities associated with housing, including renting, leasing, and purchasing. Compare the financial feasibility of these housing alternatives. Also, summarize laws that impact these housing decisions and summarize any recent changes in public policies that impact housing decisions and costs. Create a digital chart indicating consumer rights and responsibilities for each. Post your chart to the class website or e-mail it to your instructor.

Chapter 23 Assessment

9. **Writing** Use online resources and information from this chapter to compare the desirability of housing alternatives. Develop an electronic chart comparing the advantages and disadvantages of buying each of the following housing alternatives: (A) a pre-owned house; (B) a newly built house ready for occupancy; (C) a new house yet to be custom-built.
10. **Math practice** The average person can afford a house priced at 2.5 times their annual earnings. Calculate the house price each of the following families can afford based on their annual incomes.

    Family A—$32,000
    Family B—$54,000
    Family C—$75,000
    Family D—$150,000
11. **Math practice** According to the housing-to-income ratio, what total monthly housing costs are affordable to people with these yearly salaries: $38,000, $55,000, and $80,000?
12. **Math practice** Find a mortgage calculator online and enter a house purchase price, down payment amount, and interest rate. Then enter a higher interest rate and identify the monthly payment cost. How does the monthly payment change when the interest rate increases? Is it better to have a low interest rate or a high interest rate in terms of ability to pay for the home?
13. **Math practice** Determine the housing-to-income ratio and the debt-to-income ratio for the following situation. Suppose you and a sibling decide to buy a house. Your combined monthly gross income is $5,500. The proposed monthly mortgage payment for the house you like is $695. Other monthly related housing costs are $500. You pay $200 per month in credit card debt and your sibling's college loan payment is $150 per month. Will you and your sibling be able to borrow money for a mortgage based on your housing-to-income and debt-to-income ratios? What other factor(s) may determine your eligibility for a mortgage?
14. **Math practice** Suppose you want to buy a house that costs $92,000. Your mortgage lender requires a 20 percent down payment. How much money will you need for the down payment? Use the following formula:

    $$\text{Percent down payment} \times \text{House price} = \text{Down payment}$$
15. **Research, technology, and writing** Search online to locate at least two moving companies that serve the local area. What services do they provide? How are the costs calculated? Create a digital data table showing the services provided and the costs per company to share with your class. Which company would you choose and why?
16. **CTE career readiness practice** Suppose you have recently purchased your first home. You would now like to purchase a new refrigerator that costs $850. Investigate what the credit terms would be if you obtained credit from the seller, procured a cash loan, or used a credit card. Find out about finance charges, annual percentage rate, monthly payments, length of repayment period, and late payment charges. Which option gives you the best deal? Why? What benefit would you have from delaying your purchase and paying with cash?

Design Practice

17. **Create a virtual home tour** Presume your design firm has been hired to create a website design for a local real estate company's virtual home tours. As part of the analysis process, you and your team take a virtual tour on a competing real estate company's website. Is the tour realistic—prompting interested buyers to contact the company? With your teammates, put together a web design plan for virtual home tours that is attractive and engaging. Share your plan with the class.
18. **Portfolio** Develop a plan for selecting and renting an apartment. Include guidelines for conducting a search, reviewing your housing options, reviewing your housing rights and responsibilities, and examining required contracts. Save your plan in your portfolio.

Chapter 24

Home Safety and Security

Content Terms

electrical shock
carbon monoxide
radon
mold
lead paint
ventilation
asbestos
noise pollution
decibel (dB)
smoke detector
escape plan
deadbolt locks

Academic Terms

precautions
toxic
encapsulating
nuisance
combustible
asphyxiation
deter
biometrics

Learning Outcomes

After studying this chapter, you will be able to

- summarize ways to keep a home safe, including accident prevention, safety for children, keeping the air safe and clean, and controlling noise pollution.
- analyze ways to make a home secure from carbon monoxide poisoning, radon, fire, and intruders.
- determine changes that can make a home safe and secure for people with special needs.
- develop a plan for detecting safety hazards and maintaining a safe home.

Reading with Purpose

On a sheet of paper, write six reasons why the information in this chapter is important to you now and in the future. Think about how this information might help you at home or as an interior designer. When you finish reading the chapter, summarize your six reasons along with the chapter information that supports each reason.

While studying, look for the access icon  **to:**

- **Practice** the *Content* and *Academic Terms* with e-flash cards, matching activities, and vocabulary games.
- **Reinforce** what you learn by completing the *Review & Assessment* questions and e-mailing them to your instructor.

www.g-wlearning.com/housing/

Image provided courtesy of JELD-WEN Windows & Doors

You face a variety of risks as you go about your daily life. Using common sense and taking preventive measures may avoid other risks. The housing decisions you make for yourself and others can reduce the risk of home accidents. You can also make decisions that will help everyone in the home feel more secure.

A Safe Home

You, and many others, likely think of home as a safe place. Surprisingly, it is not always a safe place. More injuries take place in the home than anywhere else. Home accidents are a major cause of death and serious injury. Each year, accidents around the home, along with traffic and work accidents, hurt thousands of people each year. How safe is your home?

Preventing Accidents

In your own home and in the homes of interior design clients, you should not wait until an accident happens to take safety measures. Survey the home for danger spots. Guard the members of your household or that of a client against accidents that can have painful or even fatal results. Be sure that everyone knows and follows safety rules.

Preventing Falls

Falls are the most common type of home accidents. People of all ages suffer from falls, but the majority of those who suffer serious injury are older adults. Children also experience falls, but curiosity is generally the cause of such incidents, which usually are less serious. Taking a few simple ***precautions***, or preventive actions, can help avoid many falls. The following tips can help you prevent falls in and around the home.

- **Floors.** Wet floors can cause people to slip and fall. Wipe up water or other spilled liquids immediately.
- **Rugs.** Loose rugs can also cause falls. Choose rugs with a nonskid backing or place a nonskid pad under the rug.
- **Tripping hazards.** Remove tripping hazards by picking up toys, shoes, or other items left on floors or stairs and encourage others to do so, too.
- **Ladders.** When using a ladder or stepladder, make sure it is securely in place before climbing (Figure 24.1). Whenever possible, a second person should support the ladder. After using a ladder, store it properly so that children will not be tempted to climb.

Daxiao Productions/Shutterstock.com

Figure 24.1 A second person holding a tall ladder is a good safety principle.

- **Stairways.** Stairways should have light switches at both the top and bottom, and a sturdy, secure handrail. When climbing or descending stairs, always keep one hand free to use the rail. Keeping stairs free of clutter will also help prevent falls.
- **Bathrooms.** The bathroom can be especially dangerous because wet surfaces cause many falls. Soap left in the bathtub creates a slippery, hazardous surface. You can reduce the danger of falling in the bathroom by using suction-type nonskid mats or safety strips in the shower and bathtub. Firmly attached grab bars can also help prevent falls.
- **Bedrooms.** The most dangerous room in the home, according to the National Safety Council, is the bedroom. Many falls take place in the bedroom, as do fires. One reason for the high rate of bedroom accidents is that people move around while half-asleep. Placing handy lamps next to the bed will help prevent falls caused by stumbling in the dark.
- **Outdoors.** Falls also occur on the outside of the home, often as a result of slipping on wet leaves, snow, or ice. Promptly removing snow and ice from sidewalks will help prevent falls. Be sure to remove toys, garden tools, and other possible tripping hazards from walks.

Preventing Burns

Burns are another major type of injury resulting from home accidents. Children under four years of age and older adults are the most likely victims.

Kzenon/Shutterstock.com

Figure 24.2 Home accidents often occur during busy periods when attention is focused somewhere else.

Hot cooking utensils can cause serious burns (Figure 24.2). Turn panhandles away from the edge of the range when cooking to avoid spills. Open steam-filled pans on the side away from your body. To move hot utensils, use pot holders or oven mitts. Be sure the mitt or pot holder is not damp because the heat from the cooking utensil could cause steam burns.

Scalding water can cause serious burns, too. Lowering the temperature of your home's hot water supply to 120°F can prevent scalding burns.

Be careful of other household heat sources, such as toasters, hair dryers, steam irons, and portable room heaters.

Preventing Electrical Shock

Electricity in homes is convenient and makes possible a high standard of living. Proper design, installation, and maintenance of the home's electrical system are crucial to prevent it from becoming a safety hazard. An electrical shock can be fatal. **Electrical shock** is an electric current passing through your body.

Most electrical shocks result from the misuse of household appliances. The following guidelines will help you avoid electrical shock accidents:

- Since water conducts electricity, do not use electrical appliances near water or with wet hands. Dry your hands before using, connecting, or disconnecting electrical equipment. Also, do not stand on a damp floor while connecting or disconnecting an appliance's power cord.
- When disconnecting a power cord, grip the plug, not the cord. Pulling on the cord can weaken wires and eventually result in a shock or fire.
- Use heavy-duty extension cords whenever possible. An extension cord should never be lighter than the appliance cord that is plugged into it.
- To avoid damage to electrical cords, do not tie knots in them or run them under rugs. Replace damaged or frayed cords and defective plugs promptly.
- Do not plug too many tools or appliances into one outlet. Overloading circuits can cause electrical fires (Figure 24.3).

The National Electric Code requires safety grounding of all outlets. Kitchens, bathrooms, laundry rooms, and other locations near water require installation of a special type of electrical outlet. The outlet includes a *ground fault circuit interrupter (GFCI)* to prevent shocks. Outlets on the exterior of your home should have weatherproof covers or caps. Circuit breakers and fuses are safety devices. They interrupt electrical power if too much current flows. Always replace a fuse with one having the same rating. Using a fuse with a higher rating could allow wires to overheat, causing a fire.

Preventing Poisonings

Another major cause of home injuries and fatalities is poisoning (Figure 24.4). Swallowing common household products causes most such accidents. Laundry and cleaning aids, medicines, and cosmetics can be ***toxic***, or poisonous. Garden

Virote Chuenwiset/Shutterstock.com

Figure 24.3 In areas where many electrical tools are used, install enough wiring and outlets to safely handle the electrical load.

MyImages-Micha/Shutterstock.com

Figure 24.4 The skull-and-crossbones symbol is a warning sign for poisonous materials. Many household and gardening products show this symbol on their labels.

chemicals, materials used in the workshop, and many items found in the garage are also toxic. The leaves or other parts of some houseplants are poisonous, too, if eaten. The list of dangerous items is long. You can probably think of others.

To help prevent poisoning, always keep products in their original containers. Read and understand the product labels, and follow directions. Then properly dispose of the container and any leftover product. Use the safety checklist for hazardous materials in Figure 24.5.

You may wish to use nontoxic alternatives for household products that contain potentially harmful ingredients (Figure 24.6).

Keeping Children Safe at Home

Children are often the victims of home accidents. When they are present, be sure to take extra precautions. To prevent falls, install gates, bars, railings, and other types of barriers. Keep children away from open windows, porches, and stairways. To help prevent falls in the dark, install night-lights.

Keep children away from electrical appliances and cords. Install safety covers on unused outlets to prevent possible electrical shocks. Guard against fire, and safely store matches and lighters out of sight. It is especially important to involve children in fire drills so they know what to do in case of a fire.

Safety Checklist for Hazardous Materials
Actions to Take
• Store hazardous materials in their original labeled containers.
• Store hazardous materials in locked cabinets that are well ventilated.
• Keep hazardous materials beyond the reach of children and pets.
• Always read the entire label before using hazardous materials.
• Follow directions carefully and use the materials only in the manner permitted by law.
• Avoid inhaling hazardous materials.
• Wear protective clothing and masks when directions for hazardous materials require it.
• Protect your skin from exposure to accidental spills, and carefully clean up spills.
• Wash your hands thoroughly after handling the hazardous materials and again before eating.
• Wash contaminated clothing immediately after use when directed to do so.
• Cover or move your pet's food and water containers when using hazardous materials nearby or upwind.
• Dispose of the empty containers so they pose no hazards to humans, animals, wildlife, or plants.

Figure 24.5 When handling a hazardous material, or any material unfamiliar to you, carefully follow these steps to take safety precautions.

Safe Alternatives for Chemical Products		
You can substitute vinegar, baking soda, borax, and soap for most of the household products you use. To make an all-purpose cleaner with nontoxic ingredients, combine 1 gallon hot water, ⅔ cup baking soda, and ¼ cup vinegar. For tough cleaning jobs, double the baking soda and vinegar. For specific household needs, use the following mixtures.		
Product	**Hazardous Chemicals**	**Safe Alternative**
Abrasive cleaners or powders	Ammonia, ethanol	Rub area with ½ lemon dipped in borax; rinse and dry.
Ammonia-based cleaners	Ammonia, ethanol	Use a mixture of vinegar, salt, and water for most surfaces; for bathrooms, use baking soda and water.
Bleach cleaners	Sodium or potassium hydroxide, hydrogen peroxide, sodium or calcium hypochlorite	For laundry, use ½ cup white vinegar, baking soda, or borax.
Disinfectants	Diethylene or methylene glycol, sodium hypochlorite, phenols	Mix ½ cup borax in 1 gallon water.
Drain cleaners	Sodium or potassium hydroxide, sodium hypochlorite, hydrochloric acid, petroleum distillates	Flush with ½ cup baking soda, ¼ cup vinegar, and boiling water.
Enamel or oil-based paints	Pigments, ethylene, aliphatic hydrocarbons, mineral spirits	Latex or water-based paints.
Floor and furniture polish	Diethylene glycol, petroleum distillates, nitrobenzene	Mix 1 part lemon juice with 2 parts olive or vegetable oil.
House plant insecticide	Methoprene, malathion, tetramethrin, carbaryl	Mix a few drops liquid soap and 1 cup water; spray on leaves.
Roach and ant killers	Organophosphates, carbamates, pyrethrins	To kill roaches, use traps or a mixture of baking soda and powdered sugar. For ants, use chili powder to hinder entry.

Figure 24.6 The alternatives listed here are less harmful to people and the environment than other well-known products.

Children can learn to identify symbols that indicate poison. Many products that can be dangerous to children, however, are not in a poison classification. For example, how many laundry and cleaning products have you seen that carry a warning label? Where do you store these products in your home? Too often, people keep them under the kitchen sink, where children can reach them easily. Be sure to store dangerous products in a safe place, such as behind doors with safety latches or locks (Figure 24.7).

Keeping dangerous products out of sight is the best safety precaution to use with children. Simply moving them out of reach is no guarantee that children will not try to reach them anyway, however. Young children cannot judge the distance to an object and the length of their reach. Many serious falls occur when children climb and stretch for distant objects that seem reachable.

A home swimming pool is another potential source of danger for children. For youngsters under five years of age, drowning is one of the leading causes of accidental deaths around the home. Local codes usually specify the type and height of fences and other enclosures that home owners must install around pools. In addition,

B Calkins/Shutterstock.com

Figure 24.7 This cabinet door lock is one option for protecting children from substances that may be harmful to them.

pool owners should observe the following safety precautions:

- Supervise young children at all times.
- Keep a phone and emergency numbers handy (Figure 24.8).
- Learn cardiopulmonary resuscitation (CPR) procedures, a lifesaving technique to use in an emergency.

Keeping the Air Safe and Clean

Clean air in the home is more of a concern now than in the past. To save energy used for heating and cooling, houses have become more airtight. Such airtight houses, however, have increased the problem of indoor air pollution.

Few people realize that air pollution can be very bad inside the average home. Indoor pollution comes from many sources. Some insulating materials give

Aleksandra Gigowska/Shutterstock.com

Figure 24.8 Keep emergency numbers directly next to your house phone or programmed into your cell phone so children can refer to them quickly.

off vapors that are pollutants. Tobacco smoke, dust, pet dander, and household cleaning and beauty products all add pollutants to the air in the home. Even stagnant water left in containers like vaporizers and humidifiers pollutes the air.

When various sources create pollutants in an airtight house, problems may arise. The air can become polluted enough to affect health. People may develop allergies or feel tired and listless. Two pollutants—carbon monoxide and radon—can cause serious illness.

Carbon Monoxide

Perhaps the most dangerous of all indoor pollutants is carbon monoxide. **Carbon monoxide** is a colorless, odorless, tasteless gas that develops from incomplete burning of fossil fuel or wood. Fossil fuels include natural gas, propane, gasoline, coal, and charcoal. Depending on how much gas a person inhales, symptoms can range from temporary headaches to permanent brain damage to death.

The body's red blood cells readily absorb carbon monoxide. The primary job of red blood cells is carrying oxygen to all parts of the body. When these cells carry carbon monoxide instead, oxygen starvation occurs in the body. The poisonous gas gradually invades all body cells. Nausea, coughing, and dizziness are the first signs of carbon monoxide poisoning. If they suspect such poisoning, people should call 911 or their local fire department immediately—especially if one or more household members, and even pets, show the same flu-like symptoms.

Most cases of carbon monoxide poisoning occur with the onset of cold weather. Restarting furnaces

ENERGY STAR Air Quality Label

Research studies show that air pollution in homes and other buildings is often two to five times that of the outdoors. People have concerns about mold, radon, carbon monoxide, and toxic chemicals found in living and working environments. Poor indoor air quality can lead to a number of health problems including allergies, headaches, and such breathing problems as asthma.

One reliable solution is the ENERGY STAR Indoor Air Package. The federal government backs this solution. Homes with this labeling effectively deal with the following problems:

- Moisture control—added protection from mold and other moisture-related challenges
- Pest management—provides defense from pests because there are fewer cracks and other ways for pests to enter the home
- Heating and cooling system and vents—help prevent moisture problems and also filter the air
- Venting of fumes and gases—a ventilation system removes carbon monoxide from the home
- Building materials—selected to reduce the release of gases and other chemicals into the air
- Radon protection—special treatments and designs are used to control radon in the indoor air

without a proper cleaning from the previous winter's use is a leading cause. Homes that are tightly caulked and weather-stripped prevent indoor air from escaping. These are ideal conditions for the creation and buildup of the poisonous gas. Entire households have been known to die within a few days of starting a poorly maintained gas furnace.

Regular maintenance of fuel-burning appliances is the best way to prevent the creation of carbon monoxide. Venting all fuel-burning appliances to the outdoors is another way. You can monitor your home's carbon monoxide levels with a carbon monoxide detector, which will be discussed later in this chapter.

Radon

Radon is a natural radioactive gas. Radon occurs in high concentrations in soils and rocks containing uranium and some other minerals. Soils with certain types of industrial wastes often contain this substance. Radon can lead to lung cancer. The risk of developing lung cancer from radon depends on the concentration and the length of exposure time to the gas.

You cannot see, smell, or taste radon. Federal and state governments are working to identify high-risk areas and provide information on handling radon exposure. The solution may be as simple as keeping the home well ventilated.

The federal government recommends that you measure the level of radon in your home. A radon test is the only way to know whether radon is present (Figure 24.9).

Mold

Sometimes harmful mold (also commonly called *mildew*) can begin growing on surfaces in homes. A **mold** is a fungus that grows on damp or decaying matter. Some molds can be harmful to humans. These harmful molds can grow anywhere there is warmth and moisture, particularly in bathrooms,

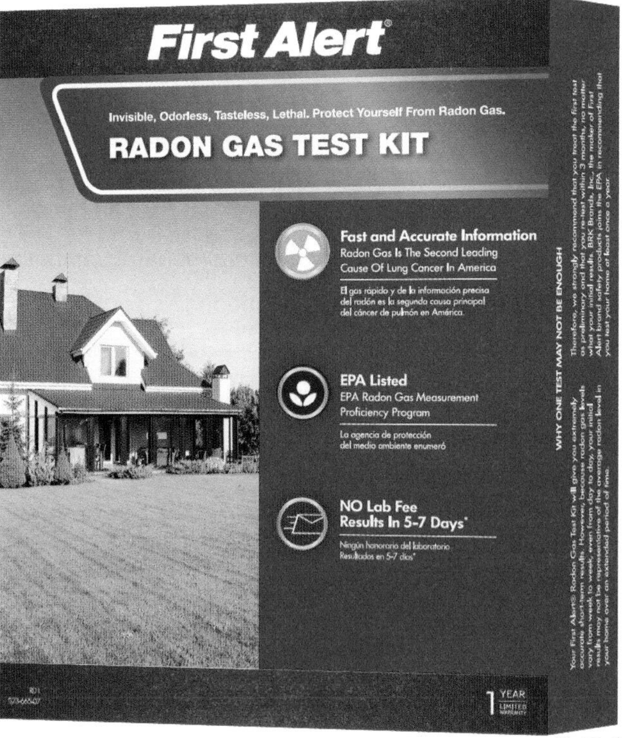

First Alert

Figure 24.9 A radon test kit is available from several companies. Radon detection services are also available.

under carpeting, or in the cavities of walls, floors, and ceilings. Whenever flooding or water problems occur in a home, preventing an environment for mold growth requires proper drying and ventilation. Common causes of water problems include leaking pipes and emergencies such as an overflow from a clogged sink.

Health problems, such as allergies and other respiratory conditions, can occur from harmful molds in the air. Continual irritation by harmful airborne mold spores keeps these reactions from going away easily. A house in which household members suffer continuing breathing difficulties and allergic reactions may require a professional inspection for mold. If an inspector finds mold, professional removal is often a requirement.

Lead Paint

Lead paint refers to lead-based paint, which was a common form of paint manufactured before 1978. When the hazards of lead poisoning became clear, the federal government banned the use of lead in paint in 1978. However, homes built or painted prior to that date often have paint that contains lead. Federal law also requires that individuals receive specific information regarding the presence of lead paint before renting, buying, or renovating pre-1978 housing.

The problem with lead-based paint occurs when the paint chips, peels, or results in excessive amounts of lead-contaminated dust. For example, opening and closing windows with lead paint creates such chips and dust, thereby allowing the lead to become airborne. Small children sometimes eat paint chips, mistaking them for candy. Lead can also be absorbed by handling of some ceramics and other items containing lead.

Lead can be harmful, especially to young children, pregnant women, and older adults. In children, lead poisoning can cause damage to the brain and nervous system, which results in behavior and learning problems. Adults can also suffer many permanent physical difficulties.

A house can be tested for lead paint and airborne lead so the occupants know about any potential hazard. Also, household members can take steps to avoid the harmful effects of the paint. These steps include professional paint removal from the walls and possibly replacing the windows.

Ventilation

Proper **ventilation**, or air circulation, greatly reduces air pollution levels. The living spaces of the house need ventilation to exchange fresh air for stale air. The attic, basement, or any crawl space under the floor also requires proper ventilation. If a house does not have built-in vents, they can be installed. Home owners can add exhaust fans to increase ventilation. With good ventilation planning, household air exchange occurs at a good rate (Figure 24.10).

Home Ventilation Checklist

Consider the following questions when evaluating the effectiveness of a home ventilation system. If a home owner answers "no" to any of the following, it may be necessary to make some changes in the home ventilation system.

- Does the home have continuous general ventilation?
- Is there spot ventilation as needed?
- Are windows clear of condensation?
- Are there lingering odors in the home?
- Are exhaust ducts insulated in an unheated space, such as a basement or crawl space?
- Does the exhaust fan over the kitchen range have a vent to the outdoors?
- Is the dryer vented outdoors?
- Does each fuel-burning device (such as a furnace, water heater, or wood-burning stove) have a separate vent to the outdoors?
- Does each bathroom have an exhaust fan vented to the outdoors (and not into a soffit, attic, or crawl space)?
- Is exhaust air free of condensation?
- Has the home been tested for radon? Were the levels high or low?

Figure 24.10 After evaluating your home ventilation, you may be able to correct problems with a few simple steps.

Eliminating or controlling the source of the pollutants can reduce air pollution. For example, ventilate the home well whenever painting, staining wood, or using chemicals that release vapors. Always follow manufacturer's instructions when using harsh chemicals. Become familiar with their negative health effects so you can recognize the symptoms if they occur.

Professional sealing or ***encapsulating*** (enclosing) for some pollutant types is necessary to prevent polluting the air. Asbestos is a prime example. **Asbestos** is a fireproof, cancer-causing mineral that can easily become airborne and inhaled. Because of its fireproof quality, asbestos was used prior to 1978 in insulation, linoleum flooring, and other building materials. When renovating an older home, any asbestos present requires professional removal or encapsulation.

Two effective solutions for eliminating pollutants in the home are proper ventilation and elimination of pollutants' sources. Another solution to consider is the use of an air cleaner. Such devices generally clean the air of particles, not vapors or gases. Before buying an air cleaner, carefully check its *clean air delivery rate (CADR)*. This is the industry measure by which air cleaner manufacturers test the performance of their appliances.

Housecleaning

Housecleaning methods also affect the indoor pollution level. Using a feather duster, for instance, merely stirs dust around to later settle on another surface. A central vacuum system helps clean the air by filtering it and exhausting it to the outside. Indoor air cleaners with good airflow and sturdy filters can clean effectively, too. Some vacuum cleaners use a compartment of water to "filter" the air before it returns to the room. Cleaning services are another housecleaning alternative (Figure 24.11). These services will handle any size job at times convenient to the home inhabitants.

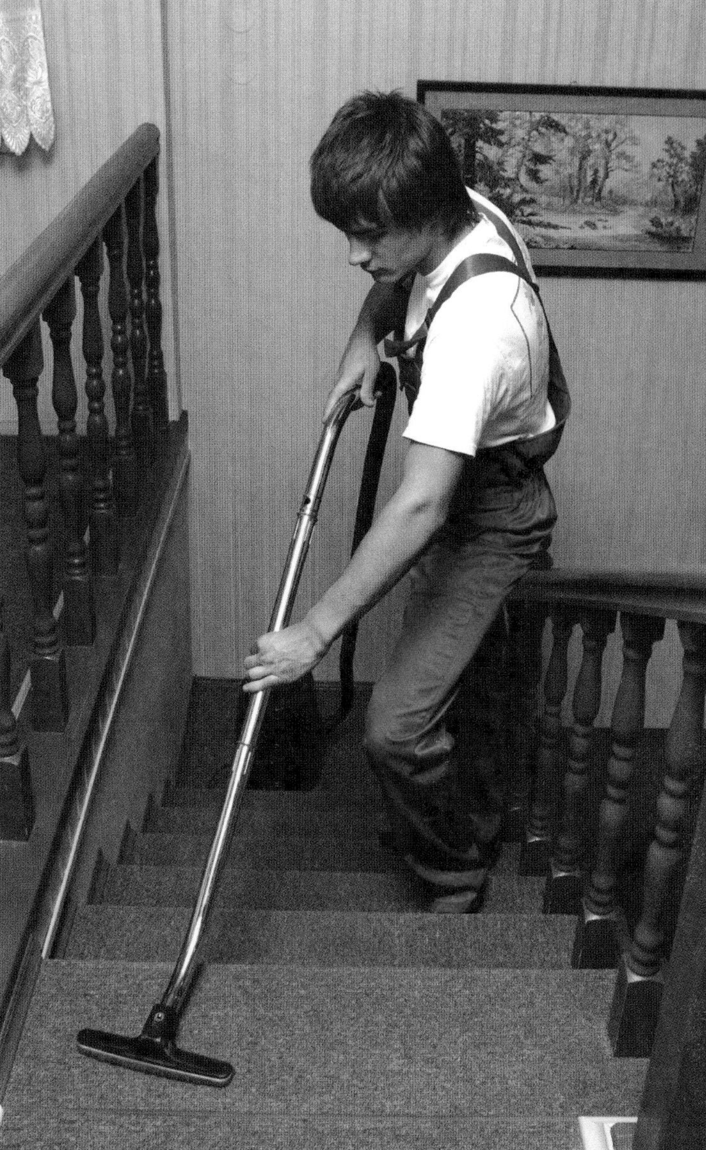

nikkytok/Shutterstock.com

Figure 24.11 The owner of this house called a professional cleaning service to remove sawdust particles that settled throughout the house during remodeling.

Controlling Noise Pollution

Noise pollution is unwanted sound that spreads through the environment. According to government studies, noise is the leading cause of neighborhood dissatisfaction, which suggests it is a widespread ***nuisance*** (annoyance). Medical research indicates that noise causes physical and psychological stress. It hampers concentration, slows work efficiency, and interferes with sleep.

Sound is the sensation the sense of hearing perceives. A **decibel (dB)** is a unit for measuring sound intensity. The quietest sound that people can hear has a rating of 0 dB. Normal conversation is about 60 dB. The loudness of a sound and the length of exposure time to it determine its effect on a person. Continual exposure to loud noise can cause permanent hearing loss.

Listen to your house. Evaluate the noises you hear. Do they interfere with conversation? Are there sounds that invade privacy or cause distractions? See Figure 24.12 for sound levels of some typical

Household Noisemakers	
Appliance	**Sound Level in Decibels**
Floor fan	38 to 70
Refrigerator	40
Automatic washer	47 to 78
Dishwasher	54 to 85
Clothes dryer	55
Hair dryer	59 to 80
Vacuum cleaner	62 to 85
Sewing machine	64 to 74
Food disposer	67 to 93
Electric shaver	75
Electric lawn edger	81
Home shop tools	85
Gasoline-powered mower	87 to 92
Gasoline-powered riding mower	90 to 95
Chain saw	100
Stereo	up to 120
Digital music players	100 to 115

Figure 24.12 These are the sound levels heard by the person operating the appliance or someone standing nearby. Normal conversation level is about 60 dB.

Photography Courtesy of Karastan

Figure 24.13 The rug on this kitchen floor helps hold down appliance noise and noise from other activities in the kitchen.

household appliances. Compare them to the level of normal conversation.

Solving some noise problems may be a simple matter. Solving others may take more effort. Indoors you can install sound-absorbing materials, such as acoustical ceiling panels. Carpets and draperies also help absorb sound (Figure 24.13). Pleasant sounds, such as music, can muffle unwanted sounds. You may want to consider closing off noisy rooms. When you buy new appliances, you may want to choose those that are designed for quieter operation.

Insulating exterior walls may control noise from outside the house. Storm windows or multiple-pane glass can keep out some of the noise. Landscaping techniques, such as building berms (earth mounds), erecting walls, and planting shrubs, can also help reduce noise.

Review & Assessment

1. Summarize three types of home accidents. Give a possible cause for each and a precaution that could prevent it.
2. What two people groups are the most likely victims of home accidents?
3. Name three health problems that may result from inside air pollution.
4. How is sound measured?
5. What is the difference between noise and sound? Name two ways noise can impact people.
6. What is the best way to keep household members secure from carbon monoxide poisoning?
7. List two guidelines children who are home alone should follow.

A Secure Home

A home should provide security, which is protection from physical harm. It should be a place where people can feel safe and sheltered from the unknown.

If you live in a well-built dwelling located in a relatively crime-free neighborhood, you are likely to feel safe. To more fully satisfy the need for security, however, include some protective devices in the home. Some of these devices monitor the surrounding conditions to make sure the home stays safe and secure.

Security from Carbon Monoxide Poisoning

Any dwelling that burns a fossil fuel or wood indoors should have a carbon monoxide detector. The chemical symbol for carbon monoxide is CO, so this device is a CO detector. Many local building codes require the installation of these detectors in new housing. Some cities require CO detectors in all housing.

This relatively inexpensive device sounds an alarm when low levels of the poisonous gas are present. It provides an early warning to occupants before harmful levels of carbon monoxide develop.

Career Focus Security Management Specialists and Systems Installers

Do you have an interest in helping people and keeping them safe? Are you a hands-on person who likes to work with systems and tools? Do you have an interest in electricity and electronics? If you have these interests and can imagine yourself in a career in public safety, perhaps a job as a security management specialist or a security and fire alarm systems installer is for you.

Interests/Skills: Security management specialists and security and fire alarm systems installers must have knowledge and skills about equipment, wiring, computer program applications, and ability to monitor such systems and those who design and install them. They must also have excellent communication skills to work with clients and industry professionals and understand their security needs. Effective problem solving, manual dexterity, and precision are also key skills. They must also understand building and construction and the tools involved in repair or construction of houses and buildings. Installers of security equipment need to think critically and solve complex problems.

Career Snapshot: Security management specialists and security and fire alarm systems installers work with individuals of private homes to estimate installation costs, install equipment, and maintain these systems. They meet with clients to prepare an estimate and effectively demonstrate how the system functions. They may also return to a client to help fix any electrical issues or expand the system as needed. In addition, installers must determine whether certain systems comply with laws, regulations, and standards.

Fh Photo/Shutterstock.com

Education/Training: Most positions require an associate's degree or training in career and technical education programs. Security management specialists and installers of security equipment may also receive on-the-job training with experienced workers or participate in an apprenticeship program.

Licensing/Examinations: Most states require licensing for any firm or individual that installs, monitors, or maintains fire and burglar alarm systems.

Professional Associations: Central Station Alarm Association (CSAA); Electronic Security Association (ESA)

Job Outlook: Jobs in this area are expected to grow slower than the average. Job opportunities may arise from professionals who retire within the industry.

Sources: The Occupational Outlook Handbook (OOH); the Occupational Information Network (O*NET)

Since most carbon monoxide poisoning occurs when people are sleeping, install CO detectors near bedrooms. The ideal location is on the hallway ceiling outside the rooms. If bedrooms are on a second floor, install the CO detector on the ceiling at the top of the stairs. For greater protection, locate carbon monoxide detectors in the kitchen and at the top of a basement stairway. If battery operated, it is important to check batteries and replace them on a regular basis (Figure 24.14).

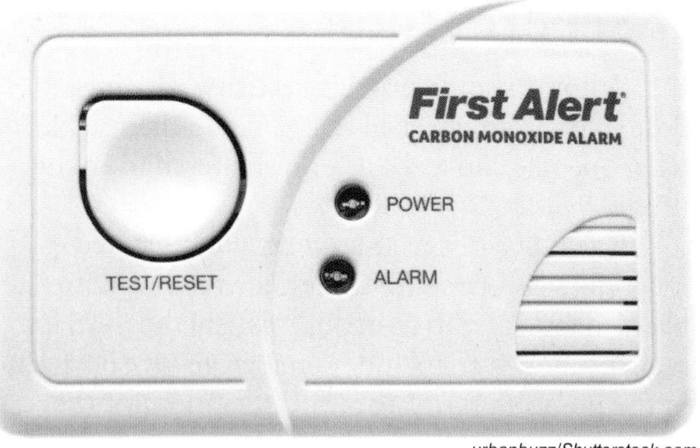

urbanbuzz/Shutterstock.com

Figure 24.14 You can buy a combination carbon monoxide and smoke detector that mounts inconspicuously on or near the ceiling.

Security from Fire

Home fires are one of the most serious types of accidents, sometimes claiming small children and the elderly as victims. Fires can cause not only bodily injury and death, but also costly damage to property. The leading causes of fire include

- cooking accidents
- operating defective electrical or heating equipment
- unintentional carelessness

Fire department officials stress that fire prevention is a matter of common sense. You can help prevent a fire in your home by following these simple rules:

- Choose upholstered furniture constructed to resist a fire caused by smoldering material. Such furniture carries a hangtag from the Upholstered Furniture Action Council (UFAC) certifying that the upholstery is resistant to sources of smoldering heat.
- Store flammable liquids properly, using only approved containers.
- Keep ***combustible*** (burnable) materials away from a source of fire.

Housing Health & Safety

Creating a Family Emergency Plan

Hurricanes. Earthquakes. Fires. Power outages. These are a few of the natural and man-made disasters that can suddenly turn lives upside down. Although some of these events are unpredictable, you can still help prepare your family for such situations. Identify the potential hazards in your area and know how local authorities will alert you to these dangers. Also, create an emergency plan with members of your household.

Check with the American Red Cross, the U.S. Department of Homeland Security, and local authorities for the most up-to-date and detailed information. Fill out the “Family Emergency Plan” form at the U.S. government's ready.gov website. The form prompts you for information about household members' medical issues, an evacuation location, and how members will contact one another if separated. Put a copy of the emergency plan in your emergency preparedness kit. Make sure everyone knows how and when to dial 911 for emergencies.

The following are general tips for emergency preparedness:

- Assemble an emergency preparedness kit. Everyone in the household should know what it contains and where it is located. Keep a copy of your emergency plan in the kit or wherever it will be handy.
- Know the locations of shut-off switches for electricity, gas, and water services, and how to shut them off. (Since improperly turning on the gas is dangerous, get assistance from the utility company to turn it back on.)
- Eliminate in-home hazards. Move heavy items to low shelves; remove items hung over beds. Strap or bolt heavy furniture and appliances, including water heaters, to walls, floors, and secured cabinets.
- Hold an emergency drill several times each year. Rehearse your plan and make changes as necessary.

The American Red Cross says one person in each household should be trained in first aid, CPR, and the operation of an automated external defibrillator (AED). With these tips and special training, you can help prepare your family for disaster.

- Keep matches in a safe place out of sight where children cannot reach them. Be sure to dispose of used matches and lighters in a safe manner.
- Do not overload electrical wires.
- Dispose of trash regularly.
- Have the heating system inspected yearly by a professional.
- Burn only seasoned (dry) wood in wood-burning stoves and fireplaces. Do not use green wood, which can cause the buildup of a dark, flammable tar in the chimney.
- Keep at least three feet of open space around any space heater and never leave one unattended around children. Keep space heaters away from bedding, curtains, papers, and other combustibles.

Some fire deaths result from burns or injuries resulting from panic. However, the deadly smoke and gases a fire releases claim most fire victims through asphyxiation. ***Asphyxiation*** is the state of unconsciousness or death resulting from inadequate oxygen or some other breathing obstruction. Some simple steps can help you escape injury. The best precaution, however, is having a fire emergency plan, which you will learn about later in this chapter.

Smoke Detectors

A **smoke detector** will send a loud warning signal if a fire starts. The detectors are easy to install. Place one on each floor of a building. The diagrams in Figure 24.15 suggest good locations for smoke detectors. Most building codes for new homes require smoke detectors.

There are two basic types of smoke detectors: ionization and photoelectric. The ionization type responds more rapidly to fires where flames are present. The photoelectric detector is quicker to detect a smoldering, slow-burning fire. Both types effectively provide an early fire warning. Most detectors use batteries for operation, but some connect directly to the home's electrical wiring. As with other appliances, check for a safety seal before choosing a smoke detector.

If a smoke detector is battery operated, install a fresh battery once each year. Most smoke detectors emit a sharp beep or have a flashing light to indicate that the battery needs replacing. It is a good idea to check smoke detectors for proper operation every month. Most units have a test button for this purpose.

Fire Extinguishers

Fire extinguishers are classified according to the type of burning material they handle. The Class A extinguisher is for fires involving paper, wood, fabric, and other "ordinary combustibles." Utilize Class B extinguishers for liquids that combust into fire, such as overheated cooking oil in a skillet on the range. Class C extinguishers are best for use on electrical fires.

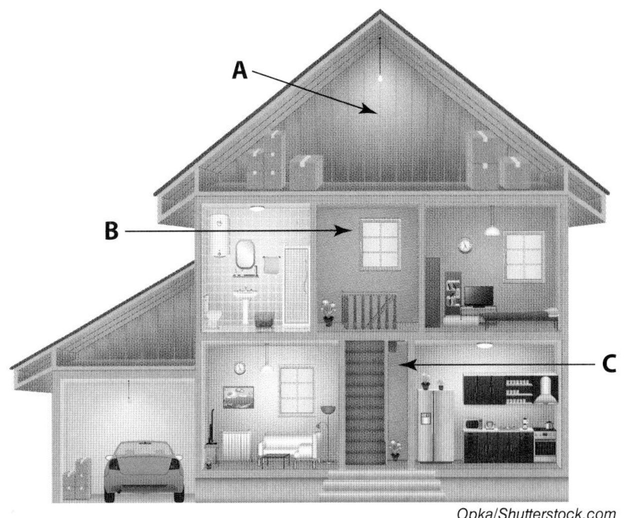

Opka/Shutterstock.com

Figure 24.15 Smoke detectors should be placed on each floor of a dwelling (A), especially near bedrooms (B). They can be mounted on a ceiling or wall (C).

Figure 24.16 describes the classes of fire extinguishers. In practice, you can use many extinguishers available today on fires of any type. These types of extinguishers are marked ABC. Locate fire extinguishers where they are easy to find and use (Figure 24.17).

Plan for Fire Emergencies

The members of your household should have a plan of action, or **escape plan**, in case a fire occurs. Draw a scale floor plan of your home. Then mark a main escape route and an alternate route from each room. Remember that children and older adults will need special assistance in escaping from a fire. Make sure that all members of the household know the sound of the fire detector alarm and any other signal that household members might use. For example, you might use a loud whistle or a bell to awaken and alert everyone in the home.

Everyone must understand that speed in leaving the burning building is essential. There is no time to waste getting dressed or collecting possessions. Be sure each person knows how to make the door test: if the knob or panels of the closed door are warm, do not open the door. Use an alternate escape route. If the doorknob or panels are not warm, open the door slowly. If no smoke or hot air blows in, it is probably safe to use that exit.

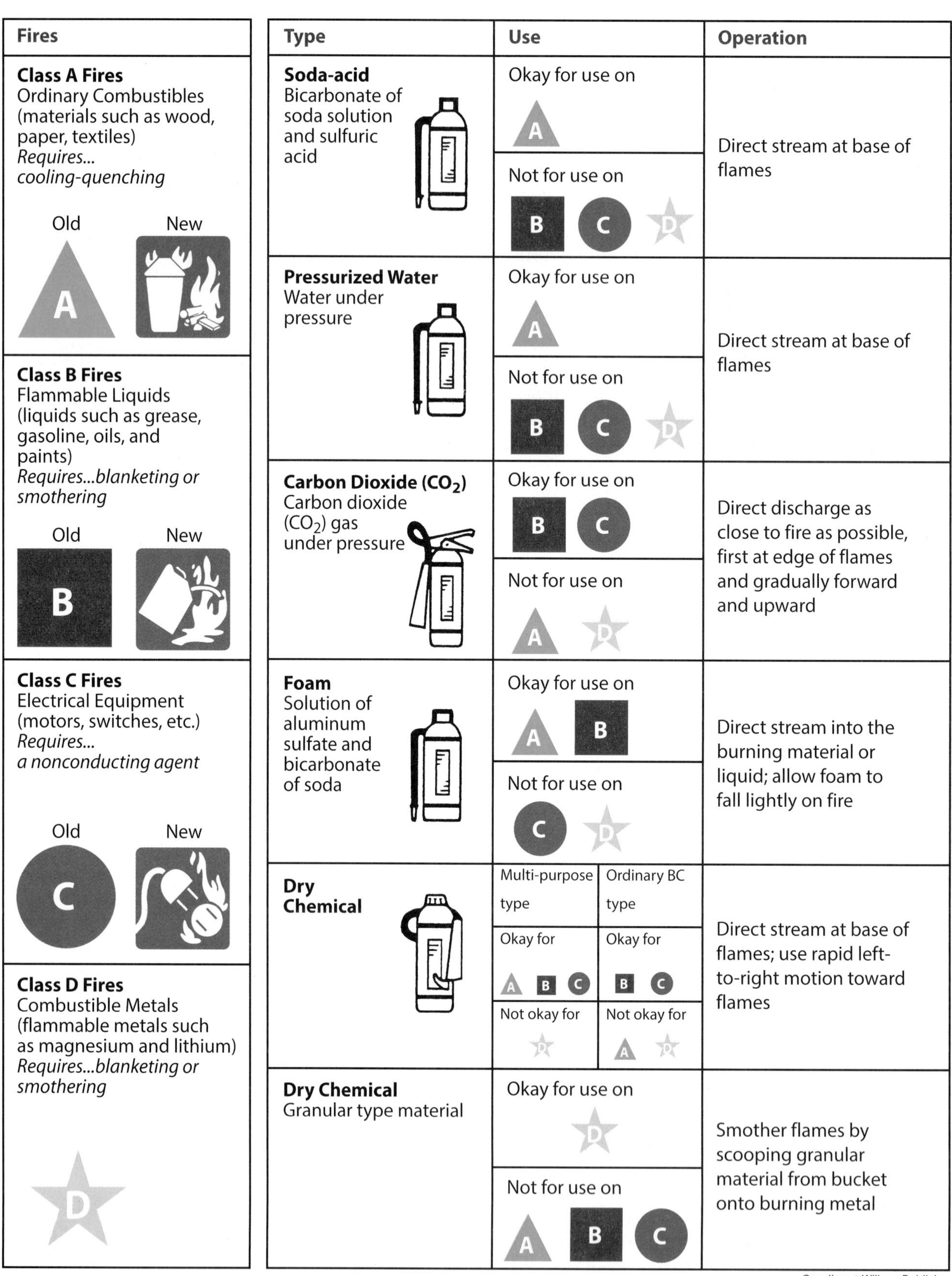

Fires
Class A Fires Ordinary Combustibles (materials such as wood, paper, textiles) *Requires... cooling-quenching* Old: A New
Class B Fires Flammable Liquids (liquids such as grease, gasoline, oils, and paints) *Requires...blanketing or smothering* Old: B New
Class C Fires Electrical Equipment (motors, switches, etc.) *Requires... a nonconducting agent* Old: C New
Class D Fires Combustible Metals (flammable metals such as magnesium and lithium) *Requires...blanketing or smothering* D

Type	Use	Operation
Soda-acid Bicarbonate of soda solution and sulfuric acid	Okay for use on: A Not for use on: B C D	Direct stream at base of flames
Pressurized Water Water under pressure	Okay for use on: A Not for use on: B C D	Direct stream at base of flames
Carbon Dioxide (CO_2) Carbon dioxide (CO_2) gas under pressure	Okay for use on: B C Not for use on: A D	Direct discharge as close to fire as possible, first at edge of flames and gradually forward and upward
Foam Solution of aluminum sulfate and bicarbonate of soda	Okay for use on: A B Not for use on: C D	Direct stream into the burning material or liquid; allow foam to fall lightly on fire
Dry Chemical	Multi-purpose type — Okay for: A B C; Not okay for: D Ordinary BC type — Okay for: B C; Not okay for: A D	Direct stream at base of flames; use rapid left-to-right motion toward flames
Dry Chemical Granular type material	Okay for use on: D Not for use on: A B C	Smother flames by scooping granular material from bucket onto burning metal

Goodheart-Willcox Publisher

Figure 24.16 This chart shows fire and fire extinguisher classifications. Use the proper extinguisher effectively to put out fires. Using the wrong extinguisher may lead to electrocution.

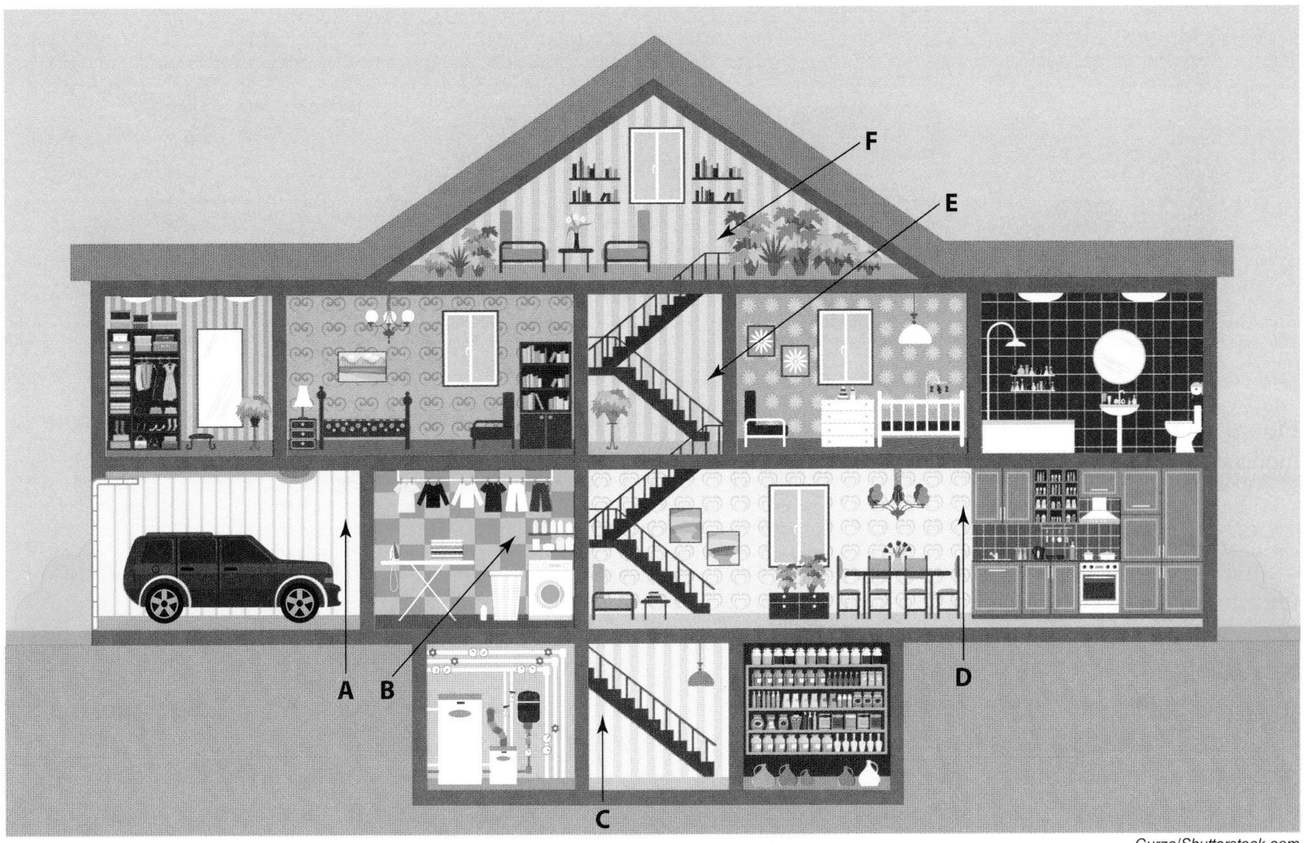

Figure 24.17 Install fire extinguishers in the garage (A), laundry room (B), basement (C), kitchen (D), and easy-to-reach locations on each floor (E and F). Ideally, they should be near exits. No corner of the floor should be more than 75 feet away from an extinguisher.

If the home has more than one floor or is high off the ground, it is a good idea to provide a fire escape ladder in each bedroom. This allows another exit from the room when other exits are unusable. Conduct a trial practice in using the ladder as part of the household escape plan.

Part of your plan should include deciding on a place to meet once everyone is outside. After everyone is safely outside, find the nearest phone and call the fire department.

Once everyone knows the emergency plan, hold a practice drill. Repeat the drills periodically. Be sure to practice the use of alternate routes as well as main escape routes.

Security from Home Intruders

Securing a home from burglary or unwanted intruders is important. Many security measures are merely common sense. For instance, do not publicize the absence of household members when away from home. Most burglaries are committed during the day, while people are away at work or shopping. Take steps to make your home look lived-in, even when you are gone. The following will give a home that lived-in look:

- leaving a vehicle in the driveway
- stopping delivery of newspapers and mail, or having a friend pick them up daily at the normal times
- returning emptied trash cans from the curb
- using a variable timer to turn lights, radio, or TV on and off
- keeping the yard mowed, or snow removed from walks
- opening drapes during the day and closing them at night
- keeping a dog that barks at strange noises

Do not let strangers into your home. You should have some way of knowing who is at the door without opening it. A peephole or a chain lock permits you to see who is there. Monitoring devices are available that permit you to see and hear the person at your door before that person sees you (Figure 24.18). If a stranger asks to use your phone, offer to make the call for him or her. Other security precautions include using outside lighting at every entrance to your home and installing secure locks on all doors and windows. You can also install a home security system with an alarm.

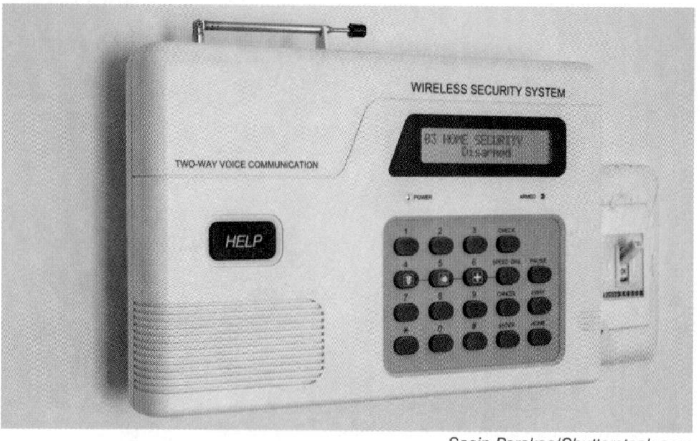

Sasin Paraksa/Shutterstock.com

Figure 24.18 This family information center helps monitor safety and security in the home.

Maxal Tamor/Shutterstock.com

Figure 24.19 A deadbolt lock makes entrances more secure. The type that requires a key to enter either side, as shown above, is best.

When home alone, children should follow additional rules. Children should know how to use the phone, and important numbers should be available nearby. When answering the phone, instruct children not to give details. For example, children should not tell a caller they are home alone or what time someone is to return.

Make the exterior of your home as visible as possible. Install a system to light exterior doors and the yard. Use automatic timers so lights are on from dusk to dawn. An alternate method is to use motion-detecting lights that go on when anything moves near the house. Trim all shrubs so that doors and windows are clearly visible from the street. If shrubs are growing under windows, make sure that they are thorny or cannot hide an intruder.

Locks and Other Security Devices

To make doors as secure as possible, install **deadbolt locks** as in Figure 24.19. These are lock bolts that unlock by turning a knob or key without action of a spring. Use a double-cylinder lock that requires a key to unlock from the inside as well as the outside. When moving to a new residence, change the lock cylinders to prevent entry by anyone who previously had a key to the door. Lock cylinders are less expensive than complete locks. Be sure to hire a reputable locksmith to make this change.

Keep all windows and exterior doors locked. If there is a door between the garage and the house, keep it locked, too. Never leave keys in the locks. Also, do not hide keys near entrances, such as under a mat. Intruders know the usual hiding places and can find them easily. Install extra locks or take other measures to make sliding doors and windows secure.

Install strong exterior doors that are made of metal or have solid wood cores. Many doors are so weak that they can be broken through with a strong kick. Hang the doors so the hinge pins are on the inside. If the pins are on the outside, a burglar can remove them and open the door. If you have a glass pane in the door, installing a rigid transparent panel is a good security measure. A panel of plastic, such as acrylic, is ideal for this purpose.

Another deterrent to burglary is to mark your valuables with an identification number. Marking valuables can ***deter*** (discourage) a thief, since marked items are more difficult to sell for quick cash than unmarked items. If a burglar steals your possessions, these items are easier to trace and identify with an identification number. Keep valuable items, such as jewelry and savings bonds, safely locked away. People may wish to store them in a home safe, a private security vault, or a safe deposit box at the bank.

Home Security Systems

Many people install electronic home security systems in their homes. The newest models use biometrics to determine who belongs in the home and who does not. ***Biometrics*** is the measurement and analysis of an individual by using unique physical characteristics. Safe, keyless entry into homes is possible with security systems that use biometric data. Fingerprints, the pattern of an eye's iris, and vein patterns in hands are some of the biometrics that can identify the members of a household.

The typical home security system uses window and door sensors. The sensors trigger an alarm when someone forces open a door or window. Some systems also have sensors that respond to vibrations, body heat, or noise. Some include smoke detectors or water-flow alarms, which signal a plumbing problem. Many home security systems will signal a burglary attempt with flashing lights, a siren, an alarm bell, or a combination. Other systems

Housing Health & Safety

Assembling an Emergency Preparedness Kit

During a natural disaster or other emergency, your home and community may lose power, heat, water, telephone, and Internet services. Emergency responders may be temporarily unavailable. You may have to evacuate your home. Roads, stores, doctor's offices, and other businesses and services may be closed. Hopefully, this will never happen to you. However, if it should, having an emergency preparedness kit in your home will be crucial. The kit should contain at least three days of supplies for each household member. Kit content recommendations vary. The following supplies are a few basic kit recommendations:

- water (at least 1 gallon of commercially bottled water per person per day)
- nonperishable food (prepackaged or precooked and canned), including infant formula and baby food if needed
- manual can opener, forks, and spoons
- prescription medicines (at least a 7-day supply)
- first aid kit and manual
- household chlorine bleach (not scented, color safe, or bleaches with cleaners)
- hand-crank or battery-powered radio and flashlight or lantern
- extra batteries
- cell phone with charger
- basic tool kit (hammer, wrenches, pliers, screwdrivers)
- blankets or sleeping bags and extra clothing (in cold climates, store warm clothes)
- face masks (N95-type masks are often recommended) to facilitate breathing

In addition, fill a large envelope with the following components: a list of emergency numbers and contact information; an area map; cash; copies of identification, credit cards, bank account information, and insurance policies; and copies of car and house keys. Put these items in one or more tightly closed containers in a cool, dry place that is inaccessible to children, pets, or pests. Check the kit several times a year and replace old, expired, or damaged items with fresh supplies.

To learn more about preparing for emergencies, visit the websites of the American Red Cross, the U.S. Department of Homeland Security, and the Federal Emergency Management Agency.

connect to a monitoring station. If you are away, the monitoring service you hire will know when the alarm goes off. This service will notify the fire department or police. You can expect to pay a monthly fee for the monitoring service in addition to the installation charge.

Often the presence of a home security system will ward off intruders. Placement of signs or stickers around the house and on doors and windows of the home indicate the presence of the home security system. A barking dog may serve the same purpose. People who live on the same street may form a *Neighborhood Watch* program. People in such a program report any suspicious activities on their street to police. Some people prefer to live in a place that has security guards in stations or gatehouses.

Personal needs and beliefs will affect the way people choose to keep their homes secure. For instance, some people feel safe with a security guard nearby. Having a guard may make other people feel restrained or uncomfortable. No matter what your situation, you will probably want to take some security measures. Choose those that make you feel comfortable and safe within your home.

Whether you own or rent, take measures to prevent home accidents and safeguard your home against intruders. You will also want your home to be safe and secure for the other household members.

Review & Assessment

1. List four ways to prevent fire in a home.
2. Name three essentials every household should have to prevent fire injury.
3. What are five ways to make a home appear occupied when household members are away?
4. What type of locks should be used on exterior doors?
5. How do biometric security systems differ from typical home security systems?

Chapter 24 Assessment

Summary

- A safe home provides freedom from accidents and offers security.
- Home accidents can occur to people of all ages. Take special precautions to assure safety for older adults, children, and people with disabilities.
- Preventive measures can eliminate many falls and can also lessen the possibility of injury as a result of fire, burns, and electrical shock.
- Understand the ways to control or reduce pollutant sources, including proper ventilation and wise use of cleaning methods and materials.
- Make a home more secure by using protection and warning devices.
- Reduce the possibility of injury or death from fire by installing monitoring devices and fire extinguishers.
- An emergency plan is important in case of the need to evacuate.

Terms in Action

1. **Visual recognition** Work in pairs to locate images online that visually describe or explain eight of the *Content Terms* listed at the beginning of this chapter. Then collaborate with another pair to compare images. Do all images visually describe the terms? Why or why not?

Think Critically

2. **Analyze responsibility** Research the effect of housing conditions on health. How important is it to be aware of harmful molds in residences? Can people unknowingly experience exposure to harmful indoor air quality? Who is responsible for investigating the presence of harmful mold: the current home owner, the previous owner, or a government agency? Explain your position.
3. **Assess accountability** Use online and print resources to research the effect of housing conditions on the severity of lead poisoning among small children. Identify evidence to support ways to prevent lead poisoning in children. Should government agencies require the testing of older homes to determine lead-paint presence before households with young children are allowed to move into the units? Why or why not?
4. **Evaluate safety** Using the list of safety tips for families, check your home for safety problems. Identify areas or equipment that could lead to potential falls, burns, electrical shocks, or poisonings. What hazards do you see? Then collaborate in groups to develop a plan for maintaining a safe home.
5. **Create safety guidelines** Create a list of safety guidelines for children around swimming pools. In addition to 911, include phone numbers to call in case of emergency. Develop a flyer to share in your community.
6. **Analyze evidence** Collaborate in supervised pairs to use one of the common household products listed in *Figure 24.6* as well as its "safe alternative." Before you begin the experiment, predict which cleaner will work more efficiently. Then conduct the experiment and compare the results of the two cleaning products. Write a report summarizing your evidence. Include any pros and cons you notice with each cleaning product.
7. **Analyze criteria** Use interior design websites to compare the costs of various types and styles of exterior doors. What criteria make certain door models strong enough to withstand a forceful kick or punch with a heavy object? Decide which door you would choose, identify the door material, check its price, print a photo, and report your choice to the class.

Core Skills

8. **Reading and writing** To research the effect of housing conditions on safety, read articles about childproofing a home on such websites as the *American Academy of Pediatrics*, *Kids Health*, or *BabyCenter*. Presume you are an interior designer who has been asked to make home safety recommendations to a young couple with two children under age three. The couple has a three-bedroom ranch style home. The back entry has a sliding glass door off the deck. Write a summary of recommendations you can give to this couple.

Chapter 24 Assessment

9. **Research and speaking** To research the effect of housing conditions on health, use a source, such as the *Environmental Protection Agency (EPA)* website, to investigate more about the impact of radon in homes and its impact on human health. What is the difference between short-term and long-term testing for radon? What recommendations exist for lowering radon levels in the home? Apply your oral communication skills to effectively explain your findings in a socially acceptable manner that others can easily understand.
10. **Listening and speaking** Investigate various types of home-security services available in your community. Select one service provider and make an appointment to interview a customer service agent about the security services this company provides. What types of systems does it use? How does home design influence the security system? Give an oral report and share your findings with the class.
11. **Research and speaking** To research the effect of housing conditions on health, search online for information on mold and mildew prevention. Identify ways to prevent mold or mildew and how to eliminate it once mold or mildew occurs. Develop a report on your findings using presentation software. If possible, locate photos of different types of mold to enhance your report. Share the report in class.
12. **Reading and writing** Research the effects of continued exposure to loud noises. How is a person's hearing affected over time? Write a summary of your findings to post on the class web page.
13. **Speaking and technology** Collaborate, contribute, and cooperate as a team member to create a public-service video about how to make a home look occupied when the family is away. Share your video with school, neighborhood, or community organizations to demonstrate your plan for maintaining a safe home.
14. **CTE career readiness practice** Assume you own an apartment building that was built in the 1970s. The building has eight units, a basement, and an attic. Part of your responsibility as property owner is to ensure that the entire building is safe from such health hazards as asbestos, radon, mold, and carbon monoxide. Create a resource list of companies that specialize in detecting and abating radon, carbon monoxide, mold, lead paint, and asbestos in residences. Confirm the services they offer. Share the list with your class.

Design Practice

15. **Fire escape plan** Develop a plan for maintaining a safe home. Use CADD software to create a floor plan showing each floor of your home or the home of someone you know. Draw the escape routes for each floor on the plan and note the locations of smoke detectors, carbon monoxide detectors, and fire extinguishers throughout the home. Share your plan in class.
16. **Design for safety** You have been asked to assess and design an indoor and outdoor environment for a young couple with two children, especially researching housing features for individuals with special needs because one of the children uses a wheelchair. Locate a floor plan for a home on one level. Evaluate the floor plan and determine features to add or remove to make this home safe and secure for the family. What safety design features should be added to the kitchen, bathroom, and child's bedroom? What outdoor features would ensure safety and a place for both children to play outdoors? Locate photographs of items you think are essential for the safety and security of your client's family. Prepare a visual and written summary that describes housing features for all people, including those with special needs. Present the summary to your clients (the class). Save a copy as an example in your portfolio.
17. **Portfolio** Develop a plan for detecting safety hazards and maintaining a safe home. Create a storyboard, photo essay, or an oral report using presentation software on health, safety, and security recommendations in the home from an interior designer's perspective. Use a digital camera to take pictures to accompany your report. Save your presentation in your portfolio.

Chapter 25
Maintaining a Home

Content Terms

disinfectant
plumbing plunger
closet auger
finish nail
box nail
short circuit
redecorate
remodeling

Academic Terms

termites
caustic

Learning Outcomes

After studying this chapter, you will be able to

- evaluate and select the cleaning tools, products, and schedule necessary to care for and to maintain a home.
- summarize how to properly maintain the landscape.
- explain how to use basic tools for common home repairs.
- summarize ways to improve storage and organize space.
- assess redecorating choices.
- evaluate the pros and cons of remodeling.
- summarize resources for home maintenance.

Reading with Purpose

Before reading the chapter, make a list of everything you already know about the chapter topic. As you read the chapter, check off the items that are covered. Take notes on the items that are not on your list.

While studying, look for the access icon  **to:**

- **Practice** the *Content* and *Academic Terms* with e-flash cards, matching activities, and vocabulary games.
- **Reinforce** what you learn by completing the *Review & Assessment* questions and e-mailing them to your instructor.

G-WLEARNING.com
www.g-wlearning.com/housing/

Juriah Mosin/Shutterstock.com

Maintaining a home involves keeping it clean, safe, and in good repair. It also involves making sure that equipment, electrical and plumbing systems, and other parts of the home are in proper working order. Adhering to regular, established home maintenance practices keeps the home environment, healthy, secure, and comfortable. Home owners can use the decision-making and problem-solving processes to choose how and to what level they maintain their homes.

Cleaning and Maintaining a Home

Every house is different, and everyone has different standards of cleanliness. One person wants every part of a room spotless and each object in its place (Figure 25.1). In contrast, another person may not mind some clutter. When people share a home, they should come to an agreement on acceptable cleaning standards. The standards should be realistic and everyone should be able to cooperate and contribute together to meet the standards.

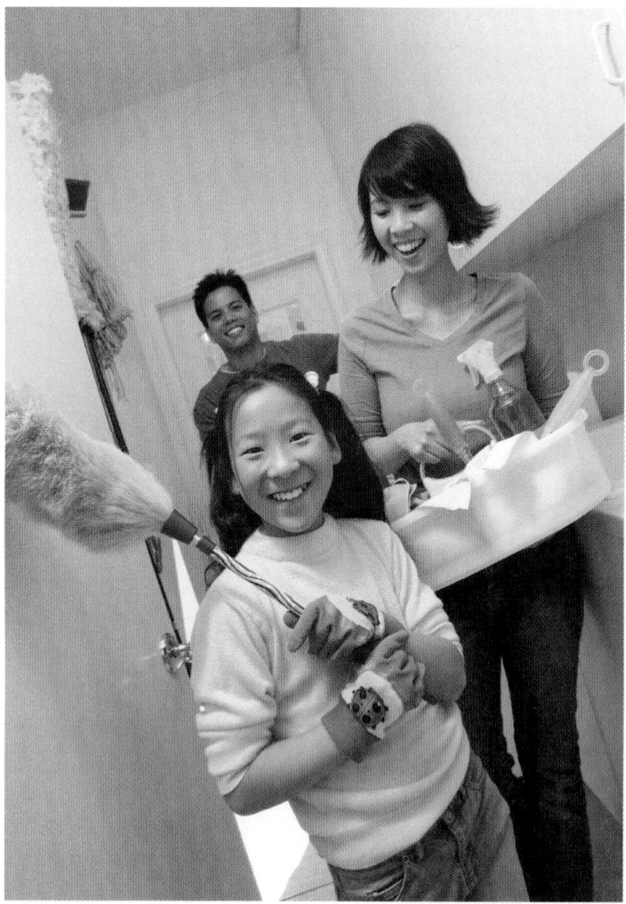

bikeriderlondon/Shutterstock.com

Figure 25.1 Cleanup is much quicker and easier when household members help keep the home tidy.

Keeping family members healthy and safe requires a certain minimum standard of cleanliness. Inhabitants of a home must contain and remove garbage from the dwelling regularly. If garbage is uncovered or left for a period of time, it can attract animals and insects. In addition, remove or properly store any items that cause odors. This helps to keep the air fresh.

Interior Home Maintenance and Cleaning

It is important to decide how much time you can devote to cleaning. Your decision affects your choices in home furnishings and accessories. For instance, if you want to devote as little time as possible to cleaning, choose furnishings that do not show soil readily or contain fine woods. Also, avoid furniture and accessories that require frequent care. These include items that must be polished, shined, or frequently dusted.

Cleaning is easier if there is little or no clutter to maneuver around. You can eliminate clutter in a number of ways. Recycle items such as newspapers and cans and other items your community designates. Discard items that are obviously old, broken, or unusable. If you are like most people, you will keep some items that you treasure, even though they produce clutter.

Cleaning Tools

Cleaning the home is easier with the right equipment or cleaning tools. There are two main types of cleaning tools. The first type, which removes loose dust and dirt, includes

- a dust mop for picking up dust on hard floors
- a broom and dustpan for sweeping hard-surface floors and steps
- a vacuum cleaner with attachments for carpets, hard floors, woodwork, furniture, upholstery, and window treatments
- cloths for dusting and polishing

The second type of cleaning tool removes soil that is stuck to surfaces. These cleaning tools include

- sponges for washing walls, woodwork, and appliances
- a pail to hold cleaning solutions
- a wet mop for cleaning floors
- a toilet bowl brush

A stepladder or stool for reaching high places, whether loosening dust and dirt or removing it is

Career Focus Professional Organizer

Does organizing items and finding the right place for them excite you? When you walk into a friend's room that is cluttered, do you immediately want to help organize and straighten the space? Does clutter often distract you from the task at hand? If so, you may want to consider exploring a career as a professional organizer.

Interests/Skills: Skills needed to become a professional organizer include problem solving and organizing materials. A professional organizer can help individuals and businesses take control over their surroundings. The ability to communicate with a client is essential in this career, as is having a good understanding of space and volume. Other important skills include ability to take measurements and plan space, strong ability in math and technology, and effective drawing and sketching skills.

Career Snapshot: Professional organizers help people in many ways. They can help people deal with everything from paper to professional responsibilities. They can give parameters on what to keep, what to toss, and where to take action. Professional organizers can also consult on interior spaces. For example, kitchen and bathroom cabinets, closets, and garages need order. Professional organizers are especially helpful when homes or offices have been taken over by clutter and junk. They teach their clients valuable techniques and conduct workshops and seminars. Their goal is to teach people how to organize their belongings.

photobank.ch/Shutterstock.com

Education/Training: No specific requirements are mandatory except for knowledge in the area of expertise. A high school diploma is recommended. Courses in computer programs, psychology, business management, accounting, and interior design are helpful.

Examination/License: Voluntary certification is available through the Board of Certified Professional Organizers (BCPO).

Professional Organizations: The National Association of Professional Organizers (NAPO)

Job Outlook: Due to demands placed on individuals, more people are turning to professionals to help get their personal and professional lives in order. The job outlook for the future is good.

Source: The National Association of Professional Organizers (NAPO)

necessary for safety. See Figure 25.2 for a variety of cleaning tools.

Cleaning Products

Cleaning products include the chemicals that aid in cleaning tasks. The basic cleaning products a home owner should always have include

- glass cleaner for mirrors, bathroom fixtures, and the surfaces of kitchen appliances
- grease-cutting liquid for fingerprints, oily stains, or soap residue
- mild abrasive powder for stubborn stains on countertops and work surfaces

Figure 25.3 shows a list of some useful cleaning agents, waxes, and polishes. Many cleaning products also contain a **disinfectant**, which is a cleaning

Laboko/Shutterstock.com

Figure 25.2 These are some tools used to get surfaces clean.

Cleaning Products	
Cleaning Agents	**Method of Action**
Water	Dilutes and flushes dirt away
Alkalies • Soaps • Washing soda • Some general purpose cleaners • Ammonia	Breaks down surface tension of water, allowing the cleaning agent to penetrate dirt better
Synthetic Detergent	Relieves surface tension to clean and cut grease better than soaps; does not react with minerals to form scum deposits as soap does
Acid • Vinegar • Lemon juice	Cuts grease and acts as a mild bleach
Fat Solvent	Dissolves soil held by grease
Fat Absorbent • Fuller's earth • Talcum • Bentonite • Cornmeal	Absorbs oils in a dry form, then brushed away with the soil
Abrasive • Silver polish • Scouring powder • Steel wool • Soap pads	Rubs dirt away in dry form or with water (depending on type)
Waxes and Polishes	**Method of Action**
Solvent-based Cleaning Wax • Liquid wax • Paste wax	Loosens soil on hard floors, removes old wax, and forms a new wax coating
Water-based Cleaning Wax • Emulsion wax • Solution wax	Loosens soil on hard floors other than wood and cork, and forms a new wax coating; won't remove old wax, which must be stripped with remover
Furniture Polish • Aerosol and pump spray • Creamy liquid • Paste polishes	Lifts soil, removes old wax, and forms a new wax coating
Multipurpose Cleaner Wax	Lifts soil from countertops, tiles, appliances, cabinets, and furniture; removes old wax and forms a new wax coating

Goodheart-Willcox Publisher

Figure 25.3 Using the proper cleaning agent for the job is important.

Eco-Friendly Cleaning Products and Tips

Some on-the-shelf cleaning products are more environmentally friendly than others. Products that are more kind to the environment are labeled with "green" on the packaging or in the product description. Using these products can help reduce strain on the environment.

One alternative to purchasing cleaning products is to use common household pantry items and create your own cleaning solutions. This method can save money and be environmentally friendly. The following are cleaning solutions you can make from common household items.

Cleaning Need	Eco-Friendly Homemade Solution
Oven	*Table salt*. Cover the area with baked on food with salt while the oven is still warm. When oven is cool, scrape away food and wipe with damp sponge.
Windows	*White vinegar and water*. Using a spray bottle, spray glass with a solution of 3 tablespoons white vinegar and 1 gallon cool water. Avoid streaks by wiping panes with newsprint.
Floors	*Liquid soap, white vinegar, and water*. Damp mop once a week with 1 gallon of water mixed with ⅛ cup liquid soap and ⅛ cup white vinegar.
Countertops	*Baking soda and water.* Add 4 tablespoons baking soda to 1 quart warm water for a nontoxic all purpose cleaner.
Clothes Drying	*Clothesline*. Hang clothes on an outdoor clothesline for fresh-smelling clothes. Let the sunshine dry the clothes.
Stains on White Clothing	*Borax and water*. Remove stains from whites by dabbing spots with a mixture of one part borax and six parts water.
Mold and Mildew in Bathroom	*Tea-tree oil and water*. Prevent mold and mildew by spraying stains with a spray bottle filled with 1 cup water and 1 drop tea-tree oil.

agent that destroys bacteria and viruses. Before you purchase any cleaning product, check your supplies. You may already have what you need. Look for products that serve more than one purpose. There are many multipurpose cleaning products. Most are available in dry and liquid forms.

You must also be aware of dangers associated with many cleaning products. Check labels to see if the products are toxic. Many cleaning compounds are poisonous or flammable. In addition, always read labels on cleaning products to make sure they will not damage the surface you are cleaning. Follow directions carefully. Finally, do not mix different cleaning products. Some products create toxic gases when mixed with other cleaning agents.

To help make cleaning easier, keep all cleaning items in an organized area (Figure 25.4). Always store cleaning products in locked cabinets out of

Africa Studios/Shutterstock.com

Figure 25.4 Storing cleaning supplies in one place helps make cleaning easier.

children's reach. Keep cleaning products away from heat sources.

Cleaning Schedule

Some people prefer to get their work done early in the day. Others like to sleep late and work at night. Some people like housework, while others do not. Whatever your energy level or your work pattern is, scheduling your cleaning tasks allows you to better use your cleaning time. Figure 25.5 shows a list of common tasks.

Cleaning schedules may vary from day to day or week to week, depending on the use of facilities. The more often facilities are used, the greater the need for cleaning. Less use usually means less cleaning. The larger the household is, the greater the cleaning task. When making a cleaning schedule, include the name of the person responsible for each task. Divide the tasks among household members.

Weekly cleaning tasks are easier if each household member helps with daily maintenance. For example, each person can be responsible for cleaning the bathtub or shower after bathing. An immediate wipe-down should leave it clean. Supply a sponge, brush, or towel. You may also need to use a glass cleaner. Keep everything needed for the task in the bathroom.

Techniques and procedures for regular and special cleaning of household items depend on their individual characteristics. There are many different types of furnishings on the market, requiring different cleaning approaches. Figure 25.6 provides guidelines for furniture care and maintenance.

Over time, walls and woodwork will need more than cleaning. If the paint begins to chip or fade, the surface must be repainted. Corners of wall coverings that begin to peel will need to be re-pasted. If wall coverings fade or become damaged, home owners should strip the walls and apply a new wall treatment.

Exterior Home Maintenance and Cleaning

Just as it is necessary to clean and maintain the interior of a home, home owners also need to establish a schedule for the house's exterior. A house represents one of the biggest lifetime investments. It is extremely important to keep the structure in good condition, both to avoid costly repairs and preserve its economic value. Home owners will need to monitor all exterior areas.

Checklist for Cleaning Tasks

Daily Tasks
- ✓ Make bed
- ✓ Straighten bedroom, bathroom, living area, and eating area
- ✓ Wash dishes
- ✓ Wipe kitchen counters and range top or other cooking surface
- ✓ Sweep or vacuum kitchen floor
- ✓ Empty wastebaskets and other garbage containers

Weekly Tasks
- ✓ Change bed linens
- ✓ Do laundry and mending
- ✓ Wash kitchen garbage can or change liner
- ✓ Wash kitchen floor
- ✓ Clean bathroom sink, tub, and toilet
- ✓ Wash bathroom floor
- ✓ Dust accessories
- ✓ Dust and polish furniture
- ✓ Vacuum lamp shades
- ✓ Vacuum carpet
- ✓ Shake out small rugs

Monthly Tasks
- ✓ Vacuum and turn mattress
- ✓ Wash mattress pad
- ✓ Vacuum drapes and wipe blinds
- ✓ Vacuum upholstered furniture
- ✓ Clean kitchen shelves
- ✓ Clean refrigerator
- ✓ Clean oven
- ✓ Clean woodwork

Semiannual Tasks
- ✓ Clean closets
- ✓ Dry-clean or wash bedding (comforter, bedspread, pillow shams, bed skirt, blankets)
- ✓ Clean drapes thoroughly (wash or dry-clean as appropriate) and wash curtains
- ✓ Wash seldom-used glassware and dinnerware
- ✓ Clean silverware (if silver and not stainless)
- ✓ Replace shelf liners
- ✓ Wash walls, including bathroom

Goodheart-Willcox Publisher

Figure 25.5 A checklist for cleaning tasks will help keep you on schedule.

Furniture Care and Maintenance

Always observe the following general cautions:

- Save care labels that come with new furniture and follow instructions.
- When using commercial cleaning products, read and follow the manufacturer's label instructions.
- When using chemicals, protect your eyes with safety goggles or glasses.

Furniture Materials	Cleaning Procedures
Wood • Used indoors	*Regular cleaning:* Vacuum and/or dust with a soft, dry cloth; do not use oil or treated cloth. *Special cleaning:* • Use a liquid furniture wax or cream polish that gives the desired gloss. • If dirty, clean with a cleaning or polishing furniture wax according to label directions. Moisten a soft cloth with the cleaner and rub briskly, changing the cloth when soiled.
Upholstery • May be on furniture with or without springs • Generally used indoors • May have a stain-repellent finish	*Regular cleaning:* Vacuum and check for any objects lodged in the folds of fabric or under cushions. *Special cleaning:* If heavily soiled, clean with a solution of two teaspoons of detergent to one pint of water. Test a small area on the back or underside for fading before proceeding with cleaning. Dip a brush or cloth in the solution and clean only small areas at a time. Rinse the cleaned area before moving to another and avoid wetting the furniture too much.
Aluminum • Generally used outdoors	*Regular cleaning:* Wash painted frames with mild soap and water. Coat the finish with auto wax to add protection. Do not use abrasive material or strong detergents. *Special cleaning:* • To brighten mildly discolored surfaces, wash with a solution of soap and water, and a small amount of a mild household acid, such as lemon juice, vinegar, or cream of tartar. (Aluminum used outdoors may darken.) • If the finish is pitted, polish with a soap-filled steel wool pan cleaner and rinse dry. All steel wool must be removed or it will rust and stain the aluminum.
Painted Metal Furniture • Often used outdoors • Also used indoors in children's rooms or casual settings	*Regular cleaning:* Wash surface with warm water and a heavy-duty liquid detergent. Rinse thoroughly with clean water to remove any detergent residue. Wipe dry or allow to air dry in a sunny or heated room. Apply automobile liquid or paste wax and polish.
Wicker, Rattan, and Bamboo • Can be used throughout the home • Is often used on enclosed porches • Is not recommended for regular outdoor use	*Regular cleaning:* Vacuum, then wipe with a rag soaked in a mild detergent and warm water solution. Use a small brush to remove stubborn dirt. *Special cleaning:* If mildew is a problem, wash the furniture with a solution of ¾ cup of chlorine bleach and one quart of water. Since bleach may lighten the surface, apply it to the entire piece of furniture.

(Continued)

Figure 25.6 For best results, always use the right cleaning agent and technique for each type of furniture surface.

Furniture Care and Maintenance *(Figure 25.6, continued)*

Furniture Materials	Cleaning Procedures
Plastic Resin • Used most often outdoors • Also used in children's rooms	*Regular cleaning:* • Use a nonabrasive all-purpose cleaner or a cleaner-polish and follow package directions. • Wipe the surface with a solution made of hand dishwashing liquid and warm water. Rinse thoroughly and dry with a clean, soft cloth.
Slipcover • Adds a new look to old furniture • Protects new furniture	*Regular cleaning:* Vacuum while still on furniture, remove, and shake out loose dirt outdoors. *Special cleaning:* If washable, wash in warm water and laundry detergent. Do not overcrowd the washer. Smooth over furniture while still a little damp. Straighten seams and cording. Do not use furniture until the covers are completely dry.
Cane • Used in the seats of dining room or occasional chairs	*Regular cleaning:* Vacuum or dust regularly. Occasionally wipe with a damp cloth.
Redwood • Used outdoors because of natural resistance to weathering and rot	*Regular cleaning:* Maintain a coating with a sealer to keep out moisture and thus retard cracks. Scrub with detergent and water. Rinse and dry thoroughly before sealing. *Special cleaning:* Colored sealers restore redness to grayed redwood.

Roof, Gutters, and Downspouts

Often home owners do not realize the importance of keeping the roof, gutters, and downspouts free of debris, such as leaves and branches. For roof construction that includes shingles or metal, it is important to protect it from moving branches that may scrape and damage the roof during a windstorm. Also, do not permit leaves and twigs to accumulate on the roof as they contribute excess moisture that eventually causes damage.

Proper maintenance of gutters and downspouts is also essential. Keep gutters and downspouts clear of anything that may block the proper flow of water off the roof. Routine cleaning and special attention after storms and in autumn after heavy leaf-fall keeps water flowing in gutters and downspouts. If rainwater cannot flow off the roof, it will back up into the attic space and wall cavities. Water can cause extreme damage and eventually contribute to problems from mold, rot, and termites.

Exterior Walls

The exterior walls of a house can be made of wood siding, manufactured siding, or masonry, such as brick or stucco. It is important to monitor wood siding for rot and replace siding as needed. Regular painting or staining is necessary to protect wood siding from the eroding effects of weather. Between paintings, pressure-wash the exterior siding to remove stains caused by mildew (Figure 25.7). Also wash and paint manufactured siding, such as fiberboard and fiber cement siding, on a regular basis.

If a house is of brick construction, routine inspection of the mortar is important. Over time, the

Beth Van Trees/Shutterstock.com

Figure 25.7 Pressure washing this siding helps keep it free of dirt and mildew.

tuck-pointing (mortar between the bricks) deteriorates and requires replacement.

Stucco walls also require washing to eliminate the growth of mildew. Use special care, however, because it is easy to damage the walls by a high-pressure washing.

Regardless of a home's exterior, it is important to have the home inspected annually for termites. ***Termites*** are pale-colored insects that feed on wood, particularly wood that is holding moisture. Termites can destroy the structure of a house. Many companies offer service contracts that provide annual inspections and effective treatments, should any termites appear.

Windows and Doors

Windows and doors are expensive investments in a house and require special attention. They need regular cleaning and careful inspections to make sure they stay properly caulked and sealed. Use caulk and sealants to fill cracks and gaps that may appear over time (Figure 25.8). Caulking prevents air leakage, which is a cause of higher heating and cooling costs. Replace weather stripping that wears out over time. Inspect windows and doors made of wood for rot, too, and replace them as needed. Wash windows regularly to keep them looking good. See *Green Choices: Eco-Friendly Cleaning Products and Tips* for an eco-friendly way to clean windows.

Driveways and Outdoor Living Spaces

Driveways and outdoor living spaces, such as patios, terraces, decks, and porches, represent expensive components of the home's exterior environment. They, too, require routine inspection and maintenance.

Greg McGill/Shutterstock.com

Figure 25.8 Proper caulking on windows can help lower heating and cooling costs.

Driveway materials consist of concrete, asphalt, brick, or a variety of other products. All are subject to heavy traffic, which eventually results in the need for repair. Periodically check driveway surfaces for cracks and other signs of deterioration. Then make timely repairs by filling cracks with a compatible product. When repairs become extensive, the home owner may need to resurface or replace the driveway.

Periodic pressure washing keeps the areas free of excess dirt and algae growth. Home owners can also apply water-sealant products to the surface to repel moisture. Likewise, take these same steps to properly maintain patios and terraces.

Inspect decks and porches for any signs of damage or rot. They, too, benefit from routine pressure washing and occasional painting or staining. Careful inspection of handrails, steps, and railings is important to make sure they are safe and secure for use.

Review & Assessment

1. What cleaning tools are basic for cleaning a home?
2. What three basic cleaning products should every home have?
3. What are two advantages of a cleaning schedule?
4. Summarize maintenance and cleaning tasks for two exterior areas of a home.

Outdoor and Lawn Care

After investing time, money, and energy in making the outdoor living space attractive and inviting, the home owner needs to maintain it. A maintenance schedule will help home owners care for their outdoor living environments. Maintaining the outdoor living space requires some special tools.

Tools for Outdoor Tasks

A lawn mower is probably the most expensive and necessary outdoor tool (Figure 25.9). Most lawn mowers use gasoline or electricity. Many not only cut grass, but also shred it for mulch. Since landfills are filling up, communities are encouraging people to use clippings as mulch throughout the landscape. Many communities charge extra to accept yard waste. Some areas will not accept it at all.

Other powered outdoor tools commonly used around a home are leaf blowers, lawn trimmers, and weed cutters. Outdoor hand tools include pruning and lopping shears, shovels, rakes, and hoes (Figure 25.10).

bikeriderlondon/Shutterstock.com

Figure 25.9 Many mowers shred the cut grass into fine pieces that sift to the soil and serve as mulch for the lawn.

Chrislofotos/Shutterstock.com

Figure 25.10 Keeping the landscape well maintained often involves enough tools to merit their own storage center in the garage or a tool shed.

Many yard tasks involve the use of tools that cut through plants or soil. This is true of all the tools mentioned thus far. The more frequently tools are sharpened; the easier they are to use. In addition, sharp tools are safer and less likely to damage plants. You may want to sharpen your tools yourself, or you can have them sharpened professionally.

Yard Maintenance

Schedule yard maintenance tasks according to the season of the year. The specific outdoor tasks will vary depending on where you live. Plant life may need special care to withstand extremely hot or cold weather. During such periods, watering continues but fertilizing stops. Applying mulch around the bases of trees, shrubs, and bushes helps insulate the roots. In addition, mulch helps to retain moisture and maintain a more moderate temperature. Home owners may need to wrap sensitive plants for protection from extreme cold or wind.

Some summer-flowering bulbs, such as gladiolus, need to be dug up after the leaves have dried. Replant these bulbs in the spring. Bulbs that bloom in the spring, such as tulips, require fall planting. Bulbs that bloom in the spring generally do not require digging up and replanting.

For people who live in an area where the ground freezes during winter, it is important to begin watering and fertilizing landscape plants when the ground thaws. At the first sign of sprouting in the spring, uncover roses and other plants that require covering during the winter. Wait until the last frost to plant summer-blooming bulbs and flower seeds. You can divide perennials into smaller clumps at this time, and trim most trees and shrubs. Long-handled lopping shears are the best tool for shaping trees and shrubs and removing dead limbs.

Keeping mulch around plants inhibits weed growth and helps retain the moisture in the ground. If plants begin to wilt, it is usually an indication that the plants need watering. The age of the plants, the soil characteristics, and the weather are all factors in determining the watering schedule. Drip irrigation is especially useful for directing water straight to a plant's roots.

A lawn requires regular care during the growing season. When watering a lawn, it is better to water thoroughly and less often than to underwater often. Thorough watering encourages deeper root growth. The soil should remain moist between 8 and 12 inches under the ground. Weeds compete for space, moisture, and nutrients in the lawn. Eliminate

VladisChern/Shutterstock.com

Figure 25.11 Green grass is usually brown near its base. For a green lawn after mowing, never cut more than one-third off the top.

these unsightly plants by hand weeding or by chemical methods. Handle any products you apply to the yard carefully. Like household cleaning products, yard care products may be poisonous. Check to see how long after treatment it is safe for children and pets to play on the lawn. Use and store them according to directions.

Mowing the grass is a critical part of lawn care. If you mow the grass in a diagonal direction, you will prevent a striped look. Change directions each time you mow. Mowing the lawn too closely will prevent the development of a healthy root system. A general rule is to cut only the top third of the grass with each mowing (Figure 25.11). Your mowing schedule will depend on the rate your grass grows.

Review & Assessment

1. Identify outdoor power and hand tools necessary for lawn-care tasks.
2. What is the danger in mowing a lawn too low?
3. Why are watering, mulching, and fertilizing necessary elements of yard maintenance?

Making Common Home Repairs

Keeping a home safe and comfortable requires regular care and maintenance. Home maintenance includes the inspection and repairs needed to keep the home safe and prolong its life. Home owners can make the repairs independently with the right tools and some basic knowledge of what to do.

When knowledge and experience is limited, home owners may want to hire a professional to do the work. This is especially important when safety is involved. Some utility companies have professional service people to handle electrical or gas repairs. Even the best do-it-yourself home owner needs to call on a skilled professional from time to time.

The Basic Tools

Tools can be expensive, so buy quality tools because they last longer. Consider shopping around or buying from discount stores. Home owners can build a supply of tools by buying only what they need. To get the right tool for the job, ask for advice from people with experience. Figure 25.12 shows some basic home-maintenance tools.

Hammer

Use a general purpose 16-ounce model hammer with a curved claw primarily for driving and pulling (removing) nails. The curved claw provides leverage when pulling nails. The medium-weight head performs finish work as well as rough work.

Screwdrivers

Use a screwdriver for driving and removing screws. A standard straight-blade screwdriver and a Phillips tip screwdriver are typical for most household repairs. Both come in various sizes. The straight-blade screwdriver must fit the slot in the head of the screw to work. The Phillips fits a screw with a T-shaped slots in the head of the screw.

Adjustable Wrench

A wrench is useful for tightening and loosening nuts and bolts. This tool is adjustable to fit nuts of different sizes. If a nut is hard to turn, apply a few drops of a lubricant. Let it soak for the recommended time period. If the wrench slips off the nut, turn the wrench over.

Pipe Wrench

The pipe wrench is a holding tool for assembling fittings on pipes. Teeth are set at an angle in one direction. The teeth are designed to grip a curved surface firmly and produce a ratchet effect. This effect forces a tight grip and prevents the grip from loosening.

Side-Cutting Pliers

This tool is useful for cutting wire and stripping the insulation and plastic coating from electrical wire. Take care to not cut into the wire when removing the insulation.

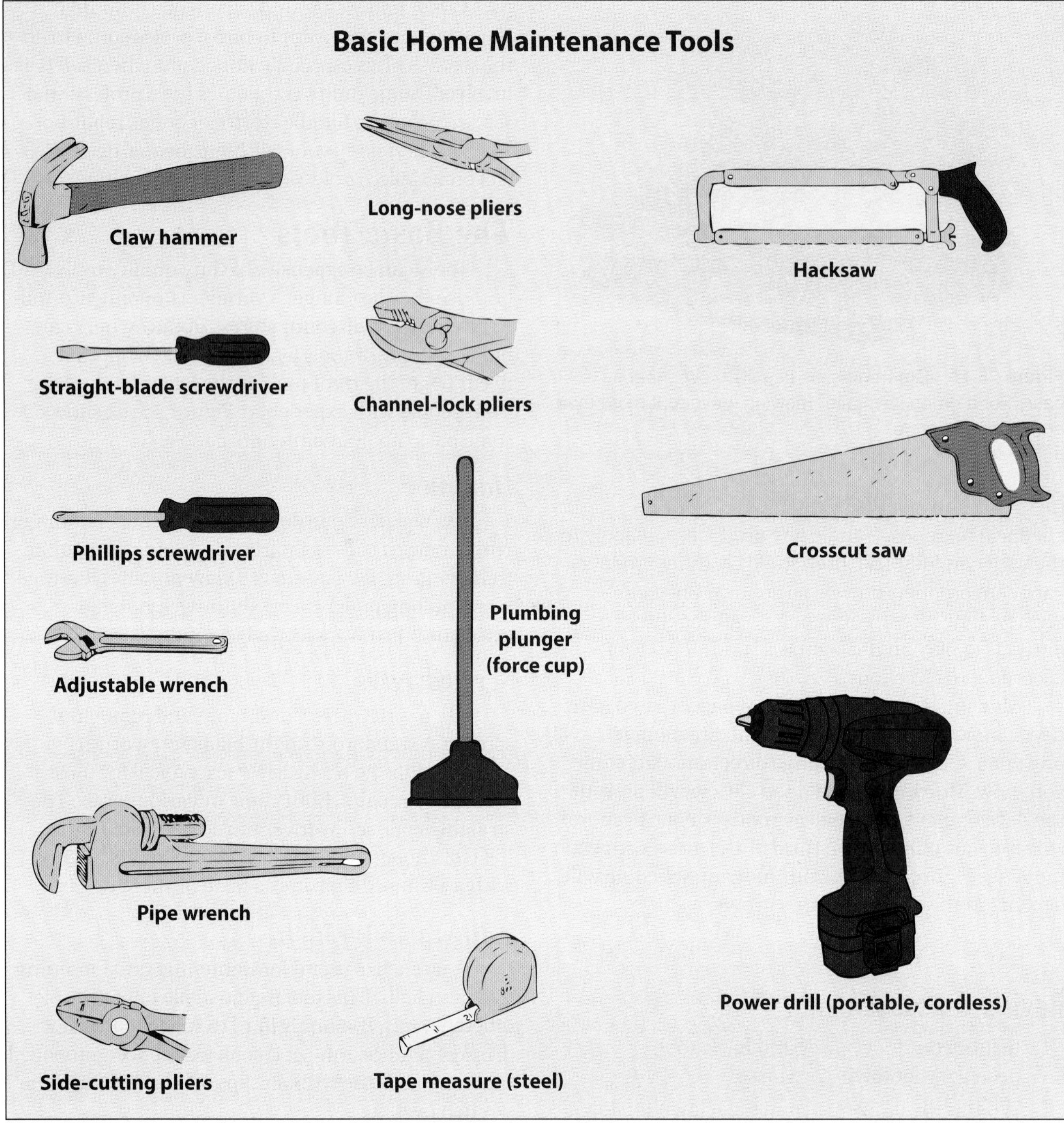

Goodheart-Willcox Publisher

Figure 25.12 These basic tools will help you handle many household maintenance tasks.

Long-Nose Pliers

These pliers are appropriate for bending wire and positioning small components into close and difficult work areas. This tool is not a substitute for a wrench. Do not use it when objects must be securely gripped and tightened.

Channel-Lock Pliers

Another name for channel-lock pliers is *slip-joint pliers.* Use this handy tool to tighten nuts and bolts. This basic plumbing tool provides a secure grip on many common materials.

Plumbing Plunger

A **plumbing plunger** is a device that creates a suction motion to clear a blocked drain. Another name for a plunger is a *force cup*. There are two types. Use a molded plunger for curved surfaces, such as the toilet bowl. The flat plunger is for level surfaces, such as sinks, showers, and tubs.

Tape Measure

Choose a retractable tape measure that is at least 16 feet long and ¾-inch wide. There are many types of measuring tapes on the market. Some have a thumb lock to prevent the tape from retracting when in use.

Hacksaw

The hacksaw is a general-purpose tool for cutting metal. The teeth of the hacksaw cut pipe when pushing the tool forward. A hacksaw has no cutting action when pulling it toward the body.

Crosscut Saw

This saw, used to cut across the grain of wood, can also serve as a general purpose saw for sheet materials such as plywood. Many types work well for a variety of purposes. A ten-point crosscut, for example, has 10 teeth per inch of saw blade.

Power Drill

A power drill is a light-duty tool to drill holes and drive or loosen nuts and screws. Both corded and cordless models are available. With a special attachment, it becomes a lightweight buffer or grinder. The drill chuck determines the size of a drill. The chuck is the clamping device that holds the drill bit. Common sizes are ¼-inch and ⅜-inch. For versatility, select a ⅜-inch chuck, variable speed, and a reversible motor. You need a variety of drill bits, which are sized by diameter in one of three systems: fractional, decimal, letters, and metrics. Straight-shank drill bits will drill holes in metal and wood.

Closet Auger

When there is blockage in the toilet caused by a washcloth or some item that is retrievable, the closet auger is a useful tool. A **closet auger** is a device used to bore through items with a twisting and turning motion to free blocked plumbing or wastewater lines. In some cases, a comb, pencil, or other object causes a blockage that is not retrievable. By alternately using the closet auger and plumbing plunger, a person usually can force the object through the pipe.

Electricity Tester

Electrical circuits can be tested safely with an electrical tester, called a *neon tester*. Most hardware stores sell this item inexpensively. The tester is designed to light up in the presence of 110 volts and 220 volts. To use, firmly press each lead against the terminals. If the circuit has electricity, the light will go on.

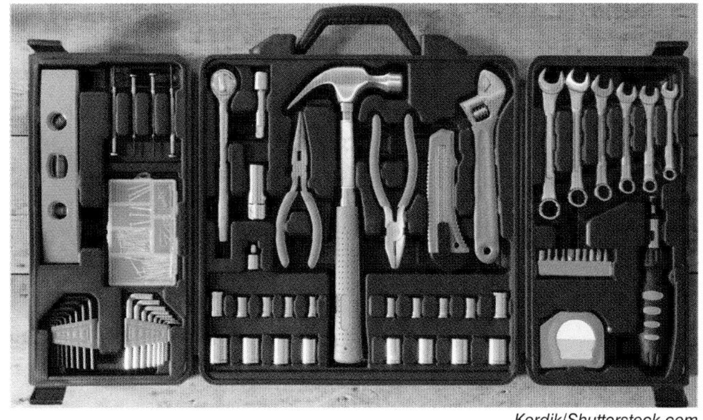

Kordik/Shutterstock.com

Figure 25.13 When shopping for toolboxes, buy one that holds all the tools you use regularly.

Flashlight

A two-cell unit is sufficient for most household needs. An industrial-rated flashlight is brighter and more durable.

Toolbox

One of the most overlooked yet vital components of a tool collection is a toolbox to hold tools. Metal or plastic toolboxes are affordable and come in a variety of sizes and shapes. The main purpose of a toolbox is to keep tools in the same location for use when repairs are necessary (Figure 25.13).

Plumbing Repairs

Plumbing problems can occur in any home at any time. Some problems appear suddenly, such as when someone accidentally drops an item into a toilet. Other problems develop over time. Drains become sluggish or faucets and pipes begin to leak. Certain problems can result in water damage to parts of the home, adding to the repair costs. If home owners can handle minor plumbing repairs themselves, they can save the expense and inconvenience of hiring a plumber.

One of the most common plumbing problems is a clogged drain. Pipes tend to clog when foreign matter finds its way into waste lines and accumulates. The most common cause of a clogged drain is foreign matter, such as grease and hair, in the drainage system. Stoppages in the drainage system rarely occur in straight, horizontal, or vertical runs of piping. They usually occur where two pipes join together with a fitting, creating a change of direction. Stoppages may also occur in the trap (Figure 25.14). Chemical drain cleaners or plumbing plungers and closet augers are most often useful for clearing these stoppages.

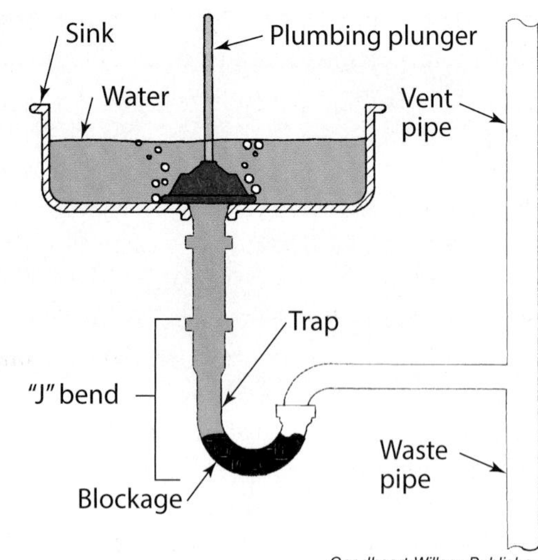

Figure 25.14 Since there is a curve in the trap, a blockage is likely to occur here.

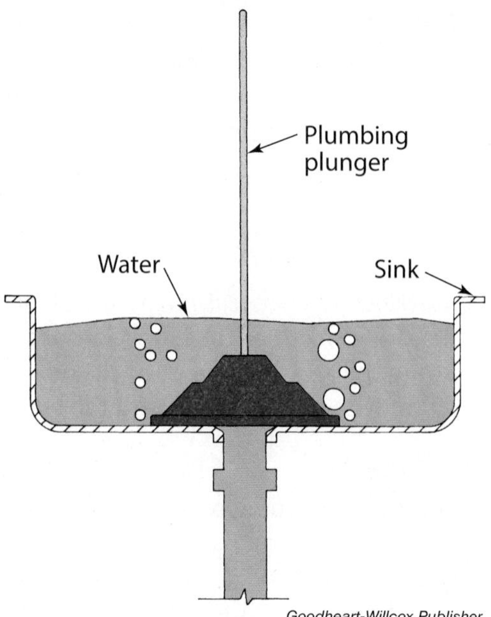

Figure 25.15 A plunger is pumped up and down to form a suction and surge in the drain.

If a drain is partially clogged, one cleaning method is to use a chemical drain cleaner. Drain cleaners are available in liquid or crystal forms. Liquid drain cleaners are heavier than water and settle into the trap to dissolve grease, food, soap, and hair. Crystal cleaners in granular form begin the chemical cleaning process when they come in contact with the water in the trap.

Use these chemicals with *caution* because they are poisonous and caustic. Many contain sodium hydroxide—or lye—which is a caustic manmade chemical. A ***caustic*** substance will burn the skin. Wear protective gloves and keep your face away from the drain opening. Carefully read the directions on each container. Use acid drain cleaners to dissolve soap and hair. Alkaline chemicals cut grease. Never mix chemical cleaners because toxic gas may form. Some of these products are combustible, meaning they will burn easily.

A more environmentally friendly option is to use a commercial enzymatic biological drain cleaner. These products are not caustic and will not combust. Another simple home remedy for the drain is to put a handful of baking soda with ½-cup vinegar in the drain and follow it with a flush of boiling water.

If a drain is completely clogged, chemical cleaners may not work. The tool to use in this case is a flat plumbing plunger (Figure 25.15). First remove the basket strainer in the sink waste outlet. If it is a double compartment sink, plug the other waste outlet with a rag to prevent loss of pressure in the drain. Place the flat force cup of the plunger directly over the drain opening. Two inches of standing water will provide the necessary seal for the force cup to take hold. Grip the plunger handle firmly with both hands and push down with a slow, even pressure. Pull up quickly and repeat the process several times. This will unstop most sink drains.

If the stoppage still exists, try an auger with a flexible spring cable. Place a container under the trap. Loosen two nuts on the trap and remove the J-bend. Use a small auger with a ¼-inch spring cable. Feed the cable slowly into the drainpipe. Rotate the cable as you feed it. Turn the handle until the obstruction is broken up (Figure 25.16). When finished, remove the cable, replace the J-bend, and tighten the nuts. Flush the drain with hot water and check for leaks.

When a toilet has a clog, try to determine the cause of the stoppage. If the substance will not cause additional blockage when forced into the drainage system, use the molded plunger. If material such as a diaper caused the stoppage, use the closet auger. Since an auger has a flexible spring cable, it can make sharp turns in a drain.

For some items, you may need to use the plunger and auger in alternating sequence. Compare the two methods in Figure 25.17. Should these methods fail, the only solution is to shut off the water to the toilet, disconnect the toilet from the floor, and retrieve the object from the toilet's underside. Whenever the seal between the toilet and floor is broken, you must replace the rubber or wax ring that serves as the seal.

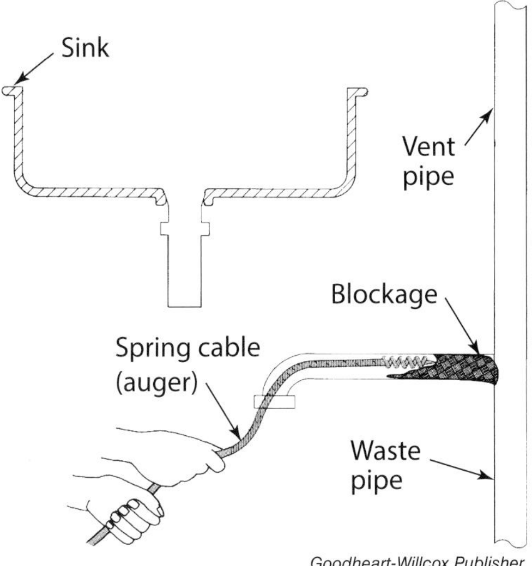

Figure 25.16 The auger, which has a flexible spring cable, may need to be placed near the blockage to remove it.

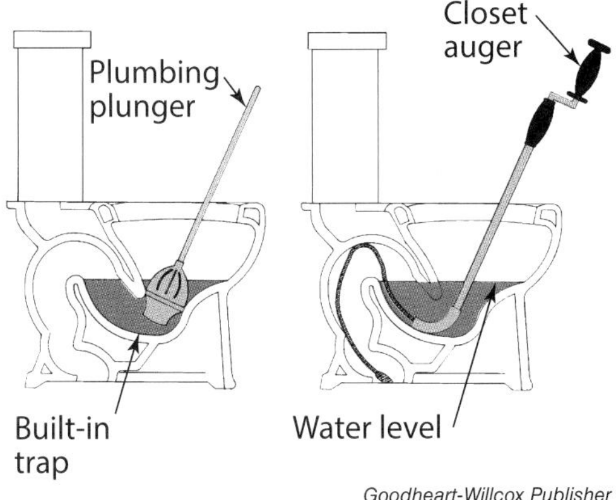

Figure 25.17 Both the plumbing plunger and the auger may be needed for a toilet blockage.

As you can see, this repair can become extensive. You may wish to hire a professional plumber to do this job.

Debris and tree roots growing into the lines can also block the sewer lines. When this occurs, professional help is required to clean out or open the lines.

Installing Nails and Screws

Nails and screws are fastening devices. Each has special uses in household repairs. Nails can be easy to drive, but may be difficult to remove. Screws can be easy to remove.

Nails come in two basic shapes. A **finish nail** has a very small head. You can drive it below the surface by using another nail or a nail set tool. Fill holes with wood filler or putty. Use finish nails when appearance is important. Installing paneling or shelves are two examples. A **box nail** has a large, flat head. Use it for rough work when appearance is less important.

When driving a nail, hammer the head until it is seated on the surface, but leaves no mark on the surface.

If you are placing nails or screws in walls, location is important. To secure heavy objects, place fasteners in line with a stud behind the wall surface. This allows you to drive the fastener into the wood of the stud for additional support. You can find studs by tapping along the walls lightly. You will hear a lower tone when you tap the walls bordering hollow spaces between studs. When you tap a stud, you will hear a noticeably higher tone. You can also purchase inexpensive stud-sensing devices at hardware stores and home improvement centers (Figure 25.18).

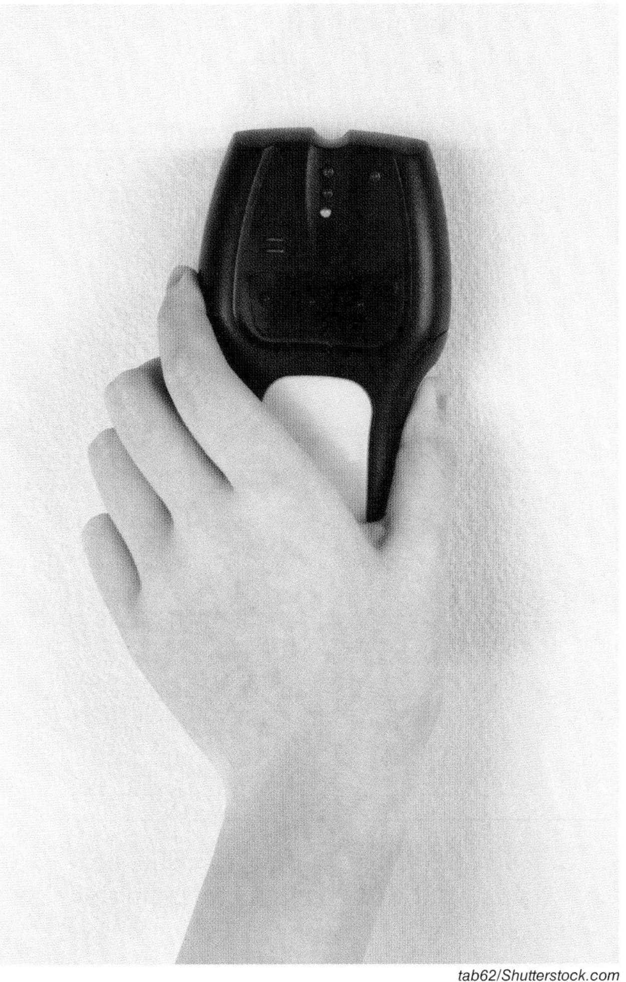

tab62/Shutterstock.com

Figure 25.18 Studs that are used to form walls are often placed 16 inches apart. Use a stud finder to locate wall studs before inserting fasteners to support heavy objects that are hung on a wall.

After you find one stud, you can usually find adjacent studs by measuring 16-inch intervals to the left or right.

To install a wood screw, drill a pilot hole. Use the proper type of screwdriver, either a Phillips or a straight screwdriver. Try to match the size of the screwdriver to the head of the screw. Using an undersized screwdriver makes the task more difficult and can damage the screw head.

Electrical Repairs

When electricity enters a house, the wires connect into the service entrance panel. Service entrance panels contain either circuit breakers or fuses. Circuit breaker entrance panels are more common than panels with fuses (Figure 25.19). When a circuit in a house is overloaded with appliances or other electrical items, the fuses or circuit breakers cut off the power. This prevents damage to wiring and possible electrical fires.

The most common cause of electrical problems is likely a short circuit. A **short circuit** is an undesirable current path that allows the electrical current to bypass the load of the circuit. Sometimes the short circuit occurs between two wires due to faulty insulation. It can also occur between a wire and a grounded object, such as a metal frame on an appliance. Sometimes a black carbon deposit indicates where the short occurred. A short circuit requires repair before resetting a breaker or replacing a fuse. If you are unfamiliar with making such repairs, call an electrician.

Lisa F. Young/Shutterstock.com

Figure 25.19 The service entrance panel monitors the electrical system for the house.

Circuit Breakers

Usually a circuit breaker trips when the circuit is overloaded. This happens when too many electrical appliances are in use on a circuit at one time. The switch on each breaker switches to the *off* position when a problem occurs. This interrupts the power.

Disconnect some appliances before restoring electricity to the circuit. Large appliances—such as refrigerators, ranges, or dishwashers—generally require their own circuit. To restore the electricity, move the handle of the circuit to the *reset* position, then to the *on* position. The reset position is usually on the opposite side of the on position.

Fuses

You must replace a blown fuse to restore power. There are two types of fuses—plugs and cartridges. Plug fuses screw into the entrance panel like lightbulbs. A plug fuse has a clear window with a metal strip—or fuse link—across it. When current level exceeds the rating of the fuse, the link melts and a gap forms. The result is a broken circuit with no flow of current.

To replace a plug fuse, remove the main fuse or turn off the connection switch. This will disconnect all power. Use a flashlight, if necessary, to locate the blown fuse. The window of a blown fuse is black or the fuse link is broken.

Spring clips hold cartridge fuses in place. These fuses often show no sign of being blown. If the power is off, follow the same steps as in replacing a plug fuse. Always replace the blown fuse with a new one of the exact size. To avoid electrical shock, stand on a dry surface and be sure your hands are dry.

Wall Switches

All types of electrical switches can wear out as they get older. Do not attempt to replace a wall switch unless you know how to work with electrical wiring. Fatal electric shocks can occur. The illustration in Figure 25.20 shows the black wires to disconnect to remove a faulty switch.

Power Cord Plugs

For the safety of members of the household, replace damaged or worn electric plugs before using them. When replacing a plug on a flat two-wire cord, use a snap-down plug.

To attach the snap-down plug, lift the top clamp. Slit the cord apart to ¼ inch from the end of the

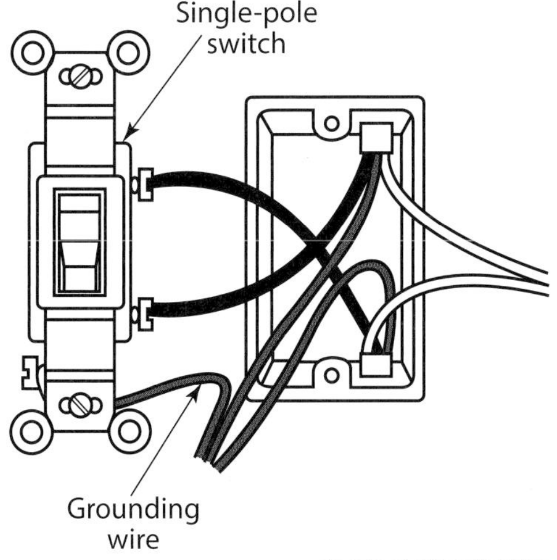

Goodheart-Willcox Publisher

Figure 25.20 Use extra precaution when repairing electrical switches.

cord. Push the cord into the plug and tightly close the clamp. Test the cord to see that it works. Feel the plug to make sure it is not overheating.

Making Replacements

Home maintenance includes more than making repairs. It includes replacing the parts of a house that wear out or become obsolete. It also includes replacing appliances that are no longer worth repairing.

A quality item should perform well for many years before replacement becomes necessary. Nothing lasts forever, though. A wise consumer, therefore, budgets for the repair and replacement costs that are certain to come. When repair parts become unavailable or costs become too high, it probably is time to make a replacement.

Review & Assessment

1. Name five basic tools needed for home repairs and summarize their uses.
2. List five common home repairs.
3. Contrast cleaning a clogged drain with chemical cleaners and mechanical methods. Which is most likely to work?
4. When would you use a finish nail and a box nail?
5. What are two causes of an electrical short circuit?
6. Contrast plug fuses with cartridge fuses.

Meeting Storage Needs

Whether a home is large or small, the inhabitants need to make the most of their space. Organized storage helps to keep clutter out of the living spaces. Finding items is easier, too, when storage space is organized.

Organize for Storage

There are many ways to reorganize closets using a variety of storage devices. Various types of storage components are available to help tailor the space to the storage needs. Many of these organizers do not require nailing to a structure, so a person can easily move them. Another option for organizing is to hire a professional organizer or purchase a custom closet organization system (Figure 25.21).

Durable cardboard, fabric, or plastic storage boxes come in many sizes, colors, and styles. Many have drawers or doors. Some fit under beds; others will fit in small spaces throughout the house. Consider using these items to organize closet storage. Boxes can be painted, papered, or covered with fabric to match room décor.

Often utility rooms and garages have poorly organized storage space. Shelves and storage containers can make storage in these areas more efficient. Attach some types of shelves to the ceiling for off-the-floor storage.

California Closets Organizational Solutions for the Whole Home. © 2009 California Closet Co. Inc. All Rights Reserved. (www.californiaclosets.com)

Figure 25.21 Closet organizers can be customized to fit any closet.

Consider placing shelves in window nooks and over radiators. Shelf arrangements on bare walls provide open storage for displays. Attach racks to doors or walls to hold magazines, books, or supplies.

Many home owners and designers choose to convert space under a stairway or at the end of a hall or room to storage. You can buy ready-to-use shelves or other storage items for this space. Purchase them in components and adapt them to the space that exists. You can also build your own storage units.

Hooks and poles are useful types of storage that are popular for hanging coats (Figure 25.22). You can also use them in bathrooms to hang towels and bathroom supplies. Also, consider attractively placing supplies in baskets or decorated buckets with handles.

John Wollwerth/Shutterstock.com

Figure 25.22 The coat storage in this hallway utilizes hooks, seating space, and storage drawers and cubbies.

Space Savers

The design of many furniture pieces helps save space. A sofa bed and a daybed are two such pieces. They double as sofas and beds. This saves room if you do not have space for both.

You can replace your regular bed frame with a platform that has drawers. This provides storage and sleeping space in the same area. You can also use stacking beds in a children's room to save space.

Stacking chairs and folding chairs are other types of space-saving furniture. Multipurpose storage and organizer units can double as small tables in the bedroom, living room, or home office. Padded chests or window seats used for seating, with storage underneath, also save space (Figure 25.23).

A drop-leaf table takes up little space when the leaves are down. Expanding it is easy when extra tabletop space is necessary. Consider building a hinged table surface or desk that attaches to the wall. It can have legs that fold out or a hinged support that swings out from the wall. The table lies flat against the wall when it is not in use. To save space, mount other household furniture and equipment to the wall.

In the kitchen, mounting small appliances on the wall or under kitchen cabinets can free valuable shelf space for other uses. Drawer trays, adjustable racks, hooks, and other shelving components keep food supplies, cooking equipment, and dinnerware orderly (Figure 25.24).

Well-organized storage helps make living easier. It keeps clutter out of living spaces. Having enough storage helps home owners make the most of their housing.

Breadmaker/Shutterstock.com

Figure 25.23 These built-in window seats are attractive and offer hidden storage in the family room.

casadaphoto/Shutterstock.com

Figure 25.24 Storage drawers for plates and cups are convenient for all household members, even those with special needs.

Review & Assessment

1. How can a home owner create more efficient storage for poorly organized storage spaces, such as utility rooms and garages?
2. List three examples of furniture that can serve as space savers.

Redecorating

Eventually a home owner will probably want to change or update the decorating scheme of a home, or **redecorate**. Parts of a home may look out of fashion. Some furnishings may show wear. Perhaps a home owner may simply want a new look. As life situations change, so do needs and values. In turn, people may redecorate part of the home or the entire home accordingly.

Redecorating is different from decorating because there is already a base from which to start. When home owners decorate wisely the first time, there should be several items to keep when redecorating. Old and new items do not need to match. They only need to complement each other.

To begin, home owners can use the same process in planning the redecoration that they used before decorating. Planning is important when blending the old with the new. Home owners need to determine what they want to keep, what they want to replace, and then evaluate why they want to eliminate certain items. Perhaps some items can fit into the new decorating plan.

Sometimes redoing what a home owner already has can meet his or her needs. For instance, a sofa may be sturdy, but the home owner may not like its color or pattern. Reupholstering may satisfy decorating needs at a lower cost than replacing the sofa. This is especially true if a home owner can do the work independently.

Redecoration may take place in a single stage or in a series of steps. People with limited time and money may prefer the step approach. After deciding what to change, divide the project into phases. For instance, the process in redecorating the living room may include painting the walls, replacing the carpet, and changing the window treatment. The first step should be repainting since the room's new color may affect other redecorating decisions (Figure 25.25). As furnishings sales

Before MR. INTERIOR/Shutterstock.com

After MR. INTERIOR/Shutterstock.com

Figure 25.25 These before and after photos demonstrate what a difference basic paint and furnishings can make. No new construction was performed in this renovation.

occur, replace some furniture and accessories. A home owner's priorities and budget help determine the sequence.

Professional services are available to help home owners decorate. As you recall, an *interior designer* is a person who specializes in applying the principles and elements of design to interiors. An interior designer can plan a decorating scheme, make purchases, and supervise the work to make sure it is correct. Most designers expect to do the bulk of the planning and let the client do some of the purchasing. Using these services will save time and help home owners avoid costly mistakes.

Some furniture stores employ designers or decorators that you can hire. There are generally no charges for this service, but store personnel expect customers to purchase some furniture.

Review & Assessment

1. How is redecorating different from decorating?
2. Identify three reasons a home owner may want to redecorate his or her home.

Remodeling

Remodeling is usually more expensive than redecorating. This is because it involves changes to the structure, such as adding a wall or a room. There are times when remodeling is more of a bargain than moving or trying to live with the house's flaws.

Remodeling can extend livable space to existing areas, such as finishing a basement, attic, or garage (Figure 25.26). Some people choose to add usable space to a structure, such as a family room addition or an attached garage. Others choose to enclose a porch or build a patio. Some remodeling jobs—such as creating a more spacious and convenient kitchen—increase the market value of a home (Figure 25.27). Other projects may not increase the value of a home, but provide great comfort and satisfaction to the household.

Weighing Options

There are many ways to measure the cost of remodeling. Home owners who are considering remodeling need to ask themselves the following questions:

- Is the cost of remodeling a better value than moving or keeping the living space the same?
- Will remodeling increase the quality of life in the home?
- Will the remodeling process cause too many inconveniences for household members? Adding

Before Jennifer Blanchard Belk, IIDA, LEED AP

After Jennifer Blanchard Belk, IIDA, LEED AP

Figure 25.26 This remodeled single car garage adds an office and children's study room to the home.

Green Choices

Remodel with REGREEN

If you are thinking about remodeling your home, consider REGREEN. This is the nation's first program for remodeling homes with "green" changes.

The American Society of Interior Designers (ASID) and the United States Green Building Council (USGBC) developed REGREEN. It is a series of guidelines that include the best ways to remodel a home using "green" ideas. The guidelines are for either room-by-room or the entire house.

Remodeling with REGREEN involves a number of responsibilities on the part of the designer to investigate practices of the manufacturers of the products and materials considered for use in the remodeling. There is concern that materials are recyclable and are made with renewable resource materials if possible. With the emphasis on protecting the environment by today's society, more clients will be interested in remodeling using green practices.

A

B

Jennifer Blanchard Belk, IIDA, LEED AP

Figure 25.27 Converting a small, outdated kitchen (A) into a more spacious and modern kitchen (B) significantly increases a home's value.

a room is not likely to be as inconvenient as remodeling the kitchen or bathroom.

- Will there be a need to move shortly after remodeling?

Home owners also need to decide whether to use professionals or do the work themselves. People who do their own remodeling can save about half the cost of hiring the work out. However, the work could take twice as long or longer for people who choose to do their own work. If a project is simple and the home owner knows what to do, handling the remodeling may be worthwhile. When tasks involve rewiring and adding plumbing, hiring a professional is generally best. In fact, local building codes may require it. Home owners may do some tasks themselves and hire professionals for others, or they may hire a remodeling service to do the whole job.

Getting the Best Value for the Money

It pays to do some homework before starting a remodeling project. This helps avoid making changes that cost more than they are worth. Home owners should start by researching information about remodeling products, trends in design, and financing. The next step is to get estimates on how much a remodeling project will cost. Will it be

Home Improvements and Increased Home Value

Projects that make a home more desirable often increase its value. A higher value means a better sales price when the owner sells the home. Sometimes the sales price is high enough to offset part or all of the improvement costs. The following figures show the average percentages of home improvement costs that are offset by a higher sales price. For example, adding a fireplace to a home will offset all of the improvement costs. The home owner may also gain a 10% increase in value on the home.

Project	Percentage of Costs Offset by Higher Sales Price
Fireplace addition	100–125%
Kitchen remodeling	75–125%
Solar greenhouse addition	90–100%
Garage or patio addition	75–100%
Bathroom remodeling	75–100%
Bathroom addition	50–100%
Room addition	40–75%
Addition of energy saving measures (such as storm windows or more insulation)	40–50%
Maintenance-free siding	40–45%

Figure 25.28 Remodeling improves the usefulness and appearance of a home and often increases its resale value.

possible to regain the costs of remodeling when selling the house? See Figure 25.28.

Some contractors specialize in remodeling projects. When home owners do not want to do the work themselves, they should use a licensed contractor who will guarantee the work. Before choosing a contractor, home owners should learn the answers to the following questions:

- Is the contractor licensed? by whom?
- How long has the contractor been in business?
- Do former clients express satisfaction with the contractor's work? Ask the contractor for references or find names of clients at the local building department.
- Can the contractor show images of a similar completed project?
- Does the contractor have insurance coverage for all workers?
- Will the contractor provide lien waivers to show payment for supplies and subcontractors used for the project? A *lien waiver* protects the home owner from liability if the contractor does not pay for items used to remodel a house.

Home owners should not pay for the entire remodeling project until all the work is finished to satisfaction. The best arrangement is to pay 25 percent of the total fee before work starts and the rest upon completion. Contractors are more likely to complete a project the way a home owner wants it if they are waiting for payment.

When making a remodeling plan, keep the neighborhood in mind. Keep improvements in line with nearby houses. Try not to raise the value of a home more than 20 percent over the value of neighboring homes. Raising the home's value by more than 20 percent may mean the home owner will not get the full value selling the house.

Consider adding features that conserve energy when remodeling. Such features are bargains because they lower monthly energy bills. They also increase the resale value of a home. Removing a drafty window and replacing it with a wall or with an insulating window adds value. Insulating windows provide a good view and insulate better than standard windows. Add insulation to walls or replace old doors with insulating doors. Also consider replacing older appliances with energy-efficient models.

Review & Assessment

1. Why is remodeling usually more expensive and complex than redecorating?
2. What questions should home owners ask themselves when considering a remodeling project?

Resources for Home Care

There are resources for home owners to use if they need help in maintaining their homes. Resource people can offer advice, or they can do the work. Consider seeking both advice and help with the work.

Help with Home Maintenance

If a home owner does not have time to maintain a home or does not know someone who can help, one option is to hire people to do the cleaning and maintenance for the home. Service companies have employees who work by the hour, the day, or the job. A home owner contracts with the service, not with individuals. In contrast, a home owner can hire an individual who provides a specific service. Individuals set their own rates (Figure 25.29).

The cost of the services varies with the job as well as the size and location of the house. When hiring a cleaning service, it is important to learn what specific tasks are done at what costs. A home owner may need to hire someone else or pay more for certain cleaning tasks. For instance, window washing is not usually part of a weekly cleaning service.

It is also possible to hire someone to help with outside maintenance. A home owner may have someone mow the lawn and trim the trees and shrubs. Employing the services of a landscaping or yard maintenance company on a regular basis is also possible. They will provide complete maintenance or just do the specific projects the home owner requests.

Other Resources

Many home owners learn more about how to do their own home maintenance. Home improvement centers offer free workshops and helpful literature. Many community colleges and technical schools offer free or inexpensive courses on home maintenance. Decorating, remodeling, and home maintenance programs are common TV programs. Search for resources online by using *home improvement*, *landscaping*, and *gardening* as search words. You can buy videos and books, or borrow them from a local library. Newspapers and magazines often feature articles on home maintenance techniques and new products. Clip the articles and start your own resource file.

Tyler Olson/Shutterstock.com

Figure 25.29 Before hiring self-employed individuals, check their references and talk with former clients. Be sure the individual does good work and upholds his or her contracts.

Review & Assessment

1. If a home owner does not have time to maintain a home, what options does he or she have for cleaning and maintenance? Locate three examples of services in your area that can help with these tasks.
2. Name three resources that help home owners maintain their homes.

Chapter 25 Assessment

Summary

- The first step in maintaining a home is to keep it clean. The proper tools, cleaning products, and a cleaning schedule are important.
- Yard maintenance also requires certain tools and products, and a maintenance schedule by the seasons.
- The right tools and knowledge of their use can speed up home repairs.
- A professional should do repairs that pose safety risks or require expert knowledge.
- Creating and organizing storage space can simplify home maintenance.
- Redecorating and remodeling require careful planning for home maintenance.
- Many helpful resources exist for redecorating and remodeling as well as home maintenance.

Terms in Action

1. **Term charades** In teams, play picture charades to identify each of the *Content Terms* listed at the beginning of this chapter. Write the terms on separate slips of paper and put the slips into a basket. Then choose a team member to be the sketcher. The sketcher pulls a term from the basket and creates quick drawings to represent the term until the team guesses the term. Rotate turns as sketcher until the team identifies all terms.

Think Critically

2. **Analyze features** The idea of "easy maintenance" usually appeals to home buyers looking for a home. Analyze types of features to seek in a home for it to deserve the title of "easy to maintain." Make a list of both interior and exterior features. What features would be at the top of your list? Why?
3. **Evaluate resources** Suppose you have been hired to help a young professional set up his or her first apartment. Using $150.00 to get started, evaluate what cleaning tools, cleaning products, and basic repair tools you would recommend this young professional buy. Check prices at a local hardware store or home improvement center to identify current costs, or research prices online. Compare the financial feasibility of some of the alternatives. What items would be on your list and why?
4. **Draw conclusions** Cleaning and maintaining a home requires human energy and so does developing a plan for maintaining a safe home. Some people, particularly some older adults, may hire someone to clean their homes or do their yard maintenance. Draw conclusions about whether you think professional cleaning services or yard maintenance services represent a growing industry because of the increasing number of older adults. Give evidence to support your thinking.

Core Skills

5. **Kitchen remodel** Visit a home improvement center that offers design assistance in remodeling kitchens and baths. Determine the square footage of the kitchen in your home (width by length) and ask a salesperson how much it typically costs to remodel a kitchen of that size. What steps are required to remodel a kitchen?
6. **Listening and writing** Watch an online video demonstration of how to use basic tools as instructed by your teacher. Write a concise summary about the demonstration that is clear and easy to understand.
7. **Research and speaking** Mix together one or more of the alternative cleaning solutions described in *Green Choices: Eco-Friendly Cleaning Products and Tips.* Use each solution to clean the appropriate surface. How well did each product work? Use online or print resources to investigate how these eco-friendly solutions function and how they benefit the environment. Share your findings in an oral report.
8. **Speaking and technology** Collaborate with your team to choose a basic home tool from this chapter. Learn how to use the tool properly by investigating online resources or by interviewing a professional. Use a web-based video application to create a brief how-to video explaining what the tool is and how

Chapter 25 Assessment

to properly use it. Be sure to exhibit all safety procedures.

9. **Reading and research** Use reliable resources to research drip irrigation. Explain what it is and how it is installed. Where is it most often used? What is the main benefit of such a system?
10. **Math practice** Use the checklist in Figure 25.5 to develop a cleaning schedule for your home. List the cleaning tools and supplies needed to perform the tasks on the schedule. Then visit the website of a local hardware and home improvement store and determine the price of these items. Tally the cost and include the tax you would pay if you purchased each item in your neighborhood. Compare price estimates with classmates.
11. **Technology, research, and writing** Use online or print resources to investigate several types of eco-friendly lawn mowers, such as solar-powered lawn mowers, battery-powered lawn mowers, or robotic lawn mowers. What technology makes these mowers unique? What are the pros and cons of the mower(s)? If you were a landscape designer, would you recommend one of these mowers to a client? Why or why not? Write a summary.
12. **CTE career readiness practice** Imagine that you are a professional blogger of housing-related topics. Your readers have asked you to write an article that compares different types of cleaning products. Select three different cleaning products to test. Then carefully test each product and write a product review for each. Be sure to read the product's safety warnings and instructions for use before you use each product. Then apply your written communication skills to write a clear, concise, and convincing article to rate the ease of use, efficiency level, and cost of all three cleaners.Include a picture of the products you test.

Design Practice

13. **Bedroom redecoration** Using a CADD software program, use your imagination to create a redecorating plan for a bedroom, including a floor plan, furniture plan, and a rendering of the final design. Apply job-appropriate computer applications to develop a preliminary budget for the project. Create a presentation board showing samples of colors and designs you plan to use. Put the items together in a binder and share the decorating plan with the class.
14. **Family room remodel** Your new clients want to remodel their basement for family room space. The family requires space for watching movies and playing video games along with space for playing games and storing toys for their children ages 3 and 5. Easy maintenance is a requirement. The current basement has two small semifinished rooms that each measure 12 ft. by 14 ft. The family prefers to have one large open room that uses furnishings to designate the space usage. Use your problem-solving skills to analyze and identify the problem and create a workable floor plan for an open-concept family room using CADD software. Research various attractive, but durable, materials for walls, floors, furnishings, and storage suitable for the client's needs. Create a presentation board to show all materials and furnishings you recommend for this project. Write a summary outlining your recommendations for the family room and indicate how this plan meets the client's requirements.
15. **Portfolio** Presume you have been hired to develop a plan for organizing bedroom closet space for a three bedroom home. One walk-in closet measures 8 ft. wide by 10 ft. long by 8 ft. high. The other two closets measure 8 ft. wide by 3 ft. deep by 8 ft. high. Use online or print resources to help develop the plan and locate photos of organizer examples. Use CADD software to provide scale floor plan drawings (1" = 1'-0") and elevations of the closets. Be sure to note placement and dimensions of new storage system components. Print (plot) your plan and write a summary explaining your choices for each closet to include in your portfolio.

Unit 7

Careers in Housing and Interiors

Chapter 26	Career Planning
Chapter 27	Preparing for Career Success
Chapter 28	Entrepreneurship for Housing and Interiors

bikeriderlondon/Shutterstock.com

Careers Related to Housing and Interiors

As you have studied the various aspects related to housing and interior design, you may have discovered your interests and skills fall into many career pathways. To narrow your career path and develop a career plan for the future, complete the FCCLA *Career Investigation* STAR Event. See the FCCLA *STAR Events* descriptions in the *Competitive Events Guide* on the FCCLA website for event details. See your adviser for information as needed.

Leadership for Career Success

Do you have the ability to inspire others around you? Do you like to take charge and lead a team toward common goals? Do you strive for new challenges and like to learn new things? If you do, you may just have the leadership skills employers look for most.

To further strengthen your leadership abilities, create an FCCLA *Career Connection* project that fits your needs in the housing and interior design career area. See your adviser for information as needed.

Chapter 26

Career Planning

Content Terms

career
occupation
aptitude
abilities
principal designer
unskilled labor
semiskilled labor
skilled labor
job shadowing
mentor
internship
apprenticeship
cooperative education
certificate
license
associate's degree
bachelor's degree
master's degree
career cluster
networking

Academic Terms

dexterity
dictate
disseminate

Learning Outcomes

After studying this chapter, you will be able to

- assess your interests, aptitudes, abilities, and personality traits to determine a good career selection.
- research and evaluate careers for job duties and responsibilities, career levels, skill levels, employment outlook, earning levels, and other factors.
- summarize education and training options and how to achieve education goals.
- demonstrate how to use sources of career information.
- determine the benefit of joining organizations to help develop your career.

Reading with Purpose

Read the summary at the end of the chapter before you begin to read the chapter. On a sheet of paper, note the main points outlined in the summary. As you read the chapter, take additional detailed notes for each main point.

G-WLEARNING.com

While studying, look for the access icon  **to:**

- **Practice** the *Content* and *Academic Terms* with e-flash cards, matching activities, and vocabulary games.
- **Reinforce** what you learn by completing the *Review & Assessment* questions and e-mailing them to your instructor.

www.g-wlearning.com/housing/

wavebreakmedia/Shutterstock.com

Have you considered the type of career you would like to pursue? The actions you take now will lay the groundwork for the career you will have in the future (Figure 26.1). Would you like to be an interior designer? Do you see yourself buying and selling real estate? Are you interested in teaching housing and design? Preparing for your career may seem overwhelming at first, but taking one step at a time will make the process easier. If you have not started to think about your future, now is a good time to begin.

Having a career means you will hold several occupations related by a common skill, purpose, or interest over your lifetime. A **career** is a series of related occupations that show progression in a field of work. The term *job* is commonly used to mean *occupation*. Strictly speaking, a *job* is a task, while an **occupation** is paid employment that involves handling one or more jobs.

An example of a career is the course followed by a construction worker over a span of several years. He or she may enter the field doing one job well, learn to do others, and eventually supervise parts or all of various construction projects. As you move from one occupation to the next, you will gain new skills and knowledge.

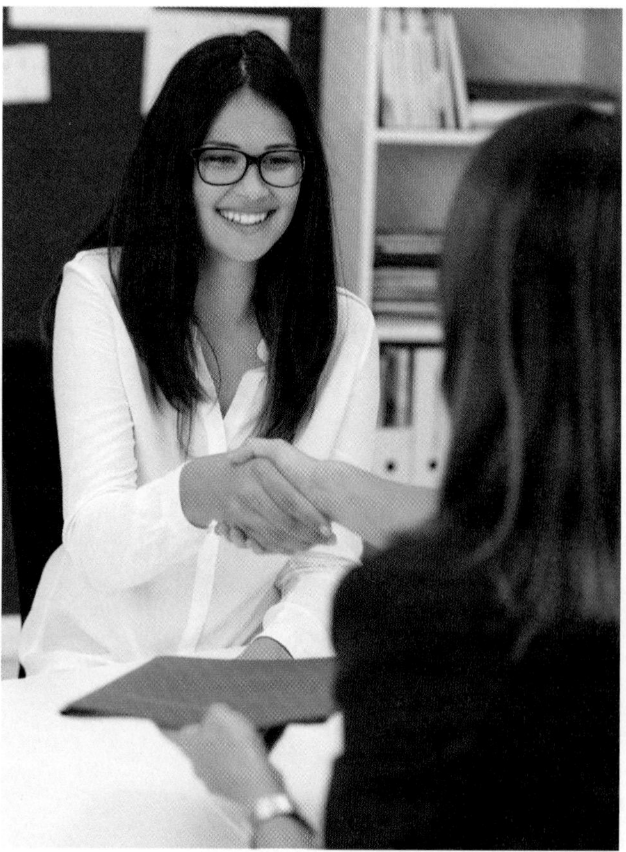

racorn/Shutterstock.com

Figure 26.1 Decisions and connections you make now can make your future career easier to attain.

Preparing yourself for a meaningful career in the workplace requires advance planning. This involves setting *goals*, which are aims or targets a person tries to achieve. Preparing yourself for the future involves performing a self-assessment, researching careers, investigating education and training options, identifying sources of career information, and joining organizations to help develop your skill sets and explore career options.

Performing a Self-Assessment

Before you can set career goals, you will need to explore the real you. Consider your *values*, or beliefs and ideas about what is important. Identify your interests, natural talents, and skills. Examine your personality traits and how they can help you identify a fitting career. Imagine the lifestyle you would like to have in the future and how your career will impact that lifestyle.

Examining Interests

Few teens know exactly what career they want. Sometimes adults who have prepared for one career decide they want to pursue another. As you grow older, you may notice that your interests change. This is perfectly normal. Active people are constantly developing new interests.

Usually a person's interests parallel his or her likes. For example, if you enjoy mowing the lawn and keeping flowerbeds well maintained, you may enjoy a landscaping career. If you enjoy part-time work at a home improvement store and working with people, you may enjoy work as a general contractor (Figure 26.2). If you dislike that type

michaeljung/Shutterstock.com

Figure 26.2 For career inspiration, look to everyday activities you enjoy. Some activities can also open doors to moneymaking opportunities that will help pay for your education and training.

of work, however, a job involving these tasks is definitely not for you.

Interests involve people, data, or objects—and sometimes all three. In the case of the construction management job, the focus is on objects: a beautiful and safe home. A person who likes to focus on data may enjoy a position estimating materials and costs for construction. In contrast, a person interested in people may enjoy a job in marketing or teaching within the field. By reviewing your likes and dislikes, you will get a better picture of the tasks you would enjoy in a career.

Determining Aptitudes and Abilities

Career planning cannot take place until you know what you can do well. What are your aptitudes? An **aptitude**, or natural talent, is an ability to learn something quickly and easily. Are some of your subjects in school much easier than others? Knowing which subjects are easier for you can help determine some of your talents. You may not be aware of all of your aptitudes if you have never been challenged to use them. A school counselor can give you an *aptitude test* to help reveal your strengths.

Abilities are skills you develop with practice. As you prepare to handle a new responsibility, you will learn that it requires certain skills. Can you develop those skills with practice? For example, can a person who is afraid of heights become a good roofer? Can someone lacking finger ***dexterity*** (ability to skillfully move) learn to manipulate precision tools? It is impossible to excel at every skill, so find out what tasks you can do well.

Considering Your Personal Traits

Some people have personality traits that are in conflict with the requirements of certain occupations. Choosing one of these occupations would not lead to career satisfaction or success. For instance, if you are outgoing, you may not enjoy work that requires working independently from home. If you prefer a routine, you may resent a job that involves constant change. Think carefully about your personality while you are exploring career choices and keep your strongest characteristics in mind.

Also consider whether your aptitudes, abilities, and traits complement each other. For instance, you may be a very detailed and technology-savvy person, but you also have great people skills and an extroverted personality. In that case, it might not be wise to pursue a career as a CADD technician even if you have the skills, because you might become frustrated with the isolation of an office and computer-based job. How do you avoid this disconnect? The more you learn about a profession and speak to professionals about their daily activities, the higher the likelihood that you will find a career that merges your traits, interests, aptitudes, and abilities.

Thinking About Lifestyle

The career you choose affects your lifestyle in many ways. It affects your income, which determines how much you can spend on housing, clothing, food, and luxury items. Your career choice may also affect where you live (Figure 26.3). You will want to identify areas where the work is plentiful. If you prefer not to live in a large city, choose work that is available in other areas.

Adwo/Shutterstock.com

f11photo/Shutterstock.com

Figure 26.3 Your career will likely determine where you live. Do you prefer a rural setting or an urban setting?

Your friendships are affected by your career choice, too. You are likely to become friends with some of your work associates. You may meet other friends through the people you know from work. Your leisure time is affected by the hours and vacation policies of your job. If you prefer to work weekdays from 9:00 a.m. to 5:00 p.m., you may want to avoid jobs that require overtime, late shifts, or working weekends.

Review & Assessment

1. What is the difference between a career and an occupation?
2. What is the difference between aptitudes and abilities?
3. How can your career impact your lifestyle?

Researching Careers

After performing a self-assessment, the next step is to research career options and learn about each occupation in-depth. As you are researching, you will find many occupations and allied careers. Notice how the job descriptions and titles vary within a field. Note the different skill levels and career levels of those occupations. Review the employment outlook, typical salaries, and several other factors to evaluate if a certain career is right for you.

Job Duties and Responsibilities

When exploring the duties and responsibilities related to different career options, it is important to understand the definition of each occupation. These definitions make a huge difference on what you can do and are qualified to do within the industry. For example, although *interior decorator* and *interior designer* sound similar, one position carries more responsibilities. Compare the job descriptions of an interior decorator, an interior designer, and an architect:

- An *interior decorator* is someone who has a love and understanding of color, textiles, spatial quality, and other aesthetic aspects of (usually) residential interiors. Interior decorators may have no formal training, but could have extensive experience in the industry. As with all housing and interiors professionals, they work closely with other tradespeople to bring interior environments to completion. Their job is not typically regulated by any type of licensure.
- An *interior designer* does all that a decorator does, but quite a bit more. In many states that have title and/or practice acts related to interior design, interior designers are required to have a degree and a license to use the *title* of interior designer and/or to practice the profession. These professionals have been trained not only in the aesthetic aspects of design, but also in the health, safety, and welfare issues within both residential and commercial environments. Some states with practice acts allow licensed interior designers to acquire building permits.
- An *architect's* responsibilities often overlap with an interior designer's responsibilities, but architects are usually more involved in the structural and aesthetic design of the building envelope. Their practice is regulated nationwide. Some interior designers eventually pursue a further degree in architecture (Figure 26.4).

It is important to find out exactly what a job or career entails. The responsibilities and daily duties as well as the educational preparation of each occupation differ. Remember, you will be fulfilling these duties every day for many years. If they do not sound appealing now, it is unlikely that you will enjoy them in future years.

Career Levels

Career opportunities in housing and interior design are sometimes grouped according to the qualifications, time within the industry, and level of responsibility linked to each specific occupation.

Rido/Shutterstock.com

Figure 26.4 Interior designers and architects may work closely together on a project.

Career Focus Interior Designer—Community Medical Complex

©2015, Tim Buchman Photography

Do you feel that certain health care interiors, such as hospitals, doctor's offices, or dentist's offices, could be designed differently? Perhaps you have thought about how waiting areas could be more comfortable and inviting. If so, then a career as an interior designer who specializes in medical complexes may be the right fit for you.

Interest/Skills: Interior designers who specialize in health-care facilities have a passion to help others and provide comfort during challenging times. Attention to detail and active listening are important skills. Strong technology skills, especially in CADD software, are important for complicated projects. Because many people are involved in developing a medical complex, exemplary communication and teamwork skills are essential in working with clients and contractors to finish the job on time. Medical interior designers also need math skills to work with a budget and calculate all job costs.

Career Snapshot: Medical interior design involves working with clients and architects. The designer develops a plan that keeps the client happy. Along with following a budget and local building codes, an interior designer is responsible for the flooring, all the fittings, decorating, and accessories. Work hours are irregular due to the nature of the work.

Education/Training: A bachelor's or master's degree is preferred. Computer courses in CADD are essential. To specialize in medical interior design, classes in psychology, biology, physiology, and medical facility management are also necessary.

Licensing/Examinations: Approximately one half of the states require interior designers to be licensed. The National Council for Interior Design Qualification (NCIDQ) administers an examination that you must pass to obtain a license.

Professional Associations: Associations for interior designers specializing in health care facilities include the American Academy of Healthcare Interior Designers (AAHID), the International Interior Design Association (IIDA), and the American Society of Interior Designers (ASID).

Job Outlook: Interior designers can expect job growth to be between four and eight percent through 2024. Designers with a broad range of skills and experiences will be in demand. Also, because of the aging U.S. population, the job market is strong for designers with knowledge of special needs for this aging demographic.

Sources: The Occupational Outlook Handbook (OOH); the Occupational Information Network (O*NET)

By these measures, work opportunities can be divided as follows:

- entry-level positions
- mid-level positions
- professional positions

Entry-Level Positions

Entry-level positions are positions that are at the base level of a career. People in entry-level positions follow the directions of those in mid-level and professional positions. The qualifications for entry-level positions vary widely. Although you will be ready to perform many tasks, this is usually a period of learning. Often there is opportunity to move up if you do your job well. Design assistants with two to three years of postsecondary training often qualify for entry-level positions.

Mid-Level Positions

People in mid-level positions often work as *support personnel* to professionals. They carry out the decisions of the professionals. Their job assignments often include supervising workers who have less authority and responsibility.

In housing construction, for example, one supervisor oversees the work of many laborers. Supervisors rarely do the wiring, plumbing, or roofing themselves, but know how to do these jobs well. Consequently, they are well qualified to evaluate workmanship and supervise those actually doing the job.

The middle level in a given career field may have sublevels. This is especially true on large or complex projects. As a result, mid-level supervisors report to a head manager with higher authority. The fact that mid-level supervisors have supervisors themselves does not make their work any less important. They also need good communication and teamwork skills to effectively manage the work of others.

Professional Positions

Jobholders in professional positions make decisions that affect the lives of individuals, families, and whole communities. Engineers, planners, project managers, and designers are some of the people with professional-level positions. Generally, a bachelor's degree is required for these jobs as well as special training and experience. Some professional positions also require an advanced degree.

Another professional position is that of principal designer. The **principal designer** is the interior designer who finalizes all design decisions on a project. In smaller businesses, this position is often the owner and perhaps the only interior designer (Figure 26.5). In larger businesses, the principal designer may be the lead designer on a project. Depending on the business size, the principal designer may also be the project manager. The project manager oversees the implementation of the project design, coordinating all units to deliver the final project.

BlueSkyImage/Shutterstock.com

Figure 26.5 Within a small business, designers must not only take care of the creative portions of a project, but also handle logistics like ordering product.

Skill Levels

In addition to categorizing occupations as entry level, mid-level, or professional level, occupations in the housing and interior design industry may also be grouped by skill level. Special skills and training are needed to carry out various tasks. For jobs related to manufacturing, for example, the following three terms are commonly used in job descriptions: unskilled labor, semiskilled labor, and skilled labor. **Unskilled labor** describes workers who fill entry-level jobs that require almost no previous knowledge or experience. **Semiskilled labor** describes workers who have some experience and/or technical training. **Skilled labor** refers to workers who have successfully completed a formal training program beyond high school. When exploring different occupations, look carefully at what each occupation involves and what is expected of the jobholder. Also study the qualifications for entering that field.

Employment Outlook

When researching occupations, be sure to learn about the employment outlook for each occupation of interest. In 10 years, will the need for a certain occupation increase, stay the same, or decrease compared to average employment trends? Are too many people choosing a field that is not growing? If the employment outlook for a career is poor, you will have fewer employment choices. It is best to focus on career areas that are growing. They will offer you greater employment options when you are ready to begin your career.

Earning Levels

You will want to check average earnings or salaries before choosing your career. What is the average beginning pay? What does it take to achieve higher earnings? Are additional degrees or training generally required to earn higher salaries?

When checking pay levels for various careers, you can expect professional positions to earn higher pay. Entry-level positions earn the least. As you work your way up from entry level, your pay generally increases. This is because your knowledge and skills also increase, and they are worth more to your employer.

When investigating earning levels, research earnings of other allied and related careers as well. You may discover a related occupation that suits you, yet earns higher pay.

RossHelen/Shutterstock.com

Figure 26.6 Travel opportunities can be an exciting benefit of employment in the design industry.

Other Factors

When considering your future career, there are many more factors to think about. Some of these may be very important to you. Others may not matter if you meet your most important criteria.

- **Rewards.** People have different ideas about what constitutes a "reward." For example, does the occupation involve frequent travel? Adventurous people would consider this job factor a reward (Figure 26.6). People who like to stay at home, however, may not be happy with so much traveling. Each job situation presents certain conditions that involve personal preferences.
- **Employer.** What companies, government offices, schools, or other workplaces employ people with the expertise? Where are these employers located? Will you be required to move?
- **Workplace.** Is the work environment a quiet office, a noisy factory, or the great outdoors? Is it near public transportation, or will you need a vehicle? Think carefully about your preferences.

Review & Assessment

1. List five factors to consider when thinking about a career.
2. In which career level are you most likely to find support personnel?
3. What is a principal designer?
4. Why is employment outlook an important factor during career research?

Investigating Education and Training Options

You need to consider what educational level is necessary for entering each career you investigate. How much training or experience does a career require? Can people enter the field with less training and acquire expertise while working on the job? Are special certificates, licenses, or credentials requirements? You can learn about education and training requirements when researching careers. Another way to learn about the necessary education and training for a particular occupation is to gain experience in the industry.

Gaining Experience

Before deciding on a specific career, you may want to shadow someone who holds the type of job you desire. **Job shadowing** is the process of observing a person in the workplace to learn more about his or her job and its requirements. In addition, you may seek to have a mentor's assistance. A **mentor** is someone with greater experience and knowledge who guides you in your career.

When you are ready to gain further experience, you may also consider assisting someone who knows how to do the job tasks well through an internship or apprenticeship program. An **internship** is an arrangement with an educational institution whereby a student is supervised while working with a more experienced jobholder within a profession. In some instances, an internship may count toward college credit. An **apprenticeship** involves on-the-job training and classroom instruction to learn a trade under the direction and guidance of an expert trade professional.

Educational Levels

Educational requirements vary among different positions. Some occupations may require certification, an associate's degree, a bachelor's degree, or an advanced degree. You can begin your career education in high school.

Cooperative education programs offer opportunities to work part-time and attend classes part-time as a high school student. These programs combine classroom instruction with paid, practical work experience. You may be able to secure a job that provides on-the-job training through this kind of program. You will also receive help from a counselor or career education teacher in your school.

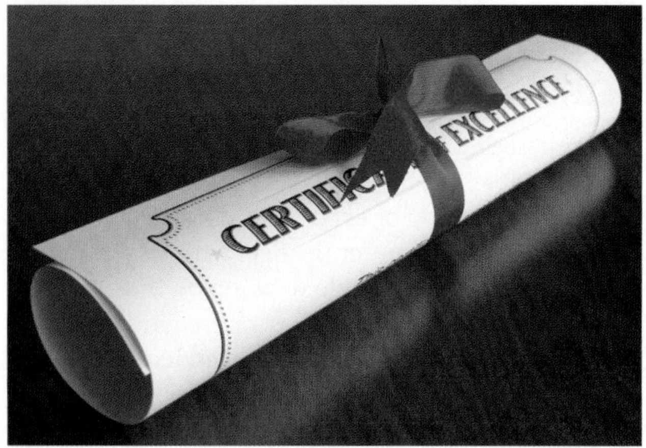

ever/Shutterstock.com

Figure 26.7 Earning a certificate is one way to prove that you are qualified for a particular occupation.

People who are seeking a hands-on profession or trade often acquire career and technical education or community college certificates or licenses. A **certificate** is a document that verifies completion of coursework or a program (Figure 26.7). Some professions require a license. A **license** certifies that an individual has undergone the proper training to perform a profession. You can receive certificate or licensure training at a traditional educational institution. You can also acquire training online or through fast-paced concentrated courses on weekends or in the evenings. Specialty construction contractors and those interested in upholstering, window coverings, and other trades often pursue a certificate or license.

Some professions require job applicants to complete a degree. An **associate's degree** is typically a two-year college program. These programs focus on the fundamentals of design, aesthetics and finishes, and business coursework. It may be at a traditional institution or be an online program. These programs often have an affiliation with bachelor's programs at colleges or universities to allow for easy transfer if a student decides to pursue a higher degree. Most graduates with an associate's degree will eventually practice in the residential design specialty and become allied members of professional associations.

Students typically achieve a **bachelor's degree** in four to five years from a college or university. Degrees may have many different titles, such as interior design, interior architecture, or interior environments. In addition to materials covered in an associate's degree, students pursuing a bachelor's degree will complete coursework that is often more technical, specialized, and commercially focused. The curriculum is also likely to require an internship and liberal arts courses. A bachelor's degree is typically the minimum requirement for an entry-level design position at a commercial design firm or for a graduate program.

People who want to specialize in a particular design area, those who want to teach in a design program, or those who want to advance to an architectural position must acquire a **master's degree** at a college or university. Programs vary in length, but usually require an extensive individualized thesis project and research.

Taking into consideration what you have read so far, imagine the following two scenarios. Two women graduated from high school together and sought design degrees. Isabela attained a four-year bachelor's degree in interior design and has just begun an entry-level position at a residential design firm. At the same time, Madison attained a two-year associate's degree and now has two years of experience at a residential design firm. Although they have different levels of experience and different degrees, their levels of responsibility in their jobs may be very similar. Isabela, however, may eventually have a greater opportunity to advance within her company due to her advanced degree.

Evaluating Postsecondary Programs

Many careers in the housing and interior design industry require job applicants to have completed at least a bachelor's degree. To obtain a bachelor's degree, you can enroll in a college or university with the program that best suits your professional interests. Most bachelor programs range from four to five years of higher education courses.

When pursuing higher education, it is important to evaluate a college or university and the programs it offers. In the past, it was common for those seeking higher education to select their favorite college or institution and then choose a major which would lead to an eventual career. With the ever-increasing cost of further education, people are beginning to realize that this may be backward thinking. There is much less risk of dropping out or failing to complete a program if a student does each of the following:

- researches and makes an educated decision about a future career
- selects a college *major* (focus of study) based on that decision
- selects an institution that offers an excellent program in the area of interest

No matter what level of higher education you are seeking, there are similar factors to consider when comparing and contrasting programs. The following is a list of topics to investigate about any learning institution (Figure 26.8).

- **Is the program accredited?** The Council for Interior Design Accreditation (CIDA) is the governing body that regulates accredited four-year interior design programs. The Council establishes minimum competency guidelines and reevaluates programs regularly to ensure continued curriculum quality. The National Kitchen & Bath Association (NKBA) offers accreditation for associate's degree, bachelor's degree, and certification programs as they relate to kitchen and bath topics. The National Association of Schools of Art and Design (NASAD) offers accreditation for all levels of postsecondary education in subjects related to design.

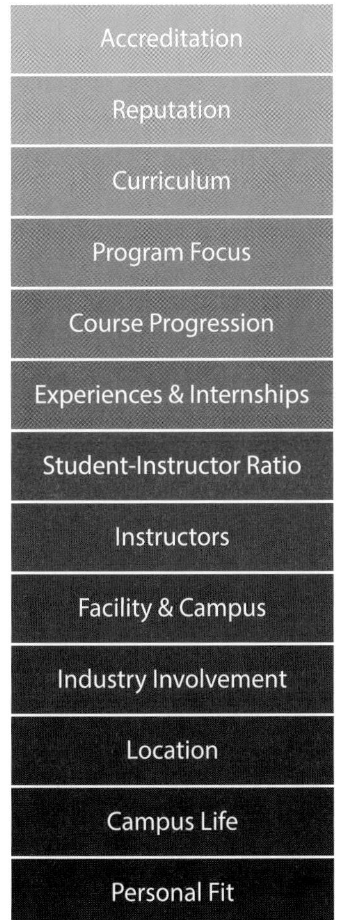

Factors to Consider in Evaluating Postsecondary Programs
Accreditation
Reputation
Curriculum
Program Focus
Course Progression
Experiences & Internships
Student-Instructor Ratio
Instructors
Facility & Campus
Industry Involvement
Location
Campus Life
Personal Fit

Jennifer Blanchard Belk, IIDA, LEED AP; Goodheart-Willcox Publisher

Figure 26.8 Consider each of these factors carefully when choosing a higher education institution and program.

- **How good is the program's reputation?** It is important to find out if a design program is well-regarded in your area and beyond. Determine how successful a program's graduates and interns are at attaining and retaining employment through discussions, college visits, and online professional networking.
- **What is the focus of the program?** Not all design programs, even those that are accredited, are similar. The origin of the program within the college or university is important. Design programs are typically located within art, architecture, or consumer affairs departments and each department affects the philosophy and concentration of the program.
- **How does the program progress?** Some programs have students start the first day of freshman year in coursework related to their majors. This allows students to test out the major before getting too far into their degree. Other programs allow students to get more general education behind them before concentrating in design. Each approach has its benefits and should be considered carefully.
- **Are internships required?** Although some students might think an internship experience is not necessary, most graduates who did not have an internship requirement wish they had that experience before graduation. An internship is an opportunity to briefly try out multiple areas of the industry with little risk or commitment while still acquiring skills and experience that will be beneficial later.
- **How large are the classes?** Some class sizes in a university can be quite large. As a rule, design-studio classes are much smaller because of the need for individualized instruction and space availability. The larger the class, however, the less one-on-one time students receive. The student-to-teacher ratio can be very important (Figure 26.9).
- **Who are the instructors?** One of the most important pieces of information relates to the background and activities of the faculty. Since faculty typically ***dictate*** (command) their course content, it is integral to have professors who are professionally licensed in design, have advanced degrees, have diverse but extensive professional backgrounds, and are professionally active. The instructor's design specialties may influence

dotshock/Shutterstock.com

Figure 26.9 Classes within interior design programs are often very interactive and rely on the helpful industry experience of the faculty.

coursework. Programs may also rely partially on part-time instructors who may offer fresh, current industry content but may not provide as much out-of-class advisement and instruction.

- **What equipment and facilities are available?** So much of a student's portfolio and employability rely on the tools and computer programs they are trained to use. Make sure teaching facilities are adequately equipped and software is continually updated to ensure your future success.
- **How much do students interact with professionals?** Is becoming connected with the design industry and having enriching experiences important to the program? If it is, faculty and staff will provide opportunities for travel, study abroad programs, volunteerism, professional events, guest speakers, and professional jurors (Figure 26.10).

Jennifer Blanchard Belk, IIDA, LEED AP

Figure 26.10 These interior design students have just finished a tour of internationally renowned architect Frank Lloyd Wright's home and studio outside of Chicago as part of a class trip.

- **Where is the campus located?** Do students have the opportunity to go to professional events because of close proximity to an urban area and professional firms? A campus that is located in an area with a higher population often offers greater options for internships, networking with alumni, and eventual employment.
- **What type of experience does the university offer?** Student success does not solely depend on the quality of the design program. Schools that offer a range of enriching opportunities, such as student organizations, volunteer events, cultural exposure, study abroad programs, and leadership development, can mean just as much to the overall development of a well-rounded student.
- **Does this college fit my needs and situation?** In the end, it does not matter if a design program is perfect if the university does not meet your needs. Seriously consider the size of the institution, costs and availability of financial aid, on-campus housing requirements, and other factors when deciding on your higher-education plans.

Review & Assessment

1. How can you gain firsthand experience before working in an entry-level position?
2. How many years of study does a bachelor's degree usually require?
3. List seven factors to research when considering a higher education institution and program.

Identifying Sources of Career Information

You can learn about career information through a variety of sources. Start your search at the career placement office of your school. Usually school counselors and teachers can direct you to helpful job information. You can also check newspaper want ads and job fairs. Good information is also available online and in libraries. The professional journals in your career field and the leading professional organizations often announce job openings. Family members and neighbors can provide help, too. Learning about careers according to categories is another good way to begin your career search.

Career Clusters

The **career clusters** are groups of occupations or career specialties that are similar or related to one another (Figure 26.11). The occupations within a cluster require a set of common knowledge and skills for career success. These are called *essential knowledge and skills*. If one or two job titles in a career cluster appeal to you, it is likely that others will, too. This is because the jobs grouped together share certain similarities. To help you narrow down your options, each

Career Clusters	
Cluster	**Type of Job Emphasis**
Agriculture, Food, and Natural Resources	Agricultural products such as food, natural fibers, wood, plants, and animal products; the production, distribution, marketing, and financing of these products
Architecture and Construction	Design, plan, or construct building structures; building management and maintenance
Arts, A/V Technology, and Communications	Visual and performing arts, journalism, and entertainment; designing, directing, exhibiting, writing, performing, and producing multimedia products
Business Management and Administration	Plan, organize, and evaluate business operations; sales, support services, and administration
Education and Training	Teach in various learning environments; educational support services and administration
Finance	Investments, banking, insurance, financial planning, and financial management
Government and Public Administration	Local, state, and national government jobs
Health Science	Health and medical services
Hospitality and Tourism	Foodservice, lodging, travel, and tourism
Human Services	Child and adult care services, counselors, therapists, home care assistants, and consumer services
Information Technology	Relate information through communication systems, computers (including hardware, software, Internet), and other media
Law, Public Safety, Corrections, and Security	Public safety and security
Manufacturing	Production of goods; sourcing and distribution
Marketing	Sale of goods; advertising, marketing, forecasting, and planning
Science, Technology, Engineering, and Mathematics	Scientific research, scientific services, and product development
Transportation, Distribution, and Logistics	Movement of people or goods through flight, rail, car, biking, trucking, walking, or by other means

Figure 26.11 The career clusters can help you determine your career area of interest.

career cluster is further divided into *career pathways*. These subgroups often require additional and more specialized knowledge and skills.

Career Pathways

Knowing the relationship between careers within a pathway is helpful when researching information about careers. The skills required for different jobs in a similar field may overlap somewhat. Preparing for more than one career in a related field allows more flexibility when you are searching for employment. If you cannot find the exact position you desire, other occupations in the same pathway will likely need your skills. The more you learn about related careers now, the more easily you will be able to adapt to changes in your occupation later.

The career clusters most closely related to the housing and interior design industries are the *Architecture and Construction* cluster and the *Arts, A/V Technology, and Communications* cluster. There are also overlapping careers and allied careers within the *Science, Technology, Engineering, and Mathematics* cluster, as well as the *Business Management and Administration* and *Human Services* clusters.

Programs of Study

Since occupations in a career pathway require similar knowledge and skills, they also require similar programs of study. A *program of study* is the sequence of instruction used to prepare students for occupations in a given career pathway. The program includes classroom instruction, co-curricular activities such as student organizations, and other learning experiences, including worksite and service learning.

Customizing a program of study for an individual learner's needs and interests results in a *personal plan of study*. A personal plan of study will help prepare you for the career direction you choose. Start by taking the appropriate classes in high school and participating in related organizations and activities such as Habitat for Humanity (Figure 26.12). A career or guidance counselor can help you create a personal plan of study.

Once you have created a personal plan of study, seek programs that address your career interests. Some dual-credit high school classes count toward college credit. Your plan of study does not expire with high school. Update your plan at least yearly, but more often if plans change.

Wendy Kaveney Photography/Shutterstock.com

Figure 26.12 Valuable experiences can be gained by volunteering within the design and construction community.

Online Resources

One of the best ways to learn about jobs is by searching reliable career websites online. You can search for open positions across the country, view job requirements, and learn about job qualifications. Many sites also offer tips for job hunting and presenting yourself in a professional manner. Other sites offer information about specific industries or careers. You can explore the following helpful sources to gain more insight into careers of interest:

- **Occupational Outlook Handbook (OOH).** The Occupational Outlook Handbook (OOH) describes major U.S. jobs and their working conditions, how to become a professional in the field, education and training requirements, average salaries, similar occupations, and job outlooks. This publication is available online and in most libraries.
- **Occupational Information Network (O*NET).** O*NET is the most complete online resource available. It provides tools for exploring careers, examining job trends, and assessing personal abilities and interests. It also includes options for finding jobs within a career cluster or searching for jobs related to specific skills.
- **CareerOneStop.** CareerOneStop has components for exploring careers, salaries, benefits, education,

training, and other resources. You can use the CareerOneStop Toolkit for exploring careers, occupational trends, wage information, and state resources. The American Job Center helps users find jobs and job-related resources in their local areas. These resources include job centers that offer assistance in job-seeking skills and various types of job training.

In addition to general career resource websites, you can learn about careers through professional organizations within the industry. The *Interior Design Educators Council (IDEC)* website includes information about what the profession entails as well as links to schools and other organizations.

Industry Publications

There are digital and print publications within the design industry that are written by professionals and respected by professionals. You can find helpful information and inspiration within the magazine pages of *Interior Design, Contract, Interiors & Sources, Dwell, Hospitality Design, Architectural Record,* and many others.

Networking

Many people find employment and learn more about an occupation through networking. **Networking** is the exchange of information or services among individuals or groups. As a newcomer to the career field, the goal of your

STEM Science & Technology — Managing Your Online Image

The Internet provides many tools that enable people to market themselves to potential employers and to search for job leads. However, pitfalls abound. Many employers also use the Internet to check job applicants as well as employees. What they are finding posted in cyberspace may cause people to lose job opportunities, promotions, and even their jobs.

A first step in managing your online image is to identify what is currently posted about you. Plug your name into one or more search engines and examine what comes up. Delete anything you wouldn't want a prospective employer to see. However, since you cannot control the flow of information online, be prepared to answer questions employers may ask. The following tips are some additional pointers:

- Do not say or do anything that is unethical or illegal.
- Do not take photos or videos that show you in a bad light. Images that depict illegal and lewd behavior have created problems for those pictured.
- Do not say anything negative about current or former employers, jobs, or coworkers. Negative comments and anything profane, sexist, or racist can result in the rejection of a job application or being named in a lawsuit.

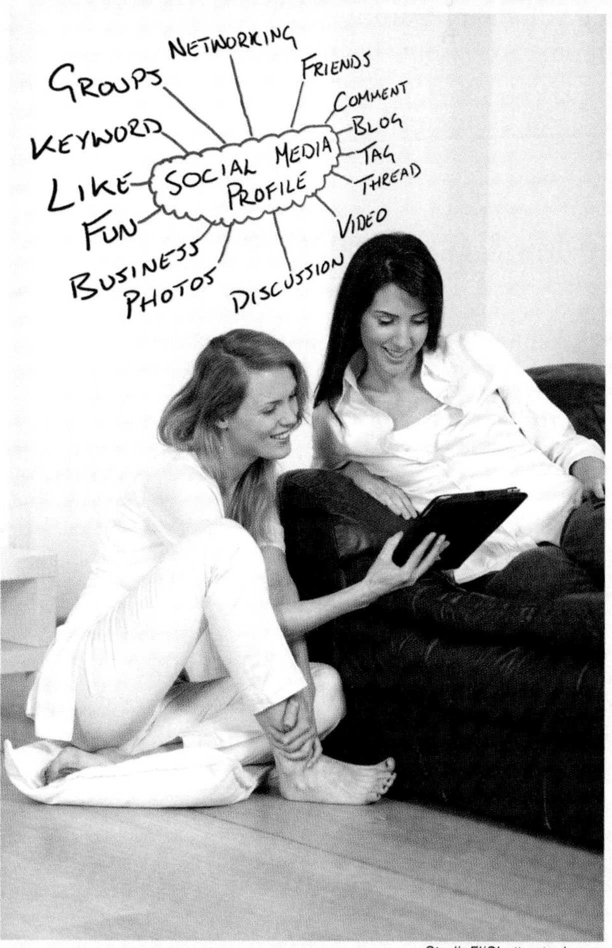

StudioFI/Shutterstock.com

Remember that cybercriminals are trolling the Internet for victims. They collect and piece together data they use to commit crimes. Avoid posting personal information, especially your address, date of birth, and phone number. Revealing your future whereabouts is also risky. For instance, one family was robbed while away on vacation because a teenage son posted the family's vacation plans on a social networking site.

networking is to meet mentors, take part in educational experiences, and learn about possible job leads.

Social-networking sites have become popular places to find information on companies and their available positions. Many companies network on these sites because it is an additional source of advertising for them. Users find that these sites expand their job search possibilities. In addition, social-networking sites allow a personal exchange between users and company representatives.

Professional-networking sites are more popular for professionals seeking to connect with other professionals, companies, or organizations. These sites can also be a way to learn about a profession, seek mentoring opportunities, view projects that professionals such as interior designers get to work on, and research the educational preparations of professionals you admire. Also, some professionals may post job-related articles that provide more insight into a career of interest.

Review & Assessment

1. Name five sources of career information.
2. What is the purpose of the career clusters?
3. Why do careers in a career pathway require similar programs of study?
4. Define networking.

Joining Organizations

You can begin getting involved in career-related organizations and learning more about career opportunities now. There are several groups that you can join. They include student organizations and student chapters of professional organizations.

Career and Technical Student Organizations

Belonging to a career and technical student organization (CTSO) can help you learn more about career options and meet other students and professionals who can help you establish a career. You will learn valuable teamwork skills that are necessary in the workplace. CTSOs that may help you in a housing or interior design career include the following:

- **Family, Career and Community Leaders of America (FCCLA).** FCCLA is an organization for students of family and consumer sciences education. Its goal is to help students develop leadership qualities with an emphasis on personal, family, work, and community activities. National programs include *Career Connections*, *Leadership Service in Action*, and *Power of One*.
- **SkillsUSA.** SkillsUSA is an organization for students preparing for technical, trade, and skilled-service occupations. Its goal is to create a strong American workforce. Programs include the Professional Development Program, which builds employability skills such as communication and teamwork. The Work Force Ready System offers assessments for career and technical education, including areas in technical drafting, residential wiring, and plumbing.
- **Business Professionals of America (BPA).** BPA is an organization of students planning for careers in business management, office administration, or information technology. Students learn workplace and leadership skills. BPA offers competitive events through its Workplace Skills Assessment program.

Professional Organizations

Professional organizations often have programs, events, and seminars to discuss current events in the industry. The International Interior Design Association (IIDA) and the American Society of Interior Designers (ASID) are the largest and longest standing professional organizations in the industry, although there are many more (Figure 26.13). Although most of these organizations do not offer high school memberships, they do provide useful information and opportunities for possible scholarships. They may also publish journals or magazines to ***disseminate*** (spread) industry information and discuss the latest industry trends.

It seems like there is a lot to do to prepare for these next stages of your life journey. This may

Professional Organizations within the Housing and Design Industry

- American Society of Interior Designers (ASID)
- International Interior Design Association (IIDA)
- Interior Design Society (IDS)
- Interior Design Educators Council (IDEC)
- International Facility Management Association (IFMA)
- International Furnishings and Design Association (IFDA)
- National Council for Interior Design Qualification (NCIDQ)
- National Kitchen & Bath Association (NKBA)
- American Institute of Architects (AIA)
- Building Office & Management Association International (BOMA)
- Construction Specifications Institute (CSI)
- National Association of Women in Construction (NAWIC)
- Illuminating Engineering Society of North America (IES)
- Leadership in Energy and Environmental Design (LEED)
- National Trust for Historic Preservation (NTHP)
- U.S. Green Building Council (USGBC)
- The Council for Interior Design Accreditation (CIDA)
- National Society of Professional Engineers (NSPE)
- American Association of Family and Consumer Sciences (AAFCS)
- National Association of Home Builders (NAHB)

Figure 26.13 You can investigate the profession by visiting these organization's websites.

be daunting or exciting for you. There are many things you can do to make your exploration of and preparation for your next stage of life more successful (Figure 26.14).

Preparing Yourself for Future Study

- Take demanding college-preparatory courses. If possible, take electives in art, art history, industrial arts, mechanical drawing or drafting, and computer sciences.
- Look for part-time jobs that will give you a chance to explore the field of design. Work for a building contractor, interior designer, or offer to do window displays for a local store. Volunteer to help set the lighting design for school plays and community theater.
- Purchase a sketchbook and practice observational drawing. Draw anything you can see.
- Keep an up-to-date record of your work in a portfolio.
- Research housing and interior design topics through libraries, bookstores, or industry magazines.
- Seek out and talk to housing and interior design professionals in your area or students at the schools that interest you.
- Attain pre-professional validation by way of the AAFCS Pre-PAC Assessment and Certification or other related certification programs.

Figure 26.14 If you are interested in pursuing an education in interior design, follow these steps to help prepare yourself for future study and jumpstart your career today.

Review & Assessment

1. What is a CTSO? How can it help you reach your career goal?
2. Name three professional organizations that would be beneficial for membership, networking, and leadership development.
3. List four actions you can take now to help you prepare for future study in the housing and interior design field.

Chapter 26 Assessment

Summary

- The first step in determining your career path is to evaluate your interests, aptitudes, abilities, personal traits, and desired lifestyle to help discover a career that is best for you.
- There are many factors to consider when researching careers. Learn about the job duties and responsibilities of each occupation, the various career and skill levels available, employment outlook, and earning levels.
- The educational level you seek depends on the level of skill needed for the position you desire.
- Education and training options include an internship, apprenticeship, cooperative education program, certification, licensure, associate's degrees, bachelor's degrees, and master's degrees.
- When you are ready to pursue higher education, carefully evaluate each program to ensure it is the best fit for you.
- Sources such as the career clusters, the Online Occupational Handbook (OOH), O*NET, and CareerOneStop can help you research career details.
- Each career cluster has career pathways that are grouped by similar knowledge and skills. Programs of study can help you plan for the education and training you need for the job you want.
- Belonging to career and technical student organizations or professional organizations can also help you learn more about a career.

Terms in Action

1. **Categorization** In teams, create categories for the *Content Terms* located at the beginning of the chapter. Classify as many of the terms as possible. Then discuss your ideas with the remainder of the class.

Think Critically

2. **Draw conclusions** Most workers can no longer expect to work for one employer for an entire lifetime. Occasionally people find themselves out of work through no fault of their own. The ideal, of course, is steady employment. After reviewing this chapter and one or more career websites, draw conclusions about which careers appear to have the strongest employment outlook. Which professions are growing? Why? Report your conclusions and your reasoning to the class.
3. **Predict consequences** Suppose a classmate posted some untrue, inappropriate remarks about you on a social-networking site. You are in the process of submitting college applications and waiting for acceptance. You know that your first-choice college examines social-networking sites to look for information about their applicants. Predict the potential consequences of these remarks on your pending college acceptance. How could these remarks impact future employment opportunities? What are some ways you safely can deal with such cyberbullying? Use your problem-solving skills to analyze this situation and solve the problem.
4. **Evaluate options** Choose a state you might like to live in. Investigate at least three colleges or universities in that state that offer interior design programs. Compare these programs according to criteria described in this chapter. What do you see as the advantages and disadvantages of each program? Does the institution offer other benefits not related to the program itself? Use your written communication skills to summarize your finds.
5. **Assess aptitude** Ask the school counselor to administer an aptitude assessment and explain your results. Based on your results, determine which types of careers in housing and interior design present the best opportunities for you to succeed. Determine whether any local employers offer these or similar jobs.
6. **Assess skills and interests** Use such online self-assessments such as the *Skills Profiler, Interest Profiler,* or *Work Importance Locator* on the CareerOneStop and O*NET websites. Take the assessments. Then evaluate how these assessments can help you locate a career that matches your skills and interests.

Chapter 26 Assessment

Core Skills

7. **Writing and speaking** Obtain a copy of a career-search book (such as the latest edition of *What Color Is Your Parachute?*). Read the book. Then write a book report identifying the important guidelines for finding meaningful employment. Select two topics you found most valuable to share with the class. Apply your written and oral communication skills to clearly, concisely, convincingly, and effectively support your evidence in a socially acceptable manner that is easily understood by others.
8. **Writing** Select two careers related to housing and interior design to research on O*NET. Read the summary reports for these careers, especially the knowledge, skills, abilities, and interests required to do the work. Analyze whether your personal interests, skills, and abilities are a logical fit with one or both careers. Write a summary explaining why you think you are well suited for either career.
9. **Research and writing** Use online resources to contrast the educational requirements for an interior decorator, an interior designer, and an architect. What is different about their job responsibilities and expertise? Find the answers by searching such professional association websites as the American Society of Interior Designers (ASID) and the American Institute of Architects (AIA). Write a summary of your findings to share with the class.
10. **Research and speaking** Search online for three sources of information about the job requirements for a housing or interior design position you might pursue. Use one or more references from the U.S. Department of Labor. Investigate the salary potential and job outlook for the profession. Is demand for the career increasing or declining? Give an oral summary of your findings and cite your sources.
11. **CTE career readiness practice** Most employers value employees that can set and achieve reasonable, attainable goals. Here are a few things you need to know about goals. Goals should be specific and positive, be measurable, and have a target deadline (either short-term—several months, or long-term—several years).

    In writing, set a career goal for five years from now. Determine how you will measure achievement of this goal, and identify a deadline for meeting it. Create a personal plan of study to outline how you can help meet your career goal.

Design Practice

12. **Class design project** Presume your school administrator is designating a space in the school media center as a career resource center that will be 30 feet by 30 feet. The administrator is requesting that your housing and interior design class submit a proposal for the space arrangement and interior design of the space. Create visual solutions by elaborating on experience and imagination to complete all necessary parts of the design process. Along with a written description of the program, your class will need to submit a CADD floor plan along with a design presentation board showing photos or samples for the following: wall, floor, and window treatments; furniture and storage options; and equipment required for career research. Strive for accuracy in your floor plan. Once the project design is complete, present it to the school administrator. Ask the administrator for critique and constructive criticism.
13. **Portfolio** A portfolio showcases your work and abilities and is essential to ultimately finding meaningful employment in your chosen career. An *introduction letter* is an important part of a portfolio. Based on your experiences and accomplishments during this course, write a letter of introduction that offers a short description of who you are and your experiences, abilities, and goals. Use word-processing software to neatly create and print your letter. Keep your letter to one page or less. Have your instructor or another experienced person proofread your letter. As you gain education and experience, periodically update your letter to document these achievements. Remember, a career portfolio is ever-evolving.

Chapter 27

Preparing for Career Success

Content Terms 

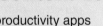

productivity apps
résumé
reference
portfolio
cover message
attitude
verbal communication
nonverbal communication
team
leadership
conflict
negotiation
ethical behavior
transferrable skills
lifelong learning

Academic Terms 

intercede
decorum
honing
elaborate
conducive
punctual
self-motivation
concisely

Learning Outcomes 

After studying this chapter, you will be able to

- determine work habits and behaviors that are important in school and career.
- demonstrate the process of applying for employment, including writing a résumé and cover message, preparing a job application and portfolio, and interviewing for a position.
- identify and practice the skills, attitudes, and behaviors important for maintaining a job and attaining career success.
- utilize appropriate communication skills for the workplace.
- discuss the importance of lifelong learning and career growth.
- summarize the procedure for leaving a job.

Reading with Purpose

Fold a sheet of notebook paper in half lengthwise before you begin to read the chapter. In the left column, write the chapter headings. In the right column, write a question you have about the topic of each heading. Then read the chapter. Note the answers to your questions while you read.

While studying, look for the access icon  **to:**

- **Practice** the *Content* and *Academic Terms* with e-flash cards, matching activities, and vocabulary games.
- **Reinforce** what you learn by completing the *Review & Assessment* questions and e-mailing them to your instructor.

www.g-wlearning.com/housing/

Darren Baker/Shutterstock.com

Planning for career success begins while you are in high school. The habits you develop now in managing your time, solving problems, and interacting with others can help you succeed in your future profession. Developing professional skills early in your life can help you successfully transition into a postsecondary program and into a career.

There are many avenues to professions in housing and interior design. The pathway to your career may be through a community college, a four-year college or university, a certification program, or another program. When you are ready to begin applying for jobs and enter the housing and interior design field, you will need to be prepared with the proper documents, including a résumé and cover message. Once in the workplace, you can achieve success by developing certain skills. This chapter focuses on ways to prepare early for professional success, apply for a job, succeed on the job, and continue your career success.

©iStock.com/monkeybusinessimages

Figure 27.1 After you graduate from high school, you have several options to further your education and acquire job skills, such as through an apprenticeship or trades program.

Preparing for Future Success

Now is the perfect time to practice behaviors and habits that will serve you well in your future career. Forming positive, professional habits while you are in high school not only makes the transition to the professional world easier, it also ensures that you will enter the industry with a positive reputation among your peers, former instructors, and industry contacts.

Many occupations in the housing and interior design field require job applicants to have successfully completed a certificate program and/or earned a degree. After high school, you can meet this requirement by attending a college or university, completing a certification or licensing program, or becoming an apprentice (Figure 27.1). Postsecondary educational experiences will differ in level of responsibility, class structure, and professional interaction; all of these experiences will shape the professional skills and qualities you possess when you apply for your first housing and interior design job.

Beginning Postsecondary Studies

Postsecondary education is an amazing time of independence and growth. If you pursue postsecondary education, it is up to you to ensure your own success. No longer will parents be able to ***intercede*** (intervene) with instructors or monitor your success completing homework. In addition to academic or technical studies, you will also have practical responsibilities, such as laundry, groceries, and often a part-time job. In this environment, time management and accountability must become self-directed.

The structure of academic classes and programs is likely to change during postsecondary studies. Unlike high school, instructors expect you to do much of the preparation yourself. Class time is often used for discussion, teamwork, exercises, project work, presentations, and project critique. Between classes, it is expected that students will make a great deal of progress and that they come to each class prepared and ready to contribute and participate. Interaction in class is imperative, as faculty want to see that you are passionate and curious. Ask questions and be open to critique. If you need to meet with an instructor outside of class, do not be afraid to ask for help, but respect your instructor's time and expertise. Before seeking help, try your best to solve the issue first.

Many students aspiring to become housing professionals or interior designers pursue a bachelor's degree. A degree in interior design is a popular type of bachelor's degree. Although interior design bachelor's programs are all different, there are particular categories of classes that typically appear within the curriculum due to the guidelines set by accreditation through the Council for Interior Design Accreditation (CIDA). Each of these courses comes with its own set of challenges and growth opportunities and requires students not only to be creative, but to be critical thinkers as well (Figure 27.2). You can take steps toward success when you make your education your top priority, treat it as your full-time job, and use the experience to establish great work habits.

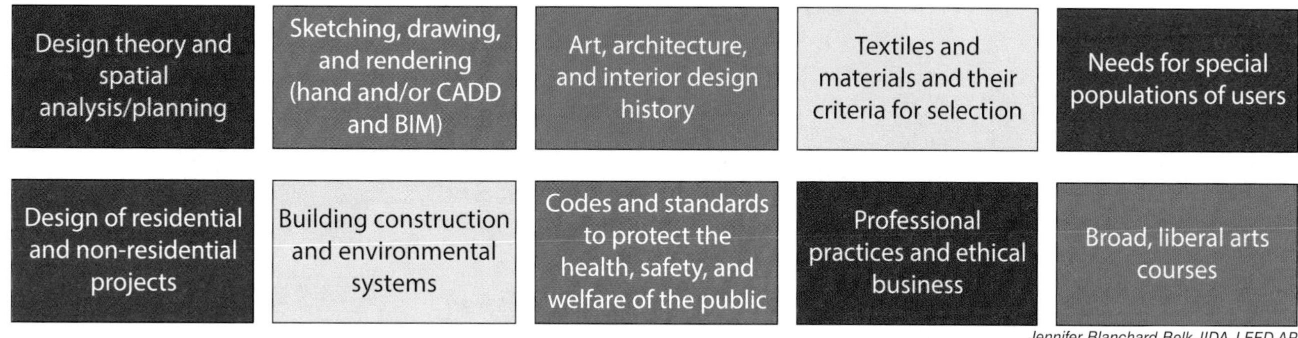
Topics Typically Covered in Interior Design Curriculum
Design theory and spatial analysis/planning
Sketching, drawing, and rendering (hand and/or CADD and BIM)
Art, architecture, and interior design history
Textiles and materials and their criteria for selection
Needs for special populations of users
Design of residential and non-residential projects
Building construction and environmental systems
Codes and standards to protect the health, safety, and welfare of the public
Professional practices and ethical business
Broad, liberal arts courses

Jennifer Blanchard Belk, IIDA, LEED AP

Figure 27.2 Although each interior design program is different, these topics are commonly covered in most programs.

Laying a Professional Foundation

Professional behavior is important when you interact with classmates, instructors, and professionals in a postsecondary program. As you interact with others, you are building your reputation and securing references and recommendations for future internships, jobs, and leadership positions. Your classmates and professors may become your future coworkers. Your attitude and ***decorum*** (proper manners and behavior) while in school will show professors and classmates what behaviors you will likely demonstrate in the workplace.

Attire is another aspect of professionalism. Although classroom situations are often casual in postsecondary education programs, avoid wearing sleepwear or dressing immodestly. How you dress can communicate how much value you place in the classes and events you are attending. Communicating through your attire, attitude, and diligence that your education is important to you can earn you a reputation as a competent, professional candidate among potential work associates.

Monitoring Your Time

Whether you are in a career or in a postsecondary program, you will face the challenge of managing your own time. Becoming calendar driven and improving your time-management skills will not only help you succeed academically, but will also help you plan for and enjoy leisure time. You can utilize **productivity apps**—apps with features such as scheduling functions, to-do lists, and task boards—and other helpful programs to help manage and relieve the stress of keeping up with deadlines and commitments.

These days, it can be difficult to control distractions due to connectivity, media, and social networking, among other daily life events. This makes monitoring how you spend your time even more important. In some professions related to housing and interior design, professionals bill clients by the hour. Thus, during work hours, these professionals should be fully engaged in their work, not checking texts or personal e-mails. Establishing organizational skills, productive patterns, and good study habits now will help you become a well-respected and productive employee later (Figure 27.3).

Demonstrating Professionalism in Communications

Much success as a professional or a student comes from ***honing*** (developing and refining) oral, written, and visual communication skills; listening skills; and critical-thinking skills. Both in a career and in a postsecondary education program, it is important to always represent yourself in a professional manner, especially in your communications with others. This means using Standard English, proper grammar, and appropriate punctuation in your written communications. Consider the following tips when communicating digitally with others:

- Use a professional-sounding e-mail address that relates to your name.
- Create an e-mail signature that contains your contact information, full name, and a brief description of your education or leadership positions.
- Compose e-mail messages in a professional manner. Avoid using acronyms and emoticons.
- Proofread your message for proper spelling, grammar, and punctuation before sending it.
- Update your information on professional networking sites on a regular basis so it remains current. This is often the first place an employer or industry contact will look to learn about you.

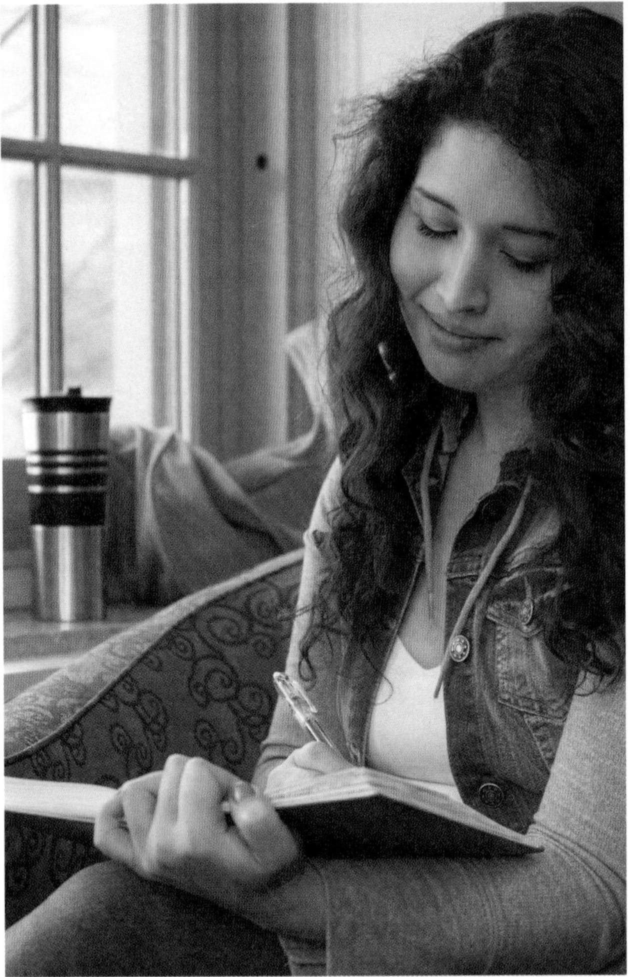

Burlingham/Shutterstock.com

Figure 27.3 By identifying which study and organizational methods are most helpful for you, you can increase your productivity.

- Pay attention to how you present yourself in your online communications, including personal e-mail and professional networking sites. If you disregard your personal image in professional communications, it is unlikely that professionals will contact you for an interview.

Engaging Early with Professionals

For optimal success, get involved in the housing and interior design community as early as you can. Do not wait to approach and job shadow different designers, take advantage of enrichment opportunities, and put your best foot forward.

One way to become involved in the housing and interior design community is to join a professional organization. Becoming involved in a professional organization now can help you learn more about an industry and land a job in your chosen field. Through networking, you can make excellent contacts for future jobs and internships

©iStock.com/BartekSzewczyk

Figure 27.4 Attending seminars, panels, or events hosted by professional organizations, is a great way to learn about industry trends and network with professionals.

(Figure 27.4). Professional organizations often have job boards posted on their websites and may have newsletters listing current job or internship listings. Your membership shows potential employers that you are already involved in the profession and are serious about a career and your future. Involvement and leadership opportunities outside of your postsecondary program of study are also essential.

When seeking employment or internship opportunities, word-of-mouth is still the best way to find opportunities in the design industry. Network with professionals you know and ask for referrals. You may also need to utilize other resources for job or internship opportunities. Your educational institution may have a career development office or website that lists internships, apprenticeships, and job opportunities. If you have laid a professional foundation and cultivated a good reputation, professors and industry members will be more eager to help you.

Review & Assessment

1. Why is it important to begin practicing good work habits and behaviors now?
2. What types of courses should you expect if you choose to pursue an interior design degree?

Applying for a Position

Eventually, as you read job boards, network with professionals, or visit company websites, you may discover a job, internship, or apprenticeship position that appeals to you. When you find an employer or

STEM Science & Technology Tips for Applying Online

Employers and many online job boards have varying requirements for posting résumés to their websites. Here are a few general tips for posting your electronic résumé.

- Acquire an e-mail address to use specifically for your job search and use it on your résumé. Choose an appropriate e-mail name. Using an inappropriate or "cutesy" e-mail name may indicate to an employer that you are a less-than-serious job seeker.
- Alter some of the contact information on your résumé to use it electronically. To keep your information out of the hands of cyber criminals, avoid using your home address and telephone number. Instead, acquire a post office box address and buy a prepaid or "pay as you go" cellular phone. Use these numbers on your electronic résumé. If an employer contacts you for an interview, you can provide your home address and telephone number at that time.
- Do not put your social security number on your résumé. If an employer shows interest in hiring you, at that time you may need to give your social security number.
- Read the privacy policies of online job boards to which you want to post your résumé. Some reserve the right to sell your personal identifiable information. Others promise never to do so.
- Choose several online job boards that seem to fit your criteria for meaningful employment and post your résumé to them.
- Consider removing your résumé from job-search sites once you find meaningful employment. Some employers may check to see if a résumé is still online once a person is on the job. The employer may want to know why he or she is still "looking" for employment.

specific position that attracts your attention, quickly express your interest. You will need to know the appropriate steps to take to apply for the position. Having a well-prepared résumé along with an organized and updated portfolio is an important first step. Knowing how to write an acceptable cover message is another goal. Finally, you will want to practice your interviewing techniques.

The best plan is to develop your résumé, portfolio, and cover message early in your high school experience. It is much easier to update a résumé or portfolio than to write one from scratch. Additionally, as you progress through school, you will have multiple opportunities to apply for scholarships, grants, awards, and leadership positions. These opportunities often require applicants to submit a cover message, résumé, or portfolio. Make sure you have the most up-to-date version of these items ready for use.

Your Résumé

A **résumé** is a brief outline of your education, work experience, and other qualifications for work. A well-written résumé can help you get an interview. You will need to include several sections on your résumé, including employment objective, career profile, education history, work history, honors and activities, community service, and special interests. Make sure your résumé is precise and without errors. Use word-processing technology to create your résumé and use a consistent format throughout.

Your résumé should include the most important, relevant items. Write a *career profile*, or a brief section on your résumé that succinctly describes your skills and abilities. Review and select educational and work history highlights that are critical to emphasize. Include dates of your employment history, education experiences, volunteer activities, and any other related special activities. When applying for an internship, include the coursework you have completed by that point in your studies. If you do not have work experience, any type of involvement that demonstrates workplace skills would be appropriate to include on your résumé. Refrain from using too much verbiage, but utilize *action verbs* when describing what you accomplished at a job or in a leadership position.

The two main types of résumé formats are the chronological résumé and the functional résumé. A *chronological résumé* organizes employment and education history according to date, with the most recent experience listed first at the top of the résumé (Figure 27.5). A *functional résumé* organizes information according to experiences that best demonstrate relevant skills and achievements. Work experiences may not be in chronological order (Figure 27.6). Select the format that best emphasizes your abilities and qualifications.

Daniela Hernandez

328 Weston Boulevard (Cell) 123.456.7890
Greensboro, North Carolina 27405 dhernandez@provider.com

EMPLOYMENT OBJECTIVE

To obtain a position assisting an interior designer and use my technology and art skills in a design studio setting

EDUCATION

Page High School graduating June 20XX
Design/Business Program Greensboro, NC
Related Courses GPA—3.5/4.0

- Four years of art classes
- Family and consumer sciences course in housing and interior design
- Computer-aided drafting design (CADD) course from Guilford Technical Community College, Summer 20XX

SKILLS and ABILITIES

- AutoCAD and AutoCAD Architecture
- SketchUp
- Hand sketching and rendering
- Social media

WORK EXPERIENCE

September 20XX–present
***Framing Specialist,* The Art Shop** Greensboro, NC

- Mount images to a variety of standard and custom-made frames and cut glass to frames using construction tools such as knives, glass-cutting tools, glues, eyes, and wire
- Work directly with customers to ensure satisfaction and implement requested modifications
- Use design experience to recommend flattering frames and treatments to customers
- Repair and revamp old or damaged frames brought in by customers

May 20XX–August 20XX
***Sales Associate,* Amy's Upholstery Fabric Shop** Greensboro, NC

- Advised customers in choosing appropriate and attractive fabrics for upholstery and for creative projects
- Answered customer requests and complaints and met customer needs in a sometimes crowded environment

HONORS and ACTIVITIES

Family, Career and Community Leaders of America

- Vice President of local chapter 20XX–20XX

Page County School District

- Second-place winner in House Plans Design Contest November 20XX
- First-place winner in Still Art Competition April 20XX

COMMUNITY SERVICE

- Habitat for Humanity volunteer Spring 20XX–present
- Youth Group soup kitchen volunteer July 20XX–present
- Page High School Literacy Program volunteer October 20XX–March 20XX
- Arts and Craft Fair for Seniors organizer February 20XX

INTERESTS

Interior design (particularly kitchen design), computer design software, sketching

REFERENCES

Available upon request

Goodheart-Willcox Publisher

Figure 27.5 A *chronological* résumé lists an applicant's education and work experience in reverse chronological order beginning with the most recent experiences. A résumé includes your employment objective, career profile or skills and abilities, education history, work history, honors and activities, community service, and special interests.

Daniela Hernandez

328 Weston Boulevard (Cell) 123.456.7890
Greensboro, North Carolina 27405 dhernandez@provider.com

CAREER PROFILE

Innovative, team-oriented, interior designer with five years experience in residential interior design. Experienced with universal and sustainable design practices. Current on residential trends, interior design codes and standards, lighting design, spatial analysis, and professional practices.

SKILLS and ABILITIES

Effective communication and interpersonal skills. Accomplished with the following:

- Autodesk Revit Architecture
- AutoCAD and AutoCAD Architecture
- Adobe Creative Suite
- SketchUp
- Social media
- Hand sketching
- Hand drafting
- Hand rendering
- 3-D model building
- Presentation techniques

DESIGN EMPLOYMENT HISTORY and ACHIEVEMENTS

Marigold Design Group, Greensboro, NC—*Junior Interior Designer* June 20XX–present

- Assist designers with creating elevations, sketches, 3-D models, renderings and material boards, both by hand and using technology
- Assist with fabric, furniture, and fixture selections and specifications for residential interiors, focusing on universal and sustainable design practices
- Interact with design clients by answering questions, collecting information, and communicating design requirements

Art Shop Design Studio, Greensboro, NC—*Interior Design Assistant* May 20XX–April 20XX

- Scheduled client meetings, tracked interior design projects, and prepared materials for client presentations
- Assisted with presentation board creation and digital presentations for various client projects
- Managed the design studio's social media site and wrote blog posts with design-studio news

PROFESSIONAL INVOLVEMENT

American Society of Interior Designers (ASID), Professional Membership 20XX–present
NeoCon—Chicago, Illinois—June 20XX
Funiture Market—High Point, North Carolina—September 20XX

CAMPUS INVOLVEMENT

Alpha Delta Pi Sorority 20XX–20XX

- President—20XX
- Vice President, Recruitment and Marketing—20XX
- Director of Social Enrichment—20XX
- American Society of Interior Designers, Carolinas Chapter, Student Member 20XX–20XX
- Secretary, Campus Chapter—20XX–20XX
- ASID Carolinas Student Day and Otto Zenke Competition—20XX

EDUCATION

Appalachian State University, Boone, North Carolina graduated May 20XX

- Bachelor of Science—Interior Design, CIDA and NASAD Accredited, GPA—3.8/4.0
- Concentration in universally and environmentally sensitive residential design

INTERESTS

Interior design, computer design software, sketching, Habitat for Humanity

REFERENCES

Available upon request

Goodheart-Willcox Publisher

Figure 27.6 A *functional* résumé is organized to show the most relevant experiences related to employer needs near the top of the résumé. The functional résumé may or may not have experiences listed in chronological order.

To apply for a position, most employers request that you e-mail your résumé or post it to the employer's job site. You can also post an electronic résumé to a number of online job-search sites. Some websites and employers may request a text-only format. To create this type of résumé, save your formatted résumé as "text only." Then review the text-only résumé to make sure lines and headers break properly. Be sure to save this in a separate file from your formatted résumé. Employers may use this file to search for key terms that match their descriptions of an ideal job candidate.

Along with the résumé, you need to develop a list of references. A **reference** is an individual who will provide important information about you regarding your traits, skills, and abilities to a prospective employer. A reference can be a teacher, school official, previous employer, or any other adult outside your family who knows you well.

You will need at least three references. Always contact professional references first and ask permission from each person to use his or her name as a reference. Your list of references, along with their titles, phone numbers, and e-mail addresses, should be kept private. Share this list only with an employer who has interviewed you and asks for your references.

You may also need to submit a *letter of recommendation*. These letters serve to validate your character, skills, and abilities. You can obtain a letter of recommendation by asking your references to write a letter for you. Choose people who know you well. Make sure you choose references who are good writers, since they will be representing you.

Your Portfolio

A well-developed, professional-looking portfolio can help you get a job. A **portfolio** is a collection of items that show your special achievements and accomplishments. The portfolio includes examples of your work that emphasize your skills, talents, and knowledge. It can show proof of your creative, imaginative skills and how you utilized them to create visual solutions.

The following items should be included in your portfolio:

- your résumé
- samples of your best work from school classes, organizations, special design projects, or your job
- documents or illustrations that demonstrate specific ability; for example, drawings or renderings that demonstrate design abilities
- certificates and licenses
- awards, honors, and recognitions
- letters of recommendation

In addition, if you have a news article about any of your accomplishments, be sure to highlight your name to place it in your portfolio. Also include reports of special projects you completed and any other credentials that prove your talent and skill. See Chapter 18 for tips on portfolio layout, design, and illustrations.

As you progress through your education, training, and work experiences, document your accomplishments along the way to help build your portfolio. When you earn a certificate, license, award, or honor, take the time to document your success and update your portfolio. Keep a record of when you complete a course or training program. Document positive work experiences, education and training experiences, and any other experiences that demonstrate your credentials. As you continue through your education and career, maintain a record of these achievements and update your portfolio often.

For some job positions, you may need to provide a take-away portion of your portfolio. Designers, for example, are visual people and seeing the work you produce is often more impressive than written descriptions. Prepare a *take-away*, or a small sample of your work, to give the employer or mail in with an application (Figure 27.7). Your take-away may have either a small sampling of work or be one complete student project. Also include your contact information.

Before you submit your résumé or portfolio to a potential employer, ask several people to proofread your résumé and critique your portfolio materials. Although a computer program can automatically double-check your spelling, it does not always help with sentence structure, repetitive language, and industry terms. Some professional organizations offer portfolio review events. You can also contact industry members and ask them if they can assist in reviewing your materials.

Your Cover Message

A **cover message**, sometimes called a *cover letter*, is often the first contact you have with a potential employer. It can make a lasting impression.

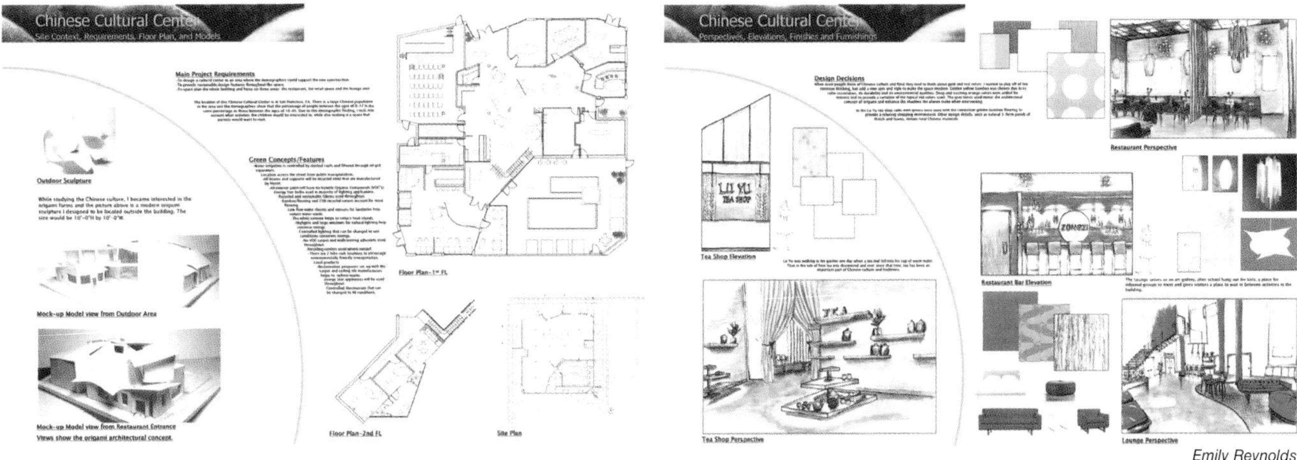

Emily Reynolds

Figure 27.7 This is a two-sided take-away portfolio sample. An internship or job applicant may leave this take-away with an employer.

Your cover message is your chance to ***elaborate*** on (explain in further detail) your positive attributes, experiences, and accomplishments. While your résumé may be fairly standard, the cover message should be customized to each job or internship for which you apply. Personalize your wording to the specific job description and employer.

A cover message should be brief and to the point and include the following items:

- title of the job you seek
- where or how you heard about the job
- your strengths, skills, and abilities for the job
- reasons you should be considered for the job
- when you are available to begin work
- request for an interview

A sample cover message appears in Figure 27.8. Most cover messages are submitted through e-mail along with your résumé. The message appears in the body of the e-mail to introduce yourself and indicate that your résumé is attached. Use a standard font to give the message a professional look. Coordinate it with your résumé and other visuals for consistency. Be sure to check spelling and punctuation. Avoid starting every sentence with "I" by varying your sentence structure throughout. Have several people read the message and offer advice for improving it. If you use a print format, follow a standard form for business letters.

Job Application Forms

A prospective employer may ask you to complete a job application form before having an interview. The job application form highlights the information the employer needs to know about you, your education, and your prior work experience. Employers often use these forms to screen applicants for the skills needed on the job. Most job application forms are available online. Some establishments may have these forms available on-site.

How you complete the form can give an employer the first opinion about you. Fill out the form accurately and completely. If you are filling out the form by hand, write neatly. How well you fill out the form can determine whether you get the job. When asked about salary, write *open* or *negotiable*. This means you are willing to consider offers.

Tips for completing a job application form appear in Figure 27.9. When filling out an online application, it is extremely important to include key terms for which the employer may search. This will help you stand out from the many other applications the employer will receive.

When preparing your application, be sure to save it in the appropriate format if given the option. If a preferred format is not given, it is best to save the application as a PDF. This will enable the employer to find specific search terms in your document. Be sure to complete all the fields of the application. Many job-search sites have sample forms on which you can practice before attempting a real application.

Some online job applications may be in fill-in-the-blank form. It is a good practice to produce the answers in another document first to be able to check your spelling before copying information into the online application. Save your progress as you go

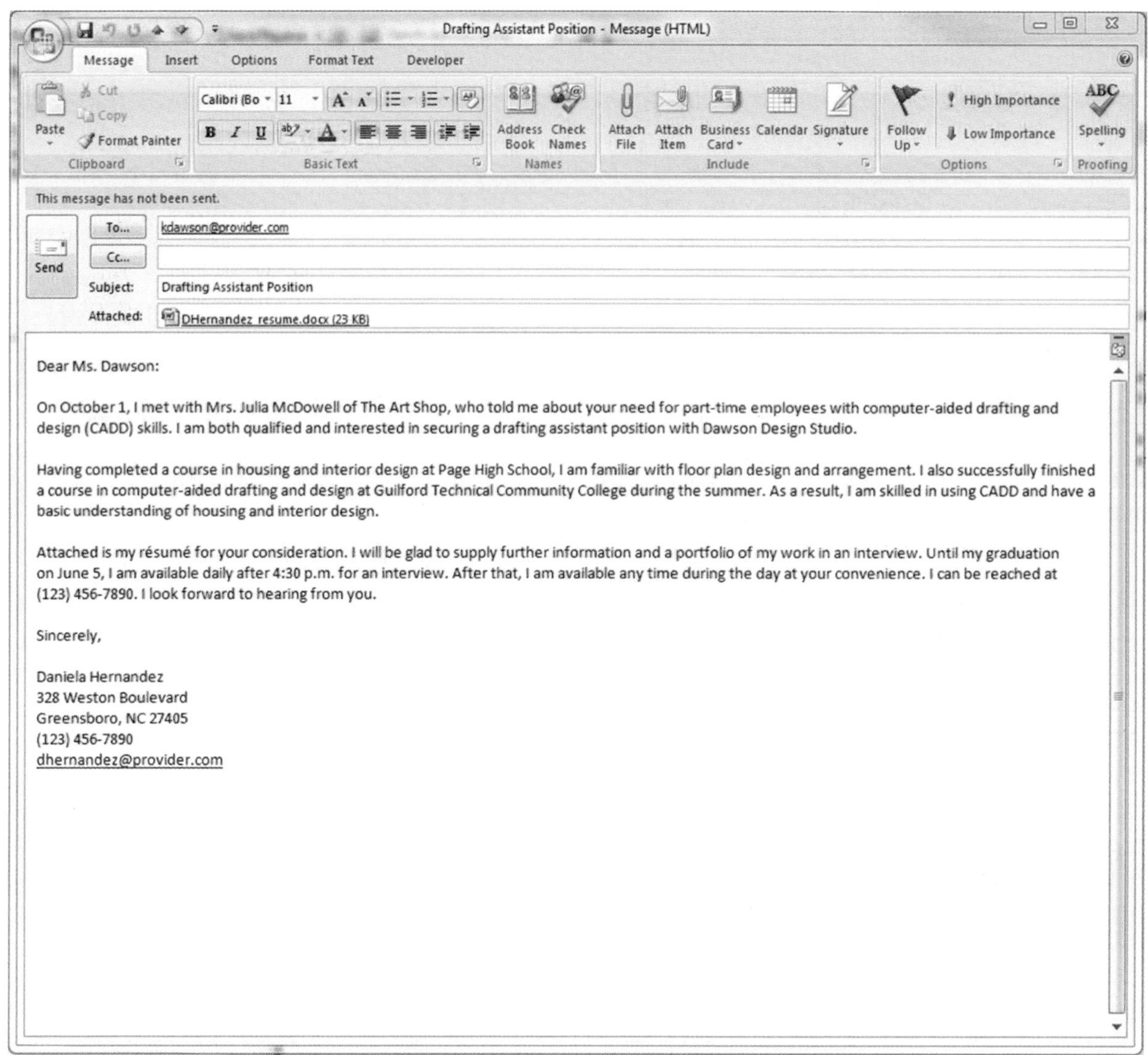

Goodheart-Willcox Publisher

Figure 27.8 Your cover message is often the first contact you have with potential employers. Before you send your message, ensure that it is well written and does not contain any errors.

Completing a Job Application Form

- Preview the form to see what information it seeks. How much space is there for writing responses? Is there a character limit? Which questions pertain to you?
- Read the directions and follow them carefully. If filling out a form by hand, print legibly using a pen with dark ink.
- When completing a form online, note that there may be a time limit. You may be timed out of your session. If possible, save your work along the way.
- Have your résumé, list of references, and other important data with you so you have all important information at your fingertips. Never submit guesses, only facts.
- Think through your responses first so you can respond to them concisely.
- When questions do not apply to you, write *N/A*, which means *not applicable*.
- If filling out an application by hand, request a new form if you make a mess. There is no penalty for filling out another form, but you may be rejected if you turn in a sloppy one.
- Review the form one last time to make sure you replied to every question and completed every space.

Figure 27.9 Take your time when you fill out a job application form and follow these tips.

Sociocultural Connections Discrimination in the Workplace

Federal and state laws protect workers from discrimination because of their race, color, religion, gender (including pregnancy), national origin, age, or disability. Federal laws cover businesses with 15 or more employees. The laws in many states, however, cover more businesses and prohibit harassment based on other characteristics.

Federal laws that deal with discrimination and harassment include the following:

- *The Fair Labor Standards Act (FLSA)* of 1938 regulates minimum wage, overtime pay, and child labor. It is updated each time the minimum wage is raised. This law limits the hours that a child under the age of 16 may work.
- *The Equal Pay Act* of 1963 requires that men and women receive the same pay for jobs with the same requirements and responsibilities. Exceptions are made if a person gets a pay raise based on seniority or merit.
- *The 1964 Civil Rights Act* bans employment discrimination based on race, color, religion, sex, or national origin. This law also created the Equal Employment Opportunity Commission (EEOC).
- *The Age Discrimination in Employment Act* of 1967 bans discrimination against workers age 40 and older. The Older Workers Benefit Protection Act of 1990 allows workers to sue employers over age discrimination. These laws are both important as the aging population continues to grow.
- *The Immigration Reform and Control Act* of 1986 prohibits the discrimination of U.S. citizens born outside the United States. The Immigration Act of 1990 made it more difficult for noncitizens to get employment in the United States.
- *The Americans with Disabilities Act* of 1990 prohibits discrimination against people with disabilities. As long as a person's disability does not interfere with the ability to do the job, he or she must be considered for the position. This law also requires places of employment to be physically accessible to people with disabilities.

Many of these laws also cover issues that do not impact the workplace. To read more about them, check out the Equal Employment Opportunity Commission's website or the U.S. Department of Labor's website.

Dig Deeper

Choose one or more of the laws mentioned and further investigate the details about the laws. Apply your written communication skills to clearly, concisely, and convincingly justify actions identified in the laws in a socially acceptable manner that is easily understood by others.

since some forms will time out and log you off should you remain inactive for an extended amount of time.

The Job Interview

At some point in the job-searching process, an employer may contact you for an interview. The interview gives you the opportunity to learn more about a company and to convince the employer that you are the best person for the position. The employer wants to know if you have the skills necessary for the job. Interview preparation is essential for making a lasting, positive impression. Here are some ways to prepare for the interview:

- **Research the employer and the job.** Know the mission of the employer and specifics about the job. Learn about former clients and projects so that you can speak in an educated manner about them and show that you have done your homework. You can usually find this information on a company's website. You may also be able to review portfolios of design professionals to gain a sense of the type of work an employer does. Also, try to learn what the company looks for when hiring new employees.
- **Be prepared to answer questions.** You can often predict some of the questions you will be asked in an interview. Review the list in Figure 27.10 and prepare answers for each commonly asked question.
- **List questions you want answered.** Just as companies show interest in you, it is a good idea to show interest in the company. For example, do you want to know if there is on-the-job training or opportunities for advancement? The interview is just as much about finding out if you want to work with them.

Common Interview Questions

- Tell me about yourself.
- What do you see yourself doing in 10 years?
- What in particular attracted you to this position?
- Why would you like to work for this organization?
- What are your greatest weaknesses? strengths?
- What type of work do you prefer—working independently or in teams?
- Can you describe a challenge that you have encountered either at work or school? How did you handle this challenge and what did you learn from it?
- What did you like most about your last job or work experience? least?
- Why did you leave your previous job?
- Why do you feel you are the most qualified person for the job?
- Which piece in your portfolio exemplifies your best work?
- Which area is your design specialty?
- Are you comfortable using CADD and other software programs?
- Do you have any questions?

Figure 27.10 Become interview ready by preparing answers to each of these questions.

- **List the materials you plan to take.** This seems simple enough. If you wait to grab items at the last minute, however, you will likely forget something important.
- **Decide what to wear.** Dress professionally, usually one step above what is worn by your future coworkers. For instance, casual clothing is acceptable for individuals who will do manual labor or wear a company uniform. If the job involves greeting the public in an office environment, a suit is more appropriate. Always appear neat and clean. Keep jewelry, accessories, cosmetics, and fragrances to a minimum. You may also want to cover tattoos and remove piercings.
- **Practice the interview.** Have a friend or family member interview you until you are happy with your responses. Many college career centers also offer mock interview or video critique services.
- **Know where to go for the interview.** Verify the address of the interview location by checking the site beforehand, if possible. Plan to arrive ready for the interview at least 10 minutes early. Call the firm beforehand to ask about parking recommendations and costs.

Good preparation will make you feel more confident and comfortable during the interview. Be polite, friendly, and cheerful during the process. Use a firm handshake. Maintain eye contact at all times. Answer all questions carefully and as completely as you can. Be honest about your abilities. Avoid chewing gum and fidgeting. Keep your cell phone turned off during the interview. Also be aware of questions you legally do not have to answer, such as those related to age, marital status, religion, or family background.

A prospective employer may ask you to take employee tests. Some employers administer tests to job candidates to measure their knowledge or skill level. Since all employers support a drug-free workplace, most will likely require you to take a drug test if hired.

After the interview, send a thank-you letter to the employer within 24 hours to thank the person or people who interviewed you. If you get a job offer, respond to it quickly. If you do not receive an offer after several interviews, evaluate your interview techniques and seek ways to improve them.

Evaluating Job Offers

If a potential employer decides after the interview that you are the best fit for the job, you may receive a job offer. When considering a job offer or comparing two or more positions, explore the following work factors:

- **Physical surroundings.** Where is the workspace located? Is the atmosphere ***conducive*** (favorable

Monkey Business Images/Shutterstock.com

Figure 27.11 When weighing job offers, consider the type of work environment in which you will be working. Does the environment emphasize collaboration or working independently?

for something to happen) to your style of working? Is parking provided? Is public transportation close by? What is the actual office like? See Figure 27.11.

- **Work schedule.** Will the workdays and work hours mesh with your lifestyle? Is occasional overtime work required? If it is, is there additional compensation or flexible time off offered?
- **Income and benefits.** Is the proposed salary fair? Will you receive benefits that are just as valuable as extra income? How much sick leave is granted during the year? Is personal or emergency leave available? What is the vacation leave policy? Are there medical and life insurance benefits? Is there a credit union? Will the company pay tuition for college courses, professional organization memberships, or special programs related to your job? Is a cafeteria on the premises? Does it offer food to employees at reduced cost?
- **Job obligations.** Will you be expected to join a union or other professional organization? If so, what are the costs? Will you be expected to attend meetings after work?
- **Advancement potential.** Is there opportunity for advancement? After demonstrating good performance, how soon can you seek a position with more responsibilities? Before you can advance, are there special expectations such as a higher degree? Are training programs provided?

Review & Assessment 

1. Briefly identify the categories of information that a résumé outlines.
2. List three examples of people who would make good references for a job applicant.
3. What items should be included in a cover message?
4. What does it mean when an applicant writes *open* or *negotiable* for salary on a job application?
5. List five steps to take to prepare for a successful interview.
6. List five work factors you should explore when evaluating job offers.

Succeeding in the Workplace

After securing employment, adjusting to your new duties and responsibilities will occupy your first few weeks. Your supervisor and coworkers will help you learn the routine. An introduction to company policies and procedures as well as the special safety rules that all employees must know is common for new employees. While your coworkers will be watching what you do, they will also pay attention to how you work. Making an effort to do your best will help you succeed. Dressing professionally, establishing positive work habits, managing your time, showing respect in speech and behavior, effectively handling stress and conflict, and demonstrating ethical behavior will set you on a positive course for your future.

Appearance and Hygiene

As an employee, you are a representative of your company. Therefore, your employer expects you to be neat and clean on the job. Taking care of yourself gives the impression that you want people to view you as a professional.

Your daily grooming habits consist of bathing or showering, using an antiperspirant, and wearing clean clothes. Regularly brushing your teeth and using mouthwash will promote healthy teeth and fresh breath. Keep your hair clean and styled in a way that will not be distracting.

Employers expect workers to dress appropriately. Many places of work have a dress code. If your employer does not have a dress code, use common sense and avoid extremes. Refrain from wearing garments that are revealing or have inappropriate pictures or sayings. Party or special-occasion attire is inappropriate for the workplace. Some employers have rules requiring that tattoos or piercings (besides pierced ears) remain covered. Good appearance is especially important for employees who have frequent face-to-face contact with customers.

The design industry is often a bit more flexible when it comes to contemporary fashions. What is acceptable is dictated by the employer, the environment, and the client type. Formal business suits are not as common, but most denim and immodest clothing is not appropriate (Figure 27.12).

Dress appropriately for your day's activities and always come prepared with clothing options. It is helpful to carry a jacket or cardigan in case of unexpected meetings or cold environments. If you will be measuring a building or doing a furniture inventory,

A Vladimir Gjorgiev/Shutterstock.com David Gilder/Shutterstock.com

B Lapina/Shutterstock.com elwynn/Shutterstock.com

Figure 27.12 Professional business attire includes suits, blazers, skirts and dresses, and business pants (A). Business casual attire includes button-up shirts, sweaters, dresses and skirts, dressy tops, and business pants (B).

bikeriderlondon/Shutterstock.com

Figure 27.13 When visiting a construction site, a designer or architect may be required to wear appropriate safety gear.

it would not be appropriate to wear high heels, a dress, expensive clothing, or dark colors. If you visit a construction or manufacturing site, you will need to dress for safety and wear a helmet; bright vest; safety goggles; and flat, protective shoes (Figure 27.13).

Work Habits

Employers want employees who are punctual, dependable, and responsible. They want their employees to be capable of taking initiative and working independently. Other desirable employee qualities include organization, accuracy, and efficiency.

A ***punctual*** employee is always prompt and on time. This means not only when the workday starts, but also when returning from breaks and lunches. Being dependable means that people can rely on you to carry through your intentions and meet your deadlines. If you are feeling sick, be sure to call in and let the employer know right away. If there are reasons you cannot be at work, discuss this with your employer and work out an alternate arrangement. Many people have lost jobs by not checking with their supervisors about time off.

Taking initiative means that you start activities on your own without being told. When you finish one task, you do not wait to hear what to do next. Individuals who take initiative need much less supervision. They have ***self-motivation***, or an inner urge to perform well. Generally, this motivation will drive you to set goals and accomplish them. All of these qualities together show that you are capable of working independently.

You are expected to be as accurate and error-free as possible in all that you do. This is why you were hired. Complete your work with precision and double-check it to assure accuracy. Your coworkers depend on the careful completion of your tasks.

Time Management

A good employee knows how to manage time wisely. This includes the ability to prioritize assignments and complete them in a timely fashion. It also involves not wasting time. Time-wasting behaviors include visiting with coworkers, making personal calls, texting, sending personal e-mail, playing games, checking social media sites, or doing other nonwork activities during work hours. You may also need to thoroughly document time spent on each individual client so you can provide accurate billing for your services.

While it is important to complete all your work thoroughly, you must also be able to gauge which assignments are most important. Avoid putting excessive efforts into minor assignments when crucial matters require your attention. Even though you are still accomplishing work, this is another way of using time inefficiently.

Attitude on the Job

Your attitude can often determine the success you have on your job. Your **attitude** is how you think and feel about a person or concept and the manner in which you project those thoughts and feelings. Your attitude is also your outlook on life. It is reflected by how you react to the events and people around you. A smile and courteous, respectful behavior can make customers and fellow employees feel good about themselves and you. Clients and customers prefer to do business in friendly environments. Friendliness may take some effort on your part, but it does pay off.

Enthusiasm spreads easily from one person to another. Usually, enthusiasm means a person enjoys what he or she is doing. In a sales environment, enthusiasm increases sales. In an office, enthusiasm builds a team spirit for working together (Figure 27.14).

People who do a good job feel pride in their work. They feel a sense of accomplishment and a desire to achieve more. This attitude can inspire others as well.

Professional Behavior

You will be expected to behave professionally on the job. Professional behavior includes showing respect for your boss and coworkers. Limit your personal conversations and phone calls to break times or lunch. Act courteously; remember that

Sociocultural Connections Manners at Work

As a housing and interior design professional, you may find employment in a variety of work environments. In all of these environments, you will come into contact with diverse clients. Knowing how to relate in these worksites and with clients of all backgrounds is critical to career success in the design profession. Whether in a worksite or meeting with clients, you should exhibit professionalism. *Professionalism* includes the behaviors, discretion, and skills characteristic of someone who has been trained to do a job well. Some signs of professionalism include *punctuality* (the ability to arrive on time), *diligence* (the commitment to doing good work), ethical conduct, and respect for others. Excellent communication skills are also a sign of professionalism. In many professions, including housing and interior design, another critical aspect of professionalism is *cultural sensitivity*.

Since housing and interior design are global industries, the clients you work with will likely come from many different countries and cultures. These clients' societal and cultural expectations will influence what they want and how they interact with you. For example, people in some cultures do not view direct eye contact as positive nonverbal communication; rather, they consider direct eye contact inappropriate. Cultural sensitivity involves recognizing and responding appropriately to your clients' cultural cues—in this case, it might mean not making direct eye contact with your client. To foster cultural sensitivity, you can learn about the societies and cultures you will encounter as a housing and interior design professional, and you can use this knowledge to help you make decisions.

Dig Deeper

Cultures and societies view interpersonal interactions and even design in vastly different ways. To learn more about how you can be culturally sensitive, choose one culture or society to research. What interpersonal and communication skills are most important in this culture or society? In this culture or society, how do people show respect? How are the industries of housing and interior design different in this culture or society? Once you have researched answers to these questions, role-play a work situation (such as a designer and a client or two designers) in which these skills come into play. Demonstrate for the class how to relate professionally and sensitively with a person from your chosen society or culture.

Photographee.eu/Shutterstock.com

Figure 27.14 Enthusiasm and a positive attitude can create a positive team environment.

others are focusing on their work. Interruptions can cause them to lose concentration.

Part of behaving professionally is responding appropriately to *constructive criticism*. Every employee, no matter how knowledgeable or experienced, can improve his or her performance. If you receive criticism from a supervisor or coworker, do not be offended. Instead, use the feedback to improve yourself. Ask thoughtful questions and be open to critique. The more you improve, the more successful you will be in your work.

Decision Making and Problem Solving

Employers value workers who have the ability to make sound decisions. The decision-making process applies in the workplace as well as other aspects of life. As you may recall from an earlier chapter, the decision-making process is a helpful problem-solving tool that can help you analyze a situation. The process will help you identify the problem to be solved, identify possible solutions, make a decision, implement the decision, and evaluate the results. By using the decision-making process, you can break a complex problem into component parts that can be analyzed and solved separately.

Having ability to solve problems on the job shows an employer that you are able to handle more responsibility. Solving problems as a group can strengthen camaraderie and help employees feel more pride in their work.

The ability to make decisions and solve problems requires *critical-thinking skills.* These are higher-level skills that enable you to think beyond the obvious. Critical-thinking skills help you learn to interpret information and make judgments. Supervisors appreciate employees who can analyze problems and think of workable solutions.

Elena Elisseeva/Shutterstock.com

Figure 27.15 Maintain a level of professionalism when speaking with clients, coworkers, and other professionals over the phone.

Communication Skills

Communicating effectively with others is important for job success. Sharing information well with others is an attribute of a good communicator. It also means you are a good listener.

Good communication is central to a smooth operation of any business. Communication is the process of exchanging ideas, thoughts, or information. Poor communication is costly to an employer, as when time is lost because directions are unclear. Poor communication can result in a loss of customers, too.

The primary forms of communications are verbal and nonverbal. **Verbal communication** involves speaking, listening, and writing. **Nonverbal communication** is the sending and receiving of messages without the use of words. It involves *body language*, which includes facial expressions, gestures, and body posture.

Listening is an important part of communication. If you do not understand the speaker's message, be sure to ask questions. Also give feedback to let others know you understand them and are interested in what they have to say. Leaning forward while a person is talking signals interest and keen listening. Slouching back in a chair and yawning give the opposite signal—that you are bored and uninterested.

When you communicate verbally, speak and write in a clear manner for your audience to understand. This is especially important when explaining or justifying actions, or giving oral presentations to clients. Communicate ***concisely***, or succinctly, to deliver your message and reasoning effectively. When you present projects, concepts, or data to others, remember to communicate convincingly, since you are the expert on the subject. Always communicate respectfully and in a manner that is socially acceptable for the setting.

The message you convey in telephone communication involves your promptness, tone of voice, and attitude. Answering the phone quickly with a pleasant voice conveys a positive image for the company (Figure 27.15). Remember to listen to the caller without interrupting his or her message.

Communication tools have advanced with the development of new technologies. To be an effective employee, you need to know how to communicate well with the common tools of your workplace. For example, when sending e-mail communications at work, remember to think through the content of each message before you write and send the message. Make sure your writing skills convey a message that is clear, concise, and effective; and that the message is written in a professional tone of voice. Often messages are sent quickly without thought of how the recipient may interpret them. The same is true of voicemail.

The development of good communication skills is an ongoing process. Attending communication workshops and practicing often can keep your skills sharp. Periodically give yourself a communications checkup by asking your supervisor to suggest areas that need improvement.

Interpersonal Skills

Communication skills are especially important for interpersonal skills. Interpersonal skills involve interacting with others. Some workplace activities that involve these skills include teaching others, leading, negotiating, working as a member of a team, and working with clients. Getting along well with others can require great effort on your part, but it is essential for accomplishing your employer's goals.

Teamwork

Employers seek employees who can effectively serve as good team members. Due to the nature of most work today, teamwork is necessary. A **team** is a small group of people collaborating together for a common purpose. Often collaboration requires flexibility and willingness to try new ways to get things done (Figure 27.16). If someone is uncooperative, it takes longer to accomplish the tasks. When people do not get along, strained relationships may occur, which get in the way of finishing the tasks.

A big advantage of a team is its ability to develop plans and complete work faster than individuals working alone. In contrast, a team usually takes longer to reach a decision than an individual worker does. Team members need some time before they become comfortable with one another and function as a unit. You will be more desirable as an employee if you know how to be a team player and are willing to contribute and cooperate as a team member.

Team development goes through various stages. In the beginning, people are excited about being on a team. Later, disagreements may replace harmony. The good result of this is that people express themselves and learn to trust the other team members. Eventually, leaders emerge and the team develops a unique pattern of interaction and goal attainment. Finally, the team becomes very productive and performs at its highest level. It takes time and a genuine desire to cooperate and collaborate to build a strong team.

wavebreakmedia/Shutterstock.com

Figure 27.16 A good team member can bring enthusiasm and cohesiveness into a work group.

Creative ideas often develop from building on another person's idea. Honesty and openness are essential. Also, trying to understand the ideas of others before trying to get others to understand your ideas is an effective skill to develop.

In most professions, you are usually part of a larger team. Sometimes teamwork means working independently, while other team members work independently. After forming a team, you will often be expected to carry out your job responsibilities independently. The team periodically comes together to check project status and discuss any issues. As part of a larger team, you must be counted on to perform your portion of the project. This does not mean, however, that you should not ask other team members or supervisors questions.

Leadership

All careers require leadership skills. **Leadership** is the ability to guide and motivate others to complete tasks or achieve goals. It involves communicating well with others, accepting responsibility, and making decisions with confidence. Those employees with leadership skills are most likely to be promoted to higher levels.

Leaders often seem to carry the most responsibility of a group. Other group members look to them for answers and direction. The most important role of leaders is to keep the team advancing toward its goal. Leaders do this by inspiring their groups and providing the motivation to keep everyone working together.

Good leaders encourage teamwork, because a team that is working together well is more likely to reach goals. They listen to the opinions of others and make sure all team members are included in projects. Leaders also want to set a good example by doing a fair share of the work. In these ways, leaders cultivate a sense of harmony in the group.

Client and Customer Relations Skills

In the housing and interior design field, working directly with clients and customers is not uncommon. Working with clients takes special communication skills. The most important aspect of client relations is always remaining courteous. This may also require patience in some situations. When clients and customers visit your business, you want them to have the best possible service

Goodluz/Shutterstock.com

Figure 27.17 Part of customer service is working *with* your clients to arrive at solutions, not just talking *to* your clients.

and to leave happy. Remember that your behavior and skills at handling clients can determine if they will return to your business (Figure 27.17). The client may spread the word about his or her experience with you to other potential clients. Make sure your clients know you appreciate their business.

Client and customer relations may also involve problem solving. If a customer needs help, you must provide answers as quickly and accurately as possible while remaining pleasant and polite. When a situation becomes stressful, you must be able to control your own level of stress without letting it affect your performance. At the same time, you must be able to lessen the client's stress and attempt to eliminate its source.

Belonging to Organizations

Joining an organization can help you improve your interpersonal skills. You may have the opportunity to work as a team member and a leader. Leading others may not be easy for some people, but everyone can improve their leadership skills with practice. Taking a role as an officer or a committee chair will give you leadership practice. Belonging to an organization can also help you develop your teamwork skills. You will learn how to work well in a group as you plan events, create projects, and accomplish goals together.

Conflict Management

When you work with others, disagreements are likely to occur. More serious disagreements are called conflicts. A **conflict** is a hostile situation resulting from opposing views. It is important to know how to handle a conflict to prevent it from becoming a destructive force in the workplace. This is called *conflict management*. A team leader has a special responsibility to prevent conflict among the team members. Several steps can be followed in managing conflict (Figure 27.18).

Sometimes the cause of a conflict is not simple or easily understood. Use a positive approach and try to understand the problem from the other party's point of view. Avoid jumping to conclusions and making snap judgments. Treat others with respect and in the same way you would like to be treated. Explore positive and negative aspects of each possible solution. If progress falls short of expectations, bring the parties back together and repeat the process.

Conflict Management	
Know When to Intervene	The time to intervene is when the team's productivity slows, several members have serious disagreements, and one or more members are obviously unhappy.
Address the Conflict	Acknowledge the conflict with those involved using an "I" approach. "You" statements tend to make people defensive.
Identify the Source of the Conflict	State the problem as clearly as possible, seeking recognition that a problem exists and not a simple misunderstanding.
Identify Possible Solutions	It is important that people involved in the conflict develop ideas for solving it. Individuals who are not involved should not participate in the discussion.
Implement and Evaluate	Make sure everyone understands his and her role in carrying out the agreed-upon solution. Check periodically to monitor the progress and the return to normal teamwork.

Jennifer Blanchard Belk, IIDA, LEED AP; Goodheart-Willcox Publisher

Figure 27.18 These steps can help you manage workplace conflicts.

Many disagreements in the workplace can lead to productive change.

Often there are times when employees and employers must negotiate on a task or work-related issue. **Negotiation** is the process of agreeing to an issue that requires all parties to give and take. The goal is a "win-win" solution in which both parties get some or all of what they are seeking.

Negotiation begins with trying to understand the other party's interests. Through communication and negotiation skills, parties can develop possible solutions that meet mutual concerns. Often the best solution becomes clear when both parties have ample time to explain what they are trying to accomplish.

Ethical Workplace Behavior

Ethical behavior on the job means conforming to accepted standards of fairness and good conduct. It is based on a person's sense of what is right to do. Individuals and society as a whole regard ethical behavior as highly important. Integrity, confidentiality, and honesty are crucial aspects of ethical workplace behavior. *Integrity* is firmly following your moral beliefs. See *Appendix A—ASID Code of Ethics and Professional Conduct* for more information about ethical standards for interior designers.

Unfortunately, employee theft is a major problem at some companies. The theft can range from carrying office supplies home to stealing money or expensive equipment. Spending time at work on personal tasks can be considered unethical because you are stealing time, and in turn money, from the employer and clients. Company policies are in place to address these concerns. In cases of criminal or serious behavior, people may lose their jobs. If the employee is found guilty, the charge of criminal behavior stays on the employee's record. Such an employee will have a difficult time finding another job.

Staying Safety Conscious

Safety on the job is everyone's responsibility. Many workplace accidents occur because of careless

Housing Health & Safety

Material Safety Data Sheets (MSDS)

About 32 million people work where they may be exposed to potentially hazardous materials and chemicals, according to the U.S. Occupational Safety and Health Administration (OSHA). Short- or long-term exposure to these substances can cause illness, injury, and even death. OSHA's Hazard Communication Standard requires employers to notify employees about these hazards and how to protect themselves. One important element of this standard requires that employees have easy access to a material safety data sheet (MSDS) for any hazardous chemical and material in their workplace.

Included in an MSDS form are the following:

- common names of a substance and name of its hazardous ingredient(s) with the physical and chemical characteristics
- fire and explosion hazards
- known health effects and exposure limits
- signs and symptoms of exposure, medical conditions aggravated by exposure
- emergency and first-aid procedures to treat those exposed
- precautions for safe handling and disposal, including use of protective clothing and equipment

More than a half-million products have an MSDS form. The producers of the materials and chemicals usually prepare and distribute these forms to their customers. Employers receiving an MSDS must ensure that employees can access a paper or online copy. If an employer does not receive an MSDS form, the employer must request it from the supplier or importer.

In case of accidents, the forms are given to emergency responders and physicians. The U.S. Environmental Protection Agency and state and local governments also require submission of all MSDS forms to local fire departments and to state and local emergency and response agencies. State and local laws may have stricter requirements.

Although there is no standard format for the MSDS, OSHA provides a sample (Form 174) on its website. For an informational booklet about OSHA's Hazard Communication Guidelines, visit OSHA's website to learn more.

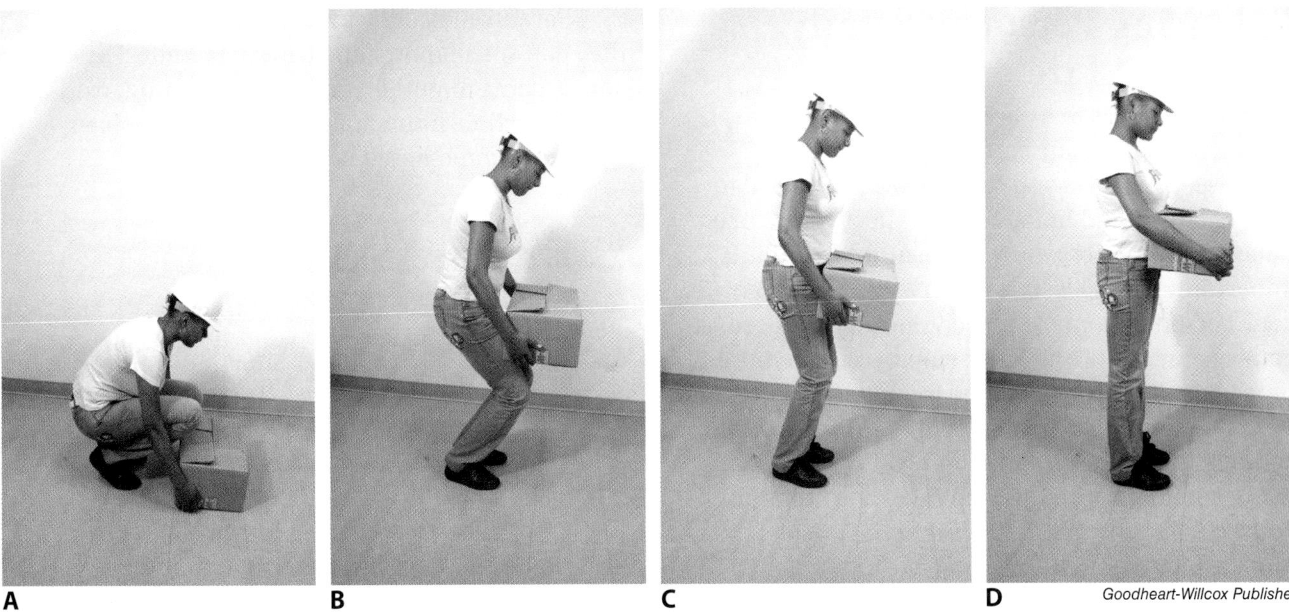

Goodheart-Willcox Publisher

Figure 27.19 Always follow proper lifting procedures to reduce strain on your back. Position feet shoulder-width apart and always bend at your knees (A). Keep the load close to you. Lift the load smoothly without any sudden movements (B). Never twist your back while lifting or holding a load. Turn your whole body by moving your feet (C). If lifting with a partner, maintain clear communication (D).

behavior. Often poor attitudes can cause unsafe behavior, too.

Practicing good safety habits is essential for preventing accidents and injuries on the job. A healthy worker is more alert and less likely to make accident-prone mistakes. Knowing how to use machines and tools and lift properly is the responsibility of both the employer and employees (Figure 27.19). Carefully read and follow written instructions or listen to and follow oral instructions to comply with health and safety rules. Wearing protective clothing and using safety equipment correctly helps keep workers safe. Your employer will emphasize the safety practices that employees must follow in your workplace. Once you learn the proper safety and health procedures, adhere to these rules.

The government agency that promotes safety in the workplace is the Occupational Safety and Health Administration (OSHA). You will be required to follow the specific OSHA regulations that apply to your workplace.

Transferable Skills

Possessing **transferable skills** can help you succeed in whatever job you choose. The transferable skills useful in all jobs include reading, writing, speaking, and basic math. The essential skills identified for a given career cluster are transferable across the careers within that cluster.

Some transferable skills are less tangible, but are no less important. The following is a list of personal and behavioral skills and traits that your future teachers, employers, teammates, and clients will recognize and encourage:

- critical thinking skills and creativity
- excellent communication skills and customer service skills
- teamwork skills
- adaptability
- goal-orientation
- energy and enthusiasm
- confidence, but ability to ask for help and take criticism
- efficiency and organization
- dependability and loyalty

Transferable skills can help employees during career transitions. Many people today do not stay in one career their entire lives. They may change career directions at some point and pursue other interests. If there is a decline in their industry, jobs may be eliminated. Innovations in the industry may present career tracks that are only now in their infancy. These employees may need additional training or education to succeed in a new career area. Having transferable skills can help smooth career transitions.

Balancing Personal, Family, and Work Life

Your success in a career will affect your satisfaction with your personal and family life. Likewise, your roles and responsibilities related to your personal and home life will affect your career. Balancing your personal, home, and career life is important in any lifestyle (Figure 27.20). When your personal, home, and work life are balanced, you become a more effective employee with more time to dedicate to family and friends.

Belonging to a family involves roles and responsibilities. As a son or daughter, your responsibilities at home may involve watching younger siblings, helping with family meals, and keeping your clothes and room clean. Usually these tasks do not interfere with your responsibilities to attend school and perform well. Adding a part-time job can complicate matters, however, and force you to manage your time more carefully.

The roles of spouse, parent, home owner, and employee are much more demanding and may conflict at times. People with multiple roles must balance their responsibilities to fully meet them all. Sometimes family responsibilities will take priority over work responsibilities, such as when a family member is ill. At other times, career demands may take time away from family life. When home owners do not have balance, housing decisions and maintenance may become neglected.

Monkey Business Images/Shutterstock.com

Figure 27.20 Balancing family time and work responsibilities can be a challenge.

Parents may adjust work responsibilities so they can spend more time with the family. These adjustments might include telecommuting, working fewer overtime hours, taking a part-time job, or starting a home-based business.

Review & Assessment

1. Why is appearance important to work success?
2. What are the parts of the problem-solving process you can use to analyze a situation? Give an example showing use of problem-solving skills.
3. What is the difference between verbal and nonverbal communication?
4. What is leadership? Describe at least two ways in which you have demonstrated your understanding of leadership skills.
5. What are the steps of conflict management?
6. What is the goal of negotiation?
7. Give three examples of transferable skills. Why are transferable skills important?

The Evolution of Your Career

As your career evolves, you will develop a specialty. Seeking professional certification can help you master a specialization. Continuing to update your knowledge of the field will help you progress in your career and stay up-to-date.

Concentrations in the housing and interior design field may be specific to an end user type, such as retail, hospitality, or educational end uses. Other concentrations may be conceptual, such as sustainable design or historic preservation, as these areas can be applied to any type of end user's space (Figure 27.21). Each specialty comes with its own set of challenges, marketing strategies, technologies, and innovations. It is a good idea for designers, either through internships or full-time employment, to seek diverse experiences before deciding to pursue a specialization.

Professional Examination and Certification

No matter what segment of the industry you decide to pursue, there are related certifications and examinations. Refer to individual *Career Focus*

Iriana Shiyan/Shutterstock.com

Figure 27.21 The interior designer who created this space specializes in creating rooms of a specific historic period, as shown in this bedroom in a historic inn.

features for specifics on various professions. Some certifications are mandatory and regulated by the profession and/or the location in which you practice. The following are some of the most pertinent examples of industry examinations:

- **NCIDQ.** The Council for Interior Design Qualifications sponsors the *National Council for Interior Design Qualification (NCIDQ)* exam is the national standard for qualification in the interior design profession. More than half of the states require the exam. It is transferrable and does not have to be retaken if you relocate. Eligibility for the exam depends on the educational and professional route you select. Applicants must first complete a certain number of college credits and work hours in the field before they are eligible to take the exam.
- **LEED.** The LEED (Leadership in Energy & Environmental Design) exams designate professionals who have knowledge and experience working with sustainable design and construction. There are several levels of LEED certification. The Green Associate exam is more general and can be taken without any formal training or documented experience. The LEED AP (Accredited Professional) exam is taken by those with significant experience with sustainable projects. Examples of exams testing specialization include LEED ID+C (interior design and construction) and the LEED ND (neighborhood development).
- **NKBA.** The National Kitchen & Bath Association has a series of exams based on a designer's concentration and expertise in kitchen and/or bath design. Passing this exam is not required to practice in the profession, but can increase employability and entrepreneur marketing efforts.
- **AAFCS Pre-Professional Assessment & Certification.** The American Association of Family & Consumer Sciences (AAFCS) offers two certification areas for secondary to postsecondary students. One area is in housing and home furnishings and the second area is in interior design fundamentals. These certifications assure that students have acquired knowledge and skills in these two areas. These exam options are important for students who plan to pursue careers and further education in housing and home furnishings or interior design.

Each exam takes a different level of educational preparation and required experience. The exams are also updated frequently due to innovations and new knowledge in the industry. Make sure to investigate these exams fully before embarking on a study plan.

Continuing Education and Lifelong Learning

No matter what career you choose, you will be expected to keep pace with the changes in your field. Continually updating your knowledge and skills is known as **lifelong learning**. The term implies that your need for learning will never end. You cannot assume that the skills you have will be all you ever need during your career. Technology, changes in laws and building codes, and other advances mean you must continue to learn to keep up with changes in the field. Employers usually provide some training. However, employees are often expected to use time outside the job to stay up-to-date in their field of expertise.

People who enjoy their work will view lifelong learning as an exciting challenge. Also, most licensure and certifications require a particular number of hours to be dedicated to applicable continuing education to stay active and current in the field. These sessions are typically made available at monthly professional association meetings or at annual conferences.

Career Focus Real Estate Appraiser

Do you have a good eye and mind for detail? Do you enjoy doing research and comparing prices of one item to another? Are you interested in laws, regulations, and standards? If you share some of these interests, you may want to consider a career as a real estate appraiser.

Stephen Coburn/Shutterstock.com

Interests/Skills: Appraisers and assessors must possess good analytical skills, mathematical skills, and attention to detail skills. They must also work well with people and independently. Politeness is a must, along with the ability to listen and thoroughly answer any questions about their work.

Career Snapshot: Real estate appraisers estimate the value of property for a variety of purposes. They often specialize in appraising certain types of real estate, such as residential buildings or commercial properties. They may also estimate the value of any type of real estate, ranging from farmland to a major shopping center.

Education/Training: The requirements to become a fully qualified appraiser vary by state and may also vary by the value or type of property. Most appraisers are required to have a bachelor's degree or the equivalent in credit hours. Most practicing appraisers have at least a bachelor's degree, sometimes in a related field such as economics, finance, or real estate. Obtaining on-the-job training is also an essential part of becoming a fully qualified appraiser and is required for obtaining a license or certification. In the past, many appraisers obtained experience working in financial institutions or real estate offices. The current trend, however, is for candidates to get their initial experience in the office of an independent fee appraiser.

Licensing/Examinations: Federal law requires that any appraiser involved in a federally related transaction must have a state-issued license or certification. Licensing requirements vary by state, but they typically include specific training requirements, a period of work as a trainee, and passing one or more examinations.

Professional Associations: American Society of Appraisers (ASA), National Association of Independent Fee Appraisers (NAIFA), National Association of Real Estate Appraisers (NAREA), and the Appraisal Institute (AI).

Job Outlook: Employment of appraisers and assessors of real estate is expected to grow as fast as the average for all occupations. Job opportunities should be favorable for those who meet licensing qualifications and have several years of experience.

Sources: The Occupational Outlook Handbook (OOH); the Occupational Information Network (O*NET)

Review & Assessment

1. What is professional examination and why is it important?
2. Why is lifelong learning important to a person striving for career success?
3. How can a professional gain access to continuing education opportunities?

Leaving a Job

There are many reasons you may eventually choose to leave your job. More money, more responsibility, and better benefits are some of the reasons for leaving a job. All job departures should be handled in a way that is considerate of the employer. Try not to leave your job with noticeable anger and hostility. Employers know that employees

Letter of Resignation

118 Thompson Boulevard
Atlanta, Georgia 30303
June 1, 20XX

Mr. John Alston
Alston Home Builders, Inc.
9923 Construction Avenue
Atlanta, Georgia 30303

Dear Mr. Alston:

I plan to leave Alston Home Builders, Inc., effective July 15, 20XX. I thoroughly enjoyed my work here and thank you for the excellent training I received. I especially appreciate the opportunity you gave me to work "up the ranks" and demonstrate my ability as an assistant construction manager.

I now plan to further my education and enter the engineering program at Georgia Tech University this fall. After careful consideration, I have decided that this is the best opportunity for me. I would be happy to help screen potential job candidates and train my replacement in the remaining weeks. Thank you again for the opportunity to work for your company.

Sincerely,
Derrick Sampson

Goodheart-Willcox Publisher

Figure 27.22 A letter of resignation should state your reason for leaving and your last day of work.

will not stay forever. However, they dislike when employees leave on short notice, especially during a busy season.

When you make the decision to leave a job, let the employer know in writing by giving at least a two-week notice. It would be helpful to give a longer notice if you can, although an employer has the right to ask you to leave immediately upon resignation. A letter of resignation should state your reason for leaving and the date you expect to leave. See Figure 27.22. The letter allows the employer to begin looking for your replacement. Perhaps there will be enough time to hire someone who can work with you during your final days. Leaving in a positive manner creates an easier transition for you and your employer. Furthermore, many people have found that a past employer became their greatest ally when they needed a good reference for a future position.

Review & Assessment 

1. Identify three reasons you may have for leaving a job.
2. How much notice should you typically give an employer before you leave a job?
3. What information should a letter of resignation contain?

Chapter 27 Assessment

Summary

- Developing professional behavior, time-management skills, and effective communication skills can help you succeed now and in the future.
- Engaging with professionals in the industry can help you learn more about job and internship opportunities in the field.
- Applying for a job involves developing a résumé, portfolio, and cover message; completing an application form; and interviewing.
- Succeeding in the workplace involves being clean and neat, having good work habits, using effective time-management skills, having a positive attitude, and behaving professionally.
- Decision-making, communication, interpersonal, and conflict-management skills are essential.
- Having ethics and integrity lead to good conduct.
- Staying safety conscious will help you follow safety procedures.
- Taking required or optional professional exams is an important part of the evolution of a career.
- Staying skilled and knowledgeable is important for career success and advancement.
- Leaving a job properly can help guarantee that your employer will give you good references.

Terms in Action

1. **Terms classification** Review the list of *Content* and *Academic Terms* and classify the list into categories. Then pair up with a classmate and compare how you classified the terms. How are your lists similar or different? Discuss your lists with the class.

Think Critically

2. **Compare and contrast** Think about how planning and presenting an interior design project is similar to and different from preparing yourself for an interview with an interior design firm. Compare and contrast the personal preparations you need to make for the interview with the design process applications you make when preparing a design for a client.
3. **Recognize ethics** In teams, brainstorm a list of ethical behaviors you have observed in real life. What characteristics help you and your team members recognize these behaviors as ethical? How do ethical behaviors in nonwork situations transfer to workplace behaviors?
4. **Create a plan** Through networking, you recently became aware of an available internship position at an interior design firm. Using a productivity app of your choice, plan a time line for creating each of the necessary components to apply for this position—a job application form, résumé, cover message, and portfolio.

Core Skills

5. **Writing** Obtain a job application form from your instructor. Read the application thoroughly. Then practice filling out the application in a precise manner. Have your instructor critique your application for areas that require improvement.
6. **Listening and speaking** Invite one or more community employers in the area of housing and interior design to conduct mock interviews with the members of your class. Video-record the interviews. Practice speaking clearly, concisely, convincingly, and effectively in your interview as you explain your experiences, skills, and abilities. Demonstrate professional behavior in your appearance, speech, and manners. Then watch and critique your recording. What were your interview strengths and weaknesses? What are some actions you can take to strengthen your interviewing skills? Write a summary of your experience.
7. **Reading** Using the CareerOneStop website, read about job interviews and informational interviews. What are the similarities and differences between the two types of interviews? Why is preparation for both essential to finding meaningful employment? Write a summary of your findings to share with the class.
8. **Writing** Review the employment listings on an online job board for jobs related to housing and interior design. Choose one of the listings and write an engaging cover message for a position. Write your message in a professional tone in a clear, concise, convincing, and effective manner.

Chapter 27 Assessment

Have your instructor or another trusted adult with experience critique your message. Make any corrections and save a copy of your cover message to use as a guide in the future.

9. **Reading and writing** Work independently and search online for examples of different types of résumés that can be used when applying for a job. Print an example of each. Analyze the similarities and differences among the documents. Then write a summary indicating when you might use each type of résumé in applying for employment related to housing and interior design.
10. **Writing** Use word-processing technology to create your personal résumé. Be sure to select relevant educational, work, and volunteer history highlights. Strive for accuracy and precision Save a copy of your résumé and print it. Then work with a partner in class to review, proofread, and critique your résumé.
11. **Writing** Contact professional references to acquire recommendations. Practice your professional communication skills by contacting these individuals to seek permission to list them as references. If they agree, verify their contact information. Then prepare an electronic list of references to give to potential employers. Also ask each reference if he or she would consider writing a letter of recommendation for you. Store these letters in your portfolio.
12. **Reading** Use reliable online sources to investigate the proper techniques for posting résumés to online job boards and completing online applications. What changes should you make to your résumé for this application? What keywords may be important for an online application for an interior design career? If possible, complete a practice application on a job-search site.
13. **Speaking** Search online for opportunities to take free interview quizzes. Practice your responses aloud. Take the quizzes and analyze your answers with the recommended responses. Practice until your score reaches 90 percent.
14. **Listening** Locate one or more educational career-related podcasts from a reliable source such as the O*NET Resource Center. Choose from such topics as career guidance, transferability of skills, creating résumés, or interviewing. Listen to one or more podcasts and write a summary of each to share.
15. **CTE career readiness practice** Talk with the manager of a local interior design firm or home improvement store about company instructions for reporting accident, safety, and security incidents. Obtain and read samples of forms used for reporting such incidents. Then, with a classmate, role-play a scenario for the class in which an employee is talking with his or her manager about an accident. Demonstrate written and oral procedures to follow when reporting such incidents.

Design Practice

16. **Business card design** Presume you are an interior designer who is making the transition from working for a design firm to working independently in your own interior design business. Use your knowledge of the elements and principles of design to create a business card for your new venture.
17. **Presentation interview** You are a new graduate and have just had your first employment interview with an interior design firm. You have their attention—the interview team liked your enthusiasm and they were impressed with your educational background. During a second interview, they have asked that you present one of your design projects to the interview team. Practice presenting one of your class projects in preparation for this interview.
18. **Portfolio** Assemble your portfolio to use for work-based learning opportunities and postsecondary education applications. Choose an attractive binder or case in which to display your work. Be sure that your portfolio documents the following items: letter of introduction, résumé, references, letters of recommendation, and design project samples (drawings, photos, and materials used) to showcase your abilities to use industry tools. In addition, include any recognition, work experiences, awards, or honors you have received for your work or academics. Include any certificates or licenses you have earned. As you gain new credentials, maintain and update your portfolio to reflect your abilities.

Chapter 28

Entrepreneurship for Housing and Interiors

Content Terms 

entrepreneur
sole proprietorship
partnership
corporation
shareholder
franchise
chain
joint venture
target market
product trends
product life cycle
market survey
business plan
expenses
revenues (sales)
profit
loss
income statement
balance sheet
assets
liabilities
equity
statement of cash flow (SCF)
channel of distribution
physical inventory
labor cost percentage
profit margin

Academic Terms 

optimistic
free market economy

Learning Outcomes

After studying this chapter, you will be able to

- summarize factors about the importance of entrepreneurship including the advantages and disadvantages of entrepreneurship, characteristics and skills entrepreneurs need, values and goals of entrepreneurs.
- compare and contrast different types of business structures.
- identify actions necessary for starting a small business.
- summarize how to develop a business plan including legal requirements for starting a business, insurance and taxes, startup expenses, and sources for assistance.
- explain three types of financial statements used by businesses and the importance of managing revenues and expenses.

Reading with Purpose

Locate three online magazine articles about successful entrepreneurs in residential and nonresidential housing and interior design careers. Before reading the articles, divide a sheet of notebook paper in four columns. At the top of the first three columns, write the name of each entrepreneur you selected. In the last column, write your name. Read the articles and note in the appropriate column what personal traits, skills, behaviors, and abilities helped make each entrepreneur successful. Review the characteristics noted for each entrepreneur. In the last column, note which traits, skills, behaviors, and abilities you have that might help you become a successful entrepreneur.

While studying, look for the access icon to:

- **Practice** the *Content* and *Academic Terms* with e-flash cards, matching activities, and vocabulary games.
- **Reinforce** what you learn by completing the *Review & Assessment* questions and e-mailing them to your instructor.

www.g-wlearning.com/housing/

© iStock.com/Wavebreakmedia

In recent years, the U.S. Bureau of Labor Statistics shows that about one in four interior designers are self-employed. As you explored the careers of housing and interior design professionals throughout this course, have you thought about working for yourself? Having your own business can be exciting and challenging at the same time. What knowledge and skills might you need to acquire *before* starting your own design business?

Entrepreneurship in Housing and Interior Design

An **entrepreneur** is a person who starts and runs their own business. Like most careers, entrepreneurship has both advantages and disadvantages. Entrepreneurs also have common characteristics, skills, values, and goals. There are many issues to research when you are starting your own business. Consider all aspects carefully before deciding that entrepreneurship is for you.

Advantages and Disadvantages of Entrepreneurship

Many people become entrepreneurs so they can be their own boss. They enjoy the ability to make all the decisions and work whatever hours they choose.

Some people start a business for the satisfaction of working with subjects they understand or enjoy. Starting a business may also provide a sense of accomplishment. Many people become entrepreneurs for monetary reasons. If a business is successful, the owner can make a sizable profit.

Chief among the disadvantages to becoming an entrepreneur is the hard work. At first, you may have to work nonstop just to get the business started. During this period, very little money—if any—is coming in. You may have to put most of your savings into the business since affordable loans for an unproven business are rare. If the business fails, you could lose everything. About 30 percent of new businesses do not last two years. Fifty percent close within 5 years. All these factors add to a heightened sense of stress. Too much stress could even affect your health.

Common Characteristics of Entrepreneurs

Certain characteristics are vital for a person to succeed as an entrepreneur. First, entrepreneurs must be ***optimistic*** (to anticipate the best possible outcome). They have to believe their business will succeed. Entrepreneurs must be self-starters who can recognize when they need to initiate action. They should be hard workers who are willing to put extreme effort into the business. They must be innovative, having interesting new ideas about doing or providing something that is not available anywhere else. Usually, a business succeeds by fulfilling a consumer need. A perceptive entrepreneur will be able to recognize a need that could become a money-making opportunity.

An entrepreneur needs to be committed to the business. This involves using his or her personal money, time, or other resources to make the business succeed. Entrepreneurs must be energetic and in good health to handle long workdays. An entrepreneur must also be willing to take risks. It is a huge risk to give up a steady paycheck for a business that may not succeed.

Common Skills Entrepreneurs Need

Entrepreneurs need to be capable of running all aspects of a business. First, they must be good managers. They must have some business acumen so they understand what is happening in the business. They may hire others to handle certain jobs, but they must be able to evaluate their employees' performance. They must be good at decision making, since the final decision on all matters lies with them. Problem-solving skills are also essential and include developing creative solutions that work.

Communication Skills

In addition, entrepreneurs need basic skills. Communication skills are important for dealing with employees as well as clients (Figure 28.1). These skills are also important for communicating with other businesses, such as suppliers. In business, it is essential that written communications are clear because miscommunication can cost money.

Interpersonal skills go hand-in-hand with oral communication skills. You must be courteous in your communications with customers if you want repeat business. Getting to know your customers well is also an important part of building a strong customer base. Entrepreneurs who are out of touch with customer needs often lose business. You should also be aware of how to best relate to employees. You will want to have cordial relationships with them, yet still remind them at all times that you are the boss.

Monkey Business Images/Shutterstock.com

Figure 28.1 Communication skills and interpersonal skills are necessary to be able to deal with employees as well as clients.

Math and Computer Skills

It is important to have good math skills. Entrepreneurs use them to keep track of their business's profits, losses, assets, and liabilities. Without math skills, you could be cheated by a supplier or underpay your taxes. More importantly, you could lose everything by making a bad deal.

Entrepreneurs also need computer skills. Most procedures today, from inventory to billing, require computers. You must have good knowledge of computers and their uses, or the wisdom to seek an expert's advice.

Values and Goals of Entrepreneurs

Many entrepreneurs have similar values and goals. They may value success, especially succeeding through their own hard work. They may value career satisfaction and want this to be a goal for their work. They may value the freedom of creativity. Expressing the value of products and services have to customers is also important to business success.

It is likely that an entrepreneur will value profit. The profit motive is a big incentive for starting a business. The success of a business is based on its ability to make a profit and grow.

Importance of Entrepreneurship

Entrepreneurship is important to a ***free market economy***. This is an economic system in which government control is limited and citizens are allowed to privately own and operate businesses. A free market economy is also called *capitalism*, a *market economy*, or *free enterprise*.

Over 95 percent of businesses in the U.S. are considered "small businesses." These businesses each have less than 500 employees. About half the people employed in the United States work for small businesses. Of the people who do not work in government jobs, more than half are employed by small businesses.

Small businesses help create jobs, and more jobs help keep the economy strong. A strong economy creates more demand for goods and services, which raises the standard of living. This, in turn, spurs the growth of small businesses that offer the goods and services desired.

Because small businesses usually produce highly specialized products, they may fulfill a focused need. To fill this need, however, they may require employees who are highly trained or experienced in one specialty. Many small businesses employ workers who are just starting their careers. This helps workers gain employment experience.

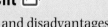

Review & Assessment 

1. List two advantages and disadvantages of entrepreneurship.
2. What are at least five characteristics of persons who might be drawn into becoming business owners?
3. Name and describe three common skills that entrepreneurs need to be successful.
4. How is entrepreneurship important to the economy?

Types of Business Structures

There are three types of business ownership or structure. A **sole proprietorship** is a business owned by only one person who has full responsibility (Figure 28.2). He or she makes all decisions, pays all the costs, and receives 100 percent of the profits.

A **partnership** is a business owned by two or more owners, usually no more than a small group of people. A partner gives an owner someone to share responsibilities and costs. All decisions, however, must be made jointly and the profits must be shared. Also, all partners are held responsible for one partner's actions.

A **corporation** is formed to represent the legal aspects of the business. This entity is separate from the individual people who own the corporation

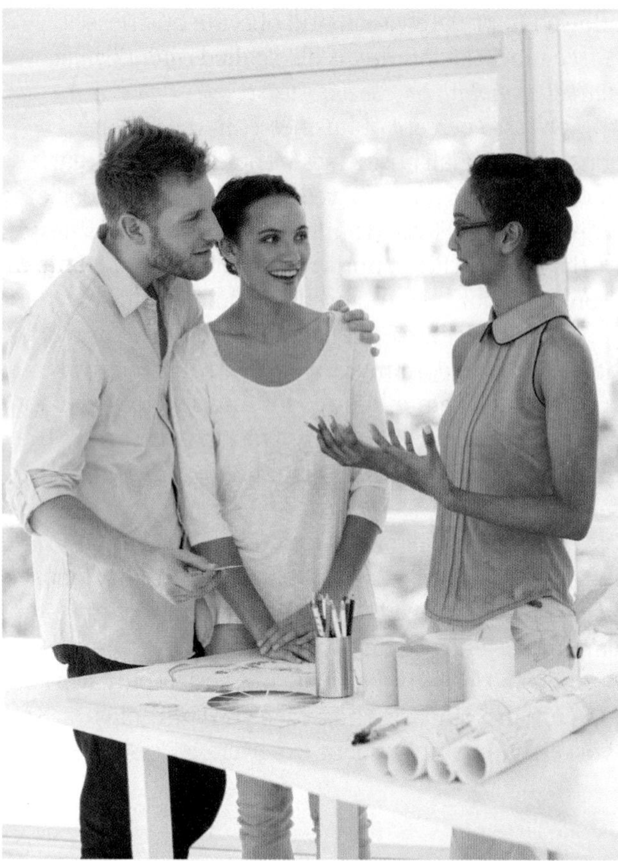

wavebreakmedia/Shutterstock.com

Figure 28.2 An interior designer who is a sole proprietor has full responsibility for running the business and well as working with clients on their design plans.

or work for it—which offers the individuals some protection. Individual **shareholders** have partial ownership in the company as a result of buying its stock. If the business fails, the shareholders may only lose their initial investment.

Instead of starting a new business, an entrepreneur may choose to buy into an existing business. One type of business is a **franchise**. A franchise is an agreement to sell another company's products or services. The person who buys the franchise, the *franchisee*, then has the exclusive right to sell the product or service in that area. A franchise can make a lot of money for an entrepreneur, but often the license can be very expensive. There may be additional ongoing fees. Also, the franchisee is legally bound to follow all the rules and guidelines of the company. For example, the owner may be required to buy supplies from a specific vendor rather than make his or her own decisions.

A **chain** is different from a franchise. A chain is a business that has many locations. Its owner is generally a corporation or partnership. The owner makes the decisions for all stores in the chain, which are run by managers.

A business option becomes a **joint venture** when an established interior design business joins with one or more companies. All companies share in the initial investment, profits, and losses. For example, suppose an interior design firm joins with an architectural/engineering firm to deliver final interior and exterior products. Each firm contributes to the investment to produce or acquire the products. Jointly, the firms handle the losses and enjoy the profits.

Review & Assessment

1. Contrast a sole proprietorship with a partnership.
2. What is a corporation?
3. What is the difference between a franchise and a chain?
4. Describe a joint venture.

Starting a Business

If starting your own business, you will have many decisions to make and questions to answer. Answering these questions requires careful research. Before beginning a business, it is a good idea to work in business with others in the field to learn the "tricks of the trade." Persons in housing and interior design related fields have opportunities to become entrepreneurs, see the list in Figure 28.3.

Entrepreneurial Careers in Housing and Interior Design	
Interior designer	Model maker
Color designer	Building contractor
Ergonomic designer	Carpenter
Historical preservationist	Electrician
Professional organizer	Painter
Real estate appraiser	Wall covering installer
Real estate broker	Plaster/drywall installer
Land surveyor	Floor covering installer
Upholsterer	HVAC installer
Landscape architect	Plumber
Architect	Roofer
Drafter	Bricklayer/stonemason

Figure 28.3 There are many entrepreneurial opportunities for housing and interior design professionals. Which opportunities interest you most?

Select a Product or Service

The first thing you must decide is what type of business is best. It is wise to pick something you already know that can use your abilities and aptitudes. Many experts also suggest sticking with something you enjoy, such as a hobby. You are more likely to put your all into making the business succeed if you enjoy the work.

You may choose to enter an area that is already established. For instance, you may open the hardware store your neighborhood wants, or you may provide a service, such as housecleaning. You may come up with an entirely new product or idea that presents good sales potential. If your passion is residential interior design, you may decide to offer design services in your community—using industry concepts and skills to meet the needs of your clients.

Analyze Potential Markets

Once you decide on a product or service, you identify your **target market**. This is the specific group of people who needs your product or service. By narrowing your target market, you have a greater chance of identifying potential buyers. This information will help you plan how to best promote your business.

Study the Competition

Find out if anyone is already making or providing your product or service. If so, how can you make your product better than the competition? Research the details of the competition. Record important facts about your competitors and update them frequently. What do they charge for their product? Where are they located? Include any other facts that will help you plan your business.

Conduct Market Research

Research the market to find usable data. Your research may include a *qualitative* work process in which you gather housing or interior design data from your own observations, surveys, or interviews with potential customers. During such research, it is important to accurately collect and review both your process (how you conducted research) and the end product. Talking with people directly is also known as *primary data.*

Secondary data comes from sources other than direct interaction with consumers. You may research business records, government information, and private databases. You may use the Internet and libraries to do much of this research. The accurate collection of secondary data (statistics) often involves *quantitative* work processes, or data that includes the use of numbers or data that can be measured such as size or quantity. For instance, an architect may research statistics regarding the weight load certain building materials can bear while an interior designer might research statistics about space needs for patients in a medical facility.

Watching trends is very important. **Product trends** relate to features of the products themselves. For instance, a current product trend is to make sure products are "green," or environmentally safe. *Social trends* relate to the consumers, but may also affect your product. For example, popular social networking sites may be an ideal advertising channel for your product. *Demographic trends* reflect changes to parts of the population, such as the growing population of older adults. Because of this trend, perhaps demand for a housecleaning business for older adults would continually increase. What design trends do you observe for various populations—younger and older?

Understand Your Product Life Cycle

Whether you plan to offer a product or service, you should understand its life cycle phases. These phases cover the life of a product or service from beginning to end (Figure 28.4). The phases of a **product life cycle** include

- **Introduction.** When you introduce the product or service to the market, the introduction phase begins. The goals of this phase include informing customers about the product or service and outlining the key benefits. Prices or fees are generally the highest during this phase.
- **Growth.** Once a product or service catches on with customers, the growth phase begins. During this phase, sales and profits for products and services rise rapidly.
- **Maturity.** When a product or service reaches the maturity phase, the sales begin to level off. At this point, the market is saturated—or the point at which customers who need, want, and can afford to buy the product or service have done so. Competition among brands is also intense at the maturity phase. Prices or fees are often lower at this phase.
- **Decline.** During the decline phase, sales begin to fall for the product or service. The prices or fees

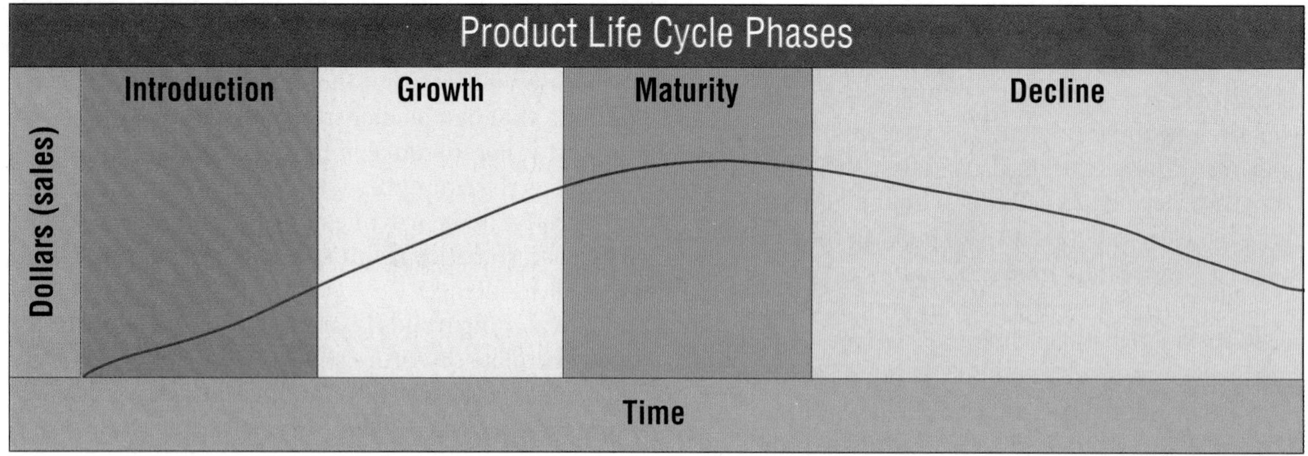

Goodheart-Willcox Publisher

Figure 28.4 Working knowledge of product life cycles is essential for all entrepreneurs.

are generally their lowest during this phase. When a product or service begins to decline, business owners and marketers must decide what to do. They may choose one of two options—either discontinue the product or service or develop new marketing strategies to increase sales.

Prepare Market Surveys

If you conduct a **market survey** (research that involves compiling market data such as client or customer preferences, market price trends, or competing products), be sure to ask the right questions. Your questions should not influence people to answer a certain way. If the questions do not really address what you need to know, the answers will not be useful to you. Use a small group as a sample, and then apply the results to a larger group. Make sure you can analyze the answers to the questions quickly. For example, it is easy to compile data from multiple choice options for responses. What types of questions might you ask a potential interior design market if you want to open your own business?

Choose a Name

The name for your business should appeal both to you and your target market. However, there may also be legal requirements. For instance, your state may require business names to reflect the business structure. You will also want to make sure the name is not trademarked by another business in your area. You may check for trademarks with the Secretary of State office in your state.

Choose the Location

Perhaps you will want to work from your own home (Figure 28.5). Keep in mind that some cities do not allow a business to operate in residential neighborhoods. Perhaps you will be moving from place to place, such as a cleaning service.

If you must choose a business location, you will need to consider several factors. Easy access is a key factor in bringing customers to your business. Also, you will need to consider the location of your competition. You do not want to be so close that customers go to your competition. You do not want to be too far away to be considered competition. How can you improve on your competition's location?

Consider the neighborhood. Is it safe? inviting? Are the people who live there likely to give your business a try? Are they likely to spend money? Check out the neighboring businesses. Will they attract customers similar to those you are targeting? Will the customer base of neighboring businesses alienate your target market?

Once you choose a neighborhood, you can start looking for a store or office space. You will want to

Sergey Nivens/Shutterstock.com

Figure 28.5 Starting a business from your home can save on startup expenses and be very fulfilling.

consider the actual features of the building. Does it have the utilities you need? What is the lease or rental fee? Make sure your business is easily accessible to traffic. Also check to make sure there is adequate parking for customers.

Find Sources of Capital

You may have the best idea for a new product or service, but you need money to start the business. Where does the money come from?

Hopefully, you will put just a portion of your own savings toward your business. (Be sure to preserve enough savings for possible emergencies outside the business.) You may plan to borrow money from friends and family, but if you do, the terms of the loans should be in writing. Make sure friends and family understand the terms—the amount loaned, the lending fee, and the payback period.

Having a sound business plan is required for getting a bank loan. The *U.S. Small Business Administration* may be able to help you secure a bank loan, too. Getting capital from outside investors is another way to obtain startup money, but the business plan must be sound.

When pulling together capital, be sure you have a little extra. You want to be sure you have enough to cover any unexpected expenses.

Establish the Price or Fee

Deciding the value of your own time or skills is usually more difficult. As you learned in Chapter 18, interior designers may use a fixed fee, hourly fee, cost plus fee method, the retail method, or per square foot methods for determining project costs. Here are some other methods to decide how to price your product or service, while considering the cost of your materials and tools.

- **Demand-based pricing.** A pricing method that is determined by what customers are prepared to pay. You may also be able to charge more if your product, service, or business is seasonal.
- **Cost-based pricing.** Pricing that is determined by calculating how much it costs you to buy or produce the item. You then add a certain percentage to that price for profit.
- **Competition-based pricing.** A type of pricing that is determined by checking the prices of similar businesses in your area. If you have no real competition, you can charge a bit more. You do not want to add so much that customers will not buy your product or service.

Review & Assessment

1. What is a target market?
2. Contrast qualitative work processes with quantitative work processes.
3. What are the phases of the product life cycle?
4. Name four items to consider when choosing a business location.
5. What is a basic requirement for getting a bank loan for a business?
6. What are three methods entrepreneurs may use to determine product or service fees?

Develop a Business Plan

The **business plan** documents how you propose to start and run your business (Figure 28.6). The business plan will also help you think through any unanswered questions about your business.

If you need a bank loan to start your business, your business plan will help you secure it. The business plan shows the bank that you have carefully considered every aspect needed to help your business succeed.

A business plan includes the following sections:

- An executive summary—a short overview
- The description of the business—gives details on your product, service, business structure, how the company will be run, and the company's goals
- Industry analysis—an overview of the market, how it fits into the economy, and detailed information about your competition as well as how you plan to beat them

Marlon Lopez MMG1 Design/Shutterstock.com

Figure 28.6 A business plan is the real starting point for a business. Extensive research and many decisions go into developing a business plan that leads to success.

- The target market—who will be buying your product or service, how many customers you might have, and how much they might spend
- Organization and operations—the structure of the company, staff members and their positions, and the way the company will be run
- Marketing strategy—how you plan to sell the product or service
- Financial plan—includes the startup costs, how much of your own money you will use, who will supply loans and how much you will need, and how you expect to pay the money back; also includes budgets, cash flow statements, and balance sheets measuring net worth

For more information on business plans, review the Small Business Administration's website.

Legal Requirements for Starting a Business

Before you start a business, you are responsible for researching the legal requirements you need to fulfill. For example, there may be zoning laws for your home or location. If you plan to work out of your home, make sure a zoning law does not restrict you from doing this in a residential neighborhood. Some laws prevent certain businesses from operating in some areas.

Some businesses need a permit, while other businesses may need a license. For instance, landscape architects, land surveyors, and real estate agents must all be licensed. You will probably have to pay a fee for both permits and licenses.

Check with the Department of Commerce for your state. This office can help inform you of any permits or licenses you will need.

Protecting your ideas and the ideas of others is important. You should also conduct research to determine whether any aspect of your potential business will infringe on copyrights, trademarks, or patents of other businesses. See Figure 28.7 for differences in intellectual property.

Insurance and Taxes

To limit the amount of risk to your business, you will need to acquire various types of insurance coverage. You will want to

- protect your business from losses due to fire or theft with property insurance.
- have commercial liability insurance in case your product or service causes injury.
- carry disability and worker's compensation insurance for yourself and your employees to avoid losses if unable to work due to injury or illness.
- carry car insurance and business trip insurance for yourself and employees when traveling among clients or to business trips or conferences.

Navigating the information necessary for tax purposes can seem daunting. Each state's

Copyright, Trademark, and Patent Basics

As an entrepreneur, you should know about others' rights related to copyrights, trademarks, and patents. All of these rights fall under the umbrella of intellectual property. Intellectual property usually refers to ideas, inventions, or processes that derive from work of the mind or intellect. What are these rights? The following briefly describes each:

- **Copyright** is the exclusive legal right to reproduce, publish, sell, or distribute the matter and form of something (literary, musical, or artistic work).
- **Trademark** is a device (such as a word) pointing distinctly to the origin or ownership of merchandise to which it is applied and legally reserved to the exclusive use of the owner as the maker or seller.
- **Patent** is an official document giving the exclusive right to make, use, or sell an invention for a term of years.

Infringing on some else's copyright, trademark, or patent can lead to severe legal penalties and fines. The best way to protect yourself and your business from unintentional infringement on the intellectual property of others is to do a search. You will not want to infringe on the designs or products created by others.

You can conduct a preliminary search yourself using the Internet and such sources as the *U.S. Patent and Trademark Office* or the *Library of Congress Copyright Office*. It is best, however, to hire an attorney who specializes in doing copyright, trademark, and patent searches.

Figure 28.7 Protecting your design ideas and the ideas of others is very important. What might happen to a housing and interior design professional who fails to understand the legal responsibilities connected to copyrights, trademarks, and patents?

Department of Commerce has assistance programs that can help you. Also check with the U.S. Small Business Administration's website.

First, you will need a tax identification number for your business because you will be paying taxes for any profit your business makes. You must also find out how much sales tax you need to charge for a product. Most personal services are not taxed, although some states are considering adding a tax.

Startup Expenses

The most expensive part of being an entrepreneur can be your startup costs. This is because it will take a while for the business to start earning money. You may feel at first that everything is a "loss."

You may spend a lot of money to start the business, but some of this will cover one-time fees. For instance, you may need to buy machines that will last for several years. In contrast, you may need to buy supplies every few months. Your operating fees will be ongoing, but you may never have the need for all the beginning costs again.

Sources of Assistance

It is unlikely that you are an expert in all areas of entrepreneurship. Where can you go for support?

First, consult the U.S. Small Business Administration (Figure 28.8). Its website has helpful answers to many common questions. It also links to the state Departments of Commerce. The states set many of the regulations that affect small businesses. You would be wise to investigate these regulations before starting a business. Your local chamber of commerce may also be able to help you check for local regulations. These sources may be free or require a small fee.

Mark Van Scyoc/Shutterstock.com

Figure 28.8 The U.S. Small Business Administration offers a wealth of information to those seeking to start their own businesses.

From time to time, you will also need support in these business areas:

- A lawyer will make sure you fulfill all legal requirements.
- An accountant can handle or check your bookkeeping and tax-related records.
- An insurance agent will determine the amount and types of insurance you need.

These professionals can be expensive, but they limit your business risk and provide peace of mind.

Although most professionals charge for their services, there may be some free types of assistance for small businesses. Consider checking with the Agricultural Extension office and local small business support groups that might provide helpful and free services.

Review & Assessment

1. What is a business plan and what information does it include?
2. Why is a business plan important for securing a bank loan?
3. List two legal requirements for starting a business.
4. What are four types of insurance necessary for a business to carry?
5. What is the primary reason entrepreneurs may need to use a lawyer, accountant, or insurance agent from time to time?

Managing for Profit

For a company to succeed, it must make enough money to pay employees, purchase materials, cover other costs, and have some left over to maintain and improve the business. The costs of doing business are called **expenses**. The money that results from customers purchasing the company's product or service is called **revenues**, or *sales*. A business calculates its *income* by subtracting its expenses from its revenues. When the revenues are greater than expenses, the company is said to make a **profit**. When a company's expenses are greater than its revenues, it is called a **loss**. The equation for calculating income is

$$\text{Income} = \text{Revenues} - \text{Expenses}$$

Financial Statements

The preceding formula is the basis for one of three fundamental financial statements used to manage a business—the **income statement**. The income statement is sometimes referred to as the *profit and loss (P&L) statement*. The income statement communicates the results of the company's operations for a given period of time such as one month or one year. See the income statement for *Ina's Interiors* (Figure 28.9).

The second financial statement used by a business is the **balance sheet**. The balance sheet shows the businesses assets, liabilities, and equity on a given date. **Assets** are items a company owns that have value, such as cash, physical inventory, buildings, and equipment. **Liabilities** are debts, or what a company owes such as bills payable to suppliers, mortgage loans, or various taxes it must pay to state or federal governments. **Equity** represents the owner's rights to the assets of the company. For example, if an owner invests $100,000.00 in a business to start it, he or she has $100,000.00 in equity in the business. A business' assets are equal to the sum of its liabilities and equity

Assets = Liabilities + Equity

Ina's Interiors
Income Statement
for Month Ending September 30, 2018

Revenue		
Interior designer services	$5,350.00	
Designer consultation fees	800.00	
Total Revenues		**$6,150.00**
Expenses		
Designer salary	$3,210.00	
Rent	1,250.00	
Utilities (heat, electric, water)	325.00	
Office supplies	78.00	
Total Expenses		**$4,863.00**
Income		**$1,287.00**

Goodheart-Willcox Publisher

Figure 28.9 An income statement is one of the three fundamental financial statements necessary for managing a business.

The **statement of cash flow (SCF)** is the third fundamental financial statement you will use. The SCF shows how cash came into the business and how it left, or was used by the business. This is different from profit or loss because only *cash* received or paid out is analyzed. The cash flow in and out of business is categorized as either from *operating activities* (for example cash received from customers or paid to suppliers), *investing activities* (for example, cash received from the sale of equipment or paid on a vehicle loan), or *financing activities* (for example, cash received from an investor or paid to stockholders as dividends).

Managing Revenues and Expenses

The equation for calculating profit demonstrates how either increasing or decreasing the revenues, expenses, or both can impact a business' income. To achieve a planned profit, both revenues and expenses must be managed. Key factors that must be addressed are marketing plans, production, inventory control, and performance analysis.

Marketing Plan

How will your customers learn that your product or service is available? You need to get the message out to them through marketing. You will need to choose which type of advertising to use (Figure 28.10). The goal is to acquaint customers with the merits of your product or service so they are persuaded to buy it. You may have to explain its value and importance. Sometimes this is accomplished by explaining how it is better than the competition. See Figure 28.11 for marketing strategies for housing professionals and interior designers.

You will need to set up a timetable for your advertising. When will you introduce the product? How often will you advertise? This may depend on your advertising budget, too.

alphaspirit/Shutterstock.com

Figure 28.10 Developing an effective marketing strategy takes time and much thought.

Marketing Strategies for Housing and Interior Design
To effectively market your housing or interior design related business, try the following:
Target Your Market
To gain the most from your marketing dollars, focus your market on a few key market segments. With *geographical segmentation*, you would focus on housing and interior design clients and customers in a certain geographical area. With *customer segmentation*, identify those customers and clients that are most likely to buy your services or products and focus on these groups.
Develop a Logo or Brand
Having a logo or brand helps create your "business identity." It should be something that your clients and potential clients can easily identify. You can use your brand for your website, business cards, stationary, and other documents.
Create a Website
Developing a website is key for marketing your business. Make sure your website is attractive and accurately reflects your business and specialty. Include portfolio images that show your work focusing on your target market. Highlight your educational achievements, credentials, awards, and any testimonials you receive from satisfied clients. Be sure to continually update project and product images and testimonials.
Use Social Media
Carefully analyze what you want to promote before signing up for and using various social media sites. Some social media sites allow businesses to create their own page; however, you must read the guidelines first. Managing multiple social media accounts can be challenging. You will want to post frequent updates and connect with friends and followers of your site to gain the best marketing advantage.
Use High-quality Photography
Effective photography skillfully showcases your completed projects to display in your professional portfolio or use on your website and in printed materials.
Prepare Printed Materials
Brochures, post cards, and newsletters can be great marketing tools for your business. Well-designed print materials should be brief and highlight your skills. Distribute these materials to real estate agents, builders, property developers, and others who can help get the word out about your business.
Maintain Good Public Relations
Share your business talents at conferences and workshops or volunteer to use your skills through such community service organizations and Habitat for Humanity or United Way.

Figure 28.11 Effective marketing strategies help lead to business success.

Channels of Distribution

Understanding distribution of products is important, too. A **channel of distribution** is the route a product takes from the manufacturer to the customer. For example, the manufacturer may sell the product to a store, which then sells to the customer. In other cases, the manufacturer may sell to a wholesaler, who sells to retailers, who then sell to the customer. Adding businesses to the channel of distribution increases price and production time. As an entrepreneur, you will want to investigate the most cost-effective channel of distribution for your product.

Production Process

No matter how the production is accomplished, you should have two goals for production. First, your product should have quality and value. If your customers do not believe the item is worth its cost, you will not be able to sell the item. The other factor to consider is efficiency. You want to be able to make your product quickly so you can sell as many as possible.

Career Focus Interior Designer—Hotels/Vacation Lodges

Can you imagine yourself as the interior designer of a hotel or vacation lodge where families spend their vacations? If you can, you'll want to read the following about this exciting career.

Interests/Skills: Do your interests include a love of or desire to travel? Do you share the value that it is important for families and individuals to have safe and fun places to tour and spend their vacation time? Skills include a talent for researching information and understanding details. The ability to work well with a team is essential. Strong math, communication, and computer skills along with an understanding of mechanical systems are critical.

Career Snapshot: Making a profit in hotel or vacation lodges is a challenge. That is why interior design is so important and must leave a lasting impression on visiting guests. Hospitality designers have special training in designing such commercial buildings. Many factors enter into the design process. First, designers must identify the people who will be using the space. Second, they must consider the location for the hotel or vacation lodge. The look and feel of the décor should speak to the surrounding environments. For example, mountain resorts might have a more rustic feel than a vacation resort at the beach. As a designer, you would work with and listen closely to the owner of the proposed resort. In order to create a design that meets all client requirements, cooperation of the entire team is essential. For a resort business to be successful, the design must be one that people enjoy and to which they want to return.

Education/Training: Completion of a bachelor's or master's degree is preferred. Classes include business management, lighting, computer technology, color theory, textiles, and CADD. Additional courses in culinary arts and psychology make the designer more competitive in the job market.

Image Worx/Shutterstock.com

Licensing/Examinations: About one half of the states require licensing of interior designers. The National Council for Interior Design Accreditation administers an examination that interior designers must pass in order to obtain a license and to be competitive in their careers.

Professional Associations: The American Society of Interior Designers (ASID); The International Interior Design Association (IIDA)

Job Outlook: The hospitality landscape is constantly changing with many older hotels renovated into new hip designs. Your hotel cannot afford to lose out to the competition as the look and feel of a luxury hotel is something that many travelers have come to expect.

Sources: The Occupational Outlook Handbook (OOH); the Occupational Information Network (O*NET)

Sacrificing quality for speed, however, will probably cost you sales in the long run.

Inventory Records

Keeping track of your inventory is very important. Having too much inventory has a few drawbacks. First, having too much inventory means you probably ordered or manufactured too much to sell at its current price. Lowering the price may not cover your expenses. Second, you may not have enough storage for your entire inventory. If you buy more space, you may have more expenses. Finally, your stock may become dated or damaged over time. The longer you keep it in inventory, the less you will be able to eventually sell.

If you have too little inventory, you can sell out your product. Getting more product available takes time. Customers will be unhappy if they cannot have the product they want when they are ready to buy. They may shop elsewhere. They may spread the word that your products are appealing, but unavailable.

bikeriderlondon/Shutterstock.com

Figure 28.12 Interior designers who run small businesses may only stock samples of materials and finishes for their clients to review.

Some businesses keep a minimal amount of stock on hand at any given time. Some businesses, especially in the interior design industry, stock only samples (Figure 28.12). Products such as drapery and upholstered furniture are not manufactured until customers place customized orders. Carrying too much inventory can affect cash flow.

Businesses may keep track of inventory by hand, also known as **physical inventory**. This means visually checking and physically counting the number of items you have available.

Today, it is most common for inventory systems to be computerized. Bar code scanners can "read" special labels and automatically update your inventory in the computer system. You may have a system that keeps constant inventory. That means whenever you add or remove stock, your needed supplies are automatically ordered. Other systems take inventory at set intervals, such as once a month.

Analyzing the Income Statement

Ratios are commonly used to analyze information on the income statement. Ratios express how one number relates to another. For example, a company might find it useful to understand how many dollars in sales are received for every dollar spent on wages (labor cost). This ratio is called the **labor cost percentage**.

$$\frac{\text{(Wages + benefits)}}{\text{Sales}} \times 100 = \text{Labor cost \%}$$

For example, in the month of April, suppose a small business paid \$6,400 in wages and \$1,260 in benefits to its employees. Total sales for the month were \$24,900. The labor cost percentage for April was 30.8 percent.

$$\frac{(\$6{,}400 + \$1{,}260)}{\$24{,}900} \times 100 = 30.8\%$$

Is a labor cost percentage of 30.8 good or bad? To understand that, this number must be compared to other numbers such as a budgeted labor cost percentage or the labor cost percentages from prior months or years. If a business has planned, or budgeted, for 32 percent labor cost, 30.8 percent would be good. If labor cost was 40 percent in March of the same year, why did it decrease? This ratio can be used to analyze expenses other than labor as well.

Another ratio is commonly used to measure a company's profitability. This ratio is called the **profit margin**. The profit-margin ratio compares a business' income (profit or loss) to its sales.

$$\frac{\text{Income}}{\text{Sales}} \times 100 = \text{Profit margin}$$

The income statement for Figure 28.9 *Ina's Interiors* shows that the business generated sales of \$6,150 and a profit of \$1,287 for the month of September 2018. The profit margin for Ina's Interiors can be calculated as follows:

$$\frac{\$1{,}287}{\$6{,}150} \times 100 = 21\%$$

Another way of stating Ina's profit margin is for every one dollar in sales, the business makes a profit of 21 cents.

Review & Assessment

1. What is the equation businesses use for calculating income?
2. What are the three fundamental financial statements used to manage business?
3. What key factors must be addressed when managing both revenues and expenses for a business?
4. List four marketing strategies for housing and interior design businesses.
5. What are the drawbacks of having too much or too little inventory?
6. Use the formula on this page to calculate the labor cost percentage for a business with the following information for one month: \$7,500 in wages, \$1,350 in employee benefits, and total monthly sales of \$30,000.

Chapter 28 Assessment

Summary

- Many housing and interior design professionals are entrepreneurs.
- Entrepreneurs have common characteristics, skills, values, and goals.
- Effective communication skills and math and computer skills are essential for entrepreneurs.
- Entrepreneurs as small business owners help create jobs and help keep the economy strong.
- Types of business structures include sole proprietorship, partnership, corporation, franchise, chain, and joint venture.
- Starting a small business requires careful research and making effective decisions to ensure success.
- Analyzing potential markets, studying the competition, and conducting market research for qualitative and quantitative data and product trends provides the necessary data for making the decision to start a business.
- Choosing a business name and locations, finding sources of capital, and establishing prices or fees are essential for starting a small business.
- An effective business plan shows that an entrepreneur has carefully considered every aspect needed to help a business succeed.
- Understanding legal requirements, insurance and taxes, startup expenses, and sources of assistance is necessary for business success.
- For a business to succeed, it must make enough money to pay employees, purchase materials, cover other costs, and improve the business.

Terms in Action

1. **Term attribute** For each of the *Content* and *Academic Terms* at the beginning of the chapter, identify a word or group of words describing a quality of the term—an *attribute*. Pair up with a classmate and discuss your list of attributes. Then, discuss your list with the whole class.

Think Critically

2. **Predict risk factors** Statistics on small business startups reveal that 30 percent of new businesses fail within two years and that 50 percent fail in five years. Review the characteristics common among entrepreneurs and predict what risk factors could contribute to failure. Create a list of reasons why some businesses fail and discuss in class.
3. **Identify interrelationships** Research and identify the interrelationship of the housing industry (particularly entrepreneurial housing and interior design businesses) with the economy. What impact do small housing and interior design businesses have on the overall economy on local, state, and national levels? Write a brief summary to post the class website.
4. **Evaluate advertisements** Review a weekend edition of your local newspaper for housing or interior design related business advertisements. Evaluate the ads for the appeal to potential buyers/users. How would you change the advertisement to what you think would be more effective for the target market?

Core Skills

5. **Research and speaking** Explore your community to determine resources available to assist new entrepreneurs in starting a business. Check with local groups such as the Chamber of Commerce and local business organizations. Categorize the ways that the groups are offering to help such as with developing the business plan. Apply your oral communication skills to report this information to the class.
6. **Speaking, listening, and writing** Contact the local Chamber of Commerce for assistance in developing a list of five successful businesses in your field in the community. Success can be defined as being in business over five years. Write a list of questions to ask these persons to determine from their perspective the factors of their success. Write a blog for the class web page summarizing your findings.
7. **Reading and writing** Locate a marketing journal online. Find an article of interest regarding entrepreneurship. Read the article and write summary of five main points of the article.

Chapter 28 Assessment

8. **Math practice** Review the monthly income statement for *Figure 28.9 Ina's Interiors*. Calculate what difference moving to a lower cost rental arrangement could make in the bottom line income. Specifically, calculate what difference a rent of $1000 and utilities of $350 would make in the income profit. What percent difference is this amount from her original income statement amount of $1,287? How does this change impact her profit margin?
9. **Research and writing** Suppose you and a team of three friends want to open an interior design business with a focus on green and sustainable design. As an initial step, you need to collect some primary data (qualitative) in your community as well as some secondary data (quantitative). Review the following questions to guide your research. Then, write a summary of the information you find.
   - What form(s) of primary data (qualitative) will you use? Develop interview questions or a survey for potential clients. Accurately review the qualitative end product of your research related to your interior design business.
   - What secondary data (quantitative) will your team use? Conduct research for several secondary sources of information including government databases, private databases, and the Internet about the interior design market in your community. Accurately review the quantitative end product of your research as related to your interior design business.
10. **Writing and technology** Presume that you and your teammates completed your market research. Your team has decided that there is a local market for a "green" interior design business. To get financial backing, your team needs to write a business plan covering the details in all specific parts of the plan. For additional help in writing your business plan, use the *Small Business Planner* tools on the Small Business Administration website.
11. **Research and speaking** As a team, research the role of ethics in business practices and procedures. Why is ethical behavior important to a profitable and successful business? How do ethics impact the legal requirements of a business owner? For information about legal responsibilities, see the Small Business Administration website. Apply your oral communication skills to clearly and concisely report your findings to the class.
12. **Research and writing** Many factors impact loss prevention and business profits. Research various inventory control strategies, laws, and workplace policies that can help entrepreneurs limit business losses and maintain profitability. Review articles about how successful entrepreneurs keep losses down and profits up. Write a summary of your findings for peer review.
13. **CTE career readiness practice** Imagine it is eight years in the future and you are starting your own interior design business. Your design work is fast-paced and demanding, and now you have the responsibility for managing the business operations as well. You have watched some friends and family members suffer the effects of workplace stress on their health and safety in recent years. Your goal is to maintain your health and safety by developing a plan for handling work stress. Investigate and evaluate resources on the *National Institute for Occupational Safety and Health* link on the Centers for Disease Control website. Write a plan for preventing and managing job stress.

Design Practice

14. **Creating marketing tools** When developing a marketing plan, it is important to use creative tools to capture client interest. For your team's "green" interior design firm, use a school-approved web application to create two or more of the following that emphasize your business identity: logo for business cards and stationary, website or page with attractive photography, brochure about the business, a newspaper or web advertisement about design services, a newsletter, or a press release. Review your completed items with your instructor and make revisions as needed.
15. **Portfolio** Save copies of your best work for item 14 above in your portfolio.

ASID Code of Ethics and Professional Conduct

AMERICAN SOCIETY OF INTERIOR DESIGNERS
AMERICAN SOCIETY OF INTERIOR DESIGNERS
AMERICAN SOCIETY OF INTERIOR DESIGNERS
AMERICAN SOCIETY OF INTERIOR DESIGNER
AMERICAN SOCIETY OF INTERIOR
AMERICAN SOCIETY
AMERICA

ASID CODE OF ETHICS AND PROFESSIONAL CONDUCT

Government & Public Affairs
www.asid.org/about/ethics

AMERICAN SOCIETY OF INTERIOR DESIGNERS
ASID

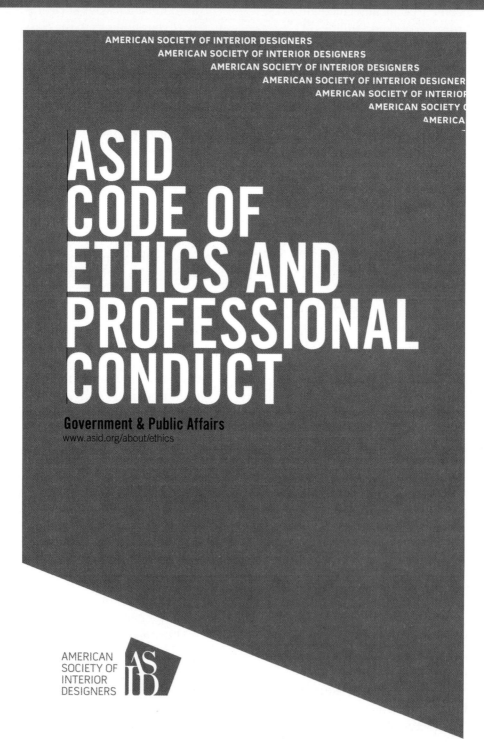

Reprinted with permission from the American Society of Interior Designers (ASID)

ASID Code of Ethics and Professional Conduct

1.0 PREAMBLE

Members of the American Society of Interior Designers are required to conduct their professional practice in a manner that will inspire the respect of the general public, their clients, fellow professional designers, as well as suppliers of goods and services to the profession. It is the individual responsibility of every member of the Society to uphold this Code of Ethics and Professional Conduct and the Bylaws of the Society.

2.0 RESPONSIBILITY TO THE PUBLIC

2.1 Members shall comply with all federal, state and local laws, rules, regulations and codes governing business procedures and the practice of interior design in the jurisdictions in which they practice ("Applicable Laws").

2.2 Members shall not seal or sign drawings, specifications, or other interior design documents except where the member or the member's firm has prepared, supervised or professionally reviewed and approved such documents, as allowed by Applicable Laws.

2.3 Members shall at all times consider the health, safety and welfare of the public in spaces they design. Members agree, whenever possible, to notify property managers, landlords, and/or public officials of conditions within a built environment that endanger the health, safety and/or welfare of occupants.

2.4 Members shall not engage in any form of false or misleading advertising or promotional activities.

2.5 Members shall neither offer, nor make any payments or gifts to any public official, nor take any other action, with the intent of unduly influencing the official's judgment in connection with an existing or prospective project in which the members are interested.

2.6 Members shall not assist or abet improper or illegal conduct of anyone in connection with a project.

3.0 RESPONSIBILITY TO THE CLIENT

3.1 Members' contracts with a client shall clearly set forth the scope and nature of the project involved, the services to be performed and the method of compensation for those services.

3.2 Members may offer professional services to a client for any form of legal compensation.

3.3 Members shall not undertake any professional responsibility unless they are, by training and experience, competent to adequately perform the work required.

3.4 Members shall fully disclose to a client all compensation which the Member shall receive in connection with the project and shall not accept any form of undisclosed compensation from any person or firm with whom the member deals in connection with the project.

3.5 Members shall not divulge any confidential information about the client or the client's project, or utilize photographs of the project except as is expressly allowed by agreement between the Member and client.

3.6 Members shall be candid and truthful in all their professional communications.

3.7 Members shall act with fiscal responsibility in the best interest of their clients and shall maintain sound business relationships with suppliers, industry and trades.

4.0 RESPONSIBILITY TO OTHER INTERIOR DESIGNERS AND COLLEAGUES

4.1 Members shall abide by common law and statutory prohibitions against tortuous interference of contract and will not unlawfully interfere with another interior designer's existing contractual relationships.

4.2 Members shall avoid making any intentionally false communication, either written or spoken, that harms another interior designer's reputation or otherwise disparages his or her character.

4.3 Members may, when requested and it does not present a conflict of interest, render a second opinion to a client, or serve as an expert witness in a judicial or arbitration proceeding.

4.4 Members shall not endorse the application for ASID membership and/or certification, registration or licensing of an individual known to be unqualified with respect to education, training, experience or character, nor shall a Member knowingly misrepresent the experience, professional expertise or moral character of that individual.

4.5 Subject to the provisions of section six, members shall only take credit for work that has actually been created by that Member or the Member's firm, and under the Member's supervision.

4.6 Members shall respect the confidentiality of sensitive information obtained in the course of their professional activities.

5.0 RESPONSIBILITY TO THE PROFESSION

5.1 Members agree to maintain standards of professional and personal conduct that will reflect in a responsible manner on the Society and the profession.

5.2 Members shall seek to continually upgrade their professional knowledge and competency with respect to the interior design profession.

5.3 Members agree, whenever possible, to encourage and contribute to the sharing of knowledge and information between interior designers and other allied professional disciplines, industry and the public.

6.0 RESPONSIBILITY TO THE EMPLOYER

6.1 Members leaving an employer's service shall not take drawings, designs, photographs, data, reports, notes, client lists, or other materials relating to work performed in the employer's service except with permission of the employer.

6.2 Members shall not divulge any confidential information obtained during the course of their employment about the client or the client's project.

7.0 ENFORCEMENT

7.1 The Society shall follow standard procedures for the enforcement of this Code of Ethics and Professional Conduct as approved by the Society's Board of Directors.

7.2 Members having a reasonable belief, based upon substantial information, that another member has acted in violation of this Code of Ethics and Professional Conduct, shall report such information in accordance with accepted procedures.

7.3 Any deviation from this Code of Ethics and Professional Conduct, or any action taken by a Member which is detrimental to the Society and the profession as a whole shall be deemed unprofessional conduct subject to discipline by the Society's Board of Directors.

(Adopted by the National Board 8/94)

PROCEDURES FOR FILING AN ETHICS COMPLAINT

ASID procedures regarding a complaint filed against a member of ASID are as follows:

1. The individual against whom an ethics complaint is made must be a current member in the Society (the "member"). The complaint must be in writing, signed by the complaining party (the "complainant"), shall state the matter complained of in detail, and be accompanied by all materials the complaining party wishes to bring to the attention of the Society (collectively referred to as "complaining materials").

2. The complaining materials must be sent to Society headquarters within two years of the occurrence of the conduct which is the subject matter of the complaining materials.

3. The complaining materials are forwarded to the Society's legal counsel for review and to determine if the conduct complained of involves a possible violation of the Society's Code of Ethics, or might otherwise constitute conduct detrimental to the Society or the profession.

4. If legal counsel decides the complaining materials do not involve a possible violation, the complainant is informed and the matter is closed. If legal counsel decides the complaining materials may involve a possible violation, the complaining materials are sent by the Society to the member with a request for a written response from the member to the complaining materials within 21 days. The response shall be in writing, signed by the member, and shall be accompanied by all materials the member wishes to bring to the attention of the Society in response to complaining materials ("responding materials").

5. The complaining and responding materials are then reviewed by the Society's Ethics Committee to determine whether there is sufficient evidence to warrant a disciplinary proceeding. In making their determination, the Ethics Committee may request additional information from either the complainant or the member. A copy of any such additional information provided by a party will, if the matter proceeds to a disciplinary hearing, be provided by the Society to the other party prior to the date of the hearing.

6. If the Ethics Committee concludes that a disciplinary hearing is not warranted, both parties are informed in writing of such determination and the matter is closed.

7. If the Ethics Committee determines that a disciplinary hearing is warranted, then the Society shall send a notice of the disciplinary hearing to the parties by certified mail, return receipt requested, (with a copy by ordinary mail) not less than 45 days prior to the date of the disciplinary hearing. The notice of disciplinary hearing shall specify the date, time and place of the hearing.

8. Either party may submit such other written materials they wish to bring to the attention of the Disciplinary Committee ("additional materials"), provided such additional materials are received at Society's headquarters no later than 20 days preceding the hearing date. A copy of additional materials submitted by a party must be sent by the submitting party to the other party by certified mail, return receipt requested, so that the same materials will be received by the other party no later than 20 days preceding the hearing date.

9. The Complainant shall be required to participate in the hearing in the manner described below. If the Complainant fails to participate in the hearing for any reason, the complaint will be dismissed as against the Complainant with prejudice to Complainant's right to file another complaint against the accused member in connection with the subject matter that was set forth in the complaint. The complainant and the accused member may appear personally and by counsel and may produce such witnesses as they determine (revised 1/98). Alternately, the complainant and the accused may elect to participate in the hearing via video teleconferencing or telephone conference call, provided such technology is available at the site of the hearing and all costs as reasonably determined by the Society are paid in advance by the party to the complaint requesting either video teleconferencing or a conference telephone call. In such regard, the complainant and the member shall each provide the Society with written notice, no later than 20 days prior to the hearing date, containing information as to how they plan to participate in the hearing, a telephone number where they may be reached on the date of the hearing, and a list of witnesses if applicable. Each submitting party must also send a copy of the written notice to the other party by certified mail, return receipt requested, so that the same information will be received by the other party no later than 20 days preceding the hearing date.

10. No stenographic transcript of such hearing shall be made unless it is specifically requested and paid for in advance by the requesting party.

(Amended 12/13)

Appendix B

Practical Math Review

Math skills are essential to the housing or interior design professional's success on the job. For example, a designer or builder uses computational skills when taking measurements or creating a bid. When a designer works from a set of plans, math is used to obtain distances or to extrapolate actual dimensions.

Could you calculate the areas of ceilings or walls, or estimate the amount of wall covering or fabric a job requires? Could you estimate how much paint is needed to cover a structure's exterior or a room's walls? What if the area to be covered is not rectangular, but a triangular- or circular-shaped space? What if measurements are given in meters instead of feet?

You learned many of these skills throughout this text. This appendix reviews some basic mathematical operations a housing and interior design professional may use.

Place Values of Whole Numbers

A *whole number* (0, 1, 2, 3, etc.) is any positive number with no fractional parts. The position of a digit (number) determines its *place value*. The positions never change, but the digits may.

The number farthest to the right occupies the ones place value, or ones position. The digit immediately to the left is in the tens position, followed by the next digit to the left that is in the hundreds position. Moving left, there are the thousands position, the ten-thousands position, and so forth.

Example
2,542,908

8 has a place value of *ones*
0 has a place value of *tens*
9 has a place value of *hundreds*
2 has a place value of *thousands*
4 has a place value of *ten-thousands*
5 has a place value of *hundred-thousands*
2 has a place value of *millions*

Addition

Addition is the combining of at least two numbers to result in a new figure, or *sum*. When adding, align numbers by place value. For instance, line up the numbers that are in the ones column beneath each other. Numbers occupying each of the other place values should also line up in columns.

Example
Use the format that follows to add these numbers: 813 + 1305 + 2137

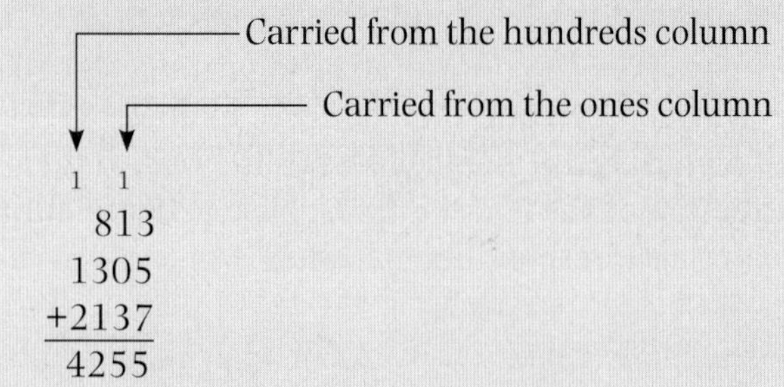

Subtraction

This mathematical process involves finding the *difference* between two numbers. You generally write the larger number (*minuend*) first, and write the smaller number (*subtrahend*) beneath it. The result of subtracting the subtrahend from the minuend is the difference. Maintain the place-value columns as in addition. For example, ones-place values should line up in a column, tens-place values in another, and so forth.

Sometimes, it is necessary to borrow in subtraction. If a digit borrows, it takes from the next higher place value column. The column borrowed from is reduced by 1 and 10 is added to the digit that required the borrow.

The following example shows how borrowing occurs when subtracting 15 from 43. When borrowing, note a "1" is borrowed from the tens column (the number 4 here). This reduces the number "4" to "3." The number "3" in the ones column now becomes "13."

This appendix is adapted with permission from Painting & Decorating by E. Keith Blankenbaker. Available through Goodheart-Willcox Publisher (www.g-w.com).

Example

$$\begin{array}{r} {}^{3}\overset{1}{4}3 \\ -15 \\ \hline 28 \end{array}$$

Multiplication

Suppose an interior designer has 6 lengths of baseboard trim, each measuring 8 ft. in length. What is the total length of baseboard trim available? One way to calculate the total length is to use addition:

Example
8 + 8 + 8 + 8 + 8 + 8 = 48 ft. (of baseboard trim)

The same result can be achieved quicker by multiplication. Multiplication uses the × (times) sign between two numbers, or *factors*. The answer to the problem is the *product*. The following example shows how to achieve the same answer for the baseboard trim with multiplication:

Example
8 ft. × 6 = 48 ft. (of baseboard trim)

Division

If you have 12 sets of house plans and want to give each of four interior designers an equal number of these house plans, division is a useful process. Division is the opposite of multiplication. The *dividend* is the number being divided. The *divisor* is the number dividing the dividend. The answer to the problem is the *quotient*. The following example reads as 12 *divided* by 4 *equals* 3.

Example
12 ÷ 4 = 3

Because you can divide the number 12 into equal parts, each of the four interior designers will receive three sets of house plans. Some division problems do not yield equal parts. For example, 13 divided by 4 equals 3 with 1 left over. The left-over number is called the *remainder*.

Fractions

A fraction is a number that represents a part of something. For example, when making calculations for wall treatments, fractions are often part of the measurements or calculations. A ¾ in. mark on a measuring tape indicates a fraction (part) of a whole inch.

The bottom number, or *denominator*, shows how many parts make up the whole. The denominator cannot be 0. The top number, or *numerator*, specifies some number of those parts. The more parts there are in the whole, the smaller the size of each part. For instance, ½ gal. of paint is more than ¼ gal. of paint. The parts created by breaking a unit into two are larger than the parts created by breaking it into four.

Proper Fractions

In a *proper fraction*, the numerator is less than the denominator.

Examples
$\frac{1}{2}$, $\frac{2}{5}$, $\frac{3}{4}$, $\frac{1}{5}$, and $\frac{5}{8}$

Improper Fractions

In an *improper fraction*, the numerator is greater than or equal to the denominator.

Examples
$\frac{4}{4}$, $\frac{7}{3}$, $\frac{8}{6}$, $\frac{12}{9}$, and $\frac{11}{8}$

If the numerator and denominator are equal, as in (4/4), the fraction is *equivalent* (equal) to the whole number 1.

Mixed Numbers

An improper fraction can be written in the form of a *mixed number*. A mixed number consists of a whole number and a fraction.

Examples
$2\frac{3}{4}$, $5\frac{7}{8}$, and $7\frac{2}{3}$

To convert an improper fraction into a mixed number, divide the numerator by the denominator. The quotient is either a whole number or a whole number with a remainder. The remainder can be written as a fraction. How is the improper fraction 14/5 converted into a mixed number?

Example
$\frac{14}{5}$ = 14 ÷ 5 = 2 with a remainder of 4, or
$2\frac{4}{5}$ (mixed number)

Reducing Fractions

Fractions are usually expressed in their *lowest terms*, or an equivalent fraction in which the numerator and denominator are the lowest possible numbers. To calculate the lowest terms of a fraction, find the largest number that divides evenly into *both* the numerator and denominator. Note how the fraction in the following example is reduced to its lowest terms.

Example

$\frac{25}{100}$

Find a number that is a factor of both 25 and 100. For example, both 25 and 100 can be divided by 5. This reduces the fraction to $5/20$.

However, $5/20$ is not in lowest terms since it can be further reduced by dividing its numerator and denominator by 5. The lowest term is $1/4$; this fraction cannot be reduced any further. The quickest way to reduce $25/100$ to its lowest terms is to use their largest common factor, or 25. Dividing the numerator and denominator by 25 yields

$\frac{25}{100} = \frac{5}{20} = \frac{1}{4}$

Adding Fractions

Adding fractions that share the same denominator is simple: add the numerators together and use the same denominator.

Example

$\frac{2}{6} + \frac{3}{6} = \frac{5}{6}$

However, fractions with different denominators require another step before the addition. You must find a *common denominator* of the fractions. One way to find a common denominator is to multiply the two denominators together.

Example

$\frac{1}{2} + \frac{6}{8}$

Find the common denominator. Multiplying the denominator 8 by 2 gives a denominator 16. Convert each fraction to an equivalent fraction with the denominator of 16.

Example

$\frac{1}{2} = \frac{8}{16}$

$\frac{6}{8} = \frac{12}{16}$

$\frac{8}{16} + \frac{12}{16} = \frac{20}{16} = 1\frac{4}{16}$

$1\frac{4}{16} = 1\frac{1}{4}$ (reduced to lowest terms)

Fractions are easier to read when using the smallest common denominator, or *lowest common denominator (LCD)*. Here is another example showing how to add and reduce fractions. First find the LCD. In this case, the LCD is 24. Convert $1/6$ to $4/24$. Then add the numerators and keep the same denominator (24). Check to see if the answer is in lowest terms. If it is not, reduce the answer to its lowest terms. In the following example, the answer is in its lowest terms.

Example

$\frac{1}{6} + \frac{3}{24}$

$\frac{1}{6} = \frac{4}{24}$

$\frac{4}{24} + \frac{3}{24} = \frac{7}{24}$

Subtracting Fractions

Subtracting fractions is a lot like adding fractions. First, convert the fractions so they have a common denominator. Second, subtract the numerators but keep the denominator the same. Finally, reduce your answer to lowest terms.

In the following example, note the LCD is 40. When you subtract the numerators (20 – 15), the difference is 5. Keep the denominator at 40. Then you must reduce the answer, $5/40$, to its lowest terms. The largest whole number that divides evenly into the numerator and denominator is 5. The final answer is $1/8$.

Example

$\frac{5}{10} - \frac{3}{8}$

$\frac{5}{10} = \frac{20}{40}$

$\frac{3}{8} = \frac{15}{40}$

$\frac{20}{40} - \frac{15}{40} = \frac{5}{40} = \frac{1}{8}$ (in lowest terms)

$\frac{5}{40} = \frac{1}{8}$ (reduced to lowest terms)

Multiplying Fractions

It is not necessary to find a common denominator when you are multiplying fractions. Simply multiply the numerators and then multiply the denominators.

Example

$\frac{2}{7} \times \frac{3}{11}$

$\frac{2}{7} \times \frac{3}{11} = \frac{6}{77}$

If the answer needs to be reduced to lowest terms, do so. In this case, you cannot reduce it any further.

Dividing Fractions

In division of fractions, the *dividend* (number being divided) is multiplied by the *reciprocal* of the *divisor* (the number dividing the dividend). The reciprocal of a number is determined by simply switching the number's numerator and denominator. A number multiplied by its reciprocal equals 1. For example, the reciprocal of 2 is $\frac{1}{2}$ because

$$\frac{2}{1} \times \frac{1}{2} = \frac{2}{2} \text{ or } 1$$

The numerators and the denominators of the fractions are then multiplied and reduced to the lowest terms.

In the following example, find the reciprocal of the divisor by inverting the divisor. Then multiply and reduce to the lowest terms.

Example

$$\frac{9}{12} \div \frac{3}{4}$$

$$\left(\frac{3}{4}\right) \text{ to } \frac{4}{3} \text{ (reciprocal)}$$

$$\frac{9}{12} \times \frac{4}{3} = \frac{36}{36} = 1$$

Decimals

Interior designers, builders, and painters may use decimals during estimating—while determining job costs or tracking hours or parts of hours for payroll. A decimal is another way of representing a fraction, or part of a unit. A decimal is made up of digits with each one representing a multiple of ten. A point (.), called a *decimal point*, is used in the decimal system. To read decimal numbers, say them out loud like fractions (0.7 = seven-tenths) or say the word point with the numbers (0.028 = zero point zero twenty-eight).

Place Values

The place value determines the value of the digit. The number written to the left of a decimal point represents the whole number. For example, in the number 487, the digit 4 has a place value of hundreds.

Digits to the right of the decimal show the number of parts required to make a whole. This is the fraction, and its value is less than 1. Read decimal numbers from left to right. For example, 0.591 would be read $^{591}/_{1000}$. Zeros are used as placeholders to keep remaining digits in their proper places, as in 0.031 = thirty-one *thousandths*. Place values are multiples of 10.

Example
0.72138 (72138/100,000)
0 has a place value of zero *ones*
. *decimal point*
7 has a place value of *seven tenths* (7/10)
2 has a place value of *two hundredths* (2/100)
1 has a place value of *one thousandths* (1/1000)
3 has a place value of *three ten thousandths* (3/10,000)
8 has a place value of *eight hundred thousandths* (8/100,000)

Adding and Subtracting Decimals

When you are adding or subtracting decimal numbers, align the decimal points before performing the operation. The decimal point in the answer drops down and into the same location.

Example
Add:

$$\begin{array}{r} 0.57 \\ 21.678 \\ +\ 0.38 \\ \hline 22.628 \end{array}$$

Subtract:

$$\begin{array}{r} 89.538 \\ -\ 7.2913 \\ \hline 82.2467 \end{array} \qquad \begin{array}{r} 89.5380 \\ -\ 7.2913 \\ \hline 82.2467 \end{array}$$

Note: The preceding subtraction problem requires a zero in the blank space to the right of 8 to allow the completion of the problem.

Multiplying and Dividing Decimals

When multiplying decimal numbers, disregard the decimal points when you perform this operation. Then count the number of places to the right of the decimal point in each factor. The sum of these numbers is the number of decimal places required in the product (the answer). Starting to the right of the product, place the decimal point by moving left by this sum. Review the following problem to multiply decimals.

Example

0.59	(2 places right of the decimal point)
× 12.8	(1 place right of the decimal point)
7.552	(2 + 1 = 3, count back 3 places from the right to the left and insert the decimal point)

If there are fewer digits to the left than you need, add zeros to the left to maintain the required decimal place values.

Example

$6\overline{)45} = 6\overline{)45.0}$ (quotient 7.5)

When dividing decimal numbers, if there is a decimal in the divisor, change it to a whole number by moving the decimal point to the far right. Count the places moved to the right, and then move the decimal point in the dividend the same number of places to the right. You may need to add zeros to keep the place values. Perform the division operation. Align the decimal point in the quotient with the position of the decimal point in the dividend.

Example

$1.5\overline{).225}$

(Move the decimal point one place to the right)

$15\overline{)2.25}$ (quotient 0.15)

Converting Inches to Feet

The following chart (Figure A) shows the conversion of inches to feet. Values are expressed as decimals and fractions.

Converting Inches to Feet		
Inches	**Feet (decimal)**	**Feet (fraction)**
1	0.08	1/12
2	0.17	1/6
3	0.25	1/4
4	0.33	1/3
5	0.42	5/12
6	0.50	1/2
7	0.58	7/12
8	0.67	2/3
9	0.75	3/4
10	0.83	5/6
11	0.92	11/12
12	1.00	12/12

Figure A Sometimes a housing and interior design professional must convert inches to feet before performing a calculation.

Squares and Square Roots

The product of a number multiplied by itself is the number's *square*. For example, the square of 3 is 9 because 3 × 3 = 9. If one side of a square measures 10 ft., the remaining three sides also measure 10 ft. The area (A) of a square is the length of one side squared. Here is the formula:

$A = S^2$

Example

If one side of the square measures 10 ft., the area of the square is

$A = S^2$

$A = 10^2$

$A = 10 \times 10$

A = 100 sq. ft.

Alternately, if the area of a square is given as 100 sq. ft., you could determine the length of a side by taking the square root of 100. A square root is written using the symbol $\sqrt{}$.

Example

$\sqrt{100}$ (square root of 100)

A number's square root is a factor of the number. When you multiply that factor by itself, the product is the number. In the above case, the square root of 100 is 10. You can find the square root of any number by using a calculator.

Metric Measurement

When designers, builders, or painters take measurements, they use the U.S. Conventional or the SI Metric system. In the U.S. Conventional system, commonly used in the U.S., basic units of measure include the inch, foot, and yard. In the SI Metric system, used in many other countries, measures are described as *millimeter, centimeter,* or *meter*. The metric system gives dimensions as decimal fractions (35.2 mm) instead of mixing units of measurement (3' 7").

The following examples are U.S. Conventional system units and their SI Metric system equivalents:

Example

1 inch = 25.40 millimeters (mm)
1 inch = 2.54 centimeters (cm)
1 foot = 0.3048 meter (m)
1 yard = 0.9144 meter
1 mile = 1.6093 kilometers (km)

U.S. Conventional with SI Metric Measurement Equivalents for Length					
Fractional Inch	**Millimeters**	**Inches**	**Centimeters**	**Feet**	**Meters**
1/32	.7938	1	2.54	1	.3048
1/16	1.588	1 1/4	3.175	1 1/2	.4572
3/32	2.381	1 1/2	3.81	2	.6096
1/8	3.175	1 3/4	4.445	2 1/2	.7620
5/32	3.969	2	5.08		
3/16	4.763	2 1/4	5.715	3	.9144
7/32	5.556	2 1/2	6.35	3 1/2	1.067
1/4	6.350	2 3/4	6.985	4	1.219
9/32	7.144	3	7.62	4 1/2	1.372
5/16	7.938	3 1/4	8.255	5	1.524
11/32	8.731	3 1/2	8.89	5 1/2	1.676
3/8	9.525	3 3/4	9.525	6	1.829
13/32	10.32	4	10.16	6 1/2	1.981
7/16	11.11	4 1/4	10.80		
15/32	11.91	4 1/2	11.43	7	2.134
1/2	12.70	4 3/4	12.07	7 1/2	2.286
17/32	13.49	5	12.70	8	2.438
9/16	14.29	5 1/4	13.34	8 1/2	2.591
19/32	15.08	5 1/2	13.97		
5/8	15.88	5 3/4	14.61	9	2.743
21/32	16.67	6	15.24	9 1/2	2.896
11/16	17.46	6 1/2	16.51	10	3.048
23/32	18.26	7	17.78	10 1/2	3.200
3/4	19.05	7 1/2	19.05	11	3.353
25/32	19.84	8	20.32	11 1/2	3.505
13/16	20.64	8 1/2	21.59	12	3.658
27/32	21.43	9	22.86	15	4.572
7/8	22.23	9 1/2	24.13		
29/32	23.02	10	25.40	20	6.096
15/16	23.81	10 1/2	26.67	25	7.620
31/32	24.61	11	27.94	50	15.24
1	25.40	11 1/2	29.21	100	30.48

Figure B Lengths are calculated using the U.S. Conventional and SI Metric systems.

Length

The metric system is convenient to use because its units can be converted from one to another by multiplying or dividing by multiples of 10 (Figure B). When a designer or contractor reads a metric measuring tape, for example, the smallest unit is the millimeter. Ten millimeters make a centimeter, and ten centimeters make a decimeter (a decimeter is seldom marked on measuring tapes). Ten decimeters make a meter.

Finding Areas

Area is a two-dimensional measurement. Calculating the area helps interior designers determine how much paint or wall covering is needed to cover a surface. Area is expressed in *square units,* such as 29 sq. ft. or 3 sq. m. To calculate area, measurements must be in the same (common) unit. For example, if a wall is 12 ft. 6 in. long and 8 ft. 6 in. high, you first convert the measurements to inches.

Example
12 ft. 6 in. = 144 in. + 6 in. = 150 in.
8 ft. 6 in. = 96 in. + 6 in. = 102 in.

To find the area of the wall, do the following calculation:

Example
150 in. × 102 in. = 15,300 sq. in.

To find the area of the wall in square feet, convert square inches into square feet by dividing the answer by 144.

Example
15,300 sq. in. ÷ 144 = 106.25 sq. ft. (area of wall)

Squares, Rectangles, and Parallelograms

A *square* has four sides that are equal in length and meet at right (90°) angles. A *parallelogram* has four sides; two pairs of parallel sides. A *rectangle* is a type of parallelogram with four sides that meet at right angles. The formulas for the areas for each of these figures follows in Figure C.

Triangles

A *triangle* is a three-sided polygon. The area of a triangle (Figure D) is calculated by taking one-half the *base* times the *height*. Use the following formula:

Area (A) = $(B \times H) \times \frac{1}{2}$
or
Area (A) = $(B \times H) \div 2$

If the base of a triangle is 14 ft. and the height is 5 ft., the area is calculated in the following ways.

Example
$A = (14\text{ ft.} \times 5\text{ ft.}) \times \frac{1}{2}$
$A = 70\text{ sq. ft.} \times \frac{1}{2}$
$A = 35$ sq. ft.
or
$A = (14\text{ ft.} \times 5\text{ ft.}) \div 2$
$A = 70\text{ sq. ft.} \div 2$
$A = 35$ sq. ft.

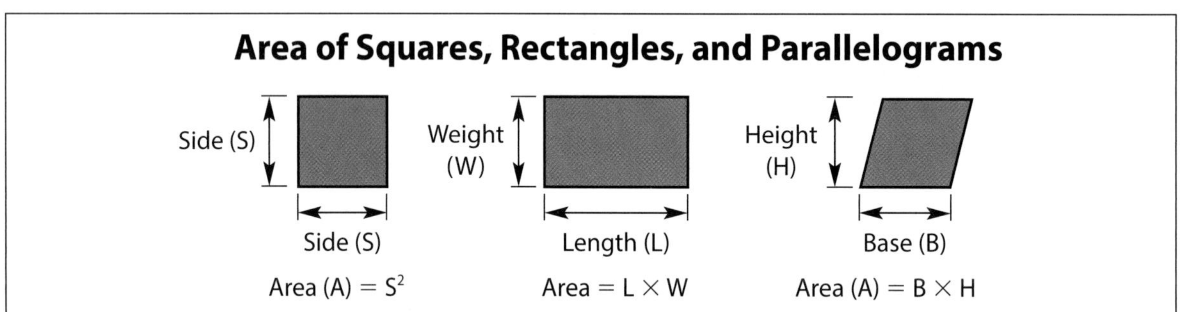

Figure C The areas of squares, rectangles, and parallelograms can be found using the formulas shown.

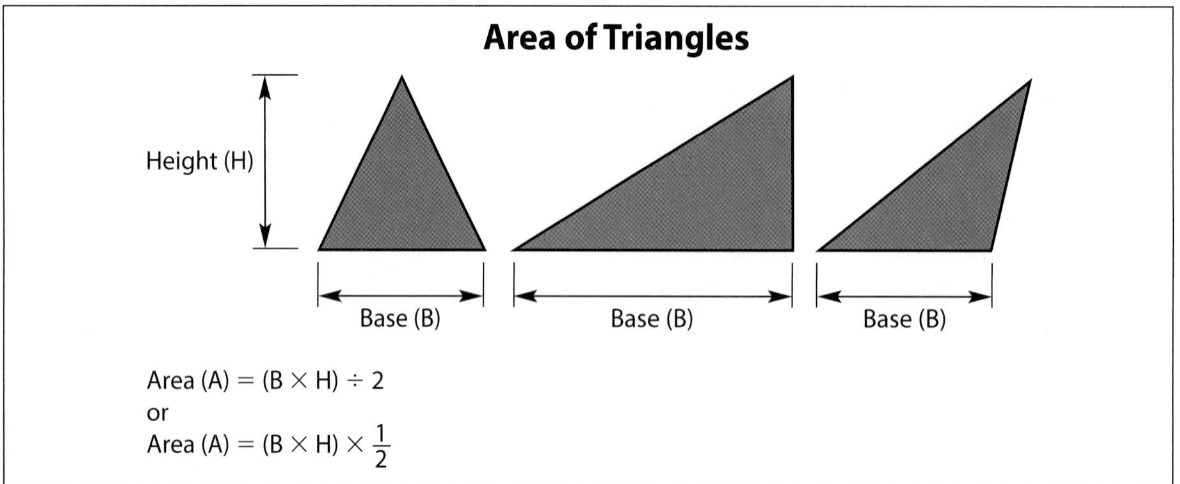

Figure D Triangular areas equal one-half of the base times the height.

Circles and Half-Circles

The *diameter* of a circle is a straight line between two points on the circle and passing through the center of the circle. The *radius* of the circle begins at the center and extends to any point in the circumference of the circle. Multiplying the radius by two gives the diameter (Figure E). The formula for finding the area of a circle is

$A = \pi \times r^2$

In the preceding formula, A = area, π (pi) = 3.1416, and r = radius. The radius is squared (^{2}), meaning the radius is multiplied by itself. The following example shows how to calculate the area of a circle with a radius of 4 in.

Example
$A = \pi \times r^2$
$A = 3.1416 \times 4^2$
$A = 3.1416 \times (4 \times 4)$
$A = 3.1416 \times 16$
$A = 50.2656$ sq. in.

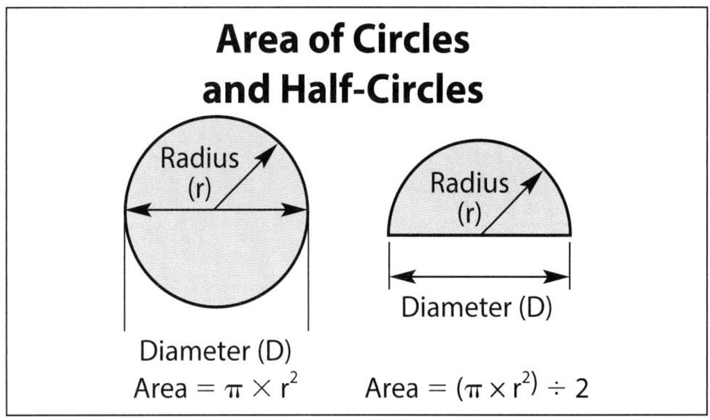

Figure E Use these formulas when calculating the areas of circles and half-circles.

The area of a half-circle is half the area of a circle. Use the following formula to calculate the area of a half-circle:

$A = (\pi \times r^2) \times \frac{1}{2}$
or
$A = (\pi \times r^2) \div 2$

Glossary

A

abilities: Skills you develop and practice. (26)

abrasion: Damage caused by wearing, rubbing, or scraping. (20)

absorbed light: Light that is drawn in by a surface. (11)

abstract form: The physical shape of an object that rearranges or stylizes a recognizable object. (14)

accent lighting: A form of lighting that serves as a highlight. (11)

accessibility: The ability to reach something and use it such as the ability of people with a wide range of disabilities to fully use an entry, especially wheelchair users. (8)

accessories: Items smaller than furnishings that accent the design of a room or area. (22)

acoustical: A material that will reduce or absorb sound. (9)

Adam style: A style of architecture that emerged during the Federal period. The houses were symmetrical with graceful details. A fanlight over the front entrance is characteristic of this style. (5)

adaptability: The ability to change or fit different circumstances such as the ability of an interior to meet the changing accessibility needs of the occupants without excessive cost or inconvenience. (8)

adaptive reuse: A renovation which involves updating an existing building for new and creative use. (5)

adhesives: Substances such as hot glue, rubber cement, and spray mount that stick materials together. (18)

adjacencies: The nearness of two or more rooms or functions. (8)

adjacency matrix: A tool that shows the desired relationship of room and space locations. (17)

adjustable rate mortgage (ARM): Mortgage in which the interest rate is adjusted up or down periodically according to a national interest rate index. (23)

adobe: A building material consisting of sun-dried earth and straw. (1)

advancing: Appearing to move forward. (15)

aesthetics: Beauty. (14)

aging-in-place: A concept that identifies the need for older adults to remain independent and live safely and comfortably in their homes regardless of age, income, or ability level. (3)

agrarian: People who earned their living from the land (farming). (2)

agreement of sale: Document that gives a detailed description of the property and its legal location and all specific terms and conditions of the real estate sale; also known as *offer to purchase, contract of purchase, purchase agreement,* or *sales agreement.* (23)

alcove: A small recessed section of a room. (7)

alignment: The quality of two or more visual elements to be in a straight line or arranged in a parallel manner. (18)

alphabet of lines: Seven different lines commonly used on architectural drawings. (6)

amortize: To pay off. (23)

ampere (amp): Measurement used to determine the amount of electricity passing through a conductor per unit of time. (10)

analogous color harmony: A color harmony created by combining related hues—those next to each other on the color wheel. (15)

anchor bolts: A series of bolts set about six feet apart into the concrete of the foundation walls. (9)

annuals: Flowers that must be replanted yearly. (13)

anthropometry: The scientific study of human body measurements on a comparative basis. (7)

antique: Pieces of furniture made over 100 years ago in the style of the period. (21)

appliance: A household device powered by gas or electricity that serves a specific use or function. (12)

applied design: Design printed onto the surface of the fabric. (19)

appraisal: An expert estimate of the quality and value of the property given by a licensed appraiser. (23)

apprenticeship: Learning a trade under the direction and guidance of an expert worker. (26)

aptitude: A natural talent; an ability to learn something quickly and easily. (26)

Note: The numbers in parentheses following definitions represent the chapter in which the terms appear.

archaeologist: A social scientist who studies ancient cultures by unearthing dwelling places of past civilizations. (1)

architect: A person who designs buildings and supervises their construction. (2)

architectural drawings: Drawings that contain information about the size, shape, and locations of all parts of a house or structure. (6)

Arts and Crafts: A housing style built between 1905 and 1930 that had its roots in the Arts and Crafts movement of the 1880s. Also called *Craftsman*, this style celebrated the use of natural materials worked by hand. (5)

asbestos: A fireproof, cancer-causing mineral that can easily become airborne and inhaled. (24)

asphyxiation: The state of unconsciousness or death resulting from inadequate oxygen or some other breathing obstruction. (24)

assets: Items that a business owns that have value such as cash, physical inventory, buildings, and equipment. (28)

assign: To transfer the entire unexpired portion of the lease to someone else. After the transaction, the original renter is not responsible for the lease. (23)

assisted-living facility: A facility that serves those who need daily living assistance but not constant care; includes meals, laundry service, and household cleanup. (3)

associate's degree: Typically a two-year college degree. (26)

asymmetrical: When objects on one side of the center point differ from the other. (5)

attached houses: Single-family houses/units that hold one household but share (are attached by) common walls with houses on each side; townhouses or row houses are examples. (3)

attitude: How a person thinks or feels about another person or concept, and the manner in which those thoughts and feelings are projected. (27)

autoclaved aerated concrete (AAC): A mixture of sand, fly ash, cement, and water with aluminum powder (an expansion agent) that is cast into a mold and then cut into blocks after a curing process. (9)

B

baby boomers: A large segment of the adult population born from 1946 to 1964 following World War II. (2)

bachelor's degree: A four- or five-year college degree. (26)

balance: The equilibrium among parts of a design. A perception of the way arrangements are seen. (16)

balance sheet: A financial statement showing the assets, liabilities, and equities of a business on a given date. (28)

bandwidth: A term that refers to the capacity for data transfer of an electronic communications system. (4)

bearing wall: A wall that supports some weight from the ceiling or roof of the structure. (9)

beauty: The quality or qualities that give pleasure to the senses. (1)

belvedere: A small room on the roof of a house used as a lookout. (5)

bid: A statement including products, work, and fees for a project. The fee or proposed cost provided by a vendor. (17, 23)

biennials: Flowers that must be replanted every two years. (13)

bill of lading: A receipt listing the goods shipped during a move. (23)

biometrics: The measurement and analysis of an individual by using unique physical characteristics. (24)

blend: When two or more different fibers are combined in making yarn. (19)

blinds: Window treatments with slats that can be tilted, raised and lowered, or moved to the side; often made of wood, metal, plastic, or fabric. (21)

body language: A form of nonverbal communication that includes communicating without words using facial expressions and gestures. (18)

bonded fabric: Two layers of fabric that are permanently joined together with an adhesive. (19)

bonded wood: The application of glue and pressure to several layers of wood. (21)

box nail: Type of nail with a large, flat head. (25)

box springs: A series of coils attached to a base and covered with padding. (21)

breach of contract: When landlords or renters are unable to fulfill promises outlined in a lease. (23)

brick: Block molded from moist clay and hardened with heat. (9)

British thermal unit (Btu): The unit of measurement used to measure the energy usage of gas burners. (12)

buffer zone: A neutral area designed to separate space from noise. (7)

building codes: Standards that establish minimum standards for materials and construction. (2)

Building Information Model (BIM): An approach to building that embraces every stage of the building's lifecycle: design, construction, maintenance, and sometimes demolition. Some software programs utilize the BIM approach. (6)

built-in storage: Storage built into a housing unit including shelves and drawers. (7)

bungalow: A one-and-one-half story house with a low-pitched roof, horizontal shape, and a covered front porch. (5)

business culture: A company's beliefs and actions that indicate how employees and management deal with clients and customers and with each other. (17)

business plan: A document that describes how a business is proposed to be started and operated. (28)

butcher block: A work surface made by fusing a stack of long, thin hardwood strips. (20)

butler's pantry: A service room between the kitchen and dining room. (8)

butt joint: Type of joint that involves gluing or nailing one board flush to another board. (21)

C

Cape Cod: A small, symmetrical, one or one-and-one-half story house with a steep gable roof and side gables. (5)

carbon monoxide: A colorless, odorless, tasteless gas that develops from incomplete burning of fossil fuel or wood. (24)

career: A series of related occupations that show progression in a field of work. (26)

career clusters: Groups of occupations or career specialties that are similar to or related to one another. (26)

case good: Furniture piece in which wood is the primary construction material. (21)

Casual style: Style that emphasizes comfort and informality in furniture. (21)

caustic: Ability to burn the skin through a chemical substance. (25)

ceiling treatment: Coating, covering, or building material applied to the ceiling area. (20)

cellulosic natural fiber: Fiber that comes from the cellulose in plants. (19)

census: An official count of the population by the government. (2)

central heat-pump system: Heating system in which an electric refrigeration unit is used to either heat or cool the house. (10)

ceramic tile: A flat piece of kiln-fired clay coated with a protective glaze. (20)

certificate: A document that verifies completion of coursework or a program. (26)

chain: A business that has many locations and is owned generally by a corporation or partnership. The owner makes all decisions for the chain, which is run by a manager. (28)

change order: A document that outlines the details and costs of unexpected plan changes in a bid. (17)

channel of distribution: The route that a product makes from the producer to the consumer. (28)

circuit: An enclosed loop that forms when electrons follow a path from the source of electricity to the device and back to the source. (10)

circuit breaker: A switch that automatically trips and interrupts the flow of electrical current in the event of an abnormal condition. (10)

circulation: Movements that impact living space. (7)

clad: Covered. (9)

classic: A design style that uses formal architectural elements that have been recognized over time for their enduring design excellence. (5)

clearance space: A measurement term for the amount of space to leave unobstructed around furniture to allow for ease of use and a good traffic pattern. (7)

closeout sale: Sale held when a store moves to another location or is going out of business. (22)

closet auger: Device used to bore through items with a twisting and turning motion to free blocked plumbing or wastewater lines. (25)

closing costs: Payment of fees and charges for settling the legal and financial matters. (23)

cogeneration: An efficient, clean, and reliable approach to generating power and thermal energy from a single fuel source; uses heat that is otherwise waste from conventional power generation to produce thermal energy; also known as *combined heat and power (CHP)*, and total energy. (4)

coil springs: Spiral-shaped springs without padding and covering. (21)

collectible: Highly valued furnishing less than 100 years old, but no longer made. (21)

color: An element or property of light; also an element of design. (15)

color harmony: A pleasing combination of colors based on their respective positions on the color wheel. (15)

color rendering index (CRI): An indicator of how well light from a source will bring out the true color of an item. (11)

color scheme: The combination of colors selected for the design of a room or house. (15)

color spectrum: The full range of all existing colors. (15)

color temperature: The color of a light, rated in kelvin (K), that impacts how items appear in light. (11)

color wheel: A particular circular arrangement of primary, secondary, and tertiary colors; the basis of all color relationships. (15)

combination yarn: Combining two or more different yarns. (19)

combustible: Burnable. (24)

comforter (duvet): Thick bed coverings that consist of two layers of fabric with filling sandwiched between them. (19)

common-use storage: Storage which is used by all who live in a house. (7)

community: A large city, small village, or rural area; part of a region. (3)

compact fluorescent lamp (CFL): A type of fluorescent lamp in which electric current runs through a tube containing argon gas and a small amount of mercury vapor. This generates invisible ultraviolet light that excites a fluorescent (or phosphor) coating on the inside of the tube. When the coating is excited, it emits visible light. (11)

comparison shopping: Comparing the qualities, prices, and services linked to similar items in different stores before making a purchase. (22)

competition-based pricing: Pricing of a product or service based on what prices other businesses are charging. (28)

complement: A hue that is directly opposite another hue on the color wheel. (15)

complementary color harmony: A color harmony made by combining two colors opposite each other on the color wheel; sometimes called contrasting colors. (15)

composting toilet: A self-contained, stand-alone toilet. (10)

computer-aided drafting and design (CADD): Software and hardware that creates designs with a computer; useful in creating housing interiors and house plans. (2)

concisely: Succinctly. (27)

concrete: A strong, durable, hard building material consisting of cement, sand, and gravel with water. (9)

condominium: A type of ownership in which the buyer owns individual living space and also has an undivided interest in the common areas and facilities of a multiunit project. (3)

conducive: Favorable for something to happen. (27)

conductor: An agent (usually a wire) that allows the flow of electricity. (10)

conduit: Metal or plastic pipe that surrounds and protects wires. (10)

conflict: A hostile situation resulting from opposing views. (27)

coniferous: Evergreen trees that do not shed their leaves. (21)

conservation: The process of protecting or saving something. (13)

construction: A design characteristic that includes materials and structure. (14)

construction drawings: Drawings with detailed instructions to the builder to obtain necessary permits and erect the structure. (6)

Contemporary style: A current housing style in which the designs are surprising and often controversial; also refers to a twenty-first century furniture style composed of designs that are the very latest introductions to the market. (5)

contingencies: Terms and conditions. (23)

Contract Administration phase: The phase of the design process in which the designer facilitates the project by issuing bid documents and receiving proposals, product purchasing, performing site visits, and oversees construction, holding project meetings for coordination, and executing project completion. (17)

Contract Documents phase: The phase of the design process in which the designer prepares documents that relate to interior construction. (17)

contractor: A person who contracts, or agrees, to supply certain materials or do certain work for a specific fee. (3)

convection oven: An oven that bakes foods in a stream of heated air. (12)

conventional mortgage: A two-party contract between a borrower and a lender. (23)

cool colors: Blue, green, and violet and the colors near them on the color wheel; also called *receding colors*. (15)

cooperative: A type of ownership in which people buy shares of stock in a nonprofit housing corporation. These shares entitle them to occupy a living unit in the cooperative building. (3)

cooperative education: A program that offers opportunities to work part-time and attend classes part-time as a high school student. (26)

cork: The woody bark tissue of a sustainable plant. (20)

corner block: Small pieces of wood attached between corner boards. (21)

cornice: A molded and projecting horizontal member that crowns architectural elements such as columns. (5)

corporation: An entity formed to represent legal aspects of a business. The entity is separate from the individuals who own the corporation or work for it. (28)

cost-based pricing: Pricing of a product or service based on what it costs to buy or produce the item. (28)

countertop: A durable work surface installed on a base cabinet. (20)

Country style: Style of furniture that traces its origins to the lifestyles of rural areas; also called *Shabby Chic*. (21)

cover message: A message written to a potential employer to introduce yourself and explain your positive attributes, experiences, and accomplishments; also called a *cover letter*. (27)

creativity: The ability to use imaginative skills to make something new. (1)

credit history: A person's past payment records, profile of outstanding debts, and credit score. (23)

criteria matrix: A tool that shows the impact of specific needs on various spaces. (17)

critical path schedule: A plan that identifies each task within the design and implementation process, the time required for each task, task relationships with other tasks, and the effect that completing tasks ahead or behind schedule has on the entire project. (17)

culture: The beliefs, social customs, and trains of a group of people. (2)

curtains: Flat fabric panels that hang to the left and right of a window or may completely cover it. (21)

curved line: Part of a circle or oval; can also take a free-form shape ranging from slightly curvy to very curvy. (14)

cutting for approval (CFA): A small sample of the actual dye lot that is used to confirm the actual color of a treatment. (17)

D

deadbolt locks: Lock bolts that unlock by turning a knob or key without action of a spring. (24)

debt-to-income ratio: Total debt (debt + housing costs) divided by gross income. (23)

decibel (dB): A unit for measuring sound intensity. (24)

deciduous: Trees that lose their leaves once each year. (20)

decision-making process: A method for selecting logical choices from available solutions to make a decision or solve a problem. (3)

declaration of ownership: Document that contains the conditions and restrictions of the sale, ownership, and use of the property within a particular group of condominium units. (23)

decompose: Break down. (10)

decorum: Proper manners and behavior. (27)

deed: Legal document that shows the transfer of title from one person to another. (23)

dehumidifier: An appliance that removes moisture from the air. (12)

demand-based pricing: Pricing of a product or service based on what the customers can pay. (28)

demographics: Statistical facts about the human population. (2)

density: The number of people in a given area. (2)

design: The entire process used to develop a specific project. (14)

Design Development phase: The phase of the design process in which the designer creates, develops, and refines drawings and specifications. (17)

design process: A series of organized phases a designer uses to carry out a project in an orderly manner. (17)

detail view: An enlargement of a construction feature that uses a larger scale than other drawings. (6)

deter: Discourage. (24)

dexterity: Ability to move skillfully. (26)

diagonal lines: Lines that angle between horizontal and vertical lines and communicate different levels of activity, ranging from a low- to high-level of energy. (14)

dictate: Command. (26)

diffused light: Light that scatters over a large area. (11)

direct lighting: Light that shines directly toward an object. (11)

disability: An attribute or functional limitation that interferes with a person's ability to carry out daily living activities. (2)

disinfectant: Cleaning agent that destroys bacteria and viruses. (25)

disseminate: Spread. (26)

dissipate: Dissolve. (9)

dormer: A structure with windows that projects through a sloping roof in the second story. (5)

double-complementary color harmony: A color harmony consisting of two colors and their complements. (15)

double-dowel joint: Type of joint in which glued wooden dowels fit into drilled holes in both pieces of wood. (21)

dovetail joint: Type of joint in which wood pieces are fastened at corner joints. (21)

down payment: A partial payment made up front to secure a purchase. (23)

downspout: A vertical pipe that connects the gutter system to the ground to carry rainwater away from the home's foundation. (9)

draperies: Fabric panels with pleats that cover windows completely or are pulled to the side. (21)

dual-career family: A family in which both adults in a family have employment outside the home. (2)

duct: Large round tube or rectangular boxlike structure that delivers heated (and air-conditioned) air to distant rooms or spaces. (10)

Dutch Colonial: A housing style with a gambrel roof. (5)

E

Early Classical Revival: A Federal style of architecture using classical details of Greek and Italian design; Monticello is an example. (5)

Early English: An architectural style built by English settlers in North America beginning in the early 1600s. (5)

earnest money: A deposit paid to a seller to show seriousness about buying a house. (23)

earth-sheltered: A house that is partially covered with soil. (5)

Earthship housing: A type of self-sufficient housing that uses passive solar and earth-sheltered design along with the use of recycled materials. (4)

Eclectic style: Style of furniture in which furniture and fabrics cross over styles and periods. (21)

elaborate: Explain in further detail. (27)

electric current: The movement of electrons along a conductor; another term for *electricity*. (10)

electric radiant-heating system: Heating system that uses resistance wiring to produce heat in the wire. Wires are placed in the ceiling, floor, or baseboards. (10)

electrical shock: An electric current passing through the human body. (24)

electricity: The movement of electrons along a conductor. (10)

electronic workflow: The process a project team uses to methodically utilize multiple software packages in a particular order for certain tasks to create successful, coordinated, and efficient design documents for a project. (18)

elevation view: Architectural drawing that shows the finished exterior appearance of a given side of the house. (6)

emphasis: A feature that creates a center of interest or focal point in a room. (16)

encapsulating: Enclosing. (24)

enclosure elements: Features that enclose a space such as walls and fences. (13)

Energy Independence and Security Act: A law passed in the United States that established energy efficiency standards for many types of lightbulbs. (11)

ENERGY STAR® label: A label that indicates that a product is at least 10 percent more energy efficient than similar products that meet minimum government energy standards. (12)

EnergyGuide label: A label that states the average yearly energy use and operating cost of an appliance. (12)

engineered quartz: Stone-like countertop material that is a combination of quartz particles with a mixture of binders. (20)

entice: To attract. (22)

entrepreneur: A person who starts or owns a business. (28)

environment: The total of all conditions, objects, places, and people that surround a person. (2)

equity: The money value of a house beyond what is owed on it. The value of the owner's right to the assets of the company. (23, 28)

ergonomics: The design of consumer products and environments to promote user comfort, efficiency, and safety. (22)

escape plan: A plan of action for escaping a home if an emergency such as a fire occurs. (24)

esteem: The respect, admiration, and high regard of others. (1)

ethical behavior: Conforming to accepted standards of fairness and good conduct. (27)

eviction: A legal procedure that forces a renter to leave the property before the rental agreement expires. (23)

expenses: Costs of doing business. (28)

extended warranty: A warranty the consumer can purchase for an extra fee which adds several years to the manufacturer's warranty. (12)

exterior elevation: Architectural drawing that shows the outside views of the house. (6)

extrusion: Process used to form and shape fibers. (19)

F

fabrication: To create or manufacture. (6)

factory-built housing: Housing constructed in a plant and moved to a site. (3)

fad: Style that is popular only for a limited amount of time. (22)

Fair Housing Act: Legislation that gives people with disabilities greater freedom to choose a place to live that meets their needs. (3)

family: Two or more people living together who are related by birth, marriage, or adoption. (1)

faux finish: Decorative wall finish created through the application of paint in different textures and patterns. (20)

Federal: A style of housing with a box-like shape, double-hung sash windows, and is symmetrical with at least two stories. (5)

FHA-insured mortgage: A three-party contract that involves the borrower, a lender, and the Federal Housing Administration (FHA). (23)

fiber: Raw material of which yarns and fabric consist. (19)

fiber optic lighting: A type of heatless light produced by passing an electric current through a cable containing very fine strands of glass. (11)

finance charge: The extra amount charged for the privilege of using credit. It includes interest and other service fees. (23)

finish nail: Type of nail with a very small head. (25)

finishes: Treatment applied to fabrics that improve the appearance, texture, or performance of the fiber, yarn, or fabric. (19)

fireplace insert: A metal device that fits into an existing fireplace and attaches to the chimney liner. (10)

flammable: Material that burns quickly. (19)

flashing: A water-resistant sheet metal used to help keep the roof watertight. (9)

flat springs: Flat, S-shaped springs that may have metal support strips banded across them. (21)

float: Segment of yarn on the surface of the fabric that is woven under one yarn and then glides over four or more yarns. (19)

floor coverings: Surfaces placed over the structural floor. (20)

floor plan: A simplified drawing that shows the size and arrangement of rooms, hallways, doors, windows, and storage areas on one floor of a home. (6)

floor treatment: Flooring materials and floor coverings. (20)

flooring materials: Materials that form the top surface of a floor. (20)

fluorescent light: Light produced in a glass tube by releasing electricity through a mercury vapor to make invisible ultraviolet rays. A coating of fluorescent material on the inside of the glass tube converts these rays into visible light rays. (11)

foam mattress: Mattress made of latex or polyurethane foam. (21)

folk: A design style that originates from the common experiences of a group of people, such as common values and concerns. (5)

foot-candle: A measurement of how much light reaches an object or a surface. One foot-candle is the amount of light a standard candle gives to an object one foot away. (11)

footing: The very bottom of the foundation which supports the rest of the house. (9)

forced warm-air system: Heating system in which the furnace heats and delivers the air to the rooms through supply ducts. (10)

foreclosure: A legal proceeding in which a lending firm takes possession of the property because the borrower fails to make monthly house payments on a timely basis or does not fulfill the agreements related to the loan. (23)

form: The physical shape of objects. (14)

formal balance (symmetry): The identical proportion and arrangement of objects on both sides of a center point; also called *symmetry*. (16)

fossil fuel: Fuel that forms in the earth from plant or animal remains. Fossil fuels include natural gas, propane, gasoline, coal, charcoal, and wood. (10)

foundation: The underlying base of the house. (9)

foundation wall: The walls supporting the load of the house between the footing and the floor. (9)

franchise: A type of business that has an agreement to sell another company's products or services. (28)

free form: The physical shape of an object that is random and flowing. (14)

free market economy: An economic system in which government control is limited and citizens are allowed to privately own and operate businesses. It is also called capitalism or free market enterprise. (28)

freestanding houses: Single-family houses that stand alone without connections to other units. (3)

French Manor: A symmetrically styled home with wings on each side and a Mansard roof on the main part of the house. (5)

French Normandy: Early French homes built by French Huguenot settlers; one-story structures with many narrow door and window openings and steeply pitched roofs. (5)

French Plantation: An architectural style built by French settlers in southern U.S. regions; an adaptation for the French Normandy design. (5)

French Provincial: A usually symmetrical style of housing that has a delicate, dignified appearance. The windows are the dominant part of the design, and the tops of windows break into the eave line. (5)

frost line: The depth to which frost penetrates soil in the area. (9)

fuel cell: An equipment system that produces electricity from the use of chemicals. (4)

full warranty: A warranty that provides the consumer with free repair or replacement of a warranted product or part if any defect occurs during the warranty period. (12)

function: How a design works, including its usefulness, convenience, and organization. (14)

functional zone: Grouping rooms together in an efficient way to organize space. (7)

fuse: A device that includes a wire or strip of fusible metal that melts and interrupts a circuit when an electrical-current overload occurs. (10)

G

gable roof: A roof that comes to a high point in the center and slopes on both sides, forming a triangle. (5)

gambrel roof: A roof with a lower steeper slope and an upper less-steep slope on both of its sides. (5)

Garrison: A style of housing with an overhanging second story which allows extra space on the second floor without widening the foundation. (5)

general lighting: Lighting that provides a uniform level of light throughout a room; also called *ambient lighting.* (11)

generic name: Name that describes a group of fibers with similar chemical compositions. (19)

geometric form: The physical shape of an object that uses squares, rectangles, circles, and other geometric figures. (14)

Georgian: A style of housing with simple exterior lines, a dignified appearance, and is symmetrical. Georgian houses have windows with small panes of glass and either gable or hip roofs. (5)

geothermal energy: Energy that comes from the earth's core. (4)

German: A settler who traveled from the region called Germany today. (5)

gilt: The application of gold or a material that looks like gold onto a surface. (21)

girder: A large horizontal member in the floor that takes the load off joists. (9)

golden mean: The division of a line midway between one-half and one-third of its length, which creates a more pleasing look to the eye than an equal division. (16)

golden rectangle: A rectangle having sides in a ratio of 1:1.618. (16)

golden section: The division of a line or form in such a way that the ratio of the smaller section to the larger section is equal to the ratio of the larger section to the whole. (16)

gradation: The type of rhythm created by a gradual increase or decrease of similar elements of design. (16)

graduated-care facility: A facility that offers more than one level of care ranging from individual apartments with no care, to assisted living. (3)

grain: The direction threads run in a woven fabric. (19)

graywater: Wastewater from washing machines, showers, and sinks that is not contaminated with human waste. (4)

Greek Revival: Architecture style that embraced and carefully duplicated the formal elements found in ancient Greek architecture. The main characteristic is the two-story entry porch. The porch is supported by columns and has a triangular pediment. (5)

gross domestic product (GDP): The value of all goods and services produced within a country during a given time period. (2)

gross income: Income before deductions. (23)

ground cover: Grasses and low-growing plants that cover the ground. (13)

ground fault circuit interrupter (GFCI): Electrical device that stops the flow of an electrical current in a circuit as a safety precaution. (10)

gutter: A horizontal open trough located under the perimeter of the roof to channel away water. (9)

gypsum wallboard: The most common building material used for interior walls and ceilings; also drywall or Sheetrock™. (9)

H

half-timbered: A form of house construction in which the wood frame (beams) of the house actually formed part of the outside wall; brick or plaster was used to fill the spaces between the beams. (5)

hand limitation: Conditions that limit movement and gripping ability. (8)

hardscape: Anything in the landscape other than vegetation and outdoor furniture. (13)

harmony: An agreement among the parts created when the elements of design are used effectively according to the principles of design. (16)

header: Small, built-up beams that carry the load of the structure over door and window openings. (9)

hearing disability: Any degree of hearing loss. (8)

hedge: Something that provides protection. (23)

heterogeneous: A term meaning *dissimilar* or culturally diverse. (3)

hierarchy: A classification or ranking in order. (1)

high mass: A term that refers to a space that is visually crowded or fabrics with a lot of pattern or lines. (14)

hip roof: A roof with sloping ends and sides. (5)

hogan: Navajo buildings made of logs and mud; windows faced west and a single door faced east. (2)

home: Any place a person lives. (1)

home automation: A way to manage and control energy use. (4)

home generators: Back-up generators. (10)

home inspection: Evaluation of the construction and present condition of a house. (23)

homogenous: A term meaning *similar*. Some neighborhoods have residents of similar age, ethnic background, income level, or occupation. (3)

honing: Developing and refining. (27)

horizon line: A line indicating the eye level of the viewer on a drawing. (18)

horizontal lines: Lines that are parallel to the ground and direct your eyes across a space. (14)

house: Any building that serves as living quarters for one or more families. (1)

household: One or more people who occupy a dwelling, both family and nonfamily members. (1)

housing: Any dwelling that provides shelter. (1)

housing market: The transfer of dwellings from producers to consumers. (2)

housing-to-income ratio: Total housing costs divided by gross income. (23)

hue: The name of a color in its purest form with no added black, gray, or white. (15)

human resources: Resources available from people including ability, knowledge, attitude, energy, and health. (3)

humidifier: An appliance that adds moisture to the air. (12)

HVAC: Heating, ventilating, and air-conditioning. (10)

hydronic heating system: Heating system that uses circulating hot water systems. (10)

hypoallergenic: Unlikely to cause an allergic reaction. (19)

I

imperative: Necessary. (6, 18)

impermeable: Material that does not allow substances to pass through. (10)

impervious: Nonporous. (20)

implement: To put thoughts into action. (3)

incandescent light: Light produced when electric current passes through a fine tungsten filament inside a bulb. (11)

income statement: A financial statement over a given period of time of a business showing the results of the business (profit and loss); also called a *profit and loss (P&L) statement*. (28)

indirect lighting: Light directed toward a surface that reflects the light into the room. (11)

induction cooktop: A cooktop that uses a magnetic field below a glass-ceramic surface to generate heat in the bottom of magnetic cookware. (12)

Industrial Revolution: A rapid major change in the economy marked by the general introduction of power-driven machinery or the prevailing types and uses of such machines. (2)

influx: Inward flow. (21)

informal balance (asymmetrical): The arrangement of different but equivalent objects on each side of a center point; also called *asymmetrical balance*. (16)

infrastructure: The underlying foundation or basic framework; the term often refers to installation of the sewer, water, gas, and electrical lines to make housing livable. (2)

innate: Belonging to the essential nature of something, such as psychological needs. (8)

innerspring mattress: Mattress that contains a series of springs covered with padding. (21)

installment buying: The process of buying something by making a series of payments during a given length of time. (23)

insulated concrete forms (ICF): Rigid polystyrene foam forms with internal plastic for ties that stack together like building blocks. The forms are reinforced with steel. Concrete is poured into the open middle forming a reinforced concrete wall with insulation on the face. (9)

insulation: Material that restricts the flow of air between a house's interior and the outdoors. (10)

integrate: Join. (10)

intensity: A term that refers to the brightness or dullness of a hue. (15)

intercede: Intervene. (27)

interest: The price you pay for the use of someone else's money. (23)

International style: A modern style of architecture and furniture design that began in the 1900s, influenced strongly by the Bauhaus, the German state school of design. (5)

internship: An arrangement with an educational institution whereby a student is supervised while working with a more experienced jobholder. (26)

inventory: A complete listing of property or belongings of a person or company, such as existing furniture, fixtures, or equipment. (18)

isometric drawing: A drawing that illustrates a space or product in three dimensions (width + length + height) at the same time, resulting in an overhead view showing depth perception at a 30-degree angle. (6)

J

job shadowing: The process of observing a person in the workplace to learn more about his or her job and its requirements. (26)

joint venture: A business option in which an established business joins with one or more companies. All companies share in the initial investment, profits, and losses. (28)

joist: Lightweight horizontal support member. (9)

jurisdiction: Governing authority. (17)

K

kelvin (K): The base unit of temperature used to measure light temperature. (11)

keystoning: The effect by which a picture seems to get larger at the top and/or bottom. (18)

kilowatt hour (kWh): A unit of measure to determine energy use per hour. (12)

kit house: A type of factory-built house that is shipped as unassembled parts or as a finished shell from the factory. (3)

knitting: The looping of yarns together. (19)

L

labor cost percentage: The ratio of how much money is received in sales for every dollar spent on wages. (28)

laminate: Product made by uniting one or more different layers, usually a decorative surface, to a sturdy core. (20)

landing space: The area on either side or across from an appliance or other functional kitchen piece that serves as a space to set cooking tools, hot food, or oversized items. (8)

landscape: The outdoor living space. (13)

landscape architect: A professional trained to create designs that function well and are aesthetically pleasing. (13)

landscape zones: The ground around a building that is divided into three areas—public zones, private zones, and service zones. (13)

landscaping: Altering the topography and adding decorative plantings to change the appearance of a site. (3)

lead paint: A term that refers to lead-based paint, which was a common form of paint manufactured before 1978 that contained lead. (24)

leadership: The ability to guide and motivate others to complete tasks or achieve goals. (27)

lease: A legal document spelling out the conditions of the rental agreement. (23)

lessee: Person who agrees to pay rent for a place to live; also called *renter.* (23)

lessor: Property owner; also called *landlord.* (23)

letter of agreement: A document that spells out the scope of project services and the responsibilities of the interior designer and the client for a project. (17)

liabilities: Debts of a business. (28)

liaison: Connecting agent. (17)

license: A document that certifies that an individual has undergone the proper training to perform a profession. (26)

life cycle: A series of stages through which an individual or family passes during its lifetime. (1)

lifelong learning: Continually updating your knowledge and skills. (27)

lifestyle: A living pattern or way of life. (1)

light-emitting diode (LED): Extremely long-lasting bulbs composed of crystals on silicon chips (about the size of a grain of salt) that produce light when a low electric current passes through them. (11)

limited warranty: A warranty that provides service, repairs, and replacements only under certain conditions. (12)

line: The most basic element of design that forms when two dots are connected. (14)

log cabin: Originally a one-room, rectangular house made from squared-off logs with notches on the top and bottom of each end. (5)

loss: When a company's expenses are greater than its revenues. (28)

loss leader: Item priced well below normal cost to entice people into a store to buy that item plus items not on sale. (22)

low mass: A term that refers to a space that is simple and sparse. (14)

lumen: A measurement of the amount of light a bulb produces. (11)

M

Mansard roof: A variation of the gambrel roof designed by a French architect named Mansard. The low slopes of the roof encircle the house, and dormers often project from the steeply pitched part of the roof. (5)

manufactured fiber: Fiber made from wood cellulose, oil products, and other chemicals. (19)

manufactured housing: Single-family homes completely built in a controlled factory environment and moved with attached wheels to a lot or housing site; after 1976. (3)

manufactured landscape elements: Landscape components that are not found in the natural environment. (13)

market survey: A research tool used to gather information about a product or service and the marketplace. (28)

marketing presentation: A presentation (like a job interview or portfolio review) in which a designer is selling the quality of future services to a potential client, clarifying experience and abilities. (18)

masonry: A hard building material, such as brick, concrete block, stucco, or natural stone, bonded together with mortar. (9)

mass: The amount of pattern or objects in a space. It also refers to how crowded or empty a space appears. (14)

master's degree: An advanced college degree often sought by people wanting to specialize in a particular area. (26)

median: The mathematical average that divides a group of numbers into two parts with half the numbers above the median and half the numbers below the median. (2)

memo sample: A sample that is large enough to show an entire pattern repeat. (17)

memory foam mattress: Type of mattress that molds to the body during sleep, but quickly returns to its original shape once a person gets out of bed. (21)

mentor: Someone with greater experience and knowledge who guides you in your career. (26)

meter: Device that monitors electrical usage. (10)

micro-adjacencies: The nearness of two or more tasks or tools within a room. (8)

microturbine: A small turbine engine that produces electricity. (4)

microwave oven: An appliance that cooks food with high-frequency energy waves. (12)

minimum property standards (MPS): Standards set by the Federal Housing Administration (FHA) that require the systems and property construction meet durability standards and building codes. (3)

mobile homes: Single-family homes completely built in a controlled factory environment and moved with attached wheels to a lot or housing site; before 1976. (3)

mobility limitation: Conditions that make it difficult for a person to walk from one location to another. (8)

model: A three-dimensional miniature of a design structure. (6)

Modern style: Style of housing developed in the United States from the early 1900s into the 1980s; also refers to the twenty-first century furniture style that uses simpler lines and abstract forms to result in pieces that can be mass produced for automated machinery. (5)

modular housing: Housing that is factory-built in a coordinated series of modules. (3)

moisture barrier: A sheet of polyethylene plastic that is spread across the filler before placing plumbing and heating systems and pouring the slab for a slab-on-grade house. (9)

mold: A fungus that grows on damp or decaying matter. (24)

monochromatic color harmony: The simplest color harmony based on tints and shades of a single hue. (15)

mortgage: A pledge of property that a borrower gives to a lender as security for a loan with which to buy the property. (23)

mortise-and-tenon joint: Type of joint in which a glued tenon fits tightly into the mortise, or hole. (21)

multifamily house: A structure that provides housing for more than one household; each household within the dwelling has its own distinct living quarters. (3)

multipurpose furniture: Furniture that serves more than one purpose. (22)

multipurpose room: A room of a house that provides space for such activities as reading, studying, watching TV, listening to music, or working on hobbies. (7)

N

nap: A layer of fiber ends that stand up from the surface of the fabric. (19)

natural landscape elements: Landscape components that are found in the natural environment. (13)

natural stone: Hardened earth or mineral matter. (9)

near environment: A small and distinct part of the total environment in which people live. (1)

needle-punching: Process of interlocking fibers by using felting needles. (19)

needs: The basic requirements that people must fill to live. (1)

negotiation: The process of agreeing to an issue that requires all parties to give and take. (27)

neighborhood: A group of houses and people; part of a community. (3)

networking: The exchange of information or services among individuals or groups. (26)

neutral color harmony: A color harmony using combinations of black, gray, and white. Brown, tan, and beige can also be used. (15)

New England: A region of North America that now includes the states of Maine, New Hampshire, Vermont, Connecticut, and Rhode Island. (5)

new town: An urban development consisting of a small to midsize city with a broad range of housing and planned industrial, commercial, educational, and recreational facilities. (2)

new urbanism: Communities that are planned to encourage pedestrian traffic, place more emphasis on the environment, and are sustainable—producing most of the energy needed and/or using minimum natural resources. (2)

noise pollution: Unwanted sound that spreads through the environment. (24)

nonbearing wall: A wall that does not support any weight from the structure beyond its own weight. (9)

noncombustible: Cannot be easily burned. (9)

nonhuman resources: Resources that are not directly supplied by people including money, property, time, and community resources. (3)

nonrenewable energy sources: Sources of energy that do not replenish themselves and are depleting in supply. (4)

nonstructural lighting: Lighting that is not a structural part of the house. (11)

nonverbal communication: The transmission of ideas without the use of words; involves *body language*. Also the sending and receiving of messages without the use of words. (14, 27)

notations: Characters, symbols, or abbreviated expressions used in math to express technical facts or quantities. (7)

nuisance: Annoyance. (24)

O

occupation: Paid employment that involves handling one or more jobs. (26)

off-gassing: The release of fumes and chemicals in the air as a result of the treatment of a product, such as carpeting. (4)

opaque: Not see-through; does not let light through. (19)

opposition: The type of rhythm in which lines meet to form right angles. (16)

optimistic: The ability to anticipate the best possible outcome. (28)

oral communication: The transmission of ideas through speech. In design, examples include verbal presentations and conversations on the phone or in person. (18)

organic matter: Compost or mulch that replenishes the soil. (13)

orientation: Placing a structure on a site in consideration of the location of the sun, prevailing winds, water sources, and scenic view. (3)

oriented strand board (OSB): A sheet formed by layering wood chips and fiber in a crosshatch pattern and gluing them together. (9)

outsource: Hire out. (17)

overcurrent protection device: Device that protects each circuit by stopping the excessive flow of electrical current in the circuit. (10)

owner-built housing: Housing built by the owner who has time, energy, and building skills, although a contractor may be hired to put up the shell of the house. (3)

P

paint: A mixture of pigment and liquid that thinly coats and covers a surface. (20)

Palladian window: A window with a large center section and two side sections, usually arched. (5)

paneling: A building material that is usually made of plywood but can be produced from synthetic material. (9)

panelized housing: Housing that involves panels of walls, floors, ceilings, or roofs that people can order separately and have assembled at the housing site. (3)

partnership: A business owned by two or more people, and usually no more than a small group. Partners share responsibilities and costs, make joint decisions, and share profits. (28)

pattern bond: The pattern formed by masonry units and the mortar joints on the face of the wall. (9)

penetrate: To enter or go through. (9)

pent roof: A small roof ledge between the first and second floors of a house. (5)

perennials: Flowers that last for many years without replanting. (13)

peril: Danger. (23)

permit: A form of documentation proving permission has been received from a local authority to build or renovate a building. (18)

photovoltaic (PV) system: An active solar system that converts sunlight into electricity. (4)

photovoltaic shingles: Shingles that convert sunlight into electricity for a facility. (4)

physical inventory: A count of the number of product items that a business has available. (28)

physical limitation: Conditions such as mobility, vision, and hearing disabilities that limit how people can use or interact with the living environment. (8)

physical needs: The most basic human needs of shelter, food, water, and rest. (1)

physical neighborhood: The land and buildings that make up a neighborhood. (3)

pigment: A coloring agent used in paint and printed materials. (15)

pilaster: A decorative crown over the top of a front door with flattened columns along each side. (5)

plan view: A view from the top of a building, as with an imaginary glass box. (6)

planned community: The design and implementation of a community, city, or neighborhood with a master plan. (2)

planned development: A master plan showing how to use land for various purposes. (2)

planned neighborhood: An area with zoning restrictions. Developers organize the subdivision and make decisions about lot size and layout of individual lots before constructing dwellings. (3)

plaster: A paste used for coating walls and ceilings that hardens as it dries. (9)

plastic wallboard: A building material with a durable decorative finish that contractors commonly used for interior walls. (9)

pliability: Ability to bend and twist. (21)

plumbing plunger: Device that creates a suction motion to clear a blocked drain. (25)

plywood sheet: Layers of thin wood veneers that have been glued and pressed together. (9)

pocket development: Planned community on a smaller scale that is more focused on the small neighborhood concept; small land areas, or "pockets" with small homes placed close together. (2)

points: Fees paid to the lender for the loan. (23)

polymer: A chemical compound that forms from the union of small molecules that contain repeating structural units. (19)

porcelain tile: The highest quality ceramic tile made; the tile has a white or light clay-colored body that is kiln-fired at a very high temperature. (20)

porous: Something that allows substances to pass through. (9)

portfolio: A collection of items that show your special achievements and accomplishments. (27)

portico: An open space covered with a roof supported by columns. (5)

Postmodern: An exterior style that deviates from strict rules in architecture, often showing different angles and varying styles. (5)

powerless language: Words that do not add depth or content to presentations and explanations. Examples include "umm, like, okay, and whatnot" and vague or simple terms such as "nice, good, and pretty." (18)

pragmatics: Dealing realistically with things that cannot change rather than using theories and artistic solutions. (8)

Prairie style: A housing style designed by Frank Lloyd Wright with strong horizontal lines, low-pitched roofs, and overhanging eaves. (5)

preapproval: Designation in which the home buyer has gone through a preliminary approval process in which the lender verifies employment and checks tax records, bank references, and the borrower's credit history. (23)

precautions: Preventive actions. (24)

precut housing: Housing components that are cut to exact size in the factory and delivered to the building site. (3)

presentation drawings: Refined drawings or renderings to use for publication or for showing the design to the client. (6)

pressed wood: Wood panel made of shavings, veneer scraps, chips, and other small pieces of wood. (21)

pressure preservative treated (PT): A treatment in which chemical preservatives are forced into the cellular structure of wood under pressure. (9)

primary colors: The colors of yellow, red, and blue from which all other colors are made. (15)

primary data (qualitative): Qualitative data gathered from observations, surveys, or interviews with potential customers. (28)

principal: The original sum borrowed. (23)

principal designer: The interior designer who finalizes all design decisions on a project. (26)

print: A copy of a drawing. (6)

prioritize: To rank goals in order of importance. (22)

private area: An area of the house, typically bedrooms and bathrooms, that offers the best setting for rest and relaxation. Generally used for sleeping, resting, grooming, and dressing. (7)

private mortgage insurance (PMI): Insurance that protects the lender if the borrower fails to pay. (23)

private zone: The part of the site hidden from public view that provides space for recreation and relaxation. (3)

product life cycle: Phases that describe the life cycle of a product from the introduction, growth, maturity, and decline. (28)

product trends: Trends related directly to the product itself that can make it attractive in the market place. (28)

productivity apps: Apps with features such as scheduling functions, to-do lists, and task boards. (27)

profile: A concise biographical sketch that portrays the key characteristics about the client. (17)

profit: The difference between the expenses and revenues of a business. (28)

profit margin: A ratio that is a comparison of the company's business income (profit or loss) to its sales. (28)

Programming phase: The phase of the design process that includes identifying client objectives and requirements, gathering information from the client, developing a client contract and overall budget, and preparing a broad concept statement to guide the actual design. (17)

project presentation: A presentation that educates the clients to obtain their approval on design choices. (18)

proportion: The ratio of one part to another part or of one part to the whole. (16)

prospective: Probably; likely. (9)

protein natural fiber: Fiber that comes from animal sources. (19)

proximity: Closeness. The nearness or closeness of two or more items or people. (7, 18)

psychological needs: Needs relating to the mind and feelings that people must meet to live a satisfying life. (1)

public zone: The part of the site people can see from the street or road and is usually in front of the house. (3)

punch list: A document the designer creates during a walk-through that lists unfinished tasks, missing items or damaged goods, or subpar craftsmanship that a contractor must complete prior to final payment. (17)

punctual: Prompt and on time. (27)

Q

qualitative needs: Characteristics (quality needs) of an object or interior that cannot be measured such as the needs for privacy, security, and control. (8)

quality of life: The degree of satisfaction a person obtains from life including satisfying surroundings. (1)

quantitative information: Characteristics of objects or interiors that can be measured with numbers such as size, quantity, or temperature. (8)

R

radiation: The type of rhythm in which lines flow outward from a central point as in a wagon wheel. (16)

radon: A natural radioactive gas that occurs in high concentrations in soils and rocks containing uranium and some other minerals. (24)

rafter: A beam (or series of beams) that supports the roof. (9)

Ranch: A style of housing characterized by a one-story house structure that may have a basement; often has an asymmetrical façade and entry and a central but not elaborate fireplace. Two-story versions are available. Other variations include the raised ranch or split-entry. (5)

realistic form: The physical shape of an object that communicates a lifelike, traditional, and familiar feeling. (14)

receding: Appearing to make objects seem smaller and walls seem farther away than they really are. (15)

reclamation: Getting back; reclaiming. (20)

rectilinear: Made with straight lines. (20)

recycle: To adapt something to a new use. (22)

redecorate: To change or update a decorating scheme. (25)

reference: An individual who will provide important information about you regarding your traits, skills, and abilities to a prospective employer. (27)

reflected light: Light that bounces off surfaces. (11)

region: A specific part of the world, country, or state in which you live. (3)

remodeling: Changing a structure, such as adding a wall or room. (25)

remotely: From a distance. (10)

rendering: A presentation drawing—usually with color, texture, and shadows—that shows a realistic view of the completed house. (6)

renew: To give something a new look. (22)

renewable energy sources: Sources of energy that replenish themselves regularly. (4)

repetition: Rhythm that forms by repeating an element of design. (16)

reproduction: Copy of an antique original. (21)

repurpose: To change the original use of an object to another use that meets an expanded or new need. (22)

resiliency: Ability to return to the original size and shape. (19)

resilient floor covering: Floor treatments that are generally nonabsorbent, durable, easy to maintain, and fairly inexpensive. (20)

resources: Objects, qualities, and personal strengths that people can use to reach a goal. (2)

restore: To return something to its original state as much as possible. (22)

résumé: A brief outline of your education, work experience, and other qualifications for work. (27)

retainer: An upfront fee the client pays to engage the services of a designer. (17)

revenues (sales): Money from customer purchases of products or services. (28)

reverse mortgage: A type of mortgage that enables older adults to convert the money tied up in their houses into income. (3)

rhythm: A sense of movement that smoothly leads the eyes from one area to another in a design; the cause of an organized pattern. (16)

ridge board: The horizontal member at which the two slopes of the roof meet. (9)

rigid: Stiff; not flexible. (9)

roles: Patterns of behavior that people display at home, in the workplace, or in the community. (1)

row houses: Continuous groups of dwellings linked by common sidewalls. (2)

R-value: Measurement of how well a material insulates. (10)

S

Saltbox: A variation of the Cape Cod style of housing created by adding a lean-to addition to the rear of the house. (5)

scale floor plan: A reduced-size drawing that is directly proportional to the actual size and shape of a space or room. (7)

scale: The relative size of an object in relation to other objects. (16)

Scandinavian: An immigrant from Sweden, Finland, Norway, or Denmark. (5)

schedule: An organized chart of detailed notes in a ruled enclosure. (6)

Schematic Design phase: The phase of the design process in which the designer creates diagrams (matrices and bubble/stacking/block diagrams) to develop solutions, creates conceptual space plans, and selects initial furniture and finishes. (17)

schematic drawings: Freehand sketches of a proposed plan the designer uses in refining the design. (6)

schematic drawings: Quick, freehand sketches and drawings to show space arrangements for the project. (17)

seasonal sale: Sale held at the end of a selling season to eliminate old stock and make room for new items. (22)

secondary colors: The colors of orange, green, and violet; made by mixing equal amounts of two primary colors. (15)

secondary data (quantitative): Quantitative data from sources other than direct interaction with consumers that includes the use of numbers or data that can be measured such as size or quantity. (28)

section view: A view taken from an imaginary slice through a part of a building such as a wall. (6)

security deposit: A payment that ensures the owner against financial loss caused by the renter. (23)

self-actualization: Developing into full potential as a person and doing what he or she does best. (1)

self-cleaning oven: An oven that operates at extremely high temperatures to burn away spatters and spills. (12)

self-esteem: Awareness and appreciation of worth. (1)

self-expression: Showing your true personality and taste. (1)

self-motivation: An inner urge to perform well. (27)

semiskilled labor: Workers who have some experience and/or technical training. (26)

sensory design: The application of design that affects the senses of sight, hearing, smell, and touch. (16)

septic tank: Underground tank that decomposes waste through the action of bacteria. (10)

service drop: Area that contains the wires connecting the utility pole transformer to the point of entry to the customer's house. (10)

service entrance panel: Large metal box that receives power from the electric company's service drop or service lateral. (10)

service zone: The part of the site that household members use for necessary activities; includes sidewalks, driveways, and storage areas. (3)

shade: The addition of black to a hue to make it a darker value. (15)

shades: An application that blocks unwanted light, such as intense sunlight in the afternoon or streetlight at night; includes roller shades, Roman shades; balloon shades, and pleated shades. (21)

shareholder: A person who buys stock in a company and therefore has partial ownership of the company. (28)

shingle: Thin pieces of building material that lay in overlapping rows on roofs. (9)

short circuit: An undesirable current path that allows the electrical current to bypass the load of the circuit. (25)

shutters: Vertical panels that are hinged together to open and close much like a folding door; constructed of wood or synthetic materials. (21)

siding: The material forming the exposed surface of the outside walls of a house. (9)

sill plate: A piece of lumber bolted to the foundation wall with anchor bolts. (9)

single-family house: A dwelling that houses one family. (3)

site: A piece of land on which a dwelling or structure is built. (3)

site-built house: Housing built on a lot, piece by piece on a foundation, using few factory-built structural components. (3)

skilled labor: Workers who have successfully completed a formal training program beyond high school. (26)

smoke detector: A device that sends out a loud warning signal if a fire starts. (24)

social area: An area of the house that provides space for daily living, entertaining, and recreation. Typically includes entrances, dining rooms, living rooms, and family rooms. (7)

soft floor covering: Floor treatments that consist of manufactured or natural fibers, such as carpets and rugs. (20)

soil conservation: Improving and maintaining the soil. (13)

soil stack: The main vertical pipe that receives waste matter from all plumbing fixtures. (10)

sole proprietorship: A business owned and operated by one person. (28)

solid wood: Term that means all exposed parts of a piece of furniture are made of whole pieces of wood. (21)

Southern Colonial: A style of housing that features a large two- or three-story brick or frame house of symmetrical design. (5)

space: A term that refers to the area around a form. (14)

space planning: The process of placing furnishings for a well-functioning and visually pleasing area. (7)

Spanish: A housing style from the south and southwest consisting of asymmetrical design with low-pitched red tile roofs, enclosed patios, wrought iron exterior décor, and stucco walls. (5)

Spanish Revival: A modern style of home built with stucco emulating features of the earlier Spanish style home. (5)

specifications: Detailed documents that tell the types and quality of materials to use and give directions for their use. (6)

spinneret: A small nozzle with tiny holes, much like a showerhead, used to extrude and solidify manufactured fibers. (19)

split-complementary color harmony: A color harmony consisting of one hue with the two hues adjacent to its complement. (15)

square footage: A measurement of house size that refers to the amount of living space in the home. (6)

staggering: Arranging plantings in various zigzags or alternations. (13)

stark: Plain, empty. (21)

statement of cash flow (SCF): A financial statement that shows how cash came into the company and how it was used by the business. (28)

stenciling: Applying paint by using a cutout form to outline a design or lettering. (20)

storyboard: A board that contains quick, small-scale sketches of the layout and components of pages within a portfolio or presentation typically in sequential order. (18)

structural design: The pattern produced by varying the yarns in a woven or knitted fabric. (19)

structural light fixture: A light fixture that is permanently built into a home. (11)

stucco: A type of plaster applied to the exterior walls of a house. (5)

stud: Vertical 2-inch by 4-inch or 2-inch by 6-inch framing member; length varies. (9)

subdivision: The division of a tract of land into two or more parcels that make it easier to sell and develop. (2)

subdued: Lacking vitality, intensity, or strength. (16)

subflooring: A covering of plywood or oriented strand board (OSB) sheets directly glued and nailed to the floor joists. (9)

sublet: The transfer of part interest in the property to someone else; both parties are responsible to the landlord for all terms of the lease. (23)

substandard: Housing is not up to the quality living standards prescribed by law that are best for people. (2)

Sunbelt: Southern and southwestern regions of the United States. (2)

sunroom: A structure that uses energy from sunlight to heat a living space; also called a *garden room*. (13)

sustainability: A term that describes human interaction with the resources in the earth's environment, including the air, water, forests, and other materials. (4)

sustainable design: A term that refers to incorporating sustainability in the built environment through use of building materials and furnishing interiors, operation of living spaces, and practices in the manufacture of materials and production of buildings. (4)

symbology: The interpretation of symbols or a system of symbols. (6)

symbols: Icons used on architectural drawings to represent plumbing and electrical fixtures, doors, windows, furniture, and other common objects in a house or structure. (6)

symmetrical: When objects on both sides of a center point or line are identical. (5)

synthetic: A manufactured material that imitates or replaces another substance. (9)

system: An interacting or interdependent group of items forming a unified whole. (10)

T

tactile texture: The way a surface feels to the touch. (14)

tangible: Capable of being precisely identified. (8)

tanning: Process that requires the use of a complex acid compound, or tannin, which causes leather to become soft and resistant to stains, fading, and cracking. (19)

target market: The specific group of people who need a product or service. (28)

task lighting: Lighting that is used in areas where specific activities require more light. (11)

team: A small group of people collaborating together for a common purpose. (27)

technology: The practical application of knowledge. (2)

telecommuting: Working at home or another site through an electronic link to a computer network at a central office. (2)

teleworking: The use of technology in various locations to avoid the need for the worker to travel to work. (2)

template: A small piece of paper or plastic scaled to the actual dimensions of the furniture piece it represents. (7)

tenement houses: Early apartments built before housing regulations existed. (2)

termites: Pale-colored insects that feed on wood, particularly wood that is holding moisture. (25)

tertiary colors: Colors made by mixing equal amounts of a primary color with a secondary color adjacent to it on the color wheel; also called *intermediate colors.* (15)

textiles: Flexible materials made of thin films or of fibers, yarns, or fabrics. (19)

texture: A term that refers to the way a surface feels or appears to feel. (14)

thermostat: A device for regulating room temperature. (10)

three-dimensional (3-D) printing: A type of printing process through which a three-dimensional object is produced without the use of molds, dies, or machining; also called *additive manufacturing.* (2)

Tidewater South: An architectural style built by early English settlers in the southern coastal regions of what is now the United States. (5)

tile: A flat piece of kiln-fired clay or natural stone that is available in a wide range of sizes, colors, finishes, and patterns. (20)

tint: The addition of white to a hue to make it a lighter value. (15)

title: A document that gives proof of the rights of ownership and possession of a particular property. (23)

title block: A box of information on drawings that at a minimum includes the project title, author, drawing name, scale, and date. (18)

tone: The result of adding gray to a hue to soften its value. (15)

tongue-and-groove joint: Type of joint formed by fitting a tongue cut on one edge of a board into a matching groove cut on the edge of another board. (21)

topography: The arrangement of physical features of the land, and its climate that influence the location and design of dwellings. (2)

toxic: Poisonous. (24)

tract homes: Groups of similarly designed houses built on a tract of land. (2)

trade name: Name a company uses to identify the specific fibers the company develops. (19)

traditional: Houses that reflect experiences and traditions of past eras. (5)

traffic patterns: The paths occupants follow when moving easily within a room, from room to room, or to the outdoors. (7)

transferrable skills: Skills that can help you succeed in whatever job you choose. (27)

transition: The type of rhythm in which curved and horizontal lines carry the eyes from one part of an object or room to another part. (16)

translucent: Clear, allowing light to pass through. (7)

trap: A bend in the pipe within or just below a plumbing fixture that catches and holds a quantity of water. (10)

triadic color harmony: A color harmony created by combining any three colors that are equally distant from each other on a standard color wheel. (15)

truss rafter: A group of members forming a rigid-triangular framework for the roof. (9)

Tudor: A style of housing with exposed heavy timbers and filled with stucco between the timbers. (5)

tufted: Process that involves looping yarns into a backing material and securing them to the backing with an adhesive. (19)

tungsten-halogen (quartz) light: A form of incandescent lighting in which halogen gas combines with tungsten molecules to activate a filament inside a quartz enclosure. (11)

U

unassembled furniture: Furniture sold in parts that require assembly. (22)

unity: Occurs when all parts of a design relate to one design idea. (16)

universal design (UD): A design concept that focuses on making living environments, and the products used to create them, without special adaptations. Such living environments meet the needs of all people when they are built so they will not require future alterations. (8)

unskilled labor: Workers who fill entry-level jobs that require almost no previous knowledge or experience. (26)

upholstery: The fabric, padding, or other material manufacturers use to make a soft covering for furniture. (19)

urban sprawl: The spreading of urban developments such as housing and shopping centers on undeveloped land near a city. (2)

utilitarian: Something that is useful or designed for a purpose. (22)

V

VA-guaranteed mortgage: A three-party loan involving the borrower (who is a veteran of the U.S. Armed Forces), a lending firm, and the Veterans Administration (VA). (23)

value: The relative lightness or darkness of a hue. (15)

values: Strong beliefs or ideas about what is important. (1)

vanishing point: The point at which parallel lines converge. (18)

vellum: A strong, translucent, cream-colored paper. (18)

veneer: A thin layer of material such as wood. (9)

veneer wall: A nonsupporting wall tied to the wall frame that is covered with sheathing. (9)

veneered wood: Three, five, or seven thin layers of wood bonded to one another, to a solid wood core, or to a pressed wood core. (21)

vent stack: A vertical pipe that extends through the roof to release gases and odors outdoors. (10)

ventilation: Air circulation. (24)

verbal communication: Form of communication involving words, including speaking, listening, and writing. (27)

verbal communication: The transmission of ideas through words. (14)

vertical lines: Lines that are perpendicular to the ground and cause your eyes to move up and down. (14)

Victorian: A style of housing named after Queen Victoria of England that has an abundance of decorative trim. Victorian styles include Italianate, Gothic Revival, American Second Empire, Stick, Richardsonian Romanesque, Eastlake Victorian, and Queen Anne. (5)

vision disability: Any degree of vision loss. (8)

visual communication: The transmission of ideas through a medium that people can see or view. In design, examples include schematic plans, construction drawings, renderings, and models, finish boards, or a combination of all. (18)

visual imagery: A type of nonverbal communication. It is the language of sight and communicates a certain personality, feeling, or mood. (14)

visual texture: Texture that you see, but cannot feel. (14)

visual weight: The perception that an object weighs more or less than it really does. (16)

volatile organic compounds (VOCs): Chemicals that evaporate into the air and can cause breathing difficulties and health problems. (4)

voltage: A measure of the pressure used to push the electrical current along a conductor. (10)

W

wale: Diagonal rib or cord pattern in fabric. (19)

wall covering: Decorative paper or vinyl applied to a wall with a special paste. (20)

wall treatment: A surface treatment that is applied to an interior wall. (20)

warm colors: Red, yellow, and orange and the colors near them on the color wheel; also called *advancing colors*. (15)

warp yarn: Yarn that runs in the lengthwise direction. (19)

warranty: A manufacturer's written promise that a product will meet certain performance and quality standards as outlined. (12)

water conservation: Reducing water use and eliminating water waste. (13)

waterbed: Bed with a mattress consisting of a plastic bag or tubes filled with water. (21)

wattage: The amount of electricity a bulb uses. (11)

watts: A measurement of the amount of electrical power used. (10)

weather stripping: A strip of material that covers the edges of a window or door to prevent moisture and air from entering the house. (10)

weaving: Interlacing two sets of yarns at right angles. (19)

weft yarn: The filling yarn that runs in the crosswise direction. (19)

window treatments: Fabric applications—such as draperies or curtains— added to window units, either for helping to control the home environment or for purely decorative purposes. (19)

wood grain: Pattern that forms as a tree grows. (21)

work area: All parts of the house that are needed to maintain and service other areas. Typical work areas include the kitchen, laundry area, utility room, and garage. (7)

work triangle: The imaginary line connecting the food preparation and storage center, cleanup center, and cooking and serving centers of a kitchen. (8)

written communication: The transmission of ideas through a medium that people can read. In design, examples include contracts, meeting minutes, e-mail correspondence, or purchase orders. (18)

X

xeriscape: A landscaping method that utilizes water-conserving techniques. (13)

Y

yarn: A continuous strand of fibers that may consist of staple fibers (short fibers) and/or filaments (long, continuous fibers). (19)

yurt: A portable hut made of several layers of felt covered with canvas. (1)

Z

Zero Energy Home (ZEH): A home that produces and uses its own energy. (4)

zoning regulation: A government requirement that controls how land is used. (2)

Index

B

C

D

E

F

G

H

J

K

L

M

N

O

P

Q

R

S

T

U

V

W

X

Y

Z